STECK-VAUGHN

S0-BEZ-319

COMPLETE

GED

PREPARATION

 STECK-VAUGHN
ELEMENTARY · SECONDARY · ADULT · LIBRARY

A Harcourt Company

www.steck-vaughn.com

 staff **credits**

Executive Editor: Ellen Northcutt
Assistant Art Director: Richard Balsam
Design Manager: Danielle Szabo
Cover Designer: Danielle Szabo
Electronic Cover Production: Alan Klemp
Electronic Production Artists: JoAnn Estrada,
 Jill Klinger, Bo McKinney
Photo Editor: Margie Foster

ISBN: 0-8114-9893-X

Contents

Unit 2 The Essay

Unit 3 Reading Strategies

Unit 4 Social Studies

Unit 5 Science

Unit 6 Literature & the Arts

Unit 7 Mathematics

What Is the GED Test?

You are taking a very big step toward changing your life with your decision to take the GED test. By opening this book, you are taking your second important step: preparing for the test. You may feel nervous about what is ahead, which is only natural. Relax and read the following pages to find out the answers to your questions.

Dave Thomas, founder of the Wendy's restaurant chain, receives his GED diploma.

The GED test, the Test of General Educational Development, is given by the GED Testing Service of the American Council on Education for adults who did not graduate from high school. When you pass the GED test, you will receive a certificate that is regarded as being equivalent to a high school diploma. Employers in private industry and government, as well as admissions officers in universities, accept the GED certificate like a high school diploma.

The GED test covers the same subjects people study in high school. The five subject areas are: Writing Skills, Interpreting Literature and the Arts, Social Studies, Science, and Mathematics. You will not be required to know all the information that is usually taught in high school. You will, however, be tested on your ability to read and process information. Certain U.S. states also require a test on the U.S. Constitution or on state government. Check with your local adult education center to see if your state requires such a test.

Each year hundreds of thousands of adults pass the GED test. The *Steck-Vaughn GED Series* and *Skill Books* will help you develop and refine the reading and thinking skills you need to pass the GED test.

After you complete the GED test, you will get a score for each section and a total score. The total score is an average of all the other scores. The highest score possible on a single test is 80. The scores needed to pass the GED test vary depending on where you live. The chart on page 2 shows the minimum state requirements. A score of *40 or 45* means that the score for each test must be 40 or more, but if one or more scores is below 40, an average of at least 45 is required. A minimum score of *35 and 45* means that the score for each test must be 35 or more and an average of at least 45 is required.

GED Score Requirements

Area	Minimum Score on Each Test		Minimum Average on All Five Tests
UNITED STATES			
Alabama, Alaska, Arizona, Connecticut, Georgia, Hawaii, Illinois, Indiana, Iowa, Kansas, Kentucky, Maine, Massachusetts, Michigan, Minnesota, Montana, Nevada, New Hampshire, North Carolina, Ohio, Pennsylvania, Rhode Island, South Carolina, Tennessee, Vermont, Virginia, Wyoming	35	and	45
Arkansas, California, Colorado, Delaware, District of Columbia, Florida, Idaho, Maryland, Missouri, New York, Oklahoma, Oregon, South Dakota, Utah, Washington, West Virginia	40	and	45
Louisiana, Mississippi, Nebraska, New Mexico, North Dakota, Texas	40	or	45
New Jersey (42 is required on Test 1; 40 is required on Tests 2, 3, and 4; 45 is required on Test 5; and 45 average on all tests.)			
Wisconsin	40	and	50
CANADA			
Alberta, British Columbia, Manitoba, New Brunswick (English and French), Northwest Territories, Nova Scotia, Prince Edward Island, Saskatchewan, Yukon Territory	45		—
Newfoundland	40	and	45
U.S. TERRITORIES & OTHERS			
Guam, Kwajalein, Puerto Rico, Virgin Islands	35	and	45
Panama Canal Area, Palau	40	and	45
Mariana Islands, Marshall Islands, Micronesia	40	or	45
American Samoa	40		—

Note: GED score requirements change from time to time. For the most up-to-date information, check with your state or local GED director or GED testing center.

THE TESTS OF GENERAL EDUCATIONAL DEVELOPMENT

This chart gives you information on the content, number of items, and time limit for each test. In some places you do not have to take all sections of the test on the same day. If you want to take all the test sections in one day, the GED test will last an entire day. Check with your local adult education center for the requirements in your area.

Test	Content Areas	Number of Items	Time Limit (minutes)
Writing Skills Part I	Sentence Structure Usage Mechanics	55	75
Writing Skills Part II	Essay	1	45
Social Studies	Geography U.S. History Economics Political Science Behavioral Science	64	85
Science	Biology Earth Science Physics Chemistry	66	95
Interpreting Literature and the Arts	Popular Literature Classical Literature Commentary	45	65
Mathematics	Arithmetic Algebra Geometry	56	90

Where Do You Go to Take the GED Test?

The GED test is offered year-round throughout the United States, its possessions, U.S. military bases worldwide, and in Canada. To find out when and where tests are held near you, contact the GED Hot Line at 1-800-62-MY-GED (1-800-626-9433) or one of these institutions in your area:

- An adult education center
- A continuing education center
- A local community college
- A public library
- A private business school or technical school
- The public board of education

In addition, the Hot Line and the institutions can give you information regarding necessary identification, testing fees, and writing implements. Schedules vary: some testing centers are open several days a week; others are open only on weekends.

Why Should You Take the GED Test?

A GED certificate can help you in the following ways:

Employment

People without high school diplomas or GED certificates have much more difficulty changing jobs or moving up in their present companies. In many cases employers will not hire someone who does not have a high school diploma or the equivalent.

Education

If you want to enroll in a technical school, a vocational school, or an apprenticeship program, you often must have a high school diploma or the equivalent. If you want to enter a college or university, you must have a high school diploma or the equivalent.

Personal

The most important thing is how you feel about yourself. You have the unique opportunity to turn back the clock by making something happen that did not happen in the past. You can attain a GED certificate that will help you in the future and make you feel better about yourself now.

How to Prepare for the GED Test

Classes for GED preparation are available to anyone who wants to take the GED. The choice of whether to take classes is up to you; they are not required. If you prefer to study by yourself, the *Steck-Vaughn GED Series* has been prepared to guide your study. *Steck-Vaughn GED Exercise Books, Skill Books,* and software are also available to give you additional practice for each test.

Most GED preparation programs offer individualized instruction and tutors who can help you identify areas in which you may need help. Many adult education centers offer free day or night classes. The classes are usually informal and allow you to work at your own pace and with other adults who also are studying for the GED. In addition to working on specific skills, you will be able to take practice GED tests (like those in this book) in order to check your progress. For information about classes available near you, contact one of the institutions in the list on page 3.

What You Need to Know to Pass the GED Test

Writing Skills

The GED Writing Skills Test is divided into two parts. Part I focuses on grammar, and Part II asks you to write an essay. The Writing Skills unit in this book teaches you the skills you need to pass Writing Skills Part I. These skills are also necessary when you write the essay for Part II. Unit 2 in this book teaches you a step-by-step approach to writing an effective GED essay for Part II of the Writing Skills Test.

Part I

Part I of the GED Writing Skills Test takes 75 minutes and has 55 items. The items will test your knowledge of three areas of grammar: mechanics, usage, and sentence structure.

Thirty percent of the test items are in the area of mechanics. These items will test your knowledge of correct punctuation, spelling, and capitalization. Items will include using commas, correct spelling of possessives, contractions, and homonyms, and proper capitalization in sentences.

Thirty-five percent of the test items ask you to correct errors in usage. Usage includes using the verb or pronoun that agrees with the subject of the sentence. Correct usage also includes determining the right verb tense for the situation.

Thirty-five percent of the test items examine the way sentences are put together. The goal of these items is to make sure you know how to write a clear and logical sentence that has a subject, a complete verb, and the correct punctuation.

Writing Skills Test, Part I, consists of paragraphs from ten to thirteen sentences long. Each item is based on one or two sentences from the paragraph. Always read the paragraph completely before you begin to answer the items. You will need to know what the paragraph is about in order to decide what subject, verb, or pronoun a sentence from the paragraph may need.

Some of the items will ask you to correct a sentence. No more than one error will appear in these sentences, and some sentences will be correct as written. Other items will give you one or two sentences from the paragraph. You will then have to select a change in the wording or punctuation, or choose to leave the sentence alone. Other items will test your skill at writing new sentences. You may be asked to rewrite a sentence from the paragraph beginning with a different set of words, or you may be given two sentences to combine.

In Part II of the Writing Skills Test, you will be asked to write an essay. An essay is a composition of more than one paragraph that gives the writer's views on a particular topic. Unit 2, The Essay, will teach you effective ways to gather and organize ideas, write your essay, evaluate it, and revise it. You will focus on developing a five-paragraph essay that includes an introductory paragraph, three body paragraphs, and a conclusion paragraph. This is an effective way to organize a GED essay.

The essay topic assignment will be brief. You will be asked to "state a view," "present an opinion," or "explain why or how" about an issue or situation familiar to adults. You will be expected to write an essay of about 200 words that clearly explains your point of view. You will not need any specialized knowledge or information to respond to the topic.

The directions for the essay test tell you the steps to take to prepare your answer. You will be allowed 45 minutes to complete your essay.

Your essay will be scored and judged on its overall effectiveness. A few misspelled words or a few grammatical errors will not cause your essay to earn a failing score. If, however, there are so many errors that your ideas are hard to understand, your score will go down. The most important element is how well you stick to the topic and support your ideas with examples.

Two different people will score your essay. Each will read your essay and decide how effective it is based on its content, organization, and control of the English language. Each scorer will use the GED Scoring Guide (see page 181) to assign a score ranging from 1 to 6. The two scores will then be added, resulting in a range of scores from 2 to 12. A third scorer will be used if the first two scores are more than one point apart.

The scores you earn on Writing Skills Parts I and II will be combined and reported as a single score on a standard score scale.

Social Studies

The GED Social Studies Test examines your ability to read and understand selections and graphics about social studies. The test items require you to think about reading the selections in several ways. To answer the items, you will be using four basic thinking skills: comprehension, application, analysis, and evaluation. These skills are fully explained and practiced in Unit 3, Reading Strategies, pages 198–219. It is strongly recommended that you complete Unit 3 before moving on to Unit 4, Social Studies, in order to have the best chance of successfully passing the actual GED test. You will not be tested on any outside knowledge about social studies. The test takes 85 minutes and has 64 items. The items are divided into five categories: geography, history, economics, political science, and behavioral science.

Fifteen percent of the test items cover geography. Geography is the study of the overall physical and cultural make-up of the world. The reading selections focus on how Earth affects humanity and how humanity affects Earth.

Twenty-five percent of the test items cover the history of the United States. Selections are drawn from events from the earliest part of American history to the present.

Twenty percent of the test items cover economics. Economics selections focus on how goods and services are produced and used by government, business, and consumers.

Twenty percent of the test items cover political science. Political science selections focus on the way government works and how citizens are involved in the way the country is run.

Twenty percent of the test items cover behavioral science. Selections are drawn from anthropology, psychology, and sociology; all study how and why people act the way they do.

Science

The GED Science Test examines your ability to read, understand, think about, and apply science information in passages, charts, diagrams, and illustrations. The test items require you to think about the information in several ways. To answer the items, you will be using four basic thinking skills: comprehension, application, analysis, and evaluation. These skills are fully explained and practiced in Unit 3, Reading Strategies, pages 198–219. It is strongly recommended that you complete Unit 3 before moving on to Unit 5, Science, in order to have the best chance of successfully passing the actual GED test. You will not be tested on your knowledge of science facts. The GED Science Test takes 95 minutes and has 66 items. The items are divided into four content areas: biology, Earth science, chemistry, and physics.

About fifty percent of the test items involve biology. There may be passages and illustrations about cells, genetics, ecology, health, nutrition, disease, and the structure and functions of plants and animals, such as reproduction and photosynthesis.

About twenty percent of the test items involve Earth science. There may be passages and illustrations about landforms, earthquakes, volcanoes, rock formation, minerals, fossils, and Earth's history. Also covered are the atmosphere, weather, oceanography, tides, the solar system, and Earth's magnetic field.

About fifteen percent of the test items involve chemistry. There may be passages and illustrations about atoms, elements, molecules, chemical bonding, chemical reactions and their energy changes, radioactivity, and hydrocarbons.

About fifteen percent of the test items involve physics. There may be passages and illustrations about energy, motion, forces, work, machines, heat transfer, change of state, waves, optics, electricity, magnetism, and nuclear fission and fusion.

Literature & the Arts

This test focuses on reading comprehension and analysis. In other words, you will be tested on how well you understand what you read and on how you can use and apply that information. You will not be tested on your knowledge of literature. The items on the test require you to think about the reading selections in several ways. To answer the items, you will be using four basic thinking skills: literal and inferential comprehension, application, analysis, and evaluation. These skills are fully explained and practiced in Unit 3, Reading Strategies, pages 198–219. It is strongly recommended that you complete Unit 3 before moving on to Unit 6, Literature & the Arts, in order to have the best chance of successfully passing the actual GED test. The test takes 65 minutes. It has 45 items divided among three types of literature: Popular Literature, Classical Literature, and Commentary.

Fifty percent of the passages you will read are from popular literature. Popular literature is recently published prose nonfiction, novels, short stories, plays, poems, and magazines.

Twenty-five percent of the passages are from classical literature. Classical literature is prose nonfiction, novels, short stories, plays, and poetry that literary experts regard as superior writing. The classics have stood the test of time.

Twenty-five percent of the passages are from commentary in current publications. Commentary includes reviews of books, movies, television, music, art, dance, or theater.

Mathematics

The GED Mathematics Test focuses on the practical use of basic arithmetic, algebra, and geometry. You will be tested on your understanding of how to solve a problem and on your ability to do the math to find a solution.

The test takes 90 minutes and has 56 items. The items are divided into three areas: arithmetic, algebra, and geometry.

Within each area, some of the items require you to solve the problem and others ask you to show how you would solve (set up) the problem. Each area tests your ability to do the basic mathematics operations: addition, subtraction, multiplication, and division. Some concepts, such as percent, ratio, proportion, and the use of formulas are tested in each of the main subject areas. You will be provided with a formula page that contains all the formulas you will need when you take the GED Mathematics test. The formulas are located on the inside back cover of this book for your use while studying for the test.

Approximately fifty percent of the test items focus on arithmetic. You will be expected to work problems involving whole numbers, fractions, decimals, and percents. Some problems require an understanding of ratio and proportion or probability. There are three topics in the arithmetic section: measurement, number relations, and data analysis.

Measurement items test your ability to use basic math skills in items about length, perimeter, circumference, area, volume, time, and in making standard measurement conversions. Some measurement items test less commonly used concepts such as square roots, exponents, and scientific notation.

Number relations items test your ability to compare numbers and draw conclusions.

Data analysis items test your ability to use information presented in graphs, charts, and tables. You decide which pieces of information you need to solve the problem, locate the information, and work the problem. You may also be asked to find the mean (average) or median of a set of data.

Approximately thirty percent of the items on the test focus on algebra. You will be tested on the use of algebraic symbols and expressions. Some items will test your ability to write equations and find the solutions.

A few items may include powers and roots, factoring, solving inequalities, graphing equations, and finding the slope of a line.

Approximately twenty percent of the items on the test focus on geometry. The geometry concepts covered are finding volume; measuring angles, triangles, and quadrilaterals; and using similarity, congruence, and the Pythagorean Theorem for indirect measurement.

Test-Taking Skills

The GED test is not the kind of test you can cram for. There are, however, some ways you can improve your performance on the test.

Answering the Test Items

♦ Never skim the directions. Read them carefully so that you know exactly what to do. If you are unsure, ask the test-giver if the directions can be explained.

♦ First read the passage to get a general idea about what it is about. Notice the overall verb tense and the way the sentences relate to each other. Then read the items once. Read each sentence carefully before answering the question about it.

♦ Read all of the answer options carefully, even if you think you know the right answer. Some of the answers may not seem wrong at first glance, but one answer will always be better than the others.

♦ Answer all the items. Wrong answers will not be subtracted from your score. If you cannot find the correct answer, reduce the number of possible answers by eliminating all the answers you know are wrong. Then go back to the passage to figure out the correct answer. If you still cannot decide, make your best guess.

♦ Fill in your answer sheet carefully. To record your answers, mark one numbered space on the answer sheet beside the number that corresponds to the item. Mark only one answer space for each item; multiple answers will be scored as incorrect.

♦ Remember that the GED is a timed test. When the test begins, write down the time you have to finish. Then keep an eye on the time. Do not take a long time on any one item. Answer each item as best you can and go on. If you are spending a lot of time on one item, skip it. If you finish before time is up, go back to the items you skipped or were unsure of, and give them more thought.

♦ Don't change an answer unless you are certain your answer was wrong. Usually the first answer you choose is the correct one.

♦ If you feel you are getting nervous, stop working for a moment. Take a few deep breaths and relax. Then begin working again.

Study Skills

Study Regularly

♦ If you can, set aside an hour to study every day. If you do not have time every day, set up a schedule of the days you can study. Be sure to pick times when you will be the most relaxed and least likely to be bothered by outside distractions.

♦ Let others know your study time. Ask them to leave you alone for that period. It helps if you explain to others why this is important.

♦ You should be relaxed when you study, so find an area that is comfortable for you. If you cannot study at home, go to the library. Most public libraries have areas for reading and studying. If there is a college or university near you, find out if you can use its library. All libraries have dictionaries, encyclopedias, and other resources you can use if you need more information while you're studying.

Organize Your Study Materials

♦ Be sure to have pens, sharp pencils, and paper for any notes you might want to take.

♦ Keep all of your books together. If you are taking an adult education class, you probably will be able to borrow some books or other study material.

♦ Make a notebook or folder for each subject you are studying. Folders with pockets are useful for storing loose papers.

♦ Keep all of your material in one place so you do not waste time looking for it each time you study.

Read Regularly

♦ Read the newspaper, read magazines, read books. Read whatever appeals to you—but read! Regular, daily reading is the best way to improve your reading skills.

♦ Use the library to find material you like to read. Check the magazine section for publications of interest to you. Most libraries subscribe to hundreds of magazines ranging in interest from news to cars to music to sewing to sports. If you are not familiar with the library, ask a librarian for help. Get a library card so that you can check out material to use at home.

Write Regularly

♦ Try to write every day. The more you write, the more comfortable you will feel writing. You will receive extensive practice in Unit 2 of this book, and some learners find that keeping a journal or writing letters to friends in other cities or countries gives valuable writing experience.

Take Notes

♦ Take notes on things that interest you or things that you think might be useful.

♦ When you take notes, do not copy the words directly from the book. Restate the information in your own words.

♦ Take notes any way you want. You do not have to write in full sentences as long as you can understand your notes later.

♦ Use outlines, charts, or diagrams to help you organize information and make it easier to learn.

♦ You may want to take notes in a question-and-answer form, such as: *What is the main idea? The main idea is . . .*

Improve Your Vocabulary

♦ As you read, do not skip a word you do not know. Instead, try to figure out what the word means. First, omit it from the sentence. Read the sentence without the word and try to put another word in its place. Is the meaning of the sentence the same?

♦ Make a list of unfamiliar words, look them up in the dictionary, and write down the meanings.

♦ Since a word may have several meanings, it is best to look up the word while you have the passage with you. Then you can try out the different meanings in the context.

♦ When you read the definition of a word, restate it in your own words. Use the word in a sentence or two.

♦ All of the words you see in **boldface** type are key terms. The key terms are important vocabulary for the content areas you are studying. We recommend that you look up any words you do not understand in a dictionary.

Make a List of Subject Areas that Give You Trouble

♦ As you go through this book, make a note whenever you do not understand something. Then ask your teacher or another person for help. Later go back and review the topic.

Taking the Test

Before the Test

- If you have never been to the test center, go there the day before the test. If you drive, find out where to park. This way you won't get lost the day of the test.

- Prepare the things you need for the test: your admission ticket (if necessary), acceptable identification, some sharpened No. 2 pencils with erasers, a watch, glasses, a jacket or sweater (in case the room is cold), and a snack to eat during breaks.

- You will do your best work if you are rested and alert. So do not cram before the test. In fact, if you prepared for the test, cramming should be unnecessary. Instead, eat a meal and get a good night's sleep. If the test is early in the morning, set the alarm.

The Day of the Test

- Eat a good breakfast. Wear comfortable clothing. Make sure that you have all of the materials you need.

- Try to arrive at the test center about twenty minutes early. This allows time if, for example, there is a last-minute change of room.

- If you are going to be at the test center all day, you might pack a lunch. If you have to find a restaurant or if you wait a long time to be served, you may be late for the rest of the test.

Using this Book

♦ Start with the Entry Test for each unit. These tests will give you an idea of what the GED test is like. Then use the Correlation Chart that follows each entry test to figure out your areas of strength and the areas you need to review. Each chart will tell you the exact pages in this book to study.

♦ As you study, read the passages and Tips carefully. Then answer the questions and check your work in the Answer Key. Use the GED Review at the end of each lesson section and the GED Cumulative Review at the end of each unit to find out if you need to review any lessons before continuing.

♦ After you complete the GED Cumulative Reviews, take the Simulated GED Test. It is identical to the actual GED test in format and length. It will give you an idea of what the real test is like and it will help you decide if you are ready for the real GED test. You do not have to take the test all at once. You can take each test separately if you choose. The Simulated GED Test Correlation Chart for each test will tell you if you need additional review.

WRITING SKILLS ENTRY TEST

Directions

The Writing Skills Entry Test is intended to measure your ability to use clear and effective English. It is a test of English as it should be written, not as it might be spoken.

This test consists of paragraphs with numbered sentences. Some of the sentences contain errors in sentence structure, usage, or mechanics (spelling, punctuation, and capitalization). After reading the numbered sentences, answer the multiple-choice questions that follow. Some questions refer to sentences that are correct as written. The best answer for these questions is the one that leaves the sentence as originally written. The best answer for some questions is the one that produces a sentence that is consistent with the verb tense and point of view used throughout the paragraph.

You should spend no more than 40 minutes answering the 28 questions on this test. Work carefully, but do not spend too much time on any one question. Do not skip any items. Make a reasonable guess when you are not sure of an answer. You will not be penalized for incorrect answers.

When time is up, mark the last item you finished. This will tell you whether you can finish the real GED Test in the time allowed. Then complete the test.

Record your answers to the questions on a copy of the answer sheet on page 922. Be sure that all required information is properly recorded on the answer sheet.

To record your answers, mark the numbered space on the answer sheet that corresponds to the answer you choose for each question on the test.

Example:

Sentence 1: **We were all honored to meet governor Phillips.**

What correction should be made to this sentence?

(1) insert a comma after honored
(2) change the spelling of honored to honered
(3) change governor to Governor
(4) replace were with was
(5) no correction is necessary   ① ② ● ④ ⑤

In this example, the word governor should be capitalized; therefore, answer space 3 would be marked on the answer sheet.

Do not rest the point of your pencil on the answer sheet while you are considering your answer. Make no stray or unnecessary marks. If you change an answer, erase your first mark completely. Mark only one answer space for each question; multiple answers will be scored as incorrect. Do not fold or crease your answer sheet.

When you finish the test, use the Correlation Chart on page 24 to determine whether you are ready to take the real GED Test, and, if not, which skill areas need additional review.

Adapted with permission of the American Council on Education.

(1) The medical profession continues to stress the effects of cholesterol and fat in the diet as they relate to heart disease. (2) Experts do not agree on the level at which cholesterol becomes a risk factor. (3) Ten years ago there wasn't concern unless a cholesterol level reached 300. (4) Since then experts say that increased risk of heart disease begins at a cholesterol level of 180.
(5) Studies show that about 70 percent of people can reduce their cholesterol 15 to 25 percent by eating less food that is high in fat and cholesterol. (6) According to Dr. John LaRosa chairman of the American Heart Association's task force on cholesterol issues keeping your cholesterol level low improves your chances of a long, healthy life. (7) The American public are encouraged to read labels and to choose products with low amounts of fat and cholesterol.
(8) Today, doctors recommends replacing whole-milk products with those made with low-fat or skim milk. (9) Eating lean meat and increasing your intake of fiber oat bran and beans help reduce cholesterol levels in the bloodstream. (10) Exercising keeps you fit and seems to help clear cholesterol from the arteries. (11) Evidence is strong that what you eat can affect your cholesterol level and therefore your risk of heart disease.

1. Sentences 3 and 4: **Ten years ago there wasn't concern unless a cholesterol level reached 300. Since then experts say that increased risk of heart disease begins at a cholesterol level of 180.**

    The most effective combination of sentences 3 and 4 would include which of the following groups of words?

    (1) reached 300; consequently, since then
    (2) reached 300; maybe since then,
    (3) reached 300, then since then,
    (4) reached 300; however, since then
    (5) reached 300; because since then,

2. Sentence 5: **Studies show that about 70 percent of people can reduce their cholesterol 15 to 25 percent by eating less food that is high in fat and cholesterol.**

    What correction should be made to this sentence?

    (1) change show to showing
    (2) insert a comma after people
    (3) change their to they're
    (4) insert a comma after fat
    (5) no correction is necessary

3. Sentence 6: **According to Dr. John LaRosa chairman of the American Heart Association's task force on cholesterol issues keeping your cholesterol level low improves your chances of a long, healthy life.**

Which of the following is the best way to write the underlined portion of this sentence? If you think the original is the best way, choose option (1).

(1) LaRosa chairman of the American Heart Association's task force on cholesterol issues keeping
(2) LaRosa, chairman of the American Heart Association's task force on cholesterol issues keeping
(3) LaRosa, chairman of the American Heart Association's task force on cholesterol issues, keeping
(4) LaRosa, chairman of the American Heart Association's task force, on cholesterol issues keeping
(5) LaRosa, chairman of the American Heart Association's task force on cholesterol issues; keeping

4. Sentence 7: **The American public are encouraged to read labels and to choose products with low amounts of fat and cholesterol.**

What correction should be made to this sentence?

(1) change American to american
(2) change are to is
(3) insert a comma after labels
(4) change to choose to have chosen
(5) no correction is necessary

5. Sentence 8: **Today, doctors recommends replacing whole-milk products with those made with low-fat or skim milk.**

Which of the following is the best way to write the underlined portion of this sentence? If you think the original is the best way, choose option (1).

(1) Today, doctors recommends
(2) Today, doctors' recommends
(3) Today, doctor's recommend
(4) Today, doctors recommend
(5) Today, Doctors recommend

6. Sentence 9: **Eating lean meat and increasing your intake of fiber oat bran and beans help reduce cholesterol levels in the bloodstream.**

Which of the following is the best way to write the underlined portion of this sentence? If you think the original is the best way, choose option (1).

(1) fiber oat bran and beans
(2) fiber, oat bran, and beans
(3) fiber, oat bran; and beans
(4) fiber oat bran, and beans
(5) fiber, oat bran and, beans

7. Sentence 10: **Exercising keeps you fit and seems to help clear cholesterol from the arteries.**

What correction should be made to this sentence?

(1) change the spelling of Exercising to Exersizing
(2) replace Exercising with Since exercising
(3) change you to your
(4) insert a comma after fit
(5) no correction is necessary

Items 8 to 15 refer to the following paragraphs.

(1) We have come a long way from the first room-size vacuum tube computers to todays purse-size laptop computers. (2) We will probably have intelligent computers like Hal in the movie <u>2001</u> when the year 2001 arrives. (3) There is computers in every part of our lives. (4) They are in our cars, supermarkets and discount stores have them, and on the desks of at least some employees in even the smallest businesses. (5) Computers are in the space shuttle and satellites. (6) They are in the thermostat on your furnace and in the burglar alarm systems of offices. (7) Computers can be very small and simple or very large and complex. (8) The one problem with computers is that, at least so far, they are very dumb. (9) Computers are only as smart as the person entering the information. (10) The main benifit of computers is that they process extremely complicated data very, very fast. (11) However, they process wrong data just as fast as correct data, which results in errors. (12) Skillful, accurate keyboarding and data entry is critical to successful computer operations.

8. Sentence 1: **We have come a long way from the first room-size vacuum tube computers to todays purse-size laptop computers.**

What correction should be made to this sentence?

(1) insert a comma after <u>way</u>
(2) change the spelling of <u>vacuum</u> to <u>vaccum</u>
(3) change <u>todays</u> to <u>todays'</u>
(4) change <u>todays</u> to <u>today's</u>
(5) no correction is necessary

9. Sentence 2: **We will probably have intelligent computers like Hal in the movie <u>2001</u> when the year 2001 arrives.**

If you rewrote sentence 2 beginning with

<u>When the year 2001</u>

the next words should be

(1) arrives, we
(2) arrives; we
(3) arrives; because, we
(4) arrives; as a result, we
(5) arrives, but we

10. Sentence 3: **There is computers in every part of our lives.**

What correction should be made to this sentence?

(1) change <u>There is</u> to <u>There was</u>
(2) change <u>There is</u> to <u>There are</u>
(3) replace <u>our</u> with <u>their</u>
(4) change <u>our</u> to <u>ours</u>
(5) no correction is necessary

11. Sentence 4: **They are in our cars, supermarkets and discount stores have them, and on the desks of at least some employees in even the smallest businesses.**

Which of the following is the best way to write the underlined portion of this sentence? If you think the original is the best way, choose option (1).

(1) supermarkets and discount stores have them,
(2) our supermarkets and discount stores have them,
(3) our supermarkets and discount stores,
(4) at the supermarkets and discount stores,
(5) on the supermarkets and discount stores,

12. Sentences 5 and 6: **Computers are in the space shuttle and satellites. They are in the thermostat on your furnace and in the burglar alarm systems of offices.**

Which of the following is the best way to write the underlined portion of this sentence? If you think the original is the best way, choose option (1).

(1) satellites. They
(2) satellites; and they
(3) satellites and they
(4) satellites, they
(5) satellites they

13. Sentence 8: **The one problem with computers is that, at least so far, they are very dumb.**

Which of the following is the best way to write the underlined portion of this sentence? If you think the original is the best way, choose option (1).

(1) is that, at least so far, they
(2) are, that at least so far, they
(3) are that at least so far they
(4) is that at least so far they
(5) are that, at least so far; they

14. Sentence 10: **The main benifit of computers is that they process extremely complicated data very, very fast.**

What correction should be made to this sentence?

(1) change the spelling of benifit to benefit
(2) change is to are
(3) replace they with it
(4) replace extremely with extreme
(5) no correction is necessary

15. Sentence 12: **Skillful, accurate keyboarding and data entry is critical to successful computer operations.**

What correction should be made to this sentence?

(1) change is to are
(2) change is to has been
(3) change the spelling of successful to successfull
(4) replace to with too
(5) no correction is necessary

Items 16 to 22 refer to the following paragraphs.

(1) Sucessful job hunting requires careful preparation. (2) First, you need to list the kinds of jobs you would like. (3) Then you need to determine what skills, training, and the required experience for these jobs. (4) One of the best ways to determine these requirements is to ask people which are now doing those jobs.

(5) Next, you need to list your qualifications and see if they match any of the jobs we have selected. (6) If not, you need to think again about what jobs you want. (7) For example, you probably cannot start as manager of a restaurant. (8) You may be able to start in one of the many other jobs in a restaurant and work your way up.

(9) When you select a job that you want, which matches your qualifications, you needed to go for an interview. (10) You need to look and act your best at the interview. (11) Try to learn about it before you go for an interview. (12) Stress your qualifications for the job, your knowledge of the job, and be interested in it.

16. Sentence 1: **Sucessful job hunting requires careful preparation.**

What correction should be made to this sentence?

(1) change the spelling of Sucessful to Successful
(2) insert a comma after hunting
(3) change requires to require
(4) change the spelling of preparation to preperation
(5) no correction is necessary

17. Sentence 2: **First, you need to list the kinds of jobs you would like.**

What correction should be made to this sentence?

(1) change need to needed
(2) change jobs to job
(3) replace you would with we would
(4) change would like to would have liked
(5) no correction is necessary

18. Sentence 3: **Then you need to determine what skills, training, and the required experience for these jobs.**

Which of the following is the best way to write the underlined portion of this sentence? If you think the original is the best way, choose option (1).

(1) training, and the required experience
(2) training, and experience are required
(3) training, and experience is required
(4) training, and experience was required
(5) training; and experience are required

19. Sentence 5: **Next, you need to list your qualifications and see if they match any of the jobs we have selected.**

What correction should be made to this sentence?

(1) remove the comma after <u>Next</u>
(2) insert a comma after <u>see</u>
(3) change <u>we have</u> to <u>you has</u>
(4) change <u>we have</u> to <u>you have</u>
(5) no correction is necessary

20. Sentences 7 and 8: **For example, you probably cannot start as manager of a restaurant. You may be able to start in one of the many other jobs in a restaurant and work your way up.**

The most effective combination of sentences 7 and 8 would include which of the following groups of words?

(1) restaurant and you
(2) restaurant but you
(3) restaurant; but, you
(4) restaurant; because you
(5) restaurant; however, you

21. Sentence 9: **When you select a job that you want, which matches your qualifications, you needed to go for an interview.**

What correction should be made to this sentence?

(1) change <u>you want</u> to <u>you will want</u>
(2) replace <u>which</u> with <u>who</u>
(3) remove the comma after <u>qualifications</u>
(4) change <u>needed</u> to <u>need</u>
(5) no correction is necessary

22. Sentence 12: **Stress your qualifications for the job, your knowledge of the job, and <u>be interested in it.</u>**

Which of the following is the best way to write the underlined portion of this sentence? If you think the original is the best way, choose option (1).

(1) be interested in it
(2) whether you are interested
(3) tell them you are interested in the job
(4) you're interest in the job
(5) your interest in the job

Items 23 to 28 refer to the following paragraphs.

(1) We have come a long way from the 1400s when j. gutenberg invented the printing press to today's fax machines that send pages of text around the world in seconds. (2) Prior to the invention of the printing press, written material was all done by hand. (3) It took an hour or more to hand print a page. (4) Days, weeks, or months to do a whole book like the Bible.

(5) There are few books and very little written information. (6) That is not true today. (7) Some people would say we have too much written material. (8) You even hear about an organization "floating on a sea of paperwork" (printed pages of information).

(9) The printing press enabled many copies of the same printed page to be made once the page of type had been set quickly and easily. (10) Once this was possible, it spread widely and rapidly, people became more educated, and civilization advanced. (11) The invention of the printing press is probably the most important single invention ever made.

23. Sentence 1: **We have come a long way from the 1400s when j. gutenberg invented the printing press to today's fax machines that send pages of text around the world in seconds.**

What correction should be made to this sentence?

(1) change j. gutenberg to J. Gutenberg
(2) change printing press to Printing Press
(3) change that send to who send
(4) change world to World
(5) no correction is necessary

24. Sentences 3 and 4: **It took an hour or more to hand print a page. Days, weeks, or months to do a whole book like the Bible.**

Which of the following is the best way to write the underlined portion of these sentences? If you think the original is the best way, choose option (1).

(1) page. Days,
(2) page; days,
(3) page; and days
(4) page; therefore, days,
(5) page and days,

25. Sentence 5: **There are few books and very little written information.**

What correction should be made to this sentence?

(1) change There to Their
(2) replace are with is
(3) replace are with were
(4) change books to book
(5) no correction is necessary

26. Sentence 8: **You even hear about an organization "floating on a sea of paperwork" (printed pages of information).**

Which of the following is the best way to write the underlined portion of this sentence? If you think the original is the best way, choose option (1).

(1) You even hear
(2) You even here
(3) We even here
(4) We even hear
(5) They even hear

27. Sentence 9: **The printing press enabled many copies of the same printed page to be made once the page of type had been set quickly and easily.**

What correction should be made to this sentence?

(1) move quickly and easily to the beginning of the sentence
(2) move quickly and easily after many copies
(3) change printing press to Printing Press
(4) move quickly and easily after to be made
(5) no correction is necessary

28. Sentence 10: **Once this was possible, it spread widely and rapidly, people became more educated, and civilization advanced.**

Which of the following is the best way to write the underlined portion of this sentence? If you think the original is the best way, choose option (1).

(1) it spread
(2) it spreads
(3) information spread
(4) information, spread
(5) information will spread

Answers are on page 734.

Entry Test Correlation Chart: Writing Skills

Name: _____ Class: _____ Date: _____

This chart can help you determine your strengths and weaknesses on the content and skill areas of the Writing Skills GED Test. Use the Answer Key on pages 734–736 to check your answers to the test. Then circle on the chart the numbers of the test items you answered correctly. Put the total number correct for each content area and skill area in each row and column. If you answered fewer than 28 questions correctly, look at the total items correct in each column and row and decide which areas are difficult for you. Use the page references to study those areas.

Content/ Item Type	Sentence Correction	Sentence Revision	Rewrite/ Combine	Total Correct	Page Reference
Mechanics *(Pages 64–87)*					
Capitalization	23			_____ out of 1	64–65
Commas	2	3, 6		_____ out of 3	68–71
Apostrophes and Quotation Marks	8			_____ out of 1	74–75
Spelling	7, 14, 16			_____ out of 3	76–84
Usage *(Pages 88–115)*					
Subject-Verb Agreement	4, 10, 15	5, 13		_____ out of 5	88–90
Verb Tenses and Irregular Verbs	17, 21, 25			_____ out of 3	91–97
Pronouns	19	26		_____ out of 2	98–101
Pronouns and Antecedents		28		_____ out of 1	102–105
Sentence Structure *(Pages 116–142)*					
Sentence Fragments		24	9	_____ out of 2	116–118
Run-On Sentences		12	20	_____ out of 2	119–121
Combining Sentences			1	_____ out of 1	122–125
Parallel Structure		11, 18, 22		_____ out of 3	126–128
Misplaced Modifiers	27			_____ out of 1	132–135
				Total correct: ___ out of 28	

1–21 → You need more review.
22–28 → Congratulations!
You're ready for the GED Test!

For additional help, see the Steck-Vaughn GED Writing Skills Exercise Book.

THE ESSAY ENTRY TEST

Directions

This part of the Writing Skills Test is intended to determine how well you write. You are asked to write an essay that explains something or presents an opinion on an issue. In preparing your essay, you should take the following steps:

1. Read carefully the directions and the essay topic given below.

2. Plan your essay carefully before you write.

3. Use scratch paper to make any notes.

4. Write your essay on separate paper.

5. Read carefully what you have written and make any changes that will improve your essay.

6. Check your paragraphs, sentence structure, spelling, punctuation, capitalization, and usage, and make any necessary corrections.

You will have 45 minutes to write on the topic below. Write legibly and use a ballpoint pen so that the evaluators will be able to read your writing. The notes you make on the blank pages (scratch paper) will not be scored. Your composition will be scored by at least two trained evaluators who will judge the paper according to its overall effectiveness. They will be concerned with how clearly you make the main point of your composition, how thoroughly you support your ideas, and how clear and correct your writing is throughout the composition. You will receive no credit for writing on a question other than the one assigned.

Topic

Each decade has its music. The 1950s brought Elvis and rock-and-roll. The 1960s were the Beatle years. Heavy metal and disco ruled the scene in the 1970s; punk rock, rockabilly, and rap emerged in the 1980s. In each decade, parents have feared that pop music would ruin their children.

Write a composition of about 200 words on the effects of pop music and culture on the young people of the late 1980s or the 1990s. You may deal with the good effects, the bad effects, or both.

When you finish your essay, see page 736 of the Answer Key to evaluate and score your essay.

Adapted with permission of the American Council on Education.

SOCIAL STUDIES ENTRY TEST

Directions

The Social Studies Entry Test is intended to measure your knowledge of general social studies concepts. This test consists of 32 multiple-choice questions that are based on short readings, graphs, maps, charts, cartoons, and diagrams. Study the information given and then answer the questions that follow. Refer to the information as often as necessary in answering the questions.

You should spend no more than 45 minutes answering the 32 items on this test. Work carefully, but do not spend too much time on any one item. Do not skip any items. Make a reasonable guess when you are not sure of an answer. You will not be penalized for incorrect answers. When time is up, mark the last item you finished. This will tell you whether you can finish the real GED Test in the time allowed. Then complete the test.

Record your answers to the questions on a copy of the answer sheet on page 922. Be sure that all required information is properly recorded on the answer sheet.

To record your answers, mark the numbered space on the answer sheet that corresponds to the answer you choose for each item on the test.

Example: Early pioneers of the western frontier looked to settle on land that had adequate access to water. To ensure access to water, many early pioneers settled on land near

  (1) forests
  (2) grasslands
  (3) rivers
  (4) glaciers
  (5) oceans   ① ② ● ④ ⑤

The correct answer is <u>rivers</u>; therefore, answer space 3 should be marked on the answer sheet.

Do not rest the point of your pencil on the answer sheet while you are considering your answer. Make no stray or unnecessary marks. If you change an answer, erase your first mark completely. Mark only one answer for each question; multiple answers will be scored as incorrect. Do not fold or crease your answer sheet.

When you finish the test, use the Correlation Chart on page 35 to determine whether you are ready to take the real GED Test, and, if not, which skill areas need additional review.

Directions: Choose the <u>best answer</u> to each item.

Items 1 to 3 refer to the following table.

TEMPERATURE TABLE										
	LENGTH OF RECORD	AVERAGE DAILY TEMPERATURE							EXTREME	
		JANUARY		APRIL		JULY		OCTOBER			
		MAXIMUM	MINIMUM	MAXIMUM	MINIMUM	MAXIMUM	MINIMUM	MAXIMUM	MINIMUM	MAXIMUM	MINIMUM
CITIES	YEAR	°F	°F	°F	°F	°F	°F	°F	°F	°F	°F
Bismarck, N. D.	30	20	0	55	32	86	58	59	34	114	-45
Boise, Idaho	30	36	22	63	37	91	59	65	38	112	-28
Brownsville, Tex.	30	71	52	82	66	93	76	85	67	104	12
Buffalo, N. Y.	30	31	18	53	34	80	59	60	41	99	-21
Cheyenne, Wyo.	30	37	14	56	30	85	55	63	32	100	-38
Chicago, Ill.	30	33	19	57	41	84	67	63	47	105	-23
Des Moines, Ia.	30	29	11	59	38	87	65	66	43	110	-30
Dodge City, Ks.	30	42	20	66	41	93	68	71	46	109	-26
El Paso, Tex.	30	56	30	78	49	95	69	79	50	109	-8
Indianapolis, Ind.	30	37	21	61	40	86	64	67	44	107	-25
Jacksonville, Fla.	30	67	45	80	58	92	73	80	62	105	10
Kansas City, Mo.	30	40	23	66	46	92	71	72	49	113	-22
Las Vegas, Nev.	30	54	32	78	51	104	76	80	53	117	8
Los Angeles, Ca.	30	64	45	67	52	76	62	73	57	110	23
Louisville, Ky.	30	44	27	66	43	89	67	70	46	107	-20
Miami, Fla.	30	76	58	83	66	89	75	85	71	100	28
Minneapolis, Mn.	30	22	2	56	33	84	61	61	37	108	-34

1. What is Chicago's average maximum temperature in April?

   (1) 30°F
   (2) 41°F
   (3) 56°F
   (4) 57°F
   (5) 84°F

2. Which is <u>not</u> a fact based on the table?

   (1) The temperature record covers a period of 30 years.
   (2) The table shows the highest and lowest temperatures recorded at each city during a 30-year period.
   (3) Bismarck is the coldest city in North Dakota.
   (4) Buffalo is the only city not to have recorded a high temperature of at least 100° F in the 30-year period.
   (5) In Indianapolis, the average daily temperatures in January are between 37° and 21°F.

3. Based on the table, which city would have the <u>largest</u> tourist industry offering people a warm winter vacation?

   (1) Bismarck
   (2) Chicago
   (3) Des Moines
   (4) Kansas City
   (5) Miami

Items 4 and 5 refer to the following paragraphs.

General Grant of the Union and General Lee of the Confederacy continued to engage in battle until April of 1865. On April 9, facing encirclement and cut off from lines of supply, Lee sent a white flag of truce to arrange for a conference with General Grant. Grant suggested that Lee's retreating and dissolving army should surrender. Lee, after great consideration, asked for terms. Grant generously suggested and Lee gladly accepted these terms of surrender:

"officers and men paroled . . . arms and materials surrendered . . . officers to keep their side arms, and let all the men who claim to own a horse or mule take the animals home with them to work their little farms."

After the surrender, Lee returned to his home in the South. He urged all Southerners to work for peace and harmony in a united country.

4. Which best states a fact that supports the opinion that Lee gladly agreed to Grant's terms?

    (1) Lee accepted them.
    (2) These were the terms Lee had asked for.
    (3) Lee had sent a flag of truce.
    (4) Lee surrendered immediately.
    (5) There is no supporting fact.

5. Which of the following statements reveals the author's opinion about Grant?

    (1) Lee respected Grant.
    (2) Grant kept fighting until the end.
    (3) Grant agreed to meet with Lee.
    (4) Grant was generous in his terms.
    (5) Grant wanted Lee to surrender.

Items 6 and 7 refer to the following paragraph.

One of the most important factors in the economy is the consumer. Every person in the country has some influence, one way or another, on the economic health of the nation. Ordinarily, people buy something almost every day. The sales of items from chewing gum to houses are a good part of what keeps the money moving. When consumers feel that they have enough money to buy more than just what they need to live, the businesses in the nation profit. Interest rates go down, and people borrow more money and spend it. But when consumers begin to feel a pinch in the pocketbook, they spend less. The decrease in spending hurts business. A decrease in business activity often results in more unemployment and people having even less money to spend. Then the question that economists face is how to keep the consumer happy.

6. Which of the following does the writer assume in the paragraph?

    (1) Economists try to keep the economy stable.
    (2) People would rather borrow money than earn it.
    (3) American consumers spend more than they can afford.
    (4) Housing is one of the most important economic factors.
    (5) Consumers are not aware of their role in the economic picture.

7. Which of the following is a result of high unemployment?

    (1) increased business activity
    (2) increased consumer spending
    (3) interest rates go down
    (4) consumer spending decreases
    (5) economic good health

Items 8 and 9 refer to the following paragraph.

One way government is involved in the economy is in its attempts to protect the consumer. In the past, shoppers had little protection. Every store should have posted large signs saying "Buyer, beware!" If a baker bought flour that was full of bugs, he could sift them out, cook with them, or toss out the flour and lose money. Now public awareness of consumer rights, increased federal controls, public relations on the part of manufacturers and store owners, and self-policing by various groups have combined to increase consumer protection. Most large supermarkets replace food that has gone stale or sour, and, in fact, include the cost of returns in the amount of markup on the groceries.

8. Which is the best example of government control for consumer protection?

   (1) articles in *Consumer Reports*
   (2) rating of movies by the Motion Picture Association of America
   (3) state laws on seat belts
   (4) neighborhood stores removing pornographic magazines from public shelves
   (5) comparison testing in advertisements

9. The manufacturer's cost of recalling defective merchandise is probably paid for by the

   (1) government
   (2) manufacturer
   (3) automobile industry
   (4) consumer
   (5) labor union

Item 10 refers to the following paragraph.

Interest is the amount earned on an investment. If an investment pays simple interest, the interest is earned only on the original amount of the investment. If an investment earns compound interest, the interest is earned on the original investment plus its earnings.

10. Alicia is trying to decide where to open a savings account with $1,000. Which of the following bank accounts would pay Alicia the most interest?

    (1) an account paying 3 percent simple interest
    (2) an account paying 3.5 percent simple interest
    (3) an account paying 4 percent simple interest
    (4) an account paying 4.5 percent simple interest
    (5) an account paying 4.5 percent interest compounded daily

Item 11 refers to the following graph.

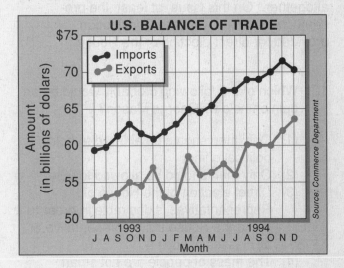

11. Over the period shown, the general trend has been

    (1) increasing exports and decreasing imports
    (2) increasing exports and increasing imports
    (3) decreasing exports and decreasing imports
    (4) decreasing exports and increasing imports
    (5) flat for both exports and imports

Items 12 and 13 refer to the following information.

There was disagreement about many issues besides the qualifications of the Vice President at the 1787 Constitutional Convention. Most members, for example, did not trust the mass of people to make wise political choices. In fact, they opposed the direct election of members of the House of Representatives by the people. However, there were several very influential men who took the opposing view. Benjamin Franklin, for example, felt that the public had shown great virtue during the Revolution and would continue to do so. George Mason of Virginia argued that direct election of the House was needed to make it "attend to the rights of every class of the people." James Madison did not want "the people to be lost sight of altogether." On this issue, at least, the pro-democracy forces won: the Constitution provided for direct election of the House.

12. Which of the following probably would be an opinion held by George Mason?

   (1) Only men should be allowed to hold political office.
   (2) Only men should be allowed to vote.
   (3) Direct election of the House of Representatives is desirable in order to make the House truly representative of all classes of society.
   (4) The mass of people are not smart enough to make sound political decisions.
   (5) Members of the House of Representatives should be appointed by the governors of each state.

13. Which of the following facts can be determined from the paragraph?

   (1) Representatives serve longer terms.
   (2) Representatives are elected by direct vote.
   (3) The Vice President is chosen by the President.
   (4) The Constitution was signed on September 7, 1787.
   (5) James Madison was the fourth President of the United States.

Items 14 to 16 refer to the following paragraphs.

One of the many religious groups that helped to settle the New World was called the Society of Friends, or Quakers. The Quakers were led by William Penn, the son of an admiral in the English Navy. Like other groups who disagreed with the teachings of the Church of England, the Quakers wanted to take advantage of the new territory. The Quakers had special luck. King Charles II owed money to Penn's family. He paid the debt with a grant of American land claimed by England.

In 1682, William Penn and the Quakers colonized some of the rich lands of the New World, which they named Pennsylvania. They met the Native Americans who lived there, paid them for the land, and made a peace treaty that was never broken. The gentle Quakers then built their main city, Philadelphia, whose name means "City of Brotherly Love."

Unlike some of their religious neighbors, the Quakers accepted people of other faiths and nationalities and encouraged them to settle on Quaker land. Catholics, Jews, and blacks answered the invitations and were offered inexpensive land and a say in the colony's government.

14. In 1682, the Quakers established the colony of

   (1) Massachusetts
   (2) Rhode Island
   (3) Pennsylvania
   (4) Virginia
   (5) North Carolina

15. Which of the following was a cause of the Quakers coming to America?

   (1) William Penn founded Pennsylvania.
   (2) The Quakers had a treaty with the Native Americans.
   (3) The Quakers wanted to practice their religion.
   (4) The Quakers wanted to get rich.
   (5) King Charles owed a debt to Penn.

16. One opinion expressed about this group of colonists is that they were

    (1) Quakers
    (2) religious
    (3) Friends
    (4) gentle
    (5) from England

Items 17 to 20 refer to the following information.

Conformity is people's tendency to adjust their thinking or behavior to that of a group. Conformity can be a positive force, as when people line up to wait their turn to board a bus. Sometimes it is a negative force, as when a "nice" child joins a group that is bullying another child.

17. Which of the following is not an example of conformity?

    (1) wearing the latest fashion fad
    (2) clapping at the end of a rock concert
    (3) drinking alcohol at a party
    (4) getting your hair cut when you join the armed forces
    (5) arguing for an opinion when others disagree with you

18. Which of the following sayings best expresses the idea of conformity?

    (1) Go along to get along.
    (2) A penny saved is a penny earned.
    (3) One rotten apple ruins the barrel.
    (4) Don't count your chickens before they hatch.
    (5) It's better to be a big fish in a little pond than a little fish in a big pond.

19. Many factors make people conform. Which of the following factors would not be likely to result in conformity?

    (1) A person feels insecure.
    (2) The group is large.
    (3) The group is unanimous.
    (4) The group is not important.
    (5) People in the group are watching.

20. In experiments that tested obedience, psychologists found that many people obeyed the order to harm another person (the harm was not real, but the subjects did not know this). About two-thirds of the subjects obeyed the experimenter. These subjects probably shared a belief in

    (1) the power of good over evil
    (2) the importance of the victims
    (3) obeying authority
    (4) their own moral standards
    (5) being kind to others

Item 21 refers to the following map.

UNITED STATES SHORELINE—
PAST, PRESENT, AND FUTURE

Future

15,000
Years
Ago

Present

Source: U.S.
Geological Survey

21. Based on the information in the map, which is most likely to happen?

    (1) The average temperature of North America will become cooler.
    (2) Present-day coastal cities of the eastern United States will disappear.
    (3) The population of the United States will decrease.
    (4) The population of the United States will increase a great deal.
    (5) America's West Coast will experience severe earthquakes.

Items 22 to 25 refer to the following paragraphs.

American government divides its governing power among three branches: legislative, executive, and judicial. Each branch is separate and independent of the others.

Legislative power to make laws is held by Congress, which is made up of two parts. The Senate has two delegates from each state, and the House of Representatives has a number of delegates based on the population of each state. The Constitution gave Congress many important powers, including the power to tax, borrow money, regulate foreign and interstate trade, coin money and punish counterfeiters, establish a post office, and declare war. Congress as a whole has the right to make laws for the United States, but only the House of Representatives may initiate bills for raising money.

Executive power to enforce the laws is held by the President. The President is also commander-in-chief of the armed forces. The President can make Supreme Court appointments with Senate approval.

The Supreme Court and lower courts have judicial power to settle disputes or cases in courts of law. The Supreme Court has original jurisdiction, or first hearing, of cases involving conflicts between states or foreign diplomats. All other cases are first heard in lower courts, but may go to the Supreme Court on appeal.

22. Based on the information in the paragraphs, which statement about Congress is not logically sound?

   (1) Congress is given the power to make laws.
   (2) Congress has been given too many powers.
   (3) The Senate cannot initiate fund-raising bills.
   (4) All states have the same number of senators.
   (5) The number of representatives is probably different from the number of senators.

23. Based on the paragraphs, which is not true about the President?

   (1) The President holds executive power.
   (2) The President, as commander-in-chief, can make decisions about the military.
   (3) The President can enforce laws because the President is the commander-in-chief.
   (4) The President can select a judge for the Supreme Court.
   (5) The President is the head of the executive branch.

24. Which of the following is not true about the presidency?

   (1) The President is the head of the executive branch of government.
   (2) The President is the commander-in-chief of the military.
   (3) The power of the President is limited by the Constitution.
   (4) A woman cannot be President.
   (5) The office of the presidency gives its holder a great deal of power.

25. Which of the following statements is supported by facts in the paragraphs?

   (1) There is a division of power among the legislative, executive, and judicial branches.
   (2) Of the three branches, the executive branch has the most power.
   (3) Foreign policy is exclusively the responsibility of the President.
   (4) Justices of the Supreme Court are elected every four years.
   (5) Congress can settle disputes between states or foreign diplomats.

Items 26 to 29 refer to the following paragraphs.

Throughout history, people from many countries colonized and settled new areas. There were several important reasons, or motives, for colonization and settlement. Five different motives are listed below.

1. economic—to gain wealth from the new area, either from its natural resources or through trade
2. religious—to practice one's religion freely or to spread one's own religion to other people
3. political—to make one's own country more powerful by gaining more land
4. scientific—to learn more about the world by exploring
5. social—to get away from one society's problems and to set up a better society

People from Spain, Portugal, England, France, and Holland colonized and settled the Americas. People from each country made the long trip for many different reasons.

Each of the following statements is an example of one of the reasons. Choose the reason for which each situation is an example.

26. Spain sent many priests to the Americas to convert Native Americans to Catholicism. In this case, Spain's motive was

    (1) economic
    (2) religious
    (3) political
    (4) scientific
    (5) social

27. Spanish explorers and settlers found and mined gold in the Americas. This gold was sent to Spain. In this case, Spain's motive was

    (1) economic
    (2) religious
    (3) political
    (4) scientific
    (5) social

28. Puritans and Quakers were often persecuted in England. Many members of these groups settled in America so they could worship freely. The motive of these English settlers was

    (1) economic
    (2) religious
    (3) political
    (4) scientific
    (5) social

29. In 1607, a group of London merchants sent an expedition team to the Americas to find gold and other resources. The motive of the group, which settled in Virginia, was

    (1) economic
    (2) religious
    (3) political
    (4) scientific
    (5) social

Item 30 refers to the following paragraph.

Psychologists and folklorists who have studied joking behavior have come to the conclusion that jokes often serve as a way to criticize something the joker does not agree with.

30. People who tell political jokes probably

   (1) are firm believers in the political system
   (2) believe that politicians are inefficient
   (3) agree with all politicians
   (4) are folklorists
   (5) study joking behavior

Item 31 refers to the following paragraph.

About 5.6 million American children under 15 years of age live in homes without a father. Only one-third of those children receive financial support from their fathers. According to one child advocacy group, only 23 percent of the child support due in 1987 was actually paid. In 1994, a law went into effect to correct this problem. Payments will automatically be taken out of the paycheck of the parent who is ordered to pay child support.

31. What is the most likely effect of the law?

   (1) There will be more divorces.
   (2) More women will go to work.
   (3) More men will gain custody of their children.
   (4) Fewer children not living with their fathers will live in poverty.
   (5) The law will be repealed because fathers will be unable to afford the child support payments.

Item 32 refers to the following information and map.

As Americans continue to move west, the population center of the United States has also moved steadily west. When the first census was taken in 1790, the population center was near Baltimore, Maryland. Today the population center is southwest of St. Louis, Missouri.

U.S. Population Shift, 1790–1990

32. Which of the following statements is supported by the information and map?

   (1) The population center of the United States has moved steadily east.
   (2) Most people lived in Baltimore, Maryland, in 1790.
   (3) The geographical center of the United States is near St. Louis, Missouri.
   (4) Many people who retire move to Florida.
   (5) Since about 1950, the population center has moved to the south and west.

Answers are on page 736.

Entry Test ◆ Social Studies

Entry Test Correlation Chart: Social Studies

Name: _____ **Class:** _____ **Date:** _____

This chart can help you determine your strengths and weaknesses in the content and skill areas of the Social Studies GED Test. Use the Answer Key on pages 736–738 to check your answers to the test. Then circle on the chart the numbers of the test items you answered correctly. Put the total number correct for each content area and skill area in each row and column. Look at the total items correct in each column and row and decide which areas are difficult for you. Use the page references to study those areas.

Cognitive Skills/Content	Comprehension (pp.198–203)	Analysis (pp. 209–212)	Application (pp. 204–206)	Evaluation (pp. 216–219)	Total Correct
Geography (pages 240–251)	1	2, 21	3	32	____ out of 5
History (pages 252–271)	14	4, 5, 15, 16	26, 27, 28, 29		____ out of 9
Economics (pages 272–283)	7, 9, 11	6	8, 10		____ out of 6
Political Science (pages 284–297)	13	12		22, 23, 24, 25	____ out of 6
Behavioral Science (pages 298–311)	18	19, 31	17	20, 30	____ out of 6
Total Correct	____ out of 7	____ out of 10	____ out of 8	____ out of 7	Total correct: ___ out of 32

> 1–25 → You need more review.
> 26–32 → Congratulations! You're ready for the GED Test!

Boldfaced numbers indicate items based on charts, graphs, illustrations, and diagrams.

For additional help, see the Steck-Vaughn GED Social Studies Exercise Book.

SCIENCE ENTRY TEST

Directions

The Science Entry Test consists of multiple-choice questions intended to measure your understanding of general concepts in science. The questions are based on short readings that often include a graph, chart, or diagram. Study the information given, and then answer the questions that follow. Refer to the information as often as necessary in answering the questions.

You should spend no more than 45 minutes answering the 33 questions on the Science Entry Test. Work carefully, but do not spend too much time on any one question. Do not skip any items. Make a reasonable guess when you are not sure of an answer. You will not be penalized for incorrect answers.

When time is up, mark the last item you finished. This will tell you whether you can finish the real GED Test in the time allowed. Then complete the test.

Record your answers to the questions on a copy of the answer sheet on page 922. Be sure that all required information is properly recorded on the answer sheet.

To record your answers, mark the numbered space on the answer sheet that corresponds to the answer you choose for each question on the test.

Example:

Which of the following is the smallest unit in a living thing?

(1) tissue
(2) organ
(3) cell
(4) muscle
(5) capillary

The correct answer is "cell"; therefore, answer space 3 should be marked on the answer sheet.

Do not rest the point of your pencil on the answer sheet while you are considering your answer. Make no stray or unnecessary marks. If you change an answer, erase your first mark completely. Mark only one answer space for each question; multiple answers will be scored as incorrect. Do not fold or crease your answer sheet.

When you finish the test, use the Correlation Chart on page 45 to determine whether you are ready to take the real GED Test, and, if not, which skill areas need additional review.

Adapted with permission of the American Council on Education.

Directions: Choose the <u>best answer</u> to each item.

Items 1 and 2 refer to the following information.

The human body contains many types of tissues and organs. These function as parts of various systems. Five of the systems are the following:

1. <u>Muscular system.</u> Moving skeletal and body parts such as the stomach and heart.
2. <u>Digestive system.</u> Eating, digesting, and absorbing foods; eliminating some wastes.
3. <u>Circulatory system.</u> Transporting nutrients, waste, oxygen, heat, carbon dioxide, hormones, and other substances.
4. <u>Nervous system.</u> Receiving stimuli from the environment, sending and interpreting data, controlling actions of other body parts.
5. <u>Reproductive system.</u> Producing sex cells for the continuation of the species.

1. The blood, which carries substances around the body, is part of which system?

   (1) muscular system
   (2) digestive system
   (3) circulatory system
   (4) nervous system
   (5) reproductive system

2. Which system is not vital to the survival of an individual human being?

   (1) muscular system
   (2) digestive system
   (3) circulatory system
   (4) nervous system
   (5) reproductive system

Items 3 and 4 refer to the following article.

Earth's crust is made of plates thousands of miles across and 30 or 40 miles thick. Scientists think that at one time all the continents formed a single land mass called Pangaea. Pangaea broke into huge pieces that drifted apart, forming the present continents.

Plate tectonics is the study of how plates form, move, and interact. Plates come together at three types of continually changing boundaries:

1. <u>Diverging boundaries</u> separate plates that are moving apart. These are generally located beneath the oceans. The Gulf of California is located over a diverging boundary.
2. <u>Converging boundaries,</u> located where plates are colliding, may form high mountains, deep ocean trenches, earthquakes, or volcanoes. The Himalayas are located at a converging boundary.
3. <u>Transform fault boundaries</u> occur where plates are sliding past one another. Like converging boundaries, they also cause earthquake activity. The San Andreas Fault in California is located along a transform fault boundary.

3. According to the theory of plate tectonics, what is true of Earth's continents?

   (1) The continents are stable in their present locations.
   (2) The continents ride on plates that move, causing new formations of land and water.
   (3) The separation of continents was caused by a rising ocean.
   (4) Earthquakes, volcanoes, and other dramatic geologic activity may stop someday.
   (5) Diverging boundaries usually occur on the continents.

4. What is likely to have caused the formation of the Andes Mountains along the west coast of South America, an area of earthquakes and volcanoes?

   (1) plates drifting apart
   (2) plates sliding past each other
   (3) two plates colliding
   (4) the lowering of sea level
   (5) the Ice Age

Items 5 and 6 refer to the following chart.

FOOD ADDITIVES		
Type	Examples	Possible Effects
Preservatives	Salt Vinegar Sugar Nitrates	High blood pressure Irritation of the stomach Tooth decay, obesity Cancer

Colorings and
flavorings
	Chlorophyll,
	Carotene
	
	Synthetic
	chemicals
	Monosodium
	glutamate
		Food may appear
		  more nutritional
		  than it actually is.
		Cancer
		
		Allergic reactions

Texturizers	Pectin Gelatin Glycerol monostearate	Unknown

Supplementary
vitamins and
minerals
	Iron
	Vitamins A,
	  B complex,
	  C, D, etc.
	Iodide
		Both deficiencies
		and excesses of
		minerals and
		vitamins can cause
		disease.

5. An example of a food that contains preservatives is

  (1) enriched flour
  (2) homogenized milk
  (3) pickles
  (4) monosodium glutamate
  (5) iodized salt

6. Why are food additives so important?

  A. They enable food to be transported long distances and to be stored for long periods of time without spoiling.
  B. They provide important minerals and vitamins.
  C. Most food additives cause disease.

  (1) A only
  (2) B only
  (3) C only
  (4) A and B
  (5) B and C

Items 7 and 8 refer to the following article.

If you drop a bar magnet into a pile of iron filings, the filings will stick to the magnet. Iron and steel and a few other metals are attracted to magnets. The force of attraction is called magnetic force. The area around a magnet where the magnetic force acts is called a magnetic field. The field is strongest at the poles, or ends, of the magnet.

Each magnet has a north and a south pole. If you hang a magnet from a string, its north pole will turn to the north. This is because Earth has a magnetic field. The magnetic north pole of Earth is located near the geographic north pole. A compass used for navigation points to the magnetic north pole and not to the geographic north pole.

Many substances that are attracted to a magnet can be magnetized, or made into a magnet. Inside these substances, groups of atoms act as tiny magnets. These groups, called magnetic domains, are usually found with their north and south poles pointing in different directions. If they can be made to line up so that their north and south poles point in the same direction, they will cause a magnetic field. The substance will be a magnet.

7. Which of the following items would not be affected by a magnetic field?

  (1) iron filings
  (2) a rubber eraser
  (3) a magnetic compass
  (4) a horseshoe magnet
  (5) a steel girder in a building

8. The magnetic needle of a compass always points to the north because

  (1) compasses are used for finding direction
  (2) Earth has a magnetic north pole
  (3) the needle touches the north pole
  (4) the magnetic domains of the needle point in different directions
  (5) Earth's magnetic field is strongest at the south pole

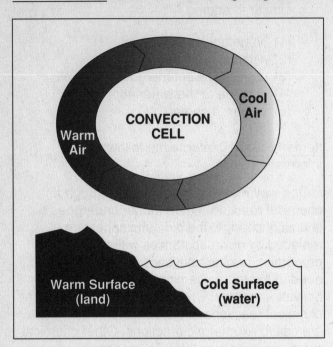

Jellyfish are invertebrate animals that live in the sea. Some of these invertebrates have a two-stage life cycle. The free-swimming jellyfish mate and produce young called polyps. Polyps generally are unable to move from place to place.

The body of a jellyfish is shaped like a bell or umbrella. A clear material that looks like jelly fills the space between the top and the bottom of the bell. The jellyfish's mouth is located in the middle of the bottom surface of the bell. Tentacles grow around the edge of the bell. Jellyfish move up in the water by contracting and relaxing muscles around the edge of the bell. They drift down and depend on ocean currents and waves to move sideways.

Jellyfish usually catch their prey by using stinging cells located on the tentacles. The sting of some jellyfish can be irritating or even dangerous to humans. The sea wasp, for example, is a well-known stinger. It has a tall, rigid bell and four two-part tentacles. It lives in tropical oceans but sometimes strays as far north as Long Island Sound. The Australian variety of the sea wasp is dangerous to humans. A sting from the Australian sea wasp can be fatal.

9. The convection cell in the diagram is an area of the atmosphere in which air movement is caused by variations in temperature. Which of the following conclusions is best supported by the diagram?

    (1) Warm air rises and cool air sinks.
    (2) Warm air sinks and cool air rises.
    (3) Warm air pushes cold air upward.
    (4) The temperature of Earth's surface has no effect on air movement.
    (5) Convection cells occur only where land meets water.

10. According to the diagram, in which direction should you face to keep the wind out of your eyes at this particular beach and at this time?

    (1) Face the water.
    (2) Face inland.
    (3) Have your left side to the water.
    (4) Have your right side to the water.
    (5) Face in any direction.

11. When a jellyfish captures food, it swims up and then drifts down onto its prey. When does a jellyfish use its muscles during this process?

    (1) when moving up
    (2) when drifting down
    (3) when drifting sideways
    (4) when drifting up
    (5) when swimming down

12. Which of the following statements is supported by the information provided?

    (1) Jellyfish stings are usually fatal to humans.
    (2) Jellyfish are closely related to mussels and clams.
    (3) Jellyfish are concentrated in tropical oceans.
    (4) Jellyfish reproduce sexually.
    (5) Polyps look like jellyfish.

Items 13 and 14 refer to the following article.

In order to be healthy, plants must take in certain minerals from the soil. These minerals contain the chemical elements that plants need to grow. Nitrogen is used for leaf and stem growth. Phosphorus helps strengthen roots and stems. Potassium helps prevent disease. Other elements are also needed but to a lesser extent. As plants grow, they use up the minerals in the soil. When plants are harvested, these chemicals are not returned to the soil. For this reason, fertilizers are added to the soil to restore its ability to support growing plants.

Artificial fertilizers consist of mined or manufactured minerals that contain the missing chemicals. These are mixed in different proportions. When the composition of the soil is analyzed, it is easy to see which chemical is missing and to select the proper mix. Fertilizer labels show the percentages of the three major ingredients. For example, 8-12-6 means that the fertilizer contains 8 percent nitrogen, 12 percent phosphorus, and 6 percent potassium. Artificial fertilizers contain these elements in compounds that are easy for plants to absorb.

Some people prefer to use organic or living matter, such as compost or manure, as fertilizer to replace the missing chemicals. These natural fertilizers contain minerals in complex compounds. Plants cannot absorb these compounds until they have been broken down by the decay process. In addition, the exact mineral content of the organic matter cannot be controlled.

13. On what basis could a farmer who uses organic fertilizers claim that it is better to buy these vegetables than vegetables grown using artificial fertilizers?

    (1) Organically grown vegetables use organic forms of minerals.
    (2) Organically grown vegetables use simple forms of minerals.
    (3) Organic fertilizers act on the soil in a manner more similar to nature than do chemical fertilizers.
    (4) Organic fertilizers can be more easily adjusted to achieve the correct balance of minerals than chemical fertilizers.
    (5) Organic fertilizers contain pesticides.

14. The addition of fertilizer to the soil is most similar to adding

    (1) vegetables to your diet
    (2) vitamin A to skim milk
    (3) artificial sweetener to a soft drink
    (4) fluoride to the water supply
    (5) sugar to cereal

Items 15 and 16 refer to the following information.

One way matter can change is through a chemical reaction. When matter undergoes a chemical change, the old substances are replaced by new substances with new properties, or characteristics. The energy needed to start a chemical reaction is called activation energy. Once they have started, some chemical reactions release heat energy. These are called exothermic reactions. Other chemical reactions absorb energy. These are called endothermic reactions.

15. Lighter fluid is poured on charcoal in a barbecue grill, and a match is used to light the coals. In this chemical reaction, the lit match is

    (1) a property of the reaction
    (2) an endothermic reaction
    (3) a physical change
    (4) the resulting form of matter
    (5) the source of activation energy

16. What is an endothermic reaction?

    (1) a chemical reaction in which the properties of matter change
    (2) a chemical reaction in which heat energy is released
    (3) a chemical reaction in which heat energy is absorbed
    (4) the application of energy to start a reaction
    (5) a reaction that does not need activation energy to start

Items 17 and 18 refer to the following information.

The density of a substance is its mass per unit of volume. The density of a gas is expressed in grams per liter.

DENSITY OF GASES	
Gas	Density (grams per liter)
Air	1.29
Hydrogen	0.09
Nitrogen	1.25
Oxygen	1.43
Carbon dioxide	1.98
Sulfur dioxide	2.93

17. The specific gravity of a gas is the ratio of its density to the density of air. For example, the specific gravity of oxygen is expressed as:

$$\frac{1.43}{1.29} = 1.11$$

This means that oxygen is 1.11 times as dense as air. Which of the following gases has the highest specific gravity?

(1) hydrogen
(2) nitrogen
(3) oxygen
(4) carbon dioxide
(5) sulfur dioxide

18. Nitrogen makes up almost 80 percent of the air. Which of the following is a result of this fact?

(1) The densities of air and nitrogen are similar.
(2) Nitrogen is more dense than air.
(3) Nitrogen is more dense than hydrogen.
(4) Sulfur dioxide is less dense than nitrogen.
(5) Nitrogen is more dense than carbon dioxide.

Items 19 and 20 refer to the following article.

Tumors grow from our own cells. Some tumors are malignant—cancers that are likely to cause death if untreated. Cancer cells are harmful because they grow abnormally and rapidly. They use up nutrients and starve normal cells. Malignant tumors can grow large, causing pressure that interferes with circulation. As the cancer grows, it may spread throughout the body.

What causes cancer? A variety of chemical and physical agents can start cancer. These include chemicals in plastics, cigarette smoke, and asbestos. Radiation can also cause cancer. Certain viruses have been shown to cause cancer in animals. Some researchers think that cancer cells may form but stay inactive for a while. Cancer cells become active only if the body's immune system—which defends against disease—breaks down. Some recognized cancer-causing agents are known to suppress the immune system. People who have had organ transplants take drugs that suppress the immune system, and they show a higher number of cancers.

19. What are malignant tumors?

(1) cancerous growths that may cause death if untreated
(2) cancerous growths that are suppressed by the immune system
(3) harmless growths that can be removed surgically
(4) harmless growths that are a side effect of organ transplants
(5) the major cause of cancer

20. Which of the following practices would be most likely to cause cancer?

(1) eating a vegetarian diet
(2) not exercising
(3) avoiding foods with chemical additives
(4) being exposed to a high level of radiation
(5) drinking water from a remote mountain stream

Items 21 and 22 are based on the following information.

The temperature at which a liquid begins to boil is called the boiling point. At the boiling point, the vapor pressure in the liquid is equal to the pressure of the atmosphere. At higher elevations, the pressure of the atmosphere decreases, and the boiling point is lowered. No matter how much more heat is applied, a liquid never gets hotter than its boiling point. It simply boils until there is no liquid left.

BOILING POINTS OF SOME LIQUIDS	
Liquid	Boiling Point at Sea Level (°C)
Chloroform ($CHCl_3$)	61.7
Ethanol (C_2H_5OH)	78.5
Water (H_2O)	100.0
Octane (C_8H_{18})	126.0

21. In New York City, which has an elevation of 0 meters, water boils at 100°C. In Denver, Colorado, at an elevation of 1,609 meters, water probably boils at

    (1) 126°C
    (2) 100°C
    (3) 95°C
    (4) 0°C
    (5) −5°C

22. Which of the following conclusions can be supported by the information provided?

    (1) Once a liquid reaches its boiling point, its temperature increases until all the liquid evaporates.
    (2) Water has a higher boiling point than octane.
    (3) Adding salt to water raises its boiling point.
    (4) The boiling point of a liquid increases as the air pressure increases.
    (5) Chloroform is used as an anesthetic because its boiling point is lower than that of water.

Items 23 to 25 refer to the following article.

Solar energy is energy from the sun. Unlike fossil fuels such as oil and coal, solar energy is a renewable resource. Fossil fuels will someday be used up. Solar energy does not produce smoke or ash and is a clean source of energy. Fossil fuels often produce smoke or ash.

One way to gather solar energy for use in a building is through a solar collector. A solar collector looks like a box with a glass or plastic top. Inside the box are tubes filled with water. The sun heats the water in the tubes, and the heated water is pumped into a storage tank. From there the hot water is piped through the building.

Another way to gather solar energy is to build houses that act as solar collectors. Sunlight comes in through the windows that face the sun. Materials inside the house absorb and release the heat. To make sure that enough heat is stored during sunny days to warm the house on cloudy days and at night, a dense material, such as stone, cement, or brick, is used to collect the energy. The dense material is called a storage mass. At night and on sunless days, the storage mass continues to release energy into the air around it.

To convert a building so that it can use solar heat may require the redesign of windows, the creation of storage masses, and the addition of collectors to the roof or surrounding areas.

23. How does a storage mass provide heat to areas of the house that are not near it?

    (1) Heated air is piped into radiators throughout the house.
    (2) Heated water is piped into radiators throughout the house.
    (3) Steam is piped into radiators throughout the house.
    (4) Heated air near the storage mass creates air currents that circulate warm air throughout the house.
    (5) The storage mass generates electricity, which is used to heat the house.

24. What is the major reason that solar heating of homes is not widespread?

    (1) Solar heating always requires large windows.
    (2) Solar heating always requires a storage mass.
    (3) Most houses do not receive direct sunlight.
    (4) It is often difficult and expensive to convert existing houses to solar energy.
    (5) Solar heating pollutes the environment.

25. The purpose of a storage mass is to

    (1) serve as the foundation of the house
    (2) provide a decorative surface for the southern wall
    (3) heat water
    (4) store cement, stone, and brick
    (5) store reserves of energy to be used on cloudy days and at night

Items 26 to 29 refer to the following article.

Ants are social insects. This means that they live in a group called a colony and that each ant has a job to do to help the whole group survive. Ants must live in a colony; an ant cannot survive alone.

You will find three kinds of ants in a typical colony:

1. There is one queen, who lays eggs.
2. There are winged males. The males develop from unfertilized eggs. Their role is to mate with the queen, after which they die.
3. There are workers. Most of the ants in a colony are worker ants. They are females who cannot lay eggs. Instead, they find food and sometimes fight to help the colony.

Ants are usually helpful to humans. Their underground tunneling mixes and enriches the soil. In some places ants turn more earth than earthworms. Ants spread plant seeds and feed on dead insects and other animals. Many ant species eat insects that are crop pests.

One species, the leaf-cutting ant, harms farmers' crops in Texas and Louisiana. Large leaf-cutting worker ants carry big pieces of leaves to the ant colony. There the smaller workers chop the leaves into tiny bits. The smallest worker ants transplant small pieces of fungus to the bits of leaves. The fungus then grows on the leaves, and the ants use the fungus for food.

26. All of the following activities performed by ants are helpful to humans except

    (1) enriching the soil
    (2) feeding on dead insects
    (3) cutting leaves
    (4) eating crop pests
    (5) spreading plant seeds

27. A sociobiologist studies the way living creatures behave with one another in a group. What would a sociobiologist most likely study about ants?

    (1) the diet of the ant
    (2) the anatomy of the ant
    (3) the location of the colony
    (4) the roles of the queen, winged males, and workers
    (5) the enrichment of the soil

28. Which of the following human behaviors is most similar to the behavior of the leaf-cutting worker ants?

    (1) following a political system with a king and queen
    (2) performing tasks one after another on an assembly line
    (3) raising crops
    (4) raising livestock
    (5) maintaining an army

29. The role of the queen ant is to produce eggs so that the colony continues. What is the most important contribution other ants make to the life of the colony?

    (1) enriching the soil
    (2) feeding other members of the colony
    (3) cutting leaves
    (4) spreading plant seeds near the colony
    (5) eating crop pests

Items 30 and 31 refer to the following information.

Matter is anything that has mass and takes up space. Matter is found in three different states—solid, liquid, and gas.

1. A solid such as iron has a definite shape and takes up a definite amount of space.
2. A liquid such as milk does not have a definite shape since it can be poured. It takes up a definite amount of space.
3. A gas such as air has no definite shape and does not take up a definite amount of space. It expands to fill whatever space is available.

Most matter can exist in any one of the three states and can change from one state to another through changes in temperature.

30. Which of the following is an example of a single form of matter in three different states?

(1) lump of sugar, grains of sugar, sugar syrup
(2) rock salt, salt crystals, salt water
(3) ice, water, water vapor
(4) glass, broken glass, molten glass
(5) dry ice, carbon dioxide, carbonated beverage with carbon-dioxide bubbles

31. What causes a form of matter to change from one state to another?

(1) changes in chemical makeup
(2) changes in position
(3) changes in color
(4) changes in amount of heat
(5) changes in hardness

Items 32 and 33 refer to the following diagram.

BUOYANCY

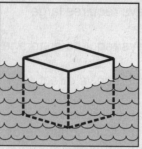 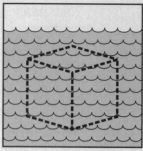

Weight of object = weight of displaced liquid (liquid pushed aside)

Weight of object is greater than weight of displaced liquid

32. An object will float if

(1) it displaces or pushes aside liquid
(2) its weight equals the weight of the liquid it displaces
(3) its weight is greater than the weight of the liquid it displaces
(4) its weight equals the weight of the liquid in which it is placed
(5) its weight is greater than the weight of the liquid in which it is placed

33. A solid steel cube will sink when placed in water, but a steel ship will float. Which of the following is the best explanation of why a steel ship will float?

(1) Steel is heavier than the water it displaces.
(2) Steel is lighter than the water it displaces.
(3) Steel and air are heavier than the water they displace.
(4) Steel and air are equal in weight to the water they displace.
(5) Steel and air are lighter than the water they displace.

Answers are on page 738.

Entry Test ◆ Science

Entry Test Correlation Chart: Science

Name: _____ **Class:** _____ **Date:** _____

This chart can help you determine your strengths and weaknesses on the content and reading skill areas of the Science GED Test. Use the Answer Key on pages 738–741 to check your answers to the test. Then circle on the chart the numbers of the test items you answered correctly. Put the total number correct for each content area and skill area in each row and column. Look at the total items correct in each column and row and decide which areas are difficult for you. Use the page references to study those areas.

Cognitive Skills/Content	Comprehension	Application	Analysis	Evaluation	Total Correct
Biology (*pages 320–339*)	19, 26	1, **5**, 14	2, **6**, 11, 20	12, 13, 27, 28, 29	____ out of 14
Earth Science (*pages 340–357*)	3, 25	**10**	4, 23	9, 24	____ out of 7
Chemistry (*pages 358–373*)	16	15, **21**, 30	**17, 18**, 31	**22**	____ out of 8
Physics (*pages 374–387*)	**32**	7	8	**33**	____ out of 4
					Total correct:
Total Correct	____ out of 6	____ out of 8	____ out of 10	____ out of 9	____ out of 33

1–27 → You need more review.
28–33 → Congratulations!
You're ready for the GED Test!

Boldfaced numbers indicate items based on charts, graphs, illustrations, and diagrams.

For additional help, see the Steck-Vaughn GED Science Exercise Book.

LITERATURE & THE ARTS ENTRY TEST

Directions

The Literature & the Arts Entry Test consists of excerpts from classical and popular literature and articles about literature or the arts. Each excerpt is followed by multiple-choice questions about the reading material.

Read each excerpt first and then answer the questions that follow. Refer to the reading material as often as necessary in answering the questions.

Each excerpt is preceded by a "purpose question." The purpose question gives a reason for reading the material. Use these purpose questions to help focus your reading. You are not required to answer these purpose questions. They are given only to help you concentrate on the ideas presented in the reading material.

You should spend no more than 35 minutes answering the 23 questions on this test. Work carefully, but do not spend too much time on any one question. Do not skip any items. Make a reasonable guess when you are not sure of an answer. You will not be penalized for incorrect answers. When time is up, mark the last item you finished. This will tell you whether you can finish the real GED Test in the time allowed. Then complete the test.

Record your answers to the questions on a copy of the answer sheet on page 922. Be sure that all required information is properly recorded on the answer sheet.

To record your answers, mark the numbered space on the answer sheet that corresponds to the answer you choose for each question on the test.

Example:

It was Susan's dream machine. The metallic blue paint gleamed, and the sporty wheels were highly polished. Under the hood, the engine was no less carefully cleaned. Inside, flashy lights illuminated the instruments on the dashboard, and the seats were covered by rich leather upholstery.

The subject ("It") of this excerpt is most likely

(1) an airplane
(2) a stereo system
(3) an automobile
(4) a boat
(5) a motorcycle

The correct answer is "an automobile"; therefore, answer space 3 would be marked on the answer sheet.

Do not rest the point of your pencil on the answer sheet while you are considering your answer. Make no stray or unnecessary marks. If you change an answer, erase your first mark completely. Mark only one answer space for each question; multiple answers will be scored as incorrect. Do not fold or crease your answer sheet.

When you finish the test, use the Correlation Chart on page 55 to determine whether you are ready to take the real GED Test, and, if not, which skill areas need additional review.

Adapted with permission of the American Council on Education.

Directions: Choose the <u>best answer</u> to each item. Items 1 to 3 refer to the following excerpt from a story.

WHY IS THIS BOY IN TROUBLE?

(5)

(10)

(15)

(20)

(25)

(30)

(35)

(40)

(45)

She was a large woman with a large purse that had everything in it but a hammer and nails. It had a long strap, and she carried it slung across her shoulder. It was about eleven o'clock at night, dark, and she was walking alone, when a boy ran up behind her and tried to snatch her purse. The strap broke with the sudden single tug the boy gave it from behind. But the boy's weight and the weight of the purse combined caused him to lose his balance. Instead of taking off full blast as he had hoped, the boy fell on his back on the sidewalk and his legs flew up. The large woman simply turned around and kicked him right square in his blue-jeaned sitter. Then she reached down, picked the boy up by his shirt front, and shook him until his teeth rattled.

After that the woman said, "Pick up my pocketbook, boy, and give it here."

She still held him tightly. But she bent down enough to permit him to stoop and pick up her purse. Then she said, "Now ain't you ashamed of yourself?"

Firmly gripped by his shirt front, the boy said, "Yes'm."

The woman said, "What did you want to do it for?"

The boy said, "I didn't aim to."

She said, "You a lie!"

By that time two or three people passed, stopped, turned to look, and some stood watching.

"If I turn you loose, will you run?" asked the woman.

"Yes'm," said the boy.

"Then I won't turn you loose," said the woman. She did not release him.

"Lady, I'm sorry," whispered the boy.

"Um-hum! Your face is dirty. I got a great mind to wash your face for you. Ain't you got nobody home to tell you to wash your face?"

"No'm," said the boy.

"Then it will get washed this evening," said the large woman, starting up the street, dragging the frightened boy behind her.

Langston Hughes, "Thank You, M'am," *The Collected Stories of Langston Hughes.*

1. How did the boy and the woman meet?

(1) The boy was trying to help the woman carry her heavy purse.
(2) The woman was the boy's teacher.
(3) The boy stole a purse the woman was carrying.
(4) The woman and the boy were neighbors.
(5) The boy tried to take something that belonged to the woman.

2. Which of the following best describes the woman's first reaction upon encountering the boy?

(1) She dragged him off behind her.
(2) She called him a liar.
(3) She kicked him in the seat of his pants.
(4) She ran after him in an attempt to retrieve her purse.
(5) She called the police.

3. Based upon the information in the excerpt, which of the following is the woman most likely to do to the boy?

(1) take the boy to his house and speak to his parents
(2) take the boy to her house to wash his face
(3) take the boy to the police station
(4) give the boy money and send him away
(5) let the boy go

Items 4 to 8 refer to the following excerpt from a play.

HOW DOES ALMA MAKE THESE PEOPLE REVEAL THEMSELVES?

MRS. BUCHANAN: You mustn't misunderstand me about Miss Alma. Naturally I feel sorry for her, too. But, precious, precious! In every Southern
(5) town there's a girl or two like that. People feel sorry for them, they're kind to them, but, darling, they keep at a distance, they don't get involved with them. Especially not in a sentimental
(10) way.

JOHN: I don't know what you mean about Miss Alma. She's a little bit—quaint, she's very excitable, but—there's nothing *wrong* with her.

(15) MRS. BUCHANAN: Precious, can't you see. Miss Alma is an *eccentric!*

JOHN: You mean she isn't like all the other girls in Glorious Hill?

MRS. BUCHANAN: There's always at least
(20) one like her in every Southern town, sometimes, like Miss Alma, rather sweet, sometimes even gifted, and I think Miss Alma *does* have a rather appealing voice when she doesn't
(25) become too carried away by her singing. Sometimes, but not often, pretty. I have seen Miss Alma when she was almost pretty. But never, never *quite*.

(30) JOHN: There are moments when she has beauty.

MRS. BUCHANAN: Those moments haven't occurred when *I* looked at her! Such a wide mouth she has, like the mouth of a
(35) clown! And she distorts her face with all those false expressions. However, Miss Alma's looks are beside the point.

JOHN: Her, her eyes are fascinating!

MRS. BUCHANAN: Goodness, yes,
(40) disturbing!

Tennessee Williams, *The Eccentricities of a Nightingale*.

4. When Mrs. Buchanan sees Alma, she will probably

(1) ignore her
(2) invite her to dinner
(3) speak politely but distantly
(4) try to gain her friendship
(5) laugh at her

5. When John sees Alma, he will probably

(1) ask her to marry him
(2) talk with her in a friendly way
(3) tell her that he cannot see her again
(4) tell her what Mrs. Buchanan has been saying about her
(5) realize that Mrs. Buchanan is right

6. The words that the author italicizes serve to emphasize

(1) Mrs. Buchanan's negative opinion of Alma
(2) Mrs. Buchanan's fear that John will continue to like Alma
(3) Mrs. Buchanan's anger at John
(4) John's negative opinion of Mrs. Buchanan
(5) John's fear of losing Alma

7. Mrs. Buchanan's own husband is most likely to be

(1) eccentric
(2) sentimental
(3) beautiful
(4) conforming
(5) stubborn

8. Mrs. Buchanan says the things she does because she

(1) admires beauty
(2) feels sorry for Alma
(3) likes talking about Alma
(4) is sentimental and indulges John
(5) is critical and a snob

Items 9 and 10 refer to the following poem.

WHAT MADE THIS POET SO HAPPY?

I WANDERED LONELY AS A CLOUD

I wandered lonely as a cloud
That floats on high o'er vales and hills,
When all at once I saw a crowd,
A host, of golden daffodils;
(5) Beside the lake, beneath the trees,
Fluttering and dancing in the breeze.

Continuous as the stars that shine
And twinkle on the milky way,
They stretched in never-ending line
(10) Along the margin of a bay:
Ten thousand saw I at a glance,
Tossing their heads in sprightly dance.

The waves beside them danced; but they
Outdid the sparkling waves in glee;
(15) A poet could not but be gay,
In such a jocund company;
I gazed—and gazed—but little thought
What wealth the show to me had brought:

For oft, when on my couch I lie
(20) In vacant or in pensive mood,
They flash upon that inward eye
Which is the bliss of solitude;
And then my heart with pleasure fills,
And dances with the daffodils.

William Wordsworth, "I Wandered Lonely As a Cloud."

9. Which of the following sentences best restates the main idea of the poem?

(1) Unexpected sights can produce endless pleasure.
(2) Daffodils grow by the water.
(3) The water makes flowers pale in comparison.
(4) Certain images are easily forgotten.
(5) Poets spend most of their lives wandering.

10. Which of the following is the best restatement of "They flash upon that inward eye / Which is the bliss of solitude" (lines 21–22)?

(1) The author looks inward to his soul.
(2) The daffodils remind the author of lightning flashes.
(3) When he is alone, the author uses his imagination to replay the sight of the flowers.
(4) The author prefers to be alone.
(5) Having left the flowers, the author cannot picture them in his mind.

Items 11 to 16 refer to the following excerpt from a review.

WHAT DID THESE MEN TAKE TO WAR?

Only a handful of novels and short stories have managed to clarify, in any lasting way, the meaning of the war in Vietnam for America and for the soldiers
(5) who served there. With *The Things They Carried,* Tim O'Brien adds his second title to the short list of essential fiction about Vietnam. As he did in his novel *Going After Cacciato* (1978), which won a National
(10) Book Award, he captures the war's pulsating rhythms and nerve-racking dangers. But he goes much further. By moving beyond the horror of the fighting to examine with sensitivity and insight the
(15) nature of courage and fear, by questioning the role that imagination plays in helping to form our memories and our own versions of truth, he places *The Things They Carried* high up on the list of best fiction
(20) about any war.

The Things They Carried is a collection of interrelated stories. . . .

In the title story, Mr. O'Brien juxtaposes the mundane and the deadly items that
(25) soldiers carry into battle. Can openers, pocketknives, wristwatches, mosquito repellent, chewing gum, candy, cigarettes, salt tablets, packets of Kool-Aid, matches, sewing kits, C rations are "humped" by the
(30) G.I.'s along with M-16 assault rifles, M-60 machine guns, M-79 grenade launchers. But the story is really about the other things the soldiers "carry": "grief, terror, love, longing . . . shameful memories" and,
(35) what unifies all the stories, "the common secret of cowardice." These young men, Mr. O'Brien tells us, "carried the soldier's greatest fear, which was the fear of blushing. Men killed, and died, because
(40) they were embarrassed not to."

Embarrassment, the author reveals in "On the Rainy River," is why he, or rather the fictional version of himself, went to Vietnam. He almost went to Canada
(45) instead. What stopped him, ironically, was fear. "All those eyes on me," he writes, "and I couldn't risk the embarrassment. . . .

I couldn't endure the mockery, or the disgrace, or the patriotic ridicule. . . . I was
(50) a coward. I went to the war." . . .

Mr. O'Brien strives to get beyond literal descriptions of what these men went through and what they felt. He makes sense of the unreality of the war—makes
(55) sense of why he has distorted that unreality even further in his fiction—by turning back to explore the workings of the imagination, by probing his memory of the terror and fearlessly confronting the way
(60) he has dealt with it as both soldier and fiction writer. In doing all this, he not only crystallizes the Vietnam experience for us, he exposes the nature of all war stories.

Robert R. Harris, "Too Embarrassed Not to Kill," *New York Times Book Review.*

11. The stories in the book are about

    (1) different men in the Vietnam war
    (2) one man who has many experiences in Vietnam
    (3) the author's day-to-day life in Vietnam
    (4) some men who went to Vietnam, some who went to Canada
    (5) men who were too embarrassed to be good soldiers

12. From the excerpt you can infer that the author of the book

    (1) went to Vietnam but did not enjoy being there
    (2) wishes he had gone to Vietnam
    (3) hopes his book will be used to train future soldiers
    (4) wrote this book while he was in Vietnam
    (5) did not make many friends while he was in Vietnam

13. The reviewer mentions two stories in detail in order to

    (1) show off his knowledge of the war
    (2) explain how the stories in the book are alike and different
    (3) give examples of the characters in the book
    (4) relate these stories to the reviewer's own experience
    (5) tell why the author did not like the war

14. The reviewer thinks that *The Things They Carried* is better than most books about war because it

    (1) describes the day-to-day routines of men in war
    (2) is a collection of short stories
    (3) is about the soldiers' feelings
    (4) is not about just one person
    (5) is written by an author with a good imagination

15. How does the reviewer feel about the author's previous novel, *Going After Cacciato?*

    (1) The reviewer thinks it was better than *The Things They Carried*.
    (2) The reviewer thinks it did not go far enough.
    (3) The reviewer thinks the two books should be read together.
    (4) The reviewer despises it.
    (5) The reviewer admires it.

16. The reviewer thinks that this book will help readers understand

    (1) the author's life
    (2) the war experience
    (3) certain battles in Vietnam
    (4) how to write a book
    (5) how to understand interrelated stories

WHY DID MICHAEL FUREY DIE?

Her hand was warm and moist: it did not respond to his touch, but he continued to caress it just as he had caressed her first letter to him that spring morning.

(5)   —It was in the winter, she said, about the beginning of the winter when I was going to leave my grandmother's and come up here to the convent. And he was ill at the time in his lodgings in Galway and

(10)   wouldn't be let out, and his people in Oughterard were written to. He was in decline, they said, or something like that. I never knew rightly.

She paused for a moment and sighed.

(15)   —Poor fellow, she said. He was very fond of me and he was such a gentle boy. We used to go out together, walking, you know, Gabriel, like the way they do in the country. He was going to study singing

(20)   only for his health. He had a very good voice, poor Michael Furey.

—Well; and then? asked Gabriel.

—And then when it came to the time for me to leave Galway and come up to the

(25)   convent he was much worse and I wouldn't be let see him, so I wrote a letter saying I was going up to Dublin and would be back in the summer and hoping he would be better then.

(30)   She paused for a moment to get her voice under control and then went on:

—Then the night before I left I was in my grandmother's house in Nun's Island, packing up, and heard gravel thrown up

(35)   against the window. The window was so wet I couldn't see so I ran downstairs as I was and there was the poor fellow at the end of the garden, shivering.

—And did you not tell him to go back?

(40)   asked Gabriel.

—I implored of him to go home at once and told him he would get his death in the rain. But he said he did not want to live. I can see his eyes as well as well! He was

(45)   standing at the end of the wall where there was a tree.

—And did he go home? asked Gabriel.

—Yes, he went home. And when I was only a week in the convent he died and he

(50)   was buried at Oughterard where his people came from. O, the day that I heard that, that he was dead!

She stopped, choking with sobs, and, overcome by emotion, flung herself face

(55)   downward on the bed, sobbing in the quilt. Gabriel held her hand for a moment longer, irresolutely, and then, shy of intruding on her grief, let it fall gently and walked to the window.

James Joyce, "The Dead," *Dubliners.*

17. What is the effect of the last two sentences?

   (1) They show that these people will never get along.
   (2) They contrast the stormy feelings of the woman with the quiet feelings of the man.
   (3) They emphasize the tragedy of Michael Furey's death.
   (4) They hint that the woman is not really grieving over Michael Furey.
   (5) They hint that the woman might kill herself over Michael Furey.

18. From the excerpt you can infer that Gabriel

   (1) is in love with the woman
   (2) was a friend of Michael Furey
   (3) thinks the woman's grief over Michael Furey is silly
   (4) is glad that Michael Furey is dead
   (5) hopes that the woman will forget about Michael Furey

19. What was the woman's response to Michael Furey's last visit?

   (1) She told him she loved him.
   (2) She sent him away.
   (3) She gave up her plans to go to the convent.
   (4) She planned to run away with him.
   (5) She rejected him and went to Gabriel instead.

20. The underlying cause of Michael Furey's death was that he

   (1) had failed to become a singer
   (2) liked to go for long walks
   (3) did not want to live without love
   (4) wanted to get back at the world
   (5) suffered from a fatal disease

WHY IS THIS BIRD SINGING?

SYMPATHY

I know what the caged bird feels, alas!
  When the sun is bright on the upland slopes;
When the wind stirs soft through the springing grass,
And the river flows like a stream of glass;
(5) When the first bird sings and the first bud opes,
And the faint perfume from its chalice steals—
I know what the caged bird feels!

I know why the caged bird beats his wing
  Till its blood is red on the cruel bars;
(10) For he must fly back to his perch and cling
When he fain would be on the bough a-swing;
  And a pain still throbs in the old, old scars
And they pulse again with a keener sting—
I know why he beats his wing!

(15) I know why the caged bird sings, ah me,
  When his wing is bruised and his bosom sore,—
When he beats his bars and he would be free;
It is not a carol of joy or glee,
  But a prayer that he sends from his heart's deep core,
(20) But a plea, that upward to Heaven he flings—
I know why the caged bird sings!

Paul Laurence Dunbar, *The Complete Poems of Paul Laurence Dunbar.*

21. On the most literal level, what is the poet describing in this poem?

 (1) a sunny day
 (2) the struggle of a bird to escape his cage
 (3) the perfume from a chalice
 (4) a song performed by a bird
 (5) the flight of a bird on a summer day

22. The phrase, "faint perfume from its chalice" (line 6) refers to the smell of

 (1) the bird
 (2) the cage
 (3) a flower
 (4) the river
 (5) grass

23. What statement below describes what the poet means by "For he must fly back to his perch and cling / When he fain would be on the bough a-swing" (lines 10–11)?

 (1) The bird willingly flies back and clings to his perch.
 (2) The bird willingly sits and swings on a bough.
 (3) The bird's cage is hung in a tree so it can enjoy nature.
 (4) The bird must sit on his perch when he desires freedom.
 (5) The bird's cage is swinging on the boughs of the tree.

Answers are on page 741.

Entry Test Correlation Chart:
Literature & the Arts

Name: _____ **Class:** _____ **Date:** _____

This chart can help you determine your strengths and weaknesses on the content and skill areas of the Literature & the Arts Entry Test. Use the Answer Key on pages 741–743 to check your answers to the test. Then circle on the chart the numbers of the test items you answered correctly. Put the total number correct for each content area and skill area in each row and column. Look at the total items correct in each column and row and decide which areas are difficult for you. Use the page references to study those areas.

Cognitive Skills/ Content	Literal Comprehension (pp. 198–203)	Inferential Comprehension (pp. 198–203)	Application (pp. 204–208)	Analysis (pp. 209–215)	Total Correct
Popular Literature *(Pages 396–437)* Fiction Poetry Drama	1, 2 21	22 8	3 4, 5, 7	23 6	_____ out of 11
Classical Literature *(Pages 438–459)* Fiction Poetry	19	18, 20 9		17 10	_____ out of 6
Commentary *(Pages 460–479)* Television Music Books	14, 16	11, 12, 15		13	_____ out of 6
					Total correct:
Total Correct	_____ out of 6	_____ out of 8	___ out of 4	___ out of 5	_____ out of 23

1–16 → You need more review.
17–23 → Congratulations!
You're ready for the GED Test!

For additional help, see the Steck-Vaughn GED Literature & the Arts Exercise Book.

MATHEMATICS ENTRY TEST

Directions

The Mathematics Entry Test consists of multiple-choice questions intended to measure your general mathematical skills and problem-solving ability. The questions are based on short readings that often include a graph, chart, or diagram.

You should spend no more than 45 minutes answering the 27 questions. Work carefully, but do not spend too much time on any one question. Do not skip any items. Make a reasonable guess when you are not sure of an answer. You will not be penalized for incorrect answers. When time is up, mark the last item you finished. This will tell you whether you can finish the real GED Test in the time allowed. Then complete the test.

Formulas you may need are given on the inside back cover. Only some of the questions will require you to use a formula. Not all the formulas given will be needed.

Some questions contain more information than you will need to solve the problem. Other questions do not give enough information to solve the problem. If the question does not give enough information to solve the problem, the correct answer choice is "Not enough information is given."

The use of calculators is not allowed.

Record your answers on a copy of the separate answer sheet provided on page 922. Be sure all required information is properly recorded on the answer sheet.

To record your answers, mark the numbered space on the answer sheet that corresponds to the answer you choose for each question on the test.

Example: If a grocery bill totaling $15.75 is paid with a $20.00 bill, how much change should be returned?

    (1) $5.26

    (2) $4.75

    (3) $4.25

    (4) $3.75

    (5) $3.25   ①②●④⑤

The correct answer is $4.25; therefore, answer space 3 would be marked on the answer sheet.

Do not rest the point of your pencil on the answer sheet while you are considering your answer. Make no stray or unnecessary marks. If you change an answer, erase your first mark completely. Mark only one answer for each question; multiple answers will be scored as incorrect. Do not fold or crease your answer sheet.

When you finish the test, use the Correlation Chart on page 61 to determine whether you are ready to take the real GED Test, and, if not, which skill areas need additional review.

Adapted with permission of the American Council on Education.

Directions: Choose the best answer to each item.

1. Kevin assembles 35 valves in one hour and works 8 hours per day. Which expression represents how many valves he can assemble in 10 days?

(1) 35(8) + 10(8)

(2) 35(8)(10)

(3) $\frac{35(10)}{8}$

(4) $\frac{35(8)}{10}$

(5) Not enough information is given.

2. To make 4 skirts, when each skirt requires $3\frac{3}{8}$ yards of material, how many yards of material are needed?

(1) $7\frac{3}{8}$

(2) $10\frac{1}{2}$

(3) $12\frac{3}{8}$

(4) $12\frac{7}{8}$

(5) $13\frac{1}{2}$

3. Working as a store clerk, James earns $17,160 per year. If his boss gives him a 6% raise, what is his new annual salary?

(1) $17,760.00

(2) $18,189.60

(3) $20,660.20

(4) $22,243.40

(5) $27,456.00

4. Which of the following represents 273,815 written in scientific notation?

(1) 2.73815×10^5

(2) 2.73815×10^6

(3) 27.3815×10^6

(4) 273.815×10^5

(5) 2738.15×10^3

Item 5 refers to the following drawing.

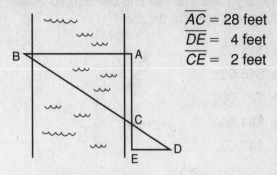

$\overline{AC}$ = 28 feet
$\overline{DE}$ = 4 feet
$\overline{CE}$ = 2 feet

5. Lines $\overline{AB}$ and $\overline{DE}$ are parallel. What is the approximate width in feet of the river $(\overline{AB})$?

(1) 20

(2) 32

(3) 40

(4) 56

(5) Not enough information is given.

6. A delivery truck is loaded with boxes of T-shirts. Of the 200 boxes on the truck, 150 contain large shirts and 50 contain extra-large. What is the probability that the first box taken off the truck will contain large shirts?

(1) $\frac{1}{200}$

(2) $\frac{1}{150}$

(3) $\frac{2}{3}$

(4) $\frac{1}{4}$

(5) $\frac{3}{4}$

7. The city of Whitesburg is 12 miles due east of Wellington. Fallsdale is 16 miles due south of Wellington. What is the straight line distance between Whitesburg and Fallsdale?

(1) 17 miles

(2) 20 miles

(3) 22 miles

(4) 25 miles

(5) 28 miles

8. Marvina sold a radio/cassette player originally priced at $70 and discounted 20%. How much was the discount?

(1) $14.00

(2) $18.00

(3) $21.00

(4) $34.50

(5) $42.00

9. Working 4 hours per day, Matt can inspect 92 computer monitors. At the same rate, which expression represents the number of monitors (N) Matt could inspect if he worked 7 hours per day?

(1) $N = \frac{4}{7}(92)$

(2) $N = \frac{7}{4}(92)$

(3) $N = 4(92)$

(4) $N = 7(92)$

(5) Not enough information is given.

10. Solve: $2(2x + 3) = -3(x + 5)$.

(1) $x = -21$

(2) $x = -3$

(3) $x = \frac{2}{7}$

(4) $x = -18$

(5) $x = 14$

11. What is the approximate volume in cubic feet of a box with a length of $2\frac{1}{2}$ ft, a width of 1 ft 6 in, and a height of 1 ft 9 in?

(1) between 3 and 4

(2) between 4 and 5

(3) between 5 and 6

(4) between 6 and 7

(5) between 7 and 8

12. Five teams are canvassing the town before an election. With two weeks to go, they compare their results. Which statement is true?

Team Results

	A	B	C	D	E
Fraction of goal reached	$\frac{2}{3}$	$\frac{1}{3}$	$\frac{3}{10}$	$\frac{1}{2}$	$\frac{3}{8}$

(1) Team E is closer to its goal than Team A.

(2) Team E is closer to its goal than Team D.

(3) Team B and Team C are exactly even.

(4) Team C is farthest from its goal.

(5) Team D is farthest from its goal.

13. For which value of y is the inequality $\frac{5}{y} > 1$ true?

(1) 4

(2) 5

(3) 6

(4) 7

(5) 8

14. What is the area in square centimeters of the triangle in the figure?
(Hint: 1 meter = 100 centimeters.)

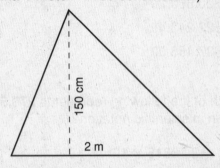

(1) 12,000

(2) 12,500

(3) 15,000

(4) 20,000

(5) 22,500

15. In a catalog, the price of a lamp is $45. A coupon reduces the price of the lamp 15%. With the coupon, what is the price of the lamp?

    (1) $ 6.75
    (2) $25.50
    (3) $32.25
    (4) $36.75
    (5) $38.25

16. Gas Station A charges $1.35 per gallon for gas and Gas Station B charges $1.39 per gallon. How much more would 18 gallons of gas cost at Station B than at Station A?

    (1) $ 0.04
    (2) $ 0.72
    (3) $ 1.17
    (4) $ 2.74
    (5) $25.02

17. What is the volume of the cylinder shown to the nearest cubic inch?

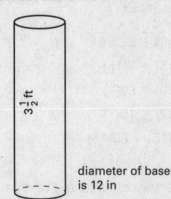

diameter of base is 12 in

    (1)   132
    (2) 2,862
    (3) 4,224
    (4) 4,748
    (5) 4,918

18. Bill Jackson teaches at two schools. In the last 30 days, he taught in one of the schools for 2 more days than in the other school. How many days did he teach at each of the two schools in the last 30 days?

    (1) 9 and 11
    (2) 13 and 15
    (3) 14 and 16
    (4) 19 and 21
    (5) 24 and 26

Item 19 refers to the following figure.

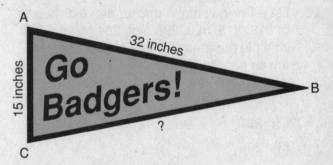

19. The pennant is an isosceles triangle. What is the perimeter (in inches) of the pennant if angles A and C are equal?

    (1) 45
    (2) 62
    (3) 64
    (4) 79
    (5) 96

20. 45% of the employees at La Plata Engineering responded to a company survey. If 126 employees responded, how many employees does the company have?

    (1) 160
    (2) 188
    (3) 210
    (4) 255
    (5) 280

21. In the figures below, what is the length of $\overline{KL}$, if $\triangle GHI$ and $\triangle JKL$ are congruent?

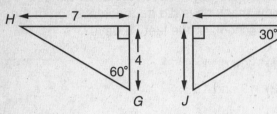

(1) 4

(2) 7

(3) 30

(4) 45

(5) 60

22. On a five-day trip, a trucker drove distances of 318, 315, 320, 298, and 264 miles. What was the mean (average) number of miles driven per day?

(1) 276

(2) 291

(3) 298

(4) 303

(5) 308

23. Doris is three times as old as her daughter Anne. If Doris is 33, which equation could be used to determine the age (*a*) of Anne?

(1) $\frac{a}{3} = 33$

(2) $a - 3 = 33$

(3) $3a = 33$

(4) $a + 3 = 33$

(5) $3(a + 3) = 33$

24. David's check for lunch was $8.80. He left a 15% tip. How much was the tip?

(1) $0.88

(2) $0.96

(3) $1.22

(4) $1.32

(5) $1.76

Item 25 refers to the following drawing.

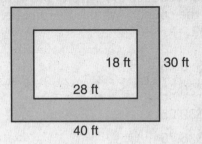

25. What is the area in square feet of the shaded part of the figure?

(1) 144

(2) 504

(3) 696

(4) 1,200

(5) 1,704

26. Corene has two jobs. She earns $7 per hour as a clerk, and $9 per hour as a receptionist. Which expression represents how much money she will earn in a week if she works 15 hours as a receptionist and 22 hours as a clerk?

(1) 15(7) + 22(9)

(2) 9(15) + 7(15)

(3) 15(9) + 22(7)

(4) 22(7) + 15(7)

(5) 15(16) + 22(16)

27. A doctor tells a nurse to give a patient 5 grains of an allergy drug. Each allergy tablet contains $1\frac{1}{4}$ grains of the drug. How many allergy tablets should the nurse give the patient?

(1) $1\frac{1}{2}$

(2) $2\frac{1}{4}$

(3) 3

(4) $3\frac{1}{2}$

(5) 4

Answers are on page 743.

Entry Test Correlation Chart: Mathematics

Name: _____ Class: _____ Date: _____

This chart can help you determine your strengths and weaknesses on the content and skill areas of the Mathematics GED Test. Use the Answer Key on pages 743–745 to check your answers to the test. Then circle on the chart the numbers of the test items you answered correctly. Put the total number correct for each content area and skill area in each row and column. Look at the total items correct in each column and row and decide which areas are difficult for you. Use the page references to study those areas.

Content	Item Number	Total Correct	Page Reference
Arithmetic *(pages 488–583)*			
Whole Number Operations	1, 26	_____out of 2	488–501
Fractions	2, 12, 27	_____out of 3	502–519
Decimals	16	_____out of 1	520–533
Percent	3, 8, 15, 20, 24	_____out of 5	534–545
Ratio, Proportion, Mean, Median, Probability	6, 9, 22	_____out of 3	556–569
Algebra *(pages 584–613)*			
Equations	10, 18, 23	_____out of 3	584–597
Graphs, Slope, Lines	13	_____out of 1	598–605
Powers and Roots	4	_____out of 1	606–609
Geometry *(pages 614–636)*			
Perimeter, Area, Volume	11, 14, 17, 25	_____out of 4	615–619
Triangles and Quadrilaterals	19	_____out of 1	624–627
Congruence and Similarity	5, 21	_____out of 2	628–630
Pythagorean Theorem	7	_____out of 1	631–632
		Total Correct: _____out of 27	

1–21 → You need more review.
22–27 → Congratulations!
You're ready for the GED Test!

© 1997 Steck-Vaughn Company. *Complete GED Preparation.* Permission granted to reproduce for classroom use.

For additional help, see the Steck-Vaughn GED Mathematics Exercise Book.

Maya Angelou uses her writing skills to express her convictions.

Test One, Part I of the GED tests your writing skills. Your understanding of the mechanics of good writing will be helpful in everything you write. Writing is easier when you know the rules for capitalization, punctuation, and spelling.

When you use capitalization, you emphasize. You show that a word is the name of a specific person, place, or thing; or you show that you are beginning a new sentence.

When you use punctuation, you show how the sentence should "sound." Punctuation is used within a sentence to indicate a pause, or to show which words are in a list or are a direct quotation. Punctuation shows where a sentence ends. Punctuation marks help the reader understand the exact meaning of what is written.

Correct spelling also makes writing clear and accurate. Some misspellings cause the reader to mistake your meaning. But even if the reader knows what you mean, he or she may notice the misspellings before noticing what you have to say.

Grammar is the rules of our language. Usage pertains to the standard ways we construct ideas and use our language. In this unit, grammar rules and usage concepts are organized so that you can study them efficiently and refer to them quickly.

You will learn how the two basic parts of a sentence, the subject and verb, relate to each other. The subject and the verb of a sentence must match, or agree, with each other.

Verbs have three principal forms: present, past, and past participle. To construct these forms, verbs change. You will learn the normal way to form these parts of a verb; you will also learn how irregular verbs are formed. Verb tenses communicate how the action of a sentence relates to the passage of time.

Pronouns take the place of nouns. Subject pronouns are used as subjects, and object pronouns take the place of noun objects. You will also learn when to use possessive pronouns. Usage rules call for agreement between pronouns and their antecedents, the nouns to which they refer. Just as subjects and verbs must agree, pronouns must match the nouns they represent.

Sentence structure is the part of writing that deals with correctly expressing related ideas in a sentence and with combining two or more sentences that have related information. A sentence is a group of words with a noun and a verb that expresses a complete thought. Whenever a subject or a verb or both are missing, what remains is a fragment. When two or more sentences are strung together into one often confusing sentence, you have a run-on. You will learn how to correct both fragments and run-ons. You'll also practice combining sentences with related ideas into compound sentences.

As you work through this unit, you'll gain confidence in your writing skills as you apply the rules of mechanics, usage, and sentence structure to your writing.

Mechanics
Lesson

Using Capitalization

> **Tip** Capitalize *I,* the first letter of proper nouns, and the first word of each sentence.

You capitalize the name of a *specific* person, place, or thing. This shows that someone, someplace, or something is one of a kind.

Always capitalize:

♦ the specific names of people, places, and organizations
♦ the specific names of days, months, and holidays
♦ the first word of a sentence
♦ the first word of a sentence in quotation marks
♦ the word *I*
♦ the first, last, and other important words in the titles of books, stories, movies, and so on. Articles (*a, the*), conjunctions (*and, or, but*), and prepositions (*on, in, to*) are not considered important words.

Titles

Titles are often part of a person's name and are capitalized when they refer to a specific person. Titles are often abbreviated.

Examples: Alice went to see <u>Dr. Jones</u>.
The <u>mayor</u> appointed a new <u>police chief</u>.

Titles, along with such family names as *mother, father, grandmother,* and *grandfather,* are capitalized when they are used to address a person directly.

Examples: When do you think you will be able to visit, <u>Mother</u>?
Do you think, <u>Doctor</u>, that she will recover?

Names

Brand names are *always* specific names, so they are capitalized.

Example: Here is a <u>Kleenex</u>.

Places

Direction words sometimes indicate a specific place. They are capitalized only when they refer to a specific area of the world, a country, a region, or a city.

Examples: Laura grew up in the <u>South</u>.
The Barnards live in the <u>Middle East</u>.
We took a tour of the <u>East</u>.
Note: A proper adjective that is formed from a specific place name is also capitalized (*Middle Eastern, American*).

ged Exercise Using Capitalization

Items 1 to 5 refer to the following sentences. Choose the best answer to each item.

(1) When Secretary of State Kissinger served under President Nixon, he went all over the world, especially to the middle East.

(2) After Nixon resigned from the office of the presidency, Vice President ford became president.

(3) On Election Day in the Fall, Americans will go to the polls, hoping to elect a president to solve both old and new problems.

(4) Many presidents, such as Bill Clinton, have been from the south.

(5) The nation's most populous State, California, has produced only two presidents, Richard Nixon and Ronald Reagan.

1. Sentence 1: **When Secretary of State Kissinger served under President Nixon, he went all over the world, especially to the middle East.**

What correction should be made to this sentence?

(1) change Secretary of State to secretary of state
(2) change Kissinger to kissinger
(3) change President to president
(4) change middle East to Middle East
(5) no correction is necessary

2. Sentence 2: **After Nixon resigned from the office of the presidency, Vice President ford became president.**

What correction should be made to this sentence?

(1) change presidency to Presidency
(2) replace Vice President ford with Vice President Ford
(3) change Vice President ford to vice President Ford
(4) change Nixon to nixon
(5) no correction is necessary

3. Sentence 3: **On Election Day in the Fall, Americans will go to the polls, hoping to elect a president to solve both old and new problems.**

What correction should be made to this sentence?

(1) change Election Day to election day
(2) change Fall to fall
(3) change Americans to americans
(4) change polls to Polls
(5) no correction is necessary

4. Sentence 4: **Many presidents, such as Bill Clinton, have been from the south.**

What correction should be made to this sentence?

(1) change Clinton to clinton
(2) change Bill to bill
(3) change the to The
(4) change south to South
(5) no correction is necessary

5. Sentence 5: **The nation's most populous State, California, has produced only two presidents, Richard Nixon and Ronald Reagan.**

What correction should be made to this sentence?

(1) change nation's to Nation's
(2) change State to state
(3) change California to california
(4) change presidents to Presidents
(5) no correction is necessary

Answers are on page 745.

Lesson 2

Using End Punctuation

Periods, question marks, and exclamation marks are used to mark the end of a sentence. **End punctuation** tells you where to pause, making the meaning much clearer. End punctuation cuts the message into "bite-size" pieces so it is more easily understood.

Read the paragraph about an upcoming wedding and notice the end punctuation marks.

(1) What time would be best for us to schedule the wedding? (2) I have always wanted to be married in a church at 8 P.M. with candlelight. (3) Do you think that is too late? (4) When the wedding is over, I want people to come to a dance. (5) Wow! (6) That's a wonderful idea, isn't it?

Question Mark

Rule: A question mark is used at the end of direct questions. A direct question requires an answer.

Examples: (Sentence 1) What time would be best for us to schedule the wedding?
(Sentence 3) Do you think that is too late?
(Sentence 6) That's a wonderful idea, isn't it?

Period

Rule: Use a period at the end of a group of words that makes a statement and expresses a complete thought or command.

Example: (Sentence 4) When the wedding is over, I want people to come to a dance.

Rule: Periods are used in abbreviations, such as A.M. and P.M.

Example: (Sentence 2) I have always wanted to be married in a church at 8 P.M. with candlelight.

Exclamation Mark

Rule: Use an exclamation mark at the end of a word or a sentence that expresses strong feelings, such as surprise, shock, or enthusiasm.

Example: (Sentence 5) Wow!

To figure out whether to use a period, question mark, or exclamation mark to indicate the end of each sentence, say the sentence to yourself and decide whether it is a statement, a question, or an exclamation.

Writing Skills ◆ Mechanics

Items 1 to 6 refer to the following note. Choose the best answer to each item.

(1) I have been looking forward to this wedding for a long time. (2) Please meet me at Brown's Department Store to help me select a wedding present? (3) On Friday I will get paid, so I can buy a wedding present then? (4) Do you think the bride and groom would like something for their kitchen! (5) I'm not going to spend $100 for towels. (6) I think I can buy a nice wedding present for about $25?

1. Sentence 1: **I have been looking forward to this wedding for a long time.**

    What correction should be made to this sentence?

    (1) change the period to a question mark
    (2) change the period to an exclamation mark
    (3) no correction is necessary

2. Sentence 2: **Please meet me at Brown's Department Store to help me select a wedding present?**

    What correction should be made to this sentence?

    (1) change the question mark to a period
    (2) change the question mark to an exclamation mark
    (3) no correction is necessary

3. Sentence 3: **On Friday I will get paid, so I can buy a wedding present then?**

    What correction should be made to this sentence?

    (1) change the question mark to a period
    (2) change the question mark to an exclamation mark
    (3) no correction is necessary

4. Sentence 4: **Do you think the bride and groom would like something for their kitchen!**

    What correction should be made to this sentence?

    (1) change the exclamation mark to a period
    (2) change the exclamation mark to a question mark
    (3) no correction is necessary

5. Sentence 5: **I'm not going to spend $100 for towels.**

    What correction should be made to this sentence?

    (1) change the period to a question mark
    (2) change the period to an exclamation mark
    (3) no correction is necessary

6. Sentence 6: **I think I can buy a nice wedding present for about $25?**

    What correction should be made to this sentence?

    (1) change the question mark to a period
    (2) change the question mark to an exclamation mark
    (3) no correction is necessary

Answers are on page 745.

Lesson 3 Using Commas

Here are some rules to help you use commas correctly.

Items in Series

When items in a list appear one after the other, the items are referred to as **items in series**. Items in series can be words or phrases.

Rule: Use commas to separate more than two items in a list. Place a comma before the conjunction. Do not use a comma after the last item in a list unless another punctuation rule requires one.

Example: Cakes, pies, and cookies will be sold.

Rule: Two adjectives that describe the same noun are separated by a comma if *and* could be used between them without changing the meaning.

Example: The president of the hall believes that this year's will be the best, biggest sale yet.

Interrupting Words or Phrases

Words or phrases that interrupt the main thought are sometimes used in sentences. A common type of interrupter that further explains a noun or pronoun is called an **appositive.** If an appositive or a nonessential phrase is left out of the sentence, the sentence still expresses a complete idea.

Rule: Use a comma to separate a descriptive word or group of words (an appositive) from the noun being described. A comma is used before and after the appositive.

Example: Chuck Garr, his neighbor, pays more rent than he.

Another common interrupter is the **parenthetical expression.** A parenthetical expression adds nothing to the meaning of the sentence, so it is set off with commas. Some common expressions are:

for example   I am sure   incidentally   of course   however

Rule: Set off expressions that are not essential to the meaning of the sentence.

Example: The grandfather clocks, for example, will be on sale.

Introductory Elements

An introductory element is a word or a group of words located at the beginning of a sentence that is not part of the main idea of the sentence. Introductory elements may be such common expressions as *yes, well, however,* and *oh*.

Writing Skills ◆ Mechanics

Rule:	Use a comma after a long introductory phrase.
Example:	As a result of overspending, Ron's funds are low.

Commas with Direct Quotations

Rule:	Use a comma to separate a quotation from the rest of a sentence. Place a comma before the quote.
Example:	Ben Franklin said, "A penny saved is a penny earned."

Commas with Dates and Place Names

Dates and names of places may have several parts. Separate the parts of a date or place name with commas.

Rule:	Use a comma to separate the name of a town from a country or state.
Rule:	Use a comma to separate the day of the week from the name of the month in a date and to set off the year from the rest of the sentence.
Example:	The reunion will be Sunday, August 3, 1997, at Miller Park in Columbus, Ohio.

Commas in Complex Sentences

Many sentences express two ideas. If an idea is a complete thought, it is an independent clause. If the idea is an incomplete thought, it is a dependent clause. When a sentence has at least one dependent and one independent clause, it is a complex sentence.

Rule:	Use a comma to separate a part of a sentence that cannot stand alone (a dependent clause) when it comes before the independent clause.
Example:	If the back door had been unlocked, I would have left the package inside your house.
Note:	A sentence that begins with *if, as,* or *when* probably has an introductory dependent clause.

Commas in Compound Sentences

When a sentence expresses two or more complete ideas that are related, it is called a compound sentence. Each complete thought is an independent clause that can stand alone as a complete sentence. In other words, an independent clause has a subject and a verb and expresses a complete thought. Although two independent clauses can be written as two separate sentences, they can also be joined as a compound sentence.

Rule:	Use a comma to join the two main parts of a compound sentence connected by a coordinating conjunction, such as *and, but, or, nor, so,* and *for.*
Example:	Sam tries to budget his money, but he has never been successful.

Items 1 to 5 refer to the following paragraph. Choose the best answer to each item.

(1) People are afraid, angry, and, confused over the news that radon gas may be in their homes. (2) Radon, a gas from uranium in the soil, can enter homes through cracks in basements, walls, and floors. (3) According to Floyd Whellan a government official, "There is a definite connection between breathing radon gas and dying from lung cancer." (4) Radon, a radioactive gas is invisible and has no color or odor. (5) We should do more research on the connection between radon gas and cancer.

1. Sentence 1: **People are afraid, angry, and, confused over the news that radon gas may be in their homes.**

   What correction should be made to this sentence?

   (1) insert a comma after people
   (2) remove the comma after afraid
   (3) remove the comma after and
   (4) insert a comma after be
   (5) no correction is necessary

2. Sentence 2: **Radon, a gas from uranium in the soil, can enter homes through cracks in basements, walls, and floors.**

   What correction should be made to this sentence?

   (1) remove the comma after Radon
   (2) remove the comma after soil
   (3) insert a comma after homes
   (4) remove the comma after basements
   (5) no correction is necessary

3. Sentence 3: **According to Floyd Whellan a government official, "There is a definite connection between breathing radon gas and dying from lung cancer."**

   What correction should be made to this sentence?

   (1) insert a comma after Whellan
   (2) remove the comma after official
   (3) insert a comma after connection
   (4) insert a comma after gas
   (5) no correction is necessary

4. Sentence 4: **Radon, a radioactive gas is invisible and has no color or odor.**

   What correction should be made to this sentence?

   (1) remove the comma after Radon
   (2) insert a comma after gas
   (3) insert a comma after color
   (4) insert a comma after or
   (5) no correction is necessary

5. Sentence 5: **We should do more research on the connection between radon gas and cancer.**

   What correction should be made to this sentence?

   (1) insert quotation marks before we and after cancer
   (2) insert commas after radon and gas
   (3) insert a comma after gas
   (4) change radon to Radon
   (5) no correction is necessary

Writing Skills ◆ Mechanics

Items 6 to 10 refer to the following paragraphs.

(1) Are firefighters, ambulance drivers, and paramedics aware of the importance of good nutrition? (2) Do they realize that their eating habits can affect their reaction time, stamina, and overall, job performance? (3) Mrs. Ruth Lahiff, a county nutritionist decided to find out. (4) After gathering data from more than 500 county employees Lahiff concluded, "Most of them get enough protein." (5) "But," she added "about one-third of them should cut down on fats and eat more fruits, vegetables, and fiber."

(6) The president of the local firefighter's union and the leader of the local paramedics agree. (7) "For most of us, it's a macho thing to live on burgers, fries, shakes, and coffee" the union leader chuckled.

(8) "We'd feel silly eating salads and juice in front of the rest of the guys," added one paramedic from station 74.

6. Sentence 2: **Do they realize that their eating habits can affect their reaction time, stamina, and overall, job performance?**

What correction should be made to this sentence?

(1) insert a comma after realize
(2) insert a comma after habits
(3) remove the comma after time
(4) remove the comma after overall
(5) no correction is necessary

7. Sentence 3: **Mrs. Ruth Lahiff, a county nutritionist decided to find out.**

What correction should be made to this sentence?

(1) remove the comma after Lahiff
(2) insert a comma after nutritionist
(3) insert a comma after decided
(4) insert a comma after to
(5) no correction is necessary

8. Sentence 4: **After gathering data from more than 500 county employees Lahiff concluded, "Most of them get enough protein."**

What correction should be made to this sentence?

(1) insert a comma after data
(2) insert a comma after 500
(3) insert a comma after employees
(4) remove the comma after concluded
(5) no correction is necessary

9. Sentence 5: **"But," she added "about one-third of them should cut down on fats and eat more fruits, vegetables, and fiber."**

What correction should be made to this sentence?

(1) remove the comma after But
(2) insert a comma after added
(3) remove the comma after fruits
(4) remove the comma after vegetables
(5) no correction is necessary

10. Sentence 7: **"For most of us, it's a macho thing to live on burgers, fries, shakes, and coffee" the union leader chuckled.**

What correction should be made to this sentence?

(1) remove the comma after us
(2) insert a comma after thing
(3) remove the comma after burgers
(4) insert a comma after coffee
(5) no correction is necessary

Tip Avoid excess commas in a series of items by counting the number of items. If there are only two items, do not use commas. For three or more items, subtract one from the number of items. That's the number of commas you need.

Answers are on page 746.

Lesson

4

Using Semicolons

Tip

Use semicolons in compound sentences to separate independent clauses. To decide if the clauses are independent, ask yourself whether each clause can stand alone as a separate sentence.

Read the paragraph. Note the semicolons and commas.

(1) Nuclear weapons are a serious issue; failure to solve this problem could have very serious consequences. (2) People are interested in avoiding nuclear war; however, they do not always agree on the best way to do so. (3) Is the answer to build up a supply of arms and prevent war through strength, or is the answer to work for disarmament? (4) World leaders, thinkers, and ordinary people have thought, of course, about these questions; but none have solved this crisis.

In the paragraph, all of the sentences contain at least two ideas and use commas and/or semicolons. Look at the following rules to see when semicolons should be used.

Rule: Use a semicolon to join clauses that can stand alone (independent clauses) and that are not joined by a connecting word.

Example: (Sentence 1) Nuclear weapons are a serious issue; failure to solve this problem could have very serious consequences.

Note: In joining these two clauses, you have the option of using the semicolon or of eliminating the semicolon and using a conjunction and a comma. Either is correct.

Rule: Use a semicolon to join two clauses that could stand alone but are joined by such linking words as *however* or *therefore*. Always use a comma following the linking word.

Example: (Sentence 2) People are interested in avoiding nuclear war; however, they do not always agree on the best way to do so.

Rule: Sometimes it is necessary to use a semicolon instead of a comma to connect two independent clauses joined with a conjunction. When there are other commas in the independent clauses that may cause the reader confusion, use a semicolon.

Example: (Sentence 4) World leaders, thinkers, and ordinary people have thought, of course, about these questions; but none have solved this crisis.

Note: Since there are several other commas in the first clause, a semicolon is used instead of a comma to separate the clauses.

Items 1 to 5 refer to the following paragraph. Choose the best answer to each item.

(1) Newborn babies are tiny and helpless they need very special care. (2) Family members and friends usually want to hold your baby, however, your baby should have some quiet time. (3) You will need to take time to consider the benefits of nursing your baby, and you will need a large supply of diapers. (4) It is the hope, dream, and wish of every parent, of course, to have a healthy baby; and it is the goal of every parent to provide the best possible life for the child. (5) First-time parents are often nervous about how to care for their newborn; therefore they often ask friends, relatives, and doctors for advice.

1. Sentence 1: **Newborn babies are tiny and helpless they need very special care.**

   Which of the following is the best way to write the underlined portion of this sentence? If you think the original is the best way, choose option (1).

   (1) and helpless they
   (2) and helpless, they
   (3) and helpless; they
   (4) and helpless; and they
   (5) and helpless, however, they

2. Sentence 2: **Family members and friends usually want to hold your baby, however, your baby should have some quiet time.**

   Which of the following is the best way to write the underlined portion of this sentence? If you think the original is the best way, choose option (1).

   (1) baby, however, your
   (2) baby however, your
   (3) baby, however; your
   (4) baby, however your
   (5) baby; however, your

3. Sentence 3: **You will need to take time to consider the benefits of nursing your baby, and you will need a large supply of diapers.**

   Which of the following is the best way to write the underlined portion of this sentence? If you think the original is the best way, choose option (1).

   (1) baby, and you
   (2) baby and you
   (3) baby; and, you
   (4) baby; and you
   (5) baby and, you

4. Sentence 4: **It is the hope, dream, and wish of every parent, of course, to have a healthy baby; and it is the goal of every parent to provide the best possible life for the child.**

   Which of the following is the best way to write the underlined portion of this sentence? If you think the original is the best way, choose option (1).

   (1) baby; and it
   (2) baby and it
   (3) baby; and, it
   (4) baby, and, it
   (5) baby, and; it

5. Sentence 5: **First-time parents are often nervous about how to care for their newborn; therefore they often ask friends, relatives, and doctors for advice.**

   What correction should be made to this sentence?

   (1) change the semicolon to a comma
   (2) insert a comma after therefore
   (3) remove the comma after relatives
   (4) insert a comma after doctors
   (5) no correction is necessary

Answers are on page 747.

Lesson ⑤ Using Apostrophes and Quotation Marks

Apostrophes

Use apostrophes to show possession and to replace missing letters in contractions.

Rule: A contraction combines two words, one of which is usually a verb. The apostrophe takes the place of missing letters.

Example: I'd like a better job because my current job doesn't pay enough money. (I'd = I would; doesn't = does not)

Rule: An apostrophe shows that an object or a characteristic belongs to a particular person or thing. The possessive of most singular nouns is formed by adding an apostrophe and *s ('s)*.

Example: My sister's idea of the ideal job is one with good wages, insurance, and an opportunity for promotion.

Note: If a singular noun ends in *-s*, form the possessive by adding *'s (witness's, boss's)*.

Rule: The possessive of most plural nouns that end in *-s* is formed by adding an apostrophe *(')*.

Example: The agencies' fees can be quite expensive.

Rule: The possessive of plural nouns that do not end in *-s* is formed by adding an apostrophe and *s ('s)*.

Example: I'd like a job with a children's day-care program.

Quotation Marks

Here are some rules to help you use quotation marks correctly.

Rule: Use quotation marks to set off someone's exact words. Notice that quotation marks are always used in pairs.

Examples: Mary replied, "I want a sales job in a retail store."
"Oh," Mark said, "you want to get into management."

Rule: A punctuation mark—such as a period, comma, exclamation point, or question mark—that is part of the quote is always placed before, or inside, the second quotation mark.

Example: "Are you willing to work on weekends?" asked Mark.

Rule: Quotation marks should not be used unless someone's exact words are given. An indirect quotation is not set off by quotation marks.

Example: He explained that most management positions require experience.

Rule: Use quotation marks to set off an unusual term or an exact phrase used by a specific person.

Example: One of management's biggest headaches is "lazy employees."

Writing Skills ◆ Mechanics

ged **Exercise** Using Apostrophes and Quotation Marks

Items 1 to 3 refer to the following paragraph. Choose the best answer to each item.

(1) I'd like to have a pet because I dont want to be alone. (2) The womens group is helping the animal shelter find homes for its cats and dogs. (3) Last month, the boys' club was successful in its program to help lost animals find their owner's. (4) I'd say its about time for our club to do something.

1. Sentence 1: **I'd like to have a pet because I dont want to be alone.**

   What correction should be made to this sentence?

   (1) change I'd to Id
   (2) replace dont with don't
   (3) change dont to do'nt
   (4) replace dont with donot
   (5) no correction is necessary

2. Sentence 3: **Last month, the boys' club was successful in its program to help lost animals find their owner's.**

   What correction should be made to this sentence?

   (1) replace boys' with boys
   (2) replace boys' with boy's
   (3) change animals to animals'
   (4) change owner's to owners
   (5) no correction is necessary

3. Sentence 4: **I'd say its about time for our club to do something.**

   What correction should be made to this sentence?

   (1) change I'd to I had
   (2) change its to its'
   (3) replace its with it's
   (4) replace our with our'
   (5) no correction is necessary

Items 4 to 6 refer to the following paragraph.

(1) A group of veterinarians recently commissioned a study to find out if dogs are still man's best friend." (2) Dick Grover, group spokesman, said "One surprise in the study is that cats are becoming more popular, while dogs' popularity is declining." (3) "Dogs will never lose their popularity as pets, especially as children's companions, predicted Grover. (4) When a dog dies, it's like a member of the family has passed away," added Grover's sister.

4. Sentence 1: **A group of veterinarians recently commissioned a study to find out if dogs are still man's best friend."**

   What correction should be made to this sentence?

   (1) change veterinarians to veterinarians'
   (2) insert a quotation mark before man's
   (3) change man's to mans'
   (4) insert a period after out
   (5) no correction is necessary

5. Sentence 3: **"Dogs will never lose their popularity as pets, especially as children's companions, predicted Grover.**

   What correction should be made to this sentence?

   (1) remove the quotation mark before Dogs
   (2) change Dogs to Dogs'
   (3) change children's to childrens'
   (4) insert a quotation mark after companions,
   (5) no correction is necessary

6. Sentence 4: **When a dog dies, it's like a member of the family has passed away," added Grover's sister.**

   What correction should be made to this sentence?

   (1) insert a quotation mark before When
   (2) change it's to its
   (3) remove the comma after away
   (4) change Grover's to Grovers
   (5) no correction is necessary

Answers are on page 747.

Lesson

Correct Spelling

Correct spelling is an important part of writing well. Spelling errors often occur in words that contain the letter combinations *ie* or *ei*, words that have special endings called **suffixes,** and words that have special beginnings called **prefixes.**

Tip

Memorize one example for each spelling rule. You can remember the rules and apply them to test items by recalling your examples.

Rule: Use *i* before *e*, except after *c*, or when sounded as *a*, as in *neighbor* and *weigh*.

Example: I believe I lost the <u>receipt</u> for the <u>sleigh</u>. (Exceptions to this rule include *either, neither, foreign, forfeit, height, leisure, seize, weird, conscience,* and *science*.)

Rule: If a word ends in *-e*, drop the *e* before adding a suffix that begins with a vowel, but keep the *e* when adding a suffix that begins with a consonant.

Examples: like + *-ed* = liked   slide + *-ing* = sliding
hope + *-ful* = hopeful   place + *-ment* = placement

Rule: If a word ends in *-ce* or *-ge*, keep the final *e* when adding a suffix that begins with *a* or *o*.

Examples: notice + *-able* = noticeable   outrage + *-ous* = outrageous

Rule: When a word ends in a consonant and the suffix begins with a consonant, just add the suffix.

Examples: art + *-ful* = artful   resent + *-ment* = resentment

Rule: When a one- or two-syllable word ends in a consonant and the suffix begins with a vowel, the consonant is usually doubled before adding the suffix. If the final consonant comes after two vowels, it is not doubled.

Examples: hop + *-ing* = hopping   rot + *-en* = rotten
read + *-ing* = reading   eat + *-en* = eaten

Rule: The spelling of a word does not change when a prefix is added to it.

Examples: *co-* + operate = cooperate   *mis-* + lead = mislead

Rule: When adding a suffix that starts with a vowel—such as *-ed, -ing, -er,* or *-est*—to a word, the spelling of most words doesn't change.

Examples: small + *-est* = smallest   find + *-ing* = finding

Rule: If a word ends in *-y* preceded by a consonant, change the *y* to *i* before adding the suffix.

Examples: happy + *-er* = happier   hurry + *-ed* = hurried
pretty + *-est* = prettiest

Contractions

A contraction combines two words. An apostrophe takes the place of the missing letters. Most contractions combine a personal pronoun and verb:

I'm = I am   you're = you are   I've = I have
you've = you have   I'd = I had, I would   you'll = you will

Other contractions combine a verb and the word *not:*

isn't = is not   aren't = are not
don't = do not   didn't = did not
won't = will not   hasn't = has not
wasn't = was not   weren't = were not
couldn't = could not

Possessives and Homonyms

Possessives are used to show ownership. Homonyms are words that sound alike but have different spellings or different meanings.

Tip

To avoid errors with homonyms, read the entire sentence before you decide how to spell the word. That way, you will know the intended meaning of the word.

Rule: Form the possessive of a noun by adding 's (or just an apostrophe if the noun is a plural and ends in -s).

Example: Is it true that <u>Bob's</u> sisters overheard a conversation about their jobs?

Rule: Do not confuse words that are homonyms. Be sure of the spelling and the meaning.

Example: Everybody <u>knew</u> they intended to hire new employees, but are dismissals necessary?
The homonyms are <u>knew</u>, the past tense of the verb <u>know</u>, and <u>new</u>, meaning "latest" or "additional."

Example: I guess you can't be <u>too</u> sure that your job is going <u>to</u> last more than <u>two</u> years.
The homonyms are <u>too</u>, meaning "very" or "also"; <u>to</u>, a preposition or part of an infinitive verb form; and <u>two</u>, a number.

Rule: Do not confuse possessive pronouns with contractions that sound the same.

Example: <u>It's</u> too bad if <u>it's</u> true that the management will fire <u>its</u> two most experienced employees.
<u>It's</u> is a contraction meaning "it is"; <u>its</u> is a possessive pronoun.

Note: Most pronouns that show possession are <u>not</u> spelled with an apostrophe. The possessive pronouns are *my, mine, your, yours, his, her, hers, its, our, ours, their, theirs, whose.*

GED Master Spelling List

With some practice and concentration you can improve your spelling ability. Study the words on the GED Master Spelling List. These are the most commonly misspelled words. Write the words as someone reads them to you. Make a list of the ones you spelled incorrectly. You may find it easier to master the ones you missed if you learn the correct spelling of ten to twelve words at a time.

 The spelling rules you have learned will help you with many difficult-to-spell words. When you come to a difficult word in a test item, recall the spelling rules and decide whether they apply to the item.

GED Master Spelling List

a lot ☐	agree ☐	arouse ☐	between ☐
ability ☐	aisle ☐	arrange ☐	bicycle ☐
absence ☐	all right ☐	arrangement ☐	board ☐
absent ☐	almost ☐	article ☐	bored ☐
abundance ☐	already ☐	artificial ☐	borrow ☐
accept ☐	although ☐	ascend ☐	bottle ☐
acceptable ☐	altogether ☐	assistance ☐	bottom ☐
accident ☐	always ☐	assistant ☐	boundary ☐
accommodate ☐	amateur ☐	associate ☐	brake ☐
accompanied ☐	American ☐	association ☐	breadth ☐
accomplish ☐	among ☐	attempt ☐	break ☐
accumulation ☐	amount ☐	attendance ☐	breath ☐
accuse ☐	analysis ☐	attention ☐	breathe ☐
accustomed ☐	analyze ☐	audience ☐	brilliant ☐
ache ☐	angel ☐	August ☐	building ☐
achieve ☐	angle ☐	author ☐	bulletin ☐
achievement ☐	annual ☐	automobile ☐	bureau ☐
acknowledge ☐	another ☐	autumn ☐	burial ☐
acquaintance ☐	answer ☐	auxiliary ☐	buried ☐
acquainted ☐	antiseptic ☐	available ☐	bury ☐
acquire ☐	anxious ☐	avenue ☐	bushes ☐
address ☐	apologize ☐	awful ☐	business ☐
addressed ☐	apparatus ☐	awkward ☐	
adequate ☐	apparent ☐		cafeteria ☐
advantage ☐	appear ☐	bachelor ☐	calculator ☐
advantageous ☐	appearance ☐	balance ☐	calendar ☐
advertise ☐	appetite ☐	balloon ☐	campaign ☐
advertisement ☐	apply ☐	bargain ☐	capital ☐
advice ☐	appreciate ☐	basic ☐	capitol ☐
advisable ☐	appreciation ☐	beautiful ☐	captain ☐
advise ☐	approach ☐	because ☐	career ☐
aerial ☐	appropriate ☐	become ☐	careful ☐
affect ☐	approval ☐	before ☐	careless ☐
affectionate ☐	approve ☐	beginning ☐	carriage ☐
again ☐	approximate ☐	being ☐	carrying ☐
against ☐	argue ☐	believe ☐	category ☐
aggravate ☐	arguing ☐	benefit ☐	ceiling ☐
aggressive ☐	argument ☐	benefited ☐	cemetery ☐

Writing Skills ◆ Mechanics

cereal ☐	corroborate ☐	disastrous ☐	exercise ☐
certain ☐	council ☐	discipline ☐	exhausted ☐
changeable ☐	counsel ☐	discover ☐	exhaustion ☐
characteristic ☐	counselor ☐	discriminate ☐	exhilaration ☐
charity ☐	courage ☐	disease ☐	existence ☐
chief ☐	courageous ☐	dissatisfied ☐	exorbitant ☐
choose ☐	course ☐	dissection ☐	expense ☐
chose ☐	courteous ☐	dissipate ☐	experience ☐
cigarette ☐	courtesy ☐	distance ☐	experiment ☐
circumstance ☐	criticism ☐	distinction ☐	explanation ☐
citizen ☐	criticize ☐	division ☐	extreme ☐
clothes ☐	crystal ☐	doctor ☐	
clothing ☐	curiosity ☐	dollar ☐	facility ☐
coarse ☐	cylinder ☐	doubt ☐	factory ☐
coffee ☐		dozen ☐	familiar ☐
collect ☐	daily ☐	dyed ☐	farther ☐
college ☐	daughter ☐		fascinate ☐
column ☐	daybreak ☐	earnest ☐	fascinating ☐
comedy ☐	death ☐	easy ☐	fatigue ☐
comfortable ☐	deceive ☐	ecstasy ☐	February ☐
commitment ☐	December ☐	ecstatic ☐	financial ☐
committed ☐	deception ☐	education ☐	financier ☐
committee ☐	decide ☐	effect ☐	flourish ☐
communicate ☐	decision ☐	efficiency ☐	forcibly ☐
company ☐	decisive ☐	efficient ☐	forehead ☐
comparative ☐	deed ☐	eight ☐	foreign ☐
compel ☐	definite ☐	either ☐	formal ☐
competent ☐	delicious ☐	eligibility ☐	former ☐
competition ☐	dependent ☐	eligible ☐	fortunate ☐
complement ☐	deposit ☐	eliminate ☐	fourteen ☐
compliment ☐	derelict ☐	embarrass ☐	fourth ☐
conceal ☐	descend ☐	embarrassment ☐	frequent ☐
conceit ☐	descent ☐	emergency ☐	friend ☐
conceivable ☐	describe ☐	emphasis ☐	frightening ☐
conceive ☐	description ☐	emphasize ☐	fundamental ☐
concentration ☐	desert ☐	enclosure ☐	further ☐
conception ☐	desirable ☐	encouraging ☐	
condition ☐	despair ☐	endeavor ☐	gallon ☐
conference ☐	desperate ☐	engineer ☐	garden ☐
confident ☐	dessert ☐	English ☐	gardener ☐
congratulate ☐	destruction ☐	enormous ☐	general ☐
conquer ☐	determine ☐	enough ☐	genius ☐
conscience ☐	develop ☐	entrance ☐	government ☐
conscientious ☐	development ☐	envelope ☐	governor ☐
conscious ☐	device ☐	environment ☐	grammar ☐
consequence ☐	devise ☐	equipment ☐	grateful ☐
consequently ☐	dictator ☐	equipped ☐	great ☐
considerable ☐	died ☐	especially ☐	grievance ☐
consistency ☐	difference ☐	essential ☐	grievous ☐
consistent ☐	different ☐	evening ☐	grocery ☐
continual ☐	dilemma ☐	evident ☐	guarantee ☐
continuous ☐	dinner ☐	exaggerate ☐	guard ☐
controlled ☐	direction ☐	exaggeration ☐	guess ☐
controversy ☐	disappear ☐	examine ☐	guidance ☐
convenience ☐	disappoint ☐	exceed ☐	
convenient ☐	disappointment ☐	excellent ☐	half ☐
conversation ☐	disapproval ☐	except ☐	hammer ☐
corporal ☐	disapprove ☐	exceptional ☐	handkerchief ☐

happiness ☐	jealous ☐	monkey ☐	pastime ☐
healthy ☐	judgment ☐	monotonous ☐	patience ☐
heard ☐	journal ☐	moral ☐	patients ☐
heavy ☐		morale ☐	peace ☐
height ☐	kindergarten ☐	mortgage ☐	peaceable ☐
herd ☐	kitchen ☐	mountain ☐	pear ☐
heroes ☐	knew ☐	mournful ☐	peculiar ☐
heroine ☐	knock ☐	muscle ☐	pencil ☐
hideous ☐	know ☐	mysterious ☐	people ☐
himself ☐	knowledge ☐	mystery ☐	perceive ☐
hoarse ☐			perception ☐
holiday ☐	labor ☐	narrative ☐	perfect ☐
hopeless ☐	laboratory ☐	natural ☐	perform ☐
horse ☐	laid ☐	necessary ☐	performance ☐
hospital ☐	language ☐	needle ☐	perhaps ☐
humorous ☐	later ☐	negligence ☐	period ☐
hurried ☐	latter ☐	neighbor ☐	permanence ☐
hurrying ☐	laugh ☐	neither ☐	permanent ☐
	leisure ☐	newspaper ☐	perpendicular ☐
ignorance ☐	length ☐	newsstand ☐	perseverance ☐
imaginary ☐	lesson ☐	niece ☐	persevere ☐
imbecile ☐	library ☐	noticeable ☐	persistent ☐
imitation ☐	license ☐		persuade ☐
immediately ☐	light ☐	o'clock ☐	personality ☐
incidental ☐	lightning ☐	obedient ☐	personal ☐
increase ☐	likelihood ☐	obstacle ☐	personnel ☐
independence ☐	likely ☐	occasion ☐	persuade ☐
independent ☐	literal ☐	occasional ☐	persuasion ☐
indispensable ☐	literature ☐	occur ☐	pertain ☐
inevitable ☐	livelihood ☐	occurred ☐	picture ☐
influence ☐	loaf ☐	occurrence ☐	piece ☐
influential ☐	loneliness ☐	ocean ☐	plain ☐
initiate ☐	loose ☐	offer ☐	plane ☐
innocence ☐	lose ☐	often ☐	playwright ☐
inoculate ☐	losing ☐	omission ☐	pleasant ☐
inquiry ☐	loyal ☐	omit ☐	please ☐
insistent ☐	loyalty ☐	once ☐	pleasure ☐
instead ☐		operate ☐	pocket ☐
instinct ☐	magazine ☐	opinion ☐	poison ☐
integrity ☐	maintenance ☐	opportune ☐	policeman ☐
intellectual ☐	maneuver ☐	opportunity ☐	political ☐
intelligence ☐	marriage ☐	optimist ☐	population ☐
intercede ☐	married ☐	optimistic ☐	portrayal ☐
interest ☐	marry ☐	origin ☐	positive ☐
interfere ☐	match ☐	original ☐	possess ☐
interference ☐	mathematics ☐	oscillate ☐	possession ☐
interpreted ☐	measure ☐	ought ☐	possessive ☐
interrupt ☐	medicine ☐	ounce ☐	possible ☐
invitation ☐	million ☐	overcoat ☐	post office ☐
irrelevant ☐	miniature ☐		potatoes ☐
irresistible ☐	minimum ☐	paid ☐	practical ☐
irritable ☐	miracle ☐	pamphlet ☐	prairie ☐
island ☐	miscellaneous ☐	panicky ☐	precede ☐
its ☐	mischief ☐	parallel ☐	preceding ☐
it's ☐	mischievous ☐	parallelism ☐	precise ☐
itself ☐	misspelled ☐	pare ☐	predictable ☐
	mistake ☐	particular ☐	prefer ☐
January ☐	momentous ☐	partner ☐	preference ☐

Writing Skills ◆ Mechanics

preferential	☐	renovate	☐	specified	☐	university	☐
preferred	☐	repeat	☐	specimen	☐	unnecessary	☐
prejudice	☐	repetition	☐	speech	☐	unusual	☐
preparation	☐	representative	☐	stationary	☐	useful	☐
prepare	☐	requirements	☐	stationery	☐	usual	☐
prescription	☐	resemblance	☐	statue	☐		
presence	☐	resistance	☐	stockings	☐	vacuum	☐
president	☐	resource	☐	stomach	☐	vain	☐
prevalent	☐	respectability	☐	straight	☐	valley	☐
primitive	☐	responsibility	☐	strength	☐	valuable	☐
principal	☐	restaurant	☐	strenuous	☐	variety	☐
principle	☐	rhythm	☐	stretch	☐	vegetable	☐
privilege	☐	rhythmical	☐	striking	☐	vein	☐
probably	☐	ridiculous	☐	studying	☐	vengeance	☐
procedure	☐	right	☐	substantial	☐	versatile	☐
proceed	☐	role	☐	succeed	☐	vicinity	☐
produce	☐	roll	☐	successful	☐	vicious	☐
professional	☐	roommate	☐	sudden	☐	view	☐
professor	☐			superintendent	☐	village	☐
profit	☐	sandwich	☐	suppress	☐	villain	☐
profitable	☐	Saturday	☐	surely	☐	visitor	☐
prominent	☐	scarcely	☐	surprise	☐	voice	☐
promise	☐	scene	☐	suspense	☐	volume	☐
pronounce	☐	schedule	☐	sweat	☐		
pronunciation	☐	science	☐	sweet	☐	waist	☐
propeller	☐	scientific	☐	syllable	☐	ware	☐
prophet	☐	scissors	☐	symmetrical	☐	waste	☐
prospect	☐	season	☐	sympathy	☐	weak	☐
psychology	☐	secretary	☐	synonym	☐	wear	☐
pursue	☐	seize	☐			weather	☐
pursuit	☐	seminar	☐	technical	☐	Wednesday	☐
		sense	☐	telegram	☐	week	☐
quality	☐	separate	☐	telephone	☐	weigh	☐
quantity	☐	service	☐	temperament	☐	weird	☐
quarreling	☐	several	☐	temperature	☐	whether	☐
quart	☐	severely	☐	tenant	☐	which	☐
quarter	☐	shepherd	☐	tendency	☐	while	☐
quiet	☐	sheriff	☐	tenement	☐	whole	☐
quite	☐	shining	☐	therefore	☐	wholly	☐
		shoulder	☐	thorough	☐	whose	☐
raise	☐	shriek	☐	through	☐	witch	☐
realistic	☐	siege	☐	title	☐	wretched	☐
realize	☐	sight	☐	together	☐		
reason	☐	signal	☐	tomorrow	☐		
rebellion	☐	significance	☐	tongue	☐		
recede	☐	significant	☐	toward	☐		
receipt	☐	similar	☐	tragedy	☐		
receive	☐	similarity	☐	transferred	☐		
recipe	☐	since	☐	treasury	☐		
recognize	☐	sincerely	☐	tremendous	☐		
recommend	☐	site	☐	tries	☐		
recuperate	☐	soldier	☐	truly	☐		
referred	☐	solemn	☐	twelfth	☐		
rehearsal	☐	sophomore	☐	twelve	☐		
reign	☐	soul	☐	tyranny	☐		
relevant	☐	source	☐				
relieve	☐	souvenir	☐	undoubtedly	☐		
remedy	☐	special	☐	United States	☐		

Items 1 to 12 refer to the following paragraph. Choose the best answer to each item.

(1) This winter a new strain of flu is goeing around. (2) Its worse than other flus, and people are sicker than ever. (3) The flu victims suffer from noticable symptoms, including runny noses, watery eyes, and coughing. (4) Theyr'e also experiencing muscle aches, chills, and high fevers. (5) Visiting the emergency room is unecessary, say many doctors. (6) Yo'ud be better off staying in bed, resting, and drinking a variety of liquids. (7) Youll be making steps toward a full recovery within a week. (8) Next year, show good judgment by geting a flu shot in November. (9) Don't wait until you already have the flu; the shot will be useless. (10) The flu is especially dangerous for children and senior citizens. (11) Start encourageing your grandparents and elderly neighbors to go to the clinic early. (12) Hurrying to get vaccinated in November means being healthyer during the flu season.

1. Sentence 1: **This winter a new strain of flu is goeing around.**

   What correction should be made to this sentence?

   (1) change winter to Winter
   (2) change is to are
   (3) change is to be
   (4) change the spelling of goeing to going
   (5) no correction is necessary

2. Sentence 2: **Its worse than other flus, and people are sicker than ever.**

   What correction should be made to this sentence?

   (1) change Its to It's
   (2) change the comma after flus to a semicolon
   (3) change the spelling of sicker to sickker
   (4) change the first than to then
   (5) no correction is necessary

3. Sentence 3: **The flu victims suffer from noticable symptoms, including runny noses, watery eyes, and coughing.**

   What correction should be made to this sentence?

   (1) change the spelling of noticable to noticeable
   (2) change victims to victim's
   (3) change the spelling of including to includeing
   (4) change the spelling of coughing to coffing
   (5) no correction is necessary

4. Sentence 4: **Theyr'e also experiencing muscle aches, chills, and high fevers.**

   What correction should be made to this sentence?

   (1) change Theyr'e to They're
   (2) change the spelling of experiencing to experienceing
   (3) change the spelling of experiencing to expereincing
   (4) remove the comma after chills
   (5) no correction is necessary

5. Sentence 5: **Visiting the emergency room is unecessary, say many doctors.**

   What correction should be made to this sentence?

   (1) change the spelling of Visiting to Visitting
   (2) replace the comma after unecessary with a semicolon
   (3) change the spelling of unecessary to unnecessary
   (4) change doctors to Doctors
   (5) no correction is necessary

6. Sentence 6: **Yo'ud be better off staying in bed, resting, and drinking a variety of liquids.**

   What correction should be made to this sentence?

   (1) change Yo'ud to Youd
   (2) change Yo'ud to You'd
   (3) change off to of
   (4) change the spelling of variety to vareity
   (5) no correction is necessary

7. Sentence 7: **Youll be making steps toward a full recovery within a week.**

   What correction should be made to this sentence?

   (1) change Youll to You'll
   (2) change the spelling of making to makeing
   (3) change steps to step's
   (4) change week to Week
   (5) no correction is necessary

8. Sentence 8: **Next year, show good judgment by geting a flu shot in November.**

   What correction should be made to this sentence?

   (1) change judgment to judgement
   (2) change geting to getting
   (3) change shot to shots
   (4) change November to november
   (5) no correction is necessary

9. Sentence 9: **Don't wait until you already have the flu; the shot will be useless.**

   What correction should be made to this sentence?

   (1) change Don't to Dont
   (2) change Don't to Do'nt
   (3) change the spelling of useless to usless
   (4) change the semicolon after flu to a comma
   (5) no correction is necessary

10. Sentence 10: **The flu is especially dangerous for children and senior citizens.**

    What correction should be made to this sentence?

    (1) change the spelling of especially to especialy
    (2) change the spelling of dangerous to dangeress
    (3) change children to childs
    (4) change senior citizens to senior Citizens
    (5) no correction is necessary

11. Sentence 11: **Start encourageing your grandparents and elderly neighbors to go to the clinic early.**

    What correction should be made to this sentence?

    (1) change the spelling of encourageing to encouraging
    (2) change grandparents to Grandparents
    (3) change the spelling of elderly to elderrly
    (4) change the spelling of neighbors to nieghbors
    (5) no correction is necessary

12. Sentence 12: **Hurrying to get vaccinated in November means being healthyer during the flu season.**

    What correction should be made to this sentence?

    (1) change the spelling of Hurrying to Hurriing
    (2) change means to mean's
    (3) change the spelling of healthyer to healthier
    (4) change season to Season
    (5) no correction is necessary

Answers are on page 748.

Items 1 to 5 refer to the following paragraph. Choose the <u>best answer</u> to each item.

(1) John and his two sons are planning to go on a fishing trip next week. (2) John's sons are planning to bring there swim trunks for swimming at the lake. (3) The whether report says that the temperature is going to be low, and it might rain, too. (4) I hope the weather report is wrong; it could spoil the whole trip four them. (5) The cold weather and rain would probably ruin the boy's plans for a great vacation.

1. Sentence 1: **John and his two sons are planning to go on a fishing trip next week.**

    What correction should be made to this sentence?

    (1) change <u>two</u> to <u>to</u>
    (2) change <u>sons</u> to <u>suns</u>
    (3) change <u>to</u> to <u>too</u>
    (4) change <u>week</u> to <u>weak</u>
    (5) no correction is necessary

2. Sentence 2: **John's sons are planning to bring there swim trunks for swimming at the lake.**

    What correction should be made to this sentence?

    (1) change <u>John's</u> to <u>Johns</u>
    (2) change <u>to</u> to <u>two</u>
    (3) change <u>there</u> to <u>their</u>
    (4) change <u>for</u> to <u>four</u>
    (5) no correction is necessary

3. Sentence 3: **The whether report says that the temperature is going to be low, and it might rain, too.**

    What correction should be made to this sentence?

    (1) change <u>whether</u> to <u>weather</u>
    (2) change <u>to</u> to <u>two</u>
    (3) change <u>might</u> to <u>mite</u>
    (4) change <u>too</u> to <u>to</u>
    (5) no correction is necessary

4. Sentence 4: **I hope the weather report is wrong; it could spoil the whole trip four them.**

    What correction should be made to this sentence?

    (1) change <u>weather</u> to <u>whether</u>
    (2) replace <u>it</u> with <u>its</u>
    (3) change <u>whole</u> to <u>hole</u>
    (4) change <u>four</u> to <u>for</u>
    (5) no correction is necessary

5. Sentence 5: **The cold weather and rain would probably ruin the boy's plans for a great vacation.**

    What correction should be made to this sentence?

    (1) replace <u>would</u> with <u>wood</u>
    (2) change <u>boy's</u> to <u>boys'</u>
    (3) change <u>plans</u> to <u>plans'</u>
    (4) replace <u>great</u> with <u>grate</u>
    (5) no correction is necessary

Answers are on page 749.

Items 1 to 5 refer to the following paragraph. Choose the best answer to each item.

(1) Managers have become interested in the veiws of their employees. (2) One new way employees can communicate with management is through an attitude survey. (3) Such surveys are usually designed and processed by experts? (4) Their purpose is to give employees a chance to tell their bosses how they feel about their jobs and the Company, while ensuring confidentiality. (5) Some questions such as those related to satisfaction with salary may receive fairly low ratings from even the most satisfied employees; few will admit that they're satisfied with their pay.

1. Sentence 1: **Managers have become interested in the veiws of their employees.**

   Which of the following is the best way to write the underlined portion of this sentence? If you think the original is the best way, choose option (1).

   (1) veiws of their employees
   (2) views of their employees
   (3) views, of their employees
   (4) views of there employees
   (5) views of their employees'

2. Sentence 2: **One new way employees can communicate with management is through an attitude survey.**

   Which of the following is the best way to write the underlined portion of this sentence? If you think the original is the best way, choose option (1).

   (1) communicate with management is
   (2) comunicate with management is
   (3) communicate with managment is,
   (4) communicate with management, is
   (5) communicate with management is;

3. Sentence 3: **Such surveys are usually designed and processed by experts?**

   What correction should be made to this sentence?

   (1) change surveys to survey's
   (2) change the spelling of usually to usualy
   (3) change experts to expert's
   (4) change the question mark to a period
   (5) no correction is necessary

4. Sentence 4: **Their purpose is to give employees a chance to tell their bosses how they feel about their jobs and the Company, while ensuring confidentiality.**

   What correction should be made to this sentence?

   (1) change Their to There
   (2) replace bosses with bosses'
   (3) change Company to company
   (4) replace confidentiality with Confidentiality
   (5) no correction is necessary

5. Sentence 5: **Some questions such as those related to satisfaction with salary may receive fairly low ratings from even the most satisfied employees; few will admit that they're satisfied with their pay.**

   What correction should be made to this sentence?

   (1) insert commas after questions and salary
   (2) change receive to recieve
   (3) change the semicolon to a comma
   (4) change they're to there
   (5) no correction is necessary

Items 6 to 10 refer to the following paragraph.

(1) Department managers receive tabulated results of the surveys, then they hold meetings with their employees and present the data. (2) During each meeting; certain problem areas are defined and employee task groups may be formed to recommend solutions. (3) Surveys can never take the place of face-to-face communication, but as one worker stated, I liked being able to tell the boss what I would change about my job if I had the chance." (4) Managers sometimes find that their employees' suggestions are workable their suggestions often improve productivity. (5) Worker morale also may be improved, along with company profits.

6. Sentence 1: **Department managers receive tabulated results of the surveys, then they hold meetings with their employees and present the data.**

Which of the following is the best way to write the underlined portion of this sentence? If you think the original is the best way, choose option (1).

(1) surveys, then
(2) surveys! then
(3) surveys. then
(4) surveys. Then
(5) surveys? Then

7. Sentence 2: **During each meeting; certain problem areas are defined and employee task groups may be formed to recommend solutions.**

What correction should be made to this sentence?

(1) change the semicolon to a comma
(2) change areas to areas'
(3) replace to with too
(4) change the spelling of recommend to recomend
(5) no correction is necessary

8. Sentence 3: **Surveys can never take the place of face-to-face communication, but as one worker stated, I liked being able to tell the boss what I would change about my job if I had the chance."**

Which of the following is the best way to write the underlined portion of this sentence? If you think the original is the best way, choose option (1).

(1) but as one worker stated, I liked
(2) but as one worker stated I liked
(3) but, "as one worker stated, I liked
(4) but as one worker stated, "I liked
(5) but, as one worker stated, "I liked

9. Sentence 4: **Managers sometimes find that their employees' suggestions are workable their suggestions often improve productivity.**

What correction should be made to this sentence?

(1) replace their employees' with there employees'
(2) change employees' to employee's
(3) insert a semicolon after workable
(4) replace suggestions with suggestions'
(5) no correction is necessary

10. Sentence 5: **Worker morale also may be improved, along with company profits.**

Which of the following is the best way to rewrite the underlined portion of this sentence? If you think the original is the best way, choose option (1).

(1) improved, along
(2) improved along
(3) improved; along
(4) improved. along
(5) improved. Along

Writing Skills ◆ Mechanics

Items 11 to 15 refer to the following paragraph.

(1) Much has been written about "displaced homemakers" and "children of divorce." (2) According to a recent publication, "Depression, Divorce, And Death," little research has been done on how divorce relates to depression. (3) "Depression probably precedes divorce," according to Dr. Stanley Livingood author of a recent book on the subject. (4) "But, he added, "we are just beginning to discover to what extent depression also follows divorce and what its effects are." (5) Teenage suicide, a growing problem is being linked to the increasing divorce rate. (6) "Being able to talk out your problems and feelings with someone who will really listen to you is very important during this time," says Dr. Livingood.

11. Sentence 1: **Much has been written about "displaced homemakers" and "children of divorce."**

    What correction should be made to this sentence?

    (1) change written to Written
    (2) insert a semicolon after written
    (3) remove the quotation mark before displaced
    (4) change children to children's
    (5) no correction is necessary

12. Sentence 2: **According to a recent publication, "Depression, Divorce, And Death," little research has been done on how divorce relates to depression.**

    What correction should be made to this sentence?

    (1) change to to too
    (2) remove the comma after publication
    (3) change And to and
    (4) change Death," to Death",
    (5) no correction is necessary

13. Sentence 3: **"Depression probably precedes divorce," according to Dr. Stanley Livingood author of a recent book on the subject.**

    What correction should be made to this sentence?

    (1) remove the quotation mark before Depression
    (2) replace to with too
    (3) insert a comma after Livingood
    (4) insert a comma after book
    (5) no correction is necessary

14. Sentence 4: **"But, he added, "we are just beginning to discover to what extent depression also follows divorce and what its effects are."**

    What correction should be made to this sentence?

    (1) insert a quotation mark after But,
    (2) remove the quotation mark before we
    (3) change the spelling of beginning to begining
    (4) change its to it's
    (5) no correction is necessary

15. Sentence 5: **Teenage suicide, a growing problem is being linked to the increasing divorce rate.**

    What correction should be made to this sentence?

    (1) change Teenage to teenage
    (2) remove the comma after suicide
    (3) insert a comma after problem
    (4) change the spelling of increasing to incresing
    (5) no correction is necessary

Answers are on page 749.

Usage Lesson 7

Subject-Verb Agreement

Subject-verb agreement means that the two parts of a sentence—the subject and the verb—match or agree.

Read the company bulletin. Notice how the subjects and verbs agree in each sentence.

(1) Once again, Ms. Lopez is busy planning the annual company party. (2) The Garrisons have offered the use of their home for the event. (3) There is a map on the bulletin board showing the way to their house. (4) If you have any questions, Pauline and Ray know what activities are planned. (5) The tug-of-war should certainly be more fun this year since neither the shipping clerks nor Mr. Paulson is planning to attend. (6) The budget committee has finally reached a decision about bringing spouses and children. (7) Everyone is welcome!

To make a subject and verb agree, decide whether the subject is singular or plural, and then make the verb form match the subject.

Tip

Most verb forms ending in *-s* are singular: *she walks, he sings.* Most verb forms not ending in *-s* are plural: *we were, they have.* Verbs following the pronouns *I* and singular *you* are exceptions: *I am, I walk, you are, you sing.*

Rule: A singular subject (one person or thing) takes a singular verb. Many singular verb forms end in *-s: talks, is, was, has.*

Example: (Sentence 1) Once again, Ms. Lopez is busy planning the annual company party.
The singular subject, <u>Ms. Lopez</u>, requires a singular verb form. The word <u>is</u> is a singular form of the verb <u>be</u>.

Rule: A plural subject (more than one person or thing) takes a plural verb. Plural forms of some commonly used verbs are *have, were,* and *are.* The plural forms of verbs do not end in *-s.*

Example: (Sentence 2) The Garrisons have offered the use of their home for the event.
The subject in this sentence, <u>Garrisons</u>, refers to more than one person. The plural verb <u>have offered</u> agrees with the plural subject.

Rule: When a sentence starts with *here* or *there,* the subject usually comes after the verb. The subject and verb must still agree.

Example: (Sentence 3) There is a map on the bulletin board showing the way to their house.
The subject of this sentence is <u>map</u>. Since <u>map</u> is singular, the verb <u>is</u> is correct.

Compound subjects can cause confusion in determining subject-verb agreement. Study the following rules to avoid errors.

Rule: Most compound subjects joined by *and* take a plural verb.

Example: (Sentence 4) If you have any questions, Pauline and Ray know what activities are planned.

The subject <u>Pauline and Ray</u> refers to two people. The plural verb form <u>know</u> agrees with the subject.

Rule: When a singular subject and a plural subject are joined by *or, either-or, neither-nor,* or *not only-but also,* the verb agrees with the nearest subject.

Example: (Sentence 5) The tug-of-war should certainly be more fun this year since <u>neither the shipping clerks nor Mr. Paulson is planning to attend.</u>

The subject in the second part of the sentence is made up of two parts joined by <u>neither-nor</u>. The first part, <u>the shipping clerks,</u> is plural; the second part, <u>Mr. Paulson,</u> is singular. The singular verb <u>is</u> is closest to the second part and so agrees with <u>Mr. Paulson</u>.

Rule: A word that refers to a group of people is usually considered singular.

Example: (Sentence 6) The budget committee has finally reached a decision about bringing spouses and children.

Although a <u>committee</u> is made up of more than one person, there is only one committee. The singular verb <u>has reached</u> agrees with the singular subject <u>committee</u>.

Rule: Some pronouns may not seem clearly singular or plural. The following list will help you in determining subject-verb agreement.

Always Singular			Always Plural	Either Singular or Plural	
one	either	anything	several	all	any
each	neither	everything	few	some	part
much	anybody	something	both	none	half
other	everybody	nothing	many	most	
another	somebody	someone			
anyone	nobody				
everyone	no one				

Example: (Sentence 7) Everyone is welcome!
The singular verb form <u>is</u> agrees with the singular pronoun <u>everyone</u>.

Items 1 to 7 refer to the following paragraph. Choose the best answer to each item.

(1) Vince hope to sign a contract with a major league baseball team. (2) The Firebirds have offered him a tryout during spring training. (3) There are a good opportunity for a spot on the team as a relief pitcher. (4) Vince and his two friends, Raul and Al, plays sandlot ball. (5) Neither Vince nor his friends have any professional experience. (6) However, the team are very positive about Vince. (7) With work, someone with his talent are bound to succeed.

1. Sentence 1: **Vince hope to sign a contract with a major league baseball team.**

   What correction should be made to this sentence?

   (1) change Vince to Vince's
   (2) change hope to hopes
   (3) change sign to signs
   (4) change baseball to Baseball
   (5) no correction is necessary

2. Sentence 2: **The Firebirds have offered him a tryout during spring training.**

   What correction should be made to this sentence?

   (1) change Firebirds to Firebird
   (2) change have to has
   (3) change offered to offers
   (4) change spring to Spring
   (5) no correction is necessary

3. Sentence 3: **There are a good opportunity for a spot on the team as a relief pitcher.**

   What correction should be made to this sentence?

   (1) change are to is
   (2) change are to be
   (3) change are to were
   (4) change the spelling of opportunity to oportunity
   (5) no correction is necessary

4. Sentence 4: **Vince and his two friends, Raul and Al, plays sandlot ball.**

   What correction should be made to this sentence?

   (1) change two to too
   (2) remove the comma after Al
   (3) change plays to play
   (4) change sandlot to Sandlot
   (5) no correction is necessary

5. Sentence 5: **Neither Vince nor his friends have any professional experience.**

   What correction should be made to this sentence?

   (1) change Vince to vince
   (2) change nor to or
   (3) change have to has
   (4) change friends to friend's
   (5) no correction is necessary

6. Sentence 6: **However, the team are very positive about Vince.**

   What correction should be made to this sentence?

   (1) change team to Team
   (2) change team to team's
   (3) change are to were
   (4) change are to is
   (5) no correction is necessary

7. Sentence 7: **With work, someone with his talent are bound to succeed.**

   What correction should be made to this sentence?

   (1) change are to is
   (2) change are to were
   (3) change are to be
   (4) change bound to bounds
   (5) no correction is necessary

Answers are on page 750.

Lesson  Irregular Verbs

Every verb has three principal parts: present, past, and past participle. An irregular verb usually changes its spelling to make the past and past participle forms.

Read the paragraph. Notice how verbs are used.

(1) In the past decade, the recycling business has grown into a multimillion-dollar industry. (2) Scientists have known for some time that we face a tremendous waste disposal problem. (3) In addition, the amount of garbage produced by the average American has risen sharply. (4) In the past, corporations often shrank from their responsibilities in waste management. (5) They gave us plastic containers and packing materials despite the growing threat to the environment. (6) They chose to ignore the problem before; now they must look for solutions.

With regular verbs, the past and past participle forms are made by adding *-d* or *-ed* to the present form. For example, the principal parts of the verb *ask* are *ask, asked,* and *asked.* Irregular verbs do not follow this pattern. The *to . . .* form of the verb is called the **infinitive.** The infinitive is formed by adding *to* in front of the present part of a verb.

The following rules will help you correctly use the present, past, and past participle forms of all verbs, including the irregular ones.

Rule: The past participle form always uses a helping verb, such as *has, have, had, is, are, was,* or *were.*

Study these sentences. The past participle form is underlined once. The helping verb in each case is underlined twice.

Examples: (Sentence 1) In the past decade, the recycling business <u>has</u> <u>grown</u> into a multimillion-dollar industry.
(Sentence 2) Scientists <u>have</u> <u>known</u> for some time that we face a tremendous waste disposal problem.
(Sentence 3) In addition, the amount of garbage produced by the average American <u>has</u> <u>risen</u> sharply.

Rule: The past form never uses a helping verb.
Examples: (Sentence 4) In the past, corporations often <u>shrank</u> from their responsibilities in waste management.
(Sentence 5) They <u>gave</u> us plastic containers and packing materials despite the growing threat to the environment.
(Sentence 6) They <u>chose</u> to ignore the problem before; now they must look for solutions.

Some irregular verbs can be grouped according to the patterns by which they change. Study the verbs in the charts below. Notice how -*n* or -*en* is added to the past form to make the past participle. (When the past form ends in a consonant, as in *bit,* the consonant is doubled before -*en* is added.)

Present	Past	Past Participle
break	broke	broken
bite	bit	bitten
choose	chose	chosen
freeze	froze	frozen

Present	Past	Past Participle
speak	spoke	spoken
steal	stole	stolen
swear	swore	sworn
wear	wore	worn

Here is another group of irregular verbs. Notice how the middle vowel changes from *i* in the present form to *a* in the past and to *u* in the past participle.

Present	Past	Past Participle
begin	began	begun
drink	drank	drunk
ring	rang	rung

Present	Past	Past Participle
sing	sang	sung
sink	sank	sunk
swim	swam	swum

In the irregular verbs that follow, notice how the vowels change to make the past form. To make the past participle, -*n* or -*en* is added to the present form. (In some verbs, such as *ridden* and *written,* the last consonant must be doubled in forming the past participle.)

Present	Past	Past Participle
blow	blew	blown
drive	drove	driven
eat	ate	eaten
give	gave	given
grow	grew	grown
know	knew	known

Present	Past	Past Participle
ride	rode	ridden
rise	rose	risen
see	saw	seen
shake	shook	shaken
take	took	taken
write	wrote	written

The irregular verbs in this chart do not follow a pattern.

Present	Past	Past Participle
come	came	come
run	ran	run
go	went	gone
make	made	made

ged Exercise Irregular Verbs

Items 1 to 7 refer to the following paragraph.
Choose the best answer to each item.

(1) Ava knowed she would be ready for the triathlon in the spring. (2) Every morning, she eaten breakfast at 6 o'clock to start her training. (3) For comfort, Ava weared loose-fitting jogging clothes. (4) She drive to the beach about five miles away. (5) There she run for one hour. (6) For the next hour she swum. (7) To finish her training, she rode her bike the length of the beach.

1. Sentence 1: **Ava knowed she would be ready for the triathlon in the spring.**

   What correction should be made to this sentence?

   (1) change knowed to knew
   (2) change knowed to known
   (3) change for to four
   (4) change spring to Spring
   (5) no correction is necessary

2. Sentence 2: **Every morning, she eaten breakfast at 6 o'clock to start her training.**

   What correction should be made to this sentence?

   (1) change eaten to eat
   (2) change eaten to ate
   (3) change eaten to eats
   (4) change eaten to eated
   (5) no correction is necessary

3. Sentence 3: **For comfort, Ava weared loose-fitting jogging clothes.**

   What correction should be made to this sentence?

   (1) change weared to wear
   (2) change weared to wore
   (3) insert had before weared
   (4) change jogging to Jogging
   (5) no correction is necessary

4. Sentence 4: **She drive to the beach about five miles away.**

   What correction should be made to this sentence?

   (1) change drive to drived
   (2) change drive to drove
   (3) change drive to driven
   (4) insert had before drive
   (5) no correction is necessary

5. Sentence 5: **There she run for one hour.**

   What correction should be made to this sentence?

   (1) change There to Their
   (2) change There to They're
   (3) change run to runned
   (4) change run to ran
   (5) no correction is necessary

6. Sentence 6: **For the next hour she swum.**

   What correction should be made to this sentence?

   (1) change swum to swimmed
   (2) change swum to swims
   (3) change swum to swam
   (4) insert was before swum
   (5) no correction is necessary

7. Sentence 7: **To finish her training, she rode her bike the length of the beach.**

   What correction should be made to this sentence?

   (1) change rode to ride
   (2) change rode to rided
   (3) change rode to ridden
   (4) change rode to had ridden
   (5) no correction is necessary

Answers are on page 751.

Lesson  Verb Tenses

There are six verb tenses: present, past, future, present perfect, past perfect, and future perfect.

Rule: There are two present tenses. One expresses something that is commonly done or generally true. The other expresses an action that is happening now.

I walk./We walk.	I am walking./We are walking.
You walk.	You are walking.
He, she, it walks./They walk.	He, she, it is walking.
	They are walking.

Example: Mike <u>walks</u> three miles each day. Mike <u>is walking</u> his dog.

Rule: The past tense expresses an action that was started and completed in the past, or a condition that was true in the past. The past tense is formed by adding *-ed* or *-d* to the present form.

	I walked.		We walked.
Singular	You walked.	**Plural**	You walked.
	He, she, it walked.		They walked.

Example: I <u>walked</u> into the room to welcome my guests.

Rule: The future tense expresses an action or condition that will take place or be true in the future. The future tense is expressed by using *shall* or *will* with the verb's present form.

	I shall/will walk.		We shall/will walk.
Singular	You shall/will walk.	**Plural**	You shall/will walk.
	He, she, it shall/will walk.		They shall/will walk.

Example: The bride and groom <u>will walk</u> down the aisle.

Rule: The present perfect tense expresses an action completed at some indefinite time in the past. It also expresses an action that began in the past and continues in the present. The present perfect is formed by using *has* or *have* with the verb's past participle.

	I have walked.		We have walked.
Singular	You have walked.	**Plural**	You have walked.
	He, she, it has walked.		They have walked.

Example: We <u>have walked</u> along this river before.

Rule: The past perfect tense expresses an action that began and ended before another past action began. The past perfect is expressed by using *had* with the verb's past participle.

	I had walked.		We had walked.
Singular	You had walked.	**Plural**	You had walked.
	He, she, it had walked.		They had walked.

Example: I <u>had walked</u> two blocks when it started to rain.

Writing Skills ◆ Usage

Rule: The future perfect tense expresses a future action that will begin and end before another definite future action begins. The future perfect uses *shall have* or *will have* with the verb's past participle.

	Singular		**Plural**
	I shall have/will have walked.		We shall have/will have walked.
	You shall have/will have walked.		You shall have/will have walked.
	He, she, it shall have/will have walked.		They shall have/will have walked.

Example: He <u>will have walked</u> ten miles when he is through.

The Verb Be

The most frequently used verb is *be*, an irregular verb.

Present Tense		**Past Tense**	
Singular	**Plural**	**Singular**	**Plural**
I am	We are	I was	We were
You are	You are	You were	You were
He, she, it is	They are	He, she, it was	They were

Future Tense: I shall/will be
Present Perfect Tense: I have been
Past Perfect Tense: I had been
Future Perfect Tense: I shall/will have been

Rule: Use *were* when a sentence expresses a wish or a thought contrary to fact.
Example: I wish I <u>were</u> better at drawing.

Rule: Use a form of *be* and the present participle (the *-ing* verb form) when a subject is doing an action.
Example: We <u>are planning</u> to build a house.

Rule: Use a form of *be* and the past participle when a subject receives the action.
Example: All the crops <u>were harvested</u> last week.

Rule: Use *be* with clauses beginning with *that* which come after the verb and express a request or recommendation.
Example: It is important that they <u>be</u> at the airport early.

Be aware of troublesome verb pairs—such as *learn/teach* and *precede/proceed*—that are commonly confused because their meanings are somewhat related.

Present	Past	Past Participle
learn (to gain knowledge)	learned	learned
teach (to give knowledge)	taught	taught
precede (to go or come before)	preceded	preceded
proceed (to continue)	proceeded	proceeded

Items 1 to 6 refer to the following paragraph. Choose the best answer to each item.

(1) Recently, Ms. Barlow has forgetting details about her work tasks. (2) She wishes she was more organized. (3) Ms. Barlow decide her old time-management system is not working out. (4) So she writes down everything she was needed to do during the month. (5) Then she proceeds to divide her work into daily and weekly tasks. (6) Finally, she has created a form to record her telephone messages. (7) She already feels more organized and decides she will have used this new plan next month too.

1. Sentence 1: **Recently, Ms. Barlow has forgetting details about her work tasks.**

   Which of the following is the best way to write the underlined portion of this sentence? If you think the original is the best way, choose option (1).

   (1) has forgetting
   (2) will be forgetting
   (3) has been forgetting
   (4) has forgot
   (5) had forgetting

2. Sentence 2: **She wishes she was more organized.**

   What correction should be made to this sentence?

   (1) change wishes to wish
   (2) change was to is
   (3) change was to were
   (4) change was to has been
   (5) no correction is necessary

3. Sentence 3: **Ms. Barlow decide her old time-management system is not working out.**

   What correction should be made to this sentence?

   (1) change decide to decides
   (2) change decide to will have decide
   (3) change decide to have decided
   (4) change is to are
   (5) no correction is necessary

4. Sentence 4: **So she writes down everything she was needed to do during the month.**

   What correction should be made to this sentence?

   (1) change writes to written
   (2) change writes to had wrote
   (3) change was to were
   (4) change was needed to needs
   (5) no correction is necessary

5. Sentence 5: **Then she proceeds to divide her work into daily and weekly tasks.**

   Which of the following is the best way to write the underlined portion of this sentence? If you think the original is the best way, choose option (1).

   (1) proceeds
   (2) has proceeded
   (3) procedes
   (4) will have proceeded
   (5) proceed

6. Sentence 7: **She already feels more organized and decides she will have used this new plan next month too.**

What correction should be made to this sentence?

(1) change feels to feeled
(2) change will have used to will use
(3) change month to month's
(4) change too to to
(5) no correction is necessary

Items 7 to 10 refer to the following paragraph.

(1) Jim has been working in the bookstore for one month. (2) When he has completed his probation period, he will have receive a promotion with a salary increase. (3) His favorite part of the job is helped customers locate books. (4) Today he are scheduled to stock shelves and to work the cash register.

7. Sentence 1: **Jim has been working in the bookstore for one month.**

What correction should be made to this sentence?

(1) remove has
(2) change working to worked
(3) change bookstore to Bookstore
(4) change one to won
(5) no correction is necessary

8. Sentence 2: **When he has completed his probation period, he will have receive a promotion with a salary increase.**

What correction should be made to this sentence?

(1) remove has
(2) change has completed to is completing
(3) remove have
(4) remove will
(5) no correction is necessary

9. Sentence 3: **His favorite part of the job is helped customers locate books.**

What correction should be made to this sentence?

(1) insert a comma after job
(2) change is to were
(3) change helped to help
(4) change helped to helping
(5) no correction is necessary

10. Sentence 4: **Today he are scheduled to stock shelves and to work the cash register.**

What correction should be made to this sentence?

(1) change are to been
(2) change are to were
(3) change are to is
(4) change work to worked
(5) no correction is necessary

Tip Use a helping verb with past and present participle forms, but never with simple past-tense forms. Note that the past and past participle forms for some irregular verbs are the same. Examples: *made, sat, laid, kept, told, read.*

Answers are on page 751.

Lesson  Pronouns

Personal Pronouns

A **personal pronoun** takes the place of a specific person, place, or thing. Personal pronouns can be used as subjects or objects.

Subject Pronouns		Object Pronouns	
Singular	**Plural**	**Singular**	**Plural**
I	we	me	us
you	you	you	you
she, he, it	they	her, him, it	them

Rule: A subject pronoun is used as the subject of a sentence.
Example: Tom is a writer. <u>He</u> is working on a new book.
(<u>He</u> is the pronoun subject of the second sentence.)
Rule: An object pronoun is used as the object of a verb or of a preposition.
Example: Tom <u>will finish it</u> soon. We are very proud <u>of him</u>.
(The pronoun <u>it</u> is the object of the verb <u>will finish</u>; the pronoun <u>him</u> is the object of the preposition <u>of</u>.)
Rule: In a compound subject or object, the pronoun is always last. When used with another pronoun, <u>I</u> or <u>me</u> is placed last.
Example: Tom <u>showed</u> <u>Ann</u> and <u>me</u> the first chapter.
(<u>Ann</u> and the personal pronoun <u>me</u> are objects of the verb <u>showed</u>.)
If you are unsure about a pronoun, see if it makes sense by itself: Tom showed <u>me</u> (not <u>I</u>) the first chapter.

Common Pronoun Errors

Rule: Use a subject pronoun when a pronoun that refers to the subject follows a linking verb.
Example: The winner of the race will be <u>she</u>. (not <u>her</u>)
Rule: When a comparison is made using the words *than* or *as*, words are often omitted from the sentence. To choose the correct pronoun, mentally fill in the missing words.
Example: Jon likes fish more than <u>she</u>. (. . . than <u>she likes fish</u>)
Rule: When a pronoun is used for a subject, use a subject pronoun.
Example: The two musicians, Mary and <u>he</u>, entertained the crowd.
(Mentally substitute the pronoun for the compound subject to decide whether the pronoun "sounds right." <u>He</u> entertained the crowd.)
Rule: When a pronoun is used for an object, use an object pronoun.
Example: I missed Raul and <u>him</u>.
(Mentally substitute the pronoun for the compound object to decide whether the pronoun "sounds right." I missed <u>him</u>.)

Writing Skills ◆ Usage

Possessive Pronouns

A **possessive pronoun** is a word that can take the place of a possessive noun. Use a possessive pronoun to show ownership.

Rule: A possessive pronoun is used before nouns or used alone to show ownership.

Examples: This is <u>Brent's</u> horse. (<u>Brent's</u> is a possessive noun.)
This is <u>his</u> horse. (The possessive pronoun <u>his</u> is used before the noun <u>horse</u>.)
This horse is <u>his</u>. (The possessive pronoun <u>his</u> is used alone.)

	Used Before Nouns	Used Alone
Singular	my, your, his, her, its	mine, yours, his, hers
Plural	our, your, their	ours, yours, theirs

Possessive personal pronouns do not use apostrophes.

Reflexive and Intensive Pronouns

Reflexive and intensive pronouns are formed by adding *-self* or *-selves* to certain pronouns.

Singular	**Plural**
myself	ourselves
yourself	yourselves
himself, herself, itself	themselves

Rule: Use a reflexive pronoun when the subject is both the doer and the receiver of the action.

Example: <u>I</u> hurt <u>myself</u> playing soccer.
(The pronoun <u>I</u> is the subject, or doer, and the pronoun <u>myself</u> is the object, or receiver, of the action.)

Rule: Use an intensive pronoun to add emphasis to another noun or pronoun. An intensive pronoun can appear either immediately after the subject or in the predicate.

Examples: <u>Dan</u> <u>himself</u> built the house.
<u>Dan</u> built the house <u>himself</u>.
(The pronoun <u>himself</u> gives emphasis to the subject <u>Dan</u>.)

Rule: Do not use a reflexive pronoun as a subject.
Example: <u>I</u> work at a fast-food restaurant. (not <u>Myself</u>)

Rule: The spellings <u>hisself</u> and <u>theirselves</u> are incorrect.
Examples: Donald painted the barn <u>himself</u>. (not <u>hisself</u>)
Leslie and Jean made the bread <u>themselves</u>. (not <u>theirselves</u>)

Items 1 to 7 refer to the following letter. Choose the <u>best answer</u> to each item.

Dear Neighbor:
   (1) We live in such a beautiful neighborhood. (2) But lately its has been marred by suggestive, and sometimes frightening, billboards. (3) Judging from the billboards that surround ours apartments, there are no guidelines that advertisers must follow. (4) Many children live in our area, and them are exposed to these offensive pictures daily. (5) Jan Sheridan, Neal Oshiro, and me are forming a committee to look into the situation. (6) If you want to join us to solve this problem, contact me at 555-3358. (7) Us are hoping to eliminate the billboards altogether.

1. Sentence 1: **We live in such a beautiful neighborhood.**

    What correction should be made to this sentence?

    (1) change <u>live</u> to <u>lives</u>
    (2) insert <u>have</u> before <u>live</u>
    (3) insert <u>had</u> before <u>live</u>
    (4) insert a comma after <u>live</u>
    (5) no correction is necessary

2. Sentence 2: **But lately its has been marred by suggestive, and sometimes frightening, billboards.**

    What correction should be made to this sentence?

    (1) change <u>its</u> to <u>they</u>
    (2) change <u>its</u> to <u>it</u>
    (3) change <u>its</u> to <u>them</u>
    (4) remove <u>has</u>
    (5) no correction is necessary

3. Sentence 3: **Judging from the billboards that surround ours apartments, there are no guidelines that advertisers must follow.**

    What correction should be made to this sentence?

    (1) change <u>surround</u> to <u>surrounds</u>
    (2) change <u>ours</u> to <u>our</u>
    (3) change <u>there</u> to <u>their</u>
    (4) change <u>there</u> to <u>they're</u>
    (5) no correction is necessary

4. Sentence 4: **Many children live in our area, and them are exposed to these offensive pictures daily.**

    What correction should be made to this sentence?

    (1) change <u>our</u> to <u>ours</u>
    (2) change <u>our</u> to <u>are</u>
    (3) change <u>them</u> to <u>theirselves</u>
    (4) change <u>them</u> to <u>they</u>
    (5) no correction is necessary

5. Sentence 5: **Jan Sheridan, Neal Oshiro, and me are forming a committee to look into the situation.**

    What correction should be made to this sentence?

    (1) change <u>me</u> to <u>mine</u>
    (2) change <u>me</u> to <u>us</u>
    (3) change <u>me</u> to <u>I</u>
    (4) change the spelling of <u>committee</u> to <u>commitee</u>
    (5) no correction is necessary

6. Sentence 6: **If you want to join us to solve this problem, contact me at 555-3358.**

What correction should be made to this sentence?

(1) change you to your
(2) change us to we
(3) change us to they
(4) change me to I
(5) no correction is necessary

7. Sentence 7: **Us are hoping to eliminate the billboards altogether.**

What correction should be made to this sentence?

(1) change Us to We
(2) change are to is
(3) change hoping to hoped
(4) change the spelling of altogether to all together
(5) no correction is necessary

Items 8 to 12 refer to the following paragraph.

(1) Joyce Webberly, a postal worker, wanted to improve hers reading speed. (2) She took a course that promised to help herself understand and remember more of what she read. (3) She learned that the average adult reads between 150 and 200 words per minute. (4) A fellow student and herself increased their reading speeds from 175 to 600 words per minute. (5) Now they can read a book in about too hours.

8. Sentence 1: **Joyce Webberly, a postal worker, wanted to improve hers reading speed.**

What correction should be made to this sentence?

(1) change wanted to has wanting
(2) change wanted to will had wanted
(3) change hers to her
(4) change hers to herself
(5) no correction is necessary

9. Sentence 2: **She took a course that promised to help herself understand and remember more of what she read.**

What correction should be made to this sentence?

(1) change She to Her
(2) change herself to her
(3) change remember to remembered
(4) insert is before remember
(5) no correction is necessary

10. Sentence 3: **She learned that the average adult reads between 150 and 200 words per minute.**

What correction should be made to this sentence?

(1) change She to Them
(2) change learned to teached
(3) change reads to was reading
(4) change reads to read
(5) no correction is necessary

11. Sentence 4: **A fellow student and herself increased their reading speeds from 175 to 600 words per minute.**

What correction should be made to this sentence?

(1) change herself to her
(2) change herself to she
(3) change their to there
(4) change their to theirselves
(5) no correction is necessary

12. Sentence 5: **Now they can read a book in about too hours.**

What correction should be made to this sentence?

(1) change they to them
(2) insert a comma after book
(3) change too to two
(4) change hours to ours
(5) no correction is necessary

Answers are on page 752.

Lesson  Pronouns and Antecedents

The noun that a pronoun stands for and refers to is the **antecedent** of that pronoun. Just as a subject and its verb must agree, a pronoun must agree with its antecedent.

Read these notes from a hotel desk clerk's records. As you read, identify the pronouns and their antecedents.

> (1) The Johnsons and their children moved to Room 215. (2) June Aryiku and Lynn Dupay will be meeting their guests in the lobby at 6:30 P.M. (3) Neither Kevin Escalante nor the Livingstons are happy with their room assignments. (4) Jon Maeda, a friend of the Livingstons, is holding a meeting in his room tomorrow at 8:30 A.M.
>
> (5) Anita Vasquez wants her luggage held at the front desk. (6) The airline may deliver it in the middle of the night. (7) We should contact the airline ourselves if the luggage does not come by morning.

Rule: A pronoun must agree with its antecedent in number—singular or plural.

Example: (Sentence 1) The Johnsons and their children moved to Room 215.
The plural pronoun <u>their</u> agrees with the plural antecedent <u>Johnsons</u>.

Rule: Use a plural pronoun with a compound antecedent (two or more nouns joined by *and*).

Example: (Sentence 2) June Aryiku and Lynn Dupay will be meeting their guests in the lobby at 6:30 P.M.
The plural pronoun <u>their</u> agrees with the compound antecedent and subject <u>June Aryiku and Lynn Dupay</u>.

Rule: When a compound antecedent is joined by *or, either-or,* or *neither-nor,* the pronoun should agree in number with the nearest antecedent.

Example: (Sentence 3) Neither Kevin Escalante nor the Livingstons are happy with their room assignments.
The plural pronoun <u>their</u> agrees with the nearest antecedent, <u>the Livingstons</u>.

Writing Skills ◆ Usage

Note:	Do not be fooled by prepositional phrases or by nonessential phrases set off by commas.
Example:	(Sentence 4) Jon Maeda, a friend of the Livingstons, is holding a meeting in his room tomorrow at 8:30 A.M. The singular pronoun <u>his</u> agrees with the antecedent <u>Jon Maeda</u>. The plural noun <u>Livingstons</u> does not affect the pronoun choice.
Rule:	A pronoun must agree with its antecedent in gender—masculine, feminine, or neuter.
Examples:	(Sentence 5) Anita Vasquez wants her luggage held at the front desk. <u>Anita Vasquez</u> is a woman's name, so the pronoun <u>her</u> is used. (Sentence 6) The airline may deliver it in the middle of the night. The neuter pronoun <u>it</u> refers to the <u>luggage</u>. In a paragraph, the antecedent may be found in an earlier sentence.
Note:	When the gender of a singular antecedent naming a person is unclear, use the masculine gender, or use *he or she, his or hers,* or *him or her;* if the unclear antecedent is plural, use *they, their, theirs,* or *them.*
Example:	Each hotel guest should return <u>his or her</u> room key by 11 A.M.
Rule:	A pronoun must agree with its antecedent in person—first, second, or third.

First person: I, we, me, us, my, mine, our, ours, myself, ourselves
Second person: you, your, yours, yourselves
Third person: he, she, it, they, him, her, them, his, hers, its, their, theirs, himself, herself, themselves

Example:	(Sentence 7) We should contact the airline ourselves if the luggage does not come by morning. The first-person intensive pronoun <u>ourselves</u> agrees with the first-person antecedent and subject <u>We</u>.

To decide which pronoun to use in a sentence, find its antecedent. Ask yourself: What is its number? What is its gender? Then choose a pronoun that agrees with its antecedent on both points.

⬡ ged Exercise Pronouns and Antecedents

Items 1 to 12 refer to the following paragraph. Choose the best answer to each item.

(1) Me and Joan discussed last Tuesday's fire drill. (2) We decided to tell you our views of it. (3) Apparently, the employees on the second floor never left his offices since the alarm did not ring on that floor. (4) I tried to exit through the fire door on the third floor and found they was locked. (5) Jason started down the south stairwell and, feeling the cold, realized he had left her coat upstairs and went back for it. (6) Neither the accountants nor Howard got up from their coffee break to leave. (7) The plant manager and the foreman didn't know which exit was closest to his offices. (8) Jenny has since decided her needs someone assigned to call the fire department. (9) Everyone should improve their knowledge of safety procedures. (10) Let's consider appointing Joan to be our fire marshal because he has such great organizational skills. (11) There's a need for each employee to make it our own responsibility to learn fire safety. (12) Us employees must realize that fire safety is very important and should be taken seriously. (13) We'll try a fire drill again on Friday.

1. Sentence 1: **Me and Joan discussed last Tuesday's fire drill.**

   What correction should be made to this sentence?

   (1) change Me to I
   (2) change Me and Joan to Joan and me
   (3) change Me and Joan to Joan and I
   (4) change Tuesday's to Tuesdays
   (5) no correction is necessary

2. Sentence 2: **We decided to tell you our views of it.**

   What correction should be made to this sentence?

   (1) change We to Us
   (2) change our to our's
   (3) change views to veiws
   (4) change it to them
   (5) no correction is necessary

3. Sentence 3: **Apparently, the employees on the second floor never left his offices since the alarm did not ring on that floor.**

   What correction should be made to this sentence?

   (1) change second to Second
   (2) change his to their
   (3) change his to his or her
   (4) change ring to rang
   (5) no correction is necessary

4. Sentence 4: **I tried to exit through the fire door on the third floor and found they was locked.**

   What correction should be made to this sentence?

   (1) change I to Myself
   (2) change through to threw
   (3) change they to it
   (4) replace they with them
   (5) no correction is necessary

5. Sentence 5: **Jason started down the south stairwell and, feeling the cold, realized he had left her coat upstairs and went back for it.**

Which of the following is the best way to write the underlined portion of this sentence? If you think that the original is the best way, choose option (1).

(1) her
(2) his
(3) him
(4) their
(5) hers

6. Sentence 6: **Neither the accountants nor Howard got up from their coffee break to leave.**

What correction should be made to this sentence?

(1) change Neither to Either
(2) change nor to or
(3) change got to get
(4) change their to his
(5) no correction is necessary

7. Sentence 7: **The plant manager and the foreman didn't know which exit was closest to his offices.**

What correction should be made to this sentence?

(1) change didn't to did'nt
(2) change was to were
(3) change his to their
(4) change his to his or her
(5) no correction is necessary

8. Sentence 8: **Jenny has since decided her needs someone assigned to call the fire department.**

What correction should be made to this sentence?

(1) change has to have
(2) change her to his or her
(3) change her to she
(4) replace her needs with she need
(5) no correction is necessary

9. Sentence 9: **Everyone should improve their knowledge of safety procedures.**

What correction should be made to this sentence?

(1) change knowledge to knowlege
(2) change their to our
(3) change their to his or her
(4) change procedures to proceedures
(5) no correction is necessary

10. Sentence 10: **Let's consider appointing Joan to be our fire marshal because he has such great organizational skills.**

What correction should be made to this sentence?

(1) change let's to lets
(2) change he to her
(3) change he to him
(4) change he to she
(5) no correction is necessary

11. Sentence 11: **There's a need for each employee to make it our own responsibility to learn fire safety.**

What correction should be made to this sentence?

(1) change There's to Theirs
(2) insert a comma after responsibility
(3) change our to their
(4) change our to his or her
(5) no correction is necessary

12. Sentence 12: **Us employees must realize that fire safety is very important and should be taken seriously.**

What correction should be made to this sentence?

(1) change is to are
(2) change seriously to serious
(3) change Us to We
(4) change realize to realizes
(5) no correction is necessary

Answers are on page 753.

Lesson  Indefinite Pronouns

An **indefinite pronoun** makes a general reference to a person, place, or thing. Some indefinite pronouns are always singular and some are always plural.

Singular Pronouns			Plural Pronouns
another	everyone	one	both
anybody	everything	other	several
anyone	much	somebody	few
anything	neither	someone	many
each	nobody	something	
either	no one		
everybody	nothing		

Rule: Use a singular pronoun when its antecedent is a singular indefinite pronoun.

Examples: <u>Everyone</u> wanted <u>his or her</u> plane ticket right away.
(The pronoun <u>Everyone</u> is a singular antecedent. Since the gender is unclear, the singular compound pronoun <u>his or her</u> correctly agrees with it.)
<u>Each</u> of the bottled waters has <u>its</u> own distinct taste.
(The indefinite pronoun <u>Each</u> is the subject and antecedent in this sentence. The third-person singular pronoun <u>its</u> correctly agrees with it. Note that the prepositional phrase <u>of the bottled waters</u> does not affect the number of the subject <u>Each</u>.)

Rule: Use a plural pronoun when its antecedent is a plural indefinite pronoun.

Example: After the shoppers heard the announcement, <u>several</u> steered <u>their</u> carts toward the bakery.
(The indefinite pronoun <u>several</u> is the subject of the second clause in the sentence. Since <u>several</u> is always plural, the pronoun <u>their</u> correctly agrees with it.)

Troublesome Pronouns

Rule: *Who* (or *whoever*) is used when it functions as the subject of a verb.

Example: <u>Who</u> gave you the notes?
(<u>Who</u> is the subject of the verb <u>gave</u>.)
One way to make sure that you have used *who* correctly is to put the subject before the verb and substitute *he* for *who*. If the sentence makes sense, *who* is used correctly.

Example: <u>Who</u> gave you the notes? He gave you the notes.

Rule:	*Whom* (or *whomever*) is used when it functions as the direct object of a verb or the object of a preposition.
Examples:	Whom did they invite?
	(<u>Whom</u> is the object of the verb phrase <u>did invite</u>.)
	<u>Whom</u> are you talking about?
	(<u>Whom</u> is the object of the preposition <u>about</u>.)
	To be sure that you have used *whom* correctly, put the subject before the verb and substitute *him* for *whom*. If the sentence makes sense, *whom* is used correctly.
Example:	<u>Whom</u> did they invite? They invited him.

Rule:	*Whose* is used to show possession.
Example:	This is the man <u>whose</u> dog bit my sister.
	(The pronoun <u>whose</u> shows that the <u>man</u> possesses a <u>dog</u>.)
	To be sure that you have used *whose* correctly, try substituting the word *his* for *whose*. If the pronoun *his* could make sense in the phrase, you have used *whose* correctly.
Example:	<u>His</u> dog bit my sister.

Rule:	Pronouns such as *neither*, *no one*, and *nobody* are sometimes incorrectly used in double negatives. Sentences with two negative words contain a double negative. In order to make a sentence mean "no" or "not," use only one negative.
Example:	<u>Nobody</u> is able to work today.
	(If you said "Nobody isn't able to work today," you would have a double negative: the pronoun <u>Nobody</u> and the <u>-n't</u> that stands for <u>not</u> in <u>isn't</u>.)

Common Pronoun Errors

Some pronouns can be confused with words that sound like them. Study the spelling and meaning of the following words.

Rule:	<u>It's</u> is a contraction of <u>it is</u>.
Example:	<u>It's</u> time to open the store.
Rule:	<u>Its</u> is a possessive pronoun.
Example:	Look for the book. <u>Its</u> cover is blue.

Rule:	<u>They're</u> is a contraction of <u>they are</u>.
Example:	<u>They're</u> in charge of promotion.
Rule:	<u>There</u> is an adverb that shows direction.
Example:	The cash register is over <u>there</u>.
Rule:	<u>Their</u> is a possessive pronoun.
Example:	The cats are longhairs. <u>Their</u> fur is thick.

Rule:	<u>Who's</u> is a contraction of <u>who is</u>.
Example:	<u>Who's</u> going with me?
Rule:	<u>Whose</u> is a possessive pronoun.
Example:	<u>Whose</u> coat is this?

ged Exercise | Indefinite Pronouns

Items 1 to 6 refer to the following paragraph. Choose the best answer to each item.

(1) Anyone who likes a challenge is welcome to add their ideas to the block-party committee. (2) Several have expressed his interest in a scavenger hunt. (3) A few have volunteered his or her yards for the barbecue. (4) Karla, whom is really creative, will help decorate. (5) We need someone to donate her time to plan games. (6) Whomever has time and energy is welcome.

1. Sentence 1: **Anyone who likes a challenge is welcome to add their ideas to the block-party committee.**

   What correction should be made to this sentence?

   (1) change likes to like
   (2) change is to are
   (3) change their to her
   (4) change their to his or her
   (5) no correction is necessary

2. Sentence 2: **Several have expressed his interest in a scavenger hunt.**

   What correction should be made to this sentence?

   (1) change have to has
   (2) change his to his or her
   (3) change his to their
   (4) change his to theirs
   (5) no correction is necessary

3. Sentence 3: **A few have volunteered his or her yards for the barbecue.**

   What correction should be made to this sentence?

   (1) change have to has
   (2) change volunteered to volunteer
   (3) change his or her to their
   (4) change his or her to theirselves
   (5) no correction is necessary

4. Sentence 4: **Karla, whom is really creative, will help decorate.**

   What correction should be made to this sentence?

   (1) remove the comma after Karla
   (2) change whom to who
   (3) change whom to whose
   (4) change is to are
   (5) no correction is necessary

5. Sentence 5: **We need someone to donate her time to plan games.**

   What correction should be made to this sentence?

   (1) change need to needs
   (2) change her to hers
   (3) change her to their
   (4) change her to his or her
   (5) no correction is necessary

6. Sentence 6: **Whomever has time and energy is welcome.**

   What correction should be made to this sentence?

   (1) change Whomever to Whoever
   (2) change Whomever to Whosever
   (3) change is to are
   (4) change is to were
   (5) no correction is necessary

Items 7 to 12 refer to the following paragraph.

(1) Dr. Merriam of the Northeast Medical Center advises everyone to add some form of exercise to their daily routine. (2) At a recent medical conference, Dr. Merriam suggested that anyone who wants to reduce stress in her life should exercise. (3) "Everybody should choose a form of exercise that suits her lifestyle," he stated. (4) "Most assume jogging and swimming are the best ways to condition theirselves. (5) I see nothing wrong with neither choice." (6) "Too much are made about the type of exercise chosen," Dr. Merriam concluded. (7) "The most important thing is the frequency of the exercise."

7. Sentence 1: **Dr. Merriam of the Northeast Medical Center advises everyone to add some form of exercise to their daily routine.**

What correction should be made to this sentence?

(1) change the spelling of <u>advises</u> to <u>advices</u>
(2) change the spelling of <u>exercise</u> to <u>exersice</u>
(3) change <u>their</u> to <u>him</u>
(4) change <u>their</u> to <u>his or her</u>
(5) no correction is necessary

8. Sentence 2: **At a recent medical conference, Dr. Merriam suggested that anyone who wants to reduce stress in her life should exercise.**

What correction should be made to this sentence?

(1) change <u>medical</u> to <u>Medical</u>
(2) change <u>who</u> to <u>whom</u>
(3) change <u>wants</u> to <u>want</u>
(4) change <u>her</u> to <u>his or her</u>
(5) change <u>her</u> to <u>their</u>

9. Sentence 3: **"Everybody should choose a form of exercise that suits her lifestyle," he stated.**

What correction should be made to this sentence?

(1) change <u>choose</u> to <u>chose</u>
(2) change <u>her</u> to <u>their</u>
(3) change <u>her</u> to <u>his or her</u>
(4) change <u>her</u> to <u>hers</u>
(5) no correction is necessary

10. Sentence 4: **"Most assume jogging and swimming are the best ways to condition theirselves.**

What correction should be made to this sentence?

(1) change <u>are</u> to <u>is</u>
(2) change <u>are</u> to <u>was</u>
(3) change <u>theirselves</u> to <u>himself</u>
(4) change <u>theirselves</u> to <u>themselves</u>
(5) no correction is necessary

11. Sentence 5: **I see nothing wrong with neither choice."**

What correction should be made to this sentence?

(1) change <u>see</u> to <u>sees</u>
(2) change <u>neither</u> to <u>either</u>
(3) insert <u>not</u> before <u>neither</u>
(4) change <u>neither</u> to <u>none</u>
(5) no correction is necessary

12. Sentence 6: **"Too much are made about the type of exercise chosen," Dr. Merriam concluded.**

What correction should be made to this sentence?

(1) replace <u>Too</u> with <u>Two</u>
(2) replace <u>are</u> with <u>is</u>
(3) remove the quotation mark after <u>chosen,</u>
(4) change <u>Dr.</u> to <u>dr.</u>
(5) no correction is necessary

Answers are on page 754.

Lesson 13

Adjectives and Adverbs

Adjectives and adverbs modify or describe other words.

Read the following advertising copy. Look for adjectives and adverbs as you read.

> **Tip**
>
> Many adverbs look the same as adjectives except for the *-ly* ending. (cautious, cautious*ly;* quiet, quiet*ly*) To decide whether to use an adverb or an adjective, look at the word being modified. If the word is a noun or pronoun, use an adjective. If the word is a verb, adjective, or other adverb, use an adverb.

(1) Our new automobile, the XP20 Sedan, is luxurious and affordable. (2) Its powerful V-6 engine has been very carefully engineered for a remarkably smooth ride. (3) In addition, the XP20 is safer and more reliable than the leading competitor. (4) If you want to drive the finest car on the market today, test drive the new XP20—a masterpiece of modern technology.

Rule: Use an adjective to describe a noun or pronoun. Adjectives tell *what kind, which one, how many,* or *how much.*

Example: (Sentence 1) Our new automobile, the XP20 Sedan, is luxurious and affordable.
The adjectives new, luxurious, and affordable modify the noun automobile. Adjectives may come before the word they modify or after a form of the verb be.

Rule: Use an adverb to describe an action verb. Also, use an adverb to describe an adjective or another adverb. Adverbs tell *when, where, how,* or *to what extent.* Many adverbs end in *-ly* but some common ones such as *very* do not.

Example: (Sentence 2) Its powerful V-6 engine has been very carefully engineered for a remarkably smooth ride.
The verb in this sentence is has been engineered. The adverb carefully tells *how* the car was engineered. The adverb very modifies the adverb carefully, telling *how* carefully. The adjective smooth describes ride. The adverb remarkably modifies the adjective, telling *how* smooth the ride is.

Note: Linking verbs, especially *feel, touch, smell,* and *taste,* are often modified by an adjective.

Example: The garbage smells bad.

Troublesome Adjectives and Adverbs

bad and badly: Bad is an adjective. Badly is always an adverb.

good and well: Good is an adjective; it usually refers to quality or appearance. Well is used as an adjective when referring to satisfactory conditions or to a person's health. Well can also be used as an adverb when describing *how* an action is performed.

Writing Skills ◆ Usage

Adjectives and adverbs can show degrees of comparison.

fewer and less: <u>Fewer</u> is an adjective used to compare things that can be counted. <u>Less</u> is an adjective used with qualities and quantities that cannot be counted. For example: I had <u>less</u> free time this weekend, so I studied <u>fewer</u> lessons.

Rule: To compare two people, places, or things, use the comparative form of the adjective or adverb. Add *-er* to one-syllable adjectives and adverbs. Use *more* or *less* before adjectives and adverbs of two or more syllables.

Example: (Sentence 3) In addition, the XP20 is safer and more reliable than the leading competitor.
The adjectives <u>safer</u> and <u>more reliable</u> compare the XP20 to the leading competitor.

Rule: To compare more than two people, places, or things, use the superlative form of the adjective or adverb. Add *-est* to one-syllable adjectives and adverbs. Use *most* and *least* before adjectives and adverbs of two or more syllables.

Example: (Sentence 4) If you want to drive the finest car on the market today, test drive the new XP20—a masterpiece of modern technology.
The superlative adjective <u>finest</u> compares the car with all other cars on the market today.

This chart lists some exceptions to the rules for forming comparative and superlative adjectives.

Adjective	Comparative	Superlative
good	better	best
many	more	most
much	more	most
bad	worse	worst
Adverb	**Comparative**	**Superlative**
badly	worse	worst
well	better	best
much	more	most

Rule: Do not make double comparisons. Never use *more, most, less,* or *least* with adjectives or adverbs ending in *-er* or *-est*.

Incorrect: The XP20 is the most finest car on the market today.

Items 1 to 6 refer to the following paragraph. Choose the best answer to each item.

(1) The Huggle baby stroller is compactly and durable. (2) The stain-resistant cloth padding is easily washable, but it fades quick in sunlight. (3) Also, the vinyl hood did not hold up good in our tests. (4) The aluminum carriage makes the Huggle much lightest than its leading competitor, the Cuddle Walkmaster. (5) Unfortunately, the Huggle brand is much more expensive. (6) Even so, of the five brands tested, we believe you will get a better value from the Huggle. (7) When it comes to producing the highest quality baby strollers, less companies can compare with Huggle.

1. Sentence 1: **The Huggle baby stroller is compactly and durable.**

   What correction should be made to this sentence?

   (1) change is to are
   (2) change is to were
   (3) change compactly to compacter
   (4) change compactly to compact
   (5) no correction is necessary

2. Sentence 2: **The stain-resistant cloth padding is easily washable, but it fades quick in sunlight.**

   What correction should be made to this sentence?

   (1) change is to was
   (2) change easily to easier
   (3) change it to they
   (4) change quick to quickly
   (5) no correction is necessary

3. Sentence 3: **Also, the vinyl hood did not hold up good in our tests.**

   What correction should be made to this sentence?

   (1) change good to better
   (2) change good to best
   (3) change good to well
   (4) change good to goodest
   (5) no correction is necessary

4. Sentence 4: **The aluminum carriage makes the Huggle much lightest than its leading competitor, the Cuddle Walkmaster.**

   What correction should be made to this sentence?

   (1) change makes to make
   (2) change much to more
   (3) change lightest to lighter
   (4) change lightest to more lighter
   (5) no correction is necessary

5. Sentence 6: **Even so, of the five brands tested, we believe you will get a better value from the Huggle.**

   What correction should be made to this sentence?

   (1) change get to got
   (2) replace a better with the best
   (3) change better to gooder
   (4) change better to more better
   (5) no correction is necessary

6. Sentence 7: **When it comes to producing the highest quality baby strollers, less companies can compare with Huggle.**

   What correction should be made to this sentence?

   (1) change highest to most highest
   (2) change strollers to stroller's
   (3) replace the comma with a semicolon
   (4) replace less with few
   (5) no correction is necessary

Items 7 to 12 refer to the following paragraph.

   (1) Of all the memory techniques, repetition is the more effective of all. (2) This idea might sound too simpler. (3) Still, it is the best helpful way to put facts into your memory. (4) A real good idea is to say the fact aloud many times. (5) The most times you say the information, the more effective it will be. (6) The key is repeating the information enough times so it becomes a part of your long-term memory. (7) Repetition will help you retain new information easy; it's a better technique than any other.

7. Sentence 1: **Of all the memory techniques, repetition is the more effective of all.**

   What correction should be made to this sentence?

   (1) change memory to Memory
   (2) change techniques to technique
   (3) change more to most
   (4) change more to best
   (5) no correction is necessary

8. Sentence 2: **This idea might sound too simpler.**

   What correction should be made to this sentence?

   (1) change sound to sounds
   (2) change simpler to simplest
   (3) change simpler to more simple
   (4) change simpler to simple
   (5) no correction is necessary

9. Sentence 3: **Still, it is the best helpful way to put facts into your memory.**

   What correction should be made to this sentence?

   (1) change best to more
   (2) change best to most
   (3) change helpful to helpfully
   (4) change helpful to helpfuller
   (5) no correction is necessary

10. Sentence 4: **A real good idea is to say the fact aloud many times.**

    Which of the following is the best way to write the underlined portion of this sentence? If you think the original is the best way, choose option (1).

    (1) real good idea
    (2) really good idea
    (3) real best idea
    (4) real better idea
    (5) more real good idea

11. Sentence 5: **The most times you say the information, the more effective it will be.**

    What correction should be made to this sentence?

    (1) change most to more
    (2) change more effective to effectiver
    (3) change more effective to more effect
    (4) change it to it's
    (5) no correction is necessary

12. Sentence 7: **Repetition will help you retain new information easy; it's a better technique than any other.**

    What correction should be made to this sentence?

    (1) replace easy with easily
    (2) replace easy with most easiest
    (3) change better to more better
    (4) change better to best
    (5) no correction is necessary

Answers are on page 755.

Items 1 to 8 refer to the following paragraph. Choose the best answer to each item.

(1) Some people thinks that working as a bank teller would be a boring job. (2) Actually, a bank teller's job might be the more challenging job you could have. (3) Since January, Althea worked as a teller at Citizen Bank. (4) Every day, she goes to work early to count the money in their cash drawer. (5) Althea need a good understanding of math. (6) She also tries to be polite and friendly to everyone, even people who are rude to her. (7) At the end of the day, she carefully review all the transactions she made. (8) If she finds a mistake, she stays until her corrects it.

1. Sentence 1: **Some people thinks that working as a bank teller would be a boring job.**

   What correction should be made to this sentence?

   (1) change thinks to thought
   (2) change thinks to think
   (3) insert a comma after thinks
   (4) change bank teller to Bank Teller
   (5) change would be to are

2. Sentence 2: **Actually, a bank teller's job might be the more challenging job you could have.**

   What correction should be made to this sentence?

   (1) remove the apostrophe in teller's
   (2) change teller's to tellers'
   (3) change more to most
   (4) change you to your
   (5) no correction is necessary

3. Sentence 3: **Since January, Althea worked as a teller at Citizen Bank.**

   Which of the following is the best way to write the underlined portion of this sentence? If you think the original is the best way, choose option (1).

   (1) Althea worked as a teller
   (2) Althea work as a teller
   (3) Althea works as a teller
   (4) Althea has been working as a teller
   (5) no correction is necessary

4. Sentence 4: **Every day, she goes to work early to count the money in their cash drawer.**

   What correction should be made to this sentence?

   (1) change goes to go
   (2) change early to earlier
   (3) change their to there
   (4) change their to her
   (5) change their to them

5. Sentence 5: **Althea need a good understanding of math.**

   Which of the following is the best way to write the underlined portion of this sentence? If you think the original is the best way, choose option (1).

   (1) Althea need a good understanding of math
   (2) Althea needs a good understanding of math
   (3) Althea has need a good understanding of math
   (4) Althea have needed a good understanding of math
   (5) no correction is necessary

6. Sentence 6: **She also tries to be polite and friendly to everyone, <u>even people who are rude</u> to her.**

   Which of the following is the best way to write the underlined portion of this sentence? If you think the original is the best way, choose option (1).

   (1) even people who are rude
   (2) even people who had been rude
   (3) even people who is rude
   (4) even people who will be rude
   (5) even people who are ruder

7. Sentence 7: **At the end of the day, she carefully review all the transactions she made.**

   What correction should be made to this sentence?

   (1) remove the comma after <u>day</u>
   (2) change <u>carefully</u> to <u>careful</u>
   (3) change <u>review</u> to <u>reviews</u>
   (4) change the spelling of <u>review</u> to <u>reveiw</u>
   (5) change <u>made</u> to <u>had made</u>

8. Sentence 8: **If she finds a mistake, she stays until her corrects it.**

   What correction should be made to this sentence?

   (1) change <u>finds</u> to <u>find</u>
   (2) remove the comma after <u>mistake</u>
   (3) change <u>stays</u> to <u>will have stayed</u>
   (4) change <u>stays</u> to <u>stay</u>
   (5) change <u>her</u> to <u>she</u>

Items 9 to 11 refer to the following paragraph.

   (1) Despite the common belief that only children can learn to play an instrument, many people whom are over sixty have become musicians. (2) Piano, guitar, and keyboard lessons have begun to grow in popularity among the elderly. (3) Many senior citizens will tell you that having time to learn an instrument is one of the most finest aspects of retirement. (4) One musically active group in our town has preceded to form a mini-orchestra.

9. Sentence 1: **Despite the common belief that only children can learn to play an instrument, many people whom are over sixty have become musicians.**

   What correction should be made to this sentence?

   (1) remove the comma after <u>instrument</u>
   (2) change <u>whom</u> to <u>who</u>
   (3) insert commas after <u>people</u> and sixty
   (4) change the spelling of <u>belief</u> to <u>beleif</u>
   (5) no correction is necessary

10. Sentence 3: **Many senior citizens will tell you that having time to learn an instrument is one of the more finest aspects of retirement.**

    What correction should be made to this sentence?

    (1) replace <u>is</u> with <u>are</u>
    (2) change <u>more finest</u> to <u>finest</u>
    (3) change <u>more finest</u> to <u>most finest</u>
    (4) change <u>aspects</u> to <u>aspect's</u>
    (5) no correction is necessary

11. Sentence 4: **One musically active group in our town has preceded to form a mini-orchestra.**

    What correction should be made to this sentence?

    (1) change <u>musically</u> to <u>musical</u>
    (2) replace <u>our</u> with <u>hour</u>
    (3) change <u>has</u> to <u>have</u>
    (4) replace <u>preceded</u> with <u>proceeded</u>
    (5) no correction is necessary

Answers are on page 756.

Sentence Structure

Lesson 14

Sentence Fragments

Fragments are incomplete sentences. They do not express a complete thought. Many fragments are corrected by just adding a missing subject or verb.

Another kind of fragment contains both a subject and a verb but may begin with a word that makes it dependent upon another sentence for a complete meaning. These fragments are called dependent clauses, and they cannot stand alone. If the fragment is a dependent clause, you can correct it by attaching it to a nearby, related independent clause. Remember to use a comma after the dependent clause if you place it in front of the independent clause. Do not use a comma if the dependent clause is *essential* information needed to understand the meaning of the independent clause. The dependent clause may limit or restrict the meaning of the independent clause in an important way. Without the added information, the thought would not be clearly expressed. Use a comma to separate the dependent clause if it is *nonessential*—that is, not needed to understand the meaning of the independent clause.

Fragments may also happen when a certain kind of pronoun is used as a subject. These pronouns—*who, that, which*—are called **relative pronouns.** They must be part of the sentence containing the noun antecedent to which they refer. Clauses that begin with a relative pronoun are dependent on another related sentence. When making a decision about commas, relative clauses should be treated the same as other dependent clauses.

The following paragraph contains different kinds of fragments. As you read, find them and consider why they are fragments.

(1) Chicken Little was wrong about the sky falling, but once in a while it may seem that he was right. (2) Although the sky itself does not come apart. (3) Rocks sometimes fall to the earth from space. (4) In fact, fall very often. (5) There is a chance that any of us could get hit by one of these rocks. (6) Which are called meteorites. (7) But do not run out and buy a steel umbrella. (8) A group of scientists has figured out that one person will get hit by a meteorite every 180 years. (9) So it's fortunate that a woman in Alabama was only bruised. (10) From being hit by one in 1954. (11) Now the odds going in your favor for another one hundred years.

Identify sentence fragments by asking three questions: Does the sentence have a subject? Does it have a complete verb? Does it express a complete thought? If the answer to one or more of these questions is no, it's a sentence fragment.

Writing Skills ◆ Sentence Structure

Now look at the rules on how to correct fragments.

Rule: A sentence must have a subject.

Example: (Sentence 4) In fact, fall very often.

To correct this fragment, add a subject: In fact, <u>they</u> fall very often.

Rule: A sentence must have a complete verb.

Example: (Sentence 11) Now the odds going in your favor for another one hundred years.

To correct this fragment, make the verb complete: Now the odds <u>are</u> <u>going</u> in your favor for another one hundred years.

Hint: Remember that verbs show action or a condition. The present participle (present form + -*ing*) must be used with a form of the verb *be* in order to be complete.

Rule: A sentence must have both a subject and a verb.

Example: (Sentence 10) From being hit by one in 1954.

To correct this fragment, either add a subject and a verb or treat it like a phrase and combine it with another complete sentence: (Sentences 9 and 10 combined) So it's fortunate that a woman in Alabama was only bruised from being hit by one in 1954.

The following words are used to begin dependent clauses:

after	before	though	whenever
although	even though	unless	where
as	if	until	wherever
because	since	when	

Example: (Sentence 2) Although the sky itself does not come apart.

To correct this fragment, join it to another complete sentence, an independent clause: (Sentences 2 and 3 combined) Although the sky itself does not come apart, rocks sometimes fall to Earth from space.

Hint: Remember that an introductory dependent clause is separated from the rest of the sentence by a comma.

Rule: A sentence cannot use a relative pronoun for a subject. The following are relative pronouns: *who, whom, which, that, what, whoever, whatever.*

Example: (Sentence 6) Which are called meteorites.

To correct this fragment, combine it with the sentence containing the noun to which the relative pronoun refers: (Sentences 5 and 6 combined) There is a chance that any of us could be hit by one of these rocks, which are called meteorites.

Items 1 to 5 refer to the following paragraph. Choose the best answer to each item.

(1) Recently, an Indiana man received a huge bill from his town's police department for cat care. (2) When he returned home from vacation. (3) Before leaving, he'd turned on his home security system. (4) To inform the local police if a break-in occurred. (5) Also, had left his lonely cat in the house. (6) Soon, the police were going to the house. (7) Several times a day. (8) The cat had quickly learned how to get attention. (9) The man has been asked to pay nearly a thousand dollars to the police. (10) Who had to check out the "cat burglar" every time the cat tripped the alarms.

1. Sentences 1 and 2: **Recently, an Indiana man received a huge bill from his town's police department for cat care. When he returned home from vacation.**

   Which of the following is the best way to write the underlined portion of these sentences? If you think the original is the best way, choose option (1).

   (1) department for cat care. When he
   (2) department for cat care, when he
   (3) department for cat care; when he
   (4) department for cat care when he
   (5) department for cat care. "When he

2. Sentences 3 and 4: **Before leaving, he'd turned on his home security system. To inform the local police if a break-in occurred.**

   Which of the following is the best way to write the underlined portion of these sentences? If you think the original is the best way, choose option (1).

   (1) system. To inform
   (2) system to inform
   (3) system. Informing
   (4) system, to inform
   (5) system; to inform

3. Sentence 5: **Also, had left his lonely cat in the house.**

   What correction should be made to this sentence?

   (1) remove the comma after Also
   (2) insert he after the comma
   (3) change had to has
   (4) change his to him
   (5) insert there after house

4. Sentences 6 and 7: **Soon, the police were going to the house. Several times a day.**

   Which of the following is the best way to write the underlined portion of these sentences? If you think the original is the best way, choose option (1).

   (1) house. Several
   (2) house. several
   (3) house, several
   (4) house several
   (5) house; several

5. Sentences 9 and 10: **The man has been asked to pay nearly a thousand dollars to the police. Who had to check out the "cat burglar" every time the cat tripped the alarms.**

   Which of the following is the best way to write the underlined portion of these sentences? If you think the original is the best way, choose option (1).

   (1) police. Who had to check
   (2) police. Who checking
   (3) police, who had to check
   (4) police; who had to check
   (5) police, whom had to check

Answers are on page 757.

Lesson  Run-On Sentences

A sentence is an independent clause. It has a subject and a verb, and it expresses a complete idea. A run-on sentence occurs when two or more independent clauses are strung together without the proper punctuation or linking words.

One way to avoid a run-on sentence is to separate the two independent clauses into two different sentences using a period. Other ways to avoid a run-on—but still keep the two sentences combined—are to join the two independent clauses (1) with a semicolon; (2) with a comma and a coordinating conjunction; or (3) with a semicolon, a conjunctive adverb, and a comma.

Read the following paragraph and find the run-on sentences.

(1) The story tells of a man at an auction who sneezed he wound up being the owner of a moth-eaten moose head. (2) In reality, those who attend auctions have time to change their minds they don't have to take the moose head home. (3) One problem in attending auctions, however, is getting caught up in the excitement of the sale it goes so quickly and so noisily. (4) You must decide how much you would be willing to pay ahead of time you won't be tempted to overbid and won't regret it later. (5) You should plan ahead, you might avoid finding a home for that moose head.

Rule: Correct a run-on sentence using a period.

> **Independent clause. Independent clause.**

Example: (Sentence 3) One problem in attending auctions, however, is getting caught up in the excitement of the <u>sale it</u> goes so quickly and so noisily.

Correct: One problem in attending auctions, however, is getting caught up in the excitement of the <u>sale. It</u> goes so quickly and so noisily.

Rule: Correct a run-on sentence using a semicolon.

> **Independent clause; independent clause.**

Example: (Sentence 2) In reality, those who attend auctions have time to change their <u>minds they</u> don't have to take the moose head home.

Correct: In reality, those who attend auctions have time to change their <u>minds; they</u> don't have to take the moose head home.

Rule: Correct a run-on sentence using a comma and a coordinating conjunction.

Independent clause	, and , but , or , nor , for , yet , so	independent clause.

Example: (Sentence 1) The story tells of a man at an auction who <u>sneezed he</u> wound up being the owner of a moth-eaten moose head.

Correct: The story tells of a man at an auction who <u>sneezed, and he</u> wound up being the owner of a moth-eaten moose head.

 Remember, joining two independent clauses with a comma but without a conjunction creates a comma splice. Never use a comma alone to fix a run-on sentence.

Rule: Correct a run-on sentence using a semicolon, a conjunctive adverb, and a comma.

Independent clause	; however, ; therefore, ; also, ; then, ; nevertheless, ; next, ; consequently, ; moreover,	independent clause.

Example: (Sentence 4) You must decide how much you would be willing to pay ahead of <u>time you</u> won't be tempted to overbid and won't regret it later.

Correct: You must decide how much you would be willing to pay ahead of <u>time; then, you</u> won't be tempted to overbid and won't regret it later.

Example: (Sentence 5) You should plan <u>ahead, you</u> might avoid finding a home for that moose head.

Correct: You should plan <u>ahead; then, you</u> might avoid finding a home for that moose head.

Items 1 to 5 refer to the following paragraph. Choose the best answer to each item.

(1) Not all on-the-job injuries involve heavy equipment some safer occupations can also cause injuries. (2) Workers who type constantly, such as data entry operators, may suffer from overstrain of muscles their fingers may literally seize up from the repetitive finger movements. (3) A few of these typists possibly have permanent nerve damage. (4) Staring for long periods at computer screens may cause severe eyestrain the studies on long-term effects continue. (5) In some offices, continuous whines or buzzes from ventilation or machines can affect workers, even though the sounds are not loud, over time, employees may experience hearing loss.

1. Sentence 1: **Not all on-the-job injuries involve heavy equipment some safer occupations can also cause injuries.**

   What correction should be made to this sentence?

   (1) insert a comma after equipment
   (2) insert a semicolon after equipment
   (3) insert and after equipment
   (4) insert however after equipment
   (5) no correction is necessary

2. Sentence 2: **Workers who type constantly, such as data entry operators, may suffer from overstrain of muscles their fingers may literally seize up from the repetitive finger movements.**

   Which of the following is the best way to write the underlined portion of this sentence? If you think the original is the best way, choose option (1).

   (1) muscles their fingers
   (2) muscles, their fingers
   (3) muscles. Their fingers
   (4) muscles. There fingers
   (5) muscles, there fingers

3. Sentence 3: **A few of these typists possibly have permanent nerve damage.**

   What correction should be made to this sentence?

   (1) change typists to Typists
   (2) change have to has
   (3) change the spelling of permanent to permenant
   (4) insert a comma after nerve
   (5) no correction is necessary

4. Sentence 4: **Staring for long periods at computer screens may cause severe eyestrain the studies on long-term effects continue.**

   What correction should be made to this sentence?

   (1) insert a semicolon after screens
   (2) insert a comma after screens
   (3) insert a semicolon after eyestrain
   (4) change effects to affects
   (5) change continue to continues

5. Sentence 5: **In some offices, continuous whines or buzzes from ventilation or machines can affect workers, even though the sounds are not loud, over time, employees may experience hearing loss.**

   What correction should be made to this sentence?

   (1) change offices to office's
   (2) insert a comma after ventilation
   (3) insert a semicolon after machines
   (4) change the comma after workers to a semicolon
   (5) no correction is necessary

Answers are on page 758.

Lesson  Combining Sentences

One way to connect two sentences is with a semicolon. When you use a semicolon, you are implying that the ideas in the two sentences are closely related without clearly showing what the relationship is.

Another way to connect two sentences is to use a **conjunctive adverb.** A conjunctive adverb connects two sentences and shows a certain kind of relationship between the two ideas. When you connect two sentences with a conjunctive adverb, you use a semicolon before the adverb and a comma following it.

Coordinating conjunctions can also show the relationship between the ideas in two sentences. Use a comma with a coordinating conjunction when combining sentences this way. Always be sure to use a conjunctive adverb or coordinating conjunction that conveys the appropriate connection between the independent clauses.

Read the paragraph and consider how these sentences can be combined.

(1) Jack is a stage director. (2) He wanted to start a community theater group. (3) He did not have enough money to start a theater. (4) His friends wanted to loan him the money. (5) Jack went to a bank for a loan. (6) The loan officer of the bank was a reasonable woman. (7) She granted the loan to Jack. (8) Jack found some good playwrights, actors, and designers. (9) Their company is working hard. (10) Their first play is an exceptionally funny comedy. (11) It is sure to be a hit.

Here are some rules of sentence combining and examples of how to show relationships between sentences when you combine them.

Rule: Combine sentences using a semicolon.
Example: (Sentences 1 and 2) Jack is a stage director. He wanted to start a community theater group.
Combine: Jack is a stage director; he wanted to start a community theater group.

 When combining two sentences, read both sentences and look for the relationship between their ideas. Then choose the punctuation and/or connecting words that best express that relationship.

Rule:	Combine sentences using a semicolon, a conjunctive adverb, and a comma.
Hint:	Choose the correct conjunctive adverb to show the relationship between the two ideas being combined.

Relationship	Conjunctive adverb
connects two ideas	also, furthermore, moreover, besides
contrasts two ideas	however, still, nevertheless, instead, nonetheless
compares two ideas	similarly, likewise
shows a result	therefore, thus, consequently
shows time passing	next, then, meanwhile, finally, subsequently

Example:	(Sentences 4 and 5) His friends wanted to loan him the money. Jack went to a bank for a loan.
Combine:	His friends wanted to loan him the money; instead, Jack went to a bank for a loan. (This shows a *contrast*.)
Example:	(Sentences 6 and 7) The loan officer of the bank was a reasonable woman. She granted the loan to Jack.
Combine:	The loan officer of the bank was a reasonable woman; therefore, she granted the loan to Jack. (This shows a *result*.)

Rule:	Combine sentences using a comma and a coordinating conjunction.
Hint:	Choose the correct coordinating conjunction to show the relationship between the two ideas being combined.

Relationship	Coordinating conjunction
connects two ideas	and
contrasts two ideas	but, yet
shows a cause	for
negates a possibility	nor
shows another possibility	or

Example:	(Sentences 8 and 9) Jack found some good playwrights, actors, and designers. Their company is working hard.
Combine:	Jack found some good playwrights, actors, and designers, and their company is working hard. (This *connects* the two ideas.)
Example:	(Sentences 10 and 11) Their first play is an exceptionally funny comedy. It is sure to be a hit.
Combine:	Their first play is an exceptionally funny comedy, so it is sure to be a hit. (This shows a *result*.)

Items 1 to 5 refer to the following paragraph. Choose the best answer to each item.

(1) Pushcart Supermarket does not sell my favorite kind of cold cut. (2) The supermarket down the block does. (3) This store has a deli department. (4) It has many kinds of cold cuts. (5) Their selection includes turkey, ham, and roast beef. (6) There are others, too. (7) The clerk at the deli counter made me a sandwich. (8) The sandwich was larger than I'd asked for. (9) The sandwich was huge, but I ate it anyway. (10) It was twice as much food as I normally eat. (11) I felt sick.

1. Sentences 1 and 2: **Pushcart Supermarket does not sell my favorite kind of cold cut. The supermarket down the block does.**

   The most effective combination of sentences 1 and 2 would include which of the following groups of words?

   (1) cold cut, but the supermarket
   (2) cold cut, so the supermarket
   (3) cold cut; likewise, the supermarket
   (4) cold cut, however, the supermarket
   (5) cold cut, the supermarket

2. Sentences 3 and 4: **This store has a deli department. It has many kinds of cold cuts.**

   The most effective combination of sentences 3 and 4 would include which of the following groups of words?

   (1) department, but it
   (2) department, it
   (3) department; meanwhile, it
   (4) department, so it
   (5) department, but, it

3. Sentences 5 and 6: **Their selection includes turkey, ham, and roast beef. There are others, too.**

   The most effective combination of sentences 5 and 6 would include which of the following groups of words?

   (1) beef; finally, there are
   (2) beef, nor are there
   (3) beef; therefore, there are
   (4) beef, and there are
   (5) beef; there being

4. Sentences 7 and 8: **The clerk at the deli counter made me a sandwich. The sandwich was larger than I'd asked for.**

   The most effective combination of sentences 7 and 8 would include which of the following groups of words?

   (1) sandwich; consequently, the
   (2) sandwich, the sandwich
   (3) sandwich; however, the
   (4) sandwich; besides, the
   (5) sandwich, or the

5. Sentences 10 and 11: **It was twice as much food as I normally eat. I felt sick.**

   The most effective combination of sentences 10 and 11 would include which of the following groups of words?

   (1) normally eat; subsequently, I
   (2) normally eat; nevertheless, I
   (3) normally eat; still, I
   (4) normally eat, or I
   (5) normally eat, I felt

Items 6 to 10 refer to the following paragraph.

(1) The saying goes that the only sure things in life are death and taxes. (2) Most people would surely agree. (3) When April 15 comes, taxpayers take note and this is the deadline for federal taxes. (4) The tax forms take time to complete. (5) Many taxpayers tend to wait until the last minute. (6) Now the Internal Revenue Service has introduced electronic filing; therefore, some taxpayers can receive their refunds in less than two weeks. (7) The majority still prefer to use the mail. (8) Their refunds may take more time to arrive. (9) The Internal Revenue Service would like more people to take advantage of electronic filing. (10) Electronic returns are easier to process.

6. Sentences 1 and 2: **The saying goes that the only sure things in life are death and taxes. Most people would surely agree.**

   The most effective combination of sentences 1 and 2 would include which of the following groups of words?

   (1) taxes, and most
   (2) taxes, but most
   (3) taxes, most
   (4) taxes; then, most
   (5) taxes or most

7. Sentence 3: **When April 15 comes, taxpayers take note and this is the deadline for federal taxes.**

   Which of the following is the best way to write the underlined portion of this sentence? If you think the original is the best way, choose option (1).

   (1) take note and this
   (2) taking note; this
   (3) take note, this
   (4) take note, and this
   (5) take note, for this

8. Sentences 4 and 5: **The tax forms take time to complete. Many taxpayers tend to wait until the last minute.**

   The most effective combination of sentences 4 and 5 would include which of the following groups of words?

   (1) complete, but many
   (2) complete; finally, many
   (3) complete; many waiting
   (4) complete; likewise, many
   (5) complete, many

9. Sentences 7 and 8: **The majority still prefer to use the mail. Their refunds may take more time to arrive.**

   The most effective combination of sentences 7 and 8 would include which of the following groups of words?

   (1) mail, their
   (2) mail, so their
   (3) mail, but they're
   (4) mail; there
   (5) mail, consequently, their

10. Sentences 9 and 10: **The Internal Revenue Service would like more people to take advantage of electronic filing. Electronic returns are easier to process.**

    The most effective combination of sentences 9 and 10 would include which of the following groups of words?

    (1) filing, electronic
    (2) filing, or electronic
    (3) filing; consequently, electronic
    (4) filing; subsequently, electronic
    (5) filing, for electronic

Answers are on page 758.

Lesson  Parallel Structure

Parallel structure is a way to express equal and related ideas and phrases in a sentence.

When a sentence contains items in a series, each item must grammatically match the others. This is called a parallel structure. Maintaining parallelism is important to the clear expression of ideas.

Read the short paragraphs below and on page 127. Look for series of words or phrases and find the item that is not parallel.

(1) We love our pets because they live with us, knowing us well, but love us anyway. (2) We need them to charm, to entertain, and they comfort us. (3) Enough to eat, daily exercise, and a safe home are all they ask of us.

Look for items in a series separated by commas and the conjunctions *and, but, or,* or *nor*. Make sure that each item represents the same part of speech.

Rule: Use parallel adjectives and nouns in a series.
Example: (Sentence 3) Enough to eat, daily exercise, and a safe home are all they ask of us.
Correct: Enough food, daily exercise, and a safe home are all they ask of us.

Not Parallel	Parallel
Enough <u>to eat</u> (adjective-infinitive)	Enough food (adjective-noun)
daily exercise (adjective-noun)	daily exercise (adjective-noun)
safe home (adjective-noun)	safe home (adjective-noun)

Rule: Use parallel verb forms in a series.
Example: (Sentence 2) We need them to charm, to entertain, and they comfort us.
Correct: We need them to charm, to entertain, and to comfort us.

Not Parallel	Parallel
to charm (infinitive)	to charm (infinitive)
to entertain (infinitive)	to entertain (infinitive)
<u>they</u> comfort (noun-verb)	to comfort (infinitive)

Rule: Use parallel verbs in a series.
Example: (Sentence 1) We love our pets because they live with us, knowing us well, but love us anyway.
Correct: We love our pets because they live with us, know us well, but love us anyway.

         Writing Skills ◆ Sentence Structure

Not Parallel	Parallel
because they live with us	because they <u>live</u> with us
(present plural verb)	(present plural verb)
(because they) <u>knowing</u> us	(because they) <u>know</u> us
(present participle)	(present plural verb)
(because they) love us	(because they) <u>love</u> us
(present plural verb)	(present plural verb)

(1) A renter must look sensibly, carefully, and with caution at new apartments. (2) The renter who wanting quiet, needs space, and likes value should take time to look carefully. (3) Look in the rooms, looking at the view, but most of all at the lease.

Rule: Use parallel adverbs in a series.

Example: (Sentence 1) A renter must look sensibly, carefully, and with caution at new apartments.

Correct: A renter must look sensibly, carefully, and cautiously at new apartments.

Not Parallel	Parallel
sensibly (adverb)	sensibly (adverb)
carefully (adverb)	carefully (adverb)
<u>with caution</u>	cautiously (adverb)
(prepositional phrase)	

Rule: Use parallel prepositional phrases in a series.

Example: (Sentence 3) Look in the rooms, looking at the view, but most of all at the lease.

Correct: Look in the rooms, at the view, but most of all at the lease.

Not Parallel	Parallel
Look in the rooms	Look in the rooms
(verb–prepositional phrase)	(verb–prepositional phrase)
<u>looking</u> at the view	(Look) at the view
(participle–prepositional phrase)	(verb–prepositional phrase)
(Look) at the lease	(Look) at the lease
(verb–prepositional phrase)	(verb–prepositional phrase)

Rule: Use parallel verbs and nouns in a series.

Example: (Sentence 2) The renter who wanting quiet, needs space, and likes value should take time to look carefully.

Correct: The renter who wants quiet, needs space, and likes value should take time to look carefully.

Not Parallel	Parallel
<u>wanting</u> quiet	wants quiet (verb–noun)
(present participle–noun)	needs space (verb–noun)
needs space (verb–noun)	likes value (verb–noun)
likes value (verb–noun)	

ged **Exercise** Parallel Structure

<u>Items 1 to 5</u> refer to the following paragraph. Choose the <u>best answer</u> to each item.

(1) Having good intentions, a lot of experience, and carrying a good résumé are not enough for a job interview. (2) If you walk in wearing jeans, a sweatshirt, and with sneakers on, you won't impress anyone. (3) Plan ahead to have a good appearance. (4) Wear clothes that are businesslike, conservatively, and attractive. (5) When you arrive late, you're smoking, and you have your groceries, you don't create a good impression either. (6) Behave normally, act rationally, and being responsible, and you will do well. (7) If you are confident, serious and pleasant, you stand every chance of getting the job. (8) Even if you aren't hired at the very first interview, the experience of preparing for it will probably improve your chances at the next one.

1. Sentence 1: **Having good intentions, a lot of experience, and carrying a good résumé are not enough for a job interview.**

   What correction should be made to this sentence?

   (1) change Having to To have
   (2) change Having to have
   (3) insert having before a lot
   (4) replace a lot with alot
   (5) insert a comma after résumé

2. Sentence 2: **If you walk in wearing jeans, a sweatshirt, <u>and with sneakers on,</u> you won't impress anyone.**

   Which of the following is the best way to write the underlined portion of this sentence? If you think the original is the best way, choose option (1).

   (1) and with sneakers on,
   (2) and wearing sneakers,
   (3) with sneakers,
   (4) and sneakers,
   (5) and sneakers on,

3. Sentence 4: **Wear clothes that are businesslike, conservatively, and attractive.**

   What correction should be make to this sentence?

   (1) change Wear to Wearing
   (2) change clothes to cloths
   (3) replace businesslike with business
   (4) change conservatively to conservative
   (5) change attractive to attractively

4. Sentence 6: **Behave normally, act rationally, and being responsible, and you will do well.**

   What corrections should be make to this sentence?

   (1) change Behave to Behaving
   (2) change normally to normal
   (3) change act to acting
   (4) change being to be
   (5) change responsible to responsibly

5. Sentence 7: **If you are confident, serious and pleasant, you stand every chance of getting the job.**

   What correction should be made to this sentence?

   (1) change confident to confidently
   (2) insert a comma after serious
   (3) replace pleasant with a pleasant person
   (4) change the spelling of getting to geting
   (5) no correction is necessary

Tip Be sure you don't combine different parts of speech in a series. Check that you have used all nouns, all verbs, all adjectives, or all adverbs.

Answers are on page 759.

Writing Skills ◆ Sentence Structure

Lesson 18

Subordination

An independent clause contains a subject and predicate, which includes the verb. It contains the main idea and can stand alone as a sentence. However, if you want to add more details about the independent clause, you can use subordinate clauses.

Subordinate clauses add either essential or nonessential information to the main idea of a sentence. They are dependent on the main sentence and cannot stand alone. Two kinds of subordinate clauses are (1) adverb clauses beginning with a subordinating conjunction and (2) adjective clauses beginning with a relative pronoun.

Adverb clauses begin with subordinating conjunctions. These conjunctions set up a specific kind of relationship between the main ideas in the independent and the subordinate clauses.

Here is a list of some subordinating conjunctions and the relationships that they show.

Time	Reason/Cause	Concession	Location
after	as	although	where
before	because	even though	wherever
once	since	though	
since			
until	**Condition**	**Result/Effect**	**Choice**
when	if	in order that	rather than
whenever	even if	so	than
while	provided that	so that	whether
	unless	that	

Adjective clauses begin with relative pronouns, such as *who, that,* and *which*. Remember that *who* and *whom* always refer to people (or animals with names, such as Lassie). *That* and *which* always refer to things and animals, not people. Adjective clauses can act as appositives. Use commas to set off an adjective clause when it appears inside a sentence unless the information is essential to the sentence. Place a comma before a nonessential adjective clause that follows an independent clause.

 Remember to use a comma after a subordinate clause if that clause comes at the beginning of the sentence.

Read the paragraph below and then look at the examples.

(1) Computer graphics has become the newest expert witness in some jury trials. (2) They can use pictures or drawings alone. (3) Some lawyers are introducing computer simulations. (4) Computer images show jurors reconstructions of accidents. (5) The images are watched on a screen. (6) Juries can picture events better. (7) They can see a moving image. (8) A lawyer may improve his or her argument. (9) A lawyer may use the simulations to do this. (10) Computers may enter more courtrooms in the future. (11) Their cost is still steep.

Rule: Use a subordinating conjunction to show a relationship between two clauses.

Example: (Sentences 2 and 3) They can use pictures or drawings alone. Some lawyers are introducing computer simulations.

Combine: Rather than use pictures or drawings alone, some lawyers are introducing computer simulations. (Relationship: choice. Type of clause: introductory.)

Example: (Sentences 6 and 7) Juries can picture events better. They can see a moving image.

Combine: Juries can picture events better because they can see a moving image. (Relationship: cause. Type of clause: essential.)

Example: (Sentences 10 and 11) Computers may enter more courtrooms in the future. Their cost is still steep.

Combine: Computers may enter more courtrooms in the future, although their cost is still steep. (Relationship: concession. Type: nonessential.)

Rule: Use a relative pronoun to begin a subordinate clause.

Example: (Sentences 8 and 9) A lawyer may improve his or her argument. A lawyer may use the simulations to do this.

Combine: A lawyer who uses the simulations may improve his or her argument. (Relationship: describes a person. Type: essential.)

Example: (Sentences 4 and 5) Computer images show jurors reconstructions of accidents. The images are watched on a screen.

Combine: Computer images, which are watched on a screen, show jurors reconstructions of accidents. (Relationship: describes a thing. Type: nonessential.)

Items 1 to 5 refer to the following paragraphs. Choose the best answer to each item.

(1) Supermarkets encourage us to buy on impulse. (2) When we enter we generally move in the direction the store chooses, down the "power" aisle. (3) This aisle is crowded with sale items, whether nonsale items may be casually displayed as well. (4) Displays that are placed midaisle will slow us down. (5) The more costly merchandise is placed at eye level when shoppers look first.

(6) The shopper which reaches the milk products in the rear of the store without picking up other items is rare. (7) We cannot leave though we pay for our purchases. (8) We stand in the checkout line. (9) We'll see more impulse buys. (10) Magazines, candy, and other small items are placed at the register.

1. Sentence 2: **When we enter we generally move in the direction the store chooses, down the "power" aisle.**

   What correction should be made to this sentence?

   (1) insert a comma after enter
   (2) change move to moving
   (3) change the spelling of generally to genrally
   (4) change chooses to chosen
   (5) no correction is necessary

2. Sentence 3: **This aisle is crowded with sale items, whether nonsale items may be casually displayed as well.**

   Which of the following is the best way to write the underlined portion of this sentence? If you think the original is the best way, choose option (1).

   (1) whether
   (2) so that
   (3) unless
   (4) because
   (5) although

3. Sentence 5: **The more costly merchandise is placed at eye level when shoppers look first.**

   Which of the following is the best way to write the underlined portion of this sentence? If you think the original is the best way, choose option (1).

   (1) when
   (2) where
   (3) until
   (4) once
   (5) which

4. Sentence 6: **The shopper which reaches the milk products in the rear of the store without picking up other items is rare.**

   What correction would be made to this sentence?

   (1) insert a comma after shopper
   (2) replace which with who
   (3) replace reaches with reach
   (4) change items to item
   (5) change is to are

5. Sentence 7: **We cannot leave though we pay for our purchases.**

   What correction should be made to this sentence?

   (1) insert a comma after leave
   (2) insert a semicolon after leave
   (3) replace though with when
   (4) replace though with until
   (5) replace though with because

Answers are on page 760.

Misplaced Modifiers

A modifier is a word or phrase that describes another word or phrase. Adjectives, which describe nouns, and adverbs, which describe verbs, are both modifiers. Entire phrases can also be used as modifiers.

When modifiers are put in the wrong place in a sentence, they can confuse or change the sentence's meaning. These are called **misplaced modifiers.** Misplaced modifiers may seem to refer to two different words or phrases at once, or they may appear to be describing the wrong word or phrase. **Dangling modifiers** are a special kind of misplaced modifier. These occur when a sentence lacks the appropriate subject for the modifying phrase.

Because we always interpret sentences when we read them, misplaced modifiers can be hard to spot. We may read what the sentence means to say, rather than what it does say. In other words, we may mentally "correct" the sentence and understand the intended meaning; however, the sentence actually says something else, according to its structure.

Read this paragraph and find the misplaced modifiers.

(1) For our vacation, we decided finally to go canoeing on the river. (2) We began our trip by renting a canoe with high spirits. (3) Our canoe was old and wooden, which was the only choice. (4) Looking down at the river, the water was muddy and brown. (5) The oars blistered our hands when we paddled painfully. (6) Then the canoe, paddling down the river, overturned.

Now look at the following examples of how to correct misplaced modifiers.

Rule:	Avoid wrong placement of words or phrases.
Example:	(Sentence 5) The oars blistered our hands when we paddled painfully.
	Does <u>painfully</u> modify <u>paddled</u> or <u>blistered</u>?
Correct:	The oars painfully blistered our hands when we paddled.
Example:	(Sentence 2) We began our trip by renting a canoe with high spirits.
	Does <u>with high spirits</u> modify <u>canoe</u> or <u>began</u>?
Correct:	With high spirits, we began our trip by renting a canoe.

Rule:	Avoid unclear placement of words or phrases.
Example:	(Sentence 3) Our canoe was old and wooden, which was the only choice.
	Does the phrase <u>which was the only choice</u> modify <u>canoe</u> or <u>wooden</u>?
Correct:	Our canoe, which was the only choice, was old and wooden.
Example:	(Sentence 1) For our vacation, we decided finally to go canoeing on the river.
	Does <u>finally</u> modify <u>decided</u> or <u>to go canoeing</u>?
Correct:	For our vacation, we finally decided to go canoeing on the river.
Note:	Avoid *split infinitives,* such as <u>to finally go</u>; an adverb should not interrupt a *to* + *verb* phrase.
Rule:	Avoid dangling modifiers.
Example:	(Sentence 4) Looking down at the river, the water was muddy and brown.
	As written, the introductory phrase modifies <u>water</u>, the subject of the sentence. Was the water looking down? Who is the subject of the phrase?
Correct:	When we looked down at the river, the water was muddy and brown.
Example:	(Sentence 6) Then the canoe, paddling down the river, overturned.
	As written, the phrase <u>paddling down the river</u> modifies <u>canoe</u>. Was the canoe paddling? Who is the subject?
Correct:	Then while we were paddling down the river, the canoe overturned.
Hint:	Creating a subordinate clause can usually fix a dangling modifier.

 Avoid misplaced modifiers by placing modifiers as close as possible to the word or words they modify.

Items 1 to 5 refer to the following paragraph. Choose the best answer to each item.

(1) Buyers should take care when buying a used car from a dealer with low mileage. (2) Someone else may have set back the odometer it shows the mileage. (3) Also, wear on the foot pedals informing you of a heavily driven car. (4) Most states have, however, "lemon laws" to protect consumers. (5) Oily spots under a car or excessive oil on the engine may indicate further problems as well. (6) When looking to buy, a car can't be too carefully examined. (7) Having the car whom you trust inspected by a mechanic is one way to avoid making a bad purchase. (8) If the dealer won't allow you to do this, there may be something seriously wrong with the car.

1. Sentence 1: **Buyers should take care when buying a used car from a dealer with low mileage.**

   What correction should be made to this sentence?

   (1) change care to caring
   (2) insert a comma after care
   (3) move with low mileage after car
   (4) change a dealer to dealers
   (5) no correction is necessary

2. Sentence 2: **Someone else may have set back the odometer it shows the mileage.**

   Which of the following is the best way to write the underlined portion of this sentence? If you think the original is the best way, choose option (1).

   (1) odometer it shows
   (2) odometer which shows
   (3) odometer, which shows
   (4) odometer, it shows
   (5) odometer, who shows

3. Sentence 3: **Also, wear on the foot pedals informing you of a heavily driven car.**

   What correction should be made to this sentence?

   (1) remove the comma after also
   (2) move on the foot pedals after you
   (3) insert a comma after pedals
   (4) replace informing with informs
   (5) replace informing with to inform

4. Sentence 6: **When looking to buy, a car can't be too carefully examined.**

   What correction should be made to this sentence?

   (1) insert your after When
   (2) insert you're after When
   (3) remove the comma after buy
   (4) change can't to cant
   (5) change too to to

5. Sentence 7: **Having the car whom you trust inspected by a mechanic is one way to avoid making a bad purchase.**

   What correction should be made to this sentence?

   (1) move whom you trust after mechanic
   (2) change whom to who
   (3) move making a bad purchase after mechanic
   (4) change bad to badly
   (5) no correction is necessary

Items 6 to 11 refer to the following paragraph.

(1) For some states, recycling has become a priority. (2) Landfills are all around our country at capacity. (3) Not realizing that they are not biodegradable, parents throw out billions of disposable diapers. (4) Under the soil, sanitation workers bury all these diapers. (5) Residents are required to separate their trash in certain states. (6) In containers, each household must separate bottles, cans, and paper. (7) When left at the curb, residents help the recycling effort.

6. Sentence 2: **Landfills are all around our country at capacity.**

   What correction should be made to this sentence?

   (1) insert a comma after <u>Landfills</u>
   (2) change <u>are</u> to <u>is</u>
   (3) move <u>capacity</u> before <u>Landfills</u>
   (4) move <u>at capacity</u> after <u>are</u>
   (5) no correction is necessary

7. Sentence 3: **Not realizing that they are not biodegradable, parents throw out billions of disposable diapers.**

   What correction should be made to this sentence?

   (1) change the spelling of <u>realizing</u> to realising
   (2) replace <u>they</u> with diapers
   (3) replace <u>throw</u> with <u>through</u>
   (4) replace the comma with a semicolon
   (5) no correction is necessary

8. Sentence 4: **Under the soil, sanitation workers bury all these diapers.**

   What correction should be made to this sentence?

   (1) move <u>under the soil</u> after <u>diapers</u>
   (2) remove the comma
   (3) change <u>workers</u> to <u>worker</u>
   (4) change the spelling of <u>bury</u> to <u>bery</u>
   (5) no correction is necessary

9. Sentence 5: **Residents are required to separate their trash in certain states.**

   What correction should be made to this sentence?

   (1) change the spelling of <u>separate</u> to <u>seperate</u>
   (2) change <u>their</u> to <u>there</u>
   (3) move <u>in certain states</u> after <u>Residents</u>
   (4) move <u>in certain states</u> after <u>separate</u>
   (5) change the spelling of <u>certain</u> to <u>certen</u>

10. Sentence 6: **In containers, each household must separate bottles, cans, and paper.**

    What correction should be made to this sentence?

    (1) move <u>in containers</u> after <u>household</u>
    (2) move <u>in containers</u> after <u>separate</u>
    (3) change <u>containers</u> to <u>containers'</u>
    (4) change the spelling of <u>separate</u> to seperate
    (5) move <u>separate</u> before <u>each</u>

11. Sentence 7: **When left at the curb, residents help the recycling effort.**

    What correction should be made to this sentence?

    (1) move <u>when left at the curb</u> after <u>effort</u>
    (2) move <u>when left at the curb</u> after Residents
    (3) insert <u>these are</u> after <u>When</u>
    (4) move <u>at the curb</u> after <u>residents</u>
    (5) no correction is necessary

Answers are on page 760.

Lesson  Revising Sentences

When you revise sentences, you apply everything that you have previously learned about putting together sentences. The goal in revising sentences is to make them express the proper relationships between ideas.

The most important point to remember when revising sentences is that each sentence expresses a main idea. That main idea must remain the main idea in the new sentence unless you are asked to make it a supporting idea. Also, when you revise a sentence, it must be grammatically correct in its new form. Therefore, everything that you have learned in the first two units of this book also must be used.

This lesson will teach you to apply what you have learned about word order and meaning in a sentence. Read this short paragraph.

(1) Halloween is celebrated by children in disguise. (2) Children are dressed as different characters. (3) They go in costumes to other houses. (4) Children knock on doors. (5) Children ask for candy from the resident.

Now look at the following examples of ways to revise sentences.

Rule: When changing the word order in a sentence, be careful to note clarity and logic.

Example: (Sentence 1) Halloween is celebrated by children in disguise.

Goal: Begin sentence 1 with: <u>Children in disguise</u>

Correct: Children in disguise celebrate Halloween.

Hint: Notice that not every word in the original sentence is used in the revised sentence. In order to form a clear, logical sentence, the verb must change to agree with <u>Children</u> and <u>by</u> must be dropped since it is no longer needed.

Rule: When combining sentences, identify the most important idea and change the sentences accordingly.

Example: (Sentences 2 and 3) Children are dressed as different characters. They go in costumes to other houses.

Goal: Combine these two sentences by using <u>who</u>.

Correct: Children, who are dressed as different characters, go in costumes to other houses.

Hint: Again, one of the sentences must change in order to combine them this way. As both sentences refer to clothing, the second sentence, which carries an additional, new idea—visiting houses—should become the main clause. It carries the sentence on into the next one in the paragraph.

Rule:	When combining sentences, establish a relationship between the two ideas in the sentences.
Example:	(Sentences 4 and 5) Children knock on doors. Children ask for candy from the resident.
Goal:	Choose a subordinating conjunction to join these two sentences in a relationship.
Correct:	After children knock on doors, they ask for candy from the resident.
Hint:	As these two ideas represent one action happening after another, after is used to set up a time relationship when combining them into one sentence. Also, notice that the second Children was replaced with they in order to avoid repeating the same noun twice in one sentence. Again, words may be dropped or changed in order to create a clearer sentence.

 Before revising a sentence, identify the main idea and the relationships between the main idea and supporting ideas. Check your revised sentence to see that you have not changed those ideas or the relationships between them.

ged Exercise Revising Sentences

Items 1 to 3 refer to the following paragraph. Choose the best answer to each item.

(1) We love seasonal change because we never notice the exact moment when it occurs. (2) The changes are so gradual. (3) They're so dramatic. (4) They always surprise us. (5) We know that they're coming.

1. Sentence 1: **We love seasonal change because we never notice the exact moment when it occurs.**

   What correction should be made to this sentence?

   (1) replace We with Everyone
   (2) insert a comma after change
   (3) replace it with they
   (4) replace because with so that
   (5) no correction is necessary

2. Sentences 2 and 3: **The changes are so gradual. They're so dramatic.**

   The most effective combination of sentences 2 and 3 would include which of the following words?

   (1) because
   (2) yet
   (3) or
   (4) so
   (5) until

3. Sentences 4 and 5: **They always surprise us. We know that they're coming.**

   The most effective combination of sentences 4 and 5 would include which of the following words?

   (1) so
   (2) even though
   (3) or
   (4) when
   (5) and

(1) Moving into a small apartment is more difficult than I imagined. (2) Moving into a small apartment requires organization. (3) I have to put away my pots and pans. (4) I have to put away all my clothes. (5) Everything is out of order. (6) I can't find anything. (7) I need a maid. (8) I need someone to help me clean everything. (9) I had thought that living in a small place would be easy. (10) Living in a small place is harder than I thought. (11) Maybe I should live in a bigger apartment. (12) A bigger apartment would give more room for my furniture. (13) But what if I don't know where to put everything? (14) Maybe I should stay with my small apartment. (15) Maybe I should get rid of many of my things. (16) My new apartment is confusing my entire life.

4. Sentences 1 and 2: **Moving into a small apartment is more difficult than I imagined. Moving into a small apartment requires organization.**

   The most effective combination of sentences 1 and 2 would include which of the following groups of words?

   (1) but it requires
   (2) imagined moving
   (3) and requires
   (4) imagined into
   (5) and a small

5. Sentences 3 and 4: **I have to put away my pots and pans. I have to put away all my clothes.**

   The most effective combination of sentences 3 and 4 would include which of the following groups of words?

   (1) pans I have
   (2) my pots and pans and my clothes
   (3) pans and away
   (4) pots, pans, clothes
   (5) pots, pans, and put all

6. Sentences 5 and 6: **Everything is out of order. I can't find anything.**

   The most effective combination of sentences 5 and 6 would include which of the following groups of words?

   (1) out of order, I can't
   (2) anything because
   (3) Being out of order,
   (4) out of order, but I
   (5) can't find nothing because

7. Sentences 7 and 8: **I need a maid. I need someone to help me clean everything.**

   The most effective combination of sentences 7 and 8 would include which of the following groups of words?

   (1) maid who will
   (2) a maid I
   (3) maid, I need
   (4) maid which will
   (5) A maid needs

8. Sentences 9 and 10: **I had thought that living in a small place would be easy. Living in a small place is harder than I thought.**

   The most effective combination of sentences 9 and 10 would include which of the following groups of words?

   (1) but it
   (2) therefore, it
   (3) and it
   (4) so
   (5) because

9. Sentences 11 and 12: **Maybe I should live in a bigger apartment. A bigger apartment would give me more room for my furniture.**

The most effective combination of sentences 11 and 12 would include which of the following groups of words?

(1) apartment that would
(2) apartment, it would
(3) apartment; giving me
(4) apartment who would
(5) apartment, and it

10. Sentences 14 and 15: **Maybe I should stay with my small apartment. Maybe I should get rid of many of my things.**

The most effective combination of sentences 14 and 15 would include which of the following words?

(1) so
(2) or
(3) yet
(4) for
(5) therefore

Items 11 to 13 refer to the following paragraph.

(1) Advances in automotive technology have increased the safety of car drivers and passengers. (2) Many new cars come equipped with dual air bags, antilock brakes, and side impact protection. (3) Some worry, however, that new car owners may feel so safe in their cars that they will drive less carefully. (4) Drivers can become overconfident. (5) As a result, they may take unnecessary chances behind the wheel. (6) The safety devices in the new cars are impressive; however, they can be neutralized by poor driving on the part of their owners.

11. Sentence 1: **Advances in automotive technology have increased the safety of car drivers and passengers.**

If you rewrote sentence 1 beginning with

The safety of car drivers and passengers

the next word(s) should be

(1) has been increased by
(2) have been increased by
(3) increased
(4) is increasing the
(5) are

12. Sentence 3: **Some worry, however, that new car owners may feel so safe in their cars that they will drive less carefully.**

If you rewrote sentence 3 beginning with

Some worry, however, that new car owners will drive less carefully

the next word(s) should be

(1) , or
(2) in order that
(3) , and
(4) , but
(5) because

13. Sentences 4 and 5: **Drivers can become overconfident. As a result, they may take unnecessary chances behind the wheel.**

The most effective combination of sentences 4 and 5 would include which of the following groups of words?

(1) Because drivers take unnecessary chances
(2) Although drivers take unnecessary chances
(3) Drivers may take unnecessary chances because
(4) Drivers become overconfident because
(5) Although drivers may take unnecessary chances

Answers are on page 761.

Items 1 to 5 refer to the following paragraph. Choose the best answer to each item.

(1) The drive-in movie was perhaps the ultimate expression of the American love of cars. (2) In the heyday of the drive-in, families would packing snacks and blankets, pile into the car, and head for a movie under the stars. (3) The car of choice, of course, being the station wagon with the fold-down back gate. (4) Some families brought the entire makings of a picnic, the barbecue grill, charcoal, cooler, and lawn chairs all were packed in with the kids. (5) Not even pesky mosquitoes, teenagers, or scratchy speakers dimmed the drive-in's appeal. (6) The only things, in fact, that now lure families away are smaller cars and larger, air-conditioned indoor theaters. (7) Dying away, moviegoers seldom attend open-air cinemas. (8) Most of these hold more nostalgic memories than customers these days.

1. Sentence 2: **In the heyday of the drive-in, families would packing snacks and blankets, pile into the car, and head for a movie under the stars.**

   What correction should be made to this sentence?

   (1) remove the comma after drive-in
   (2) insert would before packing
   (3) change packing to pack
   (4) change head to heading
   (5) no correction is necessary

2. Sentence 3: **The car of choice, of course, being the station wagon with the fold-down back gate.**

   What correction should be made to this sentence?

   (1) move of choice after gate
   (2) remove the comma after choice
   (3) remove the comma after course
   (4) replace being with was
   (5) replace being with be

3. Sentence 4: **Some families brought the entire makings of a picnic, the barbecue grill, charcoal, cooler, and lawn chairs all were packed in with the kids.**

   Which of the following is the best way to write the underlined portion of this sentence? If you think the original is the best way, choose option (1).

   (1) a picnic, the
   (2) a picnic the
   (3) a picnic; the
   (4) a picnic, but the
   (5) a picnic; also, the

4. Sentence 5: **Not even pesky mosquitoes, teenagers, or scratchy speakers dimmed the drive-in's appeal.**

   What correction should be made to this sentence?

   (1) insert a comma after even
   (2) insert rowdy before teenagers
   (3) change speakers to speaker's
   (4) insert a comma after speakers
   (5) change drive-in's to drive-ins

5. Sentence 7: **Dying away, movie-goers seldom attend open-air cinemas.**

   What correction should be made to this sentence?

   (1) move dying away after moviegoers
   (2) remove the comma after away
   (3) insert As they're before dying
   (4) insert As there before dying
   (5) insert As drive-ins are before dying

(1) A gardener's desires no longer constrained by the limits of the weather. (2) In an outdoor garden, some plants cannot withstand heavy rain or frost. (3) They are easily raised in the controlled environment of a greenhouse. (4) A gardener should consider several factors before beginning construction expense is one primary concern. (5) Any prospective greenhouse owner must anticipate large fuel bills; heating a greenhouse can be very expensive.

6. Sentence 1: **A gardener's desires no longer constrained by the limits of the weather.**

    What correction should be made to this sentence?

    (1) change gardener's to gardeners
    (2) insert are after desires
    (3) insert is after desires
    (4) insert were after desires
    (5) no correction is necessary

7. Sentences 2 and 3: **In an outdoor garden, some plants cannot withstand heavy rain or frost. They are easily raised in the controlled environment of a greenhouse.**

    The most effective combination of sentences 4 and 5 would include which of the following groups of words?

    (1) rain or frost; however,
    (2) rain or frost; similarly,
    (3) rain or frost because
    (4) rain or frost, they
    (5) rain or frost they

8. Sentence 4: **A gardener should consider several factors before beginning construction expense is one primary concern.**

    What correction should be made to this sentence?

    (1) insert a comma after factors
    (2) insert a comma after construction
    (3) insert a semicolon after construction
    (4) change is to are
    (5) no correction is necessary

(1) Cat owners are divided on the issue of whether to declaw their beloved animals. (2) On the one hand, cat owners without claws feel bad about the idea of leaving their animals. (3) Cats need their claws for climbing trees, fighting with other cats, and to catch prey. (4) On the other hand, cats can cause great damage. (5) They use the walls, furniture, and other household items as scratching posts.

9. Sentence 2: **On the one hand, cat owners without claws feel bad about the idea of leaving their animals.**

    What correction should be made to this sentence?

    (1) remove the comma after hand
    (2) move without claws after hand
    (3) move without claws after animals
    (4) change bad to badly
    (5) no correction is necessary

10. Sentence 3: **Cats need their claws for climbing trees, fighting with other cats, and to catch prey.**

    What correction should be made to this sentence?

    (1) change need to needs
    (2) change climbing trees to climb trees
    (3) change fighting with other cats to fights
    (4) change to catch prey to catching prey
    (5) no correction is necessary

11. Sentences 4 and 5: **On the other hand, cats can cause great damage. They use the walls, furniture, and other household items as scratching posts.**

    The most effective combination of sentences 4 and 5 would include which of the following groups of words?

    (1) great damage unless
    (2) great damage so
    (3) great damage before
    (4) great damage, or
    (5) great damage if

(1) The planet Mars, one of Earth's nearest neighbors, has always captured the imagination of scientists and writers. (2) Historically, the question asked was whether or not life existed on that planet by both groups. (3) When looking through a telescope lens, Mars appears to have waterways or canals crossing its surface. (4) Observers wondered for many years about possible life on that planet because of the apparent waterways. (5) Such writers as Edgar Rice Burroughs imagined a planet of exotic races, sharp swords, and strange creatures. (6) Another writer, H. G. Wells, to describe a Martian invasion of Earth as "The War of the Worlds." (7) Even later, Ray Bradbury told stories of deserted palaces and deserts that were empty. (8) Some people had had high expectations for the unmanned space flight to Mars. (9) They were disappointed when it found no signs of life. (10) However, scientists' fascination with Mars still continues.

12. Sentence 2: **Historically, the question asked was whether or not life existed on that planet by both groups.**

    What correction should be made to this sentence?

    (1) remove the comma after Historically
    (2) change the spelling of whether to wether
    (3) insert a comma after whether
    (4) move by both groups after asked
    (5) move on that planet after asked

13. Sentence 3: **When looking through a telescope lens, Mars appears to have waterways or canals crossing its surface.**

    What correction should be made to this sentence?

    (1) replace When with Whenever
    (2) replace looking with one looks
    (3) change appears to appear
    (4) change the spelling of appears to appeers
    (5) change its to it's

14. Sentence 4: **Observers wondered for many years about possible life on that planet because of the apparent waterways.**

    If you rewrote sentence 4 beginning with

    Because of the apparent waterways,

    the next word would be

    (1) observers
    (2) wondering
    (3) for
    (4) about
    (5) possible

15. Sentence 6: **Another writer, H. G. Wells, to describe a Martian invasion of Earth as "The War of the Worlds."**

    What correction should be made to this sentence?

    (1) remove the comma after writer
    (2) remove the comma after Wells
    (3) remove to
    (4) change to describe to describing
    (5) change to describe to described

16. Sentence 7: **Even later, Ray Bradbury told stories of deserted palaces and deserts that were empty.**

    Which of the following is the best way to write the underlined portion of this sentence? If you think the original is the best way, choose option (1).

    (1) and deserts that were empty
    (2) and deserts that was empty
    (3) and deserts who were empty
    (4) and empty deserts
    (5) and deserts being empty

Answers are on page 762.

Items 1 to 4 refer to the following paragraph. Choose the best answer to each item.

(1) The number of families with two working parents have increased greatly over the past 15 years. (2) This increase has brought many changes to the family and place of working. (3) Today, working parents are willing to accept a job at lower wages if it allow for increased time at home with their children. (4) Some parents may choose not to accept a job promotion if they means more time at work and less time with their families. (5) Others may take only those jobs that are near home or child care.

1. Sentence 1: **The number of families with two working parents have increased greatly over the past 15 years.**

   What correction should be made to this sentence?

   (1) insert a comma after families
   (2) change parents to parent
   (3) insert a comma after parents
   (4) change have to has
   (5) no correction is necessary

2. Sentence 2: **This increase has brought many changes to the family and place of working.**

   Which of the following is the best way to write the underlined portion of this sentence? If you think the original is the best way, choose option (1).

   (1) family and place of working
   (2) family, and working place
   (3) family and working places
   (4) families and to the workplace
   (5) family and to the workplace

3. Sentence 3: **Today, working parents are willing to accept a job at lower wages if it allow for increased time at home with their children.**

   Which of the following is the best way to write the underlined portion of this sentence? If you think the original is the best way, choose option (1).

   (1) if it allow
   (2) if it allows
   (3) if they allows
   (4) if they allow
   (5) if it allowance

4. Sentence 4: **Some parents may choose not to accept a job promotion if they means more time at work and less time with their families.**

   What correction should be made to this sentence?

   (1) change parents to parent's
   (2) insert a comma after promotion
   (3) replace they with it
   (4) change means to mean
   (5) change their to they're

Items 5 to 9 refer to the following paragraphs.

(1) The U.S. Postal Service has come a long way since its founding by ben franklin in the late 1700s. (2) Back then it took days to travel across the 13 colonies by horseback. (3) Later came the Pony Express, carrying the mail from the midwest to california. (4) Next came the railroads, trucks, and finally came the speedy airplanes. (5) The post office says that mail within the 50 states can usually be delivered within three to five days airmail to most European countries takes five to six days.

(6) The cost of first class mail has rose dramatically since Colonial days. (7) One ounce of first class mail cost less than 5 cents to mail in 1800. (8) By 1995 the cost was up to 32 cents, it appears that the cost will continue to rise.

(9) Many people are upset by the rapidly increasing cost of postage. (10) However, the U.S. Postal Service despite its faults do the finest job in the world of fast, accurate delivery of mail. (11) The relative cost in terms of dollars are less now than in 1800.

5. **Sentence 1: The U.S. Postal Service has come a long way since its founding by ben franklin in the late 1700s.**

   What correction should be made to this sentence?

   (1) change Postal Service to postal service
   (2) change Service to service
   (3) change ben franklin to Ben franklin
   (4) change ben franklin to Ben Franklin
   (5) no correction is necessary

6. **Sentence 3: Later came the Pony Express, carrying the mail from the midwest to california.**

   What correction should be made to this sentence?

   (1) change came to come
   (2) change midwest to Midwest
   (3) change california to California
   (4) change midwest to california to Midwest to California
   (5) no correction is necessary

7. **Sentence 4: Next came the railroads, trucks, and finally came the speedy airplanes.**

   Which of the following is the best way to write the underlined portion of this sentence? If you think the original is the best way, choose option (1).

   (1) finally came the speedy airplanes
   (2) finally came the airplanes
   (3) finally the speedy airplanes
   (4) finally, the airplanes
   (5) finally came the super speedy airplanes

8. **Sentence 5: The post office says that mail within the 50 states can usually be delivered within three to five days airmail to most European countries takes five to six days.**

   Which of the following is the best way to write the underlined portion of this sentence? If you think the original is the best way, choose option (1).

   (1) days airmail
   (2) days, airmail
   (3) days; and airmail
   (4) days; airmail
   (5) days; but airmail

9. **Sentence 6: The cost of first class mail has rose dramatically since Colonial days.**

   What correction should be made to this sentence?

   (1) change first class to First Class
   (2) change has to have
   (3) change rose to risen
   (4) change Colonial to colonial
   (5) change days to Days

Items 10 to 14 refer to the following paragraph.

(1) Many changes been made in the American game of baseball since its invention in the 1800s. (2) Games played before the 1930s was scheduled only during daylight. (3) Early professional players wore baggy uniforms, used unpadded gloves to catch balls, and received little or no money for their efforts. (4) A starting pitcher were expected to pitch the entire game. (5) Today baseball is played day and night in such faraway places as Europe, Asia, South America, and Australia. (6) Players wear trim uniforms, collect huge salaries, and enjoy celebrity status. (7) Everyone who watches baseball in this country realize that it has become a big business. (8) Players' salaries, owners' revenues, and concession prices have soared ever upward. (9) There a growing sense is that attending a game costs too much money. (10) Nonetheless, the popularity of baseball continues to grow around the world.

10. Sentence 1: **Many changes been made in the American game of baseball since its invention in the 1800s.**

    What correction should be made to this sentence?

    (1) replace changes with change
    (2) change been made to have been made
    (3) change American to american
    (4) insert a comma after baseball
    (5) change its to it's

11. Sentence 2: **Games played before the 1930s was scheduled only during daylight.**

    What correction should be made to this sentence?

    (1) change played to play
    (2) insert a comma after played
    (3) change was to were
    (4) change was scheduled to have been scheduled
    (5) no correction is necessary

12. Sentence 4: **A starting pitcher were expected to pitch the entire game.**

    Which of the following is the best way to write the underlined portion of this sentence? If you think the original is the best way, choose option (1).

    (1) A starting pitcher were expected
    (2) A starting pitcher have expected
    (3) A starting pitcher was expected
    (4) A Starting Pitcher was expected
    (5) A starting pitched had been expected

13. Sentence 7: **Everyone who watches baseball in this country realize that it has become a big business.**

    What correction should be made to this sentence?

    (1) insert commas after Everyone and country
    (2) change who to whom
    (3) change realize to realizes
    (4) replace it with they
    (5) no correction is necessary

14. Sentence 9: **There a growing sense is that attending a game costs too much money.**

    What correction should be made to this sentence?

    (1) change There to Their
    (2) change a growing sense is to is a growing sense
    (3) change costs to cost's
    (4) change too to to
    (5) no correction is necessary

Items 15 to 19 refer to the following paragraph.

(1) What can be used as a parachute to soften a landing, as an umbrella in a downpour, or as a way to say "hello"? (2) The answer was the bushy tail of a squirrel. (3) About seventy kinds of squirrels live throughout the world in forests, fields, parks, and city backyards. (4) Some squirrels nest in trees, while others live in their colonies underground. (5) Most squirrels store their food, which consists of acorns, nuts, leaf buds, seeds, fruit, berries, mushrooms, pine cones, insects, and bird eggs. (6) Occasionally, squirrels even "plant" new trees by forgetting to uncover them buried nuts. (7) Some people think that the squirrel is a dangerous, disease-carrying menace; others finds squirrels to be intelligent, curious, and very sociable animals. (8) Never try to capture squirrels; despite their cuteness, they should be treated as wild animals. (9) Squirrels are not naturally aggressive animals; however, squirrels may bite when threatened. (10) Although a squirrel's bite can be dangerous, this member of the rodent family plays an important role in our environment.

15. Sentence 2: **The answer was the bushy tail of a squirrel.**

    What correction should be made to this sentence?

    (1) change was to should have been
    (2) change was to is
    (3) insert a semicolon after was
    (4) insert a comma after was
    (5) change squirrel to Squirrel

16. Sentence 4: **Some squirrels nest in trees, while others live in their colonies underground.**

    What correction should be made to this sentence?

    (1) change their to his
    (2) change their to her
    (3) change colonies to Colonies
    (4) change underground to Underground
    (5) no correction is necessary

17. Sentence 6: **Occasionally, squirrels even "plant" new trees by forgetting to uncover them buried nuts.**

    What correction should be made to this sentence?

    (1) insert a comma after even
    (2) change the spelling of forgetting to forgeting
    (3) change them to their
    (4) change buried to bury
    (5) no correction is necessary

18. Sentence 7: **Some people think that the squirrel is a dangerous, disease-carrying menace; others finds squirrels to be intelligent, curious, and very sociable animals.**

    What correction should be made to this sentence?

    (1) change Some to A lot
    (2) change people to peoples
    (3) replace the semicolon with a comma
    (4) change finds to find
    (5) insert a comma after very

19. Sentence 9: **Squirrels are not naturally aggressive animals; however, squirrels may bite when threatened.**

    What correction should be made to this sentence?

    (1) change are to is
    (2) change naturally to natural
    (3) change the semicolon to a comma
    (4) replace the second squirrels with they
    (5) no correction is necessary

Items 20 to 24 refer to the following paragraphs.

(1) Controlling pesticides has become a serious problem. (2) The resistance of bugs to pesticides has caused a demand for stronger and stronger pesticides. (3) This we now know have resulted in the carry-over of pesticides into the food chain.

(4) Pesticides can cause serious illnesses in adults and children, they can cause birth defects in babies. (5) The solution to this problem involves many different efforts. (6) One approach is to breed insects that are sterile so it cannot reproduce and will gradually die out. (7) Another approach is to breed natural enemies for a selected bug that will not cause harm themselves. (8) Its also possible to breed plants that are resistant to or can even repel certain bugs.

(9) All the solutions require a long time and a lot of research and development money. (10) Unfortunately, developing a new, stronger pesticide is quicker and cheaper than the safer alternatives.

20. Sentence 2: **The resistance of bugs to pesticides has caused a demand for stronger and stronger pesticides.**

What correction should be made to this sentence?

(1) change the spelling of resistance to resistence
(2) change has to have
(3) change has caused to causes
(4) change stronger and stronger to strong and strong
(5) no correction is necessary

21. Sentence 3: **This we now know have resulted in the carry-over of pesticides into the food chain.**

Which of the following is the best way to write the underlined portion of this sentence? If you think the original is the best way, choose option (1).

(1) This we now know have
(2) This, we now know, have
(3) This, we now know, has
(4) This we now know has
(5) This we now know, have

22. Sentence 4: **Pesticides can cause serious illnesses in adults and children, they can cause birth defects in babies.**

What correction should be made to this sentence?

(1) change children to childs
(2) change children, they to children, and they
(3) change children, they to children; and they
(4) change babies to babys'
(5) no correction is necessary

23. Sentence 6: **One approach is to breed insects that are sterile so it cannot reproduce and will gradually die out.**

Which of the following is the best way to write the underlined portion of this sentence? If you think the original is the best way, choose option (1).

(1) that are sterile so it
(2) who are sterile so it
(3) that are sterile so they
(4) who are sterile so they
(5) whom are sterile so they

24. Sentence 8: **Its also possible to breed plants that are resistant to or can even repel certain bugs.**

What correction should be made to this sentence?

(1) change Its to It's
(2) change Its to Its'
(3) replace that with who
(4) change the spelling of resistant to resistent
(5) no correction is necessary

(1) Organ transplants are becoming more and more common. (2) In the past kidney transplants were about the only common organ transplants. (3) Today, we hear of heart, lung, liver, and eye transplants, in addition to kidney transplants. (4) Sources of organs for transplants are people which are killed in accidents or who die of illnesses that do not affect the organ being used.

(5) A big problem with organ transplants is that it often tries to reject the organ. (6) It sometimes requires the use of strong drugs to prevent this rejection. (7) As better transplant methods and better antirejection drugs are developed, transplants will become more common and more successful. (8) Some concerns, are heard, that organ transplants are too common now. (9) There is also concern about people selling their organs.

(10) Someday the transplanting of most body organs may become common and routine. (11) More and more people are making advance arrangements to donate its organs when they die, so that someone else can live.

25. Sentence 2: **In the past kidney transplants were about the only common organ transplants.**

    What correction should be made to this sentence?

    (1) replace past with passed
    (2) insert a semicolon after past
    (3) insert a comma after past
    (4) change were to was
    (5) no correction is necessary

26. Sentence 3: **Today, we hear of heart, lung, liver, and eye transplants, in addition to kidney transplants.**

    What correction should be made to this sentence?

    (1) replace hear with here
    (2) replace eye with I
    (3) remove the comma after eye transplants
    (4) change addition to edition
    (5) no correction is necessary

27. Sentence 4: **Sources of organs for transplants are people which are killed in accidents or who die of illnesses that do not affect the organ being used.**

    Which of the following is the best way to write the underlined portion of this sentence? If you think the original is the best way, choose option (1).

    (1) people which are
    (2) people which is
    (3) people who are
    (4) people who is
    (5) people who were

28. Sentence 5: **A big problem with organ transplants is that it often tries to reject the organ.**

    Which of the following is the best way to write the underlined portion of this sentence? If you think the original is the best way, choose option (1).

    (1) is that it
    (2) are that it
    (3) is that the body receiving the transplant
    (4) are that the body receiving the transplant
    (5) is because the body receiving the transplant

29. Sentence 6: **It sometimes requires the use of strong drugs to prevent this rejection.**

    If you rewrote sentence 6 beginning with

    The use of strong drugs

    the next words should be

    (1) is sometimes required
    (2) are sometimes required
    (3) were sometimes required
    (4) is, in any case, required
    (5) are, in any case, required

30. Sentence 8: **Some <u>concerns, are heard, that</u> organ transplants are too common now.**

Which of the following is the best way to write the underlined portion of this sentence? If you think the original is the best way, choose option (1).

(1) concerns, are heard, that
(2) concerns are heard, that
(3) concerns, are heard that
(4) concerns are heard that
(5) concerns are, heard that

<u>Items 31 to 34</u> refer to the following paragraph.

(1) The small town is back in style with new suburban planners and architects. (2) A typical suburb usually has winding streets, ranch-style homes, and big yards these new planners are using straight streets, farm-style homes, and small yards instead. (3) The homes have front porches. (4) They are set close to neighbors' homes. (5) All the new homes are within walking distance of a central square. (6) It contains a small grocery store and other shops. (7) The main goal is to bring community spirit to the suburbs planners believe that homeowners who live closer together will talk and interact more with one another.

31. Sentence 2: **A typical suburb usually has winding streets, ranch-style homes, and big <u>yards these new</u> planners are using straight streets, farm-style homes, and small yards instead.**

Which of the following is the best way to write the underlined portion of this sentence? If you think the original is the best way, choose option (1).

(1) yards these new
(2) yards, these new
(3) yards; these new
(4) yards, or these new
(5) yards unless these new

32. Sentences 3 and 4: **The homes have front porches. They are set close to neighbors' homes.**

The most effective combination of sentences 3 and 4 would include which of the following groups of words?

(1) porches, they
(2) porches they
(3) porches, yet they
(4) porches, so they
(5) porches, and they

33. Sentences 5 and 6: **All the new homes are within walking distance of a central square. It contains a small grocery store and other shops.**

The most effective combination of sentences 5 and 6 would include which of the following groups of words?

(1) square contains
(2) square who contains
(3) square, which contains
(4) square; however, it contains
(5) square it contains

34. Sentence 7: **The main goal is to bring community spirit to the <u>suburbs planners</u> believe that homeowners who live closer together will talk and interact more with one another.**

Which of the following is the best way to write the underlined portion of this sentence? If you think the original is the best way, choose option (1).

(1) suburbs planners
(2) suburbs, planners
(3) suburbs. planners
(4) suburbs. Planners
(5) suburbs but planners

Items 35 to 38 refer to the following paragraph.

(1) Badgers are the great individualists of the animal world. (2) Their fierce appearance, sharp teeth, and finger-length claws can support the badger's claim to privacy. (3) Living alone in burrows that they dig, badgers each have their own territories. (4) They dislike other animals so much. (5) Badgers don't even associate with other badgers. (6) These relatives of the weasel will challenge anything that moves, in fact. (7) The badger's loose hide enables it to turn around when caught. (8) It rakes opponents with its claws. (9) Rattlesnakes, dogs, and other animals have been stood up to by badgers that were angry. (10) Since the loser in a badger fight gets eaten, many animals are happy to give badgers plenty of space.

35. Sentence 2: **Their fierce appearance, sharp teeth, and finger-length claws can support the badger's claim to privacy.**

What correction should be made to this sentence?

(1) change Their to They're
(2) change the spelling of appearance to appearence
(3) change the spelling of length to legnth
(4) change badger's to badgers
(5) no correction is necessary

36. Sentences 4 and 5: **They dislike other animals so much. Badgers don't even associate with other badgers.**

The most effective combination of sentences 4 and 5 would include which of the following groups of words?

(1) so much because badgers
(2) Even though they dislike
(3) Because they dislike
(4) so much, but badgers
(5) so much since badgers

37. Sentences 7 and 8: **The badger's loose hide enables it to turn around when caught. It rakes opponents with its claws.**

The most effective combination of sentences 7 and 8 would include which of the following groups of words?

(1) caught it rakes
(2) caught, it rakes
(3) caught, yet it rakes
(4) caught; then, it rakes
(5) caught, nor rakes

38. Sentence 9: **Rattlesnakes, dogs, and other animals have been stood up to by badgers that were angry.**

If you rewrote sentence 9 beginning with

Angry badgers

the next words should be

(1) have been stood up to
(2) stood up to
(3) have stood up to
(4) been stood up to
(5) were stood up to

Items 39 to 43 refer to the following paragraphs.

(1) Alfred Nobel a Swedish chemist invented dynamite. (2) When he died, he left $9 million to a fund to award prizes to outstanding persons each year in the areas of world peace chemistry physics literature and medicine. (3) Nobel felt bad about creating something so destructive as dynamite, he started this fund to compensate for his guilt.
(4) The prizes, which began in 1901, are awarded by various organizations in Sweden. (5) The peace prize is awarded by a committee of five elected by the norwegian parliament. (6) A sixth prize in economics was established in 1969 by the Swedish Central Bank.
(7) The prizes are awarded each year on december 10, the anniversary of Alfred Nobel's death. (8) The Nobel prize consists of a large sum of cash and a medal. (9) The cash for each category are an equal share of the income from the original $9 million.

39. Sentence 1: **Alfred Nobel a Swedish chemist invented dynamite.**

Which of the following is the best way to write the underlined portion of this sentence? If you think the original is the best way, choose option (1).

(1) Nobel a Swedish chemist invented
(2) Nobel, a Swedish chemist invented
(3) Nobel a Swedish chemist, invented
(4) Nobel, a Swedish chemist, invented
(5) Nobel, a swedish chemist, invented

40. Sentence 2: **When he died, he left $9 million to a fund to award prizes to outstanding persons each year in the areas of world peace chemistry physics literature and medicine.**

Which of the following is the best way to write the underlined portion of this sentence? If you think the original is the best way, choose option (1).

(1) world peace chemistry physics literature and
(2) world peace chemistry, physics literature and
(3) world peace, chemistry, physics, literature, and
(4) world peace, chemistry, physics literature and
(5) world peace chemistry, physics, literature, and

41. Sentence 3: **Nobel felt bad about creating something so destructive as dynamite, he started this fund to compensate for his guilt.**

What correction should be made to this sentence?

(1) remove the comma after dynamite
(2) change dynamite, he to dynamite; he
(3) change started to starts
(4) change fund to Fund
(5) no correction is necessary

42. Sentence 4: **The prizes, which began in 1901, are awarded by various organizations in Sweden.**

What correction should be made to this sentence?

(1) remove the comma after prizes
(2) change began to begun
(3) remove the comma after 1901
(4) replace Sweden with sweden
(5) no correction is necessary

43. Sentence 5: **The peace prize is awarded by a committee of five elected by the norwegian parliament.**

What correction should be made to this sentence?

(1) change peace to piece
(2) change committee to Committee
(3) insert a comma after elected
(4) change norwegian to Norwegian
(5) no correction is necessary

Answers are on page 763.

Dave Barry's essays appear in many newspapers across the country.

In Test One, Part II, you will be asked to write an essay. An essay is a composition of more than one paragraph that gives the writer's views on a particular topic. Unit 2 will teach you effective ways to gather and organize ideas, write your essay, evaluate it, and revise it. You will focus on developing a five-paragraph essay, which is an effective way to organize a GED essay. A five-paragraph essay includes an introductory paragraph, three body paragraphs, and a conclusion paragraph.

By helping you focus on passing the GED Writing Skills Test, Part II and by giving you a step-by-step approach to writing a good five-paragraph essay, Unit 2 will give you the POWER to succeed. In fact, we call our program the POWER Program. Each step—from how to begin your essay to how to end it—is listed for you. **P** stands for **Plan, O** for **Organize, W** for **Write, E** for **Evaluate,** and **R** for **Revise.** The chart that follows summarizes the POWER Writing Program.

POWER STEPS

	Lesson	Steps	Time
P	**Planning Your Essay** (p. 154–160)	☐ Figure out the topic. ☐ Understand the instructions. ☐ Choose your main idea. ☐ Gather ideas.	5 minutes
O	**Organizing Your Essay** (p. 161–167)	☐ Group and name your ideas. ☐ Expand your groups. ☐ Order your groups.	5 minutes
W	**Writing Your Essay** (p. 168–180)	☐ Write your introduction. ☐ Write your body paragraphs. ☐ Write your conclusion.	25 minutes
E	**Evaluating Your Essay** (p. 181–187)	☐ Evaluate your ideas and organization. ☐ Evaluate your use of the conventions of English.	5 minutes
R	**Revising Your Essay** (p. 188–194)	☐ Revise your ideas and organization. ☐ Revise your use of the conventions of English.	5 minutes

In Unit 2 you will get plenty of practice with each of the POWER steps. Review the POWER steps until they become automatic for you and use them as you write the essays in this unit. Following the time limits will allow sufficient time for you to write a good essay and check it within the 45-minute time limit on the test.

Planning
Lesson 1

Planning

The first step of the POWER writing process is planning. To write a good GED essay, you have to write about the assigned topic and include a lot of good ideas. In Lesson 1, you will learn how to plan your essay so that it is about the assigned topic and includes a variety of good ideas.

Figuring Out the Topic

The GED Writing Test, Part II begins with the **writing assignment.** Completing a GED writing assignment does not require any specialized information or knowledge. Rather, the GED requires you to state your opinion. Your composition has to back up this opinion with specific examples drawn from your experience.

For example, a writing assignment on seat belt laws would not ask how many people die each year in traffic accidents because they were not wearing seat belts. Instead, it would ask whether you think that laws requiring people to wear seat belts are a good idea.

A GED writing assignment contains three parts:
   ◆ Background information on the topic
   ◆ The topic
   ◆ The instructions

Here is a typical GED writing assignment with the parts marked:

Background information on the topic }

> Recently several states have passed laws requiring the driver and passengers in a motor vehicle to wear seat belts while the vehicle is in operation. Many people believe that these laws infringe on personal freedom. Others believe that these laws are necessary to save lives.

Use the background information to give you ideas about the topic.

The topic— the subject of your essay }

> Write a composition of about 200 words that explains your opinion about (laws requiring the use of seat belts.) Tell why you agree or disagree with the seat belt laws. Be specific and use examples to support your views.

All of the ideas in your essay should relate to this topic.

The instructions —what you are to do }

The instructions state the kind of information you need to give in your essay.

Exercise Figuring Out the Topic

Read each GED writing assignment. Draw a box around the background information, circle the topic, and underline the instructions.

TOPIC 1

Because of the increase of women in the work force, finding ways to arrange adequate child care has become a major issue. To address the problem, many companies have begun to provide on-site day care for their employees' children.

Write a composition of about 200 words discussing whether or not you think employers should supply child care for their employees. Be specific and use examples to support your view.

TOPIC 2

Mandatory drug testing in the work place has been the cause for heated debate. Many people feel that testing employees is an invasion of privacy. Others see it as a way of protecting themselves and their employees.

In a composition of about 200 words, describe the effects of mandatory drug testing on employees. You may wish to describe the positive effects, the negative effects, or both. Use specific examples to support your opinion.

TOPIC 3

Most jobs today require applicants to have either a GED or a high school diploma. For many employers, these certificates are evidence of the applicant's ability to accomplish goals and perform at certain standards.

How important is having a GED or a high school diploma when you apply for a job? In an essay of about 200 words, tell your opinion. Use specific examples to support your view.

TOPIC 4

Although cigarette ads were banned from TV in the 1970s, they still appear in magazines and on billboards. Many ads seem to appeal to a very young audience.

In an essay of about 200 words, tell how you think cigarette advertising should be handled. Should all ads for cigarettes be banned? Support your opinion with specific examples.

Answers are on page 767.

Understanding the Instructions

The instructions in the writing assignment tell you how to write your essay. It is important to understand exactly what the instructions say. Usually, **key words** in the instructions will help you understand what to write.

This chart contains some of the key words that are used in GED writing instructions and tells the kind of information you should give in your composition.

Understanding the Instructions	
If the Instructions Say:	**You Should:**
1. describe the effect of... tell how this might affect...	write about causes and effects
2. explain how or why... tell how... discuss... identify... describe how... describe why...	give reasons or explain facts about an issue
3. state a view... present an opinion... state your opinion...	tell what you think about an issue

ged Exercise Understanding the Instructions

Read each GED writing assignment. Underline the instructions. Use the chart to figure out the kind of information your essay should provide. Write the kind of information on the line.

TOPIC 1

Fast food is a part of our way of life. Fast-food restaurants can be found all over the country selling hamburgers, chicken, and fish sandwiches. Many of these places have inexpensive salad bars, too.

Why are fast-food restaurants so popular today? In a composition of 200 words, state the reasons for fast food's popularity. Support your opinion with specific examples.

tell what you think about an issue

TOPIC 2

Airplanes are the fastest way to get from one place to another. Today you can eat breakfast in Chicago, lunch in Dallas, and dinner in Los Angeles. For many people this is a modern miracle, but others are afraid that rapid transportation may have negative effects on daily life.

Write a composition of 200 words that describes both the negative and the positive effects of rapid transportation on everyday life. Be specific and use examples.

TOPIC 3

In many families, both parents work outside the home. Children under the age of five are cared for by full-time baby-sitters or in day-care centers until they are old enough to go to school.

Is it harmful for both parents of a preschool child to work outside the home? In a composition of about 200 words, state your opinion. Use specific examples to support your point of view.

TOPIC 4

Climates vary greatly in different parts of the country. Some people say that they would not move to a certain place because of the effect the weather would have on their lives.

How does the climate where you live affect you and the people who live there? Write a composition of about 200 words describing the good points, the bad points, or both. Be specific, and use examples to support your views.

TOPIC 5

Young people spend as much as five or six hours a day watching TV. Anything that takes up so much of their time will affect them—for better or for worse.

In a composition of 200 words, describe the effects of watching TV on young people. You may describe good or bad effects, or both. Be specific, and use examples to support your views.

Answers are on page 767.

Gathering Ideas

Tip

All the ideas you gather should support your essay's main idea.

Once you have a main idea, you are ready to begin **gathering ideas** for your essay. This is a very important step because you need to back up your main idea with a variety of examples. An easy way to gather ideas is to think about the main idea and then start listing as many related ideas as you can.

You may worry that you won't be able to think of enough ideas to write a good essay. A good way to overcome this fear is by relaxing and writing all of the ideas that come to mind—as many as you can. The best ideas you get may not be the first ideas you think of, so don't stop with two or three ideas. If you write only a few ideas, you're stuck with those. If you write down a lot of ideas, you can pick and choose the best.

A good habit to get into when you are thinking about ideas is to make a note of the time you begin. Allow yourself at least five minutes to think of and write ideas. When you have written as many ideas as you can, stop and look at them. Are there enough ideas to work with?

Two good ways to write your ideas are lists and idea maps. When you make a **list,** you write the ideas in the order you think of them. When you make an **idea map,** you write down ideas in a way that shows their relationship to the main idea.

Look at how two students wrote their ideas about seat belt laws. One student wrote a list and the other wrote an idea map.

Student 1's List

Main Idea: *Seat belt laws are good.*

— *save lives*

— *people are more careful*

— *cities make money on fines*

— *people would not use them*

Student 2's Idea Map

can't get out of car after accident

Main Idea: Seat belt laws are bad.

people should make their own decisions

government controls too much

ged Exercise Gathering Ideas

Read each main idea. Then write a list of ideas or an idea map about it.

1. Digital pagers and portable telephones have changed how we communicate in several ways.

2. Some kinds of popular music are bad influences on young people.

3. Universal, free health care is a good idea.

4. It's very important to have a GED or a high-school diploma when you apply for a job.

Answers are on page 768.

A. Read the GED writing assignment. Draw a box around the background information, circle the topic, and underline the instructions.

> Over the past few years, many people who were living in the country have moved to the city. At the same time, many people in the city have moved to the country.
>
> In a composition of about 200 words, state whether you think life is better in the country or in the city. Give specific examples to support your view.

B. Look at the instructions. What kind of information is required? Write the kind of information.

_____

_____

C. Look at the topic and the background information. Then think of a main idea for an essay on this topic. Write your main idea.

_____

_____

D. Think about the main idea you wrote in C. Then write a list of ideas or an idea map about it.

Answers are on page 768.

The Essay ◆ Planning

Organizing
Lesson 2 Organizing

Grouping and Naming Your Ideas

Once you have some ideas about a topic, your next step is **grouping and naming ideas.** Each group of ideas will become a paragraph to support the main idea of your essay. To group ideas, see what the ideas in your list have in common. Put related ideas in a group and label or name the group to show how they relate to the main idea. If an idea doesn't fit in any group, cross it out.

Here is one student's list of ideas about the effects of watching TV. Read how she grouped them.

Main idea: Watching TV has both good and
              bad effects.

        The Effects of Watching TV
    violence seems to be everywhere
    keeps people from reading
    keeps people from family
    keeps people from doing active things
    TV's cost a lot
    informs
    escape
    entertainment
    ads make people want things

To group her ideas, she looked for ideas that were related. She knew she had listed both good and bad effects, so she circled all the ideas that were good effects and labeled them. Then she did the same for the bad effects. The labels helped her remember what each group had in common. After sorting out her effects, she realized that one idea was not an effect at all—TVs cost a lot. So she crossed that idea off her list. Her grouped ideas are on the next page.

The groups of ideas looked like this:

The Effects of Watching TV

- *violence seems to be everywhere*
- *keeps people from reading*
- *keeps people from family*
- *keeps people from doing active things*

Bad effects ~~*TVs cost a lot*~~

- *informs*
- *escape*
- *entertainment* — *Good effects*

- *ads make people want things*

It is usually not difficult to divide your list of ideas into two groups. However, since you want to write a five-paragraph essay, it is best to have three groups of related ideas for the three supporting paragraphs you will write. If you divide your largest group into two groups, each of your three groups can become a supporting paragraph for the three middle paragraphs of your essay.

To make her three groups, the writer noticed that she could make two groups from the larger group—the bad effects of TV. One group could name things that were unrealistic about TV. The other group could name things that watching TV kept people from doing.

Bad Effects

False Sense of Life	*Keeps People from Better Things*
want too many things (ads)	*reading*
violence seems to be everywhere	*family*
	doing active things

Tip

Try to make three groups of ideas. Having three groups will help ensure enough support for your main idea.

Tip

If you have divided your list into two groups, see if one of those groups can become two smaller groups of related ideas.

If the writer had used an idea map, many of her ideas would already be grouped and connected. She would only need to label the different groups, like this:

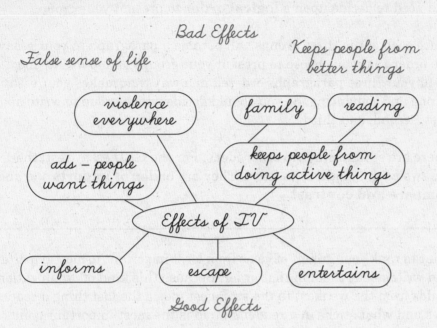

Bad Effects

False sense of life

Keeps people from better things

violence everywhere

family

reading

ads – people want things

keeps people from doing active things

Effects of TV

informs

escape

entertains

Good Effects

> **Tip**
>
> Ask yourself if the ideas in each group have something in common and if the labels tell how the ideas are related.

ged **Exercise** Grouping Ideas

Read the list of ideas for the topic "What are the pros and cons of having a hobby?" Write each idea in the group where it belongs. One idea does not fit with any of the groups. Cross out that idea.

The Pros and Cons of Having a Hobby

- have fun
- can learn things
- can develop new skills
- may spend too much time away from family
- may spend too much money

- bowling is my hobby
- relieves stress
- may neglect things that need to be done
- may meet people with similar interests, make friends
- may discover a talent

Pros

Practical Reasons

Emotional and Social Reasons

Cons

_____

_____

_____

_____

_____

_____

_____

_____

_____

Answers are on page 768.

Ordering Your Groups

There is one more step you should take before you write your essay. You need to decide upon a **logical order** to present your groups.

Since each of the three groups will become a paragraph in your essay, the order that you choose to present your groups is important. You want your three paragraphs ordered in a way that makes your essay strong and convincing. So you should decide which group to write about first, second, and third.

There are several ways to order ideas. For the GED essay test, there are two useful methods to learn. They are **order of importance** and **compare and contrast.**

Order of Importance

You can rank your groups of ideas from least important to most important and write about them in that order. Because this kind of organization builds from the weakest to the strongest ideas, the last thing a reader sees and what sticks in a reader's mind is the most important point.

The order of the paragraphs below is from least important to most important. As you read the paragraphs, notice the words in **color.** They help you understand the order of ideas.

> Seat belt laws are a source of money for cities. People ticketed for not wearing seat belts must pay fines, and this money can be used to improve traffic safety.
>
> **Even more important,** seat belt laws themselves improve traffic safety. Just by buckling up, people are reminded to drive more safely.
>
> **But the most important reason** that seat belt laws are wise is that they save lives. Countless numbers of people are alive today because they were wearing their seat belts when they had an accident. Countless more have been saved from serious injury.

Tip

These words signal that ideas are organized in order of importance: *more important, most important, better, best.*

The writer placed his reasons for supporting seat belt laws in order from least important to most important. The most important idea, saving lives, is the last one to be read. It leaves the reader with the strongest impression.

Compare and Contrast

When you **compare** things, you show how they are alike. When you **contrast** things, you show how they are different. A GED writing assignment may ask you to compare and contrast two things, such as the problems of the past and those we encounter today. Or it may ask you to contrast different sides of a topic, such as the advantages and disadvantages of pay TV.

Contrasting is the way the student organized her essay about the good and bad effects of watching TV.

> There's no doubt that watching television can have positive effects. Adults can keep informed about current events by watching the evening news. They may even gain some practical knowledge about their health and other personal concerns. Children can learn from educational shows like <u>Sesame Street</u>. In addition, everyone can be entertained and even escape a little with the cartoons, comedies, movies, and action shows.
>
> **On the other hand,** watching television has some definite negative effects. Instead of just using it as a temporary escape, some people may watch television rather than deal with their problems. TV also keeps people from spending time with their family or from reading. In fact, it turns some people into couch potatoes, keeping them from any physical activity.
>
> **In addition,** television gives people a false sense of what life is like. They see commercials on TV and feel they must have what's being advertised. They see violence on shows and think modern life is more violent than it really is, or they may even think it's all right to act violently.

These words signal that ideas are being compared: *both*, *also*, *similarly*, *like*. **These words signal that ideas are contrasted:** *on the other hand*, *in contrast*, *however*, *but*, *whereas*, *while*.

By contrasting the negative with the positive effects of watching television, the student got her main idea across effectively. She used her first paragraph to discuss the good effects. She used her second paragraph to discuss some of the bad effects signaling this contrast with the words <u>on the other hand</u>. She used her third paragraph to discuss more negative effects.

Which Organization Should You Use?

The order you choose to present your ideas should lend the greatest support for your main idea. This chart can help you decide.

If you are writing about:	Try using:
◆ reasons or causes ◆ the qualities of one thing ◆ how you feel about an issue	◆ order of importance
◆ good and bad effects ◆ advantages and disadvantages	◆ contrast
◆ the qualities of two things	◆ compare and contrast

Before you decide how to order groups for an essay, write your main idea at the top of your paper. It can help you determine the best way to support your main idea.

Here are some groups of ideas for two essays. Determine the order that would lend the most support to the main idea. Use the boxes to number the groups in that order.

1. **Essay topic**: Describe the advantages of swimming.

   Main idea: Swimming is a good sport.

   [ ]   [ ]   [ ]

   Benefits

   ◆ healthy exercise
   ◆ little stress on body
   ◆ fun
   ◆ mental relaxation

   Little Equipment

   ◆ swimming suit
   ◆ towel
   ◆ maybe swimming cap

   Ease and Convenience

   ◆ can do year round
   ◆ park district pools
   ◆ beach in summer
   ◆ easy to learn

2. **Essay topic**: What effect would passing the GED test have on a person?

   Main idea: _____

   [ ]   [ ]   [ ]

   Personal Reasons

   ◆ feel good about yourself
   ◆ learn how not to quit
   ◆ more confidence

   Job-related Reasons

   ◆ get a more satisfying job
   ◆ earn more money
   ◆ better chance for promotion

   Educational Reasons

   ◆ stronger reading and math skills
   ◆ chance to go on to college
   ◆ develop writing skills

3. Review the groups of ideas you wrote for the essay topic "The Pros and Cons of Having a Hobby" on page 163. Decide on the best order and number the groups in the order you would write about them.

Here is the GED essay question you gathered ideas for in the GED Review on page 160.

> Over the past few years, many people who were living in the country have moved to the city. At the same time, many people in the city have moved to the country.
>
> In a composition of about 200 words, state whether you think life is better in the country or in the city. Give specific examples to support your view.

Use the list of ideas or idea map you made on page 160 for these exercises.

A. Group your ideas. Make three groups of related ideas with labels. You can circle and label the groups on your list or map, or you may rewrite your ideas in groups in the space below.

_____

_____

_____

_____

_____

_____

_____

_____

_____

_____

_____

_____

B. Expand your groups. Try to add at least one idea to one or more of the groups.

C. Think about the best way to order the groups to support your main idea. Number the groups to show the order you chose.

Answers on page 768.

Writing

The third step in the POWER writing process is writing your essay. In Lesson 3, you will learn how to use your groups of ideas to write an introductory paragraph, three well-developed body paragraphs, and a concluding paragraph. Using this approach, you will be able to produce an effective five-paragraph essay.

The Three Parts of an Essay

An essay has three basic parts. The parts follow an order, and each part has a specific purpose. In a five-paragraph essay, each part also consists of a specific number of paragraphs. Look at this plan for a five-paragraph essay.

Introduction
- ◆ consists of one paragraph
- ◆ includes the essay topic
- ◆ tells the main idea

Body
- ◆ consists of three paragraphs
- ◆ develops the topic
- ◆ supports the main idea

Conclusion
- ◆ consists of one paragraph
- ◆ sums up and reviews information in the body

To write a five-paragraph essay on the importance of regular exercise, one student read the following topic assignment and then completed the first two POWER steps. Look at the student's work.

Main idea: *Regular exercise is important.*

Better Health	Look Better	Feel Better
stronger heart	lose weight	feel good about
breathe better	firm muscles	how you look
more endurance	healthier skin	more self-esteem
burns calories	and hair	reduces tension
		feel more relaxed

Then the student wrote the following essay. Read it and notice how the three parts of an essay are contained in the five paragraphs.

Many people exercise regularly, yet many others do not. If those who don't exercise knew how important it is, they would all start exercise programs. Regular exercise makes and keeps you fit. In fact, it helps you look and feel fit in addition to being fit.

Introduction

First of all, regular exercise is good for your health. When you run, bicycle, or do some other aerobic activity three times a week, your heart becomes stronger, and your breathing improves. These physical changes increase your endurance. You actually feel like you have more energy. In addition, muscles that are working burn more fat calories.

Body

Exercise can help improve not only your health but also your looks. Because your body burns more calories, you lose weight and look slimmer and trimmer. Your muscles become firm. You seem more youthful and energetic. In addition, better circulation gives your skin and hair a healthy glow.

Body Perhaps all these physical benefits lead to the most important result of regular exercise—it makes you feel better. Exercise reduces tension in your muscles and makes you more relaxed. You feel rested and ready to go during the day, and you sleep better at night. Because you look better, you also just naturally feel better about your body and about yourself. Your self-esteem increases.

Conclusion With all these benefits of regular exercise, it's hard to understand why someone would not work out. If you exercise regularly, your body and your mind will appreciate it.

Paragraphs and Topic Sentences

Before you write your essay, you need to know how to develop a good paragraph. To do so, focus on the groups of ideas you wrote in POWER Step 2. Each group of ideas will become a paragraph in your essay.

Each paragraph will have a **topic sentence** that tells the main idea of the paragraph. The other ideas become the **supporting details** of the paragraph. You can write the topic sentence at the beginning, middle, or end of a paragraph. A paragraph may be written in these three ways:

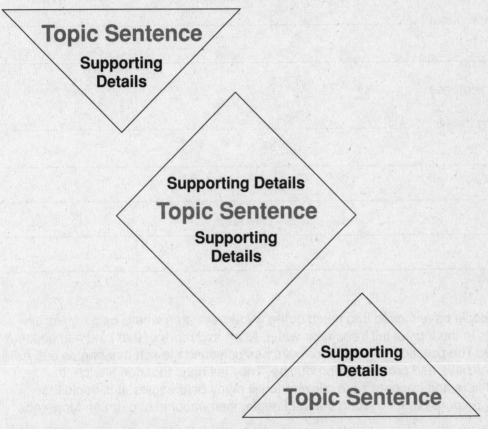

Read this paragraph. Where is the topic sentence?

> The cost of living has risen steadily over the past several decades. While a loaf of bread cost 30 cents 30 years ago, today it can cost 5 or 6 times that. Just 25 years ago, you could purchase a new car for about $4,000. Today the average cost of a new car is closer to $14,000. The price of housing is another example of rising costs. In the 1960s, an apartment rented for as little as $125 a month. With today's rents, that same apartment would cost at least $500 per month.

The first sentence of the paragraph is the topic sentence. It tells the main idea of the paragraph. The rest of the sentences support the paragraph's main idea with details that contrast the prices of bread, cars, and housing.

Read each paragraph. Then answer the questions.

1. A good worker is someone who understands how important it is not to be absent too often and who gets the job done. People seldom get fired because the quality of their work is poor. Instead, more people lose their jobs for such things as not showing up for work or not doing their job. Managers need to know that they can count on their workers to be on the job. Employers have little tolerance for workers who talk so much with their coworkers that they can't finish a job.

a. What is the paragraph about? _____

_____

b. Underline the topic sentence.

c. List some supporting details. _____

_____

_____

_____

2. Over the years people have moved into much of the wilderness area where bald eagles live. Eagles build their nests in the tops of tall trees near water. More and more of that land has become farmland or city streets. The pollution of lakes and rivers has poisoned the fish that eagles eat. As a result, the bald eagles have had problems reproducing. They lay eggs that don't hatch. In addition, until 1950 hunters and trappers were allowed to kill many bald eagles. It is ironic that Americans are directly responsible for making the bald eagle, their national bird, an endangered species.

a. What is the paragraph about? _____

_____

b. Underline the topic sentence.

c. List some supporting details. _____

_____

_____

_____

Answers are on page 768.

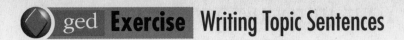

Write a topic sentence for each paragraph.

1.　　Two hundred years ago, few people could read or write. At that time, people could get jobs and make a living without having to read or to write their names. However, over the years, jobs have become more complex. Machinery has replaced workers that performed manual labor. The ability to think has become much more important. Jobs that require workers to read, write, compute, and think have become the norm.

_____

_____

2.　　Smoking cigarettes is bad for your health. In fact, tobacco use in any form has been proved harmful. Thousands of people die each year from lung cancer, and thousands more die from heart disease that is linked to smoking. In addition, smoking is an expensive habit. Heavy smokers may spend as much as $7 per day on cigarettes. That adds up to about $210 a month! Think of all the things a person could buy with that money.

_____

_____

3.　　There are consumer groups you may go to for financial help. They will review your finances and advise you on how to reduce your debt. They will help you make a budget to pay your creditors. They will even tell you if your financial situation is so complicated that you need to see an attorney. People to whom you owe money will often work with you as well. They may be willing to reduce your monthly payments so that you can afford to pay them. Most important, you can learn to live within your means.

_____

_____

4.　　Pharmacists do not generally mark a prescription drug with an expiration date, although the container usually shows the date of the prescription. Generally, if the drug is more than one year old, it should not be taken. A good rule to remember about the length of time to keep prescription drugs is, "When in doubt, throw it out."

_____

_____

Answers are on page 769.

Writing Your Introductory Paragraph

A good introductory paragraph does several things:

- It states the topic of the essay.
- It tells your reader what your main idea is.
- It gives your reader a preview of your essay.
- It provides your reader with background information.

Sometimes your main idea becomes clearer after you've planned your essay. Your thesis statement can pinpoint exactly what you want to say.

The topic of an essay is stated in a sentence called the **thesis statement.** You can write the thesis statement by rewriting the main idea (POWER Step 1). Expand the main idea by adding words or phrases that help explain or strengthen the statement. Read this example that shows how a student expanded a main idea into a thesis statement.

Main idea: Comedies are my favorite TV shows.

Thesis statement: I like comedy shows more than anything else on TV.

For a good introductory paragraph, you will also need to write one or more **preview sentences.** Preview sentences tell your reader what to expect in the essay. To write preview sentences, use your labeled groups (POWER Step 2) and tell about them in a way that might interest a reader. The ideas you present in preview sentences should be brief and general.

You can use the background information in the topic assignment to write background sentences.

Finally, you can add **background sentences** — one or two sentences that give general information about the topic. Background sentences are not necessary, but they can help introduce your reader to the topic.

Here is the introductory paragraph from the essay on pages 169–170. In the planning stage, the main idea was, "Regular exercise is important." After thinking about his ideas, the writer expanded the main idea and wrote a thesis statement. He included background information, and he wrote a preview sentence that told what his essay would be about.

Many people exercise regularly, yet many others do not. If those who don't exercise knew how important it is, they would all start exercise programs. ⎫ Background Sentences

Regular exercise makes and keeps you fit. — Thesis Statement

In fact, it helps you look and feel fit in addition to being fit. ⎫ Preview Sentence

ged Exercise Writing Introductory Paragraphs

Write introductory paragraphs for the topic assignments. Follow these steps.

a. Read each topic assignment. On your paper, use POWER Steps 1 and 2 to write a main idea, create groups of ideas, and label them. Topic 1 has been done for you. Use it as a model.

b. Then write an introductory paragraph for each essay.

TOPIC 1

Professional athletes today earn salaries in excess of $100,000 a year. Some people believe these athletes deserve the money they make, while others think athletes are paid too much.

Write an essay of 200 words discussing the high salaries of professional athletes. You may agree or disagree that salaries are too high. Be specific and use examples to support your view.

Main idea: Athletes earn their money.

Physical Work
- requires intense work
- can be hurt or hospitalized
- chance of long-term injury
- lots of effort during game

Professionals
- train for a long time
- work hard to become pro
- have to stay on a strict diet
- have no privacy

Serve the Community
- act as positive role models
- do commercials against drugs
- work for charities

TOPIC 2

Many people claim that rock music is a bad influence on young people. They feel it encourages drug use and inappropriate behavior. Others believe that rock music is good entertainment. They don't think that it causes social problems.

In an essay of 200 words, discuss the influence of rock music on young people. You may discuss positive or negative influences, or both. Be specific and use examples to support your view.

TOPIC 3

How to be a good parent has become a popular topic. Magazines and books offer parenting advice, classes teach parents how to raise children, and TV shows present parenting experts.

In a composition of about 200 words, discuss the role of being a parent. You may discuss the responsibilities, the pleasures, or both. Support your view with details and examples.

Answers are on page 769.

Writing the Body Paragraphs

Tip

You can place a topic sentence at the beginning, middle, or end of a paragraph, but it's a good idea to put it first so your reader knows what the paragraph is about.

Now you're ready to write the **body paragraphs** of your essay. The three body paragraphs develop your topic. They back up the thesis statement in your introductory paragraph with supporting ideas.

To write three body paragraphs, use your expanded groups of ideas (POWER Step 2). Use the labels you gave to each group to help you write topic sentences for the paragraphs. The topic sentences should tell the main ideas of the paragraphs.

Then use the ideas from each group to write supporting sentences for the paragraphs. To be sure your supporting sentences stay on the topic, keep your lists handy as you write. And remember to follow the order you chose for the paragraphs (POWER Step 2).

Here are the body paragraphs from the essay about exercise on pages 169–170. Compare the paragraphs with the three groups of ideas.

<u>Better Health</u>

stronger heart
breathe better
more endurance
burns calories

Topic Sentence ⟶

First of all, regular exercise is good for your health. When you run, bicycle, or do some other aerobic activity three times a week, your heart becomes stronger, and your breathing improves. These physical changes increase your endurance. You actually feel like you have more energy. In addition, muscles that are working burn more fat calories.

<u>Look Better</u>

lose weight
firm muscles
healthier skin
  and hair

Topic Sentence ⟶

Exercise can help improve not only your health but also your looks. Because your body burns more calories, you lose weight and look slimmer and trimmer. Your muscles become firm. You seem more youthful and energetic. In addition, better circulation gives your skin and hair a healthy glow.

Feel Better   Topic Sentence ⟶   _Perhaps all these physical benefits lead to the most important result of regular exercise—it makes you feel better. Exercise reduces tension in your muscles and makes you more relaxed. You feel rested and ready to go during the day, and you sleep better at night. Because you look better, you also just naturally feel better about your body and about yourself. Your self-esteem increases._

feel good about
how you look
more self-esteem
reduces tension
feel more relaxed

Did you notice that the writer added some details that weren't in the groups? While writing the body, new ideas occurred to him. You can use new ideas that occur to you during <u>any</u> of the POWER steps. Just be sure they support the thesis statement of the essay as well as the topic sentence of the paragraph.

ged **Exercise** Writing Body Paragraphs

To practice writing body paragraphs, look back at the GED Exercises on page 175. Follow these steps for each topic assignment.

a. Review the lists of ideas and the introductory paragraph you wrote.

b. Choose an order for the lists.

c. Use the labels to write topic sentences for the body paragraphs.

d. Use the ideas in each list to write supporting sentences.

e. Add details if they come to you.

1. Write three body paragraphs justifying the high salaries of professional athletes. Use the same sheet of paper that you used to write the introductory paragraph.

2. Write three body paragraphs about whether or not rock music is a bad influence on young people.

3. Write three body paragraphs about the responsibilities, pleasures, or both of being a parent.

The Concluding Paragraph

The last paragraph of your essay is the **concluding paragraph.** It gives the same information that the introductory paragraph gives, but it is written from a different perspective. Instead of previewing your essay, the concluding paragraph looks back at the ideas in your essay. This final paragraph restates your topic and reviews your ideas.

Reread the concluding paragraph from the essay about exercise.

As you write your essay, you may want to add or change phrases or sentences. Leave wide margins so that you can make changes easily.

With all these benefits of regular exercise, it's hard to understand why someone would not work out. If you exercise regularly, your body and your mind will appreciate it.

You can see that the concluding paragraph restates the topic and reviews the supporting details. It includes some advice and ends with a strong statement about what will happen when the advice is followed.

ged Exercise The Concluding Paragraph

Reread the introductory and body paragraphs you wrote for practice on pages 175 and 177. Write a concluding paragraph for each essay.

1. Write a concluding paragraph for the essay justifying the high salaries of professional athletes.

_____

_____

_____

_____

_____

_____

_____

_____

2. Write a concluding paragraph for the essay about whether rock music is a bad influence on young people.

_____

_____

_____

_____

_____

_____

_____

3. Write a concluding paragraph for the essay about the responsibilities, the pleasures, or both of being a parent.

_____

_____

_____

_____

_____

_____

_____

_____

Answers are on page 769.

Here is the topic assignment you organized ideas for in the Review on page 167.

> Over the past few years, many people who were living in the country have moved to the city. At the same time, many people in the city have moved to the country.
>
> In a composition of about 200 words, state whether you think life is better in the country or in the city. Give specific examples to support your view.

Use the ordered groups of ideas you made for these exercises. Write paragraphs on the lines that follow.

1. Write an introductory paragraph. Use your main idea sentence to write a thesis statement. Use the labels of the idea groups to write one or more preview sentences. If you want to write background sentences, use the background information from the topic assignment.

2. Write three body paragraphs. Use the labels of the idea groups to write the topic sentences. Use the ideas in each group to write supporting sentences. Develop each paragraph with details and examples. Write the paragraphs in the order you selected on page 167.

3. Write a concluding paragraph. Restate your topic and review your ideas.

_____

_____

_____

_____

_____

_____

_____

_____

_____

_____

_____

_____

Answers are on page 769.

Evaluating

Lesson 4 — Evaluating

The fourth step in the POWER writing process is evaluation. In Lesson 4, you'll learn how a GED test scorer will score your essay. Then you'll learn how to evaluate your essay.

Holistic Scoring

GED test scorers will evaluate your essay **holistically**—by judging its overall effectiveness. To the scorers, how clearly you present your thesis statement and how well you support it are the most important. A few misspelled words or a few errors in grammar will not cause your essay to receive a low score. The GED Essay Scoring Guide tells what scorers look for.

GED Essay Scoring Guide

Copyright © 1987, GED Testing Service

Papers will show *some or all* of the following characteristics.

Upper-half papers have a clear, definite purpose pursued with varying degrees of effectiveness. They have a structure that shows evidence of some deliberate planning. The writer's control of the conventions of Standard Written English (spelling, punctuation, grammar, word choice, and sentence structure) ranges from fairly reliable at 4 to confident and accomplished at 6.

6 The *6 paper* offers sophisticated ideas within an organizational framework that is clear and appropriate for the topic. The supporting statements are particularly effective because of their substance, specificity, or illustrative quality. The writing is vivid and precise, although it may contain an occasional error in the conventions of Standard Written English.

5 The *5 paper* is clearly organized with effective support for each of the writer's major points. While the writing offers substantive ideas, it lacks the fluency found in the 6 paper. Although there are some errors, the conventions of Standard Written English are consistently under control.

4 The *4 paper* shows evidence of the writer's organizational plan. Support, though adequate, tends to be less extensive or effective than that found in the 5 paper. The writer generally observes the conventions of Standard Written English. The errors that are present are not severe enough to interfere significantly with the writer's main purpose.

Lower-half papers either fail to convey a purpose sufficiently or lack one entirely. Consequently, their structure ranges from rudimentary at 3, to random at 2, to absent at 1. Control of the conventions of Standard Written English tends to follow this same gradient.

3 The *3 paper* usually shows some evidence of planning, although the development is insufficient. The supporting statements may be limited to a listing or a repetition of ideas. The 3 paper often demonstrates repeated weaknesses in the conventions of Standard Written English.

2 The *2 paper* is characterized by a marked lack of organization or inadequate support for ideas. The development is usually superficial or unfocused. Errors in the conventions of Standard Written English may seriously interfere with the overall effectiveness of this paper.

1 The *1 paper* lacks purpose or development. The dominant feature is the absence of control of structure or the conventions of Standard Written English. The deficiencies are so severe that the writer's ideas are difficult or impossible to understand.

* An asterisk code is reserved for papers that are blank, illegible, or written on a topic other than the one assigned. Because these papers cannot be scored, a Writing Skills Test composite score cannot be reported.

Reprinted with permission of the American Council on Education.

Here and on page 183 is an example of an essay and the score it received. Read the writing assignment and the essay. Then look over the explanation of the essay's score.

> Over the past few years, many people who were living in the country have moved to the city. At the same time, many people in the city have moved to the country.
>
> In a composition of about 200 words, state whether you think life is better in the country or in the city. Give specific examples to support your view.

Life in the big city, and life in a small town vary sharply. There are advantages as well as disadvantages to life in the city, just as there are good and bad things about small towns.

Some of the bad points to city life are high crime, over crowded housing, and heavy traffic. Life can also be very rewarding in the city, as there are more places of employment as well as intertainment.

Life in a small town moves at a slower rate. The people are friendlier, because of a lower crime rate. The housing is spaced more openly, and the highways are not as crowded, because there are less intertainment and employment oppurtunities.

In my oppinion life in the small town far out weighs life in the city because life at a slower pace is more rewarding.

The essay received a score of 3. It has good organization, but the topic and supporting ideas need more development; details in the body paragraphs are repetitious. There are also some errors in the conventions of English—mainly in spelling.

Evaluating an Essay

GED scorers read an essay once and then assign a score to it. However, when you evaluate your essay, you want to read it more carefully to see how to improve it and get a higher score. There are four areas to consider when evaluating your essay—**organization, support, clarity,** and **conventions of English.** You can use this check list to help you.

Organization

Yes	No		
☐	☐	(1)	Does the introductory paragraph include the essay topic and a thesis statement?
☐	☐	(2)	Does each body paragraph have a topic sentence and details related to the topic sentence?
☐	☐	(3)	Does the concluding paragraph restate the topic and review the ideas?
☐	☐	(4)	Does the essay stick to the topic?

Support

☐	☐	(5)	Do the paragraphs include specific details and examples that support the topic sentences?
☐	☐	(6)	Does the essay support the thesis statement?

Clarity

☐	☐	(7)	Is the main idea understandable?
☐	☐	(8)	Are the supporting ideas expressed clearly?

Conventions of English

☐	☐	(9)	Are the ideas written in complete sentences?
☐	☐	(10)	Is the grammar correct?
☐	☐	(11)	Are punctuation marks used correctly?
☐	☐	(12)	Are words spelled correctly?
☐	☐	(13)	Are capital letters used correctly?

To evaluate your essay, read it twice. During the first reading, concentrate on the first three areas of the check list—organization, support, and clarity. These questions help you evaluate your presentation of ideas. During the second reading, concentrate on the last area of the check list, the conventions of English.

When you evaluate your GED essay, read it carefully but not too slowly. If you read slowly, you may pay too much attention to minor details instead of your presentation of ideas.

The essays on this page and the following pages were written for the writing assignment on page 182, city living versus country living. Work independently or with a partner to evaluate the essays. Use these steps to evaluate them.

1. Read each essay once to evaluate it as a GED scorer would. Use the GED scoring guidelines on page 181 to assign a score of * to 6.

2. Evaluate each essay again to improve the presentation of ideas. Answer the questions in the first three areas of the check list on page 186.

3. Check over the essay a third time to evaluate the control of the conventions of English. Answer the questions in the last area of the check list on page 186.

Essay 1

I think that rural life is better than urban. Because you save time and money. You don't have to go to the grocery store as much. You don't have to commute back & forth on a bus. You can do your washing on hand. It is less complicated. The crime rate is very low. Less traffic. Don't worry that much about being mugged or robbed because the town is so small. The people within the community. They seem very nice. The atmosphere smells very clean.

In spite of the obvious advantages of big city life, I'll take the small town everytime. Life in a small town is superior because of the quality of ~~your~~ the relationships you can develop and because small town life is less stressful.

The quality of the relationships one can develop in a small town are far better than those that you have in a large, faceless city. People in small towns, can really get to know one another. They help each other out and share in each others' successes. They have time for one another. People in small towns don't have to fear strangers and can trust others. They can count on there being someone there for them even if they are new to town or have no family close by. People in small towns ~~have the time~~ tend to express their affection for each other. They are more open and giving. It is easier to, get to know and be known by people in a ~~small~~ rural setting.

In addition, the lifestyle in a small town ~~has~~ is much less stressful than that of a large city. ~~There~~ People seems to be in less of a hurry. There are no crowds to shove and pressure you. Traffic is not a daily nightmare. Crime is not so very plentiful. Drugs don't ~~tempt~~ your children on every corner. These things that create stress in the life of an urban dweller are just not present in the lives of people living in small towns.

Because relationships are easier to develop in a small town and stress is far less noticeable, life in the small town seems superior to living in a city. I'd pick the ~~sub~~ rural life if I had my choice.

Essay 1　　　Essay 2

Yes　No　　Yes　No
□　　□　　　□　　□　　**Organization**
　　　　　　　　　　　(1)　Does the introductory paragraph include the essay topic and a thesis statement?
□　　□　　　□　　□　　(2)　Does each body paragraph have a topic sentence and details related to the topic sentence?
□　　□　　　□　　□　　(3)　Does the concluding paragraph restate the topic and review the ideas?
□　　□　　　□　　□　　(4)　Does the essay stick to the topic?

□　　□　　　□　　□　　**Support**
　　　　　　　　　　　(5)　Do the paragraphs include specific details and examples that support the topic sentences?
□　　□　　　□　　□　　(6)　Does the essay support the thesis statement?

□　　□　　　□　　□　　**Clarity**
　　　　　　　　　　　(7)　Is the main idea understandable?
□　　□　　　□　　□　　(8)　Are the supporting ideas expressed clearly?

□　　□　　　□　　□　　**Conventions of English**
　　　　　　　　　　　(9)　Are the ideas written in complete sentences?
□　　□　　　□　　□　　(10)　Is the grammar correct?
□　　□　　　□　　□　　(11)　Are punctuation marks used correctly?
□　　□　　　□　　□　　(12)　Are words spelled correctly?
□　　□　　　□　　□　　(13)　Are capital letters used correctly?

Answers are on page 769.

Turn back to the essay you wrote on page 180 about whether life is better in the country or the city.

Score your essay from * to 6 using the GED scoring guidelines on page 181. Then evaluate your essay using this check list.

 When you write your GED essay, don't take time to score it. Spend about five minutes evaluating it with the check list in mind and decide how you can improve it.

○ ○ ○ ○ ○ ○ ○
* 1 2 3 4 5 6

Yes No **Organization**

☐ ☐ (1) Does the introductory paragraph include the essay topic and a thesis statement?

☐ ☐ (2) Does each body paragraph have a topic sentence and details related to the topic sentence?

☐ ☐ (3) Does the concluding paragraph restate the topic and review the ideas?

☐ ☐ (4) Does the essay stick to the topic?

Support

☐ ☐ (5) Do the paragraphs include specific details and examples that support the topic sentences?

☐ ☐ (6) Does the essay support the thesis statement?

Clarity

☐ ☐ (7) Is the main idea understandable?

☐ ☐ (8) Are the supporting ideas expressed clearly?

Conventions of English

☐ ☐ (9) Are the ideas written in complete sentences?

☐ ☐ (10) Is the grammar correct?

☐ ☐ (11) Are punctuation marks used correctly?

☐ ☐ (12) Are words spelled correctly?

☐ ☐ (13) Are capital letters used correctly?

Answers are on page 769.

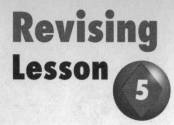

Revising
Lesson 5

Revising

The fifth step in the POWER writing process is revising. Revising an essay means changing the parts you think are weak. In Lesson 5, you will learn to use the evaluation of your essay (POWER Step 4) to revise the presentation of ideas and correct any mistakes. The result will be a stronger, more effective essay.

Revision is a two-step process:
STEP 1: Read your essay to evaluate the ideas and the organization. If necessary, revise them.
STEP 2: Proofread your essay for your use of the conventions of English. Then make necessary corrections.

A Two-Step Process

When you evaluate an essay (POWER Step 4), you identify areas that need strengthening or correcting. To revise the essay, decide how to change those areas and then make the changes.

Because evaluation is a two-step process, it's best to revise in two steps, too. First, evaluate and revise your ideas and organization. Then evaluate and revise your use of the conventions of English.

Revising Your Ideas and Organization

When you evaluated your presentation of ideas (POWER Step 4), you asked yourself three groups of questions:

When you revise, you don't need to rewrite your essay. Instead, you can use these revision methods:
- **Cross out any unwanted words.**
- **Make corrections between the lines or in the margins.**
- **Use a caret (^) to show where additions belong.**
- **Rewrite any part that is illegible.**

Yes	No		**Organization**
☐	☐	(1)	Does the introductory paragraph include the essay topic and a thesis statement?
☐	☐	(2)	Does each body paragraph have a topic sentence and details related to the topic sentence?
☐	☐	(3)	Does the concluding paragraph restate the topic and review the ideas?
☐	☐	(4)	Does the essay stick to the topic?

Yes	No		**Support**
☐	☐	(5)	Do the paragraphs include specific details and examples that support the topic sentences?
☐	☐	(6)	Does the essay support the thesis statement?

Yes	No		**Clarity**
☐	☐	(7)	Is the main idea understandable?
☐	☐	(8)	Are the supporting ideas expressed clearly?

Your answers to the questions tell you which parts of your essay need revising. For example, if your answer to question 1 is no, decide how to add a thesis statement or the essay topic. Use revision marks to add sentences. If your answer to question 4 is no, decide which sentences or phrases discuss things not directly related to the topic. Then cross them out.

Look at how one writer revised her ideas in her essay on the topic assignment "State whether you think it is better to stay in one place or to move often and live in different places."

You can revise your essay during any of the POWER steps. For example, correct a misspelled word whenever you notice it.

Main idea: *Living in one place has advantages and disadvantages.*

Many people live in one place their entire lives and enjoy it, but I prefer experiencing different places. Living in one place provides security, but there are many disadvantages to this lifestyle. Living in new places is exciting and educationel.

Living in one place for a long time does have some advantages. You know where everything is and have the security of a routine. If you need help, you can ask a friend or neighbor. ^It is easy to cash checks and conduct other business because everyone knows you.

For me these advantages are overshadowed by the disadvantages of staying in one place. Especially in a small town, you can't escape your past. ^*Educational and job opportunities are often limited.* *Everyone knows everything about you.* ^*The biggest disadvantage is that everything stays the same—to me that means boredom!*

Moving to a different city or town is an adventure. Everything will be unfamiliar to you. You will have new experiences you will have different things to see and do. Maybe you will be near mountains or on the ocean. You could learn to ski or surf. ~~But remember, long distance phone calls are expensive.~~ Moving can give you opportunities you didn't have before. Best of all, you will be able to meet a variety of people and make many new friends.

So brave! Find a place you think you'd like, then pack up and move. ~~Decide if you will move yourself or if you will hire a moving company.~~ You'll have many more exciting experiences than people who stay in one place all their lives.

Tip

When you revise your essay, compare it with your planning list of ideas. That will help you determine if you included all your ideas.

When the writer began evaluating her essay, she noted her thesis statement, "Many people live in one place their entire lives and enjoy it, but I prefer experiencing different places." As she evaluated, she looked for ideas that did not relate to the topic. She found a sentence in the fourth paragraph and one in the last paragraph that did not seem to fit, so she crossed them out.

The writer also realized she had not included her idea about the advantage of getting checks cashed. So she added a sentence to the second paragraph about checks. In addition, she felt she had not given enough support to the disadvantages of living in one place, so she added a sentence about opportunities to her third paragraph.

Revising Your Use of the Conventions of English

After you make revisions to the ideas and organization of your essay, you can evaluate and revise your use of the conventions of English. To evaluate (POWER Step 4), you asked yourself this group of questions:

Yes	No	Conventions of English
☐	☐	(9) Are the ideas written in complete sentences?
☐	☐	(10) Is the grammar correct?
☐	☐	(11) Are punctuation marks used correctly?
☐	☐	(12) Are words spelled correctly?
☐	☐	(13) Are capital letters used correctly?

Your answers to the questions tell you which parts of your essay need correcting. For example, if you've written an incomplete sentence, correct the sentence fragment by adding a noun or a verb and drawing a caret to show where it should be inserted. If you've forgotten to use a comma between items in a list, put one in. If you've misspelled a word, cross it out and write it correctly above the misspelling.

Look again at the essay about living in one place versus moving to different places. The writer has finished the second revision step and has corrected her errors in the conventions of English. Her revision marks are in color.

Main idea: *Living in one place has advantages and disadvantages.*

Many people live in one place their entire lives and enjoy it, but I prefer experiencing different places. Living in one place provides security, but there are many disadvantages to this lifestyle. Living in new places is exciting and educational*.*

Living in one place for a long time does have some advantages. You know where everything is and have the security of a routine. If you need help, you can ask a friend or neighbor. It is easy to cash checks and conduct other business because everyone knows you.

For me these advantages are overshadowed by the disadvantages of staying in one place. Especially in a small town, you can't escape your past. Educational and job opportunities are often limited. Everyone knows everything about you. ^ The biggest disadvantage is that everything stays the same—to me that means boredom!

Moving to a different city or town is an adventure. Everything will be unfamiliar to you. You will have new experiences. You will have different things to see and do. Maybe you will be near mountains or on the ocean. You could learn to ski or surf. ~~But remember, long distance phone calls are expensive.~~ Moving can give you opportunities you didn't have before. Best of all, you will be able to meet a variety of people and make many new friends.

So be brave! Find a place you think you'd like, then pack up and move. ~~Decide if you will move yourself or if you will hire a moving company.~~ You'll have many more exciting experiences than people who stay in one place all their lives.

Tip

Be sure to use all the POWER steps when you write the GED essay. You may allow more or less time for a step than the time suggested, but following the steps will help you write a better essay.

The writer noticed that she had misspelled the word <u>educational</u> in the first paragraph, so she crossed out the misspelling and rewrote the word correctly (see page 191). She found a run-on sentence in the fourth paragraph, so she added a period and capitalized the next word to make two sentences. Finally, she realized she had a sentence fragment at the beginning of the concluding paragraph, so she inserted a verb with a caret.

Her essay was now finished. By following the five POWER steps, she was able to write an effective five-paragraph essay.

The following essay was written about winning money in a lottery. Evaluate and revise the essay for both its presentation of ideas and its use of the conventions of English. Use a copy of the Evaluation Check List on page 183 if you need to. Make your revisions directly on the essay.

I usually enter every contest or sweepstake that come along, so I have given much thought to what I would do if I really won something big. I have decided that if I won the State lottery, I would help my family and the needy first, and then I would have some fun.

My family could use some financial help. I would love to pay off my parent's home so that they would never have another house payment to make. Financing a house is extremely expensive these days. I would put money aside for my sister's children to go to colege. In addition, I would buy my brother and his wife a car so that they wouldn't have to ride the bus to work.

I would also give money to needy causes that I think are important. For example, cancer and AIDS research.

With the rest of the money, I would have a great time. I would travel to places I have never been. Every time I go to the bookstore I see all these books about travel. I would never cook another meal I would eat out every day in a diffrent restaurant. I would hire a maid so that I would never have to clean the house again. Finally, I would buy tickets to every concert every sports event and every new movie that comes to town.

Winning the lottery would be great for me and everyone else. Therefore, I will keep buying those lottery tickets

Answers are on page 769.

Here is the topic assignment you wrote an essay for on page 180 and evaluated on page 187.

> Over the past few years, many people who were living in the country have moved to the city. At the same time, many people in the city have moved to the country.
>
> In a composition of about 200 words, state whether you think life is better in the country or in the city. Give specific examples to support your view.

First, revise the presentation of ideas in your essay. Use your answers to the first three groups of questions on the check list on page 187 to guide your revision.

Second, revise your use of the conventions of English. Use your answers to the last group of questions on the check list to help you find mistakes.

Answers are on page 769.

Use these topics to gain additional experience writing GED essays. Follow all the POWER Steps and take no more than 45 minutes to write each essay.

TOPIC 1

In the 1950s people began to hear about computers. Some people thought computers would never last. Others feared computers would take their jobs. Today computers are part of our lives.

Write a composition of about 200 words about how computers affect our lives. You may wish to deal with the good or bad effects, or both.

TOPIC 2

Few people ever say, "I have so much money that I just can't spend it all." More people are likely to pinch pennies. Getting by is easier if people learn wise ways of dealing with money.

Write a composition of about 200 words offering advice on stretching an income. You may want to include both "do's" and "don'ts."

TOPIC 3

Part of each TV hour is spent on ads. Newspapers and magazines are sometimes more than half ads. Ads seem to follow every song on the radio. It is not possible to avoid ads.

Write a composition of about 200 words stating the effects of ads on the buying public. You may consider the good effects or bad effects, or both.

TOPIC 4

Computer games, VCRs, large screen TVs, and cable TV have become common. More and more people have complete entertainment centers in their homes. These people have less and less need to leave the home for entertainment.

Write a composition of about 200 words stating what effects you think home entertainment has on modern life. You may talk about the good or bad effects, or both. Be specific. Use examples to support your view.

Answers are on page 769.

Robert Reich uses a chart to make a point during a news conference.

Reading plays an important part in passing the GED tests. The Mathematics and Writing Skills tests require you to read and understand word problems, passages, and questions. In the Social Studies, Science, and Interpreting Literature and the Arts tests, reading plays a major role in your potential for success. The passages in Social Studies, Science, and Interpreting Literature and the Arts will be up to 150 words long. Two or more questions will follow the passages. Some of the questions you will answer will be based on charts, tables, maps, graphs, diagrams, and cartoons.

To answer these questions correctly, you will have to use various reading and thinking skills. In many instances, you are already using these skills in your everyday reading.

In this unit you will study the reading and thinking skills necessary to help you understand questions. You will use these skills in a variety of ways as you study the Social Studies, Science, and Interpreting Literature and the Arts sections of the book.

Lesson 1 will emphasize comprehension skills. You will learn to restate information, draw conclusions, and summarize. You will also learn the difference between literal and inferential comprehension.

Lesson 2 will address the skill of application. You will learn to apply information you have read to new situations.

Lesson 3 will help you sharpen analysis skills. You will learn to distinguish fact and opinion, analyze cause-effect relationships, and understand figurative language.

Lesson 4 will present evaluation skills. You will learn to recognize the role of beliefs and values as you read and to judge the adequacy of facts.

Lesson 5 will provide you with practice in reading and understanding information on charts, tables, maps, graphs, and diagrams that are similar to those used on the Social Studies and Science section of the GED test.

Once you have completed the lessons in this section of the book, you will have a better understanding of the skills necessary to understand and answer the questions in specific GED subject areas. All questions in this unit are answered for you in the answer section of this book. You should go over all of the pages in this section and review your answers to the questions before going on to other units in the book.

Comprehension
Lesson 1

Comprehension

Topic 1: Restatement and Drawing Conclusions

Reading Comprehension requires thinking in different ways and on different levels. These ways of thinking may be defined as specific reading skills. In the pages that follow, you will be introduced to some of these skills so that you can be an active reader and thinker as you take the GED test.

One way to become a more active reader is to learn to **restate** the author's ideas in your own words. **Restatement** is an important skill because it ensures that you have understood what you have read.

Before you can make an accurate restatement, you must read carefully: notice details, think about word meanings, and see how individual facts and ideas relate to each other. Does one thing cause another? Does this fact illustrate a principle? Why did the author use this word? Does it suggest a feeling or an attitude? Asking questions like these will help you think clearly and critically as you read and reread.

To restate something, ask yourself: How could this be said more simply? What are the important facts I must include? On the GED test, you may be asked to recognize a restatement of a sentence or an idea.

Example: The so-called Wild West period lasted roughly thirty years, from the end of the Civil War to the turn of the century. No other period of American history has generated so much interest.
Restatement: The last thirty years of the nineteenth century comprise the period known as the Wild West. It was a legendary time that has excited the imagination of Americans ever since.

Another comprehension skill used by active readers is **drawing conclusions.** Information from your reading may lead you to a conclusion not directly stated by the author. You compare the author's words with your own experience; then you use reasoning to arrive at a logical conclusion or expectation. Carefully examine facts the author has given you. Do they justify a conclusion, decision, or prediction? Is your conclusion logical? Drawing conclusions requires careful reading and reasoning.

 When you restate information, make sure the facts are the same even if the words are different.

Example: Many differences in male and female behavior are learned differences based on the roles played by men and women in our culture.

Conclusion: If differences are learned (*stated in passage*), they may be "unlearned" (*logical conclusion*). Perhaps we can learn to overcome male and female stereotypes. Maybe we can teach our children different ways of behaving (*conclusion expanded, made specific*).

ged Exercise Restatement and Drawing Conclusions

Choose the best answer to each item.
Items 1 and 2 refer to the following paragraph.

Interest rates conform to the law of supply and demand. The less money available for loans, the higher the rate of interest charged by banks. Higher interest rates encourage people with money to invest or save money. This process has the effect of stockpiling dollars, from which new loans can be issued. Lower rates of interest, on the other hand, serve to stimulate the economy by encouraging buyers.

1. According to this passage, banks determine interest rates based on

   (1) government regulations
   (2) economic stimulation
   (3) the size of loans
   (4) the supply of available money
   (5) the stockpiling of new loans

2. One may conclude that falling interest rates result in

   (1) more saving and spending
   (2) more buying and borrowing
   (3) less buying
   (4) more investment
   (5) less spending and borrowing

Items 3 and 4 refer to the following passage.

Malnutrition is a poor state of health that results from an unbalanced diet. Malnutrition is often thought of as undernutrition. This problem can be caused by eating too little food or by eating too little of a particular nutrient. However, malnutrition can also be caused by overnutrition. People who eat too much food or too much of certain nutrients such as fats or vitamins also suffer from malnutrition.

3. Malnutrition is a condition in which

   (1) not enough food is eaten
   (2) too little of a specific nutrient is eaten
   (3) a person's health is affected by poor diet
   (4) a person eats too much
   (5) too much fat is eaten

4. What causes undernutrition?

   (1) not eating enough food or not eating enough of a specific nutrient
   (2) eating foods rich in fat
   (3) eating foods with very large amounts of particular vitamins
   (4) poor health
   (5) malnutrition

Answers are on page 769.

Topic 2: Summarizing

You have seen how reading comprehension can be demonstrated by restatement. When you restate ideas or information, you express them in other words. Restating is similar to translating.

Restatement is helpful in developing another comprehension skill—summarizing. Summarizing may also involve expressing thoughts in other words. However, the main purpose of summarizing is to use <u>fewer</u> words. When you summarize, you make a simpler, shorter statement. You write a "condensed version," which briefly expresses the main idea and/or the most important details.

When you describe the plot of a movie to a friend, you are summarizing. The movie may be two hours long, but you sum it up in a minute or two. You give an outline of the basic plot and some information about the main characters, but you leave out details.

When you summarize a piece of writing, you first try to determine the main idea. The author may provide a topic sentence that briefly states the main idea. Topic sentences are often (but not always) found at the beginning or the end of a passage. If there is no topic sentence, you must look for clues to the main idea. Look for the topic, or subject, first. It can usually be stated in a word or phrase, such as *earthquakes, one-celled animals, the circulatory system*. After you identify the topic, you must answer these questions: What about it? What is the writer saying about earthquakes? What is the main point?

When summarizing, it is helpful to identify the basic facts by answering the "5Ws and H" questions—*who, what, when, where, why,* and *how.* Who or what is the subject? What does it do?, etc.

Example: When you exercise, your body needs to take in increased oxygen and get rid of other gases. These two functions are handled by your respiratory and circulatory systems. When you exercise, your heart beats faster and your breathing rate increases. This speeds the flow of blood to your muscles and other tissues. The blood provides the extra food and oxygen the tissues need. The circulating blood also carries wastes from the tissues to the kidneys and lungs, where they are excreted (eliminated).

Summary: Your respiratory and circulatory systems (*what?*) step up action (*what do they do?*) when you exercise (*when?*). They provide the extra oxygen your tissues need and help to eliminate wastes (*why? how?*).

 When summarizing, make sure the summary contains the main idea of the passage and that there are no extra ideas not in the passage.

Choose the best answer to each item. Items 1 and 2 refer to the following paragraphs.

Our solar system is usually portrayed as a yellow ball (the sun) with nine planets neatly ringed around it. This picture does not really give us an accurate idea of the size of the sun, the great differences between the planets, or the vast distances between them.

The sun contains 99 percent of the mass, or material, of the solar system. The sun's diameter is more than 100 times that of Earth, and its volume is more than a million times greater than Earth's. Yet, it seems dwarfed by the quantities of empty space around it. (Tiny Mercury, only 3,000 miles across, is 36 million miles from the sun.) The remaining 1 percent of the mass of the solar system is spread out among planets and other satellites across more than 8 billion miles of emptiness.

1. Which of the following is the best summary of this passage?

    (1) The sun is like a yellow ball with nine planets around it.
    (2) The sun is vastly larger than the planets.
    (3) The solar system has more than 8 billion miles of emptiness.
    (4) It is hard to picture the vastness of our solar system, its giant sun, and millions of miles of empty space.
    (5) The sun and the planets make up the solar system.

2. The second paragraph uses details to

    (1) compare size and distance in the solar system
    (2) compare the sun with Mercury
    (3) explain the workings of the solar system
    (4) convince the reader of the importance of the sun
    (5) describe the composition of the sun

Item 3 refers to the following paragraphs.

Millions of years ago, part of North America was covered by glaciers. The movement of these glaciers helped to shape the geography of this area. A glacier is a snowfield of compressed ice. When a glacier reaches a depth of 100 feet, it becomes too heavy to stay in place. It moves down the slope it is on. As the glacier moves, it tears away masses of rock and land. Sometimes it leaves behind a lake or series of lakes. Most often, a glacier leaves behind a valley.

New England and New York were once flat land covered by glaciers. The movement of the ice carved deep valleys between what are now the Adirondack Mountains, the Green Mountains, and the White Mountains. Now this northeastern area of the United States has many lakes and valleys surrounded by mountains.

3. Which best summarizes the second paragraph?

    (1) New England's and New York's geography was affected by glaciers.
    (2) Mountains are made by glaciers.
    (3) New England is a flat area.
    (4) New York is covered by ice.
    (5) New England is a scenic region.

Answers are on page 770.

Topic 3: Literal and Inferential Comprehension

Literal comprehension involves understanding what is directly stated. **Inferential** comprehension requires you to read between the lines to understand what an author has implied or assumed. In making an inference, you use knowledge, experience, reasoning ability, and common sense to understand more than an author has said. You may, for instance, understand why he said it or how he felt about it.

You will use both kinds of comprehension in all of your reading. Sometimes a main idea will be clearly stated in a topic sentence. In other cases, the writer assumes you will be able to summarize the writing and understand the main idea on your own. Sometimes you will use both skills at the same time. First, you understand what is stated. Then you use reasoning and experience to infer a conclusion.

In reading literature, these skills are used all the time. If you understand what a character does, you can then infer something about that character's personality. If you understand a description of an event, you can infer the meaning of a word, or of poetic or figurative language. Clues in a story help you predict what might happen next.

Both skills are important. You must understand what is said *in* the lines before you can successfully read *between* them. Careful reading, questioning, and clear thinking are the keys to comprehension.

Example: The following passage describes people on a cruise ship.

The Foxens, like most of the passengers, lived in the past. But it was not, Betty noted, necessarily the real past. It was, rather, a past that was being constantly edited, smoothed, brightened, and touched up. It was a past studded with the little victories of the person who was in the process of creating it.

Literal Comprehension: The passengers lived in the past. They edited the past, changing and improving it.

Inferential Comprehension: 1. We infer that they talk about the past often. Common sense tells us we wouldn't know about the "editing" if they didn't do it aloud. 2. From experience we know that elderly people often dwell on the past. We tentatively infer that these people are elderly. 3. They feel the need to improve on the past. It seems logical to assume that they have some regrets or guilt. We know that people commonly stretch the truth to build their self-esteem and impress others. We infer that this is happening here.

Reading Strategies ◆ Comprehension

Choose the <u>best answer</u> to each item. <u>Items 1 to 3</u> refer to the following excerpt from an essay.

It is hard to predict how science is going to turn out, and if it is really good science, it is impossible to predict. This is the nature of the enterprise. If the things to be found
(5) are actually new, they are by definition unknown in advance, and there is no way of telling in advance where a really new line of inquiry will lead. You cannot make choices in this matter, selecting things you
(10) think you're going to like and shutting off the lines that make for discomfort. You either have science or you don't, and if you have it, you are obliged to accept the surprising and disturbing pieces of
(15) information, even the overwhelming and upheaving ones, along with the neat and promptly useful bits. It is like that.
   The only solid piece of scientific truth about which I feel totally confident is that
(20) we are profoundly ignorant about nature. Indeed, I regard this as the major discovery of the past hundred years in biology. It is, in its way, an illuminating piece of news. It would have amazed the brightest minds of
(25) the eighteenth-century Enlightenment to be told by any of us how little we know and how bewildering seems the way ahead. It is this sudden confrontation with the depth and scope of ignorance that represents the most significant contribution of twentieth-century science to the human intellect. We are, at last, facing up to it.

Lewis Thomas, "The Hazards of Science."

1. The topic sentence (main idea) of the first paragraph begins

   (1) "It is hard to predict . . ." (line 1)
   (2) "You either have science or you don't . . ." (lines 11–12)
   (3) "You cannot make choices . . ." (lines 8–9)
   (4) "If the things to be found . . ." (line 4)
   (5) "This is the nature . . ." (line 3)

2. Which of these best expresses the main idea of the second paragraph?

   (1) The major contribution of twentieth-century scientific study has been to show us how much we don't know.
   (2) Scientists in the eighteenth century have been proven wrong.
   (3) The future is bewildering because we don't know enough to make a prediction.
   (4) Although we are profoundly ignorant, researchers are making great advances.
   (5) The twentieth century is a depressing time in which to live.

3. We can infer from the first paragraph that the author feels that

   (1) science can be made more predictable if we work at it
   (2) scientists should concentrate on useful, practical discoveries
   (3) scientific discoveries are always disturbing
   (4) people are uncomfortable with science because its findings are unpredictable and often disturbing
   (5) people distrust scientists

Answers are on page 770.

Application
Lesson ② Application

Topic 1: Using Given Ideas in Another Context _____

Good readers are often able to use facts, principles, or concepts they learn from their reading in other situations. The ability to use your learning in other areas is called **application.** This thinking skill can only be used by a reader who first comprehends the information and ideas presented. Application is the next level of thinking—the ability to use what you have understood.

To apply new learning, you must be able to see the similarities between one situation and another. If situations are similar, the same rule or principle may apply to both. You may read about an idea stated in a general way. You may then be able to apply the idea to a specific situation. For instance, after you learn the formula for calculating the area of a rectangle, you can use this formula to figure out how much ceiling tile to order. You may also read about an occurrence in history which can provide a lesson for our time. Recognizing similarities and parallels, then applying ideas to new contexts is a valuable skill.

Example: Physical geography was a determining factor in decisions made by early American settlers. Towns most often grew up along major waterways because of access to drinking water and transportation.

Application: The city of St. Louis, Missouri, is located at the intersection of two major rivers. The founders probably chose the site because of the abundance of drinking water and the potential for water travel to the north, south, and west (*general statement applied to a specific place*).

When applying information to a new situation, look for similarities between the original situation and the new situation.

Choose the best answer to each item. Items 1 and 2 refer to the following paragraphs.

A major characteristic of many dictatorships is the tendency to manage news. Those who assume absolute control of the government seem to be sensitive about their public image. Ruling largely without the consent of the people, dictators feel a constant need to demonstrate that things are under control. They resist having their authority questioned.

Absolute authority rests upon power. Power is the ability of the dictator to make people do what he wants them to do. There is very little room in a dictatorship for opposing views. Dissenters are discouraged from voicing their opinions. In many cases they are prevented from doing so. In Nicaragua, for example, opposition parties were permitted to campaign for votes only if they shared the basic views of the Sandinista regime.

News suppression is one way to keep people uninformed about developing events. Without the news, citizens cannot stay informed about local, national, and international events. They must trust that their leaders are working on their behalf.

1. For decades the communist government of the Soviet Union controlled all the news media in the country. Government control of a national newspaper probably

   (1) allowed the government to limit the public's access to information
   (2) was an excellent source of income for the state
   (3) allowed government leaders free campaign coverage
   (4) helped the government to build trust and public confidence
   (5) encouraged citizens to participate in solving national problems

2. A dictator would likely react to a group of university students who oppose his policies by

   (1) debating publically with their leader
   (2) congratulating university administrators for encouraging critical thinking

(3) holding a national referendum on the debated issues
(4) writing an open letter to citizens to persuade or threaten them into agreement with his policies
(5) arresting the group's leaders and banning press coverage of their activities

Item 3 refers to the following paragraph.

At sea level, where the air is at standard pressure, pure water boils at 100°C. When water is heated in a closed container so that the steam cannot escape, the boiling point of the water is raised above 100°C.

3. Which of the following appliances is based on the principles described above?

   (1) a microwave oven
   (2) a washing machine
   (3) a toaster
   (4) a refrigerator
   (5) a pressure cooker

Item 4 refers to the following paragraph.

Minerals dissolved in water can be removed from water by the process of distillation. Water is added to a distilling flask and boiled. The water vapor released then passes through a cooled tube, and the condensed water flows down into a receiving container. The minerals are left behind.

4. Which of the following is an example of a use for distillation?

   (1) getting drinking water from the ocean
   (2) putting ice cubes in a cold drink
   (3) boiling water for tea
   (4) adding antifreeze to a car engine
   (5) bottling mineral water

Items 5 and 6 refer to the following paragraphs.

Most of us are exposed to some pollution every day from the exhaust fumes of hundreds of cars. Others are exposed daily, on the job, to chemicals in the air they breathe. Polluted air is harmful to the respiratory system.

Pollutants in the air affect the linings of the bronchial passages. The mucus lining in the passages is supposed to trap foreign particles and bacteria that may enter when you breathe. The mucus is then swept along by hair-like structures called cilia, and eventually eliminated from the body. Pollutants, however, interfere with the action of the cilia.

When this happens, the dust- or bacteria-filled mucus may clog the bronchial passages. This may cause swelling in the respiratory tract. A respiratory infection or the worsening of a chronic respiratory problem may result.

5. Smokers may experience more respiratory problems than non-smokers because

   (1) they often breathe through their mouths
   (2) they pollute the air they breathe with smoke
   (3) cigarette smoke thins the lining of the bronchial passages
   (4) cigarette smoke and car exhaust fumes form a deadly combination
   (5) smokers' frequent coughing overworks the lungs

6. In an area where many factories pollute the air, you might expect that

   (1) factory workers would have many respiratory problems
   (2) children would get more measles and chicken pox
   (3) asthma, colds, and bronchitis would be less frequent
   (4) people living in the area would have more than the average number of respiratory illnesses
   (5) mouth breathing would decrease

Items 7 and 8 refer to the following paragraph.

The government gets the money to pay for its programs in two ways: taxes and borrowing. The main source for the national treasury is the federal income tax. All Americans who make over a minimum income pay a part of it to the government. The Department of the Treasury borrows money from citizens by selling treasury bonds and treasury notes. In return for the use of the money spent on a bond, the Treasury pays the citizen a set interest.

7. Which is most likely to happen if the government spends more money on all of its programs?

   (1) Income taxes will go down.
   (2) Taxes will increase.
   (3) Americans will have to earn more money.
   (4) People will buy more bonds.
   (5) The Treasury will stop paying interest on bonds.

8. According to the paragraph, government programs are

   (1) free
   (2) paid for by the citizens
   (3) not dependent on the citizens
   (4) paid for with the interest from bonds
   (5) supported mainly by borrowed money

Answers are on page 770.

Topic 2: Application Skills in Literature _____

You have seen how the skill of application multiplies the effects of your learning. You apply facts, ideas, principles, or rules acquired through reading to other similar situations. This works especially well in social studies and science, where you learn new information that is clearly useful. When you read literature, however, you sometimes use application skills somewhat differently.

You will often gather information as you read a story or a novel. Historical novels and biographies, for instance, are often educational, as are essays and book reviews. It is easy to see how you can apply this learning. However, you may think that "pleasure reading" is not concerned with learning. Even if we read a mystery novel or a poem for entertainment only, these may offer ideas and new understandings. Insights into human motivations and social concerns, as well as moral or other viewpoints, are conveyed through fiction. Most popular literature offers insights and ideas to the thoughtful reader. When you read, or watch a play or movie, look for similarities between the fictional characters and situations and the people and events in your life. Don't pass up an opportunity for new understanding and applications.

Example: Read these excerpts from the poem "To be of use," by Marge Piercy.

The people I love the best
jump into work head first
without dallying in the shallows
and swim off with sure strokes almost out of sight . . . .
I love people who harness themselves, an ox to a heavy cart . . . ,
who do what has to be done, again and again . . . .
The work of the world is common as mud.
Botched, it smears the hands, crumbles to dust.
But the thing worth doing well done
has a shape that satisfies, clean and evident . . . .
The pitcher cries for water to carry
and the person for work that is real.

Application: When you read this poem, you may think of people you have known. Are there people whose good work has been important in your life? Imagine a young person who is drifting and who finds life a meaningless bore. What would the speaker say to this young person? Perhaps she would say, "Get to work. In work you will find purpose and self-respect and a place in the world."

 When applying information to a new situation, imagine what the narrator and characters would think and do in the new situation.

Choose the <u>best answer</u> to each item. <u>Items 1 to 3</u> refer to the following excerpt from a play.

JOSEPHINE: I was once courted by a young man from Harvard—before I met your grandfather. Dashing fellow. Had a Pierce-Arrow with lavender trim. There was an automobile! It was only my Yankee practicality that kept me from marrying him.

EVELYN: Were you in love with him?

JOSEPHINE: Not profoundly, but that's hard to know at twenty, and he had a rather handsome inheritance. Fortunately I had the sense to ask him how much, and he told me. Well, I did some calculations and figured he'd run through it in ten years' time. And he did! Ruined himself before the crash!

EVELYN: (*teasing but genuinely shocked*) Grandmother! How could you be so cold-blooded? Maybe you broke his heart!

JOSEPHINE: Never marry for money, girls. Ambition is better security.

EVELYN: Come on—you didn't marry for security.

JOSEPHINE: Of course I did. Love is just a fancy name for it.

EVELYN: Well, marriage is no longer a functional institution. I have a theory, based on personal observation: whatever you get married for, you'll get the opposite—if it's security, your husband will be unfaithful; if it's money, he'll lose it; if it's love, he'll end up despising you, or you'll despise him. It fits every married couple I know.

JOSEPHINE: You must know a sorry group of people! You kids are romantics. You think you're supposed to be happy, and you start fussing and fuming if someone doesn't come and hand it to you . . .

Elizabeth Diggs, *Close Ties.*

1. What would Evelyn most likely say to her daughter about marriage?

    (1) The best bet is to marry for money and security.
    (2) If your first marriage doesn't succeed, try, try again.
    (3) Marriage doesn't work well. Don't expect a husband to meet your needs.
    (4) Don't be cold-blooded. Marry for love.
    (5) Cultivate romance and your marriage will be a success.

2. Josephine's philosophy of life is probably based on

    (1) romance
    (2) practicality
    (3) religion
    (4) happiness
    (5) material possessions

3. Feminists viewing this scene today might

    (1) disapprove of Josephine's dependence on a husband for security
    (2) approve of Josephine's no-nonsense thinking
    (3) think Josephine too romantic
    (4) consider her cold-blooded
    (5) sympathize with her interest in financial security

Answers are on page 771.

Analysis
Lesson 3

Analysis

Topic 1: Fact and Opinion

You have probably heard the expression, "you can't see the forest for the trees." It is often more important to see the "big picture" or to grasp the main idea than to remember every tiny detail. However, to understand your reading in depth, it is also important to see the "trees." You should recognize the parts, ideas, or reasoning that form the whole. Breaking something into its parts or examining the working of its components is called **analysis.**

Analysis is the kind of thinking we use when we look for causes and effects of events in history. We practice analysis when we examine an author's reasoning or distinguish fact from opinion in a campaign speech.

Analysis can be practiced in different ways. You might be asked to analyze an author's reasoning by separating facts from opinions in a piece of writing. Critical thinkers are not persuaded by opinions that look like facts.

Facts can be proven by
- observation (it can be seen, heard, or experienced in some other way)
- demonstration or scientific experiment
- written records or historical documents

Opinions express what someone thinks, believes, or feels. Opinions may be based on facts. (However, people can form different opinions based on the same facts.) Opinions may be reasonable and widely held, and they are neither wrong nor right. They may be predictions, estimates, theories, or value judgments. Even if an opinion seems reasonable or morally correct, it is still an opinion, not a fact.

 Use these clues to identify opinions:

1. Opinions are often generalizations (broad, not specific). Example: People always look out for number one. (all people? always?)

2. Opinions often include words such as *probably, likely, may, perhaps.* **These words indicate uncertainty or suggest predictions. Watch for "I think," "many believe," and other similar expressions.**

3. Opinions often use words that interpret or make value judgments. Look for words such as *pretty, brilliant, best, worst, dangerous, immoral, important.* **These qualities are impossible to define or objectively measure.**

Choose the best answer to each item. Items 1 to 3 refer to the following paragraphs.

What happened to the country financially during 1929–1939 is well documented in history books. Such familiar phrases as "the stock market crashed," "Wall Street collapsed," and "banks folded" are evidence that the United States experienced great social and economic upheaval.

To this day, analysts study the causes and effects of the Great Depression. Some critics blame the government for not meeting its responsibility to preserve the nation's monetary system. Some critics go so far as to accuse federal and state officials of corruption and willful neglect. Others claim that the government, under President Herbert Hoover, simply lacked foresight. Hoover's administration failed to anticipate the negative effects of its laissez-faire policy toward business and industry. Other critics see the Great Depression as part of a global event. They find similar situations of insecurity and widespread unemployment in many European nations at that time. They also believe that the Depression hastened the start of World War II.

1. Which of the following is a fact?

    (1) The Great Depression spanned the years 1929–1939.
    (2) The Depression hastened the start of World War II.
    (3) Some federal and state officials were corrupt.
    (4) President Hoover's economic policies lacked foresight.
    (5) The Depression was caused by the government's failure to preserve the monetary system.

2. Which fact supports the generalization that the Depression was part of a global event?

    (1) The stock market crashed.
    (2) The U.S. experienced social and economic upheaval.
    (3) President Hoover followed a laissez-faire policy.

    (4) Unemployment was widespread in Europe at that time.
    (5) The Depression lasted for a decade or more.

3. Which of these words signals that an opinion is being expressed?

    (1) hastened
    (2) claim
    (3) well-documented
    (4) evidence
    (5) failed

Item 4 refers to the following paragraph.

During the Civil War, Lincoln's declared goal was not only to end slavery but to keep the Union together. He, like other Northerners, believed that the Union was created by the people and was indivisible: no state had the right to secede. Lincoln's terms for planning postwar Reconstruction were based on this belief. He wanted the nation to be reunited as quickly and painlessly as possible. The only requirements for acceptance back into the Union were to swear allegiance to the Constitution and to end slavery. The rebel states would then be pardoned and allowed to reestablish their state constitutions. However, some members of Congress were against Reconstruction.

4. According to the paragraph, Lincoln held the opinion that

    (1) the states had a right to secede
    (2) the Confederacy was legitimate
    (3) the South would win the war
    (4) slavery would be maintained
    (5) secession was not legal

Answers are on page 771.

Topic 2: Cause and Effect

Analysis involves taking something apart, examining the parts, and seeing how they work together. As you have learned, one way of analyzing your reading is to look for facts and opinions. Another form of analysis is to recognize causes and effects. In your reading, causes and effects are often part of a description or explanation.

A **cause** makes something happen. An **effect** is what happens as a result of the cause. You notice causes and effects in everyday life. An ice storm causes slippery roads. Heat turned too high causes a pot to boil over.

Below are important points to remember about cause-effect relationships.

• A cause always occurs <u>before</u> its effect, <u>but</u>
• Something that comes before is <u>not necessarily</u> a cause.
Example: When we drove downtown, it started to rain.
• Although a cause always occurs before its effect, it doesn't necessarily come first in a sentence or paragraph.
Example: Twelve minor accidents (*effect*) resulted from the icy roads (*cause*).
• Some effects can have <u>several</u> contributing causes. There may be a chain reaction where "A" causes "B," and "B" causes "C." In this case, "B" is both an effect <u>and</u> a cause.
• Some causes may result in multiple effects.
Example: The ice storm caused slippery roads, broken tree limbs, and frozen car door locks.

Sometimes the cause-effect relationship is clearly stated. In other cases, it is only implied and you must use reasoning to infer that one event caused another.

Example: Addison's disease results from an underactive adrenal gland. Symptoms include anemia, weakness, and fatigue.
Analysis: The underactive adrenal gland comes first in fact, but not in the sentence. The underactivity causes Addison's disease and its symptoms. Clue word: *results*.

 Words that often signal cause-effect relationships are: *cause, because, due to, reason, result, consequently,* and *therefore*.

Choose the best answer to each item. Items 1 to 3 refer to the following paragraphs.

The human body is under constant assault by microbes. Bacteria, viruses, and other parasites enter the bloodstream through the skin, lungs, or intestines. Microbes reproduce and grow within the body's tissues. As they attack the body's organs, they create the symptoms of disease. If the body cannot resist them, they can cause death.

In order to resist the constant invasion of microbes, the body must develop an immunity to them. The body produces special cells that attack the harmful substances, or antigens, in several ways.

T cells in the blood attack and destroy invading microbes in the body's cells. B cells respond to the microbes by producing special proteins called antibodies. Carried through the blood, these antibodies destroy the antigens. Other cells, called macrophages, surround the harmful microbes and digest them. These types of cells working together produce the body's immune response.

Although the immune response keeps people healthy, it may also work against a person. In some people, dust and pollen trigger the production of antibodies that cause a disease: allergy. When an organ is transplanted from one person to another, the new organ may cause an immune response in the recipient's body. The body responds to the new organ as if it were a harmful invader and attacks it.

1. What causes the symptoms of disease?

    (1) microbes such as bacteria and viruses
    (2) the body's organs
    (3) the immune response
    (4) antibodies
    (5) special cells that attack harmful microbes

2. The writer implies that the immune response is caused by

    (1) the symptoms of disease
    (2) antibodies
    (3) macrophages
    (4) bacteria and viruses attacking the body
    (5) special cells that surround the microbes

3. Which of these is an effect of the immune response?

    (1) an allergy
    (2) the invasion of microbes
    (3) cells working together
    (4) organ transplants
    (5) the growth of bacteria

Item 4 refers to the following paragraph.

During the more than 200 years since the United States was founded, the makeup of the labor force has changed. In the early years, most workers were farm workers and agriculture was the chief industry. After the Industrial Revolution of the late 1800s, most of the nation's workers were in manufacturing industries. By the 1990s automation had cut into the manufacturing sector. Now the fastest-growing occupations are in the service sector. The service field includes industries like health care, education, and computer services.

4. Which of the following is the most likely cause of the changes in the type of work done by the U.S. labor force?

    (1) lack of good farmland
    (2) changes in technology
    (3) increased education
    (4) decline in population
    (5) more women in the work force

Answers are on page 771.

Topic 3: Understanding Figurative Language

Analysis involves taking something apart and examining the working of its parts. There are many approaches you might take in using this skill. You have practiced distinguishing facts from opinions in social studies and identifying causes and effects in science. These skills will be helpful in analyzing literature.

A particularly helpful skill in literary analysis is identifying and understanding figurative language. Novelists, dramatists, and especially poets are fond of using figurative, as opposed to literal, language. Literal language makes a clear, direct statement. It means what it seems to mean. A heartbeat is a heartbeat. A pickle is simply a pickle. With figurative language, it's not that simple.

When we say, "Don't count your chickens," "He's getting too big for his britches," or "She's getting a big head," we know that what we mean has nothing to do with chickens, britches, or heads. The words are symbols. They represent something other than their most concrete meaning.

Many writers use this kind of language to draw a mental picture for the reader. They choose words that allow the reader to get a richer meaning than a concrete word can convey. Sometimes a writer uses figurative language to express emotion. A poet may choose words simply for the rhyme or rhythm of the language, or for the beauty of the image it creates. The use of figurative language can enrich the experience of reading.

Example:	Figurative Language	Literal Meaning
	Under veils of white lace	Under a dusting of snow
	A solid set of streets, where pigeons strut, meet, and mate	A tree where pigeons gather
	A narrow fellow in the grass	A snake

As these excerpts show, figurative language is more colorful than the literal translation. Much can be said in few words, because the image can be rich and broad.

As you read, try to get a mental picture from the words. What does this image make you think of? How does it make you feel? The author is probably suggesting a comparison. How is a tree similar to a set of streets? In relation to the rest of the piece, what does the author mean to say?

 Remember, writers often want to help their readers look at the world in a new way. To do this, they use ordinary words in figurative ways.

Choose the <u>best answer</u> to each item. <u>Items 1 to 4</u> refer to the following excerpt from an article.

WHAT'S SO SPECIAL ABOUT NEWS MAGAZINES?

Beyond the bottom line, Wall Street doesn't much care about editorial quality; journalists do and others should. Not because journalism is perfect, but because
(5) it isn't.

News magazines come at the end of the food chain of journalism. First radio reports the news hourly, then the evening television news repeats it and adds
(10) pictures. Newspapers fill out the story in greater detail. Finally the news magazine comes along to summarize and analyze it. By that time the reader may be suffering an acute case of information glut. It takes
(15) wit, reflection, a gift for compression, some fresh reporting or consultation with experts, and an original turn of mind to add something new. The real job of the news magazine is to help the reader to
(20) make sense out of his times. Those who can do this, the best of them, form a shaggy group of contentious minds.

Thomas Griffith, "What's So Special About News Magazines?", *Newsweek*.

1. What is the effect of saying "suffering an acute case of information glut" (line 14)?

   (1) It describes how the reader makes sense of his world.
   (2) It suggests that there is too much news on TV.
   (3) It reminds the reader of having an upset stomach from overeating.
   (4) It suggests that readers need to find new sources of information.
   (5) It implies that magazine readers should stop watching television news programs.

2. What point about news reporting is the author making by saying news magazines are "at the end of the food chain of journalism" (lines 6–7)?

   (1) As each news medium reports a story that has already been reported, it becomes harder to present the story in an interesting way.
   (2) News magazines have smaller lunch expense accounts than newspapers or television stations.
   (3) News magazines are given less detailed information and fewer pictures.
   (4) The quality of the food served gets better as a reporter moves up through the ranks.
   (5) Because Wall Street does not care about quality, journalism has become a dog-eat-dog world.

3. Which of the following best describes what the author means by a "shaggy group of contentious minds" (line 22)?

   (1) a group of writers
   (2) a quarrelsome group of journalists
   (3) a collection of news magazines
   (4) a variety of magazines with opposing points of view
   (5) an assembly of reporters in need of haircuts

4. Based on the excerpt, for which of the following reasons would you read a news magazine?

   (1) keeping up with news as soon as it breaks
   (2) learning all the details of a news story
   (3) a sensible summary of important news stories
   (4) a glut of information
   (5) perfect journalism

Choose the best answer to each item. Items 5 and 6 refer to the following poem.

Strange Season

    First go the birds, bound south and always south,
    And then the fox, sly-faced, among the leaves
    Sniffs the dark air; the fields released from drouth
    Sigh in the night. The great orb spider weaves
(5) His low-hung calculations, lost in fear
    That midnight might brew crystal in his veins.
    This is the end of summer; the long year
    Is settling toward November and the rains.

    First go the birds—but stubborn is the heart
(10) Responsive still to unforgotten springs,
    Hoarding its love while spinning leaves depart,
    Hearing no sound of passing or of wings.
    This is the heart's strange season—brave but lost
    Under the cold blue pole star of the frost.

Loren Eisley, *All the Night Wings.*

5. The phrase "stubborn is the heart" (line 9)
probably means

(1) man clings to thoughts of spring, in spite
of evidence of the changing season
(2) people are stubborn
(3) heartbreak will come to stubborn people
(4) a stubborn heart hoards love
(5) birds are stubborn

6. In the phrase "brew crystal in his veins"
(line 6), crystal represents

(1) plastic
(2) blood
(3) water
(4) ice
(5) glass

Answers are on page 772.

Evaluation

Evaluation

Topic 1: Beliefs and Values—Recognizing their Role _____

As an adult, you know that you cannot always accept as true everything you hear. You may not agree with other people's interpretations of events. You have developed standards to judge accuracy, completeness, logic, honesty, and prejudice. A critical reader analyzes writing in the same way.

When you judge a meal in a restaurant, you are making an evaluation. When you decide whether an editorial argument is logical, you are also evaluating. Do you agree with the writer? Why or why not? To answer these questions and make these decisions, you must read carefully. You must use other skills you have practiced, including comprehension and application. You will especially need your analysis skills to distinguish fact from opinion, and to recognize the logical steps in the development of an idea or an argument. This is why evaluation is considered a higher level of thinking. It requires the use of many skills.

An important aspect of evaluation is the ability to recognize the role of values and beliefs in determining people's attitudes, opinions, and actions. For example, you watch a group of striking employees picket for weeks through the cold of winter. You infer that these workers value their cause more than their physical comfort.

When you read, you can make similar judgments by reading between the lines to make an inference about the author's beliefs and values. To identify values and beliefs, you use the author's words and your experience of life and human nature. You try to imagine what beliefs the particular statements or actions might reflect.

Example: Government must make laws and regulations to require equal treatment for all citizens. Private businesses and public organizations must be forced to use fair employment practices. Racial and gender equity can only be achieved by aggressive government action.
Evaluation: You might infer from this passage that the author believes people and organizations will do the right thing only if they are forced. In other words, people cannot be trusted, and government must act as a watchdog. Words such as *must*, *require*, *force*, and *aggressive* are clues to strong feelings and beliefs. Reasoning: if force is necessary, people can't be trusted to be fair.

When trying to identify beliefs, look for clues that could have influenced the people's actions. This will help you evaluate the people's cultural values and to compare those values to other cultural values.

Choose the <u>best answer</u> to each item. <u>Items 1 to 3</u> refer to the following paragraphs.

A free market economy works better than a government-controlled system. Growth occurs at a faster rate under free enterprise because businesses can make their own decisions. They can adjust to changes in the marketplace. In fact, they are encouraged to do so by the rewards of the system. If a business owner improves efficiency and lowers costs, her increased profits mean higher income for herself. The profit motive is the basis of a growing economy.

Centrally controlled systems attempt to distribute profits equally throughout society. The person who works harder or "works smarter" generally receives no greater reward than his less ambitious co-workers. There is little incentive for increasing the quality or quantity of production or service. Consequently, economic growth is slower.

1. The author apparently believes

    (1) people need government control
    (2) business owners are the most important people in an economy
    (3) women should make higher salaries
    (4) people are motivated by personal gain
    (5) centrally controlled systems are fairer to workers

2. The author appears to prefer

    (1) free market economies over government-controlled systems
    (2) free market systems rather than privately owned businesses
    (3) equally distributed profits instead of individual profits
    (4) profits over efficiency
    (5) a growing economy rather than the profit motive

3. The author would probably agree with which of the following statements?

    (1) Workers should be treated equally.
    (2) Business owners are too greedy.
    (3) People will work harder only for personal profit.
    (4) People will work more efficiently for the common good.
    (5) Business owners could benefit from more government control.

<u>Item 4</u> is based on the following paragraphs.

People sometimes confront problems or situations in which some of their values conflict with other values. For example, a husband and wife who value companionship, love, and family life may also value personal growth, hard work, and success. Their home life encourages one set of values, and their jobs provide expression for the other set. When the job requires long hours, or a move to a distant city, couples compromise to try to balance their values.

One couple may decide to move to another city to pursue the work-related values of one spouse. Another couple may decide that family values are more important and refuse to move. Still another couple may decide that just one of them should move to pursue a job opportunity. They may live apart for a time, commuting to see each other on weekends. Commuter marriages are an attempt to pursue all these values.

4. A couple that decides against moving the whole family to pursue one spouse's career probably places a high value on

    (1) ambition
    (2) personal growth
    (3) personal freedom
    (4) family life
    (5) work

Answers are on page 772.

Topic 2: Judging the Adequacy of Facts _____

As you have learned, evaluation involves making a judgment. You evaluate your work, on the job or at home. Is it neat? Does it meet standards? You may evaluate your child's performance at school. Is it average or above average? You judge a movie or a TV show. Is it funny? Is it boring?

To make an evaluation, you apply a standard of some kind to make a judgment. The standard may be formally stated. In a factory, standards for product quality are spelled out. When you evaluate a movie, your standards are more personal, but you still have reasons and evidence to justify your evaluation.

In science, evaluation based on standards is an essential thinking skill. Scientists don't accept conclusions until they are tested and proven. Hard facts and evidence are necessary for proof.

You should adopt a scientific attitude when you read. Question the author's conclusions. A good mental habit is to analyze the reasoning and evaluate the conclusions. To analyze the reasoning, look at the facts and how they relate to each other. Test the author's conclusion or theory against those facts. Do the facts support the conclusion? Is the cause-effect analysis sound? Could the facts be explained as well by another theory? Judging the adequacy of facts is an important part of evaluation.

Example: When you add sugar or table salt to water, each will dissolve. You can add more sugar or salt, and each will continue to dissolve—up to a point where the solution is said to be saturated. However, if you heat the water, it will accept more of either substance. Heating increases solubility.

Evaluation: Do these facts support the general conclusion stated in the last sentence? Table salt and sugar were tested. Is this enough information to justify a general conclusion about solubility? Does heating increase the solubility of all substances? We don't know. The facts here are not sufficient. The conclusion may be correct, but the writer has not presented a complete argument. The reader may remain skeptical. (However, if the author is a recognized expert in the field, it may be reasonable to accept the conclusion.) In fact, the conclusion above is not true.

 As you read, ask yourself whether the author's statements are adequately supported by facts.

Choose the <u>best answer</u> to each item. <u>Items 1 and 2</u> are based on the following paragraphs.

   Physicists have made careful measurements of objects in motion. They have studied masses of data gathered in years of painstaking observations. They have been able to show that objects always move in certain ways, and that what is true in one case will be true in all cases. They have arrived at a set of natural "laws," which are actually descriptions or observations of the behavior of objects in motion.

   These laws describe a simplified view of objects in motion. For example, one law states that two objects that are dropped from a height will hit the ground at the same time, no matter what size and shape they are. A cannonball and a feather will fall side by side. This is true of objects falling in a vacuum. In Earth's atmosphere, however, the feather will float slowly to the ground, while the cannonball falls with a thud. The shape and lightness of the feather cause it to be resisted by the air. The cannonball, on the other hand, is streamlined, so that the air flows around it with very little resistance. The effect of air resistance can be measured and predicted when necessary. But the law of motion itself is based on the ideal situation of objects falling in a vacuum. It excludes the particular effects of any one-time conditions. It allows the physicist to concentrate on the basic relationships.

1. The "law" that states that two objects dropped from a height will hit the ground at the same time is

   (1) not supported by the evidence in the passage
   (2) supported by the evidence summarized in the first paragraph
   (3) disproved by the details in the second paragraph
   (4) supported by observing a cannonball and a feather
   (5) not supported by enough evidence

2. The law referred to in the second paragraph is most likely

   (1) not a true description of objects in motion
   (2) not valid in a vacuum
   (3) true in all circumstances
   (4) true under certain conditions
   (5) not true for all objects

Item 3 refers to the following paragraph.

   Energy is the ability to move matter from one place to another or to change matter from one substance to another. Energy is never used up. It just changes from one form to another. For example, you use the energy stored in your muscles to lift an object such as a pen. Some of the energy is changed into the motion of the pen. This energy is called <u>kinetic energy</u>, or the energy of motion. Some of your energy is changed into potential energy, or the energy of position. Potential energy is stored energy. The higher you lift the pen, the more potential energy you give it. Potential energy is released when matter moves. Drop the pen and its potential energy changes into kinetic energy as it falls.

3. A rolling ball stops moving. Which of the following conclusions is supported by the information in the passage?

   (1) The ball's energy is lost.
   (2) The ball's energy changes form.
   (3) The ball's potential energy becomes kinetic energy.
   (4) The matter in the ball changes to another substance.
   (5) The ball is made of energy.

Answers are on page 773.

Tables, Graphs, Charts, Maps

Lesson 5

Tables, Graphs, Charts, Maps

A number of questions on the GED Social Studies, Science, and Mathematics tests require you to read, interpret, and apply information that is presented in pictorial, or graphic, form. This means that you will need to gain skill and experience in reading and understanding tables, charts, and maps, as well as bar graphs, line graphs, circle graphs, and pictographs. This unit will cover each type of graphic display and provide you with exercises for practice.

Topic 1: Tables

In our daily lives, we constantly come in contact with information that is presented in the form of tables. For example, bus, train, and airplane schedules present departure and arrival times in table form. State sales tax charts also present information in table form. Boxed cake mixes list required baking times in table form to account for various types of cake pans, e.g., loaf pan, 8" or 9" rounds, and 10" x 13" sheet cake pan. Tables also are used to keep scores in sports events, compare weather reports, and list financial institutions' profits and losses over a given time period.

Tables provide the writer with a handy way to highlight essential bits of information. Facts and figures presented in table form often are easier to locate, understand, and compare than these same facts and figures presented in paragraph form. For example, a car dealer who wants to compare the gas mileage of four leading cars has a better chance of having prospective buyers read and remember the information if it is presented in graphic form, as follows:

Mileage Comparison* of Four Leading Car Models				
	Model A	Model B	Model C	Model D
City Driving	18	22	28	30
Highway Driving	26	29	39	35

*Data presented in miles per gallon (mpg) of gasoline.

Information in a table is arranged into **columns** and **rows.** The column headings in the table above are Car Models A, B, C, and D. The row headings are City Driving and Highway Driving. At the **intersection** of each row and column, there is a cell which contains information. For example, find the intersection of Model C car and Highway Driving. The data contained in this cell tells you that Model C gets 39 mpg during highway driving.

To gain information from a table, always remember the following three steps: **R**ead, **Q**uestion, **S**ummarize. First, **READ** the title of the table and the headings of the columns and rows. This will help orient you to the table and how the information is presented. Next, **QUESTION** yourself about the information in the table: Does Model A get better mileage in city or highway driving? What about Models B, C, and D? Which model gets the best mileage for city driving? For highway driving? Is one car model clearly the best in gasoline consumption for both highway and city driving? Finally, **SUMMARIZE** the information presented in the table in one or two sentences. You might say something like this: "Of the four 1992 car models, Model A reports the poorest ratio of miles per gallon, with Model B reporting the next-to-poorest. Model D reports the best mpg ratio for city driving, while Model C reports the best mpg ratio for highway driving."

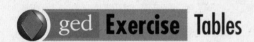 **ged Exercise** Tables

Choose the best answer to each item. Items 1 to 3 refer to the following table.

Planets of the Solar System			
Name	Mean Distance From Sun in Millions of Miles	Period of Revolution Around Sun	Diameter of Equator in Miles
Mercury	36.0	87.96 days	3,031
Venus	67.2	224.68 days	7,521
Earth	93.0	365.26 days	7,926
Mars	141.6	686.95 days	4,222
Jupiter	483.6	11.86 years	88,729
Saturn	886.7	29.46 years	74,600
Uranus	1,784.0	84.07 years	32,600
Neptune	2,794.4	164.81 years	30,200
Pluto	3,674.5	248.53 years	1,430

1. Which planet is smallest in size?

(1) Mercury
(2) Mars
(3) Venus
(4) Earth
(5) Pluto

2. Which planet has the shortest year?

(1) Mercury
(2) Jupiter
(3) Venus
(4) Saturn
(5) Earth

3. Which planet is closest to Earth?

(1) Venus
(2) Mercury
(3) Mars
(4) Jupiter
(5) None of the above

Item 4 refers to the following table.

Taxonomic Key for Classifying Vertebrate Animals	
IF	**THEN**
1 1a. Spinal column present 1b. Spinal column absent	Go to 2 Invertebrate
2 2a. Fins and gills present 2b. Fins and gills absent	Fish Go to 3
3 3a. Scales present 3b. Scales absent	Reptile Go to 4
4 4a. Feathers present 4b. Feathers absent	Bird Go to 5
5 5a. Hair or fur present 5b. Hair or fur absent	Mammal Amphibian

4. An animal with a spinal column and hair or fur is

(1) a reptile
(2) a bird
(3) a mammal
(4) an amphibian
(5) an invertebrate

Topic 2: Graphs

Answers are on page 773.

Graphs are pictorial representations of data. They often serve to highlight and clarify information contained in reading passages, particularly when the information includes many facts and figures. There are different types of graphs that can be used, depending on the nature of the information to be presented.

Line Graphs

A line graph is used to show a trend over time, such as a company's profits and losses over a five-year period. Often, a line graph is used to show a relationship between two (or more) items, such as the profits of two separate departments within the same company. In this case, two separate lines are used, each one representing one of the departments. All line graphs have both a vertical and a horizontal axis. On the following line graph, the horizontal axis represents the months of the year, and the vertical axis represents the average monthly temperature.

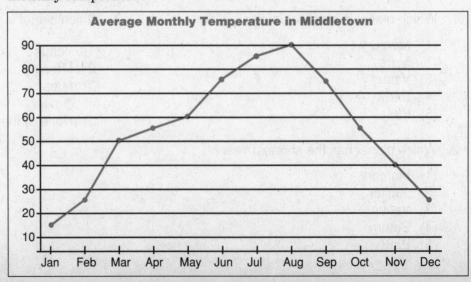

Average Monthly Temperature in Middletown

Reading Strategies ◆ Tables, Graphs, Charts, Maps

Just as you interpret tables, you should follow the same three steps to interpret line graphs: **R**ead, **Q**uestion, and **S**ummarize. **READ** the title of the line graph as well as the headings of the horizontal and vertical axes. Then **QUESTION** yourself about the graph: In what months can you expect the hottest temperatures in Middletown? How hot does it get? In what months can you expect the coldest temperatures? How cold does it get? Is Middletown likely to be as far north as Chicago? Is Middletown likely to be as far south as Miami? Now **SUMMARIZE** the data on the graph: Middletown enjoys a relatively moderate climate with average temperatures ranging from a low of 15 to 25 degrees to a high of 85 to 90 degrees. For only four months of the year (November through February) is the average monthly temperature below 50 degrees.

ged Exercise Line Graphs

Choose the best answer to each item. Items 1 to 4 refer to the following graph.

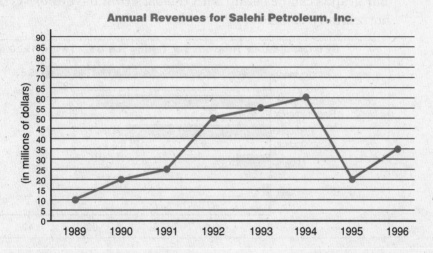

1. What were the annual revenues for Salehi Petroleum in 1989, the year the company was founded?

    (1) $10,000,000
    (2) $19,000,000
    (3) $11,000,000
    (4) $5,000,000
    (5) None of the above

2. During which two years did the company realize the greatest income?

    (1) 1991 and 1992
    (2) 1992 and 1993
    (3) 1994 and 1995
    (4) 1995 and 1996
    (5) None of the above

3. One year the company made twice as much money as it had the year before. What year was that?

    (1) 1991
    (2) 1992
    (3) 1993
    (4) 1994
    (5) 1995

4. Another year, there was a fire that destroyed most of the company's equipment. In what year do you think the fire happened?

    (1) 1996
    (2) 1995
    (3) 1994
    (4) 1992
    (5) 1991

Answers are on page 773.

Bar Graphs

Bar graphs are similar to line graphs in that both show comparisons among quantities of similar items. However, the bar graph can capture information at a **single point in time,** whereas line graphs show **trends over time.** For example, a bar graph is useful for showing the number of persons within several different age brackets in a given population at a given point in time.

As with tables and line graphs, you need to follow the three steps to interpret bar graphs: **R**ead, **Q**uestion, and **S**ummarize. **READ** the title of the bar graph as well as the heading of the horizontal and vertical axes. Then **QUESTION** yourself about the information contained in the graph. For example, in the graph below, what was the primary reason given by GED candidates in 1980 for taking the GED Tests? And in 1989? What factors may have contributed to this difference? Now try to **SUMMARIZE** the data on the graph.

Bar graphs can be set up with the bars running either vertically or horizontally, as below:

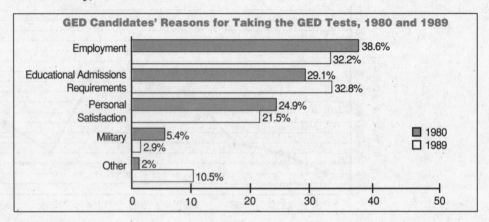

GED Candidates' Reasons for Taking the GED Tests, 1980 and 1989

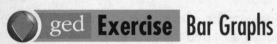 **Exercise** Bar Graphs

Items 1 to 3 refer to the following graph.

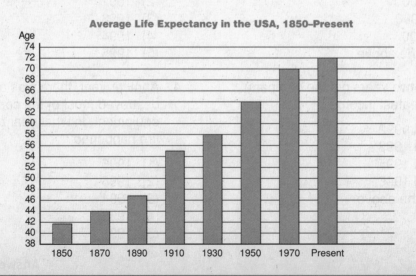

Reading Strategies ◆ Tables, Graphs, Charts, Maps

1. The average life expectancy is the average number of years that people born in a given year could be expected to live. What was the average life expectancy of persons born in 1890?

   (1) 44
   (2) 47
   (3) 51
   (4) 54
   (5) 59

2. Average life expectancy at the present time is how many years greater than in 1950?

   (1) 6
   (2) 8
   (3) 10
   (4) 12
   (5) 14

3. Between what years did the life expectancy increase most?

   (1) 1850–1870
   (2) 1870–1890
   (3) 1890–1910
   (4) 1930–1950
   (5) 1950–1970

Answers are on page 773.

Circle Graphs

The circle graph is used to compare parts with the whole, or 100%, of something. For example, the amount of Harry's weekly check represents 100% of his take-home pay of $480. One-half of Harry's paycheck, or 50%, is used to pay for food and housing. The other half is divided among the following: transportation, clothing, savings, entertainment, and insurance and medical expenses. A circle graph of how Harry spends his paycheck would look like this:

The total of the portions of a circle graph is **always** 100%. Circle graphs are also called pie graphs because the portions within the circle resemble slices of a pie. To interpret the circle graph, remember the three steps: **R**ead, **Q**uestion, and **S**ummarize. **READ** the title of the graph and the headings of each "slice of the pie." **QUESTION** yourself about the information given: What category of expenses accounts for the greatest share of Harry's take-home pay? What category accounts for the smallest share? How much money each week is spent on food and housing? Now **SUMMARIZE** the data on the pie graph.

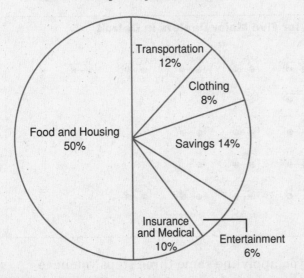

Where Harry's Paycheck Goes

Transportation 12%
Clothing 8%
Savings 14%
Food and Housing 50%
Insurance and Medical 10%
Entertainment 6%

Items 1 and 2 refer to the following graph.

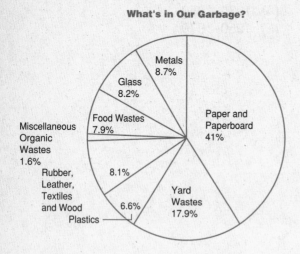

What's in Our Garbage?

Metals 8.7%
Glass 8.2%
Food Wastes 7.9%
Miscellaneous Organic Wastes 1.6%
Rubber, Leather, Textiles and Wood
Plastics
8.1%
6.6%
Paper and Paperboard 41%
Yard Wastes 17.9%

1. The largest component of garbage in America is

   (1) yard wastes
   (2) rubber, leather, textiles, and wood
   (3) glass
   (4) metals
   (5) paper and paperboard

2. Which of the following conclusions <u>cannot</u> be drawn from the information presented in the circle graph?

   (1) Almost one-fourth of our garbage is made of up metals, glass, and plastics.
   (2) Americans waste 7.9% of their food.
   (3) The smallest component of garbage in America is miscellaneous organic wastes.
   (4) The percentage of our garbage made up of rubber, leather, textiles, and wood is about the same as that made up of glass.
   (5) The percentage of our garbage consisting of yard wastes is about double that consisting of metals and glass combined.

Answers are on page 773.

Pictographs

A pictograph compares **one thing** over time or in different places. For example, to portray the number of cars sold by different dealers over a one-year period, you might construct a pictograph like the one below:

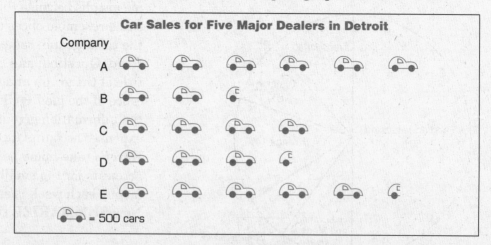

Car Sales for Five Major Dealers in Detroit

Company

A
B
C
D
E

= 500 cars

To interpret pictographs, you apply the same three steps you have learned to use for interpreting all other types of graphs: **R**ead, **Q**uestion, and **S**ummarize. By now, you should be familiar with these three steps and know how to apply them to all types of graphs.

Items 1 and 2 refer to the following graph.

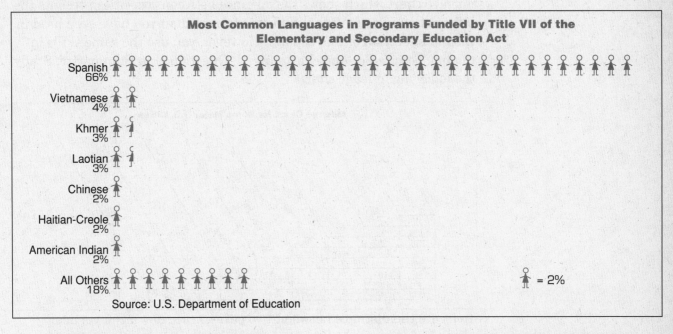

Most Common Languages in Programs Funded by Title VII of the Elementary and Secondary Education Act

Spanish 66%

Vietnamese 4%

Khmer 3%

Laotian 3%

Chinese 2%

Haitian-Creole 2%

American Indian 2%

All Others 18%

Source: U.S. Department of Education

= 2%

1. Which language is most frequently used by students in Title VII-funded education programs?

   (1) Vietnamese
   (2) Khmer
   (3) Chinese
   (4) American Indian
   (5) Spanish

2. The U.S. Congress appropriated $140 million in 1988 for Title VII programs. If funds were spent proportionately on each group, how much of the funding was used to serve students for whom Chinese was the primary language?

   (1) $28 million
   (2) $14 million
   (3) $2.8 million
   (4) $1.4 million
   (5) $140,000

Items 3 and 4 refer to the following graph.

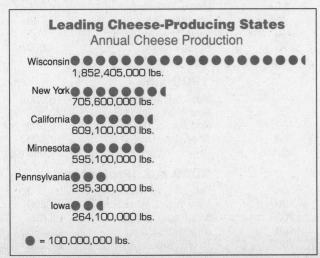

Leading Cheese-Producing States
Annual Cheese Production

Wisconsin
1,852,405,000 lbs.

New York
705,600,000 lbs.

California
609,100,000 lbs.

Minnesota
595,100,000 lbs.

Pennsylvania
295,300,000 lbs.

Iowa
264,100,000 lbs.

= 100,000,000 lbs.

3. According to the graph, which state leads the nation in cheese production?

   (1) New York
   (2) California
   (3) Minnesota
   (4) Pennsylvania
   (5) Wisconsin

4. Which is the third-ranking state in cheese production?

   (1) New York
   (2) California
   (3) Pennsylvania
   (4) Minnesota
   (5) Iowa

Answers are on page 773.

Lesson 5 ◆ Tables, Graphs, Charts, Maps

227

Topic 3: Charts

A chart is similar to a table in that it organizes many facts into a small space. Information presented in chart form often is not lined up in rows and columns as information presented in a table is. For example, a mileage chart which shows the distance between two cities presents the information in a somewhat different format than you have seen used in the tables section of this chapter. However, you use the same skills in reading both tables and charts: **R**ead, **Q**uestion, and **S**ummarize. Study the following mileage chart.

Mileage Chart for Some Major U.S. Cities

Milwaukee, WI	Minneapolis-St. Paul, MN	Nashville, TN	New Orleans, LA	New York, NY	Oklahoma City, OK	Omaha, NE	Philadelphia, PA
327							
536	858						
1037	1250	528					
924	1246	892	1325				
903	810	678	688	1508			
485	357	751	1034	1290	453		
881	1165	794	1227	98	1435	1189	
1812	1684	1676	1525	2483	1011	1327	2410

To locate the distance between two cities, trace down the vertical column of one city (Milwaukee) to the intersection with the horizontal row of the second city (Philadelphia). The figure in this intersection is the approximate distance in miles between the two cities. Ask yourself the following questions: What is the distance between Minneapolis/St. Paul and Omaha? (357 miles) How far is it from Oklahoma City to Nashville? (678 miles)

ged Exercise Charts

Population of the World's Five Largest Cities (In Thousands) 1350 B.C. to 2000 A.D. (Projected)			
1350 B.C.		**1925 A.D.**	
Babylon, Iraq	55	Berlin, Germany	4,015
Chengchow, China	40	London, England	7,740
Khattushas, Egypt	40	New York City, U.S.A.	7,775
Memphis, Egypt	75	Paris, France	4,800
Thebes, Egypt	100	Tokyo, Japan	5,250
1000 A.D.		**1980 A.D.**	
Constantinople, Turkey	450	Mexico City, Mexico	15,000
Cordova, Spain	450	New York City, U.S.A.	20,500
Kaifeng, China	400	Sao Paulo, Brazil	13,500
Kyoto, Japan	200	Shanghai, China	13,500
Sian, China	300	Tokyo, Japan	20,000
1600 A.D.		**2000 A.D. (Projected)**	
Agra, India	500	Mexico City, Mexico	31,000
Cairo, Egypt	400	New York City, U.S.A	22,800
Constantinople, Turkey	700	Sao Paulo, Brazil	25,800
Osaka, Japan	400	Shanghai, China	22,700
Peking, China	705	Tokyo, Japan	24,200
All figures are approximate.			

Reading Strategies ◆ Tables, Graphs, Charts, Maps

Choose the <u>best answer</u> to each item. <u>Items 1 to 3</u> refer to the previous chart.

1. Which of the following countries appears most often on the chart?

   (1) China
   (2) Egypt
   (3) Brazil
   (4) Mexico
   (5) U.S.A.

2. Between 1980 and 2000, which city is projected to have the slowest growth rate?

   (1) Mexico City
   (2) New York City
   (3) Sao Paulo
   (4) Shanghai
   (5) Tokyo

3. In 1600 A.D., which continent held most of the world's largest cities?

   (1) Africa
   (2) Asia
   (3) Europe
   (4) North America
   (5) Australia

Answers are on page 773.

Topic 4: Maps

Different maps can provide different kinds of information about a specific region. For example, a **political map** of Europe shows the boundaries between countries and regions and identifies major cities and waterways. A **physical map** of Europe identifies features of the land, such as mountains, lakes, and rivers. Other maps graphically represent special features of the region, such as its weather, population centers, or location of natural resources (oil, coal, etc.).

Most maps contain **legends**. The legend, or key, explains the meaning of each symbol on the map. For example, a map of Europe might have a legend explaining that ★ indicates the capital city of each country on the map. Maps frequently contain distance scales, such as the one below, which help the reader judge distances between points on the map.

0   250   500   750   1000 miles

As you learned in interpreting other graphics, careful reading of the information presented aids your understanding of the graphic. With maps, be sure you read not just the information on the map itself, but also the legend that accompanies the map. Then question yourself about the map and summarize the information presented.

Choose the <u>best answer</u> to each item. <u>Items 1 to 3</u> refer to the following weather map of the United States.

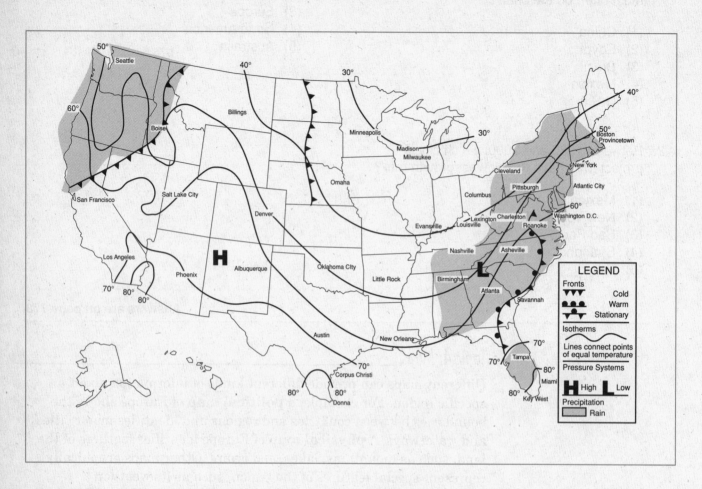

1. In which city is it raining with a temperature of 60 degrees?

   (1) Miami
   (2) Washington, D.C.
   (3) Salt Lake City
   (4) Seattle
   (5) Columbus

2. Where is there a stationary front?

   (1) from Los Angeles to San Francisco
   (2) in North Dakota, South Dakota, and Nebraska
   (3) in New England
   (4) in the Southwest
   (5) along part of the East Coast

3. Where is there a high pressure system?

   (1) the Southwest
   (2) the Southeast
   (3) the Mid-Atlantic States
   (4) the Northwest
   (5) the Great Lakes Region

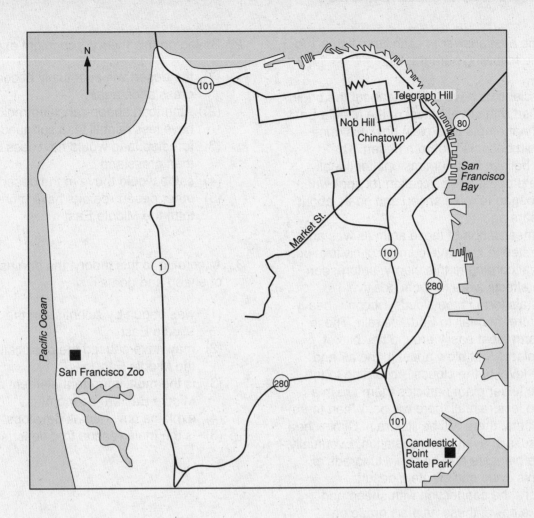

4. Off what state highway is the exit to Candlestick Point State Park?

   (1) 280
   (2) 1
   (3) 80
   (4) 101
   (5) None of the above

5. Tourist attractions such as Chinatown, Nob Hill, and Telegraph Hill are located in what area of the city?

   (1) along the west coast
   (2) in the central area
   (3) in the south
   (4) in the northwest
   (5) in the northeast

Answers are on page 773.

Choose the best answer to each item. Items 1 to 3 refer to the following paragraphs.

Some scientists have a theory about the origin of the desert that covers most of the Middle East. The theory attempts to explain how this once grassy plain became a barren desert. The scientists believe that humans unintentionally began the process of desiccation (drying) when they first began to raise sheep and goats about 10,000 years ago.

The domestication of these animals was an important step in the development of civilization. However, according to this theory, unforeseen long-term effects were far from positive.

Ice crystals form in the clouds, become heavy with moisture, and fall to Earth as rain. These crystals form most easily around tiny bits of decayed plants that blow about in the air and rise to the level of the clouds. According to the theory, the fewer plant particles there are in a region, the less rainfall there will be. When there are few plants, there will be little rain. Diminished rainfall results in even less vegetation. Eventually, there is no plant life and no rain. Hundreds of years of this cycle can create a desert.

So, what's the connection with sheep and goats? Like cows, these animals graze on grass and other plants, but they graze more destructively. Unlike cows, they bite the grass close to the ground, which removes the plant cover from the soil. Over many centuries, these animals may have turned Middle East grasslands into a desert.

1. Which of these is a statement of opinion?

   (1) Ice crystals form in clouds.
   (2) People in the Middle East domesticated sheep and goats about 10,000 years ago.
   (3) Much of the Middle East is desert.
   (4) Overgrazing by sheep and goats may have helped create the desert in the Middle East.
   (5) Ice crystals form around bits of animal matter.

2. Based on this theory, you might expect that

   (1) the desert will eventually become grasslands again
   (2) American sheep-ranching regions might have less rainfall than surrounding areas
   (3) forested land would have less rainfall than grassland
   (4) cattle would thrive in the desert
   (5) other desert regions have more rainfall than the Middle East

3. According to this theory, the domestication of sheep and goats

   (1) was begun by scientists in the Middle East
   (2) may have caused the desiccation of the Middle East
   (3) is the most important element of the Middle Eastern economy
   (4) explains how rainfall develops
   (5) is the main reason that deserts develop

Scientists believe the immediate cause of an earthquake is a sudden break in the layers of rock beneath the surface soil. In a process called faulting, rocks break under the strain of extreme pressure. Rock will yield to pressure by changing shape. Eventually, however, pressure builds to the breaking point. The rock underlying Earth's surface then tears apart and snaps back to a more unrestrained position. This snapping back is called elastic rebound.

This underground activity creates shocks felt on the surface. Tremors and minor property damage often result. Large earthquakes shake buildings and other structures at their foundations. Many buildings crumble. In addition, electrical and water systems are often disrupted. Landslides occur in some areas.

The belief that earthquakes are caused by faulting is based on observations of visible effects. In addition, laboratory tests offer evidence. In the lab, scientists have applied various pressures and distorting forces to rocks. These lab conditions are equal to the force of pressures at various depths in Earth. Under these pressures, the rocks slowly change shape. Finally, they break apart and snap back. These experiments attempt to demonstrate actual events before and during an earthquake.

4. Earthquakes are most directly caused by

   (1) extreme pressures on the rock layers beneath Earth's surface
   (2) landslides
   (3) faulting, tremors, and property damage
   (4) a sudden break in the rock layers underground
   (5) elastic rebound

5. The evidence from laboratory experiments

   (1) is unconvincing because there is no snap-back effect in an earthquake
   (2) is insufficient support for the faulting theory
   (3) provides a good model of how earthquakes cause damage
   (4) does not prove the elastic rebound theory
   (5) is convincing because lab conditions and results are very similar to those described by the faulting theory

6. Increasing pressure on the layers of rock underground causes the rock to break, creating an earthquake. This explanation is supported by observations and laboratory experiments.

   These statements

   (1) prove the faulting theory
   (2) summarize the passage
   (3) draw a conclusion from the passage
   (4) apply the faulting theory to another context
   (5) make an illogical argument

Items 7 to 9 refer to the following paragraphs.

Most of us think that childhood is a happy, carefree time of life. We don't pay much attention to children's complaints. We say, "He'll get over it," or "She's just pouting to get attention." We ignore the child to try to discourage the behavior. We scold or lecture. We offer meaningless platitudes like, "You'll feel better tomorrow," and "Everything will be all right." Sometimes we try to distract an unhappy child with candy or television. What we don't do is take our children seriously.

While many problems are minor and temporary, some are symptoms of something more serious. Children get depressed, just as adults do. The depressed child may appear sad, tired, and apathetic. Behavior problems, eating disorders, and difficulty with schoolwork are other symptoms. Instead of punishment or benign neglect, the child suffering from depression needs professional treatment.

7. The author appears to believe

   (1) children should not be scolded or ignored
   (2) adults should take children's problems seriously because they may be symptoms of depression
   (3) children's needs are more important than those of adults
   (4) adults should provide strong discipline for children
   (5) children take advantage of their parents' love

8. We might conclude from this passage that

   (1) ignoring, scolding, and lecturing are not helpful treatments for childhood depression
   (2) a growing number of children suffer from depression
   (3) children's behavior problems are always related to depression
   (4) adults do not care enough about children
   (5) most children suffer from depression at some time

9. According to the passage, depressed children

   (1) are spoiled
   (2) are victims of poor parenting
   (3) have serious behavior problems
   (4) need understanding and love most of all
   (5) may have several symptoms, including sadness, apathy, eating disorders, and school problems

Item 10 refers to the following passage.

A chemical equation uses formulas and symbols to show what happens during a chemical reaction. In chemical reactions, the substances you start out with are called the reactants. The substances that are formed are called the products. The general form of a chemical equation is: reactants $\longrightarrow$ products

10. Which of the following conclusions about the chemical equation shown below can be supported by the information provided?

$$C + O_2 \longrightarrow CO_2$$

   (1) C is a product of the chemical reaction.
   (2) CO_2 is present in the atmosphere.
   (3) CO_2 is formed when coal burns.
   (4) CO_2 is a product of the chemical reaction.
   (5) CO_2 is a reactant of the chemical reaction.

Reading Strategies ◆ Cumulative Review

Items 11 to 13 refer to the following passage.

A moving object has kinetic energy, which gives it the ability to do work. Work, in physics, has a precise definition: "the application of force through a distance." The force may be mechanical, as in lifting or pushing a heavy object. The force may also take less obvious forms, such as in a magnet lifting metal filings, or gravity pulling a thrown ball back to Earth. Thus, work includes all types of physical effort and changes.

An object may also contain potential energy. This is energy that is stored in the object, ready to be turned into other forms of energy, such as kinetic energy. A large rock teetering on the edge of a cliff has a great deal of potential energy. If it falls, the force of gravity will have turned the potential energy into kinetic energy. The kinetic energy will be turned into heat and sound energy at the moment of impact with the ground.

An example of another form of potential energy is found in the mainspring of a watch. When it is wound tightly, the spring has a great deal of potential energy. As it unwinds, the potential energy overcomes the friction that would otherwise stop the hands of the watch. As the hands move, the potential energy is turned into heat.

11. Which of these best summarizes this passage?

   (1) A moving object has kinetic energy, which gives it the ability to do work.
   (2) Kinetic and potential energy are found in all objects.
   (3) A moving object has kinetic energy, but an object may also have potential energy, which can be turned into another form of energy, such as kinetic energy.
   (4) Potential energy is stored in an object, ready to be turned into kinetic energy.
   (5) Potential energy can turn into kinetic energy and the reverse is also true.

12. In the passage above, the force of gravity

   (1) causes potential energy to turn into kinetic energy
   (2) causes potential energy to turn into heat energy
   (3) increases potential energy in the rock
   (4) has a great deal of potential energy
   (5) is the only force that releases potential energy

13. Another example of potential energy is

   (1) a wagon rolling downhill
   (2) a slingshot pulled back
   (3) heat energy
   (4) a bullet shot from a gun
   (5) sound energy

There are roughly three New Yorks. There is, first, the New York of the man or woman who was born here, who takes the city for granted and accepts its size and its
(5) turbulence as natural and inevitable. Second, there is the New York of the commuter—the city that is devoured by locusts each day and spat out each night. Third, there is the New York of the
(10) person who was born somewhere else and came to New York in quest of something. Of these three trembling cities, the greatest is the last—the city of final destination, the city that is a goal. It is this
(15) third city that accounts for New York's high-strung disposition, its poetical deportment, its dedication to the arts, and its incomparable achievements. Commuters give the city its tidal
(20) restlessness, natives give it solidity and continuity, but the settlers give it passion. And whether it is a farmer arriving from Italy to set up a small grocery store in a slum, or a young girl arriving from a small
(25) town in Mississippi to escape the indignity of being observed by her neighbors, or a boy arriving from the Corn Belt with a manuscript in his suitcase and a pain in his heart, it makes no difference: each embraces New York with the intense excitement of first love, each absorbs New York with the fresh eyes of an adventurer, each generates heat and light to dwarf the Consolidated Edison Company.

E.B. White, *Essays of E.B. White.*

14. Which of these best states the main idea?

(1) New York City has three parts.
(2) New York City is restless, solid, and passionate.
(3) In New York City, three different kinds of people form a whole.
(4) Of the three kinds of people in New York, the newcomers with a dream have brought passion to the city.
(5) There are three kinds of New Yorkers: those who were born there, those who commute daily, and those who moved to the city.

15. The expression "generates heat and light to dwarf Consolidated Edison Company" probably means that the people

(1) have a lot of energy and excitement
(2) arrive in such great numbers that they strain the city's ability to provide electricity
(3) in the third group are warm because they are active
(4) are highly intelligent
(5) work hard and acquire power

16. On the issue of restricting immigration, the author would probably

(1) support restricting the number of immigrants to the U.S.
(2) support and encourage immigration
(3) support restricting immigration from certain parts of the world
(4) encourage all immigrants to move to New York City
(5) encourage immigration of people with skills, education, or money

17. What does the author mean when he says "Of these three trembling cities, the greatest is the last" (lines 12–13)?

(1) He means that the last shall be first.
(2) He means that there are many shaky people in New York.
(3) He means that the New York of the commuter is the greatest of the three.
(4) He means that the New York of the native is the greatest of the three.
(5) He means that the New York of the settler is the greatest of the three.

Items 18 to 19 refer to the following poem.

A Song in the Front Yard

I've stayed in the front yard all my life.
I want a peek at the back
Where it's rough and untended and hungry weed grows.
A girl gets sick of a rose.

(5) I want to go to the back yard now
And maybe down the alley,
To where the charity children play.
I want a good time today.

They do some wonderful things.
(10) They have some wonderful fun.
My mother sneers, but I say it's fine
How they don't have to go in at quarter to nine.

My mother, she tells me that Johnnie Mae
Will grow up to be a bad woman.
(15) That George'll be taken to Jail, soon or late
(On account of last winter he sold our back gate).

But I say it's fine. Honest, I do.
And I'd like to be a bad woman, too,
And wear the black stockings of night-black lace
(20) And strut down the streets with paint on my face.

Gwendolyn Brooks, "A Song in the Front Yard."

18. About the speaker's age and personality, you can infer that she is

(1) a young girl who wants to play in the back yard and stay out late
(2) a teenager who feels rebellious and wants to experiment a little
(3) a teenager who is attracted to a bad crowd and is headed for trouble
(4) a little girl who wants to hang around with the big kids
(5) a nice girl who just wants to have fun

19. What does the speaker mean by "front yard" and "back yard"?

(1) She means what she says; no symbolism is intended.
(2) The front yard is childhood; the back yard is adulthood.
(3) Staying in the front yard means doing what is expected. The back yard represents the exciting, unfamiliar world where people dare to break the rules.
(4) Staying in the front yard means being a coward and a conformist. Playing in the back yard means being brave enough to fight the restrictions of society.
(5) The front yard represents law-abiding society. The back yard is the criminal element.

Answers are on page 774.

Unit 4 Social Studies

Colin Powell's diverse experiences aided him in his role as principal military adviser to the President of the United States.

Test 2 of the GED covers the social studies. Social studies is the study of social relationships and functions of society. Knowledge of the social studies will help you understand how society works and your role in society. Social studies has five main branches: history, geography, economics, political science, and behavioral science.

Geography is the study of the land and the people. Geography has three main focuses: the physical environment, the human population, and Earth and its people. The physical environment refers to the shape of the land, what grows on the land, Earth's natural resources, and the climate of the land. The human environment refers to the population, migration, and cultural distribution of people on Earth. Earth and its people refers to how people and the physical environment influence one another. The geography lessons in this unit will cover the lands and people of Earth's major regions as well as how we can protect the environment.

History records and analyzes society's past. A knowledge of America's past will help you understand the present and prepare for the future. The history lessons in this unit will cover key areas of American history: the colonization of America by Europeans, the American Revolution, the Civil War and Reconstruction, Industrialization, and the involvement of the U.S. with the world.

Economics is the study of society's use of goods and services. Economists look at how goods and services are produced, distributed, and consumed. Production refers to the labor, natural resources, and tools and equipment used in making goods. Distribution refers to the way wealth is divided among members of society. (It does not refer to the way goods are marketed, or sold.) Consumption refers to the end use of goods and services by people. The economics lessons in this unit cover general economic behavior, labor and the economy, and the government and economics.

Political science is the study of how society governs itself. Political science includes how government is organized, the theories behind the organization of government, and how political ideas are actually practiced. An understanding of political science will help you be more informed. It will help you understand your own political values and the politics of your city, state, and national governments. The political science lessons in this unit will cover the idea of government, the American political process, government money and the general welfare, and U.S. foreign policy.

Behavioral science studies how people act; it is divided into several branches. Anthropology studies how people act as members of cultures. Sociology studies how people act in smaller groups, such as family, work, religious, and social groups. Psychology is concerned with individuals rather than groups. The behavioral sciences can help us understand why people act the way they do. In the behavioral science lessons in this unit, you will learn about people as members of cultures and read about individual and group behavior.

Geography
Lesson 1

Earth's Regions I

The Far East region of the world includes the countries of Mongolia, China, Korea, Macao, Japan, and Taiwan. These countries have mostly been populated by the Mongoloid race. However, the aborigines of Japan, called the Ainu, are Caucasoid; about 15,000 of the Ainu still live on the northernmost island of Japan, Hokkaido. The climate in the Far East ranges from extremely cold winters in northeastern China and northern Japan and Korea to subtropical summers in southeastern China and Kyushu, the southernmost island of Japan. Much of Mongolia is desert, and Japan, a range of volcanic islands, has little farmable land. However, other countries of the Far East were primarily agricultural until 30 years ago. The chief crop in the area continues to be rice, a food staple in the region. Recently, great mineral resources have been discovered in North Korea and China, while Japan has developed into a major industrial power. A potential problem in this region is the rapid increase in population, which outstrips the increase in food production. Politically, China and North Korea are communist countries, while South Korea and Japan are classified as democracies. Even though these countries are grouped as a region, there are many differences among them.

ged Exercise Earth's Regions I

Choose the best answer to each item.

Items 1 and 2 refer to the previous information.

1. Which of these is a need that must be addressed by nations of the Far East?

   (1) developing more productive strains of rice
   (2) establishing medical training programs
   (3) establishing university exchange programs
   (4) designing better irrigation systems
   (5) implementing a rapid transport network

2. The passage best supports the conclusion that the Far East is

   (1) rapidly losing population
   (2) a major industrial power
   (3) politically united
   (4) diverse in climate, race, and geography
   (5) accepting many immigrants from other countries

Items 3 to 5 refer to the following paragraph.

Many countries are made up of groups of islands. One of these countries is Japan. The climate of Japan varies. Hokkaido, the northernmost island, gets very cold in winter. On the other hand, the southern island of Kyushu has subtropical summers. All of the islands were formed by volcanoes erupting from the bottom of the ocean. Japan has many mountains but not much land for farming or for building sprawling cities like Los Angeles.

3. According to the paragraph, the climate in Japan

   (1) is influenced by volcanic eruptions
   (2) is always very mild
   (3) varies from north to south
   (4) makes farming impossible
   (5) is very mountainous

4. Japan has many mountains because

   (1) it is made up of groups of islands
   (2) it has cold winters and hot summers
   (3) it was formed by volcanoes erupting from the ocean floor
   (4) it attracts many tourists
   (5) the mountains provide good areas for farming

5. Knowing that Japan has very little usable land, you can guess that sprawling in the last line means

   (1) taking up a lot of space
   (2) very businesslike
   (3) having a warm climate
   (4) mountainous
   (5) southern

Items 6 and 7 refer to the following information.

On a map, a river looks as though it follows a set line. But a river can change its course. A riverboat captain of one hundred years ago would note many changes in how the Mississippi River looks today. The water pushing against the mud and trees has changed all the bends and small islands in the river. Humans can also change the course of a river by building dams and digging channels. An extraordinary example of human change is the Chicago River. For economic reasons, engineers made the Chicago River run backward.

The changes in a river can affect the way people live. Before it was dammed in 1902, the Nile River in Egypt overflowed its banks every summer. The people who first settled near the Nile realized that the rich soil the river left behind as the water went down allowed them several harvests a year. These harvests provided extra food and eventually led to profitable trade.

6. What did the early Egyptians discover about the Nile River?

   (1) It made travel and trade easy.
   (2) They could make it run backward.
   (3) Its flooding created good farmland.
   (4) Harvesting could be done only in the summer.
   (5) Floods washed away rich soil.

7. According to the information, the course of a river can be changed by

   (1) people who travel on the river
   (2) farmers
   (3) Egyptians
   (4) the action of the water
   (5) nothing at all

Items 8 to 12 refer to the following map.

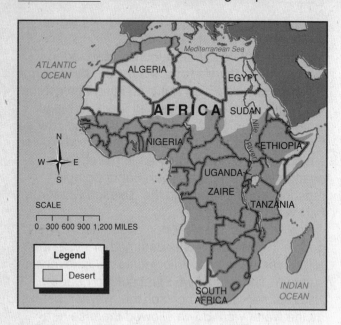

8. According to the map, the largest desert in Africa is in which part of the continent?

(1) north
(2) southeast
(3) southwest
(4) south
(5) central

9. According to the map, which of the following countries is entirely desert?

(1) Tanzania
(2) Ethiopia
(3) Egypt
(4) South Africa
(5) Zaire

10. About how many miles long from north to south is Ethiopia?

(1) 100
(2) 200
(3) 300
(4) 400
(5) 800

11. Which of the following countries has no seaport?

(1) Egypt
(2) Algeria
(3) Nigeria
(4) South Africa
(5) Uganda

12. You can conclude from the map that which of the following countries has the least rainfall?

(1) Egypt
(2) Uganda
(3) Nigeria
(4) Zaire
(5) Tanzania

Item 13 refers to the following table.

LIFE EXPECTANCY AT BIRTH, 1994		
Country	Male	Female
United States	73	79
Brazil	57	67
Sweden	75	81
Japan	76	82
Egypt	59	63

13. From the information in the table, you can conclude that

(1) the United States has the longest life expectancy in the world
(2) men in the United States live longer than men in Japan
(3) women tend to live longer than men in all the countries listed
(4) climate affects life expectancy
(5) Brazil has the longest life expectancy of countries in South America

Social Studies ◆ Geography

Items 14 and 15 refer to the following map.

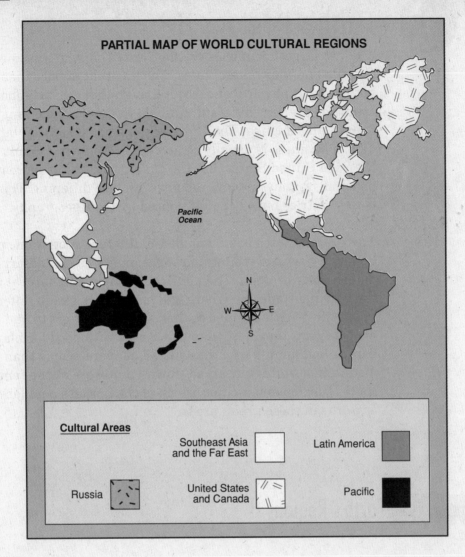

PARTIAL MAP OF WORLD CULTURAL REGIONS

Pacific
Ocean

Cultural Areas

Southeast Asia
and the Far East

Latin America

Russia

United States
and Canada

Pacific

14. From the map you can tell that

 (1) the Pacific area is north of Latin
 America
 (2) Southeast Asia and the Far East are
 not near Russia
 (3) Russia is south of the Pacific area
 (4) more than one cultural region can be on
 one continent
 (5) cultural regions are always separated
 from each other by water

15. The United States is often called the West.
If you traveled directly east across the
Pacific from Russia, which of the following
cultural regions would you most likely find?

 (1) Latin America
 (2) the Pacific area
 (3) the United States and Canada
 (4) the Far East and Southeast Asia
 (5) the North Pole

Answers are on page 775.

Lesson 2 — Earth's Regions II

The two largest countries on the North American continent are Canada and the United States. The line that divides them is a political border, not a physical one. Even though they are neighbors, the two countries are very different. Canada has two official languages: French and English. The United States has no official language, but official business is usually conducted in English. Canada is larger than the United States, but the United States has more people. Their political systems, money, and laws are also different. The histories of both countries have been influenced by their geography.

The United States has a number of different geographic regions. It is divided by several mountain ranges, major rivers, desert areas, flat plains, and farmland. The physical features and natural resources of the land have affected where and how people live in different regions. People first settled in places that were easy to get to and that could provide what they needed to live. Areas with good farmland and fishing and mining resources attracted more people than did mountainous or desert areas. Towns that were at the center of trade routes became major cities. Much of the nation's population now lives or works in these urban areas.

ged Exercise Earth's Regions II

Choose the best answer to each item. Items 1 to 3 refer to the previous information.

1. Which best summarizes the first paragraph?

    (1) The United States and Canada are separated by a political border.
    (2) There are two large countries in North America.
    (3) History can be influenced by geography.
    (4) The United States and Canada are neighboring countries, but they are not completely alike.
    (5) Some people in Canada speak French.

2. If you moved to the desert, which of the following would you expect to find?

    (1) good fishing
    (2) good farmland
    (3) large cities
    (4) mountains
    (5) very few towns

3. Major cities were settled because

    (1) the landscape was beautiful
    (2) they had mountains
    (3) they were on trade routes
    (4) they had mining resources
    (5) they had good farmland

Items 4 to 6 refer to the following map.

Military Presence in Bosnia-Herzegovina in 1995

4. According to the map, Serb forces were in which areas?

   (1) Slovenia and Croatia
   (2) Croatia and Serbia
   (3) Bosnia-Herzegovina and Yugoslavia
   (4) Bosnia-Herzegovina and Bihac
   (5) Bosnia-Herzegovina and Croatia

5. Zagreb is approximately how many miles away from Sarajevo?

   (1) 30 miles
   (2) 130 miles
   (3) 180 miles
   (4) 210 miles
   (5) 300 miles

6. By looking at this map, you can conclude that in 1995

   (1) the United Nations (U.N.) was preparing to attack Yugoslavia
   (2) Serb forces controlled the government in Bosnia-Herzegovina
   (3) Hungary planned to invade Croatia
   (4) Bosnia-Herzegovina was occupied by various armies
   (5) Serb and Croat forces were allies

Items 7 and 8 refer to the following paragraphs.

Millions of years ago, part of North America was covered by glaciers. The movement of these glaciers helped to shape the geography of this area. A glacier is a snowfield of compressed ice. When a glacier reaches a depth of 100 feet, it becomes too heavy to stay in place. It moves down the slope it is on. As the glacier moves, it tears away masses of rock and land. Sometimes it leaves behind a lake or series of lakes. Most often, a glacier leaves behind a valley.

New England and New York were once flat land covered by glaciers. The movement of the ice carved deep valleys between what are now the Adirondack Mountains, the Green Mountains, and the White Mountains. Now this area has many valleys surrounded by mountains.

7. Which best summarizes the second paragraph?

   (1) New England's and New York's geography was affected by glaciers.
   (2) Mountains are made by glaciers.
   (3) New England is a flat area.
   (4) New York is covered by ice.
   (5) New England is a scenic region.

8. Which is the main idea of the paragraphs?

   (1) Our land is always changing.
   (2) New York has many lakes.
   (3) Glaciers have helped to shape the American landscape.
   (4) Glaciers are made of ice.
   (5) Once glaciers start moving, they cannot be stopped.

Answers are on page 776.

Lesson

3

Protecting the Environment

The word **ecology** is one that most people used to hear only in a science or social studies class. Today even many children have some idea of what it means. Ecology refers to the balance between living things and the environment.

As more countries became industrialized, people took more and more resources from the land. Labor-saving inventions required energy to run them. The overall standard of living rose, and people began to see comfortable lives as a basic right. But as the land was mined and stripped of its forests and minerals, and as water was rerouted to support growing cities, people began to realize an important fact. Earth could not renew its resources as quickly as they were being used. Some of the products that made life better for humans were actually poisoning plant and animal life. Some of the things that provided good living were also causing health problems for people.

As studies were made about these discoveries, a major question came up: Which is more important, a healthy economy or a healthy environment? This question is not easy to answer. People want to have jobs and to be able to take advantage of modern conveniences. But there is a cost for both. We now need to be aware of environmental problems and search for solutions that can restore the balance between the land and the people who live on it.

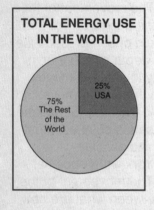

TOTAL ENERGY USE IN THE WORLD

25% USA

75% The Rest of the World

ged **Exercise** Protecting the Environment

Choose the <u>best answer</u> to each item. <u>Items 1 to 5</u> refer to the previous information.

1. You can conclude from the information that the world's ecology

   (1) is still in balance
   (2) can take care of itself
   (3) is out of balance
   (4) makes everyone comfortable
   (5) is not an important issue

   Tip **When drawing a conclusion, make sure that the facts clearly support the conclusion and that the conclusion makes sense.**

2. Which can be concluded from the information?

   (1) It will be easy to solve Earth's environmental problems.
   (2) Natural resources cannot be taken for granted.
   (3) America is a land of plenty.
   (4) No one understands much about ecology.
   (5) Industry has had little effect on the environment.

Social Studies ◆ Geography

3. You can learn from the information that

    (1) things that make people comfortable can also cause problems
    (2) mining does not hurt the land
    (3) Earth renews its resources quickly
    (4) a healthy economy is more important than a healthy environment
    (5) a healthy environment is more important than a healthy economy

4. Which is an example of people giving something back to the land?

    (1) rerouting a river
    (2) panning for gold
    (3) pulling weeds
    (4) using more electricity
    (5) planting trees

5. You can conclude from the information that Americans probably

    (1) use a lot of labor-saving devices
    (2) are not concerned about ecology
    (3) use very little energy
    (4) have well-educated children
    (5) use too much water

Items 6 and 7 refer to the following graph.

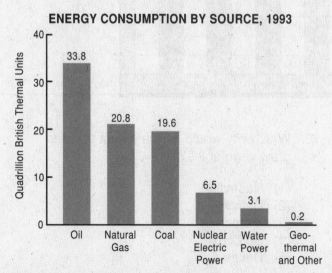

ENERGY CONSUMPTION BY SOURCE, 1993

(Source: Energy Information Administration, *Annual Energy Review*, 1993.)

6. According to the graph, which source of energy was used the most?

    (1) oil
    (2) natural gas
    (3) nuclear electric power
    (4) water power
    (5) geothermal and other power

7. According to the graph, 19.6 quadrillion British Thermal Units of energy consumed in 1993 came from

    (1) natural gas
    (2) coal
    (3) nuclear electric power
    (4) water power
    (5) geothermal and other power

Item 8 refers to the following paragraph.

   Large parts of Earth are very different now from the way they used to be. Many of the changes, like climate changes, have natural causes. Other changes are caused by people. For example, in the 1800s, much of the eastern United States was farmland. Today, much of it is urban or forested.

8. What is the main idea of the paragraph?

    (1) The United States was mainly farmland in the 1800s.
    (2) Cities now stand where farms used to be.
    (3) Changes in Earth are caused by nature and by people.
    (4) Although Earth has changed in the past, it no longer does so.
    (5) Much of the eastern United States is forested or urban today.

Items 9 and 10 refer to the following pie chart.

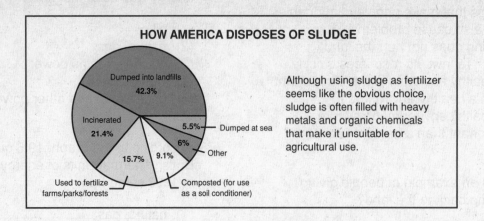

9. From the chart, you can conclude that

   (1) there is no one best way to dispose of sludge
   (2) sludge makes an excellent fertilizer
   (3) the landfills have a lot of room
   (4) sludge is messy
   (5) sludge is easy to get rid of

10. According to the chart, most of America's sludge

    (1) is burned
    (2) finds its way into the land
    (3) is dumped at sea
    (4) becomes compost
    (5) is used as fertilizer

Items 11 and 12 refer to the following bar graph.

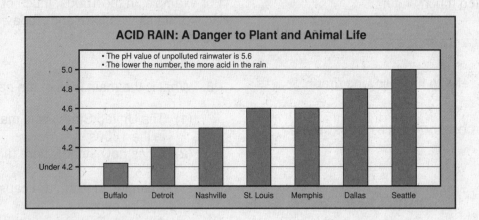

11. From the graph, rainwater acidity

    (1) is the same in all large cities
    (2) cannot be measured
    (3) is a serious problem in Texas
    (4) changes from place to place
    (5) is caused by factories

12. Which city would be the safest place to grow vegetables?

    (1) Nashville
    (2) Detroit
    (3) Memphis
    (4) St. Louis
    (5) Dallas

Item 13 refers to the following passage.

Fossil fuels are underground deposits of coal, oil, and natural gas. They are the world's main source of energy. The world's increasing demand for energy has begun to exhaust the fossil fuels.

In 1978, fossil fuels supplied 90 percent of the world's energy. Experts predict that by the year 2000, fossil fuels will supply only 75 percent of the world's growing energy needs. The use of coal will have increased by then. By 2000, coal is expected to provide 24 percent of the energy used.

13. It is predicted that by the year 2000

    (1) coal will supply all of the world's energy
    (2) there will be no more oil reserves
    (3) natural gas reserves will be gone
    (4) fossil fuels will produce a lower percentage of the world's energy
    (5) oil prices will have increased

Items 14 and 15 refer to the following cartoon.

"Have you given any thought to what you'll do with your Saturdays when the world's fossil fuels are used up?"

Drawing by Koren; © 1970 The New Yorker Magazine, Inc.

14. This cartoon is commenting on

    (1) American vs. foreign cars
    (2) the limited supply of fossil fuels
    (3) do-it-yourself car wash
    (4) the number of miles per gallon the car gets
    (5) recreational activities on weekends

15. From the cartoon you can conclude that

    (1) people take fossil fuels for granted
    (2) it's a good idea to wash the car once a week
    (3) fossil fuels will run out soon
    (4) new forms of transportation will be invented
    (5) people will walk more in the future

Answers are on page 777.

Lesson 3 ◆ Protecting the Environment

Choose the <u>best answer</u> to each item.

<u>Items 1 to 4</u> are based on the following paragraph.

   Climates on Earth are determined by three things: latitude, elevation, and closeness to a large body of water. Latitude is the distance of a place from the equator. The heat of the sun is strongest at the equator and weakest at the poles. Elevation affects climate because the higher an area is, the cooler the temperature will be. Closeness to water affects the climate because the winds are warmed or cooled by the water's temperature. In general, coastal areas have the least extreme temperatures.

1. Hot tropical climates would <u>most likely</u> be found

   (1) in mountainous regions
   (2) near the North and South poles
   (3) close to the equator
   (4) on sea coasts
   (5) halfway between the equator and the poles

2. Which <u>best</u> summarizes the paragraph?

   (1) Latitude least affects climate.
   (2) The climate at the poles is similar to the climate at the equator.
   (3) Climates are similar coast to coast.
   (4) Islands have the best climates.
   (5) Several factors affect climate.

3. Based on the paragraph, the latitude of an area

   (1) tells how high the land is above sea level
   (2) determines how hot the sun is there
   (3) influences the amount of rainfall
   (4) makes the temperature even
   (5) shows how close the land is to water

4. Elevation affects climate by making the weather

   (1) wetter
   (2) cooler
   (3) hotter
   (4) swampy
   (5) drier

<u>Item 5</u> refers to the following graph.

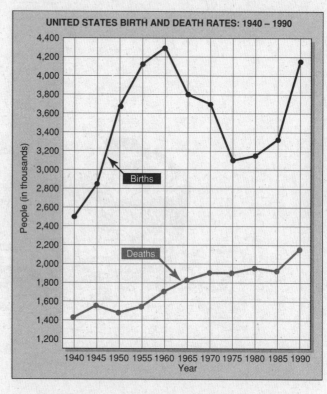

UNITED STATES BIRTH AND DEATH RATES: 1940 – 1990

5. Which can be concluded from the graph?

   (1) The death rate is lower than the birthrate.
   (2) The birth and death rate are about the same.
   (3) The death rate is higher than the birthrate.
   (4) The birth and death rates are both decreasing.
   (5) The birthrate is decreasing while the death rate is increasing.

Items 6 to 8 refer to the following paragraph.

In 1994 the world's population reached 5.6 billion people. By the year 2020, the population is expected to rise to 7.9 billion. Most of the population increase in the next 25 years will take place in the developing countries. In fact, of the 2.3 billion people added to the population, 9 out of 10 will be from developing regions.

6. By the year 2020, the world's population is expected to increase to

   (1) 2.3 billion
   (2) 5.6 billion
   (3) 7.9 billion
   (4) 10.2 billion
   (5) 13.5 billion

7. From the paragraph, you can conclude that

   (1) more people will live in Asia than in any other continent
   (2) most of the people on Earth will be children in 2020
   (3) more people are being born than are dying
   (4) the food supply will not be able to feed the growing population
   (5) most people will live in cities by the year 2020

8. Which of the following is the main idea of the paragraph?

   (1) Developing nations are growing rapidly.
   (2) The world's population is increasing.
   (3) In 1994 the world's population was 5.6 billion people.
   (4) In 2045 the world's population will be 10.2 billion people.
   (5) World population growth is a problem.

Tip Questions using *best* or *most likely* often signal that other options may appear correct or partially correct. You must choose the one that is best supported by the information.

Item 9 refers to the following cartoon.

9. Which of the following best describes what is happening in the cartoon?

   (1) A fisherman has caught the largest fish on record.
   (2) A fish is being prepared for processing.
   (3) A fish is hanging over the deck of a boat.
   (4) A fisherman has caught a fish that has eaten people's trash.
   (5) A fish was used to help clean up the ocean.

Answers are on page 778.

History Lesson 4

The Colonization of America

By the 1400s, Europe had started to trade with China and India for goods such as spices, silks, and gems. Italy dominated this trade. Other countries such as Spain and Portugal wanted to get a share of the wealth, so they sought new routes to the Orient. Christopher Columbus reasoned that since the world is round, he could get to the East by sailing west. He convinced Queen Isabella of Spain to finance this voyage. On October 12, 1492, Columbus and his crew sighted land. They naturally assumed they had reached India. They became sure of this when they were given gold by the natives of the land, whom the explorers called "Indians."

Further exploration convinced Spain and the other European nations that Columbus had in fact reached a new land. They decided they could benefit by colonizing what they came to call the New World. Colonization happens when a country sends people to live in a new area and keeps political and economic control over the area and the people.

Spain had a head start on the colonization of the Americas. Many Spanish settlements were soon located in Central America, the islands of the Caribbean, and North and South America. In North America, they settled in the area we know as the states of Florida, New Mexico, Arizona, Texas, and California. The Spaniards had two specific motives for colonizing the New World. They wanted to gain wealth by finding gold and by planting crops that could not be grown in Europe. They also wanted to introduce Christianity to the Native Americans. As one explorer said, "We came here to serve God and also to get rich."

Colonization by Spain and other European countries brought tragic events to Native Americans. The Spanish and Portuguese sometimes forced Native Americans into near slavery. Colonists also took land from the Native Americans. In addition, many Native Americans died from diseases carried by the Europeans.

The Portuguese colonized the area of South America that is now Brazil. There they set up large plantations to grow sugar, a valuable crop.

The French colonized parts of North America in what is now eastern Canada and along the Mississippi River as far south as New Orleans. They traded with the Native Americans for furs that sold for high prices in Europe.

The Dutch settled mainly in what is now New York and New Jersey because of the profit that could come from the fur trade. Both the Dutch and the French eventually lost their North American colonies to England.

Like Spain, England sent many colonists to America. The English settled in what is now Canada and the eastern United States. The English had different motives from the Spanish. The Spaniards wanted to convert the Native Americans, but the English were more concerned simply with having the freedom to practice their own religion. Also, their economy depended on activities such as farming because the English had settled in an area without gold.

ged Exercise The Colonization of America

Choose the best answer to each item. Items 1 to 5 refer to the previous information.

1. A study of death rates among Native Americans following the arrival of Europeans would most likely show a steep rise in which of the following causes of death?

   (1) poison
   (2) drowning
   (3) smallpox and influenza
   (4) starvation
   (5) accidents and natural disasters

2. Columbus's motive for traveling to the New World was to

   (1) convert "heathens" to Christianity
   (2) take some of the trade with the Orient away from Italy
   (3) find new sources of gold
   (4) obtain scientific proof that the world is round
   (5) discover unknown lands

3. The first Europeans to have extensive settlements in the New World were the

   (1) Dutch
   (2) English
   (3) French
   (4) Portuguese
   (5) Spanish

4. World history has many examples of colonization. One example is discussed in the passage. Which of the following would be another example?

   (1) The American Revolution, which began in 1776, ended England's control over its American colonies and began a new nation.
   (2) During the twentieth century, people from many different countries have settled in the United States.
   (3) In 1861, Southern states seceded from, or left, the United States.
   (4) Around 1800, England claimed the continent of Australia and sent settlers there.
   (5) During World War II, the United States sent troops to Italy and France in order to fight the Germans.

5. What is the main idea of the passage?

   (1) Columbus proved that Earth is round.
   (2) Spain had settlements in all parts of the Americas.
   (3) Many European countries colonized parts of the Americas.
   (4) Spreading Christianity was the primary reason for colonizing the Americas.
   (5) Native Americans were mistreated by the European settlers.

Items 6 and 7 refer to the following paragraphs.

The Pilgrims were persecuted in England because their beliefs differed from the teachings of the Church of England. To escape this situation, the Pilgrims decided to settle in the New World. Before their ship, the *Mayflower,* reached Massachusetts, the Pilgrims wrote and signed an agreement, the Mayflower Compact. In part, the compact reads as follows:

"We . . . the loyal subjects of our dread and sovereign Lord King James . . . having undertaken, for the glory of God, and advancements of the Christian faith and honour of our king and country, a voyage to plant the first colony in the Northern parts of Virginia, do . . . solemnly and mutually covenant and combine ourselves together into a civil body politic for our better ordering, and preservation of our ends, and by this virtue to enact, constitute and frame such just and equal laws, ordinances, acts, constitutions and offices, from time to time, as shall be thought convenient for the general good of the Colony to which we promise all due submission and obedience."

6. Based on the quotation, the Mayflower Compact was probably written to

   (1) develop a plan for dealing with the Native Americans
   (2) establish religious rules
   (3) express rebellion against the king of England
   (4) divide the land among the colonists
   (5) establish plans for governing the new colony

7. The Mayflower Compact was an important influence in American history. Based on the quotation, how was the Mayflower Compact applied?

   (1) It helped establish the right to bear arms.
   (2) It provided a basis for treaties with Native Americans.
   (3) It helped establish the principles of self-government.
   (4) It set terms for trade with foreign countries.
   (5) It was used to argue against slavery.

Items 8 and 9 refer to the following paragraph.

In the Massachusetts Bay Colony, the government and the church were closely related. To participate in government, men had to be members of the church. People who disagreed with either the government or the church were often banished. When Roger Williams was banished to England, he escaped and founded Rhode Island, where religious freedom was granted to all.

8. In this paragraph, the word "banished" means

   (1) imprisoned
   (2) confined to the home
   (3) sent away
   (4) beaten
   (5) fined

9. From the paragraph, you can conclude that Massachusetts Bay women were not allowed to

   (1) live in Massachusetts
   (2) participate in government
   (3) be banished
   (4) worship in the church
   (5) marry other colonists

By the 1730s, there were 13 colonies in what is now the United States. There were certain differences among these colonies. But there were also many things that united them all.

The colonies differed in their geography and in the way people earned their living. There were three main groups of colonies. The New England colonies included New Hampshire, Massachusetts (including Maine), Rhode Island, and Connecticut. The middle colonies were New York, New Jersey, Pennsylvania, and Delaware. Maryland, Virginia, North and South Carolina, and Georgia formed the southern colonies. The New England colonies had cold winters and poor soil. They did, however, have good harbors. The middle colonies had soil that was good for growing grains such as wheat. The southern colonies had warm weather and very rich soil. These conditions made it possible to raise crops grown on large farms, such as tobacco, cotton, and indigo, a dye.

The colonies were united by their British heritage. One important part of this heritage was the belief in democratic ideals such as self-government. This democratic British heritage indirectly led the colonists to rebel against England because the colonies were united by another factor. They increasingly saw themselves as Americans, separated from the British by their experience in the New World.

10. Which of the following features did the 13 colonies have in common?

    (1) good farmland
    (2) cold weather
    (3) excellent horses
    (4) British heritage
    (5) similar geography

Tip Words such as *in common*, *in general*, and *overall* signal that you are being asked to generalize.

11. Which of the following can be concluded from the paragraphs?

    (1) People in the middle colonies suffered economic hardships.
    (2) Plantations, or large farms, were most common in the southern colonies.
    (3) The southern colonies had trouble attracting settlers.
    (4) The three groups of colonies were often at war with one another.
    (5) Settlers in New England usually came from countries other than Britain.

12. Based on the paragraphs, why did the colonists rebel against Britain?

    (1) They came to reject their British heritage.
    (2) The colonists came to feel they should be governed only from America.
    (3) They were influenced by other groups in the New World.
    (4) The colonists came to believe in freedom of religion.
    (5) They came to feel that the British king was not ruling them with a strong enough hand.

13. In which of the following colonies was farming least likely to be successful?

    (1) North Carolina
    (2) Virginia
    (3) New Jersey
    (4) New York
    (5) Connecticut

14. On which of the following activities did the New England colonies most likely base their economy?

    (1) growing wheat
    (2) raising cattle
    (3) growing tobacco
    (4) shipbuilding
    (5) mining

Answers are on page 778.

Lesson 5 The American Revolution

As Britain's colonial empire in America grew, the English government began to have trouble controlling the settlers across the ocean. The king of England continued to treat these distant people as if they still lived in England.

Life in America required the colonists to adjust to many new challenges. The customs and traditions they brought from England were not always suited to the harsh climate and nonagricultural land of New England. A new way of life had to be developed in order to survive. Because the goods that were easily available in England could be bought only at high prices with long waits for delivery, what had been common often became a luxury. The settlers became more and more used to producing the necessities by themselves. American colonists came to be self-reliant.

When King George III passed laws such as the Stamp Act and the Townsend Act, which imposed heavy taxes, the colonists refused to obey the laws. At first, the Americans hoped to force England to give in to their demands, but when the Second Continental Congress met in 1775, the king rejected their petitions and called them rebels. Eventually the colonists decided to fight, not for their rights as Englishmen, but for complete freedom from England. The discontent was no longer limited to the issue of taxes. On July 4, 1776, representatives from all the colonies signed the Declaration of Independence. This document, written mainly by Thomas Jefferson, declared the colonies to be an independent nation. It also set out the basic principles of democratic government. The foundation of many American laws can be found in the beliefs that "All men are created equal" and that people have "certain unalienable rights" including "life, liberty, and the pursuit of happiness."

The American Revolution took seven hard years to win. It is important to remember that this small group of colonists was fighting the most powerful country in the world. Also, most Americans had close relatives in England and had to take sides against them. It took brave and determined people to continue the long war. It also took help from France. The French contributed money and soldiers, and perhaps more importantly, ships.

After Cornwallis surrendered to Washington following the battle at Yorktown, the British House of Commons voted for ending the war. Peace negotiations took over a year, but the Treaty of Paris was finally signed in September 1783. The thirteen American states were recognized as an independent nation.

Choose the best answer to each item. Items 1 to 4 refer to the previous information.

1. It can be inferred from the passage that the prices of some common goods were high because

   (1) the colonists had not developed good trading skills
   (2) goods had to be imported all the way from England
   (3) pirates were attacking many of the trade routes
   (4) the colonists would accept only the best
   (5) these goods were really luxury items

2. It can be inferred from the passage that the colonists' first reaction to King George III's taxes was to

   (1) declare their freedom from England
   (2) demand their rights as English subjects
   (3) agree to pay the taxes
   (4) ask for help from France
   (5) form a democratic government

3. According to the information, King George III

   (1) was very old
   (2) passed fair laws
   (3) understood the colonists' problems
   (4) did not understand the attitude in the colonies
   (5) was a cruel and uncaring man

   Tip **Making correct inferences depends on recognizing unstated ideas. Look for what an author implies, rather than what is directly stated.**

4. It can be concluded from the information that the colonists might not have won the war if

   (1) their British relatives had not supported them
   (2) Britain had had a better navy
   (3) Jefferson had not been such a good writer
   (4) they had listened to the French adviser
   (5) they had not received help from France

Items 5 and 6 refer to the following information.

During the American Revolution, the colonists were divided. Some were patriots and many, called loyalists, were loyal to the British crown. It is estimated that less than half the colonists were patriots who helped the American war effort.

5. The above information implies that the British

   (1) were helped by some American colonists
   (2) hired Hessian soldiers to fight the Americans
   (3) were defeated by loyalists
   (4) did not tax the loyalists before the war
   (5) punished any loyalists they captured

6. You can infer from the information that

   (1) all colonists supported the British
   (2) all colonists supported the patriots
   (3) the American army had difficulty finding soldiers
   (4) the colonists were in agreement
   (5) the loyalists had the right attitude

Answers are on page 779.

Lesson 6

The Civil War and Reconstruction

The United States was almost split in two because of disagreements about issues important to the North and the South. When the Civil War was over, the task of rebuilding the nation was very difficult.

By the mid-1800s, economic tensions between the North and the South had come to the breaking point. The Southern states relied mainly on agriculture for their financial stability, and the Northern states were mainly industrial. Because of this, the North had more actual wealth and was better able to use its natural resources. These primary economic differences also had moral and emotional overtones.

The institution of **slavery** had been an issue for many years. Even the admission of states to the Union had been restricted to maintain a balance between slaveholding and free states. Although many Southerners did not own slaves, the large plantations depended on this inexpensive labor to produce their crops. Slaveholders did not want to see their investments go down the drain with the outlawing of slavery. They were finding themselves having to argue with **abolitionists,** people who wanted to do away with slavery throughout the nation. Northern abolitionists had even set up "underground railroads," safe houses across the country for runaway slaves.

The slavery question became an issue in the presidential election of 1860. The new Republican party tended to be antislavery, while the Democratic party was supported by Southern slave states and more moderate Northerners. Although newly elected Republican Abraham Lincoln did not support slavery, he did agree to guarantee slavery in the states where it already existed. But the Southern states felt that Lincoln would do little else to support them.

By February 1861, six Southern states had seceded from the Union and founded the **Confederate States of America,** with Jefferson Davis as the president. War began when the Confederate government demanded the surrender of Union soldiers at Fort Sumter, South Carolina. The hastily organized Southern forces fired on the fort before supply ships sent by President Lincoln could reach it. Five more Southern states immediately left the Union. During the next four bloody years, friends and families had to choose which side of the divided nation they would support.

Reconstruction is the term for the years from 1865 to 1877. After the Southern states had been brought back into the Union, the South needed help rebuilding cities, farms, railroads, and schools that had been destroyed during the War Between the States. Southerners also needed to learn how to live without slavery, and newly freed blacks needed help in finding their roles in the new society.

Social Studies ◆ History

Choose the <u>best answer</u> to each item. <u>Items 1 to 8</u> refer to the previous information.

1. Following Lincoln's presidential election, six Southern states seceded from the Union. This event was based on their belief that

   (1) the Constitution became invalid
   (2) Lincoln would not represent their interests
   (3) Jefferson Davis was a Southerner
   (4) the South was not part of the Union
   (5) Southern states had to rebel

2. Which is a valid opinion based on the information?

   (1) The South was right to secede.
   (2) Abolitionists should not have helped runaway slaves.
   (3) Slaveholders were right to protect their investments.
   (4) The South probably resented the North even after the war.
   (5) Lincoln should have supported the South.

3. It can be concluded from the information that slavery was

   (1) becoming unpopular in the South
   (2) needed to keep landowners wealthy
   (3) supported by abolitionists
   (4) the only cause of the Civil War
   (5) morally wrong

4. Abolitionists were people who wanted to abolish

   (1) the U.S. Constitution
   (2) the Democratic party
   (3) the Republican party
   (4) slavery
   (5) Reconstruction

5. You can infer that the last five Southern states left the Union because

   (1) they felt they had to support the Confederacy after the Fort Sumter incident
   (2) Lincoln made them feel unwelcome
   (3) too many of their slaves were running away
   (4) they wanted to do away with slavery
   (5) they were afraid of the abolitionists

6. The information is mainly about

   (1) the evils of slavery
   (2) economic recovery
   (3) the rebuilding of the nation
   (4) Lincoln's position on secession
   (5) what led to the Civil War

7. The situation that many families of both the North and the South had to face when the war began is <u>most similar</u> to that of the families of American soldiers in

   (1) the Vietnam War
   (2) today's Army
   (3) the American Revolution
   (4) the French and Indian War
   (5) the Korean War

8. "Reconstruction" refers to

   (1) the plantation system of agriculture
   (2) people who were against slavery
   (3) the system of safe houses for runaway slaves
   (4) the Republican party of 1860
   (5) the period after the Civil War

Answers are on page 779.

Lesson 7 Industrial America

The term Industrial Revolution is often used to describe the shift in the national economy from farming to manufacturing. Although the word <u>revolution</u> suggests a sudden change, the growth of industrial America was gradual and happened in two main segments.

The Industrial Revolution began in Great Britain in the 1700s and had moved to America by the early 1800s. Steam engines and machines began to replace hand labor. People began to use products made in factories instead of ones made at home. Two important ideas for speeding the production process came from a young schoolteacher named Eli Whitney. In addition to inventing the cotton gin, which separated cotton fiber from the seeds, he came up with the related ideas of mass production and interchangeable parts. Each special part of an item could be made by a machine instead of by hand. All parts made by that machine would be the same, so a worker could produce many identical items. The different parts could be fitted together easily by people on an assembly line, thereby speeding up production. This process made America the world's leading manufacturer of goods.

Other American inventors had made important contributions to industry before the Civil War. John Deere introduced the steel plow. Charles Goodyear had discovered how to treat rubber so that it hardened enough to hold its shape. Cyrus McCormick invented a reaper that could do the work of many people. Elias Howe invented a sewing machine that could handle heavy material such as sailcloth and leather. Walter Hunt gave us the paper collar, the tricycle, and the safety pin. All these inventions helped America grow.

After the Civil War, manufacturing increased again, and the number of inventions soared. A form of energy called electricity was discovered. The American way of life began to change. In the early 1800s, most Americans had lived on farms with no electricity, no running water, no furnaces, and only the transportation available from the horse and buggy. By 1900, many people had moved to the cities where they could get factory jobs. Many homes now had electric lighting, indoor plumbing, and good heating. Trains ran frequently, and some people even had automobiles. The telegraph and telephone made long-distance communication easy.

Because most individuals did not have enough money to build factories on their own, they formed companies. Corporations formed by groups could raise large sums of money and reduce individual financial risk. To raise money, the corporations sold shares of stock to stockholders who would get dividends if the companies made a profit.

With the new machines and power sources, the developing companies could take advantage of the natural resources found all over America. America was on its way to becoming a wealthy nation.

Choose the best answer to each item. Items 1 to 6 refer to the previous information.

1. What effect did machines have on manufacturing?

   (1) Production was speeded up.
   (2) Production was slowed down.
   (3) Goods were more easily transported.
   (4) Hand labor became more costly.
   (5) Products had to be made individually.

2. Which of the following is an advantage of mass production?

   (1) Each item produced is unique.
   (2) The cost of production goes up.
   (3) Parts are identical and interchangeable.
   (4) Things are made by hand.
   (5) Each item is custom-made.

3. A heavy-duty sewing machine would make production of which of the following easier?

   (1) lace
   (2) paper goods
   (3) needles
   (4) shoes
   (5) blouses

4. What is the main idea of the third paragraph?

   (1) The Industrial Revolution started in England before the Civil War.
   (2) There were many important American inventions before the Civil War.
   (3) Charles Goodyear discovered a way to make rubber hard.
   (4) Walter Hunt invented many items.
   (5) Cyrus McCormick invented the reaper.

5. The inventions of the nineteenth century resulted in

   (1) the Civil War
   (2) a more comfortable way of life
   (3) a decrease in manufacturing
   (4) the safety pin
   (5) products of poor quality

6. The main reason the people formed corporations was to

   (1) protect their rights
   (2) make bigger profits
   (3) cheat shareholders
   (4) have enough capital
   (5) take greater risks

Item 7 is based on the following table.

AVERAGE ANNUAL EARNINGS FOR SELECTED OCCUPATIONS—1890	
Farm laborers	$233
Public school teachers	256
Bituminous coal miners	406
Manufacturing employees	439
Street railway employees	557
Steam railroad employees	560
Gas & electricity workers	687
Ministers	794
Clerical workers in manufacturing & steam RR	848
Postal employees	878

7. Based on the table, a probable reason for people to move from the country to the city in 1890 was that

   (1) railroads did not go out into the country
   (2) rural life was not interesting
   (3) city jobs paid much better wages
   (4) schoolteachers were needed in the city
   (5) many government jobs were available

Answers are on page 780.

Lesson 8

The United States and the World

By the end of the nineteenth century, the United States extended from the Atlantic to the Pacific coasts. The Alaskan and Hawaiian territories had come under U.S. jurisdiction, along with Cuba, Puerto Rico, Guam, and the Philippine Islands. The country had finally stopped growing physically and was ready to take an active role in world affairs.

The first involvement with world politics occurred in 1898, when Cubans rebelled against Spain and requested help from the United States. The assistance turned into a 115-day war after an American ship, the *Maine,* blew up in Havana harbor.

Despite this brief encounter with another nation, many Americans wanted to follow George Washington's advice to stay out of foreign countries' affairs. But when World War I began in 1914, the United States found that remaining neutral was not easy. At first, involvement was only on the level of trade. American goods were sold to the European Allies who did not have time for manufacturing. Eventually, Americans came to believe in the Allied cause. England, France, Russia, and later Italy claimed they were fighting for democracy. After three American ships were sunk in one day by the German and Austria-Hungary alliance, the United States finally joined the fight.

In 1939, Germany attacked Poland. France and Great Britain, having promised to support Poland, declared war on Germany, and World War II had begun. Again the United States wanted to stay out of European affairs. But many Americans objected to what the Axis dictators were trying to do. While Americans debated the question, on December 7, 1941, Japan attacked Pearl Harbor, Hawaii. The next day America declared war.

The peace that came in 1945 did not really settle world affairs. The Soviet Union went back on its promises to let neighboring countries be self-governing. China and many countries in Eastern Europe were dominated by communism, while Western Europe and the United States still vigorously supported democracy. The Communists and the Free World settled into a long Cold War. Communists wanted other countries to join them, and the Free World wanted to spread democratic principles.

The now economically powerful United States found itself the most influential nation in the world. Americans supported struggling countries with food, money, and people. The Cold War warmed up a bit when democratic forces in Korea and Vietnam fought against the Communist rulers. The United States supported the battle against the governments backed by the former USSR and China.

Maintaining world power is a difficult and costly process. In recent years, all of the major political powers have encountered internal upheavals. Although the United States has been paying increased attention to its own problems, it still plays an important role in world affairs.

Choose the <u>best answer</u> to each item. <u>Items 1 to 7</u> refer to the previous information.

1. What is the main idea of the first paragraph?

    (1) The United States extended all the way to the West Coast.
    (2) Alaska and Hawaii were territories of the United States in 1900.
    (3) Puerto Rico, Guam, Cuba, and the Philippines came under the jurisdiction of the United States.
    (4) The United States was involved in several wars.
    (5) By the time the United States stopped expanding, it was ready to take part in world affairs.

2. Which <u>best</u> supports the conclusion that staying out of World War I was not easy for the United States?

    (1) The encounter with Spain had been brief.
    (2) George Washington had encouraged remaining neutral.
    (3) Americans believed in fighting for democracy.
    (4) The Allies had trouble with manufacturing during the war.
    (5) Germany and Austria-Hungary were allies.

3. The details about the divisions between communism and democracy support the conclusion that

    (1) the Free World is right
    (2) the Cold War lasted a long time
    (3) Communists are right
    (4) peace came in 1945
    (5) world affairs were not settled by the war

Tip **Use key words to help you answer the questions on the GED. For example, the words *cause* and *reason* in questions 5 and 6 tell you to look for cause-effect relationships.**

4. From the information given, you can infer that "Cold War" means

    (1) the spread of communism
    (2) the spread of democracy
    (3) an alliance between nations
    (4) a conflict without fighting
    (5) a local war involving few countries

5. The immediate cause of U.S. involvement in World War II was

    (1) the bombing of Pearl Harbor
    (2) the blowing up of the *Maine*
    (3) the invasion of Poland by Germany
    (4) the European Allies' need for help
    (5) communist activity in Korea

6. A major reason the United States became involved in three wars is that

    (1) other countries requested help
    (2) American property had been attacked
    (3) America was eager to be involved
    (4) communism had to be stopped
    (5) the economy improved during war

7. Which of the following is an example of recent internal upheavals experienced by major powers?

    (1) the U.S. election of a Democratic President, Bill Clinton, in 1992
    (2) the Gulf War of 1991 in which the U.S. sent troops to remove Iraqi troops from Kuwait
    (3) the breakup of the former USSR into independent nations in 1991
    (4) the election of a Republican majority in the U.S. Congress in 1994
    (5) the joining of European nations into an economic bloc in 1993

Items 8 and 9 refer to the following paragraph.

After the end of World War I in 1918, Americans looked forward to better times. But first they had to deal with the economic problems left by the war. The 1920s began with deciding what to do with the millions of veterans who came home and had to find work. There also were many veterans who came home injured and unable to work. Thousands of domestic wartime employees no longer were needed for government work. Factories that had enjoyed increased production of wartime items shut down to retool for peacetime products. Unemployment rose. The nation was involved in struggles among factory owners, workers, farmers, and consumers, all of whom demanded an end to inflation and recession.

8. The information in the paragraph best supports the conclusion that

(1) Americans were expecting better times
(2) economic problems resulting from the war had to be solved
(3) wars cause inflation and recession
(4) thousands of Americans were out of work
(5) the 1920s were depressing times

9. Even if it had not been stated in the paragraph, you would have been able to draw which of these conclusions?

(1) Veterans had to look for work.
(2) Wartime employees lost their jobs.
(3) Factories shut down.
(4) Unemployment rose.
(5) People demanded an end to inflation.

Items 10 and 11 refer to the following information.

During the 1920s, the United States began to produce more iron, steel, cars, furniture, and other goods than the rest of the world combined. The prices of many goods fell, and millions of people were able to buy them. The incomes of businesspeople, doctors, lawyers, and salespeople rose. The average worker made about $25 or $30 a week, enough to afford some home appliances. However, in New England, local textile mills and shoe factories moved to the South. The coal-producing areas of Ohio and Pennsylvania were hurt when people began to use electricity instead of coal. Most farmers did poorly during this period as well.

10. Which of the following details supports the conclusion that the northeastern regions of the country had hard times during the 1920s?

(1) Salespeople and businesspeople made lots of money.
(2) The production of goods increased.
(3) Farmers did poorly.
(4) Factories moved from New England to the South.
(5) Prices on manufactured goods decreased.

11. Which of the following conclusions is supported by the information?

(1) The 1920s was a period of great international conflict.
(2) During the 1920s, the United States suffered from poor economic times.
(3) Farming became increasingly prosperous.
(4) The average worker was poor.
(5) The prosperity of the 1920s was not shared by all Americans.

Items 12 and 13 refer to the following paragraphs.

As the 1980s were left behind, so were some of the accepted positions of the world's powerful nations. After years of Cold War and a bitter nuclear arms race, many surprising political changes happened in a very short time. Students in China demonstrated for democracy, and for a few hours Americans were even able to watch the unrest on TV. Mikhail Gorbachev instituted liberal policies in the former USSR and paid two visits to the United States. East and West Berlin residents joined in tearing down the Berlin Wall that had divided that city since World War II.

Not all of these movements were successful. But the world powers are talking, and for the first time in years, they are also listening. The United States, a major force for peace against the injustices of communism, now has to determine its new role in world relations.

12. Based on recent world events, the writer has concluded that

    (1) the civil rights movement has been successful
    (2) freedom is right around the corner
    (3) the United States will have to take a different role
    (4) freedom movements will not succeed
    (5) the Cold War is over

13. Which is the main effect of the recent political events?

    (1) Gorbachev came to the United States.
    (2) Americans have been able to see China on TV.
    (3) The Berlin Wall is down.
    (4) All of the movements have been successful.
    (5) The world powers are having real discussions.

Items 14 and 15 refer to the following cartoon.

14. The intravenous line going into the tombstone of the Soviet Union represents

    (1) United Nations interference with the affairs of the Soviet Union
    (2) exports of wheat from the United States to the Soviet Union
    (3) Gorbachev's attempts to fix what was wrong with the Soviet Union
    (4) Gorbachev's election as president of the Soviet Union
    (5) Gorbachev's reliance on other nations to help the Soviet Union

15. What has the cartoonist concluded?

    (1) The U.S. policy toward the former Soviet Union is working.
    (2) Gorbachev was not able to keep the Soviet Union alive.
    (3) The Soviet Union is a major force in world affairs.
    (4) Other nations support the death of the Soviet Union.
    (5) Gorbachev is the finest leader of the Soviet Union since World War II.

Items 16 and 17 refer to the following map and information.

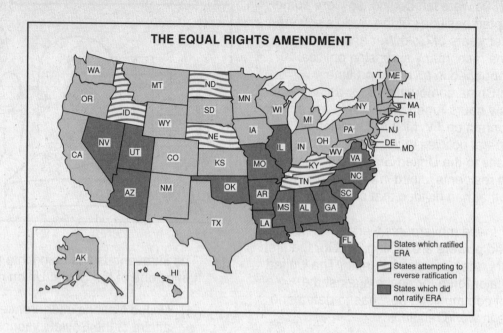

THE EQUAL RIGHTS AMENDMENT

States which ratified ERA

States attempting to reverse ratification

States which did not ratify ERA

The Equal Rights Amendment was intended to guarantee that a woman could not be legally or socially discriminated against on the basis of sex. To pass into law, an amendment needs ratification or approval by 38 states.

16. You can conclude from the map that

(1) the ERA passed
(2) the ERA had no support
(3) the country was evenly divided about the ERA
(4) the ERA was defeated by only a few states
(5) the ERA would not have helped anyone

17. Which of the major areas of the United States would be the least likely to support another bill for women's rights?

(1) New England
(2) the Great Plains
(3) the South
(4) the Northwest
(5) the Midwest

Items 18 to 27 refer to the following information.

During the 1960s to 1990s, many new terms became part of the American national vocabulary. Listed on the next page are definitions and descriptions of some of these terms. Each definition supplies support for concluding that there is a connection between a term and an important historical event or concept. Choose the term most likely to be related to the event or concept.

1. arms race—Competition between the United States and the former Soviet Union from the 1950s to the 1980s to develop nuclear weapons
2. New Frontier—President John F. Kennedy's 1960s challenge to fulfill national goals in economic development, civil rights, and space
3. Watergate—A political scandal caused by high-level cover-ups leading to the resignation of President Richard Nixon in 1974
4. Reaganomics—President Ronald Reagan's 1980s plan to cut taxes and curb federal spending in order to stimulate the economy
5. Contract with America—Republican 1990s agenda for reducing the role of the federal government

18. The Civil Rights Act and NASA

    (1) Reaganomics
    (2) arms race
    (3) Contract with America
    (4) Watergate
    (5) New Frontier

19. Strategic Arms Limitation Talks

    (1) arms race
    (2) Watergate
    (3) New Frontier
    (4) Reaganomics
    (5) Contract with America

20. A topic for discussion at summit meetings between world leaders

    (1) New Frontier
    (2) Watergate
    (3) arms race
    (4) Contract with America
    (5) Reaganomics

21. The involvement of high-level officials and accusations of obstruction of justice

    (1) Contract with America
    (2) Watergate
    (3) New Frontier
    (4) Reaganomics
    (5) arms race

22. Proposals to cut federal welfare programs and return them to the states

    (1) Reaganomics
    (2) arms race
    (3) New Frontier
    (4) Watergate
    (5) Contract with America

23. Legislation to reduce inflation and high interest rates

    (1) arms race
    (2) Watergate
    (3) Reaganomics
    (4) New Frontier
    (5) Contract with America

24. NASA's goal to land astronauts on the moon

    (1) Reaganomics
    (2) arms race
    (3) New Frontier
    (4) Watergate
    (5) Contract with America

25. U.S. Justice Department enforcing integration of Southern schools

    (1) arms race
    (2) Reaganomics
    (3) New Frontier
    (4) Watergate
    (5) Contract with America

26. A ban on atmospheric testing of nuclear weapons

    (1) Reaganomics
    (2) Contract with America
    (3) Watergate
    (4) New Frontier
    (5) arms race

27. The first President to resign under threat of impeachment

    (1) Reaganomics
    (2) Contract with America
    (3) Watergate
    (4) New Frontier
    (5) arms race

Items 28 and 29 refer to the following paragraph.

During the 1960s, U.S. involvement in the Vietnamese War grew. What started as a few military advisers helping democratic South Vietnam fight Communist North Vietnam grew to more than 500,000 troops by 1968. American casualties were high. For the first time, Americans watched a war in progress on television. These factors created doubts in many Americans' minds about the wisdom of the war. Opinions about the war divided the country.

28. From the paragraph you can infer that

    (1) there were large numbers of American troops in Vietnam in the early 1960s
    (2) few soldiers died in the war
    (3) American involvement in the Vietnam War increased gradually
    (4) Americans knew little about the war
    (5) most Americans approved of the war

29. What was a result of televising the war?

    (1) Americans received more accurate information about the war.
    (2) Americans increased their commitment to the war.
    (3) American casualties increased.
    (4) Military advisers were withdrawn.
    (5) More American troops were sent to Vietnam.

Items 30 and 31 refer to the following information and cartoon.

In the 1990s, after years of Communist dictatorship, Russia adopted democratic reforms.

30. What does the burning pot represent?

    (1) the country of Russia
    (2) a revolt of Russian citizens against the government
    (3) the difficulties of changing from a dictatorship to a democracy
    (4) Russia's relations with the United States
    (5) Russia's fallen position as a world power

31. According to the cartoonist, why is Russia having trouble making democracy work?

    (1) The economy of Russia is doing poorly.
    (2) The Russian economy is so strong that it doesn't need democracy.
    (3) Russia has no tradition of democracy so it must use a "recipe."
    (4) Russians are against democracy.
    (5) The symbol of Russia is a bear.

The beginning of the 1990s saw an unprecedented alignment of nearly all the member countries of the United Nations. They united in an effort to turn back the aggression of one country against another. In late July 1990, following a long dispute between the two countries over oil rights and the pricing of oil, several hundred thousand members of Iraq's army assembled on the border between Iraq and Kuwait. Despite assurances of only peaceful intentions from Iraqi President Saddam Hussein, Iraq invaded tiny Kuwait, claiming the entire country as its own territory. When it became evident that Iraq would not pull its forces out of Kuwait, the United Nations issued a resolution telling Iraq to leave Kuwait by January 15, 1991. Iraq refused to leave.

On January 16, bombers from the United States, Great Britain, France, and Saudi Arabia began a month-long bombing of Baghdad and other important Iraqi military cities. In mid-February, ground forces drove the Iraqi army out of Kuwait in 100 hours, inflicting heavy losses and taking hundreds of thousands of prisoners. For the first time in history, the nations of the world had successfully allied themselves under the United Nations banner to turn back an aggressor and to give a country back to its citizens.

32. The conflict with Iraq was different from previous conflicts in the world because it was the

   (1) first war Iraq had ever fought
   (2) first time that all Americans were in favor of war
   (3) first time the United Nations had been involved in a conflict
   (4) first conflict in which the U.S. had been allied with other countries
   (5) first time in United Nations history that nearly all the world's nations agreed on the effort to turn back an aggressor

33. The United Nations issued a resolution concerning Iraq's aggressive activities

   (1) when the Iraqis assembled on their border with Kuwait
   (2) when Iraq invaded Iran
   (3) after Iraq invaded Kuwait
   (4) after allied bombers bombed Iraq
   (5) after Kuwait invaded Iraq

Tip Correct answers on the GED are always based upon information stated in or implied by the passage. Therefore, when selecting an answer, make sure that it is supported by the passage. Do not depend on background information.

Answers are on page 780.

ged Review History

Choose the best answer to each item. Items 1 to 3 refer to the following information.

After World War II, the United States took part in the following programs to help rebuild Europe. All, except for the Marshall Plan, continue to help develop the economies of the underdeveloped nations of the world.

1. Marshall Plan—supplied food and equipment to European countries
2. Point Four Program—helps foreign countries gain the technical knowledge needed to develop their own resources and industries
3. International Bank for Reconstruction and Development—lends money to countries or individuals to develop economically-sound projects
4. International Monetary Fund—stabilizes the world currency exchange rates through international cooperation
5. Military Aid—given to countries allied with the United States

1. A private investor in Bangladesh has developed a financial plan for a factory. The plan has identified buyers of the finished product and sellers for the raw materials. The person cannot get a loan from a Bangladeshi bank. Where could he get a loan?

    (1) Marshall Plan
    (2) Point Four Program
    (3) International Bank for Reconstruction and Development
    (4) International Monetary Fund
    (5) Military Aid

2. A small African country asks the United States for technical assistance to start a fish-farming cooperative. Which program will provide this assistance?

    (1) Marshall Plan
    (2) Point Four Program
    (3) International Bank for Reconstruction and Development
    (4) International Monetary Fund
    (5) Military Aid

3. In response to the invasion of Kuwait by Iraq, the United States sent troops to Kuwait's neighbor, Saudi Arabia. Under which program could U.S. aid to the Saudis be justified?

    (1) Marshall Plan
    (2) Point Four Program
    (3) International Bank for Reconstruction and Development
    (4) International Monetary Fund
    (5) Military Aid

Item 4 is based on the following paragraph.

On becoming president of the Soviet Union in 1988, Mikhail Gorbachev attempted to change Soviet society with the application of glasnost and perestroika, defined in the West as "openness" and "reform."

4. An example of glasnost would be

    (1) a military buildup
    (2) jailing dissidents
    (3) allowing freedom of the press
    (4) writing a new Soviet constitution
    (5) stopping the emigration of Soviet Jews

Item 5 refers to the following map.

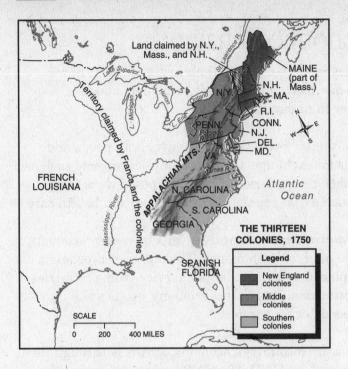

THE THIRTEEN COLONIES, 1750

Legend
- New England colonies
- Middle colonies
- Southern colonies

5. Which event can be predicted from the information in the map?

   (1) Land disputes would erupt between the colonists and the French.
   (2) Fighting would occur between the colonists and the Native Americans.
   (3) The colonists would fight the British for independence.
   (4) Slavery would become common in the Southern colonies.
   (5) France would sell the Louisiana Territory to the United States.

6. A potato blight in Ireland led to the great famine of 1846–1847. Nearly one million people died during the famine and another two million were forced to emigrate. About 1.5 million of them came to the United States. Which of the following best explains why many Irish immigrants came to America?

   (1) overcrowding in Ireland
   (2) the need for economic survival
   (3) a desire for religious freedom
   (4) a desire for political freedom
   (5) free farmland in the United States

Item 7 refers to the following 1871 cartoon.

THE "BRAINS"

7. After the Civil War, many large city governments became very corrupt. Most cities were controlled by political machines headed by a boss who remained behind the scenes. The elected officials were puppets of the "Brains," or boss. This cartoon represents Boss Tweed of New York. The cartoonist probably assumed that his readers would

   (1) disagree with his view of Boss Tweed
   (2) think that Boss Tweed was not really so corrupt
   (3) recognize Boss Tweed even without facial features
   (4) not understand the symbol of the money bag
   (5) think that Boss Tweed should be reelected as mayor of New York

Answers are on page 783.

Economics
Lesson

General Economic Behavior

The study of economics is more complex than just looking at how people use money. Remembering a few basic principles makes economics much easier to understand.

The economy of every country is based on exchange. Both goods and services form the basis for exchange. Goods are physical objects such as food, cars, houses, and clothing. Services are the types of work that a person does for you, such as car repair, house painting, and health care.

Most countries have **monetary economies.** In a monetary economy, goods and services are paid for with money. The money represents a certain value that is placed on the product or service. Some countries still have **barter economies.** In a barter economy, goods are exchanged for other goods or for services.

A common way to measure a country's economic status is through its **Gross National Product,** or **GNP.** The GNP is the total monetary value, either at current prices or at a fixed price, of everything produced and sold over the year in that country. The GNP includes manufactured goods, farm products, public services such as education, and private services such as legal advice.

Prices in the overall economy are set by two main factors. The first is the law of supply and demand. As the price of a product increases, the supplier will want to sell more in order to make money. As prices decrease, consumers will want to buy more. The second thing that influences prices is the cost of making the product. For example, a lipstick might cost $1 to make. It could be sold at a profit for $2. However, the cost of advertising and packaging can bring the price up to $6.

In order to afford goods, people need to have an income. Most people get their money by working and being paid wages. The wage for any job is usually determined in two ways. One is the value of the work performed. A doctor is paid more than a doctor's receptionist because the doctor can do specialized work that is important to the community. The other way is by considering how many people are qualified to do the work. A job that takes a lot of training will pay more than a job that takes less training. So a teacher earns a higher wage than a teacher's assistant.

Choose the best answer to each item. Items 1 to 9 refer to the previous information.

1. The writer assumes that any country's economy

   (1) operates according to certain principles
   (2) is well balanced
   (3) cannot be understood
   (4) is based on money
   (5) is set at fixed prices

2. The use of GNP as a measure of a country's economy assumes that

   (1) all economic exchanges have a monetary value
   (2) the same amount of products are made each year
   (3) everyone uses the barter system
   (4) the economy is improving
   (5) the economy is stable

3. In following the law of supply and demand, manufacturers most likely assume that consumers

   (1) will buy only inexpensive products
   (2) will demand high quality
   (3) can be persuaded to pay high prices
   (4) can save a lot of money
   (5) can be easily fooled

4. According to the information, advertising most affects

   (1) the consumer's income
   (2) the packaging of a product
   (3) the GNP
   (4) the price of a product
   (5) normal profits

5. According to the information, it can be inferred that the value of work is

   (1) always the same
   (2) always changing
   (3) determined by the community
   (4) not important to economics
   (5) up to the individual

6. Which of the following is the best example of the barter system?

   (1) exchanging a sweater for a larger one at a department store
   (2) giving a friend an IOU for a loan
   (3) buying a used car from a neighbor
   (4) getting a meal at a restaurant
   (5) trading some of your garden vegetables for your neighbor's quilt

7. According to supply and demand, when the price of a product goes down, the

   (1) demand for the product goes up
   (2) quality of the product decreases
   (3) demand for the product goes down
   (4) quality of the product improves
   (5) demand for the product remains steady

8. Which of the following is the best example of a monetary system?

   (1) baking your own bread
   (2) trading a car for a pickup truck
   (3) inheriting a house from a relative
   (4) paying your phone bill by check
   (5) exchanging a tape for a CD

9. Which of the following is not true of both barter and monetary economies?

   (1) The people work.
   (2) Goods and services are produced.
   (3) Good and services are consumed.
   (4) Goods and services have value.
   (5) Money is used to pay for goods and services.

Choose the best answer to each item.

Items 10 to 15 refer to the following paragraphs.

When more goods are being made, we say that the economy is expanding. In an expanding economy, manufacturers must find more people to buy their goods. They use advertising to let people know something special about the product. They also provide coupons that lower the price and make buyers feel they are getting a bargain. Another way manufacturers attract customers is through rebates. A rebate is a refund of part of the purchase price. Buyers who take the time to send in rebates feel they are spending their money wisely.

When the manufacturer's normal market is already buying as much as it can, the manufacturer starts to look for new customers. One way to find a new market is to change the packaging of the product in order to appeal to other groups of people. For example, in the 1970s many single people had their own households. Before then, food companies had packaged their products mainly for couples and families. To attract this new market, manufacturers began to sell food in single-serving packages. Another way to find new markets is to sell goods to another country. This practice is called exporting and can double or triple a company's sales.

10. According to the paragraphs, a new cost for a manufacturer in an expanding economy could be the cost of

    (1) labor problems
    (2) packaging
    (3) producing the product
    (4) early retirement plans
    (5) finding new markets

11. A manufacturing company will begin a new advertising campaign when it

    (1) has more customers than goods
    (2) has more goods than customers
    (3) wants to limit markets
    (4) manufactures food packages
    (5) wants to appeal to old customers

12. Information in the paragraphs indicates that in an expanding economy

    (1) exports will increase
    (2) imports will increase
    (3) exports will decrease
    (4) imports will decrease
    (5) exports and imports will stay the same

13. The writer assumes that the use of advertising to expand markets is

    (1) an economic fact of marketing
    (2) a trick played on consumers
    (3) wasteful and ineffective
    (4) damaging to the economy
    (5) helpful to the economy

14. Which of the following is the best example of a manufacturer finding a new market for a product?

    (1) mailing a special offer to loyal customers
    (2) advertising a product in the local newspaper
    (3) advertising an office product to home users
    (4) giving a rebate to someone who purchases the product
    (5) changing and updating the design of a product

15. The writer assumes that you know

    (1) what an expanding economy is
    (2) advertising helps sell products
    (3) a rebate is a refund
    (4) there were many single people in the 1970s
    (5) selling goods overseas is exporting

Items 16 and 17 refer to the diagram.

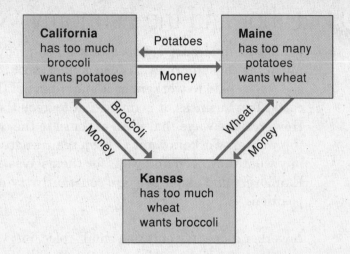

16. According to the diagram, California disposes of its surplus of broccoli by

   (1) throwing it away
   (2) selling it to Kansas
   (3) bartering it for wheat
   (4) selling it to Maine
   (5) bartering it for potatoes

17. The diagram assumes that

   (1) bartering is easier than using money
   (2) wheat is grown in Maine
   (3) people want the same products everywhere
   (4) people want different things
   (5) money has no value

Items 18 to 20 refer to the following paragraph.

   The American economy is said to go through an eight- to ten-year business cycle. This cycle has four phases: expansion, peak, recession, and trough. During expansion, business activity increases until it reaches a peak, or a high point. During recession, business activity decreases until it reaches a low point, or trough. Although minor upswings and downswings happen all the time, the overall pattern is a rise followed by a fall followed by a rise.

18. The best description of the American business cycle would be

   (1) positive
   (2) negative
   (3) unchanging
   (4) always changing
   (5) huge

19. The writer of the paragraph assumes that the American economic cycle is

   (1) seriously affected by minor variations in the pattern
   (2) not seriously affected by minor variations in the pattern
   (3) currently on the rise
   (4) falling
   (5) at a peak

20. The writer of the paragraph assumes that you know the definition of which of the following terms?

   (1) economy
   (2) expansion
   (3) peak
   (4) recession
   (5) trough

Answers are on page 783.

Labor and the Economy

Profit, the difference between how much production costs and how much the consumer pays, is the goal of most businesses. Companies see wages paid to workers as a major part of the expense in production costs. To a business, it is important to keep the cost of labor down. However, the wage that is an expense to the company is an income to the worker. Workers want to keep their wages high so that they can buy what they need and want for themselves and their families. Employers and employees are constantly trying to improve their own positions.

A worker alone has only one small voice, but workers who are union members can be heard because they have a loud collective voice. The organization of workers can influence a company's decisions about wages, benefits, and working conditions. When a large group of laborers strike, or refuse to work, the company is forced to pay attention to the demands of the union.

When unions were first established, labor's power was limited by law and by the lack of financial support for striking workers. Now American law recognizes the worker's right to join a union, to organize others, and to strike. The National Labor Relations Act (NLRA) of 1935 requires employers to bargain with a union favored by a majority of the workers and defines certain labor practices as unfair. These unfair and illegal labor practices include firing because of union activity, discrimination against union members in favor of nonunion members, and interference with employees trying to organize unions or bargain collectively. Many concerned citizens felt that the NLRA was excessively pro-labor. The Labor Management Relations Act of 1947 (Taft-Hartley Act) was passed to balance the power of company management and the power of labor; it requires labor to bargain with employers, thus setting the stage for collective bargaining.

Collective bargaining is the discussion between management and union leaders who speak for all the employees. The two groups negotiate, or present and agree on, terms for employment contracts. Often each side has to compromise in order to arrive at an agreement. Since the 1930s, collective bargaining has increased wages and salaries, health and vacation benefits, and company liability for accident and health hazards. If a union comes to the bargaining table and management and the union cannot agree on a new contract, the union may choose to strike. Sometimes the threat of a strike causes management to agree to a wage increase. Sometimes the threat is put into action before management agrees to raise wages.

Choose the best answer to each item. Items 1 to 8 refer to the previous information.

1. According to the information, profit is

   (1) necessary in an economy
   (2) the root of all evil
   (3) earned only by management
   (4) unnecessary, as long as everyone has a job
   (5) the difference between the cost of production and an item's price

2. Which is not an effect of the conflict between labor and management?

   (1) Laws had to be made to protect both sides.
   (2) Labor unions were established.
   (3) Labor has one voice and management has many.
   (4) Management and labor practice collective bargaining.
   (5) Workers have the right to strike.

3. What probably would happen first if a city did not want to increase teacher salaries?

   (1) The teachers would strike.
   (2) Teachers would take a cut in pay.
   (3) The teachers' union would picket the school board building.
   (4) The city would close the schools.
   (5) The teachers' union would bargain with the school board.

4. According to the information, labor unions

   (1) have no power
   (2) are too powerful
   (3) allow workers a voice in their jobs
   (4) have no financial support
   (5) are betraying workers' trust

Tip **Words such as *effect*, *happen*, and *because* often signal cause-effect relationships.**

5. Which is an important effect of collective bargaining?

   (1) Management and labor have social gatherings.
   (2) More tables are being manufactured.
   (3) Unions have gotten many benefits for laborers.
   (4) No labor contract can be broken.
   (5) Strikes have been made illegal.

6. It can be concluded from the information that labor and management will probably

   (1) join forces
   (2) never agree
   (3) usually have tension between them
   (4) make collective bargaining illegal
   (5) destroy the business world

7. Which best supports the concern that the NLRA was too pro-labor?

   (1) The act specified only the rights of labor.
   (2) The act made some practices illegal.
   (3) The act prevented management from firing someone because of union affiliation.
   (4) The act recognized union rights.
   (5) The act prohibited labor unions.

8. In recent years the power of labor unions in the United States has decreased because employers have moved many operations overseas. Which of the following is the most likely effect of a decrease in union power?

   (1) higher wages for workers
   (2) better negotiating position for unions during collective bargaining
   (3) better benefits for workers
   (4) smaller wage increases
   (5) more vacation days per year

Answers are on page 785.

Lesson  11 Government and Economics

The United States government spends more money and has a larger payroll than any business in the world. Its budget runs into billions of dollars. About 22 percent of the budget is spent on Social Security. Almost 21 percent is spent on national security and defense. About 15 percent is spent on interest on the public debt. The rest is spent on health, labor, welfare, education, the conservation of natural resources, commerce, agriculture, and administration. The amount of government spending affects the economy.

Whenever there is spending, there must be income. Government spending is paid for by borrowing money and by taxes paid by citizens and businesses. The federal income tax pays for much federal spending. Traditionally, the federal income tax has been a graduated income tax. People with higher incomes pay a higher percentage of their income to the government in taxes; people with lower incomes pay a lower percentage of their income in taxes.

For citizens to be taxed, they must have income, or money, coming into the household. This income may be salaries or wages from employment, interest or dividends from investments, or rental income from properties. Income also can come from benefits like welfare, Social Security, and unemployment compensation.

In this century, the government has steadily increased its control of the economy. It limits monopolies, regulates interstate commerce, restricts or expands the amount of money in the economy, uses the Federal Reserve System as a central bank, and sets up international trade agreements.

Through borrowing, spending, taxation, and regulation, the government touches the economic life of every citizen.

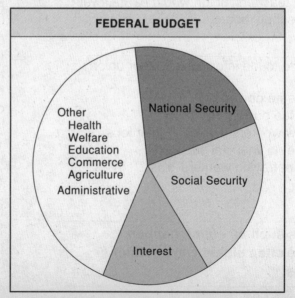

FEDERAL BUDGET

Other
Health
Welfare
Education
Commerce
Agriculture
Administrative

National Security

Social Security

Interest

ged Exercise Government and Economics

Choose the best answer to each item. Items 1 to 7 refer to the previous information.

1. In order to draw a conclusion from the pie chart on page 278, a reader must first

   (1) know the total figure for the federal budget
   (2) read the first paragraph
   (3) understand how the government gets its money
   (4) read the entire passage
   (5) know the exact figures for each expense

2. Until 1986, the United States had an income tax with many tax shelters. In practice, the tax law offered many benefits and loopholes to higher-income individuals. However, the Tax Reform Act of 1986 eliminated tax shelters. Why did Congress pass the Tax Reform Act of 1986?

   (1) The government needed more money.
   (2) The government needed less money.
   (3) The income tax was not practiced fairly.
   (4) The income tax was too difficult to enforce.
   (5) The income tax was hated by the citizens.

3. Budget legislation that promises a balanced budget would cut down on government spending. One effect of this legislation would be

   (1) more support for Star Wars defense plans
   (2) higher taxes for people in every tax bracket
   (3) more financial support for public education
   (4) less financial support for welfare programs
   (5) less income for the government

4. The type of business most influenced by the government budget is

   (1) restaurant
   (2) agriculture
   (3) child care
   (4) publishing
   (5) arms manufacturing

5. During the early 1940s, the national debt increased dramatically. This high debt was most likely caused by

   (1) unemployment
   (2) taxation
   (3) defense spending
   (4) budgeting
   (5) high income levels

6. Thomas Jefferson said that "government governs best which governs least." The information in this passage is enough to support the conclusion that modern Americans disagree with Jefferson because they have chosen a government that

   (1) spends a lot of money
   (2) taxes all its citizens
   (3) is heavily involved in the economy
   (4) taxes luxury items
   (5) has a welfare program

7. In the early 1990s, defense spending became a smaller portion of the budget. This is most likely the result of

   (1) increased overseas activity of the armed forces
   (2) the end of the Cold War
   (3) antiwar feelings in the country
   (4) less efficient operation of the armed forces
   (5) the combining of the Army, Navy, and Air Force

Items 8 and 9 refer to the following information.

Many state governments collect a state income tax or a sales tax or both. However, most states need more money than they can raise through taxes. Some get extra money by having lotteries, but at one time Montana planned to issue its own credit card. By sponsoring the card, the state would have received part of the annual fee paid by the user. Between that and a percentage of the value of the purchases charged, Montana expected to take in as much as $12.2 million a year.

8. The information supports the conclusion that

   (1) all states should issue credit cards
   (2) Montana's plan would have increased state income
   (3) lotteries raise more money than credit cards do
   (4) credit card fees are too high
   (5) Montana would have no money problems

9. The state of Montana assumed that

   (1) people would pay their annual fees
   (2) people in Montana use credit cards
   (3) its citizens no longer played the lottery
   (4) Montana did not want to raise its taxes
   (5) more people moved to Montana

Items 10 and 11 refer to the following cartoon.

Non Sequitur by Wiley

© 1995, Washington Post Writers Group.
Reprinted with permission.

10. The cartoonist assumes that you know that the Internal Revenue Service (IRS)

    (1) provides Social Security payments
    (2) runs the armed forces
    (3) sets policy on education
    (4) pays interest on the public debt
    (5) collects taxes

11. With which statement would the cartoonist disagree?

    (1) The U.S. has a free enterprise system.
    (2) Businesses can earn high incomes.
    (3) The IRS is fair in its dealings.
    (4) Taxes are too high.
    (5) People who earn money should pay taxes.

Answers are on page 785.

Choose the <u>best answer</u> to each item. <u>Items 1 and 2</u> are based on the following paragraph.

A common idea in economics is the wage-price spiral. When union bargaining results in increased wages for workers, prices of products also go up. Corporations want to keep their profits steady. If wages go up, the increase in the cost of production is passed on to the consumer as an increase in the cost of the item. Since the company continues to profit, labor demands even higher wages. Again production costs go up and so does the price. The result is inflation. However, unions oppose limiting wage increases and companies do not want to limit price increases.

1. An economist who wanted to stop the wage-price spiral would probably be in favor of

    (1) unionization
    (2) higher profits
    (3) government control of prices
    (4) socialism
    (5) price increases

2. According to the paragraph, if the wage-price spiral continues, the result will be

    (1) good for the consumer
    (2) lower profits for companies
    (3) rising prices
    (4) lower prices
    (5) labor-management deadlocks

<u>Items 3 to 5</u> refer to the following information.

Movement of the economy is classified by many different terms that explain the effects that wages, production, and cost-of-living expenses have on one another at a given time. Listed in the next column are five of these terms and brief descriptions of the economic trends they indicate.

1. <u>inflation</u>—continuing rise in prices
2. <u>demand-pull inflation</u>—caused by a demand for goods that are in short supply
3. <u>cost-push inflation</u>—caused by a push for higher wages resulting in higher prices; also called the wage-price spiral
4. <u>recession</u>—production declines and people have less money
5. <u>depression</u>—severe reduction or slowing of business activity and cash flow

3. When an oil embargo was imposed in the 1970s, Americans had to wait in long lines to get fuel for their cars. The higher prices paid for this fuel demonstrate

    (1) cost-push inflation
    (2) demand-pull inflation
    (3) inflation
    (4) recession
    (5) depression

4. In 1980, it cost more than $2 to purchase an item that had cost less than $1 in 1970. This is an example of

    (1) demand-pull inflation
    (2) cost-push inflation
    (3) inflation
    (4) depression
    (5) recession

5. In the 1930s, there was a sharp slowdown of the U.S. economy. This is an example of

    (1) inflation
    (2) demand-pull inflation
    (3) cost-push inflation
    (4) recession
    (5) depression

Tip **When applying an example in a new context, ask yourself: What is similar about these two things? Are the events similar? Are the results similar?**

Items 6 and 7 refer to the following graph.

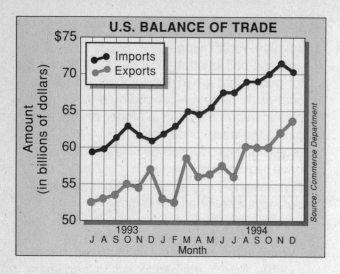

U.S. BALANCE OF TRADE

Amount (in billions of dollars)

Imports
Exports

1993   1994
J A S O N D J F M A M J J A S O N D
Month

Source: Commerce Department

6. Over the period shown, the general trend has been

   (1) increasing exports and decreasing imports
   (2) increasing exports and increasing imports
   (3) decreasing exports and decreasing imports
   (4) decreasing exports and increasing imports
   (5) flat for both exports and imports

7. Which of the following statements supports the conclusion that the United States has an unfavorable balance of trade?

   (1) Exports have risen since the beginning of 1994.
   (2) Imports peaked in the autumn of 1994.
   (3) Imports are higher than exports.
   (4) Both imports and exports have risen since June 1993.
   (5) The general trend for imports is upward.

Tip When reading a line graph or a bar graph, be sure you understand the information on the bottom and along the side. Then look at how the lines or bars compare to each other. Finally, note whether the lines or bars are going up, going down, or staying level.

Items 8 to 10 refer to the following information.

Each year the Tax Foundation figures out when Tax Freedom Day is. This is the date on which the average worker "stops" paying taxes and "starts" earning money for himself or herself. In other words, assume that all money the average American worker earns goes to pay taxes starting on January 1. In 1993, the worker started "keeping" his or her wages on May 3. In 1994, that date moved to May 5.

8. From the information, you can infer that Tax Freedom Day

   (1) usually falls on a Monday in May
   (2) is a day on which people in jail for not paying taxes go free
   (3) has fallen later each year for the last ten years
   (4) is a way of illustrating how much taxes the average worker pays
   (5) is a day on which taxes are not withheld from paychecks

9. From the information, you can conclude that the average worker

   (1) pays about one-tenth of his or her wages for taxes
   (2) does not receive any money until May
   (3) pays about one-third of his or her wages for taxes
   (4) pays more in federal than in state and local taxes
   (5) pays more in state and local than in federal taxes

10. Which of the following is most likely to have caused Tax Freedom Day to move from May 3 to May 5?

   (1) an error in calculation
   (2) increased taxes
   (3) a tax cut
   (4) lower wages
   (5) higher wages

Social Studies ♦ Economics

Items 11 to 15 refer to the following information.

All economic systems must answer five basic questions in using resources to satisfy people's needs. These questions underlie typical business decisions. The five basic questions are:

1. How much should be produced?
2. What is to be produced?
3. How is it to be produced?
4. Who is to receive it?
5. How can the economy adapt to change?

11. Sam's company made a profit on baseballs last year, but now he's wondering whether footballs might sell better next year. Which question is Sam asking?

   (1) How much should be produced?
   (2) What is to be produced?
   (3) How is it to be produced?
   (4) Who is to receive it?
   (5) How can the economy adapt to change?

12. Elena uses an electric typewriter to create documents for her clients. She's thinking about buying a computer with word-processing software to make her work easier. Which question is Elena asking?

   (1) How much should be produced?
   (2) What is to be produced?
   (3) How is it to be produced?
   (4) Who is to receive it?
   (5) How can the economy adapt to change?

13. Parker's company has been selling machine parts to U.S. companies for years. Now they are thinking of selling their parts overseas. Which question is Parker's company asking?

   (1) How much should be produced?
   (2) What is to be produced?
   (3) How is it to be produced?
   (4) Who is to receive it?
   (5) How can the economy adapt to change?

14. Many American workers have more than one job or work nights and weekends. They cannot do their banking during normal bank hours. So most banks have installed ATM machines that operate 24 hours a day. Which question does this answer?

   (1) How much should be produced?
   (2) What is to be produced?
   (3) How is it to be produced?
   (4) Who is to receive it?
   (5) How can the economy adapt to change?

15. Patricia's low-fat potato chips have really caught on. They are crispy, tasty, and good for you. She is thinking of expanding her factory so she can sell more chips next year. What question is Patricia asking?

   (1) How much should be produced?
   (2) What is to be produced?
   (3) How is it to be produced?
   (4) Who is to receive it?
   (5) How can the economy adapt to change?

Item 16 refers to the following information.

In 1992, the number of people who were officially considered poor by the U.S. government was 39.6 million. Of the total number of poor people, about 40 percent were children under 18 and 10 percent were elderly.

16. Which of the following could you figure out with the information provided?

   (1) the percent of the nation's population that was poor in 1992
   (2) the total population of the U.S. in 1992
   (3) the number of two-parent families that were poor in 1992
   (4) the number of U.S. children who were poor in 1992
   (5) the number of single-parent families that were poor in 1992

Answers are on page 786.

Political Science

Lesson 12   Modern Government

Most of us take the idea of a nation for granted, but the complex organization of a nation-state is relatively new in the history of humanity. Most modern countries are not governed by family groups, religious groups, or business groups. Instead, most of today's governments are based on one or more basic political principles.

The first principle is that of **centralized government.** Political power used to be divided among military rulers, church authorities, and aristocrats. Over the years, the state took over the functions performed by all these groups. The central government also has the duty of making sure the young are educated and that the elderly are cared for. Trade, warfare, agriculture, scientific research, public transportation, and other social issues have also become the concern of government.

The second principle is that of **legal authority.** Under traditional rule, a leader was thought of as having power because his or her family had always been powerful. Under a legal system, a leader's power comes from the authority of the political office. It is based upon and permitted by law, not by family background. Citizens in a modern state expect the leader to govern according to the laws they have established.

The third principle is called **mass political participation.** Several hundred years ago, most political decisions were made by a small group of wealthy people. Today, people of all income levels can have a say in how the government is run.

The three major types of government structures traditionally have been classified by the political principles they use to govern. **Authoritarian** governments are centralized, but they are not based on legal authority and are not supported by mass participation. The word of the leader, or small group of leaders, is the only law in an authoritarian government. Political opposition is not permitted. Idi Amin, the violent leader of Uganda, is a recent example of an authoritarian dictator.

Totalitarian governments are also centralized. However, their leaders usually do not have the same type of personal control as in authoritarian governments. In fascist totalitarianism, the dictator must have the support of the party leaders, and his power lasts only as long as he can maintain that support. Hitler, Mussolini, and Saddam Hussein of Iraq are examples of this type of power. Totalitarian governments such as the former Soviet Union and mainland China do not have dictators. The single political party is the power that regulates all aspects of the citizens' lives.

Democracies are centralized, are run according to law, and their power lies in the hands of the people. The United States is an example of a democracy.

Choose the <u>best answer</u> to each item. <u>Items 1 to 8</u> refer to the previous information.

1. An opinion is expressed in the passage about which of the following?

   (1) mainland China
   (2) the Soviet Union
   (3) democracy
   (4) Mussolini
   (5) Idi Amin

2. The descriptions about the three major government types are supported by

   (1) opinions about how well they work
   (2) opinions about the role of citizens in government
   (3) examples of political leaders in each type of system
   (4) facts about basic political principles
   (5) facts about the history of each type of government

3. Which conclusion has adequate support in the passage?

   (1) Government has changed over the years.
   (2) Principles of government have remained the same.
   (3) All governments have the same basic structures.
   (4) Military rulers no longer have any power.
   (5) Dictators are evil people.

4. If the single leader in an authoritarian government dies, what is the <u>most probable</u> effect?

   (1) The government continues as usual.
   (2) The government fails.
   (3) The people demand democracy.
   (4) The opposite political party comes to power.
   (5) The people elect a new leader.

5. Saudi Arabia has no constitution. The king is the leader of the government, and his sons fill many important positions. Free elections are not held, and dissent is not permitted. The government of Saudi Arabia is an example of

   (1) mass political participation
   (2) legal authority
   (3) authoritarian government
   (4) totalitarian government
   (5) democracy

6. After the former Soviet Union broke up, Russia elected a legislature and a president, Boris Yeltsin. Although some forms of totalitarianism still exist in Russia, its new form of government is an example of

   (1) mass political participation
   (2) legal authority
   (3) authoritarian government
   (4) totalitarian government
   (5) democracy

7. Although the official head of the British government is the king or queen, an elected Parliament makes the laws. Great Britain was one of the first nations to create rights and laws to form the basis of a constitution. This government is an example of

   (1) mass political participation
   (2) legal authority
   (3) authoritarian government
   (4) totalitarian government
   (5) democracy

8. Which of the following is <u>not</u> an aspect of American democracy?

   (1) political parties
   (2) compulsory education for all children
   (3) labor unions
   (4) gun control laws
   (5) government censorship of the media

Items 9 and 10 refer to the following paragraph.

Democracies, authoritarian governments, and totalitarian governments have different goals as well as different structures. The admirable goal of a democracy is to ensure freedom and dignity for individuals. The repressive goal of an authoritarian government is to maintain state control of the political thought and actions of individuals. The goal of a totalitarian government is for the state to control all parts of an individual's life, nonpolitical as well as political.

9. According to the paragraph, the writer thinks that

   (1) all governments are alike
   (2) authoritarian governments are best
   (3) totalitarian governments are best
   (4) democratic governments are best
   (5) the state should control the individual's life

Tip **When trying to figure out an author's opinion, look for words with an emotional content. For example, the words *admirable* and *repressive* signal the writer's feelings about kinds of governments.**

10. If you lived under a totalitarian government, you probably could expect to

    (1) be able to choose the leader
    (2) be told where you could or could not travel
    (3) make your own choices about your career
    (4) educate your children in the manner of your choice
    (5) retire early

Items 11 to 15 refer to the following information.

The United States follows the Western concept of democracy. The emphasis is on the process of government, or how government works. In a democracy, the process of government is carried on by the people. There are four foundations for the process:
1. following the rule of law
2. freedom of political activity
3. participation of the majority (the winners of an election) and the minority (the losers of an election) in the government
4. belief in the democratic tradition, freedom of choice, and the acceptance of responsibility

By following these guidelines, American citizens can pretty much rule themselves.

In fact, for Americans, democracy has become more than a political system; it has become a way of life. Liberty, human rights, and human dignity are now basic values. We expect to be able to choose our own way of doing things in day-to-day living. Because personal freedom is taken for granted by so many Americans, there is a danger of imposing our own values on someone else. One individual's choice might not be suitable for another person. Also, Americans must be aware that freedom of choice does not mean freedom to do anything that seems like a good idea. It must be remembered that living up to the democratic ideal requires that we all give up some degree of freedom in order to maintain the freedoms of our society as a whole.

11. Which of the following is not true of a democracy?

    (1) People obey the law.
    (2) People are free to engage in political activity.
    (3) Personal freedom has no limit.
    (4) Political values affect daily life.
    (5) People believe in the democratic tradition.

12. The writer holds the opinion that freedom

    (1) has its responsibilities
    (2) is a natural right
    (3) is not really possible
    (4) is leading the country into danger
    (5) has no limits

13. Abraham Lincoln defined democracy as "of the people, by the people, and for the people." His summary of the process assumes that "the people" will

    (1) respect all reasonable laws
    (2) give all people political freedom
    (3) encourage the people in power to respect the rights and needs of the people who are not in power
    (4) guarantee freedom of choice as long as it does not interfere with other people's freedom
    (5) do all of the above

14. John F. Kennedy's famous words, "My fellow Americans, ask not what your country can do for you; ask what you can do for your country," are an appeal to citizens to

    (1) act as responsible citizens
    (2) pay their taxes on time
    (3) send a ten-dollar donation to the government
    (4) support his presidency
    (5) vote for Democrats

15. Public demonstrations like those against the war in Vietnam measure the force of public opinion because people must actively participate in a public action. However, such demonstrations do not indicate that

    (1) some people feel strongly about the issue
    (2) some people agree with government policy
    (3) there is dissatisfaction with government policy
    (4) Americans have the right to express their opinions
    (5) individuals will act publicly to express their opinions

Items 16 to 18 refer to the following information.

Americans are used to hearing that they have certain rights. Just what are rights? In political terms, rights are benefits to which a person has a legal or moral claim. All U.S. citizens have certain rights just because they are citizens. For example, all citizens have the right to a fair trial and to freedom of speech.

In contrast to rights are privileges. Privileges are also benefits, but they are limited in time and can be taken away as easily as they can be given. Examples of privileges are a Social Security pension or a license to work as a nurse. These are privileges that the government can grant or take away.

In addition, laws are things that people must or must not do. If people break the laws, they usually are punished.

16. Which of the following is an example of a right?

    (1) freedom of religion
    (2) two-term limit on the presidency
    (3) federally guaranteed student loans
    (4) paying taxes
    (5) unemployment insurance

17. Which of the following is a privilege?

    (1) freedom of religion
    (2) freedom of speech
    (3) the right to a fair trial
    (4) freedom of the press
    (5) obtaining a broadcast license

18. Which of the following is an example of obeying a law?

    (1) voting for president
    (2) wearing seat belts
    (3) having a trial by jury
    (4) taking the subway to work
    (5) borrowing a book from the library

Items 19 to 23 refer to the following paragraphs.

Power is the ability to control people's behavior. There are three basic ways to get power over people: through influence, through force, and through authority. Influence is a form of persuasion. People can be persuaded to do things by someone's personal appeal, by someone's social importance or wealth, by force of numbers, or by good organization. Force is based on making people do things against their will. Because physical force makes people afraid, they will do things they do not want to do. Authority is based on people's belief that those in power have the right to rule.

A stable government is based on what is called legitimate power. Legitimate power is considered proper and acceptable by the people who obey it. The power of a government comes from having a leader who has the authority to make decisions that the people will follow, even if they do not always agree with the decisions. Influence is not usually enough in itself to provide the power to govern. Force is called an illegitimate power. It does not have the consent or support of the governed people.

19. In the 1992 presidential election, Ross Perot ran against the Republican President George Bush and the Democratic candidate Bill Clinton. Because of his wealth and good organization, Perot was able to communicate his ideas widely. Even though he did not win the presidency, he set the agenda for much of the campaign. Perot's power can best be described as coming from

(1) influence
(2) the use of physical force
(3) the right to rule
(4) political authority
(5) winning the election

20. In the 1970s, Nguyen Van Thieu ruled South Vietnam because of his military strength, which was backed up by U.S. forces. When American troops were withdrawn in 1975, Thieu fell from power because the people did not support him. Thieu's regime can best be described as

(1) influential
(2) authoritarian
(3) decisive
(4) legitimate
(5) illegitimate

21. After the death of King George VI in 1952, his daughter, Elizabeth II, became queen of England. Queen Elizabeth's rule can best be described as an example of

(1) influence
(2) the use of physical force
(3) persuasion
(4) legitimate power
(5) elected office

22. Nations whose leaders rule by force usually do not have an orderly way to pass power from one leader to another. Power often passes by means of a military coup. In a democratic republic the orderly transfer of power is accomplished primarily by

(1) elections
(2) inheritance
(3) appointments
(4) revolution
(5) campaign contributions

23. According to the paragraphs, the people's opinion is

(1) not at all important
(2) important to having legitimate power
(3) easy to change
(4) influenced by force
(5) the basis for all types of power

Items 24 and 25 refer to the following paragraphs.

Governments help people organize their lives. Groups of people have goals and need to be able to agree on what actions to take in order to achieve those goals. It would take individuals much too long to achieve those goals alone. According to Abraham Lincoln, government should do the things that people cannot do for themselves.

Governments have four basic functions in a social system. First, a government takes the responsibility for making laws and enforcing them. The laws of a society reflect the general ways people are expected to behave. A law against theft means that stealing is not regarded as proper behavior. Second, a government can help to settle arguments between conflicting interests. It sets up a process to decide how a conflict will be resolved. The government acts somewhat as an umpire. Third, a government develops plans and direction. It coordinates ideas into policies for the society. Fourth, a government deals with other governments.

24. Abraham Lincoln's statement is

   (1) false
   (2) true
   (3) a fact
   (4) an opinion
   (5) out-of-date

25. The opinion that a government acts like an umpire is

   (1) not supported
   (2) supported by the fact that it settles disputes
   (3) supported by the fact that governments make laws
   (4) supported by the fact that governments make policies
   (5) supported by the fact that governments deal with other governments

Items 26 and 27 refer to the following paragraph.

Some people think that the American government has been successful in solving social and economic problems in the last few decades. In this view, government is seen as having reduced racial injustice, inequality, and poverty, although many problems still remain. Others think that American government has not improved the lives of the poor and racial-ethnic minorities. In this view, government represents the interests of the wealthy few. Poverty, racial injustice, and inequality continue to be major problems.

26. In the paragraph, one opinion that is expressed is that American government

   (1) is superior to other forms of government
   (2) has solved all the nation's problems
   (3) represents the interests of the wealthy
   (4) has reached its peak in the last few decades
   (5) is responsible for the problems of society

27. The opinion that American government has not improved the lives of the poor is supported by the fact that

   (1) racial injustice has been reduced
   (2) inequality is not a major problem
   (3) the wealthy do not have major representation in the government
   (4) poverty still is a major problem
   (5) the government is responsible for solving all of society's problems

Tip **When trying to distinguish between facts and opinions, look for these words and phrases that signal opinions: *think, is thought to be, belief, view, probably,* and *may be.***

Answers are on page 788.

Lesson 13 — The American Political Process

A basic part of the political process in a democracy is the party system. The U.S. system tends to be limited to two major parties with one or two other small parties. Each party represents certain beliefs about important government issues. The policies that a party supports are called its platform. The parties that we are familiar with today have grown out of the traditions of several others. Up until the Civil War period, parties came in and out of existence as national issues changed.

For example, the debate over the acceptance of the Constitution led to the formation of the first two political parties in the United States. The Federalists formed a party that supported the new Constitution, while the Anti-Federalists feared that the Constitution would create a national government that was too strong. George Washington was elected President in 1792 on the Federalist ticket. In the mid-1790s, Thomas Jefferson headed the Democratic-Republican party in opposition to the Federalists. This new party supported a stricter interpretation of the Constitution and a weak central government. The election of 1828 saw the rise to power of another party. Andrew Jackson won as the Democratic candidate, defeating the National Republican John Quincy Adams. The Republican party then disappeared from the political scene until 1854, when various groups opposed to slavery picked up the old name to form a new party. This party became a major political force with the election of Abraham Lincoln in 1860.

No candidate from a third party has ever won a presidential election. Because of this, many minor parties have come and gone over the years. Often their names reflected the platform that they promoted. Some of these parties included the Abolitionist, Free Soil, Greenback-Labor, Prohibition, Union Labor, Socialist, and States' Rights candidates parties. The United States even had a Communist party whose most famous candidate, Gus Hall, ran in several presidential elections from the late 1960s to the early 1980s.

In an election, candidates who are not chosen by the two major parties often describe themselves as "Independents." In 1980, John Anderson ran as an Independent against Democratic President Jimmy Carter and the Republican Ronald Reagan. Ross Perot, the billionaire businessman, ran a strong campaign against Bill Clinton and George Bush in 1992. Though third parties and independent candidates have never attained national power, they have influenced the platforms of the two major parties by raising issues that otherwise might not have been discussed.

ged Exercise The American Political Process

Choose the <u>best answer</u> to each item. <u>Items 1 to 7</u> refer to the previous information.

1. Which can be said about third parties in America?

   (1) Third parties fail because they have strange names.
   (2) Minority parties have no support.
   (3) Third-party members are really Socialists.
   (4) Third parties have no place in a two-party system.
   (5) Third parties tend to represent special interests.

2. Over the years, Americans have elected candidates from different parties because

   (1) Democrats are better than Republicans
   (2) Republicans are better than Democrats
   (3) it is the fair thing to do
   (4) the needs of the nation change
   (5) people can't make up their minds

3. The best explanation for the disappearance of the Anti-Federalist party is that

   (1) George Washington was a Federalist
   (2) Thomas Jefferson formed a better party
   (3) ratification of the Constitution was no longer an issue
   (4) the supporters became Federalists
   (5) it wanted to ruin the Constitution

4. To which political party did Abraham Lincoln belong?

   (1) Anti-Federalist
   (2) Federalist
   (3) Democratic-Republican
   (4) Democratic
   (5) Republican

5. According to the information, the real differences between each of the major political parties are in

   (1) their platforms
   (2) their names
   (3) their financial support
   (4) the success of their candidates
   (5) their interpretation of the Constitution

6. Independent candidates have recently gained more supporters. Which is the <u>most likely</u> reason for people to vote for an independent candidate?

   (1) fear of taking a political stand
   (2) laziness
   (3) failing to register to vote
   (4) feeling the major parties do not offer solutions to important problems
   (5) indifference to politics

7. One of the current beliefs of the Republican party today is that power should be shifted from the federal government to the states. This position is <u>most similar</u> to the platform of which earlier party?

   (1) Democratic-Republican
   (2) Abolitionist
   (3) Federalist
   (4) Union Labor
   (5) Third

Tip **When you have to learn information in a long passage, first read the entire passage and figure out the main idea. Then go back and read each paragraph, looking for details to support the main idea.**

Answers are on page 789.

Lesson

14

Government Money and the General Welfare

In a capitalist system, there will always be people who find themselves in financial trouble. A single parent may be unable to manage a full-time job because there is no one to take care of the children. The head of a household may suddenly become unemployed because employers are laying off workers or requiring workers to have more skills or training. The savings from a lifetime of working might not be enough to support a person during retirement. Parents might not be able to afford to send their children to college. Whole towns can be shattered by a natural disaster such as a tornado. The government has stepped in to help in situations like these by setting up social welfare programs under the supervision of various federal agencies.

Some programs affect all Americans, and some programs are designed for special groups. The following agencies and programs are used by many Americans at one time or another.

1. Social Security—a federal insurance plan that pays benefits to retired persons or their spouses, based on their income while working

2. Veterans Administration—provides people who have served in the armed forces with money for education, job training, and hospital care, as well as special rates for housing loans and life insurance

3. Department of Housing and Urban Development—provides funding for rental housing for low-income families, the handicapped, and the elderly; it also provides funds for rehabilitating urban areas

4. Food Stamp Program—issues food stamps to individuals and families having serious temporary or long-term financial difficulties

5. Medicare—pays for some or all medical costs for a U.S. citizen of 65 or over who has worked long enough to qualify for Social Security benefits

6. Unemployment Insurance—pays weekly cash benefits to unemployed workers who have lost their jobs involuntarily. Benefits usually last for up to 26 weeks and may be continued for another 13 weeks in cases of severe economic need.

Choose the best answer to each item. Items 1 to 4 refer to the previous information.

1. William Foster, a 45-year-old who fought in Vietnam, has quit his job in a small town and moved with his family to a large city. His wife has found a good job, but William has discovered that he needs more skills to be hired at a local factory. William's best course of action would be to apply to the

   (1) Department of Housing and Urban Development
   (2) Food Stamp Program
   (3) Social Security Program
   (4) Unemployment Insurance Program
   (5) Veterans Administration

2. David Honda, a construction worker for 45 years, died recently. His wife, Wendy, had worked only a few years, spending most of her time taking care of the children. Their son, Harvey, has advised his mother to apply for government benefits. Harvey probably told her to contact the

   (1) Department of Housing and Urban Development
   (2) Food Stamp Program
   (3) Social Security Program
   (4) Unemployment Insurance Program
   (5) Veterans Administration

3. Mark Thompson has operated his own business since he was 30. Even though he just turned 68, he is still active in the company. Mark has been receiving treatment for severe headaches, but his insurance will not cover all the costs. Mark should see if he can get help from the

   (1) Food Stamp Program
   (2) Medicare Program
   (3) Social Security Program
   (4) Unemployment Insurance Program
   (5) Veterans Administration

4. The automobile parts company that Pete Hoyt worked for laid him off. Pete should apply for benefits from the

   (1) Food Stamp Program
   (2) Medicare Program
   (3) Social Security Program
   (4) Unemployment Insurance Program
   (5) Veterans Administration

Item 5 refers to the following paragraph.

Many industries benefit from government programs. For example, research, county extension agents, and crop subsidies are all paid for by the U.S. government. Each year the U.S. spends millions of dollars to research new crops, pest control, soil erosion, fertilizers, and animal management. The benefits of such research are usually given away free to farmers as a contribution to the nation's welfare.

5. Which of the following is the main idea of the paragraph?

   (1) Agriculture is one industry that benefits from government programs.
   (2) Government sponsors research, county extension agents, and crop subsidies.
   (3) Pest control is an important area of research for farmers.
   (4) The results of government research are often given away free.
   (5) Government research contributes to the nation's welfare.

Answers are on page 790.

Lesson 15 The United States and Foreign Policy

Every nation is affected by what happens in the rest of the world. A nation's behavior toward other nations is called its <u>foreign policy</u>. American foreign policy has developed over the years, based on changes in the world and in the nation itself. Because of the geographic position of the United States and its economic, political, and military strength, the United States now plays a major role in international affairs.

At first, the citizens of the United States believed that they were far enough from Europe and Asia that they could simply grow as a country without being concerned with the troubles of other nations. Washington and Jefferson even warned Americans to be wary of "permanent and entangling alliances." The concept of freedom from a superior power formed the basis for the country's initial foreign policy. For over one hundred years, isolationism, or separation from other countries, was the policy supported by Americans. Nonetheless, as the United States grew and established trade with other nations, it gradually became involved in world affairs.

Even within the framework of an isolationist policy, the United States developed policy for dealing with other countries. The Monroe Doctrine of 1823 warned European countries that interference in American affairs was not welcome. Because of industrialization, the end of the nineteenth century saw the beginning of the Open Door Policy. Communication and trade were encouraged between the United States and China and any other interested nations.

World War I ended America's policy of isolation. Citizens realized the importance of a political commitment to the rest of the world. In 1933, President Franklin D. Roosevelt established the Good Neighbor Policy which supported the right of Latin American countries to develop their own governmental systems without foreign interference. In 1947, President Harry Truman introduced the Marshall Plan and the Truman Doctrine. The Marshall Plan helped war-torn Europe to rebuild economies after the destruction of World War II. The Truman Doctrine stated that the United States would help any government that requested support against Communist influence.

Social Studies ◆ Political Science

ged Exercise The United States and Foreign Policy

Choose the <u>best answer</u> to each item. <u>Items 1 to 8</u> refer to the previous information.

1. The statement that United States foreign policy has always been one of complete isolation or complete involvement is <u>best</u> disproved by the

   (1) Monroe Doctrine
   (2) Open Door Policy
   (3) Good Neighbor Policy
   (4) Marshall Plan
   (5) Truman Doctrine

2. The recent changes in the former Communist nations and their friendliness toward the West show that

   (1) Communists will never change
   (2) communism will never resurface
   (3) communism no longer works
   (4) communism may no longer be a major threat
   (5) communism will become popular again

3. America finally became seriously involved in world affairs because

   (1) it had been too isolated before
   (2) ignoring the world had been easy
   (3) it had to honor its political commitments
   (4) it had to be involved or be destroyed
   (5) Americans tried to be the best that they could be

4. For years, China had been seen as a Communist opponent of the United States. In 1972, however, President Nixon visited that country and reopened diplomatic relations. This action was <u>most closely</u> related to the

   (1) Monroe Doctrine
   (2) Open Door Policy
   (3) Good Neighbor Policy
   (4) Marshall Plan
   (5) Truman Doctrine

5. South Vietnam asked for help against Communist guerrillas in North Vietnam. The policy that led to U.S. involvement in the Vietnam War was the

   (1) Monroe Doctrine
   (2) Open Door Policy
   (3) Good Neighbor Policy
   (4) Marshall Plan
   (5) Truman Doctrine

6. Even though Germany's economy was ruined during World War II, it became very strong in the 1970s and 1980s. One reason for this recovery was probably the

   (1) Monroe Doctrine
   (2) Open Door Policy
   (3) Good Neighbor Policy
   (4) Marshall Plan
   (5) Truman Doctrine

7. The former Soviet Union tried to establish a missile base in Cuba in the early 1960s. The United States insisted that the missiles be withdrawn. The United States was enforcing the

   (1) Monroe Doctrine
   (2) Open Door Policy
   (3) Good Neighbor Policy
   (4) Marshall Plan
   (5) Truman Doctrine

8. With the breakup of the former Soviet Union, the United States became the only truly global power. The <u>most likely</u> result is that

   (1) the United States will repeal the Truman Doctrine
   (2) the Marshall Plan will be reestablished
   (3) U.S. foreign policy will become even more important to other nations
   (4) the United States will enter a period of isolationism
   (5) the United States will build up its defenses against a strong enemy

Answers are on page 790.

Choose the best answer to each item. Items 1 to 4 refer to the following paragraph.

A special type of political leader can emerge in any of the basic political structures. These leaders have an extraordinary quality called "charisma." The force of such individuals' personalities is enough to inspire entire countries to follow them. Revolutions are often led by charismatic figures who appear to represent the principles of the revolt. Some famous charismatic leaders were the visionary Joan of Arc, France's Napoleon, the Nazi leader Hitler, India's gentle Gandhi, Mao of China, England's Churchill, and Cuba's Castro.

1. An opinion expressed by the writer of the paragraph is that

   (1) Joan of Arc said she had visions
   (2) Napoleon was from France
   (3) Hitler was a Nazi
   (4) Gandhi was gentle
   (5) Churchill was English

2. The best example of a stereotype is that charismatic leaders

   (1) have a special quality
   (2) are all revolutionaries
   (3) often represent revolutionary principles
   (4) can occur in any political system
   (5) are inspirational

3. The writer makes the assumption that

   (1) revolutions are necessary movements
   (2) the political figures listed will be familiar
   (3) having charisma is good
   (4) all revolutions have inspiring principles
   (5) the readers already know what charisma is

4. According to the paragraph, the power of certain leaders comes from their

   (1) willingness to sacrifice themselves
   (2) brilliant speeches
   (3) military leadership
   (4) government
   (5) characters

Item 5 refers to the following paragraph.

One result of a very decentralized government, according to some, is that standards of public service vary greatly from area to area. Areas that maintain high standards benefit their regions. However, areas with low standards affect their neighbors and the region as a whole. An example of this is public education. Local control of education increases inequality, according to this view. Some communities maintain high educational standards, and others maintain low standards. The result is that equality of educational opportunity is not available to all citizens.

5. Which of the following is an example of a public service of a strong centralized government?

   (1) local school board control of public education
   (2) zoning restrictions on commercial building in residential areas
   (3) federal food stamp program for the poor and unemployed
   (4) state regulation of the banking industry
   (5) local public housing projects

6. Terrorism is the use of terror as a political weapon. Violent acts are used to force governments to conform to terrorist demands. Often terrorists operate in countries other than their own. Which of the following acts of violence could not be described as an act of terrorism?

(1) A Lebanese guerrilla drives a truck armed with explosives into the American embassy in Beirut.
(2) An Irish woman, at the request of her Syrian boyfriend, carries a package of explosives onto a Pan Am airplane.
(3) The American ambassador to Afghanistan is abducted and shot in a hotel.
(4) A peaceful protester is critically injured in a demonstration against nuclear power plants in North Dakota.
(5) A Greek cruise ship is hijacked in the Mediterranean and an American is shot.

7. In 1965, President Lyndon Johnson created Medicare, a program that offers health insurance for the elderly. Currently the financial benefits for this program are no longer enough to insure adequate care for the eligible citizens. It can be concluded that

(1) the government no longer cares about the elderly
(2) there has been a rapid decline in the number of elderly citizens
(3) there has been a dramatic increase in the number of elderly citizens
(4) citizens should have a medical checkup yearly
(5) no one can rely on government programs

Items 8 and 9 refer to the following table.

THE TOP TEN STATES IN LOTTERY REVENUE, 1992		
State	Gross Revenue (in millions)	Proceeds After Prizes and Administration (in millions)
Florida	$ 2,072	$ 870
New York	1,881	865
Ohio	1,701	731
Massachusetts	1,611	483
Illinois	1,476	605
Pennsylvania	1,315	644
New Jersey	1,287	579
California	1,278	473
Michigan	1,121	482
Virginia	826	289

Source: U.S. Bureau of the Census, *State Government Finances*.

8. Which statement is supported by the information in the table?

(1) Lotteries provide enough revenue for the states that use them.
(2) Lotteries may supply millions of dollars in revenue for some states.
(3) Only ten states operate legal lotteries.
(4) California has the best lottery system.
(5) States now have to rely only on lotteries for their revenue.

9. It can be concluded from the table that gross revenue from lottery tickets is usually

(1) at least twice the amount the states get after prizes and administration
(2) the same in all states
(3) lowest in the Northeast
(4) higher than those of the previous year
(5) higher in California than in Pennsylvania

Answers are on page 791.

Behavioral Science

Lesson 16
People as Members of Cultures

All people of the world grow up in a culture. A <u>culture</u> is the sum of the knowledge, beliefs, arts, morals, laws, and customs of members of a society. Because each society's culture is determined by its physical environment and the makeup of its people, no one culture is exactly like any other. Each culture develops its own values. Societies that are near each other and exchange goods and residents will have many similarities, but they will each have special characteristics.

For many years, cultural behavior was thought to be biologically determined; that is, the way people acted was thought to be inherited like hair color or bone structure. In the early twentieth century, anthropologists Margaret Mead and Ruth Benedict did studies that supported the idea that culture was instead a learned way of behaving. They also said that each culture's behavior as a whole reflected a general personality for that group.

Within a particular culture, children learn what is expected of them. Children find out that there are acceptable and unacceptable ways of behaving. They learn that there are rules of conduct that govern how a person should think and act. Most of these rules are so old that we do not even think about them. We simply know that certain actions are right, at least, right in the eyes of the people we live with.

Some customs of one culture may look very strange to the members of another culture. However, customs that might seem to have no reason actually have functional bases. According to one anthropologist, all customs come from a way of fulfilling an emotional or biological need of the society. A general example of this idea is that a belief in magic is a way to explain things that cannot be explained by looking at facts. More specific ways of behaving are also influenced by culture. In many Christian societies, women used to wear hats or veils to church. The cultural background for such action lies in the Biblical statement that a woman's hair is her crown of glory and should be covered when worshipping in church. Another example can be seen in Asian children, trained from infancy to have an unquestioning respect for their parents and their ancestors and to uphold the reputations of their families.

ged Exercise People as Members of Cultures

Choose the best answer to each item. Items 1 to 7 refer to the previous information.

1. Women wearing hats in church are expressing a cultural value that can best be stated as

   (1) a person should be humble when worshipping
   (2) fashion is very important
   (3) women should not be jealous of each other's hairstyles
   (4) all women are vain
   (5) women are not as good as men

2. In the past few years, many of the winners of academic contests have been the American children of Asian parents. These children have studied very hard because they have been taught the value of

   (1) showing respect for their families' reputations
   (2) education as a means to success
   (3) winning contests
   (4) obeying rules
   (5) being right

3. According to the information, cultural values are

   (1) inherited
   (2) learned
   (3) the same in all societies
   (4) similar
   (5) unimportant

4. According to the information, customs are developed because

   (1) everyone believes in magic
   (2) emotional and biological needs have to be fulfilled
   (3) the Bible has set out cultural rules
   (4) life would be strange without them
   (5) children have to be taught something

5. Which of the following is most likely to be a custom among traditional Japanese?

   (1) Even after marriage, one son lives with his parents until they die.
   (2) Children leave home at age eighteen.
   (3) Old people are sent to live in the mountains.
   (4) Young children are sent to live with relatives until grown.
   (5) Children are not allowed to visit their grandparents.

6. The most likely reason that Alaskan Eskimos developed a culture which might seem strange to other people is that

   (1) Eskimos are strange people
   (2) they never came in contact with other people
   (3) they had to wear heavy furs all the time
   (4) their harsh environment made certain behavior necessary
   (5) they were the only Indian groups to remain in the North

7. Immigrant parents of American-born children often complain that their children do not respect their culture. The basis of this complaint is likely to be their children's

   (1) exposure to the culture of their parents
   (2) adopting customs of the American culture
   (3) doing poorly in American schools
   (4) choice of friends
   (5) rebellious behavior during adolescence

Tip Actions often reveal values better than speech. When reading about cultural values, pay attention to how people behave. Sometimes words and actions differ.

Items 8 to 13 refer to the following paragraph.

An individual's personality is made up of the special way that person thinks, feels, and behaves. Although each person is born with unique inherited characteristics, the culture in which that person lives has a powerful influence on personality development. Behavioral scientists say that certain general personality traits are the result of what is called <u>cultural conditioning</u>. In other words, each culture tends to produce a certain range of characteristics. For example, in traditional Arab societies, most women behave in a shy and withdrawn manner, but women in some Polynesian groups tend to be very outgoing. Such aspects of personality are learned from life experiences in the family. So, much of a child's personality is shaped by the culturally "correct" way the parents behave.

8. What is highly valued in traditional Arab societies as described in the paragraph?

   (1) family life
   (2) girl children
   (3) boy children
   (4) quiet women
   (5) aggression

9. The Marquesan tribe of the South Pacific believes that prolonged nursing of infants makes a child difficult to raise. The Chencho people of India do not wean their children until they are five or six years old. What explains this difference?

   (1) Marquesan women do not know how to nurse.
   (2) The Chencho culture encourages prolonged nursing behavior in their children.
   (3) Marquesan women are more civilized and liberated.
   (4) Chencho women are born to be better mothers.
   (5) Climate differences affect how families raise their children.

10. According to the paragraph, what is the relationship of a person's personality to his or her culture?

    (1) Personality is a cause of culture.
    (2) The relationship between culture and personality depends upon the individual.
    (3) Culture is the result of personality.
    (4) Personality is influenced by culture.
    (5) Culture has no influence on personality.

11. Which statement is <u>best</u> supported by evidence presented in the paragraph?

    (1) Early influences on personality cannot be measured.
    (2) Persons raised in the same culture eventually look alike.
    (3) Polynesian women are bashful.
    (4) Persons raised in the same culture tend to have similar characteristics.
    (5) Many Arab women wear veils.

12. Which of the following would be the <u>best</u> title for the paragraph?

    (1) The Behavioral Sciences
    (2) Culture and Personality
    (3) Characteristics of Our Culture
    (4) The Culture of Childhood
    (5) Children and Personality

13. Which of the following behaviors is <u>most</u> likely a result of cultural conditioning?

    (1) going to sleep at night
    (2) eating when you are hungry
    (3) using a fork, knife, and spoon
    (4) talking with a friend
    (5) seeking shelter from a storm

Items 14 to 18 refer to the following paragraphs.

The first great civilizations of the world developed along the banks of great rivers. From the beginning, conditions in the Nile River Valley in Egypt, and in areas like the Nile River Valley in what is now the Middle East, were favorable for agriculture. It was in river valleys that early people first worked out rules for living together in communities. The earliest rules dealt with irrigation. Cooperation was needed to build systems of dams and canals, leaders were needed to supervise the building, and laws were needed to ensure fair use of materials and water.

The well-watered, fertile soil produced abundant harvests. So fertile was the soil of the Nile Valley that farmers could produce more than enough food for themselves and their families. As a result, surplus goods could be sold. This resulted in the development of trade and commerce, and with these came the exchange of ideas and inventions between people of different regions.

Since there was ample food available, not everyone had to be engaged in farming. Some people left farming to develop arts and crafts. Potters learned to shape clay to make decorative vases; weavers learned to make fabrics and patterns of intricate designs; carpenters learned to build different types of furniture; and architects learned to construct elaborate buildings for government and worship. Thus, civilization and culture grew and prospered in the river valleys of the Middle East.

14. Which of the following tells why civilization first developed in the Nile River Valley and in the Middle East?

   (1) It was a major center for trade.
   (2) The soil was fertile and produced abundant harvests.
   (3) The area had a large population.
   (4) People were deeply religious.
   (5) It was customary to live near rivers.

15. According to the paragraphs, what was most likely highly valued by the early Egyptians who left farming?

   (1) beauty
   (2) agricultural knowledge
   (3) water rights
   (4) law and order
   (5) individual freedom

16. The rise of trade in the ancient world most likely resulted in

   (1) development of a number system with which to keep business records
   (2) the domestication of animals
   (3) widespread use of irrigation systems
   (4) the building of large temples to the gods
   (5) development of better food crops

17. Early laws were established as a result of the need to

   (1) build enough housing
   (2) limit surplus goods
   (3) create a just system of water distribution
   (4) govern commerce and trade
   (5) educate craftspeople

18. The early Egyptians as a group apparently placed a high value on

   (1) competition
   (2) cooperation
   (3) selfishness
   (4) education
   (5) independence

A recent study by a Harvard-educated sociologist born in India sought to explain why poor people in India tend to have large families. As one illiterate laborer said, despite the fact that he had no land and very little money, he considered his eight children to be his greatest wealth. He said, "It's good to have a big family. They don't cost much and when they get old enough to work, they bring in money. And when I am old, they will take care of me."

Because this is a view that millions of Indians share, it represents a major obstacle in the effort to curb the rapid growth of India's population. The report states, "People are not poor because they have large families. Quite the contrary, they have large families because they are poor."

Some of the reasons that poor people are reluctant to reduce the size of their families relate to social customs that the Indian government is trying to abolish. The dowry system, for example, often forces a couple to try to produce sons to offset the economic liability they face in providing money to marry off their daughters. Many Indians think they must have at least eight children to allow for those who may die during youth. Most Indians also want to ensure they will still have at least two adult sons to provide for them in their old age.

19. The main reason for this study was to

    (1) understand the reason for the size of Indian families
    (2) describe birth-control methods
    (3) describe the dowry system
    (4) explain why poor people live in India
    (5) caution people about overpopulation

Tip When reading about beliefs, look for clues that indicate what could have influenced people's actions. This will tell you the people's cultural values.

20. According to the paragraphs, many poor Indians do not like the idea of limiting family size because of

    (1) anti-government sentiment
    (2) the country's low birthrate
    (3) the desire to marry off their daughters
    (4) social and economic customs
    (5) religious beliefs

21. Which is a cultural value of India?

    (1) The old take care of the young.
    (2) A large family costs too much.
    (3) The dowry system produces only sons.
    (4) Indians all have eight children.
    (5) Having children is a great wealth.

22. Why is it important that the sociologist was born in India?

    (1) The sociologist was one of many children.
    (2) It supports the sociologist as an expert.
    (3) Indians can go to Harvard.
    (4) Illiterate people can become sociologists.
    (5) Not all sons die in childhood.

23. In many U.S. families, the economic role of the two adult sons who support an Indian couple in their old age is likely to be taken over by

    (1) pensions and social security
    (2) younger sons
    (3) adult daughters
    (4) an inheritance
    (5) salary from a job

A FOLKLORIST'S COLLECTION OF BELIEFS ABOUT THE WEATHER

Urban	**Rural**
John Smith (two beliefs)	Joe Green (eleven beliefs)
red sky in morning (rain)	red sky in morning (rain)
ground hog appears Feb. 2 (early spring)	birds roosting in middle of day (rain)
	cows rolling over in the dirt (rain)
Ellen Freeman (seven beliefs)	cuckoos making lots of noise (rain)
arthritis acting up (rain)	arthritis acting up (rain)
birds roosting in middle of the day (rain)	salt placed on onion peels will predict rainy months
cats claw up furniture (rain)	
persimmon seed shaped like spoon (mild winter) fork (cold winter)	fish settling near bottom of lake in early fall (cold winter)
if the geese fly early and in tight formation (winter will be cold)	the shape of a persimmon seed will tell you if the winter will be mild or severe
fish swimming deep in water in fall (cold winter)	thickness of the breastbone of a wild goose killed in early fall will predict mild or severe winter
if January first is warm (the whole month of January will be warm)	a warm Christmas (rich harvest)
	persimmon seed shaped like spoon (wet summer, good crops); shaped like fork (dry summer and crop failures)

24. Which can be concluded from the information?

    (1) Urban people have no beliefs about the weather.
    (2) Rural people have no beliefs about the weather.
    (3) Both urban and rural people have beliefs about the weather.
    (4) Urban beliefs are based on facts.
    (5) Rural beliefs are based on facts.

25. What is true about causes and effects in these beliefs?

    (1) The action of fish causes cold winters.
    (2) The action of birds causes rain.
    (3) Red morning skies cause rain.
    (4) Fruit-seed shapes affect the weather.
    (5) None of the beliefs involves causes.

26. Which proverb is most similar to the beliefs given in the information?

    (1) April showers bring May flowers.
    (2) Every cloud has a silver lining.
    (3) An apple a day keeps the doctor away.
    (4) A bird in the hand is worth two in the bush.
    (5) If March comes in like a lion, it goes out like a lamb.

27. People who believe they can predict the weather from natural signs assume that

    (1) the U.S. weather service makes more reliable predictions
    (2) predicting the weather must be done outdoors
    (3) there are relationships between weather and other natural happenings
    (4) their predictions are always correct
    (5) only rain can be predicted in this way

Answers are on page 791.

Individual and Group Behavior

People do not just behave as they please. Their actions and attitudes are the products of both their own personalities and cultural influences. The values and beliefs of large and small groups and of other individuals can influence the way a person thinks and acts.

A group is two or more people who have regular interaction and who identify, or feel something in common with each other. Humans have probably always lived in groups. A group can protect an individual from dangers that come from other people, or from natural disasters. A group also allows people to share the responsibility for providing all the basic needs of life, such as food, shelter, and clothing.

Everyone associates with many groups. The first group anyone joins is the family. The family group gives love and support and teaches the basic values of the culture. The family group is where a person learns to become a social human being. A child who is isolated from the caring of a family grows up to be less aware of responsibility and cooperation than other people. As people grow older, they get involved with play groups, friends, schoolmates, work groups, and hobby groups—such as people who are all interested in racing or who all collect baseball cards. These groups influence how the individual will act in various situations.

Sociologists have discovered that people often act differently in groups than they do when they are alone. For example, a single woman who spends much of her time at home working on carpentry projects and tinkering with her car might go out for the evening with friends. Instead of wearing her jeans and t-shirt, she dresses in a silky blouse and long flowing skirt. People also will act differently with one group than they do when they are with another group. A supervisor at a factory might be very strict and distant with his crew but be casual and relaxed when out with his buddies.

ged Exercise Individual and Group Behavior

Choose the best answer to each item. Items 1 to 3 refer to the previous information.

1. A doctor, lawyer, mechanic, clerk, and potter have been meeting every Friday night for ten years to play a friendly game of cards. They sometimes talk about their work but are not bothered by the differences in their occupations. These people probably share the belief that

   (1) gambling is necessary
   (2) friends are more important than money
   (3) they have to get away from their spouses
   (4) money makes all the difference
   (5) some people are better than others

2. According to the information, groups affect an individual's behavior. This effect probably occurs because

   (1) individuals have no real personality
   (2) we react to other people's opinions
   (3) groups practice mind-control
   (4) all people are essentially lonely
   (5) sociologists say it does

3. Ed is having trouble fitting in with the people he has met since leaving his hometown. The best explanation for this is that

   (1) he is not good at fitting in
   (2) big cities are hard to live in
   (3) he has not yet met people with common interests
   (4) he has no social skills
   (5) he gets along well with everyone

Items 4 and 5 refer to the following paragraphs.

Can a cat be the mother of rabbits? Sure, if she wants to she can, answers Vivian Gussin Paley, teacher and author of *Mollie is Three: Growing Up in School.* In Paley's preschool classroom, such imagination is valued highly. Three-year-old Mollie and her classmates play out their thoughts and feelings under the supportive and unobtrusive direction of their teacher, who realizes that "the strongest incentives a preschool classroom can offer are friendship and fantasy."

Fantasy play, Paley believes, is a way for children to share and connect with others, to begin making sense of the real world. It is an outlet for expression, and provides a channel for uncomfortable emotions such as sadness, fear, and jealousy. Fredrick, for example, works through feelings surrounding a frightening near-drowning episode: "The Incredible Hulk jumps into some water and he gets his head wet. . . . I'm the Hulk. . . . I can swim fast. . . . And then I'm home."

4. According to the paragraphs, a child who pretends something is real

   (1) is learning to deal with the real world
   (2) should be discouraged
   (3) has a serious problem with adjustment
   (4) will never understand real emotions
   (5) is too young to go to school

5. The information in the paragraphs provides evidence that fantasy play

   (1) is limited to children
   (2) has a positive social role
   (3) comes from watching TV cartoons
   (4) has no role in the classroom
   (5) has nothing to do with emotion

Items 6 and 7 refer to the following information.

Over the years, many people have told of experiences similar to the ones recorded below.

"The summer before last (1965), my daughter and I were looking out the back door here and we noticed a silver object coming up very slowly over the hill. It was just sundown so we couldn't really see how large it was. It had red, blue, green, and white lights which kept blinking on and off, and it hovered directly between the huge tree and the power lines. It would hover there for about forty minutes each time we saw it. We both saw this object go through the same act ten nights in a row."

"My husband said that about three years ago, he and some of his fraternity brothers drove to Florida for spring vacation. They drove straight through from Muncie to Fort Lauderdale, with each boy taking a turn driving. On the way down at about three o'clock in the morning, one of them saw a lighted saucer-shaped object flying a little above and directly behind the car. He was really afraid, as there were no other cars on the road at that time of night, and he told the others. He said they were all simply petrified. They went faster and faster until they were going about 120 miles per hour, but the thing stayed with them. He said this went on for about ten minutes, and then the thing finally disappeared. He said all the boys saw it and will swear it's true."

6. The people who had these experiences probably share a belief in

    (1) electricity
    (2) family values
    (3) the power of suggestion
    (4) UFOs
    (5) scientific proof

7. The speakers provide evidence for their beliefs by

    (1) giving exact descriptions of the objects
    (2) saying that the experience was shared by at least two people
    (3) referring to scientific evidence
    (4) describing the physical effects of the experience
    (5) telling about official reactions

Item 8 refers to the following information.

Once people have a belief, they often cling to it even when there is evidence that their belief is not true.

8. Which of the following is an example of the information given above?

    (1) a person who gradually overcomes a fear of flying
    (2) a child who did poorly in a substandard school believes that she is not smart
    (3) Columbus's belief that the world was round, not flat
    (4) a jury that acquits a defendant after hearing evidence of her innocence
    (5) a consumer who switches to a new brand of detergent after trying a sample

Item 9 refers to the following information.

In contrast to beliefs is knowledge, a collection of facts and ideas about the world. Knowledge is relatively objective, reliable, and can be proved true or false.

9. Which of the following is the best example of knowledge in use?

    (1) technology
    (2) magic
    (3) religion
    (4) music
    (5) art

Items 10 to 15 refer to the following information.

Many people worry, or are anxious, about what happens in their lives. Psychologists have classified the main ways people try to avoid anxiety.

1. denial—refusing to believe that something unpleasant or painful has actually happened
2. displacement—blaming one's own frustration on someone or something else that really did not cause the problem
3. projection—believing that someone else has the problem or bad habit that is actually one's own
4. rationalization—pretending that something else is the real reason for failing to do something important
5. reaction formation—acting in a way that is the opposite of how one feels or believes
6. repression—storing painful or disturbing memories involuntarily in the unconscious mind

10. A young member of a street gang is arrested for spray painting a school building. When asked why he destroyed public property, he answers that it is all his father's fault for dying in the war. The boy's answer is an example of

(1) denial
(2) displacement
(3) projection
(4) rationalization
(5) reaction formation

11. Many adults who were abused as children do not remember long periods of their child-hoods. This memory loss is an example of

(1) displacement
(2) projection
(3) rationalization
(4) reaction formation
(5) repression

12. Davy Bloch is afraid of doctors. Davy's friends have urged him to have a checkup to find out the cause of his constant stomach pains, but Davy says he just has not been able to find the time. Davy's answer is an example of

(1) displacement
(2) projection
(3) rationalization
(4) reaction formation
(5) repression

13. Mike O'Leary broke off his engagement to Anne Pallas. Anne still loves Mike, but when she runs into him, she acts as if they are almost strangers. Anne's attitude is an example of

(1) denial
(2) displacement
(3) rationalization
(4) reaction formation
(5) repression

14. Vivian has trouble being on time for anything. She accuses her prompt husband of always being late. This is an example of

(1) displacement
(2) projection
(3) rationalization
(4) reaction formation
(5) repression

15. Lester's mother recently died after a long illness. Lester refuses to get rid of any of his mother's clothes or furniture, insisting that she will soon be home from the hospital. Lester's behavior is an example of

(1) denial
(2) displacement
(3) projection
(4) rationalization
(5) reaction formation

Item 16 refers to the following cartoon.

Items 17 to 18 refer to the following cartoon.

BLONDIE

"Are you sure you won't quit after a year
or two to get married?"

16. A social scientist might use this cartoon to illustrate which concept?

    (1) peer groups—informal groups of approximately the same ages and interests

    (2) phobias—unreasonable fears

    (3) sex roles—the beliefs, attitudes, and behaviors expected of a man or a woman

    (4) prejudice—strong emotional opposition to members of a group

    (5) introversion—a tendency to keep to oneself

17. The cartoonist is poking fun at an argument often used by corporations for not hiring a certain minority group. What is that argument?

    (1) Men quit work to get married.

    (2) Teenagers quit work to get married.

    (3) Women quit work to get married.

    (4) Men quit work to have children.

    (5) Women quit work to have children.

18. Affirmative action programs were begun by the government to make sure that companies would increase the number of minority groups, such as women, African Americans, Hispanics, and people with disabilities in their employ. The government probably took this action because of evidence that company executives believed that

    (1) all people deserved a chance

    (2) minorities would be good employees

    (3) minorities were not reliable employees

    (4) women were more responsible than men

    (5) people with disabilities were dedicated workers

Many theories and principles explain how people learn. Five of these are described below.

1. <u>positive transfer</u>—earlier learning makes the learning of new skills easier.
2. <u>negative transfer</u>—earlier learning interferes with the learning of new skills.
3. <u>cognitive dissonance</u>—new facts do not agree with earlier learning and are ignored.
4. <u>cognitive consonance</u>—new facts agree with earlier learning and are accepted.
5. <u>reinforcement</u>—learning that is rewarded through self-satisfaction or by social approval will be repeated.

The following questions describe or relate to one of the five principles described above. Choose the principle that would most likely apply.

19. A confirmed smoker sees a newspaper headline saying "Medical Study Denies That Smoking Is Linked to Early Death." Because of the article she decides to continue to smoke cigarettes. This is an example of which principle?

    (1) positive transfer
    (2) negative transfer
    (3) cognitive dissonance
    (4) cognitive consonance
    (5) reinforcement

20. A teacher awards a gold star to the class for every ten minutes of quiet working. For ten gold stars the class will have an extra ten minutes of recess time. This is an example of which theory?

    (1) positive transfer
    (2) negative transfer
    (3) cognitive dissonance
    (4) cognitive consonance
    (5) reinforcement

Items 21 and 22 refer to the following graph.

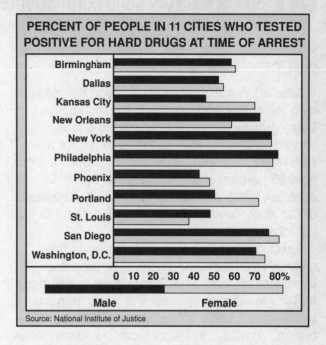

PERCENT OF PEOPLE IN 11 CITIES WHO TESTED POSITIVE FOR HARD DRUGS AT TIME OF ARREST

Source: National Institute of Justice

21. The graph supports which hypothesis?

    (1) Drug users are the only victims of drug abuse.
    (2) Addicts steal money to buy drugs.
    (3) There is a link between hard-drug use and criminal behavior.
    (4) Male drug abusers are more likely than female drug abusers to commit violent crimes.
    (5) Law enforcement officials see no relationship between drug use and crime.

22. Which of the following is a statement of opinion, rather than a fact based on the graph?

    (1) The statistics shown are from 11 large American cities.
    (2) Most drug addicts commit crimes.
    (3) In New York, more than 70 percent of those arrested tested positive for hard drugs.
    (4) In San Diego, more women than men tested positive for hard drugs at their time of arrest.
    (5) In many cities, more women than men tested positive for hard drugs at their time of arrest.

Answers are on page 793.

Choose the best answer to each item. Items 1 to 4 refer to the following information and graph.

After 30 years of affirmative action designed to help minorities and women in the workplace, these groups are still barred from top jobs, according to a federal commission. White men, who make up about 29 percent of the work force, hold 95 percent of top management jobs. In contrast, white women, who make up 40 percent of the work force, hold less than 5 percent of the top jobs.

Although many women and minorities have entered middle management, their progress usually stops there. The commission concluded that the fears and prejudices of white men were largely responsible for the so-called "glass ceiling." Although in theory women and minorities can reach the top, they often hit an invisible, or "glass," ceiling. A comparison of pay by sex and race also reveals inequalities at all levels.

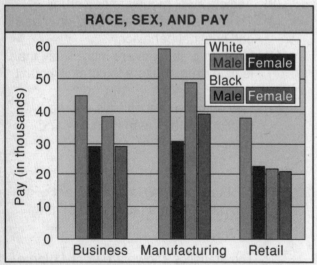

RACE, SEX, AND PAY

Pay (in thousands)

White — Male, Female
Black — Male, Female

Business   Manufacturing   Retail

Source: The Glass Ceiling Commission

1. According to the graph, the lowest-paid workers in manufacturing jobs are

    (1) white men
    (2) white women
    (3) black men
    (4) black women
    (5) Hispanic men

2. According to the commission, 30 years of affirmative action have resulted in

    (1) large numbers of black men in top-management jobs
    (2) many women breaking through the "glass ceiling"
    (3) more women and minorities in middle-management jobs
    (4) many white men in top-management jobs
    (5) equal pay for men and women in all industries

3. Which of the following is true of all three industries shown in the graph?

    (1) Black women make more than white women.
    (2) White women make more than black men.
    (3) Black men make more than white women.
    (4) Black men make more than black women.
    (5) White men make twice as much as white women.

4. According to the commission, the "glass ceiling" exists because white men fear that

    (1) minorities and women are a threat to their power
    (2) minorities and women do not have the experience for top-management jobs
    (3) minorities and women do not have the personal qualifications for top-management jobs
    (4) minorities and women are undependable workers
    (5) minorities and women do not work as hard as white men

Anthropologists and other behavioral scientists see culture as having two main parts: material culture and nonmaterial culture. Material culture consists of the tools, artifacts, and other objects that a culture produces. Nonmaterial culture includes the ways members of a society think and how they do things.

5. Which is the best example of nonmaterial culture?

   (1) pollution
   (2) a car
   (3) Native American baskets
   (4) clothing styles
   (5) courtship behavior

6. Which is the best example of material culture?

   (1) adobe ovens for baking
   (2) religious practices
   (3) Hinduism
   (4) marriage
   (5) firsthand observations

7. Which is the main idea of the paragraph?

   (1) Anthropologists are behavioral scientists.
   (2) Anthropologists study cultures.
   (3) The two parts of a culture are material and nonmaterial.
   (4) Material culture includes tools.
   (5) Nonmaterial culture includes beliefs.

Items 8 and 9 are based on the following paragraph.

An unusual but fascinating study of cultural patterns was carried out by anthropologist Hortense Powdermaker. Her personal interest in movies led her to do fieldwork in Hollywood for a year. Powdermaker thought that the social structure in the filmmaking town influenced the content of the movies made there. She found, among other things, a self-imposed moral code and a constantly changing population of artists and businesspeople.

8. Which of the following is an opinion expressed in the paragraph?

   (1) Powdermaker studied cultural patterns.
   (2) Powdermaker made a fascinating study.
   (3) Powdermaker was an anthropologist.
   (4) Powdermaker was interested in movies.
   (5) Powdermaker worked in Hollywood.

9. A group of anthropologists objected to Powdermaker's study on the grounds that the proper focus for study should be non-Western cultures. Which argument would have been a convincing one for them to use?

   (1) She would either fail to meet the proper people or would get too involved in the movie scene.
   (2) Hollywood types are just a bunch of self-interested actors.
   (3) It is difficult to make an objective study of one's own culture.
   (4) Studying filmmakers is not important because movie audiences are interested in the glamorous stars.
   (5) There are no cultural patterns in Hollywood.

Tip When evaluating answer options, think about the answer's logic. Ask: Does this answer make sense? Is this what the facts show?

10. During the 1960s, anthropologists and psychologists studied the culture of a poor rural area in Minnesota. They found that people who were poorest and who had the fewest relatives and friends were more often depressed. Those active in religious groups showed less depression. Which of the following factors is least likely to be associated with depression?

   (1) rural setting
   (2) many social contacts
   (3) isolation
   (4) poverty
   (5) unemployment

Answers are on page 795.

Choose the best answer to each item.

Items 1 to 4 refer to the following maps.

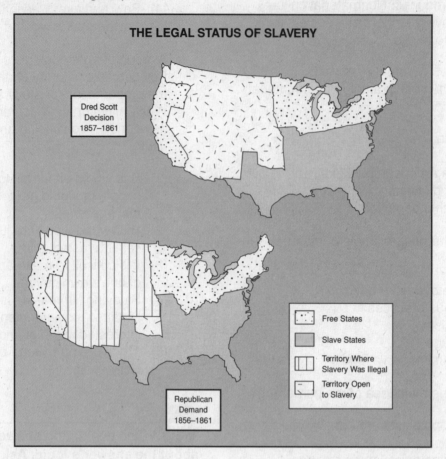

1. The maps support the conclusion that Republicans

   (1) were in favor of slavery
   (2) were successful in getting what they wanted
   (3) lived mainly in the South
   (4) never owned slaves
   (5) were opposed to legal slavery in the territories

2. According to the map of Republican demand, in which of the following states was slavery legal?

   (1) Oregon
   (2) California
   (3) Minnesota
   (4) Texas
   (5) Wyoming

3. If the Civil War had not happened and the Dred Scott decision was upheld, which would probably be true?

   (1) Any new state could have slaves.
   (2) No new states could have slaves.
   (3) Only one new state could have slaves.
   (4) The slaves would have rebelled.
   (5) The Republicans would have changed their minds.

4. The positions of the two sides of the slavery issue are most like the positions of

   (1) Quakers and Jews
   (2) two parents arguing over money
   (3) two children, each claiming all the toys
   (4) England and France during World War I
   (5) Germany and Japan during World War II

Items 5 and 6 refer to the following paragraphs.

Democracy means that the people rule themselves. The greater the voice of the people, the more democratic the system. In a true democratic system, all people have a voice in the government. Systems of government can be democratic in different ways. The thirteen colonies developed three basic systems of government that applied democratic principles in different ways.

In self-governing colonies, the colonists themselves elected the governor and all members of the legislature. Connecticut and Rhode Island were self-governing colonies. In proprietary colonies, the proprietor, or owner, of the colony selected the governor. The colonists elected all members of the legislature. Maryland, Pennsylvania, and Delaware were proprietary colonies. The other eight colonies were royal colonies. In royal colonies, the governor was selected by the king of England. The legislature was divided into two branches. The colonists elected the members of one branch, but the king chose the members of the other.

5. Some parts of colonial government were democratic; others were not. Which of the following parts was democratic?

   (1) In the southern colonies, local officials were appointed by the governor, rather than elected by the people.
   (2) In all colonies, people had to own land in order to vote.
   (3) In the proprietary colonies, governors could veto, or reject, laws that the elected legislature had passed.
   (4) In the New England colonies, people ran their own towns through meetings in which they discussed and voted on issues.
   (5) The king of England had final say about laws passed in the colonies.

6. Given the definition of democracy and of a true democratic system, which of the following lists the types of colonial government from most democratic to least democratic?

   (1) self-governing, proprietary, royal
   (2) proprietary, self-governing, royal
   (3) royal, self-governing, proprietary
   (4) proprietary, royal, self-governing
   (5) self-governing, royal, proprietary

Items 7 and 8 refer to the following paragraph.

The French expanded their holdings in North America through fur trading. Traders moved beyond the Great Lakes, into the Ohio Valley, and then west to the Mississippi River. Using the tributaries of the Mississippi, the French spread from the Gulf of Mexico to the base of the Rocky Mountains.

7. From the paragraph you can conclude that the French fur traders

   (1) established large towns throughout North America
   (2) sold furs to English colonists on the East Coast
   (3) sold furs to the Native Americans
   (4) reached the west coast
   (5) traveled largely by water

8. At the time the French controlled the middle part of North America, the most important use of the Mississippi River and its tributaries was for

   (1) fishing
   (2) transportation
   (3) natural boundary
   (4) hydroelectric power
   (5) irrigation

Tip **When applying information to a new context, look to see how key terms in the passage have been defined. Use these definitions to help you decide how they would apply in a new context.**

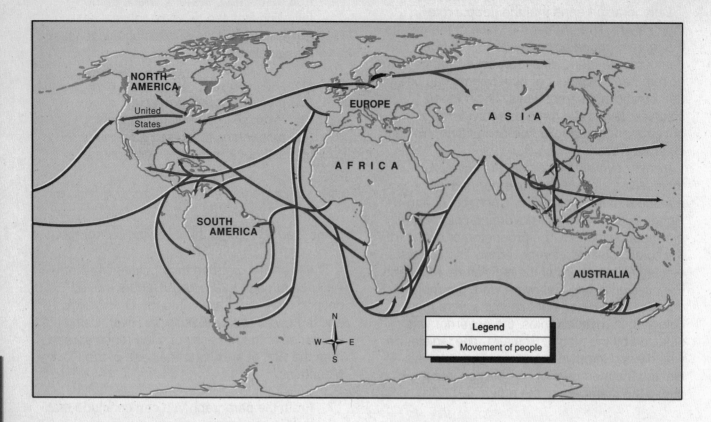

9. According to the map, which area has the fewest immigrants?

   (1) United States
   (2) South America
   (3) Europe
   (4) Australia
   (5) Africa

10. Within the United States, the movement of people has been generally to the

   (1) north
   (2) west
   (3) south
   (4) east
   (5) south and east

11. Which of the following would be the best title for this map?

   (1) Worldwide Movement of People
   (2) Immigration in the 1800s
   (3) Immigration to the United States
   (4) Future Population Trends
   (5) Patterns of European Settlements

12. From this map, you can conclude that

   (1) the number of immigrants has decreased in recent years
   (2) immigration to the United States peaked in 1900
   (3) immigration affects all continents
   (4) most immigrants from Asia go to Africa
   (5) people move to improve their economic situations

Items 13 to 15 refer to the following paragraphs.

Income in the United States is distributed unequally. Although the United States is considered a middle-class society, the poorest fifth of our country earns only 5 percent of the income while the richest fifth earns 44 percent of the income. In 1991, 11 percent of U.S. adults and 21 percent of U.S. children were at poverty levels. Many of these people lack the education necessary to hold a job in this technological society.

The difference in income between the wealthy and the poor has increased in recent years. Prices for necessities like food and housing have increased more rapidly than the minimum wage. Consequently, the poor have become poorer in terms of their ability to pay for necessities. The percentage of people living in poverty has also increased from 11 percent in 1987 to 14 percent in 1991.

13. What percent of the entire U.S. population lived in poverty in 1991?

   (1) 5 percent
   (2) 11 percent
   (3) 14 percent
   (4) 21 percent
   (5) 44 percent

14. According to the writer, what is a partial cause of unequal distribution of income?

   (1) The cost of food has become higher than the cost of housing.
   (2) There is a lack of appropriate schooling.
   (3) People pretend to be middle-class.
   (4) Prices have increased more rapidly than wages.
   (5) Many people are at poverty level.

15. According to the writer, which is an effect of the more rapid increase in prices?

   (1) increased inequality of income
   (2) more equal income
   (3) less money for social welfare programs
   (4) more poor children
   (5) more people in the middle-class

Items 16 and 17 refer to the following paragraphs.

Congress has created several regulatory commissions that protect citizens from certain economic problems. Regulatory commissions make rules and come to decisions that affect banking, transportation, labor unions, communications, and other corporations. These commissions make rules about what businesses can and cannot do. They also help to settle disputes between opposing parties.

One of these commissions is the Federal Communications Commission, or FCC. The FCC licenses all radio and television stations. It decides how broadcasting wavelengths and channels are used based on whether "public convenience, interest, or necessity" is well served. If the FCC doesn't think that a station is operating for the public benefit, it can take away the station's license to broadcast.

When Congress establishes a commission, it makes sure that the commission is independent. The President is not allowed to fire commission members or chairpersons. In this way, Congress keeps the commissions from being pressured by political issues. Instead, the commission is free to act in the public interest.

16. A regulatory commission would probably rule in a dispute between

   (1) a public-interest group and a toy manufacturer
   (2) Congress and the President
   (3) a TV station and an advertiser
   (4) two political parties
   (5) a supermarket and an employee

17. According to the paragraphs, Congress has assumed that a committee that is free of political pressure will

   (1) listen more carefully to the President
   (2) act only for the public good
   (3) seek political support
   (4) be reappointed
   (5) not be independent

Items 18 and 19 refer to the following cartoon.

Clay Bennett, North America Syndicate.

18. The man in the black suit represents

   (1) members of Congress
   (2) senators
   (3) taxpayers
   (4) business executives
   (5) lobbyists

19. Which of the following is an opinion expressed by the cartoonist?

   (1) Members of Congress present themselves as independent even though they follow the advice of special-interest groups.
   (2) In order to get elected, members of Congress must raise enough money to finance their campaigns.
   (3) Members of Congress have assistants who do research on particular bills and issues.
   (4) Members of Congress have speech writers who tell them what to say.
   (5) Most members of Congress and lobbyists are middle-aged white men.

20. The Agency for International Development is responsible for foreign aid programs. Much of the food the agency sends to Africa and Asia to feed political refugees and people in famine areas rots on the docks or in warehouses before it reaches people who are starving. The most effective response of the Agency for International Development would be to

   (1) send more food
   (2) spray all foods with preservatives
   (3) offer technical assistance in food distribution
   (4) send money instead of food
   (5) refuse to send foreign aid to countries suffering from famine

21. At the time of the 1980 Moscow Olympic games, the former USSR had sent invasion troops to Afghanistan. President Jimmy Carter decided that a withdrawal of United States teams from the international games would be powerful evidence of United States

   (1) disapproval of the Soviet action
   (2) military strength
   (3) athletic superiority
   (4) acceptance of the Soviet action
   (5) inability to compete

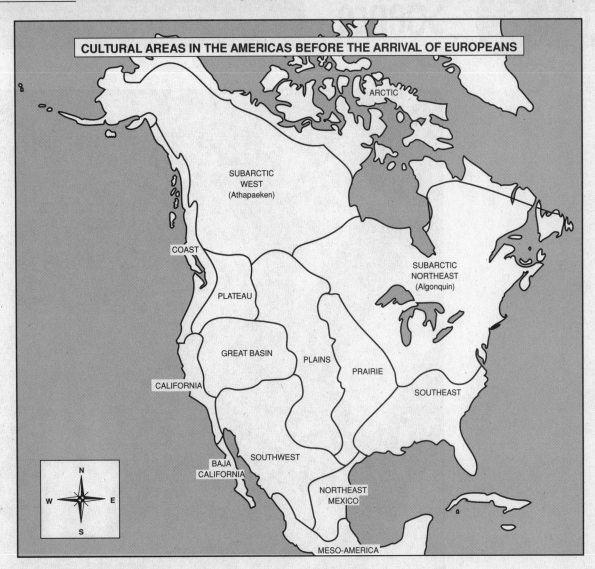

CULTURAL AREAS IN THE AMERICAS BEFORE THE ARRIVAL OF EUROPEANS

ARCTIC

SUBARCTIC
WEST
(Athapaeken)

SUBARCTIC
NORTHEAST
(Algonquin)

COAST

PLATEAU

GREAT BASIN

PLAINS

PRAIRIE

CALIFORNIA

SOUTHEAST

BAJA
CALIFORNIA

SOUTHWEST

NORTHEAST
MEXICO

MESO-AMERICA

22. According to the map, some Native American cultural areas are named after

    (1) tribes
    (2) famous chieftains
    (3) objects
    (4) geographical features
    (5) rivers

Tip When reading a map, be sure to read the map's title, the labels, and the compass rose. They will give you important information on how to interpret the map.

23. When Europeans first arrived in the Americas, many of them thought that the natives were uncivilized savages. According to the map, which was a fact at that time?

    (1) Native Americans had many distinct societies.
    (2) Native Americans were very disorganized.
    (3) Native Americans had cultures but no governments.
    (4) European cultures were better than Native American cultures.
    (5) The eastern Native American cultures were superior to the ones in the West.

Answers are on page 796.

Sally Ride's knowledge of physics was very important in her career as an astronaut and professor.

Test 3 of the GED presents you with questions that measure your general understanding of important scientific themes. These questions are based on passages and other forms of information drawn from the areas of Biology, Earth Science, Chemistry, and Physics.

Biology is the field of science that studies organisms, or living things, and how they interact with one another and their environments. Understanding biology helps us understand ourselves and the world around us.

Cells, the microscopic units of which all living things are made, are discussed in the first lessons of the biology section. Cell parts and how cells pass on hereditary information from one generation to the next, through the process of reproduction, are passage topics.

Photosynthesis, the process through which plants make their own food, is explained. As a by-product of photosynthesis, plants release oxygen into the air. All animals need oxygen to survive.

Some of the other topics covered pertain to the human body. You will read about the digestive system, bacteria and viruses, how bacteria and viruses cause diseases, and scientific developments used to fight infectious diseases.

Earth Science is the branch of science that studies Earth and the space around it. You will discover how weather is caused by air masses. You will read about Earth's resources, such as petroleum, and the challenges humans face looking for new resources to replace those that will not last forever.

Chemistry is the study of matter and changes in matter. You may think that chemistry exists only in a laboratory, but chemistry is all around you and within you. In fact, a chemical reaction within your brain enables you to understand and remember these words as you read them. Matter is what everything in the world is made up of. Matter can exist in any one of three physical states—solid, liquid, or gas.

Physics is the study of matter and energy. It is the branch of science that looks for answers to these questions: What is matter? What is energy? How are energy and matter related? Motion, speed, and the effect of forces are discussed in this section. You will also read about how an electric current is produced.

The reading and thinking skills used in the other units of this book apply to the Science unit. Be sure to allow time for careful reading of the science passages. Meanings of new terms and the relationships among facts and concepts will be apparent from the passages.

The Biology of Cells

All organisms are made up of microscopic units called <u>cells</u>. Some organisms consist of only a single cell. Other organisms are made up of many cells. Almost all cells have certain things in common, and their basic structure is similar. All cells take in food. They break down food to get energy, and then they give off waste. Cells also grow, reproduce, and die.

Most cells are divided into two general parts, the <u>nucleus</u> and the <u>cytoplasm</u>. The nucleus controls the cell's activities, and the cytoplasm carries out these activities.

The nucleus of a cell is a round body inside the cell. The three parts of the nucleus include:

1. <u>Nucleolus</u>. The nucleolus is a structure that plays a role in making protein.
2. <u>Chromatin</u>. The chromatin is the genetic material contained in the nucleus. When the cell divides, the chromatin forms chromosomes, which carry the hereditary information for the cell.
3. <u>Nuclear membrane</u>. The nuclear membrane divides the nucleus from the cytoplasm.

The cytoplasm contains the other cell structures which are called <u>organelles</u>. Some organelles found in the cytoplasm include:

1. <u>Mitochondria</u>. Mitochondria are rod-shaped organelles that produce almost all the energy a cell needs. Some cells have hundreds of mitochondria.
2. <u>Endoplasmic reticulum</u>. The endoplasmic reticulum (ER) is a system of membranes running through the cytoplasm. It is thought that the ER carries materials throughout the cell.
3. <u>Ribosomes</u>. Ribosomes are tiny structures that are attached to some of the ER and scattered throughout the cytoplasm. They help make proteins.
4. <u>Vacuoles</u>. Vacuoles are storage spaces in the cytoplasm. They may contain food or water, or they may collect and excrete waste.

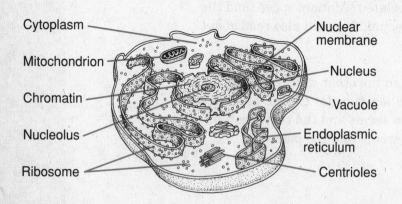

Cytoplasm

Mitochondrion

Chromatin

Nucleolus

Ribosome

Nuclear membrane

Nucleus

Vacuole

Endoplasmic reticulum

Centrioles

Items 1 to 6 refer to the previous passage and diagram. Choose the <u>best answer</u> to each item.

1. Which of the following sums up the main idea of the first paragraph?

    (1) All cells need energy to live.
    (2) Most cells have things in common and have a similar structure.
    (3) Food gives the cell energy.
    (4) The nucleus is the center of the cell.
    (5) The nucleus is an organelle.

2. Which detail most completely supports the main idea of the first paragraph?

    (1) All cells grow, reproduce, and die.
    (2) Most cells have things in common and have a similar structure.
    (3) Some organisms consist of a single cell.
    (4) The nucleus is the center of the cell.
    (5) The nucleus is an organelle.

3. What is the main idea of the second paragraph?

    (1) Most cells have a nucleus.
    (2) The nucleus controls the activities of the cell.
    (3) Most cells are divided into two basic parts.
    (4) All cells have cytoplasm.
    (5) The activities of the cell are carried out by the cytoplasm.

4. What is the main idea of the third paragraph?

    (1) The nucleus is round.
    (2) The nucleolus is part of the nucleus.
    (3) The nucleus contains a nucleolus, chromatin, and a nuclear membrane.
    (4) The nuclear membrane divides the nucleus from the cytoplasm.
    (5) Chromatin forms chromosomes during cell division.

5. Which of the following sums up the main idea of the fourth paragraph?

    (1) Cytoplasm contains all the structures inside the cell membrane except the nucleus.
    (2) Organelles are cell structures.
    (3) Mitochondria produce the energy a cell needs for its activities.
    (4) Vacuoles are storage spaces in the cytoplasm.
    (5) Cytoplasm includes the nucleus.

6. Which detail most completely supports the main idea of the fourth paragraph?

    (1) Organelles are cell structures.
    (2) Mitochondria produce most of the energy needed by a cell.
    (3) The ER is used to transport material through the cell.
    (4) A cell may contain hundreds of mitochondria.
    (5) The cytoplasm contains mitochondria, the ER, ribosomes, and vacuoles.

Tip When identifying supporting details, watch for names, numbers, dates, and examples. Also look for key words and phrases such as *like, such as*, and *for instance.*

Items 7 to 12 refer to the following passage and diagram.

The process by which a cell divides is called mitosis. During mitosis, the chromosomes in the original cell, or parent cell, duplicate and divide into two identical sets. One set will go to each of two new cells, or daughter cells. The process of cell division (mitosis) is divided into five phases.

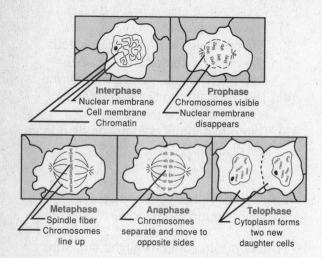

Interphase
Nuclear membrane
Cell membrane
Chromatin

Prophase
Chromosomes visible
Nuclear membrane disappears

Metaphase
Spindle fiber
Chromosomes line up

Anaphase
Chromosomes separate and move to opposite sides

Telophase
Cytoplasm forms two new daughter cells

During the first phase, called interphase, the chromatin (hereditary material) in the nucleus duplicates itself. This is the longest phase of mitosis.

During the second phase, called prophase, the chromatin shortens and thickens to form the chromosomes. Each chromosome is made of two identical parts that are attached at their centers. Protein fibers called spindle fibers come from opposite poles, or ends, of the cell toward the chromosomes The membrane around the nucleus disappears.

During the third phase, called metaphase, the chromosomes line up across the middle of the cell. A spindle fiber attaches to each chromosome. This is the shortest phase of mitosis.

During the fourth phase, called anaphase, the identical parts of chromosomes separate. They move toward opposite sides of the cell, pulled by the spindle fibers.

During the final phase, called telophase, the chromosomes again become threads of hereditary material (chromatin) and the spindle fibers disappear. A new membrane forms around each nucleus. After division of the nucleus is complete, the cytoplasm of the cell divides, producing two daughter cells. The two daughter cells have exactly the same hereditary material.

The two daughter cells are now in interphase. The cells grow and the chromatin duplicates itself again.

7. According to the diagram, when do the spindles first attach to the chromosomes?

    (1) interphase
    (2) prophase
    (3) metaphase
    (4) anaphase
    (5) telophase

8. What appears to be pulling the chromosomes apart during anaphase?

    (1) cell membrane
    (2) cytoplasm
    (3) nuclear membrane
    (4) nucleus
    (5) spindle fibers

9. Which phase makes sure that both daughter cells will receive all hereditary material?

    (1) interphase
    (2) prophase
    (3) metaphase
    (4) anaphase
    (5) telophase

10. What is the passage about?

    (1) In telophase, the parent cell finally forms two new cells.
    (2) Mitosis is the process by which cells divide.
    (3) Spindle fibers are important to the process of the division.
    (4) Chromosomes divide in half during mitosis.
    (5) The cytoplasm divides during mitosis.

11. According to the diagram, what do the spindle fibers seem to do in mitosis?

    (1) guide the chromosomes
    (2) produce the nucleus
    (3) form the nuclear membrane
    (4) form the hereditary material
    (5) form a cell plate

12. If the number of chromosomes in the parent cell is 46, how many chromosomes will there be in each daughter cell?

    (1) 12
    (2) 18
    (3) 23
    (4) 46
    (5) 60

Items 13 to 17 refer to the following passage.

Sexual reproductive cells are formed by a process called meiosis. This process differs from mitosis in that the resulting cells, called gametes, have half the number of chromosomes as the parent cell. Human gametes are sperm and eggs. During sexual reproduction, the two gametes combine to form a new cell called a zygote. Because the zygote contains the chromosomes from both gametes, the original number of chromosomes is restored.

Chromosomes occur in pairs. A parent cell contains a complete set of paired chromosomes. A gamete receives only one chromosome from each pair in the parent cell. Thus, a gamete has half the number of chromosomes found in the parent cell.

13. The chromosome number for human body cells is 46. What is the chromosome number for human gametes?

    (1) 12
    (2) 23
    (3) 32
    (4) 46
    (5) 48

14. The chromosome number of a cell produced by meiosis differs from the chromosome number of a cell produced by mitosis in that the cell produced by meiosis has

    (1) half the number
    (2) no chromosomes
    (3) the same number
    (4) one-fourth the number
    (5) twice the number

15. The zygote is formed during

    (1) meiosis
    (2) mitosis
    (3) sexual reproduction
    (4) cell division
    (5) gamete production

16. Some people have 47 chromosomes in their cells, rather than the usual 46. What could cause this error?

    (1) Extra hereditary material was produced during meiosis.
    (2) Some hereditary material was destroyed during sexual reproduction.
    (3) One chromosome pair did not separate properly during meiosis.
    (4) The zygote has one extra chromosome.
    (5) Three gametes, not two, combined during sexual reproduction.

17. What portion of one's chromosomes come from one's father?

    (1) 25 percent
    (2) 33 percent
    (3) 50 percent
    (4) 75 percent
    (5) 100 percent

Answers are on page 797.

Lesson 2 Photosynthesis

Almost all animal life depends on plants for food. Plants, however, produce their own food through a process called <u>photosynthesis</u>. In photosynthesis, green plants take water, carbon dioxide, and energy from sunlight and use these items to make sugar, oxygen, and water. The sugar is used as food and to build other substances that the plant needs, such as starches and protein. Oxygen is a by-product of photosynthesis. Plants release oxygen into the atmosphere, where animals breathe it.

Photosynthesis can be shown as a chemical equation. In the equation shown below, the arrow means <u>yields</u>.

$$\text{water + carbon dioxide} \xrightarrow[\text{chlorophyll}]{\text{light}} \text{sugar + oxygen + water}$$

This equation is a summary of all the reactions that make up photosynthesis. The diagram below shows photosynthesis in more detail. Notice that the reactions are grouped into two phases—the light reactions and the dark reactions.

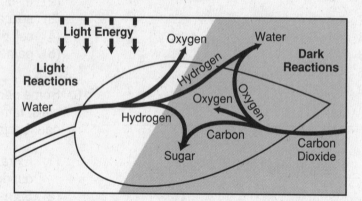

The first phase of photosynthesis is called the light reactions. The light reactions take place in sunlight. Light energy from the sun is trapped by the plant's chlorophyll, or green coloring. The chlorophyll changes light energy to chemical energy, which is used to split particles of water into hydrogen and oxygen.

The second phase of photosynthesis is called the dark reactions. Light is not needed for the dark reactions to take place. During this phase, the hydrogen produced in the light reactions combines with carbon (from carbon dioxide taken from the atmosphere) to form sugar. The rest of the hydrogen combines with oxygen to form water.

Items 1 to 6 refer to the previous passage and diagram. Choose the <u>best answer</u> to each item.

1. Which substance produced in the light reactions of photosynthesis combines with the carbon found in carbon dioxide to produce sugar in the dark reactions?

    (1) oxygen
    (2) carbon
    (3) hydrogen
    (4) chlorophyll
    (5) water

2. What substance produced during photosynthesis does the plant use for food?

    (1) sugar
    (2) oxygen
    (3) water
    (4) carbon dioxide
    (5) chlorophyll

3. Which of the following restates the equation for photosynthesis?

    (1) Water plus carbon dioxide, in the presence of light and chlorophyll, yields sugar, oxygen, and water.
    (2) Water plus carbon dioxide, in the presence of chlorophyll, yields sugar, oxygen, and water.
    (3) Water plus carbon dioxide, in the presence of light and chlorophyll, yields sugar, hydrogen, and water.
    (4) Water plus oxygen, in the presence of light and chlorophyll, yields sugar, carbon dioxide, and water.
    (5) Water plus carbon dioxide, in the presence of sunlight, yields sugar, oxygen, and water.

4. Which of the following restates the main idea of the passage?

    (1) Animals eat plants for food.
    (2) Plants make their own food through photosynthesis.
    (3) Photosynthesis takes place in green plants.
    (4) Photosynthesis replaces the oxygen in the atmosphere that is used by animals.
    (5) Sunlight is needed for photosynthesis to occur.

5. Which of the following supports the statement, "The first phase of photosynthesis is called the light reactions"?

    (1) Chemical energy splits water into hydrogen and oxygen.
    (2) The plant's green coloring is called chlorophyll.
    (3) Oxygen is a by-product of photosynthesis.
    (4) Carbon dioxide is absorbed from the atmosphere.
    (5) The light reactions take place in sunlight.

6. Which of the following restates the main idea of the fourth paragraph?

    (1) Light energy from the sun is absorbed by chlorophyll.
    (2) Chlorophyll makes chemical energy from light energy.
    (3) Chemical energy splits water into hydrogen and oxygen.
    (4) The light reactions make up the first phase of photosynthesis.
    (5) Sunlight is needed for the light reactions.

Answers are on page 799.

Lesson 3

Evolution

Evolution means change over time. In science, the theory of evolution holds that all organisms living today have a common ancestor that evolved from the first living cells. These first cells developed about 3.5 billion years ago.

There is much evidence to support the theory of evolution. One piece of evidence is the presence of similar structures in different organisms. Called homologous structures, these body parts from different organisms have similar structures but perform different functions. For example, a whale's flipper, a human's arm, a dog's front leg, and a bird's wing are homologous structures. Each of these limbs is used in a different way. When you first look at these limbs, they appear different. But if you look closely, you will see that the bones of each limb are very similar. For this reason, they have been given the same names. The similarity of these four different limbs suggests that these four organisms evolved from a common ancestor. The differences are the result of adaptation to different environments.

Another piece of evidence that supports the theory of evolution is that the embryos of different organisms are similar. An embryo is an early stage in the development of an organism from a fertilized egg. The embryos of a fish, a bird, and a human are similar at first. For example, at one stage all of these embryos have gill slits and tail buds. As the embryos develop, the differences among the organisms become more clear. However, the similarities in the early embryos suggest that fish, birds, and humans evolved from a common ancestor.

BONES

A Humerus
B Radius
C Ulna
D Carpals and
    Metacarpals
E Phalanges

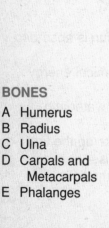

Whale

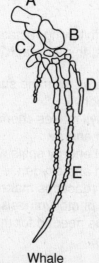

Human

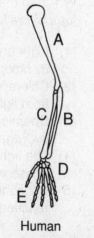

Dog

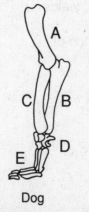

Bird

Homologous Structures

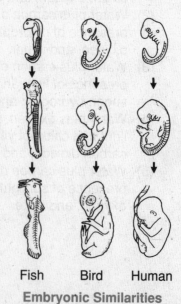

Fish   Bird   Human

Embryonic Similarities

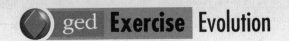
Items 1 to 6 refer to the previous passage and diagram. Choose the best answer to each item.

1. According to the diagram, what is similar about the radius and ulna bones of whales, humans, dogs, and birds?

   (1) They form fingerlike structures.
   (2) They form footlike structures.
   (3) They are positioned side by side below the humerus.
   (4) They are part of an arm, leg, and wing.
   (5) They are evidence of similarity among embryos.

2. What is one reason that scientists support the theory of evolution?

   (1) Humans are the most highly developed organisms on Earth.
   (2) Different types of organisms have homologous structures.
   (3) All organisms developed 3.5 billion years ago.
   (4) All embryos have gill slits and tail buds.
   (5) All organisms function in the same way.

3. What caused the ancestors of whales and birds to develop into different types of animals?

   (1) homologous structures
   (2) similarity between embryos
   (3) a common ancestor
   (4) the fact that they are unrelated
   (5) their evolution in different environments

4. Why does a human embryo have a tail bud?

   (1) Human ancestors had tails.
   (2) Fish and bird embryos have tail buds.
   (3) Tails are homologous structures.
   (4) Humans have evolved.
   (5) The early stages of the human embryo are similar to the early stages of the fish embryo.

5. What is the main idea of the passage?

   (1) Homologous structures are evidence supporting the theory of evolution.
   (2) Similarity among embryos exists in organisms with a common ancestor.
   (3) Birds, whales, humans, and dogs had a common ancestor.
   (4) Homologous structures and similarity among embryos are evidence supporting the theory of evolution.
   (5) Humans are related to birds.

6. How will the passage of a million years affect today's plant and animal species?

   (1) Plants and animals will continue to evolve.
   (2) Fertilization of the egg will no longer be required.
   (3) Plants and animals will develop into a single life form.
   (4) Animals will continue to change, but plants will remain the same.
   (5) Birds and whales will become land animals.

Answers are on page 799.

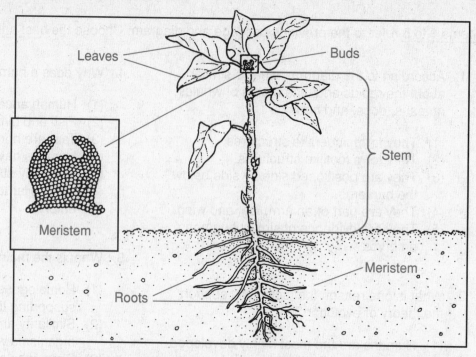

All living things grow when their cells divide, making the organism larger. In seed plants, growth occurs in specific places called meristems. During the growing season, cells in these areas divide rapidly, causing the plant to increase in size. Meristem cells are found at the tips of stems and roots.

The meristem cells of stems are found in the buds. The top bud of the stem is where the plant increases its height. Other buds on the side of the stem cause the plant to grow outward, or branch. Stem buds produce branches, flowers, and leaves.

Like stems, roots grow longer by adding cells at their tips. The meristem of a root is covered by a root cap, a layer of thick dead cells. This protects the meristem cells as the root pushes through the soil.

In woody plants, another kind of meristem cell adds to the thickness of the plant. These cells form the cambium, a one-cell-thick layer in stems, branches, and roots. As the cells in the cambium layer divide, they add to the diameter of the plant.

New cells developed in the meristems eventually become different kinds of cells. Some change by becoming elongated, whereas others develop thick walls. Each cell adapts for a specific purpose, such as reproduction, support, absorption, or storage. One type of cell that develops from a meristem cell is an epidermis cell. Epidermis cells cover the plant body and help prevent water loss. Another type of cell is the vascular cell, which supports the plant and helps transport fluids through it.

Items 1 to 8 refer to the previous passage and diagram. Choose the best answer to each item.

1. Which of the following is implied by the passage?

   (1) Growth of stems does not take place between buds.
   (2) Leaves contain meristem cells.
   (3) Meristem cells in the roots are tough.
   (4) All plants have cambium.
   (5) Branches do not have cambium.

2. The fact that meristems in stems produce branches, flowers, and leaves suggests that

   (1) all meristem cells develop into the same type of structure
   (2) meristem cells become specialized as they develop
   (3) all plants have flowers
   (4) roots do not have meristem tissue
   (5) stems grow only in length

3. The immediate short-term effect of cutting off the top bud of a stem is that the

   (1) plant would stop getting taller
   (2) lower buds on the stem would stop growing
   (3) cambium cells would stop dividing
   (4) roots would branch
   (5) root caps would stop developing

4. What is the main idea of the passage?

   (1) Only living things grow by cell division.
   (2) Growth of seed plants takes place in special areas called meristems.
   (3) Roots have meristems.
   (4) Cambium is a layer of meristem cells in woody plants.
   (5) Animals and seed plants grow in similar ways.

5. The pattern of plant growth suggests that after thirty years

   (1) the bottom branch of a tree will be considerably higher than it was when it first formed
   (2) the bottom branch of a tree will be the same height above the ground as when it first formed
   (3) most new growth will take place between buds
   (4) a tree trunk will have the same diameter as after two years
   (5) a tree trunk will have a smaller diameter than after two years

6. Where can meristem cells be found in woody plants but not in most nonwoody plants?

   (1) root cap
   (2) buds at the top of the stem
   (3) buds at the sides of stems
   (4) leaves
   (5) cambium

7. If all the meristem cells in a plant were destroyed, what would most likely happen to the plant?

   (1) It would stop growing.
   (2) It would become bushy.
   (3) It would grow faster.
   (4) It would produce more leaves.
   (5) Its roots would start to branch.

8. The word apical describes the apex, or tip of a structure. Where would you expect to find apical meristems?

   (1) along stems between buds
   (2) at the ends of stems and roots
   (3) in buds on the sides of stems
   (4) in the cambium
   (5) in the leaves

Answers are on page 800.

The Human Digestive System

The human digestive system consists of a long tube called the alimentary canal. It is made up of the mouth, esophagus, stomach, small intestine, and large intestine. In a human adult, the alimentary canal is about 30 feet long. The liver and pancreas, which also have a role in digestion, are connected to the alimentary canal by small tubes.

Mouth and Esophagus. In the mouth, food is ground and moistened with saliva. Saliva contains a substance that begins to break down the starches in food. Saliva also contains mucus, which makes the food slippery enough to pass easily through the body. The tube that connects the mouth and stomach is called the esophagus.

Stomach. In the stomach, the breakdown of fats begins. Minerals are dissolved, and bacteria in food are killed by acid produced by the stomach. The stomach makes mucus to protect the lining from the acid.

Small Intestine. The small intestine is about 1 1/4 inches wide and 23 feet long. Most of the digestive process takes place here. Nutrients from digested food pass from the small intestine into the bloodstream.

Pancreas and Liver. The pancreas secretes substances that help break down proteins, starches, and fats. Bile from the liver breaks up fats into smaller droplets. All the substances from the pancreas and liver enter the small intestine by means of tubes called ducts.

Large Intestine. The undigested material from the small intestine contains a lot of water. One of the main functions of the large intestine is to absorb this water. As a result, the undigested material becomes more solid before it passes out of the body.

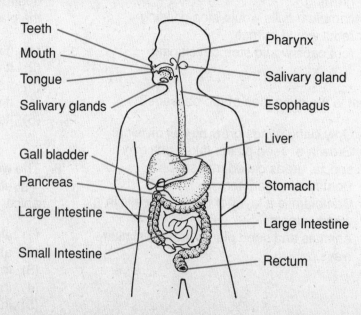

Items 1 to 8 refer to the previous passage and diagram. Choose the best answer to each item.

1. What is the purpose of the digestive system?

   (1) to move food from the mouth to the stomach
   (2) to break down food into substances the body can absorb and to get rid of wastes
   (3) to protect the lining of the organs from harmful substances swallowed with food
   (4) to protect the body against disease
   (5) to absorb oxygen from the air and release carbon dioxide

2. How is food ground up and mixed with saliva?

   (1) by contractions in the esophagus
   (2) by chemical action in the stomach
   (3) by swallowing
   (4) by absorption of water
   (5) by chewing

3. What is one of the main functions of the large intestine?

   (1) to break down proteins
   (2) to break down fats
   (3) to absorb water
   (4) to produce bile
   (5) to kill bacteria swallowed with food

4. Which organ makes up most of the length of the alimentary canal?

   (1) mouth
   (2) esophagus
   (3) stomach
   (4) small intestine
   (5) large intestine

5. Nutrients from the small intestine enter the bloodstream and go to the

   (1) large intestine
   (2) pancreas
   (3) liver
   (4) stomach
   (5) rest of the body

6. How would damage to the liver affect digestion?

   (1) Foods would not be ground up.
   (2) Proteins would not be broken down.
   (3) Starches would be changed to sugars.
   (4) Fats would not be digested properly.
   (5) Too much water would be absorbed by the large intestine.

7. What is the result of chewing and swallowing too quickly?

   (1) Food absorbs too much saliva.
   (2) Food is not ground up enough and so starches are not properly processed.
   (3) Food passes through the esophagus into the stomach.
   (4) Nutrients are not absorbed through the small intestine.
   (5) More minerals are dissolved in the stomach.

8. Through what structure does solid waste pass out of the body?

   (1) pancreas
   (2) liver
   (3) small intestine
   (4) stomach
   (5) rectum

Answers are on page 800.

Disease

Diseases that can be spread from one person to another are called <u>infectious diseases</u>. Today, we know that infectious diseases are caused by microscopic agents called <u>pathogens</u>. The most common pathogens are bacteria and viruses.

Long ago, people thought that disease was caused by evil spirits that entered the body. The disease could be cured if the spirits were driven out by prayer or foul-tasting medicines. The invention of the microscope allowed scientists to see microorganisms, but over two hundred years passed before scientists started to connect microorganisms and disease. Louis Pasteur, a French scientist working in the nineteenth century, proved that yeasts cause fermentation of beet juice. He also thought that the rod-shaped organisms he found in sour juice were responsible for its souring. If such organisms could sour juice, Pasteur thought, perhaps they could also cause disease in humans.

About the same time, a German scientist named Robert Koch discovered that a specific kind of bacterium caused anthrax in sheep, cattle, and humans. While examining organs of animals that had died of anthrax, Koch found many rod-shaped bacteria in the blood vessels. He transferred some of these into the cut skin of a healthy mouse, which then developed anthrax and died. Koch found many of the same bacteria in the blood of the dead mouse.

Anthrax bacillus

However, Koch was not satisfied until he could watch the bacteria multiply. He set up an experiment to grow the bacteria and infect laboratory animals. His experiments provided significant proof for Pasteur's idea that microorganisms can cause disease. Koch's procedure for studying disease-causing organisms is still used today. The steps in his method, known as Koch's postulates, are listed below.

1. Isolate the organism believed to cause the disease.
2. Grow the organism outside the animal in a sterile food medium. A group of organisms grown in this way is called a <u>culture</u>.
3. Produce the same disease by injecting a healthy animal with organisms from the culture.
4. Examine the sick animal and recover the organisms that caused the disease.

Most bacteria that cause disease do so by producing toxins. A toxin is a substance that keeps body cells from functioning as they normally do. For example, the disease tetanus is caused by bacteria that enter the body through deep puncture wounds. These bacteria produce a toxin that attacks nerve cells and can cause muscle contractions.

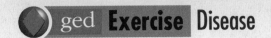

Items 1 to 7 refer to the previous passage. Choose the best answer to each item.

1. Before Louis Pasteur, what opinion was held about the nature of disease?

   (1) Diseases are caused by evil spirits.
   (2) Diseases are caused by microscopic agents called pathogens.
   (3) Anthrax is caused by rod-shaped bacteria.
   (4) Diseases are caused by yeast.
   (5) Diseases are caused by viruses.

2. At the time he thought of it, Pasteur's idea that microorganisms caused disease was an opinion. What contributed to this idea being accepted as fact today?

   (1) the development of foul-tasting medicines
   (2) the invention of the microscope
   (3) Pasteur's experiments with yeast and fermentation
   (4) Koch's experiments with anthrax bacteria
   (5) the discovery of microorganisms

3. Based on Koch's discovery of the microorganism that causes anthrax, what can you conclude?

   (1) All diseases are caused by microorganisms.
   (2) Improved types of yeasts would improve fermentation.
   (3) Yeast can be used to ferment juice.
   (4) Some diseases are not contagious.
   (5) The spread of anthrax can be stopped by stopping the spread of anthrax bacteria.

4. Which of the following was Pasteur's main contribution to the study of disease?

   (1) the invention of the microscope
   (2) the discovery that yeast causes fermentation
   (3) the discovery of microorganisms
   (4) the idea that microorganisms cause disease
   (5) a cure for anthrax

5. If the fourth step of Koch's postulates were not carried out during an experiment, what would be the result?

   (1) The injected animal would not get sick.
   (2) The injected animal would not die.
   (3) The cause of the disease would not be proved.
   (4) The culture would become contaminated.
   (5) The injected animal would die.

6. Why did Koch think that a specific kind of bacteria was responsible for anthrax?

   (1) Humans also get anthrax.
   (2) He found many of the bacteria in animals that had died of anthrax.
   (3) He knew that yeast causes fermentation of juice.
   (4) He knew that anthrax was highly contagious.
   (5) He was able to grow anthrax bacteria in the laboratory.

7. What is a culture?

   (1) a type of pathogen
   (2) a type of bacteria
   (3) a group of microorganisms grown in a sterile food medium
   (4) a laboratory with animal subjects
   (5) the result of fermentation

Tip **When answering questions about fact or opinion, look for clue words such as *think*, *believe*, or *feel* in the question and the passage.**

Answers are on page 801.

Lesson 6 ◆ Disease

333

Mendel and Genetics

How often have you heard someone say of a child, "She has her mother's eyes and her father's chin"? Statements like this refer to traits, or characteristics, that we inherit from our parents. The study of traits and how they are inherited is called genetics.

Gregor Mendel, an Austrian monk, has been called the father of genetics. He began his experiments in 1857. He bred pea plants because they have many traits that are easy to identify.

First, Mendel developed purebred pea plants. These plants always produced the same traits. Next, he crossed, or bred, plants with opposite traits. For example, he crossed purebred tall plants with purebred dwarf plants. He referred to this parental generation of plants as the P generation. Much to Mendel's surprise, all the plants that resulted were tall! Mendel called this F_1 generation of plants hybrids because they contained a mixture of the traits for tallness and dwarfness.

Then Mendel crossed tall hybrid plants from the F_1 generation. He found that some plants in the resulting F_2 generation were tall and some were dwarf. Each time he repeated the experiment, he found that, on average, there were three tall plants for one dwarf plant.

How did Mendel explain his results? He reasoned that the offspring inherited traits from both parents. However, some traits were more powerful than others. He called these traits dominant. The traits that did not show up in the F_1 generation he called recessive. In the F_2 generation, the plants that show the recessive trait must be plants that did not inherit any dominant trait for tallness.

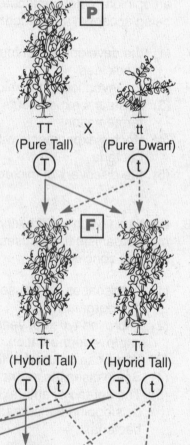

Science ◆ Biology

Items 1 to 6 refer to the previous passage and diagram. Choose the best answer to each item.

1. How did Mendel make sure that the results of his breeding experiments would be accurate?

   (1) He started with purebred plants.
   (2) He used hybrid plants having opposite traits.
   (3) He selected plants with several opposite traits.
   (4) He used only dwarf plants.
   (5) He used only tall plants.

2. If you cross purebred pea plants having inflated pods with purebred pea plants having wrinkled pods, all the F_1 generation will have inflated pods. Which statement about the F_1 generation is true?

   (1) The plants are all hybrids.
   (2) The plants are all purebred.
   (3) Inflated pods is a recessive trait.
   (4) Wrinkled pods is a hybrid trait.
   (5) Wrinkled pods is a dominant trait.

3. What is a dominant trait?

   (1) a trait that will appear only in purebred offspring
   (2) a trait that will appear only in hybrid offspring
   (3) a trait that will appear in some purebred and all hybrid offspring
   (4) a trait that will appear in every offspring
   (5) a trait that will disappear when bred

4. What evidence supports Mendel's conclusion that the recessive trait was carried by the F_1 generation even though none of these plants showed the recessive trait?

   (1) All of the F_1 generation plants showed the dominant characteristic.
   (2) Some of the F_2 generation plants showed the recessive trait.
   (3) Some of the F_2 generation plants showed the dominant trait.
   (4) All of the F_2 generation plants showed the recessive trait.
   (5) Some of the F_1 generation plants showed the recessive characteristic.

5. Why did Mendel use pea plants in his experiments?

   (1) They are the only type of plant that shows how genetics works.
   (2) They have characteristics that are easy to identify.
   (3) The rules of genetics apply only to plants.
   (4) They were the only plants available in Austria at that time.
   (5) They were available in dwarf varieties.

6. When two hybrid plants are bred, what is the chance that one offspring will show the recessive trait?

   (1) no chance
   (2) 1 out of 4
   (3) 2 out of 4
   (4) 3 out of 4
   (5) 4 out of 4

Answers are on page 801.

Lesson 8 — Ecosystems

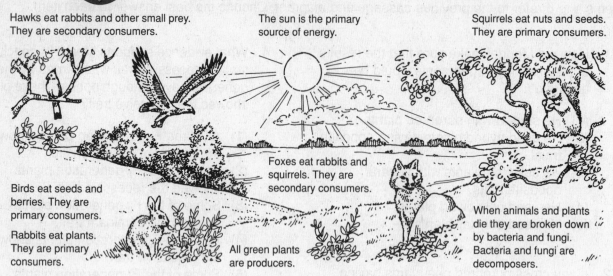

Hawks eat rabbits and other small prey. They are secondary consumers.

The sun is the primary source of energy.

Squirrels eat nuts and seeds. They are primary consumers.

Birds eat seeds and berries. They are primary consumers.

Rabbits eat plants. They are primary consumers.

All green plants are producers.

Foxes eat rabbits and squirrels. They are secondary consumers.

When animals and plants die they are broken down by bacteria and fungi. Bacteria and fungi are decomposers.

An ecosystem is a natural community in which the living and nonliving things interact. Lakes, rivers, meadows, ponds, and swamps are all ecosystems. The most important relationships in an ecosystem involve the flow of food and energy.

Food and the Ecosystem. The movement of food through a series of organisms is called a food chain. A food chain begins with producers, which in most ecosystems are green plants. Animals that eat plants are called primary consumers. Animals that eat primary consumers are called secondary consumers. Some ecosystems have tertiary consumers, which are animals that eat secondary consumers.

When plants and animals die, bacteria and fungi in the soil break them down into substances that can be used by plants. Organisms that break down plants and animals are called decomposers. Decomposers recycle the matter in an ecosystem.

Energy and the Ecosystem. The sun is the main source of energy for an ecosystem. The sun's energy enters the ecosystem through green plants, which store some of the energy. The stored energy is passed along the food chain as consumers eat producers and other consumers. However, since living things use energy to carry out life processes, less and less energy is available to each level of consumer. For example, only 10 out of 1,000 units of energy are transferred from plants to primary consumers. Only 1 out of every 10 units of energy is transferred from primary consumers to secondary consumers.

Items 1 to 7 refer to the previous passage and illustration. Choose the best answer to each item.

1. Of the sentences below, which is a conclusion, not a supporting statement?

   (1) Plants produce food.
   (2) Matter in an ecosystem is being constantly recycled.
   (3) Decomposers break down dead plants and animals into substances that can be used by plants.
   (4) Secondary consumers eat primary consumers.
   (5) Primary consumers eat plants.

2. What would be the immediate result if all the primary consumers were removed from the ecosystem?

   (1) Plants would stop producing food.
   (2) Decomposers would increase their activity.
   (3) Secondary consumers would have nothing to eat.
   (4) Tertiary consumers would have more to eat.
   (5) A new source of energy would be needed.

3. Some birds eat insects as well as seeds and berries. Which of the following most accurately describes their role in the ecosystem?

   (1) producers
   (2) primary consumers
   (3) primary and secondary consumers
   (4) secondary consumers
   (5) producers and primary consumers

4. An insect that feeds on other insects that are crop pests is a

   (1) producer
   (2) primary consumer
   (3) secondary consumer
   (4) tertiary consumer
   (5) decomposer

5. Based on the information given, it is assumed that the reader already knows which of the following?

   (1) All living things are part of an ecosystem.
   (2) Only humans are not part of an ecosystem.
   (3) The sun is the main source of energy in an ecosystem.
   (4) All matter is being constantly recycled.
   (5) Squirrels are secondary consumers.

6. What is the role of decomposers in an ecosystem?

   (1) to produce food for primary consumers
   (2) to break down dead plants and animals into substances plants can use
   (3) to provide food for secondary consumers
   (4) to provide food for tertiary consumers
   (5) to provide energy

7. Which organisms are the highest-level consumers in a food chain?

   (1) hawks
   (2) seed-eating birds
   (3) rabbits
   (4) squirrels
   (5) primary consumers

Answers are on page 802.

Directions: Choose the best answer to each item.

Items 1 to 6 are based on the following passage.

Herbicides are chemicals that kill plants. When herbicides are used on crops, it is important that the herbicide kill only the weeds and not the crops. Scientists have been developing crops that are not affected by specific herbicides, enabling farmers to use herbicides to control weeds. For example, scientists have developed a strain of cotton that is resistant to the herbicide bromoxynil. When this herbicide is used, it kills weeds but not the resistant cotton plants. Other crops that have varieties resistant to certain herbicides are soybeans, tobacco, tomatoes, and sugar beets.

Some environmental groups are opposed to the development of herbicide-resistant crops. They say that these crops encourage farmers to continue to use chemicals that pollute the environment and that may be unsafe. These groups favor practices such as improved cultivation techniques and creative planting plans to make chemicals unnecessary. They prefer scientists to concentrate on developing strains of crops that are naturally resistant to disease and pests.

1. What is a herbicide-resistant crop?

   (1) a variety of crop that cannot have a herbicide applied to it
   (2) a variety of crop that is resistant to disease
   (3) a variety of crop that is resistant to insect pests
   (4) a variety of crop that is resistant to weeds
   (5) a variety of crop that is not affected by particular chemical plant killers

2. Applying chemical herbicides to herbicide-resistant crops is likely to

   (1) kill the crops
   (2) damage the crops
   (3) result in herbicides remaining on the crops after harvest
   (4) kill more crop plants than weeds
   (5) kill insects that are crop pests

3. Based on the information given, which of the following is not a fact?

   (1) Herbicides are used to kill weeds.
   (2) Tobacco and soybean varieties are resistant to certain herbicides.
   (3) Bromoxynil is a chemical herbicide.
   (4) Improved cultivation techniques are preferable to herbicides in controlling weeds.
   (5) Scientists have developed strains of herbicide-resistant crops.

4. Based on the information given, it is assumed that the reader already knows which of the following?

   (1) Herbicides are safe to use.
   (2) Crops cannot be grown without herbicides.
   (3) Weeds are a problem in large farming areas.
   (4) All cotton plants are resistant to herbicides.
   (5) Most crops are naturally resistant to pests.

5. Which of the following would not be considered a more natural way to kill unwanted weeds in fields?

   A. improved cultivation techniques
   B. creative planting of crops
   C. new chemicals specific to certain weeds

   (1) A only
   (2) B only
   (3) C only
   (4) A and B
   (5) A and C

6. The term "resistant" as used in this passage means

   (1) not wanting to do something
   (2) opposing
   (3) striving against
   (4) withstanding the effect of
   (5) killing

Living things get the energy they need in different ways. Grasses get energy from sunlight through photosynthesis. Rabbits get energy by eating grasses. Foxes get energy by eating rabbits. This transfer of energy from the sun to various organisms in an ecosystem is known as a food chain. Ecosystems contain many food chains.

Organisms that make their own food are called producers. Food chains always begin with producers, like the grass shown in the diagram. Notice that the levels above the producer consist of consumers. A consumer is an organism that gets its food by eating other organisms.

FOOD CHAIN

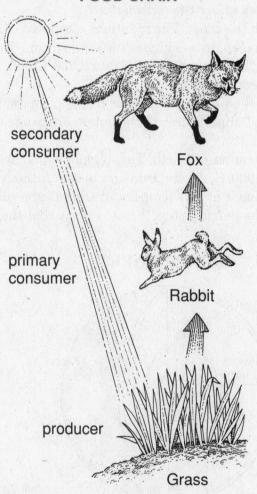

7. The correct order of the transfer of energy in the food chain described above, from the original source to the final consumer, is

   (1) rabbit, grass, fox
   (2) fox, grass, rabbit, sun
   (3) grass, rabbit, fox
   (4) sun, grass, fox, rabbit
   (5) sun, grass, rabbit, fox

8. If a predator of the fox were added to the diagram, it would

   (1) be a producer
   (2) appear at the bottom of the diagram
   (3) be a primary consumer
   (4) appear at the top of the diagram
   (5) be a secondary consumer

9. If disease killed off an ecosystem's population of rabbits, how would the food chain shown most likely be affected?

   (1) A new producer would become part of the food chain.
   (2) The food chain would consist of foxes feeding on grass.
   (3) The amount of grass would decrease.
   (4) The fox population would decrease.
   (5) It would not be affected.

10. Which of the following statements is most accurate?

   (1) Some food chains consist only of organisms that feed on other organisms.
   (2) An organism that eats only plants cannot be a secondary consumer.
   (3) Producers are organisms that get energy by eating other organisms.
   (4) Consumers eat only plants.
   (5) Consumers eat only animals.

Answers are on page 803.

Earth Science
Lesson

The Planet Earth

For many years, scientists have been gathering information about Earth's interior. Intense heat and high pressure make human exploration of this region impossible. Thus, most of what is known about the interior structure of Earth has been learned by studying the movement of seismic waves, or vibrations, produced by earthquakes. From this indirect evidence, scientists have concluded that Earth is made up of four different layers: the crust, the mantle, the outer core, and the inner core.

1. The crust is the part of Earth that is familiar to us, for it includes Earth's surface. This layer is made up of many kinds of rock. The crust ranges from about 8 kilometers thick under the oceans to about 40 kilometers thick under the continents.

2. The mantle lies beneath the crust. The mantle is composed of rock that contains mainly oxygen, iron, magnesium, and silicon. The temperatures in this region range from 870°C to 2,200°C and cause some of the solid rock to flow.

3. The outer core is below the mantle. The outer core is composed of molten iron and nickel. Temperatures in the outer core range from 2,200°C to 5,000°C.

4. The inner core is at the center of Earth. This region, which has a temperature of about 5,000°C, is solid iron and nickel. Although iron and nickel usually melt at this temperature, great pressure in the inner core pushes the particles together so tightly that they remain solid.

EARTH'S LAYERS

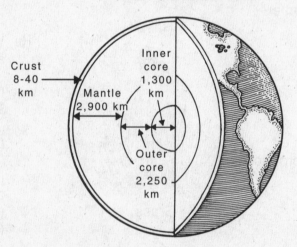

Crust
8-40 km

Mantle
2,900 km

Inner core
1,300 km

Outer core
2,250 km

ged **Exercise** The Planet Earth

Items 1 to 7 refer to the previous passage and diagram. Choose the <u>best answer</u> to each item.

1. What is the most likely thickness of Earth's crust under Africa?

   (1)   8 kilometers
   (2)   40 kilometers
   (3) 1,300 kilometers
   (4) 2,250 kilometers
   (5) 2,900 kilometers

2. What led scientists to conclude that Earth is made up of four different layers?

   (1) direct evidence from human observation
   (2) rock samples from all four layers
   (3) unchanging seismic wave patterns
   (4) changing behavior of seismic waves as they reach each layer of Earth's interior
   (5) temperature readings from Earth's interior

3. Which layer of Earth has been explored directly by humans?

   (1) crust
   (2) mantle
   (3) outer core
   (4) inner core
   (5) all four layers

4. Like a magnet, Earth has a magnetic field. What is the most likely cause of Earth's magnetism?

   (1) high temperatures in the core
   (2) oxygen in Earth's crust
   (3) iron in the inner and outer cores
   (4) high pressure on the core
   (5) continents

5. What are seismic waves?

   (1) vibrations produced by earthquakes
   (2) light waves from the sun that penetrate Earth's surface
   (3) movements of liquid rock in Earth's mantle
   (4) deep ocean waves
   (5) volcanic eruptions

6. Based on the information given, which of the following does the author of the passage assume to be true?

   (1) It is reasonable to draw scientific conclusions from indirect evidence.
   (2) Indirect evidence is superior to human observation.
   (3) Someday humans will explore the inner core.
   (4) Earth is made of five different layers.
   (5) Each of Earth's layers is thicker than the one above it.

7. One type of seismic wave, called a secondary wave, can only travel through solids. A secondary wave traveling from Earth's surface toward its center would

   (1) travel straight through Earth
   (2) travel through the crust, mantle, and outer core and stop at the inner core
   (3) travel through the crust and mantle and stop at the outer core
   (4) travel through the crust and stop at the mantle
   (5) not be able to penetrate rocks below the surface

Items 8 to 12 refer to the following passage.

A fossil is the evidence or remains of a living thing. Most fossils form when plants or animals die and are buried in layers of crumbled rock particles called sediments, which later harden.

The chances of an organism leaving a fossil are actually small. The soft parts of a dead organism usually decay or are eaten before a fossil can form. Fossils that do form are often incomplete. The organisms most likely to be preserved as fossils are ones that lived in or near water. There, sand and mud provide quick burial for these organisms.

Some fossils show only the mark or evidence of a living thing. Called trace fossils, these include footprints, tracks, and burrows. Much of what is known about dinosaurs has come from footprints found in rock.

Fossils can show changes in Earth's surface and climate. For example, fossils of coral found in Antarctica show that the climate of this region was once much warmer.

Fossils can also help date layers of rock. If a particular type of organism lived on Earth for only a brief period of time, the rock containing its fossil must be from approximately the same time period.

8. In a mountainous region of Canada, fossils of fish are found. Which is the most likely explanation?

(1) The region was once much colder.
(2) The region was once much warmer.
(3) The region was once under water.
(4) Fish that lived in mountain streams formed fossils.
(5) Dead fish were taken up the mountain.

9. Which of the following would be most similar to a trace fossil?

(1) human footprints made in concrete before it hardened
(2) a fly trapped in concrete before it hardened
(3) tire tracks in the sand
(4) footprints of a deer in the snow
(5) a leaf frozen in ice

10. If a well preserved fossil of a complete bird were discovered, it could be concluded that

(1) the bird's soft parts were eaten
(2) the bird was killed by a predator
(3) there are also trace fossils made by a bird nearby
(4) the bird lived in a wet climate
(5) the bird was buried soon after dying

11. Which of the following is not an example of a fossil?

(1) tracks of a snake made in mud that later hardens to mudstone
(2) an insect trapped in sap that becomes amber
(3) the imprint of a fern preserved in siltstone
(4) grooves carved in rock by a glacier
(5) a woolly mammoth frozen in ice

12. The fossil record is not used to show which of the following:

(1) changes in Earth's surface
(2) changes in Earth's climate
(3) dating rock layers
(4) establishing animal behavior
(5) identifying extinct life forms

Items 13 to 18 refer to the following information.

Scientists have developed a geologic time line to record the history of Earth. Geologic time is often described in terms of four eras.

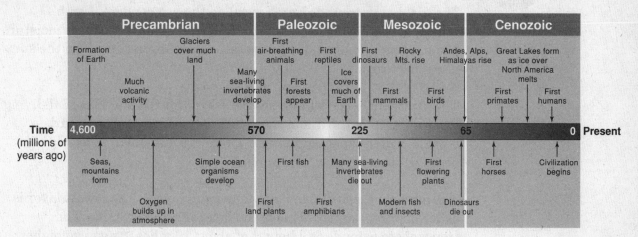

13. According to the time line, where did the first living things originate?

    (1) in the Precambrian Era
    (2) in the atmosphere
    (3) in the ocean
    (4) in the Paleozoic Era
    (5) in a swamp

14. What might have been eaten by the first fish?

    (1) flowering plants
    (2) sea-living invertebrates
    (3) insects
    (4) amphibians
    (5) land plants

15. Which of the following kinds of fossils would most likely be found in Mesozoic rocks?

    (1) only simple ocean organisms
    (2) land plants, dinosaurs, and horses
    (3) fish, land plants, and dinosaurs
    (4) primates and humans
    (5) flowering plants and primates

16. Which of the following statements is most accurate?

    (1) Human civilization has been in existence for over half the history of Earth.
    (2) Dinosaurs were the chief form of life during the Paleozoic Era.
    (3) The Great Lakes are younger than the Rocky Mountains.
    (4) Dinosaurs died out 5 million years ago.
    (5) The first life forms appeared on land.

17. For approximately how many years did dinosaurs inhabit Earth?

    (1)   160 years
    (2) 4,535 million years
    (3)   160 million years
    (4)   160 billion years
    (5)   225 million years

18. Which of the following statements <u>cannot</u> be directly supported by information on the time line?

    (1) All organisms evolved from the first living cells.
    (2) The Earth is about 4,600 million years old.
    (3) The Paleozoic Era came before the Mesozoic Era.
    (4) We are living in the Cenozoic Era.
    (5) Simple ocean organisms appeared during the Precambrian.

Answers are on page 803.

The Atmosphere

The air that surrounds Earth is called the atmosphere. Earth's atmosphere provides us with a safe environment. It gives us moisture and oxygen, a comfortable temperature, and protection from the sun's ultraviolet rays.

The atmosphere contains gases necessary for the survival of all living things. Gases in the atmosphere include nitrogen, oxygen, carbon dioxide, water vapor, and argon. There are also small amounts of neon, helium, krypton, and xenon.

The atmosphere is divided into four main layers. The lowest layer is called the troposphere. This is the layer in which we live. The troposphere extends to a height of about 10 miles. As you go higher, the air becomes colder and less dense, or "thinner." For example, at an altitude of 3.5 miles, there is only half as much oxygen as there is at Earth's surface.

Above the troposphere is the stratosphere. The stratosphere extends to a height of about 30 miles. A form of oxygen called ozone is found in the stratosphere and the mesosphere. Ozone shields Earth from the sun's harmful ultraviolet rays.

Above the stratosphere is the mesosphere. The mesosphere extends to a height of about 50 miles. The temperature in the mesosphere drops to about −100°C.

The uppermost region of the atmosphere is the thermosphere. The thermosphere does not have a well-defined upper limit. It is the hottest layer of the atmosphere, with temperatures as high as 2,000°C.

LAYERS OF EARTH'S ATMOSPHERE

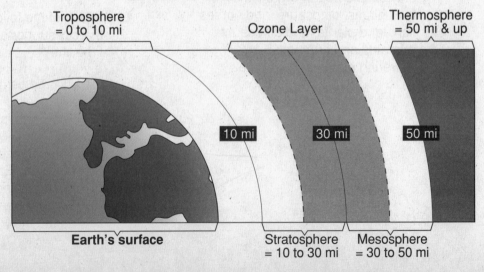

Troposphere = 0 to 10 mi

Ozone Layer

Thermosphere = 50 mi & up

10 mi

30 mi

50 mi

Earth's surface

Stratosphere = 10 to 30 mi

Mesosphere = 30 to 50 mi

ged Exercise The Atmosphere

Items 1 to 7 refer to the previous information. Choose the best answer to each item.

1. Which of the following people would need the most protection from the sun's ultraviolet rays?

   (1) a teacher
   (2) a mountain climber
   (3) an astronaut
   (4) a commercial airline pilot
   (5) a meteorologist

2. Someone at the top of Mt. Everest, which is about 29,000 feet high, would be in the

   (1) troposphere
   (2) stratosphere
   (3) ozone layer
   (4) mesosphere
   (5) thermosphere

3. Which of the following people is likely to experience dropping temperatures and thinner air during the course of a day?

   (1) a lifeguard
   (2) a mountain climber
   (3) an airline attendant
   (4) a landscape gardener
   (5) a farmer

4. What would be the effect of destroying the ozone layer?

   (1) People would have trouble breathing.
   (2) The sun's ultraviolet rays would be reflected back into space.
   (3) More ultraviolet rays would reach Earth's surface.
   (4) The stratosphere would disappear.
   (5) There would be no effect.

5. Which of the following gases is present in the atmosphere in very small amounts?

   (1) nitrogen
   (2) oxygen
   (3) carbon dioxide
   (4) water vapor
   (5) krypton

6. Based on the information given, it is assumed that the reader already knows which of the following?

   (1) Gravity holds the atmosphere in place around Earth.
   (2) The higher up you go, the denser the atmosphere becomes.
   (3) Helium does not occur naturally in the atmosphere.
   (4) The uppermost region of the atmosphere is the thermosphere.
   (5) No human being has gone higher than the mesosphere.

7. A runner from Boston, Massachusetts, at sea level, traveled to Denver, Colorado, in the Rocky Mountains. While jogging in Denver, the runner had trouble breathing. Which of the following statements is supported by this experience?

   (1) Physical activity is more difficult in tropical weather.
   (2) The mesosphere extends to about 50 miles above Earth's surface.
   (3) The higher you go in the troposphere, the less oxygen is available.
   (4) The ozone layer protects Earth from the sun's ultraviolet rays.
   (5) The air becomes colder as you go higher in the troposphere.

Changes in weather are caused by movements of air masses. An air mass has a similar temperature and humidity level throughout. An air mass may cover thousands of square miles.

Air masses are named according to where they form. There are four major types of air masses that affect the United States: maritime tropical, maritime polar, continental tropical, and continental polar. They are called maritime if they come from the sea and continental if they form over land.

A maritime tropical air mass forms over the ocean near the equator. Its air is warm and moist. In the summer it brings hot, humid weather to the United States, but in the winter it may come in contact with a cold air mass and cause rain or snow.

A maritime polar air mass forms over the Pacific Ocean in both winter and summer and over the North Atlantic Ocean in summer. It contains cool, moist air. During the summer this air mass brings fog to the western coastal states and cool weather to the eastern states. In the winter this air mass produces heavy snow and very cold temperatures.

A continental tropical air mass forms over Mexico during the summer. It brings hot, dry air to the southwestern United States.

A continental polar air mass forms over land in northern Canada. It contains cold, dry air. It brings very cold weather to the United States in winter.

8. Which of the following statements describes air masses that form over land?

   (1) They contain cold, moist air.
   (2) They contain warm, moist air.
   (3) They contain dry air.
   (4) They contain moist air.
   (5) They contain moist air in winter and dry air in summer.

9. A snowstorm in the Northern Pacific states could be caused by which of the following air masses?

   (1) maritime polar
   (2) continental tropical
   (3) continental polar
   (4) maritime polar or continental polar
   (5) continental polar or continental tropical

10. Which of the following is the best title for this passage?

   (1) Types of Air Masses
   (2) Where Air Masses Form
   (3) When Air Masses Meet
   (4) Continental Air Masses
   (5) Air and Weather

11. Air masses that form off the coast of Hawaii and over northwest Canada are likely to

   (1) be both very moist
   (2) be both very dry
   (3) cause weather changes in the contiguous 48 states
   (4) both bring warm weather to Mexico
   (5) both bring cool, dry weather to California

Tip **When selecting a title for a passage, look for the option that best summarizes the main idea of the passage. The best title should be neither too broad nor too specific.**

12. Which of the following is a <u>false</u> statement concerning air masses?

    (1) An air mass is called maritime if it originates over water.
    (2) An air mass is called continental if it originates over land.
    (3) Air masses called tropical originate over tropical seas.
    (4) The arrival of a new air mass can cause a change in humidity.
    (5) Air masses cover a very large area.

13. A maritime tropical air mass meets a continental polar air mass over the East Coast in January. What is the weather likely to be?

    (1) sunny
    (2) snowy
    (3) hurricane
    (4) dry and cold
    (5) dry and warm

14. Air masses cause changes in weather because

    (1) they bring in cooler air
    (2) they move large quantities of air
    (3) they cover thousands of square miles
    (4) they affect the temperature and humidity of the air
    (5) they move from one area to another

Items 15 to 17 refer to the following diagram.

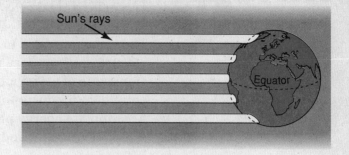

15. According to the diagram, the sun's rays

    (1) strike all parts of Earth evenly
    (2) are most direct at the North Pole
    (3) are most direct at the South Pole
    (4) are most direct in the Northern Hemisphere
    (5) are most direct at the equator

16. Based on the diagram, what change should a person traveling from the middle of the Northern Hemisphere to the equator be prepared for?

    (1) drier weather
    (2) a greater possibility of snow
    (3) cooler temperatures
    (4) a greater possibility of rainy weather
    (5) a greater possibility of sunburn

17. Climates near the equator are warmer than climates near the poles. Based on the diagram, which of the following statements could explain this observation?

    (1) Days are longer near the equator than near the poles.
    (2) The sun's rays are more concentrated near the equator than near the poles.
    (3) Weather patterns produce more sunny days near the equator than near the poles.
    (4) There are fewer oceans near the equator than near the poles.
    (5) There is less wind near the equator than near the poles.

Answers are on page 805.

Lesson 11

Earth's Resources

The things we need to live, such as water, food, and energy, are called resources. Sometimes resources are in short supply. In the 1970s, shipments of petroleum, or oil, to our country had been cut. All petroleum products—including gasoline—were in short supply. According to energy planners and Earth scientists, an oil shortage could occur again, and if so, it could become permanent.

Oil is a nonrenewable resource, one that cannot be replaced once it is used up. Earth scientists disagree about how much oil is left on Earth. Some say that, given our present rate of consumption, the United States will be out of oil by the year 2060. Others feel that there is enough oil to last another 300 years. All agree, however, that at some point the supply of oil will be gone.

Energy planners are trying to find ways to prevent a major oil shortage. Most believe that the best solution would be to look for a renewable resource that could be used in place of oil. A renewable resource is one that can be replaced. The most abundant renewable resource on Earth is energy from the sun. Scientists have developed solar cells that can convert sunlight into electricity. They have also developed ways to heat homes with solar energy. At present, solar energy cannot be produced at a low enough cost or on a large enough scale to meet much of our energy needs.

Another way to postpone an oil shortage is to use less oil. During the oil shortage of the 1970s, the United States passed laws to reduce the speed limit on highways and to lower the thermostats in public buildings. Citizens were shown ways to conserve energy, but lifelong habits are hard to break. Many people continue their old, energy-wasting habits.

ged Exercise Earth's Resources

Items 1 to 10 refer to the previous passage. Choose the best answer to each item.

1. Which of the following statements cannot be proved?

   (1) Earth's supply of oil is limited.
   (2) The reduction of speed limits conserves energy.
   (3) There is enough oil to last 300 years.
   (4) Oil became more plentiful in the 1980s than it had been in the 1970s.
   (5) Solar energy cannot currently meet our demands for energy.

2. Based on information in the passage, which of the following statements can be proved?

   (1) Americans are wasteful of energy.
   (2) An oil shortage could easily happen again.
   (3) By the year 2060, the U.S. will be out of oil.
   (4) Solar energy is a renewable resource.
   (5) Most citizens work to conserve energy.

3. Which of the following actions would help conserve a <u>nonrenewable</u> resource?

   (1) driving to work instead of taking public transportation
   (2) turning off the water while brushing your teeth
   (3) driving a small, fuel-efficient car
   (4) raising shades or blinds to let in sunlight in warm weather
   (5) converting a heating system from oil to natural gas

4. Which of the following is implied by the passage?

   (1) Vehicles will eventually be powered by something other than a petroleum product.
   (2) Oil will be the best choice for home heating in 500 years.
   (3) Oil supplies will last at least 1,000 years.
   (4) If people would conserve oil, it would last forever.
   (5) Solar energy will never be inexpensive enough to use widely.

5. What would be the effect on the supply of oil if people cut down their use of it?

   (1) The supply would be used up sooner.
   (2) The supply would be used more slowly but would eventually run out.
   (3) The supply would be used more slowly and would last forever.
   (4) The supply of oil would be used up the same as it would if people did not cut down their use.
   (5) New sources of oil would be found.

6. Which of the following is a renewable resource?

   (1) oil
   (2) natural gas
   (3) coal
   (4) gasoline
   (5) solar energy

7. Which of the following statements is the most accurate?

   (1) Solar energy is an inexpensive alternative to petroleum.
   (2) A gasoline shortage is not likely to occur again.
   (3) The supply of oil will last until the year 2060.
   (4) Conserving oil will postpone the time when supplies run out.
   (5) New sources of petroleum will be found to meet our energy needs.

8. A geologist studying Earth's layers would be most interested in which of the following resources?

   (1) sunlight
   (2) ocean water
   (3) food
   (4) nuclear energy
   (5) petroleum

9. Which of the following is the best title for this passage?

   (1) Why We Have Shortages
   (2) What Are Nonrenewable Resources?
   (3) Ways to Conserve Energy
   (4) Let's Use Renewable Resources
   (5) Oil Shortages—Can They Be Avoided?

10. Which of the following uses a renewable energy resource in place of a nonrenewable energy resource?

    (1) replacing old windows in a house with modern, double-glazed windows
    (2) using windmills instead of oil-burning power plants to generate electricity
    (3) turning off lights and the television when you leave the room
    (4) replacing an old air conditioner with a newer, more efficient model
    (5) parking your car and walking into a fast-food restaurant instead of using the drive-up window

Items 11 to 16 refer to the following passage.

The air around Earth is always moving. Moving air is called <u>wind</u>. Throughout history, people have used energy from the wind to move ships, turn mill wheels, and pump water.

Windmills began to appear on U.S. farms around 1860. The energy from these windmills was used to pump water out of the ground for crops and farm animals. In 1890, a windmill was invented that could generate, or make, electricity. Wind generators became very popular with American farmers.

One problem with wind generators was that they did not always work. On calm days, they could not work. On stormy days, they were often knocked down or blown apart. Because of this, most wind generators were set aside in the 1940s, when electricity from electric power plants became available to farmers.

The need to find energy sources other than fossil fuels such as coal, oil, and natural gas has sparked new interest in wind energy. In recent years, new materials and designs have been used to make several tough, efficient wind generators. These machines can adjust to changing wind conditions and withstand storms.

Energy planners do not expect wind energy ever to meet all our needs. However, they do think that the use of wind energy can help to conserve fossil fuels and reduce air pollution.

11. According to energy planners, what is the importance of wind energy?

    (1) Wind energy is a nonrenewable resource.
    (2) Wind energy can replace fossil fuels as the leading energy resource.
    (3) Wind energy was abandoned in the 1940s.
    (4) Wind energy can reduce the need for fossil fuels.
    (5) Wind energy can be used on farms.

12. Which of the following aspects of wind energy is <u>not</u> discussed in the passage?

    (1) how wind generators were used in the 1800s
    (2) how modern wind generators are used
    (3) the reliability of wind generators
    (4) the ability of wind energy to meet energy needs
    (5) the use of wind energy on U.S. farms

13. According to the passage, modern wind generators differ from earlier wind generators in that they are

    (1) larger
    (2) less expensive
    (3) able to generate electricity
    (4) more reliable
    (5) used mainly on farms

14. According to the passage, which of the following is <u>not</u> mentioned as a use of wind power?

    (1) moving ships
    (2) powering factories
    (3) pumping water
    (4) making electricity
    (5) turning mill wheels

15. According to the passage, what caused a new interest in wind energy?

    (1) a desire to return to a simpler lifestyle
    (2) an interest in U.S. history
    (3) a need to find more energy sources
    (4) a desire to better understand wind
    (5) an increased need for electricity on U.S. farms

16. What caused the use of most wind generators to be discontinued in the 1940s?

    (1) the need to conserve fossil fuels
    (2) the need to find energy sources other than fossil fuels
    (3) the unreliability of wind generators
    (4) an increase in storms and calm days
    (5) the invention of newer, tougher wind generators

Items 17 to 20 refer to the following passage.

One source of air pollution is the burning of coal and oil by factories and power plants. Coal and oil contain sulfur. When they are burned, sulfur is released into the atmosphere. The sulfur reacts with oxygen to form sulfur oxides. Some of these sulfur oxides combine with water in the air to form acids. Eventually these acids fall to Earth as acid rain.

Acid rain is nearly as acidic as pure lemon juice. When acid rain falls into a lake, much of the lake's plant and animal life dies. Today many lakes look clear and blue because the water is nearly empty of wildlife. Animals living near such a lake may die of starvation.

What can be done about acid rain? Factories and power plants must stop burning sulfur-containing fuels. But fuels with a low sulfur content are often expensive and hard to find.

17. The main cause of acid rain is

    (1) a lack of oxygen in the air
    (2) a lack of moisture in the air
    (3) high temperatures
    (4) the burning of certain fuels
    (5) oil released into the atmosphere

18. Based on information in the passage, which of the following statements is a fact?

    (1) Factories will stop burning coal and oil.
    (2) Research will lead to the discovery of a sulfur-free fuel.
    (3) Acid rain destroys all living things on contact.
    (4) Acid rain is formed by sulfur oxides combining with water in the air.
    (5) Dangers of acid rain are exaggerated.

19. According to the passage, some lakes look clear and blue because they have

    (1) too much oxygen
    (2) many plants and animals
    (3) had above-average rainfall
    (4) been polluted by oil
    (5) lost their wildlife as a result of acid rain

20. Based on information in the passage, which of the following statements can be assumed to be true?

    (1) Sulfur is poisonous to living things.
    (2) Plants and animals live well in water that is clear and blue.
    (3) High levels of acidity can be harmful to living things.
    (4) Plants and animals die when acid is removed from rainwater.
    (5) Plants and animals live best when sulfur is present in the air.

Answers are on page 806.

Lesson  The Changing Earth

Changes in Earth's surface can be caused when the force of gravity pulls rocks and soil down mountain slopes. This is called <u>mass wasting</u>. Sediments that come to rest at the base of a cliff form a <u>talus slope</u>.

Mass wasting can occur rapidly or slowly. One type of rapid mass wasting is a landslide. During a landslide, huge quantities of soil, small stones, and large rocks tumble down a mountain. A landslide can be caused by an earthquake, volcanic eruption, or heavy rain—any natural event that weakens the supporting rock.

Another type of rapid mass wasting is a mudflow. A mudflow is usually caused by a heavy rain. As rain mixes with soil to form mud, gravity begins to pull the mud downhill. As the mud moves, it picks up more soil and becomes thicker. It is difficult to imagine the power of a mudflow—it can move just about anything in its path, including a whole house!

Slow mass wasting can occur in an earthflow. Usually caused by a heavy rain, an earthflow consists of the slow, downhill movement of soil and plant life.

Soil creep is the slowest form of mass wasting. Soil particles that have been disturbed by heavy rain, alternate periods of freezing and thawing, or animal activity are pulled downhill by gravity. Soil creep is so slow that its effects often go unnoticed for quite some time. Evidence of a long period of soil creep includes tilted trees, fences, and telephone poles along the side of a steep slope.

ged Exercise The Changing Earth

<u>Items 1 to 12</u> refer to the previous passage. Choose the <u>best answer</u> to each item.

1. Which is <u>not</u> a cause of mass wasting?

   (1) heavy rain
   (2) animal activity
   (3) earthquakes
   (4) wind
   (5) volcanic eruptions

2. A row of tilted trees along a steep slope could be a result of

   (1) a talus slope
   (2) soil creep
   (3) a mudflow
   (4) a landslide
   (5) rapid mass wasting

3. What is the basic cause of each case of mass wasting?

   (1) heavy rain
   (2) volcanic eruption
   (3) animal activity
   (4) earthflows
   (5) gravity

Tip When answering questions that include the word *not*, be certain to evaluate each choice. Then choose the one that received no support in the passage. In this type of question, the answer that is "wrong" is the correct response.

4. Which area is likely to experience the least rapid mass wasting?

    (1) the Great Plains
    (2) the Rocky Mountains
    (3) the Allegheny Mountains
    (4) the Grand Canyon
    (5) Mt. St. Helens

5. Which of the following conditions is usually necessary in order for a mudflow to occur?

    (1) an earthquake
    (2) a volcanic eruption
    (3) heavy rain
    (4) animal activity
    (5) bare land

6. Which of the following is likely to cause the most severe property damage?

    (1) earthflow
    (2) soil creep
    (3) slow mass wasting
    (4) landslide
    (5) talus slope

7. Which of the following statements is always true?

    (1) Mass wasting is the result of earthquakes and volcanic eruptions.
    (2) Rapid mass wasting occurs only in coastal areas.
    (3) The general movement in mass wasting is from high ground to low ground.
    (4) Heavy rains are present in all cases of mass wasting.
    (5) Mountain ranges can be formed by mass wasting.

8. What is a talus slope?

    (1) a mountainside without topsoil
    (2) a mountain valley
    (3) sediments piled at the base of a cliff
    (4) a rocky outcrop on a slope
    (5) tilted landscape features

9. Which of the following is the best title for this passage?

    (1) Gravity
    (2) What is Soil Creep?
    (3) Rapid and Slow Mass Wasting
    (4) Slow Mass Wasting
    (5) Damage Caused by Mass Wasting

10. Which of the following is at the greatest risk of being damaged by a landslide?

    (1) a house at the crest of a hill
    (2) a road at the base of a steep slope
    (3) a volcano in the Cascade Mountains
    (4) a boat in a lake
    (5) a tilted tree along a river

11. Which of the following is true of an earthflow?

    (1) It is not likely to occur during a drought.
    (2) It occurs at the same rate as a mudflow.
    (3) It is an example of rapid mass wasting.
    (4) It occurs only in steep mountainous regions.
    (5) It does not result in a talus slope.

12. Which of the following is most likely to be responsible for large rocks falling onto a highway?

    (1) an earthflow
    (2) soil creep
    (3) a mudflow
    (4) rapid mass wasting
    (5) slow mass wasting

Items 13 and 14 refer to the following passage.

An earthquake is the shaking and trembling that results from the sudden movement of rock in Earth's crust. When a strong earthquake hits a populated area, there can be tremendous destruction and hundreds of deaths.

The most common cause of earthquakes is faulting. A fault is a break in Earth's crust. During faulting, rocks along the fault begin to move. They break and slide past each other. Parts of Earth's crust may be pushed together or pulled apart. During this process, energy is released.

The point beneath Earth's surface where the rocks break and move is the focus of the earthquake. Directly above the focus, on Earth's surface, is the epicenter. The most violent shaking occurs at the epicenter.

When rocks in Earth's crust break, vibrations travel out in all directions from the focus. These vibrations are known as seismic waves. There are three main types of seismic waves.

The seismic waves that travel the fastest are called primary waves. These waves can travel through solids, liquids, and gases. Primary waves are push-pull waves. They cause pieces of rock to move back and forth in the same direction as the wave is moving.

The seismic waves that travel the next fastest are secondary waves. Secondary waves can travel through solids but not through liquids or gases. Rock pieces disturbed by secondary waves move from side to side at right angles to the direction the wave is traveling.

The slowest seismic waves are surface waves. Surface waves travel from the focus directly up to the epicenter. Surface waves cause the ground to bend and twist, sometimes causing whole buildings to collapse.

The more energy an earthquake releases, the stronger and more destructive it is. The strength of an earthquake is measured on a special scale, the Richter scale. The Richter scale measures how much energy an earthquake releases by assigning the earthquake a number from one to ten. Any number above six on the Richter scale indicates a very strong earthquake.

13. According to the passage, the strength of an earthquake is directly related to which of the following?

    (1) length of the fault
    (2) amount of energy released
    (3) speed of the seismic waves
    (4) distance from the focus to the epicenter
    (5) amount of rock broken

14. From the information given, one can conclude that

    (1) surface waves are the most destructive
    (2) primary waves are the most destructive
    (3) all seismic waves except surface waves are destructive
    (4) all seismic waves are equally destructive
    (5) seismic waves are not destructive

Items 15 to 18 refer to the following passage.

Erosion is the moving and wearing away of rock materials by natural causes. A dramatic cause of erosion is a glacier.

A glacier is a large mass of moving ice. Most glaciers form in mountains where snow builds up faster than it can melt. As snow falls upon snow, year after year, the snow changes into ice. When the ice becomes heavy enough, the pull of gravity causes it to move slowly down the mountain. As the glacier moves, it picks up blocks of rock. As the rocks become frozen into the bottom of the glacier, they carve away more rock. Some of this rock is left behind at the edges of the glacier.

Sometimes, after flowing down a mountain, a glacier will enter a river valley that is narrower than the glacier. As the glacier squeezes through the valley, it erodes both the floor and sides of the valley. As a result, the valley changes from a V-shaped valley to a broad U-shaped valley.

15. Which of the following is not an effect of a moving glacier?

(1) the formation of tall mountain peaks
(2) the movement of large and small rocks
(3) deposits of rock
(4) the change in shape of a valley
(5) the carving away of rock

16. What would be the effect of several unusually long, hot summers on mountain glaciers?

(1) Glaciers would move down the mountain more rapidly.
(2) Glaciers would reach farther down the mountain.
(3) The edges of the glaciers would melt, making the glaciers smaller.
(4) The glaciers would become thicker and more dense.
(5) The glaciers would carve river valleys into U-shapes.

17. Which of the following is not an example of erosion?

(1) the washing away of sand by river water
(2) the moving of pebbles by ice in a glacier
(3) the removal of soil by wind
(4) the breaking up of granite by a jackhammer
(5) the moving of rock pieces downhill by gravity

18. Which is the best title for this passage?

(1) Glaciers
(2) Agents of Erosion
(3) How Glaciers Form
(4) How Glaciers Carve Valleys
(5) Glacial Erosion

Tip When selecting a title for a passage, look for the option that best summarizes the main idea of the passage. The best title should be neither too broad nor too specific.

Answers are on page 808.

Directions: Choose the best answer for each item.

Items 1 to 4 refer to the following diagram.

The diagram below shows the characteristics of the four main layers of the atmosphere.

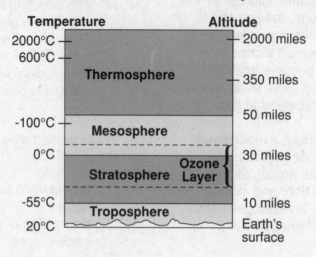

1. According to the diagram, temperature in Earth's atmosphere

   (1) remains the same as altitude increases
   (2) increases as altitude increases
   (3) decreases as altitude increases
   (4) increases, then decreases as altitude increases
   (5) decreases, then increases, then decreases, then increases as altitude increases

2. Which of the following is true of the troposphere?

   (1) It includes the ozone layer.
   (2) It is the first layer returning spacecraft encounter.
   (3) It is above the stratosphere.
   (4) It is the layer we live in.
   (5) It is thicker than the thermosphere.

3. The upper thermosphere is called the exosphere. This is where artificial satellites orbit Earth. According to the diagram, which statement must be true about these satellites?

   (1) They orbit Earth at an altitude of 62 to 124 miles.
   (2) They are protected from ultraviolet radiation by the ozone layer.
   (3) They can withstand extremely high temperatures.
   (4) They pass through thin clouds of ice.
   (5) They are used for television transmission.

4. At 50 miles above Earth's surface,

   (1) the ozone layer ends
   (2) the temperature is 600°C
   (3) the mesosphere meets the thermosphere
   (4) there are no air molecules
   (5) clouds form

The oil shortages of the 1970s set off a search for new forms of energy. At the Natural Energy Laboratory of Hawaii, scientists are producing energy without burning fossil fuels and without causing pollution. They are using cold seawater.

In one process, called <u>ocean thermal energy conversion</u>, the difference in temperature between surface and deep seawater is used to generate electricity. In experiments conducted so far, it has taken more electricity to pump up deep seawater than the process has been able to produce. Scientists and engineers are planning to use much wider pipelines in order to pump enough seawater to produce more electricity than the process uses.

A more successful test used cold seawater for air-conditioning and industrial cooling. Cold seawater was circulated through air-conditioning systems at the lab, and the electrical costs were cut by about 75 percent.

5. Which of the following does the author consider to be true about sources of energy?

   (1) Seawater will never be a practical source of energy.
   (2) Solar energy is more efficient than energy from seawater.
   (3) Seawater will eventually be used up.
   (4) It is not wise to depend only on fossil fuels for energy.
   (5) All air-conditioning systems can use cold seawater.

6. What is ocean thermal energy conversion?

   (1) a process for removing salt and other minerals from seawater
   (2) a process for farming sea plants and animals
   (3) a process that uses the difference in temperature between warm and cold seawater to produce electricity
   (4) a process to locate fossil fuel deposits under the ocean
   (5) a process for air-conditioning buildings using seawater

7. In which of the following locations would using cold seawater to produce electricity be impractical?

   (1) Hawaii
   (2) California
   (3) Florida
   (4) Puerto Rico
   (5) Kansas

8. Which of the following can be inferred from the article?

   (1) Seawater will replace fossil fuels as the main source of energy within the next ten years.
   (2) Until less electricity is used to pump up seawater than is produced by using seawater, the process will not be practical.
   (3) Using fossil fuels to produce electricity costs more than using seawater.
   (4) Seawater has been found to be more economical for producing electricity than for air-conditioning buildings.
   (5) Using seawater to produce electricity causes a lot of pollution.

Tip **When answering a question that asks you to apply information to a new context, use everything you already know about the context to help you choose the correct answer. For example, when trying to decide where using cold seawater would be impractical, use what you know about geography to figure out which states are located near the sea.**

Answers are on page 809.

Chemistry
Lesson 13

Matter

Matter can exist in any of three physical states. These states are solid, liquid, and gas.

- A solid is any form of matter that has a definite shape and volume. A bar of gold is an example of a solid. If you try to put a square bar of gold into a round hole, it will not fit. The gold has a definite shape. If you try to put the bar of gold into a space that is too small, it also will not fit. The bar of gold has a definite volume.
- A liquid has a definite volume, but it does not have a definite shape. If you pour a quart of milk into a gallon jug, the milk will fill only one-fourth of the jug. If you pour the same quart of milk into an eight-ounce glass, the milk will overflow. The volume of the milk does not change. However, its shape changes each time you pour it into a different container.
- A gas has neither definite shape nor definite volume. A gas will spread out to fill the volume of a container that it is placed in. You can understand this property of a gas if you think of how quickly the smell of an apple pie baking in the oven fills the whole kitchen.

Most matter can change from one state to another. If enough heat is removed from a liquid, it will freeze into a solid. Similarly, if enough heat is added to a solid, it will melt into a liquid. The temperature at which these changes of state occur is called the freezing point or melting point of substances. If enough heat is added to a liquid, the liquid will change into a gas. This process is called vaporization. When a gas is cooled enough, it changes into a liquid in a process called condensation. The temperature at which vaporization or condensation occurs is called the boiling point of a substance.

 Think about any experience you have had with these scientific ideas. Apply them to what you just read. This is applying knowledge to a new context, and it will help you answer questions on general or unfamiliar scientific ideas.

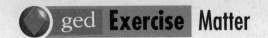

Items 1 to 8 refer to the previous passage. Choose the <u>best answer</u> to each item.

1. Which of the following situations would produce a change in the state of matter?

   (1) A drop of food coloring is added to a glass of water.
   (2) A container of ice cream is left on top of a hot stove.
   (3) A hole is pricked in a balloon.
   (4) A can of soup is placed on a scale.
   (5) A square block of wood is cut in half.

2. A heart-shaped cake is made by pouring cake batter into a heart-shaped mold. Which principle is illustrated by this situation?

   (1) A solid takes the shape of the container into which it is placed.
   (2) A solid has a definite shape but not a definite volume.
   (3) A liquid has a definite shape and volume.
   (4) A liquid has no definite shape.
   (5) A gas has a definite shape and volume.

3. What causes matter to change state?

   (1) the addition or removal of heat
   (2) its mass
   (3) the space it occupies
   (4) changes in volume
   (5) changes in shape

4. Which of the following is <u>not</u> an example of a change of state of matter?

   (1) steam condensing on a window
   (2) filling a balloon with helium
   (3) icicles melting
   (4) freezing leftover soup
   (5) boiling water until the pot is empty

5. Which of the following situations illustrates the process of condensation?

   (1) dew forming on the grass in early morning
   (2) ice cubes melting in a cold drink
   (3) rain changing to sleet
   (4) steaming vegetables
   (5) melting butter in a frying pan

6. Which of the following situations shows that gases have neither definite shape nor definite volume?

   (1) pouring a pint of orange juice into a quart container
   (2) lighting a match
   (3) adding salt to boiling water
   (4) smelling pollutants released by a nearby factory
   (5) pouring concrete into a mold

7. What are the properties that characterize a liquid?

   (1) definite shape; definite volume
   (2) definite shape; no definite volume
   (3) no definite shape; no definite volume
   (4) no definite shape; definite volume
   (5) none of the above

8. Which of the following statements is most accurate?

   (1) All matter can be found naturally in all three states.
   (2) Liquids spread out to completely fill their containers.
   (3) All matter is liquid below 100°C.
   (4) Water freezes and vaporizes at different temperatures.
   (5) Liquids melt and vaporize at different temperatures.

All matter is made up of elements. An element is a substance that cannot be broken down into simpler substances by chemical means. Oxygen, carbon, iron, and copper are examples of elements.

Can an element be broken down into smaller and smaller pieces forever and still be an element? For example, can a piece of copper be cut into smaller and smaller pieces and still be copper? The answer is <u>no</u>. Eventually, a tiny piece would be obtained that could not be divided and still be copper. This smallest piece of an element is called an atom.

An atom is the smallest physical unit of an element that still has the properties of that element. All elements are made up of atoms. The element copper is made only of copper atoms, the element iron is made only of iron atoms, and so on.

What is an atom made of? Each atom has a small, dense core called a nucleus. The nucleus contains particles called protons, which have a positive electric charge, and neutrons, which have no charge. Moving in orbits around the nucleus are tiny, negatively charged particles called electrons. A neutron and a proton have about the same mass, which is about 1,800 times greater than the mass of an electron.

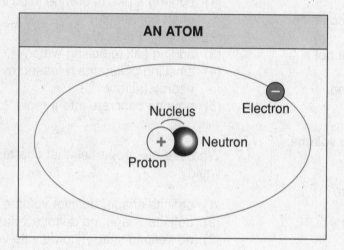

9. Which of the following statements is true of an atom of iron?

   (1) One of its electrons has the same mass as one of its protons.
   (2) Its neutrons have positive charges.
   (3) Its protons orbit the nucleus.
   (4) It is the same as an atom of copper.
   (5) It has the same properties as all other iron atoms.

10. Which of the following statements about substance X would indicate that it is <u>not</u> an element?

   (1) It breaks down when heated, producing mercury and oxygen.
   (2) It is red-orange in color.
   (3) It reacts with water to form an acid.
   (4) It is a solid at room temperature.
   (5) It can react with certain substances to form salts.

11. The total charge on an atom is zero, which means the atom is electrically neutral. Which statement explains why this is so?

  (1) The number of protons in an atom is greater than the number of electrons.
  (2) The number of protons in an atom is less than the number of electrons.
  (3) The number of protons in an atom is equal to the number of electrons.
  (4) The number of protons in an atom is equal to the number of neutrons.
  (5) The number of neutrons in an atom is equal to the number of electrons.

12. Atom X has five more protons than atom Y. Both atoms have the same mass. Which statement explains why this is so?

  (1) Atom X has more electrons than atom Y.
  (2) Atom X has fewer electrons than atom Y.
  (3) Atom X has more neutrons than atom Y.
  (4) Atom X has fewer neutrons than atom Y.
  (5) Atom X has the same number of neutrons as atom Y.

13. The structure of an atom is most similar to which of the following?

  (1) a salt crystal
  (2) a chair
  (3) an egg
  (4) the moon
  (5) the solar system

Items 14 to 16 refer to the following passage.

When two or more elements combine chemically, they form a compound. Water is a compound because it consists of the elements oxygen and hydrogen.

The smallest physical unit of a compound that still has the properties of that compound is called a molecule. A molecule is made up of two or more atoms chemically bonded together. When atoms bond together, they share or transfer electrons. If electrons are shared, the bond is said to be a covalent bond. If electrons are transferred from one atom to another, charged particles, called ions, form. A bond between two ions is said to be an ionic bond. Some atoms form bonds easily with other atoms, while some atoms hardly ever form bonds.

14. Which of the following combinations represents a compound?

  (1) two carbon atoms side-by-side in a diamond crystal
  (2) sugar and water mixed together
  (3) a hydrogen atom and a chlorine atom sharing a pair of electrons
  (4) hydrogen and nitrogen existing together in air
  (5) water and carbon dioxide mixed together in carbonated water

15. It can be inferred from the passage that atoms that do not bond easily with other atoms

  (1) have no electrons
  (2) form only ionic bonds
  (3) are present in very few compounds
  (4) are found only in water
  (5) form only covalent bonds

16. Table salt, sodium chloride, contains ionic bonds. Which of the following is true of a salt molecule?

  (1) The atoms of sodium and chloride are not bound.
  (2) Electrons are transferred from one of the atoms to another.
  (3) The sodium and chloride atoms share electrons.
  (4) Sodium and chloride do not bond easily.
  (5) The sodium atom forms bonds more easily than the chloride atom.

Answers are on page 810.

Lesson 14 Chemical Reactions

In a chemical reaction, one or more substances change, forming one or more new substances. In some chemical reactions, molecules split apart into atoms. In other reactions, atoms join together to form molecules. In yet other reactions, atoms change places with other atoms to form new molecules.

Chemical reactions either release or absorb thermal energy. A chemical reaction that releases thermal energy is called an exothermic reaction. For example, when wood or oil is burned, large amounts of thermal energy are released. A chemical reaction that absorbs thermal energy is called an endothermic reaction. Cooking an egg is an endothermic reaction, because the egg absorbs heat energy as it changes.

EXOTHERMIC REACTION   **ENDOTHERMIC REACTION**

burning wood

cooking an egg

Energy must be added to start many reactions. The energy is necessary to begin to break the bonds in the reactant molecules. The energy that must be added to start a chemical reaction is called the activation energy. When you light a match to start a charcoal grill, you are supplying activation energy.

ged Exercise Chemical Reactions

Items 1 to 9 refer to the previous passage. Choose the best answer to each item.

1. What is activation energy?

   (1) energy absorbed by a reaction
   (2) energy released by a reaction
   (3) electricity
   (4) energy needed to start a reaction
   (5) energy needed to stop a reaction

2. Which of the following is an example of an exothermic reaction?

   (1) condensing water vapor
   (2) cooking a custard
   (3) melting ice
   (4) exploding dynamite
   (5) boiling water

3. Which of the following conclusions can be supported by the information provided?

    (1) Exothermic reactions can be more useful for the energy they release than for their products.
    (2) Electricity is produced in endothermic reactions.
    (3) New chemical bonds are formed only during exothermic reactions.
    (4) Boiling water is an endothermic reaction.
    (5) Activation energy is not needed for chemical reactions.

4. Which of the following statements supports the conclusion that rusting is an exothermic reaction?

    (1) During the process of rusting, small amounts of thermal energy are released.
    (2) Activation energy produces rust.
    (3) Rusting affects only certain substances.
    (4) During rusting, metal absorbs thermal energy.
    (5) Rusting occurs in humid conditions.

5. Which of the following best describes what happens when hydrogen and oxygen combine to form water?

    (1) Molecules are breaking apart to form atoms.
    (2) Atoms are combining to form molecules.
    (3) Atoms are changing into other atoms.
    (4) Hydrogen and oxygen are undergoing a change of state.
    (5) Oxygen is a product of the reaction.

6. In the chemical reaction of photosynthesis, plants take in water and carbon dioxide and produce sugar, oxygen, and water in the presence of sunlight. What role does sunlight play in this reaction?

    (1) It is a reactant.
    (2) It is a product.
    (3) It is activation energy.
    (4) It slows the reaction.
    (5) It stops the reaction.

7. What is a chemical reaction?

    (1) a change in the state of matter
    (2) the wearing away of a substance
    (3) the change of one or more substances into a new substance with different properties
    (4) a change in the number of molecules
    (5) a change in the size of a substance

8. What is an endothermic reaction?

    (1) a reaction in which thermal energy is released
    (2) a reaction in which thermal energy is absorbed
    (3) a reaction in which energy is neither released nor absorbed
    (4) a reaction that requires activation energy to start
    (5) a reaction that changes chemical bonds

9. Which of the following is an example of a chemical reaction?

    (1) Mud hardens on a river bank.
    (2) Hydrogen combines with oxygen to form water.
    (3) Ice melts to form liquid water.
    (4) Water evaporates to form water vapor.
    (5) Rocks are ground to make gravel.

A solution is a mixture in which two or more substances are dissolved in one another. Solutions can involve solids, liquids, or gases. The substance being dissolved is called the solute. The substance doing the dissolving is called the solvent. In a sugar-water solution, sugar is the solute and water is the solvent. In carbonated water, carbon dioxide is a gas solute dissolved in water, a liquid solvent.

The greatest amount of a solute that will dissolve in a given amount of solvent at a certain temperature is called solubility. Usually, solubility increases with temperature. For gases dissolved in a liquid, however, the reverse is true—solubility increases as the temperature of the solvent decreases. The rate of solution is also affected by temperature. An increase in temperature causes molecules to move and spread apart more quickly.

10. A glass of carbonated beverage left in a warm room goes flat, while a glass of the same beverage stored in the refrigerator does not. According to the information provided, which of the following statements could explain why this happens?

   (1) Water molecules evaporate more rapidly at high temperatures.
   (2) The solubility of a gas in liquid decreases as temperature increases.
   (3) Molecules move more slowly at low temperatures.
   (4) The solubility of a gas in liquid decreases as temperature decreases.
   (5) The rate of solution is slower at low temperatures than at high temperatures.

11. If two identical mixtures of salt and water are prepared and only one is stirred, the one that is stirred dissolves the salt faster. Which of the following conclusions can be supported by the information provided?

   (1) Stirring decreases the temperature of the water.
   (2) Stirring increases solubility.
   (3) Stirring increases the amount of solute.
   (4) Stirring increases the amount of solvent.
   (5) Stirring causes molecules to move and spread apart more quickly.

12. Fish get the oxygen they need from oxygen gas dissolved in water. In this case, oxygen is

   (1) a solution
   (2) the solvent
   (3) a liquid
   (4) the solute
   (5) dissolved in a gas

Tip When reading a passage, pay careful attention to the definitions it contains. For example, the definitions of *solution*, *solvent*, and *solute* in this passage can help you answer item 12.

Items 13 to 17 refer to the following passage.

Three important groups of chemical compounds are acids, bases, and salts. When dissolved in water, these compounds produce ions. Ions are atoms or molecules with an electric charge. In water, acids produce hydrogen, or H^+ ions. In water, bases produce hydroxide, or OH^- ions. Citric acid is found in citrus fruits. Magnesium hydroxide is the base that is the active ingredient in many stomach remedies.

A strong acid, such as sulfuric acid, or a strong base, such as sodium hydroxide, is poisonous and can burn the skin. Yet a weak acid, such as citric acid, or a weak base, such as magnesium hydroxide, can be safely handled. The strength of an acid or base is measured on a scale called the pH scale. The pH scale ranges from 0 to 14. The number 7 is the neutral point. Substances with a pH below 7 are acidic, and substances with a pH above 7 are basic. The strongest acid would have a pH of 0, and the strongest base would have a pH of 14.

When an acid and a base combine chemically, the result is a neutral compound called a salt. Water is also a product of this reaction. A familiar salt is sodium chloride, table salt.

pH SCALE

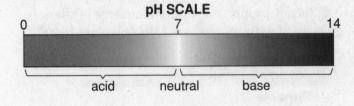

13. Which of the following statements would indicate the substance X is <u>not</u> classified as an acid?

    (1) It combines chemically with certain other compounds to produce salts.
    (2) It dissolves in water to produce OH^- ions.
    (3) It can be poisonous if swallowed.
    (4) Its pH is lower than that of water.
    (5) It can be corrosive to skin.

14. An antacid relieves indigestion by neutralizing excess acid in the stomach. Based on this information, which of the following statements is true about an antacid?

    (1) It contains salt.
    (2) It has a low pH.
    (3) It contains a base.
    (4) It produces H^+ ions.
    (5) It dissolves very rapidly.

15. Which of the following represents a correct ordering of substances from lowest to highest pH?

    (1) magnesium hydroxide, pure water, sulfuric acid, sodium hydroxide
    (2) pure water, sulfuric acid, citric acid, sodium hydroxide
    (3) sulfuric acid, sodium hydroxide, citric acid, magnesium hydroxide
    (4) sulfuric acid, citric acid, pure water, sodium hydroxide
    (5) sodium hydroxide, pure water, citric acid, sulfuric acid

16. It can be inferred from the passage that a solution of table salt and water would have a pH of approximately

    (1) 0
    (2) 4
    (3) 7
    (4) 10
    (5) 14

17. When calcium hydroxide, a base, reacts with citric acid, the reaction produces calcium citrate and water. Calcium citrate is

    (1) an acid
    (2) a base
    (3) a compound with a pH of 6
    (4) a compound with a pH of 3
    (5) a salt

Answers are on page 811.

Lesson 15

Hydrocarbons

Do you know what you have in common with trees, birds, and all living things? All living things contain carbon. Compounds that contain carbon are called organic compounds. A special kind of organic compound that contains only the two elements hydrogen and carbon is called a hydrocarbon. There are thousands of different kinds of hydrocarbons. Scientists classify these hydrocarbons into smaller subgroups called series.

The members of the alkane series are the most abundant of the hydrocarbons. You're probably already familiar with a number of these compounds. If you've ever been camping, you may have used propane or butane. These two gases are often sold in canisters for use in heating, camping stoves, lanterns, and lighters. The gasoline that fuels a car contains pentane, hexane, heptane, and octane. These and other alkanes are listed in the table below.

Since hydrocarbons consist of just two elements, you might think that there would be little variety in the properties of alkane series hydrocarbons. However, this is not the case. For example, look at the range of states and boiling points of the members of the alkane series in the table below. You can see from the formulas listed that each member of the series contains a different number of carbon and hydrogen atoms in its molecules. This difference in composition causes each compound to have different properties. Some members of the series are made up of molecules with more than 1,000 carbon atoms!

THE ALKANE SERIES			
Name	Formula	Physical State at Room Temperature	Boiling Point (°C)
Methane	CH_4	gas	−162
Ethane	C_2H_6	gas	−89
Propane	C_3H_8	gas	−42
Butane	C_4H_{10}	gas	−1
Pentane	C_5H_{12}	liquid	36
Hexane	C_6H_{14}	liquid	69
Heptane	C_7H_{16}	liquid	98
Octane	C_8H_{18}	liquid	126
Nonane	C_9H_{20}	liquid	151
Decane	$C_{10}H_{22}$	liquid	174
Eicosane	$C_{20}H_{42}$	solid	344

 Tip Charts often compare variable data for different items entered in the chart. Read across the tops of columns to see what is being compared. Read down the column on the left to see what items are being compared.

Science ♦ Chemistry

Items 1 to 8 refer to the previous information.

Choose the best answer to each item.

1. Which of the following compounds is not an organic compound?

    (1) CO_2
    (2) C_2H_6
    (3) C_2H_4O
    (4) C_3H_8
    (5) H_2S

2. Which of the following compounds is not a hydrocarbon?

    (1) C_6H_{14}
    (2) CH_4
    (3) CO_2
    (4) C_2H_2
    (5) C_6H_6

3. Which of the following statements is true of members of the alkane series?

    (1) They are living things.
    (2) They are both organic compounds and hydrocarbons.
    (3) They are all liquids at room temperature.
    (4) They contain the same number of carbon atoms.
    (5) They are made up of helium atoms.

4. Which of the following conclusions can you draw from the data in the table?

    (1) Heptane boils at a lower temperature then hexane.
    (2) Butane boils at a higher temperature than ethane.
    (3) Butane melts at a lower temperature than ethane.
    (4) Eicosane contains the fewest carbon atoms.
    (5) Pentane contains fewer carbon and hydrogen atoms than butane.

5. Which of the following is true of propane?

    (1) It is sold in canisters for use in heating.
    (2) It has the formula C_2H_8.
    (3) Its molecules contain more hydrogen atoms than butane molecules contain.
    (4) It is found in the gasoline that fuels cars.
    (5) Its boiling point is 36°C.

6. If you open the valve on the fuel tank of a gas barbecue grill, the fuel that escapes is in the gaseous state. The fuel is probably

    (1) C_3H_8
    (2) octane
    (3) nonane
    (4) decane
    (5) $C_{20}H_{42}$

7. Which of the following is true of hexane?

    (1) It is a liquid at room temperature.
    (2) It has the formula $C_4H_{10.}$
    (3) Its boiling point is −162°C.
    (4) It has the formula $C_2H_{6.}$
    (5) It has more carbon atoms than hydrogen atoms.

8. Which of the following is not true of octane?

    (1) It has a boiling point of 126°C.
    (2) It is found in gasoline used for cars.
    (3) It is a gas at room temperature.
    (4) It has a higher boiling point than pentane.
    (5) Its molecules contain more carbon atoms than those of hexane.

Items 9 to 12 refer to the following passage.

Although they may sound similar, alkanes and alkenes are very different hydrocarbon series. Like alkanes, members of the alkene series contain only hydrogen and carbon. However, unlike alkanes, alkenes contain double bonds in their molecules.

In alkanes, all bonds are single covalent bonds, in which one pair of electrons is shared. One bond in every alkene molecule is a double covalent bond, in which two pairs of electrons are shared.

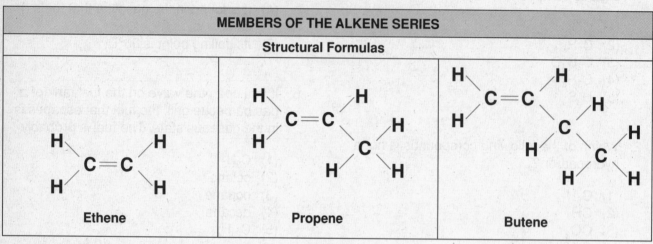

MEMBERS OF THE ALKENE SERIES

Structural Formulas

Ethene   Propene   Butene

= represents a double bond; – represents a single bond

9. Which of the following statements is true of both alkanes and alkenes?

   (1) They contain only single bonds.
   (2) They are not compounds.
   (3) They contain hydrogen and calcium.
   (4) They are hydrocarbons.
   (5) They contain ionic bonds.

10. Which of the following statements can be inferred from the information provided?

   (1) All alkenes contain the same number of carbon atoms.
   (2) Alkenes contain more hydrogen atoms than alkanes do.
   (3) Alkanes and alkenes contain different numbers of carbon atoms.
   (4) All alkenes contain an odd number of hydrogen atoms.
   (5) Double bonds occur only between the carbon atoms in alkenes.

11. Based on the information given, which of the following is the correct chemical formula of butene?

   (1) CH_4
   (2) C_4H_8
   (3) H_8
   (4) C_{12}
   (5) C_2H_4

12. The chemical formula of the alkane propane is C_3H_8. Based on the information in the table, it can be concluded that propane as compared to propene

   (1) has the same number of carbon and hydrogen atoms as propene
   (2) has more hydrogen atoms than propene
   (3) has more carbon atoms than propene
   (4) has fewer carbon atoms than propene
   (5) melts at a higher temperature than propene

Items 13 to 16 refer to the following passage.

A molecule that contains only single bonds, in which one pair of electrons is shared in each bond, is said to be saturated. In molecules that contain bonds other than single bonds, more than one pair of electrons are shared in each bond. Such molecules are said to be unsaturated. A saturated hydrocarbon contains more hydrogen than an unsaturated hydrocarbon with the same number of carbon atoms.

One example of a saturated hydrocarbon is ethane, C_2H_6. An example of an unsaturated molecule is ethene, C_2H_4. In this unsaturated hydrocarbon, two electrons of one carbon atom are paired with two electrons of another carbon atom to form a double bond.

In certain reactions, the double and triple bonds of an unsaturated hydrocarbon can be broken. Hydrogen can then be added to the molecule. A reaction in which hydrogen is added to an unsaturated hydrocarbon is called an addition reaction.

Unsaturated Hydrocarbon (Alkene)   Hydrogen   Saturated Hydrocarbon (Alkane)

13. Unlike a saturated molecule, an unsaturated molecule contains

    (1) hydrogen atoms
    (2) only single bonds
    (3) shared electrons
    (4) bonds other than single bonds
    (5) a reduction reaction

14. Which of the following conclusions is supported by the information presented?

    (1) Saturated hydrocarbons can be produced from unsaturated hydrocarbons through addition reactions.
    (2) Unsaturated hydrocarbons can be produced from saturated hydrocarbons through addition reactions.
    (3) In addition reactions, the number of carbon atoms present increases.
    (4) Alkenes cannot be made from alkanes.
    (5) Under certain conditions, hydrocarbons react with chlorine.

15. Which of the following statements is true of the addition reaction shown?

    (1) The product is C_2H_6.
    (2) The reactants are H_2 and C_2H_6.
    (3) The product contains a double bond.
    (4) One reactant is a saturated hydrocarbon.
    (5) Both reactants are unsaturated hydrocarbons.

16. Which of the following is a fact presented about ethene?

    (1) It is a saturated molecule.
    (2) Single bonding occurs between its carbon atoms.
    (3) Double bonding occurs between its carbon atoms.
    (4) Its atoms contain only two electrons.
    (5) It reacts to form an unsaturated molecule.

Two compounds whose molecules have the same number and kind of atoms but different arrangements of atoms are called isomers. Compare the isomers of butane shown. Although these isomers have the same chemical formula, they are different compounds with different properties. For example, the straight-chain butane has a higher boiling point than the branched-chain butane. The more carbon atoms contained in a hydrocarbon molecule, the more isomers that molecule can form.

H H H H
| | | |
H—C—C—C—C—H
| | | |
H H H H

Straight Chain Butane,
C₄H₁₀

H H H
| | |
H—C—C—C—H
| |
H H
|
H—C—H
|
H

Branched Chain Butane,
C₄H₁₀

17. Which of the following is true of isomers?

(1) They contain different numbers of atoms.
(2) They contain different kinds of atoms.
(3) They cannot be hydrocarbons.
(4) They have the same properties.
(5) They have different arrangements of atoms.

18. In the structural formula for the branched-chain isomer of butane,

(1) all the hydrogen atoms are bonded along a straight line
(2) all the carbon atoms are bonded along a straight line
(3) one carbon atom branches off from the middle carbon atom
(4) none of the carbon atoms are bonded along a straight line
(5) the hydrogen atoms are connected to other hydrogen atoms

19. Pentane (C_5H_{12}), a member of the alkane series of hydrocarbons, has three isomers. Another member of this series, decane ($C_{10}H_{22}$), is likely to have

(1) no isomers
(2) a lower boiling point
(3) more isomers
(4) the same number of isomers
(5) fewer isomers

20. Gasoline containing straight-chain hydrocarbons burns more quickly than gasoline containing branched-chain hydrocarbons because oxygen more easily reaches the parts of a straight-chain molecule. This, in turn, is most likely the result of

(1) the straight-chain molecule's less compact arrangement of atoms
(2) the branched-chain molecule's higher oxygen content
(3) the branched-chain molecule's chemical formula
(4) the branched-chain molecule's higher boiling point
(5) the straight-chain molecule's higher carbon and hydrogen content

Tip **When information is restated in a graph or an illustration, use the graph or illustration to help you understand the information in the passage.**

Answers are on page 812.

Directions: Choose the <u>best answer</u> for each item.

<u>Items 1 to 6</u> refer to the following passage.

All atoms and molecules are constantly in motion. The motion depends upon whether the molecules are in a solid, liquid, or gas.

Molecules in a solid move the least. They only vibrate. Forces of attraction hold the molecules of a solid very tightly in place, which is why solids have both definite volume and definite shape.

The molecules in a liquid move more freely and have more energy than the molecules of a solid. Forces of attraction among liquid molecules hold them together. That is why, when you pour a liquid, it stays together.

Molecules of a gas move freely and randomly. There are almost no forces of attraction among gas molecules. A gas will escape from an open container and "disappear."

1. In a carbonated beverage you can see bubbles of gas rising to the surface. What causes these bubbles?

   (1) vibrations of gas molecules
   (2) collisions between liquid and gas molecules
   (3) gas molecules moving rapidly through less freely-moving liquid molecules
   (4) force of attraction between liquid and gas molecules
   (5) liquid molecules pushing against less freely-moving gas molecules

2. If a tank of oxygen gas began to leak, the molecules of oxygen in the tank would

   (1) move but remain in the tank
   (2) leave the tank, but stay together
   (3) not move
   (4) escape and spread apart
   (5) stop vibrating

3. Which of the following conclusions can be supported by the passage?

   (1) Large molecules move faster than small molecules.
   (2) Molecules in gases have less energy if the gas is in a small container.
   (3) You can feel the molecules vibrating when you hold a solid.
   (4) Molecules in liquids move faster than molecules in gases.
   (5) Molecules of a gas will spread out and fill any container they are in.

4. The passage discusses a relationship between which two factors?

   (1) states of matter and movement of molecules
   (2) temperature and energy of molecules
   (3) states of matter and sizes of molecules
   (4) sizes of molecules and movement of molecules
   (5) temperature and attractions between molecules

5. A block of ice is heated, and it changes into a liquid. This shows that as temperature increases,

   (1) movement of molecules decreases
   (2) movement of molecules increases
   (3) movement of molecules becomes less random
   (4) molecules collide less often
   (5) changes of state take place more slowly

6. Rocks have a definite shape because

   (1) the molecules in a solid repel each other
   (2) the molecules in gases move about freely
   (3) their molecules vibrate
   (4) forces of attraction among liquid molecules are strong
   (5) molecules in solids are held together by forces of attraction

Items 7 to 9 refer to the following information.

If the numbers of protons and neutrons in the nucleus of an atom are very different, the atom may be radioactive. A radioactive atom decays and gives off particles until the nucleus is stable. The time needed for half the nuclei in a sample of radioactive material to decay is called its half-life. The half-life of carbon 14, for example, is 5,730 years. This means that after 5,730 years, half the carbon 14 in a given sample will have decayed into another substance.

HALF-LIFE OF CARBON 14

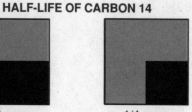

1 gram carbon 14	1/2 gram carbon 14	1/4 gram carbon 14	1/8 gram carbon 14
0 years	5,730 years	11,460 years	17,190 years

7. Using information about the half-life of radioactive substances would be of most interest to which scientist?

   (1) a metallurgist looking for ways to remove metals from ores
   (2) a geologist interested in estimating the age of rock samples
   (3) a chemist developing new products from organic compounds
   (4) an oceanographer studying wave motion
   (5) a biochemist studying photosynthesis

8. Which of the following conclusions can be supported by the information provided?

   (1) After 22,920 years, none of the carbon 14 will remain.
   (2) After 22,920 years, 1/8 gram of carbon 14 will remain of the original 1 gram.
   (3) After 22,920 years, 1/16 gram of carbon 14 will remain of the original 1 gram.
   (4) Radioactive elements can be made in the laboratory.
   (5) The number of electrons affects the radioactivity of an atom.

9. From the information given, which of the following reasons can cause an element to be radioactive?

   (1) too many protons
   (2) too many neutrons
   (3) the length of its half-life
   (4) an unstable nucleus
   (5) particles given off by the nucleus

Tip **Remember, always preview an illustration or diagram before reading the text it accompanies. Then refer back to it as frequently as necessary while you read.**

Items 10 to 12 refer to the following information.

Stalactites and stalagmites are column-shaped rocks that form in caves. A chemical reaction is responsible for their formation. This reaction begins as water dissolves minerals in rocks. This reaction can be modeled by mixing a solution of calcium chloride in water with a solution of sodium carbonate in water. Upon mixing, the ions Ca^{2+}, Cl^-, Na^+, and CO_3^{2-} are all present in the water.

When mixed, the Ca^{2+} and CO_3^{2-} ions join together to form a powdery white substance called calcium carbonate. This substance, whose chemical formula is $CaCO_3$, is what makes up stalactites and stalagmites. Because it is not soluble in water, it settles out of the solution, or precipitates. The precipitation of calcium carbonate is shown in the equation below.

$$CaCl_2 + Na_2CO_3 \rightarrow CaCO_3 + 2NaCl$$

This equation is read as: calcium chloride plus sodium carbonate yields calcium carbonate plus sodium chloride.

10. Why does $CaCO_3$ precipitate in the reaction shown?

    (1) Calcium reacts with water.
    (2) The solubility of $CaCO_3$ decreases after heating.
    (3) Sodium carbonate is not soluble in water.
    (4) Calcium carbonate is soluble in water.
    (5) Calcium carbonate is not soluble in water.

11. Which of the following is an unstated assumption of the passage?

    (1) Calcium carbonate is not soluble in water.
    (2) Calcium carbonate in soluble in water.
    (3) Calcium carbonate reacts with hydrochloric acid.
    (4) Calcium chloride and sodium carbonate are soluble in water.
    (5) Calcium chloride and sodium carbonate react with hydrochloric acid.

12. In the reaction shown in the information, why does sodium chloride, NaCl, not form a precipitate?

    (1) Na^+ ions and Cl^- ions do not react.
    (2) Sodium chloride is soluble in water.
    (3) There are more Na^+ ions than Cl^- ions.
    (4) The Na^+ ions become part of the precipitate that forms.
    (5) Cl^- ions do not react with $CaCO_3$.

Item 13 refers to the following passage and diagrams.

A dot diagram is frequently used to show the arrangement of electrons in the outer energy level of a atom. Most outer energy levels are complete with eight electrons. Then the atom is stable and tends not to enter into chemical reactions easily.

A dot diagram can be used to understand how atoms combine. Atoms seek to become stable. They do this by sharing electrons, losing electrons, or gaining electrons. A dot diagram can help you predict how an atom may react with another atom.

aluminum   sulfur   chlorine

neon   sodium

13. Which two atoms shown are likely to react most easily with each other?

    (1) aluminum and sulfur
    (2) aluminum and chlorine
    (3) sulfur and chlorine
    (4) sulfur and neon
    (5) chlorine and sodium

Answers are on page 814.

Physics
Lesson 16

Moving Objects

To describe the motion of an object, two of the things you might discuss are how far the object moved and where it moved. When someone asks you how far you've traveled or how much farther you have to go, they are asking about distance. Distance is the length of the path from one point to another. If, for example, you run home, the length of the path you run on is the distance you have traveled.

The dashed lines in the diagram below show the distances two people walked. The woman walked a distance of 10 meters from point A to point B. In other words, the length of the path she took was 10 meters long. The man also walked a total distance of 10 meters. Notice, however, that he took a path that started at point A but ended at point C. Although he traveled the same distance, where he traveled is different. Displacement is a measure of both the distance and the direction traveled. Displacement can be shown as an arrow between a starting point and an ending point. The solid arrows in the diagram show displacement. Any object that moves, but ends up at the same point it started from, has no displacement.

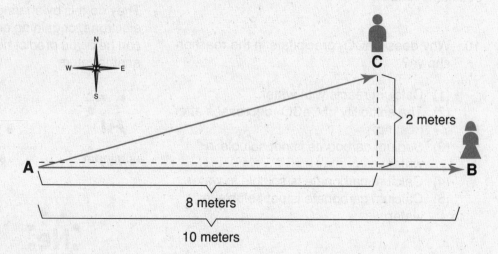

ged Exercise | Moving Objects

Items 1 to 6 refer to the previous passage. Choose the best answer to each item.

1. The displacement of the woman in the diagram is

    (1) 10 meters
    (2) 20 meters
    (3) 10 meters east
    (4) the same as that of the man
    (5) 10 meters south

2. The distance traveled by the man in the diagram is

    (1) 10 meters
    (2) 20 meters
    (3) about 8 1/4 meters northeast
    (4) greater than the distance traveled by the woman
    (5) the same as his displacement

3. The distance an object travels differs from its displacement in that

   (1) only distance includes the length of the path traveled
   (2) only distance includes the direction traveled
   (3) only displacement includes the length of the path traveled
   (4) only displacement includes the direction traveled
   (5) displacement is always greater

4. Which of the following are supporting details of the second paragraph?

   A. The woman walked a distance of 10 meters.
   B. The man and the woman traveled the same distance, but they ended up in different places.
   C. Displacement is not the same as distance.

   (1) A only
   (2) A and B
   (3) B and C
   (4) A and C
   (5) A, B, and C

5. Which of the following statements is the main idea of the second paragraph?

   (1) Displacement indicates both the direction and how far an object traveled.
   (2) Distance indicates both the direction and how far an object traveled.
   (3) The dashed lines in the diagram show the distances two people walked.
   (4) Displacement can be shown as an arrow between a starting point and an ending point.
   (5) Displacement can be measured in meters

6. If a man starts at his back door, walks in a circle around his back yard, and ends up at his back door, then

   (1) his distance traveled is zero
   (2) his displacement is zero
   (3) his distance traveled and displacement are both zero
   (4) his displacement is the length of his circular path
   (5) his displacement is greater than his distance

Items 7 and 8 refer to the following paragraph and diagram.

A person walks 30 meters east, then 5 meters north, then 20 meters west, and then 5 meters south.

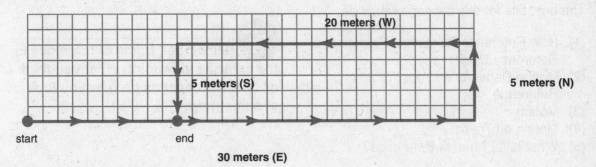

7. What is the person's displacement?

   (1) 5 meters north
   (2) 10 meters east
   (3) 15 meters north
   (4) 50 meters east
   (5) 60 meters east

8. What is the distance the person traveled?

   (1) 5 meters
   (2) 10 meters
   (3) 15 meters
   (4) 50 meters
   (5) 60 meters

Items 9 to 12 refer to the following passage.

The motion of an object doesn't look the same to everyone who sees it. How you view motion depends on your frame of reference, or your viewpoint. Think about a passenger on a train. At first, the train is standing still and the passenger is seated. To an observer standing outside the train, the passenger is not moving in relation to the train or to the train tracks. When the train begins its journey, the observer outside the train would say that the passenger is moving forward relative to the track. However, another observer sitting inside the train would say that the seated passenger is <u>not</u> moving relative to the train. This observer doesn't observe motion because the observer is moving along with the passenger and the train. The two observers have different frames of reference, so their observations of motion differ.

9. The main idea of the paragraph is

(1) To an observer standing outside a train, a passenger is not moving in relation to the train or to the train tracks.
(2) Frames of reference vary, depending on where you are.
(3) How you view motion depends on your frame of reference.
(4) Frames of reference include trains, tracks, and passengers.
(5) Two different observers can have two different frames of reference.

10. The <u>best</u> title for this passage would be

(1) How Reference Points and Frames of Reference Differ
(2) Motion Depends on Your Frame of Reference
(3) Motion
(4) Motion on Trains
(5) What Is a Frame of Reference?

11. Which of the following is a supporting detail of the paragraph?

(1) Relative to the passenger, a person outside the train is moving.
(2) Your frame of reference would include all the reference points you can see.
(3) Your viewpoint does not affect how you observe motion.
(4) Two observers have different frames of reference, so their observations of motion differ.
(5) An observer sitting inside a train next to a passenger would say that the seated passenger is moving relative to the train.

12. You are in a car stopped at a red light. Suddenly you think you are rolling into the intersection but quickly realize that the car next to you has rolled backward. Which of the following <u>best</u> explains why you thought you were moving?

(1) You can only see the other car out of the corner of your eye.
(2) Your frame of reference is the other car which you believe to be motionless; therefore, you must be moving.
(3) The traffic light appears to be getting closer.
(4) Your frame of reference is momentarily confused.
(5) Because the other car moved, you can now see the sidewalk next to you.

Tip **Remember, frame of reference is the same as viewpoint. What you think or observe depends on *how* you look at something.**

Items 13 to 16 refer to the following passage.

Every time you check the speedometer in a car to see how fast you're going, you think about the speed of motion. Speed is the distance traveled per unit of time. It is calculated by dividing the distance traveled by the time spent traveling that distance. The equation for calculating speed is

$$speed = \frac{distance}{time}$$

For example, if a bowling ball rolls 10 meters in 2 seconds, the ball's speed is 10 meters divided by 2 seconds, or 5 meters per second.

Whereas speed is a measure of how fast an object moves, velocity is a measure of both how fast and in what direction an object moves. In other words, velocity describes both speed and direction. If we know that the bowling ball described above is rolling due south, then its velocity is 5 meters per second south.

13. Which of the following statements is the main idea of the first paragraph?

    (1) You think about speed when you check a car's speedometer.
    (2) Speed is the distance traveled per unit of time.
    (3) The equation used to calculate speed includes speed, velocity, and time.
    (4) A bowling ball that rolls 10 meters in 2 seconds has a speed of 5 meters per second.
    (5) Velocity describes both speed and direction.

14. Speed differs from velocity in that

    (1) only velocity describes direction
    (2) only velocity describes how fast an object moves
    (3) only speed describes direction
    (4) only speed describes how fast an object moves
    (5) only speed is connected to distance and time

15. A hiker traveling northwest covers 12 kilometers of road in 3 hours. The hiker's speed is

    (1) 12 kilometers per hour
    (2) 12 kilometers per hour northwest
    (3) 4 kilometers per hour
    (4) 4 kilometers per hour northwest
    (5) 3 kilometers per hour

16. A driver must reach a destination 400 kilometers away by 6 P.M. If she leaves at 2 P.M. and drives her car at a speed of 80 kilometers per hour, she will arrive

    (1) 1 hour early
    (2) 1/2 hour early
    (3) just in time
    (4) 2 hours late
    (5) 1 hour late

Item 17 refers to the following paragraph and map.

A driver left Smallville at 9:00 A.M., and drove south on route 70 until 11:00 A.M. Then the driver turned east on route 3, and drove the remaining distance to Center City, arriving at noon.

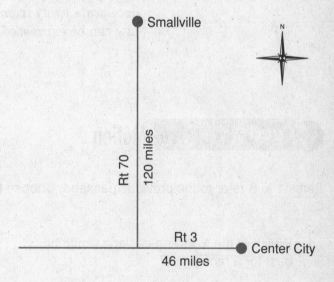

17. If velocity describes both speed and direction, what was the driver's velocity at 11:30 A.M.?

    (1) 46 miles per hour south
    (2) 46 miles per hour east
    (3) 55 miles per hour south-east
    (4) 60 miles per hour east
    (5) 60 miles per hour

Answers are on page 815.

Lesson

17 Motion

A force is a push or pull that acts on matter, causing it to speed up, slow down, or change direction. A change in the speed or direction of motion is called <u>acceleration</u>.

The English scientist Sir Isaac Newton formulated laws about motion. The First Law of Motion states that an object at rest tends to remain at rest, and an object in motion tends to keep moving in a straight line at the same speed, until acted upon by outside forces. For example, when you throw a ball, it eventually falls to the ground and stops rolling. It stops moving because the force of gravity has pulled it down, and the friction from the air and the ground has slowed it down. Without gravity and friction, the ball would continue moving in a straight line.

The tendency of an object to keep moving or remain at rest is called <u>inertia</u>. You become aware of inertia when you are riding in a car that suddenly stops. Because of inertia, you will keep moving forward until a force stops you.

Newton's Second Law of Motion states that an object will accelerate in the direction of the force that acts upon it. The mass of an object and the force that acts upon it will affect how the object accelerates. For example, a large truck requires more force than a small car to accelerate away from a stoplight at the same rate. Newton's second law can be expressed by the formula:

$$\text{force} = \text{mass} \times \text{acceleration}$$

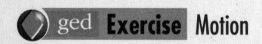 ged Exercise Motion

Items 1 to 8 refer to the previous passage. Choose the <u>best answer</u> to each item.

1. Which of the following designs would be best for a racing car?

   (1) small engine and lightweight body
   (2) large engine and lightweight body
   (3) small engine and heavy body
   (4) large engine and heavy body
   (5) small engine and large gas tank

2. Once a spacecraft reaches outer space, its inertia would keep it moving in a straight line at a constant speed, even if its engine is not used. What is most likely to cause the spacecraft to change direction?

   (1) running out of fuel
   (2) energy from the sun
   (3) the force of friction
   (4) the force of gravity
   (5) acceleration

3. If a force of 8 N is applied to a 2-kilogram ball, and a force of 6 N is applied to a 3-kilogram ball, how will the accelerations of the balls compare?

   (1) Both accelerations will be the same.
   (2) The acceleration of the second ball will be twice that of the first.
   (3) The acceleration of the first ball will be twice that of the second.
   (4) The acceleration of the first ball will be four times that of the second.
   (5) The acceleration of the second ball will be four times that of the first.

4. According to Newton's laws, an outside force would be required to make which of the following situations occur?

   (1) A cyclist traveling at 15 miles per hour continues to travel at the same speed in the same direction.
   (2) A person who stood through the first hour of a sold-out concert stands through the second hour.
   (3) A passenger sits on the subway while the train travels four miles in four minutes.
   (4) A rocket traveling through space continues to move in a forward direction.
   (5) A car traveling at 40 miles per hour goes around a curve at the same speed.

5. Which of the following is an example of Newton's Second Law of Motion?

   A. a pitcher throwing a fast ball
   B. a seat belt preventing a person from hitting the windshield
   C. a parked car

   (1) A only
   (2) B only
   (3) C only
   (4) A and B
   (5) B and C

6. Which of the following situations is an example of Newton's First Law of Motion?

   (1) A man finds that pushing a full wheelbarrow takes more force than pushing an empty one.
   (2) A package on the seat of a car going 60 miles per hour slides forward when the car stops suddenly.
   (3) Passengers notice that a bus rides more smoothly at 50 miles per hour than at 25 miles per hour.
   (4) A car stuck on an ice patch is able to move when a blanket is placed under the back wheels.
   (5) A football player intercepts a pass and runs in the opposite direction from which the ball was thrown.

7. Football teams use large players in the defense lines and smaller players in the backfield to run and catch passes. What is an advantage of this strategy?

   (1) Small players can accelerate quickly, while large players can apply force to stop the motion of opponents.
   (2) Large players remain at rest, while light players remain in motion.
   (3) Light players can catch passes, while large players can tackle.
   (4) Large players tend to move in a straight line, while light players can change direction easily.
   (5) The force needed to stop a large player is much greater than the force needed to stop a small one.

8. Newton's Second Law of Motion describes the relationship among which factors?

   (1) mass and acceleration
   (2) direction and force
   (3) direction, force, and acceleration
   (4) mass, force, and acceleration
   (5) mass, direction, and acceleration

Answers are on page 817.

Lesson 18

Electricity and Magnetism

Have you ever heard the saying "opposites attract"? People usually use this phrase to describe opposite personalities. But this phrase can also describe the forces in two important areas of physics—electricity and magnetism.

You may think of electricity as turning on the lights or starting an electric motor. Certainly these are important uses of electricity—but what exactly is electricity? Where does it come from? And how does it power the appliances that you use every day?

To answer these questions, you must first go back to the atom that you studied in lesson 13. You will recall that atoms are made up of protons, electrons, and neutrons. Protons and electrons have a property called electric charge. Protons are positively charged (+1) and electrons are negatively charged (–1). Neutrons have no charge—as their name implies, they are neutral (0).

The force of attraction between the positively-charged protons and the negatively-charged electrons helps hold an atom together. The structure of an atom shows the basic rule of electric charge: Unlike charges attract each other, while like charges repel each other. You can remember this rule easily if you just think of the old saying "opposites attract."

The area of force that surrounds a charged particle is called an electric field. The strength of an electric field depends on the distance from the charged particle—as the distance increases, the strength of the field decreases. The electric field of a charged particle exerts a force on any other charged particle. The force will be one of attraction if the particles are of unlike charge, and repulsion if the particles are of like charge.

THE HELIUM ATOM

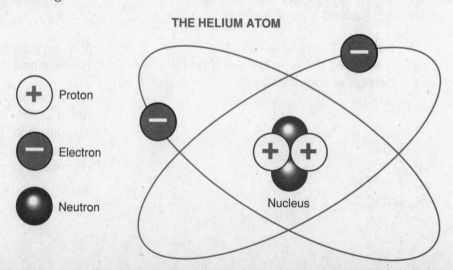

Proton

Electron

Neutron

Nucleus

Items 1 to 8 refer to the previous passage and diagram. Choose the best answer to each item.

1. A negatively-charged strip of metal is suspended from the ceiling. When another strip of metal is brought close to it, the first strip bends away. Which statement explains why this happens?

   (1) The second strip is positively charged.
   (2) The second strip is negatively charged.
   (3) The second strip contains fewer electrons than the first strip.
   (4) The second strip has a larger electric field than the first strip.
   (5) The atoms in the second strip repel the atoms in the first strip.

2. Which of the following particles always has a negative charge?

   (1) proton
   (2) neutron
   (3) electron
   (4) atom
   (5) field

3. What is an electric field?

   (1) a group of electrons
   (2) a group of protons
   (3) an area of force
   (4) a charged particle
   (5) positively-charged atoms

4. Which of the following is not affected by the electric field of a charged particle?

   A. a particle with the same charge
   B. a particle with an opposite charge
   C. an uncharged particle

   (1) A only
   (2) B only
   (3) C only
   (4) A and B only
   (5) B and C only

5. Atoms and molecules with an electric charge are called ions. What is likely to happen when positively-charged ions are mixed with negatively-charged ions?

   (1) The negative and positive ions will attract each other.
   (2) The negative ions and positive ions will remain separate.
   (3) The negative ions produce a larger electric field than the positive ions.
   (4) The negative and positive ions will repel each other.
   (5) Positive ions will remain grouped together.

6. What holds an atom together?

   (1) force of gravity
   (2) chemical bonds
   (3) its nucleus
   (4) force of attraction between protons and electrons
   (5) force of attraction between neutrons and electrons

7. If an atom contains 3 protons, 4 neutrons, and 2 electrons, what is the charge on the atom?

   (1) +2
   (2) +1
   (3) 0 (neutral)
   (4) −1
   (5) −2

8. Decreasing the distance between two unlike charged particles would

   (1) decrease their electric charges
   (2) increase their electric charges
   (3) increase the flow of electricity
   (4) decrease their force of attraction
   (5) increase their force of attraction

Items 9 to 12 refer to the following passage.

A magnetic field is formed around a wire conducting an electric current. This relationship between electricity and magnetism is known as electromagnetism.

Because of electromagnetism, powerful temporary magnets called electromagnets can be made by wrapping coils of wire around soft iron and passing an electric current through the wire. When the current passing through the wire is turned off, the magnet loses its magnetic properties. When the current is turned back on, the magnet regains its magnetic properties. The strength of the electromagnet depends on the number of loops of wire and the size of the current.

9. A heavy crane used at construction sites is equipped with a large electromagnet. The electromagnet will make the machine most useful for which of the following tasks?

    (1) transporting pieces of iron to distant locations
    (2) picking up pieces of scrap metal on the site and depositing them elsewhere on the site
    (3) generating electricity for the area surrounding the site
    (4) making magnets out of pieces of scrap metal found on the site
    (5) lifting objects too heavy for other types of machines on the site

Tip When reading about a situation where there is a change, ask yourself what causes the change. Also identify any result of the change.

10. The relationship between electricity and magnetism described in the passage is best expressed by which of the following statements?

    (1) Electromagnets form magnetic fields.
    (2) Magnets cause electricity.
    (3) Wrapping wire around iron causes magnetism.
    (4) An electric current produces a magnetic field.
    (5) An electric field can be produced by an iron magnet.

11. The needle of a compass placed near the wire of an electric circuit turns away from north when the circuit is turned on. Why does this happen?

    (1) The needle has lost its ability to point north.
    (2) The wire in the circuit must be pointing north.
    (3) The needle is responding to the magnetic field produced by the current in the wire.
    (4) Electrons in the needle are repelled by electrons in the wire.
    (5) The compass needle has become an electromagnet.

12. Which hypothesis can be supported by the information given?

    (1) Magnets make electric current strong.
    (2) Electromagnets are not as strong as natural magnets.
    (3) A magnet can reverse the direction of an electric current.
    (4) The strength of an electromagnet depends upon the material used to make the magnet.
    (5) Magnetism is related to the movement of electrons.

Science ♦ Physics

Items 13 to 16 refer to the following passage.

Over 2,000 years ago, a mysterious stone was discovered that could attract bits of material containing iron. The Greeks who found this stone named it "magnetite." They had discovered an interesting property that we now call magnetism.

Magnetite is an example of a natural magnet. Most of the magnets you have probably used are artificial magnets. The simplest artificial magnet is an iron bar magnet.

If you suspend a bar magnet horizontally on a string and allow it to swing freely, one end of the magnet will always point north. This end of the magnet is called the north magnetic pole. The other end of the magnet, which points south, is called the south magnetic pole.

The area around a magnet in which magnetic forces can act is called a magnetic field. The magnetic field of a bar magnet is strongest around the poles. If a north pole of one magnet and a south pole of another magnet are brought together, they will attract each other. If two north poles or two south poles are brought together, they will repel each other. Thus the rule for magnetic poles is: Unlike poles attract each other, while like poles repel each other. Once again, "opposites attract."

13. The discovery of magnetite was important because it

(1) made artificial magnets possible
(2) was the first natural iron magnet
(3) gave scientists information about the properties of iron
(4) illustrated the property of magnetism
(5) explained why one pole of a magnet always points north

14. The point on a bar magnet where the magnetic field is likely to be weakest is

(1) at the north pole
(2) at the south pole
(3) halfway between the poles
(4) just south of the north pole
(5) just north of the south pole

15. The needle of a compass always points to the north. Which of the following must be true about compass needles?

(1) Compass needles are made of magnetite.
(2) Compass needles are made of iron.
(3) Compass needles are magnets.
(4) A compass needle has a north magnetic pole but no south magnetic pole.
(5) Two compass needles will repel each other.

16. The fact that one end of a freely suspended magnet always points north suggests that

(1) climate influences magnetism
(2) the sun has a magnetic field
(3) a deposit of magnetite is located north of the magnet
(4) Earth has a magnetic field
(5) the polar ice caps are magnetic

Item 17 refers to the following passage.

Videotape is made of a plastic material that contains tiny bits of metal. The heads that record information on the tape contain magnets. When something is recorded on a videotape, the bits of metal are arranged into specific patterns by the magnetic fields of the magnets in the heads. When you decide to record something new, the magnets in the recording heads rearrange the metal bits in the tape, and the previous recording is destroyed.

17. Which of the following care instructions is explained by this passage?

(1) Do not leave videotapes in a hot place.
(2) Always store videotapes in their boxes.
(3) Do not store videotapes near metal objects.
(4) Keep videotapes away from magnetic fields.
(5) Always rewind videotapes after playing them.

Answers are on page 817.

Waves

A wave is a disturbance that travels through space or matter. Waves transfer energy from one place to another. Some familiar types of waves include sound waves, light waves, radio waves, microwaves, and water waves. All waves, no matter what their type, have certain basic characteristics.

The amplitude of a wave is how high it rises from its rest position. When the sea is absolutely calm, the water is at its rest position. As a wave rises, the water reaches a high point, and then falls back down again. This high point is called the <u>crest</u>. The distance from the rest position to the crest is the amplitude. The greater the amplitude, the greater the energy of the wave.

The shape of a wave is created as the wave moves from its rest position to a high point, or crest, then back through the rest position to a low point. The low point of a wave is called the <u>trough</u>, and it is the same distance from the rest position as is the crest.

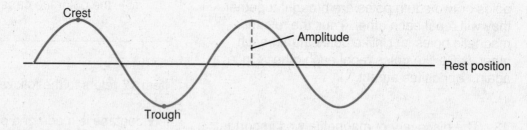

ged Exercise Waves

Items 1 to 3 refer to the previous passage and diagram. Choose the <u>best answer</u> to each item.

1. Which of the following statements <u>cannot</u> be supported by the information provided?

   (1) The amplitude of an ocean wave is equal to the distance from the rest position to the trough.
   (2) A three-foot high wave has a trough three feet deep.
   (3) The depth of the trough of a wave is double the distance from the rest position to the crest.
   (4) The higher the crest of a wave, the deeper its trough.
   (5) Crests and troughs alternate in a wave.

2. What is a wave?

   (1) a movement of water
   (2) a disturbance that travels through matter
   (3) energy in space
   (4) a disturbance that travels through space or matter
   (5) energy in space or matter

3. Which characteristic of an ocean wave would be of most interest to a surfer?

   (1) amplitude
   (2) rest position
   (3) trough
   (4) disturbance
   (5) spray

Items 4 to 8 refer to the following passage.

If you have ever watched the ocean, you have probably noticed that sometimes the waves seem to come very close together, while at other times they seem very far apart. What you were noticing was a difference in wavelength. Wavelength is the distance between the crests of two consecutive waves. Waves that appear very close together have a shorter wavelength, while those that appear far apart have a longer wavelength.

Frequency is the number of waves that pass a given point in a specific unit of time. For example, if you watched an object in the ocean bob up and down ten times in one minute, the frequency of the wave would be ten cycles per minute. In order to count one complete cycle, both a crest and a trough of the wave must pass.

If you know the wavelength and frequency of a wave, you can find its speed. If the frequency of the wave is measured in Hertz, and the wavelength is measured in meters, then the speed in meters per second is given by this equation:

$$\text{speed} = \text{wavelength} \times \text{frequency}$$

4. A wave's frequency is the relationship between

(1) height and weight
(2) height and distance between crests
(3) distance between crests and amplitude
(4) number of crests that pass a given point and unit of time
(5) unit of time and distance

5. What is the result of decreased wavelength and frequency?

(1) decreased speed
(2) the same speed
(3) increased speed
(4) increased distance
(5) decreased distance

6. To calculate the frequency of a wave you must

(1) multiply wavelength times frequency
(2) divide speed by wavelength
(3) multiply speed times wavelength
(4) divide wavelength by speed
(5) multiply speed times frequency

7. What is the speed of a wave with a wavelength of 3 meters and a frequency of 6 Hertz?

(1) 2 meters per second
(2) 3 meters per second
(3) 9 meters per second
(4) 18 meters per second
(5) 36 meters per second

8. Which of the following would be the best title for this passage?

(1) What Causes Waves?
(2) Parts of a Wave
(3) Ocean Waves
(4) Properties of Waves
(5) Frequency and Speed

Item 9 refers to the following paragraph.

A wave traveling through water disturbs the water molecules as it passes, causing them to move in an up-and-down motion. The water molecules do not move with the wave. Once the wave passes, the water molecules become still until another disturbance occurs.

9. From the information given, what would you expect a small rowboat to do when the waves from a large motor boat strike it?

A. drift away from its position
B. bob up and down
C. drift away and then return to its original position

(1) A only
(2) B only
(3) C only
(4) A and B
(5) B and C

Tip **When drawing a conclusion, keep in mind all the facts presented in a passage or diagram. Then rule out any conclusions that clearly contradict these facts.**

Answers are on page 819.

Directions: Choose the best answer to each item.

Items 1 and 2 refer to the following passage.

Atoms of the same element with different numbers of neutrons are called isotopes. Isotopes that have unstable nuclei are radioactive. Radioactive isotopes can change into other isotopes or elements by a spontaneous process known as radioactive decay. In radioactive decay, the unstable nucleus of a radioactive atom breaks down until it becomes the stable nucleus of another isotope, (of the same element) or of a different element. For example, an atom of uranium may go through 13 changes until it becomes a stable atom of lead.

As it breaks down, an atom gives off radiation. There are three types of radiation. Alpha radiation consists of two positively-charged protons and two neutrons released together in what is known as an alpha particle. Beta radiation consists of negatively-charged beta particles that are actually electrons. Gamma radiation is made up of high-energy electromagnetic waves called gamma rays.

Some radioactive elements undergo alpha decay, while others undergo beta decay. Both alpha and beta decay are nearly always accompanied by the release of gamma rays. Of the three types of radiation, gamma rays are the most harmful. With tremendous penetrating power, gamma rays have the ability to destroy the cells of living things.

1. According to the passage, an atom of a radioactive element does all of the following except

    (1) release energy
    (2) increase in size
    (3) change its identity
    (4) release subatomic particles
    (5) give off gamma rays

2. Which of the following would be most useful in separating alpha particles from beta particles?

    (1) a microscope
    (2) an electric field
    (3) a powerful lamp
    (4) a mirror
    (5) a block of lead

Items 3 and 4 refer to the following passage.

Large amounts of energy are released by atoms in a process called nuclear fission. Nuclear fission is the splitting of an atomic nucleus into two smaller, approximately equal-sized nuclei. Nuclear fission can occur naturally or be forced. The first sustained and controlled fission reaction was engineered in 1942.

The rapid splitting of many nuclei is called a nuclear chain reaction. This process produces the energy generated at a nuclear power plant. If uncontrolled, a chain reaction can result in a nuclear explosion. For this reason, fission reactions take place in a device called a nuclear reactor. The purpose of a reactor is to control the speed of the reaction and to prevent the escape of radioactive materials.

3. Which of the following statements about nuclear fission is not true?

    (1) It occurs spontaneously in nature.
    (2) It releases energy and matter.
    (3) It can be controlled.
    (4) It involves changes in the nucleus of an atom.
    (5) It never took place before the twentieth century.

4. What would be the most likely long-term effect of an accident at a nuclear power plant?

   (1) a nuclear explosion
   (2) contaminating the environment
   (3) speeding up of the nuclear chain reaction
   (4) stopping of the nuclear chain reaction
   (5) There would be no long-term effect.

6. One light bulb in a kitchen circuit burns out, but the other lights still work. Which statement supports the conclusion that the kitchen uses a parallel circuit?

   (1) The current has stopped in the entire circuit.
   (2) The current continues in all but one path of the circuit.
   (3) The current was automatically shut off by a fuse.
   (4) The burned-out light bulb was on its own series circuit.
   (5) A power shortage caused the light to go out.

Items 5 and 6 refer to the following diagrams.

SERIES CIRCUIT   **PARALLEL CIRCUIT**

A series circuit has only one path for the electric current. When the circuit is broken, the current stops.

In a parallel circuit, the current flows in two or more separate paths. If the current in one path stops, it still flows in the other branches.

Tip Read questions carefully to find important qualifying statements. Use these statements to eliminate wrong options. For example, in item 4 the words *long-term* can help you eliminate three options which are not long-term effects.

5. Which of the following is likely to use a series circuit?

   (1) the wiring for a house
   (2) a string of decorating lights
   (3) heavy duty transmission lines
   (4) the wiring in a car
   (5) the wiring for several computers in an office

Answers are on page 819.

Directions: Choose the best answer to each item.

Items 1 to 5 refer to the following passage.

When disease-causing agents enter the body, white blood cells called phagocytes find them. Phagocytes surround, or engulf, microorganisms, much as an amoeba eats its food. One kind of phagocyte can enlarge to become a macrophage. Macrophages can engulf a hundred or more bacteria at one time.

Other kinds of white blood cells, called lymphocytes, produce antibodies. Antibodies are protein substances that react with specific foreign organisms in the body and make them ineffective. Lymphocytes produce many different antibodies to attack different disease organisms.

Each antibody is specific against a single disease organism. Lymphocytes do not make the antibody unless the body has been exposed to the disease organism. This exposure may be in the form of a vaccine. A vaccine contains weakened or dead disease organisms. Exposure to it causes the body to begin antibody production without making the person sick.

1. How do phagocytes destroy disease-causing organisms?

   (1) by producing antibodies
   (2) by preventing them from entering the body
   (3) by engulfing them
   (4) by splitting them
   (5) by piercing their cell walls

2. Which of the following statements is not true?

   (1) Macrophages are a kind of phagocyte.
   (2) All white bloods cells are the same.
   (3) Lymphocytes help the body fight disease.
   (4) Some white blood cells can destroy many microorganisms at a time.
   (5) Antibodies are made of protein.

3. HIV (human immunodeficiency virus), which causes AIDS, destroys certain kinds of lymphocytes. As a result, a person with HIV is likely to

   (1) have a reduced ability to fight off disease
   (2) produce an excess of antibodies
   (3) have a reduced number of phagocytes
   (4) have an excess of white blood cells
   (5) have a reduced pulse rate

4. How is being vaccinated like getting a disease?

   A. Both cause the person's lymphocytes to start making the antibodies that attack the disease organism.
   B. Both cause the person to develop the symptoms of the disease.
   C. Both cause the person to produce a large number of macrophages and phagocytes.

   (1) A only
   (2) B only
   (3) C only
   (4) A and C
   (5) A, B, and C

5. Why does the number of phagocytes and lymphocytes in the body increase during an infection?

   (1) More phagocytes and lymphocytes are needed to fight the infection.
   (2) Disease-causing microorganisms produce phagocytes and lymphocytes.
   (3) Antibodies produce more phagocytes and lymphocytes.
   (4) Red blood cells are decreasing.
   (5) The body has become immune to the infection.

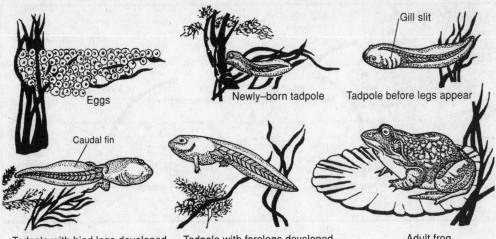

Eggs

Newly–born tadpole

Gill slit

Tadpole before legs appear

Caudal fin

Tadpole with hind legs developed

Tadpole with forelegs developed

Adult frog

The life cycle of the frog is an example of the process of metamorphosis. The word <u>metamorphosis</u> means change. In this process, the immature form, called a tadpole, gradually changes into an adult frog. The tadpole lives in water and breathes through gills. As it matures, the tadpole loses the gills and develops lungs. The adult frog can survive out of the water because it can breathe through its lungs.

6. Which of the following is the best title for the paragraph and diagram?

    (1) Metamorphosis in the Frog
    (2) The Structure of the Tadpole
    (3) The Life Cycle of Water-Dwelling Animals
    (4) Metamorphosis in Animals
    (5) Reproduction in Frogs

7. Which of the following statements does the author take for granted?

    (1) All animals go through metamorphosis.
    (2) All plants go through metamorphosis.
    (3) Different animal structures are suited to different types of environments.
    (4) Almost all eggs develop into adults.
    (5) Metamorphosis occurs in humans.

8. What is metamorphosis?

    (1) the process of reproduction
    (2) the process by which an immature form changes into a different adult form
    (3) the growth of any young organism into an adult
    (4) changes in an adult organism caused by aging
    (5) the process by which tadpoles absorb oxygen from water

9. Which of the following must develop before a tadpole becomes a land-dwelling adult?

    (1) arms
    (2) lungs
    (3) gills
    (4) tail
    (5) mouth

Items 10 to 13 refer to the following diagram and paragraph.

THE WATER CYCLE

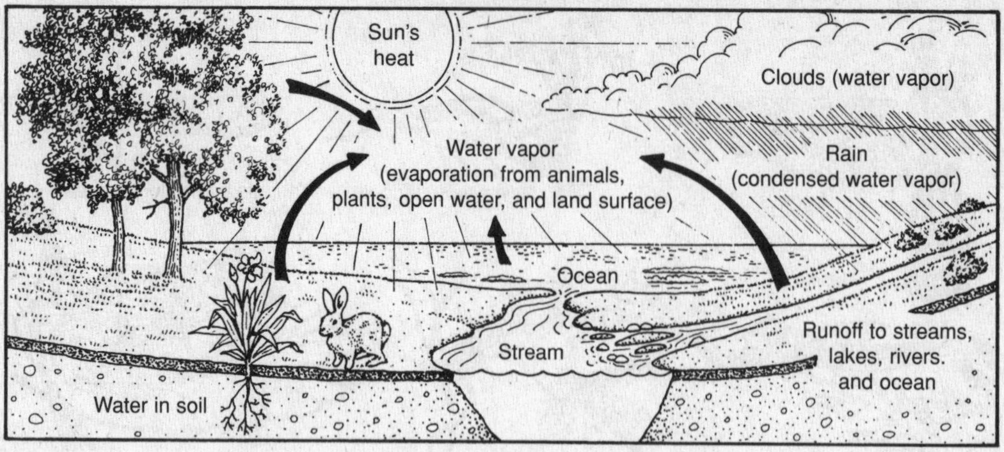

All plants and animals must have water in order to live. Cells are made mostly of water, and the chemical reactions in living things must take place in water. However, the amount of Earth's water is limited. It must be used again and again. The constant circulation of Earth's water is called the water cycle.

10. Which of the following statements is the most accurate?

   (1) Animals return water to the air only by eliminating liquid wastes.
   (2) The only water vapor in the air is found in clouds.
   (3) Plants take in water mostly by breathing.
   (4) On Earth, water is found mainly in the soil.
   (5) Water in animals' breath is returned to the air.

11. Which of the following statements supports the conclusion that water is used again and again?

   (1) Water is recirculated.
   (2) The water cycle circulates Earth's water supply.
   (3) Evaporation from the ocean returns water to the atmosphere.
   (4) Cells are composed mainly of water.
   (5) Water is needed to carry on life processes.

12. What causes water to evaporate in the water cycle?

   (1) clouds
   (2) the sun
   (3) runoff
   (4) oceans
   (5) soil

13. Which of the following statements is an opinion?

   (1) Since the supply of water is limited, it must be used again and again.
   (2) Water conservation is not useful since Earth will never run out of water.
   (3) All living organisms must have water in order to live.
   (4) The circulation of Earth's water is called the water cycle.
   (5) The chemical reactions in living things require water.

Items 14 to 18 refer to the following diagram and passage.

EARTH'S REVOLUTION AROUND SUN

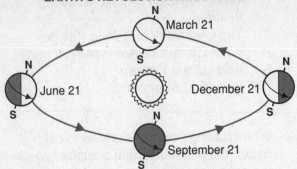

The movement of Earth around the sun is called revolution. It takes Earth 365.24 days to make one complete revolution around the sun. As it revolves, Earth also spins on its axis. This spinning is known as rotation. Earth rotates on an axis that is inclined at an angle of 23.5°.

Because Earth revolves and its axis is inclined, different parts of Earth lean toward the sun at different times of the year, resulting in seasons. When the northern hemisphere leans toward the sun, it has long periods of daylight and warm temperatures. As a result, this hemisphere gets the most energy from the sun and it experiences summer. At the same time, the southern hemisphere experiences shorter days and cooler temperatures, so it has winter. On March 21 and September 21, neither hemisphere leans toward the sun, so one hemisphere experiences spring while the other experiences autumn.

14. Which of the following is the cause of Earth's seasons?

    A. Earth's revolution
    B. Earth's rotation
    C. Earth's inclined axis

  (1) A only
  (2) B only
  (3) C only
  (4) B and C only
  (5) A and C only

15. What is rotation?

  (1) Earth's movement around the sun
  (2) the moon's movement around the Earth
  (3) the cause of the seasons
  (4) the result of the seasons
  (5) Earth's spinning on its axis

16. Which of the following is true in December?

  (1) The southern hemisphere experiences winter.
  (2) The northern hemisphere is tilted away from the sun.
  (3) Neither hemisphere leans toward the sun.
  (4) The hemispheres get the same amount of energy from the sun.
  (5) The northern hemisphere has longer days than the southern hemisphere.

17. If Earth revolved as it does now but rotated on an axis that wasn't inclined,

  (1) there would be no seasons
  (2) there would be only two seasons
  (3) half of Earth would always have night
  (4) nothing would be different
  (5) the year would be shorter

18. Which of the following is a fact presented in the passage?

  (1) It takes Earth 23.5 days to revolve around the sun.
  (2) The angle of tilt of Earth's axis is 365.24°.
  (3) Throughout the year, all parts of Earth get the same amount of the sun's energy.
  (4) Different parts of Earth get different amounts of the sun's energy at different times of the year.
  (5) The southern hemisphere experiences spring on March 21.

Items 19 to 23 refer to the following passage.

You may not think of the kitchen as being a chemistry lab, but many chemicals can be found right on your kitchen shelf. One substance that contains several interesting chemicals is baking powder, which is used to make cake batter rise.

The principal ingredient in baking powder is sodium bicarbonate, $NaHCO_3$. When sodium bicarbonate reacts with an acid, it produces the gas carbon dioxide (CO_2) and water. When sodium bicarbonate is heated strongly, it breaks down to form carbon dioxide and sodium carbonate (Na_2CO_3). Baking powder also contains a substance that will react with water to form acids. This substance is usually a type of compound called a tartrate.

19. It can be inferred from the passage that the purpose of the tartrate in baking powder is to

(1) provide an acid for sodium bicarbonate to react with
(2) break down to form carbon dioxide
(3) react with carbon dioxide
(4) provide a salt that will make dough rise
(5) react with water to form sodium bicarbonate

20. Sodium bicarbonate reacts with vinegar to produce carbon dioxide and water. Which of the following must be true about vinegar?

(1) It contains sodium carbonate.
(2) It makes bread dough rise.
(3) It decomposes when heated.
(4) It contains an acid.
(5) It contains a salt.

21. The best title for the passage would be

(1) The Chemical Formula of Baking Powder
(2) The Chemistry of Baking Powder
(3) What Chemicals Are in the Kitchen?
(4) Acids in the Kitchen
(5) Sodium Carbonate

22. When baking powder is added to cake batter, the substance that actually makes the cake rise is

(1) salt
(2) oxygen
(3) water
(4) tartrate
(5) carbon dioxide

23. When baking powder is left uncovered in damp or humid weather, it quickly loses its effectiveness. Based on the passage, which of the following statements could explain why this happens?

(1) Moisture in the air causes sodium bicarbonate to break down.
(2) Oxygen in the air causes the tartrate to break down.
(3) Moisture in the air reacts with the tartrate.
(4) Oxygen in the air reacts with carbon dioxide.
(5) Oxygen in the air reacts with sodium bicarbonate.

Tip When looking for an explanation of an observation, review the facts you know about the topic. Ask yourself how the facts could explain what has been observed.

Items 24 to 27 refer to the following passage.

Have you ever rubbed a balloon against your sleeve and stuck it to the wall? You were able to do this because the balloon became electrically charged.

Electrons in atoms are free to move. As you rub a balloon on your sleeve, electrons from the cloth move onto the balloon. The extra electrons give the balloon a negative charge. When the balloon comes near the wall, it repels the electrons in the wall, leaving the wall positively charged. Thus, the negatively charged balloon and the positively charged wall attract each other.

The ability of electrons to move from one place to another makes electric current possible. Electric current is the flow of electrons through a wire, and it is what powers your appliances.

Electrons flow through a wire in much the same way as water flows through a hose. Just as water pressure pushes water through a hose, a source of energy pushes electrons through a wire. This source of energy is called voltage. Voltage is measured in units called volts. A battery marked "9V" supplies nine volts of energy to move electrons through a wire.

24. If you scuff your feet across a wool carpet, you may feel a shock when you touch a metal object. Which statement explains why this happens?

(1) An electric charge builds up on the rug and then is transferred to the metal object.
(2) Electrons from the carpet move onto your feet, causing you temporarily to have an electric charge.
(3) Electrons flow from your feet to the carpet, causing the carpet to have an electric charge.
(4) Electrons in the metal object are repelled by electrons on the carpet.
(5) Scuffing across the carpet causes an increase in voltage, which then produces a shock.

25. Which of the following statements cannot be supported by the information provided?

(1) Protons flowing onto an object cause the object to become positively charged.
(2) Low voltage could cause a power "brownout" in a town or city.
(3) If two balloons that had been rubbed on cloth were brought close together, they would probably repel each other.
(4) A torn wire could cause a loss of electricity, just as a leaky hose would cause a loss of water.
(5) Current flow increases as voltage increases.

26. Extra electrons on an electrically charged object eventually leave the object, returning it to its neutral state. A person who wishes to stick balloons to the wall as party decorations should

(1) place the balloons on the wall just before the party begins
(2) place the balloons far apart
(3) place the balloons on the wall at least a day ahead of time
(4) rub the balloons on several different types of cloth
(5) place the balloons as close to the ceiling as possible

27. In the passage, water pressure is compared to voltage because

(1) both provide energy to move electrons
(2) both make possible the flow of a substance from one place to another
(3) both are measured in units called volts
(4) both involve the transfer of electrically charged particles
(5) both can be used to power a battery

Answers are on page 820.

Sandra Cisneros is a popular Mexican-American writer who is praised for her portrayal of Chicano life.

Test 4 of the GED covers literature and the arts. It includes several forms of the written word. It includes popular literature, classical literature, and commentary.

Popular literature is what people are reading today. When you read books, articles, short stories, or poems that have been written recently, you are reading popular literature. If you see a play that has been written in the last few years, the play, in its written form, is popular literature.

The difference between classical literature and good popular literature is often hard to tell. One major difference is that classical literature has proven itself good enough to be read over and over by many people. A novel or poem has to be more than just well written to become classical literature. It also must be about experiences that are important to all people, not just to those of one culture or one time period.

The word *classic* means a standard of excellence. It does not mean that something is old or hard to understand. A Model T Ford might be called a classic because it was well made to begin with and can still be easily driven and taken care of today. But how many of us remember a car called the Roamer? Like the Model T, classical literature endures.

Both popular and classical literature are divided into several categories or types. As you use this book to prepare for the GED test, you will read various kinds of literature. You will see prose fiction and prose nonfiction. Prose is the ordinary language that is used in most writing. Fiction is a form of writing that tells a story. A fiction writer creates a world from imagination. The most common works of fiction are short stories and novels. Fiction may be about any subject: romance, sports, mystery, science, history. In nonfiction, the writer tells about real people and events. However, they may color their descriptions with their own feelings.

You will also be reading and interpreting poetry and drama in this unit. Poetry is a special kind of writing that uses descriptive language to create images or feelings. It appeals to the emotions, the senses, or the imagination of the reader. Drama is a form of story which is meant to be performed by actors on a stage. The story is revealed through the dialogue and actions of the players. These forms of writing may be less familiar to you, but the skills you learn through the lessons in this book will help you understand them.

When writers talk about a work of literature or art, we call what they say commentary. The purpose of a commentary often is to help the reader by giving some information about a work that the reader has not seen yet. One form of commentary that you will be familiar with is the review. A review is intended to tell you what the reviewer, or critic, thinks of the book, television show, movie, play, or artwork. Reviews may be written in an informal, sometimes humorous, style or they may be very serious. The subject matter and the intended audience affect the writer's approach.

Reviews are usually found in newspapers and magazines, but may also be found in books. Reviews and commentaries are not limited to works recently produced. At times, older works or artists are discussed because they are once again of public interest.

Popular Literature
Lesson ① Fiction

Choose the <u>best answer</u> to each item. <u>Items 1 to 7</u> refer to the following excerpt from a novel.

WHY DO THESE WOMEN DISAGREE?

Naomi let the cardboard fan from Gilchrist's Funeral Home fall into her lap and assessed her daughter, stretched out on the bed, wrapped in the too-neat
(5) tranquil repose that precedes upheaval. She wanted to ask simply and boldly, "Who is he?" but she could not bear the thought of hearing a lie and the sensation that had come upon her informed Naomi
(10) that Esther would interpret curiosity as trespass. Naomi picked up the fan and felt the warm air against her cheek as forlorn as a goodbye kiss.

The phone rang and Esther said, "If it's
(15) Bruce, tell him I'm not here."

"I'm not gonna lie for you, young lady. You're big enough to do that for yourself."

The phone rang several times with a persistence that Esther associated with
(20) Bruce. She had met him at Howard. He was a mannerly young junior from Newark, New Jersey, who wanted to be a lawyer and who bored Esther more than she'd imagined possible. The phone was finally
(25) silent after the twelfth ring.

"What's wrong with this Bruce anyway?" Naomi asked.

"He's so young."

"Young, well, *you're* young. What do you
(30) want? A man? You're not ready for that. A man right now wouldn't do you nothing but harm."

"You married at seventeen."

"Yeah and I wish I hadn't. And that don't
(35) mean I was ready for it. That was the only thing a girl could do, where I come from, to prove herself."

"I just can't stand Bruce. He's got no imagination."

(40) "Sometimes I'm sorry you're in college. You come home throwing around all those words like they've got something to do with life. Man don't need imagination to love a woman. He needs to look her in the
(45) eye and see her for everything she is when he finds her, forget about fantasies and dreams and what he thinks he got to have, man has to look at a woman like she is and love her anyway."

(50) "Imagination got you everything you have."

"Being hungry got me what I own. When you're hungry you'll do almost anything, when it's imagination that's driving you,
(55) you get picky."

Marita Golden, *Long Distance Life*.

1. Based on the information given, it can be inferred that Naomi and Esther

   (1) dislike each other
   (2) share a close relationship
   (3) agree on most points
   (4) have shared similar experiences
   (5) have no respect for each other

2. Which of the following best describes the underlying conflict between the two women?

   (1) Naomi doesn't like Bruce.
   (2) Esther is going to college.
   (3) Esther doesn't want to talk to Bruce.
   (4) Naomi suspects that Esther has met a man.
   (5) Naomi has forbidden Esther to see anyone but Bruce.

3. Which of the following adds to the tension between the two women?

   (1) Esther's lying on the bed
   (2) Naomi fanning herself
   (3) the ringing of the telephone
   (4) Bruce's lack of imagination
   (5) the dreams of men

4. Based upon Naomi and Esther's discussion, which of the following is the best conclusion that can be drawn about Naomi?

(1) She does not want Esther to be happy.
(2) She is afraid that Esther will make the same mistakes she made.
(3) She is angry that Esther no longer seems to listen to her.
(4) She is not supportive of Esther's college education.
(5) She does not know what she is talking about.

5. Which of the following is the best conclusion that can be drawn about Esther?

(1) She is willing to listen to her mother.
(2) She is playing games with Bruce.
(3) She wants to stay in college.
(4) She is unwilling to listen to her mother's opinion.
(5) She thinks she is smarter than her mother.

6. If Bruce were to come to the house, Naomi would most likely

(1) lie and say that Esther was not at home
(2) try to force Esther to talk to him
(3) send him away
(4) ask him to marry Esther
(5) inquire about his dreams

7. Which of the following would be the best resolution of the events in this excerpt?

(1) Esther's willingness to give Bruce a chance
(2) Naomi's acceptance of her past mistakes
(3) the settling of differences between Esther and Naomi
(4) Esther's marriage to a man with no imagination
(5) Naomi's enrollment in college

Items 8 and 9 refer to the following excerpt from a novel.

WHAT HAS HAPPENED TO HIM?

Edward was now in total darkness. The glow of the oil lamps through the high windows of the Atrium had been extinguished, wrapped up in an obscurity
(5) which was like some black velvet textile or soft inky stuff which filled space and touched Edward's face like ectoplasm. His feet, lacking confidence in this deprivation of sensory guidance, moved slowly and
(10) uncertainly, and he had lost his sense of direction. . . . The night sky, the arching trees, could as well have been the walls of a tiny black lightless room, an oubliette in the centre of which he was now standing.
(15) He reached out again but could touch nothing. Then suddenly something took him by the throat, a frightful sensation that made him stagger and gasp harshly. . . . The sensation which had suddenly felled
(20) him was fear, pure contentless fear such as he had never experienced before.

Iris Murdoch, *The Good Apprentice*.

8. When the author says "something took him by the throat" (lines 16–17), she is

(1) describing the dark night
(2) describing the windows of the atrium
(3) describing fear as if it were a person or an animal
(4) describing the smoke from the oil lamps
(5) trying to frighten the reader

9. The phrase "an obscurity which was like some black velvet textile or soft inky stuff" (lines 4–6) describes

(1) the feeling of terror
(2) what cloth feels like
(3) the smoke from the oil lamps
(4) the way the darkness feels
(5) ectoplasm

Items 10 to 13 refer to the following excerpt from a novel.

WHAT IS A PIG IN A POKE?

It was not surprising at all that most of these trumpeters of the Vice-Presidential nominee really had only the haziest idea of what he was all about. It was not surprising
(5) that this sudden and overwhelming flood of praise should have come quite automatically, simply because he was the running mate of the man they wanted for President. It was not surprising that they
(10) should thus give this lavish and enormous buildup to a man who was, for many of them, a pig in a poke. He was their pig in their poke, and it was not the first time in American History that the self-same
(15) process had occurred. And this time, of course, he was on the Right Side of everything. That really made it perfect.

Allen Drury, *Come Nineveh, Come Tyre.*

10. The author uses the phrase "a pig in a poke" (line 12) to suggest that the Vice-Presidential nominee

    (1) reminded voters of a pig
    (2) did not deserve praise
    (3) was selected in a way that concealed his true nature
    (4) was selected after great thought
    (5) came from a rural background

11. Which of the following best summarizes the main idea of the passage?

    (1) Vice-Presidential candidates are usually unknowns.
    (2) Most of the supporters of the Vice-Presidential nominee did not know what he stood for.
    (3) The Vice-Presidential candidate was selected because his views coincided with those of the Presidential candidate.
    (4) Americans prefer unknowns as candidates for high office.
    (5) The office of Vice-President is not very important, so the candidate's views do not matter much.

12. All of the following captions might be written below a picture of the Vice-Presidential nominee except

    (1) We Know Him Well
    (2) He's Our Guy
    (3) Who Is This Guy?
    (4) A Stranger in Our Midst
    (5) Mystery Man

13. Which of the following nicknames might be applied to the narrator of this passage?

    (1) The Happy Go Lucky Guy
    (2) Mr. Right
    (3) The Professor
    (4) Mr. Cynical
    (5) Boy Wonder

Items 14 to 19 refer to the following excerpt from a novel.

WHAT DID GRANDPA BLAKESLEE'S WILL SAY?

"Now I want my burying to remind folks that death aint always awful. God invented death. Its in God's plan for it to happen. So when my time comes I do not want no trip
(5) to Birdsong's Emporium or any other. Dressing somebody up to look alive don't make it so. . . .

"I don't want no casket. Its a waste of money. What I would really like is to be
(10) wrapped up in two or three feed sacks and laid right in the ground. But that would bother you all, so use the pine box upstairs at the store that Miss Mattie Lou's coffin come in. I been saving it. And tho I
(15) just as soon be planted in the vegetable patch as anywhere, I don't think anybody would ever eat what growed there, after. Anyhow, take me right from home to the cemetery.
(20) "Aint no use paying Birdsong for that hearse. Get Loomis to use his wagon. Specially if it is hot weather, my advisement is dont waste no time."

Mama, scandalized, had both hands up
(25) to her mouth. Mary Toy had turned white
as a sheet. I held her tight. Aunt Loma
seemed excited, like when watching a
spooky stage play. I felt excited myself. I
wondered was this Grandpa's idea of a
(30) practical joke or was it a sermon. Maybe
after he made his point, he'd put a
postscript saying that when he was dead it
really wouldn't matter to him what kind of
funeral he had. But I doubted it. . . .
(35) Papa read on. "I want Loomis and them
to dig my grave right next to Miss Mattie
Lou. I don't want no other preacher there
but him, but don't let him give a sermon. It
would go on for hours. Just let him pray for
(40) God to comfort my family. . . ."
Papa read on. "I don't want nobody at
the burial except you all and them at the
store that want to come. Don't put *Not
Dead But Sleeping* on my stone. Write it
(45) *Dead, Not Sleeping.* Being dead under six
foot of dirt wont bother me a-tall, but I hate
for it to sound like I been buried alive.

Olive Ann Burns, *Cold Sassy Tree*.

14. Which of the following best expresses the
main idea of the selection?

(1) The speaker does not want a fuss
made at his funeral.
(2) Death eventually happens to everyone.
(3) Birdsong's Emporium is too expensive.
(4) Funerals should be simple and
dignified.
(5) The speaker does not want to be
dressed up after he dies.

15. Which of the following best supports
Grandpa Blakeslee's idea of saving money?

(1) using the box a coffin came in
(2) storing things upstairs
(3) going to a cheap funeral home
(4) making clothes out of feed sacks
(5) having an unmarked grave

16. The main idea in the second paragraph

(1) is very different from the main idea in
the first paragraph
(2) explains why dressing up a dead
person is wrong
(3) is a good example of common sense
(4) gives an example of the main idea of
the excerpt
(5) explains the reason for the man's belief

17. Grandpa Blakeslee is probably

(1) conventional
(2) very vain
(3) mindful of others' expectations
(4) not concerned about what society
thinks
(5) in the funeral business

18. Which of the following would Grandpa
Blakeslee most likely enjoy?

(1) attending a formal dinner
(2) spending a quiet evening at home
(3) having a large party thrown in his honor
(4) shopping at a local department store
(5) wearing a tuxedo

19. Which of the following best expresses why
the women were shocked at the contents of
the will?

(1) They thought Grandpa Blakeslee was
playing a practical joke on them.
(2) They thought Grandpa Blakeslee's
comments and wishes were strange.
(3) Grandpa Blakeslee refused to let any
preacher but Loomis give the sermon.
(4) They wanted a more traditional funeral.
(5) They were upset about what he wanted
on his stone.

Items 20 to 28 refer to the following excerpt from a novel.

WHY DOES THE WAR STILL LIVE FOR THE AUTHOR?

Everyone has a moment in history which belongs particularly to him. It is the moment when his emotions achieve their most powerful sway over him, and
(5) afterward when you say to this person "the world today" or "life" or "reality" he will assume that you mean this moment, even if it is fifty years past. The world, through his unleashed emotions, imprinted itself
(10) upon him, and he carries the stamp of that passing moment forever.

For me, this moment—four years is a moment in history—was the war. The war was and is reality for me. I still instinctively
(15) live and think in its atmosphere. These are some of its characteristics: Franklin Delano Roosevelt is the President of the United States, and he always has been. The other two eternal world leaders are
(20) Winston Churchill and Josef Stalin. America is not, never has been, and never will be what the songs and poems call it, a land of plenty. Nylon, meat, gasoline, and steel are rare. There are too many jobs
(25) and not enough workers. Money is very easy to earn but rather hard to spend, because there isn't very much to buy. Trains are always late and always crowded with "servicemen." The war will
(30) always be fought very far from America, and it will never end. Nothing in America stands still for very long, including the people who are always either leaving or on leave. People in America cry often.
(35) Sixteen is the key and crucial and natural age for a human being to be, and people of all other ages are ranged in an orderly manner ahead of and behind you as a harmonious setting for the sixteen-year-
(40) olds of the world. When you are sixteen, adults are slightly impressed and almost intimidated by you. This is a puzzle finally solved by the realization that they foresee your military future, fighting for them. You
(45) do not foresee it. To waste anything in America is immoral. String and tinfoil are treasures. Newspapers are always crowded with strange maps and names of towns, and every few months the earth
(50) seems to lurch from its path when you see something in the newspapers, such as the time Mussolini, who had almost seemed one of the eternal leaders, is photographed hanging upside down on a
(55) meathook. Everyone listens to news broadcasts five or six times every day. All pleasurable things, all travel and sports and entertainment and good food and fine clothes, are in the very shortest supply,
(60) always were and always will be. There are just tiny fragments of pleasure and luxury in the world, and there is something unpatriotic about enjoying them. All foreign lands are inaccessible except to
(65) servicemen; they are vague, distant, and sealed off as though behind a curtain of plastic. The prevailing color of life in America is a dull, dark green called olive drab. That color is always respectable and
(70) always important. Most other colors risk being unpatriotic.

John Knowles, *A Separate Peace*.

20. Which statement best describes the main idea of the first paragraph?

    (1) History is made by emotional people.
    (2) People should not dwell on the past.
    (3) People should be more interested in history.
    (4) Yesterday is more real than today.
    (5) Every person's life has a special moment.

21. According to the author, the war was

    (1) only four years ago
    (2) a dim memory
    (3) an immoral waste
    (4) proof that America is a land of plenty
    (5) a time that shaped his reality

22. The excerpt suggests that the war years affected the author as they did because

    (1) he was young and impressionable
    (2) he admired Roosevelt's policies
    (3) money was easy to get
    (4) everyone was very sad
    (5) people left America to fight

23. The main idea of the second paragraph is best described as

    (1) much different than the main idea of the first paragraph
    (2) more general than the main idea in the first paragraph
    (3) the same as the main idea in the first paragraph
    (4) unrelated to the main idea of the first paragraph
    (5) an example of the main idea in the first paragraph

24. The author helps the reader understand how he feels about the war by

    (1) explaining how the world imprints itself on people
    (2) talking about the war as if it were happening now
    (3) referring to well-known world leaders
    (4) specifically stating his emotions in clear terms
    (5) making it sound romantic and appealing

25. Which of the following details is not used to support the second paragraph?

    (1) Roosevelt is the President of the United States.
    (2) There isn't very much to buy.
    (3) Olive is the only patriotic color.
    (4) News broadcasts are very important.
    (5) A sixteen-year-old is exempt from war-time worries.

26. With which of the following statements would this author be most likely to agree?

    (1) Politics makes strange bedfellows.
    (2) There is no time like the present.
    (3) Time is something we will never understand.
    (4) Every person sees the world from a personal point of view.
    (5) Time stands still for no one.

27. This excerpt is primarily a

    (1) biography
    (2) description of the United States during World War II
    (3) complaint about wartime living conditions
    (4) humorous commentary
    (5) picture of a sixteen-year-old's world

28. Why does the author think that "To waste anything in America is immoral" (lines 45–46)?

    (1) because America is not a land of plenty
    (2) because the war has made almost everything in short supply
    (3) because everything needs to be saved for the "servicemen"
    (4) because of the "olive drab" mood of the country
    (5) because everything costs so much

Items 29 to 31 refer to the following excerpt from a novel.

WHAT IS THERE FOR NANCY TO WORRY ABOUT?

Hannah Gruen, coming into the dining room, knew from Nancy's expression that something was wrong.

"What is it?" she cried, "Not bad news, I
(5) hope."

Nancy showed her the warning note. "I can't imagine who could have sent it," she said, "unless it was the pickpocket."

"Oh, Nancy, I'm so worried!" the
(10) housekeeper exclaimed after she had read the anonymous message. "It must have something to do with the case you're working on. Please give up trying to help Mrs. Struthers!"

(15) "I can't let a little note like this frighten me," said Nancy. "Anyway, I think the person who sent it merely means he wants me to stay away from Wrightville."

"Then promise me you will," begged
(20) Hannah Gruen.

"All right," Nancy laughed, giving the housekeeper an affectionate hug. "By the way, any telephone calls for me while I was in the shower?"

(25) "One from the yacht club. A friend of yours said she was to let you know about picking up some clothes over there."

"Oh, yes," Nancy said absently. "I got a new locker and left some things in the old
(30) one. Well, I'll run out and get them now."

"Do be careful," Mrs. Gruen urged, as Nancy went out the door.

"I'll be all right," Nancy called cheerily, as she hopped into her car.

Carolyn Keene, *The Clue in the Old Album.*

29. Which of the following statements best describes the main idea of the excerpt?

(1) Nancy never listens to what Hannah says.
(2) Hannah is worried about something that does not seem to bother Nancy.
(3) Nancy had forgotten to pick up the clothes she had left in a locker.
(4) Nancy has been frightened by a person who picked her pocket.
(5) Nancy is always cheerful and friendly.

30. Based on the information in the excerpt, which of the following is Nancy most likely to do?

(1) follow the instructions in the note
(2) stay at home to avoid trouble
(3) stop helping Mrs. Struthers
(4) continue to help Mrs. Struthers
(5) stop reading her mail

31. Which of the following details does not support the main idea?

(1) Hannah worries about Nancy.
(2) Nancy belongs to the yacht club.
(3) Nancy is not frightened by the warning note.
(4) Nancy overlooks Hannah's worries.
(5) Hannah tries to change Nancy's behavior.

Tip When identifying the main idea of a passage, look at how the paragraphs in the passage are related. Each paragraph usually adds information about one central theme. If you determine the most important information in each paragraph, you can then identify the main idea of the passage.

Items 32 to 36 refer to the following excerpt from a novel.

HOW DO IDENTICAL TWINS BEHAVE?

"Anyhow, years ago Huysman got interested in the study of monozygotic twins. Identical twins. He did some important work, good research. There are
(5) anomalies in twin behavior that have yet to be understood completely. If they are separated at birth and raised separately, there are often similarities in their lives that are hard to understand. For instance, say
(10) Carol and Karen are born in New York and Karen is taken a few months later to grow up in California. They both marry a man named George on a June day in the same year at the same time. They both have two
(15) sons born at the same time. They have the same illnesses and the same accidents. And so on. This is repeated over and over. They don't know about each other, don't know they are twins. In fact, when twins
(20) are raised together this pattern is less likely to occur."

Drew felt at a loss. "There must be some reason. I mean, it isn't just Carol and Karen. It's also the Georges and the
(25) people driving the other cars involved with their accidents. Or not clearing snow off their sidewalks, whatever the accidents are. In fact, it's like an infinite regression of what ifs. You know, the what if I hadn't
(30) been on that corner at the time you came out, we'd never have met. And so on, back through their entire lives."

Kate Wilhelm, *Huysman's Pets.*

32. The best meaning for the word "anomalies" (line 5) as it is used in this context is

   (1) irregularities
   (2) discoveries
   (3) illnesses
   (4) accidents
   (5) monozygotic

33. The author helps the reader understand the meaning of the word "pattern" (line 20) by doing which of the following things?

   (1) The author defines the word in the next paragraph.
   (2) The author gives examples of twins raised together before using the word.
   (3) The author gives examples of identical twins who are raised apart but repeatedly act alike.
   (4) The author says that twins can be raised apart.
   (5) The author never gives any examples before using the word.

34. The best meaning for the word "regression" (line 28) as it is used in this context is

   (1) forward movement
   (2) backward movement
   (3) absence of movement
   (4) rapid movement
   (5) circular movement

35. The excerpt refers to which two people as monozygotic twins?

   (1) Karen and June
   (2) Karen and Carol
   (3) Carol and June
   (4) George and Karen
   (5) George and Carol

36. The excerpt states that when twins are raised together they are more likely to

   (1) follow similar patterns
   (2) marry people with the same names at the same time
   (3) have two male children
   (4) follow different patterns
   (5) have accidents and be ill

Items 37 to 42 refer to the following excerpt from a novel.

HOW DO THE REPUBLICANS AND FEDERALISTS DIFFER?

During the last session of the Third Congress I led the battle in the Senate against ratification of Jay's treaty with England. The treaty was clumsily drawn
(5) and to our disadvantage. It actually contained a clause forbidding us to export cotton in *American* ships. In effect, the treaty made us a colony again. It also revealed for the first time the deep and
(10) irreconcilable division between the Republican and Federalist parties—and they were now actual political parties, no longer simply factions. One was pro-French; the other pro-British. One wanted
(15) a loose confederation of states, the other a strong central administration; one was made up of independent farmers in alliance with city workers; the other was devoted to trade and manufacturing. One
(20) was Jefferson; the other was Hamilton.

Gore Vidal, *Burr: A Novel.*

37. Which of the following is the most probable meaning of "ratification" (line 3) as it is used in the context of this excerpt?

(1) advantage
(2) approval
(3) forbidding
(4) disapproval
(5) colonization

38. Which of the following is the most probable meaning of "confederation" (line 15) as it is used in the context of this excerpt?

(1) interpretation
(2) split
(3) association
(4) graduation
(5) division

39. You can figure out that the phrase "in alliance with" (lines 17–18) means "joined up with" by seeing that the words "farmers" and "city workers" (lines 17–18) are linked together in the same way as

(1) the treaty and the clause
(2) pro-French and pro-British
(3) Jefferson and Hamilton
(4) trade and manufacturing
(5) parties and factions

40. Which of the following is the most probable meaning of "irreconcilable" (line 10)?

(1) impossible to bring together
(2) solvable
(3) impossible to choose
(4) reconsidered
(5) irresponsible

41. Which of the following is the most probable meaning of "factions" (line 13)?

(1) fractions
(2) allies
(3) friends
(4) relatives
(5) groups

42. Based on the excerpt, which of the following is not a true statement?

(1) The treaty revealed the division between Republicans and Federalists.
(2) The treaty forbade Americans from exporting cotton in American ships.
(3) The treaty pitted farmers against manufacturing and trading.
(4) Jefferson and Hamilton disagreed about the treaty.
(5) Americans were unanimously in support of the treaty.

Items 43 to 47 refer to the following excerpt from a novel.

WHAT INFECTED RICHMOND?

A carnival of hope infected Richmond. McClellan stayed at Harrison's Landing. He plopped there like a frog full of buckshot. He moved neither forward nor
(5) backward, but seemed imprisoned by his own weight. Richmond was saved. Churches offered up services, people shouted, "Gloria in Excelsis," and Lee, instead of being the goat, was now the
(10) hero.

While Lutie, like everyone around her, offered up prayers of thanksgiving to Almighty God, she thought of the weeks of battles as the slaughterhouse of heroes.
(15) The death lists were appalling. The best families of the South lost their husbands, sons, and brothers. Hardly anyone was untouched, especially since the upper classes led the regiments, brigades, and
(20) divisions. The leaders, the wealthy and the gifted, were cut down by the scythe of war no less than the small farmer, the shopkeeper, even the vagrant seeking to redeem himself by military service. They
(25) died alike, and Death, as always, impartially selected his victims. She used to think of Death as a personal force, the god of the underworld, Hades or Pluto. Odd, too, that Pluto was the god of riches.
(30) Each day you bargained with this god, but in the end he got the better of the deal. She put aside that embroidered, mythical notion. Death these days was a threshing machine. Someone started the blades
(35) whirling, and it wouldn't cut off.

Rita Mae Brown, *High Hearts*.

43. Which of the following is <u>not</u> a restatement of the author's description of McClellan at Harrison's Landing?

   (1) resembling a frog
   (2) motionless
   (3) hopeful and exuberant
   (4) being held prisoner
   (5) wounded

44. Most of the details in the second paragraph are restatements of

   (1) the saving of Richmond by McClellan's troops
   (2) Lutie's prayers of Thanksgiving
   (3) Lee's heroism in battle
   (4) the appalling death lists
   (5) the decline of the South

45. If Lutie's final image of Death were to be modernized, which of the following might she have chosen?

   (1) a Wall Street success
   (2) a bulldozer
   (3) a lawn mower
   (4) a computer game
   (5) a wealthy politician

46. What does the author mean when she says "Death, as always, impartially selected his victims" (lines 25–26)?

   (1) She is showing that Death is always final.
   (2) She is showing that rich men as well as poor men were killed.
   (3) She is showing that Death is generous and brings its victims peace.
   (4) She is showing the horror of Death.
   (5) She is showing that Death is a threshing machine or a sweeping scythe.

47. "The vagrant seeking to redeem himself by military service" (lines 23–24) fights to

   (1) protect the best families of the South
   (2) support his family
   (3) aid the small farmer and shopkeeper
   (4) raise his social status
   (5) avoid the slaughterhouse

Items 48 to 51 refer to the following excerpt from a novel.

WHY DID THE WIFE EAT IN THE LOFT?

She seldom did eat with them. It
bothered July a good deal, though he
made no complaint. Since their little table
was almost under the loft he could look up
(5) and see Elmira's bare legs as he ate. It
didn't seem normal to him. His mother had
died when he was six, yet he could
remember that she always ate with the
family; she would never have sat with her
(10) legs dangling practically over her
husband's head. He had been at supper in
many cabins in his life, but in none of them
had the wife sat in the loft while the meal
was eaten. It was a thing out of the
(15) ordinary, and July didn't like for things to
be out of the ordinary in his life. It seemed
to him it was better to do as other people
did—if society at large did things a certain
way, it had to be for a good reason, and he
(20) looked upon common practices as rules
that should be obeyed. After all, his job
was to see that common practices were
honored—that citizens weren't shot, or
banks robbed.
(25)   Joe didn't share July's discomfort with
the fact that his mother seldom came to
the table. When she did come it was
usually to scold him, and he got scolded
enough as it was—besides, he liked
(30) eating with July. So far as he was
concerned, marrying July was the best
thing his mother had ever done. She
scolded July as freely as she scolded him,
which didn't seem right to Joe. But then
(35) July accepted it and never scolded back,
so perhaps that was the way of the world.

Larry McMurtry, *Lonesome Dove*.

Tip To find the main idea, examine all the
details in the excerpt. Most—but not always
all—of the details will support the excerpt's
main idea.

48. Which statement best reflects the main idea of the first paragraph?

  (1) July believes that common practices should be followed.
  (2) Children have no right to complain about their parents.
  (3) A wife should eat with her family.
  (4) Bank robbers should be caught.
  (5) Elmira should wear stockings during meals.

49. Which of the following details does not support the main idea in the first paragraph?

  (1) July's mother had always eaten with the family.
  (2) Elmira sat in the loft while her husband ate dinner.
  (3) July's mother died when he was six.
  (4) Most wives did not sit in the loft during a meal.
  (5) July's job was to see that customs were honored.

50. Based on the information given in the excerpt, which of the following is July most likely to do?

  (1) leave Elmira and Joe
  (2) refuse to eat dinner with the family
  (3) demand that Elmira begin to eat with the family
  (4) accept that Elmira will never eat dinner sitting at the table
  (5) show his acceptance of Elmira's behavior by eating dinner with her in the loft

51. From the information given in the excerpt, July is most likely a

  (1) law enforcement officer
  (2) minister
  (3) businessman
  (4) cowboy
  (5) farmer

Items 52 to 57 refer to the following excerpt from a novel.

WHAT WISDOM CAN TWO BITS BUY?

Well, let me tell you about that. As a
youth I was faced with an awful crisis in
my mental life when it came over me that I
had no call to know what I knew. . . . Yet I
(5) knew how everything worked. I could look
at something and tell you how it worked
and probably show you how to make it
work better. But I was no intellectual, you
see, and I had no patience with the two-
(10) dollar words.
Morgan listened. He felt that he mustn't
move.
Well then, Ford continued, I happened to
pick up a little book. It was called *An*
(15) *Eastern Fakir's Eternal Wisdom,* published
by the Franklin Novelty Company of
Philadelphia, Pennsylvania. And in this
book, which cost me just twenty-five cents,
I found everything I needed to set my mind
(20) at rest. Reincarnation is the only belief I
hold, Mr. Morgan. I explain my genius this
way—some of us have just lived more
times than others. So you see, what you
have spent on scholars and traveled
(25) around the world to find, I already knew.
And I'll tell you something, in thanks for
the eats, I'm going to lend that book to
you. Why, you don't have to fuss with all
these Latiny things, he said waving his
(30) arm, you don't have to pick the garbage
pails of Europe and build steamboats to
sail the Nile just to find out something you
can get in the mail order for two bits!

E. L. Doctorow, *Ragtime.*

52. What does the speaker say was the awful crisis of his youth?

(1) He did not know enough.
(2) He was not an intellectual.
(3) He knew how everything worked.
(4) He did not understand how he knew the things he knew.
(5) He had a limited vocabulary.

53. How does Ford explain his ability to know what he knows?

(1) intelligence
(2) scholarship
(3) reincarnation
(4) world travel
(5) knowledge of Latin

54. The author helps the reader understand the meaning of "reincarnation" (line 20) by

(1) calling it a belief
(2) saying "lived more times"
(3) referring to traveling
(4) specifically explaining the term
(5) saying it set his mind at rest

55. The phrase "Latiny things" (line 29) probably refers to which of the following things?

(1) garbage pails
(2) steamboats
(3) scholarly books
(4) the eats
(5) mail order catalogs

56. How does the author provide a clue to the meaning of the term "two bits"?

(1) by putting it in the last sentence
(2) by referring to mail order
(3) by contrasting the book to one of Mr. Morgan's
(4) by comparing it to the cost of steamboats
(5) by saying the book cost twenty-five cents

57. The speaker probably also believes that getting a college degree in philosophy

(1) improves one's mind
(2) involves examining garbage
(3) would be a waste of time
(4) leads to having enough to eat
(5) leads to reincarnation

WHAT'S DIFFERENT ABOUT THIS THANKSGIVING?

They had lasagna for Thanksgiving dinner that year. The meatless kind. From a can.

(5) "Nothing like the smell of a good bird in the oven," Mike Senior announced, scraping his boots on the doormat, inhaling.

"Uh, Pop?" Janet whispered.

"Yes, ma'am?"

(10) "Never mind. Happy Thanksgiving, Pop. Let me help you with your coat. There are a few things in the kitchen I've got to see to yet. Mike should be back any minute. I'll leave you and Shawn to get

(15) reacquainted."

He smelled it all morning. He smelled it when he woke up in the cramped, stuffy bedroom he rented near the school in South Boston where he worked as a

(20) custodian part-time—fresh, brought in from the woodshed where it had been kept during the night to keep it moist. He smelled it as the bus crossed the state line into Maine—skin turning brown, the first

(25) drippings running down the sides. He smelled it at the rest stop where he bought Shawn an Indian tomahawk made in Taiwan, smelled it during the walk from the abandoned railroad bridge where the bus

(30) let him off—almost done now, the gravy bubbling in the pan, its aroma taking him past the boarded-up stores of the old mill town, the overgrown orchards, the brief view of the lake which meant he was

(35) halfway there . . . a rich, fragrant distillation of sixty Thanksgivings past, so strong that none of the changes in the house could stain it; not the plastic stretched tight over the windows to keep

(40) out drafts, not the towels stuffed tight against cracks the plastic missed, not the ugly black wood stove jutting out from the fireplace, appropriating all the space near the couch . . . not even the garlic and

(45) parmesan cheese Janet was sprinkling over the top of the casserole dish in a last desperate attempt to make it all palatable.

"And just how heavy is it this year, Shawn?" he asked, playing to memories

(50) and traditions he felt it was his duty to impart.

"Seven. Seven and a half in May."

Shawn was busy chopping up the coffee table. He thought his grandfather had

(55) asked him his age.

"Seven pounds, eh? Kind of on the scrawny side, isn't it?"

W. D. Wetherell, "If a Woodchuck Could Chuck Wood."

58. Which of the following is the best explanation for the author's repeated use of the word "smelled"?

(1) to describe the smell of the turkey
(2) to emphasize the importance of the holiday to Mike Senior
(3) to explain the aroma of the lasagna
(4) to explain Shawn's reaction to his grandfather
(5) to illustrate that Janet was a wonderful cook

59. Based on the information given in the excerpt, which of the following statements can be inferred?

(1) Mike Senior does not see his family very often.
(2) Mike Senior has a close relationship with Shawn.
(3) Mike Senior lives nearby.
(4) Janet enjoys spending time with Mike Senior.
(5) The family did not eat meat.

60. If Janet served frozen dinners, Mike Senior's response would most likely be?

(1) to refuse to eat
(2) to offer to take the family to dinner
(3) to pretend that it was lasagna
(4) to continue pretending it was turkey
(5) to say it was delicious and ask for another helping

Items 61 to 63 refer to the following excerpt from a novel.

HOW DOES THIS FAMILY GET ALONG?

"Hi, Daddy!" Feather screamed. She was so excited to see me after all those hours asleep that she ran right for me, banging her nose against my knee. She
(5) started to cry and I picked her up. Jesus slipped into the room as silent as mist. He was small for fifteen, slight and surefooted. He was the star long-distance runner at Hamilton High School. He smiled at me,
(10) not saying a word.

Jesus hadn't said a thing in the thirteen years I'd known him. He wrote me notes sometimes. Usually about money he needed and events at school that I should
(15) attend. The doctors said that he was healthy, that he could talk if he wanted to. All I could do was wait.

Jesus took over the breakfast while I cooed to Feather and held her close.
(20) "You hurt me," she whined.

"You want peanut butter or salami for lunch?" I answered.

Feather's skin was light brown and fleshy. Her stomach rumbled against my
(25) chest. I could see in her face that she didn't know whether to cry or run for the table.

"Lemme go! Lemme go!" she said, pushing at my arms to get down to her chair.
(30) The moment she was on her stack of phone books Jesus put a slice of bread covered with strawberry jam in front of her.

"I dreamed," Feather said, then she stared off into space lost for a moment.
(35) Her amber eyes and crinkled golden hair were both made almost transparent from the light through the kitchen window. "I dreamed, I dreamed," she continued. "There was a scary man in the house last
(40) night."

"What kind of man?"

She held out her hands and opened her eyes wide to say she didn't know. "I didn't see him. I just hearded him."

Walter Mosley, *Black Betty*.

61. Which of the following is the most likely reason for Feather's first response to seeing her father?

(1) Feather hasn't seen her father for awhile, and she is happy to see him.
(2) Feather is sad because she was missing her father.
(3) There was a strange man in the house the night before.
(4) She is waking up and is hungry for breakfast.
(5) Feather wants her father to make lunch for her.

62. From the details in the excerpt, it is possible to infer that Jesus

(1) has a problem with his vocal cords which keeps him from speaking
(2) is responsible for making breakfast for his family every morning
(3) chooses not to talk to other people
(4) is in danger of failing high school
(5) does not budget his money well

63. Which of the following best describes the conflict between Feather and her father?

(1) Feather thinks she is too old to be held by her father.
(2) The father does not know what is happening in his daughter's life.
(3) Feather has a bad temper.
(4) Feather feels her father is not paying enough attention to her after she gets hurt.
(5) The father does not understand that his daughter is frightened by her dream.

Tip **When identifying the plot of a story, look for the important characters and any conflict that may be influencing the sequence of events.**

Items 64 to 67 refer to the following excerpt from a novel.

WHAT WAS GRANDPA TWEEDY LIKE?

Then there was Grandpa Tweedy, my daddy's daddy out in Banks County. He talked hard times morning, noon, and night. Called himself a farmer, but you
(5) never saw him behind a plow or driving a team. Lazy, great goodness. Like the lilies of the field in the Bible, he toiled not, neither did he spend his own money. He was always asking Papa to help him out.
(10) All he ever did was sit on the porch and swat flies, and like I said, even had him a pet hen to peck them up.

When Papa left the farm at sixteen to go work for Grandpa Blakeslee, he made
(15) twenty dollars a month and had to send half of it home to pay the field hand who took his place. That was the custom. But even after Papa married at nineteen, making forty dollars a month, he still had
(20) to send Grandpa Tweedy ten of it, till the day he was twenty-one. My mother never said she didn't like her father-in-law, but I could tell she didn't, and that may of been why.
(25) What started me hating him, he wouldn't let me fish on Sunday. Said it was a sin. I remember I put out some set hooks late one Saturday, thinking if I caught a fish, it wouldn't be a sin to take him off the hook
(30) next morning. End his suffering, you know. Early Sunday I ran down to the river and one of the lines was just a-jiggling! But when I ran up the hill and asked Grandpa's permission to get my fish off the hook, he
(35) said, "Hit'll still be thar t'morrer, Lord willin'. The Lord ain't willin', it'll be gone. Now git in the house and study yore catechism till time to leave for preachin'."

Of course the fish was gone Monday
(40) morning. But I got back at Grandpa Tweedy. I'd noticed a big hornet's nest in the privy, just under the tin roof, so I bided my time behind a tree till I saw him go in there. Giving him just long enough to get
(45) settled good, I let fly a rock and it hit that tin roof like a gunshot. . . .

I just couldn't hardly stand him. One time when he was fussing about tenants stealing out of his woodpile, I watched
(50) while he drilled holes in several sticks of stovewood, filled the holes with gunpowder, sealed them over with candlewax, and put them on top of the woodpile. "What if somebody gets kilt?" I
(55) asked him.

I was just a little bitty boy, so I believed him when he said, "Ain't go'n hurt nobody. Hit'll jest scare the livin' daylights out of'm."

Olive Ann Burns, *Cold Sassy Tree*.

64. Which statement reflects the most likely reason that Papa sent money home to Grandpa Tweedy?

(1) Papa was paying back his father for money loaned to him for school.
(2) Children have a moral obligation to support parents who cannot support themselves.
(3) Papa felt guilty for having left the farm.
(4) Papa felt guilty for not having brought his wife back to the farm to live.
(5) Grandpa Tweedy did not like to spend his own money, so he asked Papa to help out.

65. The statement "All he ever did was sit on the porch and swat flies" (lines 10–11) is a restatement of

(1) "he toiled not"
(2) "he talked hard times"
(3) "called himself a farmer"
(4) "neither did he spend his own money"
(5) "even had him a pet hen to peck them up"

66. Which of the following actions would you expect Grandpa Tweedy to take?

   (1) He would be the first man to fix anything that needed fixing.
   (2) He would tend his lilies night and day just like in the Bible.
   (3) He would talk for hours on end about his incredible good fortune.
   (4) He would be glad to lend a helping hand to any of his children.
   (5) He would let a fence fall down before he would repair it.

67. What happened when the speaker told Grandpa Tweedy about the fish?

   (1) Grandpa said it was a gift from God.
   (2) Grandpa refused permission to take the fish off the hook.
   (3) Grandpa gave his permission to get the fish.
   (4) Grandpa said to wait until after the preaching.
   (5) Grandpa got angry at the speaker.

Items 68 and 69 refer to the following excerpt.

WHAT IS THE TRUTH ABOUT THE BOMBINGS?

John Osborne and the captain stared at him. "The Russians never bombed Washington," Dwight said. "They proved that in the end."
(5) He stared back at them. "I mean, the very first attack of all."

"That's right. The very first attack. They were Russian long-range bombers, II 626's, but they were Egyptian manned.
(10) They flew from Cairo."

"Are you sure that's true?"

"It's true enough. They got the one that landed at Puerto Rico on the way home. They only found out it was Egyptian after
(15) we'd bombed Leningrad and Odessa and the nuclear establishments at Kharkov, Kuibyshev, and Molotov. Things must have happened kind of quick that day."

"Do you mean to say, we bombed
(20) Russia by mistake?" It was so horrible a thought as to be incredible.

John Osborne said, "That's true, Peter. It's never been admitted publicly, but it's quite true. The first one was the bomb on
(25) Naples. That was the Albanians, of course. Then there was the bomb on Tel Aviv. Nobody knows who dropped that one, not that I've heard, anyway. Then the British and Americans intervened and
(30) made that demonstration flight over Cairo. Next day the Egyptians sent out all the serviceable bombers that they'd got, six to Washington and seven to London. One got through to Washington and two to London.
(35) After that there weren't many American or British statesmen left alive."

Nevil Shute, *On the Beach.*

68. Which of these is <u>not</u> a cause or effect that led to the war?

   (1) The Albanians bombed Naples, then somebody bombed Tel Aviv.
   (2) The Americans bombed Leningrad and Odessa and the nuclear facilities of the Russians at Kharkov.
   (3) The Russians bombed Cairo.
   (4) The British and Americans sent planes over Egypt.
   (5) The Egyptians bombed London.

69. What was the most important result of the events in the excerpt?

   (1) Americans thought Egyptians had bombed Tel Aviv.
   (2) Russia gave airplanes to Egypt.
   (3) Many American and British statesmen were killed.
   (4) A series of mistakes and misunderstandings caused a world war.
   (5) Things happened very quickly on the day the war started.

Items <u>70 to 78</u> refer to the following excerpt from a novel.

WHAT IS THE STORY OF ADNIX?

Years before, he had invented a module that, when a television commercial appeared, automatically muted the sound. It wasn't at first a context-recognition
(5) device. Instead, it simply monitored the amplitude of the carrier wave. TV advertisers had taken to running their ads louder and with less audio clutter than the programs that were their nominal vehicles.
(10) News of Hadden's module spread by word of mouth. People reported a sense of relief, the lifting of a great burden, even a feeling of joy at being freed from the advertising barrage for the six to eight
(15) hours out of every day that the average American spent in front of the television set. Before there could be any coordinated response from the television advertising industry, Adnix had become wildly popular.
(20) It forced advertisers and networks into new choices of carrier-wave strategy, each of which Hadden countered with a new invention. Sometimes he invented circuits to defeat strategies which the agencies
(25) and the networks had not yet hit upon. He would say that he was saving them the trouble of making inventions, at great cost to their shareholders, which were at any rate doomed to failure. As his sales
(30) volume increased, he kept cutting prices. It was a kind of electronic warfare. And he was winning.

They tried to sue him—something about a conspiracy in restraint of trade. They had
(35) sufficient political muscle that his motion for summary dismissal was denied, but insufficient influence to actually win the case. The trial had forced Hadden to investigate the relevant legal codes. Soon
(40) after, he applied, through a well-known Madison Avenue agency in which he was now a major silent partner, to advertise his own product on commercial television. After a few weeks of controversy his
(45) commercials were refused. He sued all three networks and in *this* trial was able to prove conspiracy in restraint of trade. He received a huge settlement, that was, at the time, a record for cases of this sort,
(50) and which contributed in its modest way to the demise of the original networks.

There had always been people who enjoyed the commercials, of course, and they had no need for Adnix. But they were
(55) a dwindling minority. Hadden made a great fortune by eviscerating broadcast advertising. He also made many enemies. . . .

As he further developed context-
(60) recognition chips, it became obvious to him that they had much wider application—from education, science, and medicine, to military intelligence and industrial espionage. It was on this issue
(65) that lines were drawn for the famous suit *United States v. Hadden Cybernetics.* One of Hadden's chips was considered too good for civilian life, and on recommendation of the National Security
(70) Agency, the facilities and key personnel for the most advanced context-recognition chip production were taken over by the government. It was simply too important to read the Russian mail. God knows, they
(75) told him, what would happen if the Russians could read our mail.

Carl Sagan, *Contact.*

Tip **If you are having trouble trying to define a word or group of words, it is helpful to look carefully at the surrounding words. Often, the context will give you clues that will help you to figure out the meaning.**

70. Which of the following words in the excerpt is the best clue for figuring out the meaning of "amplitude" (line 6)?

(1) automatically
(2) monitored
(3) louder
(4) context-recognition
(5) module

71. Which of the following is the most probable meaning of the word "strategies" (line 24) as it is used in this paragraph?

(1) plans
(2) advertisements
(3) inventions
(4) burdens
(5) responses

72. Which of the following best helps you understand the meaning of "insufficient" (line 37)?

(1) There were relevant legal codes.
(2) The advertisers' influence was not enough to win the case.
(3) Hadden investigated legal codes.
(4) There was a conspiracy.
(5) Hadden received a settlement.

73. What happened in the lawsuit filed by the advertisers against Hadden?

(1) They used their political muscle to destroy his product.
(2) They won their case because Hadden had insufficient evidence.
(3) Hadden won by filing a motion for summary dismissal.
(4) Hadden investigated all the relevant legal codes.
(5) Hadden won because the advertisers failed to prove their case.

74. Which of the following would be the best title for this excerpt?

(1) Success in Advertising
(2) Consumer Laws
(3) A History of Inventions
(4) A Lot of Noise About Noise
(5) Madison Avenue

75. What happened in the lawsuit filed by Hadden against the networks?

(1) Hadden proved a conspiracy and won a huge settlement.
(2) Hadden became the owner of all three networks.
(3) Hadden lost the case.
(4) Hadden entered the advertising business.
(5) Hadden's motion for dismissal was denied.

76. What was the outcome of *United States* v. *Hadden Cybernetics*?

(1) Hadden was allowed to remain in business making chips.
(2) Hadden was asked to help the U.S. government on a special project.
(3) The government took over the production of context-recognition chips.
(4) Hadden won because the government failed to prove that he did anything illegal.
(5) The case was settled out of court and in Hadden's favor.

77. Which of the following is the most likely meaning of the word "dwindling" (line 55) in the third paragraph?

(1) accumulating
(2) shrinking
(3) changing
(4) growing
(5) swelling

78. Why did Hadden file a lawsuit against all three networks?

(1) He was still angry because they had tried to sue him.
(2) He wanted a large cash settlement for the hardship they had caused him.
(3) The networks refused to accept his commercials for broadcast.
(4) He had studied the relevant legal codes.
(5) The networks no longer had as much influence as they had had previously, so he thought he could win.

Answers are on page 822.

Lesson 2 Nonfiction

Choose the best answer to each item.
Items 1 to 7 refer to the following excerpt.

WHAT HAPPENED BEFORE THE SHOW COULD START?

Here was this man, Louis Armstrong, just before the show was due to start, waiting silently. He was smartly dressed, in dinner jacket, and holding his Selmer
(5) trumpet. The band was ready—there had been no rehearsal—and he was about to perform. Then Collins suddenly said, "Where's the dough? If I don't get the dough, Louis don't play." The promoter
(10) had a huge crowd and there was no problem. He offered a cheque but Collins was adamant—no cash, no Louis. It must have been humiliating for Louis, though he showed no sign of it. He just looked at the
(15) floor and went on swinging his trumpet in his hand until such time as matters were settled. He seemed utterly detached as this pasty-faced man with the cigar in his mouth demanded the money there and
(20) then, or no show. I estimate they had some two thousand people in there, and the promoter went to his box office and came back with several bags of half-crowns, of silver anyway, and put them
(25) down in front of Collins. "There's your money," he told Collins, and I remember thinking: he doesn't know how to count it.

Max Jones and John Chilton, *Louis Armstrong Story 1900–1971*.

1. Which of the following can be concluded from this excerpt about the relationship between Louis Armstrong and Collins?

   (1) Collins is the promoter of Armstrong's show.
   (2) Armstrong and Collins often argue publicly.
   (3) Collins handles Armstrong's money.
   (4) Collins is one of Armstrong's biggest fans.
   (5) Armstrong admires Collins's ability.

2. It can be concluded from the scene in this excerpt that musicians

   (1) sometimes were not paid after their performances
   (2) get nervous in front of large crowds
   (3) always rehearse before a show
   (4) demand large sums of money
   (5) are easily embarrassed

3. What is the best conclusion about the person who is telling this story?

   (1) He thought Collins did the right thing.
   (2) He was embarrassed by Armstrong's behavior.
   (3) He was a member of Armstrong's band.
   (4) Armstrong was thinking of hiring him as a manager.
   (5) He thought Armstrong behaved better than Collins.

4. Which of the following best describes how Armstrong probably acted on most occasions?

   (1) impatiently
   (2) calmly
   (3) aggressively
   (4) awkwardly
   (5) rudely

5. Which of the following is the best meaning for the word "adamant" (line 12)?

   (1) noisy
   (2) firm
   (3) confused
   (4) polite
   (5) pleased

6. Which of the following would be the best title for this paragraph?

(1) No Cash, No Show
(2) The Silent Man
(3) A Promoter's Troubles
(4) They Came to See Louis
(5) Several Bags of Silver

7. You can conclude that this performance does not take place in the United States because
A. Armstrong was using a Selmer trumpet
B. Armstrong was paid with several bags of half-crowns
C. the pasty-faced man could not count

(1) A only
(2) B only
(3) C only
(4) A and B
(5) B and C

Tip When making conclusions, identify the plot, find the main idea, restate the information, and determine the meaning from context. These skills, combined with what you already know, will help you make your own judgments and predictions.

Items 8 and 9 refer to the following excerpt from a book.

HOW MANY SIDES ARE THERE TO A MAN?

Whiteside was right. All the characteristics of Majority Leader and President Lyndon Baines Johnson that were so unique and vivid when unveiled
(5) on a national stage—the lapel-grabbing, the embracing, the manipulating of men, the "wheeling and dealing"—all these were characteristics that the students at San Marcos had seen. And the similarity
(10) extended to aspects of the man less public. The methods Lyndon Johnson used to attain power on Capitol Hill were the same ones he had used on College Hill, and the similarity went far beyond the

(15) stealing of an election. At San Marcos, the power resided in the hands of a single older man. Johnson had begged that man for the opportunity to run his errands, had searched for more errands to run, had
(20) offered that man an audience when he felt talkative, companionship when he was lonely. And he had flattered him—flattered with a flattery so extravagant and shameless (and skillful) that his peers had
(25) marveled at it. And the friendship of that one older man had armored him against the enmity of hosts of his peers, had given him enough power of his own so that it no longer mattered to him what others
(30) thought of him. In Washington, the names of his patrons—of older men who bestowed power on Lyndon Johnson— would be more famous: Rayburn, Russell, Roosevelt. But the technique would be the
(35) same.

Robert A. Caro, *The Years of Lyndon Johnson: The Path to Power.*

8. The period in Lyndon Johnson's life that is the author's subject in this excerpt is

(1) just before his death
(2) when he was President
(3) when he was Majority Leader
(4) when he was in college
(5) when he was in high school

9. What was Lyndon Johnson's main technique for attaining power?

(1) He sought out powerful men as patrons.
(2) He "wheeled and dealed."
(3) He embraced people and made them feel loved.
(4) He was a unique and vivid personality.
(5) He ran errands.

WHAT HAPPENED TO THE WIDE, OPEN SPACES?

Cities were built, new provinces. Legislatures and governments were created with all the trappings and gold braid of an ancient system on this empty
(5) land. Innumerable wooden towns sprang up beside the railways and the red wooden grain elevators stood everywhere, with square shoulders against the sky.
Presently Regina, a Royal Northwest
(10) Mounted Police post, where Riel had been hanged in the jail yard, found itself the capital of Saskatchewan with a domed parliament building beside a slough, dammed to form an ornamental lake.
(15) Trees, shrubs, and flowers grew around it where the buffalo had grazed a few years before. Saskatoon to the north expanded out of the river bank like a mushroom.
To the edge of the Rockies the plow
(20) turned up the land, turned up the old grasses and "prairie wool" that had fed the buffalo and then the cattle—for which nature would take a terrible revenge later on in dust storm and erosion. In the
(25) foothills, in sight of the mountains, they built the rollicking ten-gallon, hair-pant, and joyous town of Calgary, where business men wore cowboy hats and high-heeled boots, and R. B. Bennett, living at
(30) the Palliser, wore cutaway coats and striped gray trousers, on his sure way to the premiership of Canada and the British House of Lords. North again, almost at the edge of the tundra, they laid out
(35) Edmonton, with Jasper Avenue running, paved, for miles into the prairies; and then built another parliament building for another province until at night its lights twinkled on the river like a Rhine castle.

Bruce Hutchinson, *The Unknown Country.*

10. Which of the following phrases from the excerpt does not help to show how this excerpt is organized?

 (1) beside the railroads
 (2) where the buffalo had grazed
 (3) to the edge of the Rockies
 (4) in the jail yard
 (5) miles into the prairies

11. Which of the following phrases from the excerpt does not suggest that the development of the land was quite sudden?

 (1) were built
 (2) sprang up
 (3) found itself the capital
 (4) like a mushroom
 (5) a few years before

12. According to the context of this excerpt, a "slough" (line 13) is probably

 (1) grassland
 (2) a grove of trees
 (3) an ancient system
 (4) a waterway
 (5) an ornamental lake

13. If the author had been talking about similar growth in the United States, he might have used the example of

 (1) a small Vermont town that is losing its young people to New York
 (2) ghost towns in the West
 (3) the 1860s gold rush that brought thousands of people to the Black Hills of South Dakota
 (4) the legalization of the lottery in Illinois
 (5) the closing of automotive parts factories in Muncie, Indiana

Items 14 to 17 refer to the following excerpt from an article.

WHERE DID THIS BOY GROW UP?

My mother kept an immaculate household. Bedspreads (chenille seemed to be very in) and lace curtains, washed at home like everything else, were hung up
(5) on huge racks with rows of tight nails. The racks were assembled in the living room, and the moisture from the wet bedspreads would fill the apartment. In a sense, that seems to be the lasting image of that
(10) period of my life. The house was clean. The neighbors were clean. The streets, with few cars, were clean. The buildings were clean and uncluttered with people on the stoops. The park was clean. The
(15) visitors to my house were clean, and the relationships that my family had with other Puerto Rican families, and the Italian families that my father had met through baseball and my mother through the
(20) garment center, were clean. Second Avenue was clean and most of the apartment windows had awnings. There was always music, there seemed to be no rain, and snow did not become slush.
(25) School was fun, we wrote essays about how grand America was, we put up hunchbacked cats at Halloween, we believed Santa Claus visited everyone. I believed everyone was Catholic. I grew up
(30) with dogs, nightingales, my godmother's guitar, rocking chair, cat, guppies, my father's occasional roosters, kept in a cage on the fire escape. Laundry delivered and collected by horse and wagon, fruits and
(35) vegetables sold the same way, windowsill refrigeration in winter, iceman and box in summer. The police my friends, likewise the teachers.

Jack Agueros, "Halfway to Dick and Jane," © 1971 by Doubleday, from *The Immigrant Experience* by Thomas C. Wheeler.

14. The author suggests the meaning of the word "immaculate" (line 1) by

   (1) describing his mother
   (2) talking about school
   (3) referring to religion
   (4) using an appositive
   (5) describing the cleanliness of the house

15. Which of the following is the best reason for the author to repeat the word "clean" so many times?

   (1) It sets up a contrast to how he lives now.
   (2) It emphasizes the lasting image he has of the time.
   (3) It shows how much his mother's habits influenced him.
   (4) It adds more detail.
   (5) It gets rid of the need for more explanation.

16. Which of the following phrases does not present an idealized view of the writer's childhood?

   (1) an immaculate household
   (2) there was always music
   (3) there seemed to be no rain
   (4) school was fun
   (5) collected by horse and wagon

17. Which of the following phrases is the best example of informal use of words?

   (1) chenille seemed to be very in
   (2) the lasting image of that period of my life
   (3) snow did not become slush
   (4) hunchbacked cats at Halloween
   (5) fruits and vegetables sold the same way

Tip **Informal style uses more casual speech than formal style. Note the way that informal speech tells you something about the author's attitude or a character's feelings toward a subject.**

Items 18 to 21 refer to the following excerpt from a book.

WHO ARE THE WHALE WATCHERS?

The song of the humpback has captured the intense interest of many biologists. Why do they sing these songs, and do they sing them all the time? Do the songs
(5) carry messages to other whales, or are they just for fun?

Jacques Cousteau says both the male and female humpback sing. He states that they sing their song "day and night during
(10) their long migration to and from the warm southern waters."

Dr. Roger Payne disagrees. For several months during 1971, Payne and his colleague, Scott McVay, recorded
(15) humpbacks off the coast of Bermuda. They found that all the humpbacks in one area sing the same underwater song. However, they also found that the whales sing only in their winter breeding ground
(20) and not while traveling.

Later, Payne's wife Katy, also a whale watcher and researcher, found that not only are humpback whales "singers" but also "composers, constantly tinkering with
(25) their song so that it changes completely in only a few years." As individual whales make minor changes in the song, others learn those changes and pass them on. The Paynes theorized that the changes
(30) take place as the breeding season progresses and not between seasons.

Jacci Cole, *Animal Communication: Opposing Viewpoints.*

18. Whales are composers in that

(1) they memorize changes in songs
(2) they sing for fun
(3) they sing day and night
(4) they tinker around with their song and change it
(5) the changes in their songs take place during the breeding season

19. Which of the following is the best explanation of why the author included the detail "also a whale watcher and researcher" (lines 21–22)?

(1) to fill up space
(2) to show that Katy Payne is an expert in her own right
(3) to explain why Katy Payne disagrees with her husband
(4) to explain why whales sing
(5) to catch the reader's attention

20. Which of the following is the best explanation for the author's use of "Later" (line 21)?

(1) to indicate the start of a new paragraph
(2) to explain that whales sing after they compose songs
(3) to indicate that Katy Payne's conclusions came after Roger Payne's
(4) to explain that whales change their songs after composing them
(5) to indicate that whales sing as the breeding season progresses

21. Dr. Payne and his colleagues found which of the following not to be true?

(1) All the humpbacks in one area sing the same song.
(2) Whales sing during their long migration.
(3) Both male and female whales sing.
(4) Whales sing while in their winter breeding ground.
(5) Whales change their songs completely over the years.

WHAT'S THERE TO SEE AT THE COUNTY FAIR?

The crafts judges form a sorority of expert peers, most from out of county. Several have been to the judging school at the Augusta Presbyterian Church, with
(5)   cards to prove it. Unwary novice judges are assigned to cookies, jellies, and jams. Hundreds of sweet things are entered: platters of brownies, cakes, jams, and jellies. You'd think it would be fun tasting
(10) them, until you thought twice. The jelly judges did stay for lunch afterwards (thanks to the Highland Girl Scouts), but they hardly ate a thing.

Sewing judges sit at a table while
(15) assistants bring them garments to inspect for fabric grain lines, stitching, suitable thread, smooth darts, pleats, tucks, gathers, and facings. One lady holds up a black-and-white checked child's jumper.
(20) "Oh, look, she's covered the buttons."

The second judge turns a sundress pocket inside out to inspect the stitching. "What do you do when they're both nice?"

The senior judge says, "You get to
(25) nitpicking," and she awards first prize to the jumper. "I don't know how it is other places, but in Highland County, covered buttons are *it*."

Many skills and crafts shown here are
(30) traditional, but not all of them. Kids' art is pretty much the same as kids' art anywhere; a few more sheep and cows, a few less McDonald's arches. Mrs. Leo Schwartz has prepared a Japanese exhibit
(35) . . . because an exchange student from Japan stayed with her family this summer. And Rafe Levien, a computer whiz, has an exhibit of computer art.

The canned vegetable judges look for a
(40) perfect seal and a nice-looking ring and label. The liquid should be free of sediment and bubbles. The color should be natural, pieces must be uniform and of good quality. Mildred Detamore holds a jar
(45) of stewed tomatoes up to the light and sighs, "The tomatoes are so much seedier this year. It's because of the drought."

Donald McCaig, "The Best Four Days in Highland County," *Country Journal.*

22. Which of the following words is the best example of informal use of words?

(1) peers
(2) garments
(3) traditional
(4) kids
(5) seedier

23. The deciding factor in giving first prize to the black-and-white child's jumper is most likely

(1) its fine stitches
(2) its smooth darts
(3) its covered buttons
(4) its overall appearance
(5) the grain lines on its fabric

24. The author uses the word "sighs" (line 46) to suggest that

(1) the judge is tired
(2) judging is hard work
(3) the jar is too heavy
(4) the judge is sorry about the problem
(5) the judge will not get paid

25. The author uses the word "nitpicking" (line 25) to suggest which of the following?

(1) The senior judge is a picky person.
(2) Covered buttons are an important feature for all garments.
(3) A prize may be awarded due to some small point.
(4) The sewing judges often like two garments equally well.
(5) Small details are not the most important aspect of a garment.

Tip **Remember, understanding how an author structures his or her work can help you understand the meaning of what you're reading.**

Items 26 to 29 refer to the following excerpt from a book.

WHAT IS THIS CAT'S ROUTINE?

Cats do, however, like routine—in fact, they love it. And, in the days—and nights—which followed the rescue my cat and I worked out many routines. Or rather

(5) he worked them out, and I, as dutifully as I could, worked at following them.

Some of these routines necessarily involved compromises. My cat, for example, liked to get up early—in fact he

(10) liked to get up at 3 A.M. That was, of course, all right with me. His hours, it had been one of our understandings, were his own. The trouble was that, at 3 A.M., he liked a midnight snack of Tender Vittles.

(15) Again, seemingly, no problem. Simply leave out a bowl of Vittles before he went to bed.

But unfortunately there was a problem. I could not just leave out a bowl of Vittles

(20) before I went to bed. He would eat them before he went to bed. He did not have, when you came right down to it, either any good old-fashioned Boston discipline—as I would have thought he would have at

(25) least begun to learn from me—or, for that matter, my good sound sensible Boston foresight. No matter how large a bowl I filled of Vittles before he retired, the bowl was empty before he retired.

(30) His hours in this routine thus became my hours. And so we compromised. Before going to bed each night, I put out an empty dish on the floor by the bed and a package of Tender Vittles on my bedside table. At

(35) 3 A.M.—and he was extraordinarily accurate about this—he would wake up, roll over, and wake me up. At 3:01 I would roll over, put some Vittles in his dish, or at least reasonably near it, and go back, or at least

(40) attempt to go back, to sleep.

Cleveland Amory, *The Cat Who Came for Christmas.*

26. Which of the following is a conclusion that can be drawn from this excerpt?

 (1) Cats are harder to please than dogs are.
 (2) The author has trouble getting his cat to eat.
 (3) The author is fond of his cat.
 (4) Boston cats are old-fashioned.
 (5) Cats can be trained to tell time.

27. The main idea of this excerpt is that

 (1) the cat finally agreed to the man's schedule
 (2) the man had to figure out an easy way to feed the cat in the middle of the night
 (3) the man had to figure out a way to get his cat to go on a diet
 (4) cats will eat any time they find food in front of them
 (5) establishing routines often means making compromises

28. Which of the following is most likely to occur if the author's cat began demanding water at 1 A.M.?

 (1) the author would give the cat away
 (2) the author would devise a plan to satisfy the cat
 (3) the author would ignore the cat
 (4) the author would get up and get the cat a drink of water
 (5) the author would punish the cat

29. According to the author, the cat has no discipline and lacks foresight because he

 (1) gets up at 3 A.M.
 (2) never leaves a bit of food in his dish to eat during the night
 (3) likes to keep his own hours
 (4) does not mind waking up his owner in the middle of the night
 (5) always wants a midnight snack

Items <u>30 to 34</u> refer to the following excerpt from a book.

IS THIS PERSON A GOOD PATIENT?

Obviously this is not the moment to be talking about operations when here we all are—in the very bloom of health. But these are troubled times, and there are
(5)   people in St. Vincent's Hospital today who, as recently as yesterday, didn't know they had a spinal disk. The thing to do, I say, is be prepared, bone up, get the facts so that your stay in the hospital will be the jolly,
(10)   satisfying interlude it ought to be.
I don't know whether or not I am speaking for convalescents everywhere, but I can tell you that *my* big mistake when I go to the hospital is being too cheerful. I
(15)   arrive the day before the operation and, while it would be stretching things to suggest that on this occasion I feel fit, I at least feel human. So I try to be agreeable. Agreeable nothing; I'm adorable to a point
(20)   just short of nausea. With my gay sayings and my air of quiet self-deprecation, I creep into the heart of one and all.
"Yes," I murmur to the night nurse, "I did ring for you an hour ago, but that's
(25)   *perfectly* all right." And I reassure the orderly who forgot to bring my dinner tray with a blithe "Don't worry about it, I'm not the least bit hungry and besides I have these delicious cherry cough drops."

Jean Kerr, *How I Got to Be Perfect.*

30.   The style this author uses is most likely intended to

(1)   suggest that she is an authority on hospital care
(2)   make the reader think twice about going to a hospital
(3)   make the reader laugh
(4)   make the reader take her advice seriously
(5)   be suitable for publication in a medical journal

31.   Which is the best meaning for the word "convalescents" (line 12)?

(1)   people who like to talk a lot
(2)   nurses
(3)   orderlies
(4)   troubled times
(5)   people recovering from an illness

32.   When the writer says that "your stay in the hospital will be the jolly, satisfying interlude it ought to be" (lines 9–10), she really means that

(1)   people can have a lot of fun in a hospital
(2)   people do not enjoy being in the hospital
(3)   hospitals are becoming entertainment centers
(4)   she is satisfied with the care she received
(5)   hospital rooms are more comfortable than they used to be

33.   Which of the following is the <u>best</u> restatement of "I'm adorable to a point just short of nausea." (lines 19–20)?

(1)   I'm so sweet it's almost sickening.
(2)   I try to make myself unbearable to be around.
(3)   I act overly cheerful.
(4)   I am so nice that everyone loves me.
(5)   I act so cute that it makes me physically ill.

34.   In the phrase "the very bloom of health" (line 3), the words "health" and "bloom" are linked to imply

(1)   that health is like a dying flower
(2)   that one in good health is radiant, like an opening blossom
(3)   well-being
(4)   something past its prime
(5)   that health is related to nature

Items 35 to 41 refer to the following excerpt.

WHAT DID THE TITANS DO TO THE EARTH?

Toward midnight the cafés and
restaurants began to fill. Parties dropped
in for those quiet little suppers that were a
part of the city's fame. The rattle of dishes
(5) and clink of glasses, a merry laugh or a
happy chuckle, a snatch of a stage joke or
a bit of repartee—this for an hour or two;
then all was still.
The city slept. A lone policeman on his
(10) rounds, the clanging bell of some owl car
anxious to be off the street, the tread of a
man hurrying home, the uncertain antics of
some befuddled fellow—scarcely more
than this anywhere. The city slept,
(15) unconscious of the manner of its
awakening.
Slowly dawn crept over the hills; some
sleepy folk were getting their wares out for
the early buyers. A sudden rumbling
(20) hurried closer and closer. The houses of
the sleeping city shook as if seized with a
sudden ague. At first came a sharp but
gentle swaying motion that grew less and
less; then a heavy jolting sidewise—then
(25) another, heaviest of all. Finally a grinding
round of everything, irregularly tumultuous,
spasmodic, jerky. It was as if some Titans,
laying hold of the edge of the world, were
trying to wrest it from each other by
(30) sudden wrenchings.
Plaster showered from the walls; nails
creaked in their sockets and pulled and
tried to free themselves. Crockery and
glassware smashed upon the floor. Doors
(35) flew open—swung round—jerked off their
hinges. Furniture toppled. Pianos rattled
their keys in untimed janglings. Chimneys
snapped and fell. Houses groaned and
twisted and reeled on their foundations.
(40) Outside, streets were seized with
writhings. Hillsides slid. The city shook
itself like a dog coming out of the water.

Frank W. Aitken and Edward Hilton, "Earthquake at San
Francisco," *Man Against Nature.*

35. Which of the following best states the main
idea of this excerpt?

(1) The peace of the city is being disturbed.
(2) A terrible fight happened after midnight.
(3) An earthquake began in the early
morning.
(4) City folk are not prepared for disaster.
(5) Sleep is the best preparation for a
crisis.

36. The author uses the figurative "slept" (line 9)
not only to suggest that the city was quiet at
night, but also

(1) to imply that the policeman was tired
(2) to point out the importance of remaining
alert
(3) to prepare the reader for what
happened next
(4) as a dramatic contrast to how the city
woke up
(5) as an explanation of the word "still"

37. The word "crept" (line 17) helps to
emphasize

(1) the slow, sleepy pace of early
awakening
(2) how unwilling the sun is to begin its day
(3) how slow people were to realize what
was happening
(4) the excitement of the parties the night
before
(5) the slow way the fight began

38. Which of the following would be the best title for this excerpt?

  (1) The Day the Earth Stood Still
  (2) The Calm Before the Storm
  (3) An Awful Surprise
  (4) When the Earth Shrugged Its Shoulders
  (5) How to React to an Earthquake

39. The author used descriptions of nails freeing themselves, pianos rattling their keys, and houses groaning to add to the horror of the situation because

  (1) these are ordinary and familiar actions
  (2) it can be frightening to imagine objects acting on their own
  (3) plaster falling is not dramatic enough
  (4) they illustrate how the hillsides slid
  (5) they explain why the streets were filled with writhings

Tip **Often, writers use figurative language to make their writing more interesting or to add dramatic emphasis. Ask yourself what possible effect an author might want to make and why he or she might want to make it. This will help you understand any figurative language in a passage.**

40. Which of the following best explains the effectiveness of the sentence "The city shook itself like a dog coming out of the water" (lines 41–42)?

  (1) There were a number of animals running wildly in the streets.
  (2) Dogs often break household objects by their roughness.
  (3) Objects were thrown like the spray flying off a dog's back.
  (4) People were terrified by the violence of what was happening.
  (5) Dogs do not like being in water.

41. Which of the following best explains the author's reference to "Titans" (lines 27–30)?

  (1) to describe fully the violent spasms of the city
  (2) to explain the stirring of the city
  (3) to suggest that something was fighting over the world
  (4) to illustrate the crime of the city
  (5) to indicate the noise that accompanied the movements

Item 42 refers to the following excerpt.

WHAT HAPPENS WHEN YOU ENCOUNTER A WILD ANIMAL?

The weasel was stunned into stillness as he was emerging from beneath an enormous shaggy wild rose bush four feet away. I was stunned into stillness twisted
(5) backward on the tree trunk. Our eyes locked, and someone threw away the key.
Our look was as if two lovers, or deadly enemies, met unexpectedly on an overgrown path when each had been
(10) thinking of something else: a clearing blow to the gut. It was also a bright blow to the brain, or a sudden beating of brains, with all the charge and intimate grate of rubbed balloons. It emptied our lungs. It felled the
(15) forest, moved the fields, and drained the pond; the world dismantled and tumbled into that black hole of eyes. . . .

Annie Dillard, *Teaching a Stone to Talk.*

42. The author asserts that her encounter with the weasel "felled the forest, moved the fields, and drained the pond" (lines 14–16) because she

  (1) wanted to show the natural setting
  (2) wanted to show what happened
  (3) wanted to heighten the importance of the scene
  (4) wanted to prove the weasel's wildness
  (5) thought that no one would believe her otherwise

Items 43 to 45 refer to the following excerpt from a book.

WHERE IS THE EDGE OF NOWHERE?

My mother was Athabascan, born around 1875 in a little village at the mouth of the Hogatza River, a long day's walk north of the Arctic Circle. The country was
(5) wild enough—blizzards and sixty-below cold all the winter months, and floods when the ice tore loose in spring, swamping the tundra with spongy muskegs so that a man might travel down
(10) the rivers, but could never make a summer portage of more than a mile or so between them.

And the people matched the land. From the earliest time in Alaska, there had been
(15) bad feeling between Indian and Eskimo, and here the two lived close together, forever stirring each other to anger and violence. If an Indian lost his bearings and tracked the caribou past the divide that
(20) separated the two hunting grounds, his people would soon be preparing a potlatch in his memory, for he was almost sure to be shot or ground-sluiced, and his broken body left for the buzzards. Naturally this
(25) worked both ways. Then, in the 1890's, prospectors found gold to the west, on the Seward Peninsula, and the white man came tearing through. Mostly he was mean as a wounded grizzly. He never
(30) thought twice about cheating or stealing from the native people, or even killing a whole family if he needed their dog team— anything to get to Nome and the gold on those beaches.

James Huntington and Lawrence Elliott, *On the Edge of Nowhere.*

43. Which of the following is the best conclusion to draw about spring coming to Alaska?

(1) Women are able to make long journeys to see their families.
(2) It is the best time for prospecting.
(3) Travel is still difficult but not quite as hard as in winter.
(4) The weather becomes pleasant.
(5) The Indians and Eskimos begin fighting.

44. What conclusion can you draw from the author's statement "And the people matched the land" (line 13)?

(1) The white man never thought twice about cheating or stealing.
(2) Even skilled hunters got lost.
(3) A man killed by an enemy was often left unburied.
(4) People's acts were as violent and uncontrollable as the weather.
(5) The people endured cold winters.

45. Which of the following is the best conclusion to draw about the discovery of gold on Seward Peninsula?

(1) Both Indians and Eskimos made great fortunes.
(2) The white man took interest in an area previously inhabited by Indians and Eskimos.
(3) The violence between the Indian and Eskimo decreased.
(4) The country was tamed.
(5) The white man began to work with the Indians and Eskimos.

Items 46 to 50 refer to the following excerpt from an article.

WHAT MAKES THIS EXPERIENCE SPECIAL?

My own awakening to the magical spirit of adventure came in my university days. In Paris, I was a student, dividing my time between law and speculation in the pure

(5) sciences. Then, one February, I had the chance to go to the Alps. I came to a village peacefully hibernating among snow-covered mountains. I started at sunrise and climbed the lower mountain

(10) slopes until I came to a small forest. Far from any inhabited place, I had only myself to count on. The solitude suddenly made me feel extremely vulnerable. I had the sensation that my life was in danger. I was

(15) venturing alone up immense snow slopes. Avalanches were a constant threat.

I was part of nature, like an animal among other animals—white hares, marmots, chamois, jackdaws, foxes. I felt

(20) my muscles acting as muscles naturally should. I was steeped in brilliant sunshine, although I fought against the piercing cold. Finally, worn and hungry, I reached the crest. I had striven against nature like a

(25) primitive man to gain that goal, and suddenly I experienced a vast exultancy.

Maurice Herzog, "Adventure—The Unending Challenge," *Man Against Nature.*

46. It can be concluded from this excerpt that the author thinks adventure consists of

(1) being in Paris
(2) studying law and science
(3) finding a peaceful village somewhere in the Alps
(4) facing the dangers of nature alone
(5) being hungry

47. Which of the following is the best conclusion to draw about the Alps?

(1) Many students go there.
(2) They are snowy, isolated mountains.
(3) Climbers often die in avalanches.
(4) The Alps are near Paris.
(5) Primitive men live there.

48. Why might the author be interested in an opportunity to sail down the Mississippi River on a raft?

(1) He likes to be alone.
(2) It would be a change from the mountains where he lives.
(3) There would not be any animals to watch out for.
(4) It would be a challenge.
(5) There would be a lot of sunshine and fresh air.

49. With which of the following would the author be most likely to identify?

(1) a science book
(2) a classroom
(3) a wolf
(4) a law textbook
(5) a university library

50. From the context you can conclude that the best meaning of "vast exultancy" (line 26) as used in this excerpt is

(1) terrible loneliness
(2) deep weariness
(3) extreme hunger
(4) great joy
(5) great disappointment

Tip **Remember that conclusions are reached through reasoning based on facts.**

Answers are on page 828.

Lesson 3 Drama

Choose the <u>best answer</u> to each item. <u>Items 1 to 4</u> refer to the following excerpt from a play.

WHAT DO DAVID AND LUKE HAVE IN COMMON?

LUKE: You play piano like I dreamed you would.

DAVID: I been finding out lately you was pretty good. Mama never let us keep a
(5)   phonograph. I just didn't never hear any of your records—until here lately. You was right up there with the best, Jellyroll Morton and Louis Armstrong and cats like that. . . .
(10)   You never come to look for us. Why?

LUKE: I started to. I wanted to. I thought of it lots of times.

DAVID: Why didn't you never do it? Did you think it was good riddance we was
(15)   gone?

LUKE: I was hoping you wouldn't never think that, never.

DAVID: I wonder what you expected me to think. I remembered you, but couldn't
(20)   never talk about you. I use to hear about you sometime, but I couldn't never say, That's my daddy. I was too ashamed. I remembered how you used to play for me sometimes. That was
(25)   why I started playing the piano. I used to go to sleep dreaming about the way we'd play together one day, me with my piano and you with your trombone.

LUKE: David. David.

(30) DAVID: You never come. You never come when you could do us some good. You come now, now when you can't do nobody any good. Every time I think about it, think about *you,* I want to
(35)   break down and cry like a baby. You make me—ah! You make me feel so bad.

LUKE: Son—don't try to get away from the things that hurt you. The things that hurt
(40)   you—sometimes that's all you got. You got to learn to live with those things—and—use them.

James Baldwin, *The Amen Corner.*

1. David mainly wants to

   (1) be a musician and leave his family
   (2) forget about his father for good
   (3) be a better musician than his father
   (4) find out what his father thinks of him
   (5) understand his father's absence

2. According to this excerpt, Luke mainly wants to

   (1) show that he can live with pain
   (2) brag about his musical success
   (3) pretend David's pain does not exist
   (4) encourage David to leave home
   (5) tell David what a good pianist he is

3. Which of the following attitudes best describes David's feelings toward Luke as a father?

   (1) admiration and respect
   (2) hurt and anger
   (3) support
   (4) friendliness
   (5) shame

4. Based on the excerpt, David and Luke will most likely

   (1) never speak to each other again
   (2) play music together
   (3) begin to respect each other
   (4) have a violent argument
   (5) forget their sorrows

Items 5 to 10 refer to the following excerpt from a play.

WHAT DOES SHIRLEY DO TO ENTERTAIN HERSELF?

JOHN: You better watch that one. She's gettin' a little big for her pants, ain't you? How old are you now? How old are you?

(5) JUNE: You wouldn't know, of course.

SHIRLEY: Age is the most irrelevant judge of character or maturity that—

JOHN: Yeah, yeah, how old are you?

JUNE: She's thirteen.

(10) SHIRLEY: I am nineteen and I will be twenty next month.

JUNE: She's thirteen.

SHIRLEY: I am eighteen years old, and it is none of your business. . . .

(15) JUNE: She's thirteen.

SHIRLEY: I'm seventeen. If you must know.

JUNE: You are not seventeen, you cretin.

SHIRLEY: I am fifteen years old!

JUNE: She's fourteen. (JOHN picks SHIRLEY

(20) up and carries her over his shoulder to the porch and slams the door on her. All through this, she is screaming: "Put me down, put me down, Rhett Butler, put me down.")

(25) JOHN: (smiles, turns back to the bedroom) Yeah? You better watch that one. (exits to his bedroom)

SHIRLEY: (comes back in, follows him to steps) I happen to, am going to be an

(30) artist, and an artist has no age. . . .

Lanford Wilson, *The Fifth of July.*

5. You can infer that which of the following is true?

(1) Shirley is pleased that June keeps insisting that she is thirteen.
(2) Shirley is an artist.
(3) John and Shirley are used to fighting.
(4) June does not like to tease Shirley.
(5) Shirley does not like to argue.

6. Shirley acts the way she does in order to

(1) antagonize everyone
(2) get experience to use in her art
(3) dramatize herself and get attention
(4) force others to keep track of her birthday
(5) make people see that age is not important

7. Which of the following best describes June's attitude towards Shirley?

(1) disgust
(2) indulgence
(3) apathy
(4) humor
(5) sympathy

8. What would most likely occur if Shirley were asked her age by a stranger?

(1) she would tell the truth
(2) she wouldn't answer
(3) she would start an argument
(4) she would lie
(5) she would ask June how to answer

9. John's attitude towards Shirley can be described as

(1) impatience
(2) love
(3) dislike
(4) imitation
(5) amused concern

10. Which of the following statements best describes Shirley's attitude towards age?

(1) An artist has no age.
(2) Age is irrelevant.
(3) Twenty is the best age to be.
(4) Your age is what you say it is.
(5) Thirteen is a good age to be.

WHAT KIND OF LIVES DO MARTY AND ANGIE LEAD?

ANGIE: Well, what do you feel like doing tonight?

MARTY: I don't know. What do you feel like doing?

(5) ANGIE: Well, we're back to that, huh? I say to you: "What do you feel like doing tonight?" And you say to me: "I don't know, what do you feel like doing?" And then we wind up sitting around the

(10) house with a couple of cans of beer, watching Sid Caesar on television. Well, I tell you what I feel like doing. I feel like calling up Mary Feeney. She likes you. (MARTY *looks up quickly at*

(15) *this.*)

MARTY: What makes you say that?

ANGIE: I could see she likes you.

MARTY: Yeah, sure.

ANGIE: *(Half rising in his seat)* I'll call her

(20) up.

MARTY: You call her up for yourself, Angie. I don't feel like calling her up. (ANGIE *sits down again. They both return to reading the paper for a moment. Then*

(25) ANGIE *looks up again.*)

ANGIE: Boy, you're getting to be a real drag, you know that?

MARTY: Angie, I'm thirty-six years old. I been looking for a girl every Saturday

(30) night of my life. I'm a little, short, fat fellow and girls don't go for me, that's all. I'm not like you. I mean, you joke around, and they laugh at you, and you get along fine. I just stand around like a

(35) bug. What's the sense of kidding myself? Everybody's always telling me to get married. Get married. Get married. Don't you think I wanna get married? I wanna get married. They

(40) drive me crazy. Now, I don't wanna wreck your Saturday night for you, Angie. You wanna go somewhere, you go ahead. I don't wanna go.

ANGIE: Boy, they drive me crazy too. My

(45) old lady, every word outta her mouth, when you gonna get married?

Paddy Chayefsky, "Marty," *Television Plays.*

11. Which of the following best states the theme in this excerpt?

    (1) Marriage is a natural state.
    (2) Saturday nights can be boring.
    (3) Marty is missing opportunities.
    (4) Two people cannot decide what to do on Saturday night.
    (5) Lonely people often stop being socially active.

12. The things Marty and Angie say imply that they both

    (1) spend many evenings calling up women for dates
    (2) want to get married
    (3) spend many evenings sitting around
    (4) are under pressure from each other to get married
    (5) believe they will be married soon

13. You can infer from this excerpt that

    (1) all men want to get married
    (2) Angie is more comfortable with women than Marty
    (3) all unmarried thirty-six-year-old men are lonely
    (4) Marty and Angie dislike each other
    (5) Angie is unwilling to call women on the telephone

14. Which of the following statements about Marty best explains his problem?

    (1) He is thirty-six years old.
    (2) He is short and fat.
    (3) Girls don't go for him.
    (4) He stands around like a bug.
    (5) He is not like Angie.

Items 15 to 18 refer to the following excerpt from a play.

DO THESE ROOMMATES AGREE ABOUT MOST THINGS?

FELIX: . . . *(Gets down on his knees, picks up chips and puts them into box.)* Don't forget I cook and clean and take care of this house. I save us a lot of
(5)   money, don't I?

OSCAR: Yeah, but then you keep me up all night counting it.

FELIX: *(Goes to table and sweeps chips and cards into box.)* Now wait a minute.
(10)   We're not always going at each other. We have some fun too, don't we?

OSCAR: *(Crosses to couch.) Fun?* Felix, getting a clear picture on Channel Two isn't my idea of whoopee.

(15) FELIX: What are you talking about?

OSCAR: All right, what do you and I do every night? *(Takes off sneakers, dropping them on floor.)*

FELIX: What do we do? You mean after
(20)   dinner?

OSCAR: That's right. After we've had your halibut steak and the dishes are done and the sink has been Brillo'd and the pans have been S.O.S.'d and the
(25)   leftovers have been Saran-wrapped— what do we do?

FELIX: *(Finishes clearing table and puts everything on top of bookcase.)* Well, we read . . . we talk . . .

(30) OSCAR: *(Takes off pants and throws them on floor.)* No, no. *I* read and *you* talk! . . . I try to work and you talk. . . . I take a bath and you talk. . . . I go to sleep and you talk. We've got your life arranged
(35)   pretty good but I'm still looking for a little entertainment.

FELIX: *(Pulling upstage kitchen chairs away from table.)* What are you saying? That I talk too much?

(40) OSCAR: *(Sits on couch.)* No, no. I'm not complaining. You have a lot to say. What's worrying me is that I'm beginning to listen. . . .

Neil Simon, *The Odd Couple.*

15. Which of the following sayings comes closest to stating the theme of this excerpt?

(1) Opposites attract.
(2) Beauty is only skin deep.
(3) Do unto others as you would have others do unto you.
(4) A chicken in every pot.
(5) Every rose has its thorn.

16. Which of the following would Felix probably enjoy least?

(1) trying a new recipe
(2) lying around all day
(3) organizing his dresser drawers
(4) balancing his checkbook
(5) dusting

17. Which of the following statements comes closest to what Oscar means when he tells Felix, "Yeah, but then you keep me up all night counting it." (lines 6–7)?

(1) Felix stays up too late at night.
(2) Felix and Oscar share a bedroom.
(3) Felix always reminds Oscar of what he does around the house.
(4) Felix counts money all night long.
(5) Oscar has insomnia.

18. Based upon the information given in the excerpt, which of the following describes Oscar's fear?

(1) Felix will stop cooking and cleaning.
(2) Felix is not saving them money.
(3) Felix will leave.
(4) Oscar is getting used to Felix.
(5) Felix will cook more halibut steak.

Tip **To understand a character, ask yourself what a character does and says. Look at any stage directions involving that character. Then look for clues in the dialogue of other characters to find out how they feel about this character.**

Answers are on page 832.

Choose the <u>best answer</u> to each item.
<u>Items 1 to 8</u> refer to the following poem.

HOW DOES THIS MAN FEEL ABOUT NATURE?

EARTH AND RAIN, THE PLANTS & SUN

    Once near San Ysidro
    on the way to Colorado,
    I stopped and looked.

    The sound of a meadowlark
(5) through smell of fresh cut alfalfa.

    Raho would say,
    "Look, Dad." A hawk

    sweeping
            its wings

(10) clear through
           the blue
    of whole and pure
           the wind
              the sky.

(15) It is writhing
    overhead.
    Hear. The Bringer.
          The Thunderer.

    Sunlight falls
(20) through cloud curtains,
    a straight bright shaft.

    It falls,
        it falls,
        down
(25)   to earth,
    a green plant.

Today, the Katzina* come.
The dancing prayers.

Many times, the Katzina.
(30) The dancing prayers.
It shall not end,
son, it will not end,
this love.
Again and again,
(35) the earth is new again.
They come, listen, listen.
Hold on to your mother's hand.
They come

O great joy, they come.
(40) The plants with bells.
The stones with voices.
Listen, son, hold my hand.

Simon J. Ortiz, *A Good Journey.*

*Southwest Indian masked dancers who, during certain
ceremonial rites, impersonate ancestral spirits.

1. Which of the following is the best restatement of lines 1–3?

   (1) I've moved from San Ysidro to Colorado.
   (2) San Ysidro is on the way to Colorado.
   (3) My schedule did not allow me to stop during my last journey.
   (4) While traveling to Colorado, I stopped to look at the land around San Ysidro.
   (5) The land around Colorado is worth stopping and looking at.

2. What are the dancing prayers mentioned in lines 28 and 30?

   (1) the plants with bells
   (2) the Katzina
   (3) the stones with voices
   (4) the Bringer
   (5) the Thunderer

3. Based on the poem, it can be inferred that the speaker is

   (1) leaving his wife and son
   (2) traveling with his family
   (3) making his journey alone
   (4) recalling the time when he stopped
   (5) on his way to see the Katzina dancers

4. Which of the following phrases best reflects the author's description of the sunlight?

   (1) obscured by the clouds
   (2) reaching earth in shafts of light
   (3) too bright to look at
   (4) so strong that it is killing the plants
   (5) burning his skin

5. What is the mood of this poem?

   (1) joyful
   (2) depressed
   (3) angry
   (4) despondent
   (5) disinterested

6. The phrase "they come" in line 39 refers to

   (1) the mother and son
   (2) the hawks
   (3) the shafts of sunlight coming from the sky
   (4) the renewal of the plants and earth
   (5) the Katzina

7. Which of the following best reflects what the author is describing in this poem?

   (1) a day in the country
   (2) his experience with his son
   (3) the wonders of nature
   (4) the cycle of plant life
   (5) the Katzina dancers

8. We can infer that the poem takes place in which season?

   (1) spring
   (2) summer
   (3) winter
   (4) fall
   (5) there is not enough information to determine the season

Tip **Poems often shift both in time and place. When you read a poem, be certain you understand when and where events take place. Just because an event appears at the beginning of a poem does not necessarily mean that it is the earliest event described in the whole poem.**

Items 9 to 12 refer to the following poem.

WHAT HAS HAPPENED TO THIS PLACE?

CARMEL POINT

The extraordinary patience of things!
This beautiful place defaced with a crop of suburban houses—
How beautiful when we first beheld it,
Unbroken field of poppy and lupin walled with clean cliffs;
(5) No intrusion but two or three horses pasturing,
Or a few milch [milk] cows rubbing their flanks on the outcrop rock-heads—
Now the spoiler has come: does it care?
Not faintly. It has all time. It knows the people are a tide
That swells and in time will ebb, and all
(10) Their works dissolve. Meanwhile the image of the pristine beauty
Lives in the very grain of the granite,
Safe as the endless ocean that climbs our cliff.—As for us:
We must uncenter our minds from ourselves;
We must unhumanize our views a little, and become confident
(15) As the rock and ocean that we were made from.

Robinson Jeffers, *The Selected Poetry of Robinson Jeffers.*

9. Based upon the poem, it can be inferred that the speaker is

   (1) happy with his neighborhood
   (2) sure that everything returns to nature
   (3) impatiently waiting for the neighborhood to disappear
   (4) discussing the merits of this community
   (5) a visitor to the area

10. Which of the following is directly stated by the poem?

   (1) There used to be fields where houses now stand.
   (2) Everyone will someday return to the land.
   (3) Horses prefer empty pastures.
   (4) Man-made monuments eventually take over everything.
   (5) The new housing development includes extended gardens.

11. Which of the following best describes what the poet implies by "It knows the people are a tide/That swells and in time will ebb" (lines 8–9)?

   (1) All people eventually wash out to sea.
   (2) The human population is growing at an ever-increasing rate.
   (3) The town's population will decrease.
   (4) Populations increase and decrease in cycles.
   (5) The community is in danger of falling into the sea.

12. In which of the following locations would the speaker most likely prefer to live?

   (1) in a metropolitan area
   (2) in a highly organized suburb
   (3) in a secluded house by the sea
   (4) in a small town
   (5) in the desert

Items 13 to 16 refer to the following excerpt from a poem.

WHO WAS AFRAID OF FLYING?

MIAMI

It started with the Bay Bridge.
He couldn't take that steel vault into the blue
above the blue, so much horizon!
Then it was the road itself, the rise and fall,
(5)   the continual blind curve.
He hired a chauffeur, he took the train.
Then it was hotels, so many rooms
the same, he had to sleep with the light on.
His courage has shrunk to the size of a windowbox.

(10)   Father who scared the witches and vampires
from my childhood closets, father
who walked before me like a hero's shield
through neighborhoods where hoodlums honed their knives
on concrete, where nerve was law,
(15)   who will drive you home from Miami?
You're broke and I'm a thousand miles away
with frightened children of my own.
Who will rescue you from the garden
where jets flash like swords above your head?

Daniel Mark Epstein, *The Book of Fortune.*

13. Which of the following is the best meaning of "where nerve was law" (line 14)?

    (1) where the police were nervous
    (2) where people were very calm
    (3) where people had to be brave to survive
    (4) where hoodlums made the rules
    (5) where the law was respected

14. According to this poem, when the speaker was young, his father had been a symbol of

    (1) evil
    (2) cowardice
    (3) hatred
    (4) fearlessness
    (5) justice

15. Which of the following statements best describes the main idea of the excerpt?

    (1) Parents and children eventually change roles.
    (2) Miami is a dangerous city to drive around.
    (3) Children are unwilling to help their parents when they need it.
    (4) Miami is far away from the author.
    (5) The Bay Bridge is made of steel.

16. Based on the context, which of the following is the best meaning for "honed" (line 13)?

    (1) shined
    (2) polished
    (3) sharpened
    (4) buffed
    (5) broke

Items 17 to 19 refer to the following poem.

WHO ARE THE MIGRANTS?

MIGRANTS

Birds obeying migration maps etched in their brains
Never revised their Interstate routes.
Some of them still stop off in Washington, D.C.

This autumn evening as the lights of the Pentagon
(5) Come on like the glare of urgent trouble through surgery
      skylights,
Come on like a far-off hope of control,

I watch a peaceful V-sign of Canada Geese
Lower their landing gear, slip to rest on the slicky Potomac,
(10) Break rank and huddle with the bobbing power boats.

Wings of jets beating the air, taking turns for the landing—
Pterodactyls circling the filled-in swamps under National Airport.
There is a great wild honking

Of traffic on the bridges—
(15) The daily homing of migrants with headlights dimmed
Who loop and bank by instinct along broken white lines.

Roderick Jellema, *Something Tugging the Line.*

17. Which statement best describes what the poet is doing in the poem?

  (1) He is comparing spring and fall.
  (2) He is comparing the river and the airport.
  (3) He is contrasting boats and jets.
  (4) He is contrasting the geese and the Interstate highway.
  (5) He is comparing the commuters and the geese.

18. In lines 9–12, the poet suggests an image of the geese as

  (1) the wings of pterodactyls
  (2) bobbing power boats
  (3) airplanes landing
  (4) the swamps by the airport
  (5) a smooth river

19. What is the poet suggesting about commuters when he uses the image of the birds following a migration map?

  (1) The commuters have maps etched on their brains.
  (2) Commuters follow habits like the geese.
  (3) He does not like commuters.
  (4) Commuters wish they could fly away like the geese.
  (5) Commuters are confused about where they are going and need a map.

Items 20 to 24 refer to the following poem.

WHERE CAN YOU GO WITHOUT LEAVING HOME?

TRAVELING AT HOME

Even in a country you know by heart
it's hard to go the same way twice.
The life of the going changes.
The chances change and make a new way.
(5)   Any tree or stone or bird
Can be the bud of a new direction. The
natural connection is to make intent
of accident. To get back before dark
is the art of going.

Wendell Berry, *The Collected Poems, 1957-1982.*

20. What does the poet mean by "Any tree or stone or bird / Can be the bud of a new direction" (lines 5–6)?

    (1) Stones, trees, and birds are good guideposts.
    (2) Stones, trees, and birds are unfriendly to travelers on life's road.
    (3) A person can read hidden meaning in the world of nature.
    (4) Like trees and birds, stones are alive.
    (5) Small things can change the direction of a person's life.

21. Which of the following is the most likely reason for the poet's choice of the word "accident" (line 8)?

    (1) as a warning to be careful
    (2) to explain the art of going
    (3) to explain where new directions lead
    (4) to emphasize the idea of chance
    (5) to explain the word "intent"

22. What is the best restatement of "a country you know by heart" (line 1)?

    (1) a loving home
    (2) a distant land
    (3) a familiar place
    (4) a boring place
    (5) a memorized path

23. Which statement best reflects the main idea of this poem?

    (1) People who travel should always take maps to avoid getting lost.
    (2) Even the most experienced traveler will not be able to go exactly the same way every time.
    (3) The art of living involves shaping chance happenings to your own purposes.
    (4) People should be prepared not to reach their destinations before dark.
    (5) Travelers risk having motor vehicle accidents.

24. Why is the poem called "Traveling at Home"?

    (1) A traveler always goes home eventually.
    (2) The poem compares decisions one makes in life to those a traveler makes.
    (3) All travel starts from a traveler's home.
    (4) You can read books or watch television about travel.
    (5) Home is where the traveler's heart is.

Tip **Remember, poets often want to help their readers look at the world in a new way. To understand how they do this, look for ordinary words used in figurative ways.**

Answers are on page 833.

Choose the <u>best answer</u> to each item. <u>Items 1 to 3</u> refer to the following excerpt from a short story.

WHAT DOES THE FUTURE HOLD FOR MADGE?

Madge Dyett felt that the year 1937, which had marked for so many of her friends a turning point in the Great Depression, seemed only to confirm its
(5) permanent doom for herself and her parents. They continued to live in the shabby, four-story, red brick house on East Thirty-fourth Street, but only because they could not sell it, and the top floor was
(10) rented to an uncle and aunt. Her father was out of work and prattled all day, with a self-confidence that nothing could justify, of his financial prospects and plans. Madge had had to give up college and
(15) take a job teaching at Miss Fairfax's School, of which she and her mother were alumnae. Her only future seemed to be to stay there until she was old enough to retire.
(20) She had a vision of herself that was jarred every time she caught her reflection in an unanticipated glass. When she was prepared for the vision—gazing affectionately into her bedroom mirror,
(25) carefully turned from the garish sunlight, a long tress of brown hair pushed artfully across her high forehead, the small, full, pink lips half-open and a brooding expression in her grave brown eyes—she
(30) could at least try to see herself as an emancipated young woman of the years immediately following the war, some poetess or social worker of 1922, wasp-waisted, plainly dressed, earnest,
(35) idealistic. But the figure that she saw suddenly thrust at herself in the long mirror of a hotel lobby, even if thin and trim enough, suggested nervousness and fatigue. Nor was there any question that
(40) the left cheek on that long, perhaps lugubrious face bore two pockmarks. Oh, yes, she was angular!

Louis Auchincloss, "Charade," *Narcissa and Other Fables.*

1. Which of the following sentences best states the main idea of the first paragraph?

   (1) Madge had to help support her family by teaching.
   (2) The Great Depression forced people to sell their homes.
   (3) Madge and her parents seemed permanently doomed by the Great Depression.
   (4) Many people during the Great Depression had to live in shabby houses.
   (5) The year 1937 was a turning point in Madge's life.

2. Which of the following details does <u>not</u> support the main idea of the first paragraph?

   (1) Madge and her mother had graduated from Miss Fairfax's School.
   (2) The family was unable to sell the house.
   (3) Madge had to quit college.
   (4) Mr. Dyett was out of work.
   (5) Mr. Dyett had no reason to be confident about his finances.

3. Which of the following sentences best states the main idea of the second paragraph?

   (1) Madge has an angular body.
   (2) Madge's body and face were showing the signs of her experiences with hardship.
   (3) Madge was pleased with the way she looked.
   (4) Madge sometimes appeared tired.
   (5) Madge had a pockmarked face.

Items 4 and 5 refer to the following poem.

WHERE IS THE SPEAKER'S FAMILY FROM?

ELLIS ISLAND

Beyond the red brick of Ellis Island
where the two Slovak children
who became my grandparents
waited the long days of quarantine,
(5)   after leaving the sickness,
the old Empires of Europe,
a Circle Line ship slips easily
on its way to the island
of the tall woman, green
(10) as dreams of forests and meadows
waiting for those who'd worked
a thousand years
yet never owned their own.

Like millions of others,
(15) I too come to this island,
nine decades the answerer
of dreams.

Yet only one part of my blood loves that memory.
Another voice speaks
(20) of native lands
within this nation.
Lands invaded
when the earth became owned.
Lands of those who followed
(25) the changing Moon,
knowledge of the seasons
in their veins.

Joseph Bruchac, *The Remembered Earth.*

4. Who is the speaker referring to when he says, "the tall woman, green as dreams of forests and meadows" (lines 9–10)?

(1) the speaker's grandmother
(2) a woman who lives on an island
(3) the Statue of Liberty
(4) the mother of the two Slovak children
(5) a nurse

5. What does the speaker mean when he says, "Another voice speaks of native lands within this nation" (lines 19–21)?

(1) the Moon
(2) the captain of the Circle Line ship
(3) the Empires of Europe
(4) the speaker's Native American heritage
(5) the speaker's Slovak heritage

Answers are on page 835.

Popular Literature ◆ Review

437

Classical Literature

Lesson ⑤   Fiction/Nonfiction

Choose the best answer to each item.
Items 1 to 9 refer to the following excerpt from a biography.

WHERE WILL ISHI GO?

The black face of the white man's Demon rushed toward the platform, pouring out clouds of sparks and smoke, and filling the ears with its hollow, moaning
(5) voice. Mill Creek and Deer Creek were within range of the sound of that voice; twice a day Ishi had heard it ever since he could remember, and he had watched the train hundreds of times as it snaked along
(10) below him, bellowing and belching. His mother had reassured him as a small boy when he was afraid of it, telling him that it was a Demon who followed white men wherever they went, but that Indians need
(15) have no fear of it; it never bothered them.

Today, Ishi wondered. He had not been so near it before; it was larger and noisier and speedier than he had realized. Would the Demon know that he was Indian? He
(20) was wearing white men's clothes, and his hair was short like theirs. It might be as well to watch from a little distance, from the shelter of a tree or bush, as he was accustomed to, at least until he made sure
(25) that his friend was correct in his assurance that the Demon always stayed in its own old tracks, and that it carried people safely from place to place. He stepped behind a cottonwood tree alongside the platform.
(30) The Demon drew up beside the station and came to a halt. Ishi saw that it was as his friend had said—it did not leave its tracks. The white men who should have the most reason to be afraid, showed no
(35) signs of uneasiness, rather they climbed in and out of it, and one of them sat in its head waving to those below. Ishi came back onto the platform, and made no objection to going aboard with Waterman.

(40) He had committed himself too far to turn back, nor did he wish to do so; where his new friend led he would follow.

During the trip, Ishi sat very quiet. He found the speed of the train exciting; also
(45) the view through the window of hills and fields and houses racing in and out of sight. He averted his eyes from the strangers in the car, blotting out their nearness by not looking directly at them.
(50) The Demon carried them rapidly down its old tracks and after some hours onto a ferry boat which took them, engine, cars, and passengers, across Carquinez Straits. Waterman pointed out to him that this was
(55) where the Sacramento and San Joaquin rivers join, flow into the bay, and out the Golden Gate to the ocean. Like all inland Indians, Ishi knew that such was the destination of the creeks and rivers of his
(60) home, but, again like other inlanders, he was vague about how the river journey was actually accomplished, for his informants had known of it only traditionally and at many removes from
(65) any one who had seen either river mouth or ocean. He was sorry to leave the train at the Oakland Mole, but ahead lay further wonders—another ferry trip, this time across the bay to San Francisco; and after
(70) that, a long ride in a trolley car to the Museum of Anthropology.

Theodora Kroeber, *Ishi in Two Worlds: A Biography of the Last Wild Indian in North America.*

---

1. According to the excerpt, Ishi is

   (1) a demon
   (2) used to riding on trains
   (3) about to get on a train for the first time
   (4) not going to board the train
   (5) sure the train will leave its tracks

2. The excerpt is written

   (1) as if the author knows what the character is thinking
   (2) in Ishi's own words
   (3) in the form of a diary
   (4) by a person who did not understand Ishi
   (5) by another Indian

3. Which of the following best describes how the author feels about the subject?

   (1) fearful
   (2) confused
   (3) sympathetic
   (4) bored
   (5) angry

4. The author uses her description of the train to

   (1) explain why white men like trains
   (2) emphasize how Ishi saw the train as being alive
   (3) prove that trains are evil
   (4) make the reader uneasy
   (5) suggest the reason for the failure of the railroad

5. From the excerpt you can infer that

   (1) Ishi misses his mother
   (2) Waterman is not familiar with trains
   (3) Waterman is Ishi's brother
   (4) Ishi had never expected to ride a train
   (5) the train had arrived on schedule

6. The phrase "hollow, moaning voice" (lines 4–5) probably refers to

   (1) the noise of the passengers getting on and off the train
   (2) the clank of the train's wheels
   (3) a noise Ishi made as a child to imitate the sound of the train
   (4) the hooting of the train's whistle
   (5) the clouds of smoke and sparks that pour out of the train

7. Based upon the excerpt, Ishi will most likely have which of the following reactions to the trolley car?

   (1) resistance to experiencing another white man's invention
   (2) excitement at another new experience
   (3) disappointment that the trolley does not move as fast as the train
   (4) disgust at the replacement of older forms of transportation
   (5) a desire to get a job as a train conductor

8. The author suggests that the train route is important to Ishi because

   (1) it will be the only time he ever experiences a train ride
   (2) it gives him time to get to know Waterman
   (3) it lets him experience the journey of rivers and creeks
   (4) it allows him to experience technology
   (5) it is the means to his reaching San Francisco

9. The excerpt is told from the point of view of

   (1) Ishi
   (2) Ishi's mother
   (3) the demon
   (4) Waterman
   (5) a person who is not a character in the story

Items 10 to 13 refer to the following excerpt from a short story.

WHAT DOES ROSICKY THINK ABOUT THE GRAVEYARD?

After he had gone eight miles, he came to the graveyard, which lay just at the edge of his own hay-land. There he stopped his horses and sat still on his
(5) wagon seat, looking about at the snowfall. Over yonder on the hill he could see his own house, crouching low, with the clump of orchard behind and the windmill before, and all down the gentle hill-slope the rows
(10) of pale gold cornstalks stood out against the white field. The snow was falling over the cornfield and the pasture and the hay-land, steadily, with very little wind,—a nice dry snow. The graveyard had only a light
(15) wire fence about it and was all overgrown with long red grass. The fine snow, settling into this red grass and upon the few little evergreens and the headstones, looked very pretty.
(20) It was a nice graveyard, Rosicky reflected, sort of snug and homelike, not cramped or mournful,—a big sweep all round it. A man could lie down in the long grass and see the complete arch of the
(25) sky over him, hear the wagons go by; in summer the mowing-machine rattled right up to the wire fence. And it was so near home. Over there across the cornstalks his own roof and windmill looked so good
(30) to him that he promised himself to mind the Doctor and take care of himself. He was awful fond of his place, he admitted. He wasn't anxious to leave it. And it was a comfort to think that he would never have
(35) to go farther than the edge of his own hayfield. The snow, falling over his barnyard and the graveyard, seemed to draw things together like. And they were all old neighbors in the graveyard, most of
(40) them friends; there was nothing to feel awkward or embarrassed about. Embarrassment was the most disagreeable feeling Rosicky knew. He didn't often have it,—only with certain
(45) people whom he didn't understand at all.

Willa Cather, "Neighbor Rosicky."

10. Which of the following best states the main idea of this excerpt?

   (1) Rosicky thinks this graveyard would be a comfortable place to end up in.
   (2) Rosicky's friends and neighbors are dead and buried.
   (3) Rosicky is afraid of dying.
   (4) The graveyard is a very depressing place.
   (5) Rosicky is worried that the graveyard is too close to his barnyard.

11. The image of the snow on the graveyard and the barnyard supports the main idea by suggesting that

   (1) winter is the season of death
   (2) seasons affect how people act
   (3) everything gets buried at one time or another
   (4) the two places are not all that different
   (5) people will start burying their dead in the barnyard

12. Which of the following does not describe the graveyard?

   (1) It was next to a hayfield near his house.
   (2) There was a clump of orchard behind it.
   (3) It was surrounded by a wire fence.
   (4) It was overgrown with long red grass.
   (5) There was a comfortable feeling about it.

13. As he looks at the graveyard, Rosicky feels

   (1) peaceful
   (2) sad
   (3) awkward
   (4) cheerful
   (5) embarrassed

Items 14 to 16 refer to the following excerpt from an essay.

WHO IS THIS FINE YOUNG COUPLE?

So now at the turn of the road I saw one of these pictures. It might have been called "The Sailor's Homecoming" or some such title. A fine young sailor carrying a
(5) bundle; a girl with her hand on his arm; neighbours gathering round; a cottage garden ablaze with flowers; as one passed one read at the bottom of that picture that the sailor was back from China, and there
(10) was a fine spread waiting for him in the parlour; and he had a present for his young wife in his bundle; and she was soon going to bear him their first child. Everything was right and good and as it
(15) should be, one felt about that picture.

There was something wholesome and satisfactory in the sight of such happiness; life seemed sweeter and more enviable than before.

(20) So thinking I passed them, filling in the picture as fully, as completely as I could, noticing the colour of her dress, of his eyes, seeing the sandy cat slinking round the cottage door.

(25) For some time the picture floated in my eyes, making most things appear much brighter, warmer, and simpler than usual; and making some things appear foolish; and some things wrong and some things
(30) right, and more full of meaning than before. At odd moments during that day and the next the picture returned to one's mind, and one thought with envy, but with kindness, of the happy sailor and his wife;
(35) one wondered what they were doing, what they were saying now.

Virginia Woolf, "Three Pictures," *The Death of the Moth and Other Essays.*

14. If the author continued to "fill in the picture," which of the following would she be most likely to come up with?

(1) a fight between the sailor and his wife
(2) a quarrel between the couple and their neighbors
(3) a happy scene around the fireplace
(4) the girl cleaning the oven while the sailor watches television
(5) the sailor discovering that he cannot find a job

15. This author draws a conclusion from the four details in lines 4–7 when she says that

(1) the sight was satisfactory
(2) the scene could be called "The Sailor's Homecoming"
(3) life seemed sweeter than it had before
(4) she noticed the sandy cat at the cottage door
(5) she thought about the couple with envy and kindness

16. Which of the following best describes what the author means by "making some things appear foolish" (line 28)?

(1) The behavior of the sailor and his wife appeared foolish.
(2) All other people and events appeared foolish after the author viewed the couple.
(3) After seeing the couple, the author found it difficult to look at the world in the same way.
(4) The author felt foolish having spent so much time staring at the sailor and his wife.
(5) The author ridiculed other parts of the couple's life.

Tip **In order to make inferences about an excerpt, you should look both at what is directly stated and at what is implied by the author. Descriptive words and supporting details provide good clues for making inferences.**

IS IT POSSIBLE TO RECAPTURE THE PLEASURES OF THE PAST?

One summer, along about 1904, my father rented a camp on a lake in Maine and took us all there for the month of August. We all got ringworm from some
(5) kittens and had to rub Pond's Extract on our arms and legs night and morning, and my father rolled over in a canoe with all his clothes on; but outside of that the vacation was a success and from then on
(10) none of us ever thought there was any place in the world like that lake in Maine. We returned summer after summer— always on August 1 for one month. I have since become a salt-water man, but
(15) sometimes in summer there are days when the restlessness of the tides and the fearful cold of the sea water and the incessant wind which blows across the afternoon and into the evening make me
(20) wish for the placidity of a lake in the woods. A few weeks ago this feeling got so strong I bought myself a couple of bass hooks and a spinner and returned to the lake where we used to go, for a week's
(25) fishing and to revisit old haunts.

I took along my son, who had never had any fresh water up his nose and who had seen lily pads only from train windows. On the journey over to the lake I began to
(30) wonder what it would be like. I wondered how time would have marred this unique, this holy spot—the coves and streams, the hills that the sun set behind, the camps and paths behind the camps. I was sure
(35) the tarred road would have found it out and I wondered in what other ways it would be desolated. It is strange how much you can remember about places like that once you allow your mind to return
(40) into the grooves which lead back. You remember one thing, and that suddenly reminds you of another thing. I guess I remembered clearest of all the early mornings, when the lake was cool and
(45) motionless, remembered how the bedroom smelled of the lumber it was made of and of the wet woods whose

scent entered through the screen. The partitions in the camp were thin and did
(50) not extend clear to the top of the rooms, and as I was always the first up I would dress softly so as not to wake the others, and sneak out into the sweet outdoors and start out in the canoe, keeping close along
(55) the shore in the long shadows of the pines. I remembered being very careful never to rub my paddle against the gunwale for fear of disturbing the stillness of the cathedral. . . .
(60) I was right about the tar: it led to within half a mile of the shore. But when I got back there, with my boy, and we settled into a camp near a farmhouse and into the kind of summertime I had known, I could
(65) tell that it was going to be pretty much the same as it had been before—I knew it, lying in bed the first morning, smelling the bedroom and hearing the boy sneak quietly out and go off along the shore in a
(70) boat. I began to sustain the illusion that he was I, and therefore, by simple transposition, that I was my father. This sensation persisted, kept cropping up all the time we were there. It was not an
(75) entirely new feeling, but in this setting it grew much stronger. I seemed to be living a dual existence. I would be in the middle of some simple act, I would be picking up a bait box or laying down a table fork, or I
(80) would be saying something, and suddenly it would be not I but my father who was saying the words or making the gesture. It gave me a creepy sensation.

E. B. White, "Once More to the Lake," *Essays of E. B. White*.

17. We know that this excerpt is from an informal essay because it

    (1) is very serious and dignified
    (2) reads like a scientific report
    (3) deals with abstract principles
    (4) has an easygoing, chatty style
    (5) takes a cool, impersonal tone

18. The author decided to return to the lake in order to

    (1) visit his elderly father
    (2) enjoy some saltwater fishing
    (3) visit the cathedral there
    (4) teach his son canoeing
    (5) re-experience its peacefulness

19. Before going to the lake, the author was afraid "the tarred road would have found it out" (line 35). By this he means he feared that

    (1) the road would no longer be there
    (2) civilization had come to this secluded spot of nature
    (3) a tar factory would have been started there
    (4) there would have been little change there
    (5) no one had paved the road yet

20. Which of the following details was not part of the author's memories of the lakeside camp?

    (1) fishing for bass
    (2) riding horses
    (3) the scent of the pine woods
    (4) the stillness of the lake
    (5) getting up very early

21. By "incessant wind" (line 18), the author means that the wind

    (1) never stopped blowing
    (2) was polluted
    (3) brought thunderstorms
    (4) blew in gale-force gusts
    (5) could not be counted on

22. The main implication in this excerpt, which the author does not state directly, is his

    (1) religious feeling about nature
    (2) disapproval of all signs of progress
    (3) longing to recapture the joys of youth
    (4) disillusionment with vacations by the sea
    (5) passion for freshwater fishing

23. By stating that his son "never had any fresh water up his nose" (lines 26–27), the author means that

    (1) his son was very good at swimming
    (2) his son hated the water
    (3) his son had never been in the water
    (4) his son had never experienced swimming in a lake
    (5) his son was used to swimming pools

24. Which of the following best describes what the author means by "dual existence" (line 77)?

    (1) he was developing two personalities
    (2) he was experiencing the lake as both himself and as his father
    (3) he was becoming both a salt-water and a fresh-water man
    (4) he and his son were living together
    (5) his son was becoming more like the author while at the lake

25. The best meaning of "placidity" (line 20) is

    (1) warmth
    (2) calm
    (3) shade
    (4) freshness
    (5) excitement

Items 26 to 30 refer to the following excerpt from an autobiography.

WHAT DOES BLACK ELK DO ON THE HUNT?

I was well enough to go along on my pony, but I was not old enough to hunt. So we little boys scouted around and watched the hunters; and when we would see a
(5) bunch of bison coming, we would yell "Yuhoo" like the others, but nobody noticed us.

When the butchering was all over, they hung the meat across the horses' backs
(10) and fastened it with strips of fresh bison hide. On the way back to the village all the hunting horses were loaded, and we little boys who could not wait for the feast helped ourselves to all the raw liver we
(15) wanted. Nobody got cross when we did this.

During this time, women back at camp were cutting long poles and forked sticks to make drying racks for the meat. When
(20) the hunters got home they threw their meat in piles on the leaves of trees.

Then the advisers all went back into the council tepee, and from all directions the people came bringing gifts of meat to
(25) them, and the advisers all cried "Hya-a-a-a!," after which they sang for those who had brought them the good gifts. And when they had eaten all they could, the crier shouted to the people: "All come
(30) home! It is more than I can eat!" And people from all over the camp came to get a little of the meat that was left over.

The women were all busy cutting the meat into strips and hanging it on the
(35) racks to dry. You could see red meat hanging everywhere. The people feasted all night long and danced and sang. Those were happy times.

Black Elk, as told through John G. Neihardt (Flaming Rainbow), *Black Elk Speaks*.

26. At the time this person is telling his story, he probably is

(1) a boy
(2) a hunter
(3) a grown man
(4) very happy
(5) quite healthy

27. The style of this excerpt is

(1) very formal
(2) simple and direct
(3) complex and confusing
(4) wordy but lively
(5) informal and humorous

28. Which of the following is not true according to this excerpt?

(1) Everyone in camp gets some of the bison meat.
(2) The meat is prepared on drying racks.
(3) The advisers receive the first meat from the hunt.
(4) Everyone in the village goes on the hunt.
(5) The boys are allowed to watch the hunt.

29. The author remembers the hunt as

(1) an extended time to work for hunters, advisers, and women
(2) the opportunity to prove his maturity
(3) a time when he could do things that would otherwise not be permitted
(4) the period of time during which his mother would be absent from the camp
(5) a dreaded event—one to avoid and be fearful of

30. Which of the following is an effect of the author telling his own life's story?

(1) an emotional distance from the topic
(2) a scientific observation
(3) an impartial history
(4) a sense of intimacy
(5) an unbelievable story

Items 31 to 34 refer to the following excerpt from a book.

WHAT IS THE SIGNIFICANCE OF CARTER DRUSE'S DECISION?

The sleeping sentinel in the clump of laurel was a young Virginian named Carter Druse. He was the son of wealthy parents, an only child, and had known such ease
(5)   and cultivation and high living as wealth and taste were able to command in the mountain country of western Virginia. His home was but a few miles from where he now lay. One morning he had risen from
(10) the breakfast-table and said, quietly but gravely: "Father, a Union regiment has arrived at Grafton. I am going to join it."
       The father lifted his leonine head, looked at the son a moment in silence, and
(15) replied: "Well, go, sir, and whatever may occur do what you conceive to be your duty. Virginia, to which you are a traitor, must get on without you. Should we both live to the end of the war, we will speak
(20) further of the matter. Your mother, as the physician has informed you, is in a most critical condition; at the best she cannot be with us longer than a few weeks, but that time is precious. It would be better not to
(25) disturb her."
       So Carter Druse, bowing reverently to his father, who returned the salute with a stately courtesy that masked a breaking heart, left the home of his childhood to go
(30) soldiering. By conscience and courage, by deeds of devotion and daring, he soon commended himself to his fellows and his officers; and it was to these qualities and to some knowledge of the country that he
(35) owed his selection for his present perilous duty at the extreme outpost.

Ambrose Bierce, *A Horseman in the Sky*.

Tip   One way to find an unstated main idea in fiction is to list facts about the main character. Use these facts to make a general description of the character or the character's actions. The description should help lead you to the main idea.

31. The best statement of the main idea of this excerpt is

    (1) Carter Druse is a coward and a traitor to his country
    (2) Carter Druse acts on his beliefs no matter what the consequences
    (3) Carter's mother died of a broken heart
    (4) War is an evil thing
    (5) Carter Druse is a soldier in the Union Army

32. Which of these details supports the main idea?

    (1) Carter's father salutes his son.
    (2) Carter comes from Virginia.
    (3) Carter leaves although his mother is dying.
    (4) Carter leaves although his father will never speak to him again.
    (5) Carter returns to Virginia when he is in the army.

33. Which of the following do you think Carter would be most likely to do?

    (1) run away from a battle
    (2) lie to one of his officers
    (3) keep a difficult promise
    (4) desert to the Southern army
    (5) steal from his father

34. Which of the following statements best describes Carter's father?

    (1) a man who cares little for his wife and son
    (2) a demanding individual who wants Carter to follow in his footsteps
    (3) a coward who wants to avoid his responsibilities
    (4) a man of honor who respects his son's beliefs
    (5) a poor man with simple tastes

IS ELOPING WITH DIAMELEN WORTH ANY SACRIFICE?

　　　　We ran down to the water. I saw a low hut above the black mud, and a small canoe hauled up. I heard another shot behind me. I thought, "That is his last

(5)　charge." We rushed down to the canoe; a man came running from the hut, but I leaped on him, and we rolled together in the mud. Then I got up, and he lay still at my feet. I don't know whether I had killed

(10)　him or not. I and Diamelen pushed the canoe afloat. I heard yells behind me, and I saw my brother run across the glade. Many men were bounding after him. I took her in my arms and threw her into the

(15)　boat, then leaped in myself. When I looked back I saw that my brother had fallen. He fell and was up again, but the men were closing round him. He shouted, "I am coming!" The men were close to him. I

(20)　looked. Many men. Then I looked at her. Tuan, I pushed the canoe! I pushed it into deep water. She was kneeling forward, looking at me, and I said, "Take your paddle," while I struck the water with mine.

(25)　Tuan, I heard him cry. I heard him cry my name twice; and I heard voices shouting, "Kill! Strike!" I never turned back. I heard him calling my name again with a great shriek, as when life is going out together

(30)　with the voice—and I never turned my head. My own name! . . . My brother! Three times he called—but I was not afraid of life. Was she not there in that canoe? And could I not with her find a

(35)　country where death is forgotten—where death is unknown?

Joseph Conrad, *The Lagoon*.

35. The narrator let his brother be killed because the narrator

(1) relied on others to save him
(2) was busy saving the woman he loved
(3) did not realize he was in trouble
(4) wanted to get him out of the way
(5) did not really care about him

36. Letting his brother die has made the narrator feel

(1) secretly glad
(2) self-justified
(3) guilt-ridden
(4) nonchalant
(5) resentful

37. The brother dies while helping the narrator

(1) escape from enemy prison
(2) rescue a maiden in distress
(3) kill his enemy
(4) complete a spying mission
(5) run away with his beloved

38. The narrator probably hopes that he will be able to

(1) completely forget about his brother
(2) join his brother again when he dies
(3) avenge his brother's death
(4) stop feeling guilty about the death of his brother
(5) convince Diamelen to stop feeling bad about the death of his brother

39. What probably would have happened if the narrator had waited for his brother?

(1) Both brothers would have escaped with Diamelen.
(2) Both brothers would have escaped, but Diamelen would have been caught.
(3) The narrator would have been killed, and his brother would have left with Diamelen.
(4) Both brothers would have been killed.
(5) Diamelen would have left both brothers behind.

Items 40 to 43 refer to the following excerpt from an essay.

WHAT DID LOUIE ACHIEVE IN LIFE?

Louie left Recco in 1905, when he was close to eighteen. "I loved my family," he says, "and it tore me in two to leave, but I had five brothers and two sisters, and all
(5)   my brothers were younger than me, and there were already too many fishermen in Recco, and the bathhouse brought in just so much, and I had a fear kept persisting there might not be enough at
(10)   home to go around in time to come, so I got passage from Genoa to New York scrubbing pots in the galley of a steamship and went straight from the dock to a chophouse on East 138th Street in the Bronx that was operated by a man named
(15)   Capurro who came from Recco. Capurro knew my father when they both were boys." . . . For the next twenty-three years, [Louie] worked as a waiter in restaurants all over Manhattan and Brooklyn. . . . In
(20)   the winter of 1930, he decided to risk his savings and become his own boss. "At that time," he says, "the stockmarket crash had shook everything up and the depression was setting in, and I knew of
(25)   several restaurants in midtown that could be bought at a bargain—lease, furnishings, and good will. All were up-to-date places. Then I ran into a waiter I used to work with and he told me about this old
(30)   run-down restaurant in an old run-down building in the fish market that was for sale, and I went and saw it, and I took it. The reason I did, Fulton Fish Market reminds me of Recco. There's a world of
(35)   difference between them. At the same time, they're very much alike—the fish smell, the general gone-to-pot look, the trading that goes on in the streets, the roofs over the sidewalks, the cats in
(40)   corners gnawing on fish heads, the gulls in the gutters, the way everybody's on to everybody else, the quarreling and the arguing."

Joseph Mitchell, "Up in the Old Hotel," *Read to Write.*

40. Which is the best conclusion about why Louie left Recco (an Italian town)?

    (1) He was eighteen, of legal age.
    (2) There was no room in the house.
    (3) He did not want to support his younger brothers and sisters.
    (4) There was not enough work in Recco to support his family.
    (5) He did not want to live much longer with the problems of five brothers and two sisters.

41. Which is the best reason for the use of Louie's own words in this essay?

    (1) It helps make the character of Louie come alive.
    (2) It contrasts with the informal style of the essay.
    (3) It hides the fact that the author did not understand Louie.
    (4) It emphasizes the formal tone.
    (5) It shows how Louie disagrees with the author.

42. Which of the following is not stated in the excerpt?

    (1) Louie's restaurant opened during the Depression.
    (2) The first restaurant Louie worked in was in Brooklyn.
    (3) The Fulton Fish Market reminds Louie of Recco.
    (4) Everyone quarrels at the Fulton Fish Market.
    (5) Louie opened his own restaurant in 1930.

43. From Louie's choice of a restaurant to buy, you can infer that he

    (1) is a smart businessman
    (2) likes fish
    (3) is sentimental
    (4) likes to argue
    (5) couldn't afford to buy a restaurant that was in good condition

Items 44 to 47 refer to the following excerpt from an autobiography.

WILL THIS AUTHOR EVER GO BACK TO SCHOOL?

The morning came, without any warning, when my sisters surrounded me, wrapped me in scarves, tied up my bootlaces, thrust a cap on my head, and stuffed a baked
(5) potato in my pocket.

"What's this?" I said. . . .

They picked me up bodily, kicking and bawling, and carried me up to the road.

"Boys who don't go to school get put into
(10) boxes, and turn into rabbits, and get chopped up Sundays."

I felt this was overdoing it rather, but I said no more after that. I arrived at the school just three feet tall and fatly wrapped
(15) in my scarves. The playground roared like a rodeo, and the potato burned through my thigh. Old boots, ragged stockings, torn trousers and skirts, went skating and skidding around me. The rabble closed in;
(20) I was encircled; grit flew in my face like shrapnel. Tall girls with frizzled hair, and huge boys with sharp elbows, began to prod me with hideous interest. They plucked at my scarves, spun me round like
(25) a top, screwed my nose, and stole my potato. . . .

"What's the matter, Loll? Didn't he like it at school, then?"

"They never gave me the present!"
(30) "Present? What present?"

"They said they'd give me a present."

"Well, now, I'm sure they didn't."

"They did! They said: 'You're Laurie Lee, ain't you? Well, just you sit here for the
(35) present.' I sat there all day but I never got it. I ain't going back there again!"

But after a week I felt like a veteran and grew as ruthless as anyone else. Somebody had stolen my baked potato, so
(40) I swiped somebody else's apple. . . . This tiny, white-washed Infants' room was a brief but cosy anarchy. In that short time allowed us we played and wept, broke things, fell asleep, cheeked the teacher,
(45) discovered the things we could do to each other, and exhaled our last guiltless days.

Laurie Lee, *Cider with Rosie.*

44. The theme of this excerpt is

    (1) school is dreadful
    (2) school is wonderful
    (3) schooling should not be forced
    (4) people adapt to new situations
    (5) young teachers are understanding

45. The author now regards his early schooling with

    (1) fear and distaste
    (2) anger and disbelief
    (3) fond amusement
    (4) reluctant admiration
    (5) bitter resentment

46. Which of the following is the best meaning for "rabble" (line 19)?

    (1) disorderly mob
    (2) quiet, shy individual
    (3) young child
    (4) orderly group of scholars
    (5) tall girls with frizzled hair

47. Which of the following best describes what the author means by "last guiltless days" (line 46)?

    (1) The author feels guilty for how he treated his teacher.
    (2) The author is remembering his early childhood as free of remorse.
    (3) The author's sisters felt bad for dragging him to school.
    (4) The excerpt is the author's apology to his schoolmates.
    (5) The author is confessing his theft of an apple.

Items 48 to 52 refer to the following excerpt from an essay.

WOULD YOU HIRE THIS MAN?

As for my own business, even that kind of surveying which I could do with most satisfaction my employers do not want. They would prefer that I should do my
(5) work coarsely and not too well, ay, not well enough. When I observe that there are different ways of surveying, my employer commonly asks which will give him the most land, not which is most correct. I
(10) once invented a rule for measuring cordwood, and tried to introduce it in Boston; but the measurer there told me that the sellers did not wish to have their wood measured correctly—that he was
(15) already too accurate for them, and therefore they commonly got their wood measured in Charlestown before crossing the bridge.

The aim of the laborer should be, not to
(20) get his living, to get "a good job," but to perform well a certain work; and, even in a pecuniary sense, it would be economy for a town to pay its laborers so well that they would not feel that they were working for
(25) low ends, as for a livelihood merely, but for scientific, or even moral ends. Do not hire a man who does your work for money, but him who does it for love of it.

Henry David Thoreau, "Life Without Principle," from *Major Writers of America.*

48. The author sometimes feels unsatisfied with his work because

   (1) he is not paid well enough
   (2) he does not need the money
   (3) his clients do not always want his best effort
   (4) the customers often go to other surveyors
   (5) he has not been able to invent a better measuring rule

49. Which of the following is the best meaning of "pecuniary" (line 22)?

   (1) peculiar
   (2) inaccurate
   (3) having to do with measuring
   (4) having to do with money
   (5) a means of surveying

50. This excerpt is told

   (1) in the first person
   (2) by a person who sells wood
   (3) in the words of the surveyor's wife
   (4) in the third person
   (5) by someone who had hired a surveyor

51. If the narrator were offered a job doing something that he did not like, he would probably

   (1) accept the job because of the money
   (2) turn down the job
   (3) accept it but do a bad job
   (4) argue with the client regarding the money
   (5) hire someone else to do the work

52. The narrator thinks some of his clients

   (1) criticize his work too much
   (2) like Charlestown better than Boston
   (3) don't pay him enough
   (4) are a little dishonest
   (5) are very lazy

Tip **To identify point of view, ask yourself who is telling the story. Remember that the opinions that a character expresses may or may not be the same as the author's.**

Answers are on page 835.

Lesson 6 Drama

Choose the best answer to each item. Items 1 to 4 refer to the following excerpt from a play.

IS THIS MAN ACTING LIKE AN ADULT?

WALTER: I'm going out!

RUTH: Where?

WALTER: Just out of this house somewhere—

(5) RUTH: *(Getting her coat)* I'll come too.

WALTER: I don't want you to come!

RUTH: I got something to talk to you about, Walter.

WALTER: That's too bad.

(10) MAMA: *(Still quietly)* Walter Lee—*(She waits and he finally turns and looks at her)* Sit down.

WALTER: I'm a grown man, Mama.

MAMA: Ain't nobody said you wasn't grown.

(15) But you still in my house and my presence. And as long as you are— you'll talk to your wife civil. Now sit down.

RUTH: *(Suddenly)* Oh, let him go out and

(20) drink himself to death! He makes me sick to my stomach! *(She flings her coat against him)*

WALTER: *(Violently)* And you turn mine too, baby! (RUTH *goes into their bedroom*

(25) *and slams the door behind her)* That was my greatest mistake—

MAMA: *(Still quietly)* Walter, what is the matter with you?

WALTER: Matter with me? Ain't nothing the

(30) matter with *me!*

MAMA: Yes there is. Something eating you up like a crazy man. Something more than me not giving you this money. The past few years I been watching it

(35) happen to you. You get all nervous acting and kind of wild in the eyes— (WALTER *jumps up impatiently at her words*) I said sit there now, I'm talking to you!

WALTER: Mama—I don't need no nagging

(40) at me today.

Lorraine Hansberry, *A Raisin in the Sun.*

1. As portrayed in this scene, Walter is

   (1) loud and drunk
   (2) acting like a criminal
   (3) lazy and cowardly
   (4) angry and defensive
   (5) depressed and withdrawn

2. Walter's mother comes across as

   (1) patient and long-suffering
   (2) hard and domineering
   (3) passive and easygoing
   (4) whiny and complaining
   (5) strong and caring

3. Which of the following best describes the relationship between Ruth and Walter?

   (1) Walter is devoted and loving with Ruth.
   (2) Walter does not want to be with Ruth.
   (3) Ruth is planning to leave Walter.
   (4) The couple are tired of the interference of Walter's mother.
   (5) Walter would rather spend time with his mother than with Ruth.

4. If Walter asks Ruth to go with him, Ruth's response would most likely be

   (1) to refuse to speak to Walter
   (2) to get sick to her stomach
   (3) to accompany Walter so that they could speak
   (4) to ask if his mother could come along
   (5) to nag at Walter regarding his behavior

WHAT HAS NORA DONE FOR HER HUSBAND?

MRS. LINDE: . . . A wife can't borrow without her husband's consent.

NORA: *(tossing her head)* Ah, but when it happens to be a wife with a bit of a
(5) sense of business . . . a wife who knows her way about things, then . . .

MRS. LINDE: But, Nora, I just don't understand. . . .

NORA: You don't have to. I haven't said I
(10) did borrow the money. I might have got it some other way. *(throws herself back on the sofa)* I might even have got it from some admirer. Anyone as reasonably attractive as I am . . .

(15) MRS. LINDE: Don't be so silly!

NORA: Now you must be dying of curiosity, Kristine.

MRS. LINDE: Listen to me now, Nora dear— you haven't done anything rash, have
(20) you?

NORA: *(sitting up again)* Is it rash to save your husband's life?

MRS. LINDE: I think it was rash to do anything without telling him. . . .

(25) NORA: But the whole point was that he mustn't know anything. Good heavens, can't you see! He wasn't even supposed to know how desperately ill he was. It was me the doctors came
(30) and told his life was in danger, that the only way to save him was to go South for a while. Do you think I didn't try talking him into it first? I began dropping hints about how nice it would
(35) be if I could be taken on a little trip abroad, like other young wives. I wept, I pleaded, I told him he ought to show some consideration for my condition, and let me have a bit of my own way.
(40) And then I suggested he might take out a loan. But at that he nearly lost his temper, Kristine. He said I was being frivolous, that it was his duty as a husband not to give in to all these
(45) whims and fancies of mine—as I do

believe he called them. All right, I thought, somehow you've got to be saved. And it was then I found a way.

Henrik Ibsen, *A Doll's House.*

5. From the speeches in this scene, Nora could be described as

   (1) humble and obedient
   (2) hysterical and panicky
   (3) arrogant and evil
   (4) resourceful and determined
   (5) childish and impulsive

6. When Nora's husband called her "frivolous" (line 43), he meant she was

   (1) the life of the party
   (2) impractical
   (3) scatterbrained
   (4) hard to say no to
   (5) flirtatious

7. In her interaction with Nora, Mrs. Linde comes across as

   (1) cautious and unadventurous
   (2) boring and dull
   (3) young and wild
   (4) lying and deceitful
   (5) charming and flirtatious

8. Why does Nora want to go South?

   (1) She wants to travel.
   (2) Going South would be good for her husband's health.
   (3) Going South would make her husband stop losing his temper.
   (4) Going South would help them save money.
   (5) She wants to leave her home.

Tip **To better understand the effects of what characters say and do, examine the relationship between characters.**

Items 9 to 18 refer to the following excerpt from a play.

CAN THIS CHILD BE TRUSTED?

MARY: *(without looking up)* I'm not lying. I went out walking and I saw the flowers and they looked pretty and I didn't know it was so late.

(5) KAREN: *(impatiently)* Stop it, Mary! I'm not interested in hearing that foolish story again. I *know* you got the flowers out of the garbage can. What I do want to know is why you feel you have to lie out

(10) of it.

MARY: *(beginning to whimper)* I *did* pick the flowers near Conway's. You never believe me. You believe everybody but me. It's always like that. Everything I

(15) say you fuss at me about. Everything I do is wrong.

KAREN: You know that isn't true. *(Goes to MARY, puts her arm around her, waits until the sobbing has stopped)* Look,

(20) Mary, look at me. *(Raises MARY's face with her hand)* Let's try to understand each other. If you feel that you *have* to take a walk, or that you just *can't* come to class, or that you'd like to go into the

(25) village by yourself, come and tell me— I'll try and understand. *(Smiles)* I don't say that I'll always agree that you should do exactly what you want to do, but I've had feelings like that, too—

(30) everybody has—and I won't be unreasonable about yours. But this way, this kind of lying you do, makes everything wrong.

MARY: *(looking steadily at KAREN)* I got the

(35) flowers near Conway's cornfield.

KAREN: *(looks at MARY, sighs, moves back toward desk and stands there for a moment)* Well, there doesn't seem to be any other way with you; you'll have to

(40) be punished. Take your recreation periods alone for the next two weeks. No horseback-riding and no hockey. Don't leave the school grounds for any reason whatsoever. Is that clear?

(45) MARY: *(carefully)* Saturday, too?

KAREN: Yes.

MARY: But you said I could go to the boat-races.

KAREN: I'm sorry, but you can't go.

(50) MARY: I'll tell my grandmother. I'll tell her how everybody treats me here and the way I get punished for every little thing I do. I'll tell her. I'll—

MRS. MORTAR: Why, I'd slap her hands! . . .

(55) KAREN: *(turning back from door, ignoring MRS. MORTAR's speech. To MARY)* Go upstairs, Mary.

MARY: I don't feel well.

KAREN: *(wearily)* Go upstairs now.

(60) MARY: I've got a pain. I've had it all morning. It hurts right here. *(pointing vaguely in the direction of her heart)* Really it does.

KAREN: Ask Miss Dobie to give you some

(65) hot water and bicarbonate of soda.

MARY: It's a bad pain. I've never had it before.

KAREN: I don't think it can be very serious.

MARY: My heart! It's my heart! It's stopping

(70) or something. I can't breathe. *(She takes a long breath and falls awkwardly to the floor.)*

Lillian Hellman, *The Children's Hour.*

9. Which of the following phrases best describes Karen?

   (1) prim and proper
   (2) harsh and demanding
   (3) kindly and forgiving
   (4) reasonable and firm
   (5) easily intimidated

10. Which of the following phrases best describes Mary?

   (1) lonely and misunderstood
   (2) pathetic and victimized
   (3) friendly and open
   (4) slow-witted and dull
   (5) sneaky and uncooperative

11. Which of the following is Mary most capable of?

   (1) admitting mistakes
   (2) helping others
   (3) getting her own way
   (4) accepting punishment
   (5) obeying orders

12. The excerpt creates a sense of

   (1) harmony
   (2) suspense
   (3) conflict
   (4) sorrow
   (5) amusement

13. Karen, as the teacher, is responsible for Mary. This fact

   (1) makes it easy for Karen to control Mary's behavior
   (2) explains why Mary is being so difficult
   (3) makes the whole conflict of wills unnecessary
   (4) makes it easy for Mary to manipulate Karen's responses
   (5) makes Karen's job seem carefree and appealing

14. Given what we know about Mary, we can anticipate that later in the play she will

   (1) experience a change of heart
   (2) take revenge on Karen
   (3) become class president
   (4) become an honors student
   (5) become best friends with Karen

15. If Mrs. Mortar were in charge of Mary, she would most likely

   (1) behave towards Mary in a similar way
   (2) treat Mary with more leniency
   (3) assign Mary a harsh punishment
   (4) try to reason with Mary
   (5) send Mary from the school

16. Based on the excerpt, what can be inferred about Karen's relationship with Mrs. Mortar?

   (1) Karen does not value her opinions.
   (2) Mrs. Mortar is a close and trusted friend.
   (3) Karen is careful not to hurt Mrs. Mortar's feelings.
   (4) Karen respects Mrs. Mortar.
   (5) Mrs. Mortar was Karen's teacher.

17. Which of the following is not one of Mary's tactics?

   (1) whining
   (2) lying
   (3) making threats
   (4) pretending to be ill
   (5) pretending to like Karen

18. Which of the following is Karen most likely to do next?

   (1) call Mary's grandmother
   (2) call a doctor
   (3) scold Mrs. Mortar
   (4) wait for Mary to decide to get up
   (5) ask Miss Dobie to carry Mary up to her room

Answers are on page 839.

Lesson 7 Poetry

Choose the best answer to each item.

Items 1 to 8 refer to the following poem.

WHY WON'T THESE PEOPLE ANSWER THEIR DOOR?

THE LISTENERS

"Is there anybody there?" said the Traveler,
    Knocking on the moonlit door;
And his horse in the silence champed the grasses
    Of the forest's ferny floor:
(5) And a bird flew up out of the turret,
    Above the Traveler's head:
And he smote upon the door again a second time;
    "Is there anybody there?" he said.
But no one descended to the Traveler;
(10) No head from the leaf-fringed sill
Leaned over and looked into his gray eyes,
    Where he stood perplexed and still.
But only a host of phantom listeners
    That dwelt in the lone house then
(15) Stood listening in the quiet of the moonlight
    To that voice from the world of men:
Stood thronging the faint moonbeams on the dark stair,
    That goes down to the empty hall,
Hearkening in an air stirred and shaken
(20) By the lonely Traveler's call.
And he felt in his heart their strangeness,
    Their stillness answering his cry,
While his horse moved, cropping the dark turf,
    'Neath the starred and leafy sky;
(25) For he suddenly smote on the door, even
    Louder, and lifted his head:—
"Tell them I came, and no one answered,
    That I kept my word," he said.
Never the least stir made the listeners,
(30) Though every word he spake
Fell echoing through the shadowiness of the still house
    From the one man left awake:
Ay, they heard his foot upon the stirrup,
    And the sound of iron on stone
(35) And how the silence surged softly backward
    When the plunging hoofs were gone.

Walter de la Mare, "The Listeners."

1. Based upon the poem, what is the best meaning for "smote" (line 7)?

    (1) tapped
    (2) banged
    (3) opened
    (4) broke down
    (5) closed

2. Which of the following is the best restatement of "No head from the leaf-fringed sill / Leaned over and looked into his gray eyes" (lines 10–11)?

    (1) The occupants of the house did not open the door.
    (2) The listeners did not look directly at the narrator.
    (3) The house was enclosed among the trees.
    (4) The residents of the house did not look out at the Traveler.
    (5) The sound of the wind in the trees made it hard to hear the Traveler's knocks.

3. Which of the following does not support the author's description of the house?

    (1) remote
    (2) quiet
    (3) vacant
    (4) isolated
    (5) tranquil

4. Which of the following statements best reflects the main idea of this poem?

    (1) People are always willing to give you comfort when you are traveling.
    (2) It was not the time for the Traveler to be welcomed into the house.
    (3) Strangers are not accepted at this house.
    (4) The traveler was dreaming.
    (5) People should avoid strange houses in the middle of the forest.

5. Based upon the poem, it can be concluded that

    (1) the house was haunted
    (2) the Traveler was unfriendly
    (3) it is best not to travel at night
    (4) horses prefer to eat ferns
    (5) the Traveler tried again at the next house

6. Which of the following best describes the mood of the poem?

    (1) sad rejection
    (2) eerie expectation
    (3) burning hatred
    (4) warm friendliness
    (5) admiring respect

7. The poet refers to the Traveler as "the one man left awake" (line 32) because

    (1) the events of the poem take place late at night
    (2) he is looking for a place to fall asleep
    (3) those inside the house are no longer alive
    (4) his horse wakes everyone up
    (5) the poem is only a dream

8. Why is the poem called "The Listeners"?

    (1) because the poem is meant to be read aloud
    (2) to involve readers in the action of the poem
    (3) because the poem focuses on the people inside the house
    (4) because the Traveler doesn't play an important part in the poem
    (5) because the poem ends with the sound of the Traveler's horse leaving

Tip When reading a poem, try to identify the examples used by an author to restate information. Usually, analyzing the information provided in the details helps you better understand all kinds of literature.

WHERE DO THESE ROADS LEAD?

THE ROAD NOT TAKEN

Two roads diverged in a yellow wood,
And sorry I could not travel both
And be one traveler, long I stood
And looked down one as far as I could
(5) To where it bent in the undergrowth;

Then took the other, as just as fair,
And having perhaps the better claim,
Because it was grassy and wanted wear;
Though as for that the passing there
(10) Had worn them really about the same,

And both that morning equally lay
In leaves no step had trodden black.
Oh, I kept the first for another day!
Yet knowing how way leads on to way,
(15) I doubted if I should ever come back.

I shall be telling this with a sigh
Somewhere ages and ages hence:
Two roads diverged in a wood, and I—
I took the one less traveled by,
(20) And that has made all the difference.

Robert Frost, *The Poetry of Robert Frost.*

9. Which of the following best describes the general topic of the poem?

   (1) life decisions
   (2) travel options
   (3) unknown routes
   (4) outdoor walks
   (5) childhood stories

10. Which of the following best describes the theme of the poem?

   (1) regrets over choices not made
   (2) the ability to accomplish anything
   (3) how decisions define people's lives
   (4) traveling as a positive experience
   (5) the negative effects of choosing the less popular way of doing things

11. Which of the following best defines "diverged" (line 1)?

   (1) ran parallel
   (2) separated
   (3) merged
   (4) overlapped
   (5) appeared

12. Which of the following would the poet most likely do if asked to relive the events described in the poem?

   (1) try the busier road
   (2) forge a new road
   (3) make the same decision
   (4) run back and forth between both roads
   (5) turn around and leave the area

Items 13 to 16 refer to the following poem.

HOW DOES THIS AUTHOR FEEL ABOUT HER LOVE?

SONNET 43

How do I love thee? Let me count the ways.
I love thee to the depth and breadth and height
My soul can reach, when feeling out of sight
For the ends of Being and ideal Grace.
(5)　I love thee to the level of every day's
Most quiet need, by sun and candlelight.
I love thee freely, as men strive for Right;
I love thee purely, as they turn from Praise.
I love thee with the passion put to use
(10)　In my old griefs, and with my childhood's faith.
I love thee with a love I seemed to lose
With my lost saints—I love thee with the breath,
Smiles, tears, of all my life!—and, if God choose,
I shall but love thee better after death.

Elizabeth Barrett Browning, "Sonnet 43."

13. Which of the following does not support the author's description of her love?

    (1) free and liberated
    (2) without any reservations
    (3) purely and innocently
    (4) with her body and soul
    (5) with hesitation

14. Which of the following sentences is the best restatement of "I love thee with the breath, / Smiles, tears, of all my life!" (lines 12–13)?

    (1) I love you so much you take my breath away.
    (2) Just thinking of you makes me smile.
    (3) I love you with every part of my self.
    (4) When I am not with you I cannot be happy.
    (5) Things are not the same between us anymore.

15. Which of the following would the author most likely do if her love were to leave?

    (1) find another lover
    (2) love more intensely
    (3) lose her ability to laugh and cry
    (4) try to get her love back
    (5) lose her passion for anything

16. Most of the details in the poem are restatements of

    (1) the contents of a love letter
    (2) the author's powerful feelings for someone
    (3) the positive points of the author's lover
    (4) the author's mourning of her lover's death
    (5) the author's fear of love

Answers are on page 841.

Choose the best answer to each item. Items 1 to 5 refer to the following excerpt from a novel.

WHY IS RABBIT RUNNING?

If he could only get away from the holes in the banks, he thought, there would be no more faces. He swung off the path and plunged into the untrodden places of the
(5) wood.
Then the whistling began.
Very faint and shrill it was, and far behind him, when first he heard it; but somehow it made him hurry forward.
(10) Then, still very faint and shrill, it sounded far ahead of him, and made him hesitate and want to go back. As he halted in indecision it broke out on either side, and seemed to be caught up and passed on
(15) throughout the whole length of the wood to its farthest limit. They were up and alert and ready, evidently, whoever they were! And he—he was alone, and unarmed, and far from any help; and the night was
(20) closing in.
Then the pattering began.
He thought it was only falling leaves at first, so slight and delicate was the sound of it. Then as it grew it took a regular
(25) rhythm, and he knew it for nothing else but the pat-pat-pat of little feet, still a very long way off. Was it in front or behind? It seemed to be first one, then the other, then both. It grew and it multiplied, till from
(30) every quarter as he listened anxiously, leaning this way and that, it seemed to be closing in on him. As he stood still to hearken, a rabbit came running hard towards him through the trees. He waited,
(35) expecting it to slacken pace, or to swerve from him into a different course. Instead, the animal almost brushed him as it dashed past, his face set and hard, his eyes staring. "Get out of this, you fool, get
(40) out!" the Mole heard him mutter as he swung round a stump and disappeared down a friendly burrow.

Kenneth Grahame, *The Wind in the Willows*.

1. The speaker felt nervous because

   (1) he liked holes in the bank
   (2) he heard whistling
   (3) he was late for an appointment
   (4) the sounds were too faint
   (5) he wanted to see the faces he had imagined

2. The pattering made Mole feel

   (1) more relaxed
   (2) sick
   (3) delighted
   (4) even more nervous
   (5) as if he were at home

3. Based on the information given in the excerpt, it can be inferred that

   (1) Mole will stay where he is
   (2) the whistling will stop
   (3) Mole will take the rabbit's advice
   (4) the rabbit will join Mole
   (5) Mole will wake up and realize it is all a dream

4. Which of the following is not one of the reasons Mole feels frightened?

   (1) He is all alone.
   (2) He has no weapons to protect himself.
   (3) There is no help close by.
   (4) He is lost in the woods.
   (5) It is turning dark.

5. What is the best reason the burrow is described as "friendly" (line 42)?

   (1) It muffles the frightening sounds.
   (2) It is warm and cozy inside.
   (3) It is a safe place to hide.
   (4) There are friends in the burrow.
   (5) It is the rabbit's home.

Items 6 to 10 refer to the following excerpt from an autobiography.

WHAT WAS IT LIKE TO BE A SLAVE DURING THE WAR?

I had no schooling whatever while I was a slave, though I remember on several occasions I went as far as the schoolhouse door with one of my young
(5) mistresses to carry her books. The picture of several dozen boys and girls in a schoolroom engaged in study made a deep impression upon me, and I had the feeling that to get into a schoolhouse and
(10) study in this way would be about the same as getting into paradise.

So far as I can now recall, the first knowledge that I got of the fact that we were slaves, and that freedom of the
(15) slaves was being discussed, was early one morning before day, when I was awakened by my mother kneeling over her children and fervently praying that Lincoln and his armies might be successful, and
(20) that one day she and her children might be free. In this connection I have never been able to understand how the slaves throughout the South, completely ignorant as were the masses so far as books or
(25) newspapers were concerned, were able to keep themselves so accurately and completely informed about the great National questions that were agitating the country. From the time that Garrison,
(30) Lovejoy, and others began to agitate for freedom, the slaves throughout the South kept in close touch with the progress of the movement. Though I was a mere child during the preparation for the Civil War
(35) and during the war itself, I now recall the many late-at-night whispered discussions that I heard my mother and the other slaves on the plantation indulge in. These discussions showed that they understood
(40) the situation, and that they kept themselves informed of events by what was termed the "grape-vine" telegraph.

Booker T. Washington, *Up From Slavery.*

6. During the Civil War, the author was

   (1) starting school
   (2) an old man
   (3) a soldier
   (4) a young man
   (5) still a child

7. This excerpt is told

   (1) by a biographer
   (2) in the present tense
   (3) in the first person
   (4) by a newspaper reporter
   (5) in the third person

8. The author thought of school as

   (1) a form of slavery
   (2) a terrifying challenge
   (3) the gateway to society
   (4) a kind of heaven
   (5) an arena for protest

9. The author remains impressed by

   (1) how religious his mother was
   (2) how kind his masters were
   (3) his schooling as a slave
   (4) how hard slaves had to work
   (5) how informed the slaves were

10. What is the meaning of "agitate" (line 30)?

    (1) reject
    (2) fight
    (3) agree
    (4) fear
    (5) repress

Tip When reading an autobiography, ask yourself how the author's experiences affect the author's opinions and beliefs. This will give you insight into the author's point of view.

Answers are on page 842.

Choose the <u>best answer</u> to each item.
<u>Items 1 to 3</u> refer to the following review.

WHAT DOES THIS FILM SAY ABOUT THE PAST?

     Spike Lee's *Crooklyn* feels very much like a first film—which I mean as a compliment. Having long resisted the impulse to be sincere and

(5)   autobiographical, Lee has now taken the risk, at rather an advanced age, of filming a rambling memoir about his family and neighbors in Brooklyn during the early 1970s. The author of the screen story is

(10)   his sister, Joie Susannah Lee; the screenplay is by Joie Susannah, Spike and their brother Cinque. A cozy collaboration, you might think—certainly too cozy for the majority of film reviewers,

(15)   who have greeted *Crooklyn* with a yawn and a puzzled question: "But what's it *about?*" Friends, readers, colleagues: *Crooklyn* is about emotional situations that should be familiar to a great many

(20)   viewers, and that Spike Lee himself has brought up before, in *Mo' Better Blues,* a film that played out as one long evasion of the issue. In *Crooklyn,* though, he has opened up these feelings with an unforced

(25)   honesty and warmth that not only set the picture apart from most others in the theaters today but also establish this movie as a new beginning.

     . . . And yet the critics insist: "What's it

(30)   *about?*" To them, and to you, I advise, "Go see *Crooklyn.*" At first sight, you'll find it handsome to look at. Upon second thought, you'll realize that its meanderings are only apparent, concealing an elegantly

(35)   constructed design. Then, after mulling it over for a day or two, you may begin to feel grateful for the self-confidence with which Spike Lee has directed *Crooklyn,* allowing the film to stand back slightly

(40)   rather than jumping down your throat. You get the pleasure of discovering on your own what this movie is about.

Stuart Klawans, "Films," *The Nation.*

1. Which of the following is a fact about *Crooklyn?*

   (1) It is a difficult film to understand.
   (2) Its screen story was written by the director's sister.
   (3) It contains unnecessary scenes of violence.
   (4) It is Spike Lee's first film.
   (5) It is more successful at portraying Lee's life than his earlier films.

2. Which statement best describes the reviewer's opinion of *Crooklyn?*

   (1) It is noteworthy because of the director's earnest approach to his topic.
   (2) It is a good attempt by Lee to document the lives of a fictional family.
   (3) Its success with the majority of film reviewers is well deserved.
   (4) Watching the film is not a pleasurable experience.
   (5) Lee's collaboration with his sister and brother was an artistic mistake.

3. Which of the following is the best conclusion that can be made based upon the review's use of fact and opinion?

   (1) It is always good to believe what any reviewer says.
   (2) *Crooklyn* is too complex a film to understand.
   (3) *Crooklyn* requires its viewers to take their time discovering its meaning.
   (4) This film isn't about anything.
   (5) Film reviewers need to have this film explained to them.

Items 4 to 7 refer to the following excerpt from a review.

WHAT MAKES THIS FILM WORK SO WELL?

Many people yearn for Broadway shows of the 1920s—they want the perfect merging of high and low art that marked the best works of that era. Woody Allen's (5) new film, *Bullets over Broadway* (which he cowrote with Douglas McGrath), is what they're asking for: Crafted in an unpretentiously crowd-pleasing way, buoyant in its sophistication, it's an ode to (10) swizzle-stick comedy.

John Cusack plays the Woody Allen role—a playwright cursed with artistic scruples who gets gangster backing. . . .
Cusack's the straight man who sets off (15) the fizziness of the rest of the cast. He's a sly performer, holding his own while seeming to let others take over a scene. He has mastered the Woody Allen head bobs and hand twists, but he isn't imitating (20) Allen. Cusack has the physical elasticity of the early film comedians. He seems to change shape, Gumby-like, before your eyes; he can recede into his own features, and his black hair frames a face that's (25) waiting to be formed. He's like a kid brother who takes his cue from the older women in his family, innocently eager for them to shape him—or is it to corrupt him? . . . There may be no other current actor (30) who partners women as gracefully onscreen. Actresses should count themselves lucky to play opposite him. He's the acting equivalent of Fred Astaire.

Polly Frost, "Film," *Harper's Bazaar.*

4. Which of the following is not an example of the reviewer's opinions?

   (1) stories based on Broadway are popular
   (2) *Bullets over Broadway* is sophisticated
   (3) Woody Allen wrote and directed *Bullets over Broadway*
   (4) John Cusack plays a good straight man
   (5) Cusack and Astaire are similar

5. Which of the following is an example of a fact contained in the excerpt?

   (1) John Cusack learns from women in the cast.
   (2) John Cusack acts as well as Fred Astaire.
   (3) John Cusack is cast as a playwright.
   (4) John Cusack is graceful around actresses.
   (5) John Cusack moves like early Hollywood comedians.

6. Which of the following can be inferred from this review?

   (1) The reviewer likes movies based on the lives of Broadway playwrights.
   (2) The movie is a thriller.
   (3) The movie is similar to all of Woody Allen's other movies.
   (4) The reviewer loves Cusack's acting.
   (5) The movie did not need the addition of actresses.

7. Based on the information given in the excerpt, it can be concluded that if Cusack had not acted in the film

   (1) he would be working in better films
   (2) the film would not have been made
   (3) he would have directed the film rather than Allen
   (4) the reviewer may have been less positive about the film
   (5) Fred Astaire would have been cast for the role

Tip When identifying fact and opinion in a review, remember that a fact is a piece of information that can be proven. Opinions, on the other hand, are examples of the reviewer's personal judgments or beliefs. While opinions may be based on facts, they are more difficult to prove.

Items 8 to 10 refer to the following excerpt from an article.

WHAT IS NOTABLE ABOUT THIS PRODUCTION?

Pasadena, Calif.—Not long ago, they held a press conference here about the black migration to The Promised Land. But it was 50 years too late, and 2,000 miles
(5) astray. "The reason is that when this migration took place, nobody held a press conference. Nobody said the most important demographic event in mid-20th-century [American] history is now
(10) happening," said Nicolas Lemann, who wrote "The Promised Land," the best-selling 1991 history of the African-American diaspora. From 1940 to 1970, 5.5 million black Americans journeyed
(15) from the rural South to the cities of the North, with consequences still felt in cities like Chicago, Cleveland and Detroit.

Lemann's book is now a five-hour documentary series, co-produced by the
(20) BBC and the Discovery Channel . . . Not just TV history but sociology with a sting, "The Promised Land" also represents big stakes for cable's Discovery, which last year achieved substantial ratings and a
(25) place on many critics' year-end Top 10 lists with its mini-series "Watergate."

Overall, the new series is an accomplished showcase for the emergence of Discovery as a cable
(30) channel that Greg Moyer, its president, calls a "mixed metaphor"—overtly commercial television that makes money from both advertisers and cable-TV subscribers, but is "driven by a certain
(35) public-spirited commissioning" of programming previously seen almost wholly on PBS.

PBS, of course, is free TV. But it is also fighting for its life on Capitol Hill.
(40) Meanwhile, cable networks like Discovery are funding increasingly accomplished productions. "This is the kind of television that we've aspired to for quite a while," Moyer said. "It was not until 1989, five
(45) years after we launched, that we produced our first hour of television. But it's nice to be able to say that we can now afford to follow our intentions and put them on the screen."
(50) PBS confirms that it wanted to air "The Promised Land" but couldn't afford its share of the $2.5 million production cost.

Frederic M. Biddle, "Keeping the Promise of 'Land,' " *The Boston Sunday Globe.*

8. Which of the following is <u>not</u> a fact from the excerpt?

(1) "The Promised Land" is a history book.
(2) Discovery is a cable channel.
(3) Greg Moyer is the head of Discovery.
(4) Discovery was founded in 1984.
(5) "The Promised Land" is an exact adaptation of the book.

9. From this excerpt, you can conclude that the author

(1) prefers that people read books rather than watch television
(2) thinks that the Discovery Channel is producing quality programs
(3) wishes PBS would invest in its own programs
(4) believes that Discovery will not succeed as a cable network
(5) thinks that Discovery would be more successful if it were to show sports events

10. Which of the following statements best reflects the main idea of this excerpt?

(1) The Discovery Channel has established itself as a leading television producer.
(2) "The Promised Land" is a good television show.
(3) The Discovery Channel should follow the lead of PBS.
(4) Migration is not a worthy topic for a five-hour documentary series.
(5) Documentary shows are more interesting than comedy.

Items 11 to 13 refer to the following review.

IS THIS THE MAN WHO WROTE THAT FAMOUS SONG?

The story goes that Irving Berlin, desperate to get a new song down during a rehearsal, burst into a backstage room and asked for a piece of paper. A musician
(5) working there handed him a blank sheet of musical manuscript. "This is *music* paper," the songwriter said. "What am I supposed to do with that?"

Berlin may not have known how to write
(10) music, but there wasn't a thing he didn't know about songs. He understood instinctively that the popular song is a kind of tuning fork for the best traits in the American character: vivacity, industry,
(15) openheartedness, grit, sentiment. Berlin himself lived the American dream. He was a poor kid who achieved fame and fortune, an unschooled craftsman who rose to the top of his profession, a patriot who loved
(20) his adopted country as only an immigrant can. So always, he aimed for the heart of the average American: "Not the highbrow nor the lowbrow," he once said, "but that vast intermediate crew which is the real
(25) soul of the country." When he died . . . at 101, Berlin left behind an astonishing number of great American songs: "Blue Skies," "Always," "Cheek to Cheek," "Isn't This a Lovely Day," "God Bless America,"
(30) "White Christmas," "Let's Face the Music and Dance," "A Pretty Girl is Like a Melody," "Easter Parade," "There's No Business Like Show Business" and "What'll I Do?" And more than 1,000
(35) others.

Born Israel Baline in the Russian village of Temun on May 11, 1888, he fled the pogroms and settled with his parents and seven siblings on New York's Lower East
(40) Side. . . .

Bill Barol, "Irving Berlin, 1888–1989," *Newsweek.*

11. The excerpt as a whole is presented from the point of view of

(1) a Russian immigrant
(2) a fellow songwriter
(3) a formal biographer
(4) a jealous musician
(5) a respectful admirer

12. The reviewer probably began with the story about Berlin (lines 1–8) to

(1) get the reader's interest with an unusual detail
(2) explain why Berlin could not read music
(3) present Berlin in a bad light
(4) show how an immigrant can succeed in America
(5) show why Americans liked his songs

13. Which of the following does not represent the author's opinion of Berlin?

(1) Berlin's songs suffer because of his inability to read music.
(2) Berlin's songs capture the American character.
(3) Berlin's songs are popular because they appeal to a large section of the population.
(4) Berlin was an immigrant who lived the American dream.
(5) Berlin created a vivacity and energy in his songs.

WHAT IS THE "PALE BLUE DOT"?

After swinging by Jupiter, Saturn, Uranus and Neptune and shooting spectacular pictures of the planets and their moons, the U.S. spacecraft Voyager 2

(5) had by 1990 completed its Grand Tour of the planets and was speeding out into deep space on its way to the stars. But the temptation of one last backward look was irresistible. Swinging its camera around, it

(10) took snapshots of the now distant planets as they might appear to an alien craft approaching the solar system.

And there was Earth, barely discernible against the background of stars, an image

(15) that inspired the title of *The Pale Blue Dot* . . . the ninth book by astronomer and planetary scientist Carl Sagan. Voyager's homeward glance was his idea, and the sight was humbling. "There is perhaps no

(20) better a demonstration of the folly of human conceits," he writes, "than this distant image of our tiny world." To say nothing of the folly of wars, which from space would appear to be little more than

(25) "the squabbles of mites on a plum."

Having placed the Earth in proper perspective, Sagan launches his own Grand Tour of just about everything in space that surrounds it. Elegantly and

(30) appealingly, he surveys the current state of knowledge about the solar system, nearby stars, distant galaxies and even the very edge of the universe. As he describes each heavenly body or cosmic

(35) phenomenon, the author imparts a healthy dose of science, making it palatable to the lay reader by using jargon-free English buoyed by emotion and humor.

Sagan traces the history of space flight

(40) and looks ahead to the time when humans will fly from a dying or imperiled Earth to other worlds, "terraforming" them to make them livable and inhabiting them to preserve the species.

(45) It is Sagan's optimistic vision, however, rather than any foreboding of apocalypse, that shines through every chapter of this handsomely illustrated book.

Leon Jaroff, "What's Up With the Universe," *Time*.

Tip **Remember that if you understand a cause-and-effect relationship, you will have no difficulty determining the results, or consequences, of certain actions or decisions. When reading any kind of review or commentary, ask yourself what were the factors leading up to a certain result, or what were the consequences of particular actions or decisions. Understanding causes and consequences will both help you identify how the reviewer feels about a book and allow you to decide whether you would like to read the book.**

14. According to this review, what was the consequence of Sagan's idea to have Voyager 2 look back at Earth?

(1) The pictures that it took made great illustrations.
(2) It allowed Sagan to discuss Earth in relation to the rest of the universe.
(3) It meant that Sagan could take full credit for Voyager's discoveries.
(4) It prevented Voyager from taking pictures of the planets as they might appear to aliens.
(5) Sagan felt humbled by the sight of the solar system.

15. What is the consequence of the author's choice to use simple and plain language?

    (1) It oversimplifies difficult information.
    (2) It makes Sagan's points harder to understand.
    (3) It fails to describe the magnitude of the universe.
    (4) It succeeds in communicating to people who are not scientists.
    (5) It weakens the book.

16. From this excerpt, you can conclude that Sagan

    (1) does not know what he is talking about
    (2) is not interested in space exploration
    (3) is interested in the idea of living on other planets
    (4) does not believe that humans can live on Mars
    (5) doesn't think the Voyager 2 is important

17. The reviewer says, "Sagan launches his own Grand Tour" (lines 27–28) in order to

    (1) show Sagan retracing the steps of Voyager
    (2) compare Sagan's examination of the solar system to Voyager's
    (3) discuss Sagan's most recent vacation
    (4) suggest the size of the universe
    (5) indicate the organization of the book

18. Which of the following would Sagan most likely do if offered a trip to Mars?

    (1) turn down the offer
    (2) accept the offer only if he could live there permanently
    (3) accept the offer to join the expedition
    (4) wait until others had explored first
    (5) offer his place to one of his readers

19. Which of the following best explains Sagan's comparison of Earth with a plum?

    (1) to suggest the size of Earth in comparison with the rest of the universe
    (2) to discuss the differences and similarities in the color of the two
    (3) to examine the similar shapes between the two
    (4) to illustrate the massive size of Earth in comparison to a piece of fruit
    (5) to examine the dangers of insects to fruit

Tip When reading a book review, it is helpful to ask yourself the following two questions. First, if a reviewer discusses a result, ask yourself what events happened or what decisions were made that led to the result. Secondly, if the review examines certain decisions made by the book's author or characters in the book, try to identify what will happen or has happened because of them. Asking yourself these two questions will help you to understand the consequences of an author's or character's actions and decisions.

HOW IS CHAPIN COUNTRY DEFINED?

Chapin country is a pretty, melancholy place; sadness hides behind the lace curtains. It's on the borderline between love and loss, where a lover's rancor is so
(5) delicately phrased that it sounds like sisterly advice. Everyone is tyrannized by memories—of a lonely childhood, of words said and chances missed, of a first love whose sweetness makes everything that
(10) follows seem both tame and tawdry. Around here, folks smile to keep from screaming.

The setting created by the songs of Mary Chapin Carpenter is more haunting
(15) than your typical country-singer territory. Yet that's her landscape, and Carpenter looks fetching in it. Three years running, she has won a Grammy for wrapping her dusky alto around, respectively, *Down at*
(20) *the Twist and Shout, I Feel Lucky* and *Passionate Kisses.* She could easily make it four with her current single, the slow-rockin', Bonnie Raitt-ish *Shut Up and Kiss Me,* in which a take-charge woman
(25) whispers those five magic words to a too-well-behaved beau.

There are other impish moments on Carpenter's new album, *Stones in the Road,* but this is a seductively pensive set.
(30) It works the dark corners, where troubled souls spend lonely evenings. Because Carpenter enunciates clearly and even uses *whence* properly, she seems an English teacher's dream student; at school
(35) she'd be the quiet girl, scribbling in her diary, who wins the Sylvia Plath Prize for the most achingly sensitive poem. Even her anthems (the up-tempo *House of Cards* and *Jubilee*) have the feel of
(40) requiems. . . .

The new CD has few tunes that will grab an AM-dial twirler by the ear. But there's music aplenty in Carpenter's voice, in the emotional precision of her words, in the
(45) world she weaves. Take *Where Time Stands Still,* which will get no radio play but sounds like a piano-bar classic about the haven of love. . . .

In a music business that relentlessly
(50) merchandises machismo, there has to be room for a woman's wit and heart. It's our good luck that Mary Chapin Carpenter has made that place a room of her own.

Richard Corliss, "A Woman's Wit and Heart," *Time.*

20. In the author's opinion, the album *Stones in the Road* is sometimes flawed by

    (1) too much emotion
    (2) a lack of catchy songs
    (3) Carpenter's voice
    (4) too many love songs
    (5) not enough feeling

21. The purpose of equating Carpenter's music with a landscape is to

    (1) make the connection with the fact that she is a country singer
    (2) indicate how many of Carpenter's songs are about a real place
    (3) suggest how Carpenter creates her own world through her music
    (4) to show the influence of the country on Carpenter's songs
    (5) to explain why Carpenter is more popular in the United States than abroad

22. By stating "It works the dark corners, where troubled souls spend lonely evenings," (lines 30–31) the author wants to

    (1) indicate how disturbed Carpenter is
    (2) emphasize Carpenter's sadness
    (3) suggest the emotional depths of Carpenter's new album
    (4) explain the emptiness of Carpenter's world
    (5) describe the first time he heard Carpenter sing

23. Based on the information given in the excerpt, it can be concluded that the author

    (1) knows nothing of Carpenter's music
    (2) dislikes country music
    (3) prefers piano-bar classics
    (4) is biased against woman performers
    (5) respects Carpenter

24. Which of the following phrases best states the reviewer's conclusion about Carpenter?

    (1) a talented and emotional singer
    (2) limited in her approach to music
    (3) understandably unsuccessful
    (4) a writer of upbeat and cheerful music
    (5) a new and promising talent

25. Which of the following phrases best describes what the author means by "even her anthems have the feel of requiems" (lines 37–40)?

    (1) All of Carpenter's songs are full of memories.
    (2) Carpenter's happier songs can also feel melancholy.
    (3) Carpenter doesn't know how to be cheerful.
    (4) Carpenter's new album reminds the author of a funeral.
    (5) Some of Carpenter's songs are uplifting.

Items 26 to 28 refer to the following excerpt from a review.

WILL HIGH-TECH CHANGE TAP?

Hines dances on a specially miked platform-stage about seven by five feet, constructed to amplify the taps. Hines is trying to figure out how to bring tap up-to-
(5) date with technology, to tune the sounds of the percussions by experimenting with different surfaces and amplification. As an improviser, Hines's choices are *always* surprising and wild. He takes you in
(10) unpredictable directions, cutting into phrases in unexpected places, alternating rest periods with full-blown movement as he skitters over the surface of his soundstage. A tough, get-down
(15) tapper who hunches over his feet, Hines keeps his head low like a fighter, listening, focusing himself and us on the sound of his feet. Neither graceful nor light (although he makes his feet whisper sweet
(20) nothings when he wants to) Hines is something better and rarer in the tap dance world, a sexy and compelling performer. Of all the tappers I know, Hines is perhaps the most inventive because he
(25) is fearless. Almost single-handedly he is pushing tap's technology and is a true modernist in how he uses rhythms. Frequently, he'll wrench phrases out of rhythm to create tension. On the feet of a
(30) lesser performer it could be chaotic. On Hines, it is exhilarating.

Sally R. Sommer, "Superfeet," *The Village Voice.*

26. Hines is an unusual tap dancer because

    (1) he improvises
    (2) of his height
    (3) of his interest in high technology
    (4) his work is chaotic
    (5) he hunches over his feet

27. Why does Hines dance with his head down?

    (1) to show toughness
    (2) to gain momentum
    (3) because he is an ex-boxer
    (4) because he is slightly deaf
    (5) to focus attention on his feet

28. Which of the following phrases from the excerpt does not indicate that the reviewer knows a lot about tap dance?

    (1) Almost single-handedly he is pushing tap's technology
    (2) Of all the tappers I know
    (3) Hines dances on a specially miked platform-stage
    (4) Hines is something better and rarer in the tap dance world
    (5) On the feet of lesser performers

Items 29 to 31 refer to the following essay.

HOW DOES THIS MAN KEEP THE SHOW RUNNING?

Any visitor to the Burbank production offices of "E.R.," the NBC medical drama series, could quickly discern who is the guiding force behind the biggest network
(5) hit in several years.

It is not Michael Crichton, the novelist and screenwriter, who created the show, wrote its pilot episode—and departed almost immediately to write new novels. It
(10) is not Steven Spielberg, whose Amblin Television company took the project to a big studio, Warner Brothers. It is not Leslie Moonves, the president of Warner Brothers Television, which produces the
(15) show for NBC.

It is a man named John Wells, a veteran television scriptwriter, most notably for "China Beach."

At any one moment, Mr. Wells is
(20) supervising the content and execution of at least four one-hour episodes in various stages of development—from script to filming to editing to post-production. Future story lines of the series are also his
(25) responsibility: on the walls of the conference room next to his office are whiteboards covered, in felt-tip markers, with dozens of handwritten dramatic situations and plot twists, approved by him
(30) and cleared for use in episodes as yet unwritten. In the terms of the trade, Mr. Wells is "E.R." 's show runner.

For the last 10 years at least, the person with that unofficial title has been the true
(35) auteur [creator] of series television. Day to day, a show runner makes all important decisions about the series' scripts, tone, attitude, look and direction. He or she oversees casting, production design and
(40) budget. This person chooses directors and guest stars, defends the show against meddling by the network or production company and, when necessary, changes its course.
(45) Even in this notoriously collaborative medium, show runners are responsible for what viewers see on the screen. Yet the show runner's true position and influence are unknown to nearly everyone on the
(50) other side of the picture tube.

Andy Meisler, "The Man Who Keeps *E.R.*'s Heart Beating," *The New York Times*.

29. The most important person in the production of a television series is the person

    (1) writing the pilot episode
    (2) taking the project to a major studio
    (3) who is president of the production company
    (4) referred to as the show runner
    (5) writing the script

30. Based on this excerpt, you can conclude that

    (1) show runners and screenwriters share responsibility for a show's success
    (2) production companies always interfere with a show's management
    (3) show runners are among the most anonymous, but most important, people in television
    (4) NBC has failed in its efforts to produce a hit television series
    (5) show runners have always been responsible for series television shows

31. Which of the following would a show runner probably not do?

    (1) direct individual shows
    (2) hire actors
    (3) approve the story for an episode
    (4) decrease actors' salaries
    (5) change the set location

Items 32 to 35 refer to the following excerpt from a review.

HOW DID WONDER PERFORM IN CONCERT?

At 44, Stevie is still a Wonder. Digging deep into his treasure trove of hits, the master blaster rocked and romanced an ecstatic, sold-out crowd for more than two

(5) hours at Constitution Hall Thursday.

On his first tour in several years, Wonder performed 28 songs almost non-stop. He augmented his sextet with an orchestra and the pretty-yet-earthy vocal

(10) back-up of female quartet For Real.

Though the strings were sometimes drowned out by drums and synthesizers, the symphonic players were spotlighted on songs such as *Village Ghetto Land* and

(15) *Overjoyed*, heightening their beauty.

The night's repertoire spanned Wonder's eclectic three-decade career, from his sentimental version of Bob Dylan's *Blowin' in the Wind* and funky classic *Master*

(20) *Blaster* to the hip-hop jazz of the new *Sensuous Whisper* (from his upcoming album, *Conversation Peace* . . .), an instant hit.

Despite a cold, Wonder hit the high

(25) notes of his early days. He tested his vocal limits on a passionate, piano-only *You and I* that brought the audience of 3,700 to its feet. . . .

"No, you ain't gonna hear *Fingertips*," he

(30) joked, referring to his first hit, from 1963. "Little Stevie Wonder is resting right now. He had to go to bed."

That's OK. Big Stevie was up and jammin'.

James T. Jones IV, "Signed and sealed, Stevie Wonder delivers," *USA Today*.

32. It can be concluded from this review that Stevie Wonder

    (1) is probably near retirement age
    (2) has lost the support of his fans
    (3) is better at writing songs than performing
    (4) is performing as powerfully as when he started in music
    (5) refuses to perform older songs

33. In the reviewer's view, the overall performance was sometimes flawed by

    (1) Wonder's back-up singers
    (2) the unappreciative audience
    (3) the excessive volume of some instruments
    (4) Wonder's refusal to acknowledge the crowd
    (5) Wonder's diminished vocal range

34. Which of the following phrases best explains the author's use of the phrase "the master blaster" (line 3)?

    (1) he wanted to confuse his readers
    (2) to add a casual tone to the review
    (3) to introduce Wonder's childhood nickname
    (4) he wanted to make the review more formal
    (5) to indicate how noisy Wonder's music is

35. Which of the following is the best meaning for "augmented" (line 8)?

    (1) replaced
    (2) added to
    (3) fired
    (4) reduced
    (5) liked

Tip **When identifying point of view, look for clues that suggest the reviewer's knowledge of the subject matter. Study the use of vocabulary and ask yourself if the words used to describe something indicate experience in the field.**

Items 36 to 38 refer to the following excerpt from a review.

WHAT DID HUGHES DO WITH COMPLEX IDEAS?

Langston Hughes (1902–67) was able to turn sophisticated and complex ideas into very simple language. A lifelong fan of jazz and blues, Hughes shared with musicians
(5) the gift of flow. His words could ride above you, breeze by or lift you like Aladdin's magic carpet. He often wrote in the AAB style of blues lyricists: the first line repeated for emphasis, the third line
(10) providing the payoff or switch. . . .

In the literary world, poetry with simple rhymes is almost always looked down upon. In his lifetime, Hughes was often derided as not holding African-American
(15) arts and letters up to "intellectual" standards. Children, however, love a good rhyme. So it seems only natural that at some point in a 40-year career, which produced books of poetry, plays, novels
(20) and short stories, Hughes wrote for children, giving them just a simple but seductive taste of the blues.

"The Sweet and Sour Animal Book" is an alphabet primer for the very young. A "lost"
(25) manuscript completed in 1936, according to George P. Cunningham, a scholar who contributed the afterword, it was rejected by publishers repeatedly and rediscovered only recently among Hughes's papers at
(30) Yale's Beinecke Rare Book Library by Nancy Toff, executive editor of children's books at Oxford University Press. From Ape to Zebra, the short poems reflect Hughes's childlike wonder as well as his
(35) sense of humor. . . .

This edition of "The Sweet and Sour Animal Book" is especially charming because of the illustrations by students in the lower grades at the Harlem School of
(40) the Arts. Though Langston Hughes was born in Joplin, Mo., Harlem was the mecca where he spent most of his adult life. . . .

The language is as skeletal and yet as monumental as a dinosaur's bones.
(45) Langston Hughes tells us what black misery is, even while the alchemy of his writing turns that misery into literature.

Veronica Chambers, *The New York Times Book Review.*

36. The reviewer suggests that one consequence of Hughes's style has been

(1) an oversimplification of difficult ideas
(2) criticism for his chosen style
(3) to take away from its artistic merits
(4) overwhelming accolades of the highest praise
(5) the rejection of his books for publication

37. A musician would most likely praise Hughes's poetry because

(1) it is easily understood
(2) it can be easily transformed into songs
(3) it uses rhythms similar to some musical forms
(4) it is usually performed in small nightclubs
(5) it floats through the air like a magic carpet

38. Which of the following best explains what the author means by "The language is as skeletal and yet as monumental as a dinosaur's bones" (lines 43–44)?

(1) plain words and sentences often communicate difficult ideas
(2) Hughes's language is as extinct as the dinosaurs
(3) the larger the words, the greater the meaning
(4) literature is only successful if it is very simple
(5) Hughes's poetry is in need of many details to flesh out its meaning

Items 39 to 43 refer to the following excerpt from a review.

HOW DID THIS SCIENTIST SUCCEED?

"Go to the ant, thou sluggard," counsels the book of Proverbs, "consider her ways and be wise." Edward O. Wilson took that advice early. Scouring the swamps and
(5) woodlands of the deep South hunting for bugs, Wilson followed an insect trail right out of an impoverished childhood and into the halls of Harvard, where he is University Professor, curator in
(10) entomology at the Museum of Comparative Zoology, and one of America's most distinguished biologists.
In *Naturalist,* Wilson puts his own life under a microscope, examining in clear,
(15) candid prose his formative years, his rapid rise as an evolutionary biologist, and his later battles as the controversial prophet of sociobiology. Wilson's career has been central enough for his autobiography to
(20) entail a discussion of many of the major scientific issues of our age—while also telling the story of a boy's outdoor education that has the mythic American appeal of *The Adventures of Huckleberry*
(25) *Finn.*

Jonathan Rosen, "Lord of the Ants," *Commentary.*

39. According to the review, reading Wilson's childhood memoirs has the same effect as reading

   (1) *The Adventures of Huckleberry Finn*
   (2) a historical discussion of zoology
   (3) a field book on the collection of insects
   (4) the book of Proverbs
   (5) the story of one man's ruin

40. Based on the information given in the excerpt, which of the following is the best meaning for "entomology" (line 10)?

   (1) the study of human beings
   (2) the study of science
   (3) the study of insects
   (4) the study of literature
   (5) the study of swamps

41. Which of the following is a consequence of Wilson's scientific training?

   (1) enjoying collecting insects
   (2) becoming known for his controversial views
   (3) studying his life as he would an organism
   (4) establishing himself as a writer
   (5) relating his childhood experiences

42. Which of the following is a consequence of Wilson's following "an insect trail" (line 6)?

   (1) He got lost in the swamps and woodlands of the deep South.
   (2) He had a successful career as a biologist.
   (3) He became a great hunter.
   (4) He continued to live an impoverished life.
   (5) He invented a new, powerful microscope.

43. If Wilson were given the choice to relive his life, he would most likely

   (1) choose to write books rather than be a scientist
   (2) change no part of his life
   (3) attend another college
   (4) study animals rather than bugs
   (5) ask someone else to write his life story

Tip Often in reviews of fiction, reviewers will discuss both the author's style and the character's actions. Be careful not to confuse the two. The reviewer might like the book but criticize the character's actions.

Items 44 to 47 refer to the following review.

WHAT IS ONE OF THE MOST OVERESTIMATED PAINTINGS?

Unquestionably the most glittering personality of the high renaissance in Italy and the pioneer in its new and magnificent form of expression was Leonardo da Vinci.
(5)   Even as a youth he displayed an aptitude for all manner of achievement, a winning charm, and a personal strength and beauty which have become almost legendary. In time this brilliant boy would
(10) become not only one of the leading artists of the sixteenth century, but its greatest contributor to the advancement of modern ideas as well. Leonardo possessed a variety of artistic talents—he was
(15) architect, sculptor, musician. He also mastered and did original work in the fields of mathematics, geology, engineering, anatomy, and every other science known in his day. More than anyone else he had
(20) "taken all knowledge as his sphere." Leonardo spent the early part of his life in Florence and then stayed in Milan for a number of years working on many important projects, including the *Madonna
(25) of the Rocks* and the *Last Supper.* The latter (perhaps the best known painting in the world) offers one of the finest instances of a rigid geometric enclosure. Everything turns inward toward the head
(30) of Christ, even the expressive gestures of His own hands. In spite of the great excitement within the work, complete formal control is maintained. . . .
In the *Mona Lisa,* one of the most
(35) overdiscussed and overrated pictures of all time (through no fault of its own), the same balance of monumental form and lyrical feeling is evident. This poetic sense, here as in many other works, is a definite
(40) Leonardo quality. It has little to do with portraiture, that is, with analysis of the sitter. If it is considered part of the painter's own personality, and not that of the somewhat smug lady, the picture takes
(45) on a different meaning. Certainly it is

mysterious, but so are Leonardo's other paintings. To this artist, all things, human and divine, were fit subjects for the searching analysis of his extraordinary
(50) mind.

Bernard Myers, *Fifty Great Artists.*

44. According to the review, Leonardo is considered brilliant because

    (1) he painted the *Last Supper*
    (2) he designed a flying machine
    (3) people were dazzled by his beauty
    (4) he was gifted in art and science
    (5) his anatomical sketches were superb

45. That Leonardo took "all knowledge as his sphere" means that he

    (1) was a nervous person
    (2) felt confused
    (3) had varied interests
    (4) felt unhappy being a painter
    (5) had trouble concentrating on one subject

46. In the writer's opinion, the importance of the *Mona Lisa* has been exaggerated because

    (1) Leonardo was a pioneer in art
    (2) Leonardo lived during the Renaissance
    (3) he is not to blame for the portrait's fame
    (4) Leonardo had an extraordinary mind
    (5) all his works have depth

47. Leonardo would most likely paint

    (1) any subject that caught his imagination
    (2) any subject he was hired to do
    (3) portraits of medieval nobles
    (4) religiously significant scenes
    (5) mathematically based studies

Items 48 to 51 refer to the following excerpt from a review.

HOW DOES THIS NOVELIST FIND HER STORIES?

Bebe Moore Campbell has a knack for giving both sides of the story—in black and white.

"I'm telling it as I see it without putting
(5) my emotions on it," says the author of the new racially charged novel *Brothers and Sisters*.

As in her first novel, *Your Blues Ain't Like Mine* (1992), Campbell tells her latest
(10) story from different racial points of view. This pleases some of her readers but disturbs others. . . .

Campbell, 44, a regular contributor to National Public Radio's *Morning Edition*,
(15) listens to a lot of talk radio, especially psychological shows that get into people's heads. This helps her do the viewpoint flip-flop.

Her ability to switch thinking modes
(20) carries over to the diverse choice of authors she reads. . . .

But her "favorite, favorite writer" is Toni Morrison, who shares her birthday, Feb. 18. "It was such a wonderful experience
(25) when I first read her," she says of Morrison. "I fell in love with her writing, the poetry of it."

The Philadelphia native and former schoolteacher now lives in Los Angeles,
(30) the setting of *Brothers and Sisters,* with her banker husband, Ellis Gordon Jr. She has a 24-year-old stepson and a 17-year-old daughter.

Campbell is pondering the topic for her
(35) next novel but, in the meantime, thinks about the state of relations among different people in the world.

Barbranda Lumpkins, "Campbell Moved by Urgency of Discord," *USA Today.*

48. If Campbell were to move back to Philadelphia, she would most likely

(1) continue to write about Los Angeles
(2) return to teaching
(3) set her next novel there
(4) stop listening to talk radio
(5) leave her husband and children

49. Which of the following is a consequence of Campbell's habit of listening to talk radio?

(1) She is more aware of different opinions.
(2) She has trouble completing her work.
(3) She spends less time reading to herself.
(4) She understands her children better than before.
(5) She gets inspiration for her novels.

50. According to this article, what is the consequence of Campbell's use of different racial points of view?

(1) It adds depth and variety to her novels.
(2) It confuses the reader.
(3) It has resulted in criticism of Campbell by some of her readers.
(4) It does not make a difference to her novels.
(5) Campbell has decided not to use this technique in her next novel.

51. Which of the following does not influence Campbell's writing?

(1) radio programs
(2) living in Los Angeles
(3) the writing of Toni Morrison
(4) her emotions
(5) psychological talk shows

Tip **To identify when a reviewer is expressing his or her opinion, look for words or phrases that make an evaluation, such as *the best of* or *mediocre*, or which suggest a strong emotional response, such as *dislikes* or *loved*. Facts are usually expressed in more neutral language.**

Items 52 to 54 refer to the following excerpt from an article.

WHAT DOES THARP THINK ABOUT ART?

Twyla Tharp is working these days without a company of her own and, until tax structures change, without a permanent base of support. When she
(5) gives a performance, as she is now doing at the Brooklyn Academy, the stage is bare, the dancers wear practice clothes and dance to taped music, and the ticket prices are scaled down. A "poverty" format
(10) becomes Twyla Tharp as it does few choreographers. But the economic picture that dancers face today is not pretty. At lunch in a downtown coffee shop recently, Tharp refused to discuss it. "Everybody
(15) knows how bad it is and how bad it's going to get. It's boring. I'll have the chicken soup, please. And, by the way, when was it ever good?"

Certainly things have been worse for
(20) Twyla Tharp. So far, only a half-dozen choreographers have been given MacArthur fellowships; she is one of them. The main benefit it has conferred on her, she says, is "unstructured time." "It means
(25) I can practically live in the studio," she explained. "If I call a rehearsal for 1 P.M. and I'm not ready to begin until one-fourteen, I don't feel guilty about those lost fourteen minutes. I'm grateful for the
(30) money, but I don't feel I'm entitled to it. I'm entitled to nothing but a second chance if I fail. That's all anyone's entitled to, I think."

To get a second chance, you have to have taken a first one. Every new dance
(35) begins with the choreographer assembling the dancers and saying to them, in effect, "Take a chance with me." The first step in the collaboration is always a leap of faith—for the choreographer as much as
(40) for the dancers. Tharp insists that she does not necessarily know where she is going when she starts a piece. "I have a desire to do it, and that gets me through. A whole lot of things get decided in the
(45) making. At some point in the piece, I begin to feel which movements belong and which don't. But the luxury of using up rehearsal time deciding how to proceed

isn't given to me with every commission. In
(50) commercial work, I'm hired to get results, and I rehearse differently: I enact an effect that has been prescribed by the conditions of the contract. It isn't art. Art is about finding things out."

Arlene Croce, "Twyla Tharp Looks Ahead and Thinks Back," *The New Yorker*.

52. Which of the following statements is an opinion?

   (1) Tharp does not have a company of her own.
   (2) Tharp's performances benefit from a lack of money.
   (3) Tharp's company performs at the Brooklyn Academy.
   (4) Tharp has recently been awarded a MacArthur fellowship.
   (5) Tharp's dancers do not wear extravagant costumes.

53. Which of the following best describes the effect of the fellowship on Tharp's way of working?

   (1) It has made rehearsing less worrisome.
   (2) Tharp has been able to find more commissions.
   (3) Tharp's performances have moved from the Brooklyn Academy.
   (4) It has allowed Tharp to spend less time in the studio.
   (5) Tharp has to use taped music.

54. Which of the following is the best conclusion that can be drawn from the article?

   (1) Tharp feels she deserves the MacArthur fellowship.
   (2) Receiving a MacArthur fellowship has given Tharp more freedom to create dances.
   (3) The future of dance is not hopeful.
   (4) Dancers can only eat chicken soup.
   (5) Tharp does not have faith in her dancers.

Items 55 and 56 refer to the following excerpt from an article.

WHAT'S NEXT FOR THIS PAIR?

Since joining forces 10 years ago, producers George Jackson and Doug McHenry have been playing the Hollywood game—and winning. Their string of hits
(5) includes *Krush Groove, New Jack City,* and *Jason's Lyric,* with which McHenry made his directorial debut. Next up is *The Walking Dead,* a Vietnam War movie about the lives of four black marines: Allen
(10) Payne, Eddie Griffin, Joe Morton, and Vonte Sweet. "Everyone from Oliver Stone to Francis Ford Coppola has made films on Vietnam," says Jackson. "But even though we died in the war in
(15) disproportionately high numbers, African-Americans have been left out of the documentation." Until now . . . .
The Walking Dead is Jackson and McHenry's first film under a landmark
(20) three-year production deal with Savoy Pictures. The pact make them the first African-Americans in the history of the film industry with the power to greenlight their own projects (with budgets of up to $15
(25) million each). "We were looking for an agreement that would allow us to short-circuit the tedious process of developing a film project, then shopping it to studios and trying to convince a bunch of executives to
(30) make it," says McHenry, a California native and 14-year film-biz veteran. "This is a real milestone for us as a people."
While Jackson and McHenry—who both hold graduate degrees from Harvard—are
(35) proud of their successes, they're eager to spread it around. That's why they hired Preston A. Whitmore II to write and direct *The Walking Dead* even though he didn't have any film credits, according to
(40) Jackson, a Harlem native who began his career as a production assistant at Paramount. "We want to nurture a *diverse* pool of black talent and bring their vision to the screen too." With the Savoy deal,
(45) they've got the time and the money to do just that.

Deborah Gregory, "Film: Producers McHenry and Jackson," *Vibe.*

55. It can be concluded from this excerpt that McHenry and Jackson

(1) lack artistic talent
(2) are unwilling to help others get started in the film business
(3) possess great promise for future endeavors
(4) are talented first-time film directors
(5) need money to finance their films

56. Which of the following best describes the consequences of McHenry's and Jackson's latest decisions?

(1) They have less money with which to make films.
(2) McHenry has given up directing.
(3) They've lost the power to decide what films to make.
(4) McHenry and Jackson are no longer working together.
(5) They will be able to concentrate on making films.

Tip **When reading a film review, examine the material quoted directly from the producers, directors, and other artists. Their words and phrases will further indicate the tone and images found in the film.**

Items 57 to 59 refer to the following excerpt from a theater review.

WHAT'S WRONG WITH THIS PLAY?

Part bawdy comedy, part dark elegy, part mystery, August Wilson's rich new play, *Seven Guitars,* nicely eludes categorization. It begins with a prologue in
(5) which a group of friends are mourning the death of Floyd Barton, a blues guitarist and singer whose career was on the verge of taking off. The action that follows is a flashback leading up to Floyd's death. But
(10) though full and strong in its buildup, the play loses its potency as it reaches its climax. Floyd's death may be plausible, even inevitable, but it becomes tangled in a confusing thicket of mysticism and
(15) subplots. Though Floyd is as charming and sympathetic a protagonist as we could want, the surprising truth is that his death has little effect on us. We leave the theater entertained and admiring but not truly
(20) moved.

That is hardly the fault of the nearly flawless production that *Seven Guitars* is being given in its world premiere at Chicago's Goodman Theatre. It has been
(25) directed with both theatricality and honesty by Walter Dallas, an experienced interpreter of Wilson who was brought in when Lloyd Richards, who has directed the premiere of every other Wilson play,
(30) had to bow out because of a health problem. Scott Bradley's soaring set—the backyard of a ramshackle tenement building, complete with earnest little garden and the tallest, steepest stairway
(35) since Jacob's ladder—is abundant in telling detail. Along with Constanza Romero's flamboyant costumes, it brings to vivid life the 1948 Pittsburgh that is the locale of the play.
(40) *Seven Guitars* (whether or not it refers to the play's seven characters—the title is a mystery too) is the sixth in an ambitious series. Wilson intends to set a work in each decade of the 20th century, with each
(45) play reflecting on aspects of the black experience. Though his previous efforts have enjoyed great critical success and have won two Pulitzer Prizes, only *Fences*
(1987) achieved a run of any length on
(50) Broadway, and that was probably owing to the presence of a star, James Earl Jones. If Broadway is inhospitable to straight plays of all sorts, it is especially so to so-called black plays.

William Tynan, "Death and the Blues," *Time.*

57. Which of the following best describes the reviewer's opinion of *Seven Guitars?*

   (1) dreadful
   (2) magnificent
   (3) flawed
   (4) moving
   (5) badly directed

58. Which of the following statements is a fact?

   (1) Floyd's death is inevitable.
   (2) The play is part of an ambitious series.
   (3) Broadway isn't friendly to plays unless they are musicals.
   (4) *Fences* was popular because of James Earl Jones.
   (5) August Wilson has received two Pulitzer Prizes.

59. Which of the following best describes the point of view of this excerpt?

   (1) extreme dislike for anything Wilson writes
   (2) an even-handed appreciation for Wilson's endeavors
   (3) a willingness to overlook problems at all costs
   (4) lack of knowledge of Wilson's previous works
   (5) a disregard for any work appearing on Broadway

Literature & the Arts ◆ Commentary

Items 60 to 63 refer to the following excerpt from a review.

WHY DOES THIS 73-YEAR-OLD PAINT?

The American folk artist Howard Finster once announced that God had shown him how to paint a picture of a fabulous factory. This industrial plant, said Finster, will be
(5) "the world's 8th wonder. . . . It will run until it wears out without one single employee. . . . It will store one square mile of our largest aircraft. . . . The picture will be beautiful even if rejected."
(10) Not many of Finster's pictures have been rejected. By his own count this 73-year-old former revivalist preacher from Georgia has created more than 10,000 works of "sacred art." He's been
(15) interviewed by an amazed Johnny Carson, has designed rock-music albums, is the subject of an eye-popping retrospective at New York's Paine Webber Art Gallery, and is one of the hottest properties in the field
(20) of folk art. As the quotation above indicates, Finster is a painter of visions. His pictures combine almost every kind of graphic medium with words ranging from Bible quotations to snatches of his own
(25) wisdom. In *Four Presidents* (1983), he depicts Washington, Lincoln, Jefferson and Kennedy beneath a message that reads: "Our great nation came up through great leaders. Shall we stand by and let it
(30) turn to monsters?"
Finster's work is riding the current accelerated expansion of interest in 20th-century folk art. Say "folk art" and most Americans will think of Grandma Moses
(35) landscapes, duck decoys, quilts, and weather vanes. But the innocuous term "folk" masks many problems that have spawned additional labels including, in one scholar's list: "primitive, native, amateur, . . .
(40) country, popular, . . . innocent, provincial, anonymous, visionary, homemade, . . . ethnic, nonacademic." As Robert Bishop, director of the Museum of American Folk Art in New York, puts it: "When you have
(45) something that difficult to classify, it makes you nervous."

Jack Kroll, "The Outsiders Are In," *Newsweek*.

60. Based on the excerpt, which of the following best summarizes Howard Finster's artistic works?

(1) He created the design for an aircraft factory.
(2) He mainly paints country landscapes.
(3) He likes to go on talk shows.
(4) His painting covers a wide range of issues.
(5) His art was discovered by major art museums across the country.

61. It can be inferred from the long list of terms for folk art that

(1) art critics are not quite sure what folk art is
(2) folk art is complicated and slick
(3) folk artists are highly trained
(4) anyone can become a folk artist
(5) folk art does not really belong in museums and galleries

62. Which would you be most likely to find in a folk art museum?

(1) a painting by an art student
(2) a hand-painted Easter egg
(3) an architect's blueprint
(4) a factory-made teapot
(5) a child's first drawing

63. What is an effect of an increased interest in twentieth-century folk art?

(1) People now ignore the work of Grandma Moses.
(2) Many of Howard Finster's pictures have been rejected.
(3) There has been an increase in religious art.
(4) It has become easier to decide what folk art is.
(5) More people have paid attention to Howard Finster's work.

Answers are on page 842.

Choose the best answer to each item.
Items 1 and 2 refer to the following excerpt.

HOW DID POP ART GET ITS NAME?

Pop suggests popular. The movement
got a lot of publicity from the media who
saw that it was news, easy to enjoy and
easy to write about. It was the time when
(5)   pop stars like Elvis Presley and the
Beatles were emerging, and this art in
many instances was responding to that
world rather than the world of deep human
feelings and problems. Its idiom was in
(10)   many cases borrowed from the media:
whereas art normally proceeded by taking
ideas from art and making something new
of them, this came from commercial art
and so was speaking a language created
(15)   by experts to reach the whole consumer
society. For the same reason many
commentators, especially in the United
States, hated it. It denied, or seemed to
deny, all seriousness and attached itself to
(20)   commonplace fantasies and the hard sell.

Norbert Lynton, *A History of Art.*

1. According to the excerpt, the term "pop art"
    means that it

    (1) appealed only to fans of rock and roll
    (2) was not expensive
    (3) was easy to understand
    (4) dealt with important issues
    (5) was favored by religious groups

2. One reason that some people objected to
    pop art was that

    (1) it was too romantic
    (2) it lacked serious content
    (3) pop artists copied Picasso
    (4) it had no humor
    (5) the subject matter was unpleasant

Items 3 and 4 refer to the following review.

WHO IS JOHN MARTIN?

Fifty years ago it was possible to buy a
painting by John Martin for next to nothing.
As for the books that he illustrated, they
turned up on book barrows all over
(5)   England and cost only pennies. Born in
the year of the French Revolution, Martin
lived until 1854, had moments of celebrity
in his lifetime, and then somehow fell
through the floorboards of art history. The
(10)   fact that he was a visionary artist who
could match himself against the Old
Testament and go the distance without
apparent effort counted for nothing in the
1920s and 1930s.
(15)   But in our own time, John Martin has
come all the way back again. Curators,
connoisseurs and book collectors stand in
line for his work when it appears on the
market.

John Russell, *The New York Times.*

3. Anyone could have bought a Martin painting
    fifty years ago

    (1) for millions of dollars
    (2) with great difficulty
    (3) for practically nothing
    (4) for a moderate price
    (5) by lining up at auctions

4. Which of the following best explains why
    Martin "fell through the floorboards of art
    history"?

    (1) Martin's paintings were cheap.
    (2) Martin painted religious pictures.
    (3) Art collectors of the 1920s and 1930s
         were not interested in visionary art.
    (4) Martin died very young.
    (5) Painters do not become popular until
         they have been dead for fifty years.

Items 5 to 9 refer to the following quotation from an article.

WHAT WAS WRONG WITH CHRISTINA?

"When I painted it in 1948, *Christina's World* hung all summer in my house in Maine and nobody particularly reacted to it. I thought, 'Boy, is this one ever a flat
(5) tire.' Now I get at least a letter a week from all over the world, usually wanting to know what she's doing. Actually there isn't any definite story. The way this tempera happened, I was in an upstairs room in the
(10) Olson house and saw Christina crawling in the field. Later, I went down to the road and made a pencil drawing of the house, but I never went down into the field. You see, my memory was more of a reality
(15) than the thing itself. I didn't put Christina in till the very end. I worked on the hill for months, that brown grass, and kept thinking about her in her pink dress like a faded lobster shell I might find on the
(20) beach, crumpled. Finally I got up enough courage to say to her, "Would you mind if I made a drawing of you sitting outside?" and drew her crippled arms and hands. Finally, I was so shy about posing her, I
(25) got my wife Betsy to pose for her figure. Then it came time to lay in Christina's figure against that planet I'd created for her all those weeks. I put this pink tone on her shoulder—and it almost blew me
(30) across the room."

Richard Meryman, "Andrew Wyeth: An Interview."

5. Andrew Wyeth talks about his own work in this excerpt. His point of view helps the reader to understand

   (1) how painful being an artist can be
   (2) how an artwork is developed
   (3) why memory cannot be depended on
   (4) why artists get fan mail
   (5) that artists have courage

6. According to this artist, the pink tone

   (1) amazed him
   (2) was not very important
   (3) was carefully planned
   (4) was not effective
   (5) was the result of a pencil drawing

7. Why did Wyeth get all those letters about Christina?

   (1) People had seen the painting of her and were touched.
   (2) Christina had stopped writing to her fans.
   (3) People were angry at Wyeth for painting her.
   (4) People did not want to see the painting anymore.
   (5) People wanted to criticize her.

8. What emotional effect is suggested by Wyeth's reference to the faded lobster (lines 18–20)?

   (1) sadness
   (2) anger
   (3) happiness
   (4) fear
   (5) shyness

9. Based on information in the excerpt, which of the following statements is not true?

   (1) *Christina's World* is an oil painting.
   (2) Wyeth painted the picture over many months.
   (3) Wyeth was reluctant to pose Christina for the painting.
   (4) Wyeth painted the background mostly from memory.
   (5) The figure of Christina was the last element painted.

Answers are on page 847.

Choose the best answer to each item. Items 1 to 4 refer to the following excerpt from a short story.

WHAT IS THE BOY'S SECRET FEAR?

"Don't think," I said. "Just take it easy."

"I'm taking it easy," he said and looked straight ahead. He was evidently holding tight onto himself about something.

(5)   "Take this with water."

"Do you think it will do any good?"

"Of course it will."

I sat down and opened the *Pirate* book and commenced to read, but I could see

(10)   he was not following, so I stopped.

"About what time do you think I'm going to die?" he asked.

"What?"

"About how long will it be before I die?"

(15)   "You aren't going to die. What's the matter with you?"

"Oh, yes, I am. I heard him say a hundred and two."

"People don't die with a fever of one

(20)   hundred and two. That's a silly way to talk."

"I know they do. At school in France the boys told me you can't live with forty-four degrees. I've got a hundred and two."

(25)   He had been waiting to die all day, ever since nine o'clock in the morning.

"You poor Schatz," I said. "Poor old Schatz. It's like miles and kilometers. You aren't going to die. That's a different

(30)   thermometer. On that thermometer thirty-seven is normal. On this kind it's ninety-eight."

"Are you sure?"

"Absolutely," I said. "It's like miles and

(35)   kilometers. You know, like how many kilometers we make when we do seventy miles in the car?"

Ernest Hemingway, "A Day's Wait," *Winner Take Nothing.*

1. The absence of descriptive images in this excerpt gives it

    (1) a cold, scientific effect
    (2) a dull, ho-hum feeling
    (3) a direct, factual impact
    (4) a dry, scholarly quality
    (5) a dreamy, poetic mood

2. Like the boy's fear, the excerpt

    (1) remains mysterious throughout
    (2) fails to reach a climax
    (3) awakens little sympathy
    (4) is about something trivial
    (5) builds up and relaxes

3. Which of the following best describes the narrator's attitude towards the boy?

    (1) anger
    (2) love
    (3) pity
    (4) frustration
    (5) resentment

4. Why does the narrator use the word "poor" (line 27)?

    (1) The boy's family is poor.
    (2) The narrator is poor.
    (3) He feels sorry that the boy is going to die.
    (4) He feels sorry that the boy has been worrying all day.
    (5) He feels sorry that the boy is sick.

Tip When reading to identify tone, pay attention to the characters. *How* characters say something and *what* they say may indicate the tone of an excerpt.

Items 5 to 8 refer to the following poem.

WHY IS THE POET CALLING THE CHILD?

CALLING THE CHILD

From the third floor I beckon to the child
Flying over the grass. As if by chance
My signal catches her and stops her dance
Under the lilac tree;
(5) And I have flung my net at something wild
And brought it down in all its loveliness.
She lifts her eyes to mine reluctantly,
Measuring in my look our twin distress.

Then from the garden she considers me
(10) And gathering joy, breaks from the closing net
And races off like one who would forget
That there are nets and snares.
But she returns and stands beneath the tree
With great solemnity, with legs apart,
(15) And wags her head at last and makes a start
And starts her humorous marching up the stairs.

Karl Shapiro, *Collected Poems 1940–1978.*

5. What is suggested by the child's "flying over the grass" (line 2)?

(1) The child can actually fly.
(2) The little girl has a lot of energy.
(3) The speaker is imagining things.
(4) The girl thinks she can fly.
(5) The girl is trying to get to the safety of the sidewalk.

6. Which of the following best describes what the poet means by "Measuring in my look our twin distress" (line 8)?

(1) The child looks up and sees twins.
(2) The poet observes happiness in the child's eyes.
(3) The child is a twin.
(4) The poet and the child have similar feelings of regret.
(5) The poet and the child are equally reluctant to stop their play.

7. The little girl returns because

(1) she likes being by the tree
(2) she is tired of racing
(3) she realizes it is time to go inside
(4) it is getting dark
(5) the garden is too solemn a place to play in

8. What is the effect of the image of the net in the poem?

(1) It emphasizes the child's wild, free nature.
(2) It shows that the speaker is a skilled hunter.
(3) It shows that parents trap their children.
(4) It shows that the speaker is heartless.
(5) It shows that movement adds meaning to the poem.

Items 9 to 13 refer to the following review.

WHAT ARE THIS SINGER'S STRENGTHS?

Listening to Nancy Wilson's latest release, *Love, Nancy* (Columbia), I'm struck by two things. One is how much she says while saying so little. Nancy Wilson

(5) came up at a time when men and women knew the power of suggestion. In an age when you couldn't go around saying four-letter words in a song, artists developed the power to move people's minds with

(10) understatement, innuendo, nuance. . . .
The second thing that strikes you is the Voice. Testing emotional limits is what Wilson calls "my forte—the big, powerful, emotional ballad." And with naked emotion

(15) as her fuel, Wilson's voice usually blasts through her orchestral ballads like a blowtorch through candle wax.
When she takes on songs like "First Time on a Ferris Wheel" . . . , her

(20) interpretive powers turn the words into breathless explorations of ecstasy. In "I Remember," she conveys more feelings with the single word *sky* than other vocalists do with entire songs, or even

(25) albums. Listening to Nancy, I get the same feeling I get when hearing, for example, Organized Konfusion's giga-rhythmic "Let's Organize." I get overwhelmed by the sudden realization that, man, these people

(30) can pretty much do *anything*.

Harry Allen, "Legends," *Vibe*.

9. To demonstrate the power of Wilson's voice, the reviewer describes it as

(1) full of suggestion
(2) emotionless
(3) endowed with superhuman strength
(4) understated
(5) not being used to its fullest abilities

10. Which of the following words best defines "innuendo" (line 10)?

(1) quiet
(2) beautiful
(3) skillful
(4) hint
(5) misleading

11. Based on the excerpt, how can we best describe the approach of this reviewer?

(1) objective
(2) appreciative
(3) involved
(4) mistaken
(5) ecstatic

12. When the reviewer says that Wilson "conveys more feelings . . . than other vocalists do . . ." (lines 22–24), he is stating

(1) his personal opinion
(2) the results of a vote among his friends
(3) facts
(4) what Wilson told him in an interview
(5) public opinion

13. Based upon the excerpt, it can be concluded that the reviewer is approaching his subject

(1) never having heard of Wilson before
(2) with the belief that Wilson and Organized Konfusion perform similar types of music
(3) disliking anything Wilson has ever recorded
(4) with a respect for Wilson's musical abilities
(5) having the desire for Wilson to say more in her songs

HOW CAN ANNIE AND HELEN WORK TOGETHER?

ANNIE: It's hopeless here. I can't teach a child who runs away.

KELLER: *(nonplused)* Then—do I understand you—propose—

(5) ANNIE: Well, if we all agree it's hopeless, the next question is what—

KATE: Miss Annie. I am not agreed. I think perhaps you—underestimate Helen.

ANNIE: I think everybody else here does.

(10) KATE: She did fold her napkin. She learns, she learns, do you know she began talking when she was six months old? She could say "water." Not really— "wahwah." "Wahwah," but she meant

(15) water, she knew what it meant, and only six months old, I never saw a child so— bright, or outgoing—It's still in her, somewhere, isn't it? You should have seen her before her illness, such a

(20) good-tempered child—

ANNIE: *(agreeably)* She's changed.

KATE: Miss Annie, put up with it. And with us.

KELLER: Us!

(25) KATE: Please? Like the lost lamb in the parable, I love her all the more.

ANNIE: Mrs. Keller, I don't think Helen's worst handicap is deafness or blindness. I think it's your love. And pity.

(30) KELLER: Now what does that mean?

ANNIE: All of you here are so sorry for her you've kept her—like a pet, why, even a dog you housebreak. No wonder she won't let me come near her. It's useless

(35) for me to try to teach her language or anything else here. I might as well—

KATE: *(cuts in)* Miss Annie, before you came we spoke of putting her in an asylum.

William Gibson, *The Miracle Worker*.

14. Which of the following best explains why Kate says what she does?

(1) She is jealous of Helen.
(2) She believes Annie can help.
(3) She does not want to take care of Helen anymore.
(4) She is angry at Mrs. Keller.
(5) She feels like a lost lamb.

15. Based upon the information given in the excerpt, which of the following best describes Helen's behavior?

(1) uncooperative
(2) shy
(3) enthusiastic
(4) helpful
(5) friendly

16. Which of the following lines from the excerpt best indicates that Annie does not think Helen is hopeless?

(1) "I think everybody else here does." (line 9)
(2) "She's changed." (line 21)
(3) "Mrs. Keller, I don't think Helen's worst handicap is deafness or blindness." (lines 27–29)
(4) "I think it's your love." (line 29)
(5) "No wonder she won't let me come near her." (lines 33–34)

17. With which of these statements about children with handicaps would Annie agree?

(1) They cannot be taught language.
(2) They should be given everything they want.
(3) They must be taught, not pitied.
(4) They are better off in an asylum.
(5) They should be treated like pets.

Items 18 to 21 refer to the following excerpt from a book.

IS WASHINGTON'S NOMINATION SURPRISING?

John worked hard. By the middle of June, he decided the moment was ripe. On a dull, muggy morning, he walked alone to Congress, determined to
(5) nominate Washington before the noon bell sounded from the tower. As soon as the members were seated, John rose and spoke briefly for the establishment of a Continental army, outlining the present
(10) dangers, chief of which was that the forces at Cambridge might dissolve entirely. What was to prevent the British from profiting by this delay, marching out of Boston and "spreading desolation as far as they could
(15) go"? For commander-in-chief of a Grand American Army he would like, John finished, to suggest *"a gentleman whose skill as an officer, whose independent fortune, great talents and universal*
(20) *character would command the respect of America and unite the full exertions of the Colonies better than any other person alive."*

All the time he was speaking, Hancock
(25) wore a look of pleased, even radiant, expectancy. Facing the room in his chair behind the President's table, he was plainly visible to everyone, including John, who stood near the front. No one loved
(30) glory more than Hancock; he had the vanity of a child, open and vulnerable. John saw his face and hastened on, raising his voice a little: "A gentleman *from Virginia,* who is among us here, and well
(35) known to all."

Hancock shrank as at a blow. ("I never," John wrote later, "remarked a more sudden and striking change of countenance. Mortification and resentment
(40) were expressed as forcibly as his face could exhibit them.") Washington, who was on the south side of the room, left his seat at the word *Virginia* and slipped quietly out the door before his name was
(45) pronounced.

Catherine Drinker Bowen, *The Young John Adams.*

18. The incident in this excerpt is described

   (1) from Hancock's viewpoint
   (2) in the third person
   (3) from Washington's viewpoint
   (4) in the first person
   (5) in the interviewer's words

19. What tells us how Hancock's face looked in response to the nomination?

   (1) Adams's own words
   (2) Washington's memoirs
   (3) a newspaper account
   (4) a painting of the event
   (5) the biographer's imagination

20. The nomination speech is communicated

   (1) in the third person
   (2) in Hancock's words
   (3) in the biographer's words
   (4) in Washington's words
   (5) in the first person

21. The fact that Washington left just before Adams said his name indicates that
   (A) Washington could not take the job.
   (B) Washington knew he was about to be offered the job.
   (C) Washington was too modest to enjoy hearing himself praised.

   (1) A only
   (2) C only
   (3) A and B
   (4) B and C
   (5) A, B, and C

WHAT MAKES TV MORE INTERESTING THAN MOVIES?

Television remains a stepchild of the movie business. Movie stars and top directors often refuse to work in it, and they rarely admit to watching it. Movie

(5) agents advise clients that it's the last resort for careers in distress. Writers and intellectuals patronize it.

But for a while now, the movie business has been confronted with an

(10) uncomfortable fact of life: In terms of dramatic value, relevance and humor, prime-time television—much of it, anyway—is far better than what's on at the movies.

(15) Admissions of this come grudgingly for the most part, but they do come, especially this past week, when the film industry struggled to find five films to nominate for the Academy Awards . . . .

(20) No such difficulties face television. Once or twice a night there are TV shows that are vivid or powerful or funny— sometimes all three—and that do not insult the intelligence of viewers beyond

(25) the age of consent. . . .

Perhaps the most significant reason television has surpassed movies, many people in Hollywood say, is that it is a writer's medium, while films are dominated

(30) by directors.

Bernard Weintraub, "Pssst: TV Nudging Movies Aside as High Art. Pass It On," *The New York Times.*

22. Which of the following does the reviewer give as a cause for television moving ahead of movies?

(1) The film industry could not find five films to nominate for the Academy Awards.
(2) Movie stars and top directors often refuse to work in television.
(3) Movies are controlled by directors while TV is controlled by writers.
(4) Intellectuals do not think very highly of television.
(5) Television is an offshoot of the movie industry.

23. What does the reviewer believe is an effect of TV being better than movies?

(1) More movie stars will try to work in television.
(2) There are TV programs shown every night that do not insult their viewers.
(3) The Academy Awards will not be held this year.
(4) Movies will become more humorous and dramatic.
(5) Top directors will give up some of their control over movies.

24. If given a choice, the author would most likely

(1) read a book
(2) go to a theater to watch a new movie
(3) stay home and watch television
(4) attend a theater performance
(5) go to a museum to look at paintings and sculpture

25. Which of the following can be concluded from this excerpt?

(1) Movies are better than TV shows.
(2) Actors do not care if they work in movies or television.
(3) Television has been consistently producing better shows than the movie industry.
(4) Most television shows presume that viewers will not understand them.
(5) The television industry is controlled by directors.

Tip **To help you draw conclusions, try to identify the main idea. Then ask yourself what other ideas support it. Identifying necessary information helps you interpret and understand what the author is saying and make decisions about that information.**

Answers are on page 848.

Mathematics

The architect I.M. Pei has designed many buildings that have broad, irregular geometric shapes.

The GED Mathematics test focuses on the basic concepts of several areas of mathematics, including arithmetic, algebra, and geometry.

In this unit you will learn how to use arithmetic facts to solve a variety of problems. You will also learn how to estimate to narrow your options or check your answers.

For whole numbers, you will learn about place value and how to use it to read, write, compare, and order numbers. You will also learn to perform the four basic arithmetic operations: adding, subtracting, multiplying, and dividing.

Two lessons will help you understand how to approach and solve word problems. They will help you know when to add, subtract, multiply, and divide. The concepts in these lessons will be built upon throughout the unit.

Next you will practice computing with fractions. First you will understand the concept of fractions. Then you will learn to perform the four arithmetic operations with fractions. Finally, you will apply the operations to practical problems to test your understanding.

Decimals are another way to write fractions. Perhaps the most common use of decimals is our system of dollars and cents.

Percent is still another way we express a fraction. Just as 50 cents or $0.50 is one-half of a dollar, 50% is one-half of a whole.

Understanding basic graphs, charts, and tables is very helpful to your work with numbers. A great deal of information can be presented on a graph. Deciding what information you need to solve a problem is an important skill.

Your skills in using ratio and proportion, finding an average, and probability help you compare information and make decisions. Is Brand X cheaper per ounce than Brand Y? This type of everyday decision can be made more confidently using these skills.

Next you will learn about two common measurement systems: the standard and the metric systems. You will learn how to solve problems about distance, weight, time, and volume. You will also learn to find the perimeter, area, and circumference of basic shapes.

Algebra is a form of mathematics that uses letters called variables to stand for numbers. This unit covers how to write algebraic expressions and how to use them to solve problems. In geometry you will study shapes that you see and use every day.

Throughout this unit, you will be introduced to many useful problem-solving strategies. Using estimation and mental math are two strategies that can save you time as you work. Identifying needed information and weeding out unnecessary information are two other very important skills. Combine these strategies with your arithmetic skills and you will greatly improve your mathematics abilities.

Whole Numbers

Lesson ① Number Values and Facts

Place Value

hundred billions	ten billions	billions	hundred millions	ten millions	millions	hundred thousands	ten thousands	thousands	hundreds	tens	ones
							3	0,	3	9	6

Whole numbers are written using ten **digits: 0, 1, 2, 3, 4, 5, 6, 7, 8, and 9.** The number 3,820 has four digits. The **place value** of a digit is found by its position in a number. The chart shows the names of the first 12 whole-number places. To write a number, use a comma to group every three digits, counting from the right. Read each group, or period, together, ending with the name of the period. The number 30,396 is read "thirty thousand, three hundred ninety-six." Zeros are written to fill up a three-place period, but they are not read.

The value of the 9 in 30,396 is 9 x 10, or 90. The sum of the values of the digits in a number equals the total value of the number.

Comparing Numbers

Sometimes you need to compare numbers to find the largest or the smallest number in a group. Your knowledge of place value will help you when you compare numbers. Use these symbols to compare numbers:

=	**equals**
>	**is greater than**
<	**is less than**

140 = 140   One hundred forty **equals** one hundred forty.
25 > 23   Twenty-five **is greater than** twenty-three.
4 < 5   Four **is less than** five.

The greater and less than symbols *always point to the smaller number.*

To compare numbers, follow these rules:

Rule 1: The whole number with the most digits is greater.
Example: 7,235 > 848

Rule 2: For numbers with the same number of digits, compare digits from left to right.
Examples: 6,746 > 6,699 because 700 > 600
588,210 < 589,429 because 8,000 < 9,000

Rounding

Rounding makes numbers easier to remember. It also makes difficult calculations easier. A number can be rounded when the exact amount is not needed.

Use these steps to round whole numbers:

Step 1: Find the digit you want to round to. It may help to circle this digit. 2④,902
Step 2: Look at the digit immediately to the right of the circled digit. 2④,902
Step 3: If the digit to the right is 5 or more, add 1 to the circled digit. If the digit to the right is less than 5, do not change the circled digit. Change all digits to the right of the circled digit to zeros. 2⑤,000

◇ ged Exercise Number Values and Facts

Directions: Write the value of the underlined digit in words.

Example: 6̲27   six hundred

1. 5,5̲17   _____

2. 3̲,742,691   _____

3. 2̲6,154   _____

4. 18̲,063,500,000   _____

5. 4,7̲00,510   _____

6. 9̲64,211   _____

7. 1̲86,502,110   _____

8. What is the value of each digit in **679,308**?

6 _____

7 _____

9 _____

3 _____

0 _____

8 _____

Directions: Match each number in Column A with its word form in Column B.

Column A

_____ 9. 8,416

_____ 10. 8,420,106

_____ 11. 84,200,160

_____ 12. 842,016

Column B

a. Eighty-four million, two hundred thousand, one hundred sixty
b. Eight thousand, four hundred sixteen
c. Eight hundred forty-two thousand, sixteen
d. Eight million, four hundred twenty thousand, one hundred six

Column A

_____ 13. 10,250,900

_____ 14. 12,509

_____ 15. 1,259

_____ 16. 125,090

Column B

a. One hundred twenty-five thousand, ninety
b. Twelve thousand, five hundred nine
c. Ten million, two hundred fifty thousand, nine hundred
d. One thousand, two hundred fifty-nine

Directions: Compare the following numbers. Write $>$, $<$, or $=$ between the numbers.

17.   1,305   1,503

18.   34,000   29,989

19.   102,667   102,657

20. 5,690,185   5,690,185,100

21. 7,650,300   7,649,950

22.   875,438   875,438

23. 3,492,012,558   3,492,012,558

24. 75,390,000   75,391,540

25.   9,500,000   9,500,000,000

26.   45,100   45,099

27. 7,456,795   7,500,000

28. 319,002,110   319,002,110

Directions: Round the number to the given place.

29. **8,621** to the hundreds place _____

30. **675,924** to the nearest hundred thousand _____

31. **5,099,620** to the nearest million _____

32. **49,962,750** to the millions place _____

33. **10,562** to the nearest thousand _____

34. **46,055** to the nearest ten thousand _____

35. **64,000,000** to the nearest ten million _____

36. **73,895** to the nearest thousand _____

Items 37 to 41 refer to the following chart.

Daily Sales Totals Week Ending March 4	
Monday	$18,756
Tuesday	12,316
Wednesday	13,940
Thursday	13,772
Friday	21,592
Saturday	28,795

37. The manager of the store must report daily sales to her supervisor. The supervisor wants the sales reported to the nearest thousand dollars. What amount will the manager report for each day shown?

Monday _____   Thursday _____

Tuesday _____   Friday _____

Wednesday _____   Saturday _____

38. Which day had the greater sales, Wednesday or Thursday? _____

39. Which day of the week had the lowest sales? _____

40. Which day had the highest sales? _____

41. Arrange the sales on the chart in order from lowest to highest.

_____

_____

_____

Answers are on page 850.

Lesson  Whole Number Operations

There are four whole number operations: addition, subtraction, multiplication, and division. One key to success in mathematics is knowing how to do these four operations accurately.

Addition

Use these steps to add, or combine quantities or find a total:

$$\begin{array}{r} {}^{11} \\ 169 \\ + 683 \\ \hline 852 \end{array}$$

Step 1: Line up the numbers so that each column has digits with the same place value.

Step 2: Starting with the ones column and working to the left, add the numbers in each column.

Step 3: When a column of digits has a sum greater than 9, you will need to carry to the next column on the left.

Step 4: Check by adding up instead of down.

Subtraction

Use these steps to subtract or find the difference between numbers:

$$\begin{array}{r} {}^{911}_{4\ \ 1\ 1\ 1} \\ 5{,}025 \\ - 2{,}438 \\ \hline 2{,}587 \end{array} \qquad \begin{array}{r} \textbf{Check:} \\ 2{,}587 \\ + 2{,}438 \\ \hline 5{,}025 \end{array}$$

Step 1: Write the smaller number below the greater number, lining up the place value columns.

Step 2: Starting with the ones column and working to the left, subtract each column.

Step 3: When a digit in the bottom number is greater than the digit in the top number, "borrow" to subtract the column.

Step 4: Check your answer by adding the result and the bottom number.

Multiplication

Use these steps to multiply, or find the product of two numbers:

$$\begin{array}{r} 912 \\ \times\ 43 \\ \hline 2\ 736 \\ 36\ 48 \\ \hline 39{,}216 \end{array}$$

Step 1: Work from the right-hand digit of the number on the bottom. Multiply the ones column and continue to the left. Multiply the top number by each digit in the bottom number.

Step 2: Line up the result under the digit you multiplied by. Add the results of each multiplication.

Step 3: Check by multiplying again.

Division

To find out how many times one number goes into another number (divide), use the steps for long division:

$$\begin{array}{r} 406\text{r}2 \\ 18\overline{)7{,}310} \\ \underline{7\ 2} \\ 110 \\ \underline{108} \\ 2 \end{array} \qquad \begin{array}{r} \textbf{Check:} \\ 406 \\ \times\ 18 \\ \hline 3248 \\ 406 \\ \hline 7308 \\ +\quad 2 \\ \hline 7{,}310 \end{array}$$

Step 1: Divide (18 into 73). Write the quotient above the 3.

Step 2: Multiply (4 times 18).

Step 3: Subtract (72 from 73).

Step 4: Bring down the next digit (the 1, then the 0).

Step 5: Repeat steps 1–4 with all the digits.

Step 6: Check your solution by multiplying.

Directions: Solve.

1.   305
   + 463

3.   6,795
   + 132

5.   56,439
   + 4,796

7.   19,067
   + 35,196

2.   4,172
   + 4,510

4.   193
     317
   + 629

6.   36,075
      1,936
    189,006
   + 17,950

8.   65,196
      6,725
    114,021
   + 27,716

---

9. 81,427 + 3,584 + 24,625 =

13. Add 176 and 54,095.

10. Add 76 and 58.

14. 35,100 + 49,257 + 7,566 =

11. What is the total of 36, 9, 74, 48, 6, and 15?

15. What is the total of 950, 308, 77, 29, and 50?

12. 588,394 + 61,042 + 109,014 =

16. 6,019 + 85,200 + 116,896 =

---

17.   86
    - 51

19.   494
    - 167

21.   680
    - 268

23.   800
    - 219

18. 51,964
   - 20,651

20. 1,258
   - 295

22. 3,205
   - 2,276

24. 5,067
   - 3,795

---

25. 10,508 − 3,679 =

29. Subtract 16,567 from 20,000.

26. Subtract 3,695 from 5,000.

30. 375,000 − 186,425 =

27. 419,003 − 12,018 =

31. Subtract 4,768 from 510,000.

28. Find the difference of 10,000 and 8,975.

32. Find the difference of 100,000 and 75,510.

---

33.   432
    ×   2

35. 15,663
    ×   8

37.   36
    × 23

39. 1,193
    ×   45

34.   746
    ×   5

36. 30,409
    ×   9

38. 5,084
    ×   76

40. 3,276
    ×   24

41. $2,584 \times 2,700 =$

42. $25,097 \times 60 =$

43. $8,050 \times 509 =$

44. $1,247 \times 3,014 =$

45. $65 \times 885 =$

46. $190 \times 2,186 =$

47. $775 \times 775 =$

48. $3,056 \times 2,500 =$

49. $7\overline{)3,206}$

50. $4\overline{)23,984}$

51. $6\overline{)254,178}$

52. $16\overline{)130,112}$

53. $6\overline{)3,502}$

54. $12\overline{)76,402}$

55. $13\overline{)100,000}$

56. $24\overline{)219,315}$

57. $35\overline{)38,430}$

58. Divide 30,321 by 46.

59. $360,537 \div 68 =$

60. $139,400 \div 205 =$

61. Divide 159,035 by 155.

62. $606,450 \div 15 =$

63. Divide 712,000 by 25.

64. $419,357 \div 163 =$

65. Divide 508,320 by 120.

Answers are on page 850.

Lesson 3

Steps to Solving Word Problems

Solving word problems requires an organized approach. These ideas will help you organize your work.

Four-Step Plan

Read
Plan
Solve
Check

Read: Make sure you understand the problem. Identify what it is that you need to find out. Think of how the information in the problem can help you find the answer.

Plan: Choose the operation (addition, subtraction, multiplication, or division) you will use to solve the problem.

Solve: You may think you can solve the problem in your head. This may be possible, but you will make fewer errors if you write the problem out.

Check: Make sure your answer makes sense. Does it answer the question posed by the problem? Does it seem reasonable? Check your answer.

Estimation

To **estimate** means to find an approximate solution to a problem. Use estimation to solve problems that do not require an exact solution. One way to estimate is to use rounding.

Example: The city of Southampton has 11,968 registered voters. In a recent election, only 4,787 of the people registered actually voted. Approximately how many registered voters did not vote?

(1) between 4,500 and 5,500

(2) between 5,500 and 6,500

(3) between 6,500 and 7,500

(4) between 7,500 and 8,500

(5) between 8,500 and 9,500

To compare the number of registered voters with the number of people who voted, you need to subtract. However, the problem does not require an exact solution. The word approximately tells you to estimate the answer. To estimate, round the numbers to the nearest thousand and subtract.

$$\begin{array}{r} 12,000 \\ -\ 5,000 \\ \hline 7,000 \end{array}$$ Estimated solution

The best answer is **(3) between 6,500 and 7,500.**

Estimation can also be used to decide if an exact answer is reasonable.

Mathematics ◆ Whole Numbers

Identifying Necessary Information

Some problems may not include all the information you need to solve them. Other problems may include information that is not necessary to solve them. When you solve problems, think carefully about the situation. Be sure you have the information you need and are considering only the necessary information.

Missing Information

Example: A stockroom manager needs to send a truck to the warehouse to get 200 cartons of housewares, 150 cartons of men's clothes, and 75 cartons of bedding. How many trips must the truck make to transport all cartons to the stockroom?

Do you see that something is missing? You need to know how many cartons the truck can hold. You cannot solve the problem with only the information from the problem. When you cannot solve a problem because some of the necessary information is missing, mark an answer such as "Not enough information is given."

A common error is to perform an operation using the numbers from the problem even though there may not be a reason for using them. For instance, if you added the numbers in the problem, 200 + 150 + 75, you would get the answer 425, which may be among the choices but is not correct. Does it seem reasonable that a truck would need to make 425 trips to transport the cartons? Adding gives the total number of cartons to be shipped, not the number of trips.

Extra Information

For some problems, a table or chart of information is given. You may be asked several questions about the information. Before solving each problem, identify the information you need.

Example: The public library kept records on book circulation.

January	February	March	April
10,256	7,542	7,625	9,436

How many more books were borrowed in April than in February?

(1)   83

(2)   820

(3) 1,811

(4) 1,894

(5) 16,978

You need **only** the numbers for February and April. Subtract to find the difference. The correct answer is **(4) 1,894** (9,436 − 7,542 = 1,894). Check the answer using addition.

Directions: Choose the <u>best answer</u> to each item.

1. Quan Le sells hot dogs at the park seven days a week. He uses 15 bags of buns each day. There are 6 buns in a bag. How many buns does he use a day?

   (1) 90
   (2) 105
   (3) 180
   (4) 450
   (5) 630

2. Meg needs to have her car radiator repaired. Used parts will cost $85 and labor on the job will be $125. How much will it cost to get her car fixed if new parts are used?

   (1) $ 40
   (2) $160
   (3) $364
   (4) $584
   (5) Not enough information is given.

3. Dave can drive 160 miles on a tank of gas. Approximately how many tanks of gas will he need to drive 880 miles?

   (1) between 4 and 5
   (2) between 5 and 6
   (3) between 6 and 7
   (4) between 7 and 8
   (5) Not enough information is given.

4. Today's sales of the 20-inch HiTech television total $5,760. If each set sells for $320, how many were sold?

   (1) 15
   (2) 16
   (3) 17
   (4) 18
   (5) 19

Items 5 to 7 are based on the following information.

Marina Outboard Motors

	Work Quotas	
	Goal	Actual
Monday	100	103
Tuesday	95	136
Wednesday	120	117
Thursday	110	122
Friday	90	180

5. What was the total goal for the week?

   (1) 500
   (2) 515
   (3) 555
   (4) 620
   (5) 658

6. The workers missed the quota one day during the week. Which day was it?

   (1) Monday
   (2) Tuesday
   (3) Wednesday
   (4) Thursday
   (5) Friday

7. How many more motors were built on Friday than on Thursday?

   (1) 12
   (2) 58
   (3) 70
   (4) 90
   (5) Not enough information is given.

Answers are on page 853.

Lesson 4

Solving Multistep Word Problems

Multistep Problems

A multistep problem requires more than one calculation to find the solution. The key to solving multistep problems is to identify each step and the operation needed for each step.

Example:

Carpet Sale ....$16 per square yard
Carpet Pad Special ....$3 per square yard

Jana wants to take advantage of the sale prices in this ad. She measures her room and finds that it is 12 feet wide and 18 feet long. How much will it cost to buy the pad and carpet for her room?

(1) $ 72

(2) $216

(3) $384

(4) $456

(5) Not enough information is given.

There are several steps to solving this problem.

Step 1: Find the area of the room in square feet by **multiplying** the length and width of her room: $12 \times 18 = 216$ square feet.

Step 2: Change the area from square feet to square yards by **dividing** by 9, the number of square feet in 1 square yard: $216 \div 9 = 24$ square yards.

Step 3: Find the cost of the carpet by **multiplying** the number of square yards (from Step 2) by $16, the price of 1 square yard of carpet: $24 \times \$16 = \$384$.

Step 4: Find the cost of the carpet pad by **multiplying** the number of square yards (from Step 2) by $3, the price of 1 square yard of carpet padding: $24 \times \$3 = \$72$.

Step 5: Find the total cost by **adding** the cost of the carpet (from Step 3) and the cost of the carpet pad (from Step 4): $\$384 + \$72 = \$456$.

The correct answer option is **(4) $456.**

Directions: Choose the best answer to each item.

Items 1 and 2 refer to the following information.

Felicia and Jay Oser buy a new refrigerator. They must make eight payments of $115 each and one final payment of $162.

1. Which combination of operations would you need to find the total amount the Osers will spend on the refrigerator?

   (1) addition and subtraction
   (2) addition and division
   (3) subtraction and division
   (4) multiplication and addition
   (5) multiplication and subtraction

2. How much will the Osers spend to buy the refrigerator?

   (1) $ 477
   (2) $ 889
   (3) $ 920
   (4) $ 998
   (5) $1,082

3. Hugh Coles pays $312 every six months for insurance for his car. Brenda Coles pays $866 per year for insurance for her car. How much do the Coles pay for car insurance in one year?

   (1) $ 624
   (2) $1,178
   (3) $1,490
   (4) $1,732
   (5) Not enough information is given.

Items 4 and 5 refer to the following information.

An electronics company advertises a 24-inch stereo color television set for $460 cash or $45 per month for 12 months on credit.

4. Which combination of operations would you need to find how much a customer will save by paying cash?

   (1) addition and subtraction
   (2) subtraction and division
   (3) multiplication and addition
   (4) multiplication and subtraction
   (5) division only

5. How much will a customer save by paying cash instead of buying on credit?

   (1) $40
   (2) $45
   (3) $80
   (4) $85
   (5) $90

6. Susan Landow paid $3,794 for medical insurance and hospital and doctor's bills last year. If her insurance company refunded $2,382 of her money, how much did she spend in medical bills last year?

   (1) $ 908
   (2) $1,294
   (3) $1,412
   (4) $2,786
   (5) $3,290

Items 7 to 9 refer to the following table.

Item	Price	Sale Price
T-shirt	$8	$7
Jersey	10	8
Pants	18	15

Items 10 to 12 refer to the following table.

Daily Production Report	
Cynthia Bonales	56
Sadie Johns	50
Ariste Sanchez	48

7. On Friday, the store sold 24 pairs of pants at the sale price. How much money did the store take in on pants?

(1) $270
(2) $360
(3) $405
(4) $432
(5) $518

8. Two parents are buying school clothes for their five boys. They buy 12 T-shirts, 5 jerseys, and 10 pairs of pants. How much do they save buying at the sale prices instead of the regular prices?

(1) $28
(2) $30
(3) $36
(4) $48
(5) $52

9. After the sale, the store has only 12 pairs of pants in stock. If they take an additional $3 off the sale price, what would be the cost of 4 pairs of pants?

(1) $36
(2) $48
(3) $60
(4) $72
(5) Not enough information is given.

10. Ms. Bonales earns $1 for each item produced. If she continues to produce the same number for each of the next 5 days, how much will she earn for the 5 days?

(1) $280
(2) $300
(3) $336
(4) $356
(5) Not enough information is given.

11. Al Butler, a new worker not shown on the chart, produced fewer items than Ariste Sanchez on the same day. How much did Mr. Butler earn for the day?

(1) $132
(2) $176
(3) $204
(4) $352
(5) Not enough information is given.

12. Ms. Johns worked only 5 hours during the day shown on the chart. On the average, how many items did she produce per hour?

(1) 10
(2) 13
(3) 14
(4) 15
(5) Not enough information is given.

Answers are on page 853.

Directions: Choose the <u>best answer</u> to each item.

1. If 50,302 fans attended the Friday night game and 34,196 attended the game on Tuesday, how many more fans saw the Friday night game?

   (1) 15,601

   (2) 16,106

   (3) 17,114

   (4) 26,421

   (5) 84,498

2. Grace charges $15 for a haircut and $45 for a permanent. If she does 10 haircuts and 3 permanents on Tuesday, how much money will she earn that day from haircuts?

   (1) $15 + $45

   (2) 10 − 3

   (3) $15 × 10

   (4) $15 × 3

   (5) $45 × 10

3. Barbara discovered she was supposed to pay only $4,516 in federal income taxes last year. She actually paid $5,752. How much did she overpay?

   (1) $ 988

   (2) $1,056

   (3) $1,137

   (4) $1,236

   (5) Not enough information is given.

4. Janet has a $1,800 dental bill for herself and her children. If she pays $150 each month, how many months will it take her to pay off the bill?

   (1) 12

   (2) 13

   (3) 120

   (4) 1,650

   (5) 1,950

5. Jaime is taking inventory at the hardware store. He counts the number of $\frac{3}{8}$-inch bolts in stock and finds he has 3,325 on hand. His records show he received 21 boxes of $\frac{3}{8}$-inch bolts on his last order. If each box contained about 506 bolts, approximately how many bolts did Jaime receive on his last order?

   (1) between 9,000 and 11,000

   (2) between 11,000 and 13,000

   (3) between 13,000 and 15,000

   (4) between 15,000 and 17,000

   (5) Not enough information is given.

6. Marcia buys a box of 1,000 writing pads for office meetings. She gives out 188 pads on Tuesday and 234 pads on Wednesday. How many writing pads does she have left?

   (1) 422

   (2) 578

   (3) 766

   (4) 812

   (5) 1,422

7. Westside Car Rental held an awards banquet for its 65 employees. The company paid a hotel $125 for the use of a conference room and $9 per person for food. How much did the company pay for the room and food?

   (1) $ 199

   (2) $ 398

   (3) $ 585

   (4) $ 710

   (5) $1,125

The tenants in two apartment buildings agree to hire a private trash collector to serve their buildings. The total yearly cost of the service will be $3,096. There are 18 apartments in one building and 25 apartments in the other.

8. Which combination of operations would you need to find out how much each apartment will pay per year for the service if each apartment pays an equal share of the cost?

   (1) addition and multiplication

   (2) addition and division

   (3) subtraction and division

   (4) multiplication and subtraction

   (5) multiplication only

9. How much is each apartment's share of the annual cost?

   (1) $43

   (2) $56

   (3) $65

   (4) $68

   (5) $72

Items 10 to 14 refer to the following chart.

Employee	Hourly Wage	Hours Worked						
		S	M	T	W	T	F	S
F. Blau	$7		8	7	8	8	6	3
M. Bodine	8		8	8	9	8	8	8
T. Ortiz	8		6	6	8	9	8	
R. Perez	6		8	8	8	8	8	

10. How much money did F. Blau earn for the week?

    (1) $280

    (2) $301

    (3) $320

    (4) $329

    (5) Not enough information is given.

11. How many more hours did M. Bodine work than T. Ortiz?

    (1) 9

    (2) 12

    (3) 16

    (4) 49

    (5) 86

12. R. Perez earned $240 this week. How many more hours would he have had to work to earn $252?

    (1) 2

    (2) 3

    (3) 8

    (4) 12

    (5) 40

13. If T. Ortiz were given a $2 hourly raise, how much would he earn for the same number of hours worked?

    (1) $ 74

    (2) $296

    (3) $370

    (4) $490

    (5) Not enough information is given.

14. The following week, F. Blau worked 8 hours each day, Monday through Saturday. How much more money did he earn than the week before?

    (1) $ 48

    (2) $ 56

    (3) $280

    (4) $336

    (5) Not enough information is given.

Answers are on page 853.

Fractions

Fractions can be used to show a part of a whole: "Add $\frac{1}{2}$ cup of milk to the mixture." They can also be used to show part of one group: "One-third of our employees have used all their sick leave."

Lesson 5 covers the basic facts about fractions. You will learn to recognize **proper fractions, improper fractions,** and **mixed numbers.** You will also learn to change between improper fractions and mixed numbers.

Lesson 6 explains how to compare fractions. You will learn how to tell when two fractions are equal. You will also learn how to write a fraction in lower terms and in higher terms.

The four operations you used with whole numbers are also used to solve problems involving fractions. Lesson 7 covers addition and subtraction of fractions. Lesson 8 shows how to multiply and divide fractions.

Lesson Introduction to Fractions

Facts About Fractions

$$\frac{2}{3} \begin{array}{l} \leftarrow \underline{\text{numerator}} \\ \leftarrow \text{denominator} \end{array}$$

Every **fraction** has a **numerator** and a **denominator.** The denominator is the bottom number. It tells the number of equal parts that are in the whole object or group. The numerator is the top number. It tells the number of equal parts or things you are referring to. The numerator and denominator are the **terms** of the fractions.

Fractions have three special uses.

1. Fractions show a part of one whole thing.

Example: At a restaurant, a chef divides a cheesecake into 8 equal pieces. By the end of the evening, 5 of the pieces are sold. What part of the cheesecake is sold?

$$\frac{5}{8} \begin{array}{l} \leftarrow \text{number of pieces sold} \\ \leftarrow \text{number of equal parts in the whole cheesecake} \end{array}$$

One whole object represents 8 parts out of 8, or $\frac{8}{8}$. Any fraction with the same numerator and denominator equals 1.

5 of the 8 parts are shaded.

The fraction $\frac{5}{8}$ represents the shaded part.

2. Fractions show part of a group.

Example: At the shop where Nicco works, 18 orders were received one day. There were 11 phone orders. What fraction of the orders came by phone?

$$\frac{11}{18} \begin{array}{l} \leftarrow \text{number of orders that came by phone} \\ \leftarrow \text{number of orders received in one day} \end{array}$$

3. Fractions also mean division.
   The fraction $\frac{12}{3}$ means $12 \div 3$ or $3\overline{)12}$. $\frac{12}{3} = 4$

Proper Fractions

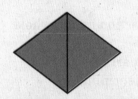

A **proper fraction** shows a quantity that is less than 1. The numerator of a proper fraction is always less than the denominator.

Example: $\frac{3}{4}$ The numerator, 3, is less than the denominator, 4. $\frac{3}{4}$ represents a quantity less than 1.

Improper Fractions

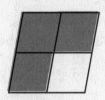

An **improper fraction** shows a quantity equal to or greater than 1. The numerator of an improper fraction is equal to or greater than the denominator.

Examples: $\frac{2}{2}$ The figure is divided into 2 equal parts, and both parts are shaded. $\frac{2}{2}$ is an improper fraction because it is equal to 1 whole and the numerator and the denominator are equal.

$\frac{7}{5}$ Each circle is divided into 5 equal parts. 7 parts are shaded. Because the numerator is greater than the denominator, $\frac{7}{5}$ is an improper fraction. This fraction shows a quantity greater than 1.

Mixed Numbers

A **mixed number** is another way to show a fraction that is greater than 1. A mixed number is a whole number and a proper fraction. Although the plus sign (+) is not written, the whole number is added to the fraction part of the mixed number.

Example: $2\frac{1}{4}$ means "two and one-fourth" or $2 + \frac{1}{4}$. Each figure is divided into 4 equal parts. Two figures are completely shaded. One-fourth of the last figure is shaded.

Rewriting Improper Fractions and Mixed Numbers

An improper fraction can be rewritten as a mixed number or a whole number. Remember that a fraction is a division problem. Follow these steps:

Step 1: Divide the numerator of the improper fraction by the denominator. The whole number answer becomes the whole number part of the mixed number.

Step 2: Write the remainder over the original denominator. This is the fraction part of the mixed number.

Example: Change $\frac{14}{3}$ to a mixed number.

$\frac{14}{3}$ means $14 \div 3$. Divide:

$$\text{denominator} \rightarrow 3\overline{)14} \quad \begin{array}{l} 4 \leftarrow \text{whole} \\ \text{number} \end{array}$$

$$\frac{12}{2} \leftarrow \text{numerator}$$

Write as a mixed number. $4\frac{2}{3}$.

A mixed number can also be rewritten as an improper fraction. Follow these steps:

Step 1: Multiply the denominator of the fraction by the whole number part of the mixed number.

Step 2: Add the numerator of the fraction part.

Step 3: Write the result over the original denominator.

Example: Rewrite $2\frac{3}{8}$ as an improper fraction.

Multiply 8 by 2. $\qquad\qquad 8 \times 2 = 16$

Add the numerator, 3. $\qquad\quad 16 + 3 = 19$

Write over the denominator, 8. $\qquad \frac{19}{8}$

Using Estimation

Rounding fractions to the nearest whole number is a good way to estimate answers to problems that involve fractions. To round a fraction to the nearest whole number, compare the fraction to $\frac{1}{2}$.

- If the fraction is less than $\frac{1}{2}$, the whole number stays the same.
- If the fraction is $\frac{1}{2}$ or more, add 1 to the whole number.

Example: Kikko and Maria each jog two times a week. Kikko jogged $4\frac{3}{4}$ miles on Monday and $3\frac{1}{6}$ miles on Tuesday. Maria jogged $3\frac{1}{4}$ miles on Tuesday and $4\frac{1}{8}$ miles on Thursday. Who jogged farther?

Estimate Kikko's total:

$\quad 4\frac{3}{4}$ is about 5

$+ \ 3\frac{1}{6}$ is about 3

$\overline{}$

8 miles rounded

Estimate Maria's total:

$\quad 3\frac{1}{4}$ is about 3

$+ \ 4\frac{1}{8}$ is about 4

$\overline{}$

7 miles rounded

Kikko jogged approximately 1 mile farther than Maria.

1. On Tuesday, 9 of Steve's 16 customers paid using credit cards. What fraction of his customers used credit cards?

2. Out of the 10 people in Carla's office, 7 regularly watch the evening news on TV. What fraction of the office workers watch the evening news?

3. Joy Chan arrived over half an hour early on 3 of the last 50 workdays. What fraction of the time has she been over half an hour early?

4. In the election for union representative, Carlos received 19 votes. What fraction of the union's 45 members voted for Carlos?

Directions: Write each improper fraction as a whole or a mixed number.

5. $\frac{7}{2}$

6. $\frac{15}{5}$

7. $\frac{10}{3}$

8. $\frac{31}{8}$

9. $\frac{17}{6}$

10. $\frac{42}{6}$

Directions: Write each mixed number as an improper fraction.

11. $6\frac{1}{2}$

12. $3\frac{5}{6}$

13. $2\frac{1}{5}$

14. $11\frac{3}{4}$

15. $10\frac{1}{2}$

16. $9\frac{2}{5}$

Directions: Solve.

17. Lorna has a $5\frac{1}{3}$-foot wood board. She needs to cut $1\frac{7}{8}$ feet from the board. After she cuts the length she needs, approximately how many feet of board will Lorna have left?

    (1) 3
    (2) 4
    (3) 5
    (4) 6
    (5) 7

18. Tara walked $2\frac{1}{4}$ miles from her home to the office. She walked $1\frac{7}{8}$ miles from the office to the store. Then she walked $2\frac{1}{4}$ miles home. Approximately what is the total number of miles she walked?

    (1) 4
    (2) 5
    (3) 6
    (4) 7
    (5) 8

Answers are on page 854.

Lesson 6 Comparing Fractions

Equal Fractions

Different fractions can have the same value.
There are 100 pennies in a dollar.   There are 20 nickels in a dollar.
20 pennies out of 100 $= \frac{20}{100}$.   4 nickels out of 20 $= \frac{4}{20}$.

Both $\frac{20}{100}$ and $\frac{4}{20}$ are worth 20 cents or $\frac{1}{5}$ of a dollar.

$$\frac{20}{100} = \frac{4}{20} = \frac{1}{5}$$

Fractions that have the same value are called **equal fractions.**

You can tell if two fractions are equal by **cross multiplying.** If the products are equal, the fractions are equal.

Example: Are $\frac{4}{8}$ and $\frac{3}{6}$ equal fractions?

Multiply: $\frac{4}{8} \diagup\!\!\!\!\diagdown \frac{3}{6}$ $4 \times 6 = 24$ The products are the same,
                              $8 \times 3 = 24$ so $\frac{4}{8}$ and $\frac{3}{6}$ are equal.

Reducing Fractions

Reducing a fraction to **lowest terms** means finding an equal fraction for which there is no number other than 1 that will divide evenly into both the numerator and the denominator. To reduce a fraction, divide the numerator and denominator by the same number.

Example: Reduce $\frac{6}{10}$ to its lowest terms.

$$\frac{6}{10} = \frac{6 \div 2}{10 \div 2} = \frac{3}{5}$$ No number other than 1 will
                                                divide evenly into 3 and 5.

Building Equal Fractions

Sometimes you need to find an equal fraction with higher terms (numerator and denominator) than those of the original. You can build or raise a fraction by multiplying both the numerator and the denominator by the same number (except 0).

$$\frac{5}{8} = \frac{5 \times 4}{8 \times 4} = \frac{20}{32}$$ $\frac{5}{8}$ and $\frac{20}{32}$ are equal fractions.

Often you need to find an equal fraction with a given denominator.

Example: $\frac{3}{4} = \frac{?}{24}$ Because $4 \times 6 = 24$, multiply the numerator 3 by **6.**

$$\frac{3 \times 6}{4 \times 6} = \frac{18}{24}$$ $\frac{3}{4}$ and $\frac{18}{24}$ are equal fractions.

Comparing Fractions

When fractions have the same number as the denominator, they are said to have a **common denominator** and the fractions are called **like fractions.** When comparing two like fractions, the fraction with the greater numerator is the greater fraction.

To compare **unlike fractions**—fractions with different denominators—you must change them to fractions with a common denominator. The common denominator must be a multiple of both of the original denominators.

Example: Which fraction is greater, $\frac{5}{6}$ or $\frac{3}{4}$?

The number 24 is a multiple of both 6 and 4 ($6 \times 4 = 24$). However, 12 is the smallest multiple of 6 and 4. Using 12, the **lowest common denominator,** build equal fractions.

$$\frac{5 \times 2}{6 \times 2} = \frac{10}{12}$$

$$\frac{3 \times 3}{4 \times 3} = \frac{9}{12}$$

Compare the like fractions. $\frac{10}{12}$ is greater than (>) $\frac{9}{12}$, so $\frac{5}{6}$ is greater than $\frac{3}{4}$.

ged Exercise Comparing Fractions

Directions: Write each fraction in lowest terms.

1. $\frac{2}{4}$

2. $\frac{6}{9}$

3. $\frac{6}{15}$

4. $\frac{18}{27}$

5. $\frac{8}{10}$

6. $\frac{12}{30}$

Directions: Find an equal fraction with the given denominator.

7. $\frac{1}{2} = \frac{?}{8}$

8. $\frac{2}{3} = \frac{?}{12}$

9. $\frac{5}{8} = \frac{?}{32}$

10. $\frac{7}{9} = \frac{?}{63}$

11. $\frac{3}{4} = \frac{?}{36}$

12. $\frac{4}{9} = \frac{?}{81}$

Directions: Compare the fractions. Write >, <, or = between the fractions.

13. $\frac{1}{3}$ $\frac{1}{4}$

14. $\frac{3}{4}$ $\frac{7}{8}$

15. $\frac{5}{6}$ $\frac{15}{18}$

Directions: Choose the best answer to each item.

16. At 10 A.M., $\frac{9}{10}$ of the shirts manufactured at Crown Shirt passed inspection. At 5 P.M., $\frac{7}{8}$ passed inspection. Which statement is true?

    (1) A greater fraction of shirts passed inspection at 10 A.M.

    (2) A greater fraction of shirts passed inspection at 5 P.M.

    (3) The same fraction of shirts passed at each time.

17. Morley's Paint Store ran an ad on television. On Thursday, 4 out of 12 customers said they saw the ad. On Friday, 6 out of 18 customers said they saw it. Which statement is true?

    (1) A greater fraction of customers saw the ad on Thursday.

    (2) A greater fraction of customers saw the ad on Friday.

    (3) The same fraction of customers saw the ad each day.

Answers are on page 855.

Lesson Adding and Subtracting Fractions

Like Fractions

Like fractions have the same or **common denominators.** You can add or subtract like fractions by adding or subtracting the numerator and writing the answer over the common denominator. If necessary, reduce the answer to lowest terms.

Example: Subtract $\frac{2}{12}$ from $\frac{11}{12}$.

$\frac{11}{12}$ Since the common denominator is 12, $\frac{11}{12}$ and $\frac{2}{12}$ are like fractions.

$-\frac{2}{12}$ Subtract the numerators $(11 - 2 = 9)$.

$\frac{9}{12}$ Write the answer using the common denominator.

Reduce the answer to lowest terms.

$$\frac{9 \div 3}{12 \div 3} = \frac{3}{4}, \quad \frac{11}{12} - \frac{2}{12} = \frac{9}{12} \text{ or } \frac{3}{4}$$

Unlike Fractions

Unlike fractions have different denominators. Use these steps to add or subtract unlike fractions:

Step 1: Find the least common denominator and change one or both of the fractions to make like fractions.

Step 2: Add or subtract the like fractions.

Step 3: Reduce the answer if necessary.

Example: Add $\frac{1}{2}$ and $\frac{2}{8}$.

Step 1: Find the least common denominator and change to like fractions. The least common denominator is 8, so you do not need to rewrite $\frac{2}{8}$.

$$\frac{1 \times 4}{2 \times 4} = \frac{4}{8}$$

Step 2: Add: $\dfrac{1}{2} = \dfrac{4}{8}$

$+\dfrac{2}{8} = \dfrac{2}{8}$

$\dfrac{6}{8}$

Step 3: Write in lowest terms: $\dfrac{6 \div 2}{8 \div 2} = \dfrac{3}{4}$; $\quad \dfrac{1}{2} + \dfrac{2}{8} = \dfrac{6}{8}$ or $\dfrac{3}{4}$

Adding and Subtracting Mixed Numbers

Follow these steps to add or subtract mixed numbers.

Step 1: Write the fractions with common denominators.

Step 2: Add or subtract the fractions, then add or subtract the whole numbers.

Step 3: If the sum of the fractions is an improper fraction, change it to a mixed number and combine it with the whole number.

Step 4: Write in lowest terms if necessary.

Example: Add $3\frac{3}{4} + 6\frac{1}{3}$.

Step 1:   Write the fractions with common denominators.

$$3\frac{3}{4} = 3\frac{3 \times 3}{4 \times 3} = 3\frac{9}{12}$$
$$+ 6\frac{1}{3} = 6\frac{1 \times 4}{3 \times 4} = 6\frac{4}{12}$$

Step 2:   Add the fractions, then the whole numbers.

$$3\frac{3}{4} = 3\frac{9}{12}$$
$$+ 6\frac{1}{3} = 6\frac{4}{12}$$
$$9\frac{13}{12}$$

Answer contains an improper fraction.

Step 3:   Change $\frac{13}{12}$ to a mixed number: $\frac{13}{12} = 1\frac{1}{12}$

Add this to the whole number answer: $9 + 1\frac{1}{12} = 10\frac{1}{12}$

So, $3\frac{3}{4} + 6\frac{1}{3} = 10\frac{1}{12}$

Step 4:   Make sure the fraction is reduced to lowest terms. In this case, $\frac{1}{12}$ cannot be reduced.

Sometimes the number you are subtracting from does not have the larger fraction. In this case, you will need to borrow 1 from the whole number.

Example: Subtract $3\frac{2}{3}$ from 6.

The whole number 6 needs a fraction part in order to subtract. Borrow 1 from the whole number and write it as the fraction. Remember, a fraction where the numerator and denominator are the same equals 1. So, 6 can be written as $5\frac{3}{3}$.

Subtract.
$$6 = 5\frac{3}{3}$$
$$- 3\frac{2}{3} = 3\frac{2}{3}$$
$$2\frac{1}{3}$$

Example: Subtract $2\frac{5}{6}$ from $5\frac{1}{3}$.

Find the common denominator.
$$5\frac{1}{3} = 5\frac{2}{6}$$
$$- 2\frac{5}{6} = 2\frac{5}{6}$$

Because $\frac{2}{6}$ is less than $\frac{5}{6}$, you need to borrow. Borrow 1 from the whole number 5 and write it as a fraction using the common denominator of 6. Add $\frac{6}{6}$ to the fraction part.

$$5\frac{2}{6} = 4\frac{6}{6} + \frac{2}{6} = 4\frac{8}{6}$$ Subtract. $$5\frac{1}{3} = 5\frac{2}{6} = 4\frac{8}{6}$$
$$- 2\frac{5}{6}\qquad\qquad - 2\frac{5}{6}\qquad\qquad - 2\frac{5}{6} = 2\frac{5}{6} = 2\frac{5}{6}$$

Reduce to lowest terms. $2\frac{3}{6} = 2\frac{1}{2}$

Directions: Add or subtract. Write answers in lowest terms.

1. $\frac{2}{3}$
   $+\frac{1}{3}$

6. $\frac{2}{5}$
   $+\frac{1}{3}$

11. $\frac{3}{4}$
    $-\frac{1}{2}$

16. $\frac{5}{9}$
    $-\frac{1}{12}$

2. $\frac{1}{6}$
   $+\frac{3}{6}$

7. $2\frac{1}{4}$
   $+5\frac{5}{8}$

12. $\frac{2}{3}$
    $-\frac{1}{6}$

17. 14
    $-3\frac{1}{2}$

3. $\frac{3}{4}$
   $+\frac{1}{8}$

8. $3\frac{5}{6}$
   $+10\frac{2}{3}$

13. $\frac{5}{6}$
    $-\frac{1}{2}$

18. $27\frac{1}{4}$
    $-15\frac{3}{8}$

4. $\frac{1}{6}$
   $+\frac{1}{2}$

9. $2\frac{4}{5}$
   $+8\frac{3}{10}$

14. $\frac{3}{4}$
    $-\frac{1}{3}$

19. $3\frac{1}{5}$
    $-1\frac{4}{5}$

5. $\frac{3}{8}$
   $+\frac{1}{5}$

10. $18\frac{1}{6}$
    $+24\frac{2}{3}$

15. $\frac{9}{10}$
    $-\frac{1}{2}$

20. $26\frac{1}{4}$
    $-18\frac{3}{8}$

---

21. $\frac{5}{8} + \frac{1}{6} + \frac{1}{4}$

22. $1\frac{1}{4} + 3\frac{1}{10} + 5\frac{2}{3}$

23. $3\frac{1}{2} + 1\frac{2}{8} + 2\frac{3}{4}$

24. $1\frac{3}{4} + \frac{7}{8} + 3\frac{5}{6}$

25. $4\frac{1}{6} + 3\frac{2}{3} + 1\frac{5}{12}$

26. $\frac{7}{10} - \frac{1}{4}$

27. $3\frac{2}{3} - 1\frac{1}{4}$

28. $4 - 2\frac{4}{5}$

29. $9\frac{1}{2} - 2\frac{5}{8}$

30. $13\frac{3}{4} - \frac{15}{16}$

31. Melissa kept records of her gasoline purchases for one month. She bought $8\frac{5}{10}$ gallons, $9\frac{3}{10}$ gallons, 8 gallons, and $7\frac{7}{10}$ gallons. How many gallons did she buy that month?

    (1) $32\frac{1}{2}$
    (2) $32\frac{7}{10}$
    (3) $33\frac{1}{10}$
    (4) $33\frac{2}{5}$
    (5) $33\frac{1}{2}$

32. Paul earns 10 vacation days per year. He has used $4\frac{1}{2}$ days this year. How many vacation days does he have left?

    (1) 5
    (2) $5\frac{1}{2}$
    (3) 6
    (4) $6\frac{1}{2}$
    (5) 7

33. Mary planned to spend $3\frac{1}{2}$ hours organizing the stock room. She has been working for $1\frac{3}{4}$ hours. How many more hours does she plan to work?

    (1) $1\frac{3}{4}$
    (2) $2\frac{1}{4}$
    (3) $2\frac{3}{4}$
    (4) $3\frac{1}{4}$
    (5) $5\frac{1}{4}$

34. Paul prepared $2\frac{2}{3}$ cups of salad dressing. He used $\frac{3}{4}$ cup of the dressing. About how many cups of salad dressing are left?

    (1) 1
    (2) 2
    (3) 3
    (4) 4
    (5) 5

35. A tailor bought $12\frac{1}{2}$ yards of brown wool, $8\frac{7}{8}$ yards of blue tweed, and $6\frac{3}{4}$ yards of brown plaid. How many yards did he buy in all?

    (1) $26\frac{7}{8}$
    (2) $27\frac{1}{2}$
    (3) $28\frac{1}{8}$
    (4) $28\frac{1}{2}$
    (5) $28\frac{3}{4}$

36. Carmine worked $5\frac{2}{5}$ hours on Monday, $6\frac{1}{2}$ hours on Tuesday, and $8\frac{4}{5}$ hours on Wednesday. How many hours did he work for the three days?

    (1) $19\frac{7}{10}$
    (2) $19\frac{4}{5}$
    (3) $20\frac{1}{5}$
    (4) $20\frac{7}{10}$
    (5) $21\frac{1}{2}$

37. Ed needs to shorten an $8\frac{1}{3}$-foot pole to a length of $5\frac{3}{4}$ feet. How much should he cut off?

    (1) $2\frac{7}{12}$ feet
    (2) $2\frac{3}{4}$ feet
    (3) $3\frac{1}{8}$ feet
    (4) $3\frac{1}{3}$ feet
    (5) $3\frac{1}{2}$ feet

Answers are on page 855.

The Easton Hotel gives an employment test that lasts $1\frac{3}{4}$ hours. Two-thirds of the time is spent on math and reading questions. How long are the math and reading parts?

To solve this problem, you need to answer this question:

$$\text{What is } \frac{2}{3} \text{ of } 1\frac{3}{4}?$$

The word "of" means multiply. Use these steps to multiply fractions:

Step 1: Change a mixed number to an improper fraction. Write a whole number as a fraction with a denominator of 1. $\left(3 = \frac{3}{1}\right)$

$$\frac{2}{3} \times 1\frac{3}{4} = \frac{2}{3} \times \frac{7}{4}$$

Step 2: Multiply the numerators. This is the numerator of the answer.

$$\frac{2}{3} \times \frac{7}{4} = \frac{14}{} \quad (2 \times 7 = 14)$$

Step 3: Multiply the denominators. This is the denominator of the answer.

$$\frac{2}{3} \times \frac{7}{4} = \frac{14}{12} \quad (3 \times 4 = 12)$$

Step 4: Write the fraction in lowest terms. Write improper fractions as mixed numbers.

$$\frac{14 \div 2}{12 \div 2} = \frac{7}{6} = 1\frac{1}{6}$$

Remember, reducing a fraction means to divide the numerator and the denominator by the same number. Using this principle, you can reduce as you work the problem.

$$\frac{1}{3} \times \frac{3}{2} = \frac{1 \times \overset{1}{\cancel{3}}}{\underset{1}{\cancel{3}} \times 2} = \frac{1}{2}$$ The numerator and the denominator are both divided by 3.

Drawing a slash through the 3 and writing 1 shows that 3 divided by 3 equals 1. This reducing process is called **cancellation.**

As a shortcut, you can divide without rewriting the problem. Make sure you divide a number in both the numerator and the denominator by the same number. Step 4 becomes Step 2!

Correct:

$$\frac{1}{\underset{3}{\cancel{6}}} \times \frac{\overset{1}{\cancel{2}}}{3}$$ The numerator and the denominator are both divided by 2. The answer is $\frac{1}{9}$.

Incorrect:

$$\frac{1}{\underset{2}{\cancel{6}}} \times \frac{2}{\underset{1}{\cancel{3}}}$$ Although 6 and 3 can both be divided by 3, both numbers are in the denominator.

Example: Multiply $1\frac{2}{3}$ by $7\frac{1}{2}$.

Use these steps:	1. Change to improper fractions.	2. Divide by the same number.	3. Multiply.	4. Write as a mixed number.

$$1\frac{2}{3} \times 7\frac{1}{2} \;=\; \frac{5}{3} \times \frac{15}{2} \;=\; \frac{5}{\overset{}{3}_{1}} \times \frac{\overset{5}{\cancel{15}}}{2} \;=\; \frac{25}{2} \;=\; 12\frac{1}{2}$$

(15 and 3 are divided by 3.)

Example: A coffee shop had 125 customers during the lunch rush hour on Monday. One-fifth of the customers ordered the lunch special. How many customers ordered the special?

This problem asks you to find a fractional part of a whole number. Use the same steps.

$$125 \times \frac{1}{5} = \frac{125}{1} \times \frac{1}{5} = \frac{\overset{25}{\cancel{125}}}{1} \times \frac{1}{\cancel{5}_{1}} = \frac{25}{1} = 25$$

Dividing Fractions

A candy company receives a shipment of 12 pounds of lemon drops. If the company sells the lemon drops in $\frac{1}{4}$-pound bags, how many bags can they make from the shipment?

Divide 12 by $\frac{1}{4}$ to solve the problem. The number being divided, 12, is written first: $12 \div \frac{1}{4}$ means "how many $\frac{1}{4}$s are there in 12?"

Follow these steps to divide fractions:

Step 1: Change any mixed numbers to improper fractions. Write a whole number as a fraction with a denominator of 1.

$$12 \div \frac{1}{4} = \frac{12}{1} \div \frac{1}{4}$$

Step 2: Invert the divisor (the fraction you are dividing by) and change the operation to multiplication. For example, when you invert the fraction $\frac{1}{4}$, it becomes $\frac{4}{1}$.

$$\frac{12}{1} \div \frac{1}{4} = \frac{12}{1} \times \frac{4}{1}$$

Step 3: Complete the problem as you would any multiplication problem and reduce to lowest terms.

$$\frac{12}{1} \times \frac{4}{1} = \frac{48}{1} = 48$$

There are 48 one-fourths in 12. The candy company can make 48, $\frac{1}{4}$-pound bags from 12 pounds of lemon drops.

Directions: Multiply or divide. Write answers in lowest terms.

1. $\frac{1}{2} \times \frac{2}{3}$

2. $\frac{7}{8} \times \frac{4}{5}$

3. Find $\frac{2}{15}$ of $\frac{3}{8}$.

4. What is $\frac{8}{9}$ of $\frac{5}{6}$?

5. What is $\frac{7}{8}$ of 24?

6. $\frac{4}{5} \times 1\frac{2}{3}$

7. $9 \times 5\frac{1}{3}$

8. $2\frac{2}{5} \times 2\frac{1}{2}$

9. $3\frac{1}{3} \times 4\frac{1}{8}$

10. $2\frac{3}{4} \times 6$

11. $\frac{1}{3} \div \frac{5}{6}$

12. $\frac{7}{10} \div 2$

13. $\frac{5}{8} \div \frac{5}{24}$

14. Divide $\frac{4}{9}$ by $\frac{2}{3}$.

15. What is 12 divide by $1\frac{1}{2}$?

16. $6\frac{1}{2} \div \frac{1}{4}$

17. $18 \div \frac{2}{3}$

18. $4\frac{9}{10} \div 1\frac{1}{6}$

19. $6\frac{1}{9} \div 1\frac{5}{6}$

20. $3\frac{5}{8} \div 4$

21. A restaurant ordered $15\frac{3}{4}$ pounds of almonds. The nut supplier sent only $\frac{1}{2}$ the order. How many pounds of almonds did the supplier send?

    (1) $3\frac{11}{16}$
    (2) $5\frac{1}{4}$
    (3) $7\frac{7}{8}$
    (4) $16\frac{1}{4}$
    (5) Not enough information is given.

22. A short-order cook uses $\frac{1}{3}$ pound of hamburger to make the lunch special. How many specials can he make from 15 pounds of hamburger?

    (1) 5
    (2) 15
    (3) 30
    (4) 45
    (5) Not enough information is given.

23. Of the 60 animals at an animal shelter, $\frac{4}{5}$ are dogs. How many of the animals at the shelter are dogs?

    (1) 28
    (2) 32
    (3) 36
    (4) 48
    (5) Not enough information is given.

24. Elio works for a construction company. His boss recently gave him a raise. If the raise is $\frac{1}{8}$ of his present yearly salary, what is the dollar amount of the raise?

    (1) $2,750
    (2) $3,125
    (3) $3,500
    (4) $3,875
    (5) Not enough information is given.

25. Each board in a stack is $\frac{3}{4}$ inch thick and 8 feet long. If the stack is 24 inches high, how many boards are in the stack?

    (1) 3
    (2) 18
    (3) 32
    (4) 44
    (5) Not enough information is given.

26. A hiking trail in a national park is $6\frac{1}{4}$ miles long. If Steve averages $2\frac{1}{2}$ miles per hour, how many hours will it take him to reach the end of the trail?

    (1) 1
    (2) $2\frac{1}{2}$
    (3) $5\frac{1}{2}$
    (4) $6\frac{1}{4}$
    (5) $12\frac{3}{4}$

Answers are on page 857.

Directions: Choose the <u>best answer</u> to each item.

1. Nick has a part-time job. One week, he worked $2\frac{3}{4}$ hours on Monday, $4\frac{1}{2}$ on Tuesday, $3\frac{1}{2}$ on Wednesday, $5\frac{1}{4}$ on Thursday, and $2\frac{3}{4}$ hours on Friday. How many hours did Nick work during the week?

   (1) $16\frac{3}{4}$
   (2) $17\frac{1}{2}$
   (3) $18\frac{3}{4}$
   (4) $19\frac{1}{4}$
   (5) $20\frac{1}{4}$

2. A uniform shop has contracted to make 120 uniforms that require $4\frac{1}{2}$ yards of fabric each. The shop buys the fabric in 60-yard bolts. How many bolts should they buy to make this order?

   (1) 8
   (2) 9
   (3) 10
   (4) 11
   (5) 12

3. Phil is given $\frac{1}{3}$ of the company's display space for his department's products. He uses $\frac{3}{4}$ of his space for posters and the rest for samples. What fraction of the entire display space is used for Phil's samples?

   (1) $\frac{3}{16}$
   (2) $\frac{1}{12}$
   (3) $\frac{1}{6}$
   (4) $\frac{1}{4}$
   (5) $\frac{3}{8}$

Items 4 to 6 refer to the following information. Colson builds kitchen cabinets. He offers five different wood finishes.

Customer Selection Information
$\frac{1}{8}$ of his customers choose dark walnut.
$\frac{3}{8}$ of his customers choose golden oak.
$\frac{1}{4}$ of his customers choose natural grain.
$\frac{3}{16}$ of his customers choose fruitwood.
$\frac{1}{16}$ of his customers choose cherry.

4. Which finish do most customers choose?

   (1) dark walnut
   (2) golden oak
   (3) natural grain
   (4) fruitwood
   (5) cherry

5. What fraction of his customers choose golden oak, natural grain, and fruitwood finishes?

   (1) $\frac{7}{16}$
   (2) $\frac{1}{2}$
   (3) $\frac{13}{16}$
   (4) $\frac{3}{4}$
   (5) Not enough information is given.

6. Of 200 customers, how many would Colson expect to choose dark walnut?

   (1) 25
   (2) 30
   (3) 35
   (4) 40
   (5) Not enough information is given.

7. A recipe calls for $\frac{2}{3}$ cup of butter. How much butter should be used in order to make $\frac{1}{2}$ the recipe?

(1) $\frac{1}{4}$ cup

(2) $\frac{3}{10}$ cup

(3) $\frac{1}{3}$ cup

(4) $\frac{3}{8}$ cup

(5) $\frac{1}{2}$ cup

8. Elena needs $1\frac{3}{4}$ yards of silk to make a blouse and $2\frac{1}{8}$ yards to make matching pants. Approximately how many yards of silk does she need?

(1) 1

(2) 2

(3) 3

(4) 4

(5) 5

9. A printing company printed 3,510 tickets for a concert. One-third of the tickets were printed incorrectly and could not be used. How many of the tickets had to be reprinted?

(1) 885

(2) 1,170

(3) 1,404

(4) 1,755

(5) 2,340

10. A recent study shows that approximately $\frac{3}{5}$ of the cars driving south on Canyon Road exceed the speed limit. Of 250 cars driving on the road, which expression shows approximately how many exceed the speed limit?

(1) $\frac{3}{5} + 250$

(2) $250 - \frac{3}{5}$

(3) $250 \times \frac{3}{5}$

(4) $250 \div \frac{3}{5}$

(5) Not enough information is given.

11. Tony can pick $14\frac{1}{2}$ baskets of berries per hour. How many baskets of berries can he pick in $5\frac{1}{2}$ hours?

(1) 70

(2) $72\frac{1}{2}$

(3) $79\frac{3}{4}$

(4) $82\frac{1}{2}$

(5) 87

12. Geoff is a potter. For every 35 mugs he makes, 7 are damaged during glazing and cannot be sold. What fraction of the mugs can be sold?

(1) $\frac{3}{8}$

(2) $\frac{3}{7}$

(3) $\frac{1}{2}$

(4) $\frac{5}{7}$

(5) $\frac{4}{5}$

13. Henry is carpeting three rooms. He needs $12\frac{1}{2}$ square yards of carpet for one room, $20\frac{3}{4}$ square yards for the next room, and $13\frac{1}{3}$ square yards for a third room. If he has 50 square yards of carpet on hand, how many square yards will he have left after he finishes the job?

(1) $2\frac{7}{12}$

(2) $3\frac{1}{12}$

(3) $3\frac{5}{12}$

(4) $3\frac{3}{4}$

(5) $4\frac{1}{6}$

14. A plant grows at a rate of $5\frac{1}{2}$ inches per week. At this rate, which expression shows how many inches the plant will grow in $2\frac{1}{2}$ weeks?

(1) $5\frac{1}{2} + 2\frac{1}{2}$

(2) $5\frac{1}{2} - 2\frac{1}{2}$

(3) $2\frac{1}{2} \times 5\frac{1}{2}$

(4) $2\frac{1}{2} \div 5\frac{1}{2}$

(5) $5\frac{1}{2} \div 2\frac{1}{2}$

Items 15 to 17 refer to the following information. Liza and Bill Saenz have a combined income of $2,080 per month.

Liza and Bill's Monthly Budget	
Rent	$\frac{1}{4}$ of income
Food	$\frac{1}{5}$ of income
Clothes	$\frac{1}{8}$ of income
Bills	$\frac{3}{8}$ of income
Savings and Miscellaneous	$\frac{1}{20}$ of income

15. Which expression shows what fraction of their income Liza and Bill spend on food and clothes?

(1) $\frac{1}{5} + \frac{1}{8}$

(2) $\frac{1}{5} - \frac{1}{8}$

(3) $\frac{1}{8} - \frac{1}{5}$

(4) $\frac{1}{8} \times \frac{1}{5}$

(5) $\frac{1}{8} \div \frac{1}{5}$

16. How much do they spend on rent per month?

(1) $416

(2) $520

(3) $658

(4) $700

(5) Not enough information is given.

17. How much of their monthly earnings do they put in savings?

(1) $ 20

(2) $ 68

(3) $104

(4) $416

(5) Not enough information is given.

18. A piece of art paper is $18\frac{1}{4}$ inches long. If you cut off $3\frac{7}{16}$ inches, how many inches are left?

(1) $12\frac{9}{16}$

(2) $13\frac{1}{4}$

(3) $13\frac{3}{4}$

(4) $14\frac{13}{16}$

(5) $14\frac{15}{16}$

19. Each Friday, Emily walks $1\frac{2}{3}$ miles from her home to work and $1\frac{2}{3}$ miles back. She also walks an additional $3\frac{3}{4}$ miles in the evening. How many miles does Emily walk on Friday?

(1) $5\frac{5}{12}$

(2) $6\frac{1}{4}$

(3) $6\frac{2}{3}$

(4) $7\frac{1}{12}$

(5) Not enough information is given.

20. How many servings can be cut from 6 cheesecakes if each serving is $\frac{1}{8}$ of a cheesecake?

(1) 24

(2) 36

(3) 48

(4) 75

(5) Not enough information is given.

21. Carin builds bird feeders that are sold in craft shops. She is working on an order for 21 feeders. It takes her $\frac{3}{4}$ of an hour to make one feeder. She has already worked $8\frac{1}{2}$ hours. How many more hours will it take her to complete the order?

(1) $6\frac{3}{8}$

(2) $7\frac{1}{4}$

(3) $15\frac{3}{4}$

(4) $19\frac{1}{2}$

(5) $24\frac{1}{4}$

Mathematics ◆ Fractions

Recipe for Grits

2 servings ($\frac{2}{3}$ cup per serving)

Uncooked Grits	Water	Salt	Butter
$\frac{1}{2}$ cup	$1\frac{3}{4}$ cup	$\frac{1}{2}$ tsp	$\frac{1}{2}$ tbsp

22. Adam plans to double the recipe. How many cups of water will he need?

(1) $3\frac{1}{2}$

(2) $2\frac{3}{4}$

(3) $2\frac{1}{2}$

(4) $2\frac{1}{4}$

(5) 2

23. Kit plans to make 30 two-third cup servings of grits. After cooking, how many cups of grits will she have?

(1) 12

(2) 15

(3) 18

(4) 20

(5) 24

24. Francisco plans to make $1\frac{1}{2}$ times the recipe. Which expression can be used to find how many cups of uncooked grits Francisco will need?

(1) $1\frac{1}{2} \div \frac{1}{2}$

(2) $1\frac{1}{2} \left(\frac{1}{2}\right)$

(3) $1\frac{1}{2} \left(1\frac{1}{2}\right)$

(4) $\frac{1}{2} \div 1\frac{1}{2}$

(5) $1\frac{1}{2} + \frac{1}{2}$

25. A store owner wants to have continuous music during store hours. The store is open for 10 hours daily. If each music tape lasts $1\frac{1}{4}$ hours, how many tapes will she need for 1 day?

(1) $6\frac{2}{3}$

(2) 8

(3) $9\frac{1}{2}$

(4) 40

(5) Not enough information is given.

26. Last year $\frac{3}{4}$ of Bert's employees gave to the Help Fund. This year $\frac{7}{8}$ gave to the fund. If Bert had the same number of employees both years, how many more gave this year than last year?

(1) 32

(2) 46

(3) 58

(4) 65

(5) Not enough information is given.

27. In April, a florist made $\frac{3}{10}$ of its deliveries to homes, $\frac{2}{5}$ to hospitals, $\frac{1}{5}$ to restaurants, and $\frac{1}{10}$ to other places. What fraction of the deliveries were made to homes and hospitals?

(1) $\frac{1}{10}$

(2) $\frac{3}{25}$

(3) $\frac{1}{5}$

(4) $\frac{7}{10}$

(5) $\frac{5}{15}$

28. An insurance company estimates that 4 out of every 100 renters do not have any insurance on their personal belongings. What fraction is this?

(1) $\frac{1}{25}$

(2) $\frac{3}{50}$

(3) $\frac{1}{10}$

(4) $\frac{1}{4}$

(5) $\frac{2}{5}$

Answers are on page 857.

Decimals

$\frac{1}{10}$ = 0.1

$\frac{7}{10}$ = 0.7

$\frac{1}{100}$ = 0.01

$\frac{9}{100}$ = 0.09

Another way to express fractions is with decimal numbers. A **decimal** is a fraction expressed using a place value system. With decimals the whole is divided into multiples (powers) of 10 such as 10, 100, 1,000, and so on. This means the denominator of the fraction equivalent is always a power of 10. The most common use of decimals is our system of money: a dollar (the whole) is divided into 100 cents. Every time you use money you must compare decimals and apply the four basic mathematical operations to decimals. Lessons 9, 10, and 11 review working with decimals.

Lesson 9 Decimals

Place Value, Comparing, and Rounding

Study the chart. Notice that decimal fractions are to the right of the decimal point. As with whole numbers, the sum of the values of the digits equals the total value of the number.

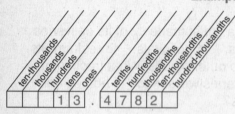

Example: What is the value of each digit in 13.4782?

1 is in the tens place.	1×10	= 10
3 is in the ones place.	3×1	= 3
4 is in the tenths place.	4×0.1	= 0.4
7 is in the hundredths place.	7×0.01	= 0.07
8 is in the thousandths place.	8×0.001	= 0.008
2 is in the ten-thousandths place.	$+ 2 \times 0.0001$	= 0.0002
		13.4782

Reading Decimals

Follow these steps to read a number with part as a decimal:

Step 1: Read the whole number part.

Step 2: Say the word "and" to indicate the decimal point.

Step 3: Read the digits to the right of the decimal point as a whole number.

Step 4: Say the place name of the last digit on the right.

Examples: What is the word form of 65.034?

Sixty-five and thirty-four <u>thousandths</u>

What is the word form of 1.82?

One and eighty-two <u>hundredths</u>

Comparing and Ordering Decimals

To compare decimals with the same number of decimal places, compare them as though they were whole numbers.

Example: Which is greater, 0.364 or 0.329?

364 is greater than 329, so 0.364 is greater than 0.329.

Use these steps to compare decimals with a different number of digits.

Step 1: Write zeros to the right of the decimal with fewer digits so that the numbers have the same number of decimal places. This does not change the value of the decimal.

Step 2: Compare the decimals as though they were whole numbers.

Example: Which decimal is greater: 0.518 or 0.52?

Add a zero: 0.518   0.520

Compare: 0.518   0.520   0.52 is greater than 0.518

Notice that the decimal with more decimal places may not be the greater decimal. When you compare numbers that have a whole number and a decimal, always compare the whole numbers first.

Example: Compare 32.001 and 31.999

Compare the whole numbers: 32   31

32.001 is greater than 31.999 because 32 is greater than 31. It does not matter that 0.999 is greater than 0.001. The whole number parts 31 and 32 determine which number is greater.

Rounding

Decimals are rounded according to the same rules as whole numbers.

Example: Round 16.959 to the nearest tenth.

Circle the digit in the tenths place.	16.⑨59
Look at the digit to the right.	16.⑨59
The digit is 5, so add 1 to the tenths place.	+ 1
Drop the remaining digits. Since 9 + 1 is 10,	16.9
put a zero in the tenths place and add one	17.0
to the ones place.	

Using Estimation with Money

To estimate means to find an approximate amount. Many money situations do not require exact amounts. In such cases, you can use amounts rounded to the nearest whole dollar (the ones place).

Auto Parts Price List

Outside Wide-Angle Mirror	$13.45
Steering Wheel Cover	$15.95
Oil Drip Pan	$8.73
Windshield Washer Fluid	$2.85
Brake Fluid	$6.35

Example: Using the price list, about how much would Pat pay for a steering wheel cover, a wide-angle mirror, and an oil drip pan?

(1)   between $31 and $33

(2)   between $33 and $35

(3)   between $35 and $37

(4)   between $37 and $39

(5)   between $39 and $41

Round the cost of each item to the nearest whole dollar and find the total of the estimates.

Item	Cost	Estimate
Steering wheel cover	$15.95	$16
Wide-angle mirror	13.45	13
Oil drip pan	8.73	+ 9
Total:		$38

The best answer is **(4) between $37 and $39.**

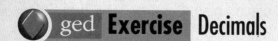 ged **Exercise** Decimals

Directions: Write the value of the underlined digit in words.

Example: 1.5<u>4</u>09 _____ **four hundredths** _____

1. 10.92<u>5</u>1 _____   3. 255.0<u>7</u> _____

2. 7.8<u>5</u> _____   4. 36.002<u>9</u> _____

Directions: Compare the following numbers. Write >, <, or = between the numbers.

5. 0.32   0.3109   8. 0.006   0.06   11. 2.38   2.83

6. 0.98   1.9   9. 1.075   1.57   12. 1.09   1.009

7. 0.5   0.50   10. 0.18   0.108   13. 3.60   3.600

Directions: List these numbers in order from least to greatest.

14. 3.4   3.09   3.9   3.901 _____

15. 0.08   0.8   0.89 _____

16. 0.95   0.954   0.9054 _____

17. 12.608   12.001   12.8   12.04 _____

Directions: Round these numbers.

18. Round **3.5719** to the tenths place. _____

19. Round **125.0699** to the thousandths place. _____

20. Round **5.132** to the hundredths place. _____

21. Round **17.0813** to the tenths place. _____

22. Round **0.6415** to the hundredths place. _____

Directions: Choose the best answer to each item.

Items 23 to 25 refer to the following information.

Computer Game Sales		
Game	Regular Price	Sale Price
Fast Pitch	$11.79	$8.99
Par 4	8.85	6.29
Dugout Derby	17.25	12.78
Crown of Power	13.72	10.09
Thunderclap Mine	12.99	9.25
Batwing	10.77	7.98

23. Lee wants to buy Fast Pitch, Crown of Power, and Dugout Derby. About how much will the three games cost on sale?

(1) between $21 and $24

(2) between $24 and $27

(3) between $27 and $30

(4) between $30 and $33

(5) between $33 and $36

24. Ana can spend $20 on computer games. She plans to buy Par 4 for $6.29 and Batwing for $7.98. At the sale price, which other game can she also afford?

(1) Fast Pitch

(2) Dugout Derby

(3) Crown of Power

(4) Thunderclap Mine

(5) She cannot afford any other game.

25. Mark wants to buy Dugout Derby and Crown of Power. About how much will he save by buying the games on sale?

(1) $ 7

(2) $ 8

(3) $ 9

(4) $10

(5) $11

26. Hank's Hardware sells a carbon monoxide detector for $38.82 and a smoke detector for $12.39. Which is the nearest estimate of the total cost of the 2 items?

(1) $26

(2) $27

(3) $50

(4) $51

(5) $52

27. Hank's Hardware sells 6 packages of nails that cost $5.75 for each package. Which is the nearest estimate of the total cost of the nails?

(1) $ 5

(2) $ 6

(3) $25

(4) $30

(5) $36

28. Pete pays $185.60 each month on the loan for his delivery van and $46.36 each month for the insurance. Which is the nearest estimate of the combined total Pete pays for his van loan and insurance?

(1) $139

(2) $140

(3) $226

(4) $232

(5) $240

29. Mark wants to buy a sofa for the recreation center that costs $685. He has saved $110. About how much more money does he need to buy the sofa?

(1) $200

(2) $300

(3) $400

(4) $500

(5) $600

Answers are on page 859.

Lesson  Decimal Operations

Adding and Subtracting Decimals

Examples: Anna assembles machine parts. One part comes in two sections with lengths of 4.875 and 3.25 centimeters. What is the total length of the two sections?

Cesar has $213 in a checking account. If he writes a check for $36.68, how much will be left in the account?

Follow these steps to add and subtract decimals:

Step 1: Write the numbers so that the decimal points are in line. If necessary, write zeros to the right of the last digit so that all the numbers have the same number of decimal places. A number without a decimal point is understood to have one to the right of the ones place.

$$\begin{array}{r} 4.875 \\ +\,3.250 \end{array}$$

$$\begin{array}{r} \$213.00 \\ -\quad 36.68 \end{array}$$
(\$213 is written as \$213.00)

Step 2: Add or subtract as you would with whole numbers.

$$\begin{array}{r} {}^{1\ 1} \\ 4.875 \\ +\,3.250 \\ \hline 8.125 \end{array}$$

$$\begin{array}{r} {}^{10\,2}\ {}^{9}\ {}^{11} \\ \$213.00 \\ -\quad 36.68 \\ \hline \$176.32 \end{array}$$

Step 3: Line up the decimal point in the answer with the decimal points in the problem. Check as with whole numbers.

$$\begin{array}{r} 4.875 \\ +\,3.250 \\ \hline 8.125 \end{array}$$

$$\begin{array}{r} \$213.00 \\ -\quad 36.68 \\ \hline \$176.32 \end{array}$$

The total length of Anna's machine part is **8.125** centimeters. Cesar will have **$176.32** left in his checking account.

Multiplying Decimals

Example: In the meat department at a grocery store, a cut of meat weighs 1.6 pounds and costs $1.79 per pound. To the nearest whole cent, what is the cost of the meat?

This problem can be solved by multiplying the weight of the meat by the cost per pound. The problem tells you to round your answer.

To multiply decimals, follow these steps:

Step 1: Multiply as you would with whole numbers. The decimal points do <u>not</u> need to line up. Ignore the decimal points until you are finished.

$$\begin{array}{r} \$1.79 \\ \times\quad 1.6 \\ \hline 1074 \\ 179 \\ \hline 2864 \end{array}$$

Step 2: Count the decimal places in the original problem to find how many places are needed in the answer.

$$\begin{array}{r} \$1.79 \;\text{2 decimal places} \\ \times\quad 1.6 \;\text{1 decimal place} \end{array}$$

There are three decimal places in the problem.

| Step 3: | Place the decimal point in the answer. Starting on the right, count three decimal places. | **$2.**864
$2.864 rounded to the nearest hundredth is $2.86 |

The cut of meat costs **$2.86.**

Dividing Decimals

Use these steps to divide a decimal by a whole number:

| Step 1: | Place the decimal point in the answer directly above the decimal point in the problem. |

$$\begin{array}{r} \$5.379 \\ 12\overline{)\,\$64.550} \\ \underline{60} \\ 4\,5 \\ \underline{3\,6} \\ 95 \\ \underline{84} \\ 110 \\ \underline{108} \\ 2 \end{array}$$

Step 2:	Divide as you would with whole numbers.
Step 3:	When a problem shows a remainder, write a zero to the right of the number you are dividing and continue. Keep dividing and writing zeros until either there is no remainder or you reach the place value you need. Carry out the division to one place to the right of the desired place value, then round.
Example:	Marvin bought a dual cassette player for $64.55, which he will pay for in 12 equal payments. How much will each payment be? Round your answer to the nearest cent.

$5.379 rounds to $5.38. Each payment is **$5.38.**

To divide by a decimal, you must make the divisor (the number you are dividing by) a whole number. Move the decimal point in the divisor all the way to the right. Move the decimal point in the number you are dividing the <u>same</u> number of places to the right. Then divide as you would by a whole number.

| Example: | A druggist is preparing a medication. Each capsule requires 0.007 grams of aspirin. She has 14 grams of aspirin. How many capsules can she prepare? |

$$\begin{array}{r} 2,000. \\ 0.007\overline{)\,14.000} \\ \underline{14} \end{array}$$

Move the decimal point 3 places to the right in both numbers. Write zeros to the right of the number you are dividing.

$$14 \div 0.007 = 2,000$$

Multiplying and Dividing by Powers of Ten

The powers of 10 are 10, 100, 1,000 and so on. When you are multiplying or dividing by a power of ten, a special rule will make your work easier. Use this rule to multiply and divide by powers of ten:

Count the number of zeros in the power of ten.
- To **multiply,** move the decimal point the same number of places to the **right.**
- To **divide,** move the decimal point the same number of places to the **left.**

Example: Multiply 78.5 by 1,000.

There are three zeros in 1,000. Move the decimal point three places to the right. You will need to write zeros as placeholders.

$78.5 \times 1,000 = 78.500 = 78,500$

Example: Divide 0.5 by 1,000.

There are three zeros in 1,000. Move the decimal point three places to the left. You will need to write zeros in front of the 5.

$0.5 \div 1,000 = 0\ 000.5 = 0.0005$

⬤ ged **Exercise** Decimal Operations

1. 1.85
    0.03
    19.007
    + 62
    ‾‾‾‾‾‾

4. $14.01 + 8.6 + 0.058$

5. $56.8 - 24.95$

2. 16,004.1
    − 6,972.1
    ‾‾‾‾‾‾‾‾

6. $0.95 + 1.843 + 3.008 + 0.9$

3. 3.8
    − 1.006
    ‾‾‾‾‾‾

Directions: Multiply.

7.   1.07
    × 12
    ‾‾‾‾

9.   5.04
    × 15
    ‾‾‾‾

11. 0.012
    ×   12
    ‾‾‾‾‾

8.   0.09
    × 6.1
    ‾‾‾‾

10. 0.008
    × 2.5
    ‾‾‾‾

12. 7.15
    × 0.03
    ‾‾‾‾‾

Directions: Divide.

13. $8\overline{)20.48}$

14. $0.07\overline{)4.34}$

15. $1.5\overline{)0.45}$

Directions: Divide. Round to the nearest hundredth.

16. $7\overline{)2}$

17. $13\overline{)6}$

18. $12\overline{)5}$

Directions: Choose the <u>best answer</u> to each item.

Items 19 and 20 refer to the following information.

Wilma has $35. She buys a blouse for $12.98, a belt for $10.67, and a poster for $5.98.

19. Which expression can be used to find how much Wilma has left?

   (1) $35 – $12.98 + ($10.67 + $5.98)
   (2) $35 – ($12.98 + $10.67 + $5.98)
   (3) ($35 + $12.98) – ($10.67 + $5.98)
   (4) ($35 – $10.67) + ($12.98 – $5.98)
   (5) $35 – $12.98 + $10.67 – $5.98

20. How much does Wilma have left?

   (1) $8.67
   (2) $7.85
   (3) $6.33
   (4) $5.37
   (5) $5.14

Items 21 and 22 refer to the following information.

The Computer Center sells 3.5-inch disks for $0.89 each. Computer Warehouse sells them for $1.05 each. A customer wants to buy 25 disks.

21. Which expression can be used to find how much the customer will save by shopping at the Computer Center?

   (1) 25($1.05 – $0.89)
   (2) 25($1.05 + $0.89)
   (3) 25 – ($1.05 + $0.89)
   (4) 25 + ($1.05 – $0.89)
   (5) ($1.05 – $0.89) – 25

22. How much will the customer save by shopping at the Computer Center?

   (1) $ 0.41
   (2) $ 2.80
   (3) $ 3.48
   (4) $ 4.00
   (5) $10.25

Items 23 and 24 refer to the following information.

Getting ready for a trip, Mr. Valdez bought two tires for $45.79 each. He also paid $18.25 for an oil change.

23. Which expression can be used to find how much Mr. Valdez spent?

   (1) 2($45.79) + $18.25
   (2) 2($45.79) – $18.25
   (3) 2($45.79 + $18.25)
   (4) 2($45.79 – $18.25)
   (5) 2($45.79) + 2($18.25)

24. How much did Mr. Valdez spend?

   (1) $ 73.33
   (2) $ 91.58
   (3) $109.83
   (4) $119.53
   (5) $128.08

25. Angelo's salary was $18,575 a year. It was raised to $21,000. What was the monthly increase to the nearest dollar?

   (1) $ 202
   (2) $1,548
   (3) $1,750
   (4) $2,021
   (5) $2,425

Answers are on page 860.

Lesson 10 ◆ Decimal Operations

527

Decimals and Fractions

Both decimals and fractions can be used to show part of a whole. Sometimes it is easier to calculate using fractions. At other times, decimals are more useful. The ability to change a number from one form to the other is an important skill.

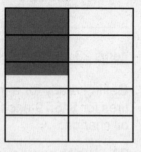  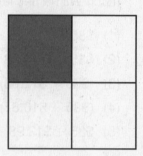

$$0.2\tfrac{1}{2}\ (2\tfrac{1}{2}\ \text{tenths}) \quad = \quad \frac{25}{100}\ \text{or}\ 0.25 \quad = \quad \frac{1}{4}$$

Writing Decimals as Fractions

Example: Write 0.375 as a fraction.
To write a decimal as a fraction, follow these steps:

Step 1: Write the number without the decimal point as the numerator of a fraction.

$$0.375 = \frac{375}{?}$$

Step 2: The denominator of the fraction is the place value of the decimal digit on the right. Hint: The number of decimal places will be the number of zeros in the denominator.

$$0.375 = \frac{375}{1,000}$$

Step 3: Reduce the fraction to lowest terms.

$$0.375 = \frac{375 \div 125}{1,000 \div 125} = \frac{3}{8}$$

Example: Write $0.33\tfrac{1}{3}$ as a fraction.
This decimal has a fraction part. To write this type of decimal as a fraction, follow these steps:

Step 1: Write the fraction as you did in steps 1 and 2 above.

$$0.33\tfrac{1}{3} = \frac{33\tfrac{1}{3}}{100}\quad \text{This means } 33\tfrac{1}{3} \div 100.$$

Step 2: Follow the steps to divide mixed numbers.

1. Change to improper number.
2. Invert the divisor.
3. Reduce and multiply.

$$33\tfrac{1}{3} \div \frac{100}{1} = \frac{100}{3} \div \frac{100}{1} = \frac{100}{3} \times \frac{1}{100} = \frac{\overset{1}{\cancel{100}}}{3} \times \frac{1}{\cancel{100}_{1}} = \frac{1}{3}$$

Writing Fractions as Decimals

Example: Write $\frac{3}{5}$ as a decimal.

To write a fraction as a decimal, divide the numerator by the denominator: $5\overline{)3}$.

Step 1: Set the decimal point in the problem.

Step 2: Set the decimal point in the answer directly above the decimal point in the problem.

Step 3: Add zeros to make extra decimal places.

Step 4: Divide.

$$\begin{array}{r} \cdot \leftarrow 2. \\ 5\overline{)3.0} \leftarrow 3. \\ 1.\uparrow \end{array}$$

$$\begin{array}{r} 0.6 \\ 5\overline{)3.0} \\ \underline{3\,0} \end{array}$$

Some problems may require you to divide to two, three, or four decimal places. Some problems will always have a remainder. When this happens, you can write the remainder as a fraction (for an exact answer), or you can round the answer to a chosen decimal place.

Example: Write $\frac{2}{9}$ as a decimal. Divide to three decimal places. Write the remainder as a fraction by writing the remainder, 2, over the divisor, 9.

$$\frac{2}{9} = 0.222\frac{2}{9}$$

To write $\frac{2}{9}$ as a decimal, round to a chosen decimal place:

0.222 rounds to 0.22

$$\begin{array}{r} 0.222\frac{2}{9} \\ 9\overline{)2.000} \\ \underline{1\,8} \\ 20 \\ \underline{18} \\ 20 \\ \underline{18} \\ 2 = r \end{array}$$

Working with Money

The unit price of an item is often stated as a decimal with a fraction. The fraction expresses a part of one cent.

Example: The unit price of orange juice is $4\frac{1}{2}$ cents per ounce. What is the cost of 32 ounces of juice?

Multiply 32 by $4\frac{1}{2}$ cents, or $\$0.04\frac{1}{2}$, to solve the problem. Write the fraction part of the decimal as a decimal. The fraction $\frac{1}{2}$ is equal to 0.5 ($1 \div 2 = 0.5$). So $4\frac{1}{2}$ cents could also be written 4.5 cents, or $\$0.045$. Multiply 32 by $\$0.045$.

$$\begin{array}{r} 32 \\ \times\ \$0.045 \\ \hline 160 \\ 128 \\ \hline \$1.440 \end{array}$$

At $4\frac{1}{2}$ cents per ounce, the cost of 32 ounces is **$1.44.**

Conversion Table

To rewrite fractions and decimals more quickly, memorize this table.

Halves	Thirds	Fourths	Fifths	Eighths
$0.5 = \frac{1}{2}$	$0.33\frac{1}{3} = \frac{1}{3}$	$0.25 = \frac{1}{4}$	$0.2 = \frac{1}{5}$	$0.12\frac{1}{2}$ or $0.125 = \frac{1}{8}$
	$0.66\frac{2}{3} = \frac{2}{3}$	$0.75 = \frac{3}{4}$	$0.4 = \frac{2}{5}$	$0.37\frac{1}{2}$ or $0.375 = \frac{3}{8}$
			$0.6 = \frac{3}{5}$	$0.62\frac{1}{2}$ or $0.625 = \frac{5}{8}$
			$0.8 = \frac{4}{5}$	$0.87\frac{1}{2}$ or $0.875 = \frac{7}{8}$

Directions: Write these decimals as fractions. Reduce to lowest terms.

1. 0.25

5. $0.31\frac{1}{4}$

9. 0.675

2. 0.875

6. $0.93\frac{3}{4}$

10. $0.10\frac{5}{6}$

3. 0.375

7. $0.91\frac{2}{3}$

11. 0.55

4. 0.76

8. $0.16\frac{2}{3}$

12. $0.05\frac{1}{3}$

Directions: Write these fractions as decimals. Round to three decimal places.

13. $\frac{4}{5}$

15. $\frac{2}{3}$

17. $\frac{7}{12}$

14. $\frac{3}{8}$

16. $\frac{5}{12}$

18. $\frac{3}{16}$

Directions: Write these fractions as decimals. Divide to two decimal places and write the remainder as a fraction. Reduce.

19. $\frac{5}{6}$

21. $\frac{7}{15}$

23. $\frac{7}{8}$

20. $\frac{8}{9}$

22. $\frac{1}{16}$

24. $\frac{5}{12}$

Directions: Choose the best answer to each item.

25. One of the sewing machines at Dreyer's Dress Company broke down. The replacement part for the broken part should be 0.007 inch thick. The part on hand is $\frac{1}{100}$ inch thick. What part of an inch too thick is the part that is on hand?

    (1) 0.0093
    (2) 0.009
    (3) 0.003
    (4) 0.09
    (5) 0.3

26. At Wherry Bat Company, $\frac{7}{8}$ of the bats passed inspection on Monday. On Tuesday, only 0.75 of the bats passed inspection. What fraction more passed on Monday than on Tuesday?

    (1) $\frac{1}{16}$
    (2) $\frac{1}{8}$
    (3) $\frac{3}{16}$
    (4) $\frac{1}{4}$
    (5) $\frac{5}{8}$

27. Unleaded gasoline sells for $1.36 per gallon at U-Save Gas. How much would $12\frac{1}{2}$ gallons cost?

    (1) $12.62
    (2) $15.65
    (3) $16.32
    (4) $17.00
    (5) $17.75

28. In a union poll, $\frac{3}{8}$ of those surveyed agreed with Mr. Samuels. Of those surveyed, 0.4 agreed with Ms. Havel. If 400 people were surveyed, how many more people agreed with Ms. Havel than with Mr. Samuels?

    (1) 10
    (2) 35
    (3) 80
    (4) 150
    (5) 160

29. Alicia needs to know how many cans of corn to open for dinner. First, she figures how many servings are in one can. A can of corn contains $35\frac{3}{4}$ ounces. If one serving is 3.25 ounces, how many servings are in the can?

    (1) 13
    (2) 11
    (3) 9
    (4) 7
    (5) 5

30. Frank jogs each evening to stay fit. He jogged 2.75 miles on Monday, $3\frac{1}{2}$ miles Tuesday, $3\frac{7}{8}$ miles Wednesday, $2\frac{3}{4}$ miles on Thursday, and 3.375 miles on Friday. How many miles did he jog in the five days?

    (1) $15\frac{7}{8}$
    (2) $16\frac{1}{4}$
    (3) $16\frac{3}{4}$
    (4) $17\frac{3}{8}$
    (5) $17\frac{1}{2}$

Answers are on page 861.

Directions: Choose the best answer to each item.

1. A delivery truck logged the following trips: to Hoptown, 12.3 miles; to Mendon, 15.8 miles; to Canton, 21.7 miles; return to office, 8.9 miles. What was the total mileage?

    (1) 30.6 miles
    (2) 40.9 miles
    (3) 49.8 miles
    (4) 58.7 miles
    (5) 71.3 miles

2. A brand of hair conditioner contains 0.52 grams of special ingredients. There are 0.06 grams of ingredient A and 0.1 gram of ingredient B in the conditioner. Which expression can be used to find how many grams of ingredient C are in the conditioner?

    (1) 0.52 + 0.06 + 0.1
    (2) 0.52 − (0.06 + 0.1)
    (3) (0.52 − 0.06) + 0.1
    (4) 0.52 − (0.06) (0.1)
    (5) 0.52 − (0.1 − 0.06)

3. A package of ground beef costs $6.98. The price per pound is $1.86. To the nearest hundredth, how many pounds of ground beef are in the package?

    (1) 3.55
    (2) 3.64
    (3) 3.75
    (4) 3.86
    (5) 3.92

Items 4 and 5 refer to the following information.

It costs the Quality Company $0.14 per mile to run its van. The van's mileage for the week was as follows: Monday, 87.6 miles; Tuesday, 17.3 miles; Wednesday, 14 miles; Thursday, 102.2 miles; Friday, 42.7 miles.

4. What was the van's total mileage for the week?

    (1) 263.8 miles
    (2) 268.9 miles
    (3) 277.8 miles
    (4) 281.6 miles
    (5) 284.8 miles

5. To the nearest whole cent, what was the cost to run the van on Monday?

    (1) $ 1.23
    (2) $ 6.57
    (3) $12.26
    (4) $13.14
    (5) Not enough information is given.

6. The Cheese Works sells cheddar cheese for $3.85 per pound. How much will a package cost that weighs $1\frac{3}{5}$ pounds?

    (1) $ 5.45
    (2) $ 6.16
    (3) $ 8.78
    (4) $10.01
    (5) Not enough information is given.

7. The gold filling on a finished ring is to be 0.03 millimeters thick. The gold already on the ring has a thickness of 0.021 millimeters. How many more millimeters of gold should be added to the ring?

(1) 0.9
(2) 0.18
(3) 0.09
(4) 0.018
(5) 0.009

Items 8 and 9 refer to the following information.

Smith's Berry Barn Weekend Sales	
Saturday Morning	$ 82.37
Saturday Afternoon	136.29
Sunday Morning	51.04
Sunday Afternoon	127.76

8. Approximately how much more did the Berry Barn earn on Sunday afternoon than on Sunday morning?

(1) between $60 and $65
(2) between $65 and $70
(3) between $70 and $75
(4) between $75 and $80
(5) between $80 and $85

9. Which expression can be used to find how much more the Berry Barn earned on Saturday than on Sunday?

(1) ($82.37 + $136.29) − ($51.04 + $127.76)
(2) ($136.29 − $82.37) + ($127.76 − $51.04)
(3) ($136.29 + $127.76) − ($82.37 + $51.04)
(4) ($136.29 − $127.76) − ($82.37 − $51.04)
(5) 2($136.29 − $127.76)

10. A metal plating process covers metal parts with 0.005 inch of aluminum chrome. A second step covers each part with 0.01 inch more of aluminum. What is the total thickness of the aluminum after the second step?

(1) 0.0051 inch
(2) 0.006 inch
(3) 0.015 inch
(4) 0.06 inch
(5) 0.15 inch

11. Kim works as a salesperson for a photo studio. To find his earnings for the week, he multiplies his total sales by 0.175. His sales for the week of October 10 total $2,507.47. To the nearest whole cent, what did he earn for the week?

(1) $388.06
(2) $438.81
(3) $449.83
(4) $880.60
(5) Not enough information is given.

12. Andre's weekly pay is $226.40. His boss plans to give him a raise that is 0.1 of his present salary. Which of the following expressions can be used to find Andre's new weekly pay?

(1) $226.40 − (0.1) ($226.40)
(2) $226.40 + ($226.40 − 0.1)
(3) 0.1($226.40 + 0.1)
(4) 0.1($226.40) + 0.1
(5) 0.1($226.40) + $226.40

Answers are on page 862.

Percent

Percent is another way to show part of a whole. With fractions, the whole can be divided into any number of equal parts—this number is shown as the denominator. With decimals, the number of parts is 10, 100, 1,000, 10,000, or another power of 10. With percents, the whole is always divided into **100** equal parts.

This square is divided into 100 equal parts. The entire square represents 100%. Fifty parts, or one-half of the whole square, are shaded. The shaded part is 50% of the whole. The percent sign, %, means "out of 100." Fifty out of 100 parts are shaded.

Percents greater than 100% are like mixed numbers. A percent greater than 100% is greater than one whole.

This drawing represents 125%. One hundred twenty-five parts are shaded. Since 100 parts equals 1 and 25 out of 100 parts is $\frac{1}{4}$, $125\% = 1.25 = 1\frac{1}{4}$.

This drawing shows $\frac{1}{2}\%$. Only one-half of one part is shaded. A percent that is less than 1% is less than $\frac{1}{100}$: $\frac{1}{2}\% = \frac{\frac{1}{2}}{100} = \frac{0.5}{100} = 0.005$.

To solve percent problems, you need to write the percent as a decimal, a fraction, a mixed number, or a whole number.

Lesson 12 — The Meaning of Percent

Writing a Percent as a Decimal

Follow these steps to change a percent, such as 45%, to a decimal.

Step 1:   Drop the percent sign.
Step 2:   Move the decimal point two places to the left.   **45**
          Remember, a number without a decimal point is   **0.45**
          understood to have a decimal point to the right of the
          ones place. Write the zero in the ones place (to the
          left of the decimal point) to serve as a placeholder.
Example: Write 7.5% as a decimal.   **7.5% = 0.075**

ged Exercise — The Meaning of Percent

Directions: Write each percent as a decimal or whole number.

1. 60%

2. 4.8%

3. $5\frac{1}{2}\%$

4. 200%

5. $9\frac{1}{4}\%$

6. 5.6%

Answers are on page 863.

Writing a Decimal as a Percent

Follow these steps to write a decimal, such as 0.15 as a percent.

Step 1:   Move the decimal point two places to the right. $0.15. = 15$

Step 2:   Write the percent sign.

Example: Write $0.33\frac{1}{3}$ as a percent. $0.33\frac{1}{3} = 33\frac{1}{3}\%$

Directions: Write each decimal or whole number as a percent.

7. 0.85   9. 0.4   11. 8.75   13. 1.5

8. 0.36   10. 4.5   12. 0.375   14. $0.16\frac{2}{3}$

Writing a Fraction or Mixed Number as a Percent

You can use the following steps to write a fraction as a percent:

Step 1:   Multiply the fraction by $\frac{100}{1}$. Reduce and divide as needed.

Step 2:   Write the percent sign.

Example: Change $\frac{1}{4}$ to a percent. $\frac{1}{\cancel{4}_1} \times \frac{\cancel{100}^{25}}{1} = \frac{25}{1} = 25 = \mathbf{25\%}$

Example: Change $\frac{2}{3}$ to a percent. $\frac{2}{3} \times \frac{100}{1} = \frac{200}{3} = 66\frac{2}{3} = 66\frac{2}{3}\%$

Use these steps to write a mixed number, such as $3\frac{1}{5}$, as a percent:

Step 1:   Multiply the whole number by 100 and write the percent sign. $3 \times 100 = 300\%$

Step 2:   Change the fraction to a percent. $\frac{1}{\cancel{5}_1} \times \frac{\cancel{100}^{20}}{1} = \frac{20}{1} = 20\%$

Step 3:   Add the two percents. $300\% + 20\% = 320\%$

Directions: Write each fraction as a percent.

15. $\frac{2}{5}$ 17. $\frac{1}{3}$ 19. $1\frac{5}{8}$ 21. $1\frac{7}{8}$

16. $\frac{3}{4}$ 18. $2\frac{7}{20}$ 20. $4\frac{2}{3}$ 22. $3\frac{1}{10}$

Writing a Percent as a Fraction or Mixed Number

Answers are on page 863.

Follow these steps to change a percent to a fraction or mixed number:

Step 1:   Drop the percent sign and write the number with a denominator of 100.

Step 2:   Reduce the fraction, if necessary.

Example: Change 35% to a fraction. $\frac{35}{100} = \frac{35 \div 5}{100 \div 5} = \frac{7}{20}$

23. 20%   24. 12%   25. 39%   26. 65%   27. 140%   28. 275%

Percents with a fraction part are harder to write as fractions.

Example: Write $41\frac{2}{3}$ % as a fraction.

Drop the % sign and divide by 100.

$$\frac{41\frac{2}{3}}{100} = 41\frac{2}{3} \div 100 = \frac{\overset{5}{\cancel{125}}}{3} \times \frac{1}{\underset{4}{\cancel{100}}} = \frac{5}{12}$$

Percents with a decimal part must be written as a decimal and then changed to a fraction.

Example: Change 37.5% to a fraction.

Change the percent to a decimal by moving the decimal point two places to the left. $37.5\% = 375 = 0.375$

Write as a fraction and reduce.
Notice the denominator is 1,000 $\frac{375 \div 125}{1{,}000 \div 125} = \frac{3}{8}$
because 0.375 has three decimal places.

Memorize these common percent/fraction equivalents.

Halves	Thirds	Fourths	Fifths
$50\% = \frac{1}{2}$	$33\frac{1}{3}\% = \frac{1}{3}$ $66\frac{2}{3}\% = \frac{2}{3}$	$25\% = \frac{1}{4}$ $75\% = \frac{3}{4}$	$20\% = \frac{1}{5}$ $40\% = \frac{2}{5}$ $60\% = \frac{3}{5}$ $80\% = \frac{4}{5}$

Sixths	Eighths	Tenths
$16\frac{2}{3}\% = \frac{1}{6}$ $83\frac{1}{3}\% = \frac{5}{6}$	$12\frac{1}{2}\%$ or $12.5\% = \frac{1}{8}$ $37\frac{1}{2}\%$ or $37.5\% = \frac{3}{8}$ $62\frac{1}{2}\%$ or $62.5\% = \frac{5}{8}$ $87\frac{1}{2}\%$ or $87.5\% = \frac{7}{8}$	$10\% = \frac{1}{10}$ $30\% = \frac{3}{10}$ $70\% = \frac{7}{10}$ $90\% = \frac{9}{10}$

29. Fill in the missing numbers on the chart.

	Decimal	Fraction	Percent
1.	0.1		
2.			20%
3.		$\frac{1}{4}$	
4.	0.3		
5.		$\frac{1}{3}$	
6.			40%

	Decimal	Fraction	Percent
7.	0.5		
8.			60%
9.	$0.66\frac{2}{3}$		
10.		$\frac{7}{10}$	
11.		$\frac{3}{4}$	
12.			80%

Answers are on page 863.

Solving Percent Problems

There are three basic elements in a percent problem,—the base, the part, and the rate. Think about this statement:

15%, or 30, of the 200 job applicants cannot work on weekends.

♦ The **base** is the whole amount. The other numbers in the problem are compared to the base. In this statement, 200 is the base amount.

♦ The **part** is a piece of the whole or base. In this statement the number 30 tells what part of the 200 applicants (the base) are not available on weekends.

♦ The **rate** is always followed by the percent (%) sign. The rate tells the relationship of the part to the base.

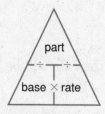

In a percent problem, one of these three elements is missing. Find the missing element, using the percent formula. The relationship of these three elements is shown in the triangle. Use the triangle to determine which operation to perform. Cover the element you need to find; perform the indicated operation on the remaining two elements.

Finding the Part

Example: Aretha puts 5% of her weekly paycheck in her savings account. If her weekly paycheck is $286.00, how much will she put in savings?

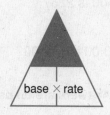

base × rate = part

The base, or whole amount is $286.00. The rate is 5%. You need to solve for the part by multiplying.

Write the rate as a decimal: 5% = 0.05

Multiply:
$$\begin{array}{r} \$286 \\ \times\,0.05 \\ \hline \$14.30 \end{array}$$

Aretha will put **$14.30** of the $286.00 in her savings account.

In some problems, the rate may be greater than 100%. In such a case, the part will be greater than the base.

ged **Exercise** Solving Percent Problems

1. Find 15% of $950.

2. Find 125% of $220.

3. Find $5\frac{1}{2}$% of $200.

4. What is 4% of $1,200?

5. What is 210% of 150?

6. What is $33\frac{1}{3}$% of 120?

Answers are on page 864.

Finding the Rate

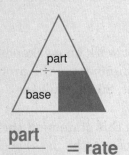

$$\frac{\text{part}}{\text{base}} = \text{rate}$$

Example: Joel earns $1,500 per month. If he spends $375 on rent each month, what percent of his income does he spend on rent?

In this problem, the base is $1,500—Joel's "whole" salary for the month. The part is $375—the part of his salary that is spent on rent.

You need to find the rate or percent. The problem can be solved by dividing:

Divide:
```
            0.25
$1,500) $375.00
         300 0
          75 00
          75 00
              0
```

Write: $0.25 = 25\%$

Joel spends **25%** of his salary on rent.

Note: If the part is greater than the base, the rate will be greater than 100%.

Directions: Solve.

7. 123 is what percent of 820?

8. 125 is what percent of 625?

9. $3.50 is what percent of $175.00?

10. What percent of $180 is $252?

11. What percent of 5,000 is 225?

12. What percent of $40.00 is $72.00?

Answers are on page 864.

Finding the Base

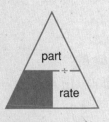

$$\frac{\text{part}}{\text{rate}} = \text{base}$$

Example: Of the employees who work at Stalling Printing, 90% attended the safety procedures meeting. If 63 employees attended the meeting, how many employees work at Stalling Printing?

The base or whole amount is the number of employees at Stalling Printing. The base is not given in the problem. The number 63 is part of the whole group of employees. The 63 employees are 90% of the base. 90% is the rate. Solve for the base by dividing.

Write the rate as a decimal: $90\% = 0.9$

Divide:
```
          70.
  0.9) 63.0
       63
        0 0
```

There are **70** employees at the printing company.

If the rate is greater than 100%, the part will be greater than the base. If Regina's new salary is $326.40 and her previous salary is $272, her new salary is 120% of her previous salary.

Problems that require you to solve for the base frequently have more than one step. Make sure you know what you are to solve for. Decide what operations you will need to solve the problem. Then do the work.

13. 6% of what amount is $1.92?

14. 115% of what number is 207?

15. 3.8% of what amount is $0.76?

16. 720 is 9% of what number?

17. 22.5% of what number is 36?

18. $679.35 is $5\frac{1}{4}$% of what amount?

Finding Percent of Increase or Decrease

Sometimes when finding the rate, you will be asked to solve for the percent of increase or decrease. To solve, follow these steps:

Step 1: Subtract the original amount from the new amount.
Step 2: Divide the difference by the original amount.
Step 3: Convert the decimal to a percent.

Example: Last month, Marty's Discount Store sold $1,375 in small appliances. This month, $1,540 worth of small appliances were sold. What is the rate of increase in the sale of small appliances?

Step 1: Subtract: $1,540 − $1,375 = $165.
Step 2: Divide: $165 ÷ $1,375 = 0.12 $\left(\frac{\$165}{\$1,375} = 0.12 \right)$.
Step 3: Write the decimal as a percent: 0.12 = 12%.
Note: Use the same method to find rate of decrease. Subtract the new amount from the original amount.

Directions: Find the percent of increase or decrease.

	Original Amount	New Amount		Original Amount	New Amount
19.	$1,500	$1,725	21.	280	70
20.	$520.00	$582.40	22.	$1,200	$1,140

Answers are on page 864.

Directions: Choose the best answer to each item.

23. During the winter, Green's Lawn Care Service contacted 325 homeowners. Of these contacts, 36% hired the lawn care service. How many homeowners hired Green's Lawn Care Service?

    (1) 72
    (2) 91
    (3) 117
    (4) 253
    (5) 300

24. The Coaches Corner sporting goods store had a sale on athletic shoes. Their top-of-the-line basketball shoe usually sells for $90. During the sale, the same model sold for $72. What percent did the store discount the shoe for the sale?

    (1) 10%
    (2) 15%
    (3) 18%
    (4) 20%
    (5) 22%

25. A cereal coupon saved Rita $0.75. If $0.75 is 20% of the cereal's original price, what was the original price?

    (1) $0.95
    (2) $1.50
    (3) $2.75
    (4) $3.75
    (5) $6.00

26. Ahmad's car insurance last year was $630. This year he had two accidents, so the insurance company raised his yearly bill to $1,008. What was the percent of increase in Ahmad's car insurance?

    (1) 160%
    (2) 60%
    (3) 50%
    (4) 40%
    (5) 6%

27. In May an automobile manufacturer produced 1,280 cars. In June the manufacturer produced 125% more cars. How many cars were produced in June?

    (1) 320
    (2) 400
    (3) 520
    (4) 670
    (5) 1,600

28. At the warehouse where Rathena works, 140 cartons had to be loaded into a truck for delivery. By lunchtime, 119 cartons had been loaded. What percent of the cartons had been loaded?

    (1) 15%
    (2) 21%
    (3) 79%
    (4) 85%
    (5) 119%

29. A serving of soup supplies 9 grams of carbohydrates. If this is 3% of the carbohydrates Keisha needs daily, how many grams of carbohydrates does Keisha need daily?

    (1) 0.27
    (2) 27
    (3) 300
    (4) 900
    (5) 2,700

30. Mr. Cortez asked Jorge to stock the store shelves with 25 cases of soft drinks: 10 cola, 8 root beer, and 7 orange. Of the total cases of soft drinks, what percent were cola?

    (1) 40%
    (2) 35%
    (3) 25%
    (4) 15%
    (5) 10%

Answers are on page 864.

Lesson 14 More Percent Problems

Interest is a fee charged for using someone else's money. **Interest rates** are familiar to anyone who borrows money for a purchase or puts money into a savings account. The borrower needs to pay back the interest in addition to the **principal** (the amount borrowed).

The formula for finding the amount of **simple interest** due after a certain number of years is $i = prt$.

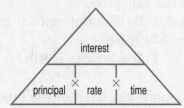

i = interest
p = principal, the amount borrowed or invested
r = interest rate, written as a percent
t = time of the loan, written in years

The formula is similar to the percent formula you have been using: part = base × rate. The interest formula can be written in a triangle.

To find simple interest, follow these steps:

Step 1: Write the rate as a decimal or a fraction.

Step 2: Write the time in terms of years. If the problem states the time in months, write the months as the numerator and the number 12 as the denominator. Reduce the fraction to lowest terms.

Step 3: Multiply: principal × rate × time. The result is the interest.

Example: Lynn Alvarez borrows $2,500 for 3 months at an 8% rate of interest. How much interest will Lynn pay on the loan?

The principal is $2,500. The rate is 8%, which can be written as 0.08. The time is 3 months, or $\frac{3}{12}$ of a year, which reduces to $\frac{1}{4}$. You may choose to change $\frac{1}{4}$ to 0.25.

Multiply $p \times r \times t$:

$$\$2,500 \times 0.08 \times \frac{1}{4} = \$200 \times \frac{1}{4} = \frac{\overset{50}{\cancel{200}}}{1} \times \frac{1}{\underset{1}{\cancel{4}}} = \$50$$

Lynn will owe **$50** in interest.

Sometimes you will need to find the **amount paid back.** This is the total amount of money the borrower must pay back to the lender. It includes the principal and any interest owed.

Lynn borrowed $2,500 and paid $50 interest. To find the pay back amount, add the principal and the interest: $2,500 + $50 = $2,550. Lynn must pay back **$2,550.**

Solving Multistep Problems

Sometimes you will use percents to solve problems that have more than one step. These problems are not difficult to solve if you organize the information you are given, decide what information you need to solve the problem, and break the problem down into steps. Remember to look for key words that tell you which operation to use.

Example: Wendy bought an $80 dress on sale for 40% off. How much did she pay for the dress?

Step 1: Find the discount amount.
Multiply the base by the rate. $80 × 0.4 = $32
Step 2: Find the sale price.
Subtract the discount amount from the original price:
$80 − $32 = $48
The sale price is **$48.**

Example: John made a small bookshelf using $8 worth of materials. John now wants to sell the bookshelf to make a 15% profit. How much should he sell the bookshelf for?

Step 1: Find the amount of profit.
Multiply base by rate:
$8.00 × 15% = $8.00 × 0.15 = 1.2 = $1.20
Step 2: Find the price of the bookshelf by adding the original cost to the profit: $8.00 + $1.20 = $9.20
John should sell the bookshelf for **$9.20.**

Example: The discount price of a sofa at a 40%-off sale is $348. What is the original price of the sofa?
Step 1: Find the rate that represents the sale price of the sofa:
100% − 40% = 60%
Step 2: Find the base or original price. Divide the part by the rate:
$348 ÷ 0.6 = $580
The original price of the sofa is **$580.**

Using Mental Math

10% is 0.1: To multiply by 10%, move the decimal point one place to the left. 10% of $40.00 = $4 0.00 = $4.00

5% is half of 10%: To multiply by 5%, find 10% and divide by 2.
5% of $900.00 = $90 0.00 ÷ 2 = $90.00 ÷ 2 = $45.00

15% is 10% + 5%: To multiply by 15%, add 10% to 5%.
15% of $20.00 = $2 0.00 + ($2 0.00 ÷ 2) = $2.00 + $1.00 = $3.00

20% is 2 times 10%: To multiply by 20%, find 10% and multiply by 2.
20% of $82.00 = $8 2.00 × 2 = $8.20 × 2 = $16.40

Mathematics ◆ Percent

Directions: Choose the best answer to each item.

1. Murray's Bargain Basement is having a sale on household goods. A $20 king-size blanket is on sale for 15% off. What is the sale price of the blanket?

   (1) $ 3.00
   (2) $ 5.00
   (3) $ 7.50
   (4) $17.00
   (5) $18.67

2. Mr. Bradford bought a delivery van. He borrowed $10,000 at $10\frac{1}{4}$% interest for 3 years. How much will he pay in interest on the loan?

   (1) $2,925
   (2) $3,000
   (3) $3,075
   (4) $3,150
   (5) $3,200

3. Alfredo bought a used car for $1,500. He replaced the engine and repaired and painted the body. He sold the car for $4,500. What was the rate of increase in the price of the car?

   (1)   67%
   (2) 133%
   (3) 200%
   (4) 300%
   (5) 400%

4. Boyd bought some fishing equipment for $150 and paid 5% sales tax. How much sales tax did he pay?

   (1) $75.00
   (2) $35.00
   (3) $15.00
   (4) $12.00
   (5) $ 7.50

5. The Yamatos borrow $900 for 3 months to pay the hospital bill for their daughter's birth. The interest rate is 18%. What is the total amount they will pay back in 3 months?

   (1) $ 904.15
   (2) $ 940.50
   (3) $ 996.00
   (4) $1,018.75
   (5) $1,020.00

6. Lavina wants to buy a rocking chair for $160. She will pay 10% down and pay the rest in 6 monthly installments. What will be the amount of each monthly payment?

   (1) $24
   (2) $26
   (3) $27
   (4) $30
   (5) $32

7. Of Zoila's $1,500 monthly earnings, 20% is paid for rent. How much does she pay each month for rent?

   (1) $240
   (2) $270
   (3) $300
   (4) $360
   (5) $412

Answers are on page 865.

Directions: Choose the <u>best answer</u> to each item.

1. On an employment test, George scored 80%. He had 16 correct answers. Which expression can be used to find the number of questions on the test?

   (1) 16(0.8) + 16
   (2) 16 ÷ 0.8
   (3) 16 ÷ 0.08
   (4) 16(0.8)
   (5) 16(0.08)

2. At a playoff game, paid attendance was 39,900. The total attendance was 42,000. What percent of those attending had free tickets?

   (1) 2%
   (2) 3%
   (3) 4%
   (4) 5%
   (5) 6%

3. Of the people attending a concert, 40% received a 50%-off coupon for next month's concert. How many received the coupon if there were 1,840 people at the concert?

   (1) 368
   (2) 460
   (3) 613
   (4) 736
   (5) 920

4. The personnel department reported total employment is 120% of last year's total. If the total number employed last year was 1,735, what is this year's employment figure?

   (1) 1,388
   (2) 1,446
   (3) 1,615
   (4) 2,082
   (5) 20,820

5. Louise makes a purchase of $19.49 and pays 6% sales tax. To the nearest whole cent, what is the amount of the sales tax on her purchase?

   (1) $0.79
   (2) $0.84
   (3) $0.92
   (4) $1.03
   (5) $1.17

6. Brigham loans his brother-in-law $690 at 8% interest for 8 months. How much will the brother-in-law pay back when the loan is due?

   (1) $718.08
   (2) $726.80
   (3) $750.00
   (4) $764.25
   (5) $775.50

7. Merrill receives a fixed salary of $165 per week and a $4\frac{1}{2}$% commission on the merchandise he sells. In a week when his sales are $5,320, how much does he earn?

    (1) $239.40
    (2) $359.12
    (3) $404.40
    (4) $473.80
    (5) Not enough information is given.

8. Jason pays $6\frac{1}{2}$% sales tax on a purchase of $15.60. Which expression can be used to find the total cost of his purchase?

    (1) $0.065($15.60 + $6.50)$
    (2) $0.6\left(\frac{1}{2}\right)($15.60) + 15.60
    (3) $0.06\left(\frac{1}{2}\right)($15.60) + 15.60
    (4) $0.065($15.60) + 6.50
    (5) $0.065($15.60) + 15.60

9. Ruth and Barry Souther borrow $3,500 at 18% for 2 years. How much interest will they pay on the loan?

    (1) $1,242
    (2) $1,260
    (3) $1,340
    (4) $1,356
    (5) $1,470

10. The sales tax in the state where Alonzo lives is $5\frac{1}{4}$%. What is the total amount he pays for a radio with the price $40?

    (1) $42.20
    (2) $42.16
    (3) $42.10
    (4) $42.04
    (5) $42.00

11. The discounted price of a new TV set at a 25%-off sale is $375.00. What was the original price of the TV?

    (1) $400
    (2) $450
    (3) $500
    (4) $550
    (5) $600

12. Ana Tew invests $3,500 for one year in a credit union account where her investment will earn $9\frac{1}{2}$% annual interest. How much will she have in the account at the end of 1 year?

    (1) $3,832.50
    (2) $3,804.17
    (3) $3,782.40
    (4) $3,697.50
    (5) $3,650.00

13. Jay buys a microwave regularly priced at $394.00. The microwave is on sale for 40% off the regular price. How much does Jay pay for the microwave?

    (1) $226.95
    (2) $232.60
    (3) $236.40
    (4) $240.25
    (5) $250.00

14. Alina saved $12 on a pair of jeans that had been marked 60% off. What was the original price of the jeans?

    (1) $ 4.80
    (2) $ 7.20
    (3) $12.00
    (4) $20.00
    (5) $36.00

Answers are on page 865.

Graphs and Tables

Lesson 15

Graphs, Charts, and Tables

Data analysis is one of the three major concepts of mathematics. One of the most common and graphic ways to present data is in the form of **graphs, charts,** and **tables.** The advantage of using these forms is that the relationships among the data can be seen quickly and easily. The disadvantage is that in order to make comparisons stand out, the data are usually condensed, rounded, or incomplete. Using graphs and tables requires the ability to decide which pieces of information are needed, to determine if they are available on the graph, and then to find the data in the graph or table. This lesson reviews the skills used for understanding graphs and tables.

Graphs

Graphs are used to give data a visual meaning. They are used to compare data from different sources, to show change over a period of time, and to make projections about the future.

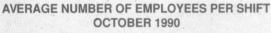

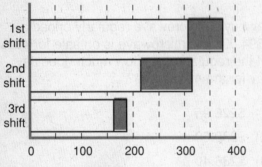

To make a visual impact, the data in graphs are often condensed, rounded, or incomplete. Yet the comparisons should stand out.

Example: The personnel manager at Morton Products wants to emphasize the difference in employment levels for each of the company's three shifts. She makes the **bar graph** at the left.

Notice these parts of the graph:
1. **Title**—labeled clearly to indicate the type of information found on the graph.
2. **Axis lines and scales**—graph has two axis lines.
   * **Horizontal axis** runs across the bottom of the graph. The sample graph shows the average number of employees.
   * **Vertical axis** runs up the side of the graph. The sample graph shows the number of shifts.
   * **Scale** is like a ruler. Each mark represents units. Some graphs have scale lines on only the vertical axis. Other graphs have a scale on both the horizontal and vertical axis.
3. **Key**—gives you any information you need to read the graph. The key is also called the legend.

To read the graph, follow across any of the three bars representing the three shifts from left to right. Examine where the endpoint of the bar falls with relation to the scale on the horizontal axis.

What information can you get from the graph?
♦ The first shift has the most employees.
♦ On the second shift, there are more part-time employees than on any other shift.
♦ The third shift has the smallest crew of full-time employees, with very few part-time employees.

What information is *not* available from the graph?
♦ The exact number of employees on any shift
♦ How these employment figures compare with a previous month
♦ The comparison between office, manufacturing, and shipping department employees

The bars in the graph below are vertical. By looking at the title and the horizontal axis at the bottom, we see that each bar represents sales from a different month from January through June. The sales amount for any month can be found from the numbers on the vertical scale at the left.

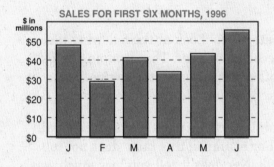

Notice the labels "$ in millions." This means that $10 on the vertical axis means $10 million. The scale runs from $0 to $50 million.

A graph can be misleading when the scale does not begin at zero.

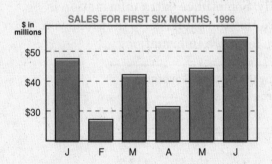

Compare the graph at the right with the one above. Which sales amounts seem the most impressive? Look carefully at the scale. It begins at $30 and ends at $50. The information is exactly the same as in the graph above.

Circle graphs show percentages. The whole circle is 100%.

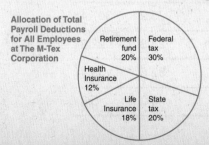

The various percentages are shown in pie-shaped pieces. A half-circle is 50%. A quarter-circle is 25%. This graph shows how deductions from paychecks are used.

Most **line graphs** are made up of connected points. A point connects a horizontal value and a vertical value. The circled point below connects "10 A.M." with "55 degrees." The line converts the points into a "picture" of the data easier to analyze. It lets you easily see that the highest temperature occurred at 4 P.M. You can also see that the temperature changed the least during the two hours between 6 A.M. and 8 A.M.

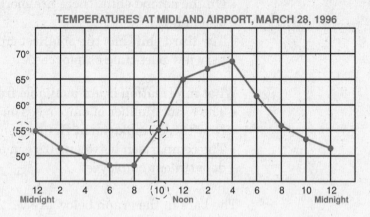

TEMPERATURES AT MIDLAND AIRPORT, MARCH 28, 1996

Tables and Charts

Another way to organize information is in a **table** or **chart.** Unlike a graph, tables show numbers instead of bar lines, pie-shaped pieces, or lines connecting points.

Tables group data into similar categories. Look at the following table. The table groups the amounts received by year. This grouping helps you to compare one year to the other for the same tax source (see A) or the amounts received from different sources in the same year (see B).

Remember, like graphs, tables and charts do not always give you all the information you may need. For example, this table does not tell you the amounts received in 1993. Nor does it tell you how much was received from Estate Taxes alone. You must remember to interpret data presented in tables carefully. Sometimes extra information is given in footnotes to the table. Notice the asterisk (*) that tells you to look at the bottom of the table for more information.

Money Received by the Federal Government from Taxes		
Tax Sources	1994	1995
Income Taxes		
Corporations	104.8*	117.2
Individuals	364.0	392.8
Social Security Taxes	(A) 273.2	307.4
Unemployment Taxes	23.8	(B) 22.2
Excise Taxes	32.6	33.4
Estate and Gift Taxes	6.0	5.8

*Billions of dollars

Information can be organized into lists or tables to help solve problems. Organizing information this way helps you find the data you need quickly.

Example: Gordon and Sue are looking for a new apartment. At the Alpenrose apartment complex, three of the available apartments face east and four face south. Five of the apartments at the Briarwood complex face north and two face west. Six apartments face east at the Cornish Arms Apartments, two face north, and four face south. Gordon and Sue prefer an apartment that faces east or south. How many choices do they have?

(1) 12

(2) 15

(3) 17

(4) 20

(5) Not enough information is given.

One way to solve this problem is to make a table. Using the table, it is easy to see that 8 apartments face south and 9 face east. Total facing south or east: $8 + 9 = 17$. The correct answer is option **(3) 17.**

	N	S	E	W
Alpenrose		4	3	
Briarwood	5			2
Cornish Arms	2	4	6	

Example: Joleen works in a clothing store. She is preparing a window display featuring summer sportswear. Tank tops come in three colors: red, black, and green. Shorts also come in three colors: tan, white, and yellow. How many possible combinations are there of tops and shorts?

To solve the problem, make a table of all the possible combinations. Start with one color top and pair it with each color of shorts before considering the next top. The possible combinations are:

Tops \ Shorts	Tan	White	Yellow
Red	R-T	R-W	R-Y
Black	B-T	B-W	B-Y
Green	G-T	G-W	G-Y

She can make **nine** possible combinations.

Directions: Choose the <u>best answer</u> to each item.

<u>Items 1 to 3</u> refer to the bar graph below.

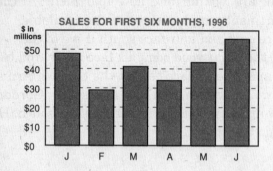

SALES FOR FIRST SIX MONTHS, 1996

1. In which two months were sales the lowest?

    (1) January and April
    (2) February and March
    (3) February and April
    (4) February and May
    (5) March and May

2. Estimate the total sales for January.

    (1) between $30 and $35 million
    (2) between $35 and $40 million
    (3) between $40 and $45 million
    (4) between $45 and $50 million
    (5) between $50 and $60 million

3. The average monthly sales for the time period shown on the graph is $40 million. Which month's sales were closest to the average?

    (1) February
    (2) March
    (3) April
    (4) May
    (5) June

<u>Items 4 to 6</u> refer to the following information.

Hiking Trail Distances			
	Crow's Point	Morning Peak	Rock Face
Eagle's Nest	3.8 mi	5.6 mi	2.1 mi
Rock Face	7.2 mi	3.3 mi	—
Morning Peak	3.4 mi	—	3.3 mi

4. The Weekend Hiking Club hiked from Eagle's Nest to Morning Peak and on to Rock Face. After lunch they hiked back the same trail. How many miles did they cover?

    (1) 7.8
    (2) 8.9
    (3) 15.6
    (4) 16.8
    (5) 17.8

5. In comparing the lengths of the shortest and longest trails, it is correct to say the longest is

    (1) about $3\frac{1}{2}$ times as long as the shortest.
    (2) $\frac{1}{3}$ the length of the shortest.
    (3) about twice the length of the shortest.
    (4) more than 4 times the length of the shortest.
    (5) less than twice as long as the shortest.

6. Charles hiked from Rock Face to Crow's Point and then to Eagle's Nest. How long did this hike take?

    (1) about 3 hr
    (2) about 4 hr
    (3) about 5 hr
    (4) about 6 hr
    (5) Not enough information is given

Items 7 to 10 refer to the circle graph below.

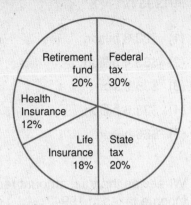

Average Deductions from Paychecks for The M-Tex Corporation

7. Which deduction takes the highest percent of the total paycheck deductions?

  (1) Federal tax
  (2) State tax
  (3) Life insurance
  (4) Health insurance
  (5) Retirement fund

8. What is the total percent of deductions allocated to health and life insurance?

  (1) 18%
  (2) 20%
  (3) 28%
  (4) 30%
  (5) 50%

9. If an employee's deductions for a pay period totaled $500, what amount on average would go to state and federal taxes?

  (1) $ 50
  (2) $100
  (3) $175
  (4) $225
  (5) $250

10. What percent of an employee's earnings is deducted for life insurance?

  (1) 30%
  (2) 20%
  (3) 18%
  (4) 12%
  (5) Not enough information is given.

Items 11 to 15 refer to the line graph below.

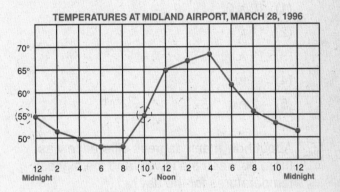

TEMPERATURES AT MIDLAND AIRPORT, MARCH 28, 1996

11. At what time was the highest temperature recorded for the day?

  (1) 12 noon
  (2) 1 P.M.
  (3) 2 P.M.
  (4) 3 P.M.
  (5) 4 P.M.

12. In which 2-hour time period did the temperature rise the most?

  (1) 8 A.M. to 10 A.M.
  (2) 10 A.M. to 12 noon
  (3) 12 noon to 2 P.M.
  (4) 2 P.M. to 4 P.M.
  (5) 4 P.M. to 6 P.M.

13. About how many degrees did the temperature fall between 4 P.M. and 6 P.M.?

    (1) 2
    (2) 4
    (3) 6
    (4) 10
    (5) 12

14. At approximately what time did the temperature first reach 60°?

    (1) 10 A.M.
    (2) 11 A.M.
    (3) 12 A.M.
    (4) 1 P.M.
    (5) 2 P.M.

15. About how many degrees difference was there between the lowest and the highest temperatures for the day?

    (1) between 10° and 14°
    (2) between 15° and 19°
    (3) between 20° and 24°
    (4) between 25° and 29°
    (5) between 30° and 34°

Items 16 to 19 refer to the table below.

Money Received by the Federal Government from Taxes		
Tax Sources	1994	1995
Income Taxes		
Corporations	104.8*	117.2
Individuals	364.0	392.8
Social Security Taxes	273.2	307.4
Unemployment Taxes	23.8	22.2
Excise Taxes	32.6	33.4
Estate and Gift Taxes	6.0	5.8

*Billions of dollars

16. What amount was received in excise taxes in 1995?

    (1) $32.6 billion
    (2) $33.4 billion
    (3) $36 billion
    (4) $38.6 billion
    (5) $66 billion

17. What was the total amount received from income taxes in 1994?

    (1) $222 billion
    (2) $468.8 billion
    (3) $510 billion
    (4) $756.8 billion
    (5) Not enough information is given.

18. To the nearest whole percent, what was the percent of increase in social security taxes from 1994 to 1995?

    (1) 10%
    (2) 12%
    (3) 13%
    (4) 15%
    (5) 18%

19. How much more was received from unemployment taxes in 1994 than in 1995?

    (1) $ 1,600,000
    (2) $ 16,000,000
    (3) $ 160,000,000
    (4) $ 1,600,000,000
    (5) $16,000,000,000

Directions: Make a table. Choose the best answer to each item.

Items 20 to 25 refer to the following information.

Sheila and Paul Jackson are looking for an apartment.

♦ One apartment on Mulberry Lane rents for $565 a month. There is also a $30 monthly parking fee, a $580 deposit, and $60 lease fee.

♦ The second apartment on Parke Boulevard rents for $485 a month, but they have to pay a $970 deposit and $50 for a key to the laundry room. There is no lease fee.

♦ A third apartment on Meridan Street rents for $525 per month. They would have to pay a $1,000 deposit and a $50 lease fee. There is also a $25 parking fee per month.

♦ A fourth apartment at 680 W. Tenth Avenue is only $495 per month, but they have to pay two months' rent as a deposit. They also have to pay a lease fee of 10% of one month's rent.

♦ The Jacksons would have to buy rugs for either the Mulberry Lane or Parke Boulevard apartment. They would need to buy drapes for either the Mulberry Lane or Meridan Street apartment. The Jacksons estimate that rugs would cost $450 and drapes would cost $250.

20. How much rent would the Jacksons pay per year if they rent the Parke Boulevard apartment?

   (1) $4,950
   (2) $5,280
   (3) $5,550
   (4) $5,820
   (5) $6,300

21. Which apartment does not require a lease fee?

   (1) Mulberry Lane
   (2) Parke Boulevard
   (3) Meridan Street
   (4) Tenth Avenue
   (5) Not enough information is given.

22. Which apartment requires the highest deposit?

   (1) Mulberry Lane
   (2) Parke Boulevard
   (3) Meridan Street
   (4) Tenth Avenue
   (5) Not enough information is given.

23. Including the first month's rent, any deposits and fees, and costs for rugs and/or drapes, what is the total move-in cost for the Mulberry Lane apartment?

   (1) $1,695
   (2) $1,935
   (3) $2,015
   (4) $2,265
   (5) $2,400

24. Not counting the cost of rugs or drapes, how much more is the move-in cost for the Tenth Avenue apartment than the Parke Boulevard apartment?

   (1) $6.00
   (2) $29.50
   (3) $30.00
   (4) $34.50
   (5) $62.10

25. Which apartment would be least expensive to move into?

   (1) Mulberry Lane
   (2) Parke Boulevard
   (3) Meridan Street
   (4) Tenth Avenue
   (5) Not enough information is given.

Answers are on page 866.

Directions: Choose the best answer to each item.

Items 1 to 6 refer to the following graph.

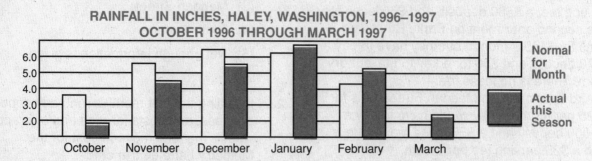

RAINFALL IN INCHES, HALEY, WASHINGTON, 1996–1997
OCTOBER 1996 THROUGH MARCH 1997

1. For which months was the rainfall less than normal?

   (1) October, November, and December
   (2) October, November, and January
   (3) October, December, and March
   (4) October, February, and March
   (5) January, February, and March

2. For how many months was the actual rainfall over 5.0 inches?

   (1) 2
   (2) 3
   (3) 4
   (4) 5
   (5) 6

3. For how many months was the actual rainfall less than 4.0 inches?

   (1) 2
   (2) 3
   (3) 4
   (4) 5
   (5) 6

4. About how many more inches of rain actually fell in January than in March?

   (1) 2.6
   (2) 3.5
   (3) 4.0
   (4) 4.4
   (5) 5.8

5. What is the approximate average normal rainfall for November, December, and January?

   (1) 4.5
   (2) 5.0
   (3) 5.5
   (4) 6.0
   (5) 6.5

6. About how many fewer inches of rain actually fell in October than in November?

   (1) 1.5
   (2) 1.7
   (3) 2.7
   (4) 3.7
   (5) 4.1

Items 7 to 10 refer to the following graph.

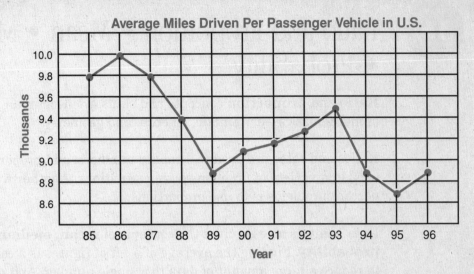

Average Miles Driven Per Passenger Vehicle in U.S.

7. What is the range of miles driven, from the lowest to the highest?

   (1) from 8,400 to 10,200
   (2) from 8,700 to 9,800
   (3) from 8,700 to 10,000
   (4) from 8,800 to 10,000
   (5) from 9,800 to 10,000

8. A turn-around is a point on the graph where the direction changes. How many turn-arounds are shown on this graph?

   (1) two
   (2) three
   (3) four
   (4) five
   (5) six

9. Which year did *not* show a decline in miles driven per vehicle?

   (1) 1986 to 1987
   (2) 1987 to 1988
   (3) 1993 to 1994
   (4) 1994 to 1995
   (5) 1995 to 1996

10. What was the percent of increase (to the nearest whole percent) in miles driven from 1989 to 1993?

   (1) 4%
   (2) 5%
   (3) 6%
   (4) 7%
   (5) 8%

Item 11 refers to the following graph.

Persons Employed in U.S. in Wholesale, Retail and Service Occupations, 1996

Business, Legal, Prof. 22%
Other 3%
Entertainment 1%
Wholesale 20%
Health and Education 12%
Retail 42%

11. Which group has about $\frac{1}{2}$ of the total amount of workers as Retail occupations?

   (1) Entertainment occupations
   (2) Health and Education occupations
   (3) Other
   (4) Business, Legal, and Professional occupations
   (5) Not enough information is given.

Answers are on page 867.

Graphs and Tables ◆ Review

Ratio and Proportion

Lesson 16

Ratio and Proportion • Mean • Median • Probability

Ratio and **proportion** concepts and skills are used in all three areas of mathematics—arithmetic, algebra, and geometry.

Ratios and rates are used to compare numbers, and proportions are used in a variety of problem-solving situations. Another way to solve percent problems is to use proportions.

Data analysis also involves the concepts of **mean, median,** and **probability.** Finding the average of a set of figures is a common way to reduce a large amount of data to a single number. And probability is used constantly in daily life. Every decision you make, whether to cross a busy street, to go on a hike, or to buy one product instead of another, involves evaluating the likelihood (probability) that some event will occur. Will I get across the street without getting hit? Will it rain? Will this product last longer than the other one?

Lesson 16 reviews your understanding of ratio, proportion, mean, median, and probability, as well as your ability to apply these concepts to solving problems.

Ratio and Proportion

A **ratio** is a comparison of two numbers. When two ratios are written as equal ratios, the equation is called a **proportion.**

Example: In a mixture of 4 quarts of red paint and 2 quarts of blue paint, the ratio of red paint to blue paint is 4 to 2, 4:2, or $\frac{4}{2}$. The fraction $\frac{4}{2}$ equals $\frac{2}{1}$ when reduced to lowest terms, so for every 2 quarts of red paint, there is 1 quart of blue paint. The ratios $\frac{4}{2}$ and $\frac{2}{1}$ are **equal ratios.**

Ratios are often used to express **rates.**

Example: If Paul earns $60 in 8 hours, what is the rate of earnings to hours?

Divide to find the unit rate: $\dfrac{\text{dollars earned}}{\text{hours}} = \dfrac{60}{8} = \dfrac{60 \div 8}{8 \div 8} = \dfrac{7.5}{1}$

When the denominator of a ratio is 1, the ratio is called a **unit rate.** The unit rate $\frac{7.5}{1}$ tells us that Paul earns **$7.50** each (per) hour.

If cross-products are equal, then the ratios are equal. If two ratios are equal, they form a **proportion.**

Examples:

Are $\frac{8}{12}$ and $\frac{12}{18}$ equal ratios?

$$\frac{8}{12} \overset{?}{\times} \frac{12}{18}$$

$$8 \times 18 \overset{?}{=} 12 \times 12$$

$$144 = 144$$

The cross-products are equal, so $\frac{8}{12} = \frac{12}{18}$ are equal ratios. Thus, $\frac{8}{12} = \frac{12}{18}$ is a proportion.

Are $\frac{15}{25}$ and $\frac{7}{10}$ equal ratios?

$$\frac{15}{25} \overset{?}{\times} \frac{7}{10}$$

$$15 \times 10 \overset{?}{=} 25 \times 7$$

$$150 \neq 175$$

The cross-products are not equal, so $\frac{15}{25} = \frac{7}{10}$ are not equal ratios. Thus, $\frac{15}{25} = \frac{7}{10}$ is not a proportion.

In a proportion problem, one of the four values is missing. The proportion can be solved using this rule:

$$\frac{N_1}{D_1} \times \frac{N_2}{D_2}$$
$$N_1 \times D_2 = N_2 \times D_1$$

Cross-product Rule: To find the missing number in a proportion, cross multiply and divide the product by the third number.

Example: Paula can drive her car 350 miles on 14 gallons of gasoline. How many gallons of gasoline will Paula need to drive 875 miles?

Solve this problem by writing a proportion. Use the cross-product rule:

Write a proportion. $\qquad \frac{350 \text{ miles}}{14 \text{ gallons}} \nearrow \frac{875 \text{ miles}}{? \text{ gallons}}$

Cross multiply. $\qquad\qquad\qquad 14 \times 875 = 12{,}250$

Divide by the third number. $\qquad 12{,}250 \div 350 = 35$

Paula will need to buy **35 gallons** of gasoline.

ged Exercise Ratio and Proportion • Mean • Median • Probability

Directions: Write each ratio as a fraction in lowest terms.

1. 16 to 12

2. 15 to 45

3. 6 to 36

4. 25 to 10

5. 24 to 36

6. 12 to 9

7. 18 to 6

8. 35 to 7

9. 80 to 100

Directions: Find each unit rate.

10. 400 miles in 5 hours

11. 5 pounds for 85 cents

12. $225 in 12 hours

13. 112 calories in 28 grams of cheese

14. 512 people for 8 teams

15. 5,400 oranges in 24 bags

16. 1,032 feet in 16 seconds

17. 16 ounces for $2.40

Directions: Solve each proportion problem. (Hint: Cross multiply.)

18. $\frac{2}{3} = \frac{?}{15}$

19. $\frac{14}{?} = \frac{28}{12}$

20. $\frac{?}{20} = \frac{3}{10}$

21. $\frac{?}{18} = \frac{3.5}{9}$

22. $\frac{4.2}{3} = \frac{?}{10}$

23. $\frac{5}{?} = \frac{15}{24}$

24. $\frac{12}{15} = \frac{24}{?}$

25. $\frac{14}{6} = \frac{7}{?}$

26. $\frac{?}{6} = \frac{11.5}{23}$

27. $\frac{7}{?} = \frac{3.5}{16}$

28. $\frac{4.9}{7} = \frac{?}{10}$

29. $\frac{?}{15} = \frac{3.2}{8}$

30. $\frac{3}{?} = \frac{1.8}{6}$

31. $\frac{6}{1.2} = \frac{5}{?}$

32. $\frac{6}{2.1} = \frac{?}{7}$

Directions: Choose the best answer to each item.

33. A recipe that serves 8 people calls for 2 cups of milk. How many cups of milk will be needed for 36 servings?

    (1) 8
    (2) 9
    (3) 10
    (4) 12
    (5) 18

34. A person uses about 315 calories to jog 3 miles. How many calories will be used in a 10-mile jog?

    (1) 945
    (2) 1,005
    (3) 1,050
    (4) 3,150
    (5) 9,450

35. Roger worked 9 hours on Friday and 6 hours on Saturday. What is the ratio of the work done on Friday to the total hours worked on both days?

(1) $\frac{2}{5}$

(2) $\frac{3}{5}$

(3) $\frac{2}{3}$

(4) $\frac{3}{2}$

(5) $\frac{5}{3}$

36. An architect is planning a city parking lot. For every 12 commuters, the parking lot will need 5 parking spaces. How many parking spaces will be needed by 132 commuters?

(1) 7

(2) 12

(3) 17

(4) 55

(5) 60

Answers are on page 867.

Using Proportion to Solve Percent Problems

Percents are ratios: 15% means 15 out of 100. Every percent problem can be set up as a proportion by writing two ratios that are equal.

$$\frac{\text{part}}{\text{base}} = \frac{\text{rate}}{100}$$

To find the missing number in the proportion, cross multiply and divide by the third number.

Example: Find 40% of 2,500.
Set up the proportion: $\frac{?}{2,500} \nearrow \frac{40}{100}$

Cross multiply: $2,500 \times 40 = 100,000$
Divide by 100: $100,000 \div 100 = 1,000$

40% of 2,500 is **1,000.**

Example: 12 is 75% of what number?
Set up the proportion: $\frac{12}{?} \searrow \frac{75}{100}$

Cross multiply: $12 \times 100 = 1,200$
Divide by 75: $1,200 \div 75 = 16$

12 is **75%** of 16.

Example: 16 is what percent of 80?
Set up the proportion: $\frac{16}{80} \searrow \frac{?}{100}$

Cross multiply: $16 \times 100 = 1,600$
Divide by 80: $1,600 \div 80 = 20$

16 is **20%** of 80.

To solve percent of increase or decrease problems, set up the proportion as follows:

$$\frac{\text{difference between the amounts}}{\text{original amount}} = \frac{\text{rate}}{100}$$

Example: Last year Sheila earned $6.40 per hour. This year she earns $7.36 per hour. What is the percent of increase?

Find the difference: $7.36 − $6.40 = $0.96

Set up the proportion: $\dfrac{\$0.96}{\$6.40} = \dfrac{?}{100}$

Cross multiply: $0.96 × 100 = 96.

Divide: $96 ÷ 6.4 = 15$ so $\dfrac{\$0.96}{\$6.40} = \dfrac{15}{100} = .15 = 15\%$.

There was a **15% increase** from last year to this year.

Directions: Choose the best answer to each item.

37. Masoud bought a used car for $1,200. Later he sold the car for $1,800. What was the percent of increase in the price of the car?

    (1) 5%

    (2) 25%

    (3) $33\frac{1}{3}$%

    (4) 50%

    (5) 75%

38. A sweater was originally priced $35. If the sweater is on sale for 20% off, how much would you save by buying it on sale?

    (1) $ 7

    (2) $ 9

    (3) $12

    (4) $14

    (5) $15

39. Sidney's insurance paid 90% of the cost of getting his car fixed. If the repair bill was $625, how much did the insurance pay?

    (1) $437.50

    (2) $468.75

    (3) $500.00

    (4) $562.50

    (5) $605.15

40. On a test, a student got 80% of the items correct. If the student got 56 items correct, how many items were on the test?

    (1) 64

    (2) 70

    (3) 72

    (4) 84

    (5) 90

41. The Bulldogs won 18 games out of 45. What percent of their games did the Bulldogs win?

    (1) 40%

    (2) 45%

    (3) 50%

    (4) 55%

    (5) 60%

42. A telephone was originally priced $112.80. Now it is on sale for $84.60. What is the percent of decrease from the original price?

    (1) 15%

    (2) 18%

    (3) 25%

    (4) 28%

    (5) $33\frac{1}{3}$%

Answers are on page 868.

Mathematics ◆ Ratio and Proportion

Proportion is also used for **indirect measurement** problems. Indirect measurement is shown on a **scale drawing,** for example, a map or a floor plan. All measurements in the sketch are in proportion to the corresponding actual measurements. The **scale** gives the relationship between two sets of measurements: the ratio of the sketch measurements to the corresponding actual measurements. On the map below, the scale shows that 1 centimeter on the map represents 5 kilometers on the actual land represented by the map.

Example: The distance on the map between Taylorville and Davis is 4.5 cm. What is the actual distance between the two towns?

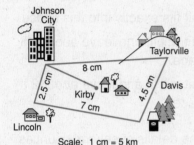

Use the scale to write a proportion using the ratio of map distance to actual distance.

$$\frac{\text{scale (map) distance}}{\text{scale (actual) distance}} = \frac{\text{map distance}}{\text{actual distance}}$$

$$\frac{1 \text{ cm}}{5 \text{ km}} = \frac{4.5 \text{ cm}}{? \text{ km}}$$

Cross multiply. $5 \times 4.5 = 22.5$

Divide by the third number. $22.5 \times 1 = 22.5$

The actual distance is **22.5 kilometers.**

Example: In the floor plan of the Martin's cabin, the living room measures 2 inches by $4\frac{1}{2}$ inches. Every 2 inches of the floor plan represents 9 actual feet. How many square feet of carpet are needed to cover the living room floor?

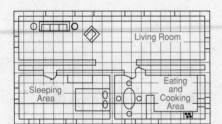

First, use proportions to find the dimensions of the living room.

$$\frac{2}{9} = \frac{2}{\text{width}} \qquad\qquad \frac{2}{9} = \frac{4.5}{\text{length}}$$

Cross multiply. $9 \times 2 = 18 \qquad 9 \times 4.5 = 40.5$

Divide by the third number. $18 \div 2 = 9 \qquad 40.5 \div 2 = 20.25$

The dimensions are 9 ft by 20.25 ft. (Note: The words *width* and *length* represent the missing amount, the unknown. You are applying algebra and geometry in this proportion problem.)

To find the area, multiply the length by the width:

$$9 \times 20.25 = 182.25$$

The living room floor will need **$182\frac{1}{4}$ square feet** of carpet.

Directions: Circle the <u>best answer</u> to each question.

<u>Items 43 and 44</u> refer to the following drawing.

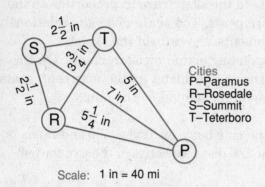

Cities
P–Paramus
R–Rosedale
S–Summit
T–Teterboro

Scale: 1 in = 40 mi

43. The distance on the map between Rosedale and Teterboro is $3\frac{3}{4}$ inches. What is the actual distance in miles between the two cities?

(1) 120 mi

(2) 150 mi

(3) 160 mi

(4) 180 mi

(5) 200 mi

44. Chloe drove from Paramus to Summit, then from Summit to Teterboro, and back to Paramus. How many miles did she drive?

(1) 460 mi

(2) 480 mi

(3) 540 mi

(4) 580 mi

(5) 620 mi

45. The floor plan of a family room is drawn to a scale of 1 inch = 8 feet. It shows that the short wall of this room is $1\frac{3}{4}$ inches long. The owner wants to place an entertainment unit that is 14 feet long on this short wall. Will the unit fit?

(1) No, the unit is about 2 ft too long.

(2) No, the unit is about 1 ft too long.

(3) Yes, the unit fits exactly into this space.

(4) Yes, the unit will fit and leave about 1 ft of extra space.

(5) Yes, the unit will fit and leave about 2 ft of extra space.

46. A map shows the details of several counties. The scale is 1 inch = 1.8 miles. If the distance from one town to the city center is 3.5 inches on the map, how far is the actual distance?

(1) 0.5 mi

(2) 1.9 mi

(3) 3.5 mi

(4) 6.3 mi

(5) 35 mi

Answers are on page 868.

Mean and Median

A list of numbers is sometimes called **data.** The average, or **mean,** is the sum of the data divided by the number of items on the list. When the data are arranged in order, the middle number is called the **median.**

Follow these steps to find an average:

Step 1: Add the data you need to average.

Step 2: Divide by the number of data items.

Example: For five days Paula recorded the time it took to drive to work. Her data are shown on the chart. What is her average driving time?

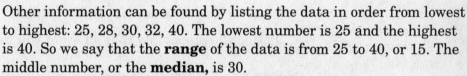

Day 1	28 minutes
Day 2	40 minutes
Day 3	30 minutes
Day 4	25 minutes
Day 5	32 minutes

Add the five values:

28 + 40 + 30 + 25 + 32 = 155

Divide by 5 the number of data items:

$$\frac{31}{5\overline{)155}}$$

Paula's average, or mean, driving time is
31 minutes.

Other information can be found by listing the data in order from lowest to highest: 25, 28, 30, 32, 40. The lowest number is 25 and the highest is 40. So we say that the **range** of the data is from 25 to 40, or 15. The middle number, or the **median,** is 30.

Paula's median driving time is **30 minutes.**

If there is an even number of data items, the median is the average of the two middle numbers.

Example: George bowled four games and had scores of 128, 157, 155, and 160. He computed his average correctly at 150. What is his median score?

List the scores from lowest to highest: 128, 155, 157, 160. Because there is an even number of scores, average the two middle numbers to find the median score.

155 + 157 = 312
312 ÷ 2 = 156

George's median score is **156.**

Directions: Find the range, mean, and median for the following data sets.

47. Test scores: 85, 100, 65, 100, 94, 80, 85

48. Weekly pay: $215.35, $219.82, $245.82, $227.83, $199.48

49. Average temperatures: 61.5°F, 64.8°F, 69.0°F, 67.3°F, 65.6°F, 60.8°F, 61.1°F

50. Grams of vitamin C in a group of cereal samples: 0.06, 0.04, 0.055, 0.052, 0.048

---

51. Attendance figures: 135, 174, 128, 215

52. Number of video tapes rented each day for a week: 27, 24, 12, 35, 120, 150, 87

53. Running times for 5 days: 41 minutes, 65 minutes, 67 minutes, 52 minutes, 35 minutes

Probability

Answers are on page 868.

Probability tells how likely it is that an event will happen. In a probability situation, there are always two numbers to consider:

1. The total number of possible results.
2. The number of favorable results.

To find the probability that an event will happen, follow these steps:

Step 1: Write this ratio: $P = \dfrac{\text{number of favorable results}}{\text{total number of possible results}}$

Step 2: Reduce the ratio to lowest terms.

Example: If you buy 4 tickets in a drawing and 1,000 total tickets are sold, what is the probability that you will win?

$$P = \frac{\text{number of favorable results}}{\text{total number of possible results}} = \frac{4}{1,000} = \frac{1}{250} = 0.004$$

Thus, probability can be expressed three ways:

- as a ratio—1 out of 250
- as a fraction—$\frac{1}{250}$
- as a decimal—0.004

Items 54 and 55 refer to the following dart board.

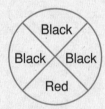

54. What is the probability of hitting red?

   (1) 0.1

   (2) 0.2

   (3) 0.25

   (4) 0.4

   (5) Not enough information is given.

55. What is the probability of hitting black?

   (1) $\dfrac{1}{4}$

   (2) $\dfrac{1}{3}$

   (3) $\dfrac{1}{2}$

   (4) $\dfrac{2}{3}$

   (5) $\dfrac{3}{4}$

Items 56 to 59 refer to the following information.

An appliance store has identical boxes containing electric mixers on a stockroom shelf. There are 5 of Model A, 8 of Model B, 10 of Model C, and 2 of Model D. A stock person takes one box from the shelf to fill an order.

56. What is the probability that the box chosen contains the Model A mixer?

(1) $\frac{1}{10}$

(2) $\frac{1}{5}$

(3) $\frac{2}{5}$

(4) $\frac{1}{2}$

(5) $\frac{3}{4}$

57. Which model has a probability of 0.08 of being chosen?

(1) Model A

(2) Model B

(3) Model C

(4) Model D

58. Which model has the greatest probability of being chosen?

(1) Model A

(2) Model B

(3) Model C

(4) Model D

59. What is the probability that the box chosen contains the Model C mixer?

(1) 0.04

(2) 0.2

(3) 0.25

(4) 0.35

(5) 0.4

Items 60 through 62 refer to the following table.

Melendez Family Utilities	
Period	Amount
Jan – Feb	$89.36
Mar – Apr	$90.12
May – Jun	$74.47
Jul – Aug	$63.15
Sep – Oct	$59.76
Nov – Dec	$84.31

60. What was the total amount spent on utilities for the first six months of the year?

(1) $179.48

(2) $193.53

(3) $224.08

(4) $253.95

(5) $461.17

61. What is the median of the amounts on the table?

(1) $84.31

(2) $79.39

(3) $74.47

(4) $63.15

(5) Not enough information is given.

62. What is the average amount spent on utilities for a 2-month period?

(1) $76.86

(2) $79.28

(3) $79.39

(4) $230.58

(5) Not enough information is given.

Items 63 and 64 refer to the following information.

Gross Earnings for Manuel Botta 1986 through 1990				
1986	1987	1988	1989	1990
$16,907	$17,756	$19,174	$19,558	$20,730

63. Find the mean gross earnings for the five-year period.

(1) $17,824

(2) $18,205

(3) $18,750

(4) $18,825

(5) $19,174

64. Manuel Botta's earnings for 1985 were $17,204. Find the median gross earnings for the six-year period from 1985 to 1990.

(1) $16,907

(2) $17,756

(3) $18,465

(4) $18,825

(5) $19,174

65. The manager of the Ear-Ring Boutique recorded the number of sales during the week: Monday: 21; Tuesday: 42; Wednesday: 34; Thursday: 45; Friday: 51; Saturday: 47. What was the average number of sales per day for the week?

(1) 39

(2) 40

(3) 41

(4) 43

(5) 45

66. Attendance for the first three days of a 15-day fair was 19,600. If attendance continues at this rate, what will be the total attendance for the fair?

(1) 78,400

(2) 98,000

(3) between 100,000 and 200,000

(4) more than 200,000

(5) Not enough information is given.

67. There are 50 marbles in a jar. They are all alike except for their color. There are 12 red marbles, 28 blue ones, and 10 green ones. If they are mixed thoroughly and one is drawn at random, what is the probability that it is red?

(1) 0.02

(2) 0.08

(3) 0.2

(4) 0.24

(5) 0.32

68. Last year the Hawks soccer team won 2 out of every 3 games it played. By the end of the season it had lost only 6 games. How many games were won?

(1) 4

(2) 9

(3) 12

(4) 16

(5) 18

69. Luke buys 4 raffle tickets at the County Fair. If a total of 200 raffle tickets are sold, what is the probability that one of Luke's tickets will win?

(1) $\frac{1}{20}$

(2) $\frac{1}{25}$

(3) $\frac{1}{50}$

(4) $\frac{1}{100}$

(5) $\frac{1}{200}$

Answers are on page 869.

Directions: Choose the best answer to each item.

1. Juanita used 2 quarts of blue paint, 3 quarts of green, and 5 quarts of white to make a paint mixture for her home. If it takes 25 quarts of paint to cover her home, how many quarts of green paint must Juanita use?

   (1) 5
   (2) 7
   (3) 7.5
   (4) 10
   (5) 15

2. A baseball team has won 16 games and lost only 4 games. If the team plays 30 games, how many more games must they win to keep the same winning ratio?

   (1) 2
   (2) 4
   (3) 6
   (4) 8
   (5) 10

3. Gail, a hairdresser, kept a record of her sales for 5 days: Monday, $120; Tuesday, $120; Wednesday, $170; Thursday, $140; Friday, $160. She reported that her average sales were $142. Which of the following is true?

   (1) Only the median is $142.
   (2) Only the mean is $142.
   (3) Neither the median nor mean is $142.
   (4) Both the median and mean are $142.
   (5) More information is needed.

Items 4 and 5 refer to the following information.

A used car lot has 12 cars in 5 different colors:					
Blue	Black	Red	Red	Yellow	Green
Black	Blue	Yellow	Green	Red	Red

4. One car is picked at random. What is the probability that the car is red?

   (1) $\frac{1}{3}$
   (2) $\frac{1}{4}$
   (3) $\frac{1}{5}$
   (4) $\frac{1}{6}$
   (5) $\frac{1}{12}$

5. Three more yellow cars are brought to the lot. One car is picked at random. What is the probability that the car is yellow?

   (1) $\frac{1}{2}$
   (2) $\frac{1}{3}$
   (3) $\frac{1}{4}$
   (4) $\frac{1}{5}$
   (5) $\frac{1}{6}$

6. Nancy received 150 votes for union president. Stanley received 56 votes and Marc received 34. What is the ratio of Nancy's votes to the total number of votes?

   (1) $\frac{3}{5}$
   (2) $\frac{5}{8}$
   (3) $1\frac{3}{5}$
   (4) $1\frac{5}{8}$
   (5) $1\frac{2}{3}$

7. In Northville, 2 out of 5 adults have part-time jobs. If the city of Northville has an adult population of 4,500, how many adults work part-time?

   (1)   900
   (2) 1,250
   (3) 1,800
   (4) 2,250
   (5) 4,500

8. Mario runs each morning before going to work. His recorded times for 7 days are 45 minutes, 35 minutes, 30 minutes, 42 minutes, and 55 minutes on the other 3 days. What is the mean (average) of his running times?

   (1) about 30 minutes
   (2) between 30 minutes and 42 minutes
   (3) between 42 minutes and 46 minutes
   (4) between 46 minutes and 50 minutes
   (5) more than 50 minutes

___

Items 9 to 11 refer to the following information.

Gem City Volleyball League

	Games Won	Games Lost	Total Games Played
Team A	3	11	14
Team B	5	9	14
Team C	12	2	14

9. What is the ratio of Team A wins to Team C wins?

   (1) $\frac{3}{11}$
   (2) $\frac{1}{4}$
   (3) $\frac{5}{12}$
   (4) $\frac{11}{14}$
   (5) $\frac{11}{15}$

10. Which team has the highest ratio of games won to games played?

   (1) Team A with $\frac{3}{11}$
   (2) Team A with $\frac{3}{14}$
   (3) Team B with $\frac{5}{14}$
   (4) Team C with $\frac{12}{2}$
   (5) Team C with $\frac{12}{14}$

11. Team B will play a total of 42 games this season. How many of these must they win to keep the same ratio of games won to games played as they now have?

   (1)   8
   (2)   9
   (3) 12
   (4) 15
   (5) 35

___

12. A vocational school admits 4 out of every 10 people who apply for admission. One year, 640 students were admitted. How many people applied for admission?

   (1)   256
   (2)   1,600
   (3)   2,560
   (4)   6,400
   (5) 12,800

13. A computer printer prints 1,000 characters every 3 seconds. If there are approximately 3,300 characters on a page, how many seconds will it take to print 5 pages?

   (1)   4.95
   (2)   9.9
   (3)   30
   (4)   49.5
   (5) 495

Items 14 to 16 refer to the following information.

A number cube has 6 sides, labeled with the numbers 1 to 6.

14. What is the probability that you will roll an even number?

(1) $\frac{5}{6}$

(2) $\frac{4}{5}$

(3) $\frac{3}{4}$

(4) $\frac{1}{2}$

(5) $\frac{1}{3}$

15. What is the probability that you will roll a number less than 5?

(1) $\frac{1}{3}$

(2) $\frac{2}{3}$

(3) $\frac{1}{2}$

(4) $\frac{4}{5}$

(5) $\frac{5}{6}$

16. What is the probability that you will roll a 4 or a 5?

(1) $\frac{1}{5}$

(2) $\frac{1}{4}$

(3) $\frac{1}{3}$

(4) $\frac{2}{3}$

(5) $\frac{5}{6}$

17. Alicia drove 220 miles in 4 hours. How far can she drive in 7 hours at the same speed?

(1)   227 mi

(2)   385 mi

(3)   660 mi

(4)   880 mi

(5) 1,080 mi

18. Jamal earned the following amounts in the last 3 years:
$21,200 $24,500 $25,100
What is the mean (average) amount he earned?

(1) $21,000

(2) $22,000

(3) $23,600

(4) $24,500

(5) $25,000

19. The scale on a map is $\frac{1}{2}$ inch = 15 miles. What is the distance between two towns that are 3 inches apart on the map?

(1)   30 mi

(2)   45 mi

(3)   60 mi

(4)   90 mi

(5)   180 mi

20. Alison earned $35 in tips in 7 hours of work at the diner. How much can she expect to earn in 10 hours if she continues to earn at the same rate?

(1) $17

(2) $42

(3) $45

(4) $50

(5) $52

21. Fred spends $15 out of every $20 he earns, and he saves the rest. His weekly take-home pay is $560. How much money does he save each week?

(1) $ 5

(2) $ 28

(3) $112

(4) $140

(5) $160

Answers are on page 870.

Measurement

Measurement is the process of determining the size or dimensions of objects by comparing them to a standard. **Standards** are systems of **interchangeable units** used by everyone.

The qualities of an object that are most commonly measured are **weight, length,** and **width.** These dimensions may then be used to determine the **perimeter, circumference, area,** and **volume** of the object. Time is a nonphysical quality that is also measured by a standard set of interchangeable units.

You will need to understand the two common measurement systems—the **standard system** and the **metric system**—to solve problems about length and weight. In Lesson 17 you will review these two measurement systems. Since both systems are commonly encountered, you must be familiar with the units of both. You must also be able to convert units into other units and be able to apply the four basic operations to these units.

Lesson 18 reviews the **formulas** that are used to find perimeter, circumference, and area of each major shape: squares, rectangles, triangles, and circles. Correct application and manipulation of these formulas is heavily tested on the GED examination. The formulas are provided on the formulas page of the exam, so you do not need to memorize them. However, you must understand and know how to use them. (Note: Computing volume is reviewed in Lesson 23.)

Lesson 17   Measurement Systems

The Standard System

You are probably most familiar with the standard system. This is the system that is used in the United States. The basic units of measure used in this system are shown in the chart below. You should learn the values on this chart.

Standard Measurement System		
Length	**Volume**	**Time**
1 foot (ft) = 12 inches (in)	1 cup (c) = 8 fluid ounces (fl oz)	1 minute (min) = 60 seconds (sec)
1 yard (yd) = 3 ft	1 pint (pt) = 2 c	1 hour (hr) = 60 min
	1 quart (qt) = 2 pt	1 day = 24 hr
Weight	1 gallon (gal) = 4 qt	1 week = 7 days
1 pound (lb) = 16 ounces (oz)		1 year = 12 months
1 ton = 2,000 lb		or 365 days

When solving problems you must always keep in mind what units are being used. Converting measurements involves using ratios correctly to change from one unit to another.

Example: How many seconds are there in one year?

This is a problem that takes several steps to solve. You must know the number of days in a year (365), the number of hours in a day (24), the number of minutes in an hour (60) and the number of seconds in a minute (60).

Most of this information can be written as ratios or rates to solve the problem.

$$\frac{365 \text{ days}}{1 \text{ year}} \quad \frac{24 \text{ hours}}{1 \text{ day}} \quad \frac{60 \text{ minutes}}{1 \text{ hour}} \quad \frac{60 \text{ seconds}}{1 \text{ minute}}$$

In all these ratios, the numerator equals the denominator, so the ratios are all equal to 1. Multiplying by 1 does not change the value of an expression.

$$1 \text{ year} \times \frac{365 \text{ days}}{1 \text{ year}} \times \frac{24 \text{ hours}}{1 \text{ day}} \times \frac{60 \text{ minutes}}{1 \text{ hour}} \times \frac{60 \text{ seconds}}{1 \text{ minute}} = \frac{?}{} \text{ seconds}$$

We need to calculate $365 \times 24 \times 60 \times 60$ to find the correct number of seconds. We have changed the quantity 1 year into the equivalent quantity 31,536,000 seconds. Notice the technique here: We built a chain of numerators and denominators so that all units would divide out except seconds, which is what we were looking for.

Example: How many inches are in 4 feet? [larger (feet) to smaller (inches)]

There are 12 inches in 1 foot. Make a conversion ratio and multiply: $4 \text{ feet} \times \frac{12 \text{ inches}}{1 \text{ foot}} = 48 \text{ inches}$

There are **48 inches** in 4 feet.

Example: Roger threw a rock 48 feet. How many yards was that?

There are 3 ft in 1 yard. You are converting smaller (feet) to larger (yards) so your conversion ratio is $\frac{1 \text{ yard}}{3 \text{ feet}}$.

$$\overset{16}{48} \text{ feet} \times \frac{1 \text{ yard}}{3 \text{ feet}} = 16 \text{ yards}$$

Notice that when you are converting from a larger unit to a smaller unit (feet to inches), the smaller unit is on the top of the conversion ratio.

When converting from a smaller unit to a larger unit, the larger unit is on the top of the ratio. Just remember to set up your ratio so the units cancel leaving the unit you want on top.

Not all conversions come out even. Often you will have a remainder. The remainder can be written as a whole number and labeled with a smaller unit name, or it can be written as a fraction and labeled with the larger unit name.

Example: Convert 56 ounces to pounds.

There are 16 ounces in 1 pound. You want to convert smaller units (ounces) to larger units (pounds) so the pounds go on top of the conversion ratio: $\frac{1 \text{ pound}}{16 \text{ ounces}}$.

Multiply: $56 \text{ ounces} \times \frac{1 \text{ pound}}{16 \text{ ounces}}$;

$$16 \overline{)\,56} \quad \begin{array}{r} 3 \\ \underline{48} \\ r = 8 \end{array}$$

The remainder can be written as a whole number, 8 ounces, or as a fraction:

$$\overset{1}{8} \text{ ounces} \times \frac{1 \text{ pound}}{\underset{2}{16} \text{ ounces}} = \frac{1}{2} \text{ pound}$$

The answer is **3 lb 8 oz, or $3\frac{1}{2}$ lb.**

Operations with Measurements

You can add and subtract measurements. But **all** measurements **must** be in the **same** units. You cannot add feet and inches (unlike units). You must first convert one measurement into the other. Then you can perform the operation.

Remember that smaller units are fractions of the larger unit (1 inch = $\frac{1}{12}$ of a foot). Often you will have an improper fraction in your answer that you will need to reduce:

$$15 \text{ inches} = \frac{15}{12} \text{ foot} = 1\frac{3}{12} \text{ foot} = 1 \text{ foot } 3 \text{ inches}$$

Example: John's son weighed 11 pounds 11 ounces at 2 months of age. At 4 months he weighed 14 pounds 8 ounces How much weight has he gained?

Subtract:
$$\begin{array}{r} \overset{13}{14} \text{ lb } \overset{24}{8} \text{ oz} \\ -\ 11 \text{ lb } 11 \text{ oz} \\ \hline 2 \text{ lb } 13 \text{ oz} \end{array}$$

Borrow 1 lb from the 14 lbs and convert it to 16 oz. Add 16 oz to 8 oz, and then subtract.

John's son has gained **2 lb 13 oz** in two months.

You can also multiply and divide measurements. As before, use like units and reduce when necessary.

Example: Mel has a pipe that is 14 feet 2 inches long. If he cuts the pipe into five equal pieces, what will be the length of each piece?

Convert to the smaller unit (inches):

$$14 \text{ ft } 2 \text{ in} = 14 \cancel{\text{ ft}} \times \frac{12 \text{ in.}}{1 \cancel{\text{ ft.}}} + 2 \text{ in} = 168 \text{ in} + 2 \text{ in} = 170 \text{ in}$$

Divide by 5: $170 \text{ in} \div 5 = 34 \text{ in}$
Simplify: $34 \text{ in} \div 12 \text{ in/ft} = 2 \text{ r10 or } 2 \text{ ft } 10 \text{ in}$

The Metric System

milli- means $\frac{1}{1,000}$

centi- means $\frac{1}{100}$

deci- means $\frac{1}{10}$

deka- means 10

hecto- means 100

kilo- means 1,000

A milligram is $\frac{1}{1,000}$ of a gram.

A centimeter is $\frac{1}{100}$ of a meter.

A deciliter is $\frac{1}{10}$ of a liter.

A dekagram is 10 grams.

A hectoliter is 100 liters.

A kilometer is 1,000 meters.

The metric system is used throughout most of the world. It uses these basic metric units:

Length: meter (m) A meter is a few inches longer than one yard.
Weight or Mass: gram (g) It takes 28 grams to make one ounce.
Volume: liter (L) A liter is slightly more than one quart.
Other units of measure are made by adding the prefixes shown in the margin to the basic units listed above.

Because the metric system is based on the powers of ten, you can convert metric units by moving the decimal point. Use this chart to make metric conversions.

kilo 1,000	hecto 100	deka 10	meter gram liter	deci $\frac{1}{10}$	centi $\frac{1}{100}$	milli $\frac{1}{1,000}$

To convert to smaller units $— — — — — — — — — \rightarrow$
$\leftarrow — — — — — — — — —$ To convert to larger units

Follow these steps to convert from one metric unit to another.
Step 1: Count from the unit given to the unit to which you are converting.
Step 2: Move the decimal point that number of places in the direction shown on the chart.

Operations

Operations with metric units are performed as you would with decimals. Remember, you can add and subtract <u>like</u> units only.

Example: Troy walked 2 kilometers on Monday. On Tuesday, he walked 1.575 kilometers. How many total kilometers did he walk on the two days?

You can add 2 kilometers and 1.575 kilometers.

```
   2     km
+ 1.575 km
  3.575 km
```

Troy walked **3.575 km.**

Directions: Solve.

1. Change $3\frac{1}{2}$ yd to feet and inches.

2. Change 4 min to seconds.

3. Change 18 c to pints.

4. Change 7,500 lb to tons.

5. Change $2\frac{1}{3}$ hr to minutes.

6. Change 72 fl oz to cups.

7. Change $5\frac{3}{4}$ gal to quarts.

8. Change 6 ft 9 in to yards.

9. Which is greater, 3 ft or 30 in?

10. Which is greater, $1\frac{1}{2}$ gal or 13 pt?

11. Change 500 mg to grams.

12. Change 8.4 kL to liters.

13. Which is less, $3\frac{1}{4}$ hr or 200 min?

14. Which is less, $4\frac{1}{4}$ lb or 75 oz?

15. Add 3 gal 3 qt and 2 gal 2 qt.

16. Add 8 ft 8 in, 3 ft 5 in, and 4 ft 9 in.

17. Subtract 20 min 45 sec from $\frac{1}{2}$ hr.

18. Subtract 1 ft 7 in from 2 ft 2 in.

19. Multiply 3 lb 4 oz by 5.

20. Multiply 2 yd 1 ft by 8.

21. Divide 1 yd 4 in by 5. Write your answer in inches.

22. Divide 3 gal by 4. Write your answer in quarts.

23. Add 5 km and 5,890 m.

24. How much more is 8.2 cm than 55 mm?

Directions: Choose the best answer to each item.

25. Dorie is canning raspberry jam. She makes 2 gallons of jam. If she plans to keep 6 pints for herself, how many pints will she have to give away?

(1) 8
(2) 9
(3) 10
(4) 11
(5) 12

26. Zola buys $3\frac{1}{4}$ yards of fabric to make a blouse. She actually uses 2 yards 2 feet 9 inches of fabric. How many inches of fabric are left?

(1) 12
(2) 13
(3) 14
(4) 15
(5) 16

27. Hank has three lengths of wire: 75 centimeters, 126 centimeters, and 460 centimeters. What is the total length in centimeters of the wire?

(1)   0.661
(2)   6.61
(3)   66.1
(4)   661
(5)   6,610

28. Meg needs 15 lengths of wood to make the railings for a stairway bannister. If each railing is 2 feet 9 inches, what is the total length of wood (in feet) that Meg will need?

(1) $11\frac{1}{4}$
(2) $36\frac{1}{4}$
(3) $41\frac{1}{4}$
(4) $48\frac{1}{2}$
(5) $53\frac{3}{4}$

29. Three shipments weigh 3 tons 750 pounds, 1 ton 150 pounds, and 4 tons 100 pounds. What is the total weight of the shipments in tons?

(1) $7\frac{3}{4}$
(2) 8
(3) $8\frac{1}{2}$
(4) $9\frac{1}{4}$
(5) $9\frac{1}{2}$

30. Marco can assemble one cabinet in 25 minutes. How many cabinets can he assemble in $3\frac{3}{4}$ hours?

(1)   7
(2)   8
(3)   9
(4) 10
(5) 11

31. A package of soup mix makes 24 ounces of soup. If $1\frac{1}{2}$ cups of soup equals one serving, how many servings will 5 packages of soup mix make?

(1)   9
(2) 10
(3) 11
(4) 12
(5) 13

32. Gregg Pharmaceuticals makes cough syrup. If 60 milliliters of the cough syrup contains 15 milliliters of the medication, how many milliliters of the medication are there in 1,000 ml of the syrup?

(1) 135
(2) 160
(3) 200
(4) 220
(5) 250

Answers are on page 871.

Lesson 18

Perimeter, Circumference, and Area

Perimeter measures the distance around the edge of any flat object. **Circumference** is the perimeter of a circle. **Area** measures the surface inside any flat object.

Perimeter

To find the perimeter of <u>any</u> figure, add the lengths of its sides.

Example: The county supervisor plans to fence in the area shown below for a playground. How much fencing is needed?

The fence will go around the perimeter of the playground. Find the perimeter by adding the lengths of the sides.

$$15 + 13 + 15 + 20 + 25 = 88$$

It will take **88 ft** of fencing to enclose the playground.

A **rectangle** has 4 sides, square corners, and <u>opposite</u> sides of equal length. Here is a formula for finding the perimeter (P) of a rectangle:

$$P = 2l + 2w, \text{ where } l = \text{length and } w = \text{width.}$$

(Note: $P = 2l + 2w$ is the same as $P = l + l + w + w$, which is the sum of the 4 sides.)

Example: What is the perimeter of this rectangle?

l = 12.25 in

w = 7.5 in

$$P = (2 \times l) + (2 \times w)$$
$$= (2 \times 12.25) + (2 \times 7.5)$$
$$= 24.5 + 15$$
$$= 39.5 \text{ in}$$

The perimeter of the rectangle is **39.5 in.**

The formula works for any unit: standard or metric. Note that <u>all</u> measurements must be the same units.

A **square** has four sides and square corners with <u>all</u> sides <u>equal</u> in length. This special formula is used to find the perimeter of a square:

$$P = 4s, \text{ where } s = \text{side}$$

Example: What is the perimeter of this square?

5.25 ft

5.25 ft   5.25 ft

5.25 ft

$$P = 4(5.25)$$
$$= 21 \text{ feet}$$

The perimeter of the square is **21 ft.**

A **triangle** has three sides. The formula for finding the perimeter of a triangle is $P = a + b + c$, where a, b, and c are the sides of the triangle. (For all other figures [with 5 or more sides] there is no special formula. Simply add the lengths of all the sides.)

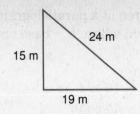

$$P = a + b + c$$
$$= 15 + 19 + 24$$
$$= 58 \text{ m}$$

The perimeter of the triangle is **58 m.**

Circumference

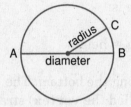

The shapes you have already learned about all have straight sides. A **circle** has a curved edge. The distance around the circle is called the **circumference.** To find the circumference, you need to know either the diameter or the radius of the circle.

The **diameter** of a circle is a line segment drawn through the center of the circle.

The **radius** is a line segment connecting the center of the circle to a point on the circle. The length of the radius is $\frac{1}{2}$ the diameter. The length of the diameter is 2 times the radius.

For all circles, the ratio of the circumference (C) to the diameter (d) is the same. The Greek letter π (pi) is used to represent this constant ratio whose value is <u>approximately</u> 3.14 or $\frac{22}{7}$ $\left(\pi = \frac{C}{d}\right)$.

Using this ratio, a formula can be written for finding circumference. The circumference of a circle can be found using this formula:
$$C = \pi d, \text{ where } \pi = 3.14 \text{ and } d = \text{diameter}$$

Example: Joe plans to put a low railing around a circular fish pond. The diameter of the pond is 20 meters. What will be the length of the railing?

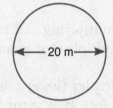

$$C = \pi d$$
$$= 3.14 \times 20$$
$$= 62.8$$

The railing will be about **62.8 m.**

Area

Area measures the surface inside an object. Area is measured in square units, such as square inches, square yards, or square meters.

A formula that tells the number of square units in any rectangular or square figure is:
$$\textbf{Area} = \textbf{\textit{l}} \times \textbf{\textit{w}}, \text{ where } l = \text{length and } w = \text{width.}$$
In a 6-inch by 5-inch rectangle, area = $6 \times 5 = $ **30 sq in.**

A **parallelogram** has four sides and the opposite sides are parallel. The area of a parallelogram is found by multiplying the length of the base by the height. **Height** is the distance straight down from a point on one nonslanting side to its opposite side, or the **base.**

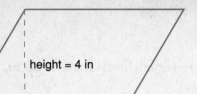

height = 4 in

base = 10 in

The formula for the area of a parallelogram can be written:
$A = bh$, where b = base and h = height

$A = bh$
$\quad = 10 \times 4$
$\quad = 40$ sq in

The area of the parallelogram in the drawing is **40 sq in.**

The formula used to find the area of a triangle is:

$$A = \frac{1}{2}bh,$$ where b = base and h = height

The **base** of a triangle is the measurement along the bottom. The **height** is the distance from the top corner (called the **vertex**) straight down to the base line.

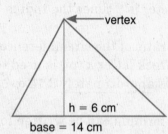

vertex

h = 6 cm

base = 14 cm

$A = \frac{1}{2}bh$
$\quad = \frac{1}{2} \times 14 \times 6 = 7 \times 6$
$\quad = 42$ sq cm

The area of the triangle in the drawing is **42 sq cm.**

The formula for finding the area of a circle is:

$$A = \pi r^2,$$ where $\pi = 3.14$ and r = radius

In other words, the area of a circle is found by multiplying π (3.14) by the square of the radius. To square a number, multiply that number by itself.

Example: Javier plans to buy fertilizer for a circular flower bed. One bag of fertilizer will cover 25 square feet. How many bags will Javier need to buy?

r = 6 ft

First find the area of the garden.

$A = \pi r^2$
$\quad = 3.14 \times 6 \times 6$
$\quad = 3.14 \times 36$
$\quad = 113.04$ sq ft

$$\begin{array}{r} 4.52 \\ 25\overline{)\,113.00} \\ \underline{100} \\ 13\,0 \\ \underline{12\,5} \\ 50 \\ \underline{50} \end{array}$$

The area of the flower bed is about **113 sq ft.**

To find the number of bags of fertilizer Javier must buy, divide 113 by 25.

Round to the nearest whole number: 4.52 rounds to 5. Javier needs to buy **5 bags** of fertilizer.

<u>Items 1 to 6</u> refer to the following information.

Identify each figure as a square, rectangle, triangle, circle, or parallelogram. Give the perimeter and area for each figure. All measurements are in inches.

1.
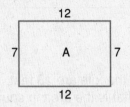

Figure name _____

Perimeter _____

Area _____

2.

Figure name _____

Perimeter _____

Area _____

3.

Figure name _____

Perimeter _____

Area _____

4.
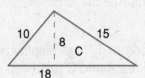

Figure name _____

Perimeter _____

Area _____

5.
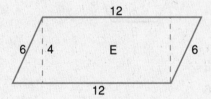

Figure name _____

Perimeter _____

Area _____

6.
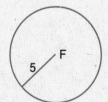

Figure name _____

Circumference _____

Area _____

Directions: Choose the best answer to each item.

Items 7 and 8 refer to the following figure.

A rectangular room is 8.5 feet by 25 feet.

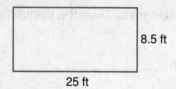

25 ft

7. What is the perimeter in feet of the room in the drawing?

   (1) 59
   (2) 63
   (3) 67
   (4) 71
   (5) 74

8. What is the area in square feet of the room in the drawing?

   (1) 105.5
   (2) 144
   (3) 192.5
   (4) 212.5
   (5) Not enough information is given.

9. What is the area in square feet of the shaded portion of the parallelogram?

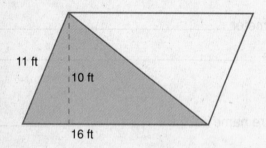

   (1) 60
   (2) 72
   (3) 75
   (4) 80
   (5) 96

10. What is the area in square inches of a triangle with a base of 18 inches and a height of 15 inches?

   (1) 135
   (2) 138
   (3) 140
   (4) 141
   (5) 144

11. The three sides of a triangle are 18 feet, 20 feet, and 24 feet. What is the area in square feet of the triangle?

   (1) 360
   (2) 400
   (3) 432
   (4) 480
   (5) Not enough information is given.

12. The design for a company logo display is shown below. If sides A and C are 14.3 centimeters long, sides D and E are 13.5 centimeters long, and side B is 12.4 centimeters long, what is the perimeter in centimeters of the logo?

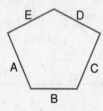

   (1) 40.2
   (2) 52.6
   (3) 58.6
   (4) 68
   (5) 70.6

Items 13 to 15 refer to the following diagram.

The city is planning to improve a section of Beverly Park. A cement area will be constructed in a grassy area for basketball and other sports.

Design for Beverly Park—SE Section

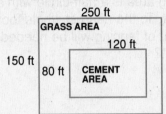

13. The city plans to build a fence around the grass area shown in the drawing. What is the perimeter of the grass area in feet?

   (1) 500
   (2) 600
   (3) 650
   (4) 700
   (5) 800

14. What is the area in square feet of the cement area?

   (1) 8,600
   (2) 8,800
   (3) 9,460
   (4) 9,600
   (5) 9,840

15. What is the area in square feet of the grass area?

   (1) 25,900
   (2) 26,400
   (3) 27,900
   (4) 30,100
   (5) 33,500

16. What is the circumference (to the nearest whole centimeter) of a circle with a diameter of 10 centimeters?

   (1) 29
   (2) 30
   (3) 31
   (4) 32
   (5) 33

Items 17 to 19 refer to the following drawing.

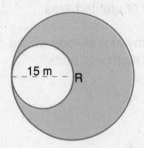

17. What is the diameter in meters of the larger circle?

   (1) 7.5
   (2) 12
   (3) 15
   (4) 30
   (5) 33

18. What is the area of the inner circle to the nearest square meter?

   (1) 165
   (2) 177
   (3) 184
   (4) 189
   (5) 195

19. What is the area of the shaded area of the larger circle to the nearest square meter?

   (1) 507
   (2) 526
   (3) 530
   (4) 577
   (5) 589

Answers are on page 872.

Directions: Choose the best answer to each item.

Items 1 to 3 refer to the following information.

A gardener has planted three square flower beds, each 6 feet on a side. In each square he plants a bush that needs an area of 5 square feet. The rest of each flower bed is planted with flowers. All three flower beds will be sprayed with liquid plant food. One pint of plant food will feed 5 square feet of planted area.

1. How many feet of rope will he need to fence off all three flower beds?

   (1) 18
   (2) 24
   (3) 36
   (4) 72
   (5) 108

2. How many pints of plant food will he need for all three flower beds?

   (1) 7
   (2) 8
   (3) 18
   (4) 19
   (5) 22

3. How many square feet are left for planting flowers in each flower bed after leaving space for the bush?

   (1) 25
   (2) 30
   (3) 31
   (4) 88
   (5) 120

4. A planting area is a half-circle with a radius of 63 feet. To the nearest whole foot, how many feet of fencing will be needed to enclose it?

   (1) 396
   (2) 324
   (3) 315
   (4) 261
   (5) 224

5. Which expression can be used to find the area in square feet of the parallelogram?

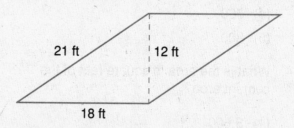

   (1) 21 + 21 + 12 + 12
   (2) 21 + 21 + 18 + 18
   (3) 2(12 + 18)
   (4) 12 × 18
   (5) 21 × 18

6. What is the perimeter of a rectangular flower bed that is 25 feet by 3 feet?

   (1) 56
   (2) 60
   (3) 65
   (4) 66
   (5) 75

7. What is the area in square meters of this parallelogram?

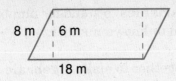

8 m / 6 m
18 m

(1) 48
(2) 54
(3) 72
(4) 108
(5) 144

Items 8 and 9 refer to the following figure.

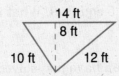

14 ft
8 ft
10 ft   12 ft

8. What is the perimeter of the triangle?

(1) 22
(2) 24
(3) 26
(4) 36
(5) Not enough information is given.

9. What is the area of the triangle?

(1) 56
(2) 63
(3) 72
(4) 112
(5) 126

---

10. The length of a rectangle is 36 centimeters. What is its area in square centimeters?

(1) 324
(2) 432
(3) 504
(4) 576
(5) Not enough information is given.

Items 11 and 12 refer to the following figure.

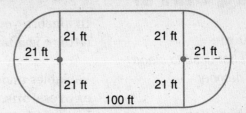

21 ft   21 ft
21 ft   21 ft
21 ft   21 ft
100 ft

11. This aerial view of a running track shows that it is really a rectangle with two half circles at the ends. To the nearest whole foot, what is the distance around the track?

(1) 282 ft
(2) 316 ft
(3) 332 ft
(4) 364 ft
(5) 388 ft

12. The inside of the track is planted with grass. What is the area (to the nearest square foot) of grass?

(1) 4,735 sq ft
(2) 4,925 sq ft
(3) 5,295 sq ft
(4) 5,585 sq ft
(5) 5,750 sq ft

---

13. What is the perimeter in centimeters of the figure in the drawing?

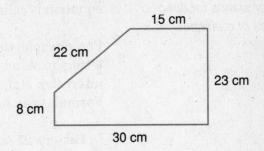

15 cm
22 cm
23 cm
8 cm
30 cm

(1) 95
(2) 98
(3) 104
(4) 112
(5) 138

Answers are on page 873.

Algebra

variable
*any letter used to stand
for a number*

algebraic expression
*a mathematical
expression that uses
letters and numbers
instead of words*

equation
*a statement that says two
expressions are equal*

solving an equation
*finding a number that
makes the equation true
when the number is put
in the place of the
variable*

formula
*an equation in which the
letter stands for specific
kinds of quantities*

In algebra you use letters called **variables** to stand for numbers. The letter x is often used to stand for an unknown number.

Variables and numbers are used together to make **algebraic expressions.** An algebraic expression uses letters and numbers instead of words to express mathematical information. In Lesson 19 you will learn about algebraic expressions. You will learn how to add, subtract, multiply, and divide with variables and numbers. You will also learn how to write an algebraic expression.

Algebraic expressions can be used to solve problems. When an algebraic expression equals some number, you can write an equation. An **equation** is a statement that says two expressions are equal.

Think about this example:
A certain number added to 5 equals 9. What is the number?

If you answered 4 because $5 + 4 = 9$, you have just solved an algebra problem. You can write an equation to solve the problem by using x to represent the unknown number.

$$\begin{aligned} \text{A certain number} \quad & x \\ \text{added to 5} \quad & 5 + x \\ \text{equals 9.} \quad & 5 + x = 9 \end{aligned}$$

$5 + x = 9$ is an equation. You will learn how to solve equations in Lesson 20. You will also learn how to translate word problems into algebraic expressions and equations.

Actually, any letter of the alphabet can be used as a variable. When the letters in an equation stand for specific kinds of quantities, the equation is called a **formula.**

For example, the formula for finding simple interest $i = prt$ uses letters to stand for specific quantities. The variable i stands for interest, p stands for principal, r stands for rate, and t stands for time. Formulas can be used to solve many algebra problems.

In Lessons 21 and 22, you will learn about some special topics in algebra.

Lesson Signed Numbers • Algebraic Expressions

Integers

Signed numbers can be used to show quantity, distance, and direction. **Positive numbers** show an increase, a gain or upward motion. **Negative numbers** show the opposite: a decrease, a loss or downward direction. All whole numbers, both the positive numbers and the negative numbers, and zero are called **integers.**

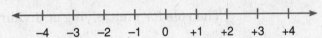

The distance an integer is from zero is called its **absolute value,** which is shown by enclosing the number between two vertical bars. The absolute value is the number value without the sign.

Examples: Absolute value of +3 is 3. We write $|+3| = 3$.
Absolute value of −7 is 7. We write $|-7| = 7$.
Absolute value of 0 is 0. We write $|0| = 0$.

We can show the addition of integers on a **number line.** Move to the right for positive numbers and to the left for negative numbers.

Example: Add: $(+6) + (-4)$

1. Start at 0 and move 6 units to the right.
2. From +6, move 4 units to the left to add −4.

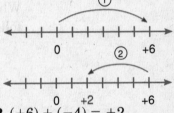

The answer is **+2.** $(+6) + (-4) = +2$

Addition

Use these rules to add signed numbers:

Rule 1: To add two integers with like signs:
Add the absolute value $(+3) + (+5) = |+3| + |+5| = +8$
and keep the same sign. $(-2) + (-6) = |-2| + |-6| = -8$

Rule 2: To add two integers with unlike signs:
Subtract the absolute $(-9) + (+3) = |-9| - |+3| = -6$
value of the lesser $(-4) + (+7) = |+7| - |-4| = +3$
integer from the absolute value of
the greater. Keep the sign of the integer with the greater
absolute value.

Subtraction

To subtract integers, use this rule:
Subtraction rule:
1. Change the subtraction operation to addition.
2. Change the sign of the number to be subtracted.
3. Complete the problem as addition.

Example: Subtract $(+5) - (-2)$
Change the operation to addition, and change -2 to $+2$.
$(+5) - (-2) = (+5) + (+2) = +7$

Study these examples to see how the subtraction rule is applied.
$(-5) - (-2)$ becomes $(-5) + (+2)$, which equals -3.
$(-5) - (+2)$ becomes $(-5) + (-2)$, which equals -7.
$(+5) - (+2)$ becomes $(+5) + (-2)$, which equals $+3$.
Notice that the sign of the <u>first</u> number in the expression does not change.

Multiplication and Division

The rule for multiplying or dividing integers is:

Multiplication/Division rule:
If the signs are the same, the answer is positive.
If the signs are different, the answer is negative.

Examples: $3 \times 5 = 15 \quad -3 \times 5 = -15 \quad 3 \times -5 = -15 \quad -3 \times -5 = +15$
$24 \div 6 = 4 \quad -24 \div 6 = -4 \quad 24 \div -6 = -4 \quad -24 \div -6 = +4$
Note: Positive numbers can be written without the plus sign. Negative numbers are <u>always</u> written with the minus sign.

Order of Operations

When an algebraic expression contains several operations, you must follow the order of operations rule to **simplify** it.

Order of operations rule:
1. If there are parentheses, do all work in them first in order: multiply, divide, add, or subtract.
2. Then, multiply and divide in order from left to right through the expression.
3. Last, add and subtract through the expression from left to right.

Example: $3 + (4 + 6 \times 3)$

1. Do the work in the parentheses first. Multiply, then add.

$3 + (4 + 6 \times 3)$
$3 + (4 + 18)$
$3 + (22)$

2. Then do the operations in order (multiply, divide, add, subtract). So add $3 + 22$.

25

If there is a fraction bar, work on the numerator and denominator separately, applying the order of operations rule to each. Then do the final division.

Example: $\dfrac{3 + 5 \div 5}{(6 - 4) \div 2} = \dfrac{3 + 1}{2 \div 2} = \dfrac{4}{1} = 4$

Mathematics ◆ Algebra

Directions: Write the absolute value for each.

1. +6   2. −7   3. −14.6   4. $+\frac{2}{3}$ 5. 0

Directions: Add or subtract.

6. (+7) + (+5)

7. (−10) + (−6)

8. (−6) + (+5)

9. (+10) − (+7)

10. (−3) − (+7)

11. (−1) − (+5)

12. (+6) + (−8)

13. $\left(+3\frac{1}{2}\right) + (−2)$

14. (+10) − (+17)

15. (+2) − (−7)

16. (+8) − (−4)

17. (−4) + (+9)

18. (−4.5) + (−1.5)

19. (+4) − (−1)

20. (−6.1) − (+2.6)

Directions: Multiply.

21. (−2) (+3)

22. (−2.5) (+2)

23. (−4) (−7)

24. (+7) (0)

25. (+5) (−3)

26. (−4) (−1) (+2)

27. (0) (−2)

28. $(+6) (−2) \left(−\frac{1}{3}\right)$

Directions: Divide.

29. (−64) ÷ (+4)

30. (+15) ÷ (−3)

31. (+20) ÷ (+5)

32. (−42) ÷ (−3)

33. (+36) ÷ (−12)

34. (−55) ÷ (+11)

35. (−49) ÷ (−7)

36. (+126) ÷ (−9)

Directions: Simplify each expression.

37. 6 + 8 × 4

38. $\frac{−2 − (+8)}{(6) ÷ (−6)}$

39. (4 × −9) − (2 × −3)

40. 10 + (−3 + 4 × (−2))

41. (−25) − 4 × 3

42. $\frac{(−4) + (−6)}{(+4) − (−1)}$

43. 6 − (4 × 8 + (−1))

44. (10 × −2) + (6 × −3)

Answers are on page 874.

Algebraic Expressions

An **algebraic expression** is a group of numbers, operation signs, and variables.

Examples: $2x + 3$ $\dfrac{4x + 1}{3}$ $3x - 4$ $3(6x)$

Expressions like these are formed by translating number relationships into symbols. Analyze the following expressions carefully.

4 times a number $4x$
6 more than a number $x + 6$
2 less than a number $x - 2$
one-half a number increased by 7
$\dfrac{x}{2} + 7$ or $\dfrac{1}{2}x + 7$

the product of 6 and x $6x$
the quotient of x and 5 $\dfrac{x}{5}$ or $x \div 5$
the product of x and 8 added to the sum of 2 and x
$8x + (2 + x)$

An algebraic expression always contains **variables.** Variables are letters that are used to represent numbers. Whenever the value of x changes, the expression also changes its value.

x	$4 + x$	becomes		value
3	$4 + x$	$4 + 3$	$=$	7
-8	$4 + x$	$4 + (-8)$	$=$	-4
8	$4 + x$	$4 + 8$	$=$	12
-3	$4 + x$	$4 + (-3)$	$=$	1

This table shows how the value of the expression $4 + x$ changes as the value of x changes. An algebraic expression has a value only when all the variables are replaced by numbers.

Example: Find the value of $3 - x + y$, when $x = -1$ and $y = +5$.

Substitute -1 for x and $+5$ for y. $3 - (-1) + (+5)$
Apply the subtraction rule. $3 + (+1) + (+5)$
Complete by adding. $+9$

Simplifying an Expression

Simplifying an expression means performing all the operations you can within the expression containing a variable. Without knowing the values of the variables, you can add and subtract **like terms. Terms** are the number and variable combinations separated by addition and subtraction signs. Like terms contain exactly the same variables.

Examples of like terms: $3x, 5x, x, -4x$
Examples of unlike terms: $2x, 3y, z, -2xy, 4$

Example: Simplify the following expression: $4x + y - 2x + 2y$
Combine like terms: $4x - 2x = 2x;\ y + 2y = 3y$
(The number part of the variable by itself is understood to be one. So, $y + 2y$ is the same as $1y + 2y$.) $2x + 3y$

Directions: Simplify each expression.

45. $5x + y - 3x + 2y$

46. $8x + 3 + 2x - 5$

47. $a + 6b + a - 8b + 2a$

48. $14 - 7x - 4x$

49. $4z + z + 5y - 3$

50. $3x + 12y - 5x - 10y$

Directions: Find the value of each expression.

51. $x - (+5) + (+3)$, when $x = +2$

52. $(+3) + x + (+5) - x$, when $x = +5$

53. $(-1) + x + (+8)$, when $x = -4$

54. $(+2) - x - x - (-3)$, when $x = -0.5$

55. $5x + y - 4 + 2y$, when $x = 3$ and $y = 2$

56. $3xy + 2x + y$, when $x = -2$ and $y = 4$

57. $\frac{6xyz}{x}$, when $x = -3$, $y = 2$, $z = -1$

58. $\frac{a + 5b}{2a - 1}$, when $a = 4$ and $b = 2$

Directions: Translate the following into mathematical expressions.

59. a number minus 2

60. a number divided by 7

61. twice a number, then increased by -4

62. twice a number subtracted from three times that same number

63. three times a number, then minus 9

64. four times a number, then divided by 3

65. Darcia has $11. She gets a certain amount more, then spends $2.

66. Richard has 19 points in a game. He loses 5 points, gains a certain number more, and then loses 2 points.

Answers are on page 874.

Lesson 20 Equations

An **equation** is a mathematical statement that shows that two quantities are equal. When an equation contains a variable, we use algebra to find the value of the variable. To solve an equation means to find the number that makes the statement true.

Look at this equation: $2x - 1 = 9$
When x equals 5, $2(5) - 1 = 9$
the statement is true. $10 - 1 = 9$

Any other value of x makes the equation false. Only 5 makes the equation $2x - 1 = 9$ true. So 5 is the **solution** of the equation. The variable x must equal 5.

One-Step Equations

To solve an equation, you must keep the sides of the equation equal. Whatever you do to one side of the equation you must do to the other.

* The basic strategy in solving an equation is to isolate the variable. **Isolating the variable** means to have the variable alone on one side of the equation.

* In an equation with only one operation, perform the **inverse** (opposite) operation on both sides of the equation.

    Addition and subtraction are inverse operations.

    Multiplication and division are inverse operations.

In the equation $x - 13 = 25$, the operation is subtraction. By performing its inverse, adding 13 to both sides, we can isolate the variable and solve the equation.

Example: Solve: $x - 13 = 25$

When 13 is subtracted from some number, the result is 25. Think what this means: If 13 is subtracted from some number and the result is 25, then by adding 13 to 25 we should be able to find the missing number.

$$x - 13 = 25$$

Add 13 to both sides: $x - 13 + 13 = 25 + 13$

$$x = 38$$

Check: $38 - 13 \overset{?}{=} 25$ $25 = 25$

Example: Solve: $x + 40 = 75$

What number added to 40 equals 75?
The operation is addition: $x \oplus 40 = 75$
Perform the inverse operation:
subtract 40 from both sides: $x + 40 - 40 = 75 - 40$

Solve the equation: $x = 35$

Check: $35 + 40 \overset{?}{=} 75$ $75 = 75$

Mathematics ◆ Algebra

Example: Solve: $5x = 35$

What number multiplied by 5 equals 35?

The operation is multiplication: $\qquad\qquad 5x = 35$

To isolate the variable,
divide both sides by 5: $\qquad\qquad \dfrac{5x}{5} = \dfrac{35}{5}$

Solve: $\qquad\qquad\qquad\qquad\qquad x = 7$

Check: $5(7) \overset{?}{=} 35 \qquad\qquad\qquad 35 = 35$

Example: Solve: $\dfrac{x}{9} = 4$

What number divided by 9 equals 4?

The operation is division: $\qquad\qquad \dfrac{x}{9} = 4$

To isolate the variable,
multiply both sides by 9: $\qquad\qquad \overset{1}{(9)}\dfrac{x}{\underset{1}{9}} = 4(9)$

Solve: $\qquad\qquad\qquad\qquad\qquad x = 36$

Check: $\dfrac{36}{9} \overset{?}{=} 4 \qquad\qquad\qquad\qquad 4 = 4$

Multistep Equations

Some equations require more than one step in order to find the solution. When solving equations, *reverse* the normal order of operations.
- Perform the inverse operations for addition and subtraction first.
- Perform multiplication and division operations second.

Example: Solve: $5x - 10 = 35$

Add 10 to both sides: $\qquad 5x - 10 + 10 = 35 + 10$
Add and subtract first. $\qquad\qquad\qquad 5x = 45$

Divide both sides by 5:
Multiply and divide second.

Solve the equation: $\qquad\qquad\qquad x = 9$

Check by substituting 9 for x $\qquad 5(9) - 10 = 35$
in the original equation. $\qquad\qquad 45 - 10 = 35$
$\qquad\qquad\qquad\qquad\qquad\qquad 35 = 35$

Some equations have variable terms on both sides. The basic strategy is to isolate the variable on one side of the equation.

Example: Solve: $12x - 9 = 10x - 1$

Subtract $10x$ from both sides:
$\qquad\qquad\qquad\qquad 12x - 10x - 9 = 10x - 10x - 1$

Now the variable is only on one
side of the equation. $\qquad\qquad\qquad 2x - 9 = -1$
Add 9 to both sides: $\qquad\qquad 2x - 9 + 9 = -1 + 9$
$\qquad\qquad\qquad\qquad\qquad\qquad 2x = 8$

Divide both sides by 2: $\qquad\qquad\qquad \dfrac{2x}{2} = \dfrac{8}{2}$

Solve the equation: $\qquad\qquad\qquad\qquad x = 4$

Check by substitution:

$$12(4) - 9 \stackrel{?}{=} 10(4) - 1$$
$$48 - 9 \stackrel{?}{=} 40 - 1$$
$$39 \stackrel{?}{=} 39$$

Some equations contain parentheses. To solve these equations, you need to remove the parentheses by multiplying each number within the parentheses by the multiplier.

Example: Solve: $2(x + 1) = -8$

Multiply both numbers inside the parentheses by 2:

$$2(x + 1) = -8$$
$$2x + 2 = -8$$

Subtract 2 from both sides:

$$2x + 2 - 2 = -8 - 2$$
$$2x = -10$$

Divide both sides by 2:

$$\frac{2x}{2} = \frac{-10}{2}$$

Solve the equation:

$$x = -5$$

Check by substitution:

$$2(-5 + 1) = -8$$
$$2(-4) = -8$$
$$-8 = -8$$

To simplify an equation, we often combine like terms. We add variable terms and then add number terms.

Examples: $2x + 3x = 5x$ $x + 3x = 4x$ $x + x = 2x$ $4x - 2x = 2x$

$5x - x = 4x$ $6x - 6x = 0$ $x - x = 0$ $4x - 7x = -3x$

Solve: $8x + 4 - 5x - 4 = 6x + 9 - 6x$

$$3x + 0 = 0 + 9$$

Simplify each side:

$$3x = 9$$

Divide both sides by 3:

$$\frac{3x}{3} = \frac{9}{3}$$

Simplify: $1x = 3$
Solution: $x = 3$

Special Words

Sometimes algebraic equations are presented in words. Remember the special words that tell you which operation to use. Let x (or any letter) represent the unknown number. Then solve the equation to find the value of the variable.

Examples: Word Problem	Equation
The **sum of** a number and 9 is 14.	$x + 9 = 14$
6 **less than** a number is 10.	$x - 6 = 10$
The **product** of a number and 4 is 12.	$4x = 12$
The **quotient** of 12 divided by x is 3.	$\frac{12}{x} = 3$
9 **more than twice** a number is 15.	$2x + 9 = 15$

ged **Exercise** Equations

Directions: Solve each equation.

1. $x - 7 = 3$

2. $2x = 12$

3. $-6x = -42$

4. $x + 12 = 22$

5. $x - 8 = -10$

6. $-3x = 18$

7. $5x = -45$

8. $6x + 7 = 37$

9. $4x + 5x - 10 = 35$

10. $3x - 6x + 2 = -4x$

11. $6 - x + 12 = 10x + 7$

12. $9x + 6x - 12x = -7x + 2x - 12 + 5x$

13. $7x + 3 = 31$

14. $3x - 8 = 28$

15. $8x + 6 = 5x + 9$

16. $11x - 10 = 8x + 5$

17. $-2x - 4 = 4x - 10$

18. $5x + 8 = x - 8$

19. $11x - 12 = 9x + 2$

20. $5(x + 1) = 75$

21. $5(x - 7) = 5$

22. $6(2 + x) = 5x + 15$

Directions: Translate each statement into an algebraic equation. Then solve.

23. Add a number and -5. Multiply by 8. The result is 2 more than the number.

24. Six less than twice a certain number is 24.

25. Multiply a number by 2 and add 2. The result is 20.

26. The sum of 8 and a certain number is increased by 12. The result is the same as that number multiplied by 3.

Answers are on page 875.

Now you can use the skills you developed to solve word problems.

Example: A busboy in a sandwich shop noticed that there were 8 more women than men in the shop. If there were 32 people in the shop, how many men were there?

Using this example we can develop steps for placing the words into the equation to be solved:

Step 1:   **Identify the unknown amount, x.** Let x equal the number of men.

Step 2:   **Label the other quantities in terms of x.** Since there were 8 more women than men, let $x + 8$ equal the number of women.

Step 3:   **Write the equation.** The number of men added to the number of women equals 32, so $x + (x + 8) = 32$.

Step 4:   **Solve for x.**
$$x + (x + 8) = 32$$
$$2x + 8 = 32$$
$$2x + 8 - 8 = 32 - 8$$
$$2x = 24$$
$$\frac{2x}{2} = \frac{24}{2}$$
$$x = 12$$

Step 5:   **Solve the problem.** Since $x =$ the number of men, 12 is the answer to the problem. However, sometimes the problem asks a different question. For this example, the question might have been "how many women were there?" The answer to the problem would be $x + 8$, or 20.

Step 6:   **Check your answer.** Read the problem again, substituting your answer, to make sure the answer makes sense. There were 12 men and 20 women (12 + 8). The total is 32. The answer makes sense.

In many problems, a chart is useful to clarify the information and to show necessary relationships.

Example: Ralph is three times as old as his daughter Suellen. In 10 years, he will be only two times as old. How old are Ralph and Suellen now?

There are four unknowns: two present ages and two future ages.

Box 1:   Let x equal the smallest unknown quantity (Suellen's age now).

Box 2:   Ralph is now three times as old as Suellen, so his age is $3x$.

Box 3:   In ten years Suellen's age will be 10 years more: $x + 10$.

Box 4:   In ten years Ralph's age will be 10 years more: $3x + 10$.

	Suellen's Age	Ralph's Age
Now	¹ x	² $3x$
In 10 years	³ $x + 10$	⁴ $3x + 10$

We also know that Ralph's age in ten years will be two times Suellen's age in 10 years. Use this fact to write the equation: the expression in box 4 is equal to two times the expression in box 3.

$$3x + 10 = 2(x + 10)$$
$$3x + 10 = 2x + 20$$
$$x = 10$$

Now return to the chart to find the answer to the problem: Suellen's age now is 10; Ralph's age now is 30. As a check, note that in 10 years, Suellen will be 20 years old and Ralph will be 40 years old ($20 \times 2 = 40$).

Formulas are another kind of equation. A formula tells you how to use information to solve a certain kind of problem. For example, the formula for finding distance (d) is $d = rt$; where r = rate and t = time. To use formulas, just substitute the known quantities and solve.

Note: The three variables must use the <u>same</u> units of measure. If the rate is in <u>miles per hour</u>, the distance will be in <u>miles</u> and the time will be in <u>hours</u>.

Example: Kiel's model rocket traveled 250 feet in 10 seconds. What was the rate of travel?

$$d = rt$$

Substitute the known quantities: $250 = r(10)$

Solve for r. Divide both sides of the equation by 10. $\dfrac{250}{10} = \dfrac{r(10)}{10}$

$$25 = r$$

The rocket traveled at a rate of **25 ft/sec.**

The formula for finding total cost (c) is $c = nr$; where n = number of units and r = cost per unit.

Example: The total cost of a shipment of chairs is $2,250. If each chair costs $75, how many chairs are in the shipment?

$$c = nr$$

Substitute the known quantities: $\$2{,}250 = n(\$75)$

Solve for n. Divide both sides of the equation by $75. $\dfrac{\$2{,}250}{\$75} = \dfrac{n(\$75)}{\$75}$

$$30 = n$$

There are **30** chairs in the shipment.

We have already used formulas for interest ($i = prt$), perimeter, area, and circumference. We will use more formulas in geometry.

27. A certain number is added to 9. This sum is multiplied by 5, and then 15 is subtracted from the result. The answer is 40. What is the number?

    (1) 2
    (2) 8
    (3) $9\frac{1}{5}$
    (4) 11
    (5) 17

28. The sum of two consecutive numbers is 49. What is the lesser number? (Note: If x is one number, the next greater consecutive number is just one more than x, namely $x + 1$.)

    (1) 16
    (2) 18
    (3) 24
    (4) 27
    (5) 33

29. The formula for the perimeter of a triangle is $P = a + b + c$. The perimeter P is 53. Which equation should you use to find the value of b?

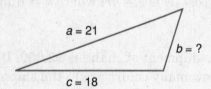

    (1) $53^2 = a + b + c$
    (2) $53 + 21 + b$
    (3) $53 - 21 - 18 = b$
    (4) $53 + 21 + 18 = b$
    (5) $53 - 18 + 21 = b$

30. Birnham Mills has 360 employees. Twelve more than 3 times the number of employees who work in management work in production. How many employees work in management?

    (1) 68
    (2) 87
    (3) 103
    (4) 112
    (5) 124

31. The formula for finding the perimeter of a rectangle (P) is $P = 2l + 2w$, where l = length and w = width. Which equation could be used to find the length of a rectangle with a perimeter of 30 centimeters and a width of 6 centimeters?

    (1) $\frac{30 - 12}{2} = l$
    (2) $30 + 12 = 2l$
    (3) $2(30) + 2(6) = l$
    (4) $30 - (2)(6) = l$
    (5) $30 - 12 - l$

32. Bonnie's weekly income is $150 less than twice her husband's weekly earnings. Together the couple earns $750. How much does her husband earn per week?

    (1) $280
    (2) $300
    (3) $315
    (4) $320
    (5) $345

33. Eight times a number, decreased by five, equals seven times that number. What is the number?

(1) 2
(2) 3
(3) 4
(4) 5
(5) 6

34. At a gym Frank did a certain number of pushups. Tom did 12 more than Frank. The total number both men did was 66. How many did Tom do?

(1) 27
(2) 29
(3) 34
(4) 39
(5) 41

35. Al got two parking tickets. The fine for the second ticket was twice as much as the fine for the first ticket. If the total fines were $54, what was the fine for the first ticket?

(1) $ 9
(2) $15
(3) $18
(4) $20
(5) $22

36. George is 5 times as old as his son. In 19 years he will be only twice as old as his son. Let x represent the son's present age. Which equation shows the correct age relationship?

(1) $x = 5x + 19$
(2) $5x = 2(5x + 19)$
(3) $2(x + 19) = 5x + 19$
(4) $x + 19 = 2(5x + 19)$
(5) $x + 19 = 2(5x)$

37. Nora is 4 years older than Diana. Two years from now Nora will be twice as old as Diana. How old is Diana now?

(1) 2
(2) 4
(3) 5
(4) 8
(5) 12

38. A plane travels 2,125 miles in 5 hours. Using the formula $d = rt$, find the plane's rate of travel.

(1) 315 mi/hr
(2) 385 mi/hr
(3) 425 mi/hr
(4) 455 mi/hr
(5) 500 mi/hr

39. A hardware store purchased 6 dozen hammers for a total cost of $104.40. Using the formula $c = nr$, what was the cost of one dozen hammers?

(1) $ 1.45
(2) $ 8.30
(3) $12.55
(4) $17.40
(5) $18.90

40. The formula $F = \frac{9}{5}C + 32$ shows the relationship between the Fahrenheit (F) and Celsius (C) temperature scales. Using the formula, what is the Celsius temperature that equals 212° Fahrenheit?

(1) 82°
(2) 85°
(3) 90°
(4) 95°
(5) 100°

Answers are on page 875.

Lesson 20 ◆ Equations

597

Lesson 21 Special Topics

Solving Inequalities

An **inequality** says that two algebraic expressions are *not* equal. The inequality symbols are:

> "greater than"   ≥ "greater than or equal to"
< "less than"   ≤ "less than or equal to"

When a variable appears in an inequality, many numbers make the statement true. Consider this inequality: $x < 5$.

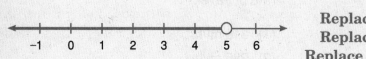

		$x < 5$	
Replace x by 2:		$2 < 5$	True
Replace x by 0:		$0 < 5$	True
Replace x by –12:		$-12 < 5$	True

Every number to the left of 5 on the number line is a solution. We show the solution by drawing a solid line on the number line.

Notice that 5 itself is represented by an empty circle. This shows that the number 5 is not included. Five is not "less than" 5.

The solution of the inequality $x \geq -3$ is the number -3 and all numbers to the right of -3 on the number line.

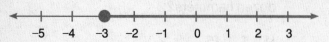

The circle at -3 is filled in because -3 is included in the solution.

Inequality signs are also used to show "between." If a number is between -1 and 3, it is greater than -1 and it is also less than 3:

$$-1 < x < 3$$

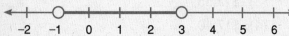

An inequality can be solved much like an equation. The same number can be added to or subtracted from both sides of an inequality. However, if you multiply or divide by a negative number, you must reverse the inequality.

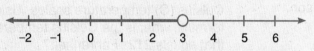

Example:	Solve:	$2x + 7 < x + 10$
	Subtract x:	$x + 7 < 10$
	Subtract 7:	$x < 3$

Check: Pick a number in the solution part $2x + 7 < x + 10$
        of the graph, like 1, and substitute $2(1) + 7 < (1) + 10$
        it in the inequality. $2 + 7 < 11$
                                                    $9 < 11$ **True**

Example:	Solve:	$3x - 4 < 5x$
	Subtract $5x$:	$-2x - 4 < 0$
	Add 4:	$-2x < 4$
	Divide by -2:	$x > -2$

Check by picking a number in the solution and substituting.

Mathematics ◆ Algebra

Word problems are sometimes solved by using an inequality.

Example: Sandy has three tasks to complete. The second will take three times as long as the first, and the third will take 30 minutes. If Sandy wants to be finished with all three tasks in less than 90 minutes, what is the longest amount of time the first task can take?

Let x stand for the time of the first task. Then $3x$ stands for the time of the second task. Since all three tasks must take less than 90 minutes, the inequality can be written:

$$x + 3x + 30 < 90$$

Solve:
$$4x + 30 < 90$$
$$4x < 60$$
$$x < 15$$

As long as the first task takes **less than 15 minutes,** Sandy will finish the three tasks in less than 90 minutes.

◆ ged **Exercise** Special Topics

Directions: Solve the following inequalities.

1. $5x + 2 > 4x + 1$

2. $6x - 4 < 3x + 2$

3. $3(x + 1) > x + 4x - 5$

4. $x + 12 < 5(x + 8)$

5. $2x + (4 - 3x) < 21$

6. $7x - 3x - x < 3x + 2x + 10$

Directions: Choose the best answer to each item.

7. If five times a number is added to 6, the result is less than 4 times that same number added to 10. Which of the following is the solution?

(1) $x < 3$

(2) $x < 4$

(3) $x > 3$

(4) $x > 4$

(5) $x < -4$

8. The perimeter of a triangle must be less than or equal to 65 inches. One side is 21 inches. The second side is 18 inches. What is the longest the third side can be (in inches)?

(1) 22

(2) 23

(3) 25

(4) 26

(5) 28

Answers are on page 877.

Factoring

Factors are numbers that are multiplied together. For instance, the factors of 12 are 3 and 4, 2 and 6, and 1 and 12. In the algebraic term $7x$, 7 and x are factors.

The algebraic expression $4x + 10$ has two terms. Both terms can be divided by the number 2, so 2 is one factor of $4x + 10$. Divide both terms by 2 to find the other factor.

$$\frac{4x + 10}{2} = 2x + 5 \quad \text{Check: } 2(2x + 5) = 4x + 10$$

Follow these steps to factor an algebraic expression with two terms:

Step 1: Find a number and/or a variable that divides evenly into both terms.

Step 2: Divide to find the other factor.

Example: Factor $x^2 + 2x$.
The term x^2 means $x \cdot x$. The term $2x$ means $2 \cdot x$. The variable x divides evenly into both terms. Divide to find

the other factor: $\dfrac{x^2 + 2x}{x} = x + 2$

$$\text{Check: } x(x + 2) = x^2 + 2x$$

A quadratic expression is one that contains the variable raised to the second power, or squared, as in $x^2 + 2x$. Quadratic expressions will always have the variable *(x)* in <u>both</u> factors—in this case, x and $x + 2$ are the factors.

You may be asked to factor a quadratic expression with <u>three</u> terms: for example, $x^2 - 3x - 4$. Both factors for this kind of expression will have <u>two</u> terms: the variable and an integer.

To factor a quadratic expression with three terms, follow these steps:

Step 1: Find all possible factors of the whole number third term.

Step 2: Find the integer factors from Step 1 that can be combined to make the number part of the middle term.

Step 3: Write the two factors with the variable as the first term in each factor.

Step 4: Check your work. Multiply both terms of the second factor by each term in the first factor.

Example: Factor $x^2 - 3x - 4$.

Step 1: The possible factors for -4 are: $-4 \cdot 1$, $4 \cdot -1$, $-2 \cdot 2$, and $2 \cdot -2$.

Step 2: Combining -4 and 1 will give you the number part of the middle term: $-4 + 1 = -3$.

Step 3: Write the factors. Put the variable as the first term in both factors: $(x \quad)(x \quad)$. Then add the integers from Step 2, -4 and 1: $(x - 4)(x + 1)$.

Step 4: Check: $(x - 4)(x + 1) = x^2 + x - 4x - 4 = x^2 - 3x - 4$.

Directions: Factor each expression.

9. $5x + 30$
10. $6y + 15$
11. $8x - 2$
12. $4z - 14$
13. $b^2 + 9b$
14. $y^2 + 3y$
15. $2x^2 + 4x$
16. $3x^2 + 9x$
17. $7y^2 - y$
18. $4x^2 + 2x$
19. $x^2 + 9x + 20$
20. $x^2 - 5x + 6$
21. $x^2 + 5x - 6$
22. $x^2 - 3x - 28$
23. $x^2 - 2x - 3$
24. $x^2 + 8x + 12$
25. $x^2 - 7x + 12$
26. $x^2 + 7x - 8$
27. $x^2 + 3x - 10$
28. $x^2 + 10x + 21$
29. $x^2 - 13x + 40$
30. $x^2 - x - 12$
31. $x^2 - 8x - 20$
32. $x^2 - 11x + 18$
33. $x^2 - 6x - 55$
34. $x^2 + 16x + 48$
35. $x^2 + 7x - 18$
36. $x^2 - 10x + 24$
37. $x^2 + 10x + 25$
38. $x^2 - 6x - 7$

Answers are on page 877.

Graphs

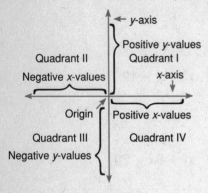

A set of points on a **graph** is called a **coordinate system.** By using a fixed starting point, called the **origin,** we can find any point by using two numbers, called the **coordinates** of that point.

On a **grid,** a horizontal line is called the ***x*-axis** and a vertical line is called the ***y*-axis.** The two axes cross at a point called the **origin.** The grid is divided into four quadrants, labeled as shown in the diagram.

Starting from the origin, we count positive numbers to the right on the *x*-axis and count negative numbers to the left. On the *y*-axis, we count up to locate positive numbers, and we count down to locate negative numbers.

Each point on the grid is named by two numbers, an *x*-coordinate (always written first) and a *y*-coordinate (always written second). They are called an **ordered pair** and are enclosed in parentheses, separated by a comma: (x, y).

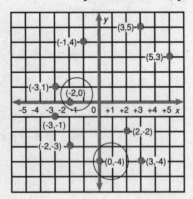

Plot a point with *x*-coordinate 0, like $(0, -4)$:
1. Start at the origin, move 0 on the *x*-axis (no move).
2. Then move -4 on the *y*-axis. The point $(0, -4)$ is 4 units down on the *y*-axis.

Plot a point with *y*-coordinate 0, like $(-2, 0)$:
1. Start at the origin, move 2 units to the left on the *x*-axis.
2. Then move 0 units on the *y*-axis (no move).

Note: The ordered pair $(5, 3)$ has a different location than the point $(3, 5)$. Remember, the point on the *x*-axis is *always* named first.

Graphing Equations

An equation with two variables might look like this: $2x - y = 4$. Graphing techniques help us to understand and solve such equations.

To solve an equation with two variables, we need to find a value for *x* and a value for *y* that makes the equation true. Follow these steps:

Step 1: Choose any value for one variable and substitute it into the equation. Substitute -2 for *x*: $2(-2) - y = 4$.

Step 2: Solve the equation for the other variable.
$$2(-2) - y = 4 \qquad -4 - y = 4 \qquad -y = 8 \qquad y = -8$$

Step 3: Write the solution as an ordered pair (x, y): $(-2, -8)$

There are many ordered pairs that are solutions to an equation with two variables.

Now find a second solution to the same equation:

Substitute 0 for *y* $\qquad 2x - y = 4$

Solve for *x*: $\qquad 2x - 0 = 4; \ x = 2$

So, **(2, 0)** is another solution.

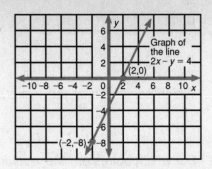

Locate both ordered pairs, $(-2, -8)$ and $(2, 0)$ on a grid, and draw a line through them. The result is the graph of the equation $2x - y = 4$.

The graph of a **linear equation** is a straight line. Every point on the line satisfies ("solves") the equation.

A graph of the linear equation $x + y = 5$ is shown below. As we have just seen, every pair of coordinates on the line solves the equation, that is, the value for x and y add up to 5.

Graphing Inequalities

An inequality with two variables can be solved by plotting points on the grid.

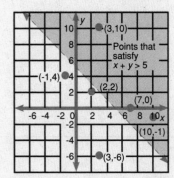

The shaded portion <u>above</u> the line shows the points that satisfy the inequality

$$x + y > 5$$

$(3, 10)$:	$3 + 10 = 13$
$(7, 0)$:	$7 + 0 = 7$
$(10, -1)$:	$10 + (-1) = 9$

All coordinate pairs result in numbers greater than 5.

Slope

Slope is a number that measures the steepness of a line. To find the slope of a line, choose any two points on the line. Then use this formula to find the slope (m):

$m = \dfrac{y_2 - y_1}{x_2 - x_1}$ Note: Either ordered pair can be thought of as (x_1, y_1), but you must be consistent.

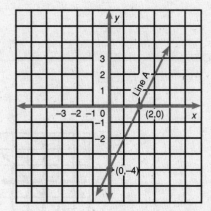

Example: Find the slope of line A.

Choose 2 points on the line. The coordinates of the two points are: $(2, 0)$ and $(0, -4)$.

Use the formula: $m = \dfrac{y_2 - y_1}{x_2 - x_1}$

$$m = \frac{-4 - 0}{0 - 2}$$

$$m = \frac{-4}{-2} = 2$$

The slope of line A is positive 2. All lines that rise as they move from left to right have a positive slope. All lines that fall as they move from left to right have a negative slope. All lines with the same slope are parallel.

Directions: Name the points and the ordered pairs for each point.

Items 39 to 48 refer to the following graph.

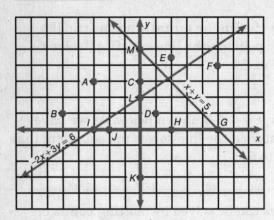

39. Which points have positive *x*-values and positive *y*-values?

40. Which points have negative *x*-values and positive *y*-values?

41. Which points are on the *y*-axis?

42. For which points are the *x*-values equal to the *y*-values?

43. For which points are the *x*-values greater than the *y*-values?

Directions: Name the points that satisfy each equation or inequality.

44. Points on the line $-2x + 3y = 6$.

45. Points in the region $-2x + 3y > 6$.

46. Points in the region $x + y < 5$.

47. Points in the region $x + y > 5$ and also in the region $-2x + 3y > 6$.

48. Points in the region $x + y < 5$ and also in the region $-2x + 3y > 6$.

Directions: Find the slope of each line.

49.

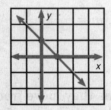

50.

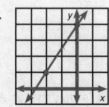

51.

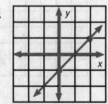

52. The points graphed satisfy which of the following equations?

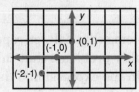

   (1) $x - y = 1$

   (2) $x - y = -1$

   (3) $2y - x = 0$

   (4) $x = 0$

   (5) $y = 0$

53. What is the missing y-value if (2, ?) is a solution of $3x - 4y = 10$?

   (1) $y = -4$

   (2) $y = -3$

   (3) $y = -1$

   (4) $y = 1$

   (5) $y = 4$

54. The ordered pair (2, 1) is a solution of which of these equations?
   A: $x + y = 3$
   B: $2x - y = 3$
   C: $-10x + 15y = -5$

   (1) A

   (2) B

   (3) C

   (4) A and B

   (5) A, B, and C

55. Which ordered pair is a solution of $x - y = 1$?

   (1) $(-3, -4)$

   (2) $(-3, -2)$

   (3) $(-1, 0)$

   (4) $(0, 1)$

   (5) $(1, -2)$

56. The point $(-4, 2)$ belongs to the graph of which of the following?
   A: $2x - 3y = 5$
   B: $2x - 3y < 5$
   C: $2x - 3y > 5$

   (1) A

   (2) B

   (3) C

   (4) both A and B

   (5) $(-4, 2)$ is not part of any of them.

57. Which of these points, A, B, or C, is not a solution of $2x - y = 1$?
   A: (3, 5) B: (1, −3) C: (0, 1)

   (1) A

   (2) B

   (3) C

   (4) Neither A nor B is a solution.

   (5) Neither B nor C is a solution.

58. What is the missing x-value if (?, 1) is a solution of $-4x + 7y = 15$?

   (1) $\frac{-11}{2}$

   (2) -2

   (3) $\frac{19}{7}$

   (4) 2

   (5) $\frac{11}{2}$

59. What is the equation of the line graphed here?

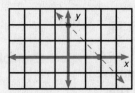

   (1) $x + y = -4$

   (2) $x + y = -2$

   (3) $x + y = 0$

   (4) $x + y = 2$

   (5) $x + y = 4$

Answers are on page 878.

Lesson 22   Exponents and Roots

Exponents

Multiplication is used to simplify problems that call for repeated addition. **Exponents** are used to simplify problems that call for repeated multiplication. The raised 3 in the expression 5^3 is an exponent. The exponent (or "power") tells how many 5's are to be multiplied.

$10^1 = 10$
$10^2 = 10 \times 10 = 100$ (10 squared)
$10^3 = 10 \times 10 \times 10 = 1,000$ (10 cubed)
$10^4 = 10 \times 10 \times 10 \times 10 = 10,000$
$10^5 = 10 \times 10 \times 10 \times 10 \times 10 = 100,000$
$10^6 = 10 \times 10 \times 10 \times 10 \times 10 \times 10 = 1,000,000$

Note: The exponent is the same as the number of zeros. For example:

$10^6 = 1,000,000$

Example: $5^4 = 5 \times 5 \times 5 \times 5 = 625$

We say, "the fourth power of 5 is 625," or "five to the fourth power is 625," or "625 is the fourth power of 5."

An exponent can also be 1, 0, or a negative number.

* Any number to the first power is itself.

$2^1 = 2 \qquad 56^1 = 56 \qquad 10^1 = 10$

* Any number (except 0) to the zero power is 1.

$4^0 = 1 \qquad 3^0 = 1 \qquad 10^0 = 1$

* Any number to a negative power represents a fraction.

Scientific notation is a way of writing these very large or very small numbers. A number written in scientific notation is expressed as a product of a number between one and ten and a power of ten.

Example: Write 5,260,000 in scientific notation.

$10^1 = 10$
$10^0 = 1$
$10^{-1} = \frac{1}{10} = 0.1$
$10^{-2} = \frac{1}{10 \times 10} = 0.01$
$10^{-3} = \frac{1}{10 \times 10 \times 10} = 0.001$

To find a number between one and ten, move the decimal point six places to the left.

$1,000,000 = 10^6$

$5,260,000 = 5.260000 \times 1,000,000$

$= 5.26 \times 10^6$

Note: The "negative exponent" and the number of decimal places are the same.

$10^{-4} = 0.0001$

Example: Write 3.1156×10^{-7} in standard notation.

Write the given number with a string of zeros in front of it. This does not change its value. 00000000003.1156

Move the decimal point to the left as many places as the exponent number. 00000000003.1156
Discard any extra zeros.

Therefore, $3.1156 \times 10^{-7} = 0.00000031156$.

Mathematics ◆ Algebra

Example: What is the side of a square if the area is 25 square inches?

$$x = ?$$

$$A = 25 \text{ sq in}$$

Remember that the area of a square is found by multiplying the length of one side by itself: $A = 5 \times 5$. If the side is 5 inches long, the area is $5^2 = 5 \times 5 = 25$, or 25 square inches.

Since $5^2 = 25$, the length of each side of the square in the example is 5 inches. The number 5 is called a square root of 25. A **square root** is a number that when multiplied times itself equals the given number. The symbol for square root is $\sqrt{\ }$.

$$5^2 = 25 \quad \sqrt{25} = 5$$

To find the square root of a number, ask yourself "What number times itself equals the number?"

Remember, if you know the squares you can find many square roots.

$1^2 = 1$	$5^2 = 25$	$9^2 = 81$
$2^2 = 4$	$6^2 = 36$	$10^2 = 100$
$3^2 = 9$	$7^2 = 49$	$11^2 = 121$
$4^2 = 16$	$8^2 = 64$	$12^2 = 144$

Example: What is $\sqrt{144}$? (Say, "What is the square root of 144?")

$$\text{Since } 12^2 = 144, \sqrt{144} = 12.$$

Sometimes a square root is not a whole number.

Example: What is $\sqrt{55}$?

What number times itself equals 55? You know that 7^2 is 49 and 8^2 is 64. So the square root of 55 must be **between 7 and 8** because 55 is between 49 and 64.

You can use trial and error or a calculator to estimate $\sqrt{55}$. Since $(7.3)^2 = 53.29$, $(7.4)^2 = 54.76$, and $(7.5)^2 = 56.25$, the square root of 55 is about 7.4.

When a number comes before the square root symbol, that number is multiplied by the square root.

Example: What is $2\sqrt{81}$?

$2\sqrt{81}$ means "2 times the square root of 81."

Since the square root of 81 is 9, the expression equals 18.

$$2\sqrt{81} = 2(9) = \textbf{18}$$

Directions: Find each value.

1. 2^4 3. 5^2 5. 5^3 7. 6^2 9. 10^4

2. 1^3 4. 4^5 6. 2^6 8. 5^4 10. 8^2

11. 6×10^3 13. 56×10^4 15. $5^2 - 3^2 - 1^2$

12. 3×10^2 14. $2^2 + 2^3$ 16. $3^2 + 2^2$

Directions: Find these values involving special exponents.

17. 10^0 18. 5^1 19. 10^{-4} 20. 10^{-2} 21. 2^0

Directions: Apply your knowledge of exponents to evaluate the following.

22. $(6 \times 10^3) + (3 \times 10^2)$ 24. $(3.1 \times 10^3) - (1.3 \times 10^1)$

23. $(4 \times 10^2) - (5 \times 10^1)$ 25. $(6.25 \times 10^3) + (5 \times 10^2)$

Directions: Evaluate these fractional and decimal values.

26. $\left(\frac{1}{2}\right)^2$ 27. $\left(\frac{1}{2}\right)^3$ 28. $(0.2)^2$ 29. $(0.05)^2$

Directions: Complete this chart to evaluate each number.

	Scientific Notation		Decimal Form		Value
30.	4.1×10^{-1}	$=$	4.1×0.1	$=$	
31.		$=$	6.1×0.01	$=$	0.061
32.	4.65×10^{-2}	$=$		$=$	0.0465

Directions: Write the square roots.

33. $\sqrt{16}$ 35. $\sqrt{81}$ 37. $\sqrt{169}$

34. $\sqrt{0}$ 36. $\sqrt{49}$ 38. $\sqrt{1}$

Directions: Choose the best answer to each item.

39. The distance across the sun, in scientific notation, is 8.65×10^5 miles. What is this distance in standard notation?

    (1) 86,500,000 mi
    (2)   8,650,000 mi
    (3)   865,000 mi
    (4)   0.00000865 mi
    (5)   0.00865 mi

40. Decide which of these are true and which are false.
    $3^4 = 64$ $8^2 = 64$ $4^3 = 64$

    (1) All are true.
    (2) Only $8^2 = 64$ is true.
    (3) Only $4^3 = 64$ is true.
    (4) Only $3^4 = 64$ is false.
    (5) All are false.

41. The square root of 22 is between which of the following pairs of numbers?

    (1) 2.2 and 2.3
    (2) 3 and 4
    (3) 4 and 5
    (4) 5 and 6
    (5) 21 and 22

42. Which of the following has the numbers in order from least to greatest?

    (1) 4.7×10^{-1}, 2.34×10^2, 5.2×10^2
    (2) 4.7×10^{-1}, 5.2×10^2, 2.34×10^2
    (3) 2.34×10^2, 4.7×10^{-1}, 5.2×10^2
    (4) 2.34×10^2, 5.2×10^2, 4.7×10^{-1}
    (5) 5.2×10^2, 4.7×10^{-1}, 2.34×10^2

43. Since $10^2 = 100$ and $10^4 = 10,000$, what power of 10 represents $10^2 \times 10^4$?

    (1) 10^3
    (2) 10^4
    (3) 10^5
    (4) 10^6
    (5) 10^7

44. Arrange these numbers in order from least to greatest value: 10^2, 2^7, 3^4.

    (1) 2^7 is the least and 10^2 is the greatest.
    (2) 3^4 is the least and 10^2 is the greatest.
    (3) 3^4 is the least and 2^7 is the greatest.
    (4) 10^2 is the least and 2^7 is the greatest.
    (5) All are false.

45. Mario and Lucia disagree on the meaning of the expression $3^2 - 2^3$. Mario says it means $9 - 6$, or 3. Lucia says it means $6 - 6$, or 0. Who is right?

    (1) Mario is right.
    (2) Lucia is right.
    (3) They are both right.
    (4) They are both wrong, since the expression equals 1.
    (5) They are both wrong, since the expression equals 2.

46. If you know that $2^{10} = 1,024$, how would you find 2^{12}?

    (1) Add 2.
    (2) Add 4.
    (3) Multiply by 12.
    (4) Multiply by 2.
    (5) Multiply by 2, and then multiply by 2 again.

Answers are on page 879.

ged Review Algebra

Directions: Choose the <u>best answer</u> to each item.

1. Write an equation for the following: The product of a number and −4 is 8 more than 2 added to −5 times that number.

   (1) $-4x = -5x + 2 + 8$
   (2) $-4x - 8 = 2x + (-5x)$
   (3) $-4x + 8 = -5x + 2$
   (4) $-4x = 8 + 2 + (-5)$
   (5) $-4x = 8 + (-5 + 2)x$

2. What are the factors of $x^2 - 8x + 15$?

   (1) $(x - 3)(5 - x)$
   (2) $(x - 3)(x + 5)$
   (3) $(x + 3)(x + 5)$
   (4) $(x + 3)(x - 5)$
   (5) $(x - 3)(x - 5)$

3. The pair $(-1, -2)$ is a solution of which of these equations?
   A. $x + 2y = -3$
   B. $2x - y = -2$
   C. $x + y = -3$

   (1) A and B
   (2) A and C
   (3) B and C
   (4) B only
   (5) C only

4. Which inequality is graphed here?

   -3 -2 -1 0 1 2 3 4 5 6 7 8 9

   (1) $1 < x < 4$
   (2) $1 > x > 4$
   (3) $1 > x < 4$
   (4) $1 < x > 4$
   (5) None of the options is correct.

5. Simplify: $2 - (x + 7)$.

   (1) $x - 9$
   (2) $x - 9$
   (3) $-x - 5$
   (4) $-x - 9$
   (5) $-x + 9$

6. Find the value of $4x - 2y + xy$ if $x = -1$ and $y = 5$.

   (1) -26
   (2) -19
   (3) -9
   (4) -1
   (5) 1

7. What is the missing number?
   $7(x + 3) = 7x +$ _____

   (1) 7
   (2) 3
   (3) 21
   (4) $3x$
   (5) $10x$

8. Solve: $-6(x + 1) + 4 = 8x - 9$.

   (1) $\frac{1}{2}$
   (2) $-\frac{1}{2}$
   (3) -1
   (4) -3
   (5) -5

9. Solve the following inequality:
   $3x + 7 < -2x + 2$.

   (1) $x < -1$
   (2) $x < 1$
   (3) $x < -\frac{1}{5}$
   (4) $x < \frac{1}{5}$
   (5) $x < -5$

10. Which of the following expresses this equation?
$$x - 2 = \frac{x}{4} + 7$$

(1) Two less than x equals 7 more than 4 divided by x.

(2) Two less than x is the same as 7 more than the quotient of x and 4.

(3) Two subtracted from x equals 4 into 7 more than x.

(4) x less than 2 is the same as x divided by 4 plus 7.

(5) x subtracted from 2 equals 4 divided by x, increased by 7.

11. Which of the following shows the product of -6 and x, subtracted from the sum of -6 and y?

(1) $-6x - (-6 + y)$

(2) $(-6 + x) - (-6 + y)$

(3) $(-6 + x) - (-6y)$

(4) $(-6 + y) - (-6x)$

(5) $(-6y) - (-6x)$

12. Which expression is correct for the following: two less than the quotient of x and 6?

(1) $\frac{x - 2}{6}$

(2) $\frac{2 - x}{6}$

(3) $2 - \frac{x}{6}$

(4) $x - \frac{2}{6}$

(5) $\frac{x}{6} - 2$

13. Simplify this expression:
$7x + 5 - 3x - 8$.

(1) $-4x - 13$

(2) $1x$ or x

(3) $4x - 3$

(4) $10x - 3$

(5) $7x - 2x - 8$

14. Solve: $2(2x + 3) = -3(x + 5)$.

(1) $x = -21$

(2) $x = -3$

(3) $x = \frac{2}{7}$

(4) $x = -18$

(5) $x = 14$

15. "Three more than the number I'm thinking of is 30," says Joe. "Then 10 less than your number," says Jill, "is the number ? ."

(1) 17

(2) 23

(3) 33

(4) 37

(5) 43

16. Coop and Carni are two cats. Coop is 4 months older than Carni. Three months ago, 5 times Coop's age in months was the same as 7 times Carni's age in months. Complete the chart. What is the entry for box 4?

	Coop's Age in Months	Carni's Age in Months
Now	1 x	2 $x - 4$
3 months ago	3	4

(1) $(x - 4) - 3$

(2) $5(x - 4)$

(3) $7(x - 4)$

(4) $\frac{7}{5}(x - 4)$

(5) $\frac{5}{7}(x - 4)$

17. Multiply: $(x + 9)(x - 2)$.

    (1) $x^2 + 11x - 18$

    (2) $x^2 - 11x - 18$

    (3) $x^2 + 7x - 18$

    (4) $x^2 + 7x + 18$

    (5) $x^2 - 7x + 18$

18. Which inequality is graphed on the number line?

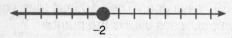

    (1) $x \leq -2$

    (2) $x < -2$

    (3) $-2 \leq x$

    (4) $-2 > x$

    (5) $2 = x$

19. In solving this inequality, $-7x < 10$, what is the next step?

    (1) $x < \frac{10}{7}$

    (2) $x < \frac{-10}{7}$

    (3) $-x < \frac{7}{10}$

    (4) $x > \frac{10}{7}$

    (5) $x > \frac{-10}{7}$

20. Ten less than a number is equal to the same number divided by 2. What is the number?

    (1)   8

    (2) 10

    (3) 14

    (4) 20

    (5) 28

21. Factor: $8x^2 + 12x$.

    (1) $x(4x + 3x)$

    (2) $4(x + 3x)$

    (3) $4x(2x + 3)$

    (4) $4x(2 + 3x)$

    (5) $4x(2x + 3x)$

Items 22 to 25 refer to the following graph.

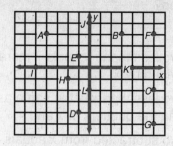

22. Which points have positive x-values and negative y-values?

    (1) A, E

    (2) A, E, I

    (3) C, G

    (4) C, G, L

    (5) C, G, L, K

23. Which points have a y-value equal to 0?

    (1) K

    (2) J and L

    (3) I and K

    (4) I, J, K, L

    (5) None have a y-value of 0.

24. If the line for $x - y = 8$ were drawn on the graph, which of the following points would be on the line?

    (1) A

    (2) B

    (3) C

    (4) D

    (5) E

25. What would be the slope of a line passing through points J and K?

    (1) $\frac{1}{2}$

    (2) 0

    (3) $-\frac{1}{2}$

    (4) -1

    (5) -2

26. Which statement is true?
    A. $-5 < -6$
    B. $3 < -2$
    C. $0 < -7$

    (1) A
    (2) B
    (3) C
    (4) All are true.
    (5) All are false.

27. The square root of 70 is found between which pair of numbers?

    (1) 5 and 6
    (2) 6 and 7
    (3) 7 and 8
    (4) 8 and 9
    (5) 9 and 10

28. Becky's mother is twice as old as Becky. Eleven years ago her mother was three times as old as Becky. Let x represent Becky's present age. Which equation shows their age relationship?

    (1) $x - 11 = 3(2x - 11)$
    (2) $x - 11 = 2x - 11$
    (3) $2(x - 11) = 2x - 22$
    (4) $3(x - 11) = 2x - 11$
    (5) $3(x - 11) = 3x - 33$

29. Two of the following have the same value. Which two are they?
    A. $4 + (1 - 4)$ C. $6 - (3 + 2)$
    B. $(7 - 3) + 1$ D. $8 - (1 - 2)$

    (1) A and B
    (2) A and C
    (3) B and C
    (4) B and D
    (5) C and D

30. Divide -12 by the sum of 4 and -2. The result is:

    (1) -6
    (2) -2
    (3) 1
    (4) 2
    (5) 6

31. Which value for x makes the following inequality true: $x > 1,000$?

    (1) 2^5
    (2) 4^3
    (3) 4^5
    (4) 5^4
    (5) 6^3

32. Express 9,800,000 in scientific notation.

    (1) 9.8×10^3
    (2) 9.8×10^4
    (3) 9.8×10^5
    (4) 9.8×10^6
    (5) 9.8×10^7

33. The pair $(-1,1)$ is a solution of which of the following equations?

    (1) $2x - 3y = 1$
    (2) $3x - 2y = -5$
    (3) $4x + 2y = 6$
    (4) $-2x - 3y = 1$
    (5) $-3x + 2y = -1$

34. Which of the following represents 0.0024 written in scientific notation?

    (1) 2.4×10^4
    (2) 2.4×10^{-2}
    (3) 2.4×10^2
    (4) 2.4×10^{-4}
    (5) 2.4×10^{-3}

Answers are on page 879.

Geometry

line segment
part of a line

arc
part of a circle

angle
a pair of rays meeting at a point

right angle
an angle that makes a "square corner" that measures 90 degrees

dimension
a measurement of length, width, or thickness

plane
a set of points that forms a flat surface

geometry
the study of points, lines, angles, and figures in space

triangle
a figure with 3 sides and 3 angles

scale
a relationship between two sets of measurements

Pythagorean Theorem
in a right triangle, the square of the hypotenuse equals the sum of the squares of the other two sides

In geometry you will study shapes that you see and use every day. These shapes are made of simple geometric ingredients—**line segments, arcs,** and **angles,** many of which are **right angles.**

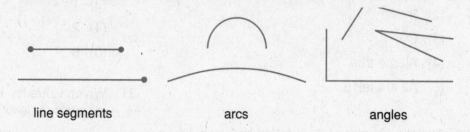

line segments   arcs   angles

Look around your home at the rooms, furniture, clothing, and household objects, and outside at buildings, streets, and bridges. All around us are examples of these simple **two-dimensional** forms. We will learn about these figures in our study of **plane geometry.**

A **plane** is a set of points that forms a flat surface. A plane figure has only two dimensions. Some examples of plane figures are circles, squares, rectangles, and triangles.

The word **geometry** means "earth measure" (*geo:* earth, *metry:* measure). The three-dimensional, or solid, objects all around us are made up of plane figures: a cube is made up of squares; a sphere, or ball, is a circle that has been spun around its diameter. In Lesson 23 you will learn how to measure the inside space, or volume, of solid objects.

In Lesson 24 you will learn about angles. Many of the plane figures are made from angles. One of the most important figures is the **triangle.** It is formed from three lines and contains three angles. You will learn more about triangles and other plane figures in Lesson 25.

Lesson 26 will show you how to tell when two figures have the same shape and size. Of course, you can always use a tape measure, but many things in our world are simply too large to measure in the mechanical way. In this lesson, you will learn how to use an object's shadow to find its height. You will also learn to interpret maps and **scale** drawings.

The early Egyptians are given credit for observing the first geometric relationships. In Lesson 27 you will study one of their most famous discoveries, the **Pythagorean Theorem.** This theorem shows the relationship of the three sides of a right triangle. The discovery grew from the needs of the early Egyptians to survey their lands each year after the annual floods on the Nile River. While you may not need to survey land, an understanding of geometry is important and of practical application to modern life.

Volume

Volume measures the amount of space inside a three-dimensional object. It is measured in cubic units—cubic inches, cubic feet, cubic yards. Each of these units is a cube made up of square sides, all the same size. To visualize volume, think of space filled with neat layers of ice cubes.

Rectangular Solid
all square corners
$V = A \times h$
$V = l \times w \times h$

Three of the most common solid shapes are the **rectangular solid** (cereal box), the **cube** (ice cube), and the **cylinder** (soup can). Formulas for finding their volumes are the same.

Volume = (area of the base) × height

The area of the base may be given as part of the data, or it may have to be calculated.

Example: What is the volume of a rectangular solid that is 14 inches long, 8 inches wide, and 4 inches high?

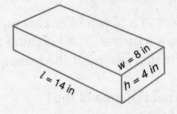

First find the area of the base:
$A = l \times w = 14 \times 8 = 112$ square inches

Now substitute this value into the volume formula:
$V = (\text{area of the base}) \times \text{height}$
$\quad = 112 \text{ sq in} \times 4 \text{ in}$
$\quad = 448 \text{ cu in}$

From this example you can see that for a rectangular solid:
Volume = length × width × height

Cube
rectangular solid
all sides square
$V = s \times s \times s$
or $V = s^3$

A **cube** is a special rectangular solid, so the same formula holds.

Example: Find the volume of a cube that is 3 feet along each side.

Volume = side × side × side
$\quad = 3 \text{ ft} \times 3 \text{ ft} \times 3 \text{ ft}$
$\quad = 27 \text{ cu ft}$

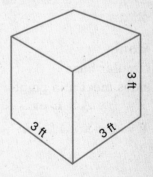

From this example, you can see that the volume of a cube is equal to the length of one side multiplied times itself three times, or cubed.

Cylinder
circular base
straight sides
$V = $ **Area of base** $\times h$
or
$V = \pi \times r^2 \times h$

Example: Find the approximate volume of a cylinder if the radius of the base is 2 feet and the height of the cylinder is 10 feet.

First find the area of the base.
$$A = \pi r^2$$
Use 3.14 for π.
$$= 3.14 \times 4$$
$$= 12.56 \text{ sq ft}$$

Use the area in the formula for volume.
$$V = A \times h$$
$$= 12.56 \times 10$$
$$= 125.6 \text{ cu ft,}$$
which rounds to
126 cu ft

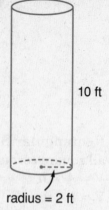
10 ft
radius = 2 ft

Two other shapes, **pyramids** and **cones,** have volume formulas that are the same. The volume of each solid is $\frac{1}{3}$ as great as its corresponding rectangular solid or cylinder.

$$V = \frac{1}{3} \times A \,(\text{area of base}) \times h \,(\text{height})$$

Pyramid
base has equal sides

Example: The base of a pyramid is a triangle with height 12 inches and base 4 inches. The height of the pyramid is 16 inches. What is the volume of the pyramid?

First find the area of the base of the pyramid.
$$A = \frac{1}{2}bh$$
$$= \frac{1}{2}(12)(4)$$
$$= 24 \text{ sq in}$$

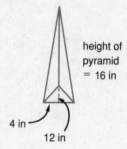
height of
pyramid
= 16 in
4 in
12 in

Use the area in the formula for volume.
$$V = \frac{1}{3} \times \text{area of base} \times h$$
$$= \frac{1}{3} \times 24 \times 16$$
$$= 128 \text{ cu in}$$

Cone
circular base
sides meet at a point
$V = \frac{1}{3} \times A \times h$ or
$V = \frac{1}{3} \times \pi \times r^2 \times h$

Example: Find the volume of a cone if the area of the base is 4 square inches and the height is 9 inches.

$$V = \frac{1}{3} \times \text{area of base} \times h$$
$$= \frac{1}{3} \times 4 \times 9$$
$$= 12 \text{ cu in}$$

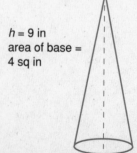
h = 9 in
area of base =
4 sq in

The units of measurement you use in formulas must be the same. So *before* you calculate your answer, remember to *convert to like units.*

Example: What is the volume of the rectangular solid?

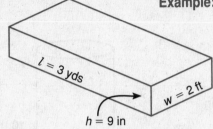

The formula you will need to solve the problem is $V = lwh$. But before you multiply you will need to convert the measurements given in the figure to the same unit of measurement.

Here the problem is solved by converting to inches.
$$\text{Volume} = \text{length} \times \text{width} \times \text{height}$$
$$= 108 \text{ in} \times 24 \text{ in} \times 9 \text{ in}$$
$$= \mathbf{23,328} \text{ cu in}$$

Convert to feet:
$$\text{Volume} = \text{length} \times \text{width} \times \text{height}$$
$$= 9 \text{ ft} \times 2 \text{ ft} \times \tfrac{3}{4} \text{ ft}$$
$$= 13\tfrac{1}{2} \text{ cu ft}$$

Convert to yards:
$$\text{Volume} = \text{length} \times \text{width} \times \text{height}$$
$$= 3 \text{ yds} \times \tfrac{2}{3} \text{ yd} \times \tfrac{1}{4} \text{ yd}$$
$$= \tfrac{1}{2} \text{ cu yd}$$

Each answer represents the same quantity:
$$23,328 \text{ cubic inches} = 13\tfrac{1}{2} \text{ cu ft} = \tfrac{1}{2} \text{ cu yd}$$

How do you decide which unit to choose? Generally, it is easiest to convert to the smallest unit of measure so that you will not have to work with fractions. Another factor to consider is the answer options. Always convert to the unit of measure given in the answer options.

A figure may be made up of several shapes. To find the volume of a combined figure, find the volume of each of the parts and add the results.

Example: Find the volume of the object shown below.

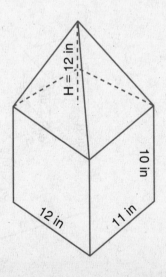

Find the volume of the pyramid.
First, find the area of the base:
$$A = lw$$
$$= 12(11)$$
$$= 132 \text{ sq in}$$
Next find the volume of the pyramid:
$$V = \tfrac{1}{3} Ah$$
$$= \tfrac{1}{3}(132)(12)$$
$$= 44(12)$$
$$= 528 \text{ cu in}$$
Then find the volume of the rectangular solid:
$$V = lwh$$
$$= 12(11)(10)$$
$$= 132(10)$$
$$= 1,320 \text{ cu in}$$
Add the results: $528 + 1,320 = \mathbf{1,848 \text{ cu in}}$

Directions: For <u>items 1 to 3</u>, name the figure and find its volume.

1.

6 in
8 in
15 in

2.

5.1 in
5.1 in   5.1 in

3.

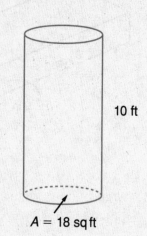

10 ft

$A = 18$ sq ft

Directions: For <u>items 4 to 6</u>, find the volume of each figure. Round your answers to the nearest whole number.

4.

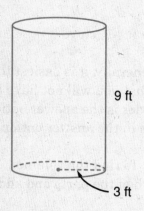

9 ft

3 ft

5.

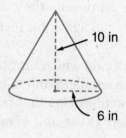

10 in

6 in

6.

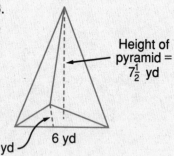

Height of pyramid = $7\frac{1}{2}$ yd

2 yd   6 yd

Directions: Each object below is made of two or more solid shapes combined into one. Name the shapes and find the volume of the object.

7.

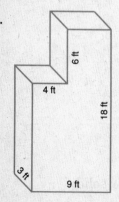

6 ft
4 ft
18 ft
3 ft
9 ft

8.

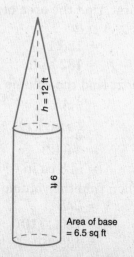

h = 12 ft

9 ft

Area of base
= 6.5 sq ft

9.

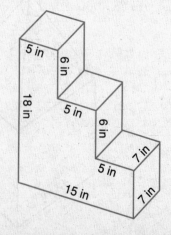

5 in
6 in
18 in
5 in
6 in
7 in
5 in
15 in
7 in

10. What is the volume in cubic inches of a rectangular solid with these measurements: length = 15 inches, width = 24 inches, and height = 4 inches?

    (1) 1,280
    (2) 1,410
    (3) 1,440
    (4) 1,520
    (5) 1,640

11. What is the volume in cubic yards of a cube that measures 2 yards on one side?

    (1) 6
    (2) 7
    (3) 7.5
    (4) 8
    (5) 9

12. The city is going to build a swimming pool. The hole needs to be 100 feet long by 25 feet wide. The depth needs to be 1 yard 2 feet. How many cubic feet of dirt will have to be removed to dig the hole?

    (1)   1,250
    (2)   2,500
    (3)   5,000
    (4) 12,500
    (5) 50,000

13. A contractor building a group of houses has a large amount of trash to be removed. The trash containers are 4 yards long, 8 feet wide, and 2 yards high. How many cubic feet of trash can each container hold?

    (1)   48
    (2)   72
    (3)   96
    (4) 192
    (5) 576

14. A cylindrical tank has a base area of 9.1 square feet and a height of 6 feet. What is the volume of the tank in cubic feet?

    (1)   5.46
    (2) 27.3
    (3) 54.6
    (4) 273
    (5) 546

15. What is the volume in cubic centimeters of a cone with height 8 centimeters and base area 12.6 square centimeters?

    (1)   3.36
    (2) 10.08
    (3) 33.6
    (4) 100.8
    (5) Not enough information is given.

16. The base of a pyramid is a triangle with height 3 feet and base 6 feet. The height of the pyramid is $12\frac{1}{2}$ feet. What is the volume of the pyramid in cubic feet?

    (1)   18
    (2) $37\frac{1}{2}$
    (3)   75
    (4) $112\frac{1}{2}$
    (5) 117

17. The base of a cone is a circle with a radius of 2 inches. The height of the cone is 6 inches. What is the approximate volume of the cone in cubic inches?

    (1) 12
    (2) 19
    (3) 25
    (4) 50
    (5) 75

Answers are on page 881.

Lesson 24   Angles

Angles

Ray

Vertex

An **angle** is the space between a pair of lines, called **rays,** which extend away from a common point, the **vertex.** Angles are named by the three letters that label the rays and the vertex or the letter of the vertex alone. The sign for angle is ∠. Thus, at left, point *B* is the vertex of ∠*ABC* (or ∠*B*.)

Degree

Angles are identified by their measure in **degrees**.

Right
Acute
Obtuse
Straight
Reflex

A **right angle** measures 90°.	An **acute angle** measures less than 90°.	An **obtuse angle** measures more than 90° but less than 180°.	A **straight angle** measures 180°.	A **reflex angle** measures more than 180° but less than 360°.

This symbol shows that the angle measures 90°.

Congruent

Angles that have equal measures are called **congruent angles.**

Angle *ABC* is congruent to angle *XYZ*.

∠*ABC* ≅ ∠*XYZ*

This symbol means "is congruent to."

60°   60°

Intersect
Vertical angles

Angles have special relationships because of their location. When two lines intersect or cross, the angles that are across from each other are called **opposite angles** or **vertical angles.** Each pair of opposite angles is **congruent**.

∠5 ≅ ∠6   ∠7 ≅ ∠8

m∠5 = *m*∠6   *m*∠7 = *m*∠8

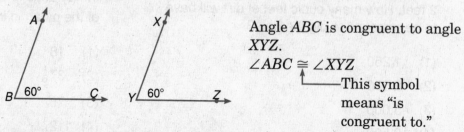

Adjacent
Nonadjacent

Adjacent angles have a common vertex and a common ray. ∠1 and ∠2 are adjacent angles.

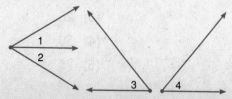

∠3 and ∠4 are examples of **nonadjacent angles.**

620

Mathematics ◆ Geometry

Perpendicular

If two lines form congruent adjacent angles, that is, two right angles, the lines are **perpendicular.** We write $l \perp m$.

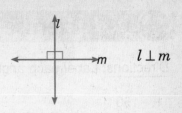

$l \perp m$

Parallel
Transversal

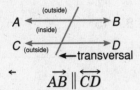

$\overrightarrow{AB} \parallel \overrightarrow{CD}$

Parallel lines are two lines on the same plane that do not intersect. The symbol used is $\parallel$. A line that crosses two or more parallel lines is called a **transversal.** Special pairs of angles are formed when two parallel lines are cut by a transversal.

Corresponding

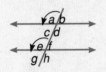

♦ **Corresponding angles** are those angles that are on the same side of the transversal and are either both above or both below the two parallel lines. They are always *equal* in measure.

$\angle a$ and $\angle e$ $\angle c$ and $\angle g$
$\angle b$ and $\angle f$ $\angle d$ and $\angle h$

Alternate exterior

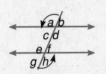

♦ **Alternate exterior angles** are always outside the parallel lines. They are on opposite sides of the transversal. One is above the top parallel line. The other is below the bottom parallel line. They are always *equal* in measure.

$\angle a$ and $\angle h$ $\angle b$ and $\angle g$

Alternate interior

♦ **Alternate interior angles** are always inside the parallel lines. They are on opposite sides of the transversal. One is below the top parallel line. The other is above the bottom parallel line. They are always *equal* in measure.

$\angle c$ and $\angle f$ $\angle d$ and $\angle e$

Complementary

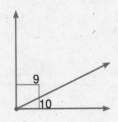

Angles are also named because of the sum of their measures.

♦ If the sum of the measures of two angles is 90°, they are called **complementary angles.**

Example: If the measure of $\angle 10$ is 25°, what is the measure of $\angle 9$?

$$m\angle 9 + m\angle 10 = 90°$$
$$m\angle 9 + 25° \quad = 90°$$
$$m\angle 9 \qquad = 90° - 25° = 65°$$

The measure of $\angle 9$ is **65°**.

Supplementary

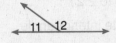

♦ If the sum of the measures of two angles is 180°, they are called **supplementary angles.**

Example: If the measure of $\angle 11$ is 35°, what is the measure of $\angle 12$?

$$m\angle 11 + m\angle 12 = 180°$$
$$35° + m\angle 12 = 180°$$
$$m\angle 12 = 180° - 35° = 145°$$

The measure of $\angle 12$ is **145°**.

---

ged Exercise Angles

Directions: Label each angle as acute, obtuse, right, or straight.

1. 150°
2. 35°
3. 90°
4. 180°
5. 7°
6. 95°
7. 175°
8. 45°

Directions: Answer each item.

Items 9 to 17 refer to the figure at the right.

9. Name an angle adjacent to ∠3.
10. Name the angle that is the vertical angle to ∠2.
11. Name the angle that is the vertical angle to ∠6.
12. Name the angle that is the vertical angle to ∠1.
13. Name two angles that are adjacent to ∠1.
14. Name two angles that are adjacent to ∠5.
15. Name the angle congruent to ∠5.
16. Name the angle congruent to ∠4.
17. Name the angle congruent to ∠3.

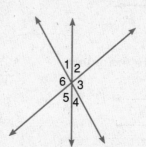

Items 18 to 21 refer to the figure at the right. ∠AXB and ∠BXC are complementary.

18. What is m∠BXC?
19. What is m∠DXC?
20. What is m∠BXD?
21. Which angle forms a supplementary angle with ∠DXC?

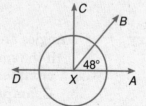

Items 22 to 31 refer to the following figure.

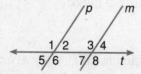

22. Name the interior angles.
23. Name the interior angle on the same side of the transversal as ∠6.
24. Name the exterior angles.
25. Name the exterior angle on the same side of the transversal as ∠4.

26. Which angle corresponds to ∠1?
27. Which angle corresponds to ∠7?
28. Which angle corresponds to ∠8?
29. Which angle corresponds to ∠2?
30. Which angle is an alternate interior angle with ∠2?
31. Which angle is an alternate exterior angle with ∠5?

32. How many acute angles are there in this figure?

    (1) 2
    (2) 4
    (3) 5
    (4) 6
    (5) 8

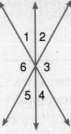

33. The measure of ∠A is 28°. The measure of ∠B is 62°. Which of the following is true?

    (1) ∠A is complementary to ∠B.
    (2) ∠A and ∠B are congruent.
    (3) ∠A and ∠B are obtuse angles.
    (4) ∠A is adjacent to ∠B.
    (5) ∠B is adjacent to ∠A.

34. ∠M and ∠R are complementary angles. The measure of ∠M is 40°. What is the measure of ∠R?

    (1) 40°
    (2) 50°
    (3) 90°
    (4) 140°
    (5) 180°

35. Line A is parallel to line B. Which statement is true?

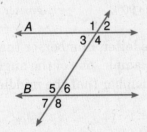

    (1) ∠1 = ∠7
    (2) m∠2 + m∠6 = 90°
    (3) ∠5 is complementary to ∠B.
    (4) m∠6 − m∠7 = 180°
    (5) m∠1 + m∠7 = 180°

Items 36 to 38 refer to the following figure.

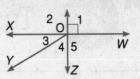

36. An angle that is supplementary, but not adjacent to, ∠2 is

    (1) ∠1.
    (2) ∠5.
    (3) ∠XOZ.
    (4) ∠WOY.
    (5) ∠WOX.

37. The measure of ∠3 is 25°. What is the measure of ∠WOY?

    (1) 65°
    (2) 115°
    (3) 135°
    (4) 155°
    (5) 165°

38. An angle that is supplementary to ∠XOZ must also be

    (1) an acute angle.
    (2) a right angle.
    (3) an obtuse angle.
    (4) a vertical angle.
    (5) congruent to ∠3.

39. ∠Q is congruent to its vertical angle, ∠R. Which of the following must be true?

    (1) ∠Q and ∠R are complementary angles.
    (2) ∠Q and ∠R are both acute angles.
    (3) ∠Q and ∠R are both obtuse angles.
    (4) ∠Q and ∠R are supplementary angles.
    (5) ∠Q and ∠R have the same degree measure.

Answers are on page 882.

Triangles and Quadrilaterals

Triangles

A geometric figure with three sides and three angles is called a **triangle.** A triangle is named by writing the vertices in any order. Triangles are identified in two ways: by the lengths of their sides and by the measure of their angles.

By the length of their sides: are any two sides equal, or congruent?

Equilateral Triangle	Isosceles Triangle	Scalene Triangle

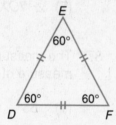 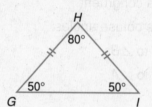 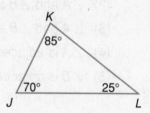

Note: The symbol ‖ is used to denote which sides are congruent. Sometimes the marks | or ||| are also used.

All sides and all angles are congruent. Two sides and their opposite angles are congruent. No sides and no angles are congruent.

By the measure of their angles:

Right Triangle	Acute Triangle	Obtuse Triangle

 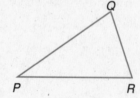 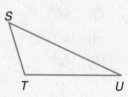

One angle is a right angle (90°). All three angles are acute angles (less than 90°). One angle is an obtuse angle (greater than 90°).

Recall that an angle is named by one letter, number, or the three letters that form it. In △MNO, for example, one of the angles can be called ∠O or ∠MON or ∠NOM. Remember that the middle letter is the vertex point.

In any triangle, the sum of the measures of the angles is 180°. To show this, cut out a triangle, tear off the corners, and arrange the corners to make a straight line. We can use this fact to find certain missing angle measures of a triangle.

In any triangle:
$m\angle 1 + m\angle 2 + m\angle 3 = 180°$
In a right triangle:
$m\angle 1 = 90°$
$m\angle 2 + m\angle 3 = 90°$

Example: If the larger acute angle of a right triangle is twice the measure of the smaller acute angle, what is the measure of the smaller acute angle?

Draw a picture. Remember: a right triangle has a right angle (90°).

Let x = measure of the smaller acute angle

Then $2x$ = measure of the larger acute angle

$$x + 2x + 90° = 180°$$
$$3x = 90°$$
$$x = 30°$$

The smaller acute angle is **30°.**

Geometry problems are often solved using logic. Draw conclusions from the information given in the problem.

Example: The sum of the measures of angles 1 and 2 is 180°. The sum of the measures of angles 2 and 3 is 180°. Which of the following statements is true?

(1) $m\angle 1 = 120°$
(2) $m\angle 2 = 60°$
(3) $m\angle 3 = 100°$
(4) $m\angle 1 > m\angle 2$
(5) $m\angle 1 = m\angle 3$

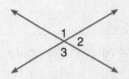

Options (1), (2), (3), and (4) are incorrect because the assumptions given do not provide any information about the measures of each angle. Use only the information in the problem and any labels on the figure.

Consider the facts: $m\angle 1 + m\angle 2 = 180°$
$$m\angle 2 + m\angle 3 = 180°$$
$$m\angle 1 + m\angle 2 = m\angle 2 + m\angle 3$$

Then:
Subtract $m\angle 2$ from
both sides: $m\angle 1 = m\angle 3$
Option (5) is correct.

Quadrilaterals

Any geometric figure with four sides is called a **quadrilateral.** A line segment drawn between the vertices of two nonadjacent sides is called a **diagonal** of the quadrilateral. The sum of the four angles of a quadrilateral is 360°. Quadrilaterals have special names.

Parallelogram	**Rectangle**	**Rhombus**	**Square**	**Trapezoid**
		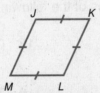		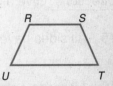
A quadrilateral with opposite sides parallel and congruent, and opposite angles equal.	A special parallelogram with four right angles.	A parallelogram with four sides of equal length.	A rectangle with sides of equal length, or a rhombus with right angles.	A quadrilateral with only one pair of parallel sides; the parallel sides are called **bases.**

ged Exercise Triangles and Quadrilaterals

Directions: Provide the correct answer to each item.

Items 1 to 5 refer to the figure at the right. (Hint: There are 5 triangles.)

1. Name an equilateral triangle.
2. Name an isosceles triangle.
3. Name an obtuse triangle.
4. Name an acute triangle.
5. Name a scalene triangle.

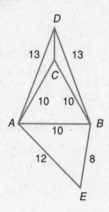

Items 6 to 14 refer to the figure at the right.

6. Name the triangle that has a right angle at *B*.

7. Name two triangles that have right angles at *D*.

8. Name two triangles that have right angles at *C*.

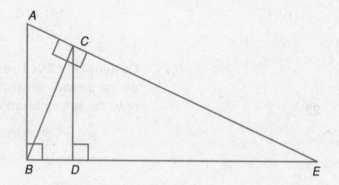

For items 9 to 14, $m\angle A = 55°$. (Hint: Label the angles as you compute their measures.)

9. If $m\angle A = 55°$, then what is $m\angle E$?

10. What is $m\angle ABC$?

11. What is $m\angle DCE$?

12. What is $m\angle CBD$?

13. What is $m\angle BCD$?

14. How are the four triangles in the figure similar?

Directions: Give all possibilities for the names of the following four-sided figures.

15. All sides have lengths of 10 inches.

16. All corners are right angles.

17. Opposite sides are parallel.

18. Only two sides are parallel.

19. There are no right angles.

20. Only one pair of opposite sides is equal.

Mathematics ◆ Geometry

Directions: Choose the best answer to each item.

21. In a right triangle the measure of one acute angle is 4 times the measure of the other acute angle. What is the measure of the smaller angle?

    (1) less than 10°
    (2) between 10° and 15°
    (3) between 15° and 20°
    (4) between 20° and 25°
    (5) greater than 25°

22. A four-sided figure has sides in order of 8, 12, 8, 12. There are no right angles. What is the figure?

    (1) triangle
    (2) square
    (3) trapezoid
    (4) rhombus
    (5) parallelogram

23. Which statement is true of the following figure?

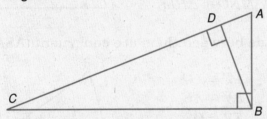

    (1) △ABC is an equilateral triangle.
    (2) △ABC is an obtuse triangle.
    (3) △ABC is an acute triangle.
    (4) There are exactly two right triangles.
    (5) There are exactly three right triangles.

24. A triangle has sides 10, 10, and 8. What type of triangle is it?

    (1) isosceles
    (2) scalene
    (3) equilateral
    (4) obtuse
    (5) right

25. In a triangle the measure of one angle is 15° more than the measure of the smallest, and the measure of the third is twice the measure of the smallest. If x is the measure of the smallest angle, then what is the equation to find the three angle measures?

    (1) $(x) + (x + 15°) = 2x$
    (2) $(x) + (x + 15°) + (2x) = 180°$
    (3) $(x) + (15°) + (2 \cdot 15°) = 180°$
    (4) $(x) + (x - 15°) + (2x) = 180°$
    (5) $(15°) + (x + 15°) + (2x) = 180°$

26. How many triangles are in the figure?

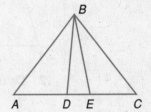

    (1) 1
    (2) 3
    (3) 4
    (4) 6
    (5) 7

27. How many isosceles triangles are there in the figure?

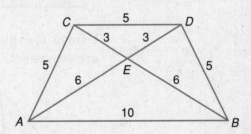

    (1) 1
    (2) 2
    (3) 3
    (4) 4
    (5) 5

Answers are on page 883.

Lesson 26 Congruence and Similarity

Congruence

Congruent figures are the same shape and size. One figure will fit perfectly on top of the other. Triangles that are exactly the same shape and size are called **congruent triangles** (symbol: ≅). Congruent triangles have matching or corresponding vertices, congruent corresponding sides, and congruent corresponding angles. Marks show which parts correspond. Below are three ways to show that two triangles are congruent.

(1) Three sides are congruent (SSS).

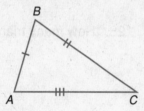

$$\overline{AB} \cong \overline{DE}$$
$$\overline{BC} \cong \overline{EF}$$
$$\overline{CA} \cong \overline{FD}$$
$$\triangle ABC \cong \triangle DEF$$

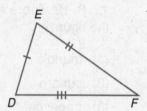

(2) Two sides and the angle between them are congruent (SAS).

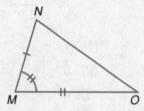

$$\overline{MN} \cong \overline{HI}$$
$$\overline{MO} \cong \overline{HJ}$$
$$\angle M \cong \angle H$$
$$\triangle MNO \cong \triangle HIJ$$

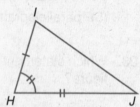

(3) Two angles and the side between them are congruent (ASA).

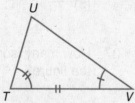

$$\angle T \cong \angle Q$$
$$\angle V \cong \angle S$$
$$\overline{TV} \cong \overline{QS}$$
$$\triangle TUV \cong \triangle QRS$$

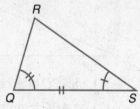

Using the explanations above, study why these pairs of triangles are congruent.

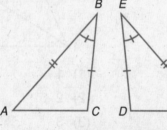 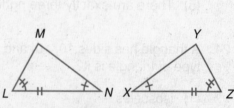

$\triangle ABC \cong \triangle FED$
Using Rule 2 or SAS,
$$\overline{AB} \cong \overline{FE}$$
$$\angle B \cong \angle E$$
$$\overline{BC} \cong \overline{ED}$$

$\triangle LMN \cong \triangle ZYX$
Using Rule 3 or ASA,
$$\angle L \cong \angle Z$$
$$\overline{LN} \cong \overline{ZX}$$
$$\angle N \cong \angle X$$

Mathematics ◆ Geometry

Two triangles are **similar** (symbol: ~) if the corresponding angles have equal measure and the corresponding sides are in proportion. They have the same shape, but they are *not necessarily* the same size.

When two figures are similar, the smallest angle of one corresponds to the smallest angle of the other, and the longest side of one corresponds to the longest side of the other, and so on. To identify corresponding parts, match up the parts of the figures that are the same.

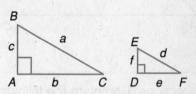

Similar triangles have the following relationships.

(1) They have the same shape.

$$\triangle ABC \sim \triangle DEF$$

(2) Corresponding angles are congruent (equal).

$$\angle A \cong \angle D \quad \angle B \cong \angle E$$
$$\angle C \cong \angle F$$

(3) Corresponding sides are proportional. (The ratio of the lengths of the sides are in proportion.)

$$\frac{a}{d} = \frac{b}{e} = \frac{c}{f}$$

A variety of practical problems can be solved using similar triangles. Similar triangles are often used when there is no way to actually perform the measurement of the missing length.

Example: What is the height of the flagpole?

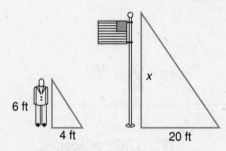

We can find the height of the flagpole in the diagram at the left. The diagram shows that the flagpole casts a shadow of 20 feet while a 6-foot person casts a shadow of 4 feet. We use the fact that the triangles formed by the objects and their shadows are similar. We set up a proportion and solve.

$$\frac{\text{height of the person}}{\text{shadow of the person}} = \frac{\text{height of the flagpole}}{\text{shadow of the flagpole}}$$

$$\frac{6}{4} = \frac{x}{20}$$
$$4x = 6(20)$$
$$4x = 120$$
$$x = 30$$

The height of the flagpole is **30 ft.**

Directions: Name the corresponding parts of the two congruent triangles by completing the tables.

$\triangle ABE \cong$
$\triangle CBD$

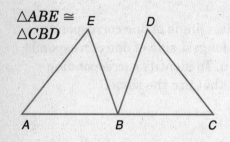

	In $\triangle ABE$	In $\triangle CBD$
1.	$\angle A$	__?__
2.	$\angle ABE$	__?__
3.	__?__	$\angle D$

	In $\triangle ABE$	In $\triangle CBD$
4.	__?__	$\overline{BC}$
5.	$\overline{AE}$	__?__
6.	$\overline{BE}$	__?__

Directions: Complete the following corresponding parts and ratios.

Items 7 to 15 refer to the diagram at the right.

7. $\angle A \cong$ __?__

$\triangle AEC \sim \triangle BGD$

8. $\angle ACE \cong$ __?__

9. $\angle CEA \cong$ __?__

10. $\overline{AC}$ corresponds to __?__ .

11. $\overline{AE}$ corresponds to __?__ .

12. $\overline{CE}$ corresponds to __?__ .

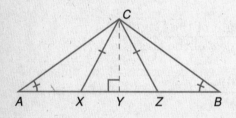

13. $\dfrac{AC}{BD} = \dfrac{CE}{?}$

14. $\dfrac{AE}{BG} = \dfrac{AC}{?}$

15. $\dfrac{CE}{DG} = \dfrac{AE}{?}$

Items 16 and 17 refer to the following figure.

16. $\triangle ACB$ is isoceles.
Therefore, $\overline{AC} \cong$ __?__
$\angle B \cong$ __?__
$\overline{AY} \cong$ __?__
$\angle ACY \cong$ __?__

17. $\triangle XCZ$ is isoceles.
Therefore, $\overline{XC} \cong$ __?__
$\angle CXY \cong$ __?__
$\overline{XY} \cong$ __?__
$\angle XCY \cong$ __?__

Item 18 refers to the following figure.

18. What is the distance across the longest part
of the lake shown in the diagram at the right?

(1) 300

(2) 225

(3) 100

(4) 60

(5) 36

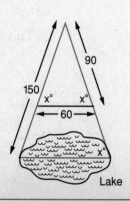

Lake

Answers are on page 884.

Lesson 27   Pythagorean Relationships

Pythagorean Theorem

The ancient Egyptians used an indirect method to resurvey their fields after the yearly flooding of the Nile River. The ancient Greeks proved the method will always work, and they named it the **Pythagorean Theorem** after the Greek mathematician Pythagoras.

hypotenuse

legs

A special relationship exists between the sides of a right triangle. The side opposite the right angle is called the **hypotenuse.** The other sides are called **legs.** The special relationship, proved by the Greeks, is called the **Pythagorean Theorem.** It states that in a right triangle, the square of the length of the hypotenuse is equal to the sum of the squares of the lengths of the legs.

> Pythagorean Theorem
> (the hypotenuse)^2 = (leg 1)^2 + (leg 2)^2
> $c^2 = a^2 + b^2$

Remember, the square of a number is the number multiplied by itself.

Example: Joan places a 13-foot ladder so that the top of the ladder touches the roof of the house. Joan measures the distance from the house to the bottom of the ladder and finds it to be 5 feet. What is the distance from the ground to the roof?

Sometimes the problem and the picture say nothing about whether the triangle is a right triangle. You have to recognize the triangle is a right triangle.

Now think of Joan's ladder as the hypotenuse, the distance from the house as one leg, and the height to the roof as the other leg.

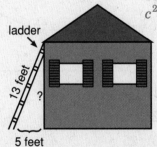

$$c^2 = a^2 + b^2, \text{ or } a^2 + b^2 = c^2$$
$$(5)^2 + b^2 = (13)^2$$
$$25 + b^2 = 169$$
$$b^2 = 169 - 25$$
$$b^2 = 144$$
$$b = 12$$

The roof is **12 feet** from the ground.

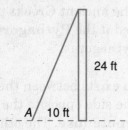
Directions: Solve.

Items 1 and 2 refer to the following diagram.

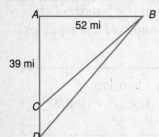

24 ft

A 10 ft

1. How many feet of wire are needed to reach from the top of the pole to point *A?*

2. Now point *A* is moved 8 feet further away from the pole. How much more wire will be needed?

Items 3 and 4 refer to the following diagram.

A ———— B
52 mi

39 mi

C

D

3 How far is it from Point *C* to Point *B?*

4. Point *D* is 11 miles from Point *C*. To the nearest whole mile, how far is it from Point *D* to Point *B?*

Directions: Choose the best answer to each item.

5. In a right triangle the short leg is 6 and the hypotenuse is 20. The other leg can be found by completing which calculation?

   (1) $\sqrt{20 + 6}$

   (2) $\sqrt{20 - 6}$

   (3) $\sqrt{20 + 36}$

   (4) $\sqrt{400 - 36}$

   (5) $\sqrt{400 + 36}$

6. In a right triangle, the hypotenuse measures 10 meters and one leg measures 6 meters. What is the length in meters of the other leg?

   (1) 5

   (2) 6

   (3) 7

   (4) 8

   (5) 9

7. Which of the following is a right triangle?

   (1) triangle with sides of 4, 5, and 6

   (2) triangle with sides of 5, 7, and 9

   (3) triangle with sides of 5, 12, and 13

   (4) triangle with sides of 6, 8, and 11

   (5) triangle with sides of 7, 9, and 12

8. Which is closest to the distance from *A* to *B?*

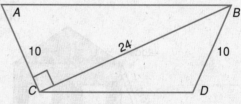

A   B
10   24   10

C   D

   (1) 27

   (2) 26

   (3) 25

   (4) 24

   (5) 23

Answers are on page 884.

Directions: Choose the best answer to each item.

1. A photograph shows Mel to be $3\frac{1}{2}$ inches tall. In the same photograph Tom, who is 6 feet tall and standing next to Mel, appears to be 4 inches tall. How tall is Mel?

   (1) 5 ft 10 in
   (2) 5 ft 8 in
   (3) 5 ft 6 in
   (4) 5 ft 4 in
   (5) 5 ft 3 in

2. The third-floor windows are 22 ft from the ground. If the ladder is positioned 7 ft out from the building, about how long would the ladder need to be to reach a third-floor window?

   (1) 18 ft
   (2) 20 ft
   (3) 22 ft
   (4) 23 ft
   (5) 25 ft

3. Similar marks on line segments and angles show congruent parts. $\triangle ABC \cong \triangle DCB$ Which of the following are not corresponding parts?

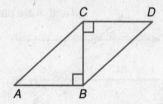

   (1) $\overline{AB}$ and $\overline{DC}$
   (2) $\triangle DCB$ and $\triangle ABC$
   (3) $\angle A$ and $\angle D$
   (4) $\overline{AC}$ and $\overline{DC}$
   (5) $\overline{DB}$ and $\overline{CA}$

4. $\angle A$ and $\angle B$ are supplementary. If $m\angle A$ is twice $m\angle B$, what is the measure of $\angle B$?

   (1) 40°
   (2) 60°
   (3) 90°
   (4) 120°
   (5) 130°

5. A wooden rectangular frame is 15 by 25 inches. If diagonal braces are added to the back of the frame, how long (to the nearest whole inch) will each brace need to be?

   (1) 18
   (2) 23
   (3) 27
   (4) 29
   (5) 32

6. In a right triangle, one leg is $7\frac{1}{2}$ feet and the other leg is 10 feet. What is the length in feet of the hypotenuse?

   (1) $10\frac{1}{2}$
   (2) $12\frac{1}{2}$
   (3) 13
   (4) $13\frac{1}{2}$
   (5) 15

7. In a right triangle, the measure of one acute angle is 5 times the measure of the other acute angle. The measure of the smaller angle is

   (1) 10°.
   (2) 15°.
   (3) 20°.
   (4) 25°.
   (5) 30°.

Items 8 to 10 refer to the following figure.

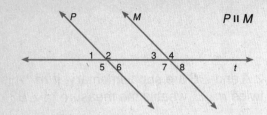

P ∥ M

8. Which of the following statements is true about angles 4 and 5?

   (1) They are alternate exterior angles.
   (2) They are supplementary angles.
   (3) They are complementary angles.
   (4) They are corresponding angles.
   (5) They are alternate interior angles.

9. If $m\angle 8 = 45°$, which of the following statements is false?

   (1) $m\angle 8 = m\angle 1$
   (2) $m\angle 4 = 135°$
   (3) $m\angle 6 = 45°$
   (4) $m\angle 7 = 135°$
   (5) $m\angle 3 = 135°$

10. Which angle corresponds to $\angle 5$?

   (1) $\angle 3$
   (2) $\angle 4$
   (3) $\angle 6$
   (4) $\angle 7$
   (5) $\angle 8$

11. A 3-feet post casts a $4\frac{1}{2}$-feet shadow at the same time that a telephone pole casts a shadow of 33 feet. What is the length of the telephone pole?

   (1) 18 ft
   (2) 22 ft
   (3) 28 ft
   (4) 33 ft
   (5) 99 ft

12. If $\triangle ABF \sim \triangle ACG$, then which is a true proportion?

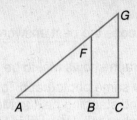

   (1) $\dfrac{\overline{AF}}{\overline{AB}} = \dfrac{\overline{AB}}{\overline{AC}}$
   (2) $\dfrac{\overline{AB}}{\overline{AC}} = \dfrac{\overline{FB}}{\overline{GC}}$
   (3) $\dfrac{\overline{AF}}{\overline{AC}} = \dfrac{\overline{AC}}{\overline{AB}}$
   (4) $\dfrac{\overline{AB}}{\overline{GC}} = \dfrac{\overline{AC}}{\overline{FB}}$
   (5) $\dfrac{\overline{AG}}{\overline{AC}} = \dfrac{\overline{AB}}{\overline{AF}}$

13. A cone-shaped candle mold has a base area of 4.5 square inches. The mold is 5 inches high. How many cubic inches of candle wax are needed to make 200 candles?

   (1)   375 cu in
   (2)   1,125 cu in
   (3)   1,500 cu in
   (4)   4,500 cu in
   (5) 13,500 cu in

14. If $\angle 8$ measures 50°, name two angles that measure 130°.

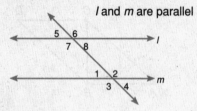

l and m are parallel

   (1) $\angle 6$ and $\angle 2$
   (2) $\angle 6$ and $\angle 4$
   (3) $\angle 7$ and $\angle 1$
   (4) $\angle 7$ and $\angle 4$
   (5) $\angle 7$ and $\angle 5$

15. Triangle *ECD* is a right triangle. Which angle is obtuse?

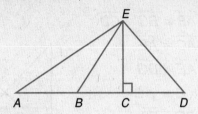

(1) ∠*AED*

(2) ∠*ACE*

(3) ∠*BCE*

(4) ∠*DAE*

(5) Not enough information is given.

16. The measure of ∠*DAB* is 70°. Which statement is true?

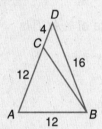

(1) *m*∠*ABC* = 55°

(2) *m*∠*D* = 30°

(3) *m*∠*ABC* = 70°

(4) *m*∠*ACB* = 70°

(5) *m*∠*CBD* = 30°

17. A post is 12 feet high. A wire is secured to the top of the post and anchored to the ground 5 feet from the base of the post. How long is the wire?

(1)   9 ft

(2)   10 ft

(3)   12 ft

(4)   13 ft

(5)   17 ft

18. The measure of ∠*CDE* is 160°. $\overline{CF} \parallel \overline{BG}$. Which other angle has the same measure as ∠*CDE*?

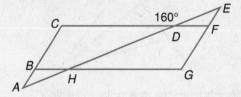

(1) ∠*BCD*

(2) ∠*EGH*

(3) ∠*AHG*

(4) ∠*ABH*

(5) ∠*DFE*

19. An ancient Mexican pyramid has a volume of 82,600 cubic feet. It is 177 feet high and has a square base. What is the area of the base of the pyramid?

(1)   155.5 sq ft

(2)   466.6 sq ft

(3)   1,400 sq ft

(4)   4,200 sq ft

(5)   More information is needed.

20. Rod, the manager of Cine-Max Theater, is changing the size of the popcorn box. He has made three choices shown below. Which statement is true about these three choices?

Box X   Box Y   Box Z

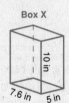 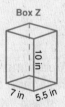

(1) Box X has the greatest volume.

(2) Box Y has the greatest volume.

(3) Box Z has the greatest volume.

(4) Box X and Box Z have the same volume.

(5) All three boxes have the same volume.

Items 21 to 23 refer to the following figure.

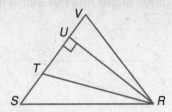

21. Which triangle is a right triangle?

    (1) △TRS
    (2) △TUR
    (3) △SRV
    (4) △VRT
    (5) △STR

22. △RTS is

    (1) an acute triangle.
    (2) a right triangle.
    (3) a scalene triangle.
    (4) an isosceles triangle.
    (5) an equilateral triangle.

23. How many right triangles can be found?

    (1) one
    (2) two
    (3) three
    (4) four
    (5) five

24. A perfume manufacturer has a gift box in the shape of a pyramid with a square base that is 3 inches on each side. The total volume of the box is 21 cubic inches. How high is the tallest bottle that can be packaged in this box?

    (1) < 4 in high
    (2) > 4 < 5 in high
    (3) > 5 < 6 in high
    (4) > 6 ≤ 7 in high
    (5) > 7 in high

25. △AEC and △BDG are isosceles. What conclusion can be drawn?

    (1) $\overline{AB} \cong \overline{BC} \cong \overline{CD}$
    (2) $\overline{AC} \cong \overline{AE}$
    (3) $\overline{AE} \cong \overline{DG}$
    (4) ∠E ≅ ∠G
    (5) $\overline{BF} \cong \overline{FC}$

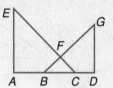

Items 26 to 28 refer to the following figure.

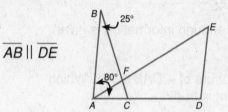

$\overline{AB} \parallel \overline{DE}$

26. The measure of ∠ACB is

    (1) 20°.
    (2) 60°.
    (3) 75°.
    (4) 105°.
    (5) 110°.

27. Angle D is

    (1) the same size as ∠BAC.
    (2) the same size as ∠BCD.
    (3) the same size as ∠B + ∠BAC.
    (4) the supplement of ∠BAC.
    (5) the complement of ∠B.

28. The measure of ∠BCD is

    (1) 105°.
    (2) 110°.
    (3) 120°.
    (4) 125°.
    (5) 130°.

Answers are on page 885.

Mathematics ◆ Geometry

All formulas needed to solve these problems can be found on the inside cover of this book.

Directions: Choose the best answer to each item.

1. To make four seat covers, when each cover requires $4\frac{2}{3}$ yards of material, how many yards of material are needed?

   (1) $8\frac{2}{3}$

   (2) $13\frac{1}{3}$

   (3) $16\frac{1}{3}$

   (4) $16\frac{2}{3}$

   (5) $18\frac{2}{3}$

2. An early radar device (Model A) is operated at a maximum frequency of 3×10^3 megahertz. With improvements, a new device (Model B) was able to operate at 3×10^5 megahertz. Which statement is true?

   (1) The maximum frequency of Model B is less than that of Model A.

   (2) The maximum frequency of Model B is 2 times as great as that of Model A.

   (3) The maximum frequency of Model B is 3 times as great as that of Model A.

   (4) The maximum frequency of Model B is 10 times as great as that of Model A.

   (5) The maximum frequency of Model B is 100 times as great as that of Model A.

3. Janice works for a collection agency. She is paid a 5% commission on the amounts she collects. Last week she collected $1,900, $2,350, and $5,800. What is the total commission she earned for the week?

   (1) $ 177.50

   (2) $ 212.50

   (3) $ 290.50

   (4) $ 502.50

   (5) $1,550.50

4. Leonard gives swimming lessons at the community center. He is paid $5 per half-hour lesson and $9 per full-hour lesson. He has 20 students per week for a half-hour lesson and 12 students per week for a full-hour lesson. Which expression represents how many dollars Leonard will earn per week?

   (1) 20(5) + 12(9)

   (2) 5(12) + 20 (9)

   (3) 12(20) + 5(9)

   (4) 5(20) + 12(20)

   (5) 12(9) + 20(9)

5. In 1994 an airline hired an aircraft company to manufacture 80 new planes. The aircraft company can complete 16 planes per year. At this rate, in what year will the airline's order be completed?

   (1) 1995

   (2) 1997

   (3) 1999

   (4) 2001

   (5) 2004

6. Mr. Fayle owns 1,200 acres of forest land. He plans to donate 75% of the land to the county for a wildlife preserve. How many acres of land is he planning to donate?

   (1)   90

   (2)   450

   (3)   750

   (4)   900

   (5) 1,050

Item 7 refers to the following number line.

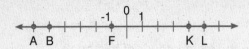

7. Which letter on the number line represents −5?

   (1) *A*

   (2) *B*

   (3) *F*

   (4) *K*

   (5) *L*

Items 8 and 9 refer to the following information.

MARIA'S TAXES

Taxable Income	$19,000
TAX	**% OF INCOME**
Federal Tax Withheld	24
State Tax Withheld	3
Federal Tax Still Owed	4
State Tax Still Owed	1

8. After she pays all the tax she owes, what percent of her income will Maria have paid for federal and state income taxes?

   (1) 34%

   (2) 32%

   (3) 27%

   (4) 16%

   (5) 8%

9. Maria must also pay a state disability tax of $475. What percent of her taxable income is the disability tax?

   (1) 4%

   (2) 3%

   (3) 2.5%

   (4) 1.5%

   (5) 1%

10. Traveling at 55 miles per hour, approximately how long will it take Mona to drive 305 miles?

   (1) between 2 and 3 hours

   (2) between 3 and 4 hours

   (3) between 4 and 5 hours

   (4) between 5 and 6 hours

   (5) between 6 and 7 hours

11. The square root of 14 is between which pair of numbers?

   (1) 1.4 and 1.5

   (2) 2 and 3

   (3) 3 and 4

   (4) 4 and 5

   (5) 13 and 15

Item 12 is based on the following information.

THINGS TO DO LIST	
A. Complete work schedule	$\frac{1}{2}$ hour
B. Clean storeroom	2 hours
C. Order new supplies	$\frac{3}{4}$ hour
D. Staff meeting	$1\frac{1}{2}$ hours
E. Restock shelves	$1\frac{1}{4}$ hours
F. Type memo	$\frac{1}{2}$ hour

12. Cliff works 6 hours per day at a restaurant. The list shows the tasks he needs to get done and the amount of time each task will take. He has already spent two hours totaling last night's receipts and $2\frac{1}{2}$ hours completing the payroll. Which combination of tasks does he still have time to complete today?

   (1) A and E

   (2) B and E

   (3) C and D

   (4) C and F

   (5) B only

13. A local market advertises tomatoes at 79 cents per pound. How much will it cost to buy 6 tomatoes?

(1) $3.16

(2) $3.88

(3) $4.74

(4) $5.82

(5) Not enough information is given.

Items 14 and 15 refer to the following information.

CARDSTON'S DEPARTMENT STORE EMPLOYEES	
Managers	15
Buyers	8
Accounting	12
Salespeople	45

14. What percent of Cardston's employees work in accounting?

(1) 12%

(2) 15%

(3) 26%

(4) 45%

(5) Not enough information is given.

15. Cardston's is holding a contest to improve employee morale. A computer will choose one employee at random to win a trip to Hawaii. What is the probability that a buyer will win the contest?

(1) $\frac{1}{2}$

(2) $\frac{1}{4}$

(3) $\frac{1}{8}$

(4) $\frac{1}{10}$

(5) $\frac{1}{80}$

16. On a map two cities are $3\frac{3}{4}$ inches apart. The map has a scale of 1 inch = 40 miles. What is the actual distance, in miles, between the two cities?

(1) 90

(2) 120

(3) 150

(4) 180

(5) 210

17. Preston bought an antique bookcase for $90 and refinished it. He sold the bookcase for 125% of the price he paid. How much did he get for the bookcase?

(1) $ 81.00

(2) $112.50

(3) $156.25

(4) $202.50

(5) Not enough information is given.

Item 18 refers to the following diagram.

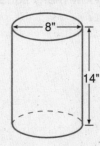

18. A can in the shape of a cylinder is 8 in. across and 14 in. tall. Which expression represents the approximate volume of the can in cubic inches?

(1) $(3.14)(4)(14)^2$

(2) $(3.14)(8)(14)^2$

(3) $(3.14)(8)^2(14)$

(4) $(3.14)(16)^2(14)$

(5) $(3.14)(4)^2(14)$

19. At Fabric Unlimited, adult patterns are $4 each and children's patterns are $3 each. A customer wants to buy 6 adult patterns and 2 children's patterns. Which expression represents how many dollars the customer will pay for the patterns?

(1) $(4 + 6)(2 + 3)$

(2) $2(6) + 3(4)$

(3) $2(4) + 3(6)$

(4) $3(2 + 4 + 6)$

(5) $6(4) + 2(3)$

20. Wayne can mow his back lawn in 45 minutes. What part of it can he mow in $\frac{1}{2}$ hour?

(1) $\frac{1}{4}$

(2) $\frac{1}{3}$

(3) $\frac{3}{8}$

(4) $\frac{2}{3}$

(5) $\frac{3}{4}$

21. A gallon of interior latex paint will cover 200 square feet. How many square feet will 8 gallons cover?

(1) 25

(2) 160

(3) 1,000

(4) 1,600

(5) 1,800

22. Which of the following expresses 2,062,493 in scientific notation?

(1) 2.062493×10^6

(2) 2.062493×10^7

(3) 20.62493×10^7

(4) 206.2493×10^6

(5) $2,062.493 \times 10^4$

Items 23 and 24 refer to the following graph.

NELL MANUFACTURING ANNUAL BUDGET

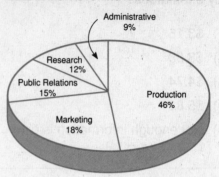

23. According to the graph, what percent of the company budget was spent on production and marketing?

(1) 33%

(2) 36%

(3) 57%

(4) 64%

(5) 67%

24. What percent of the budget is left after public relations and administrative expenses are paid?

(1) 91%

(2) 88%

(3) 85%

(4) 82%

(5) 76%

25. Max plays basketball. During the past four weeks, his team has scored 72, 66, 74, and 68 points. Which expression represents the team's mean score (average) for the month?

(1) $\frac{72+66+74+68}{4}$

(2) $4(72 + 66 + 74 + 68)$

(3) $\frac{(72)(66)(74)(68)}{4}$

(4) $\frac{4(72+66+74)}{68}$

(5) Not enough information is given.

26. A charity raises $500,000 to build shelters for the homeless. If 4% is spent on administrative costs, how much is left for building shelters?

(1) $200,000

(2) $260,000

(3) $420,000

(4) $450,000

(5) $480,000

27. An inspector at Watts-Up Light Bulb Company discovered that there were 5 defective light bulbs in every case of 150 light bulbs. What is the probability that a light bulb will be defective?

(1) $\frac{1}{3}$

(2) $\frac{1}{15}$

(3) $\frac{1}{30}$

(4) $\frac{1}{50}$

(5) $\frac{1}{100}$

28. A zoo built a circular platform with a 16-foot diameter for its sea lion exhibit. What is the approximate area (in square feet) of the platform?

(1) 50

(2) 201

(3) 252

(4) 804

(5) Not enough information is given.

29. A gardener plans to plant 12 tomato plants in each row of a garden. If there are 15 rows, how many plants will he need?

(1) 180

(2) 150

(3) 120

(4) 90

(5) 60

Item 30 refers to these diagrams.

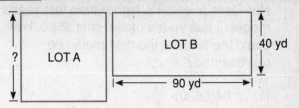

30. Lot A and Lot B have the same area. If Lot A is square, what is the length in yards of one of its sides?

(1) 40

(2) 50

(3) 60

(4) 90

(5) Not enough information is given.

31. A can of spaghetti sauce has 70 calories per serving. If 18 of the calories come from fat, to the nearest whole percent, what percent of the sauce's calories come from fat?

(1) 13%

(2) 26%

(3) 34%

(4) 52%

(5) Not enough information is given.

32. Arturo buys a computer desk for $398. If he pays $6\frac{1}{2}$ % sales tax on the purchase, what is the total cost of the desk?

(1) $258.70

(2) $404.50

(3) $423.87

(4) $433.24

(5) $656.70

33. A new computer monitor manufactured by Net-Co is priced 4% higher than last year's model. If last year's model cost $500, how could the price of the new model be represented?

(1) 0.04($500)

(2) $\frac{\$500}{0.04}$

(3) 0.04($500) + 0.04

(4) 0.04 ($500) + $500

(5) $\frac{\$500}{0.04}$ + $500

Item 34 refers to the following diagram.

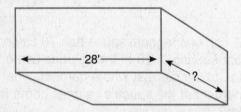

34. The rectangular storage tank has a volume of 3,920 cubic feet. If the length of the tank is 28 feet, what is the width of the tank?

(1) 7 feet

(2) 10 feet

(3) 14 feet

(4) 20 feet

(5) Not enough information is given.

---

35. Simplify: $6x + 2y - x + 3y$.

(1) $6x + 6y$

(2) $36xy$

(3) $5x + 5y$

(4) $7x^2 + 5y^2$

(5) $x^5 + y^5$

36. Oranges are priced at 6 for $1.08. What is the cost of $3\frac{1}{2}$ dozen oranges?

(1) $0.54

(2) $3.78

(3) $6.30

(4) $6.48

(5) $7.56

37. 620 clerks and cashiers register for a 2-day workshop on a new inventory system. Of the clerks and cashiers, 15% could not attend the banquet on the last day because they had to return to work. How many cashiers and clerks could not attend the banquet?

(1) 93

(2) 186

(3) 372

(4) 527

(5) 605

38. Given the formula $p = 3x(y + 2)$, find p if $y = 3$ and $x = 4$.

(1) 35

(2) 36

(3) 54

(4) 60

(5) 72

39. Nolan walks 5 miles in $1\frac{1}{4}$ hours. Which equation can be used to find how many miles Nolan can walk in 5 hours?

(1) $1\frac{1}{4}x = 25$

(2) $5x = 6\frac{1}{4}$

(3) $6\frac{1}{4}x = 5$

(4) $5x = 25$

(5) $25x = 5$

40. The perimeter of a rectangular garden is 74 feet. If the length of the garden is 22 feet, which equation could be used to find the width of the garden?

(1) $2w + 74 = 2(22)$

(2) $w^2 + 22^2 = 74$

(3) $\frac{74}{2(22)} = \frac{2}{w}$

(4) $\frac{w}{2} + 74 = 22$

(5) $74 - 2(22) = 2w$

41. Jaelle pays $12.80 per month to subscribe to the local newspaper. How much will it cost her to subscribe to the paper for 12 months?

(1) $ 76.80

(2) $128.00

(3) $153.60

(4) $230.40

(5) $256.00

42. Simplify: $2m + 2n + m - 3n$.

(1) $3m - n$

(2) $2m^2 - n^2$

(3) $m^3 - n^5$

(4) $12mn$

(5) $3m + 5n$

43. Aviva, an office manager, got a department store certificate from her staff. She wants to buy a shirt for $24.95 and a necklace for $18.65. If p represents the original amount of the gift certificate, how much will she have left to spend after buying the shirt and necklace?

(1) $p + \$24.95 - \$18.65$

(2) $p - \$24.95 - \$18.65$

(3) $p - \$24.95 + 18.65$

(4) $p + \$24.95 + \$18.65$

(5) $p(\$24.95 + \$18.65)$

44. For which value of z is the inequality $3z < 12$ true?

(1) 3

(2) 4

(3) 5

(4) 6

(5) 7

Item 45 is based on the following figure.

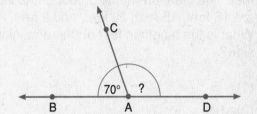

45. Angle *BAC* measures 70 degrees. How many degrees does angle *CAD* measure?

(1) 20°

(2) 50°

(3) 70°

(4) 90°

(5) 110°

Item 46 is based on the following figure.

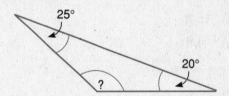

46. The triangle has three internal angles. One angle measures 25°; another measures 20°. How many degrees are in the third angle?

(1) 45°

(2) 105°

(3) 135°

(4) 315°

(5) Not enough information is given.

47. A pole 3 feet tall casts a shadow 5 feet long. At the same time, a building casts a shadow 120 feet long. How tall is the building?

    (1)   72 ft
    (2)   150 ft
    (3)   175 ft
    (4)   200 ft
    (5) 1,800 ft

48. The perimeter of a five-sided figure is 72 feet. The measurements of four of the sides are 16 feet, 15 feet, 20 feet, and 9 feet. What is the length in feet of the remaining side?

    (1)   9
    (2) 12
    (3) 42
    (4) 60
    (5) Not enough information is given.

49. Bobbi walked 8 feet up a ramp and was 6 feet from the ground. How far from the ground was Bobbi after she walked 12 feet farther up the ramp?

    (1) 12 ft
    (2) 18 ft
    (3) 14 ft
    (4) 15 ft
    (5)   4 ft

Item 50 refers to the diagram below.

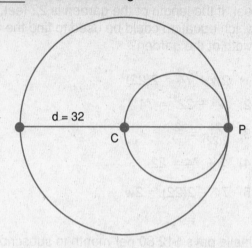

50. Two circles intersect at point P. If C is the center of the larger circle, and the diameter of the larger circle is 32, then the radius of the smaller circle must be

    (1) 32.
    (2) 24.
    (3) 16.
    (4)   8.
    (5) Not enough information is given.

Item 51 refers to the following drawing.

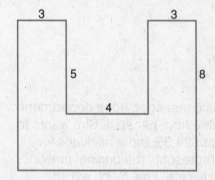

51. What is the perimeter of the figure?

    (1) 18
    (2) 23
    (3) 36
    (4) 41
    (5) 46

Item 52 refers to the following drawing.

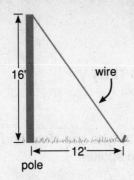

pole

52. A wire is supporting a 16-foot pole. The wire is staked to the ground a distance of 12 feet from the bottom of the pole. How long is the wire?

(1)   4 ft
(2)   8 ft
(3) 10 ft
(4) 16 ft
(5) 20 ft

Items 53 and 54 refer to the following figure.

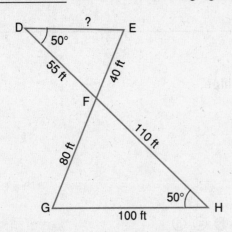

53. Triangles *DEF* and *FGH* are similar. Which side in triangle *FGH* corresponds to side $\overline{DF}$ in triangle *DEF*?

(1) side $\overline{EF}$
(2) side $\overline{FG}$
(3) side $\overline{FH}$
(4) side $\overline{GH}$
(5) Not enough information is given.

54. What is the length in feet of side $\overline{DE}$ in the figure?

(1) 20
(2) 33
(3) 40
(4) 50
(5) 55

Item 55 refers to the following figure.

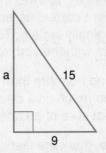

55. According to the Pythagorean Theorem, which statement is true for the triangle?

(1) $a^2 + 9^2 = 15^2$
(2) $a^2 - 9^2 = 15^2$
(3) $a^2 - 15^2 = 9^2$
(4) $a^2 + 15^2 = 9^2$
(5) $9^2 + 15^2 = a^2$

Item 56 refers to the following diagram.

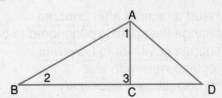

56. In triangle *ABC*, angle 2 is 35 degrees and angle 1 is 55 degrees. How many degrees is angle 3 of the same triangle?

(1) 145°
(2) 125°
(3) 100°
(4)   90°
(5)   55°

Answers are on page 886.

Simulated GED Tests

WRITING SKILLS SIMULATED GED TEST

Directions

The Writing Skills Simulated GED Test is intended to measure your ability to use clear and effective English. It is a test of English as it should be written, not as it might be spoken.

This test consists of paragraphs with numbered sentences. Some of the sentences contain errors in sentence structure, usage, or mechanics (spelling, punctuation, and capitalization). After reading the numbered sentences, answer the multiple-choice questions that follow. Some questions refer to sentences that are correct as written. The best answer for these questions is the one that leaves the sentence as originally written. The best answer for some questions is the one that produces a sentence that is consistent with the verb tense and point of view used throughout the paragraph.

You should spend no more than 75 minutes answering the 55 questions on this test. Work carefully, but do not spend too much time on any one question. Do not skip any items. Make a reasonable guess when you are not sure of an answer. You will not be penalized for incorrect answers.

When time is up, mark the last item you finished. This will tell you whether you can finish the real GED Test in the time allowed. Then complete the test.

Record your answers to the questions on a copy of the answer sheet on page 922. Be sure that all required information is properly recorded on the answer sheet.

To record your answers, mark the numbered space on the answer sheet that corresponds to the answer you choose for each question on the test.

Example:

Sentence 1: **We were all honored to meet governor Phillips.**

What correction should be made to this sentence?

(1) insert a comma after <u>honored</u>
(2) change the spelling of <u>honored</u> to <u>honered</u>
(3) change <u>governor</u> to <u>Governor</u>
(4) replace <u>were</u> with <u>was</u>
(5) no correction is necessary   

In this example, the word <u>governor</u> should be capitalized; therefore, answer space 3 would be marked on the answer sheet.

Do not rest the point of your pencil on the answer sheet while you are considering your answer. Make no stray or unnecessary marks. If you change an answer, erase your first mark completely. Mark only one answer space for each question; multiple answers will be scored as incorrect. Do not fold or crease your answer sheet.

When you finish the test, use the Correlation Chart on page 662 to determine whether you are ready to take the real GED Test, and, if not, which skill areas need additional review.

Adapted with permission of the American Council on Education.

Directions: Choose the best answer to each item.

Items 1 to 5 refer to the following paragraph.

(1) Legalized gambling is a controversial. (2) Contradictory and sometimes emotional subject. (3) Betting on horse races at state-run betting parlors are legal but private betting through a bookie is not. (4) There is some charitable organizations that have "casino nights" with roulette, blackjack, and craps. (5) These games are illegal in all states except nevada, when run by private individuals. (6) Poker, a card game is popular, but a high-stakes game in your home could be illegal.

1. Sentences 1 and 2: **Legalized gambling is a controversial. Contradictory and sometimes emotional subject.**

   The most effective combination of sentences 1 and 2 would include which of the following groups of words?

   (1) controversial; contradictory and
   (2) controversial, contradictory, and
   (3) controversial, and contradictory and
   (4) controversial, as a result of a contradictory and
   (5) controversial; as a result of a contradictory and

2. Sentence 3: **Betting on horse races at state-run betting parlors are legal but private betting through a bookie is not.**

   Which of the following is the best way to write the underlined portion of this sentence? If you think the original is the best way, choose option (1).

   (1) parlors are legal but private
   (2) parlors are legal, but private
   (3) parlors are legal; but private
   (4) parlors is legal but private
   (5) parlors is legal, but private

3. Sentence 4: **There is some charitable organizations that have "casino nights" with roulette, blackjack, and craps.**

   What correction should be made to this sentence?

   (1) change There is to There were
   (2) change There is to There are
   (3) change There is to They are
   (4) change charitable to Charitable
   (5) no correction is necessary

4. Sentence 5: **These games are illegal in all states except nevada, when run by private individuals.**

   What correction should be made to this sentence?

   (1) change states to States
   (2) replace except with accept
   (3) change nevada, to Nevada
   (4) change nevada, to Nevada,
   (5) no correction is necessary

5. Sentence 6: **Poker, a card game is popular, but a high-stakes game in your home could be illegal.**

   What correction should be made to this sentence?

   (1) remove the comma after Poker
   (2) change is to was
   (3) insert a comma after card game
   (4) insert a comma after home
   (5) no correction is necessary

Items 6 to 12 refer to the following paragraphs.

(1) Daydreaming is a popular pastime. (2) Songs, fiction stories, and movies often contain passages about daydreaming. (3) Daydreaming is not bad if you controlled it and do not let it control your life.

(4) Daydreaming can help you relax and improve your mood when your having a bad day. (5) You need to be sure your daydreams do not get to the point where you will begin to confuse dreams with reality.

(6) Sometimes we daydream while doing a boring, repetitive job. (7) Pushed a lawn mower around and around the yard. (8) You might find yourself daydreaming. (9) While you are driving alone along a straight road for a long time. (10) It can be very dangerous to daydream while using machinery, operating electrical controls, or when you drive a car. (11) Daydreaming, like many other things, is often okay if not done to excess.

6. Sentence 1: **Daydreaming is a popular pastime.**

    What correction should be made to this sentence?

    (1) replace Daydreaming with daydreaming
    (2) change is to was
    (3) replace is with are
    (4) change popular to Popular
    (5) no correction is necessary

7. Sentence 3: **Daydreaming is not bad if you controlled it and do not let it control your life.**

    Which of the following is the best way to write the underlined portion of this sentence? If you think the original is the best way, choose option (1).

    (1) if you controlled it and do not
    (2) if you control it and do not
    (3) if you control it; and do not
    (4) if you control it and Do Not
    (5) if you control it, and, you do not

8. Sentence 4: **Daydreaming can help you relax and improve your mood when your having a bad day.**

    Which of the following is the best way to write the underlined portion of this sentence? If you think the original is the best way, choose option (1).

    (1) mood when your
    (2) mood, when you're
    (3) mood, when your'
    (4) mood when you're
    (5) mood, when your

9. Sentence 5: **You need to be sure your daydreams do not get to the point where you will begin to confuse dreams with reality.**

   What correction should be made to this sentence?

   (1) change will begin to began
   (2) change will begin to begin
   (3) change your to you're
   (4) change will begin to has begun
   (5) no correction is necessary

10. Sentences 6 and 7: **Sometimes we daydream while doing a boring, repetitive job. Pushed a lawn mower around and around the yard.**

    The most effective combination of sentences 6 and 7 would include which of the following groups of words?

    (1) job, push a lawn mower
    (2) job such as push a lawn mower
    (3) job, such as pushing a lawn mower
    (4) job; such as push a lawn mower
    (5) job; push a lawn mower

11. Sentences 8 and 9: **You might find yourself daydreaming. While you are driving alone along a straight road for a long time.**

    Which of the following is the best way to write the underlined portion of this sentence? If you think the original is the best way, choose option (1).

    (1) daydreaming. While you are
    (2) daydreaming while you are
    (3) daydreaming; while you're
    (4) daydreaming while your
    (5) daydreaming; while your

12. Sentence 10: **It can be very dangerous to daydream while using machinery, operating electrical controls, or when you drive a car.**

    What correction should be made to this sentence?

    (1) change operating to operation of
    (2) change electrical to electricity
    (3) change when you drive a car to driving a car
    (4) change when you drive a car to when a car is driven
    (5) change drive to drove

(1) Yes anyone can learn to be a handy person around the house. (2) Start with simple things like changing a light bulb, oiling a lock, and the screws in the door can be tightened. (3) A reference guide, *The Handyman's Book of Tricks* is full of helpful hints.

(4) As you try more difficult jobs, you first need to analyze the job. (5) It often helps to consider what advance preparations is necessary and to make a list before you start. (6) For example, if you decide to paint the walls in your bedroom, what do you need to do? (7) Painting can be messy, and you will need to cover the floor. (8) You need to decide on the color and the type of paint to use. (9) There is oil-base and latex paints on the market. (10) Are a paintbrush to do the trim and, a roller to do the large flat areas adequate?

(11) If you want to try more technical jobs, you should first consult someone who has experience. (12) No one was born a handy person, the best way to learn is by doing.

13. Sentence 1: **Yes anyone can learn to be a handy person around the house.**

Which of the following is the best way to write the underlined portion of this sentence? If you think the original is the best way, choose option (1).

(1) Yes anyone
(2) Yes Anyone
(3) Yes, anyone
(4) Yes, Anyone
(5) Yes; anyone

14. Sentence 2: **Start with simple things like changing a light bulb, oiling a lock, and the screws in the door can be tightened.**

Which of the following is the best way to write the underlined portion of this sentence? If you think the original is the best way, choose option (1).

(1) and the screws in the door can be tightened
(2) and the door screws can be tightened
(3) and tightening the screws in the door
(4) and tighten the screws in the door
(5) and how to make the screws in the door tighter

15. Sentence 3: **A reference guide, *The Handyman's Book of Tricks* is full of helpful hints.**

    What correction should be made to this sentence?

    (1) remove the comma after guide
    (2) change Book to book
    (3) add a comma after Tricks
    (4) change is to are
    (5) no correction is necessary

16. Sentence 5: **It often helps to consider what advance preparations is necessary and to make a list before you start.**

    What correction should be made to this sentence?

    (1) insert a comma after necessary
    (2) change is to are
    (3) change is to were
    (4) change is to was
    (5) no correction is necessary

17. Sentence 7: **Painting can be messy, and you will need to cover the floor.**

    If you rewrote sentence 7 beginning with

    Because painting can be

    the next words should be

    (1) messy; you will
    (2) messy, you will
    (3) messy; and, you will
    (4) messy you will
    (5) messy, you, will

18. Sentence 9: **There is oil-base and latex paints on the market.**

    What correction should be made to this sentence?

    (1) change There is to There are
    (2) change oil-base to Oil-Base
    (3) change latex paints to Latex paints
    (4) change latex paints to latex Paints
    (5) no correction is necessary

19. Sentence 10: **Are a paintbrush to do the trim and, a roller to do the large flat areas adequate?**

    What correction should be made to this sentence?

    (1) change Are to Is
    (2) add a comma after trim
    (3) remove the comma after and
    (4) change the question mark to a period
    (5) no correction is necessary

20. Sentence 12: **No one was born a handy person, the best way to learn is by doing.**

    Which of the following is the best way to write the underlined portion of this sentence? If you think the original is the best way, choose option (1).

    (1) one was born a handy person, the
    (2) one is born a handy person, the
    (3) one is born a handy person; the
    (4) one was born a handy person; the
    (5) one is born a handy person the

Items 21 to 28 refer to the following paragraphs.

(1) AIDS is a deadly disease, it is also a very misunderstood disease. (2) There is a lot of hysteria, ignorance, and some people get emotional about AIDS. (3) It is important to learn all the facts.

(4) You won't get AIDS just by being around someone with the disease. (5) You won't get AIDS from sharing an office with an infected person; you can't get AIDS from being coughed or sneezed on. (6) You won't get AIDS from shaking hands with, hugging, or even kissing someone with the disease. (7) We won't get AIDS from using public toilets, telephones, drinking fountains, or swimming pools.

(8) You can get AIDS by coming into direct contact with the HIV virus. (9) The virus is carried in the blood and other bodily fluids of someone already infected. (10) You risk contact with the HIV virus if contaminated blood or other bodily fluids get into a cut on your skin, in your mouth, or in your eyes. (11) In the past, you could get AIDS from receiving contaminated blood in a transfusion, but now all blood is carefully screened so you're risk is very small.

(12) You can be exposed to the HIV virus if you have unprotected sex. (13) Always use condoms during sex if either you or your partner is unsure of having been exposed to the HIV virus. (14) You can be exposed to the virus by using a contaminated needle. (15) Never share needles; always wear a face mask, gloves, and long-sleeved top when giving medical care to a person with AIDS or someone suspected of being HIV positive.

(16) If you think you may have been exposed to the virus that causes AIDS, get tested. (17) You won't have to give the health clinic your name. (18) There is still no cure for AIDS, but there are treatments to slow the disease and lessen it's symptoms. (19) These medicines work best if the infection is diagnosed early.

21. Sentence 1: **AIDS is a deadly disease, it is also a very misunderstood disease.**

Which of the following is the best way to write the underlined portion of this sentence? If you think the original is the best way, choose option (1).

(1) disease, it
(2) disease; and
(3) disease; it
(4) disease; and,
(5) disease it

22. Sentence 2: **There is a lot of hysteria, ignorance, and some people get emotional about AIDS.**

What correction should be made to this sentence?

(1) replace is with are
(2) change the spelling of ignorance to ignorence
(3) replace some people get emotional with emotion
(4) replace ignorance with ignorant
(5) no correction is necessary

23. Sentence 5: **You won't get AIDS from sharing an office with an infected person; you can't get AIDS from being coughed or sneezed on.**

If you rewrote sentence 5 beginning with

You can't get AIDS from being coughed or sneezed on,

the next word should be

(1) and
(2) though
(3) but
(4) although
(5) however

24. Sentence 7: **We won't get AIDS from using public toilets, telephones, drinking fountains, or swimming pools.**

What correction should be made to this sentence?

(1) change We to You
(2) change We to They
(3) change We to Them
(4) change get to got
(5) no correction is necessary

25. Sentences 9 and 10: **The virus is carried in the blood and other bodily fluids of someone already infected. You risk contact with the HIV virus if contaminated blood or other bodily fluids get into a cut on your skin, in your mouth, or in your eyes.**

The most effective combination of sentences 9 and 10 would include which of the following groups of words?

(1) infected; and you
(2) infected; you
(3) infected you
(4) infected, you
(5) infected, because

26. Sentence 11: **In the past, you could get AIDS from receiving contaminated blood in a transfusion, but now all blood is carefully screened so you're risk is very small.**

Which of the following is the best way to write the underlined portion of this sentence? If you think that the original is the best way, choose option (1).

(1) you're
(2) your'
(3) their
(4) your
(5) my

27. Sentence 15: **Never share needles; always wear a face mask, gloves, and long-sleeved top when giving medical care to a person with AIDS or someone suspected of being HIV positive.**

What correction should be made to this sentence?

(1) remove the comma after mask
(2) insert a comma after top
(3) insert a semicolon after top
(4) change the spelling of needles to needels
(5) no correction is necessary

28. Sentence 18: **There is still no cure for AIDS, but there are treatments to slow the disease and lessen it's symptoms.**

What correction should be made to this sentence?

(1) change symptoms to symtoms
(2) remove the comma after AIDS
(3) change it's to its
(4) change there to their
(5) no correction is necessary

Items 29 to 35 refer to the following paragraphs.

(1) The Berlin Wall was built in 1961, and a shadow of despair was cast over the whole world. (2) It was the ultimate symbol of persecution separating the stark, harsh dictatorship of the Communist East from the booming economy of the democratic West.

(3) Virtually countless hundreds of people risked death to cross over, under, and through the wall. (4) Many of these people lost their lives seeking the freedom that we Americans take for granted.

(5) The harder the Communist countries tried to stop the flow of people to the West, the harder they tried to succeed. (6) We have never known what it is like to live under a harsh dictatorship with secret police looking over your shoulder, with constant shortages of food and other consumer goods, and in crowded living conditions.

(7) The sudden, dramatic shift in political conditions throughout the Communist East in 1989 that resulted in the destruction of the Berlin Wall had gave birth to hope. (8) Perhaps we were beginning an era of world cooperation, and understanding that would rise above politics and communism. (9) Maybe those who gave their lives escaping from persecution did not die in vain. (10) The free world celebrated as the Berlin Wall came tumbling down.

29. Sentence 1: **The Berlin Wall was built in 1961, and a shadow of despair was cast over the whole world.**

If you rewrote sentence 1 beginning with

A shadow of despair was cast over the whole world

the next word should be

(1) when
(2) but
(3) for
(4) therefore
(5) and

30. Sentence 3: <u>**Virtually countless hundreds**</u> **of people risked death to cross over, under, and through the wall.**

Which of the following is the best way to write the underlined portion of this sentence? If you think the original is the best way, choose option (1).

(1) Virtually countless hundreds
(2) Virtually hundreds
(3) Countless hundreds
(4) Hundreds
(5) Countless, virtually, hundreds

31. Sentence 5: **The harder the Communist countries tried to stop the flow of people to the West, the harder they tried to succeed.**

What correction should be made to this sentence?

(1) change they to these
(2) change they to it
(3) change they to the people
(4) change the spelling of succeed to suceed
(5) no correction is necessary

32. Sentence 6: **We have never known what it is like to live under a harsh dictatorship with secret police looking over your shoulder, with constant shortages of food and other consumer goods, and in crowded living conditions.**

What correction should be made to this sentence?

(1) change known to knowed
(2) change your shoulder to their shoulder
(3) change your shoulder to our shoulders
(4) change your shoulder to his shoulder
(5) no correction is necessary

33. Sentence 7: **The sudden, dramatic shift in political conditions throughout the Communist East in 1989 that resulted in the destruction of the Berlin Wall had gave birth to hope.**

What correction should be made to this sentence?

(1) change East to east
(2) insert a comma after East
(3) change resulted to will result
(4) change Berlin Wall to berlin wall
(5) change had gave to gave

34. Sentence 8: **Perhaps we were beginning an era of world cooperation, and understanding that would rise above politics and communism.**

Which of the following is the best way to write the underlined portion of this sentence? If you think the original is the best way, choose option (1).

(1) cooperation, and understanding
(2) cooperation; and understanding
(3) cooperation and understanding
(4) cooperation; and, understanding
(5) cooperation and; understanding

35. Sentence 10: **The free world celebrated as the Berlin Wall came tumbling down.**

If you rewrote sentence 10 beginning with

As the Berlin Wall came tumbling down,

the next words should be

(1) but the free world
(2) the free world
(3) because the free world
(4) consequently the free world
(5) and the free world

Items 36 to 39 refer to the following paragraphs.

(1) Lifestyles change greatly from generation to generation. (2) Our lifestyles are becoming more casual today then in the past.

(3) There is still many people with the "me first" instant gratification lifestyle. (4) However, on account of this we are beginning to be concerned about such things as the environment and our impact on it. (5) We, as a nation, is becoming more health conscious and aware of the importance of diet, exercise, low cholesterol, and high fiber. (6) We are more casual; our dress and activities are less formal than in the past.

(7) Where would we be without our jeans, denim jackets, leather jackets, and tennis shoes? (8) Not only fast food places but also the expensive restaurants now welcome customers without a suit coat and necktie.

36. Sentence 2: **Our lifestyles are becoming more casual today then in the past.**

Which of the following is the best way to write the underlined portion of this sentence? If you think the original is the best way, choose option (1).

(1) today then in
(2) today, than in
(3) today or in
(4) today, then in
(5) today than in

37. Sentence 3: **There is still many people with the "me first" instant gratification lifestyle.**

What correction should be made to this sentence?

(1) change There is to There are
(2) replace There with Their
(3) change lifestyle to Lifestyle
(4) replace me with myself
(5) no correction is necessary

38. Sentence 4: **However, on account of this we are beginning to be concerned about such things as the environment and our impact on it.**

Which of the following is the best way to write the underlined portion of this sentence? If you think the original is the best way, choose option (1).

(1) However, on account of this we
(2) However on account of this we
(3) However we
(4) However, we
(5) However, We

39. Sentence 5: **We, as a nation, is becoming more health conscious and aware of the importance of diet, exercise, low cholesterol, and high fiber.**

What correction should be made to this sentence?

(1) remove the comma after nation
(2) change nation, is to nation, are
(3) replace conscious with conscience
(4) change aware to awares
(5) no correction is necessary

Items 40 to 47 refer to the following paragraphs.

(1) The social security system was back in the beginning originally created to supplement retirement income. (2) The social security act of 1935 never intended for social security to be the only source of retirement income. (3) When enacted it did not provide for our widows, orphans, and those whom have disabilities.

(4) The system grew over the years; and the costs jumped sharply due to added benefits and inflation. (5) Also, since people now live longer due to improved health care. (6) The number of people receiving benefits has grown faster than the number of people paying into social security. (7) This caused the system to run out of money, required major changes, and increased taxes on those people which were working to support those who were retired.

(8) The social security system is now sound again. (9) In fact, it has large surpluses, which the government is using to fund other programs, temporarily. (10) This practice could lead to more problems in the future.

(11) We have to keep in mind that everything has a cost. (12) If we want the government to provide for us in our old age, we will have to pay for it in our youth.

40. Sentence 1: **The social security system was back in the beginning originally created to supplement retirement income.**

What correction should be made to this sentence?

(1) remove the word back
(2) remove the phrase in the beginning
(3) remove the phrase back in the beginning
(4) remove the word originally
(5) no correction is necessary

41. Sentence 2: **The social security act of 1935 never intended for social security to be the only source of retirement income.**

What correction should be made to this sentence?

(1) change social security act to Social security act
(2) change social security act to Social Security Act
(3) change the spelling of intended to entended
(4) change retirement income to Retirement Income
(5) no correction is necessary

42. Sentence 3: **When enacted it did not provide for our widows, orphans, and those whom have disabilities.**

Which of the following is the best way to write the underlined portion of this sentence? If you think the original is the best way, choose option (1).

(1) those whom have disabilities
(2) those who have disabilities
(3) those which have disabilities
(4) those whom are disabled
(5) disabilities

43. Sentence 4: **The system grew over the years; and the costs jumped sharply due to added benefits and inflation.**

Which of the following is the best way to write the underlined portion of this sentence? If you think the original is the best way, choose option (1).

(1) years; and the
(2) year's; and the
(3) years, and the
(4) years; and, the
(5) year's, and the

44. Sentences 5 and 6: **Also, since people now live longer due to improved health care. The number of people receiving benefits has grown faster than the number of people paying into social security.**

Which of the following is the best way to write the underlined portion of this sentence? If you think the original is the best way, choose option (1).

(1) health care. The number
(2) health care, the number
(3) health care; the number
(4) health care, while the number
(5) Health Care, the number

45. Sentence 7: **This caused the system to run out of money, required major changes, and increased taxes on those people which were working to support those who were retired.**

What correction should be made to this sentence?

(1) change money to Money
(2) change taxes to Taxes
(3) change which to who
(4) change which to whom
(5) no correction is necessary

46. Sentence 9: **In fact, it has large surpluses, which the government is using to fund other programs, temporarily.**

What correction should be made to this sentence?

(1) remove the comma after fact
(2) change the spelling of which to witch
(3) change the spelling of government to goverment
(4) change using to used
(5) move temporarily between the words using and to

47. Sentence 12: **If we want the government to provide for us in our old age, we will have to pay for it in our youth.**

If you rewrite sentence 12 beginning with

We will have to pay in our

the next words should be

(1) youth, if we want
(2) youth if we want
(3) youth; if, we want
(4) youth if, we want
(5) youth; if we want

Items 48 to 51 refer to the following paragraphs.

(1) The Academy Awards, or Oscars, are awarded each year by the academy of Motion Picture Arts and Sciences. (2) These are the oldest and best known awards in the entertainment industry. (3) Oscars are awarded for best picture, best director, best actor, best actress, and best supporting actress, as well as several other categories.

(4) What does an Oscar look like? (5) It is a gold-plated bronze statue that is about 10 inches high and weighs about 7 pounds.

(6) The Academy Awards ceremony has become a popular TV show each Spring. (7) It is a showcase of personalities and talent in the entertainment industry. (8) The Oscars are sought after and valued highly by every actor and actress, and they are a real prize. (9) Any film that wins one or more Oscars is just about guaranteed a good box office income.

48. Sentence 1: **The Academy Awards, or Oscars, are awarded each year by the academy of Motion Picture Arts and Sciences.**

What correction should be made to this sentence?

(1) change academy to Academy
(2) change Oscars to oscars
(3) change Arts and Sciences to arts and sciences
(4) change the spelling of Sciences to Sceinces
(5) no correction is necessary

49. Sentences 4 and 5: **What does an Oscar look like? It is a gold-plated bronze statue that is about 10 inches high and weighs about 7 pounds.**

The most effective combination of sentences 4 and 5 would include which of the following groups of words?

(1) An Oscar looks like it is a gold-plated
(2) An Oscar looks like a gold-plated
(3) An Oscar is a gold-plated
(4) It is a gold-plated
(5) An Oscar is like a gold-plated

50. Sentence 6: **The Academy Awards ceremony has become a popular TV show each Spring.**

What correction should be made to this sentence?

(1) change Academy Awards to academy awards
(2) change the spelling of become to becume
(3) replace has with have
(4) change Spring to spring
(5) no correction is necessary

51. Sentence 8: **The Oscars are sought after and valued highly by every actor and actress, and they are a real prize.**

Which of the following is the best way to write the underlined portion of this sentence? If you think the original is the best way, choose option (1).

(1) actress, and they are
(2) actress; and they are
(3) actress, and the Oscars are
(4) actress, and they is
(5) actress; and, they are

Items 52 to 55 refer to the following paragraphs.

(1) The supermarket scanner, a device that reads the prices on groceries at the checkout and records them, is a fairly new application of computer technology. (2) The technical name for these devices are "optical character readers." (3) The scanner is the input part of a computer system. (4) It is often connected to a computer voice who names the item being scanned.

(5) The scanner shines a light on the bar code on an item and reads the code. (6) The bar code is the small box or block with the rows of vertical lines on the package with different widths and spacing. (7) This code identifies what the item is and what it costs. (8) To change the price on an item, someone enters the code for the item in the computer and changes the price.

52. Sentence 1: **The supermarket scanner, a device that reads the prices on groceries at the checkout and records them, is a fairly new application of computer technology.**

What correction should be made to this sentence?

(1) remove the comma after scanner
(2) change scanner to Scanner
(3) remove the comma after them
(4) change them, is to them; is
(5) no correction is necessary

53. Sentence 2: **The technical name for these devices are "optical character readers."**

Which of the following is the best way to write the underlined portion of this sentence? If you think the original is the best way, choose option (1).

(1) these devices are
(2) which these devices are
(3) these devices will be
(4) these devices is
(5) these devices were

54. Sentence 4: **It is often connected to a computer voice who names the item being scanned.**

What correction should be made to this sentence?

(1) replace It with They
(2) change is to was
(3) change is to are
(4) replace who with that
(5) no correction is necessary

55. Sentence 6: **The bar code is the small box or block with the rows of vertical lines on the package with different widths and spacing.**

What correction should be made to this sentence?

(1) replace bar code with Bar Code
(2) change is to were
(3) change is to are
(4) move on the package after spacing
(5) no correction is necessary

Answers are on page 888.

Simulated GED Test Correlation Chart: Writing Skills

Name: _____   **Class:** _____   **Date:** _____

This chart can help you determine your strengths and weaknesses on the content and skill areas of the Writing Skills GED Test. Use the Answer Key on pages 888–893 to check your answers to the test. Then circle on the chart the numbers of the test items you answered correctly. Put the total number correct for each content area and skill area in each row and column. If you answered fewer than 55 questions correctly, look at the total items correct in each column and row and decide which areas are difficult for you. Use the page references to study those areas.

Content/ Item Type	Sentence Correction	Sentence Revision	Rewrite/ Combine	Total Correct	Page Reference
Mechanics *(Pages 64–87)*					
Capitalization	4, 41, 48, 50			_____ out of 4	64–65
Commas	5, 15, 19, 27, 52	13, 34, 43	47	_____ out of 9	68–71
Semicolons		21		_____ out of 1	72–73
Apostrophes and Quotation Marks	28	8, 26		_____ out of 3	74–75
Usage *(Pages 88–115)*					
Subject-Verb Agreement	3, 16, 18, 37, 39	2, 53		_____ out of 7	88–90
Verb Tenses and Irregular Verbs	6, 9, 33	7	10	_____ out of 5	91–97
Pronouns	24, 32, 45, 54	42		_____ out of 5	98–101
Pronouns and Antecedents	31	51		_____ out of 2	102–105
Sentence Structure *(Pages 116–142)*					
Sentence Fragments		11, 44	1	_____ out of 3	116–118
Run-On Sentences		20		_____ out of 1	119–121
Combining Sentences			25, 49	_____ out of 2	122–125
Parallel Structure	12, 22	14		_____ out of 3	126–128
Subordination		23, 36	17, 29, 35	_____ out of 5	129–131
Misplaced Modifiers	46, 55			_____ out of 2	132–135
Revising Sentences	40	30, 38		_____ out of 3	136–140
Total Correct				Total correct: _____ out of 55	

1–43 → You need more review.
44–55 → Congratulations! You're ready for the GED Test!

For additional help, see the Steck-Vaughn GED Writing Skills Exercise Book.

THE ESSAY SIMULATED GED TEST

Directions

This part of the Writing Skills Test is intended to determine how well you write. You are asked to write an essay that explains something or presents an opinion on an issue. In preparing your essay, you should take the following steps:

1. Read carefully the directions and the essay topic given below.

2. Plan your essay carefully before you write.

3. Use scratch paper to make any notes.

4. Write your essay on separate paper.

5. Read carefully what you have written and make any changes that will improve your essay.

6. Check your paragraphs, sentence structure, spelling, punctuation, capitalization, and usage, and make any necessary corrections.

You will have 45 minutes to write on the topic below. Write legibly and use a ballpoint pen so that the evaluators will be able to read your writing. The notes you make on the blank pages (scratch paper) will not be scored. Your composition will be scored by at least two trained evaluators who will judge the paper according to its overall effectiveness. They will be concerned with how clearly you make the main point of your composition, how thoroughly you support your ideas, and how clear and correct your writing is throughout the composition. You will receive no credit for writing on a question other than the one assigned.

TOPIC

In the 1950s people began to hear about computers. Some people thought computers would never last. Others feared computers would take their jobs. Today computers are part of our lives.

Write a composition of about 200 words about how computers affect our lives. You may wish to deal with the good or bad effects, or both.

When you finish your essay, see page 893 of the Answer Key to evaluate and score your essay.

SOCIAL STUDIES SIMULATED GED TEST

Directions

The Social Studies Simulated GED Test is intended to measure your knowledge of general social studies concepts.

This test consists of 64 multiple-choice questions that are based on short readings, graphs, maps, charts, cartoons, and diagrams. Study the information given and then answer the questions that follow. Refer to the information as often as necessary in answering the questions.

You should spend no more than 85 minutes answering the 64 questions on this test. Work carefully, but do not spend too much time on any one question. Do not skip any items. Make a reasonable guess when you are not sure of an answer. You will not be penalized for incorrect answers. When time is up, mark the last item you finished. This will tell you whether you can finish the real GED Test in the time allowed. Then complete the test.

Record your answers to the questions on a copy of the answer sheet on page 922. Be sure that all required information is properly recorded on the answer sheet.

To record your answers, mark the numbered space on the answer sheet that corresponds to the answer you choose for each question on the test.

Example: Early pioneers of the western frontier looked to settle on land that had adequate access to water. To ensure access to water, many early pioneers settled on land near

    (1) forests
    (2) grasslands
    (3) rivers
    (4) glaciers
    (5) oceans

The correct answer is "rivers"; therefore, answer space 3 should be marked on the answer sheet.

Do not rest the point of your pencil on the answer sheet while you are considering your answer. Make no stray or unnecessary marks. If you change an answer, erase your first mark completely. Mark only one answer for each question; multiple answers will be scored as incorrect. Do not fold or crease your answer sheet.

When you finish the test, use the Correlation Chart on page 681 to determine whether you are ready to take the real GED Test, and, if not, which skill areas need additional review.

Adapted with permission of the American Council on Education.

Directions: Choose the best answer to each item.

Items 1 and 2 refer to the following information.

The First Amendment to the U.S. Constitution says that Congress shall make no law about an establishment of religion, or prohibiting the free practice of religion; or reducing the freedom of speech or of the press; or the right of the people to assemble peaceably, and to request that the government listen to their complaints.

1. This amendment supports which of the following rights?

    (1) marching in a pro-choice rally
    (2) voting in presidential elections
    (3) receiving a trial by jury
    (4) traveling freely between states
    (5) owning a gun

2. By the addition of the First Amendment to the Constitution, the writers demonstrated that they placed a high value on

    (1) a free-market economy
    (2) the powers of Congress
    (3) representative democracy
    (4) the rights of individual citizens
    (5) the division between federal and state governments

Item 3 refers to the following paragraph.

A worldwide survey conducted in 1988 by the United Nations found no evidence that capital punishment was a deterrent to crime. In addition, innocent people have been, and no doubt will continue to be, executed by mistake. Yet the United States, alone among the Western democracies, maintains an active death sentence, with public opinion polls showing that 79 percent of Americans favor the death penalty.

3. According to the paragraph, Americans appear to place the highest value on

    (1) mercy
    (2) human life
    (3) punishment
    (4) democratic principles
    (5) protection of the innocent

Item 4 refers to the following information.

The way people behave in groups can have important consequences. For example, in 1961 President Kennedy and his advisers planned and implemented an invasion of Cuba by 1,500 CIA-trained Cuban exiles. When the Bay of Pigs invasion failed and the American government was blamed, President Kennedy asked, "How could we have been so stupid?" In fact, the high morale of Kennedy and his advisers after the recent election had led them to believe they would succeed. To keep the good group feeling, opposing views were suppressed, especially after Kennedy showed his enthusiasm for the plan.

The following year, President Kennedy and his advisers had to deal with the Cuban missile crisis. The former Soviet Union was building missile bases in Cuba. By asking for opinions and discussing problems before acting, Kennedy was able to get the Soviets to withdraw without armed conflict.

4. The different outcomes of the two group efforts described above were partly the result of

    (1) an improvement in Kennedy's ability to lead a group
    (2) a change of administration
    (3) an entirely new group of advisers
    (4) the Civil Rights movement at home
    (5) increased input from the American public

Items 5 to 7 refer to the following map.

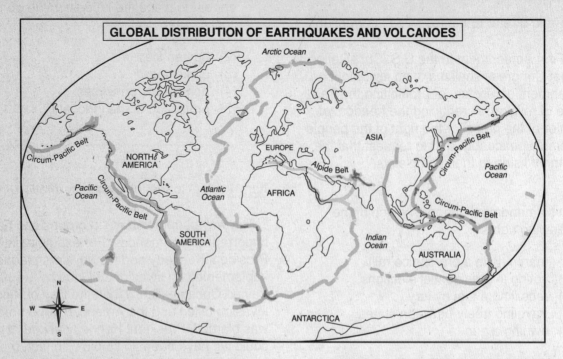

GLOBAL DISTRIBUTION OF EARTHQUAKES AND VOLCANOES

5. According to the map, in which region would you expect an increased use of earthquake-resistant architecture?

   (1) northern Africa
   (2) the eastern coast of South America
   (3) the western coast of the United States
   (4) northern Europe
   (5) Australia

6. All of the following statements are true. Which one is supported by evidence in the map?

   (1) There are an estimated one million earthquakes a year, but most are so minor that they are not noticed.
   (2) Volcanic eruptions cannot be accurately predicted.
   (3) There are about 500 active volcanoes, 20 or 30 of which erupt each year.
   (4) Soils from volcanic rocks are extremely fertile.
   (5) Compared to dry land, the ocean floor is thin and easily pierced by the underlying hot molten rock.

7. Which statement is an opinion rather than a fact according to the map?

   (1) A large earthquake will occur along the West Coast of the United States.
   (2) There have been large concentrations of volcano and earthquake activity in the Pacific Ocean.
   (3) Large concentrations of volcano and earthquake activity have been recorded in Central America.
   (4) There have been few recorded earthquakes or volcanoes in the Great Lakes region of the United States.
   (5) More earthquakes or volcanoes occur in the oceans than on the land.

Item 8 refers to the following paragraph.

During the Vietnam War, some American soldiers tortured and killed Vietnamese civilians. When this was first reported in the press, many Americans refused to believe the reports.

8. The paragraph suggests that, even in war, many Americans believe in

    (1) individual liberty
    (2) religious freedom
    (3) free speech
    (4) hard work
    (5) protection of innocent people

Items 9 and 10 refer to the following paragraph.

In the 1932 presidential election, Franklin D. Roosevelt won a landslide victory with his promise of a "New Deal" for a United States suffering from a severe economic depression. His program included public works, welfare legislation, and aid to agriculture. Almost as important as his programs was his confident, personal style. Continuing a practice begun when he was governor of New York, Roosevelt broadcast a number of "fireside chats" over the radio in which he spoke to the people as a neighbor who had just dropped by for a talk. These "chats" were designed to keep the public informed and to reassure them that government was acting in their interests.

9. The purpose of Roosevelt's "fireside chats" was to

    (1) persuade the public to support legislation
    (2) win votes in the 1932 presidential election
    (3) recruit people into public works programs
    (4) tell the people that government was working for them
    (5) inform government about what people wanted

10. It is the writer's opinion that

    (1) Franklin D. Roosevelt was once governor of New York
    (2) Roosevelt was elected President in 1932
    (3) Roosevelt promised the country a "New Deal"
    (4) Roosevelt's confident, personal style was almost as important as his programs
    (5) Roosevelt gave a number of "fireside chats" over the radio

Item 11 refers to the following paragraph.

When President Dwight Eisenhower became convinced that Fidel Castro was allied with the Soviet Union, he put in motion a plan to overthrow Castro's government. John F. Kennedy inherited the plan when he became President, and shortly after his inauguration, he launched the disastrous Bay of Pigs invasion. On April 17, 1961, 1,500 Cuban exiles, trained and equipped by the United States, landed at the Bay of Pigs on Cuba's southern coast. Every member of the invasion force was quickly killed or captured. Kennedy at first denied U.S. involvement, but soon accepted responsibility.

11. What was the most likely reason for trying to overthrow Castro?

    (1) anti-Communist sentiment among Americans
    (2) anti-Cuban sentiment among Americans
    (3) pressure from Cuban exiles
    (4) President Kennedy's fear that Cuba would invade the United States
    (5) President Eisenhower's alliance with the Soviet Union

Items 12 to 14 refer to the following information.

The highest official in state government is the governor. The governor's executive powers include enforcing state laws and heading the National Guard and the state police forces. Listed below are other executive officers that exist in most states. These officials are either appointed by the governor or elected by the people.

1. lieutenant governor—serves as governor when the governor is out of the state. Becomes governor if the elected governor leaves office before his or her term is up.

2. attorney general—legal officer who advises the governor on matters of law and represents the state in important court cases.

3. secretary of state—the chief clerk of the state who keeps the documents of the state and records all official actions taken by the state government.

4. comptroller—the chief financial officer of the state who keeps track of the accounts of those who collect and spend state money. The comptroller makes sure that state money is being spent legally.

5. treasurer—receives and keeps state money and maintains accurate records of all money received and spent. The treasurer can pay out money only on checks written by the comptroller.

12. In some states, most of the above officials are elected by the people. The best reason for this would be to

   (1) give more people a chance to run for office
   (2) make sure the governor does not have too much power
   (3) make sure all minority groups are represented
   (4) make sure the governor does not spend too much money
   (5) get more people interested in voting

13. The state treasurer receives a check requesting that an unusually large sum of money be paid out. Which course of action would the treasurer most likely choose?

   (1) call the governor for approval
   (2) pay out the money
   (3) look for the attorney general's signature
   (4) look for the comptroller's signature
   (5) ask the secretary of state to record the transaction

14. Kim is looking for a job in which she can use her accounting skills and her knowledge of the legal system. She should apply for a job with the

   (1) lieutenant governor
   (2) attorney general
   (3) secretary of state
   (4) comptroller
   (5) treasurer

Items 15 to 17 refer to the following paragraphs.

In 1787, delegates from 12 states met to write the Constitution of the United States. Among the issues they faced was how many representatives each state should have in the new legislature.

The Virginia Plan, introduced by Edmund Randolph, proposed a legislature of two houses. Members of the first house were to be elected by the people. Members of the second house were to be elected by members of the first house. States would be represented in proportion to their populations.

States with small populations were naturally worried. Their alternative was the New Jersey Plan, introduced by William Paterson. It proposed that each state have an equal voice in the legislature and that each state elect an equal number of representatives.

Delegates remained split on the issue for months. At last, a committee was formed that worked out the final compromise. Congress would be made up of two houses. Each state would elect two representatives to the Senate. States would elect representatives to the House of Representatives in proportion to their population.

15. Which idea underlies the final compromise made by the writers of the Constitution?

    (1) Government should be by consent of the people.
    (2) A weak central government is best.
    (3) Representatives should be property owners.
    (4) Voters must be white, male property owners.
    (5) States should not have their own legislatures.

16. Under this plan for representation, if Maine loses population, it will be represented in Congress by

    (1) fewer senators
    (2) fewer representatives
    (3) fewer state senators
    (4) more representatives
    (5) more senators, to make up for losing representatives

17. Which most likely resulted from the decision on representation?

    (1) Congress's power to impeach the President
    (2) the census, a regular count of the population
    (3) the lifetime appointment of Supreme Court justices
    (4) the two-thirds vote needed to override a President's veto
    (5) making the President commander-in-chief of the armed forces

Items 18 and 19 refer to the following cartoon.

"Made in Hong Kong! Made in Hong Kong! How can we compete with their cheap labor?"

18. An appropriate government response to protect the U.S. economy in the situation pictured would be to

    (1) increase sales taxes
    (2) increase export quotas
    (3) institute price controls
    (4) increase import tariffs
    (5) advertise "Buy American"

19. The most probable solution to the situation pictured in the cartoon is to

    (1) buy more radios
    (2) buy radios made in the U.S.
    (3) buy radios made in Hong Kong
    (4) avoid buying radios
    (5) buy televisions instead of radios

Items 20 to 22 refer to the following paragraph.

The most common animals in the Arctic and subarctic are reindeer and caribou, and vast herds of them roam the arctic pastures. But lemmings and voles compete with caribou and reindeer for the arctic grass. A single pair of these mouselike creatures may have more than a hundred descendants a year. Their number reaches a high point every three or four years. This cycle in the lemming and vole populations affects other animals and people. Snowy owls and other birds, together with foxes, eat the creatures. The birds fly north in great numbers when there are many lemmings and voles to eat. The foxes raise large families because of the abundant food supplies. Then the Eskimos can trap more foxes and sell their furs. But the lemmings and voles use up the grasses as their numbers increase, and this forces the caribou to move away. The whole cycle begins again as the grasses grow once again, and the lemmings and voles increase.

20. Which statement is the best summary of the paragraph?

   (1) Lemming and vole populations reach a high point every three or four years.
   (2) Snowy owls, other birds, and foxes eat lemmings and voles.
   (3) Foxes raise large families because of the abundant food supply.
   (4) The lemming and vole population cycles affect other animals and people.
   (5) Lemmings and voles compete with caribou and reindeer for the arctic grasses.

21. What might Eskimos do in years when the lemmings and voles are most plentiful?

   (1) live by trapping
   (2) turn to fishing
   (3) hunt more caribou
   (4) move to better grassland
   (5) move to subarctic regions

22. A geographer might use this information to illustrate which concept?

   (1) urbanization—the proportion of people living in cities increases
   (2) mixed farming—crop rotation and mixed land use for conservation
   (3) ecosystem—an ecological community, the relationship of living things to each other and their environment
   (4) acculturation—people becoming accustomed to a new environment
   (5) domestication—adapting of plants and animals to human use

Item 23 refers to the following cartoon.

"We plan to bargain all night until an agreement is reached."

23. The main idea of the cartoon is

   (1) collective bargaining is exhausting
   (2) management always lies
   (3) labor always lies
   (4) the media have a right to know the facts
   (5) labor and management agreed to maintain the image of round-the-clock negotiations

Items 24 and 25 refer to the following paragraph.

"A politician in this country must be the man of a party," wrote John Quincy Adams in 1802. Just five years after George Washington left office, political parties were a fact of American life. Also a fact, then as now, was the dominance of two major parties. Today it is Republicans versus Democrats; in the past it was Republicans challenging Federalists, and Democrats against Whigs. Third parties appeared as early as 1832. They have backed presidential candidates, some as well known as Theodore Roosevelt. But no third-party candidate has ever been elected. Since 1860, fewer than one vote in 20 has been cast for a third-party presidential candidate. It may be the power of the major parties' machinery—their organization and money—that keeps them on top. Or perhaps voters are hesitant to vote for a person, or a party, that they see as having little chance of winning.

24. Which statement about the paragraph is the best summary?

    (1) Because third parties get so few votes, the United States remains a two-party system.
    (2) Third parties have always existed in the American political system.
    (3) Third parties have failed to offer popular candidates for President.
    (4) American voters are either Democrats or Republicans.
    (5) Because third parties get so few votes, the Republican and Democratic parties have always been dominant.

25. The writer of the paragraph has the opinion that

    (1) a politician in this country must be the man of a party
    (2) third parties appeared in 1832
    (3) since 1860, fewer than one vote in 20 has been cast for third-party candidates
    (4) voters possibly hesitate to vote for someone they think cannot win
    (5) Theodore Roosevelt once ran as a third-party candidate for President

Item 26 refers to the following paragraph.

Between 1892 and 1943, Ellis Island in New York Harbor was the major U.S. immigration station. More than 12 million arrivals were recorded there, often having their names Americanized or changed entirely. Today, Ellis Island is a national historic site.

26. From the information, it can be inferred that

    (1) the United States is no longer accepting immigrants
    (2) immigrants are no longer received and processed in New York
    (3) the United States is populated largely by immigrants and their descendants
    (4) immigration policy now favors people with professional skills
    (5) no more immigrants were accepted after World War II

Item 27 is based on the following cartoon.

ED STEIN
Reprinted courtesy of the Rocky Mountain News.

27. From the cartoon you can infer that the 2nd Amendment

    (1) guarantees freedom of speech
    (2) gives people the right to bear arms
    (3) protects against unreasonable searches and seizures
    (4) prohibits cruel and unusual punishment
    (5) grants women the right to vote

Items 28 to 30 refer to the following paragraphs.

In defining economic systems, it is important to determine who owns the means of production (factories, businesses, etc.) and who, as a result, makes most economic decisions.

Under capitalism, private persons own most businesses, and individual producers and consumers decide what to produce, how to produce it, and for whom it should be produced. To earn more money, producers use their resources to manufacture goods that consumers want. Consumers tell producers what they want when they buy certain goods in the marketplace. Under capitalism, government plays a very small role in economic decision making: it regulates more than controls.

Under socialism, the government owns more of the natural and industrial resources, especially large-scale resources such as steel mills and utilities, so government makes most of the important economic decisions. Under socialism, government sets goals for the society as a whole and controls the economy to try to reach those goals. Scandinavia and many European countries have socialist economies. But they differ greatly from each other in the degree to which their governments own businesses and make economic policy.

28. Which is not an effect of capitalism?

   (1) Consumers influence prices by buying or not buying products.
   (2) Government controls the price of water and electricity.
   (3) Producers make as much profit as they can.
   (4) Producers make more of an item when consumers demand it.
   (5) Individuals buy factories.

29. What is most likely to happen in a socialist economy?

   (1) The owner of a textile mill decides to sell stock in his company.
   (2) National Motor Works makes air bags standard equipment on all its cars because drivers want air bags.
   (3) A dairy farmer sells his milk to the bottler who offers the highest price.
   (4) Government planners ask the nation's farmers to produce 10 percent more wheat this year.
   (5) A railroad drops its unprofitable passenger service between two small cities.

30. Which generalization is supported by the paragraphs?

   (1) There are no poor people in capitalist countries.
   (2) Everyone has a job in socialist countries.
   (3) Self-interest is the motive that drives most socialists.
   (4) The United States is the world's leading capitalist economy.
   (5) Many modern economies have both capitalist and socialist elements.

Item 31 refers to the following information.

In Canada police officers stop cars every night at roadblocks to examine drivers for signs of drinking. People do not seem to mind, and most say that they are grateful. In 1988 the Supreme Court of Canada ruled that roadside stops by police looking for drunk drivers were not an invasion of the rights of drivers who were not drinking. In the United States the police would need probable cause (a good reason to be suspicious) in order to stop a particular driver.

31. Which of these is more highly valued by Canadians than by Americans?

   (1) individual rights
   (2) public safety
   (3) police control
   (4) free speech
   (5) trial by jury

Items 32 and 33 refer to the following information.

U.S. POPULATION: 1950 TO 1990			
		Increase over preceding census	
Census	Population	Number	Percent
1950	151,325,798	19,161,229	14.5
1960	179,323,175	27,997,377	18.5
1970	203,302,031	23,978,856	13.4
1980	226,545,805	23,243,774	11.4
1990	248,709,873	22,167,674	9.8

32. What is the main idea of the table?

   (1) The number of people who answer the census does not increase according to the increase in population.
   (2) The population is increasing.
   (3) People do not like to answer the census.
   (4) Fewer people answered the census in 1990 than in 1980.
   (5) The population decreased from 1980 to 1990.

33. The census is taken every 10 years. If this table had new information, it probably would be

   (1) different figures for 1950
   (2) the census figures for 2000
   (3) a lower percentage for 1960
   (4) a higher percentage for 1970
   (5) a different population count for 1980

Items 34 and 35 refer to the following paragraphs.

In 1974, Congress passed the Equal Credit Opportunity Act (ECOA). This act bans any discrimination based on sex or marital status in the granting of credit.

Before this act, a married woman could get credit only if her husband's credit was good. A credit card had to be issued in the husband's name. When a woman divorced, she usually had no credit history and was often denied credit because of it.

Since passage of the ECOA, a lender may not ask about marital status unless the borrower

   (1) is applying jointly with a spouse,
   (2) is letting a spouse use the account, or
   (3) lives in a community-property state.

Nor may a lender ask about alimony, child support, or separate maintenance, unless the borrower is depending on those to repay the loan.

The lender must issue the card or account in the name of the applicant and give the reasons if credit is denied.

34. Before the Equal Credit Opportunity Act, lenders were able to give or deny credit based on which assumption?

   (1) Many women work.
   (2) Women are good credit risks.
   (3) Single men earn more than single women.
   (4) Married people are better credit risks than single people.
   (5) Married women are economically dependent on their husbands.

35. By passing the Equal Credit Opportunity Act, Congress recognized the value of

   (1) marriage
   (2) children
   (3) economic fairness
   (4) equal educational opportunity
   (5) women in the work force

Items 36 and 37 are based on the following map.

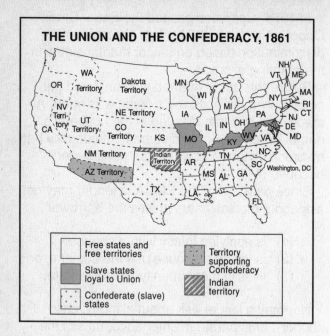

THE UNION AND THE CONFEDERACY, 1861

Legend:
- Free states and free territories
- Slave states loyal to Union
- Confederate (slave) states
- Territory supporting Confederacy
- Indian territory

36. Which information in the map <u>best</u> supports the fact that slavery was not the only issue of the Civil War?

   (1) Texas and the Arizona Territory supported the Confederacy.
   (2) Indian Territory was not yet the state of Oklahoma.
   (3) The nation's capital was located in a slave state.
   (4) Slavery existed in the border states between the Confederacy and the Union, but these states remained loyal to the Union.
   (5) There were 18 free and 15 slave states in 1861.

37. Which is a statement of opinion rather than a statement of fact according to the map?

   (1) By 1861, Texas had become a state.
   (2) By 1861, Kansas had become a state.
   (3) Kansas entered the Union as a free, or anti-slave, state.
   (4) The Confederate states were in the South, the Union states in the North.
   (5) The border states probably remained in the Union because most of their populations believed slavery was wrong.

Items 38 and 39 refer to the following quotation.

"We are determined to enforce the law, to make our streets and neighborhoods safe. . . . We won't have safe neighborhoods unless we are tough on drug criminals, much tougher than we are now. Sometimes that means tougher penalties, but more often it just means punishment that is sure and swift."
—President George Bush

38. Based on the quotation, which <u>most likely</u> would have been supported by the former President?

   (1) legalizing marijuana use
   (2) more drug-treatment programs
   (3) mandatory jail terms for convicted drug dealers
   (4) decreased federal funds for the Drug Enforcement Agency
   (5) fewer police

39. Which assumption appears to have been behind President Bush's statement?

   (1) All criminals take drugs.
   (2) Drugs contribute to crime.
   (3) Judges are too hard on drug addicts.
   (4) Drug addicts can be treated medically.
   (5) There are not enough prisons to hold all of the country's drug criminals.

Items 40 and 41 refer to the following paragraph.

Mergers between companies and the takeover of one company by another have become a fact of American business life. Some large department stores have run into financial trouble and have put themselves up for sale. Some retail managers and suppliers who have been employed by such companies are now worried about job security. New owners may want to hire an entirely different management staff or reorganize the existing team. The goods that a supplier had previously sold might not be what the new owners want to feature in their stores. Even stores that are not undergoing change can be affected by the companies that are. The financially troubled companies might get into price wars to cut prices and increase immediate sales. On the other hand, some people can benefit from the shifting business scene. The newly formed companies are often more independent and more financially secure than the old ones. Top executives can be fairly sure that their special knowledge is needed to keep the companies running smoothly. In addition, secure companies are taking advantage of the shake-ups by offering jobs to the skilled employees of the companies in transition.

40. Which of the following is the most probable cause of a new owner hiring a new staff and/or new suppliers?

    (1) to correct the financial problems the old company had
    (2) as a goodwill gesture
    (3) to hire his or her relatives
    (4) to please the top executives
    (5) to save money

41. Which of the following is most likely to result when two companies merge?

    (1) operating with less efficiency
    (2) letting some employees go
    (3) lowering salaries
    (4) raising salaries immediately
    (5) completely changing the product line

Items 42 and 43 refer to the following paragraphs.

Families have varying abilities to get, save, and pass on economic resources. Low-income families pool the resources of a large network of people. This network becomes "family," even though some members may not be related by blood. These families depend on this large network for help when work is scarce.

Middle-income families have secure resources. The traditional nuclear family—father, mother, and children—is most common in this bracket. The independence of the family results from better-paid jobs. When middle-income families need help, they tend to go to non-family sources: banks, credit cards, insurance.

Among wealthy people, family again expands to the extended family. Their kinship ties preserve inherited wealth. Marriage is a way to keep and extend the resources of the family. To help maintain their lifestyle, these families have a national network of institutions: boarding schools, colleges, clubs, charities, and vacation resorts.

42. According to the paragraphs, what family form is typical of low-income families?

    (1) traditional nuclear family
    (2) network of relatives and nonrelatives
    (3) institutional
    (4) dual-earner couples with children
    (5) stepfamilies with children

43. From the viewpoint of the writer, the values underlying family forms are

    (1) moral and ethical
    (2) related to romantic love
    (3) child-centered
    (4) economic
    (5) idealistic

Items 44 and 45 refer to the following pie charts.

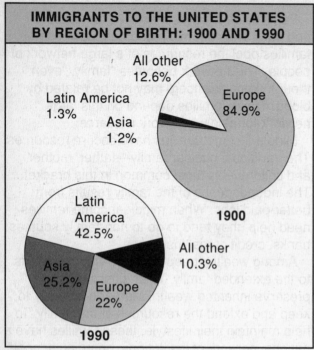

IMMIGRANTS TO THE UNITED STATES BY REGION OF BIRTH: 1900 AND 1990

All other 12.6%
Latin America 1.3%
Asia 1.2%
Europe 84.9%
1900

Latin America 42.5%
Asia 25.2%
Europe 22%
All other 10.3%
1990

Source: U.S. Bureau of the Census

44. According to the pie charts, which of the following would most likely be found in the United States today?

(1) cultural diversity in food, education, the media, and other aspects of life
(2) a concentration of Latin American immigrants in the Midwest
(3) more European immigrants than Asian immigrants
(4) the same cultural values in all regions of the country
(5) more immigrants settling in rural than in urban areas

45. Which of the following statements is best supported by the charts?

(1) The percent of European immigrants has risen sharply since 1900.
(2) Latin Americans make up the largest group of immigrants in the United States today.
(3) The children of immigrants adapt more easily to American life than their parents do.
(4) Each year, the United States accepts 20,000 immigrants from each country.
(5) Most immigrants become American citizens within 15 years of their arrival.

Item 46 refers to the following paragraph.

Dr. Louis W. Sullivan, former Secretary of Health and Human Services, spoke out against the plan of one tobacco company to test-market a new cigarette, called Uptown, aimed primarily at African Americans. Dr. Sullivan, who is African American, said: "At a time when our people desperately need the message of health promotion, Uptown's message is more disease, more suffering, and more death for a group already bearing more than its share of smoking-related illness and mortality."

46. From the paragraph, it can be inferred that

(1) smoking will soon become illegal
(2) test-marketing encourages children to begin smoking
(3) African Americans as a group have a high percentage of smokers
(4) smokers as a group are no more inclined to disease than nonsmokers
(5) cigarette ads are not allowed on television

Item 47 is based on the following advertisement.

CONSTRUCTION
Roofers & Carpenters
South suburban company needs experienced roofers. Must have own tools and car. Also carpenters. Apprentices with 4 years experience. Laborers 1 year experience. Must have own tools and car. Call for appointment. 707-555-6767

47. Which applicant is best qualified for one of the jobs described in the ad?

(1) Brenda has done some lawn and yard maintenance.
(2) Glen graduated with honors from high school.
(3) Bob has done some roofing, but he does not have a driver's license.
(4) Pedro has worked as a carpenter for three years and has his own tools and car.
(5) Jan would like to work with his hands, has a car, and lives in the south suburbs.

Items 48 and 49 refer to the following information.

Dollars are used as currency in the United States, and yen are used in Japan. Dollars and yen can be exchanged for each other. Their values in relation to each other change over time.

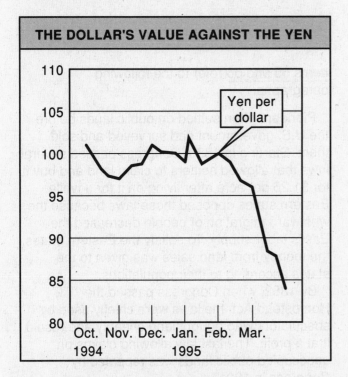

THE DOLLAR'S VALUE AGAINST THE YEN

Yen per dollar

48. To get the most for your dollar in Japan, you would have been best off traveling there in

   (1) November 1994
   (2) December 1994
   (3) January 1995
   (4) February 1995
   (5) March 1995

49. Which of the following statements is supported by the information?

   (1) The dollar was at its lowest value in relation to the yen in October 1994.
   (2) The dollar's value increased against the yen for the period shown.
   (3) Right after World War II, you could get more than 300 yen per dollar.
   (4) The dollar's value against the yen fell steadily in February and March 1995.
   (5) If the trend continues, Japanese products will cost less for American consumers.

Item 50 refers to the following paragraph.

Earth's outer shell consists of moving plates, some of which carry the continents. As some plates move apart and collide with continental plates, the material gets crushed up into mountain chains. The Himalayas were formed by the collision of continental plates. The Andes were formed by a collision between a continental and an oceanic plate.

50. Based on the paragraph, one can conclude that Earth's surface is

   (1) unchanging
   (2) constantly being reformed
   (3) mostly covered by water
   (4) set in motion by earthquakes
   (5) gradually being smoothed by erosion

Item 51 refers to the following paragraph.

The main units of local government include counties, townships, municipalities (villages, towns, and cities), and special districts. Special districts usually govern a single service, such as parks or flood control, in a geographical area.

51. According to the information, all of the following are responsibilities of local government except

   (1) redesigning and rebuilding a dangerous intersection of a U.S. highway
   (2) installing street lights in the village of Wayne
   (3) providing ambulance service to the Tri-City area
   (4) taxing the users of a county airport
   (5) funding School District 303

Items 52 and 53 are based on the following information.

The sixth amendment of the U.S. Constitution says, in part, that a person accused of a crime

"shall enjoy the right to a speedy and public trial, by an impartial jury of the state and district wherein the crime shall have been committed . . . and to be informed of the nature and cause of the accusation; to be confronted with the witnesses against him; . . . and to have the assistance of counsel for his defense."

52. According to the information, which situation is prohibited by the 6th Amendment?

(1) Someone is accused of a crime.
(2) A home is searched by police who have no warrant.
(3) Arrested for murder, the accused is denied bail.
(4) A person is jailed for a year before being brought to trial.
(5) A person is tried twice for the same crime.

53. The 6th Amendment affirms belief in the

(1) protection of accused people
(2) supremacy of federal over state government
(3) rights of minorities
(4) right of citizens to petition the government
(5) powers of the presidency

Item 54 refers to the following paragraph.

The Samali are Moslem camel herders. Often family groups feud with other groups and steal their camels on raids. If a man or woman is hurt during one of these encounters, the offending family group has to pay fines. For injuries to the eye, ear, arm, or leg, the payment is 25 to 50 camels. For an injury that causes death, the fine can be up to 100 camels.

54. The Samali apparently place a high value on

(1) family life
(2) religion
(3) human life
(4) money
(5) peace

Items 55 and 56 refer to the following paragraphs.

Pioneers often settled on public lands before the U.S. government had surveyed and sold them. Starting in 1830, Congress passed several laws that allowed settlers to claim land and buy it for $1.25 per acre after living on it for a while. Eastern states opposed these laws because the westward migration of people decreased the East's labor supply. To satisfy the Eastern states, the money from land sales was given to the states according to their populations.

By 1862, when Congress passed the Homestead Act, the laws were chiefly used by speculators who bought land cheaply and resold it at a profit. The last law allowing claims on unoccupied public lands was repealed by Congress in 1891.

55. Pioneers who settled on unclaimed land are most similar to

(1) urban homesteaders who become owners of abandoned buildings that they fix up
(2) soldiers who are placed in regular units after basic training
(3) nomads who move from place to place with their animals and belongings
(4) people who inherit property from their parents
(5) couples buying their first home or apartment

678

56. Settlers who moved west to claim land most likely assumed that

    (1) all the land was suitable for farming
    (2) eventually they would own the land they claimed
    (3) renting the land from the government was more economical
    (4) they would own only the buildings but not the land itself
    (5) only desert land was left to claim

Items 57 and 58 refer to the following map.

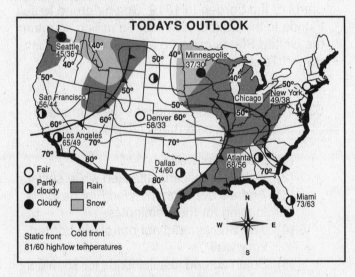

57. What is the most likely effect of the weather?

    (1) Snow delays flights at Minneapolis airports.
    (2) The Denver schools have a snow day.
    (3) Pollution closes Los Angeles beaches.
    (4) Smog disrupts air travel in New York.
    (5) Hurricane Alice threatens Miami.

58. Which statement is supported by the information in the map?

    (1) Temperatures in Denver will not reach the expected high of 58°F.
    (2) There should be fair skies for several days throughout the Southwest.
    (3) Partly cloudy skies and highs in the 70s are expected in Dallas today.
    (4) Rain-slick roads will cause traffic accidents in New York.
    (5) Isolated flash-flood warnings are expected in the Chicago area.

Items 59 and 60 refer to the following paragraph.

The Industrial Revolution refers to the period of great economic and social change brought on by the use of machines. Beginning in the mid-1700s in England, the machine age then spread throughout western Europe and the United States in the eighteenth and nineteenth centuries. As people turned from making things by hand at home to making them by power-driven machines, often in huge factories, production increased a great deal. Mechanization brought great wealth to some and made others lose their jobs. The mechanical reaper, for example, displaced thousands of farm workers.

59. The author states that the Industrial Revolution caused social upheaval. Which evidence from the paragraph best supports this?

    (1) The Industrial Revolution began in England.
    (2) The Industrial Revolution spread throughout western Europe and the United States in the eighteenth and nineteenth centuries.
    (3) People once made things by hand at home.
    (4) Mechanization increased production.
    (5) The mechanical reaper left thousands of farm workers without jobs.

60. According to the paragraph, what was the direct cause of increased production during the Industrial Revolution?

    (1) making things by hand
    (2) making things at home
    (3) power-driven machines
    (4) great wealth
    (5) displaced farm workers

Items 61 and 62 refer to the following paragraph.

Congress outlawed the manufacture and sale of liquor with the passage of the 18th Amendment. It was quickly ratified by the states and became law in 1919. Support for Prohibition, as it was called, was strong among rural and small-town people but weak in the cities. Widespread refusal to obey the law led to dishonesty among public officials, courts that did not function properly, and the rise of criminals who profited from illegal liquor sales. The law was repealed in 1933 by the passing of the 21st Amendment.

61. The purpose of Prohibition was to

    (1) prevent the making and selling of liquor
    (2) prevent public officials from becoming dishonest
    (3) ratify the 18th Amendment
    (4) repeal the 21st Amendment
    (5) keep liquor away from children

62. One effect of Prohibition was

    (1) the corruption of small-town America
    (2) a better court system
    (3) the passage of the 18th Amendment
    (4) an increase in urban crime
    (5) support among rural people

Items 63 and 64 refer to the following paragraphs.

After the American Revolution, the United States stretched from the East Coast to the Mississippi River. However, Florida was still owned by Spain. Spain was too weak to threaten the United States, but Florida was a problem to President James Monroe. In 1817 the Seminole tribe in Florida began to attack white settlers in nearby Georgia. Monroe told U.S. Army officer Andrew Jackson to deal with them. He also gave Jackson secret orders to find the Seminoles in Florida and eliminate them as a threat. Jackson did so, capturing two Spanish outposts.

This caused a diplomatic crisis with Spain. The United States blamed the incident on Spain's lax patrol of the border. In 1819, Spain agreed to sell Florida to the United States for $5 million. In return, the United States gave up all claims on Spanish-owned Texas.

63. Which of the following was the immediate cause of the diplomatic crisis with Spain?

    (1) Spain was weak.
    (2) Native Americans attacked white settlers.
    (3) Andrew Jackson invaded Florida while looking for the Seminoles.
    (4) The Spanish did not patrol the border very well.
    (5) Spain agreed to sell Florida for $5 million.

64. The 1819 agreement with Spain is most similar to which of the following agreements?

    (1) the 1763 Peace of Paris, in which France gave up the Mississippi Valley and Canada
    (2) the agreement between Generals Ulysses S. Grant and Robert E. Lee that ended the Civil War
    (3) the 1945 meeting at Yalta, in which the Allies decided to divide Germany into four zones for occupation
    (4) the 1953 agreement in which Korea was divided into the Communist north and democratic south
    (5) the Strategic Arms Limitation Treaty in which the United States and Russia agreed to end the nuclear arms buildup

Answers are on page 893.

Simulated GED Test Correlation Chart: Social Studies

Name: _____   Class: _____   Date: _____

This chart can help you determine your strengths and weaknesses in the content and skill areas of the Social Studies GED Test. Use the Answer Key on pages 893–898 to check your answers to the test. Then circle on the chart the numbers of the test items you answered correctly. Put the total number correct for each content area and skill area in each row and column. Look at the total items correct in each column and row and decide which areas are difficult for you.

Cognitive Skills/Content	Comprehension *(pp. 198–203)*	Analysis *(pp. 209–212)*	Application *(pp. 204–206)*	Evaluation *(pp. 216–219)*	Total Correct
Geography *(pages 240–251)*	21, **32**, 50	**7**, 20, 56, **57, 58**	5, 22, **33**	**6**	____ out of 12
History *(pages 252–271)*	9, 11, 26, 61	10, 15, **37**, 60, 62, 63	16, 17, 55, 64	**36**, 59	____ out of 16
Economics *(pages 272–283)*	**23**, 30, 42	28, 40, 41	**18, 19**, 29, **48**	43, **49**	____ out of 12
Political Science *(pages 284–297)*	12, 24, **27**	13, 25, 39	1, 38, 51, 52	2, 3, 14, 53	____ out of 14
Behavioral Science *(pages 298–311)*	46	4, 34	**44, 47**	8, 31, 35, **45**, 54	____ out of 10
Total Correct	____ out of 14	____ out of 19	____ out of 17	____ out of 14	Total correct: ____ out of 64

1–54 → You need more review.
55–64 → Congratulations! You're ready for the GED Test!

Boldfaced numbers indicate items based on charts, graphs, illustrations, and diagrams.

© 1997 Steck-Vaughn Company. *Complete GED Preparation.* Permission granted to reproduce for classroom use.

For additional help, see the Steck-Vaughn GED Social Studies Exercise Book.

SCIENCE SIMULATED GED TEST

Directions

The Science Simulated GED test consists of multiple-choice questions intended to measure your understanding of general concepts in science. The questions are based on short readings that often include a graph, chart, or diagram. Study the information given, and then answer the questions that follow. Refer to the information as often as necessary in answering the questions.

You should spend no more than 95 minutes answering the 66 questions. Work carefully, but do not spend too much time on any one question. Do not skip any items. Make a reasonable guess when you are not sure of an answer. You will not be penalized for incorrect answers.

When time is up, mark the last item you finished. This will tell you whether you can finish the real GED Test in the time allowed. Then complete the test.

Record your answers to the questions on a copy of the answer sheet on page 922. Be sure that all required information is properly recorded on the answer sheet.

To record your answers, mark the numbered space on the answer sheet that corresponds to the answer you choose for each question on the test.

Example:

Which of the following is the smallest unit in a living thing?

(1) tissue
(2) organ
(3) cell
(4) muscle
(5) capillary

The correct answer is "cell"; therefore, answer space 3 should be marked on the answer sheet.

Do not rest the point of your pencil on the answer sheet while you are considering your answer. Make no stray or unnecessary marks. If you change an answer, erase your first mark completely. Mark only one answer space for each question; multiple answers will be scored as incorrect. Do not fold or crease your answer sheet.

When you finish the test, use the Correlation Chart on page 702 to determine whether you are ready to take the real GED Test, and, if not, which skill areas need additional review.

Adapted with permission of the American Council of Education.

Directions: Choose the <u>best answer</u> to each item.

<u>Items 1 and 2</u> refer to the following map.

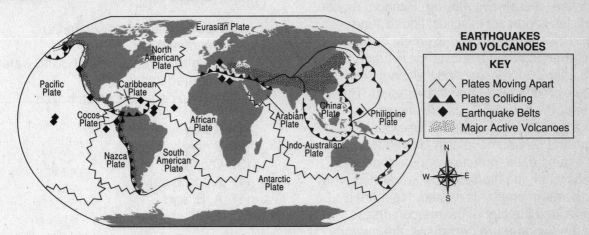

1. Large sections of Earth's crust that move slowly across Earth's surface are called plates. When two plates collide, one of the effects is the

   (1) formation of large ocean areas
   (2) creation of islands
   (3) formation of continents
   (4) formation of volcanoes
   (5) creation of rivers

2. Which of the following areas would provide a good opportunity for studying volcanoes and earthquakes?

   (1) northern Europe
   (2) southern Africa
   (3) Australia
   (4) eastern North America
   (5) western South America

<u>Item 3</u> refers to the following information.

   All matter is composed of basic substances called elements. An element is a substance that cannot be broken down into simpler substances by chemical reactions. Some common elements are iron, carbon, and oxygen. The smallest particle of an element that still has the properties of that element is called an atom. The smallest particle of the element iron is an iron atom, and a sample of the element iron contains only iron atoms.

   When two or more different elements react chemically, a compound is produced. For example, iron oxide, or rust, is a compound made when iron and oxygen react together.

3. Which of the following is an unstated assumption by the author?

   (1) Elements can be broken down into simpler substances by methods other than chemical reactions.
   (2) All compounds are made of some combination of the elements iron and oxygen.
   (3) Compounds are usually solids.
   (4) Elements have at least two different types of atoms.
   (5) Compounds are more interesting than elements.

Items 4 to 6 refer to the following article.

The basic particles of matter—atoms and molecules—are always moving. Random motion of particles is present in solids, liquids, and gases. The energy of this movement is called kinetic energy. When a substance is heated, the kinetic energy increases, and the atoms and molecules move faster and farther apart. The volume of the substance usually increases. When a substance is cooled, it loses kinetic energy, and its volume usually decreases.

For example, the mercury in a thermometer expands when the thermometer is warmed. The more the thermometer is heated, the more it expands, and the higher the mercury rises. When the temperature decreases, the mercury contracts and moves down the thermometer.

Different substances expand by different amounts when heated. Engineers must account for these differences when designing buildings, roads, and other structures. Steel bridges, for example, have special structures at each end to allow for expansion in warm weather. Concrete bridges have expansion joints between slabs. These joints prevent the concrete from buckling when it expands.

Water behaves unlike most other substances. When it cools and freezes, it does not contract; it expands.

4. Which of the following can be concluded from the information provided?

   (1) All substances expand when heated and contract when cooled.
   (2) All substances contract when heated and expand when cooled.
   (3) Most substances expand when heated and contract when cooled.
   (4) Most substances contract when heated and expand when cooled.
   (5) Most substances do not change volume when heated or cooled.

5. Given the behavior of matter when heated and cooled, which of the following would be likely to happen?

   A. Telephone wires sag in the summertime.
   B. A glass breaks when boiling water is poured into it.
   C. Soup contracts when frozen.

   (1) A only
   (2) B only
   (3) C only
   (4) A and B only
   (5) A, B, and C

6. When enough thermal energy is added, substances change from solids to liquids and then to gases. What can be concluded about the molecules and atoms in solids, liquids, and gases?

   (1) The molecules and atoms of gases are the farthest apart and the most mobile.
   (2) The molecules and atoms of liquids are the farthest apart and the most mobile.
   (3) The molecules and atoms of solids are the farthest apart and the most mobile.
   (4) The molecules and atoms of matter behave in the same way in solid, liquid, and gas forms.
   (5) The molecules and atoms of a solid do not move.

Items 7 and 8 are based on the following information.

Density is the relationship between the mass of a substance and its volume. For example, a substance of great mass and small volume is very dense. One substance can be distinguished from another if you know the density of each. The following chart shows the densities of some metals.

DENSITY OF SELECTED METALS	
Metal	Density in Grams per Cubic Centimeter
Aluminum	2.7
Iron	7.9
Copper	8.9
Lead	11.3
Mercury	13.6
Gold	19.3

7. An object will sink in a liquid if it is more dense than the liquid. Which of the following metals will sink in liquid mercury?

   (1) iron
   (2) copper
   (3) lead
   (4) gold
   (5) aluminum

8. Pure gold is 24-karat gold. Since pure gold is too soft to hold its shape, jewelers almost always mix copper with gold to make jewelry. For example, 14K gold contains 14 parts of pure gold by weight to 10 parts of pure copper. Which of the following would have the greatest density?

   (1) 24K gold
   (2) 18K gold
   (3) 14K gold
   (4) 10K gold
   (5) They would all have the same density.

Items 9 and 10 refer to the following article.

Tides are the alternate rise and fall of the sea level in oceans. They are caused primarily by the moon's gravitational pull. The sun's gravitational pull also contributes to the tides. At any one time, there are two high tides—one on the side of Earth facing the moon and one on the opposite side. The average time between high tides at any one location is 12 hours and 25 minutes.

The typical difference in sea level between high and low tides is two feet in the open ocean. Near the coast, the difference can be much greater. The greatest difference between high and low tides occurs in the Bay of Fundy in eastern Canada, where the sea level changes by 40 feet.

As the tides change, currents flow to redistribute the ocean's water. Near the coast, the direction of the current changes every 6 1/4 hours. The current first flows toward the shore in what is called a flood current. Then the current flows away from the shore in what is called an ebb current.

9. What is the primary cause of tides on Earth?

   (1) ocean currents
   (2) the gravitational pull of the sun
   (3) the gravitational pull of the moon
   (4) the positions of the planets relative to Earth
   (5) the rotation of Earth

10. When the moon, Earth, and sun are in a straight line, tides are higher than usual. What is the most likely cause of this?

   (1) The sun's gravitational pull is added to that of the moon, which increases the height of the tides.
   (2) The moon is in a position in which its gravitational pull is weaker.
   (3) The positions of the three bodies cause an increase in rainfall, thereby raising the sea level.
   (4) The positions of the three bodies cause an increase in the amount of polar ice melting, thereby raising the sea level.
   (5) Tides are higher during the spring.

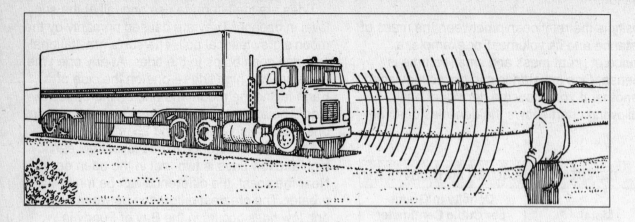

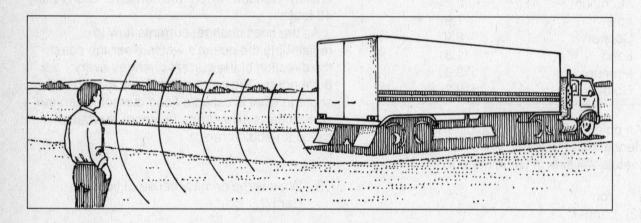

The Doppler effect describes the apparent changes that take place in waves, such as sound waves, as a result of the movement of the source or receiver of the waves. If the source of a sound and the receiver are moving closer together, the frequency seems to increase and the sound seems higher to the receiver. If the sound and the receiver are moving apart, the frequency seems to decrease and the sound seems lower.

11. Which of the following conclusions can be supported by the information given?

(1) The Doppler effect works only with sound waves.

(2) The Doppler effect can be used to determine whether a source of sound is moving away from or toward someone.

(3) The Doppler effect works only when the source of sound is close.

(4) The Doppler effect is a change in the actual frequency of sound waves as they are sent by the source.

(5) The Doppler effect is used to overcome interference from other sources of sound.

Items 12 to 17 refer to the following article.

Many insects have a wormlike stage called a larva before becoming adults. The screwworm is the larva of a fly that lays its eggs in the open sores of cattle and other animals. Hundreds of worms can develop in a single sore and kill the host animal. In warm climates, the screwworm does millions of dollars of damage each year.

Controlling the screwworm has long been a problem. Chemical control using insecticides could kill the insects. However, applying insecticides to individual animals is too expensive. A biological control method was first tried in 1958 on the island of Curaçao in the West Indies. Large numbers of sterile male flies raised in laboratories were released on the island. The theory was that if there were more sterile males that could not fertilize female flies than fertile males, many females would mate with the sterile males. Since the females mate only once, most of the eggs would not be fertilized. The number of young produced would eventually reach zero.

The Curaçao project was successful, and screwworm flies were eliminated from the island. Since then, sterile-male release has been used to control the screwworm in the southwestern United States. However, the screwworm also lives in Mexico, where it is not well controlled. Therefore, release of sterile males must be continued along the border.

12. According to the article, which method of controlling screwworms continues to be used today?

    (1) spraying insecticides
    (2) treating wounded cattle
    (3) sterilizing the males in the wild
    (4) releasing laboratory-bred sterile males
    (5) sterilizing the eggs laid by the females

13. Why was the decision made to try to control screwworm damage on cows in Curaçao by biological rather than chemical methods?

    (1) Chemical insecticides were hard to obtain.
    (2) Treating cattle individually with chemical insecticides was too expensive.
    (3) The chemical methods were less effective than biological control.
    (4) Biological methods do not harm the environment.
    (5) Biological methods can be easily developed by individual farmers.

14. Which of the following is an unstated assumption made by the author of this article?

    A. A change in the ecology of an area is permissible if the results can be helpful.
    B. Getting rid of an agricultural pest has more advantages than disadvantages.
    C. Chemical pesticides may be suitable for other insect-control problems.

    (1) A only
    (2) B only
    (3) C only
    (4) A and B only
    (5) A, B, and C

15. Based on the article, you can conclude that biological control

    (1) works best on insect populations that cover a wide geographical area
    (2) works best on isolated insect populations
    (3) is always better than chemical insecticides
    (4) does not work because insects evolve different ways of reproducing
    (5) is more expensive than chemical pesticides in the long run

16. Another type of biological control is to release males that have been exposed to radiation. The sperm of these males carry deadly genetic defects. In such a situation, you would expect that the population would

    (1) die out in one generation because none of the eggs would be fertilized
    (2) die out in several generations because most of the eggs would not be fertilized
    (3) decrease in several generations because many fertilized eggs would be seriously defective and would die
    (4) stay the same because the females would continue to mate
    (5) increase because more eggs would be fertilized

17. Which of the following is most similar to the sterile-male release method of controlling insects?

    (1) releasing chemical insecticides in areas such as swamps
    (2) spaying animals to prevent their reproduction
    (3) introducing predators to feed on the pest
    (4) introducing viruses or bacteria that are harmful to the pest
    (5) setting traps for animal pests such as rats and mice

Items 18 and 19 refer to the following chart.

PULSE RATE AFTER ONE MINUTE OF EXERCISE			
Subject's Physical Condition	Pulse Rate (beats per minute)		
	Light Exercise	Moderate Exercise	Heavy Exercise
Excellent	66	73	82
Very good	78	85	96
Average	90	98	111
Below average	102	107	126
Poor	114	120	142

18. After one minute of moderate exercise, the pulse rate of a person in average physical condition is faster than the pulse rate of a person in

    (1) below average condition after one minute of moderate exercise
    (2) below average condition after one minute of light exercise
    (3) very good condition after one minute of heavy exercise
    (4) average condition after one minute of heavy exercise
    (5) poor condition after one minute of light exercise

19. Which of the following statements is supported by the information in the chart?

    (1) The pulse rate increases with additional minutes of exercise.
    (2) People in poor physical condition should not do heavy exercise.
    (3) As the pulse rate rises during exercise, so does the number of breaths per minute.
    (4) For people in excellent physical condition, the pulse rate increases from light to moderate exercise and decreases from moderate to heavy exercise.
    (5) There is a greater difference in the pulse rate between moderate and heavy exercise than between light and moderate exercise.

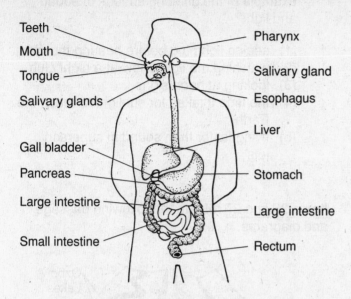

Teeth
Mouth
Tongue
Salivary glands
Gall bladder
Pancreas
Large intestine
Small intestine

Pharynx
Salivary gland
Esophagus
Liver
Stomach
Large intestine
Rectum

20. The entire digestive system consists of a long main tube called the alimentary canal. The liver and pancreas are connected to the alimentary canal by small tubes. The alimentary canal ends at the

(1) liver
(2) pancreas
(3) rectum
(4) large intestine
(5) small intestine

21. The stomach produces an acid that helps digest food. Heartburn is a painful feeling in the chest caused by stomach acids irritating the

(1) salivary glands
(2) esophagus
(3) large intestine
(4) small intestine
(5) rectum

Carbon monoxide is a gas produced by coal stoves, furnaces, or gas appliances when they do not get enough air. It is present in the exhaust of internal combustion engines, such as the ones in cars and lawn mowers.

Carbon monoxide is a deadly poison. Since it is colorless, odorless, and tasteless, it is very difficult to detect. Victims of carbon monoxide poisoning become drowsy and then unconscious. Death can occur in minutes.

22. Which of the following actions is likely to be dangerous?

(1) operating a well-vented coal furnace
(2) mowing the lawn
(3) using a properly installed gas stove
(4) running a car engine in a closed garage
(5) using a barbecue grill outdoors

23. What is the first symptom of carbon-monoxide poisoning?

(1) a bad taste
(2) convulsions
(3) choking
(4) unconsciousness
(5) drowsiness

Items 24 and 25 refer to the following article.

Sound waves are produced by rapid back-and-forth movements called vibrations. The vibrations cause disturbances in the particles of matter near them. The particles bump into one another and transmit the sound waves over distance. Because sound waves need particles of matter to transmit the disturbance caused by vibration, sound waves cannot travel through outer space.

Two factors that influence the speed of sound waves are the matter through which they travel and the temperature. Matter with particles more tightly packed, such as a solid, transmits sounds the fastest. Matter with particles loosely packed, such as a gas, transmits sound waves more slowly. In general, the higher the temperature, the faster sound travels through a given medium. The higher the temperature, the faster the particles of matter move, and the faster they bump into one another, transmitting sound waves.

Light waves, however, are produced by electric and magnetic forces. Light waves differ from sound waves in that they can travel through outer space as well as through matter. Light waves travel faster than sound waves. The speed of sound waves in air at 32°F is 1,085 feet per second. The speed of light is 186,282 miles per second.

24. Why do sound waves travel faster through solids than through gases?

(1) Gases are farther from the source of the vibration.
(2) Particles of solids are tightly packed and transmit disturbances quickly.
(3) Particles of gases are loosely packed and transmit disturbances quickly.
(4) Gases are empty space and do not transmit sound waves.
(5) Solids are warmer than gases.

25. Which of the following situations is an example of the differing speeds of sound and light?

(1) seeing lightning before hearing thunder
(2) watching the light show at a night club
(3) looking at neon signs
(4) the time it takes for sunlight to reach the Earth
(5) flying faster than sound in supersonic jets

Items 26 and 27 refer to the following passage and diagrams.

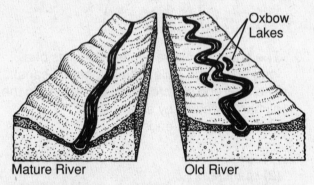

Mature River   Old River

The diagrams show a river at different stages of its life cycle. During the millions of years between the two stages, the river valley became wider and the river slower. It now winds in S curves called meanders.

26. What best accounts for the widening of the river valley?

(1) annual melting of winter snow
(2) earthquakes
(3) tides
(4) windstorms
(5) erosion by the river

27. Which of the following generalizations is supported by the diagrams?

(1) All rivers drain into an ocean.
(2) Oxbow lakes are found near old rivers.
(3) Flooding is caused by mature rivers.
(4) The valley of an old river is generally steep.
(5) Waterfalls are features of old rivers.

Items 28 and 29 refer to the following diagram.

CELL DIVISION

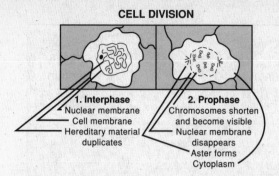

1. **Interphase**
Nuclear membrane
Cell membrane
Hereditary material
duplicates

2. **Prophase**
Chromosomes shorten
and become visible
Nuclear membrane
disappears
Aster forms
Cytoplasm

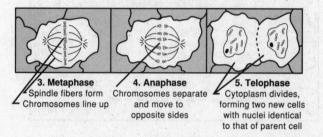

3. **Metaphase**
Spindle fibers form
Chromosomes line up

4. **Anaphase**
Chromosomes separate
and move to
opposite sides

5. **Telophase**
Cytoplasm divides,
forming two new cells
with nuclei identical
to that of parent cell

28. In cell division, one cell becomes two. Each cell must have chromosomes exactly like those of the parent cell. What step ensures that the chromosomes are the same?

    (1) duplication of hereditary material (Interphase)
    (2) disappearance of the nuclear membrane (Prophase)
    (3) formation of the aster (Prophase)
    (4) chromosomes shorten and become visible (Prophase)
    (5) division of the cell material (Telophase)

29. According to the diagram, where does the material that was inside the nucleus go when the nuclear membrane disappears?

    (1) It joins the cell membrane.
    (2) It links to the asters.
    (3) It enters the cytoplasm.
    (4) It makes up the spindles.
    (5) It is part of the nuclear membrane.

Item 30 refers to the following article.

Electric currents flowing through wires produce areas of magnetic force called electromagnetic fields. These electromagnetic fields are similar to the magnetic fields produced by magnets. The stronger the electric current, the stronger is the electromagnetic field surrounding it.

Very strong currents produce very strong fields. The force of a strong field can be felt several yards away from the wire. For example, fluorescent lamps held below a 161,000-volt transmission line light up without being plugged into an electric circuit. Many transmission lines are even more powerful.

Wires are not the only producers of electromagnetic fields. All electric appliances produce fields. Appliances with motors, such as hair dryers and washing machines, produce stronger fields than appliances without motors, such as lights and toasters.

Scientists are starting to question the effect of electromagnetic fields on our health. People living near power lines have long complained of headaches, fatigue, memory loss, and more illness than usual. There also seem to be more cases of particular types of cancer among people exposed to strong electromagnetic fields. Although the evidence is inconclusive, it raises some serious public health questions.

30. If high-power transmission lines that carry electricity from generating plants to homes and businesses are proved to be health hazards, what would be a likely solution to this problem?

    (1) Move all transmission lines to areas where few people live.
    (2) Move people away from high-power transmission lines.
    (3) Switch to another source of power for everyday use.
    (4) Cover the lines with material that blocks the electromagnetic fields.
    (5) Install small generators in each home and business.

Items 31 and 32 refer to the following information.

SINGLE FIXED PULLEY

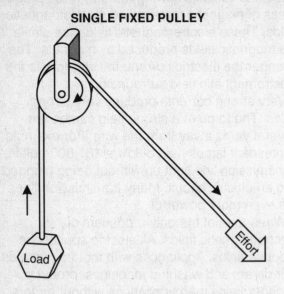

In an ideal pulley, the effort required to pull the rope is equal to the weight of the load.

31. When you pull down on the rope of a single pulley, what happens?

    (1) The load remains stationary.
    (2) The load moves downward.
    (3) The load moves upward.
    (4) The rope moves, but the pulley wheel does not turn.
    (5) The pulley wheel turns, but the rope does not move.

32. Which of the following conclusions is supported by the diagram?

    (1) A single fixed pulley changes the direction in which force must be exerted.
    (2) A single fixed pulley does not change the direction in which force must be exerted, but it decreases the force required.
    (3) A single fixed pulley does not make it easier to lift a very heavy object.
    (4) The distance in which the rope is pulled is half as long as the distance in which the load is lifted.
    (5) The distance in which the rope is pulled is twice as long as the distance in which the load is lifted.

Items 33 and 34 refer to the following diagram.

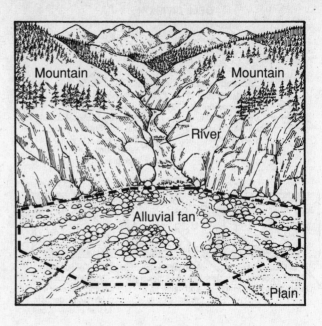

33. From the diagram you can conclude that alluvial fans

    (1) are ancient land formations
    (2) are formed by the action of glaciers
    (3) are formed by sediment or soil carried by rivers from mountains to the plain
    (4) contain rich soil that is good for agriculture
    (5) occur in regions of volcanic activity

34. When the river comes out of the mountains and into the plain, it

    (1) speeds up and becomes colder
    (2) becomes narrower and slows down
    (3) becomes narrower and speeds up
    (4) spreads out and slows down
    (5) goes underground

Simulated GED Test ◆ Science

Items 35 to 39 refer to the following article.

The path taken by an electric current is called a circuit. For electricity to flow, the circuit must be complete. In a flashlight, the electric current flows from one end of a battery through a wire to the bulb. From the bulb, the current returns along another wire to the other end of the battery. A switch is a device that enables you to break or complete the circuit, thereby stopping or restarting the flow of electric current.

Batteries used in toys and portable radios are called dry cells. These batteries are a common source of electric current for objects that must be portable. Dry cell batteries produce electricity by chemical reaction. This chemical reaction increases whenever the circuit is complete. When the circuit is broken, the current stops flowing and the chemical action continues, only more slowly. When the supply of chemicals is used up, the dry cell battery is dead.

A storage battery is often used to power larger devices. Chemical reaction is also the source of electric current in the storage battery. As long as the circuit is complete, the chemical reaction continues at an increased rate. When the chemicals are used up, the production of current stops. A storage battery does not need to be thrown away; its chemicals can be restored by recharging it with electric current from an outside source.

35. You pick up a flashlight that uses dry cell batteries and press the switch. Nothing happens. From your observations, which of the following is a valid conclusion?

    A. The chemical reaction in the batteries has increased.
    B. The chemicals in the batteries may have been used up.
    C. Storage batteries are better than dry cell batteries.

    (1) A only
    (2) B only
    (3) C only
    (4) A and B only
    (5) B and C only

36. A portable CD player stopped working. When its batteries were recharged, it worked again. Why did recharging help?

    (1) The chemical reaction continued at a reduced rate when the circuit was broken, and the chemicals were used up.
    (2) The chemical reaction continued at a steady rate when the circuit was broken, and the chemicals were used up.
    (3) An outside electric current restored the chemicals in the battery so that they could produce current again.
    (4) The CD player needed to be plugged in to operate.
    (5) The batteries were new.

37. A boy left his toy flashlight on, but the father told him to turn it off. Why did the father think it should be off?

    (1) The battery produces the same amount of current whether the light is on or off.
    (2) The battery can produce electric current as long as it is being recharged.
    (3) The life of the battery is the same whether the flashlight is left on or off.
    (4) The life of the battery is shorter when the flashlight is left on.
    (5) The battery will not wear out when the flashlight is left off.

38. Which of the following items is best suited for getting electric current from a dry cell battery?

    (1) a washing machine
    (2) a car
    (3) a motorized wheelchair
    (4) a toy truck
    (5) a doorbell

39. You need a large amount of electric current to start a car's engine. A car's internal combustion engine uses a large storage battery to produce this current. It does not take all this current to keep the car running. In fact, the battery is constantly being recharged while the car's engine is running. As a result, batteries do not have to be plugged into an electric outlet for recharging. Which of the following is a conclusion from this information?

    (1) A car battery is not powerful enough to provide electric current to start the motor.
    (2) Car batteries frequently need to be jump-started.
    (3) The car's engine generates electricity that recharges the battery as the car runs.
    (4) A car battery does not need external recharging for the first 25,000 miles.
    (5) A car battery does not need external recharging for the first 100,000 miles.

Items 40 to 43 are based on the following information.

    The animal kingdom is made up of thousands of species of animals. They are divided into several groups called phyla. Five of the phyla are described below:

1. Chordata. Animals have a notochord, or stiff rod of cells, as the primary skeletal support during some stage of development. Most members of this phylum are vertebrates, animals with backbones.
2. Mollusca. Animals have soft bodies and usually prominent shells.
3. Arthropoda. Animals have sectioned bodies covered by a jointed external skeleton.
4. Annelida. Soft-bodied, segmented animals are bilaterally symmetrical, or the same on both sides.
5. Cnidaria. Unsegmented animals are symmetrical around a central point and lack a true body cavity.

Each of the following animals belongs to one of the five phyla described. For each item, choose the appropriate phylum. Each phylum may be used more than once in items 40 to 43.

40. The earthworm, a cylindrical segmented worm, belongs to the phylum

    (1) Chordata
    (2) Mollusca
    (3) Arthropoda
    (4) Annelida
    (5) Cnidaria

41. The clam, a soft-bodied marine animal with a shell, belongs to the phylum

    (1) Chordata
    (2) Mollusca
    (3) Arthropoda
    (4) Annelida
    (5) Cnidaria

42. A cat, an animal with a backbone, belongs to the phylum

    (1) Chordata
    (2) Mollusca
    (3) Arthropoda
    (4) Annelida
    (5) Cnidaria

43. A grasshopper, a long, slender-winged insect with an external jointed skeleton, belongs to the phylum

    (1) Chordata
    (2) Mollusca
    (3) Arthropoda
    (4) Annelida
    (5) Cnidaria

Acquired immune deficiency syndrome (AIDS) is a disease that destroys the body's ability to protect itself from infection. It is an infection caused by the human immunodeficiency virus (HIV). The AIDS virus is transmitted in semen, vaginal secretions, and blood. The groups most at risk for contracting the disease are homosexual men, intravenous drug users, and their sex partners and their babies. Also at risk are people who received transfusions before blood supplies were screened for HIV.

This disease progresses slowly. During the first stage of AIDS, when the body is exposed to HIV, the person may or may not have flu-like symptoms. Within two months, antibodies to protect against HIV are produced. During the second stage, the virus is not active and the person feels fine. The second stage can last for years. In the third stage, swelling of the lymph nodes occurs, but the person is still relatively healthy. During the fourth stage, symptoms gradually appear. AIDS-related infections, tumors, and neurological diseases attack the body, eventually resulting in death.

Presently there is no way to destroy HIV once it is in the body. However, the spread of the virus can be prevented by "safer sex" techniques such as using condoms. The spread of AIDS can also be prevented by not sharing drug needles.

44. What causes AIDS?

(1) taking drugs intravenously
(2) engaging in homosexual activity
(3) receiving a blood transfusion
(4) HIV
(5) antibodies

45. What causes the production of HIV antibodies?

(1) exposure to HIV
(2) blood transfusions
(3) tumors
(4) swelling of the lymph nodes
(5) neurological diseases

RADIOACTIVE SUBSTANCES AND THEIR USES	
Substance	**Use**
Carbon 14	Estimating age of material that was once living
Arsenic 74	Finding brain tumors
Cobalt	Radiation treatment for cancer
	Tracing leaks or blockages in pipelines
Iodine 131	Treatment of thyroid gland problems
Radium	Radiation treatment for cancer
Uranium 235	Production of energy in nuclear reactors
	Atomic weapons

46. If a scientist were interested in determining the dating of a human bone from an ancient civilization, what radioactive substance could the scientist use?

(1) carbon 14
(2) arsenic 74
(3) cobalt
(4) iodine 131
(5) radium

47. Which of the following conclusions can be drawn from the information in the chart?

(1) All radioactive substances are expensive.
(2) Uranium 235 is used only for production of weapons.
(3) Radioactive substances are always beneficial to humans.
(4) Radioactive substances have many uses.
(5) Radioactive substances can be produced by humans.

Item 48 refers to the following information and diagram.

Methane is a colorless, odorless gas that is found in nature. It is a product of the breaking down of organic matter in marshes. It is also found in coal mines and natural gas deposits. When methane burns, it combines with oxygen to form carbon dioxide and water vapor, as shown in the following equation:

$$CH_4 \ + \ 2O_2 \ \rightarrow \ CO_2 \ + \ 2H_2O$$

In the reaction, atoms are rearranged to form different substances. The reaction begins with one molecule of methane (CH_4)—made up of one carbon and four hydrogen atoms—and one molecule of oxygen (O_2)—made up of two oxygen atoms. These recombine to form the new substances of carbon dioxide and water. The carbon dioxide (CO_2) molecule is made up of one carbon atom from the methane and two oxygen atoms from the oxygen molecules. Each water (H_2O) molecule is made up of two hydrogen atoms taken from the methane and another oxygen atom from the oxygen molecules. The atoms have formed new molecules, but the total number of each kind of atom remains the same. For example, there are four hydrogen atoms at the beginning of the reaction and four at the end.

The reaction of methane and oxygen can be hazardous to humans; the quantities of the gases and the speed of the reaction must be carefully controlled.

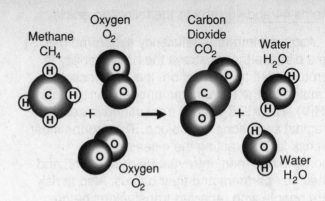

48. In order to write or express a chemical reaction in the form of an equation such as the one in the passage, what must be true?

(1) The result of the reaction must be a gas.
(2) The atoms must be made of one or more molecules.
(3) There must be an equal number of atoms from each element on each side of the equation.
(4) The same molecules must appear on each side of the equation.
(5) Each molecule in the equation must be either divided or multiplied by two.

Items 49 to 51 refer to the following article.

Pathogens are microorganisms that cause disease. To spread disease, a pathogen must leave the body of its host and enter another body. Many pathogens enter the body through a specific route. For instance, pathogens that cause respiratory diseases usually enter through the nose.

The manner in which a pathogen travels from one person to another is related to where the pathogen lives in the host. For example, an intestinal pathogen is likely to be found in the host's feces. Respiratory pathogens can be spread by droplets sneezed or coughed into the air. Such droplets may also be carried on objects. Body fluids, such as saliva, pus, mucus, and urine carry pathogens outside their hosts. Some pathogens that live in the blood are spread by bloodsucking insects such as mosquitoes.

49. A pathogen carried by droplets coughed or sneezed into the air is likely to infect the

(1) respiratory system
(2) intestines
(3) urinary system
(4) blood
(5) respiratory system and urinary system

50. You can prevent the spread of some pathogens by frequently washing your hands. With which pathogens is this effective?

A. respiratory pathogens
B. intestinal pathogens
C. pathogens in the blood

(1) A only
(2) B only
(3) C only
(4) A and B
(5) A and C

51. Malaria is a disease spread from one person to another through the bite of a female *Anopheles* mosquito. This implies that malaria affects the

(1) blood
(2) respiratory system
(3) skeleton
(4) digestive system
(5) brain

Items 52 and 53 refer to the following information.

About 8 percent of men and 0.5 percent of women are color-blind; that is, they have trouble distinguishing colors. Most color-blind people cannot distinguish red from green. Completely color-blind people see only black, white, and shades of gray; this condition is extremely rare.

52. The fact that many more men than women are color-blind implies that

(1) color is less important to men than to women
(2) color blindness is an illness
(3) color blindness is related to whether a person is male or female
(4) color blindness is associated with poor vision
(5) color blindness is a harmless visual defect

53. If a man cannot distinguish red from green, for what occupation would he be unsuitable?

(1) auto mechanic
(2) computer operator
(3) salesperson
(4) railroad engineer
(5) plumber

Items 54 to 57 refer to the following article.

Many kinds of ladybird beetles, or ladybugs, spend their time hunting insects to eat. They favor aphids and scale insects. Ladybugs can clean these harmful insects off plants, leaving the plants with energy to grow. Ladybugs have ample supplies of foul-tasting substances that repel insect-eating birds. Thus, ladybugs can spend the day in plain sight while hunting for insects.

The ladybug's appetite for harmful insects has been put to good use by farmers. An Australian variety of ladybug was imported into California to help control another Australian insect, the cottony cushion scale. This pest was accidentally introduced into America, and it quickly became a major pest in citrus orchards. The Australian ladybugs lay their eggs next to the eggs of the scale insect in citrus trees and other plants. Since a female lady bug lays about a thousand eggs and each hatchling eats about three thousand young scale insects, the benefits to citrus trees are enormous.

Ladybugs hunt until late fall when the cold limits their food supply. Then they take shelter in large groups until the spring. During the sheltering period, ladybugs can be collected in boxes and kept chilled until the spring. Then they can be sold to gardeners and farmers and released into the environment.

54. When do ladybugs hunt?

(1) twenty-four hours a day
(2) at night
(3) at dawn and dusk
(4) from spring to fall
(5) during the winter

55. An unstated assumption of the author is that

(1) ladybugs are hunters
(2) ladybugs are not active all year round
(3) most ladybugs are harmful to plants
(4) there are varieties of ladybugs that feed on different types of insects
(5) ladybugs are a type of beetle

56. Which of the following conclusions is supported by the information in the article?

(1) All varieties of ladybugs are hunters.
(2) Female ladybugs do not provide food for their young.
(3) Many ladybugs are beneficial to humans.
(4) Ladybugs have a life expectancy of less than two months.
(5) Ladybugs mate for life.

57. The winter behavior of ladybugs is most similar to

(1) frogs burying themselves in pond bottoms for the winter
(2) the migration of monarch butterflies south for the winter
(3) hares turning white in winter and brown in summer
(4) trees shedding leaves in the fall
(5) animals growing thicker fur for the winter

Items 58 and 59 refer to the following article.

Earthquakes start deep in Earth's crust. The point where an earthquake starts is called its focus. From the focus, energy moves outward in all directions, causing the ground to vibrate. These vibrations are called seismic waves.

In 1935, the American scientist Charles F. Richter developed a scale that measures the amplitude, or amount of back-and-forth movement, of the seismic waves at the focus of an earthquake. On the Richter scale, the amplitude of seismic waves increases ten times between each whole number. For example, an earthquake that measures 5 has waves with an amplitude ten times greater than one that measures 4.

The amount of energy released by an earthquake can be calculated from its Richter scale rating. Earthquakes that measure 4.5 or greater can cause serious damage if they occur in populated areas. Earthquakes that measure 7 or greater are considered severe. The famous 1906 San Francisco earthquake measured 8.3, and the 1989 San Francisco earthquake measured 7.1.

The Mercalli scale is also related to earthquakes. This scale uses Roman numerals to rate earthquakes according to their effects on a particular place where the quake is felt. For example, an earthquake felt only by scientific monitors would have a rating of I. An earthquake that destroyed all the buildings in a wide area would have the highest rating of XII. Since the effects of an earthquake differ from place to place, the Mercalli scale ratings in each place can differ.

58. The Mercalli scale measures

    (1) the amplitude of seismic waves on Earth's surface during an earthquake
    (2) the amplitude of seismic waves at the focus of an earthquake
    (3) the effect of an earthquake on the area precisely over the focus
    (4) the effects of an earthquake on a particular place
    (5) the seismic wave direction in an earthquake

59. What does the Richter scale measure?

    (1) the amplitude of seismic waves on Earth's surface during an earthquake
    (2) the amplitude of seismic waves at the focus of an earthquake
    (3) the direction of seismic waves in an earthquake
    (4) the amount of damage done by an earthquake
    (5) the distance between the focus of an earthquake and Earth's surface

Items 60 to 62 are based on the following article.

A gardener often builds a compost pile in a corner of a garden because the compost pile produces a mixture called humus. To create the compost pile, the gardener collects materials that were living, including kitchen waste (vegetable parings) and garden waste (lawn clippings and leaves). In the compost pile, microscopic organisms change this waste into humus. The gardener can then spread the humus on the soil to help plants grow well.

The most important microscopic organisms in compost are bacteria that specialize in breaking down organic matter. They thrive in temperatures up to 170°F and need air to survive. As the compost decomposes and cools, these bacteria give way to other microorganisms.

The new microorganisms include actinomycetes. These are a form of bacteria. As they become more active, they produce antibiotics, chemicals that kill the original bacteria. Protozoans are also present in compost. Their role in composting is less important than that of bacteria. Other compost organisms are fungi. They are primitive plants without chlorophyll. They are active during the final stages of composting.

60. Which microorganisms are active at the start of composting?

    (1) bacteria
    (2) actinomycetes
    (3) protozoa
    (4) fungi
    (5) All of the microorganisms are active at the start of composting.

61. All of the following material would be suitable for a compost pile except

    (1) manure
    (2) straw
    (3) lawn clippings
    (4) sawdust
    (5) plastic wrap

62. The removal of which of the following would have the greatest impact on the decomposition occurring in the compost pile?

    (1) bacteria
    (2) actinomycetes
    (3) protozoa
    (4) fungi
    (5) The impact would be the same, regardless of which are removed.

Items 63 and 64 refer to the following map.

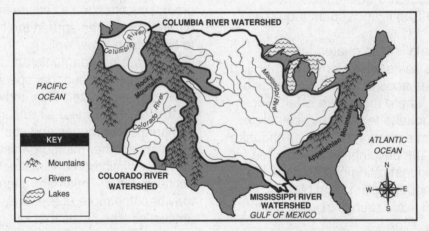

63. The area of land drained by a river is known as a watershed. Why does water in most watersheds eventually drain into an ocean?

    (1) The oceans are the largest bodies of water on Earth.
    (2) Each land mass is surrounded by an ocean.
    (3) Water flows toward the equator.
    (4) Water flows from high elevations, such as mountains, to sea level.
    (5) Too much water flows into the ocean too quickly.

64. How did early explorers of the Northwest use knowledge of watersheds to know they were approaching the Pacific Ocean?

    (1) They conserved water for the journey over the Rocky Mountains.
    (2) They saw that the Columbia River was flowing to the west.
    (3) They found the source of the Columbia River.
    (4) They encountered flooding in the Columbia River watershed.
    (5) They determined that the elevation of the Columbia River was too high to make it a major watershed.

Items 65 and 66 refer to the following diagram.

LAYERS OF EARTH'S ATMOSPHERE

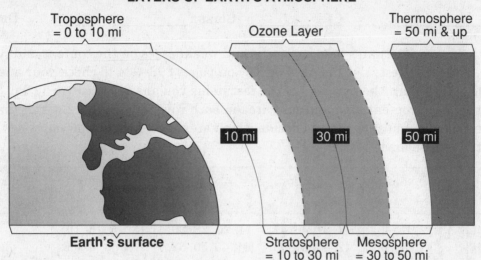

Troposphere = 0 to 10 mi

Ozone Layer

Thermosphere = 50 mi & up

10 mi | 30 mi | 50 mi

Earth's surface

Stratosphere = 10 to 30 mi   Mesosphere = 30 to 50 mi

65. As the distance from Earth's surface increases, Earth's gravitational pull decreases. In addition, the air becomes less dense. Gradually the air thins until the atmosphere merges with the near-emptiness of space. In which layer of the atmosphere would a spacecraft operate most efficiently?

(1) troposphere
(2) stratosphere
(3) ozone layer
(4) mesosphere
(5) thermosphere

66. Which of the following generalizations is supported by the diagram?

(1) The ozone layer is part of both the stratosphere and the mesosphere.
(2) The ozone layer is part of both the mesosphere and the thermosphere.
(3) The troposphere extends to a height of 30 miles.
(4) The total height of the atmosphere is 50 miles.
(5) Breathing is difficult in the lower troposphere.

Answers are on page 898.

Simulated GED Test Correlation Chart: Science

Name: _____ **Class:** _____ **Date:** _____

This chart can help you determine your strengths and weaknesses on the content and reading skill areas of the Science GED Test. Use the Answer Key on pages 898–904 to check your answers to the test. Then circle on the chart the numbers of the test items you answered correctly. Put the total number correct for each content area and skill area in each row and column. Look at the total items correct in each column and row and decide which areas are difficult for you. Use the page references to study those areas.

Cognitive Skills/Content	Comprehension	Application	Analysis	Evaluation	Total Correct
Biology *(pages 320–339)*	12, **18**, 49, 54, 60	17, **21**, 40, 41, 42, 43, 51, 53, 57	14, **20, 28, 29,** 44, 45, 50, 52, 55, 61, 62	13, 15, 16, **19,** 56	*26* out of 30
Earth Science *(pages 340–357)*	9, 58, 59, **66**	**2, 64, 65**	**1,** 10, **26, 33, 34, 63**	27	*14* out of 14
Chemistry *(pages 358–373)*	23	**8,** 22, **46**	3, **7,** 48	4, 5, 6, **47**	*11* out of 11
Physics *(pages 374–387)*	31	25, 36, 38	24, 35, 37, 39	**11, 30, 32**	*10* out of 11
Total Correct	____ out of 11	____ out of 18	____ out of 24	____ out of 13	Total correct: *61* out of 66

1–54 → You need more review.
55–66 → Congratulations!
You're ready for the GED Test!

Boldfaced numbers indicate items based on charts, graphs, illustrations, and diagrams.

For additional help, see the Steck-Vaughn GED Science Exercise Book.

LITERATURE & THE ARTS SIMULATED GED TEST

Directions

The Literature & the Arts Simulated GED Test consists of excerpts from classical and popular literature and articles about literature or the arts. Each excerpt is followed by multiple-choice questions about the reading material.

Read each excerpt first and then answer the questions that follow. Refer to the reading material as often as necessary in answering the questions.

Each excerpt is preceded by a "purpose question." The purpose question gives a reason for reading the material. Use these purpose questions to help focus your reading. You are not required to answer these purpose questions. They are given only to help you concentrate on the ideas presented in the reading material.

You should spend no more than 65 minutes answering the 45 questions on this simulated test. Work carefully, but do not spend too much time on any one question. Do not skip any items. Make a reasonable guess when you are not sure of an answer. You will not be penalized for incorrect answers. When time is up, mark the last item you finished. This will tell you whether you can finish the real GED Test in the time allowed. Then complete the test.

Record your answers to the questions on a copy of the answer sheet on page 922. Be sure that all required information is properly recorded on the answer sheet.

To record your answers, mark the numbered space on the answer sheet that corresponds to the answer you choose for each question on the test.

Example:

It was Susan's dream machine. The metallic blue paint gleamed, and the sporty wheels were highly polished. Under the hood, the engine was no less carefully cleaned. Inside, flashy lights illuminated the instruments on the dashboard, and the seats were covered by rich leather upholstery.

The subject ("It") of this excerpt is most likely

(1) an airplane
(2) a stereo system
(3) an automobile
(4) a boat
(5) a motorcycle

The correct answer is "an automobile"; therefore, answer space 3 would be marked on the answer sheet.

Do not rest the point of your pencil on the answer sheet while you are considering your answer. Make no stray or unnecessary marks. If you change an answer, erase your first mark completely. Mark only one answer space for each question; multiple answers will be scored as incorrect. Do not fold or crease your answer sheet.

When you finish the test, use the Correlation Chart on page 721 to determine whether you are ready to take the real GED Test, and, if not, which skill areas need additional review.

Adapted with permission of the American Council on Education.

Directions: Choose the best answer to each item.

Items 1 to 5 refer to the following excerpt from an article.

WHY DID SUCCESS SPOIL ERNEST HEMINGWAY?

In 1928 Hemingway's mother mailed him a chocolate cake. Along with it she sent the .32-cal. Smith & Wesson revolver with which Hemingway's father had just killed
(5) himself. Hemingway dropped the pistol into a deep lake in Wyoming "and saw it go down making bubbles until it was just as big as a watch charm in that clear water, and then it was out of sight."
(10) The story is minutely savage in its details and haunting in its outcome: perfect Hemingway. And of course, there is the water. . . . —lake water and trout stream and Gulf Stream and the rains after
(15) Caporetto and the endless washes of alcohol refracting in his brain. His style was a stream with the stones of nouns in it and a surface of prepositional ripples. . . .
. . . Ernest Hemingway's books are
(20) easier to know, and love, than his life. He wrote, at his early best, a prose of powerful and brilliant simplicity. But his character was not simple. In one of his stories, he wrote: "The most complicated
(25) subject that I know, since I am a man, is a man's life." The most complicated subject that he knew was Ernest Hemingway.
. . . His life belonged as much to the history of publicity as to the history of
(30) literature. He was a splendid writer who became his own worst creation, a hoax and a bore. He ended by being one of the most famous men in the world, white-bearded Mr. Papa. He stopped observing
(35) and started performing. . . .
Still, a long mythic fiesta between two explosions may not be a bad way to have a life. The first explosion came in Fossalta di Piave in northeastern Italy at midnight
(40) on July 8, 1918. A shell from an Austrian trench mortar punctured Hemingway with 200-odd pieces of shrapnel. . . . The second explosion came 25 years ago this summer. Early one morning in Ketchum,
(45) Idaho, Hemingway (suffering from diabetes, nephritis, alcoholism, severe depression, hepatitis, hypertension, impotence and paranoid delusions, his memory all but ruined by electroshock
(50) treatments) slid two shells into his double-barreled Boss shotgun . . . the last creature Hemingway brought down was himself.
Hemingway was mourned mostly as a
(55) great celebrity, his worst side, and not as a great writer, which he was.

"A Quarter-Century Later, the Myth Endures," *Time*.

1. According to the excerpt, Hemingway underwent marked changes in later life because

   (1) he had difficulty writing
   (2) he lived in Cuba
   (3) he won the Nobel Prize for Literature
   (4) he began acting out a role
   (5) he suffered serious injuries in a plane crash

2. The reviewer uses the story mentioned in the first paragraph to

   (1) explain why Hemingway's father killed himself
   (2) criticize Hemingway's behavior
   (3) introduce a discussion of Hemingway's life and style of writing
   (4) explain Hemingway's relationship with his mother
   (5) explain why Hemingway became a celebrity

3. The public reacted to Hemingway in his later years as

   (1) the most distinguished writer of his time
   (2) an expert on big-game hunting
   (3) a war correspondent
   (4) an expert on bullfighting
   (5) an international star

4. The reviewer would most likely enjoy

   (1) a play about Hemingway's life
   (2) a biography about Hemingway's later years
   (3) an early Hemingway story
   (4) a newspaper article about Hemingway's fame
   (5) a picture of Hemingway performing

5. The author uses the phrase "a hoax and a bore" (lines 31–32) to

   (1) describe Hemingway's later style of writing
   (2) describe what became of Hemingway in his later years
   (3) describe the publicity that surrounded Hemingway
   (4) explain the kinds of things Hemingway wrote about
   (5) describe those who mourned Hemingway as a celebrity

Items 6 to 10 refer to the following poem.

HOW DOES THIS WOMAN FEEL ABOUT HER NEW HOME?

MOVING IN

The telephone-installer was interested
In the students helping me.
He said he had a father of 93, plus a mother 77
And his wife kept running her heart out.
(5) Students could help, what a good idea! Let me know
If at any time this telephone needs adjusting.

As he left, the upstairs apartment entered
With some slices of chocolate angel food cake
To make herself acquainted.
(10) She was a retired librarian and it turned out
The one librarian I knew in the town I came from
Was an old friend of hers, they both came
From South Dakota mining country.

The telephone-installer returned to ask
(15) If students were dependable? They can be.
Even more than a good chocolate cake, even more
Than a good telephone.
This could mean a new life for my wife and me, he said,
I think I'll bring you a longer cord for that phone.
(20) Don't let this last piece of cake go begging, begged the upstairs apartment.

Josephine Miles, "Moving In," *Collected Poems 1930–83.*

6. Which of these activities is the speaker actually doing?

    (1) installing a telephone
    (2) baking a cake
    (3) teaching school
    (4) moving into a new apartment
    (5) reading a book

7. Which of the following best reflects how the speaker describes her neighbor?

    (1) the upstairs apartment
    (2) the telephone installer
    (3) a woman of 77
    (4) from the same town as she
    (5) one of her students

8. Based on the poem, it can be inferred that the speaker

    (1) is unhappy with her apartment
    (2) dislikes her upstairs neighbor
    (3) is new to the apartment building
    (4) does not eat chocolate cake
    (5) doesn't have any friends

9. Which of the following best describes what the speaker and the upstairs apartment have in common?

    (1) the same telephone number
    (2) they are both from South Dakota
    (3) a friend who is a librarian
    (4) their appreciation of chocolate cake
    (5) the enjoyment of reading

10. Which of the following best describes what the speaker means by "And his wife kept running her heart out" (line 4)?

    (1) the installer's wife likes to exercise
    (2) the installer's wife is exhausted
    (3) the students like the installer's wife
    (4) the installer can't keep up with his wife
    (5) the installer's wife has a bad heart

HOW DOES THIS MAN'S IDENTITY RELATE TO THE PLACE HE CALLS HOME?

One of my most vivid memories is of coming back west from prep school and later from college at Christmas time. Those who went farther than Chicago

(5) would gather in the old dim Union Station at six o'clock of a December evening with a few Chicago friends already caught up into their own holiday gayeties to bid them a hasty goodbye. I remember the fur coats of

(10) the girls returning from Miss This or That's and the chatter of frozen breath and the hands waving overhead as we caught sight of old acquaintances and the matchings of invitations: "Are you going to

(15) the Ordways'? the Herseys'? the Schultzes'?" and the long green tickets clasped tight in our gloved hands. And last the murky yellow cars of the Chicago, Milwaukee & St. Paul Railroad looking

(20) cheerful as Christmas itself on the tracks beside the gate.

When we pulled out into the winter night and the real snow, our snow, began to stretch out beside us and twinkle against

(25) the windows, and the dim lights of small Wisconsin stations moved by, a sharp wild brace came suddenly into the air. We drew in deep breaths of it as we walked back from dinner through the cold vestibules,

(30) unutterably aware of our identity with this country for one strange hour before we melted indistinguishably into it again.

That's my middle west—not the wheat or the prairies or the lost Swede towns but

(35) the thrilling, returning trains of my youth and the street lamps and sleigh bells in the frosty dark and the shadows of holy wreaths thrown by lighted windows on the snow. I am part of that, a little solemn with

(40) the feel of those long winters, a little complacent from growing up in the Carraway house in a city where dwellings are still called through decades by a family's name. I see now that this has

(45) been a story of the West, after all—Tom and Gatsby, Daisy and Jordan and I, were all Westerners, and perhaps we possessed some deficiency in common which made us subtly unadaptable to

(50) Eastern life.

Even when the East excited me most, even when I was most keenly aware of its superiority to the bored, sprawling, swollen towns beyond the Ohio with their

(55) interminable inquisitions which spared only the children and the very old—even then it had always for me a quality of distortion. West Egg especially still figures in my more fantastic dreams. I see it as a night

(60) scene by El Greco: a hundred houses, at once conventional and grotesque, crouching under a sullen, overhanging sky and a lustreless moon. In the foreground four solemn men in dress suits are walking

(65) along the sidewalk with a stretcher on which lies a drunken woman in a white evening dress. Her hand, which dangles over the side, sparkles cold with jewels. Gravely the men turn in at a house—the

(70) wrong house. But no one knows the woman's name, and no one cares.

F. Scott Fitzgerald, *The Great Gatsby*.

11. The main point of the first paragraph can be summed up as

    (1) the author's sadness at no longer being young and hopeful
    (2) the fun of taking a train home on vacation, instead of a plane
    (3) the author's happy memories of returning west from school
    (4) the excitement of meeting old friends on the way home
    (5) the importance of attending the best schools in the East

12. Which of the following best states the main point about the trip?

    (1) It was a difficult and disturbing journey.
    (2) It was a chance to learn about the Middle West.
    (3) It was the start of everyone's Christmas vacation.
    (4) It was an exciting way to travel in midwinter.
    (5) It made people aware of their regional identity.

13. Which of the following best sums up the main idea of the excerpt?

    (1) The story describes the middle-west.
    (2) The journeys home at Christmas changed the author's life.
    (3) The author's later life has been sad and disappointing.
    (4) The author and his friends were all from the middle-west.
    (5) Westerners are somehow unadaptable to life in the East.

14. Which one of the following is not a supporting detail in the first paragraph?

    (1) The students waved to each other.
    (2) Everyone clutched red tickets.
    (3) The girls wore fur coats.
    (4) People discussed invitations.
    (5) The railroad cars looked cheerful.

15. Upon returning to West Egg, the narrator will probably feel

    (1) somewhat ill at ease
    (2) surprised as if seeing it for the first time
    (3) caught up in many visits
    (4) thrilled to see the prairies and wheat again
    (5) happy to be home again

16. In the last paragraph, the narrator's description of a fantastic dream is effective because it

    (1) emphasizes how the narrator hates the middle-west
    (2) describes what happened one night in the East
    (3) emphasizes the cold, impersonal nature of the East
    (4) echoes the experience of train trips to the middle-west
    (5) emphasizes a desire to move back to the middle-west

Items 17 to 22 refer to the following excerpt from a review.

HOW DID THESE DIRECTORS MAKE THEIR FILM?

Not too many filmmakers are determined enough, or crazy enough, to devote seven years of their lives to the making of a movie. A movie that has no stars, no

(5) script, and was made on a budget that would barely cover the catering costs on "True Lies." Indeed, the odds against "Hoop Dreams" ever seeing the light of day were overwhelming, for it is a

(10) documentary, and the term itself carries such a commercial stigma that only a few are lucky enough to get a theatrical release.

But "Hoop Dreams" has more than good

(15) luck on its side: it's one of the richest movie experiences of the year, a spellbinding American epic that holds you firmly in its grip for nearly three hours. Chicago filmmakers Steve James,

(20) Frederick Marx and Peter Gilbert spent four and a half years following two inner-city kids with dreams of NBA glory, William Gates and Arthur Agee, basketball prodigies whose hopes of escaping the

(25) hazards of the ghetto rest on their hardwood performance. With an intimacy that never seems intrusive, "Hoop Dreams" tracks them through high school up to the brink of college. We watch two

(30) boys turn into young men before our eyes. And we see a portrait of inner-city struggle and survival shorn of the sound-bite clichés of TV and the sensationalist reductionism of Hollywood 'hood flicks.

(35) "Hoop Dreams" has all the suspense of a soap opera, but without the manipulation. It lets us draw our own conclusions, never forcing the story to fit a preordained agenda, never making easy

(40) generalizations out of the lives it examines with such cleareyed generosity. . . .

When James and Marx—later joined by cinematographer Gilbert—conceived of this project, in 1987, they thought it would

(45) be a 30-minute film about the culture of inner-city playground basketball. With $2,500 in grants and the producing help of Kartemquin Films, they began to look for their subjects. The first week of shooting

(50) they met Agee and Gates, and quickly realized that their plans had to be drastically revised: these were kids they had to follow, wherever it led.

It led them eventually to shoot 250 hours

(55) of film, almost every game and major event in the boys' lives. The project struggled through the first three years on only $2,500. . . . Everyone had a second job. Marriages were strained, debts

(60) accumulated and the filmmakers grew more and more attached to their subjects. . . .

"There were times when it was difficult to separate the roles of filmmaker/observer

(65) and extended family friend," admits Steve James. When the Agees' power was shut off, the filmmakers pulled some money together to restore it. It was the one moment when they clearly stepped

(70) beyond their roles as documentarians. "We weren't just going to exploit their pain and suffering. They say that to be a great documentary filmmaker you have to be cutthroat and not get involved. But if that's

(75) what it takes, then we don't want to be great documentary filmmakers."

"Hoop Dreams" had its triumphant premiere at the Sundance Film Festival, where it won the audience award and

(80) found a distributor, Fine Line Features. It was the first documentary ever chosen for closing night at the New York Film Festival.

David Ansen and Peter Annin, "Battered Dreams of Glory," *Newsweek.*

17. The reviewer thinks that "Hoop Dreams" is

    (1) a badly made documentary
    (2) a serious look at the issues facing inner-city teens
    (3) a shameful example of sensationalism
    (4) a one-sided attempt at looking at a subject
    (5) a film that does not compare to "True Lies"

18. The reviewer mentions the relationship between the filmmakers and their subjects in order to

    (1) indicate how the filmmakers got close to the two boys
    (2) suggest that the filmmakers did not interact with their subjects
    (3) accuse the filmmakers of interfering with the boys' lives
    (4) provide an example of bad documentary filmmaking
    (5) indicate the ease with which the project was completed

19. The reviewer does not say that the movie

    (1) took seven years to make
    (2) is set in Chicago
    (3) shot 250 hours worth of film
    (4) premiered at the New York Film Festival
    (5) is about two teenagers' dreams of playing professional basketball

20. Which of the following statements best explains the reviewer's description of the movie as having no stars, no script, and low budget (lines 4–7)?

    (1) The reviewer was trying to offer reasons for the bad quality of the film.
    (2) The reviewer was suggesting the obstacles that the filmmakers had to overcome.
    (3) The reviewer wanted to suggest that other filmmakers should follow the example of "Hoop Dreams."
    (4) The reviewer was providing a list of the film's positive attributes.
    (5) The reviewer was describing the odds all filmmakers have to face.

21. According to the review, if you went to see "Hoop Dreams," you would see a film that

    (1) succeeds in exploring the lives of people living in urban areas
    (2) uses interesting camera techniques in order to tell its story
    (3) bores you because of its extremely long length
    (4) loses track of its story half way through
    (5) offers alternatives to living in the city

22. Based on the information given in the review, it can be inferred that documentary movies

    (1) are very popular
    (2) are not usually commercially successful
    (3) are only shown on public television
    (4) are less interesting than fictional movies
    (5) are similar to soap operas

Items 23 to 27 refer to the following excerpt from a play.

WHAT DECISION HAS MRS. BROOKS MADE AND WHY?

RUBY: (RUBY *and* MRS. BROOKS *enter through the front door.*) Girl, I sure wish I could get my hands on whoever that is keeps pushing every one of them

(5)   buttons on the elevator before they get off. The old elevator door banging shut on every floor just about drove me out of my mind. I don't see how you can be so good-natured about it, Gladys.

(10) MRS. BROOKS: Sometimes I think that's my trouble, I'm too good-natured about everything.

RUBY: Ah, girl.

MRS. BROOKS: It's true, and you know it. I

(15)   just let everybody push me around.

RUBY: Don't be so hard on yourself, Gladys.

MRS. BROOKS: But, girl, this morning I made up my mind, I'm leaving Mr. Brooks.

(20) RUBY: Gladys, it's not that bad, is it? Remember it ain't the easiest thing in the world to leave a man after all these years.

MRS. BROOKS: Humph. Telling me I couldn't

(25)   buy a new dress for Gail's wedding; that was the last straw.

RUBY: You know, Gladys, there is such a thing as going from the refrigerator into the frying pan.

(30) MRS. BROOKS: Oh, Ruby, be serious.

RUBY: I am just as serious as cancer. I mean, it's not as though the man won't work. Everybody knows that he ain't known to mess up a piece of money.

(35) MRS. BROOKS: A lot of good it does me. Everything in the house is in his name. My name don't appear on nothing except the income tax deductions. . . .

MRS. BROOKS: Last week I overspent

(40)   buying groceries, and talking about a man carrying on! You'd have thought that seventeen cents was going to cause a panic down on Wall Street.

RUBY: Now, Gladys, you know sometimes

(45)   he does have good intentions.

MRS. BROOKS: My granny always said that the road to hell is paved with good intentions.

RUBY: My granny always said that there's

(50)   some good in everybody.

MRS. BROOKS: If there's some good in Mr. Brooks he's done done a Houdini with it, and made it disappear. 'Cause you sure can't see it.

Charlie Russell, *Five on the Black Hand Side.*

23. Based on the excerpt, Mrs. Brooks would most likely stay with her husband if

    (1) they did more things together
    (2) Ruby would stop interfering in their lives
    (3) Mr. Brooks would allow her more freedom
    (4) Mr. Brooks would buy her a new frying pan
    (5) she were allowed to invest some of their money

24. Which of the following best describes Ruby's position?

    (1) She is worried about Mrs. Brooks's future.
    (2) She wholeheartedly approves of Mrs. Brooks's plan.
    (3) She thinks Mr. Brooks is an admirable man.
    (4) She plans to help Mrs. Brooks as much as she can.
    (5) She thinks that Mrs. Brooks is ungrateful to her husband.

25. The sentence "Everybody knows that he ain't known to mess up a piece of money" (lines 33–34) means that Mr. Brooks

    (1) does not know how to make money
    (2) spends money only on himself
    (3) is very neat with all his possessions
    (4) does not spend money readily
    (5) spends money on having fun

26. Which of the following best describes what Mrs. Brooks's grandmother meant by "the road to hell is paved with good intentions" (lines 47–48)?

    (1) never trust people that mean well
    (2) bad things can result even when someone means well
    (3) Mr. Brooks was always an evil person
    (4) spending too much money will get you into trouble
    (5) all good things disappear over time

27. From what Mrs. Brooks says, you can infer that

    (1) she has thought about leaving Mr. Brooks for a long time
    (2) she needs Ruby's approval before she will leave Mr. Brooks
    (3) she will not leave Mr. Brooks until she has found a job
    (4) she probably will not leave Mr. Brooks at all
    (5) she will move in with Ruby

Items 28 to 32 refer to the following excerpt from a novel.

WHAT DOES SCROOGE SEE AND HEAR AT THE CHRISTMAS PARTY?

There was first a game of blind-man's bluff. And I no more believe Topper was really blinded than I believe he had eyes in his boots. Because the way in which he
(5) went after that plump sister in the lace tucker was an outrage on the credulity of human nature. Knocking down the fire-irons, tumbling over the chairs, bumping up against the piano, smothering himself
(10) among the curtains, wherever she went, there went he. He always knew where the plump sister was. He wouldn't catch anybody else. If you had fallen up against him, as some of them did, he would have
(15) made a feint of endeavoring to seize you, which would have been an affront to your understanding; and would instantly have sidled off in the direction of the plump sister.
(20) "Here is a new game," said Scrooge. "One half hour, Spirit, only one!"

It was a Game called Yes and No, where Scrooge's nephew had to think of something, and the rest must find out
(25) what; he only answering to their questions yes or no as the case was. The fire of questioning to which he was exposed, elicited from him that he was thinking of an animal, rather a disagreeable animal, a
(30) savage animal, an animal that growled and grunted sometimes, and talked sometimes, and lived in London, and walked about the streets, and wasn't made a show of, and wasn't led by anybody, and
(35) didn't live in a menagerie, and was never killed in a market, and was not a horse, or an ass, or a cow, or a bull, or a tiger, or a dog, or a pig, or a cat, or a bear. At every new question put to him, this nephew burst
(40) into a fresh roar of laughter; and was so inexpressibly tickled, that he was obliged to get up off the sofa and stamp. At last the plump sister cried out:

"I have found it out! I know what it is,
(45) Fred! I know what it is!"

"What is it?" cried Fred.

"It's your uncle Scro-o-o-oge!"

Which it certainly was. . . .

"He has given us plenty of merriment, I
(50) am sure," said Fred, "and it would be ungrateful not to drink his health. Here is a glass of mulled wine ready to our hand at the moment; and I say, 'Uncle Scrooge!'"

"Well! Uncle Scrooge!" they cried. . . .
(55) Uncle Scrooge had become so gay and light of heart, that he would have pledged the unconscious company in return, and thanked them in an inaudible speech, if the Ghost had given him time. But the
(60) whole scene passed off in the breath of the last word spoken by his nephew; and he and the Spirit were again upon their travels.

Charles Dickens, *A Christmas Carol*.

28. The author's style is

    (1) simple and direct
    (2) dry and scholarly
    (3) wordy but lively
    (4) solemn but profound
    (5) flat and unemotional

29. In the excerpt, Scrooge is described as

    (1) a cheat at blindman's bluff
    (2) a Spirit
    (3) a disagreeable and savage animal
    (4) a cow, a bull, or a tiger
    (5) a roar of laughter

30. Why does Fred drink a toast to Scrooge?

    (1) Everyone at the party likes Scrooge.
    (2) Scrooge has given the party and set up
        the games.
    (3) Scrooge has made them laugh by being
        the object of a game.
    (4) Everyone is glad that Scrooge is dead.
    (5) He is glad that Scrooge has become
        lighthearted.

31. From the last paragraph of the excerpt, you
    can infer that Scrooge is

    (1) invisible
    (2) all-powerful
    (3) furious
    (4) drunk
    (5) a magician

32. From his behavior at the end of the excerpt,
    you can infer that

    (1) Scrooge will never have a sense of
        humor
    (2) Scrooge will be able to change his
        grumpy ways
    (3) Scrooge will punish Fred and the others
        if he ever can
    (4) Scrooge will never understand why
        Fred toasts him
    (5) Scrooge and the Spirit will become
        good friends

Items 33 to 37 refer to the following excerpt from a story.

WHAT ARE THE VIEWS OF THIS FATHER?

I am not unsympathetic, Jack, to your views on the war. I am not unsympathetic to your views on the state of the world in general. From the way you wear your hair
(5) and from the way you dress I do find it difficult to decide whether you or that young girl you say you are about to marry is going to play the male role in your marriage—or the female role. But even
(10) that I don't find offensive. And I am not trying to make crude jokes at your expense. You must pardon me, though, if my remarks seem too personal. I confess I don't know you as well as a father *ought* to
(15) know his son, and I may seem to take liberties. . . .

I don't honestly know when I decided to go into college teaching, Jack. I considered doing other things—a career in
(20) the army or navy. Yes, I might have gone to Annapolis or West Point. Those appointments were much to be desired in the Depression years, and my family did still have a few political connections. One
(25) thing was certain, though. Business was just as much out of the question for me as politics had been for my father. An honest man, I was to understand, had too much to suffer there. Yes, considering our family
(30) history, an ivory tower didn't sound like a bad thing at all for an honest man and a serious man. . . .

After I had been dean of men for two years, I was made academic dean of the
(35) college. In two more years, I was president of the college. Even with as little time as you have spent with me through the years, Jack, you have seen what a successful marriage my second marriage has been,
(40) and what a happy, active life I have had. One sacrifices something. One sacrifices, for instance, the books one might have written after that first one. More important, one may sacrifice the love, even the
(45) acquaintance of one's children. One loses something of one's self even. But at least I am not tyrannizing over old women and small children. At least I don't sit gazing into space while my wife and perhaps
(50) some kindly neighbor woman waits patiently to see whether or not I will risk a two-heart bid. A man must somehow go on living among men, Jack. A part of him must. It is important to broaden one's
(55) humanity, but it is important to remain a mere man, too. But it is a strange world, Jack, in which an old man must tell a young man this.

Peter Taylor, "Dean of Men," *The Collected Stories of Peter Taylor.*

33. The speaker most likely sent this excerpt to his son in the form of a

    (1) telegram
    (2) short story
    (3) newspaper article
    (4) diary entry
    (5) letter

34. Which statement best reflects the implications drawn from the excerpt as a whole concerning the speaker's relationship with Jack?

    (1) The speaker's relationship with Jack has been a happy and active one.
    (2) The speaker's relationship with Jack is deeply troubled.
    (3) He is sorry that he tyrannized Jack as a young child.
    (4) He spurns having any relationship with Jack because he thinks Jack is not a real man.
    (5) He cannot accept Jack's political views.

35. The first paragraph of the excerpt shows that the father is

    (1) unsympathetic to his son's views on the war
    (2) somewhat uncomfortable trying to communicate with his son
    (3) trying to set the stage for some bad news
    (4) trying to help his son with his problems
    (5) hoping to get his son out of his life at last

36. The use of the phrase "ivory tower" (line 30) is effective because it

    (1) emphasizes that the writer wanted to escape into a safer world
    (2) shows how much he reveres the college where he works
    (3) shows how he admits he has not been a good father
    (4) reflects his opinion that Jack is not facing real life
    (5) helps him describe his second wife

37. If Jack invites his father to his wedding, the father will probably be

    (1) disappointed
    (2) offended
    (3) amused
    (4) glad
    (5) afraid

Items 38 to 42 refer to the following excerpt from a play.

WHY DO TROY AND CORY DISAGREE?

TROY: I'm through with it now. You go on and get them boards. *[Pause.]* Your mama tells me you got recruited by a college football team? Is that right?

(5) CORY: Yeah. Coach Zellman say the recruiter gonna be coming by to talk to you. Get you to sign the permission papers.

TROY: I thought you supposed to be

(10) working down there at the A&P. Ain't you suppose to be working down there after school?

CORY: Mr. Stawicki say he gonna hold my job for me until after the football

(15) season. Say starting next week I can work weekends.

TROY: I thought we had an understanding about this football stuff? You suppose to keep up with your chores and hold that

(20) job down at the A&P. Ain't been around here all day on a Saturday. Ain't none of your chores done . . . and now you telling me you done quit your job.

CORY: I'm gonna be working weekends.

(25) TROY: You damn right you are! And ain't no need for nobody coming around here to talk to me about signing nothing.

CORY: Hey, Pop . . . you can't do that. He's coming all the way from North Carolina.

(30) TROY: I don't care where he coming from. The white man ain't gonna let you get nowhere with that football no way. You go on and get your book-learning so you can work yourself up in that A&P or

(35) learn how to fix cars or build houses or something, get you a trade. That way you have something can't nobody take away from you. You go on and learn how to put your hands to some good

(40) use. Besides hauling people's garbage.

CORY: I get good grades, Pop. That's why the recruiter wants to talk with you. You got to keep up your grades to get recruited. This way I'll be going to

(45) college. I'll get a chance . . .

TROY: First you gonna get your butt down there to the A&P and get your job back.

CORY: Mr. Stawicki done already hired somebody else 'cause I told him I was

(50) playing football.

TROY: You a bigger fool than I thought . . . to let somebody take away your job so you can play some football. Where you gonna get your money to take out your

(55) girlfriend and whatnot? What kind of foolishness is that to let somebody take away your job?

CORY: I'm still gonna be working weekends.

TROY: Naw . . . naw. You getting your butt

(60) out of here and finding you another job.

CORY: Come on, Pop! I got to practice. I can't work after school and play football too. The team needs me. That's what Coach Zellman say . . .

(65) TROY: I don't care what nobody else say. I'm the boss . . . you understand? I'm the boss around here. I do the only saying what counts.

August Wilson, *Fences.*

38. Troy accuses Cory of

    (1) receiving failing grades in school
    (2) refusing to speak to the recruiter
    (3) spending too much money
    (4) not doing his chores
    (5) working too many hours at the A&P

39. Troy's words show that he

    (1) is extremely happy with Cory's decision
    (2) is happy for Cory, but worries about his studies
    (3) is opposed to Cory's desire to play football
    (4) thinks Cory should spend more time with his girlfriend
    (5) believes Cory should quit school and work full-time at the A&P

40. Cory's words show that he wants to

    (1) become the manager of the A&P
    (2) go to college
    (3) marry his girlfriend
    (4) do whatever Troy thinks is best
    (5) find another job

41. Which of the following statements best describes the relationship between Troy and Cory?

    (1) Troy and Cory respect each other.
    (2) Troy and Cory are best friends.
    (3) Troy wants Cory to respect his authority.
    (4) Troy does not care for Cory.
    (5) Cory does not respect Troy.

42. Based on the evidence provided by the excerpt, which of the following best describes its overall mood?

    (1) happy and carefree
    (2) angry and bitter
    (3) forbidding
    (4) sorrowful
    (5) tense and full of conflict

Items 43 to 45 refer to the following excerpt from an article.

WHAT IS HAPPENING AT THE ROOSEVELT HOTEL?

By seven o-clock I was dead tired and soaked with rain and perspiration. I walked to the Roosevelt, hoping to get a room for a brief rest. Instead of taking guests,
(5)   however, the hotel was busy evacuating them. There were no lights, and the threat of explosion from escaping gas had increased throughout the demolished area. Another warning of the possibility of
(10)   a second tornado had been issued. Fearful persons jammed the lobby in silent wait for the next blow.

The Roosevelt switchboard had one telephone circuit in operation. The
(15)   operator called the Raleigh Hotel up the street and reserved rooms for Roy Miller and me, although I did not know Roy's whereabouts at the time. Next time I saw him he said he had driven to Hillsboro,
(20)   about thirty-five miles away, to telephone his wife and reassure her of his safety. He was fuming.

"I drive seventy miles to call my wife," he said; "I says, 'Honey, I'm all right. I'm safe.
(25)   You don't need to worry any longer.' And what do I get? She says, 'Who's worried? You always have been all right. Why do you have to call me long distance to tell me so? Roy Miller,' she says, 'what have
(30)   you been up to?'" Mrs. Miller had not heard of the storm.

Ira A. J. Baden as told to Robert H. Parham, "Forty-five Seconds Inside a Tornado," *Man Against Nature.*

43. Which of the following is the most accurate conclusion to draw about the general situation in this excerpt?

(1) Men worry about what their wives will think.
(2) The Raleigh Hotel's business improved during the storm.
(3) People were reacting to the effects of a tornado.
(4) The tornado had shut down phone service within seventy miles of the town.
(5) Tornadoes can cause gas leaks.

44. You can conclude from this excerpt that Mrs. Miller

(1) was not afraid of tornadoes
(2) was too worried about the tornadoes where she was to think about her husband
(3) did not care about her husband
(4) had slept through the tornado
(5) did not understand why her husband had called

45. You can conclude from the excerpt that the Roosevelt Hotel was being evacuated primarily because

(1) there had been a tornado
(2) there were no lights
(3) there was danger of an explosion
(4) a second tornado was expected
(5) of the soaking rain

Answers are on page 904.

Simulated GED Test Correlation Chart: Literature & the Arts

Name: _____ **Class:** _____ **Date:** _____

This chart can help you determine your strengths and weaknesses on the content and skill areas of the Literature Simulated GED Test. Use the Answer Key on pages 904–907 to check your answers to the test. Then circle on the chart the numbers of the test items you answered correctly. Put the total number correct for each content area and skill area in each row and column. Look at the total items correct in each column and row and decide which areas are difficult for you. Use the page references to study those areas.

Cognitive Skills/ Content	Literal Comprehension (pp. 198–203)	Inferential Comprehension (pp. 198–203)	Application (pp. 204–208)	Analysis (pp. 209–215)	Total Correct
Popular Literature (Pages 396–437) Poetry Fiction Nonfiction Drama	9 38	6 34 43, 44 23, 24, 25, 26, 27, 39, 40	37	7, 8, 10 33, 35, 36 45 41, 42	____ out of 23
Classical Literature (Pages 438–459) Fiction	14, 29, 30	11, 12, 13, 31, 32	15	16, 28	____ out of 11
Commentary (Pages 460–479) Film Fiction	19, 21 1	17, 22 3	4	18, 20 2, 5	____ out of 11
Total Correct	____ out of 8	____ out of 19	____ out of 3	____ out of 15	Total Correct: ____ out of 45

1–36 → You need more review.
37–45 → Congratulations!
You're ready for the GED Test!

For additional help, see the Steck-Vaughn GED Literature & the Arts Exercise Book.

MATHEMATICS SIMULATED GED TEST

Directions

The Mathematics Simulated GED Test consists of multiple-choice questions intended to measure general mathematical skills and problem-solving ability. The questions are based on short readings that often include a graph, chart, or figure.

You should spend no more than 90 minutes answering the 56 questions. Work carefully, but do not spend too much time on any one question. Be sure you answer every question. You will not be penalized for incorrect answers.

Formulas you may need are given on the inside back cover. Only some of the questions will require you to use a formula. Not all the formulas given will be needed.

Some questions contain more information than you will need to solve the problem. Other questions do not give enough information to solve the problem. If the question does not give enough information to solve the problem, the correct answer choice is "Not enough information is given."

The use of calculators is not allowed.

Record your answers on the separate answer sheet provided. Be sure all requested information is properly recorded on the answer sheet. You may make extra copies of page 922. To record your answers, mark the numbered space on the answer sheet that corresponds to the answer you choose for each question on the test. Mark only one answer space for each question; multiple answers will be scored as incorrect.

Example: If a grocery bill totaling $15.75 is paid with a $20.00 bill, how much change should be returned?

(1) $5.26

(2) $4.75

(3) $4.25

(4) $3.75

(5) $3.25

The correct answer is $4.25; therefore, answer space 3 would be marked on the answer sheet.

Do not rest the point of your pencil on the answer sheet while you are considering your answer. Make no stray or unnecessary marks. If you change an answer, erase your first mark completely. Mark only one answer for each question; multiple answers will be scored as incorrect. Do not fold or crease your answer sheet.

When you finish the test, use the Correlation Chart on page 733 to determine whether you are ready to take the real GED Test, and, if not, which skill areas need additional review.

1. In 1994 an airline hired an aircraft company to manufacture 80 new planes. The aircraft company can complete 16 planes per year. At this rate, in what year will the airline's order be completed?

   (1) 1995
   (2) 1997
   (3) 1999
   (4) 2001
   (5) 2004

Item 2 is based on the following figure.

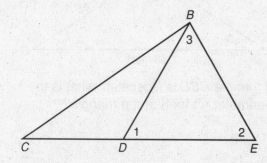

2. If angles 1 and 2 in triangle *BDE* are each 60-degree angles, what is the measure of angle 3?

   (1) 180 degrees
   (2) 120 degrees
   (3) 90 degrees
   (4) 60 degrees
   (5) 40 degrees

3. Michela has worked for McKenzie Publishing 4 years longer than Stuart. Stuart has worked there 3 years less than Sofia. If Sofia has worked at the company for 8 years, how long has Michela worked there?

   (1) 9
   (2) 10
   (3) 11
   (4) 12
   (5) Not enough information is given.

Item 4 refers to the following drawing.

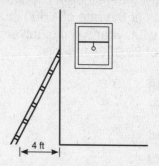

4. Approximately how high up on the wall does the 12-foot ladder in the drawing reach if the bottom of the ladder is 4 feet from the wall?

   (1) between 8 and 9 feet
   (2) between 9 and 10 feet
   (3) between 10 and 11 feet
   (4) between 11 and 12 feet
   (5) Not enough information is given.

5. Richenda wants to buy a new car priced at $9,500. If she makes a 20% down payment, which expression shows how much she will owe?

   (1) $(0.20)(\$9,500)$
   (2) $\$9,500 - (0.20)(\$9,500)$
   (3) $(0.20)(\$9,500) - 0.20$
   (4) $\$9,500 - 0.20$
   (5) $(0.20)(\$9,500) + \$9,500$

6. Traveling at 55 miles per hour, approximately how long will it take Arvin to drive 420 miles?

   (1) between 4 and 5 hours
   (2) between 5 and 6 hours
   (3) between 6 and 7 hours
   (4) between 7 and 8 hours
   (5) between 8 and 9 hours

7. In 1995, 14,000 students enrolled at State University. If the student population increases at the rate of 1,500 students per year, in what year will the university reach its goal of 20,000 students?

(1) 1996
(2) 1997
(3) 1998
(4) 1999
(5) 2000

8. Sandra's monthly salary is $1,660. If 24% is deducted for taxes, what is the amount of her take-home pay?

(1) $ 398.40
(2) $ 630.80
(3) $1,261.60
(4) $1,494.20
(5) $1,636.00

9. Evaluate $4x^3 - 2y$, if $x = 2$ and $y = 10$.

(1)   4
(2)   8
(3) 10
(4) 12
(5) 20

10. The 48 employees of the Young Construction Company were given a choice of two different retirement plans. If Plan A was chosen by twice as many employees as Plan B, how many employees chose Plan A?

(1)   8
(2) 16
(3) 25
(4) 32
(5) 44

11. In an apartment complex, 85% of the 400 residents voted for a proposal to increase parking fees. How many residents voted against the proposal?

(1) 16
(2) 30
(3) 60
(4) 80
(5) 96

Item 12 is based on the following figure.

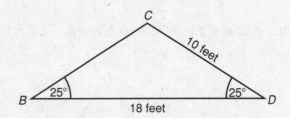

12. If triangle *BCD* is isosceles, what is the perimeter (in feet) of the triangle?

(1) 10
(2) 18
(3) 29
(4) 38
(5) 46

Item 13 refers to the following diagram.

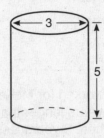

13. A cylindrical oil drum is 3 feet across and 5 feet tall. Which expression represents the approximate volume in cubic feet?

(1) $(3.14)(1.5)^2(5)$
(2) $(3.14)(1.5)(5)^2$
(3) $(3.14)(3)(5)$
(4) $(3.14)(3)^2(5)$
(5) $(3.14)(6)^2(5)$

14. Toni and Dan need to buy a weekly expense register, 50 file folders, 3 notebooks, and 6 adding machine paper rolls. The costs of the supplies are as follows:

notebooks	$4 each or 3 for $10
adding machine paper rolls	$1 each or 3 for $2
file folders	10 for $5
weekly expense register	$15

What is the least amount they can spend to buy the supplies they need?

(1) $34

(2) $42

(3) $48

(4) $54

(5) $58

Item 15 refers to the following diagram.

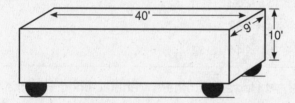

15. The inside dimensions of a rectangular freight car are shown in the diagram. What is the volume of the freight car in cubic feet?

(1) 1,800

(2) 2,400

(3) 3,600

(4) 18,000

(5) Not enough information is given.

16. Of Zoila's $1,500 monthly earnings, 20% is paid for rent. How much does she pay each month for rent?

(1) $240

(2) $270

(3) $300

(4) $360

(5) $412

17. It takes $3\frac{3}{8}$ yards of fabric to make a pillowcase. How many pillowcases can you make from $13\frac{1}{2}$ yards of fabric?

(1) 3

(2) 4

(3) 5

(4) 6

(5) Not enough information is given.

18. Given the formula $x = 3a(b^2 - 8)$, find x if $a = 5$ and $b = 4$.

(1) 0

(2) 24

(3) 40

(4) 72

(5) 120

Item 19 refers to the following information.

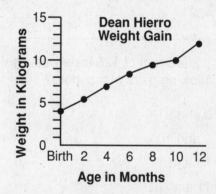

19. The Hierro infant showed the greatest weight gain over which two-month period?

(1) birth to 2 months

(2) 4 to 6 months

(3) 6 to 8 months

(4) 8 to 10 months

(5) 10 to 12 months

Items 20 and 21 refer to the following figure.

```
┌──────────────────────┐
│1 ft                  │
│      33 in           │
└──────────────────────┘
```

20. What is the perimeter in feet of the rectangle shown in the figure?

    (1) $6\frac{1}{2}$

    (2) $7\frac{1}{2}$

    (3) 8

    (4) $8\frac{1}{4}$

    (5) $8\frac{1}{2}$

21. What is the area of the rectangle in the figure in square inches?

    (1) 364

    (2) 386

    (3) 396

    (4) 412

    (5) 432

22. The square root of 125 is between which of the following pairs of numbers?

    (1) 8 and 9

    (2) 9 and 10

    (3) 10 and 11

    (4) 11 and 12

    (5) 12 and 13

23. An architect is planning a city parking lot. For every 12 commuters, the parking lot will need 5 parking spaces. How many parking spaces will be needed by 132 commuters?

    (1)   7

    (2) 12

    (3) 17

    (4) 55

    (5) 60

Items 24 and 25 refer to the following figure.

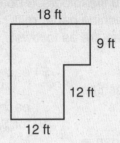

24. What is the perimeter of the figure in feet?

    (1) 78

    (2) 72

    (3) 66

    (4) 60

    (5) 57

25. What is the area of the figure in square feet?

    (1) 378

    (2) 306

    (3) 252

    (4) 162

    (5) 144

26. At Howard Brothers Manufacturing, $\frac{5}{8}$ of the employees take the bus to work. Of these, $\frac{2}{5}$ take the express bus. What fraction of the employees take the express bus?

    (1) $\frac{5}{8} + \frac{2}{5}$

    (2) $\frac{5}{8} - \frac{2}{5}$

    (3) $\frac{5}{8} \times \frac{2}{5}$

    (4) $\frac{5}{8} \div \frac{2}{5}$

    (5) $\frac{2}{5} - \frac{5}{8}$

27. The square root of 24 is between which pair of numbers?

    (1) 2.4 and 2.5

    (2) 3 and 4

    (3) 4 and 5

    (4) 5 and 6

    (5) 12 and 13

28. A computer printer prints 1,000 characters every 3 seconds. If there are approximately 3,300 characters on a page, how many seconds will it take to print 5 pages?

(1)   4.95

(2)   9.9

(3)   30

(4)   49.5

(5) 495

29. A flight from San Francisco to Seattle took $3\frac{1}{4}$ hours. The return flight took only $2\frac{4}{5}$ hours. How much shorter was the return flight?

(1) $3\frac{1}{4} + 2\frac{4}{5}$

(2) $3\frac{1}{4} - 2\frac{4}{5}$

(3) $3\frac{1}{4} \times 2\frac{4}{5}$

(4) $3\frac{1}{4} \div 2\frac{4}{5}$

30. Which of the following expresses 18,592 in scientific notation?

(1) 1.8592×10^3

(2) 1.8592×10^4

(3) 1.8592×10^5

(4) 18.592×10^2

(5) 18.592×10^4

31. Marta scored 93 points on her English test. She scored 5 points lower on the writing part of the test than on the reading part. What were her scores on each of the parts of the test?

(1) 43 and 48

(2) 44 and 49

(3) 45 and 50

(4) 47 and 52

(5) 54 and 59

32. On a map Sunnyview is 2.5 inches from Taylor. Actually these towns are 50 miles apart. What is the scale on this map?

(1) Scale: 1 in = $\frac{1}{5}$ mi

(2) Scale: 1 in = 2 mi

(3) Scale: 1 in = 2.5 mi

(4) Scale: 1 in = 20 mi

(5) Scale: 1 in = 25 mi

33. Three consecutive odd numbers total 33. What are the three numbers?

(1) 9, 11, and 13

(2) 11, 13, and 15

(3) 13, 15, and 17

(4) 15, 17, and 19

(5) 19, 21, and 23

Item 34 refers to the following figure.

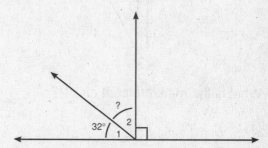

34. If angle 1 measures 32 degrees, what is the measure of angle 2?

(1)   32 degrees

(2)   45 degrees

(3)   58 degrees

(4)   90 degrees

(5) 148 degrees

35. Roger worked 9 hours on Friday and 6 hours on Saturday. What is the ratio of the hours worked on Friday to the total hours worked on both days?

(1) $\frac{2}{5}$

(2) $\frac{3}{5}$

(3) $\frac{2}{3}$

(4) $\frac{3}{2}$

(5) $\frac{5}{3}$

Items 36 and 37 refer to the following diagram.

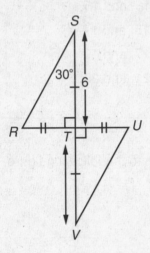

36. What is the measurement of $\angle V$?

(1) 6°

(2) 30°

(3) 60°

(4) 90°

(5) Not enough information is given.

37. What is the measurement of $\angle U$?

(1) 6°

(2) 30°

(3) 60°

(4) 90°

(5) Not enough information is given.

Item 38 refers to the diagram below.

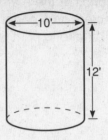

38. A cylindrical water tank is 10 feet across and 12 feet tall. Which expression shows the approximate volume of the water tank in cubic feet?

(1) $(3.14)(5)^2(12)$

(2) $(3.14)(10)^2(12)$

(3) $(3.14)(5)(12)^2$

(4) $\frac{(3.14)(12)}{5^2}$

(5) $(3.14)(10)(12)^2$

39. The Perrones made a 25 percent down payment on a new car costing $11,960. How much do they still owe?

(1) $ 299

(2) $ 897

(3) $2,990

(4) $3,289

(5) $8,970

40. Alicia borrowed $900 for two years. She paid $252 in interest. Which expression represents the annual rate of interest she was charged?

(1) $\frac{252}{900(2)}$

(2) $\frac{252(2)}{900}$

(3) $\frac{252(900)}{2}$

(4) $252(900)(2)$

(5) $\frac{(900)(2)}{252}$

41. The two triangles in the figures below are congruent. What is the measurement of ∠D?

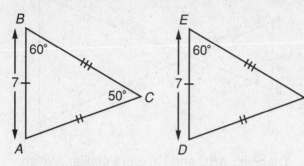

(1) 50°

(2) 70°

(3) 110°

(4) 180°

(5) Not enough information is given.

42. Denise earns $9.50 for each hour of overtime she works. How much overtime pay did she earn during the week if she worked 5 hours of overtime on Monday, 3 hours on Wednesday, and $1\frac{1}{2}$ hours on Friday?

(1) $70.75

(2) $75.00

(3) $80.75

(4) $85.50

(5) $90.25

43. Out of every 400 television sets produced at a factory, 8 are defective. What is the probability that a television will be defective?

(1) $\frac{1}{8}$

(2) $\frac{1}{40}$

(3) $\frac{1}{50}$

(4) $\frac{1}{80}$

(5) $\frac{1}{150}$

Item 44 refers to the following information.

Toys and Games	Price
A. Funny Faces Game	$ 8.95
B. Doll	$16.75
C. Sing-Along Videotape	$ 9.99
D. Building Blocks	$18.60
E. Wading Pool	$ 9.45
F. Doll Furniture	$25.37

44. Linda has $50 to spend on birthday gifts for her daughter. She has already chosen two items: a dress-up gown ($14.50) and a toy helicopter ($16.80). Which combination of toys and games can she also buy without spending more than $50?

(1) A and C

(2) A and E

(3) B and E

(4) C and E

(5) F only

45. Oscar pays for these things at the drug store: soap for $1.99, toothpaste for $2.19, tissues for $1.14, and a razor for $.85. He pays with a 10-dollar bill. Which is the nearest estimate of how much change he should get back?

(1) $2

(2) $3

(3) $4

(4) $5

(5) $6

Item 46 is based on the following graph.

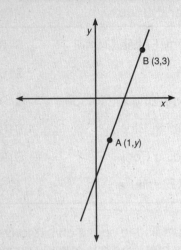

46. In the graph, what is the *y*-coordinate of point *A* if the slope of line $\overline{AB}$ is 3?

   (1) 12
   (2)   9
   (3)   5
   (4) −3
   (5) −5

Item 47 is based on the following graph.

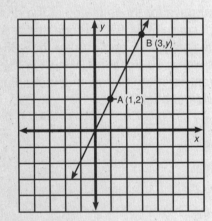

47. What is the *y*-coordinate of point *B* if the slope of line $\overline{AB}$ is +2?

   (1) −3
   (2)   4
   (3)   6
   (4)   8
   (5) 12

Items 48 and 49 refer to the following figure.

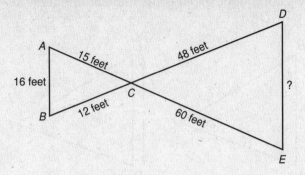

48. Triangles *ABC* and *CDE* are similar. Which side of triangle *ABC* corresponds to side $\overline{CE}$?

   (1) side $\overline{BC}$
   (2) side $\overline{AC}$
   (3) side $\overline{CD}$
   (4) side $\overline{AB}$
   (5) Not enough information is given.

49. What is the length in feet of side $\overline{DE}$ in the figure?

   (1)   49
   (2)   52
   (3)   64
   (4)   88
   (5) 120

50. In a golf tournament, there are twice as many amateur golfers as professional golfers. Altogether, 96 golfers are in the tournament. How many of them are amateurs?

   (1) 24
   (2) 32
   (3) 43
   (4) 60
   (5) 64

Item 51 refers to the following diagram.

Building

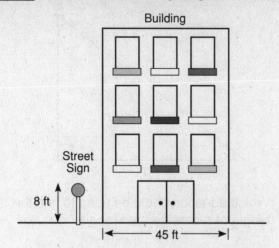

Street
Sign

8 ft

|← 45 ft →|

51. A landlord needs to find out the height of the apartment building. At 4 P.M. he takes several measurements. The shadow of the building is 30 feet long. He also determines the width of the building (45 feet) and the height of a street sign (8 feet). What additional measurement does he need to be able to determine the height of the building?

(1) the angle of the sunlight

(2) the distance from the building to the corner

(3) the volume of the building

(4) the width of the street

(5) the length of the shadow of the street sign

52. At Benlow's Shirt Factory, it takes $2\frac{1}{4}$ yards of cotton fabric to make 1 shirt. How many yards will it take to make 3 shirts?

(1) 4

(2) $4\frac{1}{2}$

(3) 5

(4) 6

(5) $6\frac{3}{4}$

53. A tailor needs 4 yards 6 inches of material to make a pair of men's pants. How many pairs of pants could he make from 21 yards?

(1) 4

(2) 5

(3) 6

(4) 7

(5) 8

Item 54 refers to the following information.

Driving Distances

	Bank	Day Care	Work
Home	3.2 mi	1.5 mi	4.7 mi
Work	2.6 mi	6.3 mi	
Day Care	2.5 mi		6.3 mi

54. Yesterday morning Sarah drove her daughter from home to day care and then drove to work. At five o'clock that evening, she drove home the same way. How many miles did Sarah drive in all?

(1) 7.8

(2) 9.5

(3) 14.6

(4) 15.6

(5) 19

Item 55 refers to the following diagram.

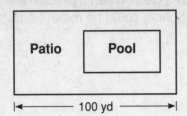

Patio   Pool

|◄————— 100 yd —————►|

55. A fenced area encloses a pool with a patio. If the area of the patio is 4,500 square yards, and the area of the pool is 1,500 square yards, what is the width of the fenced area?

(1) 100 yards

(2) 60 yards

(3) 45 yards

(4) 30 yards

(5) Not enough information is given.

Item 56 is based on the following drawing.

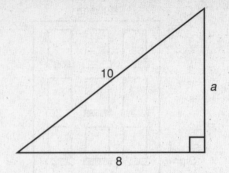

56. Which equation could be used to find the length of side a for the triangle?

(1) $8^2 + 10^2 = a^2$

(2) $a^2 - 10^2 = 5^2$

(3) $a^2 + 10^2 = 5^2$

(4) $a^2 - 8^2 = 10^2$

(5) $a^2 + 8^2 = 10^2$

Answers are on page 907.

Simulated GED Test Correlation Chart: Mathematics

Name: _____ **Class:** _____ **Date:** _____

This chart can help you determine your strengths and weaknesses on the content and skill areas of the Mathematics GED Test. Use the Answer Key on pages 907–909 to check your answers to the test. Then circle on the chart the numbers of the test items you answered correctly. Put the total number correct for each content area and skill area in each row and column. Look at the total items correct in each column and row and decide which areas are difficult for you. Use the page references to study those areas.

Content	Item Number	Total Correct	Page Reference
Arithmetic *(pages 488–583)*			
Whole Number Operations	1, 3, 7, 33	____ out of 4	488–501
Fractions	17, 26, 29, 52	____ out of 4	502–519
Decimals	42, 45	____ out of 2	520–533
Percent	5, 8, 11, 16, 39, 40	____ out of 6	534–545
Graphs and Charts	19, 44, 54	____ out of 3	546–555
Ratio, Proportion, Mean, Median, Probability	6, 23, 28, 31, 32, 35, 43, 53	____ out of 8	556–569
Algebra *(pages 584–613)*			
Equations	9, 10, 14, 18, 50	____ out of 5	584–597
Graphs, Slope, Lines	46, 47	____ out of 2	598–605
Powers and Roots	22, 27, 30	____ out of 3	606–609
Geometry *(pages 614–636)*			
Perimeter, Area, Volume	13, 15, 20, 21, 24, 25, 38, 55	____ out of 8	615–619
Angles	34	____ out of 1	620–623
Triangles and Quadrilaterals	2, 12, 36, 37	____ out of 4	624–627
Congruence and Similarity	41, 48, 49	____ out of 3	628–630
Pythagorean Theorem	4, 51, 56	____ out of 3	631–632
Total Correct		Total Correct: ____ out of 56	

1–44 → You need more review.
45–56 → Congratulations! You're ready for the GED Test!

For additional help, see the Steck-Vaughn GED Mathematics Exercise Book.

Answers & Explanations

Entry Tests

Writing Skills (page 16)

1. **(4) reached 300; however, since then** (Sentence structure/Clarity) Option (4) is correct because it combines the two related sentences using <u>however</u>. Options (1), (2), (3), and (5) are incorrect because they do not show the contrast in the relationship between the two ideas. Option (3) also creates a comma splice.

2. **(5) no correction is necessary** (Usage/Verb forms; Mechanics/Punctuation—overuse of commas and spelling—homonyms) <u>Showing</u> in option (1) is an incorrect verb form because it needs a helping verb. Option (2) is incorrect because a comma would separate subject and verb in the dependent clause. Option (3) is incorrect because <u>their</u> is the correct plural possessive pronoun referring to <u>people</u>; <u>They're</u> is the contraction for "they are." Option (4) is incorrect because a comma is not used where two items are joined with <u>and</u>.

3. **(3) LaRosa, chairman of the American Heart Association's task force on cholesterol issues, keeping** (Mechanics/Punctuation—appositives) Commas are used to separate a descriptive phrase (appositive) from the noun being described when the description is not essential to the meaning of the sentence. Notice that the commas are used on both sides of the phrase. Therefore, option (3) is correct and options (1), (2), and (5) are incorrect. In option (4), the second comma is placed incorrectly.

4. **(2) change are to is** (Usage/Subject-verb agreement) <u>Public</u> is a group word and is considered singular, so the singular verb <u>is</u>, as in option (2), is correct. There is no reason for the changes in options (1), (3), and (4).

5. **(4) Today, doctors recommend** (Usage/Subject-verb agreement; Mechanics/Capitalization) Option (4) is correct because <u>doctors</u> is a plural noun and must have a plural verb, <u>recommend</u>. Possession is not shown, so options (2) and (3) are incorrect. In option (5), there is no reason to capitalize <u>doctors</u> because it is not used as a proper noun.

6. **(2) fiber, oat bran, and beans** (Mechanics/Punctuation—commas between items in series) Option (2) is correct because commas are needed between each of the items in a simple list. Option (3) incorrectly uses a semicolon instead of a comma. Options (4) and (5) have commas placed incorrectly.

7. **(5) no correction is necessary** (Mechanics/Spelling and punctuation; Sentence structure/Fragments; and Usage/Pronoun reference) In option (1), <u>Exercising</u> is spelled correctly. <u>Since exercising</u> creates a sentence fragment, making option (2) incorrect. The sentence does not show possession, so the pronoun <u>you</u> should not be changed to <u>your</u>, as in option (3). Option (4) is incorrect because no comma is needed after the word <u>fit</u>.

8. **(4) change todays to today's** (Mechanics/Possessives) Option (4) is correct because the singular possessive <u>today's</u> is required in this sentence. Option (3) is incorrect because it shows the plural possessive <u>todays'</u>. There is no reason for the changes in options (1) and (2).

9. **(1) arrives, we** (Sentence structure/Sentence fragments; Mechanics/Punctuation—commas after introductory elements) Option (1) is correct because the rewritten sentence starts with a dependent clause; a comma, not a semicolon, as in option (2), should follow a dependent clause at the beginning of the sentence. Options (3) and (4) are incorrect because the semicolons create sentence fragments and because these options contain the unnecessary words <u>because</u> and <u>as a result</u>. The conjunction <u>but</u> in option (5) is also unnecessary.

10. **(2) change There is to There are** (Usage/Subject-verb agreement—expletive) Option (2) is correct because the subject of the sentence, <u>computers</u>, is plural, so the plural verb <u>are</u> is correct. There is no reason for the changes in options (1), (3), and (4).

11. **(4) at the supermarkets and discount stores,** (Sentence structure/Parallelism) Option (4) is correct because all three items in this series should start with prepositions: <u>in</u>, <u>at</u>, and <u>on</u>. Options (1), (2), and (3) do not maintain parallel structure. Option (5) uses the preposition <u>on</u> incorrectly.

12. **(1) satellites. They** (Sentence structure/Run-on sentence and comma splice) Option (1) is correct because the two independent clauses can stand alone as two sentences. Option (2) is incorrect because a semicolon is not used with a coordinating conjunction. Option (3) is incorrect because a comma is needed to join two independent clauses with the conjunction and. Option (4) is incorrect because it creates a comma splice. Option (5) is incorrect because it creates a run-on sentence.

13. **(1) is that, at least so far, they** (Usage/Subject-verb agreement; Mechanics/Punctuation—commas with parenthetical expressions) Option (1) is correct because the subject of the sentence is problem. Problem is singular and requires the singular verb is. Options (2), (3), and (5) are incorrect because the plural verb are does not agree with the singular subject problem. Option (4) is incorrect because the parenthetical phrase at least so far should be set off with commas.

14. **(1) change the spelling of benifit to benefit** (Mechanics/Spelling) Option (1) is correct because the correct spelling is benefit. There is no reason for the changes in options (2), (3), and (4).

15. **(1) change is to are** (Usage/Subject-verb agreement and verb tense) Option (1) is correct because this sentence has a compound subject, keyboarding and data entry, which requires a plural verb are. Option (2) is incorrect because the paragraph is written in present tense and is is present tense. There is no reason for the changes in options (3) and (4).

16. **(1) change the spelling of Sucessful to Successful** (Mechanics/Spelling) The correct spelling is successful, so option (1) is correct. There is no reason for the changes in options (2), (3), and (4).

17. **(5) no correction is necessary** (Usage/Verb tense, clarity, and pronoun reference—pronoun shift) Option (1) is incorrect because the present tense is used throughout the paragraphs. The plural jobs, in option (2), is needed because of the plural kinds, to which it refers. Option (3) is incorrect because the pronoun you should be used for consistency. Option (4) changes the meaning and does not make sense.

18. **(2) training, and experience are required** (Sentence structure/Parallelism; Usage/Subject-verb agreement and verb tense;

Mechanics/ Punctuation) Option (2) is correct because the three items in series should be of parallel structure; the first two items, skills and training, are nouns, so the last one should be a noun, experience. Are required is the correct verb because it agrees with the plural subject, skills, training, and experience, and maintains the present tense. Options (1), (3), and (4) are incorrect because they do not include the needed verb form. Items in series should be separated by commas, not semicolons, as in option (5).

19. **(4) change we have to you have** (Usage/Pronoun reference—pronoun shift) The pronoun you is used throughout the passage. We should be changed to you for consistency, so option (4) is correct. There is no reason for the changes in options (1), (2), and (3).

20. **(5) restaurant; however, you** (Sentence structure/Run-on sentences and fragments; Mechanics/Punctuation) Independent clauses may be joined by a comma and a conjunction or by a semicolon. Option (5) is correct because however is a conjunctive adverb and requires a semicolon before and a comma after it. Options (1) and (2) would create run-on sentences. A comma is not required after the conjunction but, as in option (3). In option (4), because is not logical and creates a sentence fragment.

21. **(4) change needed to need** (Usage/Verb tense—sequence of tense in sentence and paragraph) Option (4) is correct because the verb tense throughout these paragraphs is present tense. Needed is past tense and should be changed to present-tense need for consistency. There is no reason for the changes in options (2) and (3).

22. **(5) your interest in the job** (Sentence structure/Parallelism) Option (5) is correct because the list of things to stress should have a parallel structure. Option (2) is not clear in its meaning. Option (3) does not result in parallel structure. In option (4), you're, meaning "you are," is incorrect.

23. **(1) change j. gutenberg to J. Gutenberg** (Mechanics/Capitalization) J. Gutenberg is a person's name and should be capitalized. There is no reason for the changes in options (2), (3), and (4).

24. **(5) page and days,** (Sentence structure/Fragment) The phrase days, weeks, or months is a modifier of the verb took and

should not be separated from the verb by punctuation. Therefore, options (1), (2), (3), and (4) are incorrect.

25. **(3) replace are with were** (Usage/Verb tense—word clues to tense in paragraphs) The previous sentences are written in the past tense. For consistency and clarity, this sentence should also be written in past tense, using were. There is no reason for the changes in options (1), (2), and (4).

26. **(4) We even hear** (Usage/Pronoun reference—pronoun shift; Mechanics/Spelling—homonyms) The rest of the paragraph is written with the pronoun we; changing to you, or to they as in options (1), (2), and (5), is a pronoun shift. Hear means "to gain information through the ear"; here refers to a location, making option (3) incorrect.

27. **(4) move quickly and easily after to be made** (Sentence structure/Misplaced modifier) The type has not been set quickly and easily; the printed page is made quickly and easily. The modifier quickly and easily should be placed as close as possible to the phrase to be made. Therefore, options (1) and (2) are incorrect. There is no reason for the change in option (3).

28. **(3) information spread** (Sentence structure/Parallelism; Usage/Pronoun reference—vague reference) There is no antecedent for the pronoun it, so options (1) and (2) are wrong. The pronoun should be replaced with a noun, such as information. The three items in series should be of parallel structure; the last two, people and civilization, start with a noun, so the first one should also start with a noun, information. Option (4) incorrectly places a comma between the subject and verb. Option (5) incorrectly shifts to future tense.

Writing Skills Part II, The Essay (page 25)

Evaluating and scoring your essay can be done by you or by someone else. If you are taking a class, have your teacher evaluate your essay. If you are working independently, ask a friend or relative to read your essay. If this is not possible, evaluate your writing yourself. After finishing an essay, put it aside for a day. Then read it as objectively as possible. No matter who checks your writing, make sure that person follows the Scoring Guide on page 181 and uses the check list on page 187 as scoring evaluation guides.

Write the date on your completed essays and keep them together in a folder or notebook. This way, you will be able to keep track of your progress, note your strengths, and figure out areas in which you want to improve.

Social Studies (page 27)

1. **(4) 57°** (Comprehension) Find Chicago in the left column, and read across until you come to the column which gives the maximum average temperature for April. The number in that column is 57°. The information in the table does not support any of the other options.

2. **(3) Bismarck is the coldest city in North Dakota.** (Analysis) Nothing in the table allows you to compare Bismarck's temperatures with those of any other North Dakota city. Options (1), (2), (4), and (5) can be verified by information in the table.

3. **(5) Miami** (Application) According to the table, Miami has the warmest January temperatures, between 76° and 58° F, of any of the cities listed. This is likely to attract people looking for warm weather in winter. Options (1), (2), (3), and (4) are cities where the average temperature in January was 40° and lower.

4. **(5) There is no supporting fact.** (Analysis) There is no evidence other than the word gladly which reflects opinion, not fact. Lee probably would have surrendered and accepted the terms no matter how he felt, so options (1) and (4) are incorrect. Option (2) is not true. Option (3) happened before the terms were offered.

5. **(4) Grant was generous in his terms.** (Analysis) A comment on Grant's attitude would reveal the author's opinion. There is no evidence of how Lee felt about Grant, so option (1) is incorrect. Options (2), (3), and (5) are facts, not opinions.

6. **(1) Economists try to keep the economy stable.** (Analysis) The writer sees the economist as someone who is supposed to diagnose and solve the problems of the economy. There is no evidence that the writer assumes options (2), (3), (4), or (5) to be true.

7. **(4) consumer spending decreases** (Comprehension) When people are unemployed, their spending level drops. Options (1), (2), (3), and (5) usually accompany periods of high employment, not unemployment.

8. **(3) state laws on seat belts** (Application) This is the only example of specific government regulation. Option (1) is nonprofit advice. Options (2), (4), and (5) are private-sector efforts at consumer protection.

9. **(4) consumer** (Comprehension) This answer is implied by the statement that supermarkets often pass the cost of returned merchandise on to the consumer in product markup. Options (1), (2), (3), and (5) are not supported or implied in the paragraphs.

10. **(5) an account paying 4.5 percent interest compounded daily** (Application) Because the percent interest of options (4) and (5) is the highest, one of these must be correct. Option (4) is incorrect because Alicia will earn 4.5 percent only on the original $1,000. With option (5), Alicia will earn interest on her $1,000 plus earnings. Over time, this account will make the most money.

11. **(2) increasing exports and increasing imports** (Comprehension) This is shown by the general upward trend of both lines on the graph. Option (1) is incorrect because imports are also increasing. Option (3) is incorrect because both lines are moving upward, not downward. Option (4) is incorrect because exports are increasing, not decreasing. Option (5) is incorrect because both lines show a definite upward movement.

12. **(3) Direct election of the House of Representatives is desirable in order to make the House truly representative of all classes of society.** (Analysis) Mason was concerned about representing all parts of society, not only the educated and wealthy elite. Options (1) and (2) are incorrect because although many people agreed with these statements, they are not mentioned as Mason's opinion. Options (4) and (5) are opinions held by Mason's opponents.

13. **(2) Representatives are elected by direct vote.** (Comprehension) The passage states that the Constitution provides for direct election of those members. Options (1), (3), (4), and (5), although true, are not supported by the passage.

14. **(3) Pennsylvania** (Comprehension) Pennsylvania was named for William Penn, its Quaker founder. Options (1), (2), (4), and (5) are colonies not mentioned in the paragraphs.

15. **(3) The Quakers wanted to practice their religion.** (Analysis) Option (3) is correct because the first paragraph states that the Quakers disagreed with the Church of England. Options (1) and (2) are incorrect because they are effects of the Quakers settling here. Option (4) is not supported by the paragraph; also, it is not true. Option (5) is incorrect because although the debt helped the Quakers, it was not the cause of their settling in America.

16. **(4) gentle** (Analysis) This option is a judgment about the group, not a fact. Options (1), (2), (3), and (5) are all facts.

17. **(5) arguing for an opinion when others disagree with you** (Application) Of all the choices listed, this is the only one in which an individual acts contrary to a group.

18. **(1) Go along to get along.** (Comprehension) This saying sums up the idea of conformity. Option (2) refers to thrift. Option (3) refers to the influence of a serious flaw. Option (4) is about being too optimistic. Option (5) refers to small-town versus big-city life.

19. **(4) The group is not important.** (Analysis) If the group is not important to you, you are more likely to stick to your own standards. Option (1) is incorrect because an insecure person would welcome the security of conforming to a group. Options (2) and (3) are incorrect because people have difficulty standing alone against large and unanimous groups. Option (5) is incorrect because having people watch increases the pressure to conform.

20. **(3) obeying authority** (Evaluation) Two-thirds of the subjects chose obeying the experimenter over not harming another person. Options (1), (2), (4), and (5) are incorrect because if they believed strongly in these ideas, they would not have harmed the others.

21. **(2) Present-day coastal cities of the eastern United States will disappear.** (Analysis) The map shows the United States' eastern and Gulf of Mexico shorelines. Today's shoreline, according to the map, will be under water in the future. As a result, today's East Coast cities will be under water. Nothing on the map suggests temperature changes or earthquakes, ruling out options (1) and (5). A changing shoreline will not necessarily affect the growth of population, so options (3) and (4) are incorrect.

22. **(2) Congress has been given too many powers.** (Evaluation) There is no way to judge if the powers listed are too many. The statement is a hasty generalization. Options (1), (3), and (4) are true according to the

passage. Option (5) is a reasonable conclusion because state populations vary.

23. **(3) The President can enforce laws because the President is the commander-in-chief.** (Evaluation) This statement is an oversimplification of the President's duties, not a true cause and effect relationship. Options (1), (2), (4), and (5) all state real cause and effect relationships.

24. **(4) A woman cannot be President.** (Evaluation) The exercise of power is stereotypically associated with men, but that does not mean that a woman cannot be President. Options (1), (2), (3), and (5) are all facts.

25. **(1) There is a division of power among the legislative, executive, and judicial branches.** (Evaluation) The paragraphs give many examples of such a division of power. Options (2), (3), (4), and (5) are not true.

26. **(2) religious** (Application) Wanting to convert other people is a religious reason. Since the priests had no economic, social, political, or scientific motives, options (1), (3), (4), and (5) are incorrect.

27. **(1) economic** (Application) Getting gold means gaining wealth. Gold has nothing to do with options (2), (3), (4), or (5).

28. **(2) religious** (Application) People who want to worship as they choose have a religious motive. Options (1), (3), (4), and (5) are not based on religion.

29. **(1) economic** (Application) Finding gold and other resources is an economic motive. Gold has nothing to do with options (2), (3), (4), and (5).

30. **(2) believe that politicians are inefficient** (Evaluation) Telling political jokes most likely indicates a negative belief. Therefore, options (1) and (3) are incorrect. Options (4) and (5) refer to behavioral scientists, not to the joke teller.

31. **(4) Fewer children not living with their fathers will live in poverty.** (Analysis) More support money should go to children now that the law is in force, so fewer children will be poor. The information does not give support for the law resulting in more divorces, more women going to work, or more men gaining custody of their children, so options (1), (2), and (3) are incorrect.

Nothing in the paragraph suggests that fathers will be unable to afford the payments, ruling out option (5).

32. **(5) Since about 1950, the population center has moved to the south and west.** (Evaluation) The population centers since 1950 have moved south as well as west, as more people move to the Sunbelt states. Option (1) is the opposite of what the map shows. Option (2) is incorrect because Baltimore was the population center of the United States in 1790, not where most people lived. Option (3) is not supported by the map, which does not give information about the geographical center. Option (4) is true, but it is not given in the information.

Science (page 37)

1. **(3) circulatory system** (Application) The blood carries substances to all the tissues in the body through the circulatory system. Although the blood circulates through the other systems, it is part of the circulatory system. None of the other systems listed in options (1), (2), (4), and (5) transport substances around the body.

2. **(5) reproductive system** (Analysis) If the reproductive system of an individual is not working properly, the individual will still survive. Options (1), (2), (3), and (4) are incorrect because failure of these systems would cause death.

3. **(2) The continents ride on plates that move, causing new formations of land and water.** (Comprehension) Option (2) indicates that the movement of plates is changing the location of continents and oceans. Option (1) is incorrect because plate movement will continue moving land masses. Option (3) is incorrect because the separation of continents happened when the land mass, Pangaea, broke into huge pieces. Option (4) implies that plate movement has stopped, which is incorrect. Option (5) is false because diverging boundaries are usually beneath the oceans.

4. **(3) two plates colliding** (Analysis) The collision of plates causes earthquakes, volcanic activity, and the formation of high mountains. Mountain formation does not happen in options (1) and (2). Options (4) and (5) only indirectly relate to the study of Earth's plates.

5. **(3) pickles** (Application) Vinegar and salt are used to preserve cucumbers, a process that results in pickles. Option (1) is flour containing supplementary minerals and vitamins. Option (2) is milk processed so that the cream is distributed throughout rather than just remaining on the top; the process does not preserve the milk. Option (4) is added to change the taste of food; it is not a food. Option (5) is a product with a supplementary mineral.

6. **(4) A and B** (Analysis) Since most people no longer grow their own food, food additives are important in preventing the spoiling of food that is transported long distances and stored for long periods (Statement A). In addition, some food additives provide minerals and vitamins that may otherwise be lacking in the diet (Statement B). Options (1) and (2) are incorrect because they are incomplete. Most food additives do not cause disease (Statement C), so options (3) and (5) are incorrect.

7. **(2) a rubber eraser** (Application) The article mentions that objects containing iron and steel are affected by magnets. Options (1), (3), (4), and (5) all contain iron or steel. Options (3) and (4) describe two kinds of magnets which are affected by magnetic fields. Option (5), the steel girder, is large and may not visibly shift but would be affected by magnetism. A magnet would certainly stick to it!

8. **(2) Earth has a magnetic north pole** (Analysis) Earth, with a magnetic north pole, causes the suspended compass needle to point north. Option (1) is a result of the compass's behavior, not a cause. Option (3) is not true. Option (4) is incorrect because if the domains pointed in different directions, the needle would not be a magnet. Option (5) is not true because one pole is not stronger than another.

9. **(1) Warm air rises and cool air sinks.** (Evaluation) The diagram shows warm air rising. As the warm air becomes cooler, it sinks. Options (2) and (3) are incorrect because they describe the opposite of what actually happens. Option (4) is incorrect because the diagram suggests that the heat of the different types of surfaces influences air movement above them. The truth of option (5) cannot be determined from the diagram. Although the diagram shows a convection cell where land and water meet, there may be other situations in which convection cells occur.

10. **(2) Face inland.** (Application) According to the diagram, the wind is coming off the ocean onto the beach. Facing inland will keep the wind out of your eyes. Option (1) would have the wind coming directly at you. Options (3) and (4) would expose either side of your face to the wind. Option (5) is incorrect because the wind in the diagram is coming from one particular direction.

11. **(1) when moving up** (Analysis) The article states a jellyfish uses its muscles to move up in the water. Options (2) and (5) are not possible because when the jellyfish moves down to capture food, it drifts and does not use its muscles. Option (3) is not possible because jellyfish do not use their muscles to drift sideways. Option (4) is not possible because jellyfish swim up when capturing food.

12. **(4) Jellyfish reproduce sexually.** (Evaluation) The article states in the first paragraph that jellyfish mate and produce polyps. Sexual reproduction is another term for mating. Option (1) is not supported by the information provided, which is that jellyfish stings can be irritating and sometimes fatal. Option (2) is not true since mussels and clams are not mentioned and they are not closely related to jellyfish. Option (3) is incorrect because the article states only that sea wasps, a type of jellyfish, are usually found in tropical oceans. Option (5) may or may not be true; however there is not enough information to determine this.

13. **(3) Organic fertilizers act on the soil in a manner more similar to nature than do chemical fertilizers.** (Evaluation) Since the action of compost and manure imitates the process of decay in nature, the farmer can claim that this crop is produced naturally and is therefore better for the environment. Option (1) is untrue since the article states that minerals are not used by the plants until they have decayed into a simpler form. Option (2) is true but is incorrect because the article states that plants use simple forms from both natural and artificial fertilizers. Option (4) is not true. Option (5) is also untrue; neither kind of fertilizer contains pesticides.

14. **(2) vitamin A to skim milk** (Application) When fat is removed from milk to produce skim milk, most of the vitamin A content is lost. Vitamin A is added to replace it, and its addition is listed on the milk carton. Option (1) is too general to be correct. Option (3) is similar to adding fertilizer to soil, but the

sweetener has no nutritional value. Fertilizer adds nutritional value to the soil. Option (4) is also similar to adding fertilizer to soil, except that the fluoride does not replace something lost in the water. The water is just a convenient place to put fluoride for human consumption. Option (5) is simply a matter of taste. Most cereals contain natural sugars.

15. **(5) the source of activation energy** (Application) In this case, the match provides the energy to start coals burning. Option (1) is incorrect because the match is not a property, it is a form of matter. Option (2) is incorrect since the burning of the match is an exothermic reaction, releasing energy. Option (3) is incorrect because the lit match is part of a chemical reaction, not a physical change. Option (4) is incorrect; the resulting forms of matter in this reaction are ashes and gases.

16. **(3) a chemical reaction in which heat energy is absorbed** (Comprehension) Option (1) is incorrect because it defines all chemical reactions, not just endothermic reactions. Option (2) is incorrect because it defines an exothermic reaction. Option (4) is incorrect because it defines activation energy. Option (5) is incorrect because all chemical reactions need activation energy to start.

17. **(5) sulfur dioxide** (Analysis) Since sulfur dioxide has the highest density of the gases listed, it also has the highest specific gravity:

$$\frac{2.93}{1.29} = 2.27$$

The other gases all have specific gravities of less than 2.

18. **(1) The densities of air and nitrogen are similar.** (Analysis) Since nitrogen makes up almost 80 percent of air, its density has a great influence on the density of air. Option (2) is not true; at 1.25, nitrogen is less dense than air. Option (3) is true, but it is not related to the proportion of nitrogen in the air. Options (4) and (5) are not true.

19. **(1) cancerous growths that may cause death if untreated** (Comprehension) This definition appears in the first paragraph of the article. Option (2) is incorrect because if the immune system were successful in suppressing the cancerous growth, the growth would not be malignant. Options (3) and (4) are incorrect because malignant tumors are not harmless. Option (5) is incorrect because

malignant tumors are cancers; they are not the cause of cancer.

20. **(4) being exposed to a high level of radiation** (Analysis) Radiation is a known cancer-causing agent. Options (1), (3), and (5) are incorrect because they are practices that lessen the body's intake of artificial substances. Option (2) is incorrect because lack of exercise is not a chemical or physical agent that might cause cancer.

21. **(3) 95°C** (Application) Since the boiling point of a liquid decreases with a drop in air pressure, the boiling point of water in Denver must be less than the boiling point of water in New York. This is so because Denver, at a higher elevation than New York, has a lower atmospheric pressure. Option (1) is incorrect because it is a higher temperature than the boiling point of water in New York, which is 100°C. Option (2) is incorrect because the boiling point of water will differ at different elevations. The boiling point of water at sea level is 100°C. Options (4) and (5) are incorrect because they are the freezing and below-freezing temperatures of water.

22. **(4) The boiling point of a liquid increases as the air pressure increases.** (Evaluation) The information provided indicates a direct relationship between air pressure and the boiling points of liquids. In other words, as one increases, so does the other. Option (1) is incorrect because the passage indicates that once the boiling point is reached, the liquid does not get any hotter. It just boils until it evaporates. Option (2) is incorrect because the boiling point of water, 100°C, is lower than that of octane, 126°C, as is indicated in the chart. Option (3) is true but is not supported by the information provided. The passage and the chart do not deal with the effect on the liquid's boiling point of adding other substances. It is therefore incorrect. No information is given to support or disprove option (5). Although the boiling point of chloroform is lower than that of water, this fact does not necessarily have any bearing on the use of chloroform in anesthesia.

23. **(4) Heated air near the storage mass creates air currents that circulate warm air throughout the house.** (Analysis) Since warm air rises, a pattern of air flow is established in a well-designed solar house. Options (1), (2), and (3) are incorrect because houses that receive all their heat by means of

solar energy do not have radiators throughout the house. Option (5) is incorrect because the storage mass generates radiant energy, or heat, not electrical energy.

24. **(4) It is often difficult and expensive to convert existing houses to solar energy.** (Evaluation) The redesigning of windows and addition of solar collectors can be very expensive. Options (1) and (2) are incorrect because solar heating does not always involve these designs. Option (3) is not true in most areas. Option (5) is not true since solar energy is a very clean source of energy.

25. **(5) store reserves of energy to be used on cloudy days and at night** (Comprehension) The density of the materials used allows for the absorption and the gradual release of stored energy. Options (1), (2), and (4) are not purposes of a storage mass. Solar collectors—not storage masses—are generally used to heat water, option (3).

26. **(3) cutting leaves** (Comprehension) According to the article, leaf-cutting ants harm crops in Texas and Louisiana. The other activities of ants in options (1), (2), (4), and (5) help make food for humans. These are described in the third paragraph of the article.

27. **(4) the roles of the queen, winged males, and workers** (Evaluation) Each type of ant has a specific role to play in the colony. This would most interest a sociobiologist. Options (1), (2), (3), and (5) describe only physical aspects of ant life, not the way ants act in a group.

28. **(2) performing tasks one after another on an assembly line** (Application) In assembly line work, each worker performs a task in the manufacture of a product. This is most like the behavior of the leaf-cutting worker ants that divide the labor according to size. Option (1) is not correct because ants do not have political systems. Options (3) and (4) are similar to the function of one kind of leaf-cutting worker, not to all leaf-cutting ants. Option (5) is incorrect because the main job of the workers is to feed the colony, not fight for it.

29. **(2) feeding other members of the colony** (Evaluation) This is the primary job of worker ants. Options (1), (4), and (5) describe effects of ant activities that might benefit farmers. Option (3) describes an activity, cutting leaves, that can benefit one kind of ant, the leaf-cutter. In the article cutting leaves is viewed mainly as a problem for farmers.

30. **(3) ice, water, water vapor** (Application) These are three forms of water: solid, liquid, and gas. Option (1) is incorrect because both lumps and grains of sugar are solids; the option provides no gas. Option (2) is incorrect because rock salt and salt crystals are both solids and the option provides no gas; and salt water is a mixture of salt and water, not a form of salt. Option (4) is incorrect because glass and broken glass are both solids, and the option provides no gas. Option (5) is incorrect because a carbonated beverage is not a form of carbon dioxide. It contains bubbles of carbon dioxide gas.

31. **(4) changes in amount of heat** (Analysis) Matter melts and boils at different temperatures, changing from one state to another. Option (1) is incorrect because a change in chemical makeup would result in an entirely different kind of matter, not another state of matter. Options (2), (3), and (5) may result from a change of state, but they do not cause it.

32. **(2) its weight equals the weight of the liquid it displaces** (Comprehension) According to the diagram, the cube floats when its weight is the same as the weight of the liquid it pushes aside, or displaces. Option (1) is incorrect because objects that sink also displace water. Option (3) is incorrect because, if the weight of the object is greater than that of the displaced liquid, the object sinks as shown in the second diagram. Options (4) and (5) are incorrect because the total weight of the liquid does not matter. What is important is the weight of the object in relation to the weight of the liquid pushed aside.

33. **(4) Steel and air are equal in weight to the water they displace.** (Evaluation) Steel ships float because they are not made of solid steel, but of steel and air (hollow parts of the ship). Thus, they weigh less than an equal volume of solid steel, which would sink. Although option (1) is true, it is not correct because ships contain air as well as steel. Option (2) is not true since steel sinks. Option (3) is not true since steel ships float. Option (5) is not true since floating objects are equal in weight to the liquid they displace, not lighter.

Literature & the Arts (page 47)

1. **(5) The boy tried to take something that belonged to the woman.** (Literal Comprehension) The meeting between the

woman and the boy occurred when the boy tried, and failed, to steal the woman's purse. Option (1) is incorrect because the boy was attempting to steal from, not help, the woman. Option (3) is incorrect because the boy was not able to steal the purse from the woman. While options (2) and (4) may be true, they are not supported by the excerpt.

2. **(3) She kicked him in the seat of his pants.** (Literal Comprehension) The woman's initial reaction to the boy's attempt at snatching her purse is discussed at the end of the first paragraph. Options (1) and (2) do occur, but take place later in the excerpt. Options (4) and (5) do not happen.

3. **(2) take the boy to her house to wash his face** (Application) Before starting up the street with the boy in tow, the woman tells him that he will have his face washed that evening. While it is possible that any of the remaining options could occur, none are supported by the excerpt.

4. **(3) speak politely but distantly** (Application) Throughout the excerpt, Mrs. Buchanan makes a point of being polite about Alma and not insulting her outright; therefore, options (1) and (5) are incorrect. But Mrs. Buchanan does not want to be her friend, option (4), and therefore will not be likely to invite Alma to dinner, option (2).

5. **(2) talk with her in a friendly way** (Application) John does not seem to know Alma that well, so options (1) and (4) are incorrect. Options (3) and (5) are not supported by the excerpt.

6. **(1) Mrs. Buchanan's negative opinion of Alma** (Analysis) Mrs. Buchanan emphasizes such words as "eccentric" and "quite" (in "not quite") to show that she does not think much of Alma. Mrs. Buchanan is not angry at, or fearful for, John in the excerpt; so options (2) and (3) are incorrect. Options (4) and (5) are not supported by the excerpt.

7. **(4) conforming** (Application) Since Mrs. Buchanan is concerned about appearances, she is not likely to be married to an eccentric man, option (1). Because she tries to convince John not to be sentimental or stubborn, she would probably not want these qualities in a husband, so options (2) and (5) are incorrect. There is no support for option (3).

8. **(5) is critical and a snob** (Inferential Comprehension) This is correct because her

every word is judgmental and proud. Options (1), (2), and (4) are not supported by the excerpt. Option (3) is incorrect because she talks about Alma only to try to turn John from Alma.

9. **(1) Unexpected sights can produce endless pleasure.** (Inferential Comprehension) The author stresses his surprise and pleasure at the sight of the field of daffodils, so option (4) is incorrect. Option (2) is a supporting detail for the main idea. Option (3) is the opposite of what is implied by the poem. There is no support for option (5).

10. **(3) When he is alone, the author uses his imagination to replay the sight of the flowers.** (Analysis) The "inward eye" makes reference to what the author can see inside his head, or in his imagination, therefore option (5) is incorrect. Options (1) and (2) are literal interpretations of figurative language. There is no direct evidence for option (4).

11. **(1) different men in the Vietnam war** (Inferential Comprehension) The reviewer discusses two stories: one about a group of soldiers, the other about the fictional version of the author's experience. Therefore, it is about more than one man, making options (2) and (3) incorrect. Options (4) and (5) are not supported by the excerpt.

12. **(1) went to Vietnam but did not enjoy being there** (Inferential Comprehension) The author writes about firsthand experiences in Vietnam, so option (2) is incorrect. There is no evidence in the excerpt to support options (3), (4), and (5).

13. **(2) explain how the stories in the book are alike and different** (Analysis) The reviewer does not boast about knowledge of war or say he was ever in one, so options (1) and (4) are incorrect. There is no discussion of specific characters in the first example, so option (3) is incorrect. Option (5) does not explain the structure of the review.

14. **(3) is about the soldiers' feelings** (Literal Comprehension) The answer is found in lines 32–36. Options (1), (2), (4), and (5) are mentioned in the review, but not as factors that make this book better than others.

15. **(5) The reviewer admires it.** (Inferential Comprehension) The reviewer mentions that the earlier book also "captures the war's pulsating rhythms and nerve-racking dangers" (lines 10–12), and he includes both books on his "short list of essential fiction"

(lines 6–8) on the war. This admiring statement is the opposite of option (4). There is no evidence for options (1), (2), and (3).

16. **(2) the war experience** (Literal Comprehension) The answer is found in lines 61–63. The book may help the reader understand the author's life, option (1), but this is not the point the reviewer makes. There is no evidence for options (3), (4), and (5).

17. **(2) They contrast the stormy feelings of the woman with the quiet feelings of the man.** (Analysis) These two sentences record how the characters' actions reflect their feelings. Options (1), (4), and (5) are not supported by the last two sentences. Although we know that the woman feels that Michael Furey's death was tragic, option (3), this is not the point being made here.

18. **(1) is in love with the woman** (Inferential Comprehension) We can infer Gabriel's love from the information in the first paragraph. There is no evidence for options (2), (3), and (4). Although option (5) may be true, we cannot know that from the excerpt.

19. **(2) She sent him away.** (Literal Comprehension) The answer can be found in line 41 which states that she "implored of him to go home at once." Though options (1) and (5) may be true, there is not enough evidence to support them. Options (3) and (4) are the opposite of what happened in the excerpt.

20. **(3) did not want to live without love** (Inferential Comprehension) Options (1), (2), and (4) are untrue. Although he was sick, option (5), the woman's story implies that he lost his will to live when she went away.

21. **(2) the struggle of a bird to escape his cage** (Literal Comprehension) The focus of this poem is on the bird's struggle and inability to escape the bonds of its cage. While options (1), (3), and (4) appear in the poem, they are not its focus. Option (5) is not supported in the poem.

22. **(3) a flower** (Inferential Comprehension) The "its" from line 6 refers to the flower bud of line 5; therefore, the flower's perfume would be its smell. While details of options (1), (2), (4), and (5) appear in the poem, they are not discussed with regard to their smell.

23. **(4) The bird must sit on his perch when he desires freedom.** (Analysis) Based on lines 8 and 9, the caged bird has been beating his wings on the bars of the cage in order to be free. Lines 10 and 11 indicate that he cannot escape, and instead must sit in his cage when he would rather be in the trees. The bird sits on its perch unwillingly, so options (1) and (2) are incorrect. The poem does not discuss the location of the bird's cage, thus options (3) and (5) are also incorrect.

Mathematics (page 57)

1. **(2) 35(8)(10)** Multiply 35 by 8 to find the number of valves made in one day. Multiply by 10 to find the number made in 10 days.

2. **(5) $13\frac{1}{2}$** Multiply $3\frac{3}{8}$ by 4.

3. **(2) $18,189.60** Find the amount of the raise ($17,160 \times 0.06 = \$1,029.60$) and add it to the original salary ($17,160 + \$1,029.60 = \$18,189.60$)

4. **(1) 2.73815×10^5** Move the decimal point to the right 5 places to multiply by 10^5.

5. **(4) 56** $\triangle ABC$ and $\triangle CDE$ are similar triangles and have proportional sides. Set up a proportion:

$$\frac{\text{Side } \overline{AC}}{\text{Side } \overline{CE}} = \frac{\text{Side } \overline{AB}}{\text{Side } \overline{DE}}$$

$$\frac{{}^{14}\cancel{28}}{{}_{1}\cancel{2}} = \frac{x}{4}$$

$$\frac{14}{1} = \frac{x}{4}$$

$$x = (14)(4)$$

$$x = 56$$

6. **(5) $\frac{3}{4}$** Set up a ratio and reduce:

$$\frac{\text{large}}{\text{total}} = \frac{150}{200} = \frac{3}{4}$$

7. **(2) 20 miles** "Due east" and "due south" form a right triangle. These distances are the legs. Use the Pythagorean formula to solve for the hypotenuse:

$$c^2 = a^2 + b^2$$
$$c^2 = 12^2 + 16^2$$
$$c^2 = 144 + 256$$
$$c^2 = 400$$
$$c = \sqrt{400}$$
$$c = 20$$

8. **(1) $14.00** Find 10% by moving the decimal point one place to the left:
$70.00 = $7

Multiply by 2 to find 20%:
$7.00 × 2 = $14.00

9. **(2) $N = \frac{7}{4}(92)$** Set up a proportion and solve for N:

$$\frac{4 \text{ hours}}{92 \text{ monitors}} = \frac{7 \text{ hours}}{N}$$
$$4N = (7)(92)$$
$$N = \frac{(7)(92)}{4} \text{ or}$$
$$N = \frac{7}{4}(92)$$

10. **(2) $x = -3$**
$$2(2x + 3) = -3(x + 5)$$
$$4x + 6 = -3x - 15$$
$$7x = -21$$
$$x = -3$$

11. **(4) between 6 and 7**
Convert the width and height to feet:

$1 \text{ ft } 6 \text{ in} = 1\frac{6}{12} = 1\frac{1}{2}$ ft

$1 \text{ ft } 9 \text{ in} = 1\frac{9}{12} = 1\frac{3}{4}$ ft

Find the volume of the box:
$$V = lwh$$
$$= 2\frac{1}{2}(1\frac{1}{2})(1\frac{3}{4})$$
$$= \frac{5}{2} \times \frac{3}{2} \times \frac{7}{4}$$
$$= \frac{105}{16}$$
$$= 6\frac{9}{16}$$

12. **(4) Team C is farthest from its goal.**
Change the fractions to decimals for easier comparisons and evaluate each answer choice:

A $\frac{2}{3}$ = $0.66\frac{2}{3}$

B $\frac{1}{3}$ = $0.33\frac{1}{3}$

C $\frac{3}{10}$ = 0.30

D $\frac{1}{2}$ = 0.50

E $\frac{3}{8}$ = $0.37\frac{1}{2}$

Team C is farthest from its goal because it has reached the <u>smallest</u> portion of its goal.

13. **(1) 4** Solve for y. Cross multiply. $5 > y$. Only option (1) satisfies this equation.

14. **(3) 15,000** Convert the base measurement to centimeters:

$2\text{m} \times 100 \frac{\text{cm}}{\text{m}} = 200$ cm

$$A = \frac{1}{2}bh$$
$$= \frac{1}{2}(200)(150)$$
$$= 15,000 \text{ sq cm}$$

15. **(5) $38.25** Use base × rate = part to find the amount of the discount: $45 × 0.15 = $6.75. Subtract the amount of the discount from $45: $45 − $6.75 = $38.25.

16. **(2) $0.72** To find the actual answer, subtract to find the difference between the two prices for one gallon. Multiply the difference by 18 to find the total difference.
18($1.39 − $1.35)
18($0.04) = $0.72
To use estimation to narrow down the choices, round 18 to the nearest ten: 20. Work the problem using the rounded number.
20($1.39 − $1.35)
20($0.04) = $0.80 estimated solution
Options (1), (3), (4), and (5) are far from the estimated solution. Option (2) is the most likely answer.

17. **(4) 4,748** Convert $3\frac{1}{2}$ feet to inches:
$3\frac{1}{2} \times 12 = 42$ inches. Find the area of the base: The radius is $\frac{1}{2}$ the diameter.
$$A = \pi r^2$$
$$= 3.14(6^2)$$
$$= 113.04 \text{ square inches}$$
Find the volume of the cylinder:
$$V = Ah$$
$$= 113.04(42)$$
$$= 4,747.68, \text{ which rounds}$$
to 4,748 cubic inches

18. **(3) 14 and 16** Write an equation: n + n + 2 = 30; 2n = 28; n = 14. Only option (3) totals 30: 14 + 16 = 30.

19. **(4) 79** In an isosceles triangle the sides opposite the equal angles must be equal. Therefore, side AB and side BC are both 32 inches. The perimeter is $P = a + b + c =$ 15 + 32 + 32 = 79.

20. **(5) 280** Divide the number who responded (126) by the rate (45% = 0.45). Or set up a ratio: $\frac{45\%}{126} = \frac{100\%}{x}$
$$12,600 = 45x$$
$$280 = x$$

21. **(2) 7** $\angle J = 180° - (90° + 30°)$
$$\angle J = 60°$$
$$\angle J = \angle G$$
$$\angle H = 180° - (90° + 60°)$$
$$\angle H = 30°$$
$$\angle H = \angle K$$
$$\overline{HI} = \overline{KL}$$
$$\overline{HI} = 7$$
$$\overline{KL} = 7$$

22. **(4) 303** Add the distances $(318 + 315 + 320 + 298 + 264 = 1{,}515)$ and divide $(1{,}515 \div 5 = 303)$.

23. **(3) $3a = 33$** Let a represent Anne's age, $3a$ equals Doris's age (33); therefore $3a = 33$.

24. **(4) $1.32** Find 10% by moving the decimal point one place to the left:
$8.80 = $0.88.
Divide $0.88 by 2 to find 5%:
$0.88 \div 2 = $0.44.
Add 10% and 5%:
$0.88 + $0.44 = $1.32.

25. **(3) 696** Find the area of the two rectangles. Subtract the area of the smaller rectangle from the area of the larger rectangle.
$A = lw = 30 \times 40 = 1{,}200$ square feet
$A = lw = 28 \times 18 = 504$ square feet
$1{,}200 - 504 = 696$ square feet

26. **(3) $15(9) + 22(7)$** Multiply the hours worked by the wage rate for each job, then add.

27. **(5) 4** Divide 5 grains by $1\frac{1}{4}$ grains per tablet:
$1\frac{1}{4} = \frac{5}{4}. \quad \frac{5}{1} \div \frac{5}{4} = \frac{\cancel{5}}{1} \times \frac{4}{\cancel{5}} = 4$

Unit 1: Writing Skills

Mechanics

Lesson 1: Using Capitalization

GED Exercise: **Using Capitalization (page 65)**

1. **(4) change middle East to Middle East** (Capitalization) Option (4) is correct because Middle East is a specific area of the world, so both words should be capitalized. Options (1) and (3) are incorrect because titles attached to specific names are properly capitalized. Option (2) is incorrect because Kissinger should be capitalized; it is the name of a specific person.

2. **(2) replace Vice President ford with Vice President Ford** (Capitalization) Option (2) is correct because a person's name, Ford, is a proper noun and should be capitalized. For the same reason, option (4) is incorrect. Option (1) is incorrect because there is no reason to capitalize the common noun presidency here. Option (3) is incorrect because Vice is part of the title and should be capitalized.

3. **(2) change Fall to fall** (Capitalization) Option (2) is correct because seasons of the year are not capitalized. Option (1) is

incorrect because Election Day is a national holiday and should be capitalized. Option (3) is incorrect because Americans, the name of a specific nationality, should be capitalized. Option (4) is incorrect because polls should not be capitalized here.

4. **(4) change south to South** (Capitalization) Option (4) is correct because South needs to be capitalized; it refers here to a specific region of the country, not a direction. In option (3), there is no reason to capitalize the word the. In options (1) and (2), Bill and Clinton are proper names and must be capitalized.

5. **(2) change State to state** (Capitalization) Option (2) is correct because since state is not the name of a specific region, it does not need to be capitalized. Option (1) is incorrect because there is no need to capitalize the common noun nation. Option (3) is incorrect because California is the name of a specific place and should be capitalized. Option (4) is incorrect because presidents is not a proper noun and should not be capitalized.

Lesson 2: Using End Punctuation

GED Exercise: **Using End Punctuation (page 67)**

1. **(3) no correction is necessary** (Punctuation/ End punctuation) Option (3) is correct because this is a statement that expresses a complete thought; it does not ask a question or require emphasis, so it should end with a period.

2. **(1) change the question mark to a period** (Punctuation/End punctuation) Option (1) is correct because this is a statement that expresses a complete thought; it does not ask a question or require emphasis, so it should end with a period.

3. **(1) change the question mark to a period** (Punctuation/End punctuation) Option (1) is correct because this is a statement that expresses a complete thought; it does not ask a question or require emphasis, so it should end with a period.

4. **(2) change the exclamation mark to a question mark** (Punctuation/End punctuation) Option (2) is correct because this sentence asks a question that requires an answer.

5. **(2) change the period to an exclamation mark** (Punctuation/End punctuation) Option

(2) is correct because this sentence expresses a strong feeling or emotion; therefore, it should end with an exclamation mark.

6. **(1) change the question mark to a period** (Punctuation/End punctuation) Option (1) is correct because this is a statement that expresses a complete thought; it does not ask a question or require emphasis, so it should end with a period.

Lesson 3: Using Commas

GED Exercise: Using Commas (page 70)

1. **(3) remove the comma after and** (Punctuation/Commas between items in series) Option (3) is correct because a comma should not be placed after the conjunction and; it goes only before the conjunction. Option (1) is incorrect because the subject people should not be separated from the verb are. Option (2) is incorrect because afraid is the first item in the list and should be followed by a comma. Option (4) is incorrect because the prepositional phrase in their homes should not be set off by a comma.

2. **(5) no correction is necessary** (Punctuation/Appositives, overuse of commas between items in series) Options (1) and (2) are incorrect because the phrase a gas from uranium in the soil further explains Radon; therefore, the phrase is an appositive and should be set off by commas. Option (3) is incorrect because the prepositional phrase through cracks should not be set off by a comma. Option (4) is incorrect because basements is an item in series and should be followed by a comma.

3. **(1) insert a comma after Whellan** (Punctuation/Appositives) Option (1) is incorrect because the phrase a government official further explains who Floyd Whellan is; therefore, the phrase is an appositive and should be set off by commas. Option (2) is incorrect because the comma is needed both after the appositive and before the direct quote. Option (3) is incorrect because a prepositional phrase should not be set off by a comma. Option (4) is incorrect because a comma should not separate two items that are joined by the conjunction and.

4. **(2) insert a comma after gas** (Punctuation/Appositives) Option (2) is correct because the phrase a radioactive gas further explains radon; therefore, the phrase is an appositive and should be set off by commas. Option (1) is incorrect because the appositive should be set off by a comma from the noun that it describes. Option (3) is incorrect

because a comma is not needed before the conjunction or when it joins only two items. There is no reason for the change in option (4).

5. **(5) no correction is necessary** (Punctuation) Option (1) is incorrect because these are not anyone's exact words. Option (2) is incorrect because this is not a series of three items; radon gas is one item. Option (3) is incorrect because a comma is not needed to separate two items in series. Option (4) is incorrect because radon is a common noun and should not be capitalized.

6. **(4) remove the comma after overall** (Punctuation/Commas between items in series) Option (4) is correct because overall job performance is one term, which should not be broken by punctuation. Options (1) and (2) are incorrect because there is no reason to use a comma after realize or habits. Option (3) is incorrect because commas are needed to separate items in series.

7. **(2) insert a comma after nutritionist** (Punctuation/Appositives) Option (2) is correct because nutritionist is part of the descriptive phrase (appositive) that describes the noun Mrs. Ruth Lahiff and should be set off by commas. Option (1) is incorrect because the comma sets off the appositive. Option (3) is incorrect because there is no reason to use a comma after decided. Option (4) is incorrect because the comma would divide the verb to find.

8. **(3) insert a comma after employees** (Punctuation/Commas after introductory elements) Option (3) is correct because a comma is needed to set off an introductory clause that cannot stand alone. Option (1) is incorrect because there is no reason for a comma after data. Option (2) is incorrect because 500 county employees is one item and should not be broken by punctuation. Option (4) is incorrect because a comma is needed before a direct quotation.

9. **(2) insert a comma after added** (Punctuation/Commas with direct quotations) Option (2) is correct because a direct quotation should be set off from the rest of the sentence by a comma. Therefore, option (1) is incorrect. Options (3) and (4) are incorrect because commas are needed to separate all three items in the series.

10. **(4) insert a comma after coffee** (Punctuation/Commas with direct quotations) Option (4) is correct because a direct quotation should be set off from the rest of the sentence

by a comma. Option (1) is incorrect because a comma is needed after an introductory phrase. Option (2) is incorrect because the comma would separate the dependent clause in the direct quotation. Option (3) is incorrect because a comma is needed between burgers and fries in the series.

Lesson 4: Using Semicolons

GED Exercise: Using Semicolons (page 73)

1. **(3) and helpless; they** (Punctuation/Semicolon) Option (3) is correct because a semicolon is used to join two independent clauses that could stand alone and are not joined by a linking word. Options (1) and (2) are incorrect because the two independent clauses must be joined by either a semicolon or a comma and a coordinating conjunction. Option (4) is wrong because a semicolon is not normally used with the conjunction and. Option (5) is wrong because the linking word however requires a semicolon before it and a comma after it.

2. **(5) baby; however, your** (Punctuation/Semicolon) Option (5) is correct because the two clauses are joined by the linking word however. A semicolon is needed before the linking word, and a comma is needed after the linking word. Options (1), (2), (3), and (4) use semicolons and commas incorrectly.

3. **(1) baby, and you** (Punctuation/Commas and semicolons between independent clauses) Option (1) is correct because the two clauses that could stand alone are joined by a comma and the conjunction and. A comma is needed before and, so options (2) and (5) are incorrect. Semicolons are not normally used with and, so options (3) and (4) are wrong.

4. **(1) baby; and it** (Punctuation/Commas and semicolons between independent clauses) Normally a semicolon would not be needed with the conjunction and; however, other commas are used in the first independent clause, so a semicolon should be used before the conjunction. Punctuation is not needed after and, so options (3), (4), and (5) are incorrect. Option (2) would create a run-on sentence.

5. **(2) insert a comma after therefore** (Punctuation/Semicolon) A semicolon joins two independent clauses joined by the linking word therefore; a comma is required after the linking word. Option (1) is incorrect because a comma alone cannot join two independent clauses. Option (3) is incorrect because the

comma is necessary to separate items in a series. Option (4) is incorrect because the last item in a series does not require a comma.

Lesson 5: Using Apostrophes and Quotation Marks

GED Exercise: Using Apostrophes and Quotation Marks (page 75)

1. **(2) replace dont with don't** (Punctuation/Apostrophe) Option (2) is correct because don't, meaning "do not," should have an apostrophe in place of the missing letter. Options (1), (3), and (4) do not show correct contractions.

2. **(4) change owner's to owners** (Punctuation/Apostrophe) Option (4) is correct because owners should not show possession. Boys is a plural noun ending in -s, so the possessive is formed by adding an apostrophe after the s. Option (1) is incorrect because possession is meant; the club belongs to the boys. Option (2) is incorrect because the word club implies that more than one boy is meant. Option (3) is incorrect because the possessive isn't necessary.

3. **(3) replace its with it's** (Punctuation/Apostrophe) Option (3) is correct because its is a possessive pronoun; a contraction is needed here. It's means "it is." Option (1) is incorrect because I'd is a contraction meaning "I would," not "I had," here. The sentence needs the verb is, so option (2) is incorrect. Option (4) is incorrect because our is a possessive pronoun that does not use an apostrophe.

4. **(2) insert a quotation mark before man's** (Punctuation/Quotation marks) Option (2) is correct because the phrase to be quoted is "man's best friend." Option (1) is incorrect because the possessive isn't necessary. Option (3) is incorrect because man is a singular noun; the correct possessive is formed by adding 's. Option (4) is incorrect because a period is end punctuation.

5. **(4) insert a quotation mark after companions,** (Punctuation/Quotation marks) Option (4) is correct because companions, ends the direct quotation that begins with Dogs; quotation marks are used in pairs. Option (1) is incorrect because this sentence contains a direct quote. Option (2) is incorrect because the possessive isn't necessary. Option (3) is incorrect because children is a plural word not ending in -s; the possessive is formed by adding 's.

6. **(1) insert a quotation mark before When**
(Punctuation/Quotation marks) Option (1) is correct because the complete quotation begins with the first word in the sentence, so a quotation mark should be inserted before When. Option (2) is incorrect because it's is a contraction meaning "it is," which is the subject and verb of the main clause. Option (3) is incorrect because a direct quotation should be set off from the rest of the sentence by a comma. Option (4) is incorrect because Grover's tells whose sister it is, so an apostrophe is needed.

Lesson 6: Correct Spelling

GED Exercise: Correct Spelling (page 82)

1. **(4) change the spelling of goeing to going**
(Spelling) Option (4) is correct because you don't add an e when you add the suffix -ing. Option (1) is incorrect because seasons are not capitalized. Options (2) and (3) are incorrect because the singular subject strain takes the singular verb is.

2. **(1) change Its to It's** (Contractions) Option (1) is correct because It's is a contraction of It is. Option (2) is incorrect because a semicolon separates independent clauses. Option (3) is incorrect because you don't double the last consonant when it is preceded by a consonant. Option (4) is incorrect because then means "at a certain time."

3. **(1) change the spelling of noticable to noticeable** (Spelling) Option (1) is correct because the final e is kept when adding the suffix -able to notice. Option (2) is incorrect because the plural victims should not be a possessive. Options (3) and (4) are incorrect because including and coughing are spelled correctly.

4. **(1) change Theyr'e to They're**
(Contractions) Option (1) is correct because the apostrophe replaces the a in they are. Options (2) and (3) are incorrect because experiencing is spelled correctly. Option (4) is incorrect because a comma is needed after each item in a series.

5. **(3) change the spelling of unecessary to unnecessary** (Spelling) Option (3) is correct because the spelling of necessary does not change when the prefix un- is added. Option (1) is incorrect because the last consonant is not doubled when the first syllable of a word is stressed, as in VIsit. Option (2) is incorrect because a semicolon separates independent clauses. Option (4) is incorrect because people's professions are not capitalized.

6. **(2) change Yo'ud to You'd** (Contractions) Option (2) is correct because an apostrophe should replace the letters woul when forming the contraction of you would. Option (1) is incorrect because an apostrophe is needed when forming a contraction. Options (3) and (4) are incorrect because off and variety are spelled correctly.

7. **(1) change Youll to You'll** (Contractions) Option (1) is correct because an apostrophe is needed to replace the letters wi when forming the contraction you will. Option (2) is incorrect because making is spelled correctly. Option (3) is incorrect because steps is plural, not possessive, and so does not need an apostrophe. Option (4) is incorrect because there is no reason to capitalize week.

8. **(2) change geting to getting** (Spelling) Option (2) is correct because the t is doubled when the suffix -ing is added to get. Option (1) is incorrect because judgment is spelled correctly. Option (3) is incorrect because shot is the correct singular noun; the plural shots would not agree with the singular article a. Option (4) is incorrect because the names of months are capitalized.

9. **(5) no correction is necessary** (Spelling and contractions) Options (1) and (2) are incorrect because an apostrophe is needed to replace the second o in the contraction of Do not. Option (3) is incorrect because the e is not dropped when adding the suffix -less to the word use. Option (4) is incorrect because the semicolon separates two independent clauses.

10. **(5) no correction is necessary** (Spelling and contractions) Options (1) and (2) are incorrect because especially and dangerous are spelled correctly. Option (3) is incorrect because the plural of child is children. Option (4) is incorrect because senior citizens is not a proper noun.

11. **(1) change the spelling of encourageing to encouraging** (Spelling) Option (1) is correct because the e is dropped when adding a suffix that starts with a vowel. Option (2) is incorrect because grandparents is not a proper noun. Options (3) and (4) are incorrect because elderly and neighbors are spelled correctly.

12. **(3) change the spelling of healthyer to healthier** (Spelling) Option (1) is incorrect because the y in hurry is not changed to an i when the suffix -ing is added. Option (2) is incorrect because means is not possessive. Option (4) is incorrect because season is not a proper noun.

1. **(5) no correction is necessary**
(Spelling/Homonyms) Option (1) is incorrect because two, the number, is the correct word in this sentence. Option (2) is incorrect because sons, meaning "male children," is the correct word in this sentence. Option (3) is incorrect because to is part of the infinitive form of the verb to go. Option (4) is incorrect because week, meaning "seven days," is the correct word in this sentence.

2. **(3) change there to their** (Spelling/ Homonyms; Possessives) Option (3) is correct because the sons own the swim trunks, so the possessive pronoun their is needed. Option (1) is incorrect because 's is added after a singular noun to show possession. Option (2) is incorrect because to is part of the infinitive form of the verb to bring. Option (4) is incorrect because the preposition for is the correct word in the sentence.

3. **(1) change whether to weather** (Spelling/Homonyms) Option (1) is correct because weather, meaning "the climate," is the correct word in the sentence. Option (2) is incorrect because to is part of the infinitive form of the verb to be. Option (3) is incorrect because might, meaning "possible," is the correct word in the sentence. Option (4) is incorrect because too, meaning "also," is the correct word in the sentence.

4. **(4) change four to for** (Spelling/Homonyms) Option (4) is correct because the preposition for is the correct word in this sentence. Option (1) is incorrect because weather, referring to the climate, is correct in this sentence. Option (2) is incorrect because the possessive isn't necessary. Option (3) is incorrect because whole, meaning "entire," is correct in this sentence.

5. **(2) change boy's to boys'** (Spelling/ Homonyms; Possessives) Option (2) is correct because there are two boys so the plural possessive boys' is needed. Option (1) is incorrect because the verb would is the correct word in this sentence. Option (3) is incorrect because the possessive isn't necessary. Option (4) is incorrect because great, meaning "very good," is the correct word in this sentence.

GED Review: Mechanics (page 85)

1. **(2) views of their employees** (Spelling; Punctuation/Overuse of commas; Possessives) Option (2) is correct because the correct spelling is views, following the i before e rule. Option (3) is incorrect because there is no reason to set off the prepositional phrase of their employees with a comma. Option (4) is incorrect because the possessive pronoun their is needed. Option (5) is incorrect because the possessive isn't necessary.

2. **(1) communicate with management is** (Spelling; Punctuation/Semicolon and overuse of commas) Option (1) is correct because all words are spelled correctly and there is no need for any punctuation in this sentence. Option (2) is incorrect because comunicate is a misspelling. Options (3) and (5) are incorrect because the phrase through an employee . . . is essential to the meaning of the sentence and should not be set off with a comma or semicolon. Option (4) is incorrect because the comma would separate the subject way from the verb is.

3. **(4) change the question mark to a period** (Punctuation/End punctuation) Option (4) is correct because this is a statement and does not require an answer. Options (1) and (3) are incorrect because surveys and experts should be plural, not possessive. Option (2) is incorrect because usually is spelled correctly.

4. **(3) change Company to company** (Capitalization) Option (3) is correct because company is not part of a proper name and should not be capitalized. Option (1) is incorrect because the possessive pronoun Their is correct in the sentence. Option (2) is incorrect because the possessive isn't necessary. Option (4) is incorrect because confidentiality is a common noun and should not be capitalized.

5. **(1) insert commas after questions and salary** (Punctuation/Commas; Semicolons; Spelling) Option (1) is correct because a nonessential phrase is set off from a sentence with commas. Option (2) is incorrect because receive is spelled correctly. Option (3) is incorrect because a semicolon separates independent clauses. Option (4) is incorrect because the contraction they're is the correct word in this sentence.

6. **(4) surveys. Then** (Punctuation/End punctuation; Capitalization) Option (4) is correct because a nonessential phrase is set off from a sentence with commas.

7. **(1) change the semicolon to a comma** (Punctuation/Commas after introductory

elements) Option (1) is correct because a comma is used after an introductory phrase. Option (2) is incorrect because the possessive isn't necessary. Option (3) is incorrect because to is used with the infinitive verb form; too means "also." Option (4) is incorrect because recommend is spelled correctly.

8. **(4) but as one worker stated, "I liked** (Punctuation/Quotation marks, commas with quotation marks, and overuse of commas) Option (4) is correct because quotation marks are needed at the beginning of an exact quotation. All other punctuation is correct. Option (2) is incorrect because a direct quotation is set off by a comma. Option (3) is incorrect because it includes within the quotation marks the words that identify the speaker. There is no reason for the comma after but in option (5).

9. **(3) insert a semicolon after workable** (Punctuation/Semicolon) Option (3) is correct because a semicolon is used to join two independent clauses without a conjunction. Option (1) is incorrect because the possessive pronoun their is correct. Option (2) is incorrect because employees is meant in the plural and the plural possessive is formed by the apostrophe following the s. Option (4) is incorrect because the possessive isn't necessary.

10. **(1) improved, along** (Punctuation/Commas, semicolons, end punctuation) Option (1) is correct because a comma separates a nonessential dependent and an independent clause. Option (2) is incorrect because it removes the comma. Option (3) is incorrect because a semicolon separates two independent clauses. Options (4) and (5) create fragments; also, in option (4), a sentence must start with a capital letter.

11. **(5) no correction is necessary** (Capitalization; Punctuation/Semicolon, quotation marks, and apostrophe) Option (1) is incorrect because there is no reason to capitalize written. Option (2) is incorrect because there is no reason to put a semicolon after written. Option (3) is incorrect because special terms, such as displaced homemakers, are often put in quotes, and quotation marks are used in pairs. Option (4) is incorrect because the possessive isn't necessary.

12. **(3) change And to and** (Capitalization) Option (3) is correct because such words as and, in, of, on, and for are not capitalized unless they are the first or last word of the title. Option (1) is incorrect because to is used as a

preposition in this sentence; too means "also." Option (2) is incorrect because the comma after publication is needed to set off the title, as an appositive, from the rest of the sentence. Option (4) is incorrect because punctuation should go before the quotation mark.

13. **(3) insert a comma after Livingood** (Punctuation/Appositives) Option (3) is correct because a comma is used to set off a nonessential descriptive phrase (appositive) from the rest of the sentence. Option (1) is incorrect because a quotation mark is needed before Depression, which begins the doctor's exact words. Option (2) is incorrect because the preposition to is correct in this sentence. Option (4) is incorrect because a prepositional phrase should not be separated from the rest of the sentence by a comma.

14. **(1) insert a quotation mark after But,** (Punctuation/Quotation marks) Option (1) is correct because quotation marks should set off the exact words quoted; the quotation mark comes after the punctuation (comma) that follows the words quoted. Option (2) is incorrect because we is part of the direct quotation and quotation marks are used in pairs. Option (3) is incorrect because the correct spelling is beginning. Option (4) is incorrect because the possessive pronoun its is correct here.

15. **(3) insert a comma after problem** (Punctuation/Appositives) The phrase a growing problem is an appositive and should be set off by commas from the rest of the sentence; therefore, option (3) is correct and option (2) is incorrect. Option (1) is incorrect because Teenage is the first word in the sentence and needs to be capitalized. Option (4) is incorrect because the correct spelling is increasing.

Usage

Lesson 7: Subject-Verb Agreement
GED Exercise: Subject-Verb Agreement (page 90)

1. **(2) change hope to hopes** (Subject-verb agreement) Option (2) is correct because the subject Vince requires the singular verb form hopes. Option (1) is incorrect because the possessive isn't necessary. Option (3) is incorrect because sign is not the main verb that must agree with the subject in the sentence. Option (4) is incorrect because baseball is a common noun and should not be capitalized.

2. **(5) no correction is necessary** (Usage/ Subject-Verb Agreement; Mechanics/

Capitalization) Option (5) is correct because the plural verb form have offered agrees with the plural subject Firebirds. Option (1) is incorrect because the subject should be plural. Option (3) is incorrect because Firebirds requires a plural verb form. Option (4) is incorrect because spring is the name of a season and should not be capitalized.

3. **(1) change are to is** (Subject-verb agreement) Option (1) is correct because the subject of the sentence, opportunity, requires the third-person singular verb form is. Options (2) and (3) are not singular forms of the verb be. Option (4) is incorrect because the word opportunity is spelled correctly.

4. **(3) change plays to play** (Subject-verb agreement) Option (3) is correct because the compound subject requires the plural verb form play. Option (1) is incorrect because the word two, a number, is used correctly. Option (2) is incorrect because the phrase Raul and Al, an appositive, must be set off by two commas. Option (4) is incorrect because sandlot is a common noun and should not be capitalized.

5. **(5) no correction is necessary** (Subject-verb agreement/Capitalization) Option (1) is incorrect because proper nouns are capitalized. Option (2) is incorrect because neither and nor go together. Option (3) is incorrect because the verb have agrees with friends. Option (4) is incorrect because the possessive isn't necessary.

6. **(4) change are to is** (Subject-verb agreement/Capitalization) Option (4) is correct because team is one group acting as a whole unit; therefore, a singular verb form is required. Option (1) is incorrect because team is a common noun and should not be capitalized. Option (2) is incorrect because the possessive isn't necessary. Option (3) is incorrect because were is not a singular verb form.

7. **(1) change are to is** (Subject-verb agreement) Option (1) is correct because a singular verb form is needed to agree with the singular subject someone. Options (2) and (3) are incorrect because were and be are not singular verb forms. Option (4) is incorrect because the action verb does not need to change to make the subject and verb agree; the word bounds has a meaning different from what is meant.

Lesson 8: Irregular Verbs
GED Exercise: Irregular Verbs (page 93)

1. **(1) change knowed to knew** (Subject-verb agreement) Option (1) is correct because

knew is the correct past form of the verb know. Option (2) is incorrect because known needs a helping verb. Option (3) is incorrect because the preposition for, not the number four, is correct. Option (4) is incorrect because spring is the name of a season and should not be capitalized.

2. **(2) change eaten to ate** (Irregular verbs) Option (2) is correct because ate is the correct past form of the verb eat. Options (1), (3), and (4) are incorrect because they are not past forms of eat.

3. **(2) change weared to wore** (Irregular verbs) Option (2) is correct because wore is the correct past form of the verb wear. Options (1) and (3) are incorrect because they are not correct past forms. Option (4) is incorrect because jogging is a common noun and should not be capitalized.

4. **(2) change drive to drove** (Irregular verbs) Option (2) is correct because drove is the correct past form of drive. Options (1) and (3) are incorrect because they are not correct past forms. Option (4) is incorrect because drive is not the past participle form of drive and is not used with a helping verb.

5. **(4) change run to ran** (Irregular verbs) Option (4) is correct because ran is the correct past form of run. Option (1) is incorrect because the possessive pronoun Their is not needed. Option (2) is incorrect because They're, meaning "they are," would not make sense. Option (3) is incorrect because runned is not the past form of run.

6. **(3) change swum to swam** (Irregular verbs) Option (3) is correct because swam is the correct past form of swim. Options (1) and (2) are not past forms of swim. Option (4) is incorrect because swum cannot express a condition or be used reflexively.

7. **(5) no correction is necessary** (Irregular verbs) Option (1) is incorrect because the past tense is needed. Option (2) is incorrect because rided is not a past form of ride. Option (3) is incorrect because ridden requires a helping verb. Option (4) is incorrect because had ridden is the past perfect form of the verb, and the past tense is needed.

Lesson 9: Verb Tenses
GED Exercise: Verb Tenses (page 96)

1. **(3) has been forgetting** (Verb tenses) Option (3) is correct because a present perfect tense is needed. Options (1), (4), and (5) are incorrect because none is a correct verb form. Option (2)

is incorrect because the word recently indicates the action is past or continuing into the present, not the future.

2. **(3) change was to were** (Verb tenses) Option (3) is correct because were is correct when a wish is being expressed; therefore, options (2) and (4) are incorrect. Option (1) is incorrect because wish does not agree with the singular subject she.

3. **(1) change decide to decides** (Subject-verb agreement) Option (1) is correct because decides agrees with the singular subject Ms. Barlow. Option (2) is incorrect because it is an incorrect verb form. Option (3) is incorrect because have does not agree with the subject Ms. Barlow. Option (4) is incorrect because system is singular and requires the singular verb is.

4. **(4) change was needed to needs** (Verb tenses) Option (4) is correct because present tense is necessary. Option (1) is incorrect because written needs a helping verb. Option (2) is incorrect because wrote is not the past participle form. Option (3) is incorrect because the plural verb were does not agree with the singular subject she.

5. **(1) proceeds** (Usage/Verb tenses and subject-verb agreement; Mechanics/Spelling) Option (1) is correct because proceeds is spelled correctly, is the correct verb tense, and agrees with the singular subject she. Option (2) is incorrect because it is the wrong verb tense. Option (3) is incorrect because proceeds is spelled correctly. Option (4) is incorrect because future perfect tense changes the meaning of the sentence. In option (5), proceed does not agree with the singular subject she.

6. **(2) change will have used to will use** (Verb tenses) Option (2) is correct because future tense is necessary; the action use will occur next month. Option (1) is incorrect because feeled is not the past tense form of feel. Option (3) is incorrect because possession is not shown. Option (4) is incorrect because too, meaning "also," is used correctly.

7. **(5) no correction is necessary** (Verb tenses) Option (1) is incorrect because the present perfect progressive form requires the helping verb form has been. Option (2) is incorrect because worked cannot be used with has been. Option (3) is incorrect because bookstore is not a proper noun. Option (4) is incorrect because one, meaning the number, is the correct word in the sentence.

8. **(3) remove have** (Verb tenses) Option (3) is correct because will receive is a future tense verb and this future action will occur after the action from the first present perfect verb. Option (1) is incorrect because completion of the probation period is not a past event. Option (2) is incorrect because it changes the meaning of the sentence. Option (4) is incorrect because have receive is not a correct verb form.

9. **(4) change helped to helping** (Verb tenses) Option (4) is correct because this is an action that is ongoing, so the -ing ending is needed. Option (1) is incorrect because a comma should not separate the subject and the verb. Option (2) is incorrect because were does not agree with the singular subject part. Option (3) is incorrect because it is not a correct verb form.

10. **(3) change are to is** (Subject-verb agreement) Option (3) is correct because is agrees with the singular subject he. Option (1) is incorrect because it does not result in a correct verb form. Option (2) is incorrect because were does not agree with the singular subject. Option (4) is incorrect because the present form is needed in an infinitive.

Lesson 10: Pronouns
GED Exercise: Pronouns (page 100)

1. **(5) no correction is necessary** (Subject-verb agreement and verb tenses; Mechanics/Punctuation—overuse of commas) Option (1) is incorrect because lives does not agree with the plural subject we. Options (2) and (3) are incorrect because neither results in a correct verb form. Option (4) is incorrect because there is no reason to separate the prepositional phrase from the rest of the sentence with a comma.

2. **(2) change its to it** (Personal pronouns) Option (2) is correct because its is a possessive pronoun; a subject pronoun is needed. Option (1) is incorrect because they does not agree with the singular verb has. Option (3) is incorrect because them is not a subject pronoun. Option (4) is incorrect because the helping verb is needed to create the present perfect tense.

3. **(2) change ours to our** (Personal pronouns) Option (2) is correct because ours should be used only when the possessive stands alone. Option (1) is incorrect because surrounds does not agree with the plural subject billboards. Option (3) is incorrect because the possessive isn't necessary. Option (4) is incorrect because the contraction they're, meaning "they are," would not make sense in the sentence.

4. **(4) change them to they** (Personal pronouns) Option (4) is correct because a subject pronoun is necessary. Option (1) is incorrect because ours should be used only when the possessive stands alone. Option (2) is incorrect because are is not a possessive pronoun. Option (3) is incorrect because theirselves is not a word.

5. **(3) change me to I** (Personal pronouns) Option (3) is correct because a subject pronoun is needed in the compound subject. Options (1) and (2) are incorrect because neither is a subject pronoun. Option (4) is incorrect because committee is spelled correctly.

6. **(5) no correction is necessary** (Personal pronouns) Option (1) is incorrect because your is not a subject pronoun. Options (2), (3), and (4) are incorrect because we, they, and I are not object pronouns.

7. **(1) change Us to We** (Personal pronouns/Subject-verb agreement/Verb tenses/Spelling) Option (1) is correct because a subject pronoun is needed. Option (2) is incorrect because the plural verb are agrees with the plural subject. Option (3) is incorrect because the present progressive form requires the present participle. Option (4) is incorrect because altogether, meaning "completely" or "totally," is the correct word in this sentence.

8. **(3) change hers to her** (Personal pronouns) Option (3) is correct because hers is used only when it stands alone. Options (1) and (2) are incorrect because neither is a correct verb-tense form. Option (4) is incorrect because herself is not a possessive pronoun.

9. **(2) change herself to her** (Personal pronouns) Option (2) is correct because her is an object of the verb help. The course is the doer of the action, not Joyce, so a reflexive pronoun is incorrect. Option (1) is incorrect because a subject pronoun is needed. Option (3) is incorrect because the word understand is a clue that a present-tense form is needed. Option (4) is incorrect because it results in an incorrect verb form.

10. **(5) no correction is necessary** (Personal pronouns, irregular verbs, and verb tenses) Option (1) is incorrect because a subject pronoun is needed. Option (2) is incorrect because learned, meaning "received instruction," is the correct verb; also, teached is not the correct past form of the verb teach. Option (3) is incorrect because the sentence requires a present-tense verb. Option (4) is

incorrect because adult is singular and requires the singular verb form reads.

11. **(2) change herself to she** (Personal pronouns) Option (2) is correct because a subject pronoun is needed in the compound subject. Option (1) is incorrect because her is not a subject pronoun. Options (3) and (4) are incorrect because the possessive pronoun their is correct.

12. **(3) change too to two** (Spelling/Personal pronouns/Commas) Option (3) is correct because two, the number, is the correct word in this sentence. Option (1) is incorrect because the subject pronoun they is correct. Option (2) is incorrect because there is no reason to add a comma. Option (4) is incorrect because hours, a unit of time, is the correct word in this sentence.

Lesson 11: Pronouns and Antecedents
GED Exercise: Pronouns and Antecedents (page 104)

1. **(3) change Me and Joan to Joan and I** (Personal pronouns) Option (3) is correct because the subject pronoun I is needed and should come last in the compound subject. Options (1) and (2) are incorrect because neither makes both corrections. Option (4) is incorrect because Tuesday's is possessive and needs an apostrophe.

2. **(5) no correction is necessary** (Pronoun and antecedents) Option (1) is incorrect because We is a subject pronoun. Option (2) is incorrect because our is the correct possessive form. Our's is not a word. Option (3) is incorrect because view is spelled correctly. Option (4) is incorrect because it agrees with its singular antecedent fire drill in sentence 1.

3. **(2) change his to their** (Pronouns and antecedents) Option (2) is correct because their agrees in number with the plural antecedent employees. Option (1) is incorrect because second does not need to be capitalized since it is not part of a proper name. Option (3) is incorrect because his or her is singular and does not agree with the plural antecedent employees. Option (4) is incorrect because the past-tense form rang is not used with did.

4. **(3) change they to it** (Pronouns and antecedents) Option (3) is correct because it agrees with the singular antecedent door. Option (1) is incorrect because Myself should not be used as a subject. Option (2) is incorrect because the preposition through is used correctly; threw is the past-tense of the verb throw. Option (4) is incorrect because them

does not agree with the singular subject it. Option (5) is incorrect because the pronoun and antecedent do not agree.

5. **(2) his** (Pronouns and antecedents) Option (2) is correct because his agrees in gender with the antecedent Jason. Option (1) is incorrect because her does not agree in gender with Jason. Option (3) is incorrect because him is an object pronoun, not a possessive form. Option (4) is incorrect because their does not agree in number with Jason. Option (5) is incorrect because hers does not agree in gender with Jason.

6. **(4) change their to his** (Pronouns and antecedents) Option (4) is correct because with a compound antecedent joined by neither/nor, the pronoun should agree with the nearer antecedent. His agrees with the singular antecedent, Howard. Options (1) and (2) are incorrect because either/or and neither/nor are the correct forms. Option (3) is incorrect because the sentence is in the past tense and got is the correct past-tense form.

7. **(3) change his to their** (Pronouns and antecedents) Option (3) is correct because the antecedent is plural, the plant manager and the foreman. Option (1) is incorrect because the apostrophe replaces the o in the contraction of did not. Option (2) is incorrect because were does not agree in number with its subject exit. Option (4) is incorrect because the singular his or her disagrees with the plural antecedent.

8. **(3) change her to she** (Personal pronouns) Option (3) is correct because the subject pronoun she is needed to go with the verb needs. Option (1) is incorrect because have does not agree in number with the singular subject Jenny. Option (2) is incorrect because his or her is not a subject pronoun. Option (4) is incorrect because need does not agree in number with the subject she.

9. **(3) change their to his or her** (Pronouns and antecedents) Option (3) is correct because the antecedent he or she agrees with the singular pronoun Everyone. Option (1) is incorrect because knowledge is spelled correctly. Option (2) is incorrect because our is a first-person pronoun, and a third-person pronoun is needed to agree with Everyone. Option (4) is incorrect because procedures is spelled correctly.

10. **(4) change he to she** (Pronouns and antecedents) Option (4) is correct because she agrees in gender with the antecedent Joan.

Option (1) is incorrect because let's, a contraction for "let us," requires an apostrophe. Option (2) is incorrect because her is a possessive pronoun, not a subject pronoun. Option (3) is incorrect because him is neither a subject nor a feminine gender pronoun.

11. **(4) change our to his or her** (Pronouns and antecedents) Option (4) is correct because the plural our must be changed to the singular his or her to agree in number with the singular antecedent each employee. Option (1) is incorrect because There's is the correct contraction of There is. Option (2) is incorrect because a comma is not needed. Option (3) is incorrect because their is a plural pronoun and our must be replaced by a singular pronoun.

12. **(3) change Us to We** (Pronouns) Option (3) is correct because We is a subject pronoun and agrees with the rest of the paragraph. Option (1) is incorrect since the singular verb is agrees with the subject fire safety. Option (2) is incorrect because the verb taken needs to be followed by the adverb seriously, not the adjective serious. Option (4) is incorrect since must cannot be followed by any form of the verb but realize.

Lesson 12: Indefinite Pronouns
GED Exercise: Indefinite Pronouns (page 108)

1. **(4) change their to his or her** (Indefinite pronouns) Option (4) is correct because the antecedent Anyone is singular with unclear gender. Option (1) is incorrect because the plural verb like does not agree with the singular subject Anyone. Option (2) is incorrect because the plural verb are does not agree with the singular subject Anyone. Option (3) is incorrect because the antecedent Anyone has an unclear gender.

2. **(3) change his to their** (Indefinite pronouns) Option (3) is correct because the plural possessive pronoun their agrees with the plural antecedent and subject Several. Option (1) is incorrect because the singular verb has does not agree with the plural subject. Option (2) is incorrect because his or her is singular and does not agree with the plural subject. Option (4) is incorrect because theirs is a possessive pronoun that it used only when it stands alone.

3. **(3) change his or her to their** (Indefinite pronouns) Option (3) is correct because a plural pronoun is needed to agree with the plural antecedent few; his or her is singular. Option (1) is incorrect because has does not agree with the plural subject few. Option (2)

is incorrect because the present perfect tense is formed with the verb's past participle, not the present form of the verb. Option (4) is incorrect because theirselves is not a word.

4. **(2) change whom to who** (Indefinite pronouns) Option (2) is correct because the pronoun who is needed as the subject of the clause. Option (1) is incorrect because the commas are needed to set off a nonessential clause. Option (3) is incorrect because whose shows possession, which is not necessary in this sentence. Option (4) is incorrect because are does not agree with the singular subject Karla.

5. **(4) change her to his or her** (Indefinite pronouns) Option (4) is correct because a singular pronoun is needed to agree with the antecedent someone, but the gender is unclear. Option (1) is incorrect because we requires the plural verb form need. Option (2) is incorrect because hers is used only when it stands alone and is specifically feminine gender. Option (3) is incorrect because their is plural and does not agree with the antecedent someone.

6. **(1) change Whomever to Whoever** (Indefinite pronouns) Option (1) is correct because Whoever is used as a subject. Option (2) is incorrect because Whosever is not a correct pronoun form. Options (3) and (4) are incorrect because neither plural verb form can agree with the singular subject.

7. **(4) change their to his or her** (Indefinite pronouns) Option (4) is correct because his or her agrees with the singular antecedent everyone. Options (1) and (2) are incorrect because advises and exercises are spelled correctly. Option (3) is incorrect because him is an object pronoun, not a possessive pronoun.

8. **(4) change her to his or her** (Indefinite pronouns) Option (4) is correct because the singular pronoun antecedent anyone does not have a clear gender. Option (1) is incorrect because medical is not part of a proper name and should not be capitalized. Option (2) is incorrect because the object pronoun whom cannot be used as a subject. Option (3) is incorrect because want does not agree with the singular subject anyone.

9. **(3) change her to his or her** (Indefinite pronouns) Option (3) is correct because Everybody is singular but does not have a clear gender. Option (1) is incorrect because chose is the past form and is not used with should. Option (2) is incorrect because the plural pronoun their does not agree with the

singular antecedent Everybody. Option (4) is incorrect because hers is a possessive pronoun that must stand alone.

10. **(4) change theirselves to themselves** (Indefinite pronouns) Option (4) is correct because the plural themselves agrees with the plural antecedent most; theirselves is not a word. Options (1) and (2) are incorrect because a singular verb will not agree with the plural subject most. Option (3) is incorrect because himself is not plural and does not agree with the plural antecedent most.

11. **(2) change neither to either** (Indefinite pronouns) Option (2) is correct because a negative has already been used in the sentence, the word nothing; the word either has the same basic meaning as neither, but without the negative. Option (1) is incorrect because sees does not agree with the first-person singular subject. Options (3) and (4) are incorrect because both result in double negatives in the sentence.

12. **(2) replace are with is** (Indefinite pronouns) Option (2) is correct because the singular pronoun much requires the singular verb is. Option (1) is incorrect because Too, meaning "very," is the correct word in this sentence. Option (3) is incorrect because Too . . . chosen is an exact quote and needs to be preceded and followed by quotation marks. Option (4) is incorrect because the abbreviation for the title "Doctor" should be capitalized.

Lesson 13: Adjectives and Adverbs
GED Exercise: Adjectives and Adverbs (page 112)

1. **(4) change compactly to compact** (Adjectives and adverbs) Option (4) is correct because an adjective is needed to describe the stroller; compactly is an adverb. Options (1) and (2) are incorrect because both are plural verb forms that do not agree with the singular subject. Option (3) is incorrect because no comparison is made in this sentence; also, compacter is an incorrect comparative form.

2. **(4) change quick to quickly** (Adjectives and adverbs) Option (4) is correct because an adverb is needed to describe how the cloth fades. The word quick is an adjective; quickly is an adverb. Option (1) is incorrect because the present-tense is is consistent with the verb tense used throughout the paragraph. Option (2) is incorrect because easily is correctly used as an adverb; it tells how washable the padding is. Option (3) is incorrect because they does not agree with the singular antecedent padding.

3. **(3) change good to well** (Adjectives and adverbs) Option (3) is correct because an adverb is needed to tell how the hood held up; well is an adverb. Options (1) and (2) are incorrect because no comparison is made in this sentence. Option (4) is incorrect because goodest is not a correct adverb form.

4. **(3) change lightest to lighter** (Adjectives and adverbs) Option (3) is correct because two things are compared. Option (1) is incorrect because make does not agree with the singular subject carriage. Options (2) and (4) are incorrect because more is not needed when an ending is added to a word to show comparison.

5. **(2) replace a better with the best** (Adjectives and adverbs) Option (2) is correct because more than two things are compared. Option (1) is incorrect because got is the past form, which is not used with will. Options (3) and (4) are incorrect because neither is a correct comparative or superlative form; gooder is not a word.

6. **(4) replace less with few** (Adjectives and adverbs) Option (4) is correct because few is used with a quantity that can be counted, like companies. Option (1) is incorrect because the superlative most should not be used with adjectives ending in -est. Option (2) is incorrect because the possessive isn't necessary. Option (3) is incorrect because a semicolon connects two independent clauses.

7. **(3) change more to most** (Adjectives and adverbs) Option (3) is correct because the superlative form is needed to compare more than two techniques. Option (1) is incorrect because memory is a common noun and should not be capitalized. Option (2) is incorrect because techniques must be plural. Option (4) is incorrect because best is not the superlative form of more.

8. **(4) change simpler to simple** (Adjectives and adverbs) Option (4) is correct because no comparison is being made. Option (1) is incorrect because a singular verb is needed to agree with idea. Options (2) and (3) are incorrect because the superlative and comparative forms are not needed.

9. **(2) change best to most** (Adjectives and adverbs) This sentence requires the superlative adverb form of helpful. Option (2) gives the correct superlative form: most helpful. Options (1), (3), and (4) all give incorrect forms; helpfuller, in option (4), is not a word.

10. **(2) really good idea** (Adjectives and adverbs) Good is an adjective, which requires an adverb modifier, really; therefore, option (2) is correct. Good correctly modifies the noun idea, so options (3) and (4) are incorrect. Option (5) modifies real but does not correct the problem.

11. **(1) change most to more** (Adjectives and adverbs) Option (1) is correct because the comparative adjective is needed. What is being compared is not two or more different times, but more and fewer, which is implied. Option (2) is incorrect because more effective is the correct comparative form; effectiver is not a word. Option (3) is incorrect because effect is a noun and an adjective is needed. Option (4) is incorrect because it is the subject of the verb will be; the contraction it's, meaning "it is," would not make sense in the sentence.

12. **(1) replace easy with easily** (Adjectives and adverbs) Option (1) is correct because the word being modified is the verb retain; the adverb easily is required. Option (2) is incorrect because the superlative most should not be used with adjectives ending in -est. Option (3) is incorrect because the comparative more should not be used with adjectives ending in -er. Option (4) is incorrect because the sentence requires the comparative better rather than the superlative best.

GED Review: Usage (page 114)

1. **(2) change thinks to think** (Subject-verb agreement) Option (2) is correct because the plural subject people requires the plural verb form. Option (1) is not correct because the verb thought would make this sentence past tense; the action of the paragraph is in the present tense. Option (3) is incorrect because the dependent clause beginning with that is essential and, therefore, should not be set off by a comma. Option (4) is incorrect because bank teller is used as a common noun. Option (5) is incorrect because the verb form must agree in number with the singular subject of the clause, working.

2. **(3) change more to most** (Adjectives and adverbs) Option (3) is correct because more than two things are being compared—all possible jobs. Option (1) is incorrect because the apostrophe in teller's is needed to show possession. Option (2) is incorrect because teller is singular and correctly shows possession by adding 's. Option (4) is incorrect because your is not a subject pronoun.

3. **(4) Althea has been working as a teller** (Verb tenses) Option (4) is correct because the

words <u>Since January</u> require the verb-tense form <u>has been working</u> to show that the subject started working in the past and is still working as a teller. Option (1) is incorrect because <u>worked</u> incorrectly changes the action to past tense. Option (2) is incorrect because the verb must agree in number with the singular subject <u>Althea</u>. Option (3) is incorrect because the time reference <u>Since January</u> requires a verb form that shows time passing, not the present tense.

4. **(4) change <u>their</u> to <u>her</u>** (Pronoun antecedent agreement) Option (4) is correct because the pronoun <u>her</u> agrees with the antecedent pronoun <u>she</u>. Option (1) is incorrect because <u>go</u> does not agree in number with the singular pronoun subject <u>she</u>. Option (2) is incorrect because no comparison is being made. Option (3) is incorrect because <u>there</u> refers to a place; it is not a possessive pronoun. Option (5) is incorrect because <u>them</u> is not a possessive pronoun.

5. **(2) Althea needs a good understanding of math** (Subject-verb agreement) Option (2) is correct because the singular subject <u>Althea</u> and the verb form <u>needs</u> agree in number. Options (1) and (4) are incorrect because the verb forms do not agree in number with the singular subject <u>Althea</u>. In option (3), <u>has need</u> is not a correct verb form.

6. **(1) even people who are rude** (Verb tenses, subject-verb agreement, and adjectives and adverbs) Option (1) is correct because the present-tense verb form <u>are</u> is needed to maintain the present tense of the passage. Option (2) is incorrect because the past perfect verb-tense form <u>had been</u> requires a point-in-time reference, which is not found in this sentence. Option (3) is incorrect because the singular verb <u>is</u> does not agree with the plural subject. Option (4) is incorrect because the future tense <u>will</u> does not make sense with the present tense of the sentence. Option (5) is incorrect because no comparison is being made.

7. **(3) change <u>review</u> to <u>reviews</u>** (Subject-verb agreement) Option (3) is correct because <u>reviews</u> agrees with the singular subject <u>she</u>. Option (1) is incorrect because the comma after <u>day</u> is necessary to separate the introductory phrase from the rest of the sentence. Option (2) is incorrect because the adverb <u>carefully</u> is used correctly; <u>careful</u> is an adjective. Option (4) is incorrect because <u>review</u> is the correct spelling. Option (5) is incorrect because the past perfect <u>had made</u>

requires a point-in-time reference, which is not found in this sentence.

8. **(5) change <u>her</u> to <u>she</u>** (Personal pronouns) Option (5) is correct because <u>she</u> is the pronoun subject of the dependent clause beginning with <u>until</u>; <u>her</u> is an object pronoun. Option (1) is incorrect because <u>finds</u> agrees with the singular pronoun subject <u>she</u>. Option (2) is incorrect because the comma is needed to separate the introductory clause from the rest of the sentence. Option (3) is incorrect because the present-tense verb form <u>stays</u> maintains the present tense of the sentence. Option (4) is incorrect because <u>stays</u> agrees with the singular pronoun subject <u>she</u>.

9. **(2) change <u>whom</u> to <u>who</u>** (Indefinite pronouns) Option (2) is correct because <u>who</u> should be used as the subject of the verb <u>are</u>. Option (1) is incorrect because the comma correctly sets off the introductory dependent clause. Option (3) is incorrect because <u>who . . . sixty</u> is an essential phrase. Option (4) is incorrect because <u>belief</u> is spelled correctly.

10. **(2) change <u>more finest</u> to <u>finest</u>** (Adjectives and adverbs) Option (2) is correct because the comparative <u>more</u> should not be used with an adjective ending in -est. Option (1) is incorrect because the singular verb <u>is</u> agrees with the singular subject. Option (3) is incorrect because the superlative <u>most</u> should not be used with an adjective ending in -est. Option (4) is incorrect because the possessive isn't necessary.

11. **(4) replace <u>preceded</u> with <u>proceeded</u>** (Verb tenses) Option (4) is correct because <u>proceeded</u>, meaning "continued or went ahead," is the correct word in this sentence. Option (1) is incorrect because the adverb <u>musically</u> correctly modifies the adjective <u>active</u>. Option (2) is incorrect because the possessive <u>our</u> is the correct word in this sentence. Option (3) is incorrect because the plural verb <u>have</u> doesn't agree with the singular subject.

Sentence Structure

Lesson 14: Sentence Fragments

GED Exercise: Sentence Fragments (page 118)

1. **(4) department for cat care when he** (Fragments) Option (4) is correct because it joins the dependent clause (sentence 2) to the independent clause and eliminates the fragment. Option (2) is incorrect because a comma is used only when the dependent clause is nonessential. Option (3) is incorrect because a semicolon is not used to set off a dependent

clause. In option (5), quotation marks are not needed because this is not a direct quotation.

2. **(2) system to inform** (Fragments) Option (2) is correct because it joins a fragment missing both a subject and a complete verb to an existing sentence. Option (3) results in a fragment. Option (4) is incorrect because a comma is not used when the clause is essential information. Option (5) is incorrect because a semicolon is used only to join independent clauses.

3. **(2) insert he after the comma** (Fragments) Option (2) is correct because the subject is missing from this sentence; he is a subject pronoun. Option (1) is incorrect because the comma is needed after an introductory word. Options (3), (4), and (5) are incorrect because they do not add the needed subject to this sentence.

4. **(4) house several** (Fragments) Option (4) is correct because it joins a fragment missing both a subject and a verb to an existing sentence. Options (1) and (2) are incorrect because they do not correct the fragment; also a sentence starts with a capital letter. Option (3) is incorrect because a comma is used only when the dependent clause is nonessential. Option (5) is incorrect because a semicolon is used to join two independent clauses.

5. **(3) police, who had to check** (Fragments) Option (3) is correct because it joins the relative clause fragment beginning with who to the sentence containing its antecedent, police. The comma shows that the relative clause is nonessential. Option (2) results in a sentence fragment. Option (4) is incorrect because a semicolon is used only to join independent clauses. Option (5) is incorrect because whom cannot be used as a subject.

Lesson 15: Run-On Sentences

GED Exercise: Run-On Sentences (page 121)

1. **(2) insert a semicolon after equipment** (Sentence structure/Run-on sentences) Option (2) is correct because it joins two independent clauses with a semicolon. Option (1) is incorrect because it is a comma splice. Option (3) is incorrect because the sentences are intended to show contrast. Option (4) is a run-on sentence.

2. **(3) muscles. Their fingers** (Sentence structure/Run-on sentences) Option (3) is correct because it uses a period to separate the independent clauses of the run-on into two sentences. Options (2) and (5) are comma

splices. Option (4), like option (5), incorrectly uses the homonym there, rather than their.

3. **(5) no correction is necessary** (Mechanics/Capitalization, Usage/Subject-verb agreement, spelling, and punctuation—overuse of commas) Option (1) is incorrect because typists is a common noun and should not be capitalized. Option (2) is incorrect because typists is plural and requires the plural verb have. Option (3) is incorrect because permanent is spelled correctly. Option (4) incorrectly places a comma between an adjective and the noun it describes.

4. **(3) insert a semicolon after eyestrain** (Sentence structure/Run-on sentences) Option (3) is correct because it separates these two independent clauses by using a semicolon. Option (1) creates sentence fragments. Option (2) incorrectly separates the subject from the verb with a comma. Option (4) does not correct the run-on and uses the wrong homonym. Option (5) is incorrect because continues does not agree with the plural subject studies.

5. **(4) change the comma after workers to a semicolon** (Run-on sentences) Option (4) is correct because the semicolon corrects the run-on. Option (1) is incorrect because it does not correct the run-on, and no possession is shown. Option (2) is incorrect because it does not correct the run-on, and only two items in a series do not need to be separated by a comma. Option (3) is incorrect because it does not correct the run-on, and In . . . machines is not an independent clause.

Lesson 16: Combining Sentences

GED Exercise: Combining Sentences (page 124)

1. **(1) cold cut, but the supermarket** (Sentence combining) Option (1) is correct because but shows a contrast. Option (2) incorrectly shows a cause-and-effect relationship. Option (3) incorrectly compares the two sentences. Option (4) is incorrect because a semicolon should be used before a conjunctive adverb. Option (5) is a comma splice.

2. **(4) department, so it** (Sentence combining) Option (4) is correct because it shows a result. Option (1) shows a contrast not present in the sentences. Option (2) is a comma splice. Option (3) incorrectly implies a time sequence. Option (5) contains an unnecessary comma after but.

3. **(4) beef, and there are** (Sentence combining) Option (4) is correct because it simply joins the two related sentences. Option (1) gives a

wrong time indicator. Option (2) incorrectly negates a sentence that is meant to be a possibility. Option (3) shows a cause-and-effect relationship that does not exist. Option (5) creates a fragment.

4. **(3) sandwich; however, the** (Sentence combining) Option (3) is correct because it shows the contrast made in the second sentence. Option (1) shows a consequence that is not implied. Option (2) is a comma splice. Option (4) ignores the contrast meant. Option (5) shows the two sentences as possibilities, which they are not.

5. **(1) normally eat; subsequently, I** (Combining Sentences) Option (1) is correct because subsequently shows the correct time sequence. Options (2) and (3) are incorrect because nevertheless and still imply contrasts; there is no contrast present in the sentences. Option (4) is incorrect because or incorrectly indicates another possibility. Option (5) is a comma splice.

6. **(1) taxes, and most** (Combining sentences) Option (1) is correct because it simply links the two related independent clauses using a coordinating conjunction. Option (2) is incorrect because it incorrectly shows a contrast. Option (3) is a comma splice. Option (4) shows the second idea as happening after the first, which it does not. Option (5) incorrectly shows the two sentences as possibilities; it also omits the comma before the coordinating conjunction or.

7. **(5) take note, for this** (Combining sentences) Option (5) is correct because the coordinating conjunction for shows the second idea as a cause of the first. Options (1) and (4) are incorrect because they simply link two ideas when a cause-and-effect relationship is shown. Option (2) creates a fragment of the first independent clause. Option (3) is a comma splice.

8. **(1) complete, but many** (Combining sentences) Option (1) is correct because it uses the conjunction but to show contrast. Option (2) is incorrect because it shows a time sequence not indicated in the sentences. Option (3) creates a fragment. Option (4) is incorrect because the conjunctive adverb likewise shows a comparison not meant in the sentences. Option (5) is a comma splice.

9. **(2) mail, so their** (Combining sentences) Option (2) is correct because it correctly shows a result. Option (1) is a comma splice. In option (3), the conjunction but shows a contrast, which could be meant, but the

possessive pronoun their is needed, not the contraction they're. Option (4) is incorrect because there does not show possession. Option (5) is incorrect because a semicolon is needed before a conjunctive adverb.

10. **(5) filing, for electronic** (Combining sentences) Option (5) is correct because for shows the second sentence as the cause of the first. Option (1) is a comma splice. Option (2) is incorrect because or incorrectly indicates another possibility. Option (3) is incorrect because consequently indicates that the second sentence is a result of the first. Option (4) is incorrect because subsequently implies a nonexistent time-order relationship.

Lesson 17: Parallel Structure
GED Exercise: Parallel Structure (page 128)

1. **(3) insert having before a lot** (Parallelism) Option (3) is correct because it creates a verb phrase to match the other verb phrases in the series. Options (1) and (2) do not correct the parallel structure error. Option (4) is a misspelling of the two words a lot. Option (5) is incorrect because it separates the compound subject from the verb.

2. **(4) and sneakers,** (Parallelism) Option (4) is correct because it changes this prepositional phrase to a single noun like the other items in this series. Option (2) reintroduces wearing, which is not necessary. Option (3) is still a prepositional phrase. The preposition on, in option (5), upsets the parallel series of nouns.

3. **(4) change conservatively to conservative** (Parallelism) Option (4) is correct because it changes the adverb conservatively to an adjective to match the other adjectives in this series. Option (1) creates a fragment. In option (2), clothes is used correctly. Option (3) makes the adjective a noun and thereby unparallel. Option (5) changes an adjective to an adverb, which does not correct the unparallel structure.

4. **(4) change being to be** (Parallelism) Option (4) is correct because it changes the present participle being to the simple present verb be. The others in this series are verb-adverb combinations, but since be is a linking verb, an adjective will work in the place of an adverb. Options (1) and (3) do not correct the unparallel structure of the verbs in the series. Option (2) changes an adverb to an adjective, which incorrectly modifies the verb Behave. Option (5) changes the adjective to an adverb, which does not correct the parallel structure error.

5. **(2) insert a comma after serious** (Commas and items in a series) Option (2) is correct because a comma is necessary after serious, the second item in a series of three adjectives. Option (1) is incorrect because it would produce unparallel structure by changing an adjective to an adverb. Option (3) is incorrect because it would create unparallel structure by replacing an adjective with an adjective-noun combination. Option (4) is incorrect because the t in get is doubled when the suffix -ing is added.

Lesson 18: Subordination

GED Exercise: Subordination (page 131)

1. **(1) insert a comma after enter** (Subordination) Option (1) is correct because an introductory subordinate clause is always followed by a comma. Option (2) is incorrect because moving is an incorrect verb form here and creates a fragment. In option (3), generally is spelled correctly. Option (4) is incorrect because chosen needs a helping verb.

2. **(5) although** (Subordination) Option (5) is correct because it best expresses the relationship between these two ideas. Options (1), (2), (3), and (4) do not make sense in the sentence.

3. **(2) where** (Subordination) Option (2) is correct because the second idea refers to a location. Options (1), (3), (4), and (5) do not make sense in the sentence.

4. **(2) replace which with who** (Subordination) Option (2) is correct because this relative pronoun clause needs a pronoun referring to people, not to things. Option (1) is incorrect because it would separate the subject from the verb. Option (3) is incorrect because the verb reach does not agree with the singular subject shopper. There is no reason for the change in option (4). Option (5) is incorrect because is agrees with shopper.

5. **(4) replace though with until** (Subordination) Option (4) is correct because it uses a subordinating conjunction that indicates time to clarify the main meaning of the sentence. Option (1) is incorrect because the subordinate clause is essential to the meaning here. Option (2) creates a fragment. Options (3) and (5) are incorrect because neither makes sense in the sentence.

Lesson 19: Misplaced Modifiers

GED Exercise: Misplaced Modifiers (page 134)

1. **(3) move with low mileage after car** (Misplaced modifiers) Option (3) is correct

because it moves the misplaced phrase next to the word it modifies. Option (1) results in an incorrect verb form. Option (2) is incorrect because it separates an essential clause from the main clause with a comma. There is no reason for the change in option (4).

2. **(3) odometer, which shows** (Run-on sentences) Option (3) is correct because it changes the second independent clause in this run-on sentence into a nonessential relative clause. Option (2) is incorrect because it does not use a comma to set off the nonessential clause. Option (4) is a comma splice. Option (5) uses the wrong relative pronoun; who refers to people.

3. **(4) replace informing with informs** (Fragments) Option (4) is correct because it gives a complete verb to correct the fragment. Option (1) removes a necessary comma after an introductory word. Option (2) moves a modifier to the wrong position. The comma in option (3) is incorrect because it would separate the subject from the verb. Option (5) is still a fragment because it uses an infinitive verb phrase, not a complete verb.

4. **(2) insert you're after When** (Misplaced modifiers) Option (2) is correct because it adds a subject and a verb to the dangling modifier, transforming it to a dependent clause. Option (1) is incorrect because there is no reason for the possessive pronoun your. Option (3) removes a necessary comma after an introductory phrase. Option (4) is the wrong form of a contraction. In option (5), too, meaning "overly," is used correctly.

5. **(1) move whom you trust after mechanic** (Misplaced modifiers) Option (1) is correct because it moves the misplaced phrase next to the noun that it modifies. Option (2) is incorrect because who is a subject pronoun; whom is necessary here as object of the verb trust. Option (3) is incorrect because it moves the phrase into the wrong location. Option (4) is incorrect because badly is an adverb; the adjective bad is required here to modify the noun purchase.

6. **(4) move at capacity after are** (Misplaced modifiers) Option (4) is correct because it moves the wrongly placed phrase next to the verb that it modifies. In option (1), the comma would separate the subject from the verb. Option (2) is incorrect because is does not agree with the plural subject Landfills. Option (3) separates the preposition at from its object.

7. **(2) replace they with diapers** (Misplaced modifiers) Option (2) is correct because it clarifies they; in the original sentence, not biodegradable modified parents. Option (1) is incorrect because realizing is spelled correctly. Option (3) is incorrect because the verb throw is used correctly; through is a preposition. Option (4) creates a fragment.

8. **(1) move under the soil after diapers** (Misplaced modifiers) Option (1) is correct because it moves the wrongly placed modifying phrase next to the word it modifies. Option (2) removes a necessary comma after an introductory phrase. There is no reason for the change in option (3). In option (4), bury is spelled correctly.

9. **(3) move in certain states after Residents** (Misplaced modifiers) Option (3) is correct because it moves the wrongly placed phrase near the word it modifies. In options (1) and (5), separate and certain are spelled correctly. In option (2), the possessive pronoun their is used correctly. Option (4) moves the phrase to a location where it is still misplaced.

10. **(2) move in containers after separate** (Misplaced modifiers) Option (2) is correct because it moves this misplaced phrase next to the word it modifies. Option (1) moves the phrase next to the wrong word. Option (3) is incorrect because no possession is shown. In option (4), separate is spelled correctly. There is no reason for the change in option (5).

11. **(3) insert these are after When** (Misplaced modifiers) Option (3) is correct because it inserts a subject and a verb into the dangling modifier, transforming the phrase into a dependent clause. Options (1) and (2) are still dangling modifiers. Option (4) moves another modifying phrase into a wrong position.

Lesson 20: Revising Sentences
GED Exercise: Revising Sentences (page 137)

1. **(5) no correction is necessary** (Sentence structure/Subordination; Usage/Subject-verb agreement; Pronoun-antecedent agreement) Option (1) is incorrect because the indefinite pronoun Everyone is singular; it disagrees with the plural verb love. Option (2) is incorrect because a comma is unnecessary if the information in the dependent clause is essential to the main idea. Option (3) is incorrect because they disagrees in number with its antecedent change. Option (4) is incorrect because so that implies a relationship of effect that is not present in the sentence.

2. **(2) yet** (Sentence structure/Coordination) Option (2) is correct because it contrasts the small changes with their dramatic effect. Options (1) and (4) are incorrect because they show cause-and-effect relationships not implied by the sentences. Option (3) is incorrect because the two ideas are not alternate possibilities. Option (5) is incorrect because it suggests a time sequence between ideas that is not implied by the sentences.

3. **(2) even though** (Sentence structure/Subordination) Option (2) is correct because it shows the second idea as a concession. Option (1) is incorrect because it shows the second sentence as a result, which is not implied in the original sentence. Option (3) is incorrect because the two ideas are not alternate possibilities. Option (4) is incorrect because it shows an incorrect time relationship. Option (5) is incorrect because it simply links the two ideas; a relationship of concession is required.

4. **(3) and requires** (Sentence structure/Parallelism) Option (3) is correct because it links the second sentence to the first using a parallel verb to create a sequence; the second subject, Moving . . . , is dropped to avoid repetition. Option (1) is incorrect because it combines the two ideas by contrasting them. Option (2) creates a run-on. Option (4) eliminates the subject from the second sentence but does not link the subject of the first sentence. Option (5) is incorrect because it changes the meaning; in the original sentence 2, the subject of requires is Moving, not apartment.

5. **(2) my pots and pans and my clothes** (Sentence structure/Parallelism) Option (2) is correct because it combines the two sentences using a parallel series. Option (1) is a run-on. In options (3) and (5), the items in the series are not parallel. In option (4), the word and is missing from the series.

6. **(2) anything because** (Sentence structure/Subordination) Option (2) is correct because it shows a cause-and-effect relationship between the two sentences by creating a subordinate clause. Option (1) is a comma splice. Option (3) creates a dangling modifier. Option (4) sets up a contrast between two ideas that is not meant. Option (5) uses the double negative can't . . . nothing.

7. **(1) maid who will** (Sentence structure/Subordination) Option (1) is correct because it retains the main idea and creates a relative clause that describes the maid. Option (2) is a

run-on. Option (3) is a comma splice. Option (4) uses the wrong relative pronoun for referring to a person. Option (5) uses the wrong subject to keep the main idea intact.

8. **(1) but it** (Sentence structure/Coordination) Option (1) is correct because it coordinates the two ideas and shows their contrast. Options (2) and (4) show the second idea as the result of the first, which it is not. Option (3) ignores the contrast and only links the ideas. Option (5) shows an incorrect cause-and-effect relationship.

9. **(1) apartment that would** (Sentence structure/Subordination) Option (1) is correct because it combines the two sentences into a main clause with a relative subordinate clause modifying apartment. Option (2) is a comma splice. Option (3) creates a fragment. Option (4) uses the wrong relative pronoun to refer to a thing. Option (5) links the two ideas but ignores the relationship between them.

10. **(2) or** (Sentence structure/Coordination) Option (2) is correct because it presents the two ideas as alternative possibilities. Option (1) makes one idea the result of the other, which is incorrect. Option (3) contrasts the two ideas. Options (4) and (5) show an incorrect cause-and-effect relationship.

11. **(1) has been increased by** (Sentence structure/Subject-verb agreement) Option (1) is correct because it keeps the meaning of the original sentence and adjusts the verb to agree with the new singular subject safety. Options (2) and (5) are incorrect because the singular subject does not agree with the plural verbs have been and are. Options (3) and (4) are incorrect because the relationship between safety and advances is reversed.

12. **(5) because** (Sentence structure/ Subordination) Option (5) is correct because the subordinating conjunction because maintains the original relationship between the two ideas. Option (1) is incorrect because it presents the two ideas as alternate possibilities. Option (2) is incorrect because it shows an incorrect relationship of result. Option (3) is incorrect because it links the ideas without maintaining the relationship of cause. Option (4) is incorrect because but incorrectly contrasts the two ideas.

13. **(3) Drivers may take unnecessary chances because** (Sentence structure/ Subordination) Option (3) is correct because it maintains the relationship of cause and effect between the two ideas. Options (1) and (4) are incorrect

because the cause-and-effect relationship is reversed. Options (2) and (5) are incorrect because although indicates a relationship of concession rather than cause and effect.

GED Review: Sentence Structure (page 140)

1. **(3) change packing to pack** (Sentence structure/Parallelism) The other items in this series use a present-tense verb, not a participle. Option (1) removes a necessary comma after the introductory phrase. Option (2) creates an incorrect verb form. Option (4) does not result in parallel structure.

2. **(4) replace being with was** (Sentence structure/Fragments) Option (4) gives this fragment a complete verb. Option (1) misplaces a modifier. Options (2) and (3) each take away one of the commas needed to set off the interrupting phrase. Option (5) is an incorrect verb form.

3. **(3) a picnic; the** (Sentence structure/Comma splice) Option (3) corrects the comma splice by linking these two independent clauses with a semicolon. Option (2) is a run-on. Option (4) shows a contrast that is not meant. Option (5) incorrectly shows the second idea as additional to the first.

4. **(2) insert rowdy before teenagers** (Sentence structure/Parallelism) All items in this series are nouns preceded by adjective modifiers. There is no reason for the comma in option (1). Option (3) is incorrect because the possessive isn't necessary. Option (4) separates the subject from the verb. Option (5) is incorrect because possession is meant.

5. **(5) insert As drive-ins are before dying** (Sentence structure/Misplaced modifiers) Option (5) turns the dangling modifier into a dependent clause by adding a subordinating conjunction, a subject, and a verb. Option (1) misplaces the modifier. Option (2) removes a necessary comma after the introductory phrase. Option (3) uses only a pronoun, they, as the subject in the subordinate clause; the pronoun antecedent would be unclear, resulting in a misplaced modifier. Option (4) does not make sense.

6. **(2) insert are after desires** (Sentence structure/Fragments) Option (2) is correct because this fragment lacks a complete verb; inserting are corrects the fragment. Option (1) is incorrect because possession is shown. Option (3) is incorrect because the singular verb is disagrees with the plural subject desires. Option (4) is incorrect because the

verb were is past tense; the rest of the paragraph is in the present tense.

7. **(1) rain or frost; however,** (Sentence structure/Coordination) Option (1) is correct because the conjunctive adverb however correctly indicates the contrast between the outdoor and greenhouse environments. Option (2) is incorrect because similarly incorrectly indicates that the two environments are similar. Option (3) is incorrect because because indicates a cause-and-effect relationship not present in the two original sentences. Option (4) is incorrect because it is a comma splice. Option (5) is incorrect because the lack of punctuation creates a run-on sentence.

8. **(3) insert a semicolon after construction** (Sentence structure/Run-on sentences) Option (3) is correct because it corrects the run-on by connecting the two independent clauses with a semicolon. Option (1) is incorrect because a comma after factors does not correct the run-on. Option (2) is incorrect because it would create a comma splice. Option (4) is incorrect because the singular verb is agrees with the singular subject expense.

9. **(3) move without claws after animals** (Sentence structure/Misplaced modifiers) Option (3) is correct because it moves the misplaced phrase next to the word it modifies. Option (1) is incorrect because a comma is necessary after the introductory phrase. Option (2) is incorrect because it leaves without claws in an incorrect location. Option (4) is incorrect because bad is the correct modifier for feel.

10. **(4) change to catch prey to catching prey** (Sentence structure/Shift of focus) Option (4) is correct because it creates a parallel series of participles. Option (1) is incorrect because the singular verb needs disagrees with the plural subject Cats. Option (2) is incorrect because it changes the participle to a present-tense verb, which does not correct the parallel structure error. Option (3) is incorrect because it changes the participle to a plural noun, which does not correct the parallel structure error.

11. **(5) great damage if** (Sentence structure/Subordination) Option (5) is correct because if correctly shows the conditional relationship of the second idea. Option (1) is incorrect because it reverses the condition. Option (2) is incorrect because so indicates an effect relationship not present in the two original sentences. Option (3) is incorrect because before indicates an incorrect time relationship.

Option (4) is incorrect because or incorrectly indicates alternate possibilities.

12. **(4) move by both groups after asked** (Sentence structure/Misplaced modifiers) Option (4) moves the phrase next to the word it modifies. Option (1) removes a necessary comma after an introductory word. In option (2), whether is spelled correctly. There is no reason for the comma in option (3). Option (5) misplaces a modifying phrase.

13. **(2) replace looking with one looks** (Sentence structure/Misplaced modifiers) Option (2) inserts both a subject and a verb into this dangling modifier. Option (1) still leaves a dangling modifier. In option (3), appear does not agree with the singular subject; although it ends in an s, Mars is singular. In option (4), appears is spelled correctly. Option (5) is incorrect because the possessive pronoun its is needed.

14. **(1) observers** (Sentence structure/Clarity) Option (1) keeps the main clause and main idea intact. Option (2) creates a fragment. Options (3), (4), and (5) reorder the words of the sentence awkwardly.

15. **(5) change to describe to described** (Sentence structure/Fragments) Option (5) gives this fragment a complete verb. Options (1) and (2) each remove a necessary comma. In option (3), describe does not agree with the singular subject. Option (4) is still a fragment.

16. **(4) and empty deserts** (Sentence structure/Parallelism) Option (4) gives an adjective and a noun only, matching the other item, deserted palaces, in this series. Options (1), (2), and (3) all use a relative clause and so are not parallel. Option (2) contains a subject-verb disagreement, and option (3) uses an incorrect pronoun. Option (5) does not match the series because it uses a participle.

GED Cumulative Review: Writing Skills (page 143)

1. **(4) change have to has** (Usage/Subject-verb agreement) Option (4) is correct because the subject of the sentence is number, which is singular, so the singular verb has increased must be used. There is no reason for the changes in options (1), (2), and (3).

2. **(5) family and to the workplace** (Sentence structure/Parallelism) This sentence does not have parallel structure. Option (5) is correct because the phrases to the family and to the workplace are parallel. Options (2), (3), and (4) do not result in parallel structure.

3. **(2) if it allows** (Usage/Pronoun reference—agreement with antecedent and subject-verb agreement) Option (2) is correct because it is singular and requires the singular verb allows. The pronoun it correctly refers to job, which is singular. Therefore, options (3) and (4) are incorrect. Allowance is not a verb, so option (5) is wrong.

4. **(3) replace they with it** (Usage/Pronoun reference—agreement with antecedent) Option (3) is correct because the antecedent, a job promotion, is singular and requires the singular pronoun it. Option (4) does not correct the pronoun to singular. There is no reason for the changes in options (1), (2), and (5).

5. **(4) change ben franklin to Ben Franklin** (Mechanics/Capitalization) Option (4) is correct because the name Ben Franklin is a proper noun and each word should be capitalized. Therefore, option (3) is incorrect. Postal Service should be capitalized because it is a proper noun. Therefore, options (1) and (2) are incorrect.

6. **(4) change midwest to california to Midwest to California** (Mechanics/Capitalization) Option (4) is correct because both a section of the country, Midwest, and the name of a state, California, should be capitalized. There is no reason for the change in option (1). Options (2) and (3) each make only one of the two necessary capitalization corrections.

7. **(4) finally, the airplanes** (Sentence structure/Parallelism and clarity) Option (4) is correct because items in series should have parallel structure. The verb came should not be repeated, so option (2) is incorrect. Also, a comma is needed after finally to set it off because it interrupts the sentence. The extra words super and speedy in options (1), (3), and (5) are unnecessary; the sentence is clearer and more concise without them.

8. **(4) days; airmail** (Mechanics/Punctuation—semicolons) Option (4) is correct because these two sentences should be joined with a semicolon. Option (1) is incorrect because the original sentence is a run-on sentence; it contains two sentences with no punctuation between them. If the two sentences are joined with a comma and without a conjunction, as in option (2), a comma splice results. A semicolon should not be used with and or but, making options (3) and (5) incorrect.

9. **(3) change rose to risen** (Usage/Verb tense; Mechanics/Capitalization) Option (3) is correct because the past tense rose does not need the helping verb has; has risen is the correct present perfect tense. Option (2) is incorrect because mail is singular and requires the singular verb has. There is no reason for the changes in options (1), (4), and (5).

10. **(2) change been made to have been made** (Verb tenses) Option (2) is correct because the point-in-time reference since its invention in the 1800s calls for the present perfect form have been made. Option (1) is incorrect because the modifier many requires a plural, changes. Option (3) is incorrect because American is the adjectival form of a proper noun and should be capitalized. Option (4) is incorrect because the clause beginning with since is essential and should not be set off by a comma. Option (5) is incorrect because the possessive pronoun its is used correctly.

11. **(3) change was to were** (Subject-verb agreement) Option (3) is correct because were agrees with the plural subject Games. Option (1) is incorrect because before the 1930s establishes the past tense of the sentence. Option (2) is incorrect because there is no reason to put a comma after Games played. Option (4) is incorrect because the time reference before the 1930s shows that the action took place in the past; have been scheduled is present perfect tense and conveys that the action is continuing.

12. **(3) A starting pitcher was expected** (Subject-verb agreement) Option (3) is correct because the singular helping verb was agrees with the singular subject pitcher. Options (1) and (2) are incorrect because the plural helping verbs were and have do not agree with the singular subject. Option (4) is incorrect because starting pitcher is a common noun and should not be capitalized. Option (5) is incorrect because the past perfect had been expected would require a point-in-time reference in the sentence.

13. **(3) change realize to realizes** (Indefinite pronouns) Option (3) is correct because Everyone, a singular indefinite pronoun, requires the singular form realizes. Option (1) is incorrect because who . . . country is an essential phrase. Option (2) is incorrect because the subject form who should be used in front of watches. Option (4) is incorrect because they is plural; the antecedent is the singular baseball.

14. **(2) change a growing sense is to is a growing sense** (Parts of speech) Option (2)

is correct because the subject follows the verb in sentences beginning with there. Option (1) is incorrect because There is the correct word in this sentence. Option (3) is incorrect because costs is a verb in this sentence; it cannot be possessive. Option (4) is incorrect because too, meaning "very," is the correct word in this sentence.

15. **(2) change was to is** (Verb tenses) The answer is something that is true in the present; therefore, option (2) is correct and option (1) is incorrect. Options (3) and (4) are incorrect because there is no reason to use these punctuation marks in the sentence. Option (5) is incorrect because squirrel is a common noun and should not be capitalized.

16. **(5) no correction is necessary** (Indefinite pronouns; Mechanics/Capitalization) Option (5) is correct because the plural pronoun their agrees with the plural indefinite antecedent others. Options (1) and (2) are incorrect because his and her are singular and do not agree with others. Options (3) and (4) are incorrect because both colonies and underground are common nouns and should not be capitalized.

17. **(3) change them to their** (Personal pronouns) Option (3) is correct because the possessive pronoun their is needed; them is an object pronoun. Option (1) is incorrect because the subject and verb should not be separated by a comma. Option (2) is incorrect because forgetting is spelled correctly. Option (4) is incorrect because buried is used as an adjective modifying nuts; bury cannot be used this way.

18. **(4) change finds to find** (Subject-verb agreement) Option (4) is correct because the plural verb form find agrees with the plural subject people. Option (1) is incorrect because Some is correctly used as an adjective. Option (2) is incorrect because people is already a plural noun without adding s. Option (3) is incorrect because two independent clauses not joined by a conjunction should be separated by a semicolon. Option (5) is incorrect because very modifies sociable.

19. **(4) replace the second squirrels with they** (Parts of speech) Option (4) is correct because the pronoun they should replace the noun squirrels to avoid repetition. Option (1) is incorrect because the singular is doesn't agree with the plural subject Squirrels. Option (2) is incorrect because the adverb naturally correctly modifies the adjective aggressive; the adjective natural cannot be used to modify another adjective. Option (3) is incorrect because the

semicolon is correctly used here before however followed by an independent clause.

20. **(5) no correction is necessary** (Mechanics/Spelling; Usage/Subject-verb agreement, verb tense, and adjectives and adverbs) In option (1), resistance is spelled correctly. Option (2) is incorrect because the singular verb has agrees in number with the singular noun resistance. Option (3) is incorrect because it changes the verb tense of the passage. Option (4) is incorrect because the comparative adjective form stronger is needed.

21. **(3) This, we now know, has** (Usage/Subject-verb agreement with interrupting phrase; Mechanics/Punctuation—commas with parenthetical expressions) Option (3) is correct because the subject This is singular and requires the singular verb has. Options (2) and (5) are incorrect because they use the plural verb have. We now know is an interrupting phrase and should be set off with commas, so option (4) is incorrect.

22. **(2) change children, they to children, and they** (Sentence structure/Comma splice) The original sentence has a comma splice (two sentences improperly joined together with a comma). Option (2) is correct because the two sentences must be joined by a comma and a coordinating conjunction. Option (3) is incorrect because a semicolon is not used with the coordinating conjunction and. There is no reason for the changes in options (1) and (4).

23. **(3) that are sterile so they** (Usage/Pronoun reference—agreement with antecedent and wrong relative pronoun) Option (3) is correct because the pronoun must agree with its antecedent insects. Insects is plural, so the pronoun should be they, which is plural. Options (2), (4), and (5) are incorrect because the relative pronouns who and whom refer to people, not insects.

24. **(1) change Its to It's** (Mechanics/Apostrophes) It's is a contraction for "it is." Its is a possessive pronoun. Option (1) is correct because It is the subject of the sentence and is is the verb; no possession is being shown in the sentence. There is no reason for the changes in options (2), (3), and (4).

25. **(3) insert a comma after past** (Mechanics/Punctuation—commas after introductory elements) Option (3) is correct because a comma, not a semicolon as in option (2), should be placed after the introductory phrase In the past. Past is a noun meaning

"a time gone by"; passed, in option (1), which means "to transfer something to another person," is incorrect. There is no reason for the change in option (4).

26. **(5) no correction is necessary** (Mechanics/Spelling—homonyms and punctuation) In option (1), hear means to gain information through the ear; here refers to a location. In option (2), eye refers to the organ of the body that one sees with; I is a pronoun that refers to oneself. Option (3) is incorrect because a nonessential (unnecessary) clause should be set off with a comma. Option (4) is incorrect because addition means more; edition refers to a version of printed material.

27. **(3) people who are** (Usage/Pronoun reference—wrong relative pronoun and verb tense) Option (3) is correct because the pronoun who is used when referring to people, and since people is plural, the plural verb are is needed. Option (2) uses which, the relative pronoun that is used to refer to things, not people. Options (2) and (4) are incorrect because they use the singular verb is. Option (5) is incorrect because the sentence is written in present tense and the verb were is past tense.

28. **(3) is that the body receiving the transplant** (Usage/Pronoun reference—vague reference and subject-verb agreement; Sentence structure/improper coordination and subordination) Option (3) is correct because the pronoun it has no clear antecedent. The vague pronoun it should be replaced by the body receiving the transplant. Option (2) still has the vague pronoun reference. Options (2) and (4) are incorrect because the subject problem is singular and requires the singular verb is. Option (5) is incorrect because the word because creates an incorrect subordinate structure in this sentence.

29. **(1) is sometimes required** (Usage/Subject-verb agreement with interrupting phrase) Option (1) is correct because the subject use is singular, so the singular verb is is needed. Options (2) and (5) are incorrect because they use the plural verb are. Option (3) is incorrect because the verb were does not agree with the singular subject and is past tense; the rest of the sentence (and paragraph) is written in present tense. Options (4) and (5) are incorrect because the phrase in any case is wordy; eliminating it will make the sentence clearer.

30. **(4) concerns are heard that** (Mechanics/Punctuation—overuse of commas) Option (4) is correct because commas are not needed

before or after the verb are heard. Options (2), (3), and (5) are incorrect because commas should not separate the subject and verb or set off an essential clause.

31. **(3) yards; these new** (Sentence structure/Run-on sentences) Option (3) corrects this run-on with a semicolon. Option (2) is a comma splice. Option (4) incorrectly makes the second idea an alternative to the first. Option (5) incorrectly makes the first idea conditional upon the second.

32. **(5) porches, and they** (Sentence structure/Coordination) Option (5) simply links the two ideas. Option (1) is a comma splice. Option (2) is a run-on. Option (3) incorrectly contrasts the two ideas. Option (4) incorrectly establishes the second idea as a result of the first.

33. **(3) square, which contains** (Sentence structure/Subordination) Option (3) changes the second sentence into a subordinate clause using a relative pronoun. Option (1) lacks a conjunction to relate the second sentence to the first. Option (2) uses the wrong relative pronoun. Option (4) incorrectly contrasts the two ideas. Option (5) is a run-on.

34. **(4) suburbs. Planners** (Sentence structure/Run-on sentences) Option (4) is correct because it changes a run-on sentence into two sentences. Option (2) is incorrect because it is a comma splice. Option (3) is incorrect because a sentence must begin with a capital letter. Option (5) is incorrect because but shows contrast, which is not intended.

35. **(5) no correction is necessary** (Parallel Structure/Usage/Personal pronouns; Mechanics/Spelling and punctuation—apostrophe) Option (1) is incorrect because the possessive pronoun is needed. Options (2) and (3) are wrong because appearance and length are spelled correctly. Option (4) is incorrect because the possessive form is needed.

36. **(3) Because they dislike** (Sentence structure/Subordination) Option (3) correctly establishes the first idea as causing the second. Options (1) and (5) show the opposite cause-and-effect relationship. Option (2) incorrectly shows one idea as a concession to the other. Option (4) incorrectly contrasts two similar ideas.

37. **(4) caught; then, it rakes** (Sentence structure/Combining sentences) Option (4) correctly sets up a time sequence for these ideas. Option (1) is a run-on. Option (2) is a comma splice. Option (3) incorrectly contrasts the two ideas. Option (5) makes no sense; the

second idea cannot be negated as an alternative to the first.

38. **(3) have stood up to** (Sentence structure/ Clarity) Option (3) retains enough of the verb to keep the proper tense—present perfect. Option (1) changes the meaning; because the subject of the sentence is now badgers, the verb must change form. There is no reason for the past tense, as in options (2) and (5). Option (4) is an incorrect verb form.

39. **(4) Nobel, a Swedish chemist, invented** (Mechanics/Punctuation—appositives and capitalization) Option (4) is correct because the phrase a Swedish chemist further explains who Alfred Nobel was. It is an appositive and should be set off with commas. Options (1), (2), and (3) do not correctly show the appositive set off with commas. Option (5) is incorrect; Swedish should be capitalized because it is an adjective derived from a proper noun.

40. **(3) world peace, chemistry, physics, literature, and** (Mechanics/Punctuation— commas between items in series) Option (3) is correct because three or more items in series should be separated with commas. Options (1), (2), (4), and (5) are incorrect because they do not separate each item with a comma.

41. **(2) change dynamite, he to dynamite; he** (Mechanics/Punctuation—semicolons; Sentence structure/Comma splice and run-on sentence) Option (2) is correct because two sentences joined without a coordinating conjunction require a semicolon. Option (1) is incorrect because removing the comma after dynamite creates a run-on sentence. The original sentence is incorrectly joined by a comma, which options (3) and (4) do not correct.

42. **(5) no correction is necessary** (Mechanics/Punctuation—commas and capitalization; Usage/Verb forms) Options (1) and (3) are incorrect because the phrase which began in 1901 is a nonessential phrase and should be set off by commas. Option (2) is incorrect because the verb begun needs a helping verb; began is the correct tense. Option (4) is incorrect because the proper noun Sweden should be capitalized.

43. **(4) change norwegian to Norwegian** (Mechanics/Capitalization) Option (4) is correct because Norwegian is an adjective formed from a proper noun and should be capitalized. There is no reason for the changes in options (1), (2), and (3).

Unit 2: Essay

Lesson 1: Planning

GED Exercise: **Figuring Out the Topic (page 155)**

For each item, draw a box around the first paragraph in the writing assignment as background information.

1. **Topic:** whether or not you think employers should supply child care for their employees. **Instructions:** Write a composition of about 200 words. Be specific and use examples to support your view.

2. **Topic:** the effects of mandatory drug testing on employees. **Instructions:** In a composition of about 200 words, describe the effects. You may wish to describe the positive effects, the negative effects, or both. Use specific examples to support your opinion.

3. **Topic:** How important is having a GED or a high-school diploma when you apply for a job? **Instructions:** In an essay of about 200 words, tell your opinion. Use specific examples to support your view.

4. **Topic:** how you think cigarette advertising should be handled. Should all ads for cigarettes be banned? **Instructions:** In an essay of about 200 words, support your opinion with specific examples.

GED Exercise: **Understanding the Instructions (page 156)**

1. **Instructions:** In a composition of 200 words, state the reasons; support your opinion with specific examples. **Kind of information:** tell what you think about an issue

2. **Instructions:** Write a composition of 200 words that describes both the negative and positive effects. Be specific and use examples. **Kind of information:** write about causes and effects

3. **Instructions:** In a composition of about 200 words, state your opinion. Use specific examples to support your point of view. **Kind of information:** tell what you think about an issue

4. **Instructions:** Write a composition of about 200 words describing the good points, the bad points, or both. Be specific, and use examples to support your views. **Kind of information:** give reasons or explain facts about an issue

5. **Instructions:** In a composition of 200 words, describe the effects. You may describe the good or bad effects, or both. Be specific, and use examples to support your views. **Kind of information:** write about causes and effects

GED Exercise: Gathering Ideas (page 159)

Many answers are possible. Here are a few ideas.

1. **Ideas:** can communicate quickly; can communicate on the go; don't have to stay in one place to get messages; won't miss getting important messages on time; no excuses for not getting in touch with someone; doctors, emergency personnel, and other business people can respond to emergencies quickly

2. **Ideas:** lyrics are violent; songs promote unhealthy emotional and social attitudes; lyrics promote violence toward women; words promote drug use; lyrics promote violence toward police and authorities; music is repetitious and harsh

3. **Ideas:** everyone deserves to be healthy; health care costs have skyrocketed; unfair to some people for insurance costs to be so high; must work for a large company to have reasonable rates on health insurance; people who are sick can't get health insurance

4. **Ideas:** employers expect employees to be able to handle job tasks; can't compete with employees who are educated; jobs go to the best qualified; employers want their companies and their products to compete in world markets

GED Review: Planning (page 160)

A. **Background:** Over the past few years, many people who were living in the country have moved to the city. At the same time, many people in the city have moved to the country. **Topic:** whether you think life is better in the country or in the city. **Instructions:** In a composition of about 200 words, state what you think. Give specific examples to support your view.

B. **Kind of information:** tell what you think about an issue

C. Many answers are possible. Here is an example. **Main idea:** Life in the country is better than life in the city.

D. Many answers are possible. Here is an example. **Ideas:** life is simpler; people have closer ties to one another; houses cost less; people don't have to spend so much time in traffic; people

know their neighbors; people can depend on each other; fewer problems in schools and with gangs; fewer problems with drugs; fewer problems with violence

Lesson 2: Organizing

GED Exercise: Grouping Ideas (page 163)

Pros

Practical Reasons	Emotional/Social Reasons
can learn things	have fun
can develop new skills	relieves stress
may discover a talent	may meet people with similar interests, make friends

Cons

may spend too much time away from family
may spend too much money
may neglect things that need to be done

GED Exercise: Ordering Groups (page 166)

Many answers are possible. Here are some examples.

1. **1** Little Equipment, **2** Ease & Convenience, **3** Benefits

2. **Main Idea:** Passing the GED would give a person many advantages.

   1 Educational Reasons, **2** Job-related Reasons, **3** Personal Reasons

3. There is more than one correct response. Share your work with your teacher or another student.

GED Review: Organizing (page 167)

There is more than one way to group, expand, and order ideas. Share your work with your teacher or another student.

Lesson 3: Writing

GED Exercise: Paragraphs and Topic Sentences (page 172)

1. **a.** good work habits
   b. A good worker is someone who understands how important it is not to be absent too often and who gets the job done.
   c. people lose jobs because they don't show up for work or don't work hard enough; managers need workers they can count on to show up; employers don't tolerate workers who sit around visiting

2. **a.** the endangered bald eagle
   b. It is ironic that Americans are directly responsible for making the bald eagle, their national bird, an endangered species.
   c. people have developed land where eagles nest; they've polluted water (poisoning fish eaten by eagles; hunters and trappers killed eagles)

GED Exercise: Writing Topic Sentences (page 173)

There are many ways to write topic sentences for the paragraphs. Here are some examples:

1. More than ever before, adults need an education to succeed.

2. Smoking demands a price to one's health and one's wallet.

3. Getting out of debt may be difficult, but there are ways to do it.

4. Before you take a drug from your medicine cabinet, you should determine whether it is usable or not.

GED Exercise: Writing Introductory Paragraphs (page 175)

There is more than one correct way to write each introductory paragraph. Share your work with your teacher or another student.

GED Exercise: Writing Body Paragraphs (page 177)

There is more than one correct way to write each set of body paragraphs. Share your work with your teacher or another student.

GED Exercise: The Concluding Paragraph (page 178)

There is more than one correct way to write each concluding paragraph. Share your work with your teacher or another student.

GED Review: Writing (page 180)

There is more than one correct way to write the introductory paragraph, the body paragraphs, and the concluding paragraph for the topic assignment. Share your work with your teacher or another student.

Lesson 4: Evaluating

GED Exercise: Evaluating an Essay (page 184)

Answers will vary. Here are some possible responses.

1. A likely score is 2. The writer states a point of view and provides support for a main idea, but there is insufficient paragraph development for an essay. The sentence structure contains errors.

2. A likely score is 6. The essay has effective organization with a clear thesis statement and topic sentences. It has strong examples that support the main ideas. The writer has good control of the conventions of English. The revisions and messiness of the essay do not detract from its score.

GED Review: Evaluating (page 187)

Evaluating and scoring your essay can be done by you or by someone else. If you are taking a class, have your teacher evaluate your essay. If you are working independently, ask a friend or relative to read your essay. If this is not possible, evaluate your writing yourself. After finishing an essay, put it aside for a day. Then read it as objectively as possible. No matter who checks your writing, make sure that person follows the Scoring Guide on page 181 and uses the chart on page 187 as scoring evaluation guides.

Write the date on your completed essays and keep them together in a folder or notebook. This way, you will be able to keep track of your progress, note your strengths, and figure out areas in which you want to improve.

Lesson 5: Revising

GED Exercise: Revising an Essay (page 193)

Delete sentences off topic: "Financing a house is extremely expensive these days." (paragraph 2) "Every time I go to the bookstore I see all these books about travel." (paragraph 4)
Add more details and examples: Add to the second body paragraph.
Sentence fragment: The second sentence in paragraph 3 could be corrected like this: "For example, cancer and AIDS research are charities that I would love to donate money to."
Run-on sentence: The fourth sentence in paragraph 4 could be corrected like this: "I would never cook another meal because I would eat out every day in a different restaurant."
Grammatical usage: The verb come in the first sentence should be comes.
Commas: Add commas to this series of phrases in the last sentence in paragraph 4: "every concert, every sports event, and every new movie."
Spelling: These words are misspelled: college (paragraph 2), different (paragraph 4).
Capitalization: The word state in sentence 2 should not be capitalized.
Punctuation: In sentence two of paragraph 2 parent's should be parents'. The last sentence in paragraph 5 needs a period.

GED & Cumulative Reviews: Revising (page 194)

Share your work with your teacher or another student.

Unit 3: Reading Strategies

Lesson 1: Comprehension

GED Exercise: Restatement and Drawing Conclusions (page 199)

1. **(4) the supply of available money** (Comprehension) This restates the information in the second sentence. The amount of money available for loans is the only factor mentioned as affecting interest rates. Options (1), (2), (3), and (5) are not supported by the paragraph.

2. **(2) more buying and borrowing** (Comprehension) If lower rates of interest encourage buyers, as stated in the last sentence, option (2) is the most logical conclusion. Option (1) is not a logical choice because it contains a contradiction. If people are saving more, they cannot also be spending more. Options (3), (4), and (5) result from <u>high</u> interest rates.

3. **(3) a person's health is affected by poor diet** (Comprehension) The paragraph states that malnutrition is a poor state of health that can result from overeating as well as undereating. Options (1), (2), (4), and (5) define malnutrition as either overeating or undereating. Therefore, they are not complete definitions of malnutrition.

4. **(1) not eating enough food or not eating enough of a specific nutrient** (Comprehension) Undernutrition can be a matter of not getting enough food, or it can be a matter of a nutrient deficiency. Options (2) and (3) are incorrect because they are causes of overnutrition. Option (4) is incorrect because poor health is described as a result of undernutrition, not a cause. Option (5) is incorrect because undernutrition is a form of malnutrition; malnutrition does not cause undernutrition.

GED Exercise: Summarizing (page 201)

1. **(4) It is hard to picture the vastness of our solar system, its giant sun, and millions of miles of empty space.** (Comprehension) This statement includes the main ideas of both paragraphs. Option (1) is contradicted in the first paragraph. Options (2) and (3) are details supporting the main idea. Option (5) is true but doesn't capture the major ideas of the passage.

2. **(1) compare size and distance in the solar system** (Comprehension) The details point out the main idea—size of the sun and distance in space. Option (2) is a detail. Options (3), (4), and (5) are not supported by the content of the passage.

3. **(1) New England's and New York's geography was affected by glaciers.** (Comprehension) The main idea can be understood by reading all the details of the paragraph. Not all mountains are discussed, so option (2) is incorrect. Option (3) is the opposite of what is stated. There is no support for option (4). Option (5) may be true, but it is not the main idea of the paragraph.

GED Exercise: Literal and Inferential Comprehension (page 203)

1. **(2) "You either have science or you don't . . ."** (Comprehension) The author's point is that you have to accept all the findings of scientific study, whether you are comfortable with them or not. It is the nature of scientific inquiry. If you ask the question, you have to be willing to accept the answer. Options (1), (3), (4), and (5) are supporting points.

2. **(1) The major contribution of twentieth-century scientific study has been to show us how much we don't know.** (Comprehension) This a restatement from the second paragraph. Option (2) is a detail. Option (3) is a supporting point. Option (4) is not supported by the excerpt. Option (5) is a conclusion the reader might draw but does not appear to be the author's opinion and not the main idea.

3. **(4) people are uncomfortable with science because its findings are unpredictable and often disturbing** (Comprehension) The approach the author takes implies that he believes he has to explain and defend science. It is reasonable to infer from this that he thinks people are uncomfortable with it. Options (1), (3), and (5) are not supported by the passage. Option (2) is incorrect because the opposite is true according to the paragraph.

Lesson 2: Application
GED Exercise: Other Contexts (page 205)

1. **(1) allowed the government to limit the public's access to information** (Application) Dictatorships manage and often suppress news. Control of news media makes this easier. There is no support for options (2) and (3). Options (4) and (5) are contradicted by the information in the passage.

2. **(5) arresting the group's leaders and banning press coverage of their activities** (Application) There is no room in a dictatorship for opposing views. Authority may not be questioned. Options (1), (2), and (3) are contradicted by the passage. Option (4) is an unlikely course for a dictator concerned with demonstrating power and suppressing dissent.

3. **(5) a pressure cooker** (Application) A pressure cooker uses the buildup of steam to raise the boiling point of water. The hotter water cooks the foods faster. Options (1) and (3) are appliances that do not need water to cook foods. Options (2) and (4) involve water at temperatures lower than the boiling point.

4. **(1) getting drinking water from the ocean** (Application) Ocean water, which contains salts and other minerals, can be distilled to yield pure water for drinking. Options (2) and (3) involve uses of pure water. Although water is boiled for making tea, no water vapor is collected. Option (4) lowers the freezing point; it has nothing to do with removing minerals or other impurities. Option (5) does not involve distillation, since mineral water is sold because of its mineral content.

5. **(2) they pollute the air they breathe with smoke** (Application) This is an application of the fact that air pollution causes respiratory problems. Options (1), (3), (4), and (5) are not supported by the passage.

6. **(4) people living in the area would have more than the average number of respiratory illnesses** (Application) If air pollution causes respiratory problems, this is a reasonable application of the principle. Option (1) is not the best answer because everyone in the community would be affected. Options (2) and (5) have no support. Option (3) is contradicted by the information in the passage.

7. **(2) Taxes will increase.** (Application) The main source of government income would be the most likely to increase. Option (1) is the opposite of what would happen. Option (3) has no support. The government's need for money would not necessarily encourage people to buy bonds, so option (4) is incorrect. Option (5) is incorrect because that would discourage people from buying bonds and so decrease the government's income.

8. **(2) paid for by the citizens** (Comprehension) Both sources of government income come from the citizens. The paragraph does not support options (1), (3), (4), or (5).

GED Exercise: Application Skills in Literature (page 208)

1. **(3) Marriage doesn't work well. Don't expect a husband to meet your needs.** (Application) This is a restatement of Evelyn's words. She says that marriage is no longer functional, and whatever you expect from a husband, you will get the opposite. Options (1)

and (5) are the opposite of Evelyn's belief. Option (2) has no support. Option (4) is tempting because she is shocked at what she sees as cold bloodedness in her grandmother. However, she clearly doesn't believe in marrying for love.

2. **(2) practicality** (Application) Josephine takes a practical attitude toward romance and marriage. A natural application of this fact is to assume she takes this attitude toward life in general. Options (1) and (4) are clearly not indicated. Option (3) is not mentioned. Option (5) is suggested by her words and actions, but is not the best choice.

3. **(1) disapprove of Josephine's dependence on a husband for security** (Application) A feminist would probably argue that Josephine should find strength and security within herself. Josephine's is clearly an "old fashioned" attitude. Options (2) and (5) are good possibilities but not the best answers. Feminists might approve of these aspects of her personality but would likely not agree with her on the broader issue of dependence. Options (3) and (4) have no support.

Lesson 3: Analysis
GED Exercise: Fact and Opinion (page 210)

1. **(1) The Great Depression spanned the years 1929–1939.** (Analysis) This is a fact well-documented in history. Options (2), (3), (4), and (5) are all opinions of analysts and critics. Clue words: blame, accuse, claim, believe.

2. **(4) Unemployment was widespread in Europe at that time.** (Analysis) This is the only option that refers to an event outside the U.S. Options (1), (2), (3), and (5) refer to events in the country, which would not support the "global" theory.

3. **(2) claim** (Analysis) This word is a clue to opinions. Options (1) and (5) are not clue words as defined. Options (3) and (4) would suggest factual statements.

4. **(5) secession was not legal** (Analysis) Lincoln believed that states had no right to leave the Union. This was his interpretation of the Constitution. Options (1) and (2) are the opposite of what Lincoln believed. There is no evidence that Lincoln expected the North to lose, so option (3) is incorrect. There is no support for option (4).

GED Exercise: Cause and Effect (page 212)

1. **(1) microbes such as bacteria and viruses** (Analysis) This cause-effect relationship is

explained in the first paragraph. Options (2), (3), (4), and (5) are unsupported.

2. **(4) bacteria and viruses attacking the body** (Analysis) Bacteria and viruses cause disease symptoms and also trigger the immune response. Option (1) is incorrect because it is not the symptoms that cause the response. Options (2), (3), and (5) are elements of the immune response, not causes.

3. **(1) an allergy** (Analysis) Allergy is explained in the last paragraph as an effect of the immune response. Options (2), (4), and (5) can cause the immune response. Option (3) produces the immune response.

4. **(2) changes in technology** (Analysis) The broad changes in the labor force described in the paragraph were a result of technological advances. The ones mentioned in the paragraph are the Industrial Revolution and automation. Option (1) is incorrect because the United States still has a great deal of good farmland but very few farm workers. Option (3) is not a cause of changes in the type of work available. Option (4) is incorrect because the U.S. population continues to increase. Option (5) is partially a result of the shift to the service sector, not a cause of it.

GED Exercise: Figurative Language (page 214)

1. **(3) It reminds the reader of having an upset stomach from overeating.** (Analysis) The figurative suggestion in "acute case of information glut" is parallel to feeling uncomfortable because of hearing the same thing over and over. Option (1) has no support. Option (2) might be true in general, but other media besides television are a part of the problem discussed. More information, option (4), would only add to the problem. Option (5) is not suggested.

2. **(1) As each news medium reports a story that has already been reported, it becomes harder to present the story in an interesting way.** (Analysis) The author is suggesting that news media feed off each other. Options (2) and (4) refer to food literally, so both are incorrect. Option (3) is not true according to the excerpt. There is no support for option (5).

3. **(4) a variety of magazines with opposing points of view** (Analysis) The author is referring to a group of news magazines that are neither uniform nor in agreement about news topics. Options (1) and (2) make reference to writers and journalists, not

news magazines. Option (3) is incorrect because it does not address the descriptive language of the phrase. Option (5) is not supported by the excerpt and represents a literal, not figurative, use of language.

4. **(3) a sensible summary of important news stories** (Literal Comprehension) Lines 11–18 support this option. Option (1) describes radio or television journalism. Option (2) describes newspaper journalism. Option (4) describes the result of being exposed to several types of journalism. Option (5) is not supported by the excerpt.

5. **(1) man clings to thoughts of spring, in spite of evidence of the changing season** (Analysis) The main point of the poem seems to be that people are often out of touch with nature. They dream about spring instead of accepting the natural cycle of the seasons. Option (2) is not the best answer because it is not specific. Options (3), (4), and (5) are not supported by the poem.

6. **(4) ice** (Analysis) The spider is afraid he will die if frost comes overnight. The similarities between crystal and ice are stronger than exist with the other options. Options (1), (2), (3), and (5) are unrelated to winter or cold temperatures.

Lesson 4: Evaluation
GED Exercise: Beliefs and Values (page 217)

1. **(4) people are motivated by personal gain** (Evaluation) According to the passage, the profit motive is the basis of a growing economy. In a controlled economy, there is no incentive for extra effort. This is why these systems don't work, according to the author. His belief is clear. Option (1) is the opposite of what the author believes. Options (2) and (3) are not suggested. Option (5) appears possible. However, the author does not seem to place a high value on equal distribution of wealth.

2. **(1) free market economies over government-controlled systems** (Evaluation) As explained above, the author's preference is clear. Options (2), (4), and (5) do not present good contrasts. For instance, private business is a feature of free market systems. Option (3) is contradicted by the implications of the passage.

3. **(3) People will work harder only for personal profit.** (Evaluation) This is clearly implied in the passage. Options (1), (2), (4), and (5) are the opposite of the author's beliefs.

4. **(4) family life** (Evaluation) Moving the whole family because of job changes is very disruptive to family life. Options (1), (2), (3), and (5) are all values associated with people who consider career goals very important.

GED Exercise: Adequacy of Facts (page 219)

1. **(2) supported by the evidence summarized in the first paragraph** (Evaluation) The first paragraph describes years of study and observation that led to the laws of motion. This appears to be an adequate basis in fact. Options (1) and (5) are incorrect, as explained above. Option (3) is incorrect because the second paragraph explains the apparent contradiction. The law applies in a vacuum. Option (4) is false. If anything, this example appears to disprove the law.

2. **(4) true under certain conditions** (Evaluation) The second paragraph explains that the law is true in a vacuum, not necessarily in Earth's atmosphere. Option (1) is not a reasonable evaluation based on the information in the first paragraph. Options (2), (3), and (5) are contradicted by the facts.

3. **(2) The ball's energy changes form.** (Analysis) The paragraph states that energy is never used up; it only changes form. Therefore, when the ball stops moving, its energy changes form, and option (1) is not true. Option (3) is incorrect because the ball's kinetic energy becomes potential energy. Option (4) is not supported by the information in the paragraph. Option (5) is incorrect because energy is the ability to move or change matter; it is not matter itself.

Lesson 5: Tables, Graphs, Charts, Maps

GED Exercise: Tables (page 221)

1. **(5) Pluto** The diameter of Pluto is only 2,100 miles.

2. **(1) Mercury** A year on Mercury is 87.96 days.

3. **(1) Venus** The distance from Earth to Venus is 25.8 million miles; the distance from Earth to Mars is 48.6 million miles.

4. **(3) a mammal** The key brings you through all of the classifications to classification 5a.

GED Exercise: Line Graphs (page 223)

1. **(1) $10,000,000**

2. **(5) None of the above** The company realized its greatest income during the two-year period of 1993-1994.

3. **(2) 1992** In 1992, the company made $50 million, compared to $25 million in 1991.

4. **(2) 1995** Fire destroyed most of the company's equipment and profits plummeted in 1995.

GED Exercise: Bar Graphs (page 224)

1. **(2) 47**

2. **(2) 8**

3. **(3) 1890-1910** The life expectancy in 1890 was 47 years, and in 1910 it was 55 years.

GED Exercise: Circle Graphs (page 226)

1. **(5) paper and paperboard** This section comprises 41% of our garbage.

2. **(5) The percentage of our garbage consisting of yard wastes is about double that consisting of metals and glass combined.** This is an incorrect statement.

GED Exercise: Pictographs (page 227)

1. **(5) Spanish** Spanish is the most common language.

2. **(3) $2.8 million** Two percent of $140 million is $2.8 million.

3. **(5) Wisconsin** Wisconsin leads the nation in cheese production.

4. **(2) California** This state produces less cheese than the state of New York and more than the state of Minnesota.

GED Exercise: Charts (page 228)

1. **(1) China** China appears 6 times on the chart.

2. **(2) New York City** New York City's population is projected to grow by only 2,300,000 people. Each of the other cities projects a larger increase.

3. **(2) Asia** All of the countries on the list for 1600 A.D. are in Asia except Egypt.

GED Exercise: Maps (page 230)

1. **(2) Washington, D.C.** The 60-degree temperature line goes through this city on the map.

2. **(5) along part of the East Coast** North Dakota, South Dakota, and Nebraska are experiencing a cold front.

3. **(1) the Southwest** The large letter H is located near Albuquerque.

4. **(4) 101**

5. **(5) in the northeast**

1. **(4) Overgrazing by sheep and goats may have helped create the desert in the Middle East.** (Analysis) The clue word <u>may</u> indicates uncertainty—a guess or theory. Options (1), (2), and (3) are facts, according to the passage. Option (5) is untrue.

2. **(2) American sheep-ranching regions might have less rainfall than surrounding areas** (Application) If sheep and goats created one desert, perhaps they could also affect the climate in other areas. Options (1), (4), and (5) are unsupported. Option (3) is not a reasonable conclusion to draw from the theory.

3. **(2) may have caused the desiccation of the Middle East** (Comprehension) This is a restatement of information in the passage. Options (1) and (3) are unsupported. Option (4) is not the best choice because although the passage explains how rainfall develops, this is not a part of the theory. Option (5) is incorrect because the passage does not suggest it as the main reason.

4. **(4) a sudden break in the rock layers underground** (Comprehension) This is a restatement from the first paragraph. Option (1) is a cause but not the most direct, immediate cause. Option (2) is an effect, not a cause. Option (3) is only partially true. Option (5) is a part of the actual earthquake activity.

5. **(5) is convincing because lab conditions and results are very similar to those described by the faulting theory** (Evaluation) The lab experiments provide good evidence to support the explanation. Option (3) is incorrect because the lab experiments attempt to explain the quake, not the damage. Option (1) is not true according to the passage. Options (2) and (4) are not reasonable based on the evidence from the lab.

6. **(2) summarize the passage** (Comprehension) These statements state the main idea—the cause of earthquakes—and cite the evidence supporting the explanation of the cause. These are the two main parts of this passage. Option (1) is incorrect because these statements simply "tell"; they don't prove anything. Option (3) is incorrect because this is not a new conclusion but simply a restatement/summary. Option (4) is incorrect because it is not a new context. Option (5) is incorrect because the details of the argument are not included in these statements.

7. **(2) adults should take children's problems seriously because they may be symptoms of depression** (Evaluation) This belief is implied in the passage. Options (1) and (3) are too extreme. The author does not go this far. Options (4) and (5) are unsupported.

8. **(1) ignoring, scolding, and lecturing are not helpful treatments for childhood depression** (Comprehension) These behaviors are listed in the first paragraph. The conclusion we may infer is that these treatments are not helpful. The final sentence states that depressed children need professional help. Options (2), (3), (4), and (5) are unsupported.

9. **(5) may have several symptoms, including sadness, apathy, eating disorders, and school problems** (Comprehension) This is a restatement from the passage. Options (1), (2), (3), and (4) are unsupported.

10. **(4) CO_2 is a product of the chemical reaction.** (Evaluation) Since CO_2 is on the right side of the arrow, it is a product of the chemical reaction. Option (1) is incorrect because C is a reactant. Options (2) and (3) may be true but are not supported by the information provided. Option (5) is the opposite of the correct answer.

11. **(3) A moving object has kinetic energy, but an object may also have potential energy, which can be turned into another form of energy, such as kinetic energy.** (Comprehension) This statement includes both major ideas of the passage. Options (1) and (4) are true, but neither is a complete summary. Options (2) and (5) have no support in the passage.

12. **(1) causes potential energy to turn into kinetic energy** (Analysis) This cause and its effect are explained in the passage. Option (2) is not the best answer because the potential energy is turned into kinetic energy first. Then, on impact, heat energy is released. Options (3), (4), and (5) have no support in the passage.

13. **(2) a slingshot pulled back** (Application) This answer applies the definition of potential energy to another situation. While it is held back, there is potential energy, which turns into kinetic energy when the sling is released. Options (1) and (4) are examples of kinetic energy—moving objects. Options (3) and (5) are unsupported.

14. **(4) Of the three kinds of people in New York, the newcomers with a dream have brought passion to the city.** (Comprehension) This statement mentions three types of New Yorkers but stresses the

"immigrant" group. The author seems to be most interested in this group, as he spends a good deal of time discussing them. This is the best main idea statement. Option (1) does not say enough. Option (2) is a detail. Option (3) has no support in the passage. Option (5) is a good restatement of the first part of the passage but misses a major point.

15. **(1) have a lot of energy and excitement** (Analysis) This is the best explanation based on the ideas in the rest of the passage. There is no support for option (2). Options (3), (4), and (5) may be true statements about the people but are not suggested in the passage.

16. **(2) support and encourage immigration** (Application) Based on his attitude toward newcomers to New York, a reasonable application could be made to this situation. You might conclude that he would believe that immigrants enrich the nation. Options (1), (3), and (4) are not reasonable conclusions from the passage. There is no support for option (5).

17. **(5) He means that the New York of the settler is the greatest of the three.** (Literal Comprehension) In lines 1–11 the author describes three New Yorks. The third, or last, is that of the settler, so options (3) and (4) are incorrect. Option (1) is not supported in the excerpt. Option (2) is incorrect because the author does not say the people are "trembling."

18. **(2) a teenager who feels rebellious and wants to experiment a little** (Comprehension) The tone of the poem makes this a good inference. She is young and naïve. She is looking for a good time, and the people she has never been allowed to know appear glamorous and exciting. Option (1) is too literal. Option (3) is too strong a statement. Options (4) and (5) are too simple; they leave too much of the poem unexplained.

19. **(3) Staying in the front yard means doing what is expected. The back yard represents the exciting, unfamiliar world where people dare to break the rules.** (Analysis) Option (1) is too literal. Option (2) is a good start but doesn't go far enough. Options (4) and (5) are too strong. The tone of the poem does not support such strong statements.

Unit 4: Social Studies

Geography

Lesson 1: Earth's Regions I

GED Exercise: Earth's Regions I (page 240)

1. **(1) developing more productive strains of rice** (Comprehension) The passage states that a potential problem is the rapid increase in population that is not matched by growth in food production. Options (2), (3), (4), and (5) are all legitimate needs of any nation but are not crucial needs.

2. **(4) diverse in climate, race, and geography** (Comprehension) The first and last sentences of the information provide support for this conclusion. Options (1), (3), and (5) are not supported by the information. Option (2) is incorrect because the information states that Japan, not the entire Far East, has become a major industrial power.

3. **(3) varies from north to south** (Comprehension) The paragraph states that the climate varies. Option (1) is incorrect because no supporting evidence is given. Option (2) is incorrect because an example of cold winters is given. Option (4) is incorrect because the mountains make farming difficult, not the climate. Option (5) is incorrect because the land, not the climate, is mountainous.

4. **(3) it was formed by volcanoes erupting from the ocean floor** (Comprehension) Volcanic eruptions pushed up the islands and mountains. Options (1), (2), (4), and (5) are not supported by the paragraph.

5. **(1) taking up a lot of space** (Comprehension) The last sentence of the paragraph states that there is little land for farming or building in large cities like Los Angeles. The opposite of not much would be a lot. Options (2), (3), (4), and (5) are incorrect because these definitions are not supported by the paragraph.

6. **(3) Its flooding created good farmland.** (Comprehension) The information states that the first settlers realized the rich soil would provide extra harvests. Options (1), (2), (4), and (5) are incorrect because they are not supported by the information.

7. **(4) the action of the water** (Comprehension) The item asks only about the course of the river. The information states: "The water pushing against the mud . . . has changed all the bends . . . ." Although people can cause changes in rivers, options (1), (2), and (3) are incorrect because the information doesn't provide proof that the people listed did cause changes. Option (5) is incorrect because the land around rivers had been changed.

8. **(1) north** (Comprehension) The map shows that the largest desert area of Africa is in the northern part of the continent. You use the legend to find the desert areas and the compass rose to tell the direction. Options (2), (3), (4), and (5) are all incorrect because the largest desert is toward the top of the map, which is north.

9. **(3) Egypt** (Comprehension) The entire country of Egypt is shown as being in the desert. Options (1) and (5) are incorrect because these countries have no desert at all. Options (2) and (4) are incorrect because these countries are only partly desert.

10. **(5) 800** (Comprehension) Use the scale of miles to judge distances on the map. Use the compass rose to tell which direction is north to south. The other options are not the correct length of Ethiopia from north to south.

11. **(5) Uganda** (Comprehension) A country without a seaport is not on the ocean. Of all the countries listed, only Uganda is completely surrounded by land.

12. **(1) Egypt** (Comprehension) Egypt is the only option that is shown on the map as lying completely in the desert. Options (2), (3), (4), and (5) are all incorrect because countries not in the desert will get more rain than countries in the desert.

13. **(3) women tend to live longer than men in all the countries listed** (Analysis) The table shows that in each country, women in general outlive men. Options (1) and (2) are not true according to the table. Options (4) and (5) are incorrect because there is no information about climate or other South American countries in the table.

14. **(4) more than one cultural region can be on one continent** (Comprehension) Russia, Southeast Asia, and the Far East are all on the same continent. Options (1) and (3) are not supported by the map. Option (2) is incorrect because they are next to each other. Option (5) is incorrect because the map shows at least three regions that are not separated by water.

15. **(3) the United States and Canada** (Comprehension) The U.S. and Canada are the only areas directly east of Russia. Options (1), (2), and (4) would require travel in other directions. Option (5) is not a cultural area.

Lesson 2: Earth's Regions II
GED Exercise: Earth's Regions II (page 244)

1. **(4) The United States and Canada are neighboring countries, but they are not completely alike.** (Comprehension) This is stated in the topic sentence, the fourth sentence of the first paragraph. Options (1), (2), (3), and (5) are details that support the main idea.

2. **(5) very few towns** (Application) Towns are usually built in areas that can provide people with what they need to live. The desert cannot easily support people. Options (1) and (2) would mean that the area was not a desert. Option (3) is the opposite of what is suggested. Option (4) is incorrect because mountains are not necessarily near deserts.

3. **(3) they were on trade routes** (Comprehension) Because they were centers of trade, these areas attracted people and became major cities. Option (1) is incorrect because beauty is not a reason for locating a large city. Options (2), (4), and (5) are not usually true of cities.

4. **(5) Bosnia-Herzegovina and Croatia** (Comprehension) The map shows that the darkened areas representing the Serb forces were in the borders of Bosnia-Herzegovina and Croatia. Option (1) is incorrect because there were no Serb forces shown in Slovenia. Option (2) is incorrect because the map does not show Serb forces in Serbia. Option (3) is incorrect because there were no Serb forces shown in Yugoslavia. Option (4) is incorrect because the city of Bihac is shown within the Croat and Bosnian-held territory.

5. **(3) 180 miles** (Comprehension) Use the scale in miles in the lower part of the map to measure. By measuring the distance between the cities and comparing it to the scale, you get 180 miles. Options (1), (2), (4), and (5) are incorrect measurements.

6. **(4) Bosnia-Herzegovina was occupied by various armies** (Comprehension) Bosnia-Herzegovina is shaded on the map to represent where the two forces of troops were located in 1995. The map also shows where the U.N. troops were stationed. Option (1) is incorrect because there is no evidence that any attacks were taking place. Option (2) is incorrect because nothing on the map suggests this was true. Option (3) is incorrect because there is no evidence that this was true. Option (5) is incorrect because the map shows where the armies were located and makes no mention if they were allies or enemies.

7. **(1) New England's and New York's geography was affected by glaciers.** (Comprehension) The main idea can be understood by reading all the details of the paragraph. Not all mountains are discussed, so option (2) is incorrect. Option (3) is the opposite of what is stated. There is no support for option (4). Option (5) may be true, but it is not the main idea of the paragraph.

8. **(3) Glaciers have helped to shape the American landscape.** (Comprehension) This is stated in the topic sentence of the first paragraph. Options (1) and (5) are true, but they are not discussed in the passage. Options (2) and (4) are only supporting details.

Lesson 3: Protecting the Environment
GED Exercise: Protecting the Environment (page 246)

1. **(3) is out of balance** (Comprehension) Ecology is balance, and people are taking more than Earth can afford to give. Options (1) and (5) are the opposite of what is stated. Option (2) is not suggested. There is no support for option (4).

2. **(2) Natural resources cannot be taken for granted.** (Comprehension) Earth cannot supply all the natural resources that people have taken for granted. Options (1) and (5) are the opposite of what is suggested. Option (3) is incorrect because no one country is mentioned. There is no support for option (4).

3. **(1) things that make people comfortable can also cause problems** (Comprehension) This is stated in the text. Option (2) is incorrect because the effect of mining is not mentioned. Option (3) is the opposite of what is stated. Options (4) and (5) are incorrect because they are the two sides of an unanswered question given in the text.

4. **(5) planting trees** (Application) Tree planting helps to provide new growth. Options (1) and (2) are examples of taking from the land. Option (3) is not related to the question. Option (4) is incorrect because the energy for electricity is taken from natural resources.

5. **(1) use a lot of labor-saving devices** (Comprehension) This is based on the pie chart and the fact that labor-saving devices use energy. There is no other information about the United States, so options (2), (3), (4), and (5) are incorrect.

6. **(1) oil** (Comprehension) The graph shows that oil, at 33.8 quadrillion British Thermal Units (BTU), was the most-used energy source.

Options (2), (3), (4), and (5) are all incorrect because they provided fewer than 33.8 quadrillion BTUs of energy.

7. **(2) coal** (Comprehension) The only energy source labeled 19.6 is coal. Options (1), (3), (4), and (5) are all incorrect because they accounted for other amounts of energy.

8. **(3) Changes in Earth are caused by nature and by people.** (Comprehension) This is the general idea of the paragraph. Options (1), (2), and (5) are details that support the main idea. Option (4) is incorrect because it is not stated in the paragraph.

9. **(1) there is no one best way to dispose of sludge** (Comprehension) The number of ways sludge is disposed of leads to this conclusion. Option (2) is incorrect because the note next to the chart indicates there are problems in using sludge as a fertilizer. There is no mention of how large the landfills are, so option (3) is incorrect. There is no support for options (4) or (5).

10. **(2) finds its way into the land** (Comprehension) Over 73 percent of the sludge is disposed of in Earth in one way or another. The figures in the chart do not support options (1), (3), (4), or (5).

11. **(4) changes from place to place** (Comprehension) The levels of acid rain are different in different cities. Options (1) and (2) are the opposite of what is shown. There is not enough evidence for option (3). Option (5) is incorrect because the cause of acidity in rainwater is not indicated in the graph.

12. **(5) Dallas** (Application) The chart lists the pH levels of several cities. Dallas has the highest pH value of the cities listed, so vegetables would be the least damaged there. Options (1), (2), (3), and (4) all have lower pH values.

13. **(4) fossil fuels will produce a lower percentage of the world's energy** (Comprehension) This is a restatement of the beginning of the second paragraph. There is no support for options (1), (2), (3), and (5).

14. **(2) the limited supply of fossil fuels** (Comprehension) It is supported by the cartoon's caption. Although options (3) and (5) are aspects of the cartoon, they are not the main point. Options (1) and (4) are not supported by the cartoon or caption.

15. **(1) people take fossil fuels for granted** (Analysis) The man washing his car looks

surprised by the question. There is nothing in the cartoon to support options (2), (3), (4), and (5).

GED Review: **Geography** (page 250)

1. **(3) close to the equator** (Comprehension) The hotter the sun, the warmer the climate. Options (1) and (2) would tend to be cooler. Option (4) has no support. Option (5) refers to an area that would have fairly mild temperatures.

2. **(5) Several factors affect climate.** (Comprehension) This is the main idea stated in the first sentence. There is no support for options (1), (3), or (4). Option (2) is the opposite of what is stated.

3. **(2) determines how hot the sun is there** (Comprehension) This is stated in the paragraph. Option (1) refers to elevation, not latitude. There is no support for options (3) and (5). Option (4) is incorrect because it is closeness to water that helps to even out temperatures.

4. **(2) cooler** (Comprehension) This is stated in the paragraph. There is no evidence for options (1) or (5). Option (3) is the opposite of what is stated. Option (4) does not refer to a weather condition.

5. **(1) The death rate is lower than the birthrate.** (Comprehension) A comparison of the figures supports this conclusion. Options (2) and (3) are the opposite of what is shown by the figures. There is no support for options (4) and (5).

6. **(3) 7.9 billion** (Comprehension) This fact is stated in the second sentence. Option (1) is incorrect because it refers to the amount of the increase, not the total population. Option (2) refers to the population in 1994. Options (4) and (5) are incorrect because those figures do not appear in the paragraph.

7. **(3) more people are being born than are dying** (Analysis) In order for the population to grow, more people must be born (added) than die (subtracted). Options (1), (2), (4), and (5) are not supported by information in the paragraph.

8. **(2) The world's population is increasing.** (Comprehension) This sentence summarizes all the facts in the paragraph. Options (1), (3), and (4) are incorrect because they are details that support the main idea. Option (5) is incorrect because the paragraph does not state that population growth is a problem.

9. **(4) A fisherman has caught a fish that has eaten people's trash.** (Comprehension) This description covers the important points of the cartoon. Options (1) and (2) are not supported by the cartoon. Option (3) does not describe the whole cartoon. Option (5) is incorrect because fish do not clean the oceans.

History

Lesson 4: The Colonization of America

GED Exercise: **The Colonization of America** (page 253)

1. **(3) smallpox and influenza** (Application) These are diseases, and the passage states that many Native Americans died from diseases carried by the Europeans. Options (1), (2), (4), and (5) do not refer to disease.

2. **(2) take some of the trade with the Orient away from Italy** (Comprehension) This is stated in the text. The passage gives no evidence that Columbus had any interest in options (1), (3), (4), or (5).

3. **(5) Spanish** (Comprehension) The passage states that the Spanish had a head start. Options (1), (3), and (4) are not supported by the passage. Option (2) is incorrect because even though the English had many colonies, these came later than the Spanish colonies.

4. **(4) Around 1800, England claimed the continent of Australia and sent settlers there.** (Application) Colonization is defined as sending people to a new area to settle there. Option (1) is about the end of a colony. Option (2) is incorrect because it does not involve one country taking control of another. Option (3) has nothing to do with colonization. Option (5) refers to only a temporary movement of people.

5. **(3) Many European countries colonized parts of the Americas.** (Comprehension) This covers the discussion of the different European countries and their colonies. Options (1), (2), and (5) are details that support the main idea. Option (4) is incorrect because most colonies were founded primarily for economic, not religious, reasons.

6. **(5) establish plans for governing the new colony** (Comprehension) According to the compact, the Pilgrims agreed to set up laws needed for government. There is no mention of options (1), (2), and (4). Option (3) is incorrect because there is no suggestion of rebellion.

7. **(3) It helped establish the principles of self-government.** (Application) The statements in the compact focus on a group of people making their own laws, even when

supervised by a higher authority. Nothing in the quotation relates to options (1), (2), (4), or (5).

8. **(3) sent away** (Comprehension) You can figure this out because the paragraph says that Roger Williams was "banished to England." None of the other options makes sense in this context.

9. **(2) participate in government** (Comprehension) The paragraph states that only men who were church members could participate in government, so you can conclude that women were excluded. Options (1), (3), (4), and (5) have no evidence to support them in the paragraph.

10. **(4) British heritage** (Comprehension) According to the paragraphs, the colonies shared a common British heritage. Options (1), (2), (3), and (5) are incorrect because the paragraphs show that all the colonies were geographically different from one another.

11. **(2) Plantations, or large farms, were most common in the southern colonies.** (Comprehension) This is suggested by the text. Option (1) is the opposite of what is suggested. There is no support for options (3), (4), or (5).

12. **(2) The colonists came to feel they should be governed only from America.** (Comprehension) The colonists began to see self-government as a reality. As people living in America, not England, they felt they should not be ruled by England. Option (1) is too general. There is no support for option (3). There is no connection between option (4) and rebellion. Option (5) is the opposite of what the colonists felt.

13. **(5) Connecticut** (Comprehension) The paragraph states that New England had poor soil. Of all the options, only (5) is in New England. Options (1), (2), (3), and (4) are incorrect because those colonies had good soil.

14. **(4) shipbuilding** (Application) Option (4) is correct because the second paragraph states that New England had good harbors. Option (1) refers to the middle colonies. Options (2) and (5) are not mentioned. Option (3) is true of the southern colonies.

Lesson 5: The American Revolution
GED Exercise: The American Revolution (page 257)

1. **(2) goods had to be imported all the way from England** (Comprehension) Goods that could not be produced with the resources of the New World had to come from England.

Shipping them took a long time and was expensive. There is no support for options (1) or (3). The quality and the types of goods are not specified, so options (4) and (5) are incorrect.

2. **(2) demand their rights as English subjects** (Comprehension) The Continental Congress had sent petitions asking to be heard about the problem. Options (1), (4), and (5) all followed after the petitions were denied. Option (3) is the opposite of what is stated in the passage.

3. **(4) did not understand the attitude in the colonies** (Comprehension) The king expected the colonists to act like regular English citizens. He forgot they lived under different circumstances. Option (1) might be true, but it is not suggested in the passage. Options (2) and (3) are the opposite of what is suggested. There is no support for option (5).

4. **(5) they had not received help from France** (Comprehension) France supplied some much-needed things that could help to offset the power of England. Option (1) is not suggested. Option (2) has no support. Option (3) has nothing to do with winning or losing the war. If there were French advisers, it is likely their advice was taken, so option (4) is incorrect.

5. **(1) were helped by some American colonists** (Comprehension) People in the colonies who remained loyal to the king often helped the British. Option (2) is not supported by the paragraph. Options (3) and (5) are incorrect because the loyalists and the British were on the same side. Option (4) is incorrect because all the colonists were taxed, including the loyalists.

6. **(3) the American army had difficulty finding soldiers** (Comprehension) This can be inferred from the fact that much of the population was loyal to the British, so the pool of recruits was small. Options (1), (2), and (4) are the opposite of what is stated in the paragraph. Option (5) is not supported by the paragraph.

Lesson 6: The Civil War and Reconstruction
GED Exercise: The Civil War and Reconstruction (page 259)

1. **(2) Lincoln would not represent their interests** (Analysis) The Southern states based this opinion on the antislavery position of the Republicans. There is not enough support for options (1) and (5). Option (3) had nothing to do with the secession. Option (4) is incorrect because the Southern states were part of the Union before they seceded.

2. **(4) The South probably resented the North even after the war.** (Analysis) The South had felt it was not being treated fairly before the war, then it was defeated and left in a shambles, so there was probably little warm feeling for the North. There is not enough evidence to support the opinions in options (1), (2), (3), or (5).

3. **(2) needed to keep landowners wealthy** (Comprehension) The support for this is in the second paragraph. Options (1) and (3) are the opposite of the facts. Option (4) is incorrect because other economic factors were involved. Option (5) is incorrect because the moral aspect of slavery is not discussed.

4. **(4) slavery** (Comprehension) Option (4) is correct because the information states that abolitionists wanted to do away with, or abolish, slavery. Options (1), (2), (3), and (5) were not targets of the abolitionists.

5. **(1) they felt they had to support the Confederacy after the Fort Sumter incident** (Comprehension) It would have been clear that war was about to start, so the slave states would feel obliged to stick together. There is no support for options (2), (3), and (5). Option (4) is the opposite of what they wanted.

6. **(5) what led to the Civil War** (Comprehension) Except for the last paragraph, the information explains the cause of the war. Nothing is said about option (1). Options (2) and (3) are discussed only in the last paragraph. There is no support for option (4).

7. **(3) the American Revolution** (Application) In both cases, many families had relatives fighting on the other side. This is not the case in options (1), (2), (4), and (5).

8. **(5) the period after the Civil War** (Comprehension) This is stated in the last paragraph. Options (1), (2), (3), and (4) are incorrect because they do not mean "Reconstruction."

Lesson 7: Industrial America
GED Exercise: Industrial America (page 261)

1. **(1) Production was speeded up.** (Analysis) Machines could produce standard parts that could be quickly assembled. Options (2) and (5) are the opposite of the effect. Option (3) has nothing to do with the effect. There is no mention of option (4).

2. **(3) Parts are identical and interchangeable.** (Comprehension) With standardized parts, products can be made quickly, accurately, and inexpensively. Options (1), (4), and (5) are incorrect because unique or hand-made products are not mass produced. Option (2) is the opposite of what happens with mass production.

3. **(4) shoes** (Application) Leather goods would need a heavy needle and strong pressure to make the holes for thread. Options (1) and (5) are lightweight products. Options (2) and (3) are not made by sewing.

4. **(2) There were many important American inventions before the Civil War.** (Comprehension) This summarizes the general idea of the paragraph. Option (1) is incorrect because the subject of the paragraph is American inventions, not the Industrial Revolution. Options (3), (4), and (5) are details that support the main idea.

5. **(2) a more comfortable way of life** (Analysis) Inventions like electricity and indoor plumbing made life easier. Inventions did not cause the war, so option (1) is incorrect. Options (3) and (5) are the opposite of what is stated. Option (4) is one of the inventions, not a result of them.

6. **(4) have enough capital** (Analysis) Without a group of people, it was difficult to have enough money to build factories. Option (1) is not suggested. Option (2) is incorrect because profits do not depend on the formation of a corporation. No dishonesty is mentioned, so option (3) is incorrect. Option (5) is incorrect because a corporation reduced the financial risk.

7. **(3) city jobs paid much better wages** (Analysis) Most of the jobs listed are city-based and pay more than farm labor. There is no support for options (1) and (2). Option (4) is incorrect because teachers are not necessarily trained in cities, and the salary in the table gives no reason for a move. There is no mention of how many postal positions (the only government job listed) were available, so option (5) is incorrect.

Lesson 8: The United States and the World
GED Exercise: The United States and the World (page 263)

1. **(5) By the time the United States stopped expanding, it was ready to take part in world affairs.** (Comprehension) The paragraph talks about physical expansion and a readiness to get involved in the world. Options (1), (2), and (3) are details that support the main idea. Option (4) is not mentioned in the paragraph.

2. **(3) Americans believed in fighting for democracy.** (Analysis) It is difficult to ignore a struggle over basic beliefs. Options (1) and (2) have nothing to do with the difficulty of staying out of the war. Option (4) is related to the Allies' difficulties with manufacturing, not to staying out of the war. The principles, not the countries themselves, were important factors, so option (5) is incorrect.

3. **(5) world affairs were not settled by the war** (Analysis) The information supports the idea that many agreements still had to be reached. Options (1) and (3) are not conclusions supported by the passage. Options (2) and (4) are supporting details, not conclusions.

4. **(4) a conflict without fighting** (Comprehension) The Cold War consisted primarily of a nonmilitary conflict between nations having different political and economic ideas: the democratic and the communist nations. Options (1) and (2) were the goals of the two sides of the Cold War. Option (3) involves friendship, not conflict. Option (5) is an example of a war with open military conflict.

5. **(1) the bombing of Pearl Harbor** (Analysis) The United States did not declare war until Pearl Harbor was bombed, even though the other countries in the war had started fighting in Europe two years earlier. Option (2) was the immediate cause of the Spanish-American War. Options (3) and (4) are incorrect because the United States waited two years to enter World War II. Option (5) was a cause of the Korean War.

6. **(2) American property had been attacked** (Analysis) In three cases, America did not declare war until its ships or land was attacked. Option (1) is a reason only for the Spanish-American War. Option (3) is incorrect because the United States wanted to remain neutral. Option (4) is true only for the Cold War. Option (5) is a result of being in a war, not a reason for waging it.

7. **(3) the breakup of the former USSR into independent nations in 1991** (Application) This event is the only example of an upheaval within a major power. Options (1) and (4) are examples of normal elections, not great upheaval. Option (2) is an example of an event outside the nation. Option (5) is an example of an alliance, not an upheaval.

8. **(2) economic problems resulting from the war had to be solved** (Analysis) The supporting statements detail the financial difficulties that were caused by the shift from war to peace. Option (1) is not a conclusion that can be drawn from the supporting statements. Option (3) is a broad generalization that is not supported in the paragraph. Option (4) is a supporting detail. Option (5) is incorrect because it refers to the entire decade, not just to its start; it also is too general.

9. **(4) Unemployment rose.** (Analysis) The statements in the paragraph that come before this one support it as a conclusion. Options (1), (2), and (3) are support for the conclusion. Option (5) is an additional detail about the main idea.

10. **(4) Factories moved from New England to the South.** (Analysis) This fact supports the conclusion that the Northeast did not share in the prosperity of the 1920s. Options (1), (2), (3), and (5) are all true, but none deals with regional differences in the economy.

11. **(5) The prosperity of the 1920s was not shared by all Americans.** (Analysis) The paragraph gives details showing that some people did well and others did not during the 1920s. Options (1), (2), (3), and (4) are not supported by the information.

12. **(3) the United States will have to take a different role** (Analysis) Because of the trend toward political openness, the focus of the United States will have to change to suit the situation. Option (1) is not a possible conclusion because there is no reference to the civil rights movement. Options (2), (4), and (5) are not adequately supported.

13. **(5) The world powers are having real discussions.** (Analysis) Rapid and radical changes have made the powers realize they cannot ignore the situation. Options (1), (2), and (3) are details related to the events, not the results. Option (4) is the opposite of what is stated.

14. **(3) Gorbachev's attempts to fix what was wrong with the Soviet Union** (Comprehension) Even though the Soviet Union was dead or dying, Gorbachev tried to heal it. Options (1), (2), and (5) are incorrect because the cartoon does not show any nations or organizations other than the Soviet Union. Option (4) is incorrect because an intravenous line does not symbolize an election.

15. **(2) Gorbachev was not able to keep the Soviet Union alive.** (Analysis) Despite the intravenous injection by Gorbachev, the Soviet Union is already dead and buried in this

cartoon. Option (1) is incorrect because the cartoonist does not comment on the United States' policy toward the former Soviet Union. Option (3) is incorrect because the Soviet Union is pictured as dead. Option (4) is incorrect because the views of other nations are not shown. Option (5) is not supported by the cartoon.

16. **(4) the ERA was defeated by only a few states** (Comprehension) Even without the states that tried to reverse ratification, 30 states were in favor of it. Option (1) is clearly incorrect; only 35 states had originally ratified the amendment. Option (2) is incorrect because over half the states were clearly in favor. Option (3) is incorrect for the same reason. There is no support for option (5).

17. **(3) the South** (Application) Most southern states rejected the ERA. Options (1), (2), and (4) were primarily in favor of the bill and would probably vote for another one. Option (5) is incorrect because the states were divided but were not entirely against the ERA.

18. **(5) New Frontier** (Application) In 1960, President John F. Kennedy challenged the nation to fulfill the demands of a "New Frontier" in areas of economic development, civil rights, and space explorations. Option (5) is most closely related to these issues. Options (1), (2), (3), and (4) are not supported.

19. **(1) arms race** (Application) Strategic Arms Limitations Talks started in 1972 when United States President Nixon and USSR Premier Brezhnev first agreed to try to limit offensive weapons systems. Options (2), (3), (4), and (5) are not supported.

20. **(3) arms race** (Application) During the 1950s, the United States and Russia began to accumulate nuclear weapons. This competition became known as the arms race. It has been the theme of many summit conferences between the United States and Soviet leaders. Options (1), (2), (4), and (5) are not supported by the information.

21. **(2) Watergate** (Application) The break-in at the Democratic National Committee headquarters at the Watergate Hotel in Washington was part of a covert effort to hinder the election of Democratic party rivals. Senate investigations eventually revealed cover-ups at the highest levels of politics. For his knowledge and involvement, President Nixon resigned rather than face impeachment proceedings. Options (1), (3), (4), and (5) are not supported.

22. **(5) Contract with America** (Application) Returning welfare programs to the states reduces federal control of some social services, which is a goal of the Contract with America. Options (1), (2), (3), and (4) are not concerned with welfare.

23. **(3) Reaganomics** (Application) President Reagan felt that the nation's ills were due to excessive government spending, high taxes, inflation, and high interest rates. His economic program, called Reaganomics, called for major cutbacks in federal spending and lower interest rates, in addition to other measures. Options (1), (2), (4), and (5) do not stress monetary reform.

24. **(3) New Frontier** (Application) Option (3) is correct because the new frontier referred to space. Since the concept of having astronauts on the moon arose nearly 20 years before the Reagan presidency, option (1) is incorrect. Option (2) involves nuclear arms, which were not a part of the goal of landing astronauts on the moon. Option (4) deals with political scandals during the Nixon presidency, which did not affect the moon program. Option (5) does not apply to the issue.

25. **(3) New Frontier** (Application) Kennedy's administration helped the civil rights movement by giving government support to school desegregation efforts. There is no support for options (1), (2), (4), or (5).

26. **(5) arms race** (Application) During the arms race, the United States and the Soviet Union agreed to limit testing of weapons. Options (1), (2), (3), and (4) are not concerned with nuclear weapons.

27. **(3) Watergate** (Application) As a result of the Watergate scandal, Congress moved toward impeaching President Nixon. He resigned rather than face impeachment. Options (1), (2), (4), and (5) are not concerned with the resignation of a President.

28. **(3) American involvement in the Vietnam War increased gradually** (Comprehension) Starting with a few advisers in the early 1960s, involvement increased year by year. Options (1), (2), (4), and (5) are all contradicted by the paragraph.

29. **(1) Americans received more accurate information about the war.** (Analysis) This was the first time Americans had seen a war fought day after day, year after year. Option (2) may have been true of some Americans but

not of all. There is no evidence that options (3) and (5) were a result of television. Option (4) did not happen, according to the paragraph.

30. **(3) the difficulties of changing from a dictatorship to a democracy** (Comprehension) In trying to institute democratic reforms, Russia ran into many problems, symbolized by the burning food. Option (1) is incorrect because the bear represents Russia. Option (2) is incorrect because there is no indication of revolution in the cartoon. Option (4) is incorrect because the United States does not appear in the cartoon. Option (5) is incorrect because there is no clue about Russia's status as a world power.

31. **(3) Russia has no tradition of democracy so it must use a "recipe."** (Analysis) Without a tradition of democracy, Russia is having difficulty making the change from dictatorship to democracy. Option (1) is true, but there is no evidence for it in the cartoon. Option (2) is not true. Option (4) is not supported by the cartoon. Option (5) is true, but it is not a reason that Russia is having difficulty with democratic reforms.

32. **(5) first time in United Nations history that nearly all the world's nations agreed on the effort to turn back an agressor** (Comprehension) This clear from the first sentence of the passage. There is nothing in the passage to support options (1), (2), (3), and (4).

33. **(3) after Iraq invaded Kuwait** (Comprehension) The passage states that the UN resolution was issued <u>after</u> it was clear that Iraq would not remove its forces from Kuwait. Therefore, options (1) and (4) are incorrect. Option (2) is incorrect; the passage concerns Iraq's invasion of Kuwait, not Iran. Kuwait has never invaded Iraq, so option (5) is incorrect.

GED Review: History (page 270)

1. **(3) International Bank for Reconstruction and Development** (Application) Individuals who need money for projects can get loans from this bank if the financial plan is sound. Options (1), (2), (4), and (5) do not deal with financial assistance.

2. **(2) Point Four Program** (Analysis) This program provides the technical assistance to begin the fish-farming cooperative. Options (1), (3), (4), and (5) are not related to providing technical assistance.

3. **(5) Military Aid** (Analysis) The passage says that military aid is given to allies. Saudi Arabia is an ally of both the United States and Kuwait. Options (1), (2), (3), and (4) do not provide funds for military purposes.

4. **(3) allowing freedom of the press** (Application) Glasnost means "openness," implying more freedom of expression. Option (1) is not related to social reform. Options (2) and (5) are incorrect because they are examples of attempts to prohibit freedom of expression and movement. Option (4) is an example of reform.

5. **(1) Land disputes would erupt between the colonists and the French.** (Application) The map shows territory between the Mississippi River and the Appalachian Mountains being claimed by both France and the colonies. Using this information, you could predict that there would be disputes. The other options describe real historic events, but they could not have been predicted from information in the map.

6. **(2) the need for economic survival** (Comprehension) The paragraph implies that these people left Ireland for the United States in order to avoid starvation. In other words, they were seeking to survive. Option (1) is unlikely, since the paragraph states that almost one million people died during the famine. Options (3) and (4) are not discussed in the paragraph. Although option (5) is possible, no information indicates that free farmland was available in the United States.

7. **(3) recognize Boss Tweed even without facial features** (Analysis) Although Boss Tweed worked behind the scenes, he was well known. Fatness, the money bag head, and the huge diamond stickpin give the readers clues as to the figure's identity. Option (1) would not be true of most readers. Option (2) is incorrect because Boss Tweed's corruption was well known. Option (4) is incorrect because the money bag clearly symbolizes wealth and greed. Option (5) is incorrect because Boss Tweed was not the mayor.

Economics
Lesson 9: General Economic Behavior
GED Exercise (page 273)

1. **(1) operates according to certain principles** (Analysis) The writer states that economics has basic principles. Options (2), (3), and (5) have no support. Option (4) is incorrect because some economies are based on barter.

2. **(1) all economic exchanges have a monetary value** (Analysis) The GNP can

work as a measure only if a value in money is given to each exchange, even those that are not paid for in money. The quantity of products does not affect the accuracy of the GNP, so option (2) is incorrect. Option (3) is incorrect because the barter system would best be measured by something else. Options (4) and (5) are incorrect because the economy does not need to be improving or stable to be measured.

3. **(3) can be persuaded to pay high prices** (Analysis) Manufacturers would not try to sell even more high-priced goods if they did not believe that people would buy them. Option (1) suggests the opposite. There is no mention of quality, so option (2) is incorrect. Savings is not involved in the law of supply and demand, so option (4) is incorrect. Fooling the customer has nothing to do with the law of supply and demand, so option (5) is incorrect.

4. **(4) the price of a product** (Analysis) Advertising adds to the price of a product. Advertising has nothing to do with options (1), (2), or (3). Normal profits, option (5), probably would not increase much because the cost would go to the advertisers.

5. **(3) determined by the community** (Comprehension) If a person's work has no value to the community, it will not be in demand and will not provide that person with an income. There is no support for options (1) and (2). Option (4) is incorrect because the value of work helps to set income levels. Option (5) is incorrect because the community, not the individual, sets the value.

6. **(5) trading some of your garden vegetables for your neighbor's quilt** (Application) In this case, the value of the goods is not set by money but by how much each person wants the other's goods. Option (1) refers to exchanging one item for another of equal monetary value. Options (2), (3), and (4) are all based on monetary value.

7. **(1) demand for the product goes up** (Comprehension) As prices decrease, consumers buy more. Options (2) and (4) are incorrect because product quality is not affected by supply and demand. Options (3) and (5) do not reflect the law of supply and demand.

8. **(4) paying your phone bill by check** (Application) This is the only activity listed that involves paying money for something, the basis of a monetary system. The other options do not involve the exchange of money.

9. **(5) Money is used to pay for goods and services.** (Analysis) Option (5) is correct because only in a monetary economy do people use money. Options (1), (2), (3), and (4) are incorrect because they all describe ways barter and monetary economies are the same.

10. **(5) finding new markets** (Analysis) This can be understood from the main idea of the paragraphs: when more goods are produced, more people must be found to buy them. Options (1) and (4) would be costs when production was restricted. Options (2) and (3) will always be costs of manufacturing; therefore they are not new.

11. **(2) has more goods than customers** (Comprehension) Advertising is a way of getting people to buy more. The company wants people to buy more when it has more goods than customers. Option (1) is the opposite of what is stated. If option (3) were correct, the company would not advertise. Option (4) is irrelevant. For option (5), a new advertising campaign is not necessary.

12. **(1) exports will increase** (Comprehension) This is correct from the information on developing overseas, or export, markets. Option (2) does not necessarily follow. Options (3) and (4) are more likely in a tightening economy. Option (5) is the opposite of what is stated.

13. **(1) an economic fact of marketing** (Analysis) The writer accepts marketing products as an economic fact. Option (2) is not mentioned. Although option (3) may be true for some marketing strategies, it is not mentioned. Options (4) and (5) are not related to these paragraphs on marketing.

14. **(3) advertising an office product to home users** (Application) This is an example of trying to sell a product in a new market, the home. Options (1) and (4) are incorrect because they involve existing customers, not new ones. Option (2) is incorrect because you cannot tell whether the advertising will reach a new market. Option (5) will not necessarily attract a new market for the product.

15. **(2) advertising helps sell products** (Analysis) The first paragraph states that advertising tells something special about a product. The writer assumes you know that when people know that a product is special, many of them will buy it. Option (1) is incorrect because an expanded economy is defined in the first sentence. Option (3) is incorrect because a rebate is defined in the

first paragraph. Option (4) is incorrect because this is stated in the second paragraph. Option (5) is incorrect because exporting is defined at the end of the second paragraph.

16. **(2) selling it to Kansas** (Comprehension) The diagram shows California and Kansas exchanging broccoli for money. Options (1), (3), (4), and (5) are not supported by the diagram.

17. **(4) people want different things** (Analysis) The system works because when someone needs something, there is usually someone else who wants to sell it. Options (1), (2), (3), and (5) are not supported by the diagram.

18. **(4) always changing** (Comprehension) The pattern is one of change from activity to little activity and back to activity again. Options (1) and (2) are opinions about the cycle and are not supported in the paragraph. Option (3) is the opposite of what is stated. Option (5) has no support.

19. **(2) not seriously affected by minor variations in the pattern** (Analysis) The writer believes that the pattern remains constant. Option (1) is the opposite of what is stated. Options (3), (4), and (5) are not supported by the paragraph.

20. **(1) economy** (Analysis) Option (1) is correct because the paragraph does not tell you what an economy is; the writer assumes that you know this. Options (2), (3), (4), and (5) are all defined in the paragraph.

Lesson 10: Labor and the Economy
GED Exercise: Labor and the Economy (page 277)

1. **(5) the difference between the cost of production and an item's price** (Comprehension) Option (5) is stated in the first sentence. Options (1), (2), and (4) are not stated in the information. Option (3) is not true.

2. **(3) Labor has one voice and management has many.** (Analysis) This option is the only effect that has not come out of the conflict. Labor has unions or a collective voice, as does management. Options (1), (2), (4), and (5) are all results of the conflict.

3. **(5) The teachers' union would bargain with the school board.** (Application) This is the best option because the union would negotiate before it would strike, option (1), accept a pay cut, option (2), or picket, option (3). Cities try to avoid closing schools, option (4).

4. **(3) allow workers a voice in their jobs** (Comprehension) This is a restatement of the

information in the second paragraph. Options (1) and (2) are not supported by the information. Option (4) refers to the early unions, not the modern ones. There is no evidence for option (5).

5. **(3) Unions have gotten many benefits for laborers.** (Analysis) The last paragraph details the benefits that have resulted. Options (1) and (2) are not related to collective bargaining. Options (4) and (5) are the opposite of what is stated.

6. **(3) usually have tension between them** (Comprehension) The two groups have different and opposing goals, and they will rarely see eye to eye. Option (1) is unlikely. Options (2) and (4) would not be to either side's advantage. There is no support for option (5).

7. **(1) The act specified only the rights of labor.** (Analysis) A balance of rights would have made the act seem less biased. Options (2), (3), and (4) are true, but they are details that do not summarize the apparent impact of the act. Option (5) is not true.

8. **(4) smaller wage increases** (Analysis) With decreased power comes decreasing (or no) gains at the bargaining table. Options (1), (2), (3), and (5) are incorrect because improvements in wages and benefits are likely results of increased union power.

Lesson 11: Government and Economics
GED Exercise: Government and Economics (page 279)

1. **(2) read the first paragraph** (Evaluation) The chart alone does not give enough information for a reader to interpret it accurately; the first paragraph acts as a key to the chart. Exact figures are not necessary to draw conclusions about percentages, so options (1) and (5) are incorrect. Option (3) refers to income, not to the spending shown in the chart. Option (4) is incorrect because only the first paragraph is needed for supporting information.

2. **(3) The income tax was not practiced fairly.** (Analysis) This is correct from information about tax benefits for high-income citizens. No information is given on options (1) and (2). Option (4) is a possible inference but is not well supported. Option (5) is an unsupported opinion.

3. **(4) less financial support for welfare programs** (Analysis) This is the best choice because it would cut government spending. Options (1), (2), and (3) would increase spending. Option (5) relates to government income, not spending.

4. **(5) arms manufacturing** (Application) The supporting detail in the text is "almost 21 percent is spent on national security and defense." Any increases or decreases in the federal budget are most likely to affect businesses dependent on the budget, that is, defense-related businesses. Options (1), (3), and (4) are not mentioned in the text or listed in the graph. Option (2) refers to an area that has less government funding.

5. **(3) defense spending** (Analysis) National debt is high when government spending is high without adequate income from taxation. United States participation in World War II began in the early 1940s. The government had to finance a larger army and produce many weapons for the U.S. and its allies. Option (1) might increase spending, but unemployment was low in the early 1940s because many were involved in the war effort. Option (2) increases income, not spending. Option (4) equalizes income and spending. Option (5) has nothing to do with the national debt.

6. **(3) is heavily involved in the economy** (Evaluation) Government involvement in the economy supports the idea that government is taking an active part, not that it is standing apart—or governing less. Jefferson believed in government that governed as little as possible. Options (1), (2), (4), and (5) are all supporting details for the conclusion.

7. **(2) the end of the Cold War** (Analysis) When the United States was engaged in the Cold War with the USSR, defense spending was very high. After the USSR broke up and the Cold War ended, the need for such high spending declined. Option (1) is incorrect because increased activity would mean higher, not lower, spending. Option (3) is incorrect; antiwar feelings usually run highest during periods of war and great defense expenditure. Option (4) would result in higher spending. Option (5) is not true.

8. **(2) Montana's plan would have increased state income** (Evaluation) Even if the goal was not reached, the state's income would have increased. There is not enough information to support options (1), (3), (4), or (5).

9. **(2) people in Montana use credit cards** (Analysis) The essential element of success would have been that Montana citizens use credit cards to make purchases. If that is true, then they probably would have also done option (1), but not the other way around. There is no support for options (3) or (5). Option (4) has nothing to do with the success of the project.

10. **(5) collects taxes** (Analysis) When something is expensive, we say that it "costs an arm and a leg." The IRS is about to take this taxpayer's "arms and legs," as shown in the night deposit boxes. Options (1), (2), (3), and (4) do not make sense in the context of the cartoon.

11. **(3) The IRS is fair in its dealings.** (Analysis) Clearly the cartoonist feels the IRS is trapping people into paying huge amounts (the noose). Options (1) and (2) are incorrect because they are facts. Option (4) is something with which the cartoonist would agree. Option (5) is incorrect because the cartoonist is criticizing high taxes, not the fact that taxes have to be paid.

GED Review: Economics (page 281)

1. **(3) government control of prices** (Application) Outside control would have to be used to stop spiraling wages and prices. Option (1) is incorrect because unions would support increased wages. In order to have higher profits, option (2), manufacturers would have to charge higher prices. Option (4) is incorrect because socialism is an economic system that has nothing to do with the situation described in the paragraph. Price increases, option (5), would mean that workers would demand more money to pay for more expensive goods.

2. **(3) rising prices** (Analysis) As wages increase, prices rise. This situation means that the consumer has to pay more, so option (1) is incorrect. The increase in price is intended to prevent option (2). Option (4) is the opposite of the effect. There is no support for option (5).

3. **(2) demand-pull inflation** (Application) The scarcity of fuel caused prices to go up. There is no support for options (1), (3), (4), or (5).

4. **(3) inflation** (Application) Although the item remained the same, its cost more than doubled. The definitions for options (1), (2), (4), and (5) do not fit the example.

5. **(5) depression** (Application) A severe slowdown in business is called a depression. None of the other options fits the description of what happened in the 1930s.

6. **(2) increasing exports and increasing imports** (Comprehension) This is shown by the general upward trend of both lines on the graph. Option (1) is incorrect because imports are also increasing. Option (3) is incorrect

because both lines are moving upward, not downward. Option (4) is incorrect because exports are increasing, not decreasing. Option (5) is incorrect because both lines show a definite upward movement.

7. **(3) Imports are higher than exports.** (Analysis) The graph shows that the U.S. imports more than it exports, leading to an unfavorable balance of trade. Options (1), (2), and (5) are incorrect because you need information about both imports and exports to reach any conclusions about the balance of trade. Option (4) is incorrect because when both imports and exports go in the same direction, the overall trade balance doesn't change.

8. **(4) is a way of illustrating how much taxes the average worker pays** (Comprehension) Tax Freedom Day isn't a real day; it is simply a dramatic way to show the ratio of yearly taxes to yearly wages. Option (1) is incorrect because Tax Freedom Day is a symbol, not a real day. Option (2) is incorrect because the information refers to "freedom" from taxes, not freeing people in jail. Option (3) is incorrect because information is given for only two years, not ten years. Option (5) is incorrect because taxes are withheld from all paychecks.

9. **(3) pays about one-third of his or her wages for taxes** (Comprehension) If the worker is paying taxes for the four months of January, February, March, and April, 1/3 of his or her money goes to taxes (12 divided by 4). Option (1) is incorrect because workers pay one-third of their wages in taxes. Option (2) is incorrect because people get paid all year round. Options (4) and (5) are incorrect because there is no information about what type of taxes and how much of each type the worker is paying.

10. **(2) increased taxes** (Analysis) If it takes the worker more days of wages to pay taxes, that must be because taxes increased from one year to the next. There is no support for option (1). Option (3) is incorrect because a tax cut would have resulted in an earlier Tax Freedom Day. Options (4) and (5) are incorrect because taxes are a percent of wages. When average wages go up, average taxes go up too, so the percent remains the same though the amounts may change.

11. **(2) What is to be produced?** (Application) When deciding between baseballs and footballs, Sam is deciding what to produce. Option (1) is incorrect because Sam is deciding what, not

how much. Option (3) is incorrect because Sam is not deciding how he should make his product. Option (4) is incorrect because Sam is not thinking about who his customers are. Option (5) is incorrect because Sam is not concerned with general economic change.

12. **(3) How is it to be produced?** (Application) Elena is trying to improve the way she produces documents. Option (1) is incorrect because Elena is not dealing with quantities. Option (2) is incorrect because Elena already knows what she is producing. Option (4) is incorrect because Elena is not thinking about who her customers are. Option (5) is incorrect because Elena is not concerned with general economic change.

13. **(4) Who is to receive it?** (Application) Parker's company is considering going after new customers. Option (1) is incorrect because quantities are not being considered. Option (2) is incorrect because the product is not changing. Option (3) is incorrect because they are not considering changing production methods. Option (5) is incorrect because they are not asking a general economic question.

14. **(5) How can the economy adapt to change?** (Application) The change was workers' longer hours, and banks responded to this by installing ATM machines. Options (1), (2), and (3) are incorrect because no product is being produced. Option (4) is incorrect because bank customers didn't change.

15. **(1) How much should be produced?** (Application) Patricia is considering whether to produce more of her products, chips. Options (2) and (3) are incorrect because there is no change in the product or how it is produced. Option (4) is incorrect because the same people will buy the chips, just more of them. Option (5) is incorrect because Patricia is not concerned with general economic change.

16. **(4) the number of U.S. children who were poor in 1992** (Evaluation) To do this, you would multiply 39.6 million people by 40 percent. Option (1) is incorrect because you would need to know the total population in order to figure out the percent that were poor. Option (2) is incorrect because you would need to know the percent of people in poverty in order to figure out the total population. Options (3) and (5) are incorrect because there is no information given about poverty rate according to family type.

Political Science

Lesson 12: Modern Government

GED Exercise: Modern Government (page 285)

1. **(5) Idi Amin** (Analysis) The Ugandan dictator is called violent in the fifth paragraph. No opinions are expressed about options (1), (2), (3), or (4).

2. **(4) facts about basic political principles** (Analysis) Each description is based on how the principles fit into the government structure. There is no mention of opinions about how the systems work or about the citizens' role, so options (1) and (2) are incorrect. Option (3) is incorrect because examples are not given for all systems. No history of specific systems is mentioned, so option (5) is incorrect.

3. **(1) Government has changed over the years.** (Evaluation) The discussion of basic principles supports this conclusion. There is not enough support for options (2), (3), (4), or (5).

4. **(2) The government fails.** (Analysis) Because all the power was in that one person's hands, the government would be in chaos. Therefore, option (1) is incorrect. Option (3) might happen, but it is not a direct effect. Options (4) and (5) would not be direct effects in an authoritarian government because it has no political opposition or citizen participation.

5. **(3) authoritarian government** (Application) A government that is based on the power of the leader and his small group is authoritarian. Options (1) and (2) are incorrect because they refer to political principles, not forms of government. Option (4) is incorrect because the power of a totalitarian government comes from a single political party, not an individual. Option (5) is incorrect because a democracy is based on the power of the people.

6. **(5) democracy** (Application) Russia's reforms have been in the direction of democracy. Options (1) and (2) are incorrect because they refer to political principles, not forms of government. Option (3) is incorrect because an authoritarian government is based on the power of a dictator. Option (4) is incorrect because totalitarian is the form of government that Russia is moving away from.

7. **(5) democracy** (Application) In a democracy, the people elect the members of the government, and they are ruled by laws; these are both aspects of the British government. Options (1) and (2) are incorrect because they are principles, not forms of government. Options (3) and (4) are incorrect because authoritarian and totalitarian governments are not based on the rule of law.

8. **(5) government censorship of the media** (Application) Option (5) is correct because freedom of the press is guaranteed in the U.S. Constitution. Options (1) and (3) are incorrect because a multiparty system and the right to join a union are both a part of American democracy. Option (2) is incorrect because even though children must attend school, we consider education a right, not a duty. Option (4) is incorrect because democracies make laws to protect the majority of citizens.

9. **(4) democratic governments are best** (Analysis) The preference is shown by the words "admirable goal." Therefore, option (1) is incorrect. There is no support for options (2), (3), or (5).

10. **(2) be told where you could or could not travel** (Application) Under a government that wants to control your life, freedom of movement would be limited. Options (1), (3), and (4) would be unlikely. There is no support for option (5).

11. **(3) Personal freedom has no limit.** (Comprehension) Personal freedom is limited by the rights of others in a democracy. Options (1), (2), (4), and (5) are incorrect because they are all characteristic of democracy.

12. **(1) has its responsibilities** (Analysis) This opinion is shown in the last sentence; therefore, option (5) is incorrect. There is no support for options (2), (3), or (4).

13. **(5) do all of the above** (Analysis) Lincoln's definition rests on the foundations listed in the passage. Option (1), (2), (3), or (4) alone is not the best assumption.

14. **(1) act as responsible citizens** (Application) This concept refers to the basic principles of a democratic society. "Fellow Americans" and "what you can do for your country" are clues. Options (2), (3), (4), and (5) are incorrect because no reference is made to them in Kennedy's quoted words.

15. **(2) some people agree with government policy** (Application) People who agree with government policy would not take part in a demonstration against it. A demonstration is based on the democratic principle of having freedom of political activity and taking responsibility for the expression of opinion. Therefore, options (1), (3), (4), and (5) are not correct.

16. **(1) freedom of religion** (Application) Of all the items listed, only freedom of religion is a fundamental benefit that all citizens have. Option (2) is a Constitutional amendment (22nd) applying only to the President and limiting his or her power. Options (3) and (5) are privileges that the government can grant or take away. Option (4) is an obligation of citizens, not a right given to them.

17. **(5) obtaining a broadcast license** (Application) A license to broadcast is a privilege given by the government; it can be given or taken away. All the other options are rights that cannot be taken away.

18. **(2) wearing seat belts** (Application) It is a law that all drivers and passengers must wear seat belts. Options (1) and (3) are rights that cannot be taken away. Options (4) and (5) are privileges; the public transportation and public library systems can be taken away.

19. **(1) influence** (Application) Perot's power came from his wealth, organization, ideas, and personality, all sources of influence. Option (2) is incorrect because Perot did not use force. Options (3) and (4) are incorrect because they are sources of legitimacy that are given to elected officials by the people. Option (5) is not true; Perot did not win the election.

20. **(5) illegitimate** (Application) Thieu's reign was based on the use of force, not on support of the people. Options (1), (2), and (3) do not fit the description. Option (4) is the opposite of what is described.

21. **(4) legitimate power** (Application) In a monarchy such as England's, the royal family is recognized as having legitimate power. Options (1) and (3) are incorrect because the queen rules by virtue of her position, not from personal influence or persuasion. Option (2) is incorrect because the queen did not acquire power by force. Option (5) is incorrect because the queen was not elected.

22. **(1) elections** (Application) Elections are the means by which power is transferred in a democratic republic such as the United States. Option (2) is true of a monarchy, not a democratic republic. Option (3) is incorrect because most power resides in elected, not appointed, positions. Option (4) is incorrect because revolutions are not orderly transfers of power. Option (5) is incorrect because campaign contributions help in the election process, but they are not the means by which power is transferred.

23. **(2) important to having legitimate power** (Analysis) Because people act on their opinions, they have the ability to support or overthrow a government; support is necessary for a legitimate government. Therefore, option (1) is incorrect. There is no support for options (3) or (5). Option (4) is incorrect because force does not control people's opinions.

24. **(4) an opinion** (Analysis) Even a belief held by an authority can be an opinion, not a fact. Therefore, option (3) is incorrect. Options (1) and (2) are incorrect because an opinion cannot be either true or false. It can only be supported or unsupported. Option (5) has no support.

25. **(2) supported by the fact that it settles disputes** (Analysis) Settling disputes is the role of an umpire, so this opinion is validly supported. Therefore, option (1) is incorrect. Options (3), (4), and (5) are not reasonable supports for the opinion.

26. **(3) represents the interests of the wealthy** (Analysis) The paragraph presents two opposing opinions; this is the second opinion. Option (1) is incorrect because the U.S. government is not compared to other governments. Option (2) is incorrect because neither opinion holds that all problems have been solved. Option (4) is too general. Option (5) is not stated anywhere in the paragraph.

27. **(4) poverty still is a major problem** (Analysis) People who feel that the government has not done enough to help the poor point to the continued poverty in the United States. Options (1), (2), and (3) do not support this opinion. Option (5) is not evidence that the government has failed to solve the problem of poverty; it is an opinion about the role of government.

Lesson 13: The American Political Process
GED Exercise: The American Political Process (page 291)

1. **(5) Third parties tend to represent special interests.** (Evaluation) This statement is supported by the names of the parties. Option (1) is an oversimplification with no support; the parties' names have nothing to do with success or failure. Option (2) is a generalization that ignores the fact that a party must have some support to exist. Option (3) is a broad stereotype that lumps all third parties together under a familiar name. Option (4) is incorrect because it ignores the role that third parties do play.

2. **(4) the needs of the nation change** (Evaluation) Americans select the party they

believe will best serve whatever issues are important at the time. Options (1) and (2) are oversimplifications based on opinion. Options (3) and (5) are oversimplifications that link a political decision with ideas that have nothing to do with politics.

3. **(3) ratification of the Constitution was no longer an issue** (Evaluation) The reason for the party's existence vanished when the Constitution was adopted. Option (1) is incorrect because it did not matter which party Washington himself belonged to; what mattered was that the Federalist party received the strongest support. There is no support for the generalizations in options (2) or (4). Option (5) is a hasty generalization based on an unfounded opinion.

4. **(5) Republican** (Comprehension) This is stated in the second paragraph. Options (1), (2), (3), and (4) are not supported by the information.

5. **(1) their platforms** (Comprehension) The primary differences between each party lie in their policies. Option (2) has nothing to do with their main differences. There is no evidence of options (3) or (4). Option (5) refers only to the first two parties formed in the U.S.

6. **(4) feeling the major parties do not offer solutions to important problems** (Analysis) The only way to express dissatisfaction with the policies of both parties is to vote against them. Options (1), (2), and (5) would more likely result in not voting at all. Option (3) has nothing to do with choosing a party.

7. **(1) Democratic-Republican** (Application) The Democratic-Republicans favored a weak central government, as does the modern Republican party. Option (2) is incorrect because the Abolitionists focused on the issue of slavery. Option (3) is incorrect because the Federalists believed in a strong federal government. Option (4) is incorrect because the focus of this party was on labor issues. Option (5) is incorrect because "Third" refers to any third party, not a particular party; all third parties disagree with the major parties.

Lesson 14: **Government Money and the General Welfare**

GED Exercise: Government Money and the General Welfare (page 293)

1. **(5) Veterans Administration** (Application) William needs further job training, offered by the VA. Option (1) provides housing and would not solve the problem. William would not

qualify for options (2) or (4) because his wife has a good job and he left his job voluntarily. William is too young for option (3).

2. **(3) Social Security Program** (Application) Wendy is eligible to receive benefits from her husband's Social Security contributions. Because there is no evidence that Wendy needs housing or help with food money, options (1) and (2) are incorrect. Wendy is not eligible for help from options (4) or (5).

3. **(2) Medicare Program** (Application) Because Mark is over 65, he might be eligible for some medical benefits. Option (1) does not apply. Mark is not retired or unemployed, so options (3) and (4) are incorrect. There is no evidence that Mark was a veteran, so option (5) is incorrect.

4. **(4) Unemployment Insurance Program** (Application) Because Pete did not quit, he is eligible for unemployment insurance. There is no information about Pete's financial need, so option (1) is incorrect. Pete is probably not over 65, so options (2) and (3) are incorrect. There is no evidence that Pete was in the service, so option (5) is incorrect.

5. **(1) Agriculture is one industry that benefits from government programs.** (Comprehension) This sentence covers the main points of the paragraph. Options (2), (3), (4), and (5) are details and examples that support the main idea.

Lesson 15: **The United States and Foreign Policy**

GED Exercise: The United States and Foreign Policy (page 295)

1. **(3) Good Neighbor Policy** (Evaluation) This policy neither supports staying away nor being involved. It advocates a country's right to establish its own government. Options (1), (2), (4), and (5) indicate more involvement.

2. **(4) communism may no longer be a major threat** (Evaluation) Friendly relations reduce the possibility of threat. Option (1) is a self-contradiction. Options (2) and (3) are red herrings because they transfer the reader's attention to an unrelated emotional issue. There is no evidence to support option (5).

3. **(3) it had to honor its political commitments** (Evaluation) This is stated in the second sentence of the last paragraph. Options (1) and (2) are circular arguments. Option (4) is an either-or error that ignores other possibilities. Option (5) is a red herring

that appeals to a patriotic nature but is without a factual basis.

4. **(2) Open Door Policy** (Application) A renewed relationship suggests a willingness to deal with the other country rather than regard it only as an enemy. Options (1), (3), (4), and (5) do not apply.

5. **(5) Truman Doctrine** (Application) This policy supported aid to any nation fighting against a Communist influence. Options (1), (2), (3), and (4) do not apply.

6. **(4) Marshall Plan** (Application) This plan helped European countries to restore their economies. Options (1), (2), (3), and (5) do not apply.

7. **(1) Monroe Doctrine** (Application) Issues involving outside interference in Western Hemisphere affairs are covered by the Monroe Doctrine. None of the other options applies.

8. **(3) U.S. foreign policy will become even more important to other nations** (Analysis) Without the Soviet Union to balance U.S. influence, the United States has more power over other nations. Option (1) is incorrect because even though the Truman Doctrine has become less important, it still is in force. Option (2) is not likely, because the Marshall Plan was a disaster relief plan. Option (4) is not likely because the United States will be called on by other nations to use its influence more than ever. Option (5) is incorrect because it is unlikely that the United States will face a strong enemy.

GED Review: Political Science (page 296)

1. **(4) Gandhi was gentle** (Analysis) This is a judgment that cannot be proven as a fact. Options (1), (2), (3), and (5) are all facts that can be proven.

2. **(2) are all revolutionaries** (Evaluation) That some of the most famous charismatic leaders were indeed leaders of revolutions does not mean that all were. Options (1), (3), (4), and (5) are all reasonable statements based on the information given.

3. **(2) the political figures listed will be familiar** (Analysis) In using these people as examples of charismatic leaders, the writer assumes that they will be recognized. There is no evidence that the writer assumes option (1), (3), or (4). Option (5) is incorrect because charisma is explained in the paragraph.

4. **(5) characters** (Comprehension) This generalization is a restatement of given information. Options (1), (2), and (3) may be true but are not specified in the paragraph. There is no mention of the role of government in the paragraph, so option (4) is incorrect.

5. **(3) federal food stamp program for the poor and unemployed** (Application) This is a public service of the federal government, which is a strong centralized government. Options (1), (2), (4), and (5) all refer to services or powers of local governments.

6. **(4) A peaceful protester is critically injured in a demonstration against nuclear power plants in North Dakota.** (Application) This is correct because the protester is not acting in a violent manner. Instead, the paragraph states that the action is peaceful, although politically directed. Options (1), (2), (3), and (5) are all examples of violent political action.

7. **(3) there has been a dramatic increase in the number of elderly citizens** (Comprehension) This is the only logical conclusion. In the last few decades, medical advances plus a better standard of living have led to an increase in the number of elderly citizens. There is no support for options (1) or (5). Option (2) is the opposite of what is true. Option (4) is an opinion with no support in the paragraph.

8. **(2) Lotteries may supply millions of dollars in revenue for some states.** (Evaluation) The figures in the third column support this statement. There is not enough information to support options (1), (3), (4), and (5).

9. **(1) at least twice the amount the states get after prizes and administration** (Comprehension) This is true for all ten states according to the figures given. Option (2) is incorrect because gross revenue varies considerably from state to state. Option (3) is incorrect because four northeastern states are listed in the top ten. There is not enough information to support option (4). Option (5) is not true according to the figures in the table.

Behavioral Science
Lesson 16: People as Members of Cultures
GED Exercise: People as Members of Cultures (page 299)

1. **(1) a person should be humble when worshipping** (Evaluation) By covering their heads, women are covering their beauty,

according to the Bible. Options (2) and (3) are not suggested cultural values. Options (4) and (5) are unfounded stereotypes.

2. **(1) showing respect for their families' reputations** (Evaluation) By doing well academically, the children are maintaining the families' good names. Options (2), (3), (4), and (5) are possible but are not as specific as option (1).

3. **(2) learned** (Evaluation) This information can be concluded from the passage. Therefore, option (1) is incorrect. Option (3) is the opposite of what is stated. There is no support for options (4) or (5).

4. **(2) emotional and biological needs have to be fulfilled** (Analysis) This cause is stated in the paragraphs. There is no support for options (1) and (3). Options (4) and (5) may be generally true but are not the cause.

5. **(1) Even after marriage, one son lives with his parents until they die.** (Application) Parents are highly respected, so constant care would be an appropriate custom. Because of the importance of family in Asian cultures, options (2), (3), (4), and (5) are unlikely.

6. **(4) their harsh environment made certain behavior necessary** (Evaluation) Environment has a role in shaping culture. Harsh living conditions would require extreme adaptations. Option (1) is a circular argument that says nothing. Option (2) is an oversimplification of their relative isolation. Option (3) is a circular argument that simply describes one aspect of the culture. Option (5) is a red herring that leads away from the idea of cultural development.

7. **(2) adopting customs of the American culture** (Evaluation) This is a common situation for immigrants and their children because children adapt more easily than adults do. Option (1) would be more likely to lead to a greater awareness of their parents' culture than to cause greater disrespect for it. Option (3) would not cause parents to feel their culture was not being respected. Option (4) is incorrect because there is no reason to assume that the friends will be disrespectful. Option (5), though possible, is not as likely as option (2) since the ages of the children are not specified.

8. **(4) quiet women** (Evaluation) The women's personalities would be shaped by a cultural value that placed emphasis on being shy and withdrawn. Therefore, option (5) is the opposite of what is described. There is no information to support options (1), (2), or (3).

9. **(2) The Chencho culture encourages prolonged nursing behavior in their children.** (Evaluation) The differences between what these two groups of people consider the best approach to nursing imply that one culture values and encourages prolonged nursing, while the other culture does not. According to the information, child-rearing practices are culturally influenced. The example given provides an explanation for these differences. Options (1), (3), and (4) are opinions and are not based on any material presented. Option (5) is not a valid inference based on the information in the paragraph.

10. **(4) Personality is influenced by culture.** (Analysis) According to the paragraphs, each culture produces certain typical personality traits. Therefore, it may be said that personality is one of the effects, or results, of cultural influence. Options (1) and (3) are false cause-and-effect relationships. Option (2) might be true, but the question asks for a relationship discussed in the paragraphs. Option (5) is incorrect, based on the information given.

11. **(4) Persons raised in the same culture tend to have similar characteristics.** (Analysis) This statement is supported by both the explanation and the examples. Option (1) is incorrect because it contradicts the main idea of the paragraph. Option (2) is incorrect, since the paragraph states that persons raised in the same culture eventually act alike, not look alike. Option (3) is the exact opposite of what is stated. Option (5) may be known to be true from your general knowledge, but there is no evidence to support it here.

12. **(2) Culture and Personality** (Comprehension) The paragraph discusses the relationship of culture and personality. Option (1) is too general. Option (3) is incorrect because culture in general, not our culture, is being discussed. Options (4) and (5) are incorrect because they focus exclusively on childhood.

13. **(3) using a fork, knife, and spoon** (Application) This behavior is culturally conditioned and varies from place to place. All the other options are examples of basic human behavior that do not vary much from culture to culture.

14. **(2) The soil was fertile and produced abundant harvests.** (Comprehension) The Nile River Valley provided fertile soil for abundant harvests, which favored population growth. This was a major reason for the development of early civilization in this region. Options (1) and (3) are

results (effects) of, not reasons (causes) for, the development of civilization in the Nile Valley. Options (4) and (5) are not reasons for development of a civilization.

15. **(1) beauty** (Evaluation) Many of the people who left farming went into arts and crafts, so beauty is the most likely thing to have been valued. Options (2) and (3) would have been valued by farmers, not artists. Option (4) would apply to all early Egyptians, not just those who left farming. There is no evidence for option (5).

16. **(1) development of a number system with which to keep business records** (Analysis) Trading with others requires record keeping, which is more reliable if it is written down. Options (2) and (3) preceded the rise of trade. Option (4) is not related to trade. Option (5) is a more likely result of increased farming, not trade.

17. **(3) create a just system of water distribution** (Analysis) The last two sentences of the first paragraph state that the earliest laws were established to ensure cooperation in the building and use of irrigation dams and canals. These laws came before laws for housing, limiting surplus goods, commerce, and education. Options (1), (2), (4), and (5) do not apply to the question.

18. **(2) cooperation** (Evaluation) All of the cultural developments described rely on cooperation among members of the society. Therefore, options (1), (3), and (5) are incorrect. There is not enough evidence for option (4).

19. **(1) understand the reason for the size of Indian families** (Analysis) As stated in the first sentence (the topic sentence), the study sought to explain why poor people in India have large families. Options (2) and (4) are not mentioned in the text. Although the text mentions options (3) and (5), they are not the major reasons for the study.

20. **(4) social and economic customs** (Evaluation) As stated in the third paragraph, social and economic customs such as the dowry system and having at least two adult sons to support parents make limiting family size unpopular in India. The paragraphs do not mention antigovernment sentiment, nor do they discuss religious beliefs in India. You can infer that India has a very high birthrate, so option (2) is incorrect. Options (1), (3), and (5) have no support.

21. **(5) Having children is a great wealth.** (Evaluation) Look for facts that support the notion that having a large family is a great wealth. See the first and last paragraphs that discuss the notion that children, not land or money, are a great wealth. Options (1), (2), (3), and (4) are not substantiated by facts in the paragraphs.

22. **(2) It supports the sociologist as an expert.** (Analysis) A person who is born in the country being studied probably has a better understanding of the culture than an outsider. Options (1), (3), (4), and (5) have no support.

23. **(1) pensions and social security** (Application) Private and government savings programs for supporting the elderly in retirement have taken over the function of adult sons in the United States. Options (2), (3), (4), and (5) are incorrect because they are not the means of support for most elderly Americans.

24. **(3) Both urban and rural people have beliefs about the weather.** (Comprehension) As both columns contain beliefs, option (3) is a valid conclusion; therefore, options (1) and (2) are incorrect. Options (4) and (5) are incorrect because factual bases are not indicated for any of the information.

25. **(5) None of the beliefs involves causes.** (Analysis) The beliefs concern prediction, not cause, of certain types of weather. Therefore, options (1), (2), (3), and (4) are incorrect.

26. **(5) If March comes in like a lion, it goes out like a lamb.** (Application) This proverb predicts weather based on a sign, as do the beliefs. Options (1) and (2) are not really weather proverbs. Options (3) and (4) have nothing to do with weather.

27. **(3) there are relationships between weather and other natural happenings** (Analysis) The activities of animals, in particular, are assumed to be related to the weather. Options (1) and (4) are not supported by the table. Option (2) is not necessarily true, as the example of the cat proves. Option (5) is not true since many of the predictions have to do with cold versus mild winters.

Lesson 17: Individual and Group Behavior
GED Exercise: Individual and Group Behavior (page 305)

1. **(2) friends are more important than money** (Evaluation) As they have been meeting for so long and are comfortable together, the differences in their income do

not seem to matter. There is no indication that the people play cards for money, so option (1) is incorrect. There is no support for option (3). Options (4) and (5) are the opposite of what is shown by their relationship.

2. **(2) we react to other people's opinions** (Analysis) As humans, we care about the opinions of our friends and associates, so what they say will influence us. Option (1) is not true. There is no evidence of option (3). Option (4) might be the reason people join groups but not why groups affect behavior. Option (5) is incorrect because sociologists do not determine human behavior, they only study it.

3. **(3) he has not yet met people with common interests** (Evaluation) It is difficult to fit in with a group that does not share your interests. Option (1) is a circular argument that explains nothing. Option (2) is a red herring that introduces a topic that has nothing to do with Ed himself. Option (4) is a hasty generalization because there is no information about his social skills. Option (5) contradicts the information; if he gets along well with everyone, he should have little trouble fitting in.

4. **(1) is learning to deal with the real world** (Comprehension) This idea is stated in the second paragraph. Options (2), (3), and (4) are the opposite of what is suggested in the paragraphs. Option (5) has no support.

5. **(2) has a positive social role** (Evaluation) The classroom experience is positive and can be applied to all ages. There is no suggestion of options (1) or (3). Options (4) and (5) are the opposite of what is suggested in the paragraphs.

6. **(4) UFOs** (Evaluation) The stories indicate believed sightings of unexplainable objects in the sky. Option (1) might be suggested by the lights in each story but is not the belief indicated. There is no support for options (2), (3), or (5).

7. **(2) saying that the experience was shared by at least two people** (Evaluation) A second observer helps to document the occurrence. The speakers do not give the information stated in options (1), (3), (4), or (5).

8. **(2) a child who did poorly in a substandard school believes that she is not smart** (Application) Doing poorly in a substandard school does not necessarily mean that a student is not smart. However, her belief that she is not smart may remain even after she is out of school. Options (1) and (5)

are examples of people who do change their beliefs when given evidence. Option (3) is incorrect because Columbus's belief was true. Option (4) does not refer to people clinging to an untrue belief.

9. **(1) technology** (Evaluation) Option (1) is correct because technology is based on objective knowledge. Options (2) and (3) are beliefs that cannot be proved. Options (4) and (5) are interpretations of ideas about the world which are expressed by artists, not proven facts.

10. **(2) displacement** (Application) The boy is angry that his father is not around, but the father's death did not cause his behavior. The definitions in options (1), (3), (4), and (5) do not deal with blaming one's actions on someone else.

11. **(5) repression** (Application) By forgetting what happened, these adults do not have to face the pain of their pasts. Options (1), (2), (3), and (4) do not deal with forgetting events to avoid pain.

12. **(3) rationalization** (Application) Davy's excuse is not the real reason he hasn't had a checkup; he is afraid, not busy. Options (1), (2), (4), and (5) do not apply to using something else as an excuse for inaction.

13. **(4) reaction formation** (Application) Anne is acting the opposite of how she feels. Options (1), (2), (3), and (5) are incorrect because they do not deal with acting the opposite of how one feels.

14. **(2) projection** (Application) Vivian is accusing her husband of her own bad habit. Options (1), (3), (4), and (5) do not deal with believing someone else has your behavior.

15. **(1) denial** (Application) Lester is refusing to believe that something painful has happened. Options (2), (3), (4), and (5) do not deal with denying reality.

16. **(3) sex roles—the beliefs, attitudes, and behaviors expected of a man or a woman** (Application) The joke concerns whether it is appropriate for a man to do housework. The subject of the cartoon is sex roles, ruling out options (1), (2), (4), and (5).

17. **(3) Women quit work to get married.** (Evaluation) This is correct based on the caption. The role reversal here works so that the woman asks the man the question women have often been asked: "Are you going to quit to get married?" The argument often used by corporations is not that men quit work to get married but that women quit work to get

married; therefore, option (1) is incorrect. Option (2) is incorrect because there is no clear indication that a teenager is involved. Options (4) and (5) are incorrect because there is no reference in the caption to having children.

18. **(3) minorities were not reliable employees** (Evaluation) Because company executives routinely refused to hire qualified minorities, the government took steps to increase the number of minorities hired. Therefore, options (1) and (2) are incorrect. Option (4) is the opposite of what most employers believed. There is no support for option (5).

19. **(4) cognitive consonance** (Analysis) The smoker finds information that agrees with her prior learning and accepts that information. Therefore, options (1), (2), (3), and (5) are incorrect.

20. **(5) reinforcement** (Application) The teacher is using rewards to encourage positive behavior. Therefore, options (1), (2), (3), and (4) are incorrect.

21. **(3) There is a link between hard-drug use and criminal behavior.** (Evaluation) From the statistics in the graph, it does appear that many people who commit crimes are drug users. Option (1) is contradicted by the data. There are not enough data to support options (2), (4), or (5).

22. **(2) Most drug addicts commit crimes.** (Analysis) The graph shows only 11 cities in the entire United States. It does show that, in these cities, from 35% to 80% of the people arrested tested positive for drugs. But those arrested would be a very small percentage of total drug users. There is not enough evidence in the graph to either prove or disprove the statement that most drug addicts commit crimes. It is an opinion, whereas options (1), (3), (4), and (5) are facts illustrated in the graph.

GED Review: Behavioral Science (page 310)

1. **(2) white women** (Comprehension) According to the graph, white women earn a mean of about $30,000. All the other groups earn more in manufacturing. Options (1), (3), and (4) are contradicted by the graph. Option (5) is incorrect because the graph does not show figures for Hispanic workers.

2. **(3) more women and minorities in middle-management jobs** (Analysis) Progress has been made through affirmative action, but not beyond the middle-management level. Option (1) is incorrect because there are very few black

men in top-management jobs. Option (2) has not happened in significant numbers and is not supported by the information. Option (4) is still true, but it is not a result of affirmative action. Option (5) is not true according to the graph.

3. **(4) Black men make more than black women** (Evaluation) This is the only generalization supported by the graph. Option (1) is incorrect because black women make less than white women in business services and retail. Option (2) is incorrect because black men make more than white women in manufacturing and business services. Option (3) is incorrect because white women make more than black men in the retail industry. Option (5) is incorrect because in the retail and business services industries white men make about one-third more than white women.

4. **(1) minorities and women are a threat to their power** (Evaluation) According to the commission, the failure of minorities and women to break through the glass ceiling is a result of prejudice and stereotypical attitudes on the part of white men. Options (2) and (3) are excuses given for failing to promote women and minorities. Options (4) and (5) are stereotypes, not fears.

5. **(5) courtship behavior** (Application) Courting is something we do based on how we think, not a material item. Options (1), (2), (3), and (4) all refer to material things.

6. **(1) adobe ovens for baking** (Application) Ovens are material objects that are used to produce things. Options (2), (3), and (4) are aspects of nonmaterial culture. Option (5) is something we experience.

7. **(3) The two parts of a culture are material and nonmaterial.** (Comprehension) Option (3) sums up the entire paragraph. Options (1), (2), (4), and (5) are details that support the main idea.

8. **(2) Powdermaker made a fascinating study.** (Analysis) Option (2) is correct because fascinating is an opinion, not a fact; you cannot prove that something is fascinating. Options (1), (3), (4), and (5) are all facts mentioned in the paragraph.

9. **(3) It is difficult to make an objective study of one's own culture.** (Evaluation) Such an argument is based on the idea that an observer would not always see important cultural patterns because she was too familiar with them. Option (1) is an either-or error

that ignores other possibilities. That is, she could make errors other than these, or she could succeed. Option (2) is based on a stereotype. Option (4) is a red herring that leads to an unrelated idea; her concern was with the social structure of Hollywood, not with audience interest. Option (5) is an unfounded hasty generalization.

10. **(2) many social contacts** (Comprehension) People who were not depressed had in common a rich social life. This could include friends, relatives, or religious groups. Options (1), (3), (4), and (5) are all factors associated with a tendency to depression.

GED Cumulative Review: Social Studies (page 312)

1. **(5) were opposed to legal slavery in the territories** (Analysis) The demand map supports the Republican position. Option (1) is the opposite of what is shown. Since the end date of both maps is the same, option (2) is incorrect. There is no evidence of where Republicans lived or if any of them owned slaves, so options (3) and (4) are incorrect.

2. **(4) Texas** (Comprehension) Texas is the only listed state marked as a slave state. Options (1), (2), and (3) are all free states. Option (5) is incorrect because Wyoming was not a state at the time.

3. **(1) Any new state could have slaves.** (Application) Since all the territories were open to slavery under the Dred Scott decision, any section that wanted to be a state could come in as a slave state. Option (2) would not be true even under the Republican demand because the Oklahoma territory was open to slavery. Option (3) would have been true only under the Republican demand. There is no support in either map for options (4) and (5).

4. **(3) two children, each claiming all the toys** (Application) Each side wanted all the territories to follow its principles. Option (1) is incorrect because neither group demands that other people follow its ways. Option (2) is incorrect because slavery was a moral issue as well as a financial issue. Options (4) and (5) are incorrect because the countries in each option were on the same side.

5. **(4) In the New England colonies, people ran their own towns through meetings in which they discussed and voted on issues.** (Application) Democracy is based on involvement of the people. Options (1), (2), (3), and (5) are not concerned with the citizens' involvement in government.

6. **(1) self-governing, proprietary, royal** (Application) A self-governing colony is the most democratic, and one that is ruled mainly by a king is the least democratic. Options (2), (3), (4), and (5) are not correct according to the definitions.

7. **(5) traveled largely by water** (Comprehension) The paragraph indicates the lakes and rivers used by the French fur traders to get to the interior of the continent. Options (1), (2), (3), and (4) are incorrect because the information in the paragraph does not support them.

8. **(2) transportation** (Application) You can infer this because the only use mentioned in the paragraph is that of travel. Options (1), (3), and (5) are incorrect because they are not the most important use of the river. Option (4) is incorrect because there was no hydroelectric power at that time.

9. **(3) Europe** (Comprehension) The map shows arrows leading away from Europe, not toward Europe. Options (1), (2), (4), and (5) are incorrect because all these areas have arrows indicating that immigrants are moving there.

10. **(2) west** (Comprehension) By looking at the compass rose and the arrows in the United States, you can see the movement is westward. Options (1), (3), (4), and (5) are therefore incorrect.

11. **(1) Worldwide Movement of People** (Comprehension) This is a map showing people moving all over the world. Options (2) and (4) are incorrect because the map does not indicate the 1800s or the future. Option (3) is incorrect because the map shows places other than the United States. Option (5) is incorrect because the map shows more than European settlement patterns.

12. **(3) immigration affects all continents** (Analysis) All the continents have arrows indicating that people have moved to or from them. Options (1) and (2) are incorrect because the map does not show changing patterns over time. Option (4) is incorrect because the map does not show numbers of people. Option (5) is incorrect because the map does not say why people move.

13. **(3) 14 percent** (Comprehension) This figure is found in the last sentence of the second paragraph. The other options refer to other poverty and wealth statistics in the paragraphs.

14. **(2) There is a lack of appropriate schooling.** (Analysis) This is the best option, based on the last sentence in the first paragraph. Options (1) and (3) are not stated or implied. Options (4) and (5) relate to cost rather than distribution.

15. **(1) increased inequality of income** (Analysis) If the poor can afford even less than before, they are suffering from an even greater burden than before. Option (2) is the opposite of what is suggested. Options (3) and (4) are not related to the increase in prices. Option (5) is not a clear result from the increase in prices.

16. **(1) a public-interest group and a toy manufacturer** (Application) This answer follows from information in the paragraphs that regulatory commissions work for the general welfare of the consumer, represented by the public-interest group, when the consumer is being threatened by the manufacturer. Such a dispute might result from what parents believed to be a defective or hazardous toy. The disputes suggested in options (2), (3), (4), and (5) would be handled by other people, agencies, or a union.

17. **(2) act only for the public good** (Analysis) Political independence is believed to free the committee members to act in the public interest, not for private parties or political gain. There is no support for option (1). Options (3), (4), and (5) are all opposite to what is suggested.

18. **(5) lobbyists** (Comprehension) The lobbyist is telling the congressman what to say. Options (1) and (2) are incorrect because the member of Congress is wearing a gray suit. Options (3) and (4) have nothing to do with the cartoon.

19. **(1) Members of Congress present themselves as independent even though they follow the advice of special-interest groups.** (Analysis) The cartoon shows that the congressman can't even declare independence without help. Options (2), (3), and (5) are all facts. Option (4) is not supported by the cartoon.

20. **(3) offer technical assistance in food distribution** (Application) This would be the best way to get food to the people who need it. Option (1) would add to the problem. Option (2) would be of only minor help. Option (4) would not guarantee that the money went for food. Option (5) would defeat the purpose of the organization.

21. **(1) disapproval of the Soviet action** (Analysis) Refusal to participate in a friendly competition would be a sign of disapproval. Therefore, option (4) is incorrect. Options (2), (3), and (5) would not be the causes of such an act.

22. **(4) geographical features** (Comprehension) Examples are Plateau and Plains. Another naming technique is directional. Options (1), (2), (3), and (5) have no support.

23. **(1) Native Americans had many distinct societies.** (Analysis) A cultural area map must be based on clearly functioning social groups. There is no evidence of the opinion in option (2). There is no information about government given on the map, so option (3) is incorrect. No support is given for the opinions in options (4) and (5).

Unit 5: Science
Biology
Lesson 1: The Biology of Cells
GED Exercise: The Biology of Cells (page 321)

1. **(2) Most cells have things in common and have a similar structure.** (Comprehension) This is a statement of the main idea of the paragraph. Options (1) and (3) are true but do not state the main idea. Options (4) and (5) name structures that most cells have in common.

2. **(1) All cells grow, reproduce, and die.** (Comprehension) Option (1) gives details that all cells have in common. Option (2) is incorrect because it is the main idea, not a detail. Option (3) refers only to some cells. Options (4) and (5) are structures that cells have in common, so each only partly supports the main idea.

3. **(3) Most cells are divided into two basic parts.** (Comprehension) Option (3) is the main idea of the paragraph. Although options (1), (2), (4), and (5) are all true, they give specific information about option (3) and thus are supporting details.

4. **(3) The nucleus contains a nucleolus, chromatin, and a nuclear membrane.** (Comprehension) Option (3), which simply names the parts of the nucleus, is the main idea. Note that this is an implicit main idea; the paragraph does not contain a topic sentence. Options (1), (2), (4), and (5) provide details about the nucleus and its parts.

5. **(1) Cytoplasm contains all the structures inside the cell membrane except the nucleus.** (Comprehension) Option (1) states the main idea of the paragraph. It is about cytoplasm and the structures in it. Options (2), (3), and (4) are incorrect because they give specific information about the parts of the cytoplasm. Option (5) states the opposite of the main idea.

6. **(5) The cytoplasm contains mitochondria, the ER, ribosomes, and vacuoles.** (Comprehension) In naming several parts of the cytoplasm, option (5) supports the main idea, that the cytoplasm contains all the cell structures except the nucleus. Option (1) is a definition of organelles. Options (2), (3), and (4) are true, but they are specific details about various parts of the cytoplasm.

7. **(3) metaphase** (Comprehension) Spindle fibers first appear in the diagram representing metaphase. During interphase, option (1), the spindles have not yet appeared. In prophase, option (2), the spindles are forming. During the last two phases, options (4) and (5), the spindles are already contracting and disappearing.

8. **(5) spindle fibers** (Comprehension) By examining the diagram, you can see that the spindle fibers are the only structures attached to the chromosomes. Therefore, they must be pulling the chromosomes apart. Option (1) remains in one place and does not change its appearance. Option (2) has no way to pull the chromosomes apart. Options (3) and (4) are not seen during anaphase.

9. **(1) interphase** (Comprehension) According to the passage, the hereditary material that makes up the chromosomes is duplicated during the first phase, or interphase. The already duplicated chromosomes are present during each of the other phases, options (2), (3), (4), and (5).

10. **(2) Mitosis is the process by which cells divide.** (Comprehension) The paragraph describes the process of mitosis, which is mentioned only in option (2). Options (1), (3), (4), and (5) are all true, but they describe only specific aspects of mitosis.

11. **(1) guide the chromosomes** (Comprehension) By examining the diagram and reading the passage, you can see that the spindle fibers guide the chromosomes toward the opposite sides of the cell. They could not produce the nucleus, option (2), or form the nuclear membrane, option (3), since these structures reappear in the daughter cells after the spindle fibers have disappeared. The hereditary material, option (4), has already become chromosomes. There is no cell plate, option (5), mentioned in the passage.

12. **(4) 46** (Comprehension) According to the passage, each daughter cell will have the same number of chromosomes as the parent cell, 46 chromosomes. Options (1), (2), (3), and (5) are incorrect because they are numbers other than 46.

13. **(2) 23** (Application) According to the passage, a gamete has half the number of chromosomes found in a parent cell. Since the cells have 46 chromosomes, the gametes have half that number, or 23. Options (1), (3), (4), and (5) are incorrect because they are numbers other than 23.

14. **(1) half the number** (Comprehension) The number of chromosomes resulting from meiosis is half that of the parent cell. Options (2), (3), (4), and (5) are incorrect because they are values other than half.

15. **(3) sexual reproduction** (Comprehension) During sexual reproduction two gametes combine to form a zygote. Options (1) and (2) are incorrect because both are types of cell division that do not produce a zygote. Option (4) is incorrect because a zygote forms during the union, not division, of cells. During gamete production a cell with 23 chromosomes is formed, so option (5) is incorrect.

16. **(3) One chromosome pair did not separate properly during meiosis.** (Application) If one pair of chromosomes fails to separate during meiosis, one gamete will have an extra chromosome and one will be missing a chromosome. If the gamete with the extra chromosome combines with a normal human gamete, the zygote will have 47—not 46—chromosomes. Option (1) is incorrect because meiosis moves chromosomes to new cells, but no hereditary material is produced. Option (2) is incorrect because sexual reproduction does not destroy hereditary material. While option (4) is a true statement, it does not explain what caused this condition. If three gametes combined, option (5), the result would be 69 chromosomes, not 47.

17. **(3) 50 percent** (Comprehension) If one chromosome from each pair comes from each parent, then each parent contributes 50 percent of an individual's chromosomes.

Lesson 2: Photosynthesis

GED Exercise: Photosynthesis (page 325)

1. **(3) hydrogen** (Comprehension) The fifth paragraph states that hydrogen produced in the light reactions combines with carbon to form sugar in the dark reactions. Options (1), (2), (4), and (5) are incorrect because they are substances other than hydrogen.

2. **(1) sugar** (Comprehension) The first paragraph states that sugar is used as food and to build other substances such as starches and proteins that the plant needs. The other products of photosynthesis are waste materials, options (2) and (3). Option (4), carbon dioxide, is not a product of photosynthesis. Neither is chlorophyll, option (5).

3. **(1) Water plus carbon dioxide, in the presence of light and chlorophyll, yields sugar, oxygen, and water.** (Comprehension) This is the only statement that includes all the reacting substances and products shown in the equation. Option (2) is incorrect because it leaves out light. Option (3) is incorrect because hydrogen is not a product of photosynthesis. Option (4) is incorrect because oxygen is not used in photosynthesis; it is a product of photosynthesis. Option (5) is incorrect because it leaves out chlorophyll.

4. **(2) Plants make their own food through photosynthesis.** (Comprehension) The passage describes how photosynthesis works. Although options (1), (3), (4), and (5) are true statements, they are not the main idea of the passage. They are all supporting details.

5. **(5) The light reactions take place in sunlight.** (Comprehension) This statement explains why the light reactions are called light reactions. Options (1), (2), (3), and (4) are all true, but they do not support the statement in the question.

6. **(4) The light reactions make up the first phase of photosynthesis.** (Comprehension) This restates the topic sentence of the fourth paragraph, the sentence that gives the general idea of the paragraph. Options (1), (2), (3), and (5) are supporting details that explain the first phase of photosynthesis.

Lesson 3: Evolution

GED Exercise: Evolution (page 327)

1. **(3) They are positioned side by side below the humerus.** (Comprehension) The diagram shows that in all four animals the radius and ulna are next to each other just below the humerus. They are not part of the fingers, option (1), or the feet, option (2). Option (4) is incorrect because it lists homologous structures in different organisms. Option (5) is incorrect because the diagram does not show the bones of embryos.

2. **(2) Different types of organisms have homologous structures.** (Analysis) This fact is one piece of evidence that supports the theory of evolution. Option (1) may be true, but it does not offer support for the theory of evolution. Option (3) is not true; organisms have evolved gradually over time. Option (4) is incorrect because the passage states that fish, bird, and human embryos have gill slits and tail buds, but it does not say all embryos have these structures. Option (5) is not true.

3. **(5) their evolution in different environments** (Analysis) Differences in structure between whales and birds are the result of one species evolving in the ocean and the other evolving in the air. Options (1) and (2) are incorrect because homologous structures and similarity between embryos are a result of evolution, not a cause. Option (3) is true but does not explain why whales and birds developed differently. According to the passage, option (4) is not true, so it could not explain why whales and birds are different.

4. **(1) Human ancestors had tails.** (Analysis) The presence of a tail bud indicates that at one time the ancestors of humans had tails. Options (2), (4), and (5) are true, but they are incorrect because they do not explain why human embryos have tail buds. Option (3) may be true of some organisms, but not humans, since humans have no tails.

5. **(4) Homologous structures and similarity among embryos are evidence supporting the theory of evolution.** (Comprehension) The passage is about facts that support the idea that organisms have developed over time from a common ancestor. Options (1) and (2) are each only partly correct, since they mention only one of the sources of evidence. Options (3) and (5) are true, but they are supporting details, not the main idea.

6. **(1) Plants and animals will continue to evolve.** (Analysis) Evolution is an ongoing process; it will not stop with today's organisms. Options (2), (3), and (5) are specific events that are unlikely and cannot be predicted based on the passage. Option (4) is not true; both plants and animals will continue to change.

Lesson 4: Plant Growth

GED Exercise: Plant Growth (page 329)

1. **(1) Growth of stems does not take place between buds.** (Comprehension) The passage states that growth takes place at the buds; it implies that growth does not take place between buds. Option (2) is incorrect; the passage says nothing about growth of leaves. Option (3) is not true; meristem cells are delicate, so plants form root caps to protect them. Option (4) is not true, the passage states that woody plants have cambium. Option (5) is not true; the passage states that cambium is present in stems, branches, and roots.

2. **(2) meristem cells become specialized as they develop** (Comprehension) Meristems develop into all three structures, so they must take on the characteristics of each during growth. Option (1) is contradicted by the passage. Options (3) and (4) are not true. Option (5) is not true of woody stems.

3. **(1) plant would stop getting taller** (Analysis) Since growth from the top bud is upward growth, the effect of cutting off the top bud would be to stop upward growth, at least for a while. Cutting off the top bud would not have the effects listed in options (2), (3), (4), and (5). None of these options is stated or implied in the passage.

4. **(2) Growth of seed plants takes place in special areas called meristems.** (Comprehension) This is the general topic, or main idea, of the passage. Options (1), (3), and (4) are details in the passage. Option (5) is incorrect because animals are not mentioned in the passage.

5. **(2) the bottom branch of a tree will be the same height above the ground as when it first formed** (Comprehension) Since upward growth of a seed plant is from the top of the stem only, once branches grow along the stem, they will stay at the same height above the ground. Option (1) is not true since the tree grows from the top of the stem. Option (3) is not true since there is no growth between buds. Options (4) and (5) are not true since after thirty years the cambium cells will have added to the thickness of the trunk.

6. **(5) cambium** (Comprehension) The passage states that cambium is found in woody plants and implies that it is not found in most nonwoody plants. Options (1) and (4) are incorrect because these structures do not contain meristem cells. Options (2) and (3) are incorrect because these structures are found in both woody and nonwoody plants.

7. **(1) It would stop growing.** (Analysis) Since meristem cells form the growth regions of a plant, their destruction would stop all growth. Options (2), (3), (4), and (5) all could not happen without meristem cells.

8. **(2) at the ends of stems and roots** (Analysis) The word apical describes the tip, or end, of stems and roots. Option (1) is incorrect because there is no meristem between buds. Options (3) and (4) refer to meristem cells that are not at the tips of structures. Option (5) is incorrect because there is no meristem in leaves.

Lesson 5: The Human Digestive System

GED Exercise: The Human Digestive System (page 331)

1. **(2) to break down food into substances the body can absorb and to get rid of wastes** (Analysis) Although the passage discusses how the digestive system works, the general purpose is never stated. The purpose of the digestive system is an unstated assumption. Option (1) is true but is only part of the digestive system's function. Option (3) is not true. Option (4) is one function of the stomach. Option (5) is the function of the respiratory system, not the digestive system.

2. **(5) by chewing** (Analysis) Although the passage does not state this, we can assume that chewing is the process by which food is ground up and mixed with saliva. Since saliva is present in the mouth, options (1) and (2) are incorrect. Swallowing, option (3), is the way food is passed through the esophagus and into the stomach. Option (4) has nothing to do with grinding up food.

3. **(3) to absorb water** (Comprehension) In the paragraph about the large intestine, it is stated that one of the main functions of the large intestine is to absorb water. Options (1), (2), (4), and (5) are functions of other parts of the digestive system.

4. **(4) small intestine** (Comprehension) The passage states that the alimentary canal is about 30 feet long. Since the small intestine is about 23 feet long, it makes up most of the length of the alimentary canal. If you look at the diagram, you will see that the other organs are much shorter than the small intestine. Options (1), (2), (3), and (5) are incorrect because they are body parts other than the small intestine.

5. **(5) rest of the body** (Comprehension) Since nutrients pass into the blood and the blood travels throughout the body, the nutrients are carried throughout the body. Options (1), (2), (3), and (4) are therefore only partly correct.

6. **(4) Fats would not be digested properly.** (Analysis) The function of bile is to break down fats into small droplets. This process would be disrupted if anything were wrong with the liver. Options (1), (2), (3), and (5) are not functions of the liver.

7. **(2) Food is not ground up enough and so starches are not properly processed.** (Analysis) The mouth's function is to grind and moisten the food and to begin the breakdown of starch. If food does not spend enough time in the mouth, the result is that it is not properly processed. Option (1) is the opposite of what happens when you swallow too quickly. Option (3) is true whether or not food is chewed properly. Options (4) and (5) are not part of the action of the mouth.

8. **(5) rectum** (Comprehension) The diagram shows that the large intestine empties into the rectum, which is the passage out of the body. Options (1), (2), (3), and (4) are incorrect because they are internal organs that are not close to a body opening.

Lesson 6: Disease
GED Exercise: Disease (page 333)

1. **(1) Diseases are caused by evil spirits.** (Analysis) The relationship between microorganisms and disease had not yet been proved, so all views about disease were opinions. Options (2) and (3) are incorrect because they were discovered during Pasteur's time. Options (4) and (5) are incorrect because they were not known until after Pasteur's time.

2. **(4) Koch's experiments with anthrax bacteria** (Analysis) Koch's experiments proved that a specific kind of bacteria was the cause of anthrax. This fact supported Pasteur's idea. Option (1) has nothing to do with the cause of disease. Options (2) and (5) happened before Pasteur's time. Option (3), the yeast experiments, did not help prove the cause of disease.

3. **(5) The spread of anthrax can be stopped by stopping the spread of anthrax bacteria.** (Comprehension) Since a specific organism causes the disease in animals, if you can prevent the organism from getting into another animal, you can stop the spread of the

disease. Option (1) is not true; some diseases such as cancer are not caused by microorganisms. Options (2) and (3) are incorrect because fermentation is not a disease. Option (4) is true but does not follow from Koch's discovery of the anthrax bacteria, since anthrax is contagious.

4. **(4) the idea that microorganisms cause disease** (Comprehension) This idea forms the basis of all later discoveries about infectious diseases. Options (1), (3), and (5) are not contributions of Pasteur. Option (2) is one of Pasteur's contributions, but it is not directly related to the study of disease.

5. **(3) The cause of the disease would not be proved.** (Analysis) Since the fourth step of Koch's postulates involves confirming that the pathogens are indeed present in the diseased animal, leaving out this step means you cannot prove that the disease was caused by the pathogens. Option (1) is not true. Options (2) and (5) would be possible even without step 4 of the postulates. Option (4) is not true.

6. **(2) He found many of the bacteria in animals that had died of anthrax.** (Comprehension) Finding bacteria while examining the organs of the dead animals is what led Koch to think that the bacteria might be the cause of anthrax. Options (1), (4), and (5) are true but are not reasons for thinking anthrax is caused by a specific microorganism. Option (3) is incorrect because fermentation is not related to anthrax.

7. **(3) a group of microorganisms grown in a sterile food medium** (Comprehension) According to the passage, a culture is organisms grown in the laboratory on a sterile food medium. Options (1), (2), (4), and (5) are incorrect, since they do not describe the condition of growth in a sterile food medium.

Lesson 7: Mendel and Genetics
GED Exercise: Mendel and Genetics (page 335)

1. **(1) He started with purebred plants.** (Evaluation) By starting the experiment with plants that always produced the same characteristics, Mendel made sure that the results of cross-breeding would be reliable. If he had started with hybrid plants, option (2), he would not have been sure why he was getting a mix of traits. If he had selected plants with several contrasting traits, option (3), there would have been so many combinations of characteristics in the offspring that it would have been difficult to

keep track of what was going on. Using only one type of plant, options (4) and (5), would have meant that the experiment would not show the results of breeding plants with contrasting traits.

2. **(1) The plants are all hybrids.** (Evaluation) Since the offspring receive a different trait from each parent, they will all be hybrids. Option (2) is not correct because contrasting traits are being bred. Option (3) is not correct because all the offspring had inflated pods, making that the dominant trait. Option (4) is not true; the term hybrid trait is unclear in meaning. Option (5) is not correct because they did not show up in the F_1 generation, so wrinkled pods must be a recessive trait.

3. **(3) a trait that will appear in some purebred and all hybrid offspring** (Analysis) Since a dominant trait is more powerful than a recessive trait, it will appear in all hybrids. It will also appear when two dominant traits are combined in a purebred offspring. Option (1) is incorrect because it leaves out hybrid offspring. Option (2) is incorrect because it leaves out some purebred offspring. Option (4) is incorrect because some offspring will not inherit the dominant trait. Option (5) is incorrect because the dominant trait will always be more powerful when combined with a recessive trait.

4. **(2) Some of the F_2 generation plants showed the recessive trait.** (Evaluation) Although the recessive trait was hidden in their F_1 parents, some of the F_2 plants received two recessive traits from the parents and showed the recessive characteristic. This proved that the recessive trait was carried by the hybrid F_1 parents even though it did not show. Option (1) does not provide evidence that the recessive trait is present. Option (3) is incorrect because offspring with a dominant trait do not show that the recessive trait was present in the parents. Option (4) is not true; only one in four offspring showed the recessive trait. Option (5) is not true since no F_1 plants showed the recessive traits.

5. **(2) They have characteristics that are easy to identify.** (Comprehension) This is stated in the second paragraph of the passage. Options (1), (3), and (4) are not true. Option (5) is true but was not the reason he selected pea plants.

6. **(2) 1 out of 4** (Comprehension) As the diagram shows, when two hybrids are bred, one out of four offspring will show the recessive trait. The other three will inherit the dominant trait and will show the dominant trait. Options (1), (3), (4), and (5) are incorrect because they are not equal to a chance of 1 out of 4.

Lesson 8: Ecosystems
GED Exercise: Ecosystems (page 337)

1. **(2) Matter in an ecosystem is being constantly recycled.** (Analysis) This is the generalization that is supported by the other statements, each of which describes one step in a food chain.

2. **(3) Secondary consumers would have nothing to eat.** (Analysis) This is the immediate effect of the loss of primary consumers, because they are the food for secondary consumers. Option (1) is incorrect; plants would continue to function. Options (2) and (4) are incorrect because the activities of decomposers and tertiary consumers would not be affected immediately. Option (5) is not true; the sun would continue to provide energy.

3. **(3) primary and secondary consumers** (Comprehension) In their role as berry- and seed-eaters, birds are primary consumers (eating plants). In their role as insect-eaters, the birds are secondary consumers (eating animals). Option (1) refers to plants. Options (2) and (4) are only partly correct. Option (5) refers to plants and animals.

4. **(3) secondary consumer** (Comprehension) The crop pests, which feed on plants, are primary consumers. Anything that eats a primary consumer (the crop pest) is a secondary consumer.

5. **(1) All living things are part of an ecosystem.** (Analysis) Although the passage describes what an ecosystem is, it never explicitly states that all living things are part of an ecosystem. It is assumed that the reader understands this. Option (2) is incorrect because humans are part of many ecosystems. Options (3), (4), and (5) are not unstated assumptions because they are clearly stated in the passage or illustration.

6. **(2) to break down dead plants and animals into substances plants can use** (Comprehension) This is stated in the third paragraph of the passage. Option (1) is the role of producers. Option (3) is the role of primary consumers. Option (4) is the role of secondary consumers. Option (5) is the role of the sun.

7. **(1) hawks** (Comprehension) Of the listed organisms, all are primary consumers except

the hawk, which is a secondary consumer. Since secondary consumers are farther up the food chain, they are higher-level consumers than the others.

GED Review: Biology (page 338)

1. **(5) a variety of crop that is not affected by particular chemical plant killers** (Comprehension) This is explained in the first paragraph of the passage. As the passage is about applying herbicides to crops, option (1) is incorrect. No such crop is mentioned. Options (2), (3), and (4) describe crops that are resistant to other types of agricultural problems.

2. **(3) result in herbicides remaining on the crops after harvest** (Analysis) Herbicides are chemicals that remain in the environment until they break down; therefore they also remain on the plants. Options (1), (2), and (4) are incorrect because the crops are herbicide-resistant and would not be affected by the chemical. Option (5) is incorrect because herbicides kill plants, not insects.

3. **(4) Improved cultivation techniques are preferable to herbicides in controlling weeds.** (Analysis) This statement reflects the opinions of some environmental groups. Not everyone shares this point of view. Options (1), (2), (3), and (5) are statements of fact presented in the passage.

4. **(3) Weeds are a problem in large farming areas.** (Analysis) The passage gives both pro-herbicide and anti-herbicide points of view. Both sides agree that weeds must be controlled; they differ as to how. Option (1) is incorrect because the author presents the environmentalists' view that herbicides are not safe. Option (2) is incorrect because the passage indicates some practices that do not require the use of herbicides to grow crops. Options (4) and (5) are not true.

5. **(3) C only** (Analysis) Of the choices listed, Statement C uses only chemicals that are not found in nature. All other options include a method that manipulates nature but does not add an unnatural substance (Statements B and C).

6. **(4) withstanding the effect of** (Comprehension) An herbicide-resistant crop can withstand the killing effects of the herbicide and live. Option (1), (2), and (3) are meanings for resistant when used in other contents. Option (5) is an incorrect meaning.

7. **(5) sun, grass, rabbit, fox** (Comprehension) The passage describes and the diagram shows the original source of energy as the sun and the final consumer as the fox. Options (1) and (3) are incorrect because they leave out the sun. Options (2) and (4) are incorrect because they list the energy transfer in the wrong order.

8. **(4) appear at the top of the diagram** (Analysis) A predator of the fox would appear above the fox in the diagram. Therefore, option (2) describes the incorrect position. Options (1), (3), and (5) are incorrect because the new predator would be a tertiary (third-order) consumer.

9. **(4) The fox population would decrease.** (Analysis) If the rabbit population were destroyed, the foxes would lose their primary source of energy and likely begin to die. Option (1) is incorrect since the food chain would need a new primary consumer, not a producer, to replace the rabbits. Option (2) is incorrect because foxes are meat eaters. Option (3) is the opposite of how grass is likely to be affected. Option (5) is not true because the food chain would be affected.

10. **(2) An organism that eats only plants cannot be a secondary consumer.** (Evaluation) Since producers (or plants) are always on the bottom level of the food chain, animals that only eat plants are always primary consumers. Option (1) is incorrect since food chains always begin with producers, which don't feed on other organisms. Option (3) is incorrect because producers make their own food. Options (4) and (5) are incorrect because some consumers eat only animals, and some consumers eat both plants and animals.

Earth Science
Lesson 9: The Planet Earth
GED Exercise: The Planet Earth (page 341)

1. **(2) 40 kilometers** (Comprehension) The passage states that the thickness of the crust is about 40 kilometers under the continents. Africa is a continent, so the crust beneath it is about 40 kilometers thick.

2. **(4) changing behavior of seismic waves as they reach each layer of Earth's interior** (Comprehension) The passage indicates that the study of seismic waves led to the conclusion that Earth has four layers. If the seismic waves did not change, option (3), scientists would have concluded that Earth's interior was

basically the same all the way to the core. Options (1), (2), and (5) are incorrect; they are evidence that requires direct observation, which is impossible in Earth's interior.

3. **(1) crust** (Comprehension) Since the crust includes Earth's surface, it follows that it has been explored by people. The other parts of Earth's interior are out of reach because of high temperature and pressure. Option (5), all four layers, is incorrect because only option (1), the crust, has been explored by humans.

4. **(3) iron in the inner and outer cores** (Analysis) Since magnets are often made of iron, it follows that the iron in Earth's core would exert magnetic force. The other options have nothing to do with magnetic substances.

5. **(1) vibrations produced by earthquakes** (Comprehension) The passage clearly states that seismic waves are vibrations produced by earthquakes. The other options do not correctly define or describe seismic waves.

6. **(1) It is reasonable to draw scientific conclusions from indirect evidence.** (Analysis) The structure of Earth's interior was figured out by studying the indirect evidence of seismic waves. The author does not indicate that conclusions about Earth's interior are wrong but rather accepts them as reasonable. Option (2) is incorrect; direct evidence is better than indirect evidence. Option (3) is not likely. Option (4) is not true. Option (5) is not supported by the diagram.

7. **(3) travel through the crust and mantle and stop at the outer core** (Application) Since the secondary wave can travel only through solids, it would be stopped only when it reached the liquid (molten) outer core. Since it would be stopped, option (1) is incorrect. Option (2) is incorrect because the wave would not reach the inner core. Options (4) and (5) are incorrect because the wave would travel through both the crust and mantle, which are solid. The passage states that, although parts of the mantle flow like a liquid, it is solid rock.

8. **(3) The region was once under water.** (Comprehension) Since fossils are most likely to be formed by organisms in or near the water, the best option is (3). Options (1) and (2) have nothing to do with the location of fish. Option (4) is remotely possible, but since mountain streams are usually shallow and rocky, it is unlikely that enough soft sediment would be available to bury the organism

quickly. Option (5) does not explain how the fossils may have formed.

9. **(1) human footprints made in concrete before it hardened** (Comprehension) The best option is (1) because it describes evidence of living activity (human footprints) in a substance that hardens and becomes permanent (concrete). Options (2) and (5) are incorrect; a fly is a whole organism and a leaf is a part of an organism; they are not traces. Options (3) and (4) are incorrect; sand and snow do not hold a permanent print.

10. **(5) the bird was buried soon after dying** (Application) The passage says that many dead organisms decay or are eaten before a fossil can form and mentions quick burial as a likely means of fossil preservation. If the bird had been eaten, option (1), it could not form a complete fossil. Option (2) is incorrect because the bird could have died in any number of ways and there is no evidence to support predation. Although option (3) may be true, it is not the most likely option. Option (4) is incorrect since birds live in many different climates, and there is no evidence that this one necessarily lived in a wet climate.

11. **(4) grooves carved in rock by a glacier** (Application) The passage states that fossils are evidence or remains of living things. Since glaciers aren't living things, they can't leave behind fossils. Options (1), (2), (3), and (5) are all evidence or remains of once living things.

12. **(4) establishing animal behavior** (Comprehension) While scientists can sometimes guess about animal behavior from fossil remains, it is not a primary use and is not mentioned in the passage. All the other options are mentioned as a use of the fossil record.

13. **(3) in the ocean** (Comprehension) The first reference to living things mentions the ocean. Options (1) and (4) are incorrect because they refer to time periods, not places. Options (2) and (5) are not indicated by the time line.

14. **(2) sea-living invertebrates** (Analysis) Options (1), (3), and (4) are incorrect because the time line shows that these organisms appeared after the first fish. Option (5) is incorrect; land plants existed before the first fish, but fish would not have been able to leave the water to eat land plants.

15. **(3) fish, land plants, and dinosaurs** (Comprehension) By the Mesozoic Era, fish and land plants had already evolved.

Dinosaurs first appeared during the Mesozoic Era. Since these organisms existed, their fossils could occur in rocks of the Mesozoic Era. Option (1) is incorrect since many other organisms besides simple ocean organisms had appeared by the Mesozoic Era. Options (2), (4), and (5) are incorrect because horses, primates, and humans didn't appear until after the Mesozoic Era.

16. **(3) The Great Lakes are younger than the Rocky Mountains.** (Evaluation) The time line shows that the Rocky Mountains appeared before the Great Lakes. Option (1) is incorrect; according to the time line, human civilization arose very recently. Option (2) is incorrect; dinosaurs lived during the Mesozoic Era. Option (4) is incorrect; the time line shows that dinosaurs died out about 65 million years ago. Option (5) is incorrect; the first life forms appeared in the ocean.

17. **(3) 160 million years** (Comprehension) The time line is measured in millions of years. Dinosaurs appeared slightly less than 225 million years ago and died out about 65 million years ago. Subtracting 65 from 225 gives 160, which on the time line represents 160 million years. Options (1) and (4) are misreadings of the scale of the time line. Option (2) is incorrect because it represents time passed from the beginning of the time line to the extinction of dinosaurs. Option (5) is incorrect because it is the time from the appearance of dinosaurs to the present.

18. **(1) All organisms evolved from the first living cells.** (Analysis) While most scientists believe this and it is assumed that the reader knows this, the passage does not supply direct evidence that this is true. Options (2), (3), and (5) are shown on the time line. Option (4) can be inferred and supported by the fact that the time line ends with "present" time, under the Cenozoic Era.

Lesson 10: The Atmosphere
GED Exercise: The Atmosphere (page 345)

1. **(3) an astronaut** (Application) An astronaut travels above the ozone layer and has no natural protection against the sun's ultraviolet rays. The other options involve people whose occupations do not take them above the ozone layer.

2. **(1) troposphere** (Comprehension) Since the troposphere extends about ten miles up (52,800 feet), the top of Mt. Everest is still well below its upper limit. The other layers of the atmosphere are above the troposphere and are therefore incorrect.

3. **(2) a mountain climber** (Application) As a mountain climber goes higher, the air becomes colder and thinner. Options (1), (4), and (5) are occupations that do not require changes in altitude. Option (3) is incorrect because airline attendants work in a manmade environment, the airplane, in which temperature and air pressure are controlled.

4. **(3) More ultraviolet rays would reach Earth's surface.** (Analysis) Since the ozone layer prevents most ultraviolet rays from reaching the surface of Earth, its destruction would remove a natural barrier. Destruction of the ozone layer would not affect the breathing of oxygen in the troposphere, option (1). Option (2) describes the function of the ozone layer. Option (4) is incorrect because the ozone layer is only part of the stratosphere. Option (5) is incorrect because there would be an effect.

5. **(5) krypton** (Comprehension) The first four options are gases that make up a large portion of the atmosphere. The passage indicates that krypton is one of the gases present in small amounts.

6. **(1) Gravity holds the atmosphere in place around Earth.** (Analysis) To understand the passage one must know that the atmosphere remains around Earth because of the force of gravity. As the writer does not state or imply it, it is assumed that the reader has this knowledge. Options (2) and (3) are not true. Option (4) is stated in the passage and shown in the diagram. Option (5) is also not true; human beings have been to the moon, which is beyond the mesosphere.

7. **(3) The higher you go in the troposphere, the less oxygen is available.** (Analysis) The runner had difficulty breathing in Denver because it is much higher than Boston, and there is less oxygen. Option (1) makes no sense because neither place has tropical weather. Options (2) and (4) are true but not related to the change in altitude between Boston and Denver. Option (5) is true, but the change in temperature was not the cause of the runner's breathing problem.

8. **(3) They contain dry air.** (Comprehension) Options (1), (2), (4) and (5) are incorrect because continental air masses do not contain moist air.

9. **(1) maritime polar** (Comprehension) Options (2), (3), (4), and (5) are incorrect because,

according to this passage, continental air masses do not tend to cause precipitation. The only other type of air mass that might have caused the snowstorm would be a maritime tropical in winter.

10. **(1) Types of Air Masses** (Comprehension) The passage deals generally with the four different types of air masses. It does not mention what occurs when air masses meet, option (3). Where air masses form, option (2), and the characteristics of continental air masses, option (4), are supporting details of the passage. The passage only covers one of many topics that fall under the broad heading of Air and Weather, option (5).

11. **(3) cause weather changes in the contiguous 48 states** (Comprehension) The passage states that changes in weather are caused by air masses and that the contiguous 48 states are affected by air masses that form over northern Canada and the ocean. Option (1) is incorrect because the air mass that forms over Canada would be dry. Option (2) is incorrect because an air mass that forms near Hawaii would be moist. Option (4) is incorrect because an air mass over Canada would be cold. Option (5) is incorrect because the two air masses would bring different types of weather, not just cool, dry weather.

12. **(3) Air masses called tropical originate over tropical seas.** (Evaluation) Since a continental tropical air mass originates over land, all tropical air masses do not originate over tropical seas. Options (1) and (2) explain why the terms maritime and continental are used. Options (4) and (5) are accurate descriptions of air masses.

13. **(2) snowy** (Application) When two such air masses meet, precipitation is the likely result. Snow is the most likely form of precipitation in winter.

14. **(4) they affect the temperature and humidity of the air** (Analysis) It is the change in these two factors that causes the weather to be different. Option (1) is not always true; some air masses bring warm or hot air. Options (2), (3), and (5) are generally true but do not explain why the weather changes.

15. **(5) are most direct at the equator** (Evaluation) If you look at the diagram, you can see that, except at the equator, the sun's rays are spread over a wider area because of the curve in Earth's surface. Therefore, options (1), (2), (3), and (4) are incorrect.

16. **(5) a greater possibility of sunburn** (Application) The diagram shows that the sun's rays are more direct, and therefore more intense, at the equator. Option (3) is incorrect because direct sunlight at the equator produces warmer temperatures. Options (1), (2), and (4) cannot be predicted based on the diagram.

17. **(2) The sun's rays are more concentrated near the equator than near the poles.** (Analysis) This is shown in the diagram. Options (1) and (4) are incorrect because they are not shown in the diagram. Options (3) and (5) might be true, but there is no information about weather patterns in the diagram.

Lesson 11: Earth's Resources
GED Exercise: Earth's Resources (page 348)

1. **(3) There is enough oil to last 300 years.** (Analysis) Option (3) is one of two estimates given in the passage. Neither opinion can be proved. Option (1) is a fact because oil is known to be a nonrenewable resource. Options (2) and (4) are incorrect because they are facts. Both energy use and the availability of oil can be measured. Option (5) is also a fact.

2. **(4) Solar energy is a renewable resource.** (Analysis) This information is stated in the third paragraph. Option (1) is an opinion expressed by the author. No data is given to support it. Options (2) and (3) are opinions held by scientists. While citizens and energy conservation are mentioned, option (5) does not appear in the passage.

3. **(3) driving a small, fuel-efficient car** (Application) This would save gasoline, a nonrenewable resource. Option (1) would use more fuel, not less. Option (2) involves conserving water, a renewable resource. Option (4) does not make sense; in warm weather no fuel would be used to heat a home, and added sunlight would just make the building warmer. If air conditioners were in use, this would waste energy. Option (5) involves switching from one nonrenewable resource to another and thus would not help conserve a nonrenewable resource.

4. **(1) Vehicles will eventually be powered by something other than a petroleum product.** (Comprehension) The passage suggests that renewable resources will come to replace nonrenewable resources such as petroleum. Options (2) and (3) are contradicted by the passage. Option (4) makes no sense. Since the supply of oil is limited, it will eventually run out, even if people

conserve it. Option (5) is not implied by the passage, which states that at present solar energy is too expensive for widespread use.

5. **(2) The supply would be used more slowly but would eventually run out.** (Analysis) Cutting down on the use of oil will stretch the supply for a longer time, but since the supply is limited, it will eventually run out. Option (1) is the opposite of what happens when a resource is conserved. Option (3) is only partially correct. The supply would be used more slowly, but it would not last forever since it is limited. Option (4) is incorrect because the supply would last longer. Option (5) may be true, but it does not relate to the effect of conservation on supply.

6. **(5) solar energy** (Comprehension) Of the forms of energy mentioned, only solar energy is renewable because there is a constant supply of it from the sun. The other resources are all found on Earth in limited supply.

7. **(4) Conserving oil will postpone the time when supplies run out.** (Evaluation) Option (1) is not true at the present time. Option (2) is incorrect because another shortage could happen, since the supply of gasoline is limited. Option (3) is an opinion about the size of the oil supply. Option (5) may be true, but whatever new supplies are found, they will not be enough to meet long-term energy needs, since the new supplies will be limited also.

8. **(5) petroleum** (Application) Since petroleum is found in deposits on Earth, it would be of most interest to a geologist. Geologists are not primarily concerned with the study of sunlight, ocean water, food, or nuclear energy.

9. **(5) Oil Shortages—Can They Be Avoided?** (Comprehension) The main purpose of the passage is to discuss how shortages of the nonrenewable resource oil can be avoided by using alternate, renewable energy sources. Options (1), (2), (3), and (4) all address only a portion of the issue presented.

10. **(2) using windmills instead of oil-burning power plants to generate electricity** (Application) This idea would replace oil with the energy of wind, which is a renewable resource. All other options are ways to conserve energy resources, not to replace one with another.

11. **(4) Wind energy can reduce the need for fossil fuels.** (Analysis) This is the most important aspect of wind energy. Option (1) is

not true; wind energy is a renewable resource. Option (2) is contradicted by the passage. Option (3) is true, but it is not important. Option (5) may or may not be true, but it is not the most important aspect of wind energy.

12. **(2) how modern wind generators are used** (Comprehension) Modern wind generators are described, but their uses are not specified. The other options are incorrect because these topics are all covered in the passage.

13. **(4) more reliable** (Comprehension) The passage states that modern wind generators are tough and can withstand storms. Options (1) and (2) are incorrect because the passage makes no mention of size or cost. Options (3) and (5) are incorrect because both are characteristics of earlier wind generators.

14. **(2) powering factories** (Comprehension) All other options are mentioned in the passage as uses of wind power. Only option (2) is not mentioned and is therefore the correct answer.

15. **(3) a need to find more energy sources** (Comprehension) This option is clearly stated in the passage. The other options may be related to an interest in wind energy, but they are not mentioned in the passage.

16. **(3) the unreliability of wind generators** (Analysis) People stopped using wind generators because they didn't always work and thus were unreliable. The need to conserve fossil fuels, option (1), is the cause of new interest in wind generators. Options (2) and (5) did not occur until recently. Option (4) is incorrect since the passage doesn't mention that there was an increase in storms and calm days in the 1940s.

17. **(4) the burning of certain fuels** (Comprehension) The passage states that sulfur is released when coal and oil are burned. Options (1) and (2) are incorrect because oxygen and moisture cannot form acid rain without the burning of certain fuels. Options (3) and (5) are incorrect because they are not related to the formation of acid rain.

18. **(4) Acid rain is formed by sulfur oxides combining with water in the air.** (Analysis) This statement can be supported by information in the first paragraph. Options (1), (2), and (5) are incorrect because they are opinions that are not supported by the passage. Option (3) is not true.

19. **(5) lost their wildlife as result of acid rain** (Comprehension) This is stated in the second paragraph. Option (2) is incorrect

because it is a lack of plants and animals that makes the lake look blue. Options (1), (3), and (4) are incorrect because they have nothing to do with information given in the passage.

20. **(3) High levels of acidity can be harmful to living things.** (Comprehension) Since acidic rain can damage or kill plants and animals, you can logically make this assumption. Options (1) and (5) are incorrect because no mention is made of the effect of pure sulfur on living things. Option (2) is incorrect because the only mention of clear, blue water in this passage relates to a lake that has no plants and animals because it has been polluted by acid rain. Option (4) is incorrect because it is the presence of acid in rainwater that can kill plants and animals.

Lesson 12: The Changing Earth
GED Exercise: The Changing Earth (page 352)

1. **(4) wind** (Analysis) Option (1) is incorrect because it can cause all types of mass wasting. Option (2) is incorrect because it can cause soil creep. Options (3) and (5) are incorrect because they can cause landslides.

2. **(2) soil creep** (Analysis) This is stated in the last paragraph. Option (1) is incorrect because it is the result of mass wasting. Options (3), (4), and (5) are all incorrect because they cause rapid, not gradual, changes in the land.

3. **(5) gravity** (Analysis) No matter what other causes may be involved in mass wasting, gravity is always the basic cause. The other options are also causes, but they are not involved in each case of mass wasting, as gravity is.

4. **(1) the Great Plains** (Application) The Great Plains are least likely to suffer the effects of mass wasting because the landscape is generally flat. Options (2), (3), and (5) are mountainous areas where mass wasting occurs. Option (4), the Grand Canyon, would also be likely to have mass wasting because of the steep slopes.

5. **(3) heavy rain** (Comprehension) The third paragraph states that a mudflow is usually caused by heavy rain. The other options may or may not occur, but they are not the most common cause of a mudflow.

6. **(4) landslide** (Analysis) Since it is a form of rapid mass wasting involving a huge amount of rock, a landslide is likely to cause the most damage to things in its path. Options (1), (2), and (3) are smaller and slower

changes that cause less severe results. Option (5) is a landscape feature that results from mass wasting.

7. **(3) The general movement in mass wasting is from high ground to low ground.** (Evaluation) Since the force of gravity pulls things from high places to lower places, all forms of mass wasting follow this pattern. Option (1) is only partially correct; there are other causes of mass wasting. Option (2) is incorrect because rapid mass wasting takes place in mountainous areas. Option (4) is incorrect because heavy rains are not necessary for some forms of mass wasting. Option (5) is incorrect because mass wasting tends to lower mountains, not form them.

8. **(3) sediments piled at the base of a cliff** (Comprehension) According to the passage, a talus slope forms as a result of sediments piling up due to mass wasting. The other options do not describe a talus slope as defined in the passage.

9. **(3) Rapid and Slow Mass Wasting** (Comprehension) The general subject of the passage is the different types of mass wasting. Options (1) and (5) refer to supporting details in the passage. Options (2) and (4) leave out rapid mass wasting.

10. **(2) a road at the base of a steep slope** (Analysis) Damage from mass wasting is most likely to occur at the base of a steep slope where the force of gravity is acting to pull soil and rocks down. Option (1) is incorrect because gravity won't pull rocks up to the crest of a hill. Option (3) is incorrect because a volcano is more likely to be the cause of a landslide than the victim of one. Options (4) and (5) are incorrect because lakes and rivers are only at risk of damage by landslides if they are at the base of steep slopes.

11. **(1) It is not likely to occur during a drought.** (Evaluation) Since earthflows are usually caused by heavy rain, they would be unlikely to occur when there has been little rain. Options (2) and (3) are incorrect since earthflows are examples of slow mass wasting and are therefore slower than rapid mudflows. Option (4) is incorrect because earthflows can occur anywhere there is rain and a slope. Option (5) is incorrect since all mass wasting events eventually produce a talus slope, even though it may take a very long time to form.

12. **(4) rapid mass wasting** (Application) Rocks falling onto a highway are a type of a small

landslide, which is rapid mass wasting. Option (1) is incorrect because an earth flow is a type of slow mass wasting. Option (2) is incorrect because soil creep does not involve rocks and is the slowest form of mass wasting. Option (3) is incorrect because mudflow is not involved in the situation described. A rockfall does not match the description of slow mass wasting, option (5).

13. **(2) amount of energy released** (Comprehension) The last paragraph of the passage states that the more energy an earthquake releases, the stronger it is. Options (1), (3), and (4) are incorrect because, while they may be important in other ways, they do not determine the strength of an earthquake. Option (5) may be related to the strength of an earthquake, but this is not mentioned in the passage.

14. **(1) surface waves are the most destructive** (Comprehension) This is correct since it is the surface waves that cause the upheavals in the ground that are so destructive. As the passage does not describe the results of options (2), (3), (4), and (5), you can conclude that they must cause less damage than surface waves. If they caused more damage, that fact would most likely have been mentioned.

15. **(1) the formation of tall mountain peaks** (Analysis) A glacier wears away rocks, so it would not make a mountain peak taller. All other options are effects of a moving glacier.

16. **(3) The edges of the glaciers would melt, making the glaciers smaller.** (Analysis) Since glaciers form from the excess snow and ice that does not melt from season to season, it follows that unusually warm weather would cause more melting. This would make the glacier smaller. Options (1), (2), and (4) describe what happens when glaciers build up. Option (5) occurs whether or not the glacier is getting smaller.

17. **(4) the breaking up of granite by a jackhammer** (Application) Option (4) is an example of rock being broken up by humans. The passage states that erosion is the moving and wearing away of rock materials by natural causes. Therefore, options (1), (2), (3), and (5) are all examples of erosion.

18. **(5) Glacial Erosion** (Comprehension) The general topic of this passage is erosion caused by glaciers. Option (1) is too general; the passage focuses on just one aspect of what

glaciers do. Glaciers are only one of several agents of erosion, option (2). Options (3) and (4) are supporting details of the passage.

GED Review: Earth Science (page 356)

1. **(5) decreases, then increases, then decreases, then increases as altitude increases** (Comprehension) This is correct because the temperature decreases to −55°C at the border between the troposphere and stratosphere; then it increases to 0°C at the border between the stratosphere and mesosphere; then it decreases to −100°C at the top of the mesosphere; finally it reaches 2,000°C at the top of the thermosphere. The other options are incorrect because they do not describe the series of increases and decreases that occur as altitude increases.

2. **(4) It is the layer we live in.** (Evaluation) The troposphere covers Earth's surface, where we live. Options (1), (2), and (3) describe other layers of the atmosphere. Option (5) isn't true of any layer, since the thermosphere is the thickest layer.

3. **(3) They can withstand extremely high temperatures.** (Analysis) This is correct because the temperature in the upper thermosphere ranges from 600°C to 2,000°C. Option (1) is incorrect because the exosphere is much higher than 124 miles. Option (2) is incorrect because the ozone layer is located well below the thermosphere in the stratosphere and mesosphere. Option (4) is incorrect because ice clouds do not form where temperatures are very high. Option (5) is actually true in some cases, but this cannot be inferred from the information given in the diagram.

4. **(3) the mesosphere meets the thermosphere** (Comprehension) The diagram shows that at 50 miles above Earth's surface the mesosphere ends and the thermosphere begins. Options (1), (2), (4), and (5) are not true.

5. **(4) It is not wise to depend only on fossil fuels for energy.** (Analysis) Both short-term shortages, as in the 1970s, and long-term limits on fossil fuel supply indicate a need to develop alternate sources of energy. Therefore, the author does not think we should continue to depend on fossil fuels. Option (1) is incorrect because the author indicates that seawater may eventually be a useful source of energy. Option (2) is incorrect because nothing in the article indicates the author's opinions about solar energy. Option (3) is incorrect because seawater will never be used up. Option (5) is

incorrect because only air-conditioning systems near a supply of cold seawater would be candidates for seawater as a coolant.

6. **(3) a process that uses the difference in temperature between warm and cold seawater to produce electricity** (Comprehension) Ocean thermal energy conversion is defined in the second paragraph of the article. The other options do not explain this process. Options (1), (2), and (4) are not mentioned in the article. Option (5) describes a different process that uses seawater.

7. **(5) Kansas** (Application) Of the five options, only Kansas is located far from the ocean. It would thus be impractical to use seawater in such a location.

8. **(2) Until less electricity is used to pump up seawater than is produced by using seawater, the process will not be practical.** (Comprehension) At present, more electricity is used to pump seawater through the generator than the generator itself produces, causing a net loss in electricity. This obviously is not practical. Option (1) is not likely since the small-scale experiment has yet to produce electricity economically. Option (3) is not true. Option (4) is not true because the article indicates that cooling bills were cut by 75 percent, but that production of electricity was not economical. Option (5) is incorrect because there is no indication that generating electricity from seawater causes pollution.

Chemistry

Lesson 13: Matter

GED Exercise: Matter (page 359)

1. **(2) A container of ice cream is left on top of a hot stove.** (Application) This is correct because the solid ice cream would melt into a liquid. Options (1), (3), and (5) are incorrect because changing color, volume, or size does not involve a change of state. Option (4) is incorrect because no change of state occurs when the can of soup is weighed.

2. **(4) A liquid has no definite shape.** (Application) This is correct because liquid cake batter would take the shape of the mold. After the batter is baked, the solid that forms keeps that shape. Options (1), (2), (3), and (5) are not true.

3. **(1) the addition or removal of heat** (Comprehension) According to the passage, heating substances causes them to melt or

vaporize. Cooling substances causes them to freeze or condense. All of these changes are changes of state. Options (2), (3), (4), and (5) describe properties of matter, not causes of changes of state.

4. **(2) filling a balloon with helium** (Application) This is an example of one of the properties of gases—expanding to fill the available space in a container. Options (1), (3), (4), and (5) are all examples of matter changing from one state to another.

5. **(1) dew forming on the grass in early morning** (Application) Water vapor in the air condenses as the air cools during the night. Options (2) and (5) are incorrect because they involve melting. Option (3) is incorrect because it involves freezing. Option (4) is incorrect because it involves vaporization.

6. **(4) smelling pollutants released by a nearby factory** (Application) The gases spread out in all directions and can be smelled from a distance. Options (1) and (5) are incorrect because they involve liquids. Options (2) and (3) are incorrect because they involve solids.

7. **(4) no definite shape; definite volume** (Application) Liquids change shape and fill the container they are in, but their volume remains the same regardless of shape. Option (1) describes solids. Option (2) does not describe any of the types of matter. Option (3) describes gases. Option (5), none of the above, is incorrect because there is a correct description, option (4).

8. **(4) Water freezes and vaporizes at different temperatures.** (Application) Water freezes at 0°C and vaporizes at 100°C. Option (1) is incorrect because few substances are found naturally in all three states. Option (2) is incorrect because gases, not liquids, spread out to completely fill their containers. Option (3) is incorrect because some matter is solid and some matter is gas below 100°C. Option (5) is incorrect because liquids are already melted.

9. **(5) It has the same properties as all other iron atoms.** (Comprehension) Option (5) is the only option that is true. Option (1) is incorrect because the mass of a proton is about 1,800 times greater than that of an electron. Option (2) is incorrect because neutrons have no charge. Electrons, not protons, orbit the nucleus, so option (3) is incorrect. The third paragraph states that iron and copper atoms are different, so option (4) is incorrect.

10. **(1) It breaks down when heated, producing mercury and oxygen.** (Comprehension) This statement shows that substance X is not an element because elements cannot be broken down into other elements. Option (2) is incorrect because nothing stated in the passage refers to the color of an element. Options (3) and (5) are incorrect because elements can react with other substances. Option (4) is incorrect because many elements are solids.

11. **(3) The number of protons in an atom is equal to the number of electrons.** (Analysis) Option (1) is incorrect because the atom would have a positive charge. Option (2) is incorrect because the atom would have a negative charge. Options (4) and (5) are incorrect because neutrons do not have a charge, so they do not affect the charge of an atom.

12. **(4) Atom X has fewer neutrons than atom Y.** (Analysis) This is correct because neutrons and protons have about the same mass—thus extra neutrons in Y could balance the extra protons in X. Options (1) and (2) are incorrect because electrons make up so little of an atom's mass that they could not possibly balance the extra protons. Option (3) would make atom X even heavier. Option (5) is incorrect because atom X would still be heavier by five protons.

13. **(5) the solar system** (Application) The structure of the atom is most similar to the solar system, with the nucleus in the position of the sun and the electrons like the planets orbiting the sun. None of the other options involve objects in orbit around another object.

14. **(3) a hydrogen atom and a chlorine atom sharing a pair of electrons** (Application) This is correct because it describes a covalent bond between hydrogen and chlorine atoms. Option (1) is incorrect because the carbon is still just one element. Options (2), (4), and (5) are incorrect because they describe mixtures.

15. **(3) are present in very few compounds** (Comprehension) If an atom does not bond easily with other atoms, it cannot form many compounds. Option (1) is incorrect because it is clear from the information given that all atoms have electrons. Options (2) and (5) are incorrect because the passage does not indicate that one kind of bond is more likely to form than the other. Option (4) is incorrect because water molecules contain bonds.

16. **(2) Electrons are transferred from one of the atoms to another.** (Comprehension) Since ionic bonds involve the transfer of electrons, and sodium chloride contains ionic bonds, electrons must be transferred in sodium chloride. Option (1) is incorrect because sodium and chlorine are ionically bound. Option (3) is incorrect because covalent, not ionic, bonds involve the sharing of electrons. There is no evidence given to support options (4) and (5).

Lesson 14: Chemical Reactions
GED Exercise: Chemical Reactions (page 362)

1. **(4) energy needed to start a reaction** (Comprehension) According to the passage, chemical reactions are sometimes started by the application of energy from an outside source, called activation energy. The other options are therefore incorrect.

2. **(4) exploding dynamite** (Application) Exploding dynamite is a reaction in which energy is released, an exothermic reaction. Options (1), (3), and (5) are changes of state, not chemical reactions. Option (2) is an endothermic reaction since heat is absorbed when something is cooked.

3. **(1) Exothermic reactions can be more useful for the energy they release than for their products.** (Evaluation) The purpose of burning fuels, an exothermic reaction, is to release thermal energy for human use. Option (2) is incorrect because endothermic reactions absorb, not release, energy. Option (3) is not true; new bonds can form in exothermic reactions. Option (4) is a change of state, not a chemical reaction. Option (5) is not true, according to the passage.

4. **(1) During the process of rusting, small amounts of thermal energy are released.** (Analysis) Since the release of energy characterizes an exothermic reaction, rusting is an exothermic reaction. Option (2) is not related only to exothermic reactions. Options (3) and (5) are true but do not support the conclusion. Option (4) would support the conclusion that rusting is an endothermic reaction.

5. **(2) Atoms are combining to form molecules.** (Comprehension) When hydrogen atoms and oxygen atoms combine, they form molecules of water, H_2O. Option (1) is incorrect because it describes the process of breaking down a molecule. Option (3) is not true; atoms do not change into other atoms in

a chemical reaction. Option (4) is not true; they are undergoing a chemical change. Option (5) is not true; oxygen is a reactant.

6. **(3) It is activation energy.** (Application) Without energy from the sun, photosynthesis would not occur. Options (1) and (2) are incorrect because sunlight is not among the reactants and products described in the item. There is no information given to support options (4) and (5), and they are not true.

7. **(3) the change of one or more substances into a new substance with different properties** (Comprehension) This matches the description of a chemical reaction at the beginning of the passage. Option (1) is incorrect because changes of state do not result in new substances; they merely change the form of a substance from gas to liquid to solid. Option (2) is also a physical rather than a chemical change. Option (4) may or may not be true of any given reaction. Option (5) is incorrect because size of a substance is not part of the definition of a chemical reaction.

8. **(2) a reaction in which thermal energy is absorbed** (Comprehension) According to the passage, the absorption of thermal energy is part of an endothermic reaction. Options (1) and (3) are incorrect because they contradict the correct definition. Options (4) and (5) are incorrect because they apply to exothermic reactions as well as endothermic reactions.

9. **(2) Hydrogen combines with oxygen to form water.** (Application) Chemical reactions involve the forming of new substances, in this case, water from hydrogen and oxygen. Options (1) and (5) involve physical, not chemical, changes. Options (3) and (4) involve changes in state for water, which are physical changes. Physical changes do not result in new substances.

10. **(2) The solubility of a gas in liquid decreases as temperature increases.** (Analysis) Options (1), (3), and (5) are true statements, but they do not explain the situation, nor are they all covered in the passage. Option (4) is incorrect because it is an untrue statement.

11. **(5) Stirring causes molecules to move and spread apart more quickly.** (Evaluation) Stirring moves molecules around, causing the rate of solution to increase. Option (1) is incorrect because stirring will not significantly affect the water temperature. Option (2) is incorrect because stirring does

not increase the amount of salt that eventually dissolves; it increases the rate at which the salt dissolves. Options (3) and (4) are incorrect because stirring does not change the amount of matter in the container.

12. **(4) the solute** (Application) Since oxygen is dissolved in water, it is a solute. The water and oxygen together are the solution, option (1). The water alone is the solvent, option (2). Option (3) is incorrect since the oxygen is a dissolved gas. Option (5) is wrong because oxygen is dissolved in the liquid water.

13. **(2) It dissolves in water to produce OH⁻ ions.** (Comprehension) This could indicate that the substance is a base. Option (1) is incorrect because acids combine with bases to produce salts. Options (3) and (5) are incorrect because these properties are true if the acid is strong. Option (4) is incorrect because all acids have a pH lower than that of water.

14. **(3) It contains a base.** (Evaluation) This is correct because bases neutralize acids. Option (1) is incorrect because a neutralization reaction produces a salt. Options (2) and (4) are incorrect because they are properties of acids. Option (5) is incorrect because how fast the antacid dissolves does not depend on its ability to neutralize acids.

15. **(4) sulfuric acid, citric acid, pure water, sodium hydroxide** (Comprehension) This is correct because these compounds have been identified as strong acid, weak acid, neutral substance, and strong base, in that order. Options (1), (2), and (3) are not in order. In option (5) the correct order is exactly reversed and reads from highest to lowest.

16. **(3) 7** (Comprehension) This is correct because both salt and water are neutral substances. Options (1) and (2) are incorrect because they are pH values of acids, and options (4) and (5) are incorrect because they are pH values of bases.

17. **(5) a salt** (Application) The passage states that the reaction between an acid and a base produces water and a salt. Options (1), (3), and (4) are incorrect because salts are neutral compounds (pH = 7), not acids. Option (2) is incorrect because a salt is not a base.

Lesson 15: Hydrocarbons
GED Exercise: Hydrocarbons (page 367)

1. **(5) H₂S** (Comprehension) This compound is not an organic compound because it does not contain carbon, and the passage explains that

organic compounds contain carbon. Options (1), (2), (3), and (4) are incorrect because they are compounds that contain carbon and thus are organic compounds.

2. **(3) CO_2** (Comprehension) This compound is not a hydrocarbon because it contains oxygen, and the passage explains that hydrocarbons contain only carbon and hydrogen. Options (1), (2), (4), and (5) are incorrect because they are compounds that contain only carbon and hydrogen.

3. **(2) They are both organic compounds and hydrocarbons.** (Evaluation) The passage describes the alkane series as the most abundant of the hydrocarbons. Since a hydrocarbon is a special kind of organic compound, the members of the alkane series must be organic compounds also. Option (1) is incorrect because members of the alkane series are organic compounds, not living things. Option (3) is incorrect because the table lists members that are gases and a solid at room temperature. Option (4) is incorrect because the table lists formulas for members having all different numbers of carbon atoms. Option (5) is incorrect because members of the alkane series are made up of only carbon and hydrogen.

4. **(2) Butane boils at a higher temperature than ethane.** (Analysis) The table lists boiling points in order from lowest to highest. The boiling point of butane (–1°C) is higher than that of ethane (–89°C). Option (1) is incorrect because heptane boils at a higher temperature than hexane. Option (3) is incorrect because melting points are not provided. Option (4) is incorrect because, for those series members listed, eicosane contains the most carbon atoms. Option (5) is incorrect because pentane contains five carbon atoms and twelve hydrogen atoms, as compared to four carbon atoms and ten hydrogen atoms for butane.

5. **(1) It is sold in canisters for use in heating.** (Evaluation) This fact is stated in the passage. Option (2) is incorrect because the table reveals that propane has the formulas C_3H_8. Option (3) is incorrect because propane contains fewer hydrogen atoms than butane. Option (4) is a fact presented in the passage about pentane, hexane, heptane, and octane, but not about propane. Option (5) is incorrect because propane has a boiling point of –42°C.

6. **(1) C_3H_8** (Application) The fuel that escapes from the container is a gas, and propane,

C_3H_8, is a gas at room temperature. Options (2), (3), (4), and (5) are incorrect because these compounds are not gases at room temperature.

7. **(1) It is a liquid at room temperature.** (Comprehension) The table lists hexane as a liquid at room temperature. Options (2) and (4) are incorrect because the formula for hexane is C_6H_{14}. Option (3) is incorrect since the boiling point of hexane is 69°C. Option (5) is incorrect since hexane contains more hydrogen atoms (14) than carbon atoms (6).

8. **(3) It is a gas at room temperature.** (Evaluation) The table lists octane as a liquid at room temperature, not a gas. Option (1) is incorrect since octane does have a boiling point of 125°C. Option (2) is incorrect since octane along with pentane, hexane, and heptane are found in the gasoline that fuels cars. Option (4) is incorrect because octane's boiling point is higher than that of pentane. Option (5) is incorrect since an octane molecule contains eight carbon atoms and a hexane molecule contains six carbon atoms.

9. **(4) They are hydrocarbons.** (Evaluation) The passage states that both alkanes and alkenes are hydrocarbon series. Option (1) is true only of alkanes. Option (2) is incorrect because alkanes and alkenes are compounds. Option (3) is incorrect because alkanes and alkenes do not contain calcium. Option (5) is incorrect because alkanes and alkenes contain covalent bonds, not ionic bonds.

10. **(5) Double bonds occur only between the carbon atoms in alkenes.** (Comprehension) The occurrence of double bonds between carbon atoms can be seen in the structural formulas in the table. Options (1), (2), and (4) are not true. Option (3) is incorrect because some alkanes and alkenes do contain the same number of carbon atoms.

11. **(2) C_4H_8** (Comprehension) The structural formula of butene indicates that it consists of four carbon atoms and eight hydrogen atoms. Options (1), (3), (4), and (5) are incorrect since they do not show the correct number of carbon and hydrogen atoms.

12. **(2) has more hydrogen atoms than propene** (Comprehension) Since the chemical formula of propene is C_3H_6, as inferred from its structural formula, propane (C_3H_8) has more hydrogen atoms than propene. Options (1), (3), and (4) are not true. Option (5) is

incorrect because temperature is not mentioned in the passage or table.

13. **(4) bonds other than single bonds** (Comprehension) The passage states that unsaturated molecules contain bonds other than single bonds and saturated molecules contain only single bonds. Option (1) is incorrect because both kinds of molecules can contain hydrogen atoms. Option (2) is only true of saturated molecules. Option (3) is not true because both kinds of molecules contain shared electrons. Option (5) is not true because a molecule cannot contain a reduction reaction, although it may be formed by one.

14. **(1) Saturated hydrocarbons can be produced from unsaturated hydrocarbons through addition reactions.** (Evaluation) The chemical equation shows an addition reaction in which a saturated hydrocarbon is produced from an unsaturated hydrocarbon. Options (2), (3), and (4) are not true. Option (5) is true but is not supported by the information presented.

15. **(1) The product is C_2H_6.** (Evaluation) The product contains two carbon atoms and six hydrogen atoms, so it can be restated as C_2H_6. Option (2) is incorrect since C_2H_6 is the product. Option (3) is incorrect since the product only contains single bonds. Option (4) is incorrect since the only saturated hydrocarbon is the product. Option (5) is incorrect because H_2 is not an unsaturated hydrocarbon.

16. **(3) Double bonding occurs between its carbon atoms.** (Comprehension) The passage states that ethene is an unsaturated hydrocarbon, in which two electrons of one carbon atom are paired with two electrons of another carbon atom to form a double bond. Options (1), (2), (4), and (5) are not supported by the information given and are not true.

17. **(5) They have different arrangements of atoms.** (Comprehension) The passage states that isomers have the same number and kinds of atoms but different arrangements of atoms and different properties. Therefore, options (1), (2), and (4) are not true. Option (3) is incorrect since two isomers of the hydrocarbon butane are shown.

18. **(3) one carbon atom branches off from the middle carbon atom** (Comprehension) The structural formula shows one carbon atom forming a branched chain in this isomer. Options (1), (4), and (5) are not true, as shown

in the diagram. Option (2) is only true of straight-chain butane.

19. **(3) more isomers** (Application) The passage states that the more carbon atoms in a hydrocarbon molecule, the more isomers it can form. Decane has more carbon atoms than pentane, so it is likely to form more isomers. Therefore, options (1), (4), and (5) are incorrect. Option (2), boiling point, cannot be inferred from the information provided.

20. **(1) the straight-chain molecule's less compact arrangement of atoms** (Evaluation) The only factor that can account for a difference in the way the isomers burn is their only physical difference, a difference in atomic arrangement. Since the isomers don't differ in content, options (2), (3), and (5) are incorrect. Option (4) is incorrect because no mention is made of the branched-chain molecule's higher boiling point.

GED Review: Chemistry (page 371)

1. **(3) gas molecules moving rapidly through less freely-moving liquid molecules** (Analysis) This is correct because gas molecules have more freedom of motion than liquid molecules. Option (1) is incorrect because solid molecules, not gas molecules, move only by vibrating. Option (2) is not a good choice because, although gas molecules could collide with liquid molecules, this would not account for the gas bubbles rising to the top of the liquid. Option (4) is incorrect because no mention is made of forces of attraction between liquids and gases. Option (5) is the reverse of the correct answer.

2. **(4) escape and spread apart** (Application) The passage states that gases will escape from an open container and "disappear." Since their molecules have almost no force of attraction, they will not stay in the tank, option (1), or stay together, option (2). Options (3) and (5) are incorrect because all molecules are constantly in motion.

3. **(5) Molecules of a gas will spread out and fill any container they are in.** (Evaluation) According to the passage, molecules of a gas will move freely and randomly. Thus, they will fill any container in which they are placed. Nothing in the passage supports options (1), (2), (3), and (4).

4. **(1) states of matter and movement of molecules** (Comprehension) This is correct because the passage describes how molecular motion is different for gases, liquids, and

Unit 5

solids. Options (2) and (5) are incorrect because no mention of temperature is made in the passage. Options (3) and (4) are incorrect because no mention of molecular size is made.

5. **(2) movement of molecules increases** (Analysis) Because the passage states that molecular motion is greatest for a gas and least for a solid, you can conclude that the movement of molecules must increase as temperature increases. Option (1) is opposite to the correct answer. Options (3) and (4) are opposite to the effects of heating. Option (5) is incorrect because the passage says nothing about how quickly matter changes state.

6. **(5) molecules in solids are held together by forces of attraction** (Application) Rocks are solids, and solids have definite shapes because forces of attraction among their molecules hold them tightly in place. Therefore, option (1) is not true. Options (2) and (4) do not apply to solids. As all molecules are in constant motion, option (3) is not the reason solids have shapes.

7. **(2) a geologist interested in estimating the age of rock samples** (Application) By finding out the amount of radioactive material compared to decayed material in a rock sample, geologists can estimate the age of the rock. The other activities would not make use of radioactive half-life.

8. **(3) After 22,920 years, 1/16 gram of carbon 14 will remain of the original 1 gram.** (Evaluation) The diagram shows that every 5,730 years, half of the carbon 14 has decayed. At 17,190 years, 1/8 gram is left. After another 5,730 years, or 22,920 years altogether, half of 1/8, or 1/16, gram would be left. Option (1) is incorrect because 1/16 gram would be left. Option (2) is incorrect because 1/8 gram remains after 17,190 years. Option (4) is true, but it is not supported by the information provided. Option (5) is incorrect because the passage indicates that the number of protons and neutrons affects the radioactivity of an element.

9. **(4) an unstable nucleus** (Analysis) If a radioactive atom gives off particles until the nucleus is stable, the inference is that an unstable nucleus causes radioactivity. Options (1) and (2) are incorrect because it is the balance between the numbers, not the actual numbers, that causes an atom to be radioactive. Option (3) is not supported by the passage, so it is incorrect. Option (5) is a result of an unstable nucleus, or radioactivity, not a cause, so it is incorrect.

10. **(5) Calcium carbonate is not soluble in water.** (Analysis) The passage states that because calcium carbonate is not soluble in water; it settles out of its solution. Options (1) and (2) are not supported by the passage. Options (3) and (4) are not true.

11. **(4) Calcium chloride and sodium carbonate are soluble in water.** (Analysis) Since calcium chloride and sodium carbonate form solutions with water, they must be soluble in water. Option (1) is a fact stated in the passage. Option (2) is not true. Options (3) and (5) cannot be assumed based on the information presented in the passage.

12. **(2) Sodium chloride is soluble in water.** (Analysis) The passage states that $CaCO_3$ precipitates out because it is not soluble in water. Thus you can conclude that NaCl does not precipitate out because it is soluble in water. Option (1) is incorrect because Na+ and Cl– ions form NaCl. Option (3) is incorrect because there is nothing in the passage to indicate how many ions are present. Options (4) and (5) are incorrect because the precipitate is $CaCO_3$, which does not contain any Na+ ions or Cl– ions.

13. **(5) Chlorine and sodium** (Analysis) In their outermost energy levels, chlorine has seven electrons and sodium has one, making a total of eight. These two atoms do react with one another. Sodium gives up its one electron to chlorine, forming very stable sodium and chlorine atoms. We know this compound as sodium chloride, or table salt. Options (1), (2), and (3) would all produce unfilled outer energy levels and are not the atoms likely to react most easily. Option (4) includes neon, whose outer energy level is already full, thus it is not likely to react with any atom.

Physics

Lesson 16: Moving Objects

GED Exercise: Moving Objects (page 374)

1. **(3) 10 meters east** (Analysis) Displacement is a measure of both the distance and direction traveled. Option (3) is the only option that shows the correct distance (10 meters) and direction (east) as shown on the diagram. Option (1) is the distance. Options (2) and (5) are incorrect in terms of length or direction. Option (4) is not true.

2. **(1) 10 meters** (Comprehension) The passage states and the diagram shows that the man traveled a total distance of 10 meters. As a

result, option (2) is incorrect. Option (3) is approximately equal to the man's displacement, not his distance. Option (4) is not true, since both distances are 10 meters. The solid arrow showing the man's displacement is shorter than the dotted lines showing his distance, so option (5) is incorrect.

3. **(4) only displacement includes the direction traveled** (Comprehension) Displacement is a measure of both the distance and the direction traveled, whereas distance does not include direction. As a result, options (1), (2), (3), and (5) are not true.

4. **(2) A and B** (Comprehension) Both statements A and B give information included in the paragraph. Statement C is a generalization, not a supporting detail.

5. **(1) Displacement indicates both the direction and how far an object traveled.** (Comprehension) The main topic of the paragraph is displacement. Option (2) is not true. Options (3) and (4) are supporting details. Option (5) is not mentioned in the passage.

6. **(2) his displacement is zero** (Application) The passage states that when a moving object ends up where it started, it has no displacement. Options (1) and (3) are incorrect because, although the man's starting and ending points are the same, he has still traveled a path that has a length, so his distance traveled is not zero. Option (4) is incorrect because the man's distance traveled, not his displacement, is the length of his circular path. Since the distance is a numerical quantity and displacement includes direction, they cannot be compared directly, so option (5) is incorrect.

7. **(2) 10 meters east** (Application) Displacement is the distance and direction from the starting point to the ending point. After following the path described, the person would be 10 meters east of the starting point. All other options are incorrect calculations of either the distance, the direction, or both.

8. **(5) 60 meters** (Application) The total distance the person traveled equals 30 meters plus 5 meters plus 20 meters plus 5 meters, or 60 meters. All the other options are miscalculations.

9. **(3) How you view motion depends on your frame of reference.** (Comprehension) The general idea of the passage is how frames of reference affect how motion is viewed. Options (1) and (5) are supporting details. Option (2) is implied in the last sentence but is a supporting detail, not the main idea. Option (4) can be true, but it is not the main idea.

10. **(2) Motion Depends on Your Frame of Reference** (Comprehension) The main topic of the passage which makes the best title is the connection between motion and frame of reference. Option (1) is not mentioned in the passage. Option (3) is too general to be the best title. Although trains are mentioned in the supporting details, option (4) is not the subject of the passage. While the passage answers this question, option (5) covers only a detail of the passage.

11. **(4) Two observers have different frames of reference, so their observations of motion differ.** (Comprehension) Option (4) is the only supporting detail listed. Options (1) and (2) are not mentioned in the passage. Options (3) and (5) are not true.

12. **(2) Your frame of reference is the other car which you believe to be motionless; therefore, you must be moving.** (Evaluation) As the other car runs backward, it is farther back in relation to you. If you are assuming that it is stopped, the only explanation is that you are moving forward. Quickly, however, your frame of reference shifts and you realize that the other car has moved. Options (1) and (4) are factors in your first impression, that you are moving, but do not fully explain the situation. Option (3) is untrue because you have not moved. Option (5) is a factor that helps you see that you have not moved—you are still by the sidewalk, not in the intersection—but does not explain the situation.

13. **(2) Speed is the distance traveled per unit of time.** (Comprehension) The main idea of the paragraph is the definition of speed. Options (1) and (4) are supporting details. Option (3) is not true. Option (5) is the main idea of the second paragraph.

14. **(1) only velocity describes direction** (Comprehension) Speed describes a rate of motion, whereas velocity describes both rate of motion and the direction an object moves. Therefore, options (2), (3), and (4) are incorrect. Since both velocity and speed describe distance divided by time, option (5) is not true.

15. **(3) 4 kilometers per hour** (Application) Using the equation, speed is calculated as 12

kilometers divided by 3 hours = 4 kilometers per hour. Therefore, options (1) and (5) are incorrect. Option (2) is incorrect for speed and includes the hiker's direction, which is not included in speed. Option (4) is the hiker's velocity.

16. **(5) 1 hour late** (Application) Using the equation to calculate how long the trip will take, time = distance/speed = 400 kilometers divided by 80 kilometers per hour = 5 hours. She will arrive 5 hours after departure, or at 7 p.m., which is 1 hour late. As a result, options (1), (2), (3), and (4) are incorrect.

17. **(2) 46 miles per hour east** (Application) The driver was headed east on Route 3 between 11:00 A.M. and noon. According to the map, the distance is 46 miles, so the driver's speed was 46 miles per hour, and the direction was east. Thus the velocity was 46 miles per hour east. Option (1) gives the correct speed, but the wrong direction. Option (3) gives the incorrect speed and incorrect direction. Option (4) gives the incorrect speed, but the correct direction. Option (5) gives the incorrect speed and no direction.

Lesson 17: Motion
GED Exercise: Motion (page 378)

1. **(2) large engine and lightweight body** (Evaluation) The large engine provides a lot of force, and the lightweight body has little mass. This combination makes possible rapid acceleration, which is desirable for a racing car. Options (1), (3), and (5) are incorrect because a small engine would not provide enough force for rapid acceleration. Option (4) is incorrect because the heavy body would decrease the amount of acceleration the large engine could provide.

2. **(4) the force of gravity** (Analysis) Gravity from a celestial body is the most likely force to affect a spacecraft in outer space. Option (1) is incorrect because the spacecraft is not using fuel in outer space. Option (2) might warm the spacecraft but will not cause a change of direction. Option (3) is incorrect because the force of friction is absent in outer space where there is no matter. Option (5) is incorrect because acceleration would describe a change in direction, but it is not a cause for such a change.

3. **(3) The acceleration of the first ball will be twice that of the second.** (Analysis) According to the equation, force equals mass times acceleration. Acceleration is expressed in units of meters per second^2. Thus, the

acceleration of the first ball will be 4 meters per second^2. The second ball's acceleration will be 2 meters per second^2. The remaining options indicate a misuse of the formula.

4. **(5) A car traveling at 40 miles per hour goes around a curve at the same speed.** (Application) This is correct because force is required to change the direction of motion. All the other options are incorrect because they describe either objects at rest or objects continuing in motion in a straight line.

5. **(1) A only** (Application) By changing the force applied to the ball, a pitcher (Statement A) can alter its acceleration, which demonstrates Newton's Second Law of Motion. The other options include Statements B and C, which show inertia, Newton's First Law of Motion.

6. **(2) A package on the seat of a car going 60 miles per hour slides forward when the car stops suddenly.** (Application) This is correct because the package keeps moving forward even though the car stops. It stays in motion. Option (1) is incorrect because it is related to Newton's second law, which is concerned with force and acceleration. Options (3), (4), and (5) are incorrect. While they describe types of motion, these options do not demonstrate an object remaining in motion or at rest (Newton's first law).

7. **(1) Small players can accelerate quickly, while large players can apply force to stop the motion of opponents.** (Evaluation) This explanation is based on Newton's second law. Option (5) is a true statement according to Newton's second law, but it does not explain the strategy. Option (2) is not necessarily true. Options (3) and (4) may or may not be true, but they do not explain the strategy.

8. **(4) mass, force, and acceleration** (Comprehension) Newton's Second Law of Motion states that an object (mass) will accelerate in the direction of the force that acts on it. The other options list only two of the three factors or list an incorrect factor.

Lesson 18: Electricity and Magnetism
GED Exercise: Electricity and Magnetism (page 381)

1. **(2) The second strip is negatively charged.** (Analysis) This is correct because like charges repel each other. If the second strip were positively charged, option (1), it would be attracted to the first strip. Options (3) and (4) may or may not be true, but they do not explain the effect being described. Option

(5) is incorrect because it is positively and negatively charged particles, not atoms, that attract and repel each other.

2. **(3) electron** (Comprehension) According to the passage, electrons have a negative charge. Option (1) is incorrect because protons have a positive charge. Option (2) is incorrect because neutrons have a neutral charge. Option (4) is incorrect because atoms are usually neutral; an ion is a charged particle. Option (5) is incorrect because a field is not a particle.

3. **(3) an area of force** (Comprehension) According to the passage, an electric field is an area of force. The other options are all examples of matter, not force.

4. **(3) C only** (Evaluation) The passage states that a force is exerted on any other charged particle. Therefore, only Statement C, an uncharged particle, would not be affected. Options (1), (2), (4), and (5) are incorrect because each one contains at least one charged particle.

5. **(1) The negative and positive ions will attract each other.** (Analysis) This is true because like charges repel and unlike charges attract. Options (2), (4), and (5) are incorrect because they state the opposite. Option (3) may or may not be true, but it does not answer the question.

6. **(4) force of attraction between protons and electrons** (Comprehension) According to the passage, the attraction between protons and electrons helps hold atoms together. The other options do not explain what holds an atom together.

7. **(2) +1** (Analysis) There is one more proton than there are electrons, so the atom would have a positive charge. The number of neutrons does not matter because neutrons have no charge.

8. **(5) increase their force of attraction** (Analysis) Since the strength of an electric field decreases as distance increases, then the strength of the field must increase as distance decreases. Options (1) and (2) are incorrect because the particles' electric charges would not be affected. Option (3) is not mentioned in the passage. Option (4) is the opposite of the effect that would occur.

9. **(2) picking up pieces of scrap metal on the site and depositing them elsewhere on the site** (Evaluation) This is correct because the electromagnet will gain and lose its magnetism as the current is turned on and

off—thus it is ideal for picking up metal objects, and then dropping them again. Option (1) is incorrect because there is no way of knowing whether this machine is equipped to travel distances. Option (5) may or may not be true, depending on the relative strengths of this and other machines on the site. Options (3) and (4) are incorrect because the crane's electromagnet would not cause these effects.

10. **(4) An electric current produces a magnetic field.** (Comprehension) Option (1) is true, but it does not answer the question because it does not say anything specific about electricity. Options (2) and (5) are true, but this passage discusses only the production of a magnetic field from electric current, not the reverse. Option (3) fails to specify that the wire must be conducting an electric current.

11. **(3) The needle is responding to the magnetic field produced by the current in the wire.** (Analysis) Option (1) is incorrect because it does not adequately relate cause and effect. Also, once the current is turned off, the needle will again point northward. Option (5) is incorrect because the magnetism of the compass needle was not produced by the current in the wire. Options (2) and (4) do not explain the situation being described.

12. **(5) Magnetism is related to the movement of electrons.** (Evaluation) The correct option is (5) because a flow of electrons (electric current) produces a magnetic field. Options (2) and (4) are not discussed in the passage. There is nothing in the passage to support options (1) and (3).

13. **(4) illustrated the property of magnetism** (Comprehension) Option (3) is possible, but the discovery of magnetite did much more than just reveal the properties of one metal. Option (2) is incorrect because magnetite is not made of pure iron—it is made of an iron-containing compound. Options (1) and (5) are incorrect because the understanding of poles and artificial magnets came much later.

14. **(3) halfway between the poles** (Analysis) The magnetic field of a bar magnet is strongest around the poles, so it is likely to be weakest at the midpoint, which is the point farthest from each pole. Options (1), (2), (4), and (5) are incorrect because they are positions closer to one of the poles.

15. **(3) Compass needles are magnets.** (Evaluation) Options (1) and (2) are possible but not necessarily true; thus, they are not the

best choices. Option (4) is incorrect because any magnet must have a north and south pole. Option (5) is incorrect because it would depend upon how the compass needles were lined up—if the north pole of one needle were near the south pole of the other, they would attract each other.

16. **(4) Earth has a magnetic field** (Comprehension) The magnets must be turning so that one of their poles is pointing to one of Earth's magnetic poles. Option (1) is unlikely. Option (2) is true but does not explain the behavior of magnets on Earth. Option (3) cannot be true of all locations north of a magnet. Option (5) is incorrect because the ice caps are not magnetic.

17. **(4) Keep videotapes away from magnetic fields.** (Analysis) A magnetic field can rearrange the metal bits in the tape, which would damage or destroy the information stored on the tape. While options (1) and (2) are good advice, they are not related to the explanation of how magnetism changes a recording on videotape. Option (3) is not part of the care instructions for videotapes because ordinary metal objects cannot harm the recording. Option (5) is incorrect because it has no effect on the safety of recordings.

Lesson 19: Waves

GED Exercise: Waves (page 384)

1. **(3) The depth of the trough of a wave is double the distance from the rest position to the crest.** (Evaluation) The diagram shows, and the passage states, that the depth of the trough of a wave is equal to the distance between the rest position and the crest. The other options are all true and are based on information in the passage.

2. **(4) a disturbance that travels through space or matter** (Comprehension) This definition appears in the first paragraph of the passage. Option (1) is incorrect because not all water movements are waves. Option (2) is incorrect because it leaves out space. Options (3) and (5) are incorrect because they do not mention the transfer of energy.

3. **(1) amplitude** (Application) A surfer would be most interested in the amount of energy a wave has to carry him or her to shore. The passage indicates that the greater the amplitude, the greater the energy. Options (2) and (3) refer to properties of waves that would not be a surfer's main interest. Option (4) is incorrect because

all waves are disturbances. Option (5) is not an important factor in surfing.

4. **(4) number of crests that pass a given point and unit of time** (Comprehension) Frequency is defined in the second paragraph of the passage. The other options do not describe frequency.

5. **(1) decreased speed** (Analysis) If both wavelength and frequency decrease, it follows that when you multiply them, the resulting speed will also decrease. Option (2) is incorrect because speed is calculated by multiplying wavelength times frequency. If you change either, the speed will change. If both these figures are decreased, it is not possible for speed to increase, option (3). Options (4) and (5) are incorrect because distance is not determined by these two factors.

6. **(2) divide speed by wavelength** (Analysis) Since speed equals wavelength times frequency, to find frequency, you must divide speed by wavelength. Options (1) and (5) are incorrect because you don't know the frequency and are trying to solve for it. Options (3) and (4) are incorrect because they do not calculate frequency.

7. **(4) 18 meters per second** (Application) To find speed, multiply wavelength by frequency ($3 \times 6 = 18$).

8. **(4) Properties of Waves** (Comprehension) Option (4) is the most general of the options and it covers all the supporting details of the passage. Option (1) is not mentioned in the passage. Option (2) is incorrect because wavelength, frequency, and speed, quantities described in the passage, are not wave parts. Option (3) is incorrect because ocean waves are not the only kinds of waves to which the facts in the passage apply. Option (5) describes supporting details.

9. **(2) B only** (Analysis) The paragraph states that the water is disturbed by an up-and-down movement only. Thus, the boat will bob up and down (Statement B) but will not move any significant distance (Statements A and C), making all other options incorrect.

GED Review: Physics (page 386)

1. **(2) increase in size** (Comprehension) This is correct because, if a radioactive atom were to change size, it would get smaller as it releases subatomic particles and energy. Options (1), (3), and (4) are incorrect because during the

process of radioactive decay, energy and subatomic particles are released as a radioactive isotope changes into another isotope or element. Option (5) is incorrect because radioactive decay is usually accompanied by the release of gamma rays.

2. **(2) an electric field** (Evaluation) This is correct because alpha particles are positively charged and beta particles are negatively charged. There is no evidence from the information given that any of the other options would have an effect on these particles.

3. **(5) It never took place before the twentieth century.** (Evaluation) This is correct because the passage states that fission reactions can occur naturally, so they must have occurred long ago. For the same reason, option (1) is incorrect. Options (2) and (4) are incorrect because a fission reaction is defined as the splitting of an atomic nucleus in which two smaller nuclei (matter) and energy are released. Option (3) is incorrect because fission reactions are controlled in a nuclear reactor.

4. **(2) contaminating the environment** (Analysis) Options (1), (3), and (4), if they happened, would be short-term effects of an accident at a nuclear power plant. Option (2) is correct because the radioactive material released into the environment would continue to decay for a long time. Option (5) is incorrect because there would be a long-term effect, option (2).

5. **(2) a string of decorating lights** (Application) These are often made such that if one bulb is removed, the whole string goes out. In more important electricity uses such as options (1), (3), (4), and (5), parallel circuits are used to ensure that the whole circuit does not fail if one item on it burns out or is removed.

6. **(2) The current continues in all but one path of the circuit.** (Analysis) Because the other lights and appliances still work after the bulb burns out, this indicates that the circuit must be a parallel circuit. Option (1) would happen if it were a series circuit. Options (3) and (5) are incorrect because blown-out fuses and power shortages have the same effect on both kinds of circuits. Option (4) contradicts the conclusion that the kitchen is on a single parallel circuit.

GED Cumulative Review: Science (page 388)

1. **(3) by engulfing them** (Comprehension) The passage states that phagocytes work by surrounding or engulfing bacteria. Option (1)

is true of lymphocytes, not phagocytes. Option (2) is incorrect because the phagocytes cannot work until the disease-causing agent is in the body. Options (4) and (5) do not relate to the way phagocytes work.

2. **(2) All white blood cells are the same.** (Evaluation) The passage describes two kinds of white blood cells that fight disease in different ways. Options (1), (2), (4), and (5) are incorrect because they are facts presented in the passage.

3. **(1) have a reduced ability to fight off disease** (Analysis) Someone with HIV is likely to have a reduced number of lymphocytes. Since lymphocytes help fight disease, that person is also likely to have a reduced ability to fight disease. Option (2) is incorrect because fewer lymphocytes means a reduction in antibody production. Option (3) is incorrect because phagocytes aren't necessarily destroyed when lymphocytes are. Option (4) is the opposite of what is likely to occur. Option (5) is incorrect because no mention is made in the passage of a connection between lymphocytes and pulse rate.

4. **(1) A only** (Analysis) Both getting a disease and being given a vaccine start the production of antibodies, Statement A. Statement B is incorrect because a vaccine, under normal circumstances, does not make a person sick. Statement C is incorrect because the response to a vaccine involves lymphocytes, not macrophages and phagocytes. Thus only option (1) is correct.

5. **(1) More phagocytes and lymphocytes are needed to fight the infection.** (Analysis) When infectious agents enter the body, the body produces more phagocytes and lymphocytes in order to destroy the infection. Option (2) is incorrect because the body produces phagocytes and lymphocytes. Option (3) is incorrect because lymphocytes produce antibodies. Option (4) has nothing to do with fighting infection. Option (5) makes no sense; if the body were immune, there would be no infection.

6. **(1) Metamorphosis in the Frog** (Comprehension) The passage and diagram describe the process of metamorphosis, using the frog as an example. Option (2) is too specific. Option (3) is too general and includes animals, such as fish, that do not undergo metamorphosis. Option (4) is also too general; the passage describes metamorphosis only in terms of the frog. Option (5) is not the subject of the paragraph.

7. **(3) Different animal structures are suited to different types of environments.** (Analysis) For example, in showing the change from tadpole to frog, the author shows gill slits, which contain gills, for breathing underwater and legs for moving about on land. The author takes for granted the usefulness of these structures in their environment. Options (1) and (2) are incorrect, since many plants and animals do not undergo metamorphosis. Option (4) may or may not be true, but it does not have anything to do with the process of metamorphosis. Option (5) is not true.

8. **(2) the process by which an immature form changes into a different adult form** (Comprehension) This is the process described in the passage. Option (1) is incorrect because reproduction is a different function from growth. Option (3) is incorrect because it is too general. Option (4) is incorrect because it describes what happens to the mature adult form after metamorphosis. Option (5) refers to respiration, not to metamorphosis.

9. **(2) lungs** (Comprehension) Lungs are structures that are essential to supporting life on land, because without them the animal could not breathe. The structures in the other options are less vital for land-dwelling animals.

10. **(5) Water in animals' breath is returned to the air.** (Evaluation) When animals exhale, they release water vapor into the atmosphere. Option (1) is not true because animals also release water as they breathe. Option (2) is not true; invisible water vapor is found throughout the atmosphere. Option (3) is not true; plants take in water from their roots. Option (4) is not true; the oceans contain most of the water on Earth.

11. **(3) Evaporation from the ocean returns water to the atmosphere.** (Analysis) This statement provides evidence by giving an example of water changing form during the water cycle. Options (1) and (2) just restate the conclusion. Options (4) and (5) are true but do not offer the evidence that water is used again and again.

12. **(2) the sun** (Analysis) The diagram shows that the sun's heat causes water to evaporate from various places. Options (1), (3), and (4) are incorrect because they are forms of water. Option (5) is also incorrect; the soil serves to store water.

13. **(2) Water conservation is not useful since Earth will never run out of water.** (Analysis) Although it is true that water is recycled on Earth, water conservation can be useful because water may run low in particular places. The other options are all facts stated in the passage.

14. **(5) A and C only** (Analysis) Earth has seasons because of both Statements A and C, Earth's revolution and its inclined axis. Options (1) and (3) are incorrect because they are only part of the cause. Options (2) and (4) are incorrect because rotation, Statement B, causes day and night, not the seasons.

15. **(5) Earth's spinning on its axis** (Comprehension) The passage describes rotation as the spinning of Earth on its axis. Options (1) and (2) are two kinds of revolution. Options (3) and (4) are incorrect because rotation neither causes nor is caused by the seasons.

16. **(2) The northern hemisphere is tilted away from the sun.** (Application) In December it is winter in the northern hemisphere; therefore, we can conclude that the hemisphere is tilted away from the sun. Options (1) and (5) are true in June, not December. Options (3) and (4) are true in spring and autumn.

17. **(1) there would be no seasons** (Application) If Earth revolved as it does now but rotated on an axis that wasn't inclined, every place on Earth would get the same amount of daylight (12 hours) every day. Temperatures would vary with distance from the equator but not with time of year. As a result, there would be global variations in climate but not seasons, so option (2) is incorrect. Option (3) is incorrect because rotation wouldn't change. Option (4) is incorrect because a change would occur. Option (5) is incorrect because revolution wouldn't change.

18. **(4) Different parts of Earth get different amounts of the sun's energy at different times of the year.** (Comprehension) The passage explains that different parts of Earth lean toward the sun at different times of the year. Therefore they get differing amounts of the sun's energy. As a result, option (3) must be incorrect. Option (5) is incorrect because the southern hemisphere experiences fall on March 21.

19. **(1) provide an acid for sodium bicarbonate to react with** (Comprehension) Option (2) is incorrect because sodium bicarbonate breaks down to form carbon dioxide. Options (3) and (4) are incorrect because carbon dioxide is a product

of the reaction between sodium bicarbonate and an acid. Option (5) is incorrect because sodium bicarbonate is one of the substances in baking powder to begin with.

20. **(4) It contains an acid.** (Evaluation) This is correct because the passage states that sodium bicarbonate reacts with acids to form carbon dioxide and water. The other options are incorrect because the passage includes no other conditions that would cause carbon dioxide and water to be produced from sodium bicarbonate.

21. **(2) The Chemistry of Baking Powder** (Comprehension) The passage covers both the chemical composition and reactions associated with baking powder; in other words, it is about chemistry. Options (1) and (5) refer to supporting details of the passage. Option (3) is incorrect because other chemicals common in kitchens besides baking powder are not mentioned. Option (4) is not covered in the passage.

22. **(5) carbon dioxide** (Analysis) This is correct because it is logical that a gas produced would cause the cake to rise. Options (1), (3), and (4) are incorrect because they are not gases, and options (1) and (4) are not produced when sodium bicarbonate reacts. Option (2) is a gas, but there is no mention of oxygen in the passage.

23. **(3) Moisture in the air reacts with the tartrate.** (Analysis) This is correct because tartrate plus water produces acid, which in turn reacts with the sodium bicarbonate in baking powder to release carbon dioxide gas. Option (1) is incorrect because heat causes sodium bicarbonate to break down. Options (2), (4), and (5) are incorrect because no mention is made of reactions involving oxygen.

24. **(2) Electrons from the carpet move onto your feet, causing you temporarily to have an electric charge.** (Analysis) This is correct because the situation is similar to the rubbing of a balloon on a sleeve. Options (1) and (3) are incorrect because you, not the carpet, receive the shock—so you must have an electric charge as a result of acquired electrons. Option (4) leaves you out of the action entirely, and option (5) takes the concept of voltage out of context to create a senseless answer.

25. **(1) Protons flowing onto an object cause the object to become positively charged.** (Evaluation) This is correct because no mention is made in the passage of protons being able to move and, in fact, they cannot. Options (2) and (5) are supported by the passage because electric current is pushed through wires by voltage, and a change in voltage would cause a change in current. Option (3) could be supported because both balloons would have a negative charge, and like charges repel each other. Option (4) is supported by the analogy between the flow of electricity and the flow of water.

26. **(1) place the balloons on the wall just before the party begins** (Analysis) This option is correct because this would leave little time for the balloons to lose their negative charge and come loose from the wall. Option (3) would work exactly against this idea. Options (2), (4), and (5) would not help the balloons stick to the wall.

27. **(2) both make possible the flow of a substance from one place to another** (Comprehension) Voltage pushes electrons through a wire just as water pressure pushes water through a hose. Options (1), (3), and (4) are incorrect because they apply only to voltage. Option (5) is incorrect because voltage is supplied by a battery—and water pressure has nothing to do with powering a battery.

Unit 6: Literature & the Arts

Popular Literature

Lesson 1: Fiction (page 396)

1. **(2) share a close relationship** (Inferential Comprehension) The discussion between the two women indicates that though they differ in age, they are very familiar with each other. There is no direct evidence for option (1). Based on their discussion, you can infer that the women do not agree and have had different experiences but do respect each other. Therefore options (3), (4), and (5) are incorrect.

2. **(4) Naomi suspects that Esther has met a man.** (Literal Comprehension) The event that initially upsets Naomi is related to her belief that Esther is involved with a man. Option (1) is the opposite of Naomi's feelings for Bruce. While option (2) is true, it is not the cause of the underlying conflict. Naomi is already upset with Esther before the phone rings, so option (3) is incorrect. Option (5) did not happen.

3. **(3) the ringing of the telephone** (Literal Comprehension) Not only does the telephone ring for a long time, it is also the cause of the conversation about Bruce. Options (1), (2), and (5) have no support in the excerpt. Option (4) may be true, but it is the sound of the phone that introduces Bruce as a subject of discussion.

4. **(2) She is afraid that Esther will make the same mistakes she made.** (Inferential Comprehension) By stating her regrets (lines 34–37), Naomi is hoping to dissuade Esther from following in her footsteps. There is no evidence to support options (1) and (5). While option (3) may be true, it is not the main reason Naomi is worried. Option (4) is incorrect because even though Naomi complains about an attitude she thinks Esther learned in college, there is no indication that she is not supportive of her education.

5. **(4) She is unwilling to listen to her mother's opinion.** (Inferential Comprehension) Esther's continuous questioning of Naomi suggests that she is doubtful of her mother's beliefs, therefore option (1) is incorrect. Option (2) is only a detail of Esther's behavior. There is no support for option (3). While she does question her mother, there is nothing to indicate that Esther feels superior, so option (5) is incorrect.

6. **(2) try to force Esther to talk to him** (Application) Based on Naomi's refusal to lie to Bruce (lines 16–17), it can be inferred that she would invite him in and try to force Esther to talk to him. Therefore, option (1) is incorrect. There is no indication that Naomi dislikes Bruce or would refuse him access to her home, so option (3) is incorrect. Option (4) is incorrect because Naomi is afraid that Esther will get married too young. There is no support for option (5).

7. **(3) the settling of differences between Esther and Naomi** (Inferential Comprehension) The origin of the conflict is the differences between the women. Esther's life is different from Naomi's at the same age. There is no direct evidence that options (1), (2), (4), or (5) would end the conflict.

8. **(3) describing fear as if it were a person or an animal** (Literal Comprehension) Lines 19–21 indicate that the author is referring to fear, so options (1), (2), and (4) are incorrect. Option (5) relates to fear, but the author's purpose is to tell how Edward felt, not to frighten the reader.

9. **(4) the way the darkness feels** (Analysis) Option (1) is incorrect; the feeling of fear comes later in the excerpt. There is no support for options (2), (3), and (5).

10. **(3) was selected in a way that concealed his true nature** (Analysis) Option (3) is correct because it fits with the statement that the nominee's supporters "had only the haziest idea of what he was all about" (lines 3–4). None of the other choices is supported by the passage.

11. **(2) Most of the supporters of the Vice-Presidential nominee did not know what he stood for.** (Inferential Comprehension) Option (2) best summarizes what the passage is about. Options (1), (4), and (5) are incorrect because the information in the passage does not support such broad generalizations. Option (3) is incorrect because there is no information in the passage about the nominee's views.

12. **(1) We Know Him Well** (Application) This is the only choice that does not fit with the implication of the entire passage, especially lines 1–4. These lines make the point clear even if you don't know that the phrase "a pig in a poke" refers to a pig inside a sack so that the buyer doesn't really know what he or she is getting. Option (2) is a caption that fits because it refers to the idea that he "was their pig in their poke" (lines 12–13), meaning whether they knew him or not they would support him because he was their nominee. All the other options are various ways to say that the nominee's supporters really don't know him.

13. **(4) Mr. Cynical** (Application) Option (4) is correct because *cynical* means "mocking or scornful about the motives of others," a definition that fits the attitude the narrator displays in the passage. Option (1) is incorrect because it implies the narrator has an attitude of uncritical pleasure. Option (2) is incorrect because it more likely be applied to the nominee than the narrator. Options (3) and (5) are not supported by the passage.

14. **(1) The speaker does not want a fuss made at his funeral.** (Inferential Comprehension) All the details are about avoiding anything fancy at burial. Options (2), (3), and (5) are details that help to suggest that idea. The speaker may believe funerals should be simple but does not care about dignity, so option (4) is incorrect.

15. **(1) using the box a coffin came in** (Literal Comprehension) The box would cost the family nothing. Option (2) is too general. Options (3), (4), and (5) are not supported by the excerpt.

16. **(4) gives an example of the main idea of the excerpt** (Analysis) The problem of wasting money is a specific example of making too much fuss. Option (1) suggests the main ideas are opposite, which is incorrect. Option (2) is not related to the idea of money. The idea in the paragraph is not really practical, so option (3) is incorrect. Option (5) is incorrect because the second paragraph

does not explain Grandpa Blakeslee's beliefs; it gives examples of his beliefs.

17. **(4) not concerned about what society thinks** (Application) Option (1) is incorrect because his plans are hardly conventional. Option (2) is incorrect because his plans for his funeral are not at all vain. Option (3) is unlikely because Grandpa is so unconventional. Option (5) is contradicted by his opposition to conventional funerals.

18. **(2) spending a quiet evening at home** (Application) Grandpa Blakeslee's simple and quiet tastes are indicated throughout the excerpt. Options (1), (3), (4), and (5) are examples of activities that Grandpa Blakeslee would avoid either because they require an expenditure of money or demand that he change his normal way of doing things.

19. **(2) They thought Grandpa Blakeslee's comments and wishes were strange.** (Analysis) While option (4) is true, it is the very unusual nature of his requests that is shocking. Option (1) is an explanation the speaker, not the women, suggests. Options (3) and (5) are details of Grandpa Blakeslee's requests.

20. **(5) Every person's life has a special moment.** (Literal Comprehension) This is stated in the first sentence. There is no evidence for options (1) and (4). Options (2) and (3) may be true but are not suggested in the paragraph.

21. **(5) a time that shaped his reality** (Literal Comprehension) This is stated in the second sentence of paragraph two. Options (1), (2), and (4) are contradicted in the excerpt. Option (3) is not suggested in the excerpt.

22. **(1) he was young and impressionable** (Inferential Comprehension) He seems to have seen the events from a youthful point of view; sixteen is an age when emotions are easily influenced. Options (2) and (4) may be true but are not supported. Options (3) and (5) are mentioned, but they were not the cause of the author's feelings.

23. **(5) an example of the main idea in the first paragraph** (Literal Comprehension) The phrasing of the first sentence in paragraph two points out that it is an example. Because the ideas are similar, options (1) and (4) are incorrect. The second main idea is more specific, so options (2) and (3) are incorrect.

24. **(2) talking about the war as if it were happening now** (Analysis) The present tense makes the war seem more immediate, as close as it seems to the author. Options (1) and (3) are mentioned but do not help to explain the author's feelings. Options (4) and (5) are false.

25. **(5) A sixteen-year-old is exempt from wartime worries.** (Literal Comprehension) In lines 40–45, the author suggests the importance of his age in regard to the war. Also, the author's observations show that a sixteen-year-old is definitely affected by the war. The majority of the second paragraph is used by the author to offer his list of the war's characteristics. Options (1), (2), (3), and (4) are listed as characteristics.

26. **(4) Every person sees the world from a personal point of view.** (Application) This statement is similar to the author's belief that a person is affected by certain events in life. Because people's experiences are different, their understanding of how the world works will be different. Option (1) is not suggested by the excerpt. Option (2) suggests the present is more important than the past, but the author is talking about the importance of the past. Option (3) is too general, and option (5) has nothing to do with what the author is saying.

27. **(2) description of the United States during World War II** (Literal Comprehension) The excerpt describes in detail aspects of life during the war. While it is biographical, it is much more than biography, so option (1) is incorrect. The author is commenting on living conditions, not complaining, so option (3) is incorrect. The excerpt is not meant to be humorous, so option (4) is incorrect. Option (5) is too general, since not many sixteen-year-olds have this experience.

28. **(2) because the war has made almost everything in short supply** (Inferential Comprehension) The excerpt emphasizes how the war has caused shortages, so to waste anything is immoral. Options (1) and (4) are general statements about the country but do not explain why wasting anything would be immoral. Options (3) and (5) are not supported by the excerpt.

29. **(2) Hannah is worried about something that does not seem to bother Nancy.** (Literal Comprehension) It is stated that Hannah is worried (line 9) and wants Nancy to be careful. Nancy says she is not frightened (lines 15–16), so option (4) is incorrect. Option (1) is not supported by the excerpt. Option (3)

is a detail of the story. Option (5) may be true, but it is not the main idea.

30. **(4) continue to help Mrs. Struthers** (Application) Nancy says that the note does not frighten her, so she will probably find some way to help Mrs. Struthers and solve the case. Therefore, options (1), (2), and (3) are incorrect. There is no support for option (5).

31. **(2) Nancy belongs to the yacht club.** (Inferential Comprehension) Nancy's membership at the yacht club neither directly affects Hannah's worries nor Nancy's lack of worry. Options (1), (3), (4), and (5) explain the differing attitudes of the two women and help to support the main idea.

32. **(1) irregularities** (Inferential Comprehension) The text explains odd things about twins. Option (2) is incorrect because a discovery would probably be fairly well understood. Options (3) and (4) are details that support the research. Option (5) has already been defined as meaning "identical."

33. **(3) The author gives examples of identical twins who are raised apart but repeatedly act alike.** (Analysis) The word follows this series of examples and so probably refers to the similarities in twins' lives. Options (1), (2), and (5) are not true. Option (4) does not help to explain the meaning of the word.

34. **(2) backward movement** (Analysis) Drew's statement, "back through their entire lives," (lines 31–32) indicates a backward movement in time, therefore options (1), (3), and (5) are incorrect. In option (4), speed can be a quality of the word, though it does not describe its use in this excerpt.

35. **(2) Karen and Carol** (Inferential Comprehension) The excerpt uses these two names to give examples of behavior of monozygotic (identical) twins raised apart. June is used as the name of a month, not a person's name, so options (1) and (3) are incorrect. Identical twins are the same sex, so options (4) and (5) are incorrect.

36. **(4) follow different patterns** (Inferential Comprehension) The fact that twins who are raised together are more likely to follow different patterns can be inferred from the last sentence of the first paragraph. Option (1) is the opposite of what is implied. Options (2) and (3) are details about twins who are raised apart. Option (5) is not supported by the excerpt.

37. **(2) approval** (Inferential Comprehension) Options (1) and (5) do not make sense in the sentence; they are just words from the details. The rest of the paragraph shows that the author clearly does not like the treaty that is apparently being considered by the Senate; therefore, options (3) and (4) are incorrect.

38. **(3) association** (Inferential Comprehension) Clues such as "political parties" (line 12) suggest the creation of groups. Since confederation is linked with the phrase "of states," this context suggests a uniting of states. Options (1) and (4) do not make sense in the context of the excerpt. Options (2) and (5) suggest the opposite of the creation of political parties or groups.

39. **(4) trade and manufacturing** (Literal Comprehension) The parallel structure the writer uses is part of the clue. One party was made up of people in trade and people in manufacturing; the other party was made up of people who farmed and people who worked in the city. Restating the idea helps you see the meaning. Option (1) is incorrect because the clause is part of the treaty, not a separate thing. The pairs of words in options (2), (3), and (5) are opposites, not things linked together.

40. **(1) impossible to bring together** (Inferential Comprehension) The word "division" is a clue to the idea that parties were impossible to bring together. Options (2) and (3) suggest the opposite of this meaning, so they are incorrect. Options (4) and (5) make no sense in the sentence.

41. **(5) groups** (Inferential Comprehension) The sentence containing the word "factions" implies that the new parties are no longer parts or groups. Options (1) and (4) make no sense in the sentence. Option (2) is incorrect because it implies that the parties were working together. Option (3) is not supported by the excerpt.

42. **(5) Americans were unanimously in support of the treaty.** (Inferential Comprehension) The fact that there were so many differences between the two parties shows that the Americans were not in agreement. Options (1), (2), (3), and (4) are all true statements that are supported by the excerpt.

43. **(3) hopeful and exuberant** (Analysis) The author describes the environment of Richmond, not McClellan, as hopeful. Options (1), (2), (4), and (5) all reflect the author's description of McClellan's troops.

Unit 6

44. **(4) the appalling death lists** (Literal Comprehension) The details talk about the soldiers who have died. Options (1) and (3) are not related to the details. Option (2) is a result of the temporary end of the dying. There is no suggestion of option (5).

45. **(2) a bulldozer** (Application) Lutie's final image is of a large destructive machine. Options (1) and (5) are not related to Lutie's final image. Option (3) is close but is on too small a scale. Option (4) is modern but has nothing to do with death.

46. **(2) She is showing that rich men as well as poor men were killed.** (Analysis) Although option (1) is a true statement about death, it is not what the author means because it does not refer to the process of selection. Option (3), like option (2), treats death as a person; however, the characteristics in option (3) are not the ones the author intends. Option (4) is incorrect; the author is trying to show that death is impartial, not awful. Option (5) has support later in the excerpt, but it has nothing to do with this statement.

47. **(4) raise his social status** (Analysis) The word "redeem" suggests that by joining the military, a vagrant can get back something he has lost or given up. There is no support for the other options.

48. **(1) July believes that common practices should be followed.** (Inferential Comprehension) This is indicated in lines 16–21. Options (3), (4), and (5) are details which support the main idea stated in option (1). Option (2) is not supported in the excerpt.

49. **(3) July's mother died when he was six.** (Literal Comprehension) Options (1), (2), and (4) refer to people following social rules or people breaking them. July's job, option (5), affected his belief, which is the main idea.

50. **(4) accept that Elmira will never eat dinner sitting at the table** (Application) Based on the excerpt's description of July's thoughts and behavior towards Elmira, it is unlikely that he would take any action to change the situation. Options (1), (2), and (3) are not consistent with the excerpt's description of July. Option (5) is incorrect because July does not "like for things to be out of the ordinary," so it seems unlikely he would change his own behavior.

51. **(1) law enforcement officer** (Inferential Comprehension) Lines 21–24 imply that July upheld the law in some way. There is no support for options (2), (3), (4), and (5).

52. **(4) He did not understand how he knew the things he knew.** (Literal Comprehension) This idea is stated in the second sentence. There is no evidence for option (1). Options (2), (3,) and (5) are true but are not the reasons for his crisis.

53. **(3) reincarnation** (Inferential Comprehension) Ford clearly states that this is the way he explains his "genius." He says he is not an intellectual, so option (1) is incorrect. Options (2), (4), and (5) are things Ford tells Morgan are not necessary.

54. **(2) saying "lived more times"** (Analysis) This comes in the next sentence and so hints at its meaning. Option (1) is not a direct definition. Option (3) does not help give the meaning. The author does not explain the term, option (4). Option (5) refers to a book, not the word.

55. **(3) scholarly books** (Inferential Comprehension) This is an implied contrast of the speaker's book to what Mr. Morgan probably reads. Options (1) and (2) are mentioned in addition to "Latiny things." Option (4) is something the speaker appreciated. There is no evidence for option (5).

56. **(5) by saying the book cost twenty-five cents** (Literal Comprehension) This information is in the first sentence. Option (1) does not give any clues. Option (2) gives only information about how the book was acquired. Options (3) and (4) refer to things that are not specifically mentioned.

57. **(3) would be a waste of time** (Application) The speaker states that all one needs to know can be found in his book, so he probably does not think much of a degree of any sort. The speaker shows little respect for scholarly activity in general, so option (1) is incorrect. Option (2) refers to a joking insult, not a real belief. There is no support for either option (4) or (5).

58. **(2) to emphasize the importance of the holiday to Mike Senior** (Analysis) The author repeats his use of smell in order to emphasize how much Thanksgiving dinner meant to Mike Senior. Since there is no real turkey, option (1) is incorrect. The smell of the lasagna is not mentioned, therefore option (3) is incorrect. Option (4) does not refer to the author's use of "smelled." There is no evidence to support option (5).

59. **(1) Mike Senior does not see his family very often.** (Inferential Comprehension) Mike Senior's interaction with Janet and Shawn

suggests that his visit is a rare occurrence. There is no support for options (2) and (4). The excerpt includes a long description of Mike Senior's long journey, therefore option (3) is incorrect. Option (5) cannot be inferred from the information given in the excerpt.

60. **(4) to continue pretending it was turkey** (Application) The excerpt suggests that the memory of past turkeys and Thanksgivings was more important to Mike Senior than what was actually being served, so options (1) and (3) are incorrect. Option (2) is possible, although it is not supported by the excerpt. There is no evidence for option (5).

61. **(1) Feather hasn't seen her father for awhile, and she is happy to see him.** (Literal Comprehension) This is stated in lines 1–3. Option (2) is incorrect because she was happy, not sad. Options (3) and (5) are not supported by the excerpt. Although it may be true that Feather is hungry, option (4), it does not explain Feather's reaction when she sees her father.

62. **(3) chooses not to talk to other people** (Inferential Comprehension) The father says that although Jesus has not talked in years, there is nothing physically stopping him from talking, so option (1) is incorrect. Although Jesus is making breakfast this morning, it does not mean that he makes breakfast every morning, so option (2) is incorrect. There is no support for options (4) and (5).

63. **(4) Feather feels her father is not paying enough attention to her after she gets hurt.** (Analysis) Feather demands to be let go after her father does not respond to her being hurt. Feather ran to be picked up by her father, so option (1) is incorrect. Option (2) is incorrect because Feather tells her father about her dream in lines 33–40. While Feather is upset when she bumps her nose, it does not mean she has a bad temper, so option (3) is incorrect. Option (5) is not a good example of a conflict between the two characters.

64. **(5) Grandpa Tweedy did not like to spend his own money, so he asked Papa to help out.** (Inferential Comprehension) This is suggested by information in the first paragraph. Option (1) is incorrect because there is no indication that Grandpa loaned anyone money. Option (2) is incorrect because the excerpt does not indicate that Grandpa could not support himself. Options (3) and (4) might be true, but Grandpa's feelings about money make option (5) the most likely reason.

65. **(1) "he toiled not"** (Literal Comprehension) Grandpa Tweedy never worked, so what he did was just sit around. Options (2) and (3) suggest that he worked. Option (4) is a different idea. Option (5) is a detail that describes his sitting on the porch.

66. **(5) He would let a fence fall down before he would repair it.** (Application) Since laziness seems to be one of Grandpa's basic qualities, option (1) is unlikely. There is no support for option (2). Options (3) and (4) are incorrect; the excerpt indicates the opposite.

67. **(2) Grandpa refused permission to take the fish off the hook.** (Literal Comprehension) Grandpa's long-winded speech boils down to this. Options (1) and (4) are not what Grandpa said. Option (3) is contradicted in the excerpt. There is no evidence for option (5).

68. **(3) The Russians bombed Cairo.** (Literal Comprehension) This event did not happen. Options (1), (2), (4), and (5) are all mentioned in the excerpt, and each is given as one of the causes in a series. Note that except for the Albanians, each of the other causes is also an effect.

69. **(4) A series of mistakes and misunderstandings caused a world war.** (Analysis) The most important result was an accidental world war. Options (1) and (2) may be true, but they are not part of the chain of events described in the excerpt. Options (3) and (5) are true statements, but they are not the most important results of the events.

70. **(3) louder** (Literal Comprehension) This is one of the several words that refer to sound. Options (1) and (2) refer to how the device worked, not what it affected. Option (4) does not help because it needs to be defined, too. Option (5) is the device itself.

71. **(1) plans** (Inferential Comprehension) This is suggested by surrounding information describing the actions of the advertisers and networks. Options (2) and (3) refer to the things each party is protecting. Options (4) and (5) do not make sense in the context of the sentence.

72. **(2) The advertisers' influence was not enough to win the case.** (Inferential Comprehension) The first clue is in the contrast with the word "sufficient"; the second clue is that the advertisers failed. Options (1), (3), and (5) do not provide information about the advertisers. The

Unit 6

charge that there was a conspiracy, option (4), does not help explain "insufficient."

73. **(5) Hadden won because the advertisers failed to prove their case.** (Literal Comprehension) The fact that the advertisers had insufficient influence to win the case means that Hadden won. Options (1), (2), and (3) are all specifically contradicted in the excerpt. Option (4) is true, but it is something that happened as a result of the trial.

74. **(4) A Lot of Noise About Noise** (Inferential Comprehension) This comic title reflects all the arguing back and forth about the noise levels of TV ads. Options (1), (2), (3), and (5) are all too general.

75. **(1) Hadden proved a conspiracy and won a huge settlement.** (Literal Comprehension) The last half of the second paragraph covers the lawsuit filed by Hadden. There is no support in the excerpt for option (2). Option (3) is the opposite of what happened. Option (4) is true but happened before the lawsuit. Option (5) occurred during the first lawsuit when the advertisers brought a suit against Hadden.

76. **(3) The government took over the production of context-recognition chips.** (Literal Comprehension) This point is made in lines 70–72. Option (1) is incorrect because the government took over the business. Options (2), (4), and (5) did not happen.

77. **(2) shrinking** (Inferential Comprehension) Options (1), (4), and (5) refer to the opposite effects of Adnix and Hadden's efforts to destroy advertising. Option (3) is incorrect because it does not indicate the idea of something getting smaller.

78. **(3) The networks refused to accept his commercials for broadcast.** (Literal Comprehension) This is supported by lines 44–45 in the second paragraph. There is no evidence that options (1), (2), or (5) are reasons for Hadden's suit. Option (4) is why Hadden thought he could win the suit, not the reason he brought it.

Lesson 2: Nonfiction (page 414)

1. **(3) Collins handles Armstrong's money.** (Inferential Comprehension) Both Armstrong and the promoter accept Collins's right to demand payment, so it is probably his usual job. Option (1) is not true because Collins is talking to the promoter. Because Armstrong ignores Collins's action, there is no support for options (2) and (5). There is no mention of Collins's opinion of Armstrong, so option (4) is incorrect.

2. **(1) sometimes were not paid after their performances** (Inferential Comprehension) Collins would not have felt the need to demand payment before the show if the money were guaranteed. Options (2) and (5) are not supported by the excerpt. Lines 5–6 mention there was no rehearsal, so option (3) is incorrect. Option (4) is incorrect because here it is the manager, not the musician, who is concerned with money; also, no amount is mentioned.

3. **(5) He thought Armstrong behaved better than Collins.** (Inferential Comprehension) He describes Armstrong in positive terms but refers to Collins negatively. There is no support for options (1), (3), and (4). Option (2) is incorrect because he seems to admire Armstrong's patience.

4. **(2) calmly** (Application) Armstrong remains cool through an embarrassing moment, which suggests he is usually calm. Therefore, options (1) and (4) are incorrect. There is no evidence for options (3) and (5); those qualities describe how Collins acted.

5. **(2) firm** (Literal Comprehension) Collins won't take no for an answer and won't accept anything but what he asked for. There is no evidence for option (1). Options (3), (4), and (5) do not describe Collins's attitude.

6. **(1) No Cash, No Show** (Inferential Comprehension) The focus of the paragraph is on Collins's demand. Options (2) and (4) are incorrect because they suggest a focus on Armstrong or his audience. Option (3) is incorrect because this is only one problem a promoter might have; besides, the promoter himself is not the focus either. Option (5) refers only to a detail of the solution.

7. **(2) B only** (Inferential Comprehension) The fact that Armstrong is being paid in currency other than U.S. dollars indicates that he is not performing in the United States. Selmer is the type of trumpet Armstrong is playing and has nothing to do with where he is, so options (1) and (4) are incorrect. Option (3), C only, cannot be proven. The speaker says he thinks the man cannot count the money but he doesn't say why. Thus, options (3) and (5) are incorrect.

8. **(4) when he was in college** (Literal Comprehension) Careful reading of the passage indicates that the period of time the author is

writing about is college. There is no support in the excerpt for options (1), (2), (3), and (5).

9. **(1) He sought out powerful men as patrons.** (Literal Comprehension) Option (2) is true, but it was not his main technique. There is no support in the excerpt for options (3) or (4). Option (5) shows how Johnson manipulated and flattered powerful men, but this was not his main technique for acquiring power.

10. **(4) in the jail yard** (Analysis) Although it talks about location, this phrase refers to an event that happened to a single person. Options (1), (2), (3), and (5) refer to the expansion of settlements into what had been unclaimed land.

11. **(1) were built** (Analysis) Building is a commonplace activity and can take place at any speed. Options (2), (3), (4), and (5) imply surprise and speed.

12. **(4) a waterway** (Literal Comprehension) A slough is an inlet or a swamp. The clue here is that it was dammed to form a lake. Options (1), (2), and (3) cannot be dammed. Since the slough was dammed to form the lake, it could not have been the lake to begin with, option (5).

13. **(3) the 1860s gold rush that brought thousands of people to the Black Hills of South Dakota** (Application) The main idea is the rapid development of an uninhabited area. Until the gold rush, whites were forbidden by treaty to settle there. Options (1), (2), and (5) are about the loss of population, not its increase. Option (4) might have pleased people in Illinois but would not have much effect on the growth of population there.

14. **(5) describing the cleanliness of the house** (Inferential Comprehension) The word refers to the house. Options (1), (2), and (3) are incorrect because they do not help the reader understand what the house looks like. Option (4) is incorrect because no appositive is used near the word.

15. **(2) It emphasizes the lasting image he has of the time.** (Analysis) Options (1) and (3) are incorrect because we have no information about what he is like now. Option (4) is incorrect because repetition of a word is not adding detail. Option (5) is incorrect because more explanation is given.

16. **(5) collected by horse and wagon** (Analysis) This phrase describes an actual way laundry was collected and does not idealize the event. All the other options are incorrect because they suggest that life was

wonderful in every way, thus they idealize these events.

17. **(1) chenille seemed to be very in** (Analysis) "Very in" is a slang term, so the language is informal. All the other options are phrases using formal language.

18. **(4) they tinker around with their song and change it** (Literal Comprehension) This fact is stated in lines 24–26. Options (1), (2), and (3) show that whales are singers but not necessarily composers. You may infer from option (5) that changes occur, but option (5) emphasizes when such changes occur. Therefore, option (4) is the best choice.

19. **(2) to show that Katy Payne is an expert in her own right** (Analysis) This is an appositive that gives important information about Katy Payne. Option (1) has no support. Option (3) is incorrect because she agrees with her husband. Option (4) is incorrect because her qualifications have nothing to do with why whales sing. Option (5) is incorrect because it is only a minor detail.

20. **(3) to indicate that Katy Payne's conclusions came after Roger Payne's** (Analysis) "Later" indicates an event that follows another event. Here it refers to Katy Payne's conclusions. Option (1) is incorrect because the new paragraph could begin without the word "later." Options (2), (4), and (5) are true but refer to events in the whales' lives, not in Katy Payne's life.

21. **(2) Whales sing during their long migration.** (Analysis) This statement was made by Jacques Cousteau and Dr. Payne's research disagrees with it. Options (1), (4), and (5) are stated by either Dr. Payne or one of his colleagues so they are incorrect. Since option (1) says all the whales, that must include both male and female whales, so option (3) is incorrect.

22. **(4) kids** (Analysis) "Kid" is slang for child. Options (1) and (2) are standard English words but hint at formal use. Options (3) and (5) could occur in either formal or informal use.

23. **(3) its covered buttons** (Analysis) The fact that the judge states that "in Highland County, covered buttons are it," suggests that this is an important factor in the decision. There is no evidence that options (1), (2), and (5) are outstanding features of the jumper, so they are incorrect. The fact that the judges get nitpicky, or look at very small details,

suggests that this is not the reason, so option (4) is incorrect.

24. **(4) the judge is sorry about the problem** (Analysis) A sigh can show sympathy or regret. Option (1) may be true but has no support in the excerpt. There is no evidence for options (2) and (3). Option (5) may be true, but the excerpt does not indicate that the judge is sighing about not being paid.

25. **(3) A prize may be awarded due to some small point.** (Inferential Comprehension) The senior judge makes a choice between two "nice" garments by isolating a detail in one of them that the other one does not have, covered buttons. There is no evidence that the senior judge is, in general, a picky person, so option (1) is incorrect. Option (2) is incorrect because there is no evidence that all garments need covered buttons. They only became important when all else was equal. Option (4) is true, but is not suggested by the word "nitpicking," so it is incorrect. "Nitpicking" suggests the opposite of option (5), so it is incorrect.

26. **(3) The author is fond of his cat.** (Inferential Comprehension) The tone of the excerpt and the fact that the author attempts to please the cat support this. There is no comparison made to dogs, so option (1) is incorrect. The cat clearly likes to eat, so option (2) is incorrect. The references to Boston and old-fashioned are about the author, not the cat, so option (4) is incorrect. Option (5) is incorrect because the cat is acting on its own sense of time; it has not been trained to watch a clock.

27. **(2) the man had to figure out an easy way to feed the cat in the middle of the night** (Literal Comprehension) Option (1) is the opposite of what happens in the excerpt. The problem was about a late-night snack, not a diet, so option (3) is incorrect. Options (4) and (5) are general statements that are suggested in the excerpt but do not cover the main idea.

28. **(2) the author would devise a plan to satisfy the cat** (Application) Based upon the content of the passage, the author would most likely solve the problem in a similar manner as the food problem. As the author clearly likes the cat, there is no support for options (1) and (5). Options (3) and (4) are unlikely. Since the author did not do this with the food, there is no evidence that he would do it with the water.

29. **(2) never leaves a bit of food in his dish to eat during the night** (Inferential Comprehension) The author implies that if the cat did not eat all his food every evening, it would be unnecessary to get up and feed him. Therefore, the cat should just develop some discipline and a little foresight and save some dinner for later. Options (1), (3), (4), and (5) are not related to the lack of discipline and foresight but to a desire for a snack.

30. **(3) make the reader laugh** (Analysis) The style is informal, lighthearted, and intended to be funny. Options (1) and (5) suggest the style is formal and serious, so both are incorrect. There is no support for options (2) and (4).

31. **(5) people recovering from an illness** (Inferential Comprehension) She is talking as someone who has been in the hospital. Option (1) does not fit in the context. Options (2) and (3) are incorrect because she is referring to patients, not people who work in a hospital. Option (4) is incorrect because it does not refer to people.

32. **(2) people do not enjoy being in the hospital** (Analysis) The author uses sarcasm in saying the opposite of what she means, knowing that people will not take her literally. The rest of the excerpt does not suggest that people can have fun, so option (1) is incorrect. The author is talking about the patient's attitude, not what the hospital provides, so options (3), (4), and (5) are incorrect.

33. **(1) I'm so sweet it's almost sickening.** (Analysis) The excerpt indicates that the author is going beyond being merely agreeable. Option (2) is incorrect because the author tries to be agreeable. While options (3) and (4) may be true, they do not explain how being too adorable can be sickening. Option (5) is a literal interpretation of a figurative statement.

34. **(2) that one in good health is radiant, like an opening blossom** (Analysis) This point is made by comparing health to a new flower, so option (1) is incorrect. Options (3) and (5) do not explain the link between the two words. Option (4) is incorrect because it implies that the flower has already bloomed, which is the opposite of the author's intention.

35. **(3) An earthquake began in the early morning.** (Inferential Comprehension) The descriptions in the last two paragraphs imply the results of the earth shaking; the time is stated. Option (1) is true but much too general. Option (2) refers to a figurative image, not a literal one. There is not enough evidence for option (4). Option (5) may be true but is not suggested here.

36. **(4) as a dramatic contrast to how the city woke up** (Analysis) Option (1) is incorrect because the word does not refer to the policeman. Option (2) has no support. The word "sleep" suggests peacefulness, but what happened next was the opposite; therefore, option (3) is incorrect. The literal meaning of "still" would explain "slept," not the other way around, so option (5) is incorrect.

37. **(1) the slow, sleepy pace of early awakening** (Analysis) The word suggests slowness and is followed by the example of people beginning their day. Option (2) is incorrect because the sun has no feelings. The word describes the sun, not people's awareness, so option (3) is incorrect. The dawn has no connection to the parties, so option (4) is incorrect. Option (5) is not supported.

38. **(4) When the Earth Shrugged Its Shoulders** (Inferential Comprehension) This title not only suggests an earthquake but also uses the same type of figurative language found in the excerpt. Option (1) is incorrect because the earth moved. Option (2) refers only to the first two paragraphs. Option (3) is much too general. Proper reactions are not mentioned, so option (5) is incorrect.

39. **(2) it can be frightening to imagine objects acting on their own** (Analysis) By giving objects human actions, the author creates the atmosphere of unreality and horror. Option (1) is incorrect because objects do not usually do this. Option (3) is partially true but is not enough to explain why these images were used. Options (4) and (5) are incorrect because what happened inside the houses does not illustrate or explain what happened outside.

40. **(3) Objects were thrown like the spray flying off a dog's back.** (Analysis) The familiar image of the dog is usually amusing, but in this context it is scary. People and their possessions are being treated as impersonally as water drops. There is no evidence for option (1). Options (2) and (4) may be true but have nothing to do with the question. Option (5) is not true and also does not explain why the comparison works.

41. **(1) to describe fully the violent spasms of the city** (Analysis) The reference to the Titans is made to explain the jerky, back-and-forth movements of the city. Option (2) does not fully describe the movements. Option (3) refers to a literal image of Titans, not a figurative one as implied by the words "as if." There is no support for options (4) and (5).

42. **(3) wanted to heighten the importance of the scene** (Inferential Comprehension) Although saying the encounter "felled the forest" does show the natural setting, option (1), that is not the purpose of the statement. Option (2) may be true, but it does not refer to the specific event. There is no evidence for options (4) and (5).

43. **(3) Travel is still difficult but not quite as hard as in winter.** (Inferential Comprehension) River travel is possible, but the tundra (the land) is swampy. Options (1), (2), and (5) are incorrect because they describe events that have no direct connection with spring. Option (4) is not suggested in the excerpt.

44. **(4) People's acts were as violent and uncontrollable as the weather.** (Inferential Comprehension) This is suggested by the details. Options (1) and (3) have nothing to do with the land. Options (2) and (5) are true but do not answer the question.

45. **(2) The white man took interest in an area previously inhabited by Indians and Eskimos.** (Inferential Comprehension) The presence of the white man is not mentioned until after the discovery of gold. Options (1) and (4) might be true but they are not mentioned in the excerpt. While option (3) might be considered a logical inference, there is no actual evidence given to support this statement. Lines 29–34 mention the white man's cruelty, so option (5) is not directly supported by the excerpt.

46. **(4) facing the dangers of nature alone** (Inferential Comprehension) The author felt that he was testing his own abilities through the challenge of climbing a mountain. Options (1) and (2) refer to what he was doing before he found adventure. Option (3) is a detail about the adventure. Option (5) is a detail of the result.

47. **(2) They are snowy, isolated mountains.** (Inferential Comprehension) The details of the excerpt add up to this. Option (1) is not supported by any reference to other students. There is no evidence for options (3) and (5). Option (4) cannot be determined because there is no suggestion of distance.

48. **(4) It would be a challenge.** (Application) The author enjoyed the struggle against a

natural obstacle. Options (1) and (5) might be true, but they are only partial reasons for his enjoyment. Option (2) is incorrect because there is no evidence that he lives in the mountains. Option (3) has no support.

49. **(3) a wolf** (Application) Lines 17–19 indicate that the author identifies with being an animal. While options (1), (2), (4), and (5) are part of the author's life, after he climbs the Alps he feels a strong identification with nature.

50. **(4) great joy** (Inferential Comprehension) The ideas of "magical spirit" and "gaining a goal" support this option. Options (1), (2), and (3) are details of feelings during the adventure previous to attaining the goal. Option (5) is not supported by the excerpt.

Lesson 3: Drama (page 426)

1. **(5) understand his father's absence** (Analysis) This point is made by David's frequent questions along these lines. Option (1) is not supported. Option (2) could be true because his father has caused him pain, but it is also not supported. Option (3) may be true, but there is no evidence for it. Option (4) is true but only supports David's main motivation.

2. **(1) show that he can live with pain** (Analysis) This is correct because he has learned this himself and hopes to pass it on to David, which rules out option (3). Option (2) is not supported by the excerpt. Option (4), from what he says, is not a choice Luke would make for David. Option (5) is true but does not tell Luke's major motivation.

3. **(2) hurt and anger** (Inferential Comprehension) The last part of the excerpt reveals David's hurt and anger at Luke for being absent. Option (1) may be true for Luke's musical talent but not for his role as father. There is no evidence for options (3) and (4). While option (5) is mentioned, it is not David's strongest feeling about Luke as his father.

4. **(3) begin to respect each other** (Application) Even though David is angry at Luke, their tones suggest a desire to resolve their differences. There is no evidence for option (1). While Luke dreams about option (2), there is no evidence that it will ever happen. While there might be anger between the two, there is no indication that option (4) is correct. Option (5) is unlikely as Luke says not to "try to get away from things that hurt you."

5. **(3) John and Shirley are used to fighting.** (Inferential Comprehension) The fight is conducted good-naturedly, and Shirley's protest when John carries her off is humorous. This suggests they have fought often on a friendly level. Option (1) is obviously not true, because Shirley is annoyed with June. There is not enough evidence to support option (2). Options (4) and (5) are the opposite of what is shown throughout this scene.

6. **(3) dramatize herself and get attention** (Analysis) Shirley's actions are those of someone seeking attention. Option (1) is too strong. Though she may become an artist, her concerns are really with the present moment, ruling out option (2). Option (4) is not supported. Option (5) is incorrect because she shows that age—that is, being older—is important to her.

7. **(2) indulgence** (Inferential Comprehension) Throughout the passage, June patiently corrects Shirley without asking her to stop her actions; therefore, option (1) is incorrect. By correcting Shirley, June is taking action, so option (3) is incorrect. While the excerpt is humorous, there is no evidence for option (4). There is no evidence of sympathy, so option (5) is incorrect.

8. **(4) she would lie** (Application) Since Shirley doesn't mind lying to June and to John, people she knows, it is likely that she would lie to someone she does not know at all; therefore, option (1) is incorrect. The passage does not support option (2). Option (3) may be true but there is no evidence for it in the excerpt. Since Shirley disregards what June says, option (5) is incorrect.

9. **(5) amused concern** (Analysis) John plays around and smiles at Shirley but also expresses the view that June "better watch that one." There is no evidence to support options (1), (3), or (4), so they are incorrect. It is uncertain how John feels about Shirley, so option (2) is incorrect.

10. **(2) Age is irrelevant.** (Literal Comprehension) In line 6, Shirley states that age is irrelevant. Although Shirley states option (1), it is in a comment about becoming an artist and is not about age in general. Options (3) and (5) are not supported by the excerpt. Although she keeps changing what she says her age is, option (4) does not address her attitude toward age.

11. **(5) Lonely people often stop being socially active.** (Analysis) Even though they are together in this scene, Marty and Angie are clearly lonely and have stopped trying to do much about it. Option (1) is incorrect because the focus is not on marriage itself. Option (2) is not the main issue here. Options (3) and (4) refer to a specific person and a specific plot line; therefore, they do not express a theme.

12. **(3) spend many evenings sitting around** (Inferential Comprehension) Option (3) can be inferred from Angie's second speech, which also rules out option (1). Option (2) is incorrect because only Marty says he wants to get married. Option (4) is not supported by the excerpt. Option (5) is unlikely in their present situation.

13. **(2) Angie is more comfortable with women than Marty** (Analysis) Marty's speech in lines 32–34 implies that Angie's sense of humor helps him get along with women. While general conclusions can be drawn from the excerpt, they cannot be made about all men. Therefore, options (1) and (3) are incorrect. Option (4) is not true. Angie and Marty are clearly friends. Option (5) is not true. He wants to telephone but Marty is unwilling.

14. **(3) Girls don't go for him.** (Literal Comprehension) Marty states this fact in line 31. Options (1), (2), (4), and (5) are all details about Marty but do not explain his problem.

15. **(1) Opposites attract.** (Analysis) Despite their differences, the two men seem to like each other. The excerpt focuses on the relationship between the two; options (2), (4), and (5) have nothing to do with that idea. Option (3) is not supported in the excerpt.

16. **(2) lying around all day** (Application) From what is suggested about his character, Felix likes to stay busy. Option (1) is incorrect because he apparently likes to cook. Options (3), (4), and (5) are incorrect because he seems to enjoy having everything clean and orderly.

17. **(3) Felix always reminds Oscar of what he does around the house.** (Application) The preceding lines suggest that Felix is afraid that Oscar will forget to notice all he does around the house. Options (1), (2), and (5) are not supported by the excerpt. While option (4) may seem correct when read literally, it is unlikely that Felix actually keeps Oscar up all night with the sound of counting money.

18. **(4) Oscar is getting used to Felix.** (Inferential Comprehension) Based upon Oscar's claim that he is worried that he is beginning to listen to Felix, it can be inferred that he fears he is getting used to living with Felix. Options (1) and (3) are not supported by the excerpt. Oscar agrees that Felix saves them money, so option (2) is incorrect. Option (5) is incorrect because Oscar does not state his dislike of halibut steak.

Lesson 4: Poetry (page 430)

1. **(4) While traveling to Colorado, I stopped to look at the land around San Ysidro.** (Literal Comprehension) While option (1) may be true, it cannot be inferred from the lines. Option (2) seems to be true but does not fully restate the lines. Option (3) is incorrect because the lines indicate that the speaker did stop. Option (5) may be true, but this is not where the speaker stopped.

2. **(2) the Katzina** (Literal Comprehension) The masked dancers dance as a form of prayer at the ceremony. None of the other choices are associated with these lines.

3. **(4) recalling the time when he stopped** (Analysis) There is a time shift in the poem at line 27. The poet is at the ceremony but is recalling his earlier stop, so option (5) is incorrect. There is no support for option (1). Options (2) and (3) make sense only if the speaker is still traveling, and it is not clear that he is. The ceremony may take place where he lives.

4. **(2) reaching earth in shafts of light** (Literal Comprehension) This point is made in lines 19–26 in which the sunlight is described as falling down to earth. Option (1) is incorrect because the sunlight can be seen through the clouds. There is no indication that the sunlight is too bright or too strong, so options (3) and (4) are incorrect. There is no support for option (5).

5. **(1) joyful** (Analysis) Lines 34–42 indicate the happiness that the speaker feels about the plants and earth. There is no direct evidence for options (2), (3), (4), and (5).

6. **(4) the renewal of the plants and earth** (Analysis) This point is made in lines 39–41 and is the culmination of the speaker's observations about the land. Option (1) is incorrect because the speaker is urging mother and son to watch, not suggesting that they are arriving. There is no support for

options (2) or (3). Option (5) is incorrect because the speaker is not talking about the dancers coming to dance but about the plants coming back in the spring.

7. **(3) the wonders of nature** (Inferential Comprehension) The author's references to and awe of a variety of objects from nature are indicated throughout the poem. While options (1) and (2) may be true, they are literal interpretations of figurative meaning. There is no support for option (4). Option (5) is a detail of the poem but not the main thing the poet describes.

8. **(1) spring** (Inferential Comprehension) The earth is described as "new again," so spring is the season in which the events of the poem are most likely to occur. Therefore, options (2), (3), and (4) are incorrect, as they are seasons which are not "new again." Option (5) is incorrect because there is enough information in the poem to infer the season in which the action takes place.

9. **(2) sure that everything returns to nature** (Inferential Comprehension) This is implied by the speaker's discussion of houses and people in relation to the ocean and earth. There is no support for option (1). Option (3) is the opposite of what is implied. Option (4) is incorrect because the poet is critical of the community. Option (5) is incorrect because it is obvious that the speaker is familiar with the area.

10. **(1) There used to be fields where houses now stand.** (Analysis) This point is made in lines 2–4. There is no direct evidence for options (2), (3), or (4). Option (5) has no support in the poem.

11. **(4) Populations increase and decrease in cycles.** (Inferential Comprehension) The comparison of people with tides implies the cyclical ebb and flow of populations. Option (1) is a literal interpretation of figurative language. Options (2) and (3) only partially acknowledge what is being implied in the lines. There is no support for option (5).

12. **(3) in a secluded house by the sea** (Application) Based upon the negative references to the housing developments and the positive comments about the ocean, it can be inferred that the speaker would most likely prefer to live by the ocean, away from other houses. The poem suggests that options (1) and (2) are the opposite of what the poet would prefer. Options (4) and (5) are unlikely based on the information given in the poem.

13. **(3) where people had to be brave to survive** (Analysis) Having nerve can be the same as having courage, and "law" refers to what was respected by otherwise lawless people. Option (1) reverses the idea. Option (2) has nothing to do with nerve. Option (4) is true but is the reason that courage was required. Option (5) is the opposite of what is meant.

14. **(4) fearlessness** (Analysis) The father had faced all the real and imagined dangers of the speaker's childhood to protect his son. So options (1), (2), and (3) are incorrect. Option (5) may have been true, but it is not illustrated in the poem.

15. **(1) Parents and children eventually change roles.** (Inferential Comprehension) This point is made by the author's discussion of how his father used to protect him and now needs protection. Options (2), (4), and (5) may be true, but they are details of the poem. Option (3) is incorrect because the author expresses his desire to help his father.

16. **(3) sharpened** (Inferential Comprehension) The image of a sharp knife reinforces the author's discussion of how his father protected him from danger. Options (1), (2), and (4) do not imply danger. Option (5) is incorrect because it would be unlikely that the hoodlums would willingly break their knives.

17. **(5) He is comparing the commuters and the geese.** (Inferential Comprehension) Options (1), (2), and (3) have no support; the birds are a major part of the poem but are not mentioned in these options. Option (4) refers to the image in lines 1–2 in which there is no element of contrast.

18. **(3) airplanes landing** (Literal Comprehension) The poet uses the phrases "wings of jets," "landing gear," and "National Airport" to evoke an image of the geese as airplanes landing. Option (1) is incorrect because the poet likens the geese to airplanes, not pterodactyl wings. Option (2) is incorrect because the geese land by the boats, but the poet does not compare them to the boats. The geese are not compared to swamps, so option (4) is incorrect. Option (5) is incorrect because the geese land on the river; they are not compared to the river.

19. **(2) Commuters follow habits like the geese.** (Analysis) The idea of habit is suggested by the words "obeying," "never revised," and "still stop off" (lines 1–3). Option (1) is incorrect; it is the geese who have the

maps in their brains. There is no support for options (3) and (4). Option (5) is incorrect because the commuters are not confused and do not need a map.

20. **(5) Small things can change the direction of a person's life.** (Analysis) Here "bud" means a new beginning, influenced by what might appear to be unimportant things. Option (1) is a good choice, but the poem focuses on the accidental changes and making adjustments to them, not on finding a way by reading signs. There is no support for options (2) and (4). Option (3) is incorrect because there is no suggestion of hidden meanings.

21. **(4) to emphasize the idea of chance** (Analysis) This repeats the idea that unexpected things happen. Option (1) refers to another meaning of "accident." There is no support for options (2), (3), and (5).

22. **(3) a familiar place** (Literal Comprehension) "By heart" means committed to memory. Option (1) refers to another idea suggested by the word "heart." Options (2) and (4) misinterpret the phrase. Option (5) is incorrect because a country is not a path.

23. **(3) The art of living involves shaping chance happenings to your own purposes.** (Inferential Comprehension) There is only one option that is focused on chance, or accidental occurrences. Options (1) and (5) are incorrect because they are general observations about traveling but not the sort of travel the poet means. Option (2) is a true statement but is in support of the main idea. Option (4) is incorrect because it is literal and because it is not what the poet says.

24. **(2) The poem compares decisions one makes in life to those a traveler makes.** (Application) The poem is a comparison of a traveler's choices and those made in life. Options (1), (3), (4), and (5) are not supported by the poem.

GED Review: Popular Literature (page 436)

1. **(3) Madge and her parents seemed permanently doomed by the Great Depression.** (Literal Comprehension) This idea is stated in the first sentence. Option (1) may be true, but it is a detail, not the main idea. Options (2) and (4) may have been true, but they are not supported by the paragraph. Option (5) is untrue; it was a turning point for many of her friends but not for her.

2. **(1) Madge and her mother had graduated from Miss Fairfax's School.** (Inferential Comprehension) This detail is about the school where Madge was teaching. Options (2), (3), (4), and (5) help to explain why the family seemed doomed.

3. **(2) Madge's body and face were showing the signs of her experiences with hardship.** (Inferential Comprehension) The effects of Madge's hard life are implied in lines 35–42. Options (1), (4), and (5) are details, not the main idea. Option (3) is not supported by the excerpt.

4. **(3) the Statue of Liberty** (Inferential Comprehension) The tall green woman is the Statue of Liberty, which stands on an island near Ellis Island. It is a symbol of the freedom that immigrants seek when they come to the U.S. and is one of the first things they see when arriving in New York harbor. There is no support in the poem for options (1), (2), (4), or (5).

5. **(4) the speaker's Native American heritage** (Inferential Comprehension) When the speaker refers to "Another voice . . .," he is talking about his Native American ancestry. By stating that only one part of him loves the memory of his Slovak ancestors arriving on Ellis Island, he implies that there is a part of him that has no ties to Europe. There is no support for options (1), (2), and (3) in the poem. Option (5) is the part of his ancestry which he describes in the first half of the poem, so it is incorrect.

Classical Literature
Lesson 5: Fiction/Nonfiction (page 438)

1. **(3) about to get on a train for the first time** (Literal Comprehension) This information is given in lines 37–42. Option (1) refers to what Ishi calls the train. Options (2) and (4) are the opposite of what is stated. Option (5) refers to something Ishi finds is not true.

2. **(1) as if the author knows what the character is thinking** (Analysis) The excerpt is written in the third person. The biographer is writing as if she sees through Ishi's eyes. Option (2) is incorrect because Ishi is not telling his own story. Option (3) has no support. The author seems to know Ishi well, so option (4) is incorrect. There is no evidence for option (5).

3. **(3) sympathetic** (Analysis) The description of the man's nervousness shows understanding. Option (1) might refer to Ishi at one point, but not to the author. There is no support for options (2), (4), and (5).

4. **(2) emphasize how Ishi saw the train as being alive** (Analysis) The words in the description refer to the train as if it had human characteristics. There is no support for option (1). Option (3) is suggested by calling the train a demon, but the author is not saying that trains are evil. There is no support for option (4). Option (5) has nothing to do with the excerpt.

5. **(4) Ishi had never expected to ride a train** (Inferential Comprehension) The excerpt as a whole suggests this idea. It is supported by Ishi's mother telling him that trains had nothing to do with Indians. Option (1) might have been true, but it is not suggested in the excerpt. Option (2) is the opposite of what is suggested. Option (3) is not true; Waterman is a new friend. There is no mention of time, so option (5) is incorrect.

6. **(4) the hooting of the train's whistle** (Analysis) This phrase refers to the noise the train makes as it comes into the station. Option (1) is incorrect because it is the train's noise, not that of people. Option (2) is incorrect because a clank is different from a moan. The noise is not Ishi's, so option (3) is incorrect. A cloud does not make a sound, so option (5) is incorrect.

7. **(2) excitement at another new experience** (Application) This inference can be made based upon Ishi's initial reluctance to leave the train and then his anticipation of the ferry and trolley rides. Therefore, option (1) is incorrect. Option (3) is incorrect because, while Ishi finds the train's speed exciting, it is not a major part of his feelings about his travels. Options (4) and (5) are not discussed in the excerpt.

8. **(3) its lets him experience the journey of rivers and creeks** (Inferential Comprehension) In lines 57–66, Ishi notes that now he can see how creeks and rivers from home reach the sea. No one he knew had ever seen this route. It is not clear that Ishi will not ride a train again, so option (1) is incorrect. Option (2) is not stated in the excerpt. While option (4) may be true, it is not indicated by the author as the reason for the route's importance to Ishi. Option (5) is literally true but does not indicate why the route is important to Ishi.

9. **(5) a person who is not a character in the story** (Literal Comprehension) The story is told in the third person. All of the people in the excerpt are described in the third person, so options (1), (2), and (4) are incorrect. The demon is the train, so option (3) is incorrect.

10. **(1) Rosicky thinks this graveyard would be a comfortable place to end up in.** (Inferential Comprehension) All of his thoughts about the graveyard are pleasant. Option (2) assumes that the friends and neighbors there are the only ones he had. There is no support for options (3) and (4). Option (5) is incorrect because he observes only how close they are; he does not seem worried.

11. **(4) the two places are not all that different** (Inferential Comprehension) The drawing together (lines 36–38) applies not just to the land but to life and death. Option (1) is a figurative generalization that is not supported in this excerpt. Options (2) and (3) may be generally true but do not support the main idea. Option (5) has no support.

12. **(2) There was a clump of orchard behind it.** (Literal Comprehension) It is the narrator's house that has an orchard behind it. Options (1), (3), (4), and (5) all refer to the graveyard. It is clear the narrator finds the graveyard comfortable because he says it is snug and homelike.

13. **(1) peaceful** (Literal Comprehension) Rosicky can imagine resting peacefully in the graveyard. Rosicky does not think that the graveyard is mournful, so it does not make him sad, option (2). The excerpt says that there is nothing to make Rosicky feel awkward, option (3), or embarrassed, option (5). There is nothing in the excerpt to indicate that Rosicky is cheerful, so option (4) is incorrect.

14. **(3) a happy scene around the fireplace** (Application) The author has said they were the picture of happiness, so her image would be a happy and cozy one. Options (1), (2), and (4) are not pictures of a happy and loving home. Option (5) would turn the peaceful scene into a tragedy.

15. **(2) the scene could be called "The Sailor's Homecoming"** (Inferential Comprehension) She first infers that the girl was his wife and the cottage their home; then she connects all four details into a logical conclusion. Options (1) and (3) are the author's opinions about her conclusion, not the conclusion itself. Option (4) is an observation of fact. Option (5) is the author's feeling about her conclusion.

16. **(3) After seeing the couple, the author found it difficult to look at the world in the same way.** (Inferential Comprehension) In lines 25–31, the author notes the ways in which her outlook has been changed by her

experience. Options (1) and (5) are literal interpretations and are not expressed by the author. Since the author states that only "some things appear foolish," option (2) is incorrect. Option (4) is incorrect because there is no mention by the author regarding her feelings about herself.

17. **(4) has an easygoing, chatty style** (Analysis) The author's chatty, conversational style is typical of an informal essay. There is no evidence for options (1), (2), (3), and (5).

18. **(5) re-experience its peacefulness** (Literal Comprehension) In lines 20–25 the author states his reason for going back to the lake. Though he might also wish to teach his son canoeing, option (4), that is not his main reason. There is no evidence for options (1), (2), and (3).

19. **(2) civilization had come to this secluded spot of nature** (Inferential Comprehension) First, "the tarred road" has to be understood as being a paved highway and "found it out" as meaning "found its way there." A paved road would provide easy access; so what the author feared can be concluded. There is no support for options (1) and (3). Options (4) and (5) are the opposite of what worried the author.

20. **(2) riding horses** (Literal Comprehension) There is no mention of riding of any kind. All the other details are mentioned.

21. **(1) never stopped blowing** (Inferential Comprehension) "Incessant" means constant. The context clue is that the wind blew all afternoon and continued in the evening. Options (2), (3), (4), and (5) do not make sense in the context of the sentence or excerpt.

22. **(3) longing to recapture the joys of youth** (Inferential Comprehension) In line 25 the author refers to revisiting old haunts. In lines 42–59 he reviews memories obviously dear to him and wonders wistfully if things will still be the same. His fear that things may have changed suggests how much he wants to recapture his youth. There is some evidence for options (1), (2), (4), and (5), but option (3) is the implication best supported by the excerpt.

23. **(4) his son had never experienced swimming in a lake** (Inferential Comprehension) The author states that he took his son along to the lake because he had never experienced a lakeside vacation. There is no support for options (1) and (2). Option (3) is incorrect because the author makes reference to salt water and states that his son

hadn't experienced fresh water. Option (5) may be true, but the author's references to salt water suggest the opposite.

24. **(2) he was experiencing the lake as both himself and as his father** (Analysis) Because the author's son has developed similar behaviors to those the author had when he was a boy, the author realizes that his experience at the lake involves identifying not only with his childhood memories but also with his father. Options (1) and (4) are incorrect because they are literal interpretations of the author's words. The author does not indicate a conflict between his feelings towards the sea and the lake, therefore option (3) is incorrect. Option (5) may be correct, but it is not what the author is referring to.

25. **(2) calm** (Inferential Comprehension) The author describes the "restlessness of the tides" and "the incessant wind." These make him wish for a place that is different, or calmer. There is no support for options (1) and (4). The lake is not necessarily in the shade, option (3). The author wants to go somewhere quiet and calm, not exciting, option (5).

26. **(3) a grown man** (Inferential Comprehension) He is remembering an event from his boyhood, so option (1) is incorrect. Option (2) is incorrect because there is no evidence of what he does. Options (4) and (5) are incorrect because there is no suggestion of how he feels emotionally or physically at the time he tells the story.

27. **(2) simple and direct** (Analysis) The sentences are short and to the point, so option (3) is incorrect. The language is plain and easy to understand, so options (1) and (4) are incorrect. Although the style is informal, there is no attempt at humor, so option (5) is incorrect.

28. **(4) Everyone in the village goes on the hunt.** (Literal Comprehension) The small boys are not allowed to hunt, and the women stay behind to prepare the drying racks. Options (1), (2), (3), and (5) are stated in the excerpt.

29. **(3) a time when he could do things that would otherwise not be permitted** (Literal Comprehension) The author relates being allowed to eat before everyone else, an activity that did not follow tradition. The excerpt describes the hunt as a form of pleasure for the author, so options (1) and (5) are incorrect. Options (2) and (4) are not supported by the excerpt.

30. **(4) a sense of intimacy** (Analysis) By telling his own story, the author gives a first-hand, detailed account of the events of his life. This gives the reader a feeling of closeness to the author. Options (1), (3), and (5) are incorrect because they all suggest a lack of closeness. Although the author's account is very detailed, option (2) is incorrect because he makes no attempt to write from a scientific point of view.

31. **(2) Carter Druse acts on his beliefs no matter what the consequences** (Inferential Comprehension) Carter fought for a cause he believed in even though it hurt his parents, and the strength of his convictions apparently made his officers trust him in a dangerous situation. Druse is clearly brave and he fought against his state, not his country, so option (1) is incorrect. There is no support for option (3). Option (4) may be true, but it is a generalization that is not the main idea of the excerpt. Option (5) is a restatement of a supporting detail.

32. **(3) Carter leaves although his mother is dying.** (Literal Comprehension) Options (1), (2), and (5) are details in the excerpt, but they do not support the main idea. Option (4) is not true; his father says that they will speak again if they both live through the war.

33. **(3) keep a difficult promise** (Application) Carter is clearly an honest and honorable man, so if he made a promise, he would keep it. It is not in his character as described in the excerpt to do what is suggested by options (1), (2), and (5). As he has just made the decision in the face of opposition, option (4) is unlikely.

34. **(4) a man of honor who respects his son's beliefs** (Inferential Comprehension) His response illustrates that Carter's father respected Carter's decision even though he didn't agree with it; therefore option (2) is incorrect. Option (1) is incorrect because the excerpt indicates the father's stated concern for his wife and his unstated concern for his son. There is no evidence for option (3). The first paragraph states that Carter is the son of wealthy parents, so option (5) is incorrect.

35. **(2) was busy saving the woman he loved** (Inferential Comprehension) This inference is correct because the man looks at the woman right after hearing his brother. There is no evidence for options (1) and (4). Option (3) is incorrect because he saw his brother fall and heard him call. The passion with which he speaks of his brother indicates that option (5) is incorrect.

36. **(3) guilt-ridden** (Inferential Comprehension) The narrator's feeling of guilt is made clear in the line "My own name! . . . My brother!" There is no support, direct or implied, for options (1), (2), (4), and (5).

37. **(5) run away with his beloved** (Inferential Comprehension) Although there is no mention of exactly whom they were running away from, they were definitely running away. There is no support for options (1), (3), and (4). There is no evidence of why Diamelen was there in the first place, so option (2) is incorrect.

38. **(4) stop feeling guilty about the death of his brother** (Inferential Comprehension) The narrator feels guilty about the death of his brother and hopes he can forget about his guilt, not about his brother, option (1). Nothing in the excerpt suggests that the narrator also expects to see his brother after both are dead, option (2), or that the narrator is plotting revenge, option (3). The narrator is the one who feels guilty, not Diamelen, option (5).

39. **(4) Both brothers would have been killed.** (Analysis) The men who were chasing the narrator and his brother caught the brother, so it is logical that the narrator also would have been killed if he had waited or turned back to get his brother. Thus, options (1), (2), and (3) are incorrect. Option (5) is incorrect because, if the narrator had gone back for his brother, Diamelen would likely have been caught, too.

40. **(4) There was not enough work in Recco to support his family.** (Inferential Comprehension) Louie implies that work was scarce by talking about the fishermen and the bathhouse; that, combined with the mention of his large family, leads to the conclusion in option (4). Option (1) is a fact that does not answer the question. Option (2) may have been true but is not implied. There is no support for options (3) and (5).

41. **(1) It helps make the character of Louie come alive.** (Analysis) Using Louie's own speech makes him seem more real than just a character being described. Option (2) is incorrect because Louie's language is even more informal than the author's. The author seems to understand Louie fairly well, so option (3) is incorrect. Option (4) is incorrect because the tone is casual. Option (5) is incorrect because there is no evidence of disagreement.

42. **(2) The first restaurant Louie worked in was in Brooklyn.** (Literal Comprehension)

Louie states that the first restaurant he worked in was located in the Bronx. All other details are stated in the excerpt.

43. **(3) is sentimental** (Inferential Comprehension) Louie chose a building in a fish market because it reminded him of home. From this you can infer that he made his choice because of sentimental feelings about Recco. Option (1) is incorrect because one of the up-to-date restaurants would probably have been a better business decision. Option (2) is incorrect because it is the overall feel of the place, not only the fish, that reminds him of home. Option (4) is incorrect because there is nothing in the excerpt to suggest that Louis likes to argue. Option (5) is incorrect because Louis says that the modern restaurants in midtown "could be bought at a bargain."

44. **(4) people adapt to new situations** (Analysis) Although the author touches on options (1), (2), (3), and (5) as he tells about his early school days, the idea of adapting to new situations is the theme. Lines 37–38 support this.

45. **(3) fond amusement** (Analysis) The tone of this excerpt is humorous. The word choice and examples are designed to be funny. There is no support for options (1), (4), and (5). Although his initial reaction, when he was faced with his first day of school, was anger and disbelief, option (2), his remembrance of the experience as a whole is warm and positive.

46. **(1) disorderly mob** (Inferential Comprehension) The context is about the author's experiences with the other school children in the schoolyard. He describes the collection of unruly and badly behaved boys and girls, so options (2) and (4) are incorrect. Option (3) is incorrect because it describes the author at the time the story takes place. Option (5) describes only a detail of the group.

47. **(2) The author is remembering his early childhood as free of remorse.** (Inferential Comprehension) Through his use of the phrase "last guiltless days" the author is implying that his childhood was free from shame and remorse regarding the pranks the children played upon one another and on the teacher. The phrase implies that, as they got older, the children learned to feel remorse over doing something unkind. There is no support for options (1), (3), and (4). While the author mentions stealing an apple, his memories are not in the form of a confession, therefore option (5) is incorrect.

48. **(3) his clients do not always want his best effort** (Inferential Comprehension) The example suggests that customers are more interested in saving or making money; the author is more interested in quality. Options (1) and (2) are incorrect because money is not his main concern and because we do not know how much money he makes or needs. There is no evidence for option (4). Option (5) is not true.

49. **(4) having to do with money** (Inferential Comprehension) The context is about work and money. The sentence that follows suggests how a town should best spend its money. Options (1), (2), (3), and (5) do not make sense in that context.

50. **(1) in the first person** (Analysis) The use of "I" indicates that the excerpt is being told by the person who experienced the events, or in the first person. Therefore, the excerpt was not told by a person who sells wood, option (2); the surveyor's wife, option (3); in the third person, option (4); or by a past client, option (5).

51. **(2) turn down the job** (Application) Based on his statements in lines 26–28, the narrator would refuse to do a job before doing work that he didn't love. Money is not important to the narrator, so option (1) is incorrect. Option (3) is incorrect because the narrator is obviously proud of his good work. There is no support for options (4) and (5).

52. **(4) are a little dishonest** (Inferential Comprehension) He says that his employer "commonly asks which will give him the most land, not which is most correct." Employers do not criticize his work, option (1), or underpay him, option (3). Options (2) and (5) are not supported by the excerpt.

Lesson 6: Drama (page 450)

1. **(4) angry and defensive** (Analysis) Walter's anger shows in the way he treats his wife and in his defensive response to his mother. There is no support for options (1), (2), (3), and (5).

2. **(5) strong and caring** (Analysis) Mama's concern for her son and his wife comes through in the strong stand she takes about his behavior. Options (1) and (3) are incorrect because calm is not the same as patience or passiveness, and Mama is not simply tolerating Walter's behavior. Options (2) and (4) suggest the opposite of her character.

3. **(2) Walter does not want to be with Ruth.** (Inferential Comprehension) The first half of the excerpt concerns Walter's attempt to flee

from Ruth; therefore, option (1) is incorrect. Though Ruth leaves the room, she does not state a desire to leave Walter, so option (3) is incorrect. There is no evidence for option (4). Option (5) is incorrect because even though Walter is more respectful of his mother, this does not indicate a desire to be with her rather than Ruth.

4. **(3) to accompany Walter so that they could speak** (Application) Ruth's desire to speak to Walter and her feelings for him are both evident, even when she leaves the room. There is no evidence to support options (1) and (4). Option (2) is a literal interpretation of the figurative meaning of Ruth's words. While Walter makes reference to nagging, it is with regard to his mother, so option (5) is incorrect.

5. **(4) resourceful and determined** (Inferential Comprehension) Nora is clearly not humble and obedient, option (1); hysterical, option (2); or evil, option (3). While she may have an impulsive streak, option (5), her determination and resourcefulness are her most obvious qualities.

6. **(2) impractical** (Inferential Comprehension) When Nora's husband called her frivolous, he meant that she was being silly and impractical. There is no evidence for options (1), (3), (4), and (5).

7. **(1) cautious and unadventurous** (Inferential Comprehension) Based upon her reactions to Nora, Mrs. Linde cannot be described as wild, option (3); deceitful, option (4); or flirtatious, option (5). Mrs. Linde may seem boring in comparison to Nora, but this is a detail compared to her caution; therefore, option (2) is incorrect.

8. **(2) Going South would be good for her husband's health.** (Literal Comprehension) Nora tells Mrs. Linde that this is the way to save her husband's life. Option (1) is one way Amanda tries to get him to go South. Options (3), (4), and (5) are not supported by the excerpt.

9. **(4) reasonable and firm** (Inferential Comprehension) Karen does her best to reason with Mary, but she is also firm with her. She is not prim, option (1); harsh, option (2); or easily intimidated, option (5). Nor is she overly forgiving toward the girl, ruling out option (3).

10. **(5) sneaky and uncooperative** (Inferential Comprehension) Mary's tears and tantrums, threats, and steady refusal to tell the truth tell us that she is hard to control. She may be lonely and misunderstood as well, option (1), but those are not her chief traits. There is no evidence for options (2), (3), and (4).

11. **(3) getting her own way** (Inferential Comprehension) Mary has proved that she can get her own way; she has also proved that she cannot admit mistakes, option (1); accept punishment, option (4); or obey orders, option (5). There is no evidence that she would be good at helping others, option (2).

12. **(3) conflict** (Analysis) The clash of wills between Mary and Karen makes this a scene full of conflict. There is no evidence for options (1), (2), (4), or (5).

13. **(4) makes it easy for Mary to manipulate Karen's responses** (Inferential Comprehension) Karen's responsibility for Mary makes her vulnerable to Mary's accusations and phony heart attack; Karen must ask herself if she is being unfair or unfeeling at the same time that she is trying to discipline Mary. Therefore, option (1) is incorrect. The conflict between them is both real and unavoidable, so option (3) is incorrect. There is no support for options (2) and (5).

14. **(2) take revenge on Karen** (Application) What we already know about Mary does not suggest the possibility of her changing much, option (1). It is more likely that Mary will find a way to get revenge on Karen. There is no support for options (3), (4), and (5).

15. **(3) assign Mary a harsh punishment** (Application) Mrs. Mortar's comment (line 53) regarding how she would treat Mary indicates that she is less patient with Mary's misbehavior, so options (1), (2), and (4) are incorrect. There is no support for option (5).

16. **(1) Karen does not value her opinions.** (Inferential Comprehension) The stage directions show that Karen ignores Mrs. Mortar. This implies that Karen does not value her opinions. The fact that Karen openly ignores her shows that the two women are not close friends, option (2). It also shows that Karen is not careful to protect Mrs. Mortar's feelings, option (3), nor does she respect her, option (4). There is no evidence for option (5) in the excerpt.

17. **(5) pretending to like Karen** (Literal Comprehension) Based on Mary's behavior, it is obvious that she is not concerned with convincing Karen that she likes her. Option (1) is incorrect because Mary whimpers.

Option (2) is incorrect because we know that Mary is lying about the flowers. Option (3) is incorrect because Mary threatens to call her grandmother. Option (4) is incorrect because Mary falls to the floor pretending to be ill.

18. **(4) wait for Mary to decide to get up** (Analysis) Karen does not appear worried when Mary says she feels ill, so options (1), (2), and (5) are unlikely. Option (3) is incorrect because Karen ignores Mrs. Mortar.

Lesson 7: Poetry (page 454)

1. **(2) banged** (Analysis) This point is made by the author's reference to "knocking" (line 2) and the Traveler's repeated attempts to get someone's attention. Option (1) is incorrect because lines 25–26 refer to the increasing volume of the knocking. There is no direct evidence for options (3), (4), and (5).

2. **(4) The residents of the house did not look out at the Traveler.** (Inferential Comprehension) The first part of the poem indicates the Traveler's failed attempts to get the attention of the residents of the house. There is no support for option (1). Option (2) is a literal interpretation of figurative language. Option (3) is a supporting detail. There is no support for option (5).

3. **(3) vacant** (Literal Comprehension) Based on the author's description of the house, it is both silent and remote. The presence of "phantom listeners" (line 13) indicates that the house is not empty. Options (1), (2), (4), and (5) restate the author's description of the poem's setting.

4. **(2) It was not the time for the Traveler to be welcomed into the house.** (Analysis) Lines 27–28 imply that the Traveler's presence was not unexpected. There is no evidence for options (1) and (4). Option (3) is incorrect because the Traveler was not a stranger. Option (5) may be true, but it is not supported by the poem.

5. **(1) the house was haunted** (Literal Comprehension) Lines 15–16 indicate the differences between the Traveler and the "phantoms." Option (2) has no support. While options (3) and (4) may be true, they are not supported by the poem. The poem indicates that the Traveler had a specific purpose at this particular house, therefore option (5) is incorrect.

6. **(2) eerie expectation** (Analysis) Lines 22 and 29 indicate the listeners' strange stillness and silence as they listen to every sound. While the Traveler is rejected by the listeners,

there is no suggestion that he is emotionally affected by this; so option (1) is incorrect. There is no support for options (3), (4), and (5).

7. **(3) those inside the house are no longer alive** (Analysis) The Traveler is "awake" in contrast to the people inside, who are dead, or "asleep." Option (1) may be true, but it doesn't explain why the Traveler is the only person awake. There is no evidence in the poem to support options (2), (4), or (5).

8. **(3) because the poem focuses on the people inside the house** (Inferential Comprehension) There is no evidence in the poem to suggest it was meant to be read aloud, so option (1) is incorrect. While the title of the poem helps readers know what to look for when reading the poem, it does not necessarily involve them in the action of the poem, so option (2) is incorrect. Options (4) and (5) are incorrect because although the Traveler is important, the speaker is more concerned with the response of those inside the house.

9. **(1) life decisions** (Inferential Comprehension) The poet is describing a moment in his life when he had to make certain choices. Options (2), (3), and (4) are literal interpretations of the poem. There is no support for option (5).

10. **(3) how decisions define people's lives** (Analysis) In lines 16–20, the author indicates the effects of his decisions on his life. The author does not express regret regarding his choices, therefore option (1) is incorrect. Options (2), (4), and (5) are not supported by the poem.

11. **(2) separated** (Inferential Comprehension) This point is made by the poet's description of being able to look down each road at the same time, therefore option (1) is incorrect. Options (3) and (4) are the opposite of what the poet describes. There is no direct evidence for option (5).

12. **(3) make the same decision** (Application) The poet's lack of regrets regarding his choice suggests that he would again choose the less-traveled road. Options (1), (4), and (5) are not supported by the poem. There is no evidence for option (2).

13. **(5) with hesitation** (Literal Comprehension) The author's words show that she loves freely, option (1); without reservations, option (2); purely, option (3); and with her body and soul, option (4).

14. **(3) I love you with every part of my self.** (Analysis) This point is made by the poet's stress on different facets of her emotions and

body. Options (1) and (2) only partially reflect what is stated in the lines. While option (4) may be true, there is no direct evidence for it in the poem. Option (5) has no support.

15. **(2) love more intensely** (Application) Based upon the final lines of the poem, it can be implied that the author will not only continue loving the person, but she will do so with more intensity; therefore options (1) and (5) are incorrect. Options (3) and (4) may be true, but they have no support in the poem.

16. **(2) the author's powerful feelings for someone** (Analysis) The entire poem is used by the author to state and describe her love for someone. There is no support for options (1) and (3). There is no indication that the author's lover is deceased, so option (4) is incorrect. The poem reflects the author's deep feelings of love, not fear, therefore option (5) is incorrect.

GED Review: Classical Literature (page 458)

1. **(2) he heard whistling** (Inferential Comprehension) The whistle was something he did not understand. Options (1) and (3) are not suggested. Options (4) and (5) do not explain why the character is nervous.

2. **(4) even more nervous** (Inferential Comprehension) Mole is already tense. The pattering is unexplained, so it adds to Mole's tension. Options (1), (3), and (5) are the opposite of what is suggested. There is no evidence that Mole felt ill, so option (2) is incorrect.

3. **(3) Mole will take the rabbit's advice** (Inferential Comprehension) Mole is already trying to get away. Rabbit's advice is likely to make him even more nervous, therefore option (1) is incorrect. There is no evidence to support options (2) and (5). Mole has already watched the rabbit disappear down a burrow, so it is unlikely that option (4) will occur.

4. **(4) He is lost in the woods.** (Literal Comprehension) There is no indication that Mole is lost. However, options (1), (2), (3), and (5) are stated as facts in lines 18–20.

5. **(3) It is a safe place to hide.** (Literal Comprehension) Because of the way the rabbit is running and the warning he gives to Mole, you can conclude that the rabbit is running from something dangerous and needs a place to hide. While options (1), (2), (4), and (5) may be true, they are not the best choices in the context of the excerpt.

6. **(5) still a child** (Literal Comprehension) In line 33, the author describes himself as "a mere child" during the war; therefore, options (2), (3), and (4) are incorrect. Option (1) is incorrect because the author did not go to school when he was a slave.

7. **(3) in the first person** (Analysis) As is clear from the author's use of "I," the excerpt is told in the first person, rather than in the third, by a biographer. Therefore, options (1) and (5) are incorrect. The author uses the past tense, so option (2) is incorrect. Option (4) is incorrect because we do not know if he is a reporter.

8. **(4) a kind of heaven** (Literal Comprehension) In lines 9–11, the author says that going to school would be like "getting into paradise." There is no evidence for options (1), (2), (3), and (5).

9. **(5) how informed the slaves were** (Literal Comprehension) Although he probably was impressed by his mother's prayer, option (1), the main point he makes here is how amazing it was that the slaves managed to keep themselves informed. There is no evidence for options (2), (3), and (4).

10. **(2) fight** (Inferential Comprehension) The excerpt refers to the movement and the war to free the slaves. Thus, option (2) provides the best meaning. There is no support for options (1), (4), and (5). While a movement implies a group of people in agreement, option (3) does not make sense within the context.

Commentary
Lesson 8: Commentary (page 460)

1. **(2) Its screen story was written by the director's sister.** (Literal Comprehension) The fact that Joie Susannah Lee wrote the film's screen story can be verified by looking at the list of people credited as working on the film. Although many people share the opinion expressed in option (1), it is an opinion, not a fact. There is no evidence for option (3). The reviewer makes reference to earlier films made by Lee, therefore option (4) is incorrect. Option (5) is an opinion given by the reviewer. Others may disagree.

2. **(1) It is noteworthy because of the director's earnest approach to his topic.** (Analysis) In the first paragraph the reviewer states that the film's honesty and warmth set it apart from other films. The film is autobiographical, so option (2) is incorrect.

Since the reviewer notes the film's lack of success with most reviewers, option (3) is incorrect. There is no support for option (4). Option (5) is an implied opinion of other reviewers, not Klawans.

3. **(3) *Crooklyn* requires its viewers to take their time discovering its meaning.** (Analysis) This is implied in the second paragraph of the excerpt. The reviewer disputes what others have said about the film, so option (1) is incorrect. Option (2) is incorrect because the reviewer states that it can be understood. Option (4) has no support. While the excerpt makes reference to reviewers' desire to understand the film, it does not say that they need it explained to them, therefore option (5) is incorrect.

4. **(3) Woody Allen wrote and directed *Bullets over Broadway*** (Analysis) The fact that Woody Allen wrote the screenplay and directed the film is the only statement that can be proved. Options (1), (2), (4), and (5) reflect the reviewer's personal beliefs rather than facts.

5. **(3) John Cusack is cast as a playwright.** (Analysis) This is the only option which is a fact contained in the review. There is no support for option (1) in the excerpt. Options (2), (4), and (5) are all opinions of the reviewer.

6. **(4) The reviewer loves Cusack's acting.** (Inferential Comprehension) This is suggested by the reviewer's assessment of Cusack's performance. Option (1) has no direct support in the excerpt. The review states that the movie is a comedy, so option (2) is incorrect. There is no indication this film is similar to Allen's other movies, therefore option (3) is incorrect. Option (5) is not implied by the excerpt.

7. **(4) the reviewer may have been less positive about the film** (Application) It can be inferred from the assessment of Cusack's performance that the reviewer was positive about the film because of the actor's presence. There is no evidence for options (1), (2), or (3). Option (5) has no support.

8. **(5) "The Promised Land" is an exact adaptation of the book.** (Analysis) While the excerpt informs you that the mini-series is based upon a book of the same name, it does not suggest that it identically follows the book. Options (1), (2), (3), and (4) are referred to in the excerpt.

9. **(2) thinks that the Discovery Channel is producing quality programs** (Analysis) The author's use of words such as "accomplished" (line 41) indicates his positive view of "The Promised Land." There is no evidence to support options (1), (3), (4), and (5).

10. **(1) The Discovery Channel has established itself as a leading television producer.** (Analysis) The author uses "The Promised Land" to explain the main idea, the success of Discovery as a cable network, so option (2) is incorrect. Option (3) is incorrect because the author indicates that Discovery and PBS are different and cannot operate the same way. There is no direct support for options (4) and (5).

11. **(5) a respectful admirer** (Analysis) The reviewer clearly thinks highly of Irving Berlin's song writing and understanding of his audience. It is doubtful that such admiration would be presented by a formal biographer, option (3). There is no evidence to suggest options (1) or (2). Option (4) is incorrect because there is no evidence of jealousy or of the reviewer being a musician.

12. **(1) get the reader's interest with an unusual detail** (Analysis) That a songwriter cannot read music is definitely unusual. Option (2) is incorrect because the story presents the fact but does not explain it. This detail also emphasizes the reviewer's respect for Berlin, so option (3) is incorrect. Options (4) and (5) have nothing to do with the story.

13. **(1) Berlin's songs suffer because of his inability to read music.** (Inferential Comprehension) Since the author states that Berlin's talent was not limited by his inability to read music, option (1) is the only incorrect statement. Based on the reviewer's respect for Berlin, it can be inferred that Berlin succeeded in capturing the American character, option (2); appealing to a large number of listeners, option (3); and creating songs that are both vivacious and energetic, option (5). Option (4) is stated in lines 15–21.

14. **(2) It allowed Sagan to discuss Earth in relation to the rest of the universe.** (Literal Comprehension) This point is made by the second and third paragraphs. There is no evidence for options (1) and (3). Option (4) is incorrect because this is the opposite of what is stated. Option (5) is not supported by the excerpt.

15. **(4) It succeeds in communicating to people who are not scientists.** (Inferential

Comprehension) In lines 36–38 the reviewer indicates that Sagan's choice to use simple English allows him to describe scientific concepts to the "lay reader," therefore options (1) and (2) are incorrect. There is no support for option (3). Sagan's decision is seen as positive, so option (5) is incorrect.

16. **(3) is interested in the idea of living on other planets** (Inferential Comprehension) The discussion of "terraforming" (line 42) indicates that Sagan believes in the possibility of living on other planets, therefore option (4) is incorrect. The reviewer's identification of Sagan as an astronomer and planetary scientist suggests that Sagan is knowledgeable about his subject, so option (1) is incorrect. Options (2) and (5) are the opposite of what is implied in the excerpt.

17. **(2) compare Sagan's examination of the solar system to Voyager's** (Analysis) The reviewer uses the Grand Tour to suggest the topics that Sagan covers in his book. There is no support for options (1), (3), and (4). Option (5) may be true, but it is not implied in the excerpt.

18. **(3) accept the offer to join the expedition** (Application) From Sagan's clear interest in and awe of the universe, it is unlikely that options (1) and (4) are correct. There is no support for options (2) and (5).

19. **(1) to suggest the size of Earth in comparison with the rest of the universe** (Analysis) This point is made by Sagan's reference to a "tiny world" (line 22). There is no evidence for options (2), (3), (4), and (5).

20. **(2) a lack of catchy songs** (Literal Comprehension) This point is made at the beginning of the fourth paragraph. Options (1), (3), (4), and (5) are not mentioned as flaws of the album.

21. **(3) suggest how Carpenter creates her own world through her music** (Analysis) The place described by the author is implied to be created by Carpenter through her music. While Carpenter is a country singer, the comparison is too literal, so option (1) is incorrect. There is no support for options (2) and (4). Option (5) is incorrect because there is no discussion of Carpenter's popularity outside of the United States.

22. **(3) suggest the emotional depths of Carpenter's new album** (Analysis) The line supports the author's use of "pensive" (line 29) to describe the new album. There is no indication

that Carpenter is disturbed, option (1), or sad, option (2). Option (4) is incorrect because the author doesn't claim that Carpenter's world is empty. Option (5) is not mentioned.

23. **(5) respects Carpenter** (Analysis) The author provides a thorough and positive review of Carpenter's talent. Option (1) is incorrect because the author provides details of Carpenter's previous albums. There is no support for option (2). Option (3) describes a comparison made by the author, not the author's preferences. In the last paragraph the author suggests that the music business is biased against women performers, so option (4) is incorrect.

24. **(1) a talented and emotional singer** (Inferential Comprehension) This is suggested by the author's numerous references to Carpenter's vocal talent and feelings. There is no support for option (2). Options (3) and (5) are incorrect because Carpenter's numerous Grammys indicate that she has been successfully performing for a while. Option (4) is the opposite of what is implied by the review.

25. **(2) Carpenter's happier songs can also feel melancholy.** (Analysis) The reviewer suggests that sadness pervades Carpenter's work, so even her happier songs would suggest melancholy. Option (4) is a literal interpretation of figurative meaning. Options (1), (3), and (5) are not supported by the excerpt.

26. **(3) of his interest in high technology** (Analysis) Selecting the correct option involves figuring out the main point of the review. In the second sentence, the writer introduces technology and continues to pursue the idea that using elements of high-tech makes Hines an unusual tap dancer. Option (1) is incorrect because all tap dancers improvise. There is no support in the review for option (2). Option (4) is the opposite of what is implied in the excerpt. Option (5) is only a detail of his style.

27. **(5) to focus attention on his feet** (Literal Comprehension) Lines 15–18 mention that Hines keeps his head low to emphasize the tapping sounds, both to himself and his audience. Options (1), (2), (3), and (4) have no support in the review.

28. **(3) Hines dances on a specially miked platform-stage** (Literal Comprehension) This observation could be made by anyone who sees Hines perform. All the other options suggest a familiarity with tap dance by comparing Hines to other tap performers.

29. **(4) referred to as the show runner** (Inferential Comprehension) The fifth paragraph states this information. According to the second paragraph, options (1), (2), and (3) are incorrect. The role of script writer is not discussed, so option (5) is incorrect.

30. **(3) show runners are among the most anonymous, but most important, people in television** (Inferential Comprehension) The author states that the show runner is more influential than screenwriters or heads of production companies, therefore option (1) is incorrect. Since the excerpt does not state that production companies always intrude, option (2) is incorrect. Option (4) is the opposite of what is stated in the first paragraph. Option (5) is incorrect because the excerpt discusses the rising importance of the show runner in the last ten years.

31. **(1) direct individual shows** (Application) Of all the show runner's responsibilities listed in the excerpt, directing was not mentioned. All other options were mentioned.

32. **(4) is performing as powerfully as when he started in music** (Inferential Comprehension) This can be inferred by the reviewer's repeated references to Wonder's age and past performance history. There is no evidence for option (1). Options (2), (3), and (5) are not supported by the excerpt.

33. **(3) the excessive volume of some instruments** (Literal Comprehension) In lines 11–12, the reviewer criticizes the drowning out of the strings. Options (1), (2), (4) and (5) are not supported in the review.

34. **(2) to add a casual tone to the review** (Analysis) The reviewer's use of phrases such as "Big Stevie was up and jammin'" (lines 33–34) indicates an informal approach to the subject, so option (4) is incorrect. Options (1) and (3) have no support in the excerpt. As the reviewer admires Wonder's music, it is unlikely that option (5) is his intent.

35. **(2) added to** (Literal Comprehension) The words "with" and "and" in this context tell you something is being added. Options (1) and (4) are the opposite in meaning. Options (3) and (5) do not make sense within the context.

36. **(2) criticism for his chosen style** (Inferential Comprehension) This point is made in the reviewer's statement that Hughes was criticized for not trying to achieve higher standards (lines 13–16), therefore option (4) is

incorrect. Options (1) and (3) are the opposite of what is implied in the excerpt. While the reviewer does discuss the rejection of the manuscript, the reasons for rejection are not given, so option (5) is incorrect.

37. **(3) it uses rhythms similar to some musical forms** (Literal Comprehension) This is indicated in the first paragraph of the excerpt. Option (1) does not fully explain why musicians would like his poetry. Option (2) may be true, but it is not discussed in the excerpt. There is no evidence for option (4). Option (5) is incorrect because it is a figurative phrase which does not explain the reason.

38. **(1) plain words and sentences often communicate difficult ideas** (Analysis) In the last paragraph the reviewer sums up points made at the beginning of the excerpt regarding Hughes' simple style. There is no support for options (2) and (5). Option (3) is the opposite of what is implied by the reviewer. Option (4) may be true sometimes, but the excerpt does not imply that literature is only successful if it is simple; it suggests that Hughes's poems are both successful and simple.

39. **(1) *The Adventures of Huckleberry Finn*** (Inferential Comprehension) This point is made by the reviewer's references to myths and to another book. Option (2) is incorrect because the reviewer makes reference to Wilson's experience in other scientific fields. There is no evidence for option (3). Option (4) is incorrect because the reviewer does not compare Wilson's book with the book of Proverbs. Option (5) is the opposite of what is implied in Wilson's memoirs.

40. **(3) the study of insects** (Inferential Comprehension) This point is made by the reviewer's references to insects and bugs. There is no mention of human beings, so option (1) is incorrect. Option (2) is incorrect because it is too general. While reference is made to other books, the excerpt does not indicate that literature is the subject of Wilson's study, therefore option (4) is incorrect. Option (5) refers to a supporting detail, not to Wilson's subject.

41. **(3) studying his life as he would an organism** (Inferential Comprehension) Lines 13–18 imply that Wilson's scientific training affects the way he views his own life. Options (1), (2), (4), and (5) are not consequences of Wilson's scientific training.

Unit 6

42. **(2) He had a successful career as a biologist.** (Inferential Comprehension) The reviewer uses the idea of following an insect trail to show how Wilson developed a successful career from his childhood study of insects. Options (1), (3), and (5) are not supported by the review. Option (4) is the opposite of what can be inferred about Wilson's life.

43. **(2) change no part of his life** (Application) Based on the information given in the excerpt, it can be concluded that Wilson has lived a full, satisfying, and successful life. There is no evidence for options (1), (3), (4), or (5).

44. **(4) he was gifted in art and science** (Literal Comprehension) Each of the options gives accurate information, but option (4) is the only one that supplies a reason for his brilliance that is supported in the review. The first paragraph explains that he was considered brilliant because of his gifts in art and the sciences. Therefore, options (1), (2), (3), and (5) are incorrect.

45. **(3) had varied interests** (Inferential Comprehension) "All knowledge as his sphere" (line 20) means a desire for knowledge that knows no boundaries. Leonardo's genius was not limited to one area. Notice references in the review to "an aptitude for all manner of achievement" (lines 5–6) and "all things, human and divine, were fit subjects. . ." (lines 47–48). Options (1), (2), (4), and (5) suggest negative qualities not supported by the review.

46. **(5) all his works have depth** (Inferential Comprehension) The author feels that Leonardo's works convey depth and mystery. Therefore, he feels that it is not fair to single out the *Mona Lisa*. Options (1), (2), (3), and (4) are factual statements, but they do not reflect the reviewer's judgment.

47. **(1) any subject that caught his imagination** (Inferential Comprehension) This can be inferred from the last sentence of the excerpt. Option (2) is incorrect. It can be inferred from the review that his skill was such that he did not have to take every assignment. Options (3), (4), and (5) refer to some subjects and styles he used but not necessarily his most likely subjects.

48. **(3) set her next novel there** (Application) Based on the article, it can be inferred that Campbell writes about situations that she experiences. There is no support for options (1) and (5). Option (2) is unlikely because

of Campbell's success with writing. Since Campbell gets a lot of her subject matter from the radio, it is unlikely that she would stop listening to it; therefore option (4) is incorrect.

49. **(1) She is more aware of different opinions.** (Literal Comprehension) This is indicated in lines 13–18. There is no evidence for options (2), (3), and (4). Option (5) may be true, but it cannot be inferred from this excerpt.

50. **(3) It has resulted in criticism of Campbell by some of her readers.** (Literal Comprehension) Lines 11–12 indicate that some of her readers are disturbed by her use of both black and white perspectives. Option (1) may be true, but it is not implied by the excerpt. There is no support for options (2), (4), or (5).

51. **(4) her emotions** (Literal Comprehension) In lines 4–5, Campbell states that she does not allow her emotions to affect her writing. Options (1), (2), (3), and (5) are all cited as influencing Campbell's writing.

52. **(2) Tharp's performances benefit from a lack of money.** (Analysis) This is the only statement that cannot be proven. It reflects the author's personal belief. Options (1), (3), (4), and (5) are all facts.

53. **(1) It has made rehearsing less worrisome.** (Analysis) Tharp's reference to the benefit of "unstructured time" (line 24) suggests that one of the main effects of the fellowship has been the flexibility of rehearsal time. There is no support for options (2) and (3). Option (4) is the opposite of what is stated. Option (5) is an effect of Tharp's lack of adequate financing, not an effect of the fellowship.

54. **(2) Receiving a MacArthur fellowship has given Tharp more freedom to create dances.** (Inferential Comprehension) It can be inferred that Tharp believes that working under a contract hinders artistic freedom. Options (1) and (5) are the opposite of what is implied by the article. Option (3) is mentioned but is not the main point of the excerpt. Option (4) refers to a detail and cannot be used as the basis for larger conclusions.

55. **(3) possess great promise for future endeavors** (Analysis) The excerpt outlines the pair's successes and concludes with the speculation of more to come (lines 44–46), so option (1) is incorrect. Option (2) is incorrect because the final paragraph describes how the

pair have helped other individuals. The pair are neither first-time directors nor producers, therefore option (4) is incorrect. Option (5) does not acknowledge the pair's new production deal.

56. **(5) They will be able to concentrate on making films.** (Analysis) Because of their decision to work with Savoy Pictures, McHenry and Jackson have succeeded in giving themselves time and money with which to make films. Options (1) and (3) are the opposite of what is stated in the excerpt. There is no support for options (2) and (4).

57. **(3) flawed** (Analysis) The reviewer's suggestion that the play "loses its potency" suggests that there are parts of the play that could be improved. Option (1) is too negative. Option (2) is too exuberant. Options (4) and (5) are the opposite of what is suggested by the review.

58. **(5) August Wilson has received two Pulitzer Prizes.** (Analysis) This is a provable piece of information that is given in lines 46–48. Options (1), (3), and (4) reflect the reviewer's personal feelings rather than facts. While the play is the sixth in a series, the reviewer's use of the adjective "ambitious" makes this statement an opinion, so option (2) is incorrect.

59. **(2) an even-handed appreciation for Wilson's endeavors** (Analysis) The reviewer's attempts to point out both the strengths and weaknesses of Wilson's play indicate his attempts to be fair, therefore options (1) and (3) are incorrect. Option (4) is incorrect because the reviewer demonstrates his knowledge of Wilson's work in the third paragraph. Option (5) is incorrect because it is not supported by the excerpt.

60. **(4) His painting covers a wide range of issues.** (Inferential Comprehension) Howard Finster paints a wide range of subjects, from religion to politics, so option (2) is incorrect. Option (1) is incorrect because although it is something he did, it does not summarize his work. There is no evidence to support option (3). Option (5) is incorrect because Finster has not relied on art museums for exposure.

61. **(1) art critics are not quite sure what folk art is** (Inferential Comprehension) The words in the list suggest a number of different qualities. Options (2) and (3) are incorrect because the one thing most of the words on the list have in common is simplicity. There is no support for options (4) and (5).

62. **(2) a hand-painted Easter egg** (Application) In addition to being a traditional European folk art, egg painting would meet the requirements of being handmade, ethnic, nonacademic, and from the country. Options (1) and (3) refer to art produced by training. Option (4) is a manufactured object. Option (5) is incorrect because there is no reference to children's art being folk art.

63. **(5) More people have paid attention to Howard Finster's work.** (Analysis) As a folk artist, Howard Finster has benefited from an increased interest in folk art. There is no evidence in the excerpt to support options (1) and (3). Options (2) and (4) are the opposite of what the excerpt states.

GED Review: Commentary (page 478)

1. **(3) was easy to understand** (Inferential Comprehension) The meaning of the word "pop" is suggested throughout the paragraph. It was given a lot of publicity and was accepted by the public. There is no evidence to support options (1) and (5). The price of the art is not mentioned, so option (2) is incorrect. Many criticized pop art for not being serious, so option (4) is incorrect.

2. **(2) it lacked serious content** (Analysis) The excerpt describes how some people disliked it because it was too commercial and trivial. There is no evidence to support options (1), (3), (4), and (5).

3. **(3) for practically nothing** (Literal Comprehension) The excerpt says the artist's work sold for "next to nothing" (line 2). Options (1) and (2) state the opposite. Option (4) is not supported by the excerpt. Option (5) is true now but was not the case fifty years ago.

4. **(3) Art collectors of the 1920s and 1930s were not interested in visionary art.** (Analysis) If art collectors are not interested in a type of painting, it will often be ignored and forgotten. Martin's paintings were cheap because they were not popular, not the other way around, so option (1) is incorrect. It was lack of interest, not the subject of the paintings themselves, that was the cause, so option (2) is incorrect. Option (4) may be partly true, but it is not related to why Martin's work was forgotten for a while. Option (5) has no support.

5. **(2) how an artwork is developed** (Analysis) This excerpt shows that a painting comes about in stages. Options (1) and (5) may

be true, but they are not revealed because of the artist's point of view. There is no support for options (3) and (4).

6. **(1) amazed him** (Literal Comprehension) This is a restatement of the last line. The pink highlight was accidental but was also important, so options (2), (3), and (4) are incorrect. There is no support for option (5).

7. **(1) People had seen the painting of her and were touched.** (Inferential Comprehension) The letters reveal fascination with the woman. There is no support for option (2). Options (3), (4), and (5) suggest the opposite of the reason.

8. **(1) sadness** (Analysis) The image is of something worn out and useless. There is no support for options (2), (3), (4), and (5).

9. **(1) *Christina's World* is an oil painting.** (Literal Comprehension) In line 8, Wyeth states that the painting is a tempera, not an oil painting. Since the painter worked on painting the hill for months, option (2) is a true statement. Option (3) is true because Wyeth says he was "so shy about posing her" and he finally "got up enough courage" to ask her. Lines 11–15 indicate that Wyeth painted primarily from memory, so option (4) is a true statement. The last two sentences support option (5), so it is true.

GED Cumulative Review: Literature & the Arts (page 480)

1. **(3) a direct, factual impact** (Analysis) Because we have little more than dialogue to go on, the revelation of the boy's secret fear comes as a shock. The tense and down-to-earth nature of the scene rules out options (1), (2), (4), and (5).

2. **(5) builds up and relaxes** (Analysis) The underlying structure of the excerpt matches the buildup and resolution of the boy's fear, step for step. Options (1), (2), (3), and (4) are incorrect because the fear is explained in lines 11–12, reaches a climax in lines 22–24, awakens our sympathy, and is clearly not trivial.

3. **(3) pity** (Inferential Comprehension) The fact that the narrator says "Poor old Schatz" shows that he feels sorry for the boy. There is no evidence for options (1), (4), and (5). Option (2) may be true but the excerpt gives no indication that the author is feeling this emotion.

4. **(4) He feels sorry that the boy has been worrying all day.** (Literal Comprehension) There is nothing in the excerpt to suggest that the boy's family, option (1), or the narrator, option (2), is poor. The narrator knows that the

boy is not going to die, so option (3) is incorrect. The narrator's tone has been matter-of-fact throughout most of the excerpt, so he is not overly concerned that the boy is sick, option (5).

5. **(2) The little girl has a lot of energy.** (Analysis) The word "flying" suggests that the girl is running and leaping. Options (1), (3), and (4) assume the word is meant literally. Option (5) is incorrect because it suggests that the girl was afraid of the grass; however, she was having fun.

6. **(4) The poet and the child have similar feelings of regret.** (Analysis) The poet's use of "twin distress" indicates both his regret at interrupting the child's play and the child's regret at being interrupted. There is no mention of an actual twin, therefore options (1) and (3) are incorrect. The child is observing the poet's eyes, not the reverse; therefore, option (2) is incorrect. Option (5) is incorrect because the poet does not say he was playing.

7. **(3) she realizes it is time to go inside** (Inferential Comprehension) The speaker signals that it is time to come in, but even though children want to play just a little longer, the girl knows what the signal means. Options (1), (2), and (4) have no support in the details. Option (5) is incorrect because the child is obviously happy playing in the garden.

8. **(1) It emphasizes the child's wild, free nature.** (Analysis) A net is usually used to trap wild animals. Options (2) and (4) would be correct only if you take the image literally, but it is figurative language. Option (3) is clearly not what is meant. Option (5) has nothing to do with the image of the net.

9. **(3) endowed with superhuman strength** (Analysis) In lines 15–17, the reviewer describes Wilson's voice as a blowtorch blasting through candle wax, suggesting the strength of her voice. Options (1) and (4) refer to Wilson's songs. Options (2) and (5) are the opposite of what the reviewer states.

10. **(4) hint** (Literal Comprehension) Based on the context of the first paragraph, and the fact that the word is preceded by "understated" and followed by "nuance," "innuendo" is probably similar in a sense of subtle suggestion; therefore, "hint" is the best definition. There is no support for options (1), (2), (3), or (5) in the review.

11. **(2) appreciative** (Analysis) Throughout the excerpt, the reviewer describes his admiration

of Nancy Wilson's talent. Option (1) is incorrect because the reviewer makes no attempt to be objective. Option (3) is incorrect because although the reviewer is clearly involved in Nancy Wilson's music, "involved" does not explain his evaluation of Wilson's work. Option (5) is incorrect because the reviewer is more balanced in his discussion than he is ecstatic. There is no evidence in the excerpt for option (4).

12. **(1) his personal opinion** (Analysis) The reviewer's statement is not provable information, therefore option (3) is incorrect. There is no mention of the opinions of the reviewer's friends, so option (2) is incorrect. Options (4) and (5) are not supported by the excerpt.

13. **(4) with a respect for Wilson's musical abilities** (Analysis) Based on the reviewer's vocabulary and references, it is obvious that he respects Wilson's abilities, therefore option (3) is incorrect. There is no evidence in the excerpt to support option (1). The similarities between the two performers aren't based on the type of music they perform, so option (2) is incorrect. Option (5) is the opposite of what the reviewer praises in Wilson's recordings.

14. **(2) She believes Annie can help.** (Analysis) Kate is trying to get Annie to stay. Kate loves Helen and sees the good in her, so option (1) is incorrect. Option (3) is incorrect because there is no evidence that Kate took care of Helen. There is no support for option (4). Helen is the lost lamb, not Kate, so option (5) is incorrect.

15. **(1) uncooperative** (Analysis) The first few lines of the excerpt concern the difficulty Annie is having with Helen. There is no support for options (2) and (5). Options (3) and (4) describe the opposite of Helen's behavior.

16. **(1) "I think everybody else here does."** (line 9) (Inferential Comprehension) This line refers to everybody else underestimating Helen and her abilities. Option (2) is incorrect since it refers to the negative change since Helen's illness. Options (3), (4), and (5) do not deal with whether Helen is hopeless or not; they are details of the conversation.

17. **(3) They must be taught, not pitied.** (Application) Annie says pity stands in the way of teaching Helen. Option (1) is untrue, or she would not be a teacher of a blind and deaf child. Options (2) and (5) are the opposite of what she

has said she believes. Option (4) is obviously something they are all trying to avoid.

18. **(2) in the third person** (Analysis) The biographer describes the incident from Adams's viewpoint. Since it is someone other than Adams telling the story, we know that it is told from the third-person point of view. Therefore, options (1), (3), and (4) are incorrect. Option (5) is incorrect because the people were not interviewed.

19. **(1) Adams's own words** (Literal Comprehension) Adams's own words are quoted about the look on Hancock's face (lines 36–41). There is no evidence for options (2), (3), (4), and (5).

20. **(5) in the first person** (Analysis) The use of quotes indicates that the nomination speech is given in Adam's own words, not the biographers, therefore all the remaining options are incorrect.

21. **(4) B and C** (Analysis) Washington's quiet departure, which is contrasted with John Hancock's smug expectancy, implies that Washington's departure was due to modesty. When he heard the description of the nominee, he knew he would be offered the position. Only option (4) includes both of these inferences.

22. **(3) Movies are controlled by directors while TV is controlled by writers.** (Inferential Comprehension) Option (1) is incorrect because it is an effect of the situation, not a cause. Options (2), (4), and (5) may be true, but none is given as a cause.

23. **(2) There are TV programs shown every night that do not insult their viewers.** (Inferential Comprehension) Option (2) is the only direct effect given by the reviewer. Options (1) and (4) may be reasonable inferences to make from the excerpt, but they are not suggested as an effect by the reviewer. There is no evidence in the excerpt to support options (3) or (5).

24. **(3) stay home and watch television** (Application) The author clearly states his preference for television over movies, therefore option (2) is incorrect. There is no support for options (1), (4), and (5).

25. **(3) Television has been consistently producing better shows than the movie industry.** (Inferential Comprehension) This point is made in lines 10–14, so option (1) is incorrect. Options (2) and (5) are the opposite of what is implied by the excerpt. There is no support for option (4).

Unit 7: Mathematics
Whole Numbers

Lesson 1: Number Values and Facts
GED Exercise: Number Values and Facts (page 489)

1. **five hundred**

2. **three million**

3. **six thousand**

4. **eight billion**

5. **seven hundred thousand**

6. **sixty thousand**

7. **eighty million**

8. **6** is in the **hundred thousands place.**
   $6 \times 100,000 = \mathbf{600,000}$
   7 is in the **ten thousands place.**
   $7 \times 10,000 = \mathbf{70,000}$
   9 is in the **thousands place.**
   $9 \times 1,000 = \mathbf{9,000}$
   3 is in the **hundreds place.**
   $3 \times 100 = \mathbf{300}$
   0 is in the **tens place.**
   $0 \times 10 = \mathbf{0}$
   8 is in the **ones place.**
   $8 \times 1 = \mathbf{8}$

9. **b.** Eight thousand, four hundred sixteen

10. **d.** Eight million, four hundred twenty thousand, one hundred six

11. **a.** Eighty-four million, two hundred thousand, one hundred sixty

12. **c.** Eight hundred forty-two thousand, sixteen

13. **c.** Ten million, two hundred fifty thousand, nine hundred

14. **b.** Twelve thousand, five hundred nine

15. **d.** One thousand, two hundred fifty-nine

16. **a.** One hundred twenty-five thousand, ninety

17. **1,305 < 1,503**

18. **34,000 > 29,989**

19. **102,667 > 102,657**

20. **5,690,185 < 5,690,185,100**

21. **7,650,300 > 7,649,950**

22. **875,438 = 875,438**

23. **3,492,012,558 = 3,492,012,558**

24. **75,390,000 < 75,391,540**

25. **9,500,000 < 9,500,000,000**

26. **45,100 > 45,099**

27. **7,456,795 < 7,500,000**

28. **319,002,110 = 319,002,110**

29. **8,600**

30. **700,000**

31. **5,000,000**

32. **50,000,000**

33. **11,000**

34. **50,000**

35. **60,000,000**

36. **74,000**

37. **Monday—$19,000**
    Tuesday—$12,000
    Wednesday—$14,000
    Thursday—$14,000
    Friday—$22,000
    Saturday—$29,000

38. **Wednesday.** $13,940 is greater than $13,772.

39. **Tuesday.** $12,316 is less than all the other amounts.

40. **Saturday.** $28,795 is greater than all the other amounts.

41. **$12,316; $13,772; $13,940; $18,756; $21,592; $28,795**

Lesson 2: Whole Number Operations
GED Exercise: Whole Number Operations (page 492)

1.   **768**
      305
    +463
    ‾‾‾‾
      768

2. **8,682**
    4,172
    +4,510
    ‾‾‾‾‾
    8,682

3. **6,927**
    6,795
    + 132
    ‾‾‾‾‾
    6,927

4. **1,139**
      193
      317
    +629
    ‾‾‾‾
    1,139

5. 61,235

   56,439
 + 4,796
    61,235

6. 244,967

   36,075
    1,936
 189,006
 + 17,950
 244,967

7. 54,263

 19,067
+35,196
 54,263

8. 213,658

  65,196
   6,725
 114,021
+ 27,716
 213,658

9. 109,636

 81,427
  3,584
+24,625
 109,636

10. 134

 76
+58
 134

11. 188

 36
  9
 74
 48
  6
+15
 188

12. 758,450

 588,394
  61,042
+109,014
 758,450

13. 54,271

 54,095
+ 176
 54,271

14. 91,923

 35,100
 49,257
+ 7,566
 91,923

15. 1,414

 950
 308
  77
  29
+ 50
 1,414

16. 208,115

   6,019
  85,200
+116,896
 208,115

17. 35

 86
−51
 35

18. 31,313

 51,964
−20,651
 31,313

19. 327

 494
−167
 327

20. 963

 1,258
− 295
   963

21. 412

 680
−268
 412

22. 929

 3,205
−2,276
  929

23. 581

 800
−219
 581

24. 1,272

 5,067
−3,795
 1,272

25. 6,829

 10,508
− 3,679
  6,829

26. 1,305

 5,000
−3,695
 1,305

27. 406,985

 419,003
− 12,018
 406,985

28. 1,025

 10,000
− 8,975
  1,025

29. 3,433

 20,000
−16,567
  3,433

30. 188,575

 375,000
−186,425
 188,575

31. 505,232

 510,000
− 4,768
 505,232

32. 24,490

 100,000
− 75,510
  24,490

33. 864

 432
× 2
 864

34. 3,730

 746
× 5
3,730

35. 125,304

 15,663
×   8
125,304

36. 273,681

 30,409
×   9
273,681

37. 828

 36
×23
108
 72
828

38. 386,384

 5,084
× 76
 30 504
355 88
386,384

39. 53,685

 1,193
× 45
 5 965
47 72
53,685

40. 78,624

 3,276
× 24
13 104
65 52
78,624

41. 6,976,800

  2,584
×2,700
 0 000
 00 00
1 808 8
5 168
6,976,800

42. 1,505,820

 25,097
×   60
 00 000
1 505 82
1,505,820

43. 4,097,450

 8,050
× 509
 72 450
 00 00
4 025 0
4,097,450

44. 3,758,458

 1,247
×3,014
 4 988
12 47
000 0
3 741
3,758,458

45. 57,525

```
    885
  ×  65
  4 425
 53 10
 57,525
```

46. 415,340

```
   2,186
  ×  190
   0 000
 196 74
 218 6
 415,340
```

47. 600,625

```
    775
  × 775
  3 875
 54 25
 542 5
 600,625
```

48. 7,640,000

```
   3,056
  × 2,500
   0 000
  00 00
 1 528 0
 6 112
 7,640,000
```

49. 458

```
       458
   7) 3,206
      2 8
       40
       35
       56
       56
```

50. 5,996

```
       5,996
   4) 23,984
      20
       3 9
       3 6
        38
        36
         24
         24
```

51. 42,363

```
       42,363
   6) 254,178
      24
       14
       12
        2 1
        1 8
         37
         36
          18
          18
```

52. 8,132

```
        8,132
   16) 130,112
       128
         2 1
         1 6
          51
          48
           32
           32
```

53. 583r4

```
       583r4
   6) 3,502
      3 0
       50
       48
        22
        18
         4
```

54. 6,366r10

```
        6,366r10
   12) 76,402
       72
        4 4
        3 6
         80
         72
          82
          72
          10
```

55. 7,692r4

```
        7,692r4
   13) 100,000
       91
        9 0
        7 8
         1 20
         1 17
           30
           26
            4
```

56. 9,138r3

```
        9,138r3
   24) 219,315
       216
         3 3
         2 4
          91
          72
          195
          192
            3
```

57. 1,098

```
        1,098
   35) 38,430
       35
        3 43
        3 15
         280
         280
```

58. 659r7

```
       659r7
   46) 30,321
       27 6
        2 72
        2 30
          421
          414
            7
```

59. 5,302r1

```
        5,302r1
   68) 360,537
       340
        20 5
        20 4
          13
          00
          137
          136
            1
```

60. 680

```
         680
   205) 139,400
        123 0
         16 40
         16 40
            00
            00
```

61. 1,026r5

```
         1,026r5
   155) 159,035
        155
          4 0
          0 0
          4 03
          3 10
           935
           930
             5
```

62. 40,430

```
         40,430
   15) 606,450
       60
        6 4
        6 0
         45
         45
```

63. 28,480

```
         28,480
   25) 712,000
       50
       212
       200
        12 0
        10 0
         2 00
         2 00
```

64. 2,572r121

```
         2,572r121
   163) 419,357
        326
         93 3
         81 5
         11 85
         11 41
           447
           326
           121
```

65. 4,236

```
         4,236
   120) 508,320
        480
         28 3
         24 0
          4 32
          3 60
            720
            720
```

Unit 7

Lesson 3: Steps to Solving Word Problems

GED Exercise: Steps to Solving Word Problems (page 496)

1. **(1) 90** Multiply the number of bags by the number of buns in a bag ($15 \times 6 = 90$). You do not need the number of days Quan Le works to solve the problem.

2. **(5) Not enough information is given.** To figure the cost of the job, you need to know how much the new parts will cost.

3. **(2) between 5 and 6** If you divide 900 by 150 you get 6, which is mentioned in two choices. Try multiplying 160 by 6; the result, 960, is too high. A better estimate is less than 6.

4. **(4) 18** Divide the number of TV sets sold by the price of each set: $\$5,760 \div \$320 = 18$.

5. **(2) 515** Add the goals for each day of the week ($100 + 95 + 120 + 110 + 90 = 515$).

6. **(3) Wednesday** Review the data in the list. Only on Wednesday ($120 > 117$) is the actual number less than the goal number.

7. **(2) 58** Only the actual data for Thursday and Friday are needed for this problem. Subtract Thursday's actual number from Friday's ($180 - 122 = 58$). Check by addition ($122 + 58 = 180$).

Lesson 4: Solving Multistep Word Problems

GED Exercise: Solving Multistep Word Problems (page 498)

1. **(4) multiplication and addition** You need to multiply the number of payments by the amount of the regular payment and add the final payment.

2. **(5) $1,082** Multiply $115 by 8 to get $920 and add $162. ($920 + $162 = $1,082).

3. **(3) $1,490** Multiply to find how much Hugh pays in one year ($312 \times 2 = \$624$). Add Brenda's amount ($624 + $866 = $1,490).

4. **(4) multiplication and subtraction** Find the cost of the TV if you buy on credit by multiplying the payment amount by 12. Subtract the cash amount to find the difference.

5. **(3) $80** Multiply to find the cost of the TV if you buy on credit ($12 \times \$45 = \$540$). Subtract the cost if you pay in cash ($540 - $460 = $80).

6. **(3) $1,412** Subtract the amount the insurance company refunded from the total cost of medical bills. ($3,794 - $2,382 = $1,412).

7. **(2) $360** Multiply the number of pairs of pants sold by the sale price for pants ($24 \times \$15 = \$360$).

8. **(5) $52** Find out the amount they would spend for the items using the regular prices and the amount they spent using the sale prices.

12 T-shirts
Regular Price: $12 \times \$8 = \$96$
Sale Price: $12 \times \$7 = \$84$

5 jerseys
Regular Price: $5 \times \$10 = \$50$
Sale Price: $5 \times \$8 = \$40$

10 pairs of pants
Regular Price: $10 \times \$18 = \$180$
Sale Price: $10 \times \$15 = \$150$

Total at Regular Price:
$\$96 + \$50 + \$180 = \$326$

Total at Sale Price:
$\$84 + \$40 + \$150 = \$274$

Find the difference in the totals ($\$326 - \$274 = \$52$).

9. **(2) $48** Find the new sale price ($15 - $3 = $12). Find the cost of 4 pairs by multiplying ($12 \times 4 = \$48$). You do not need to know how many pairs they have in stock.

10. **(1) $280** Multiply the number produced by the number of days ($56 \times 5 = 280$) and multiply the result by the amount paid per piece ($280 \times \$1 = \$280$).

11. **(5) Not enough information is given.** You need the amount Mr. Butler is paid per item and the number of items he produced to find out how much he earned.

12. **(1) 10** Take the number she produced (50) and divide it by the number of hours she worked ($50 \div 5 = 10$).

GED Review: Whole Numbers (page 500)

1. **(2) 16,106** Subtract the attendance at Tuesday's game from the attendance at Friday night's game ($50,302 - 34,196 = 16,106$).

2. **(3) $15 \times 10** Multiply to find the amount she will earn from haircuts (15×10).

3. **(4) $1,236** Subtract the amount she actually owed from the amount she paid ($5,752 - $4,516 = $1,236). Check by addition ($4,516 + $1,236 = $5,752).

4. **(1) 12** Divide the total bill, $1,800, by equal payments of $150 to find the number of payments.

$$\begin{array}{r} 12 \\ \$150\overline{)\,\$1,800} \\ \underline{1\,50} \\ 300 \\ \underline{300} \end{array}$$

5. **(1) between 9,000 and 11,000** This problem calls for an estimate. Round the number of boxes to the nearest 10 (21 rounds to 20). Round the number of bolts per box to the nearest ten (506 rounds to 510). $510 \times 20 = 10,200$. The number of bolts on hand is not needed to solve the problem.

6. **(2) 578** Subtract the number of writing pads used on Tuesday from the original number of pads. From the number left, subtract the number of pads used on Wednesday.

$$\begin{array}{r} 1,000 \\ -\ \ 188 \\ \hline 812 \end{array}$$

$$\begin{array}{r} 812 \\ -234 \\ \hline 578 \end{array}$$

7. **(4) $710** Find the amount spent on food by multiplying $9 by the number of employees ($65 \times \$9 = \$585$). Add the amount spent on the room ($585 + \$125 = \$710$).

8. **(2) addition and division** Add to find the total number of apartments. Then divide the cost of the service by the number of apartments.

9. **(5) $72** There are 43 apartments ($18 + 25 = 43$). Divide the yearly cost by the number of apartments ($3,096 \div 43 = \$72$).

10. **(1) $280** Add to find the hours F. Blau worked ($8 + 7 + 8 + 8 + 6 + 3 = 40$). Then multiply by the hourly wage ($40 \times \$7 = \$280$).

11. **(2) 12** Add to find the total hours M. Bodine worked ($8 + 8 + 9 + 8 + 8 + 8 = 49$). Find the hours T. Ortiz worked ($6 + 6 + 8 + 9 + 8 = 37$). Find the difference ($49 - 37 = 12$).

12. **(1) 2** Subtract to find the difference between the amount he earned and the amount he needs to earn ($252 - \$240 = \$12$). Divide the result by his hourly wage ($12 \div \$6/hr = 2$ hr). R. Perez needs to work 2 more hours.

13. **(3) $370** T. Ortiz worked 37 hours which you originally found by adding in problem 11. Add the raise to the hourly wage ($8 + \$2 = \$10$). Multiply the hours by the new hourly wage ($37 \times \$10 = \$370$).

14. **(2) $56** Multiply 6 days by 8 hours to find the total number of hours F. Blau worked the following week ($6 \times 8 = 48$). Add to find the total number of hours worked the given week ($8 + 7 + 8 + 8 + 6 + 3 = 40$). Subtract to find the difference between the number of hours worked ($48 - 40 = 8$). Multiply by the hourly wage to find the difference in earnings ($8 \times \$7 = \$56$).

Fractions

Lesson 5: Introduction to Fractions

GED Exercise: Introduction to Fractions (page 505)

1. $\frac{9}{16}$ 2. $\frac{7}{10}$ 3. $\frac{3}{50}$ 4. $\frac{19}{45}$

5. $3\frac{1}{2}$ $7 \div 2 = 3\ r1$

6. 3 $15 \div 5 = 3$

7. $3\frac{1}{3}$ $10 \div 3 = 3\ r1$

8. $3\frac{7}{8}$ $31 \div 8 = 3\ r7$

9. $2\frac{5}{6}$ $17 \div 6 = 2\ r5$

10. 7 $42 \div 6 = 7$

11. $\frac{13}{2}$ $2 \times 6 = 12,$ $12 + 1 = 13$

12. $\frac{23}{6}$ $6 \times 3 = 18,$ $18 + 5 = 23$

13. $\frac{11}{5}$ $5 \times 2 = 10,$ $10 + 1 = 11$

14. $\frac{47}{4}$ $4 \times 11 = 44,$ $44 + 3 = 47$

15. $\frac{21}{2}$ $2 \times 10 = 20,$ $20 + 1 = 21$

16. $\frac{47}{5}$ $5 \times 9 = 45,$ $45 + 2 = 47$

17. **(1) 3** To find if $5\frac{1}{3}$ is nearer to 5 or 6, compare $\frac{1}{3}$ and $\frac{1}{2}$ using common denominators.

$\frac{1}{3} = \frac{2}{6}$ $\frac{1}{2} = \frac{3}{6}$ $\frac{2}{6} < \frac{3}{6}$

Since $\frac{2}{6} < \frac{1}{2}$ the whole number, 5, stays the same. $5\frac{1}{3}$ rounds to 5.

To find if $1\frac{7}{8}$ is nearer to 1 or 2, compare $\frac{7}{8}$ and $\frac{1}{2}$ using common denominators.

$\frac{1}{2} = \frac{4}{8}$ $\frac{7}{8} > \frac{4}{8}$

Since $\frac{7}{8} > \frac{1}{2}$, add 1 to the whole number. $1\frac{7}{8}$ rounds to 2.

Subtract to find approximately how many feet of board will be left. $5 - 2 = 3$

18. (3) 6 To find if $2\frac{1}{4}$ is nearer to 2 or 3, compare $\frac{1}{4}$ and $\frac{1}{2}$ using common denominators.
$\frac{1}{2} = \frac{2}{4}$ $\frac{1}{4} < \frac{2}{4}$
Since $\frac{1}{4} < \frac{1}{2}$, the whole number, 2, stays the same.
$2\frac{1}{4}$ rounds to 2.
To find if $1\frac{7}{8}$ is nearer to 1 or 2, compare $\frac{7}{8}$ and $\frac{1}{2}$ using common denominators.
$\frac{1}{2} = \frac{4}{8}$ $\frac{7}{8} > \frac{4}{8}$
Since $\frac{7}{8} > \frac{1}{2}$, add 1 to the whole number. $1\frac{7}{8}$ rounds to 2. Add to find the approximate total number of miles Tara walked.
$2 + 2 + 2 = 6$

Lesson 6: Comparing Fractions
GED Exercise: Comparing Fractions (page 507)

1. $\frac{1}{2}$ Divide numerator and denominator by 2.

2. $\frac{2}{3}$ Divide numerator and denominator by 3.

3. $\frac{2}{5}$ Divide numerator and denominator by 3.

4. $\frac{2}{3}$ Divide numerator and denominator by 9.

5. $\frac{4}{5}$ Divide numerator and denominator by 2.

6. $\frac{2}{5}$ Divide numerator and denominator by 6.

7. $\frac{4}{8}$ $2 \times 4 = 8$ and $1 \times 4 = 4$.

8. $\frac{8}{12}$ $3 \times 4 = 12$ and $2 \times 4 = 8$.

9. $\frac{20}{32}$ $8 \times 4 = 32$ and $5 \times 4 = 20$.

10. $\frac{49}{63}$ $9 \times 7 = 63$ and $7 \times 7 = 49$.

11. $\frac{27}{36}$ $4 \times 9 = 36$ and $3 \times 9 = 27$.

12. $\frac{36}{81}$ $9 \times 9 = 81$ and $4 \times 9 = 36$.

13. $\frac{1}{3} > \frac{1}{4}$ because $\frac{4}{12} > \frac{3}{12}$.

14. $\frac{3}{4} < \frac{7}{8}$ because $\frac{6}{8} < \frac{7}{8}$.

15. $\frac{5}{6} = \frac{15}{18}$ because $\frac{15}{18}$ reduces to $\frac{5}{6}$.

16. **(1) A greater fraction of shirts passed inspection at 10 A.M.** Compare $\frac{9}{10}$ and $\frac{7}{8}$. Change both to equal fractions with a denominator of 40: $\frac{9}{10} = \frac{36}{40}$; $\frac{7}{8} = \frac{35}{40}$. Compare numerators: 36 is greater than 35, so $\frac{9}{10}$ is greater than $\frac{7}{8}$.

17. **(3) The same fraction of customers saw the ad each day.** The fractions $\frac{4}{12}$ and $\frac{6}{18}$ are equal fractions. Both reduce to $\frac{1}{3}$.

Lesson 7: Adding and Subtracting Fractions
GED Exercise: Adding and Subtracting Fractions (page 510)

1. **1**
$$\frac{2}{3}$$
$$+\frac{1}{3}$$
$$\frac{3}{3} = 1$$

2. $\frac{2}{3}$
$$\frac{1}{6}$$
$$+\frac{3}{6}$$
$$\frac{4}{6} \div \frac{2}{2} = \frac{2}{3}$$

3. $\frac{7}{8}$
$$\frac{3}{4} = \frac{6}{8}$$
$$+\frac{1}{8} = \frac{1}{8}$$
$$\frac{7}{8}$$

4. $\frac{2}{3}$
$$\frac{1}{6} = \frac{1}{6}$$
$$+\frac{1}{2} = \frac{3}{6}$$
$$\frac{4}{6} \div \frac{2}{2} = \frac{2}{3}$$

5. $\frac{23}{40}$
$$\frac{3}{8} = \frac{15}{40}$$
$$+\frac{1}{5} = \frac{8}{40}$$
$$\frac{23}{40}$$

6. $\frac{11}{15}$
$$\frac{2}{5} = \frac{6}{15}$$
$$+\frac{1}{3} = \frac{5}{15}$$
$$\frac{11}{15}$$

7. $7\frac{7}{8}$
$$2\frac{1}{4} = 2\frac{2}{8}$$
$$+5\frac{5}{8} = 5\frac{5}{8}$$
$$7\frac{7}{8}$$

8. $14\frac{1}{2}$
$$3\frac{5}{6} = 3\frac{5}{6}$$
$$+10\frac{2}{3} = 10\frac{4}{6}$$
$$13\frac{9}{6}$$
Reduce:
$$13\frac{9}{6} = 13 + 1\frac{3}{6} = 14\frac{3}{6} = 14\frac{1}{2}$$

9. $11\frac{1}{10}$
$$2\frac{4}{5} = 2\frac{8}{10}$$
$$+8\frac{3}{10} = 8\frac{3}{10}$$
$$10\frac{11}{10}$$
Reduce:
$$10\frac{11}{10} = 10 + 1\frac{1}{10} = 11\frac{1}{10}$$

10. $42\frac{5}{6}$
$$18\frac{1}{6} = 18\frac{1}{6}$$
$$+24\frac{2}{3} = 24\frac{4}{6}$$
$$42\frac{5}{6}$$

11. $\frac{1}{4}$
$$\frac{3}{4} = \frac{3}{4}$$
$$-\frac{1}{2} = \frac{2}{4}$$
$$\frac{1}{4}$$

12. $\frac{1}{2}$
$$\frac{2}{3} = \frac{4}{6}$$
$$-\frac{1}{6} = \frac{1}{6}$$
$$\frac{3}{6} \div \frac{3}{3} = \frac{1}{2}$$

13. $\frac{1}{3}$
$$\frac{5}{6} = \frac{5}{6}$$
$$-\frac{1}{2} = \frac{3}{6}$$
$$\frac{2}{6} \div \frac{2}{2} = \frac{1}{3}$$

14. $\frac{5}{12}$
$$\frac{3}{4} = \frac{9}{12}$$
$$-\frac{1}{3} = \frac{4}{12}$$
$$\frac{5}{12}$$

15. $\frac{2}{5}$
$$\frac{9}{10} = \frac{9}{10}$$
$$-\frac{1}{2} = \frac{5}{10}$$
$$\frac{4}{10} \div \frac{2}{2} = \frac{2}{5}$$

16. $\frac{17}{36}$
$$\frac{5}{9} = \frac{20}{36}$$
$$-\frac{1}{12} = \frac{3}{36}$$
$$\frac{17}{36}$$

17. $10\frac{1}{2}$
$$14 = 13\frac{2}{2}$$
$$- 3\frac{1}{2} = 3\frac{1}{2}$$
$$10\frac{1}{2}$$

Unit 7

18. $11\frac{7}{8}$
$27\frac{1}{4} = 27\frac{2}{8} = 26\frac{10}{8}$
$-15\frac{3}{8} = 15\frac{3}{8} = 15\frac{3}{8}$
$\qquad\qquad\qquad\qquad 11\frac{7}{8}$

19. $1\frac{2}{5}$
$3\frac{1}{5} = 2\frac{6}{5}$
$-1\frac{4}{5} = 1\frac{4}{5}$
$\qquad\qquad 1\frac{2}{5}$

20. $7\frac{7}{8}$
$26\frac{1}{4} = 26\frac{2}{8} = 25\frac{10}{8}$
$-18\frac{3}{8} = 18\frac{3}{8} = 18\frac{3}{8}$
$\qquad\qquad\qquad\qquad 7\frac{7}{8}$

21. $1\frac{1}{24}$
$\frac{5}{8} = \frac{15}{24}$
$\frac{1}{6} = \frac{4}{24}$
$+\frac{1}{4} = \frac{6}{24}$
$\qquad \frac{25}{24} = 1\frac{1}{24}$

22. $10\frac{1}{60}$
$1\frac{1}{4} = 1\frac{15}{60}$
$3\frac{1}{10} = 3\frac{6}{60}$
$+5\frac{2}{3} = 5\frac{40}{60}$
$\qquad\quad 9\frac{61}{60}$
Reduce:
$9\frac{61}{60} = 9 + 1\frac{1}{60} = 10\frac{1}{60}$

23. $7\frac{1}{2}$
$3\frac{1}{2} = 3\frac{4}{8}$
$1\frac{2}{8} = 1\frac{2}{8}$
$+2\frac{3}{4} = 2\frac{6}{8}$
$\qquad\quad 6\frac{12}{8}$
Reduce:
$6\frac{12}{8} = 6 + 1\frac{4}{8} = 7\frac{4}{8} = 7\frac{1}{2}$

24. $6\frac{11}{24}$
$1\frac{3}{4} = 1\frac{18}{24}$
$\frac{7}{8} = \frac{21}{24}$
$+3\frac{5}{6} = 3\frac{20}{24}$
$\qquad\quad 4\frac{59}{24}$
Reduce:
$4\frac{59}{24} = 4 + 2\frac{11}{24} = 6\frac{11}{24}$

25. $9\frac{1}{4}$
$4\frac{1}{6} = 4\frac{2}{12}$
$3\frac{2}{3} = 3\frac{8}{12}$
$+1\frac{5}{12} = 1\frac{5}{12}$
$\qquad\quad 8\frac{15}{12}$
Reduce:
$8\frac{15}{12} = 8 + 1\frac{3}{12} = 9\frac{3}{12} = 9\frac{1}{4}$

26. $\frac{9}{20}$
$\frac{7}{10} = \frac{14}{20}$
$-\frac{1}{4} = \frac{5}{20}$
$\qquad \frac{9}{20}$

27. $2\frac{5}{12}$
$3\frac{2}{3} = 3\frac{8}{12}$
$-1\frac{1}{4} = 1\frac{3}{12}$
$\qquad\quad 2\frac{5}{12}$

28. $1\frac{1}{5}$
$4 = 3\frac{5}{5}$
$-2\frac{4}{5} = 2\frac{4}{5}$
$\qquad\quad 1\frac{1}{5}$

29. $6\frac{7}{8}$
$9\frac{1}{2} = 9\frac{4}{8} = 8\frac{12}{8}$
$-2\frac{5}{8} = 2\frac{5}{8} = 2\frac{5}{8}$
$\qquad\qquad\qquad 6\frac{7}{8}$

30. $12\frac{13}{16}$
$13\frac{3}{4} = 13\frac{12}{16} = 12\frac{28}{16}$
$-\frac{15}{16} = \frac{15}{16} = \frac{15}{16}$
$\qquad\qquad\qquad\qquad 12\frac{13}{16}$

31. (5) $33\frac{1}{2}$ Add to find the total number of gallons.
$8\frac{5}{10}$
$9\frac{3}{10}$
8
$+7\frac{7}{10}$
$32\frac{15}{10} = 33\frac{5}{10} = 33\frac{1}{2}$

32. (2) $5\frac{1}{2}$ Subtract to find how many days he "has left."
$10 = 9\frac{2}{2}$
$-4\frac{1}{2} = 4\frac{1}{2}$
$\qquad\quad 5\frac{1}{2}$

33. (1) $1\frac{3}{4}$ Subtract to find "how many more."
$3\frac{1}{2} = 3\frac{2}{4} = 2\frac{6}{4}$
$-1\frac{3}{4} = 1\frac{3}{4} = 1\frac{3}{4}$
$\qquad\qquad\qquad 1\frac{3}{4}$

34. (2) 2 To find if $2\frac{2}{3}$ is nearer to 2 or 3, compare $\frac{2}{3}$ and $\frac{1}{2}$ using common denominators.
$\frac{2}{3} = \frac{4}{6}$ $\frac{1}{2} = \frac{3}{6}$

$\frac{4}{6} > \frac{3}{6}$
Since $\frac{4}{6} > \frac{1}{2}$ add 1 to the whole number. $2\frac{2}{3}$ rounds to 3.

To find if $\frac{3}{4}$ is nearer to 0 or 1, compare $\frac{3}{4}$ and $\frac{1}{2}$ using common denominators.
$\frac{1}{2} = \frac{2}{4}$ $\frac{3}{4} > \frac{2}{4}$
Since $\frac{3}{4} > \frac{1}{2}$, add 1 to the whole number. $\frac{3}{4}$ rounds to 1.
Subtract to find about how many cups of dressing are left. $3 - 1 = 2$

35. (3) $28\frac{1}{8}$ Add to find the total yardage.
$12\frac{1}{2} = 12\frac{4}{8}$
$8\frac{7}{8} = 8\frac{7}{8}$
$+6\frac{3}{4} = 6\frac{6}{8}$
$\qquad\qquad 26\frac{17}{8} =$
$\qquad 26 + 2\frac{1}{8} =$
$\qquad\qquad\quad 28\frac{1}{8}$

36. (4) $20\frac{7}{10}$ Add to find the total hours.
$5\frac{2}{5} = 5\frac{4}{10}$
$6\frac{1}{2} = 6\frac{5}{10}$
$+8\frac{4}{5} = 8\frac{8}{10}$
$\qquad\qquad 19\frac{17}{10} =$
$\qquad 19 + 1\frac{7}{10} =$
$\qquad\qquad\quad 20\frac{7}{10}$

37. (1) $2\frac{7}{12}$ feet Subtract to find the difference between the two lengths.
$8\frac{1}{3} = 8\frac{4}{12} = 7\frac{16}{12}$
$-5\frac{3}{4} = 5\frac{9}{12} = 5\frac{9}{12}$
$\qquad\qquad\qquad\qquad 2\frac{7}{12}$

Lesson 8: Multiplying and Dividing Fractions

GED Exercise: Multiplying and Dividing Fractions (page 514)

1. $\frac{1}{3}$ $\frac{1}{\cancel{2}_1} \times \frac{\cancel{2}^1}{3} = \frac{1}{3}$

2. $\frac{7}{10}$ $\frac{7}{\cancel{8}_2} \times \frac{\cancel{4}}{5} = \frac{7}{10}$

3. $\frac{1}{20}$ $\frac{\cancel{3}^1}{\cancel{8}_4} \times \frac{\cancel{2}^1}{\cancel{15}_5} = \frac{1}{20}$

4. $\frac{20}{27}$ $\frac{5}{\cancel{6}_3} \times \frac{\cancel{8}^4}{9} = \frac{20}{27}$

5. **21**
$\frac{7}{8} \times 24 = \frac{7}{\cancel{8}_1} \times \frac{\cancel{24}^3}{1} = \frac{21}{1} = 21$

6. $1\frac{1}{3}$
$\frac{4}{5} \times 1\frac{2}{3} = \frac{4}{\cancel{5}_1} \times \frac{\cancel{5}}{3} = \frac{4}{3} = 1\frac{1}{3}$

7. **48**
$9 \times 5\frac{1}{3} = \frac{\cancel{9}^3}{1} \times \frac{16}{\cancel{3}_1} = \frac{48}{1} = 48$

8. **6**
$2\frac{2}{5} \times 2\frac{1}{2} = \frac{\cancel{12}^6}{\cancel{5}_1} \times \frac{\cancel{5}^1}{\cancel{2}_1} = \frac{6}{1} = 6$

9. $13\frac{3}{4}$ $3\frac{1}{3} \times 4\frac{1}{8} = \frac{10}{\cancel{3}_1} \times \frac{\cancel{33}^{11}}{\cancel{8}_4} =$
$\frac{55}{4} = 13\frac{3}{4}$

10. $16\frac{1}{2}$ $2\frac{3}{4} \times 6 = \frac{11}{\cancel{4}_2} \times \frac{\cancel{6}^3}{1} =$
$\frac{33}{2} = 16\frac{1}{2}$

11. $\frac{2}{5}$ $\frac{1}{3} \div \frac{5}{6} = \frac{1}{\cancel{3}_1} \times \frac{\cancel{6}^2}{5} = \frac{2}{5}$

12. $\frac{7}{20}$ $\frac{7}{10} \div 2 = \frac{7}{10} \div \frac{2}{1}$
$= \frac{7}{10} \times \frac{1}{2} = \frac{7}{20}$

13. **3** $\frac{5}{8} \div \frac{5}{24} = \frac{\cancel{5}^1}{\cancel{8}_1} \times \frac{\cancel{24}^3}{\cancel{5}_1} = \frac{3}{1} = 3$

14. $\frac{2}{3}$ $\frac{4}{9} \div \frac{2}{3} = \frac{\cancel{4}^2}{\cancel{9}_3} \times \frac{\cancel{3}^1}{\cancel{2}_1} = \frac{2}{3}$

15. **8** $12 \div 1\frac{1}{2} = \frac{12}{1} \div \frac{3}{2} =$
$\frac{\cancel{12}^4}{1} \times \frac{2}{\cancel{3}_1} = \frac{8}{1} = 8$

16. **26** $6\frac{1}{2} \div \frac{1}{4} = \frac{13}{2} \div \frac{1}{4} =$
$\frac{13}{\cancel{2}_1} \times \frac{\cancel{4}^2}{1} = \frac{26}{1} = 26$

17. **27** $18 \div \frac{2}{3} = \frac{18}{1} \div \frac{2}{3} =$
$\frac{\cancel{18}^9}{1} \times \frac{3}{\cancel{2}_1} = \frac{27}{1} = 27$

18. $4\frac{1}{5}$ $4\frac{9}{10} \div 1\frac{1}{6} = \frac{49}{10} \div \frac{7}{6} =$
$\frac{\cancel{49}^7}{\cancel{10}_5} \times \frac{\cancel{6}}{\cancel{7}_1} = \frac{21}{5} = 4\frac{1}{5}$

19. $3\frac{1}{3}$ $6\frac{1}{9} \div 1\frac{5}{6} = \frac{55}{9} \div \frac{11}{6} =$
$\frac{\cancel{55}^5}{\cancel{9}_3} \times \frac{\cancel{6}^2}{\cancel{11}_1} = \frac{10}{3} = 3\frac{1}{3}$

20. $\frac{29}{32}$ $3\frac{5}{8} \div 4 = \frac{29}{8} \div \frac{4}{1} =$
$\frac{29}{8} \times \frac{1}{4} = \frac{29}{32}$

21. **(3) $7\frac{7}{8}$** Multiply $15\frac{3}{4}$ by $\frac{1}{2}$ because you need to find $\frac{1}{2}$ "of" the order.
$15\frac{3}{4} \times \frac{1}{2} = \frac{63}{4} \times \frac{1}{2} = \frac{63}{8} = 7\frac{7}{8}$

22. **(4) 45** You need to find how many $\frac{1}{3}$ parts are in 15. Divide 15 by $\frac{1}{3}$.
$15 \div \frac{1}{3} = \frac{15}{1} \div \frac{1}{3} = \frac{15}{1} \times \frac{3}{1} =$
$\frac{45}{1} = 45$

23. **(4) 48** The word "of" means multiply. Multiply the number of animals, 60, by $\frac{4}{5}$ (the fraction that is dogs).
$60 \times \frac{4}{5} = \frac{\cancel{60}^{12}}{1} \times \frac{4}{\cancel{5}_1} = \frac{48}{1} = 48$

24. **(5) Not enough information is given.** You need to know Elio's present salary to solve the problem.

25. **(3) 32** Divide the height of the stack (24 inches) by the thickness of one board $\left(\frac{3}{4}\text{ inch}\right)$. You do not need the length of the boards to solve the problem.
$24 \div \frac{3}{4} = \frac{24}{1} \div \frac{3}{4} = \frac{\cancel{24}^8}{1} \times \frac{4}{\cancel{3}_1} =$
$\frac{32}{1} = 32$

26. **(2) $2\frac{1}{2}$** Divide $6\frac{1}{4}$ (the total length of the trail) by $2\frac{1}{2}$ (the distance Steve can cover in one hour). You need to find how many $2\frac{1}{2}$ parts are in $6\frac{1}{4}$.
$6\frac{1}{4} \div 2\frac{1}{2} = \frac{25}{4} \div \frac{5}{2} = \frac{\cancel{25}^5}{\cancel{4}_2} \times \frac{\cancel{2}^1}{\cancel{5}_1} =$
$\frac{5}{2} = 2\frac{1}{2}$

GED Review: Fractions (page 516)

1. **(3) $18\frac{3}{4}$** Add the hours worked each day:

$2\frac{3}{4} = 2\frac{3}{4}$
$4\frac{1}{2} = 4\frac{2}{4}$
$3\frac{1}{2} = 3\frac{2}{4}$
$5\frac{1}{4} = 5\frac{1}{4}$
$+2\frac{3}{4} = 2\frac{3}{4}$
$16\frac{11}{4} =$
$16 + 2\frac{3}{4} = 18\frac{3}{4}$

2. **(2) 9** Multiply then divide to find the number of bolts:
$120 \times 4\frac{1}{2} = \frac{\cancel{120}^{60}}{1} \times \frac{9}{\cancel{2}_1} = 540$
$540 \div 60 = 9$

3. **(2) $\frac{1}{12}$** Subtract to find what fraction of his space Phil uses for his samples:
$1 - \frac{3}{4} = \frac{1}{4}$. Multiply.
Phil uses: $\frac{1}{4} \times \frac{1}{3} = \frac{1}{12}$.

4. **(2) golden oak** Compare the five fractions on the list by changing $\frac{1}{8}$, $\frac{3}{8}$, and $\frac{1}{4}$ to equal fractions with the common denominator of 16.
$\frac{1}{8} = \frac{2}{16}$ $\frac{3}{8} = \frac{6}{16}$ $\frac{1}{4} = \frac{4}{16}$

Compare with the other two on the list: $\frac{3}{16}$ and $\frac{1}{16}$. The fraction $\frac{3}{8}$ represents the most customers.

5. **(3) $\frac{13}{16}$** Add $\frac{3}{8}$, $\frac{1}{4}$, and $\frac{3}{16}$.
$\frac{3}{8} = \frac{6}{16}$
$\frac{1}{4} = \frac{4}{16}$
$+\frac{3}{16} = \frac{3}{16}$
$\frac{13}{16}$

6. **(1) 25** Find $\frac{1}{8}$ of 200.
$200 \times \frac{1}{8} = \frac{\cancel{200}^{25}}{1} \times \frac{1}{\cancel{8}_1} = \frac{25}{1} = 25$

7. **(3) $\frac{1}{3}$ cup** Multiply: $\frac{2}{3} \times \frac{1}{2} = \frac{1}{3}$.

8. **(4) 4** To find if $1\frac{3}{4}$ is nearer to 1 or 2, compare $\frac{3}{4}$ and $\frac{1}{2}$ using common denominators.
$\frac{1}{2} = \frac{2}{4}$ $\frac{3}{4} > \frac{2}{4}$
Since $\frac{3}{4} > \frac{1}{2}$, add 1 to the

whole number. $1\frac{3}{4}$ rounds to 2.

To find out if $2\frac{1}{8}$ is nearer to 2 or 3, compare $\frac{1}{8}$ and $\frac{1}{2}$ using common denominators.

$\frac{1}{2} = \frac{4}{8}$ $\frac{1}{8} < \frac{4}{8}$

Since $\frac{1}{8} < \frac{1}{2}$, the whole number, 2, stays the same. $2\frac{1}{8}$ rounds to 2.

Add to find about how many yards of silk are needed. $2 + 2 = 4$

9. **(2) 1,170** Find $\frac{1}{3}$ of 3,510: $\frac{1}{3} \times 3,510$.

10. **(3) $250 \times \frac{3}{5}$** The problem states that $\frac{3}{5}$ of the cars are speeding. Since 250 cars are driving, then $\frac{3}{5}$ of 250 is the expression used to solve the problem. It can be written as $\frac{3}{5} \times 250$ or $250 \times \frac{3}{5}$.

11. **(3) $79\frac{3}{4}$** Multiply:
$14\frac{1}{2} \times 5\frac{1}{2} = \frac{29}{2} \times \frac{11}{2} = \frac{319}{4} = 79\frac{3}{4}$

12. **(5) $\frac{4}{5}$** Subtract: $35 - 7 = 28$
Write a fraction and reduce:
$\frac{28}{35} = \frac{4}{5}$

13. **(3) $3\frac{5}{12}$** First find the total square yards of carpeting he needs using addition.

$12\frac{1}{2} = 12\frac{6}{12}$
$20\frac{3}{4} = 20\frac{9}{12}$
$+13\frac{1}{3} = 13\frac{4}{12}$
$45\frac{19}{12} = 45 + 1\frac{7}{12} = 46\frac{7}{12}$

Then subtract the result from 50 square yards (the amount on hand).

$50 \quad = 49\frac{12}{12}$
$-46\frac{7}{12} = 46\frac{7}{12}$
$3\frac{5}{12}$

14. **(3) $2\frac{1}{2} \times 5\frac{1}{2}$** Multiply $5\frac{1}{2}$ (the rate of growth) by $2\frac{1}{2}$ (the number of weeks).

15. **(1) $\frac{1}{5} + \frac{1}{8}$** Add $\frac{1}{5}$ and $\frac{1}{8}$ to find the total fraction spent on food and clothes.

16. **(2) $520** Find $\frac{1}{4}$ of their monthly income of $2,080 using multiplication.

$2,080 \times \frac{1}{4} = \frac{\overset{520}{\cancel{2,080}}}{1} \times \frac{1}{\cancel{4}_1} = \frac{520}{1} = \$520$

17. **(5) Not enough information is given.** The chart tells that they spend $\frac{1}{20}$ of their income

on two items: savings and miscellaneous. You need to know the part of their income that is spent on savings alone.

18. **(4) $14\frac{13}{16}$** Subtract to find the difference.

$18\frac{1}{4} = 18\frac{4}{16} = 17\frac{20}{16}$
$-\ 3\frac{7}{16} = \ 3\frac{7}{16} = \ 3\frac{7}{16}$
$14\frac{13}{16}$

19. **(4) $7\frac{1}{12}$** Add the three distances: $1\frac{2}{3}$ (to work), $1\frac{2}{3}$ (from work), and $3\frac{3}{4}$ (her evening walk).

$1\frac{2}{3} = 1\frac{8}{12}$
$1\frac{2}{3} = 1\frac{8}{12}$
$+3\frac{3}{4} = 3\frac{9}{12}$
$5\frac{25}{12} = 5 + 2\frac{1}{12} = 7\frac{1}{12}$

20. **(3) 48** Divide: $6 \div \frac{1}{8} = \frac{6}{1} \times \frac{8}{1} = 48$.

21. **(2) $7\frac{1}{4}$** Multiply to find how long it would take to make 21 feeders: $21 \times \frac{3}{4} = \frac{21}{1} \times \frac{3}{4} = \frac{63}{4} = 15\frac{3}{4}$. Subtract the time worked:
$15\frac{3}{4} - 8\frac{1}{2} = 15\frac{3}{4} - 8\frac{2}{4} = 7\frac{1}{4}$.

22. **(1) $3\frac{1}{2}$** Multiply:
$1\frac{3}{4} \times 2 = \frac{7}{4} \times \frac{2}{1} = \frac{7}{2} = 3\frac{1}{2}$.

23. **(4) 20** There is $\frac{2}{3}$ of a cup of grits in a serving. Multiply: $30 \times \frac{2}{3} = 20$.

24. **(2) $1\frac{1}{2}$ ($\frac{1}{2}$)** Multiply the amount of uncooked grits ($\frac{1}{2}$) by $1\frac{1}{2}$ times the recipe.

25. **(2) 8** Divide 10 (the number of hours the store is open) by $1\frac{1}{4}$ (the number of hours each tape lasts).

$10 \div 1\frac{1}{4} = \frac{10}{1} \div \frac{5}{4} = \frac{\overset{2}{\cancel{10}}}{1} \times \frac{4}{\cancel{5}_1} = \frac{8}{1} = 8$

26. **(5) Not enough information is given.** You can compare the fractions, but you need to know the number of employees to compare the number who gave each year.

27. **(4) $\frac{7}{10}$** Add:
$\frac{3}{10} + \frac{2}{5} = \frac{3}{10} + \frac{4}{10} = \frac{7}{10}$.

28. **(1) $\frac{1}{25}$** Write as a fraction and reduce to lowest terms.
$\frac{4}{100} \div \frac{4}{4} = \frac{1}{25}$

Decimals

Lesson 9: Decimals

GED Exercise: Decimals (page 522)

1. **five thousandths** The 5 is in the thousandths place.

2. **eight tenths** The 8 is in the tenths place.

3. **seven hundredths** The 7 is in the hundredths place.

4. **nine ten-thousandths** The 9 is in the ten-thousandths place.

5. **0.32 > 0.3109** Add zeros: 0.3200 > 0.3109 The number 3,200 is greater than 3,109.

6. **0.98 < 1.9** The first number, 0.98, does not have a whole number part; the second number, 1.9, has a whole number part of 1, so it is larger.

7. **0.5 = 0.50** The 0 after the 5 in 0.50 does not change the value of the number. Both have the same value: five tenths.

8. **0.006 < 0.06** Add zero to the second number: 0.060. The first number, 0.006, is less because 6 is less than 60.

9. **1.075 < 1.57** Both have the same whole number part. Add a zero to the second number: 1.570. The first number, 1.075, is smaller because 75 is less than 570.

10. **0.18 > 0.108** Add a zero to the first number: 0.180. The first number, 0.18, is greater because 180 is greater than 108.

11. **2.38 < 2.83** Both have the same whole number part. The first number is less because 38 is less than 83.

12. **1.09 > 1.009** Both have the same whole number part. Add a zero to the first number: 1.090. The first number is greater because 90 is greater than 9.

13. **3.60 = 3.600** Both have the same whole number part. The zeros after the 6 in both numbers do not change the value. Both have the same value.

14. **3.09 3.4 3.9 3.901** Add zeros so that each number has three decimal places, and compare: 3.400, 3.090, 3.900, 3.901.

15. **0.08 0.8 0.89** Add zeros so that each number has two decimal places, and compare: 0.08, 0.80, 0.89.

16. **0.9054 0.95 0.954** Add zeros so that each number has four decimal places, and compare: 0.9500, 0.9540, 0.9054.

17. **12.001 12.04 12.608 12.8** Add zeros so that each number has three decimal places, and compare: 12.608, 12.001, 12.800, 12.040.

18. **3.6** The number to the right of the tenths place is 5 or more: 3.5̲719. Add 1 to the tenths place and drop the remaining digits to the right.

19. **125.070** The number to the right of the thousandths place is 5 or more: 125.0699. Since there is a 9 in the thousandths place, add 1 to the hundredths place and drop the remaining digits.

20. **5.13** The number to the right of the hundredths place is less than 5: 5.132̲. Drop the remaining digit to the right.

21. **17.1** The number to the right of the tenths place is 5 or more: 17.0̲813. Add 1 to the tenths place and drop the remaining digits to the right.

22. **0.64** The number to the right of the hundredths place is less than 5: 0.6415̲. Drop the remaining digits to the right.

23. **(4) between $30 and $33** Estimate the cost of the three games:

	Sale Price	Estimate
Fast Pitch	$8.99	$ 9
Crown of Power	10.09	10
Dugout Derby	12.78	13
Total estimate:		$32

24. **(5) She cannot afford any other game.** Find the total of the estimate:

	Sale Price	Estimate
Par 4	$6.29	$ 6
Batwing	7.98	8
Total estimate:		$14

Subtract from $20: $20 − $14 = $6 None of the other games among the choices costs $6 or less.

25. **(2) $8** Estimate the cost of the games at the regular price:

	Regular Price	Estimate
Dugout Derby	$17.25	$17
Crown of Power	13.72	14
Total estimate:		$31

Estimate the cost of the games at the sale price:

	Sale Price	Estimate
Dugout Derby	$12.78	$13
Crown of Power	10.09	10
Total estimate:		$23

Find the difference between the two estimates: $31 − $23 = $8

Unit 7

26. **(4) $51** Round the cost of each item to the nearest whole dollar and add to find the total of the estimates.
$38.82 rounds to $39.
$12.39 rounds to $12.
$39 + $12 = $51

27. **(5) $36** Round the cost of a package of nails to the nearest whole dollar. Multiply to find the total cost of six of the items.
$5.75 rounds to $6.
$6 × 6 = $36

28. **(4) $232** Round the cost of each item to the nearest whole dollar, and add to find the total of the estimates.
$185.60 rounds to $186.
$46.36 rounds to $46.
$186 + $46 = $232

29. **(5) $600** Round amounts to the nearest hundred dollars. Subtract to find the amount still needed.
$685 rounds to $700.
$110 rounds to $100.
$700 − $100 = $600

Lesson 10: Decimal Operations
GED Exercise: Decimal Operations (page 526)

1. **82.887**
```
   1.850
   0.030
  19.007
 +62.000
 -------
  82.887
```

2. **9,032**
```
  16,004.1
 -  6,972.1
 ---------
   9,032.0
```

3. **2.794**
```
   3.800
  -1.006
  ------
   2.794
```

4. **22.668**
```
  14.010
   8.600
 + 0.058
 -------
  22.668
```

5. **31.85**
```
  56.80
 -24.95
 ------
  31.85
```

6. **6.701**
```
  0.950
  1.843
  3.008
 +0.900
 ------
  6.701
```

7. **12.84**
```
    1.07
 ×    12
 -------
    2 14
   10 7
 -------
   12.84
```

8. **0.549**
```
     0.09
 ×    6.1
 --------
     00 9
    54
 --------
   0.54 9
```

9. **75.6**
```
    5.04
 ×    15
 -------
   25 20
   50 4
 -------
   75.60
```

10. **0.02**
```
   0.008
 ×   2.5
 -------
   0040
  0 016
 -------
  0.0200
```

11. **0.144**
```
   0.012
 ×    12
 -------
   0 024
  00 12
  00 0
 -------
  00.144
```

12. **0.2145**
```
    7.15
 ×  0.03
 -------
   21 45
   00 0
  0 00
 -------
  0.21 45
```

13. **2.56**
```
       2.56
 8) 20.48
    16
    ---
    4 4
    4 0
    ---
      48
      48
```

14. **62**
```
           62.
 0.07) 4.34.
       4 2
       ---
        14
        14
```

15. **0.3**
```
         0.3
 1.5) 0.4.5
      4 5
```

16. **0.29**   0.285 rounds to 0.29

$$7 \overline{) 2.000}$$
$$\underline{1\ 4}$$
$$60$$
$$\underline{56}$$
$$40$$
$$\underline{35}$$
$$5$$

17. **0.46**   0.461 rounds to 0.46

$$13 \overline{) 6.000}$$
$$\underline{5\ 2}$$
$$80$$
$$\underline{78}$$
$$20$$
$$\underline{13}$$
$$7$$

18. **0.42**   0.416 rounds to 0.42

$$12 \overline{) 5.000}$$
$$\underline{4\ 8}$$
$$20$$
$$\underline{12}$$
$$80$$
$$\underline{72}$$
$$8$$

19. **(2) $35 − ($12.98 + $10.67 + $5.98)** You need to add the prices for the three items together and then subtract the total from $35. The parentheses around the three prices in option (2) tell you to do that step first, then subtract.

20. **(4) 5.37** Carry out the operations:
$35 − ($12.98 + $10.67 + $5.98) = $35 − $29.63 = $5.37

21. **(1) 25($1.05 − $0.89)** The best way to work the problem is to find the difference between the two prices for one diskette. Then multiply the difference by 25 to find the total savings. You can get the same answer by multiplying each price by 25 and finding the difference: 25($1.05) − 25($0.89).

22. **(4) $4.00** Carry out the operations:
25($1.05 − $0.89) =
25 ($0.16)   = $4

23. **(1) 2($45.79) + $18.25** Multiply the cost of one tire by 2 and add the amount for the oil change.

24. **(3) $109.83** Carry out the operations:
2($45.79) + $18.25 =
$91.58 + $18.25 = $109.83

25. **(1) $202** Subtract to find the annual increase. Divide the annual increase by 12 months in a year.
$21,000 − $18,575 = $2,425
$2,425 ÷ 12 = $202.083, which rounds to $202.

Lesson 11: Decimals and Fractions

GED Exercise: Decimals and Fractions (page 530)

1. $\frac{1}{4}$ Write 25 over 100 and reduce to lowest terms.
$\frac{25}{100} \div \frac{25}{25} = \frac{1}{4}$

2. $\frac{7}{8}$ Write 875 over 1,000 and reduce to lowest terms.
$\frac{875}{1,000} \div \frac{125}{125} = \frac{7}{8}$

3. $\frac{3}{8}$ Write 375 over 1,000 and reduce to lowest terms.
$\frac{375}{1,000} \div \frac{125}{125} = \frac{3}{8}$

4. $\frac{19}{25}$ Write 76 over 100 and reduce to lowest terms.
$\frac{76}{100} \div \frac{4}{4} = \frac{19}{25}$

5. $\frac{5}{16}$ $\frac{31\frac{1}{4}}{100} = 31\frac{1}{4} \div 100 =$
$\frac{125^{5}}{4} \times \frac{1}{100_{4}} = \frac{5}{16}$

6. $\frac{15}{16}$ $\frac{93\frac{3}{4}}{100} = 93\frac{3}{4} \div 100 =$
$\frac{375^{15}}{4} \times \frac{1}{100_{4}} = \frac{15}{16}$

7. $\frac{11}{12}$ $\frac{91\frac{2}{3}}{100} = 91\frac{2}{3} \div 100 =$
$\frac{275^{11}}{3} \times \frac{1}{100_{4}} = \frac{11}{12}$

8. $\frac{1}{6}$ $\frac{16\frac{2}{3}}{100} = 16\frac{2}{3} \div 100 =$
$\frac{50^{1}}{3} \times \frac{1}{100_{2}} = \frac{1}{6}$

9. $\frac{27}{40}$ $\frac{675}{1,000} \div \frac{25}{25} = \frac{27}{40}$

10. $\frac{13}{120}$ $\frac{10\frac{5}{6}}{100} = 10\frac{5}{6} \div 100 =$
$\frac{65^{13}}{6} \times \frac{1}{100_{20}} = \frac{13}{120}$

11. $\frac{11}{20}$ $\frac{55}{100} \div \frac{5}{5} = \frac{11}{20}$

12. $\frac{4}{75}$ $\frac{5\frac{1}{3}}{100} = 5\frac{1}{3} \div 100 =$
$\frac{16^{4}}{3} \times \frac{1}{100_{25}} = \frac{4}{75}$

13. **0.8** Divide 4 by 5.

$$5 \overline{) 4.0}$$
$$\underline{4\ 0}$$
0.8

14. **0.375** Divide 3 by 8.

$$8 \overline{) 3.000}$$
$$\underline{2\ 4}$$
$$60$$
$$\underline{56}$$
$$40$$
$$\underline{40}$$
0.375

15. **0.667** Divide 2 by 3. Divide to four decimal places and round to the thousandths place.
0.6666 rounds to 0.667

$$3 \overline{) 2.0000}$$
$$\underline{1\ 8}$$
$$20$$
$$\underline{18}$$
$$20$$
$$\underline{18}$$
$$20$$
$$\underline{18}$$
$$2$$

16. **0.417** Divide 5 by 12 to four decimal places and round.
0.4166 rounds to 0.417

$$12 \overline{) 5.0000}$$
$$\underline{4\ 8}$$
$$20$$
$$\underline{12}$$
$$80$$
$$\underline{72}$$
$$80$$
$$\underline{72}$$
$$8$$

Unit 7

17. **0.583** Divide 7 by 12 to four decimal places and round.

$$
\begin{array}{r}
0.5833 \\
12\overline{)7.0000} \\
\underline{6\ 0} \\
100 \\
\underline{96} \\
40 \\
\underline{36} \\
40 \\
\underline{36} \\
4
\end{array}
$$

18. **0.188** Divide 3 by 16 to four decimal places and round.

$$
\begin{array}{r}
0.1875 \\
16\overline{)3.0000} \\
\underline{1\ 6} \\
1\ 40 \\
\underline{1\ 28} \\
120 \\
\underline{112} \\
80 \\
\underline{80} \\
0
\end{array}
$$

19. **$0.83\frac{1}{3}$**

$$
0.83\frac{2}{6} = 0.83\frac{1}{3}
$$
$$
\begin{array}{r}
6\overline{)5.00} \\
\underline{4\ 8} \\
20 \\
\underline{18} \\
2
\end{array}
$$

20. **$0.88\frac{8}{9}$**

$$
0.88\frac{8}{9}
$$
$$
\begin{array}{r}
9\overline{)8.00} \\
\underline{7\ 2} \\
80 \\
\underline{72} \\
8
\end{array}
$$

21. **$0.46\frac{2}{3}$**

$$
0.46\frac{10}{15} = 0.46\frac{2}{3}
$$
$$
\begin{array}{r}
15\overline{)7.00} \\
\underline{6\ 0} \\
1\ 00 \\
\underline{90} \\
10
\end{array}
$$

22. **$0.06\frac{1}{4}$**

$$
0.06\frac{4}{16} = 0.06\frac{1}{4}
$$
$$
\begin{array}{r}
16\overline{)1.00} \\
\underline{96} \\
4
\end{array}
$$

23. **$0.87\frac{1}{2}$**

$$
0.87\frac{4}{8} = 0.87\frac{1}{2}
$$
$$
\begin{array}{r}
8\overline{)7.00} \\
\underline{6\ 4} \\
60 \\
\underline{56} \\
4
\end{array}
$$

24. **$0.41\frac{2}{3}$**

$$
0.41\frac{8}{12} = 0.41\frac{2}{3}
$$
$$
\begin{array}{r}
12\overline{)5.00} \\
\underline{4\ 8} \\
20 \\
\underline{12} \\
8
\end{array}
$$

25. **(3) 0.003** Since the answer options are written as decimals, change $\frac{1}{100}$ to a decimal: $\frac{1}{100} = 0.01$.
Subtract:
$$
\begin{array}{r}
0.010 \\
\underline{-0.007} \\
0.003
\end{array}
$$

26. **(2) $\frac{1}{8}$** Since the answer options are written as fractions, change 0.75 to a fraction: $0.75 = \frac{3}{4}$.
Subtract:
$$
\begin{array}{r}
\frac{7}{8} = \ \ \frac{7}{8} \\
-\frac{3}{4} = -\frac{6}{8} \\
\hline
\frac{1}{8}
\end{array}
$$

27. **(4) $17.00** Since the answer options are written as decimals, change $12\frac{1}{2}$ to a decimal:
$12\frac{1}{2} = 12.5$.
Multiply:
$$
\begin{array}{r}
12.5 \\
\times 1.36 \\
\hline
7\ 50 \\
37\ 5 \\
125 \\
\hline
17.000
\end{array} = \$17.00
$$

28. **(1) 10** To find the difference of $\frac{3}{8}$ and 0.4, solve the problem using decimals as the faster method.
Convert $\frac{3}{8}$ to a decimal:
$\frac{3}{8} = 0.375$.
Subtract:
$$
\begin{array}{r}
0.400 \\
\underline{-0.375} \\
0.025
\end{array}
$$
Now multiply the number of people surveyed by 0.025.
$$
\begin{array}{r}
400 \\
\times 0.025 \\
\hline
2\ 000 \\
8\ 00 \\
\hline
10.000
\end{array}
$$

29. **(2) 11** You need to divide $35\frac{3}{4}$ by 3.25. You can use either method. Both methods are shown:

Fractions: $(3.25 = 3\frac{1}{4})$
$$
35\frac{3}{4} \div 3\frac{1}{4} = \frac{143}{4} \div \frac{13}{4} =
$$
$$
\frac{\cancel{143}^{11}}{\cancel{4}_1} \times \frac{\cancel{4}^1}{\cancel{13}_1} = \frac{11}{1} = 11
$$
Decimals: $(35\frac{3}{4} = 35.75)$
$$
\begin{array}{r}
11 \\
3.25\overline{)35.75} \\
\underline{32\ 5} \\
3\ 25 \\
\underline{3\ 25} \\
0
\end{array}
$$

30. **(2) $16\frac{1}{4}$** Since the answer options are fractions, change 2.75 and 3.375 to fractions. Then add and reduce.
$$
2.75 = 2 + \frac{75 \div 25}{100 \div 25} = 2\frac{3}{4}
$$
$$
3.375 = 3 + \frac{375 \div 125}{1,000 \div 125} = 3\frac{3}{8}
$$
Add:
$$
\begin{array}{r}
2\frac{3}{4} = \ \ 2\frac{6}{8} \\
3\frac{1}{2} = \ \ 3\frac{4}{8} \\
3\frac{7}{8} = \ \ 3\frac{7}{8} \\
2\frac{3}{4} = \ \ 2\frac{6}{8} \\
+3\frac{3}{8} = +3\frac{3}{8} \\
\hline
13\frac{26}{8}
\end{array}
$$
Reduce: $13\frac{26}{8} = 13 + 3\frac{2}{8} = 16\frac{2}{8} = 16\frac{1}{4}$

GED Review: Decimals (page 532)

1. **(4) 58.7 miles** Add the miles for each trip to find a total: $12.3 + 15.8 + 21.7 + 8.9 = 58.7$.

2. **(2) 0.52 − (0.06 + 0.1)** First you need to find how much of ingredient A and B are in the conditioner: add 0.06 and 0.1 grams. Then subtract that result from the total needed: 0.52 grams. The parentheses in option 2 tell you to do the addition step first.

3. **(3) 3.75** Divide $6.98 by $1.86. Divide to the thousandths place and round to the hundredths place:

$$\begin{array}{r} 3.752 \\ 1.86\overline{\smash{\big)}\,6.98.000} \\ \underline{5\ 58} \\ 1\ 40\ 0 \\ \underline{1\ 30\ 2} \\ 9\ 80 \\ \underline{9\ 30} \\ 500 \\ \underline{372} \\ 128 \end{array}$$

3.752 rounds to 3.75.

4. **(1) 263.8 miles** Add the miles for each day to find a total:

87.6	Line up the decimal points.
17.3	Write zeros as needed, then
14.0	add.
102.2	
+ 42.7	
263.8	

5. **(3) $12.26** Multiply Monday's mileage by $0.14

87.6	Since there are three decimal
×$0.14	places in the problem, there
3 504	must be three decimal places in
8 76	the answer. Round to the
$12.264	nearest whole cent: $12.264
	rounds to $12.26.

6. **(2) $6.16** Multiply $3.85 by 1.6.

$3.85	Since there are 3 decimal places
× 1.6	in the problem, there are 3 decimal
2 31 0	places in the answer.
3 85	
$6.16 0	Drop the final zero. $6.160 = $6.16

7. **(5) 0.009** Subtract the thickness of the gold from the desired thickness:

$$\begin{array}{r} \overset{2\ 1}{0.0\cancel{3}0} \\ -0.021 \\ \hline 0.009 \end{array}$$

8. **(4) between $75 and $80** Round each amount to the nearest whole number and find the difference:

$127.76 rounds to $128 $128
$51.04 rounds to $51   − 51
    $77

The difference is approximately $77.

9. **(1) ($82.37 + $136.29) − ($51.04 + $127.76)** Find the total earned on Saturday, $82.37 + $136.29, and the total earned on Sunday, $51.04 + $127.76. Subtract Sunday's total from Saturday's. The second set of parentheses is subtracted from the first.

10. **(3) 0.015 inch** Add the two thicknesses: 0.005 and 0.01.

$$\begin{array}{r} 0.005 \\ +0.010 \\ \hline 0.015 \end{array}$$

11. **(2) $438.81** Multiply $2,507.47 by 0.175. Round to the nearest whole cent.

$ 2,507.47	Since there are 5 decimal places
× 0.175	in the problem, there are 5
12 53735	decimal places in the answer.
175 5229	Round to the hundredths place.
250 747	
$438.80725	$438.80725 rounds to $438.81.

12. **(5) 0.1($226.40) + $226.40** First find the amount of the raise by multiplying 0.1 by his present salary. This step can be written 0.1($226.40). Then add the result to the present salary to find the new salary: 0.1($226.40) is added to $226.40.

Percent

Lesson 12: The Meaning of Percent
GED Exercise: The Meaning of Percent (page 534)

1. **0.6** $60\% = 60. = 0.6$

2. **0.048** $4.8\% = 04.8 = 0.048$

3. **$0.05\frac{1}{2}$ or 0.055** $5\frac{1}{2}\% = 05.\frac{1}{2} = 0.05\frac{1}{2}$

4. **2** $200\% = 200. = 2$

5. **$0.09\frac{1}{4}$ or 0.0925** $9\frac{1}{4}\% = 09.\frac{1}{4} = 0.09\frac{1}{4}$

6. **0.056** $5.6\% = 05.6 = 0.056$

7. **85%** $0.85 = 0.85 = 85\%$

8. **36%** $0.36 = 0.36 = 36\%$

9. **40%** $0.4 = 0.40 = 40\%$

10. **450%** $4.5 = 4.50 = 450\%$

11. **875%** $8.75 = 8.75 = 875\%$

12. **37.5%** $0.375 = 37.5\%$

13. **150%** $1.50 = 150\%$

14. **$16\frac{2}{3}\%$** $0.16\frac{2}{3} = 0.16\frac{2}{3} = 16\frac{2}{3}\%$

15. **40%** $\dfrac{2}{\cancel{5}_1} \times \dfrac{\overset{20}{\cancel{100}}}{1} = \dfrac{40}{1} = 40\%$

16. **75%** $\dfrac{3}{\cancel{4}_1} \times \dfrac{\overset{25}{\cancel{100}}}{1} = \dfrac{75}{1} = 75\%$

17. **$33\frac{1}{3}\%$** $\dfrac{1}{3} \times \dfrac{100}{1} = \dfrac{100}{3} = 33\frac{1}{3}\%$

18. **235%** $2 \times 100 = 200\%$

$\dfrac{7}{\cancel{20}_1} \times \dfrac{\overset{5}{\cancel{100}}}{1} = \dfrac{35}{1} = 35\%$

Add the two percents.
$200\% + 35\% = 235\%$

19. $162\frac{1}{2}$% or 162.5% $1 \times 100 = 100\%$

$$\frac{5}{\cancel{8}_2} \times \frac{\cancel{100}^{25}}{1} = \frac{125}{2} = 62\frac{1}{2} = 62\frac{1}{2}\%$$

Add the percents.
$100\% + 62\frac{1}{2}\% = 162\frac{1}{2}\%$

20. $466\frac{2}{3}$% $4 \times 100 = 400\%$

$$\frac{2}{3} \times \frac{100}{1} = \frac{200}{3} = 66\frac{2}{3} = 66\frac{2}{3}\%$$

Add the percents.
$400\% + 66\frac{2}{3}\% = 466\frac{2}{3}\%$

21. 187.5% $1 \times 100 = 100\%$

$$\frac{7}{\cancel{8}_2} \times \frac{\cancel{100}^{25}}{1} = 87.5\%$$

Add the percents.
$100\% + 87.5\% = 187.5\%$

22. 310% $3 \times 100 = 300\%$

$$\frac{1}{\cancel{10}_1} \times \frac{\cancel{100}^{10}}{1} = 10\%$$

Add the percents.
$300\% + 10\% = 310\%$

23. $\frac{1}{5}$ $\frac{20}{100} \div \frac{20}{20} = \frac{1}{5}$

24. $\frac{3}{25}$ $\frac{12}{100} \div \frac{4}{4} = \frac{3}{25}$

25. $\frac{39}{100}$

26. $\frac{13}{20}$ $\frac{65}{100} \div \frac{5}{5} = \frac{13}{20}$

27. $1\frac{2}{5}$ $\frac{140}{100} \div \frac{20}{20} = \frac{7}{5} = 1\frac{2}{5}$

28. $2\frac{3}{4}$ $\frac{275}{100} \div \frac{25}{25} = \frac{11}{4} = 2\frac{3}{4}$

29.

Decimal	Fraction	Percent
0.1	$\frac{1}{10}$	10%
0.2	$\frac{1}{5}$	20%
0.25	$\frac{1}{4}$	25%
0.3	$\frac{3}{10}$	30%
$0.33\frac{1}{3}$	$\frac{1}{3}$	$33\frac{1}{3}\%$
0.4	$\frac{2}{5}$	40%
0.5	$\frac{1}{2}$	50%
0.6	$\frac{3}{5}$	60%
$0.66\frac{2}{3}$	$\frac{2}{3}$	$66\frac{2}{3}\%$
0.7	$\frac{7}{10}$	70%
0.75	$\frac{3}{4}$	75%
0.8	$\frac{4}{5}$	80%

Lesson 13: Solving Percent Problems
GED Exercise: Solving Percent Problems (page 537)

1. **$142.50** $0.15 \times \$950 = \$142.50$

2. **$275** $1.25 \times \$220 = \$275$

3. **$11** $0.055 \times \$200 = \$11$

4. **$48** $0.04 \times \$1,200 = \$48$

5. **315** $2.10 \times 150 = 315$

6. **40** $\frac{1}{\cancel{3}} \times \frac{\cancel{120}^{40}}{1} = 40$

7. **15%** $123 \div 820 = 0.15 = 15\%$

8. **20%** $125 \div 625 = 0.2 = 20\%$

9. **2%** $\$3.50 \div \$175.00 = 0.02 = 2\%$

10. **140%** Since the part ($252) is greater than the base ($180), you know the percent will be greater than 100%. $\$252 \div \$180 = 1.4 = 140\%$

11. **4.5% or $4\frac{1}{2}$%** $225 \div 5,000 = 0.045 = 4.5\%$

12. **180%** Since the part ($72.00) is greater than the base ($40.00), you know the percent will be greater than 100%. $\$72 \div \$40 = 1.8$ or 180%

13. **$32** $\$1.92 \div 0.06 = \$32$

14. **180** $207 \div 1.15 = 180$

15. **$20** $\$0.76 \div 0.038 = \$20$

16. **8,000** $720 \div 0.09 = 8,000$

17. **160** $36 \div 0.225 = 160$

18. **$12,940** $\$679.35 \div 0.0525 = \$12,940$

19. **15%** Subtract: $\$1,725 - \$1,500 = \$225$. Divide by the original amount: $\$225 \div \$1,500 = 0.15$. Convert to a percent: $0.15 = 15\%$

20. **12%** Subtract: $\$582.40 - \$520.00 = \$62.40$. Divide by the original amount: $\$62.40 \div \$520 = 0.12$. Convert to a percent: $0.12 = 12\%$.

21. **75%** Subtract: $280 - 70 = 210$. Divide by the original amount: $210 \div 280 = 0.75$. Convert to a percent: $0.75 = 75\%$.

22. **5%** Subtract: $\$1,200 - \$1,140 = \$60$. Divide by the original amount: $\$60 \div \$1,200 = 0.05$. Convert to a percent: $0.05 = 5\%$.

23. **(3) 117** Find 36% of 325. $325 \times 0.36 = 117$

24. **(4) 20%** To find the percent of decrease, subtract: $90 − $72 = $18. Divide by the original price: $18 ÷ $90 = 0.2 = 20%.

25. **(4) $3.75** Divide the part ($0.75) by the rate (20%) to find the base: 0.75 ÷ 0.2 = $3.75

26. **(2) 60%** You need to find the percent of increase. Subtract: $1,008 − $630 = $378. Divide by the original amount, and convert to a percent: $378 ÷ $630 = 0.6 = 60%.

27. **(5) 1,600** Find 125% of 1,280. 1,280 × 1.25 = 1,600

28. **(4) 85%** This question asks "119 is what percent of 140?" Divide the part (119) by the whole (140): 119 ÷ 140 = 0.85 = 85%.

29. **(3) 300** Divide the part (9) by the rate (3%) to find the base: 9 ÷ 0.03 = 300

30. **(1) 40%** Divide the part (10) by the whole (25): 10 ÷ 25 = 0.4 = 40%.

Lesson 14: More Percent Problems

GED Exercise: More Percent Problems (page 543)

1. **(4) $17.00** Find the amount of the discount: $20 × 0.15 = $3. Subtract to find the sale price: $20 − $3 = $17.

2. **(3) $3,075** Multiply: $10,000 × 0.1025 × 3 = $3,075

3. **(3) 200%** Find the difference in the two amounts: $4,500 − $1,500 = $3,000. Divide by the original amount: $3,000 ÷ $1,500 = 2.00 = 200%.

4. **(5) $7.50** Find 10% by moving the decimal point one place to the left: $150.00 = $15 Divide by 2 to find 5%: $15.00 ÷ 2 = $7.50.

5. **(2) $940.50** Multiply: $900 × 0.18 × $\frac{1}{4}$ (or 0.25) = $40.50. Add $40.50 + 900 = $940.50

6. **(1) $24** Find the amount of the down payment: $160 × 0.1 = $16. Subtract the down payment from the cost of the chair: $160 − $16 = $144. Divide by the number of payments: $144 ÷ 6 = $24.

7. **(3) $300** $1,500 × 0.2 = $300

GED Review: Percent (page 544)

1. **(2) 16 ÷ 0.8** You need to solve for base. Divide the part, 16, by the rate 80% (0.8).

2. **(4) 5%** Find the difference between the two numbers to find how many people had free tickets: 42,000 − 39,900 = 2,100. Divide by the total attendance: 2,100 ÷ 42,000 = 0.05 = 5%.

3. **(4) 736** Multiply the rate (40%) by the base (1,840): 0.4 × 1,840 = 736.

4. **(4) 2,082** You know the result will be greater than the base, 1,735, because the rate is more than 100%. Multiply the base by the rate: 1,735 × 1.2 = 2,082.

5. **(5) $1.17** Multiply the base ($19.49) by the rate (6%) and round to the nearest whole cent. $19.49 × 0.06 = $1.1694; $1.1694 rounds to $1.17.

6. **(2) $726.80** Find the interest using $i = prt$. Multiply: $690 × 0.08 × $\frac{2}{3}$ = 36.8. Notice that 8 months or $\frac{8}{12}$ of a year reduces to $\frac{2}{3}$. Add the interest to the principal to find the total amount to be paid back: $36.80 + $690.00 = $726.80.

7. **(3) $404.40** First find the amount of commission he has earned during the week by multiplying: $5,320 × 0.045 = $239.40. Add the fixed salary, $165, and the commission, $239.40: $165 + $239.40 = $404.40.

8. **(5) 0.065($15.60) + $15.60** The multiplication step in the expression comes first and allows you to find the sales tax by multiplying the rate by the base, the purchase. The sales tax is then added to the purchase, or the base.

9. **(2) $1,260** Use the formula: $i = prt$. Multiply: $3,500 × 0.18 × 2 = $1,260.

10. **(3) $42.10** Find the amount of tax: Multiply $40 by $5\frac{1}{4}$%. $40 × 0.0525 = $2.10. Add the tax to the price: $40 + $2.10 = $42.10.

11. **(3) $500** Subtract 25% from 100% to get the rate that represents the sale price of the TV (100% − 25% = 75%). Divide the part, $375, by the rate, 0.75, to get the original price of the TV: $375 ÷ 0.75 = $500.

12. **(1) $3,832.50** Find how much her investment will earn using the formula: $i = prt$. $3,500 × 0.095 × 1 = $332.50. Add the interest to the principal: $332.50 + $3,500 = $3,832.50.

13. **(3) $236.40** Find the amount of the discount by multiplying the regular price by the

discount rate: $394 × 0.4 = $157.60. Subtract the amount of the discount from the regular price to find the sale price: $394 − $157.60 = $236.40.

14. **(4) $20** Solve for base. Divide the part ($12) by the rate (60%): $12 ÷ 0.6 = $20.

Graphs and Tables

Lesson 15: Graphs, Charts, and Tables
GED Exercise: Graphs, Charts, and Tables (page 550)

1. **(3) February and April** The two shortest bars are labeled F and A for February and April.

2. **(4) between $45 and $50 million** The bar for January reaches more than halfway to the bar marked $50. Remember that the scale is shown in millions of dollars. The bar represents approximately $48 million.

3. **(2) March** $40 million is the approximate average. March's sales were nearest the average.

4. **(5) 17.8** The top line of the table shows the distance from Eagle's Nest to Morning Peak is 5.6 miles. Reading on the bottom line of the table, from Morning Peak to Rock Face is 3.3 miles. Add the two figures: 5.6 + 3.3 = 8.9. Multiply by 2 to find the mileage going and coming back: 8.9 × 2 = 17.8.

5. **(1) about $3\frac{1}{2}$ times as long as the shortest** The shortest distance is from Eagle's Nest to Rock Face: 2.1 miles. The longest distance from Rock Face to Crow's Point, 7.2 miles, is about $3\frac{1}{2}$ times the shortest distance: $2.1 \times 3.5 = 7.35$.

6. **(5) Not enough information is given.** You would need to know how fast Charles hiked.

7. **(1) Federal tax** The federal tax sector is the largest and has the highest percent at 30%.

8. **(4) 30%** Add 12% (health insurance) and 18% (life insurance): 12% + 18% = 30%.

9. **(5) $250** Add the percents for state and federal taxes: 20% + 30% = 50%. Find 50% of $500. $500 × 0.5 = $250. You could also divide $500 by 2 because you know 50% is $\frac{1}{2}$.

10. **(5) Not enough information is given.** The whole that the graph represents is the total deductions. You are not told what percent the

deductions are of the employee's earnings. Since you do not know the relationship of the deductions to the earnings, you cannot solve the problem.

11. **(5) 4 P.M.** Find the highest point on the line. The highest temperature occurred at 4 P.M.

12. **(2) 10 A.M. to 12 noon** The space between each pair of vertical lines is a span of 2 hours. Examine each section that shows a rise in temperature. The steepest rise was between 10 A.M. and noon. In that period the temperature rose from 55 degrees to 65 degrees.

13. **(3) 6** Find the temperature at 4 P.M.: approximately 68 degrees. Find the temperature at 6 P.M.: approximately 62 degrees. Subtract: 68 − 62 = 6 degrees. Even if your reading of the graph was slightly different, the best estimate is 6 degrees.

14. **(2) 11 A.M.** The graph line first crosses the 60 degree line between 10 A.M. and noon. You are looking for the first time. The line crosses the horizontal 60 degree line halfway between 10 A.M. and noon. 11 A.M. is the best estimate.

15. **(3) between 20° and 24°** The lowest temperature (approximately 47 degrees) occurred between 6 and 8 A.M. The highest temperature, recorded at 4 P.M., is between 65 and 70 degrees—about 68 degrees. Subtract: 68 − 47 = 21 degrees.

16. **(2) $33.4 billion** Make sure you are looking in the 95 column on the row marked excise taxes. The amount is $33.4 billion. Remember the numbers on the chart represent billions of dollars.

17. **(2) $468.8 billion** Add the amounts paid by corporations and individuals for 1994: 104.8 + 364.0 = 468.8

18. **(3) 13%** Find the difference between the social security amounts from 1994 to 1995: 307.4 − 273.2 = 34.2. Divide by the original amount and round to the nearest whole percent: 34.2 ÷ 273.2 is approximately 13%.

19. **(4) $1,600,000,000** Subtract: 23.8 − 22.2 = 1.6
Remember the answer is in billions of dollars: 1.6 × $1,000,000,000 = $1,600,000,000.

20. **(4) $5,820** Multiply $485 by 12 (the number of months in a year).

21. **(2) Parke Boulevard** From the table you can see the apartment on Parke Boulevard has no lease fee.

22. **(3) Meridan Street** The $1,000 deposit for the Meridan Street apartment is the highest.

23. **(2) $1,935** Add all the costs on the table for the Mulberry apartment: $565 + $30 + $580 + $60 + $450 + $250 =$1,935.

24. **(2) $29.50**
Add the Tenth Avenue costs:
$495 + $990 + $49.50 =$1,534.50
Add the Parke Boulevard costs:
$485 + $970 + $50 =$1,505.
Find the difference:
$1,534.50 − $1505.00 = $29.50.

25. **(4) Tenth Avenue** It would cost $1,534.50 to move into the apartment on Tenth Avenue.

GED Review: Graphs and Tables (page 554)

1. **(1) October, November, and December** The actual rainfall is the right-hand bar for each month. The right-hand bar is lower than the left-hand bar (the normal rainfall) for only the first three months.

2. **(2) 3** Look only at the right-hand bar for each month. This bar is higher than the 5.0 line for December, January, and February.

3. **(1) 2** Look only at the right-hand bar for each month. This bar is lower than the 4.0 line for October and March.

4. **(4) 4.4** The right-hand bar for January is more than halfway to the line above 6.0, which would be 7.0. Estimate that the bar reaches to about 6.8 inches. The right-hand bar for March reaches over 2.0, but less than halfway to 3.0. Estimate that this second bar reaches to 2.4. Subtract: 6.8 − 2.4 = 4.4 inches.

5. **(4) 6.0 inches** To find the average normal rainfall, add the estimated normal amounts for the three months and divide by 3:
November is about   5.5
December is about   6.5
January is about   6.2
$18.2 \div 3 = 6.06$ inches.

6. **(3) 2.7** The right-hand bar for November is halfway between the lines for 4.0 and 5.0, which is 4.5. The right-hand bar for October is about $\frac{4}{5}$ of the length from the bottom line, which would be 1.0 to the line for 2.0.

Estimate that the bar reaches 1.8.
Subtract: 4.5 − 1.8 = 2.7.

7. **(3) from 8,700 to 10,000** The lowest point was in 1989 at about 8.7 thousand, or 8,700. The highest point was in 1986 at about 10 thousand, or 10,000.

8. **(3) four** The direction changes from up to down in 1986, from down to up again in 1989, from up to down again in 1993, and back up in 1995 for a total of four changes.

9. **(5) 1995 to 1996** You have to evaluate each of the choices by looking at the graph. Of the answer choices, the line moves up for only 1995 to 1996.

10. **(4) 7%** The miles driven for 1989 is 8.9 thousand. The amount for 1993 is 9.5 thousand. Subtract: 9.5 − 8.9 = 0.6, and divide by the original number. 0.6 divided by 8.9 is 0.067. Round to the nearest whole percent, 0.7 or 7%.

11. **(4) Business, Legal, and Professional occupations** Find $\frac{1}{2}$ of the percent figure for Retail occupations: $\frac{1}{2}$ of 42 is 21. Business, Legal, and Professional occupations has the closest percent figure with 22%.

Ratio and Proportion

Lesson 16: Ratio and Proportion • Mean • Median • Probability

GED Exercise: Ratio and Proportion • Mean • Median • Probability (page 557)

1. $\frac{4}{3}$ $\frac{16}{12} \div \frac{4}{4} = \frac{4}{3}$

2. $\frac{1}{3}$ $\frac{15}{45} \div \frac{15}{15} = \frac{1}{3}$

3. $\frac{1}{6}$ $\frac{6}{36} \div \frac{6}{6} = \frac{1}{6}$

4. $\frac{5}{2}$ $\frac{25}{10} \div \frac{5}{5} = \frac{5}{2}$

5. $\frac{2}{3}$ $\frac{24}{36} \div \frac{12}{12} = \frac{2}{3}$

6. $\frac{4}{3}$ $\frac{12}{9} \div \frac{3}{3} = \frac{4}{3}$

7. $\frac{3}{1}$ $\frac{18}{6} \div \frac{6}{6} = \frac{3}{1}$

8. $\frac{5}{1}$ $\frac{35}{7} \div \frac{7}{7} = \frac{5}{1}$

9. $\frac{4}{5}$ $\frac{80}{100} \div \frac{20}{20} = \frac{4}{5}$

10. **80 miles per hour** Divide 400 by 5.

11. **17 cents per pound** Divide 85 by 5.

12. **$18.75 per hour** Divide 225 by 12.

13. **4 calories per gram** Divide 112 by 28.

14. **64 people per team** Divide 512 by 8.

15. **225 oranges per bag** Divide 5,400 by 24.

16. **64.5 feet per second** Divide 1,032 by 16.

17. **$0.15 oz.** Divide $2.40 by 16.

18. **10** $2 \times 15 = 30$; $30 \div 3 = 10$

19. **6** $14 \times 12 = 168$; $168 \div 28 = 6$

20. **6** $20 \times 3 = 60$; $60 \div 10 = 6$

21. **7** $18 \times 3.5 = 63$; $63 \div 9 = 7$

22. **14** $4.2 \times 10 = 42$; $42 \div 3 = 14$

23. **8** $5 \times 24 = 120$; $120 \div 15 = 8$

24. **30** $15 \times 24 = 360$; $360 \div 12 = 30$

25. **3** $6 \times 7 = 42$; $42 \div 14 = 3$

26. **3** $11.5 \times 6 = 69$; $69 \div 23 = 3$

27. **32** $7 \times 16 = 112$; $112 \div 3.5 = 32$

28. **7** $4.9 \times 10 = 49$; $49 \div 7 = 7$

29. **6** $15 \times 3.2 = 48$; $48 \div 8 = 6$

30. **10** $3 \times 6 = 18$; $18 \div 1.8 = 10$

31. **1** $5 \times 1.2 = 6$; $6 \div 6 = 1$

32. **20** $6 \times 7 = 42$; $42 \div 2.1 = 20$

33. **(2) 9** $\frac{8}{2} \nearrow \frac{36}{?}$
Cross multiply: $2 \times 36 = 72$.
Divide by the remaining number: $72 \div 8 = 9$.

34. **(3) 1,050** $\frac{315}{3} \searrow \frac{?}{10}$
Cross multiply: $315 \times 10 = 3,150$.
Divide by the remaining number:
$3,150 \div 3 = 1,050$.

35. **(2) $\frac{3}{5}$** Write the ratio and reduce:
$\frac{\text{Friday}}{\text{Both Days}} = \frac{9}{9+6} = \frac{9}{15} = \frac{3}{5}$

36. **(4) 55** $\frac{12}{5} = \frac{132}{?}$
Cross multiply: $5 \times 132 = 660$.
Divide by the remaining number: $660 \div 12 = 55$.

37. **(4) 50%** Find the difference
($1,800 - $1,200 = 600), and set up
the proportion: $\frac{\$600}{\$1,200} \searrow \frac{?}{100}$
Cross multiply: $\$600 \times 100 = \$60,000$.
Divide by the remaining number:
$\$60,000 \div \$1,200 = 50$.

38. **(1) $7** $\frac{?}{\$35} \nearrow \frac{20}{100}$
Cross multiply: $\$35 \times 20 = \$700$. Divide by

the remaining number: $\$700. \div 100 = \$7$.

39. **(4) $562.50** $\frac{?}{\$625} \nearrow \frac{90}{100}$
Cross multiply: $\$625 \times 90 = \$56,250$.
Divide by the remaining number:
$\$56,250. \div \$100 = \$562.50$.

40. **(2) 70** $\frac{56}{?} \searrow \frac{80}{100}$
Cross multiply: $56 \times 100 = 5,600$.
Divide by the remaining number:
$5,600 \div 80 = 70$.

41. **(1) 40%** $\frac{18}{45} \searrow \frac{?}{100}$
Cross multiply: $18 \times 100 = 1,800$.
Divide by the remaining number:
$1,800 \div 45 = 40$.

42. **(3) 25%** Find the difference: $112.80 -
$84.60 = 28.20, set up a proportion and
solve: $\frac{\$28.20}{\$112.80} \searrow \frac{?}{100}$
Cross multiply: $\$28.20 \times 100 = \$2,820$.
Divide by the remaining number:
$\$2,820 \div \$112.80 = 25$.

43. **(2) 150** Set up a proportion:

$\frac{1 \text{ in}}{40 \text{ mi}} = \frac{3\frac{3}{4} \text{ in}}{? \text{ mi}}$

Cross multiply and solve:
$40 \times 3\frac{3}{4} = 150 \text{ mi}$

44. **(4) 580** Add the distances on the map
between the cities: $7 + 2\frac{1}{2} + 5 = 14\frac{1}{2}$ in. Set up
a proportion:

$\frac{1 \text{ in}}{40 \text{ mi}} = \frac{14\frac{1}{2} \text{ in}}{? \text{ mi}}$

Cross multiply and solve:
$40 \times 14\frac{1}{2} = 580 \text{ mi}$

45. **(3) Yes, the unit fits exactly into this space.**
Set up a proportion (in to ft):

$\frac{1 \text{ in}}{8 \text{ ft}} = \frac{1\frac{3}{4} \text{ in}}{? \text{ ft}}$

Cross multiply and solve:
$8 \times 1\frac{3}{4} = 14 \text{ feet}$

46. **(4) 6.3 mi.** Set up a propotion (in to mi):

$\frac{1}{1.8} = \frac{3.5}{?}$

Cross multiply: $1.8 \times 3.5 = 6.3$.

47. **Range: 65 to 100; Mean: 87; Median: 85**
The range is the lowest number to the highest:
65 to 100. To find the mean, add the scores
and divide by 7: $609 \div 7 = 87$. To find the
median, arrange the scores in order and find
the middle score: 65, 80, 85, 85, 94, 100, 100.

48. **Range: $199.48 to $245.82; Mean: $221.66; Median: $219.82** The range is the lowest number to the highest: $199.48 to $245.82. To find the mean, add the amounts and divide by 5 and find the middle amount: $1,108.30 ÷ 5 = $221.66. To find the median, arrange the amounts in order: $199.48, $215.35, $219.82, $227.83, $245.82.

49. **Range: 60.8°F to 69.0°F; Mean: 64.3°F; Median: 64.8°F** The range is the lowest number to the highest: 60.8°F to 69.0°F. To find mean, add the amounts and divide by 7: 450.1 ÷ 7 = 64.3. To find the median, arrange the numbers in order and find the middle temperature: 60.8°F, 61.1°F, 61.5°F, 64.8°F, 65.6°F, 67.3°F, 69.0°F

50. **Range: 0.04 to 0.06; Mean: 0.051; Median: 0.052** The range is the lowest number to the highest: 0.04 to 0.06. To find the mean, add the amounts and divide by 5: 0.255 ÷ 5 = 0.051. To find the median, arrange the numbers in order and find the middle weight: 0.04, 0.048, 0.052, 0.055, 0.06.

51. **Range: 128 to 215; Mean: 163; Median: 154.5** The range is the lowest number to the highest: 128 to 215. To find the mean, add the amounts and divide by 4: 652 ÷ 4 = 163. To find the median, arrange the numbers in order and find the middle figure: 128, 135, 174, 215. Average the two middle numbers: 135 + 174 = 309 ÷ 2 = 154.5.

52. **Range: 12 to 150; Mean: 65; Median: 35** The range is the lowest number to the highest: 12 to 150. To find the mean, add the amounts and divide by 7: 455 ÷ 7 = 65. To find the median, arrange the numbers in order and find the middle number: 12, 24, 27, 35, 87, 120, 150.

53. **Range: 35 to 67; Mean: 52; Median: 52** The range is the lowest number to the highest: 35 to 67. To find the mean, add the amounts and divide by 5: 260 ÷ 5 = 52. To find the median, arrange the numbers in order and find the middle time: 35, 41, 52, 65, 67.

54. **(3) 0.25** $\frac{\text{favorable outcomes}}{\text{total possible outcomes}} = \frac{1}{4} = 0.25$

55. **(5) $\frac{3}{4}$** $\frac{\text{favorable outcomes}}{\text{total possible outcomes}} = \frac{3}{4}$

56. **(2) $\frac{1}{5}$** 5 + 8 + 10 + 2 = 25 possible outcomes. 5 of the 25 are Model A. Reduce the fraction: $\frac{5}{25} \div \frac{5}{5} = \frac{1}{5}$.

57. **(4) Model D** $0.08 = \frac{8}{100}$ Set up a proportion: $\frac{8}{100} = \frac{?}{25}$. Cross multiply: 8 × 25 = 200. Divide: 200 ÷ 100 = 2. There are 2 Model D mixers, so Model D has a probability of 0.08 of being the one selected.

58. **(3) Model C** Since the total possible outcomes is the same for each model, compare the numbers of the different models. Model C has the greatest number of chances of being chosen: 10 out of 25.

59. **(5) 0.4** Model C has a 10 out of 25 probability of being chosen: $\frac{10}{25} \div \frac{5}{5} = \frac{2}{5} = 0.4$.

60. **(4) $253.95** Add the first three amounts for January through June: $89.36 + $90.12 + $74.47 = $253.95.

61. **(2) $79.39** Arrange the amounts in order: $59.76, $63.15, $74.47, $84.31, $89.36, $90.12. Since there is an even number of amounts, average the middle two: $74.47 + $84.31 = $158.78 ÷ 2 = $79.39.

62. **(1) $76.86** The "average" is the "mean." To find a mean, add the amounts: $89.36 + $90.12 + $74.47 + $63.15 + $59.76 + $84.31 = $461.17 and divide by 6, the number of amounts: $461.17 ÷ 6 = $76.86.

63. **(4) $18,825** Add and divide:

$16,907
$17,756
$19,174
$19,558
+$20,730
─────────
$94,125

$94,125 ÷ 5 = $18,825.

64. **(3) $18,465** Arrange the 6 amounts in order: $16,907, $17,204, $17,756, $19,174, $19,558, $20,730. With an even number of items, average the middle two: $17,756 + $19,174 = $36,930 ÷ 2 = $18,465.

65. **(2) 40** Find the total number of sales: 21 + 42 + 34 + 45 + 51 + 47 = 240. Divide: 240 ÷ 6 = 40.

66. **(2) 98,000** Set up a proportion:

$\frac{3 \text{ days}}{19,600} = \frac{15 \text{ days}}{?}$

Cross multiply: 19,600 × 15 = 294,000. Divide: 294,000 ÷ 3 = 98,000.

67. **(4) 0.24** Total number of marbles is: 12 + 28 + 10 = 50. Set up a ratio and divide to convert to a decimal:

$$\frac{12\,red}{50\,marbles} = 0.24$$

68. **(3) 12** If they won 2 out of 3, they lost 1 out of 3. Set up a proportion to find the total games played.

$$\frac{1\,lost}{3\,played} = \frac{6\,lost}{?}$$

Cross multiply: $3 \times 6 = 18$ games played. Divide: $18 \div 1 = 18$. Subtract 6 losses from 18 games played = 12 games won.

69. **(3)$\frac{1}{50}$** Set up a ratio and reduce.

GED Review: Ratio and Proportion (page 567)

1. **(3) 7.5** Of the 10 quarts in the paint mixture (2 + 3 + 5 = 10), 3 were green.

   Set up a proportion: $\frac{3}{10} = \frac{?}{25}$

   Cross multiply: $3 \times 25 = 75$
   Divide: $75 \div 100 = 7.5$

2. **(4) 8** The baseball team has won 16 out of 20 (16 + 4) games. Set up a proportion: $\frac{16}{20} = \frac{?}{30}$
   Cross multiply: $16 \times 30 = 480$
   Divide: $480 \div 20 = 24$ They need to win 24 to keep the same winning ratio. Find the difference between 24 and 16 and see how many more they have to win. $24 - 16 = 8$

3. **(2) Only the mean is $142.** To find out which statement is true, find the mean and the median of the amounts. Mean—Add the amounts:
   $120 + $120 + $170 + $140 + $160 = $710
   Divide by 5, the number of amounts:
   $710 \div 5 = $142
   Median—Arrange the amounts in order:
   $120, $120, $140, $160, $170
   The median or middle amount is $140.
   Only the mean is $142.

4. **(1) $\frac{1}{3}$** There are 12 cars and 4 of them are red. Set up a ratio and reduce. $\frac{4}{12} = \frac{1}{3}$
   There is a 1 in 3 chance of choosing a red car.

5. **(2) $\frac{1}{3}$** Now there are 15 cars on the lot. Five of the cars are yellow (2 before + 3 added = 5 cars). Set up a ratio and reduce: $\frac{5}{15} = \frac{1}{3}$

6. **(2) $\frac{5}{8}$** Find the total number of votes:
   150 + 56 + 34 = 240.

   Set up a ratio and reduce: $\frac{150}{240} = \frac{5}{8}$

7. **(3) 1,800**
   Set up a proportion and solve: $\frac{2}{5} = \frac{?}{4,500}$

   Cross multiply: $2 \times 4,500 = 9,000$
   Divide: $9,000 \div 5 = 1,800$

8. **(3) between 42 minutes and 46 minutes** Find the total of the times:
   45 + 35 + 30 + 42 + 3(55) =
   45 + 35 + 30 + 42 + 165 = 317
   Divide by 7: $317 \div 7 = 45.29$

9. **(2) $\frac{1}{4}$** $\frac{Team\ A\ wins}{Team\ C\ wins} = \frac{3}{12}$ reduce $= \frac{1}{4}$

10. **(5) Team C with $\frac{12}{14}$** Find the ratio of wins to games played for each team and compare the fractions.

    Team A $= \frac{3}{14}$ Team B $= \frac{5}{14}$ Team C $= \frac{12}{14}$
    This is the greatest of the three fractions.

11. **(4) 15** Set up a proportion and solve:
    $\frac{Games\ Won}{Games\ Played}$ $\frac{5}{14} = \frac{?}{42}$
    Cross multiply: $5 \times 42 = 210$
    Divide: $210 \div 14 = 15$

12. **(2) 1,600**
    Set up a proportion and solve: $\frac{4}{10} = \frac{640}{?}$
    Cross multiply: $10 \times 640 = 6,400$
    Divide: $6,400 \div 4 = 1,600$

13. **(4) 49.5** Multiply 3,300 by 5 to find how many characters will be on the 5 pages:
    $3,300 \times 5 = 16,500$.

    Set up a proportion and solve: $\frac{1,000}{3} = \frac{16,500}{?}$
    Cross multiply: $3 \times 16,500 = 49,500$
    Divide: $49,500 \div 1,000 = 49.5$

14. **(4) $\frac{1}{2}$** Of the 6 numbers, 3 numbers are even numbers. Set up a ratio and reduce: $\frac{3}{6} = \frac{1}{2}$.
    There is a 1 in 2 chance of rolling an even number.

15. **(2) $\frac{2}{3}$** Of the 6 numbers, 4 numbers are less than 5. Set up a ratio and reduce: $\frac{4}{6} = \frac{2}{3}$. There is a 2 in 3 chance of rolling a number less than 5.

16. **(3) $\frac{1}{3}$** The numbers 4 or 5 make up 2 of the 6 numbers. Set up a ratio and reduce: $\frac{2}{6} = \frac{1}{3}$.
    There is a 1 in 3 chance of rolling a 4 or a 5.

17. **(2) 385 miles** Set up a proportion and solve:
    $\frac{4}{220} = \frac{7}{?}$
    Cross multiply: $7 \times 220 = 1,540$
    Divide: $1,540 \div 4 = 385$ miles

18. **(3) $23,600** Find the total of the amounts: $21,200 + $24,500 + $25,100 = $70,800 Divide by 3: $70,800 ÷ 3 = $23,600

19. **(4) 90 miles** Set up a proportion and solve:

$$\frac{\frac{1}{2}}{15} = \frac{3}{?}$$

Cross multiply: $3 \times 15 = 45$

Divide: $45 \div \frac{1}{2} = 45 \times 2 = 90$

20. **(4) $50** Set up a proportion and solve:

$$\frac{\$35}{7} = \frac{?}{10}$$

Cross multiply: $\$35 \times 10 = \$350$

Divide: $\$350 \div 7 = \$50$

21. **(4) $140** Find the amount he saves out of every $20: $20 − $15 = $5.

Set up a proportion and solve: $\dfrac{\$5}{\$20} = \dfrac{?}{\$560}$

Cross multiply: $\$5 \times \$560 = \$2,800$

Divide: $\$2,800 \div \$20 = \$140$

Measurement

Lesson 17: Measurement Systems

GED Exercise: Measurement Systems (page 574)

1. **10 feet 6 inches** $3\frac{1}{2}$ yds $= \frac{7}{2}$ yds

$$\frac{7}{\underset{1}{\cancel{2}}}\,\text{yds} \times \frac{\overset{18}{\cancel{36}}\,\text{in}}{1\,\text{yd}} = 126\,\cancel{\text{in}} \times \frac{1\,\text{ft}}{12\,\cancel{\text{in}}} = 10\,\text{ft}\,6\,\text{in}$$

2. **240 seconds** $4\,\cancel{\text{min}} \times \frac{60\,\text{sec}}{\cancel{\text{min}}} = 240\,\text{sec}$

3. **9 pints** $\overset{9}{\cancel{18\,\text{cups}}} \times \frac{1\,\text{pint}}{\underset{1}{\cancel{2\,\text{cups}}}} = 9\,\text{pints}$

4. **$3\frac{3}{4}$ tons** $7,500\,\cancel{\text{lb}} \times \frac{1\,\text{ton}}{2,000\,\cancel{\text{lb}}} = 3\frac{3}{4}\,\text{tons}$

5. **140 minutes** $2\frac{1}{3}$ hr $= \frac{7}{3}$ hr

$$\frac{7}{\underset{1}{\cancel{3}}}\,\cancel{\text{hr}} \times \frac{\overset{20}{\cancel{60}}\,\text{min}}{1\,\cancel{\text{hr}}} = 140\,\text{min}$$

6. **9 cups** $\overset{9}{\cancel{72\,\text{fl oz}}} \times \frac{1\,\text{cup}}{\underset{1}{\cancel{8\,\text{fl oz}}}} = 9\,\text{cups}$

7. **23 quarts** $5\frac{3}{4}$ gal $= \frac{23}{4}$ gal

$$\frac{23}{\underset{1}{\cancel{4}}}\,\cancel{\text{gal}} \times \frac{\overset{1}{\cancel{4}}\,\text{qt}}{1\,\cancel{\text{gal}}} = 23\,\text{qt}$$

8. **$2\frac{1}{4}$ yards** 6 ft 9 in $= 6\,\cancel{\text{ft}} \times \frac{12\,\text{in}}{\cancel{\text{ft}}} + 9\,\text{in}$

$= 72\,\text{in} + 9\,\text{in} = 81\,\text{in}$

$$\overset{9}{\cancel{81\,\text{in}}} \times \frac{1\,\text{yd}}{\underset{4}{\cancel{36\,\text{in}}}} = \frac{9}{4}\,\text{yd} = 2\frac{1}{4}\,\text{yd}$$

9. **3 feet** $3\,\cancel{\text{ft}} \times \frac{12\,\text{in}}{\cancel{\text{ft}}} = 36\,\text{in} > 30\,\text{in}$

10. **13 pints** $1\frac{1}{2}$ gal $= \frac{3}{2}$ gal

$$\frac{3}{\underset{1}{\cancel{2}}}\,\cancel{\text{gal}} \times \frac{\overset{2}{\cancel{4}}\,\text{qt}}{1\,\cancel{\text{gal}}} \times \frac{2\,\text{pt}}{\cancel{\text{qt}}} = 12\,\text{pt} < 13\,\text{pt}$$

11. **0.5 grams** 1 mg = .001 gm: $\underset{\frown}{.500} = .5$

12. **8,400 liters** 1 kL = 1,000 liters: 8.400

13. **$3\frac{1}{4}$ hours** $3\frac{1}{4}$ hr $= \frac{13}{4}$ hr

$$\frac{13}{\underset{1}{\cancel{4}}}\,\cancel{\text{hr}} \times \frac{\overset{15}{\cancel{60}}\,\text{min}}{1\,\cancel{\text{hr}}} = 195\,\text{min} < 200\,\text{min}$$

14. **$4\frac{1}{4}$ pounds** $4\frac{1}{4}$ lb $= \frac{17}{4}$ lb

$$\frac{17}{\underset{1}{\cancel{4}}}\,\cancel{\text{lb}} \times \frac{\overset{4}{\cancel{16}}\,\text{oz}}{\cancel{\text{lb}}} = 68\,\text{oz} < 75\,\text{oz}$$

15. **6 gallons 1 quart**

3 gal 3 qt	5 gal
2 gal 2 qt	1 gal 1 qt
5 gal 5 qt	6 gal 1 qt

5 qt = 1 gal 1 qt

16. **16 ft 10 in**

```
   8 ft  8 in
   3 ft  5 in
 + 4 ft  9 in
 ───────────
  15 ft 22 in
```

$$22\,\cancel{\text{in}} \times \frac{1\,\text{ft}}{12\,\cancel{\text{in}}} = 1\,\text{ft}\,10\,\text{in}$$

```
   15 ft
 +  1 ft 10 in
 ─────────────
   16 ft 10 in
```

17. **9 min 15 sec** $\frac{1}{\underset{1}{\cancel{2}}}\,\cancel{\text{hr}} \times \frac{\overset{30}{\cancel{60}}\,\text{min}}{1\,\cancel{\text{hr}}} = 30\,\text{min}$

```
             29   5 10
             30     6  0
  1/2 hr  =  30 min 00 sec
          − 20 min 45 sec
          ──────────────
             9 min 15 sec
```

18. **7 in**

```
      1      14
      2 ft   2 in
   −  1 ft   7 in
   ─────────────
              7 in
```

19. **16 lb 4 oz**

```
    3 lb 4 oz
        × 5
   ──────────
   15 lb 20 oz
```

$$20\,\cancel{\text{oz}} \times \frac{1\,\text{lb}}{16\,\cancel{\text{oz}}} = 1\,\text{lb}\,4\,\text{oz}$$

```
   15 lb
 +  1 lb 4 oz
 ───────────
   16 lb 4 oz
```

20. **18 yd 2 ft**

```
    2 yd 1 ft
        × 8
   ──────────
   16 yd 8 ft
```

$$8\,\cancel{\text{ft}} \times \frac{1\,\text{yd}}{3\,\cancel{\text{ft}}} = 2\,\text{yd}\,2\,\text{ft}$$

```
   16 yd
 +  2 yd 2 ft
 ───────────
   18 yd 2 ft
```

21. **8 inches** Convert 1 yd 4 in to inches.

$$1\,\cancel{\text{yd}} \times \frac{36\,\text{in}}{1\,\cancel{\text{yd}}} + 4\,\text{in} = 40\,\text{in} \div 5 = 8\,\text{in}$$

22. **3 quarts** Convert 3 gal to quarts.

$$3\,\cancel{\text{gal}} \times \frac{4\,\text{qt}}{1\,\cancel{\text{gal}}} = 12\,\text{qt} \div 4 = 3\,\text{qt}$$

23. **10,890 m** 5 km = 5,000 m
5,000 m + 5,890 m = 10,890 m

24. **27 mm** 8.2 cm = 82 mm
82 mm − 55 mm = 27 mm

25. **(3) 10**

$2 \text{ gal} \times \dfrac{4 \text{ qt}}{1 \text{ gal}} \times \dfrac{2 \text{ pt}}{1 \text{ qt}} =$

$\begin{array}{r} 16 \text{ pints} \text{ made} \\ - \ 6 \text{ pints} \text{ to keep} \\ \hline 10 \text{ pints} \text{ to give away} \end{array}$

26. **(1) 12**

$3\frac{1}{4} \text{ yd} = 3 \text{ yd} + \frac{1}{4} \text{ yd} \times \dfrac{\overset{9}{\cancel{36}} \text{ in}}{1 \text{ yd}} = \overset{2}{\cancel{3}} \text{ yd} \overset{3}{\cancel{0}} \text{ ft } 9 \text{ in}$

$\qquad \begin{array}{r} - 2 \text{ yd } 2 \text{ ft } 9 \text{ in} \\ \hline 1 \text{ ft} \end{array}$

$1 \text{ ft} \times \dfrac{12 \text{ in}}{1 \text{ ft}} = 12 \text{ in}$

27. **(4) 661**

$\begin{array}{r} 75 \text{ cm} \\ 126 \text{ cm} \\ + 460 \text{ cm} \\ \hline 661 \text{ cm} \end{array}$

28. **(3) $41\frac{1}{4}$** There are two methods:

#1: $2 \text{ ft } 9 \text{ in} = 2 \text{ ft} + \overset{3}{\cancel{9}} \text{ in} \times \dfrac{1 \text{ ft}}{\underset{4}{\cancel{12}} \text{ in}} = 2\frac{3}{4} \text{ ft} = \frac{11}{4} \text{ ft}$

$\frac{11}{4} \text{ ft} \times 15 = \frac{165}{4} \text{ ft} = 41\frac{1}{4} \text{ ft}$

#2
$\begin{array}{r} 2 \text{ ft} \quad 9 \text{ in} \\ \times 15 \\ \hline 30 \text{ ft } 135 \text{ in} \end{array}$

$\overset{45}{\cancel{135}} \text{ in} \times \dfrac{1 \text{ ft}}{\underset{4}{\cancel{12}} \text{ in}} = 11\frac{1}{4} \text{ ft}$

$\begin{array}{r} 30 \quad \text{ft} \\ + 11\frac{1}{4} \text{ ft} \\ \hline 41\frac{1}{4} \text{ ft} \end{array}$

29. **(3) $8\frac{1}{2}$**

$\begin{array}{r} 3 \text{ tn} \quad 750 \text{ lb} \\ 1 \text{ tn} \quad 150 \text{ lb} \\ 4 \text{ tn} \quad 100 \text{ lb} \\ \hline 8 \text{ tn } 1,000 \text{ lb} \end{array}$

$\begin{array}{r} 8 \text{ tn} \\ + \frac{1}{2} \text{ tn} \\ \hline 8\frac{1}{2} \text{ tn} \end{array}$

$\cancel{1,000} \text{ lb} \times \dfrac{1 \text{ tn}}{\underset{2}{\cancel{2,000}} \text{ lb}} = \frac{1}{2} \text{ t}$

30. **(3) 9** $3\frac{3}{4} \text{ hr} = \frac{15}{4} \text{ hr}$

$\overset{15}{\underset{1}{\cancel{\frac{15}{4}}}} \text{ hr} \times \dfrac{\cancel{60} \text{ min}}{\text{hr}} = 225 \text{ min}$

$\dfrac{1 \text{ cabinet}}{25 \text{ min}} = \dfrac{?}{225 \text{ min}}$

$\dfrac{1 \text{ cabinet} \times \overset{9}{\cancel{225}} \text{ min}}{\underset{1}{\cancel{25}} \text{ min}} = 9 \text{ cabinets}$

31. **(2) 10** There are two solution methods.
#1: Find the number of servings in 24 oz (1 pkg) and multiply by 5 packages.

$1 \text{ serving} = 1\frac{1}{2} \text{ cups} = \dfrac{3}{\cancel{2}} \dfrac{\text{cups}}{\text{servings}} \times \dfrac{\overset{4}{\cancel{8}} \text{ oz}}{1 \text{ cup}} =$

$\dfrac{12 \text{ oz}}{\text{serving}}$

$\dfrac{24 \text{ oz}}{1 \text{ pkg}} \div \dfrac{12 \text{ oz}}{\text{serving}} = \dfrac{\overset{2}{\cancel{24}} \text{ oz}}{1 \text{ pkg}} \times \dfrac{1 \text{ serving}}{\underset{1}{\cancel{12}} \text{ oz}} =$

$\dfrac{2 \text{ servings}}{1 \text{ pkg}} \times 5 \text{ pkg} = 10 \text{ servings}$

#2: Find the total number of ounces in 5 pkg and divide by the number of ounces in 1 serving.

$\dfrac{24 \text{ oz}}{1 \text{ pkg}} \times 5 \text{ pkg} = 120 \text{ oz} \div \dfrac{12 \text{ oz}}{\text{serving}} =$

$\overset{10}{\cancel{120}} \text{ oz} \times \dfrac{1 \text{ serving}}{\underset{1}{\cancel{12}} \text{ oz}} = 10 \text{ servings}$

32. **(5) 250** Set up a proportion:

$\dfrac{60}{15} \rightleftharpoons \dfrac{1,000}{?}$

Cross multiply: $15 \times 1,000 = 15,000$
Divide: $15,000 \div 60 = 250$

Lesson 18: Perimeter, Circumference, and Area
GED Exercise: Perimeter, Circumference, and Area
(page 579)

1. **Rectangle A**
   Perimeter $= 2l + 2w$
   $\qquad = 2 \times 12 + 2 \times 7$
   $\qquad = 24 + 14 = \textbf{38 inches}$
   Area $= l \times w = 12 \times 7$
   $\qquad = \textbf{84 square inches}$

2. **Square B**
   Perimeter $= 4s$
   $\qquad = 4 \times 15 = \textbf{60 inches}$
   Area $= l \times w$
   $\qquad = 15 \times 15 = \textbf{225 square inches}$

3. **Triangle C**
   Perimeter $= a + b + c$
   $\qquad = 10 + 15 + 18 = \textbf{43 inches}$
   Area $= \frac{1}{2}b \times h = \frac{1}{2} \times 18 \times 8$
   $\qquad = \textbf{72 square inches}$

4. **Triangle D**
   Perimeter $= a + b + c$
   $\qquad = 10 + 10 + 10 = \textbf{30 inches}$
   Area $= \frac{1}{2}b \times h = \frac{1}{2} \times 10 \times 8.7$
   $\qquad = \textbf{43.5 square inches}$

5. **Parallelogram E**
   Perimeter $= a + b + c + d$ (or $2l + 2w$)
   $\qquad = 6 + 12 + 6 + 12$ or
   $\qquad (2 \times 6 + 2 \times 12)$
   $\qquad = \textbf{36 inches}$
   Area $= b \times h = 12 \times 4$
   $\qquad = \textbf{48 square inches}$

6. **Circle F**
   Circumference $= \pi d$ or $2\pi r$
   $\qquad = 2 \times 3.14 \times 5$
   $\qquad = \textbf{31.4 inches}$
   Area $= \pi r^2 = 3.14 \times 5 \times 5$
   $\qquad = \textbf{78.5 square inches}$

7. **(3) 67**
   $P = 2l + 2w$
   $\quad = 2 \times 25 + 2 \times 8.5$
   $\quad = 50 + 17$
   $\quad = 67 \text{ feet}$

Unit 7

8. **(4) 212.5**
$$A = lw$$
$$= 25 \times 8.5$$
$$= 212.5 \text{ square feet}$$

9. **(4) 80** The shaded portion is a triangle. Use the formula for finding the area of a triangle. The height of the parallelogram is also the height of the triangle.
$$A = \tfrac{1}{2}bh$$
$$= \tfrac{1}{2} \times 16 \times 10$$
$$= 8 \times 10$$
$$= 80 \text{ square feet}$$

10. **(1) 135**
$$A = \tfrac{1}{2}bh$$
$$= \tfrac{1}{2} \times 18 \times 15$$
$$= 9 \times 15$$
$$= 135 \text{ square inches}$$

11. **(5) Not enough information is given.** You need the height of a triangle to find the area.

12. **(4) 68** Add the five sides: 14.3 + 14.3 + 13.5 + 13.5 + 12.4 = 68 centimeters.

13. **(5) 800**
$$P = 2l + 2w$$
$$= 2 \times 250 + 2 \times 150$$
$$= 500 + 300$$
$$= 800 \text{ feet}$$

14. **(4) 9,600**
$$A = lw$$
$$= 120 \times 80$$
$$= 9,600 \text{ square feet}$$

15. **(3) 27,900** Subtract the area of the cement section from the total area of the park.
Cement Area: 9,600 square feet (see item 14)
Park Area:
$$A = lw$$
$$= 250 \times 150$$
$$= 37,500 \text{ square feet}$$
Subtract: 37,500 − 9,600 = 27,900.

16. **(3) 31**
$$C = \pi d$$
$$= 3.14 \times 10$$
$$= 31.4 \text{ which rounds to 31 centimeters}$$

17. **(4) 30** The diameter of the smaller circle is the radius of the larger circle. Double the radius to find the diameter: 15 × 2 = 30.

18. **(2) 177** Divide 15 by 2 to find the radius of the smaller circle: $15 \div 2 = 7\tfrac{1}{2}$ or 7.5.

$$A = \pi r^2$$
$$= 3.14 \times 7.5 \times 7.5$$
$$= 3.14 \times 56.25$$
$$= 176.625, \text{ which rounds to 177 square meters}$$

19. **(3) 530** Subtract the area of the smaller circle from the area of the larger circle to find the area of the shaded portion. See the explanation for item 18 to find the area of the smaller circle.
Larger circle:
$$A = \pi r^2$$
$$= 3.14 \times 15 \times 15$$
$$= 3.14 \times 225$$
$$= 706.5 \text{ square meters}$$
Subtract: 706.500 − 176.625 = 529.875, which rounds to 530 square meters.

GED Review: Measurement (page 582)

1. **(4) 72** Find the perimeter of one flower bed:
$P = 4s = 4 \times 6 \text{ feet} = 24 \text{ feet}$.
Multiply by 3 to find the perimeter of 3 beds: 24 feet × 3 = 72 feet.

2. **(5) 22** Find the area of one flower bed:
$A = s^2 = 6 \times 6 = 36 \text{ square feet}$.
Multiply by 3 to find the total area of the three beds: 36 × 3 = 108 square feet.
Divide by 5 (the number of square feet one pint will cover): 108 ÷ 5 = 21 r3.
He will need 22 pints.

3. **(3) 31** The area of one flower bed is 36 square feet (see the explanation for item 2). Each bush will need 5 square feet.
Subtract: 36 − 5 = 31 square feet.

4. **(2) 324** Find the circumference of a whole circle with a radius of 63. Double the radius (63 ft.) to get the diameter.
$C = \pi d = 3.14 \times 126 = 395.64$
Divide the result by 2 to find the length of the curved line. 395.64 ÷ 2 = 197.82
The length of the straight line is the diameter: 2(63) = 126.
Add it to the length of the curved line: 126 + 197.82 = 323.82, which rounds to 324.

5. **(4) 12 × 18** The area of a parallelogram is found with the formula: $A = bh$. The base in the drawing is 18 ft and the height is 12 ft.

6. **(1) 56** Use the formula to find the perimeter of a rectangle:
$$P = 2l + 2w$$
$$= 2 \times 25 + 2 \times 3$$
$$= 50 + 6$$
$$= 56 \text{ feet}$$

7. **(4) 108** Use the formula for finding the area of a parallelogram:
$A = bh$
$= 18 \times 6$
$= 108$ square meters

8. **(4) 36** Use the formula for finding the perimeter of a triangle:
$P = a + b + c$
$= 14 + 10 + 12$
$= 36$ feet

9. **(1) 56** Use the formula for finding the area of a triangle:
$A = \frac{1}{2}bh$
$= \frac{1}{2} \times 14 \times 8$
$= 7 \times 8$
$= 56$ square feet

10. **(5) Not enough information is given.** You need to know both the length and the width to find the area of a rectangle. You only know the length.

11. **(3) 332 feet** You are asked to find the perimeter of the track. If the two half-circle portions were joined you would have one whole circle. Find the circumference of that circle. Then add the lengths of the rectangle. The diameter is 2 times the radius.
$C = \pi d$
$= 3.14 \times 2(21) = 3.14 \times 42$
$= 131.88$
$131.88 + 100 + 100 = 331.88$, which rounds to 332.

12. **(4) 5,585 square feet** Find the area of the circle (see the explanation for item 11) and the area of the rectangle portion. Add the two amounts together.
$A = \pi r^2$
$= 3.14 \times 21 \times 21$
$= 3.14 \times 441$
$= 1,384.74$ square feet
$A = lw$
$= 100 \times (21 + 21)$
$= 100 \times 42$
$= 4,200$ square feet
$1,384.74 + 4,200 = 5,584.74$, which rounds to 5,585.

13. **(2) 98** Add the lengths of the sides:
$8 + 22 + 15 + 23 + 30 = 98$ cm.

Algebra

Lesson 19: Signed Numbers • Algebraic Expressions

GED Exercise: Signed Numbers • Algebraic Expressions (page 587)

1. **6**

2. **7**

3. **14.6**

4. $\frac{2}{3}$

5. **0** The absolute value of 0 is 0.

6. **+12**

7. **−16**

8. **−1**

9. **+3**

10. **−10**

11. **−6**

12. **−2**

13. $+1\frac{1}{2}$

14. **−7**

15. **+9**

16. **+12**

17. **+5**

18. **−6**

19. **+5**

20. **−8.7**

21. **−6**

22. **−5**

23. **+28**

24. **0**

25. **−15**

26. **+8**

27. **0**

28. **+4**

29. **−16**

30. **−5**

31. **+4**

32. **+14**

33. **−3**

34. **−5**

35. **+7**

36. **−14**

37. **+38** Begin by multiplying: $4 \times 8 = 32$. Then add: $6 + 32 = 38$.

38. **+10** The numerator is −10 and the denominator is −1. $-10 \div -1 = +10$.

39. **−30** The expression inside the first parentheses is −36. Inside the second parentheses is −6. $-36 - (-6) = -36 + 6 = -30$.

40. **−1** Begin inside the parentheses with $4 \times (-2) = -8$. Next add $-3 + -8 = -11$. The expression becomes $10 + -11 = -1$.

41. **−37** Begin by multiplying 4×3. Then $-25 - 12 = -37$.

42. **−2** The numerator is −10 and the denominator is +5. $10 \div +5 = -2$.

43. **−25** Begin inside the parentheses with 4×8. Next add $32 + (-1) = 31$. The expression becomes $6 - 31 = -25$.

44. **−38** The value of the expression inside the first parentheses is −20. The value inside the second parentheses is −18. Add: $-20 + -18 = -38$.

45. **$2x + 3y$**
$5x - 3x = 2x$; $1y + 2y = 3y$

46. **$10x - 2$**
$8x + 2x = 10x$; $3 - 5 = -2$

47. **$4a - 2b$**
$a + a + 2a = 4a$;
$6b - 8b = -2b$

48. **$14 - 11x$**
$-7x - 4x = -11x$

49. **$5z + 5y - 3$**
$4z + z = 5z$

50. **$-2x + 2y$**
$3x - 5x = -2x$;
$12y - 10y = 2y$

51. **0**
$+2 - (+5) + (+3)$
$+2 + (-5) + (+3) = 0$

52. **$+8$**
$(+3) + (+5) + (+5) - (+5)$
$(+3) + (+5) + (+5) + (-5) = +8$

53. **$+3$**
$(-1) + (-4) + (+8) = +3$

54. **$+6$**
$(+2) - (-0.5) - (-0.5) - (-3)$
$(+2) + (+0.5) + (+0.5) +$
$(+3) = +6$

55. **$+17$**
$5(3) + 2 - 4 + 2(2)$
$15 + 2 - 4 + 4 = +17$

56. **-24**
$3(-2)(4) + 2(-2) + 4$
$-24 + (-4) + 4 = -24$

57. **-12**
$\frac{6(-3)(2)(-1)}{-3} = \frac{36}{-3} = -12$

58. **$+2$**
$\frac{4 + 5(2)}{2(4) - 1} = \frac{4 + 10}{8 - 1} = \frac{14}{7} = +2$

59. **$x - 2$**

60. **$\frac{x}{7}$**

61. **$2x + (-4)$**

62. **$3x - 2x$**

63. **$3x - 9$**

64. **$\frac{4x}{3}$**

65. **$\$11 + x - \$2$**

66. **$19 - 5 + x - 2$**

Lesson 20: Equations
GED Exercise: Equations (page 593)

1. **10** $x - 7 = 3; x = 10$

2. **6** $2x = 12; x = 6$

3. **7** $-6x = -42; x = 7$

4. **10** $x + 12 = 22; x = 10$

5. **-2** $x - 8 = -10; x = -2$

6. **-6** $-3x = 18; x = -6$

7. **-9** $5x = -45; x = -9$

8. **5**
$6x + 7 = 37$
$6x = 30$
$x = 5$

9. **5**
$4x + 5x - 10 = 35$
$9x - 10 = 35$
$9x = 45$
$x = 5$

10. **-2**
$3x - 6x + 2 = -4x$
$-3x + 2 = -4x$
$2 = -1x$
$-2 = x$

11. **1**
$6 - x + 12 = 10x + 7$
$18 - x = 10x + 7$
$18 = 11x + 7$
$11 = 11x$
$1 = x$

12. **-4** $9x + 6x - 12x =$
$-7x + 2x - 12 + 5x$
$3x = -12$
$x = -4$

13. **4**
$7x + 3 = 31$
$7x = 28$
$x = 4$

14. **12**
$3x - 8 = 28$
$3x = 36$
$x = 12$

15. **1**
$8x + 6 = 5x + 9$
$3x + 6 = 9$
$3x = 3$
$x = 1$

16. **5**
$11x - 10 = 8x + 5$
$3x - 10 = 5$
$3x = 15$
$x = 5$

17. **1**
$-2x - 4 = 4x - 10$
$-2x = 4x - 6$
$-6x = -6$
$x = 1$

18. **-4**
$5x + 8 = x - 8$
$4x + 8 = -8$
$4x = -16$
$x = -4$

19. **7**
$11x - 12 = 9x + 2$
$2x - 12 = 2$
$2x = 14$
$x = 7$

20. **14**
$5(x + 1) = 75$
$5x + 5 = 75$
$5x = 70$
$x = 14$

21. **8**
$5(x - 7) = 5$
$5x - 35 = 5$
$5x = 40$
$x = 8$

22. **3**
$6(2 + x) = 5x + 15$
$12 + 6x = 5x + 15$
$12 + x = 15$
$x = 3$

23. **6**
$8(x + (-5)) = x + 2$
$8x + (-40) = x + 2$
$7x = 42$
$x = 6$

24. **15**
$2x - 6 = 24$
$2x = 30$
$x = 15$

25. **9**
$2x + 2 = 20$
$2x = 18$
$x = 9$

26. **10** $(8 + x) + 12 = 3x$
$x + 20 = 3x$
$-2x = -20$
$x = 10$

27. **(1) 2** Let x represent the number.
$5(9 + x) - 15 = 40$
$45 + 5x - 15 = 40$
$30 + 5x = 40$
$5x = 10$
$x = 2$

Unit 7

28. **(3) 24** Let x represent the lesser number. The expression $x + 1$ represents the next consecutive number. Write the equation.

$$x + x + 1 = 49$$
$$2x + 1 = 49$$
$$2x = 48$$
$$x = 24$$

The lesser number is 24.

29. **(3) $53 - 21 - 18 = b$** Use the formula to solve for b and substitute the values.

$$P = a + b + c$$
$$P - a - c = b$$
$$53 - 21 - 18 = b$$

or

$$P = a + b + c$$
$$53 = 21 + b + 18$$
$$53 - 21 - 18 = b$$

30. **(2) 87** Let x represent the number of employees who work in management. Let $3x + 12$ represent the number who work in production.

$$x + 3x + 12 = 360$$
$$4x = 348$$
$$x = 87$$

31. **(1) $\frac{30 - 12}{2} = l$** Use the formula to solve for l and substitute the values.

$$P = 2l + 2w$$
$$P - 2w = 2l$$
$$\frac{P - 2w}{2} = l$$
$$\frac{30 - 2(6)}{2} = l$$
$$\frac{30 - 12}{2} = l$$

32. **(2) $300** Let x represent her husband's earnings. Bonnie's earnings can be written as $2x - \$150$.

$$x + 2x - \$150 = \$750$$
$$3x - \$150 = \$750$$
$$3x = \$900$$
$$x = \$300$$

33. **(4) 5** $\quad 8x - 5 = 7x$
$$x = 5$$

34. **(4) 39** Let x represent the number Frank did, and $x + 12$ the number that Tom did.

$$x + x + 12 = 66$$
$$2x + 12 = 66$$
$$2x = 54$$
$$x = 27$$

Tom did 39 pushups.
$(27 + 12 = 39)$.

35. **(3) $18** Let x represent the fine for the first ticket and $2x$ the fine for the second ticket.

$$x + 2x = 54$$
$$3x = 54$$
$$x = 18$$

The fine for the first ticket is $18.

36. **(3) $2(x + 19) = 5x + 19$**
Make a chart. Let x represent the son's age.

	George	Son
Now	$5x$	x
In 19 years	$5x + 19$	$x + 19$

Write the equation: multiply 2 times the son's age in 19 years, and equate it with George's age in 19 years.

37. **(1) 2**
Make a chart.
Let x represent Diana's age.

	Nora	Diana
Now	$x + 4$	x
2 years from now	$(x + 4) + 2$	$x + 2$

Set up the equation so that 2 times Diana's age in 2 years equals Nora's age in 2 years.

$$2(x + 2) = (x + 4) + 2$$
$$2x + 4 = x + 6$$
$$x + 4 = 6$$
$$x = 2$$

Diana is now 2 years old and Nora is 6 years old.

38. **(3) 425 miles per hour**
Substitute the known values and solve for rate.

$$d = rt$$
$$2{,}125 = r5$$
$$\frac{2{,}125}{5} = r$$
$$425 = r$$

39. **(4) $17.40**
Substitute the known values and solve for r, the unit cost.

$$c = nr$$
$$\$104.40 = 6r$$
$$\frac{\$104.40}{6} = r$$
$$\$17.40 = r$$

40. **(5) 100 degrees** Substitute the known values and solve for C.

$$F = \frac{9}{5}C + 32$$
$$212 = \frac{9}{5}C + 32$$
$$180 = \frac{9}{5}C$$
$$\frac{\overset{20}{\cancel{180}}}{1} \times \frac{5}{\underset{1}{\cancel{9}}} = C$$
$$100 = C$$

Unit 7

1. $x > -1$ $\quad$ $5x + 2 > 4x + 1$
$$5x + 2 - 4x > 1$$
$$x + 2 > 1$$
$$x > 1 - 2$$
$$x > -1$$

2. $x < 2$ $\quad$ $6x - 4 < 3x + 2$
$$6x - 4 - 3x < 2$$
$$3x - 4 < 2$$
$$3x < 2 + 4$$
$$3x < 6$$
$$x < 2$$

3. $x < 4$ $\quad$ $3(x + 1) > x + 4x - 5$
$$3x + 3 > 5x - 5$$
$$3x + 3 - 5x > -5$$
$$-2x + 3 > -5$$
$$-2x > -5 - 3$$
$$-2x > -8$$
$$\frac{-2}{-2} < \frac{-8}{-2}$$
$$x < 4$$

Note the inequality reversal because of multiplication by a negative number.

4. $x > -7$ $\quad$ $x + 12 < 5(x + 8)$
$$x + 12 < 5x + 40$$
$$x + 12 - 5x < 40$$
$$-4x + 12 < 40$$
$$-4x < 28$$
$$\frac{-4x}{-4} > \frac{28}{-4}$$
$$x > -7$$

Note the inequality reversal because of division by a negative number.

5. $x > -17$ $\quad$ $2x + (4 - 3x) < 21$
$$2x + 4 - 3x < 21$$
$$-x + 4 < 21$$
$$-x < 17$$
$$x > -17$$

6. $x > -5$ $\quad$ $7x - 3x - x < 3x + 2x + 10$
$$3x < 5x + 10$$
$$-2x < 10$$
$$x > -5$$

Note the inequality reversal because of division by a negative number.

7. **(2) $x < 4$** $\quad$ Set up an inequality and solve:
$$5x + 6 < 4x + 10$$
$$5x + 6 - 4x < 10$$
$$x + 6 < 10$$
$$x < 10 - 6$$
$$x < 4$$

8. **(4) 26** $\quad$ Use the formula for the perimeter of a triangle: $a + b + c = P$. Set up an inequality and solve:
$$21 + 18 + x \le 65$$
$$39 + x \le 65$$
$$x \le 26$$

9. **$5(x + 6)$** $\quad$ Divide both terms by 5.

10. **$3(2y + 5)$** $\quad$ Divide both terms by 3.

11. **$2(4x - 1)$** $\quad$ Divide both terms by 2.

12. **$2(2z - 7)$** $\quad$ Divide both terms by 2.

13. **$b(b + 9)$** $\quad$ Divide both terms by b.

14. **$y(y + 3)$** $\quad$ Divide both terms by y.

15. **$2x(x + 2)$** $\quad$ Divide both terms by $2x$.

16. **$3x(x + 3)$** $\quad$ Divide both terms by $3x$.

17. **$y(7y - 1)$** $\quad$ Divide both terms by y.

18. **$2x(2x + 1)$** $\quad$ Divide both terms by $2x$.

19. **$(x + 4)(x + 5)$**
Check: $(x + 4)(x + 5)$
$$= x^2 + 5x + 4x + 20$$
$$= x^2 + 9x + 20$$

20. **$(x - 2)(x - 3)$**
Check: $(x - 2)(x - 3)$
$$= x^2 - 3x - 2x + 6$$
$$= x^2 - 5x + 6$$

21. **$(x + 6)(x - 1)$**
Check: $(x + 6)(x - 1)$
$$= x^2 - x + 6x - 6$$
$$= x^2 + 5x - 6$$

22. **$(x - 7)(x + 4)$**
Check: $(x - 7)(x + 4)$
$$= x^2 + 4x - 7x - 28$$
$$= x^2 - 3x - 28$$

23. **$(x + 1)(x - 3)$**
Check: $(x + 1)(x - 3)$
$$= x^2 - 3x + x - 3$$
$$= x^2 + 2x - 3$$

24. **$(x + 6)(x + 2)$**
Check: $(x + 6)(x + 2)$
$$= x^2 + 2x + 6x + 12$$
$$= x^2 + 8x + 12$$

25. **$(x - 3)(x - 4)$**
Check: $(x - 3)(x - 4)$
$$= x^2 - 3x - 4x + 12$$
$$= x^2 - 7x + 12$$

Unit 7

26. $(x + 8)(x - 1)$
    Check: $(x + 8)(x - 1)$
    $= x^2 + 8x - x - 8$
    $= x^2 + 7x - 8$

27. $(x - 2)(x + 5)$
    Check: $(x - 2)(x + 5)$
    $= x^2 - 2x + 5x - 10$
    $= x^2 + 3x - 10$

28. $(x + 7)(x + 3)$
    Check: $(x + 7)(x + 3)$
    $= x^2 + 7x + 3x + 21$
    $= x^2 + 10x + 21$

29. $(x - 8)(x - 5)$
    Check: $(x - 8)(x - 5)$
    $= x^2 - 5x - 8x + 40$
    $= x^2 - 13x + 40$

30. $(x - 4)(x + 3)$
    Check: $(x - 4)(x + 3)$
    $= x^2 + 3x - 4x - 12$
    $= x^2 - x - 12$

31. $(x + 2)(x - 10)$
    Check: $(x + 2)(x - 10)$
    $= x^2 - 10x + 2x - 20$
    $= x^2 - 8x - 20$

32. $(x - 9)(x - 2)$
    Check: $(x - 9)(x - 2)$
    $= x^2 - 2x - 9x + 18$
    $= x^2 - 11x + 18$

33. $(x + 5)(x - 11)$
    Check: $(x + 5)(x - 11)$
    $= x^2 - 11x + 5x - 55$
    $= x^2 - 6x - 55$

34. $(x + 12)(x + 4)$
    Check: $(x + 12)(x + 4)$
    $= x^2 + 4x + 12x + 48$
    $= x^2 + 16x + 48$

35. $(x + 9)(x - 2)$
    Check: $(x + 9)(x - 2)$
    $= x^2 + 9x - 2x - 18$
    $= x^2 + 7x - 18$

36. $(x - 4)(x - 6)$
    Check: $(x - 4)(x - 6)$
    $= x^2 - 4x - 6x + 24$
    $= x^2 - 10x + 24$

37. $(x + 5)(x + 5)$
    Check: $(x + 5)(x + 5)$
    $= x^2 + 5x + 5x + 25$
    $= x^2 + 10x + 25$

38. $(x - 7)(x + 1)$
    Check: $(x - 7)(x + 1)$
    $= x^2 - 7x + x - 7$
    $= x^2 - 6x - 7$

39. **D: (1,1), E: (2,4.5), F: (5,4)**

40. **A: (−3,3), B: (−5,1)**

41. **C: (0,3), K: (0,−3), L: (0,2), M: (0,5)**

42. **D: (1,1)**

43. **F: (5,4), G: (5,0), H: (2,0), K: (0,−3)**

44. **Points I, L**

45. **Points A, B, C, E, M**

46. **Points A, B, C, D, H, I, J, K, L**

47. **Point E**

48. **Points A, B, C**

49. **Slope = −1** Use the points (1,0) and (0,1). Find the slope using the slope formula.
    $$m = \frac{y_2 - y_1}{x_2 - x_1} = \frac{1 - 0}{0 - 1} = \frac{1}{-1} = -1$$

50. **Slope = $\frac{3}{2}$** Use the points (−2,1) and (0,4).
    Find the slope using the slope formula.
    $$m = \frac{y_2 - y_1}{x_2 - x_1} = \frac{4 - 1}{0 - (-2)} = \frac{3}{2} = 1\frac{1}{2}$$

51. **Slope = 1** Use the points (2,1) and (0,−1).
    Find the slope using the slope formula.
    $$m = \frac{y_2 - y_1}{x_2 - x_1} = \frac{-1 - 1}{0 - 2} = \frac{-2}{-2} = 1$$

52. **(2) $x - y = -1$** Substitute the three values into each equation until all three make the equation true. Only option (2) is correct.

53. **(3) $y = -1$** Substitute 2 for x in the equation:
    $3x - 4y = 10$
    $3(2) - 4y = 10$
    $6 - 4y = 10$
    $-4y = 4$
    $y = -1$

54. **(5) A, B, and C** Substitute 2 for x and 1 for y in each equation. The pair (2,1) is a solution for each equation.

55. **(1) (−3,−4)** Substitute each value into the equation:
    $(-3) - (-4) = (-3) + (+4) = 1$ (true)
    $(-3) - (-2) = (-3) + (+2) = -1$ (false)
    $(-1) - (0) = -1$ (false)
    $(0) - (+1) = 0 + (-1) = -1$ (false)
    $(+1) - (-2) = (+1) + (+2) = 3$ (false)
    Therefore, only option (1) is correct.

56. **(2) B** Substitute −4 for x and 2 for y in the equations:
    $2(-4) - 3(2) = -8 - 6 = -14$
    Because $-14 < 5$, it is found in the graph of B.

57. **(5) Neither B nor C is a solution.**
    Substitute each point value into the equation.
    $$2x - y = 1$$
    For A: (3,5) $6 - 5 \overset{?}{=} 1$ (true)
    For B: (1,−3) $2 + 3 \overset{?}{=} 1$ (false)
    For C: (0,1) $0 - 1 \overset{?}{=} 1$ (false)
    Therefore, option (5) is correct.

58. **(2) −2** Substitute the known value $y = 1$ into the equation and solve for x.
    $-4x + 7y = 15$
    $-4x + 7(1) = 15$
    $-4x + 7 = 15$
    $-4x = 8$
    $x = -2$

59. **(4) $x + y = 2$** Every point on the line will make this equation true. Pick any point, such as (0,2) and substitute the values into the equation. Only option (4) gives a true statement: $0 + 2 = 2$.

Lesson 22: Exponents and Roots

GED Exercise: Exponents and Roots (page 608)

1. **16**
$2^4 = 2 \times 2 \times 2 \times 2 = 16$

2. **1** $1^3 = 1 \times 1 \times 1 = 1$

3. **25** $5^2 = 5 \times 5 = 25$

4. **1,024**
$4^5 = 4 \times 4 \times 4 \times 4 \times 4$
$= 1,024$

5. **125** $5^3 = 5 \times 5 \times 5 = 125$

6. **64**
$2^6 = 2 \times 2 \times 2 \times 2 \times 2 \times 2$
$= 64$

7. **36** $6^2 = 6 \times 6 = 36$

8. **625**
$5^4 = 5 \times 5 \times 5 \times 5 = 625$

9. **10,000**
$10^4 = 10 \times 10 \times 10 \times 10$
$= 10,000$

10. **64** $8^2 = 8 \times 8 = 64$

11. **6,000** $6 \times 1,000 = 6,000$

12. **300** $3 \times 100 = 300$

13. **560,000**
$56 \times 10,000 = 560,000$

14. **12** $2 \times 2 + 2 \times 2 \times 2 =$
$\quad\quad 4 \;+\; 8 \quad = 12$

15. **15**
$5 \times 5 - 3 \times 3 - 1 \times 1 =$
$\quad 25 \;-\; 9 \;-\; 1 = 15$

16. **13** $3 \times 3 + 2 \times 2 =$
$\quad\quad 9 \;+\; 4 \;= 13$

17. **1** Any number to the zero power is 1.

18. **5**

19. **0.0001** $\dfrac{1}{10 \times 10 \times 10 \times 10} =$
$\dfrac{1}{10,000} = 0.0001$

20. **0.01** $\dfrac{1}{10 \times 10} = \dfrac{1}{100} = 0.01$

21. **1** Any number to the zero power is 1.

22. **6,300**
$6 \times 1,000 + 3 \times 100 =$
$\quad 6,000 \;+\; 300 \;=$
$\quad\quad\quad 6,300$

23. **350**
$4 \times 100 - 5 \times 10 =$
$\quad 400 \;-\; 50 \;= 350$

24. **3,087**
$3.1 \times 1,000 - 1.3 \times 10 =$
$\quad 3,100 \;-\; 13 \;=$
$\quad\quad\quad 3,087$

25. **6,750**
$6.25 \times 1,000 + 5 \times 100 =$
$\quad 6,250 \;+\; 500 \;=$
$\quad\quad\quad 6,750$

26. $\dfrac{1}{4}$ $\dfrac{1}{2} \times \dfrac{1}{2} = \dfrac{1}{4}$

27. $\dfrac{1}{8}$ $\dfrac{1}{2} \times \dfrac{1}{2} \times \dfrac{1}{2} = \dfrac{1}{8}$

28. **0.04** $0.2 \times 0.2 = 0.04$

29. **0.0025**
$0.05 \times 0.05 = 0.0025$

30. **0.41**

31. **6.1×10^{-2}**

32. **4.65×0.01**

33. **4** $4 \times 4 = 16$

34. **0** $0 \times 0 = 0$

35. **9** $9 \times 9 = 81$

36. **7** $7 \times 7 = 49$

37. **13**
You know $12 \times 12 = 144$.
$\quad$ Try $13 \times 13 = 169$.

38. **1** $1 \times 1 = 1$

39. **(3) 865,000 mi.** Add a string of zeros to 8.65 and move the decimal point 5 places to the right.
$8.65000.0000 = 865,000$

40. **(4) Only $3^4 = 64$ is false.**
$3^4 = 81$, not 64, so $3^4 = 64$ is false. <u>Both</u> $8^2 = 64$ and $4^3 = 64$ $(4 \times 4 \times 4)$ are true.

41. **(3) 4 and 5** You know the square of 4 is 16, and the square of 5 is 25. So, the square root of 22 must fall between 4 and 5.

42. **(1) 4.7×10^{-1}, 2.34×10^2, 5.2×10^2**
Compare the numbers and arrange them in order:
$4.7 \times 10^{-1} =$
$\dfrac{4.7 \times 1}{10} = 0.47$
$2.34 \times 10^2 =$
$2.34 \times 100 = 234$
$5.2 \times 10^2 =$
$5.2 \times 100 = 520$

43. **(4) 10^6**
Multiply:
$10^2 \times 10^4 = 100 \times 10,000 = 1,000,000 = 10^6$
(OR: $10^2 \times 10^4 = 10^{2+4} = 10^6$)

44. **(3) 3^4 is the least and 2^7 is the greatest.**
Find the value of each and then compare the values:
$10^2 = 10 \times 10 = 100$
$2^7 = 2 \times 2 \times 2 \times 2 \times 2 \times 2 \times 2 = 128$
$3^4 = 3 \times 3 \times 3 \times 3 = 81$

45. **(4) They are both wrong, since the expression equals 1.**
Recall that $3^2 = 3 \times 3 = 9$ and $2^3 = 2 \times 2 \times 2 = 8$. Therefore, $9 - 8 = 1$. Option (4) is the only correct answer.

46. **(5) Multiply by 2, and then multiply by 2 again.**
Because $12 - 10 = 2$, you need to multiply by 2 two more times:
$2^{12} = 2^{10} \times 2 \times 2$

GED Review: Algebra (page 610)

1. **(1) $-4x = -5x + 2 + 8$** The product of a number and -4 becomes $-4x$; is 8 more than 2 becomes $= 2 + 8$; added to -5 times a number becomes $= -5x + 2 + 8$. Therefore, $-4x = -5x + 2 + 8$.

Unit 7

2. **(5) $(x - 3)(x - 5)$**
   The factors of 15 are $15 \cdot 1$, $-15 \cdot -1$, $5 \cdot 3$, and $-5 \cdot -3$. Only -5 and -3 sum to -8.
   Check: $(x - 3)(x - 5)$
   $= x^2 - 5x - 3x + 15$
   $= x^2 - 8x + 15$

3. **(5) C only**   Try the pair in each equation. Only equation C is true. $-1 + -2 = -3$

4. **(1) $1 < x < 4$**   Only the section between $+1$ and $+4$ is shaded. The shaded area is greater than 1 and less than 4. Open circles mean $+1$ and $+4$ are not included.

5. **(3) $-x - 5$** $2 - (x + 7) = 2 - x - 7 = -x - 5$

6. **(2) -19** $4x - 2y + xy =$
   $4(-1) - 2(5) + (-1)(5) =$
   $(-4) - 10 + (-5) = -19$

7. **(3) 21**   Multiply both terms within the parentheses by 7: $7 \times 3 = 21$.

8. **(1) $\frac{1}{2}$**
   $-6(x + 1) + 4 = 8x - 9$
   $-6x - 6 + 4 = 8x - 9$
   $-6x - 2 = 8x - 9$
   $-14x = -7$
   $x = \frac{1}{2}$

9. **(1) $x < -1$**
   $3x + 7 < -2x + 2$
   $5x + 7 < 2$
   $5x < -5$
   $x < -1$

10. **(2) Two less than x is the same as 7 more than the quotient of x and 4.**   Compare each statement with the equation in the problem. Remember, "quotient" means divided by.

11. **(4) $(-6 + y) - (-6x)$**   "Product" means multiply. The product of -6 and x is $-6x$. "Sum" means add. The sum of -6 and y is $-6 + y$. Only option (4) shows $-6x$ subtracted from $-6 + y$.

12. **(5) $\frac{x}{6} - 2$**   The quotient of x and 6 is x divided by 6 or $\frac{x}{6}$. Two less means to subtract 2 from the quotient.

13. **(3) $4x - 3$**
    $7x + 5 - 3x - 8$
    $4x + 5 - 8$
    $4x - 3$

14. **(2) $x = -3$**
    $2(2x + 3) = -3(x + 5)$
    $4x + 6 = -3x - 15$
    $7x = -21$
    $x = -3$

15. **(1) 17**   Let x represent Joe's number. "Three more than the number I'm thinking of is 30" can be written $3 + x = 30$.
    Solve for Joe's number: $3 + x = 30$
    $x = 27$
    "Then 10 less than your number is the number _____."
    Subtract 10 from Joe's number: $27 - 10 = 17$.

16. **(1) $(x - 4) - 3$**

	Coop's Age in Months	Carni's Age in Months
Now	[1] x	[2] $x - 4$
3 months ago	[3] $x - 3$	[4] $(x - 4) - 3$

    Box 1 is x, Coop's age now. Box 2 is $x - 4$ because Carni must be 4 months younger. To complete these ages 3 months ago, subtract 3 from each expression.

17. **(3) $x^2 + 7x - 18$**
    $(x + 9)(x - 2) = x^2 - 2x + 9x - 18 = x^2 + 7x - 18$

18. **(1) $x \leq -2$**   The direction to the left shows "less than." Since the dot is filled in, you know the correct symbol is $\leq$.

19. **(5) $x > \frac{-10}{7}$**   You need to divide both sides by -7. Dividing or multiplying by a negative number changes the direction of the sign.

20. **(4) 20**   Let x equal the number. Write an equation: $x - 10 = \frac{x}{2}$. Multiply both sides by 2 to get rid of the fraction:
    $2x - 20 = x$
    $-20 = -x$
    $20 = x$

21. **(3) $4x(2x + 3)$**   Divide by $4x$.
    $\frac{8x^2 + 12x}{4x} = 2x + 3$

22. **(3) C, G**   The positive x-values are to the right of the y-axis. The negative y-values are below the x-axis. Only C and G are in the lower right quadrant.

23. **(3) I and K**   The points on the x-axis have a y-value of 0. Only I and K are on the x-axis.

24. **(3) C**   You could either graph the line or substitute the coordinates of each point into the equation. To graph the line, substitute any value for x and solve for y. If $x = 2$, $x - y = 8$;

2 − y = 8. Then y = −6. This gives you the first pair of coordinates. Repeat with a different value for x. Graph the two pairs of coordinates and draw a line through them. Point C is on the line. To prove that point C is on the line, substitute (6,−2), the coordinates of point C, and solve the statement: x − y = 8; 6 − (−2) = 8. Point C is on the line.

25. **(4) −1** The coordinates for point J are (0,4). The coordinates for point K are (4,0).

Use the formula: $m = \dfrac{y_2 - y_1}{x_2 - x_1}$

$$m = \dfrac{0 - 4}{4 - 0} = \dfrac{-4}{4} = -1$$

26. **(5) All are false.** Evaluate each statement. The symbol < means less than. None of the statements is true.

27. **(4) 8 and 9** The square of 8 is 64, and the square of 9 is 81, so the square root of 70 must be between 8 and 9.

28. **(4) 3(x − 11) = 2x − 11** Create a chart:

	Becky's Age	Her Mother's Age
Now	x	2x
11 Years Ago	x − 11	2x − 11

Eleven years ago, her mother was three times as old as Becky. Set up an equation. 3(x − 11) = 2x − 11

29. **(2) A and C** Evaluate each statement:
A. 4 + (1 − 4) = 4 − 3 = 1
B. (7 − 3) + 1 = 4 + 1 = 5
C. 6 − (3 + 2) = 6 − 5 = 1
D. 8 − (1 − 2) = 8 + 1 = 9
A and C have the same value.

30. **(1) −6**
$$\dfrac{-12}{(4 + (-2))} = \dfrac{-12}{2} = -6$$

31. **(3) 4^5** Evaluate each of the options: $2^5 = 32$, $4^3 = 64$, $4^5 = 1{,}024$, $5^4 = 625$, $6^3 = 216$. Only option (3) is greater than 1,000.

32. **(4) 9.8×10^6** 9800000. You would need to move the decimal point 6 places to the left, so 9.8×10^6 is the correct expression.

33. **(2) 3x − 2y = −5** Evaluate each equation using the coordinates (−1,1). Only option (2) is a true statement using these values.
3x − 2y = −5
3(−1) − 2(1) = −5
−3 − 2 = −5

34. **(5) 2.4×10^{-3}** 0.0024 The decimal is moved three places to the left when a number is multiplied by 10^{-3}.

Geometry

Lesson 23: Volume
GED Exercise: Volume (page 618)

1. **Rectangular solid**
$V = l \times w \times h$
$= 15 \times 8 \times 6$
$= $ **720 cubic inches**

2. **Cube**
$V = s \times s \times s$
$= 5.1 \times 5.1 \times 5.1$
$= $ **132.651 cubic inches**

3. **Cylinder**
$V = $ Area of base $\times h$
$= 18 \times 10$
$= $ **180 cubic feet**

4. **254 cubic feet**
$V = A \times h$
$= 28.26 \times 9$
$= $ **254 cubic feet**

5. **377 cubic inches**
$V = \frac{1}{3} \times$ Area of base $\times h$
$= \frac{1}{3} \times 113.04 \times 10$
$= $ **377 cubic inches**

6. **15 cubic yards**
$V = \frac{1}{3} \times$ Area of base $\times h$
$= \frac{1}{3} \times 6 \times 7\frac{1}{2}$
$= $ **15 cubic yards**

7. **414 cu ft** Think of the figure as **two rectangular solids**. Find the volume of each and add the results. The missing height for the lower solid is 18 − 6, or 12 ft. The missing length for the upper solid is 9 − 4, or 5 feet.
Lower solid:
$V = lwh$
$= 9(3)(12)$
$= 324$ cu ft
Upper solid:
$V = lwh$
$= 6(5)(3)$
$= 90$ cu ft
Volume = 324 + 90 = **414 cu ft**

8. **84.5 cu ft** The area of the base (A) of the **cylinder** (6.5 sq ft) is also the area of the base of the **cone**.
Cone:
$V = \frac{1}{3} \times A \times h$
$\quad = \frac{1}{3} \times 6.5 \times 12$
$\quad = 26$ cu ft
Cylinder:
$V = A \times h$
$\quad = 6.5 \times 9$
$\quad = 58.5$ cu ft
Volume $= 26 + 58.5 = $ **84.5 cu ft**

9. **1,260 cu in.** Think of the figure as **three rectangular solids**. The lower solid has a height of $18 - 6 - 6$, or 6 in.
Lower solid:
$V = lwh$
$\quad = 15(7)(6)$
$\quad = 630$ cu in
The middle solid has a length of $15 - 5$, or 10 in.
Middle solid:
$V = lwh$
$\quad = 10(7)(6)$
$\quad = 420$ cu in
The upper solid has a length of $15 - 5 - 5$, or 5 in.
Upper solid:
$V = lwh$
$\quad = 5(7)(6)$
$\quad = 210$ cu in
Volume $= 630 + 420 + 210 = $ **1,260 cu in**

10. **(3) 1,440**
$V = 15 \times 24 \times 4 = 1,440$ cu in

11. **(4) 8** $V = 2 \times 2 \times 2 = 8$ cu yd

12. **(4) 12,500**
$V = 100 \times 25 \times 5 = 12,500$ cu ft

13. **(5) 576**
$V = 12 \times 8 \times 6 = 576$ cu ft

14. **(3) 54.6**
$V = 9.1 \times 6 = 54.6$ cu ft

15. **(3) 33.6**
$V = \frac{1}{3} \times 12.6 \times 8 = 33.6$ cu ft

16. **(2) $37\frac{1}{2}$**
$V = \frac{1}{3} \times 9 \times 12\frac{1}{2} = 37\frac{1}{2}$ cu ft

17. **(3) 25** $V = \frac{1}{3} \times 12.56 \times 6 = 25.12 = 25$ cu in. (rounded)

Lesson 24: Angles
GED Exercise: Angles (page 622)

1. **Obtuse** Angles that measure between 90° and 180° are obtuse angles, so an angle of measure 150° is obtuse.

2. **Acute** An angle that measures between 0° and 90° is an acute angle, so an angle of measure 35° is acute.

3. **Right** An angle that measures exactly 90° is a right angle.

4. **Straight** An angle that measures exactly 180° is a straight angle.

5. **Acute**   7. **Obtuse**

6. **Obtuse**   8. **Acute**

9. **∠2 and ∠4** Adjacent angles share a common vertex and a common ray. There are two angles adjacent to, or touching, ∠3, namely ∠2 and ∠4.

10. **∠5** ∠5 is the vertical angle to ∠2. These two angles are made up of the same two intersecting lines. They are opposite angles.

11. **∠3** ∠3 is the vertical angle to ∠6.

12. **∠4** ∠4 is the vertical angle to 1.

13. **∠6 and ∠2** Both ∠6 and ∠2 are adjacent to ∠1.

14. **∠6 and ∠4** Both ∠6 and ∠4 are adjacent to ∠5.

15. **∠2** ∠2 is congruent to ∠5 because vertical angles are congruent.

16. **∠1** ∠1 is congruent to ∠4 because vertical angles are congruent.

17. **∠6** ∠6 is congruent to ∠3

because vertical angles are congruent.

18. **42°** ∠BXC and ∠AXB are complementary. That is, their sum is 90°. Therefore, 90° − 48° = 42° = m∠BXC.

19. **90°** ∠AXB and ∠BXC are complementary. These two angles form ∠AXC. Therefore, ∠AXC is 90° and ∠AXD is a straight angle of 180°. Since
∠AXC + ∠DXC = ∠AXD
90° + ∠DXC = 180°
∠DXC = 90°

20. **132°**
∠BXD = ∠BXC + ∠DXC
42° + 90° = 132°

21. **∠CXA** Supplementary angles sum to 180° or a straight angle. Therefore, ∠DXC and ∠CXA are supplementary.

22. **∠2, ∠3, ∠6, ∠7**

23. **∠7**

24. **∠1, ∠4, ∠5, ∠8**

25. **∠1**

26. **∠3**   29. **∠4**

27. **∠5**   30. **∠7**

28. **∠6**   31. **∠4**

32. **(4) 6** Each of the four angles, 1, 2, 4, and 5, are acute angles. But the angle made up of the adjacent angles 1 and 2 is an acute angle, and so is the angle made up of the adjacent angles 4 and 5.

33. **(1) ∠A is complementary to ∠B.** The sum of the measures of ∠A and ∠B is 28° + 62°, or 90°. Angles which sum to 90° are complementary.

34. **(2) 50°** To say that two angles are complementary means that their measures sum to 90°: ∠M + ∠R = 90°.

Since the measure of ∠M is 40°, 90° − 40°, or 50°, is the measure of ∠R.

35. **(5) m∠1 + m∠7 = 180°** ∠1 and ∠8 are alternate exterior angles, therefore m∠1 = m∠8. ∠8 and ∠7 are supplementary angles, therefore m∠8 + m∠7 = 180°. Since m∠1 = m∠8, then m∠1 + m∠7 = 180°.

36. **(2) ∠5** From the figure we see that both ∠2 and ∠5 are right angles, because ∠1 is a right angle. ∠XOZ is also a right angle. Therefore, any two of these four angles, ∠1, ∠2, ∠5, and ∠XOZ are supplementary. However, ∠1 and ∠XOZ are both adjacent to ∠2. Therefore, of these possible angles, only ∠5 fits the requirement that it not be adjacent to ∠2.

37. **(4) 155°** ∠WOY is made up of ∠4 and ∠5: m∠WOY = m∠4 + m∠5. Since ∠3 and ∠4 make up a 90° angle and the measure of ∠3 is 25°, ∠4 must be 90° − 25° = 65°. Since ∠5 is a right angle, the measure of ∠5 is 90°. Add m∠4 to m∠5: 65° + 90° = 155° = m∠WOY.

38. **(2) a right angle** ∠XOZ is a right angle. Its supplement must also be a right angle because "supplement" means the sum of the angles is 180°. Options (1) and (3) are eliminated because a right angle can be neither acute nor obtuse. Option (4) is not a necessary condition, and option (5) would not make an angle large enough to be supplementary.

39. **(5) ∠Q and ∠R have the same degree measure.** Option (5) is true because the meaning of "congruent" is that the angles "have the same degree of measure." Vertical angles are always congruent to each other and could be both acute, both obtuse, supplementary, or complementary. However, none of the options (1) through (4) is necessarily true.

Lesson 25: Triangles and Quadrilaterals

GED Exercise: Triangles and Quadrilaterals (page 626)

1. △ABC Each side has the same length, 10. (Note: This triangle could also be named △ACB, △BCA, △BAC, △CBA, or △CAB.)

2. △ABD Two of its sides have the same length, 13. (The equilateral triangle, △ABC, is a special case of an isosceles triangle.)

3. △ACD and △BCD In each triangle, there is one angle that is obtuse, that is, greater than 90°.

4. △ABE, △ABC, and △ABD All the angles are acute angles, that is, less than 90°.

5. △ABE, △ACD, and △BCD No sides are equal.

6. △ABE

7. △BDC and △CDE

8. △ACB and △BCE

9. **35°** The measures of all three angles must sum to 180°: m∠A + m∠ABE + m∠E = 180°. Since m∠A = 55° and m∠ABE = 90°, then m∠E = 180° − 55° − 90° = 35°.

10. **35°** In △ABC we know that ∠ACB = 90° and m∠A = 55°, which sum to 145°. Then m∠ABC = 180° − 145° = 35°.

11. **55°** In △DCE, m∠CDE = 90° and m∠E = 35° (see item 9), which sum to 125°. Then, m∠DCE = 180° − 125° = 55°.

12. **55°** In △BCE, m∠BCE = 90° and ∠E = 35° (item 9), which sum to 125°. Then, m∠CBD = 180° − 125° = 55°. Also, since ∠ABE = 90° and ∠ABC = 35° (from item 10), then ∠CBD = 90° − 35° = 55°.

13. **35°** In △BCD, m∠BDC = 90° and m∠CBD = 55° (item 12), which sum to 145°. Then ∠BCD = 180° − 145° = 35°. Also, since m∠BCE = 90° and m∠DCE = 55° (item 11), m∠BCD = 90° − 55° = 35°.

14. All four triangles are **similar, right** triangles: the angles in all four triangles measure 35°, 55°, and 90°.

15. The figure could be a **rhombus**, or a **square**. Since a rhombus is a special **parallelogram** and a square is a special **rectangle,** the figure could also be called one of those other figures.

16. The figure could be a **square** or a **rectangle**. However, since a square is a special **rhombus** and a rectangle is a special **parallelogram,** the figure could also be called one of these.

17. The figure could be a **parallelogram,** a **square,** a **rectangle** or a **rhombus**. A trapezoid has one pair of parallel lines.

18. The figure is a **trapezoid**.

19. The figure could be a **parallelogram,** a **rhombus,** or a **trapezoid.**

20. The figure is a **trapezoid**.

21. **(3) between 15° and 20°** Let x be the smaller angle in the triangle. Then 4x is the

measure of the other acute angle. The third angle is known to be 90°. The sum of these three angles is 180°. We can write this equation:

$$x + 4x + 90 = 180°$$
$$5x = 90°$$
$$x = 18°$$

22. **(5) parallelogram** The figure has four sides, so option (1) is eliminated. It has no right angles, so option (2) is eliminated. At least one pair of opposite sides in a trapezoid are not equal, so option (3) is eliminated. A rhombus has all four sides equal, so option (4) is eliminated. A parallelogram can have sides as listed, so option (5) is the correct answer.

23. **(5) There are exactly three right triangles.** There are no equilateral, obtuse, or acute triangles in the figure. But the three right triangles are △ABC, △ADB, and △BDC. For each, the right angle of the triangles is listed in the middle.

24. **(1) isosceles** The triangle has two sides that are the same length. This is the definition of an isosceles triangle.

25. **(2)** $(x) + (x + 15°) + (2x) = 180°$ Let x be the smallest angle in the triangle. Then the measure of the second is $x + 15°$. Since the measure of the third is twice the measure of the smallest, its measure is $2x$. The sum of these three expressions must equal 180°, and that is the basis for the equation.

26. **(4) 6** They are △ADB, △DEB, △ECB, △AEB, △DCB, and △ACB.

27. **(4) 4** A triangle with two sides of the same length is isosceles:
△AEB has two sides of length 6.
△CED has two sides of length 3.
△ACD has two sides of length 5.
△CDB has two sides of length 5.

Lesson 26: Congruence and Similarity
GED Exercise: Congruence and Similarity (page 630)

1. ∠A corresponds to ∠C.

2. ∠ABE corresponds to ∠CBD.

3. ∠E corresponds to ∠D.

4. $\overline{BA}$ corresponds to $\overline{BC}$.

5. $\overline{AE}$ corresponds to $\overline{CD}$.

6. $\overline{BE}$ corresponds to $\overline{BD}$.

7. ∠B or ∠GBD

8. ∠BDG

9. ∠DGB

10. $\overline{BD}$

11. $\overline{BG}$

12. $\overline{DG}$

13. $\overline{DG}$

14. $\overline{BD}$

15. $\overline{BG}$

16. $\overline{AC} \cong \overline{BC}$ because in an isosceles triangle two sides are congruent. ∠B ≅ ∠A because the base angles in an isosceles triangle are congruent. $\overline{AY} \cong \overline{BY}$ because in an isosceles triangle the line forming the right angle bisects (cuts into two equal parts) the base. ∠ACY ≅ ∠BCY, because in an isosceles triangle, this line bisects the vertex angle.

17. $\overline{XC} \cong \overline{CZ}$ $\overline{XY} \cong \overline{YZ}$
∠CXY ≅ ∠CZY   ∠XCY ≅ ∠ZCY
All three congruent parts are based on the properties of an isosceles triangle (see item 16).

18. **(3) 100** $\frac{60}{90} = \frac{x}{150}$
$$90x = 60(150)$$
$$90x = 9,000$$
$$x = 100$$

Lesson 27: Pythagorean Relationships
GED Exercise: Pythagorean Relationships (page 632)

1. **26 ft.** The figure forms a right triangle with legs of 10 and 24. The unknown side is x. Then $x^2 = 10^2 + 24^2 = 100 + 576 = 676$. A few trials with numbers near 25 show that $26^2 = 676$. The wire is 26 feet long.

2. **4 ft.** Now the triangle has legs of 18 and 24. $x^2 = 18^2 + 24^2 = 324 + 576 = 900$. $30^2 = 900$, so the new wire is 30 feet long, or 4 feet longer than before.

3. **65 miles** The triangle has legs of 39 and 52 miles.
$$c^2 = a^2 + b^2$$
$$= 39^2 + 52^2$$
$$= 1,521 + 2,704$$
$$= 4,225$$
The square root of 4,225 is 65, so it is 65 miles from Point C to Point B.

4. **72 miles** Add to find the distance from A to D: $11 + 39 = 50$. The triangle now has legs of 50 and 52 miles.
$$c^2 = a^2 + b^2$$
$$= 50^2 + 52^2$$
$$= 2,500 + 2,704$$
$$= 5,204$$
The square root of 5,204 is between 72 and 73, but it is closer to 72. It is 72 miles from Point D to Point B.

5. **(4)** $\sqrt{400 - 36}$ Because this is a right triangle, the short leg squared plus the longer leg squared equals the hypotenuse squared. Here, $6^2 + x^2 = 20^2$
$$36 + x^2 = 400$$
$$x^2 = 400 - 36$$
To find the length of the longer leg, x, find the square root of $400 - 36$, or $\sqrt{400 - 36}$.

6. **(4) 8**
$$c^2 = a^2 + b^2$$
$$10^2 = 6^2 + b^2$$
$$100 = 36 + b^2$$
$$64 = b^2$$
The square root of 64 is 8.

7. **(3) triangle with sides of 5, 12, and 13**
In any right triangle, the square of the short leg plus the square of the longer leg will equal the square of the hypotenuse.
Test each choice:
(1) $16 + 25 \neq 36$
(2) $25 + 49 \neq 81$
(3) $25 + 144 = 169$
(4) $36 + 64 \neq 121$
(5) $49 + 81 \neq 144$

8. **(2) 26** Focus on $\triangle ABC$. It is a right triangle with its right angle at C. The legs are 10 and 24, and the hypotenuse is $\overline{AB}$, the length we seek. $(\overline{AB})^2 = 10^2 + 24^2 = 100 + 576 = 676$. Now see which choice is closest: $27^2 = 729$ and $26^2 = 676$. We need go no further; 26 is exactly the distance.

GED Review: Geometry (page 633)

1. **(5) 5 ft 3 in** Set up a proportion:
$$\frac{3\frac{1}{2}}{x} = \frac{4}{6}$$
$$4x = 21$$
$$x = 5\frac{1}{4} \text{ ft} = 5 \text{ ft } 3 \text{ in}$$

2. **(4) 23 ft** Use the Pythagorean Theorem:
$$c^2 = a^2 + b^2$$
$$c^2 = 7^2 + 22^2$$
$$c^2 = 49 + 484$$
$$c^2 = 533$$
c is about 23 ft $23 \times 23 = 529$

3. **(4) $\overline{AC}$ and $\overline{DC}$** When two figures are congruent or similar, then the smallest angle of one "corresponds" to the smallest angle of the other, and the longest side of one "corresponds" to the longest side of the other. To identify corresponding sides we simply match up the parts of the figures that are the same (or proportional in the case of similar figures). In option (4) $\overline{AC}$ is the longest side, the hypotenuse, of one triangle, but $\overline{DC}$ is not the hypotenuse of the other.

4. **(2) 60°** Let $2x = m\angle A$ and $x = m\angle B$. Supplementary angles sum to 180°.
$$x + 2x = 180°$$
$$3x = 180°$$
$$x = 60°$$

5. **(4) 29** Use the Pythagorean Theorem to find the diagonal: (the diagonal is the hypotenuse)
$$c^2 = a^2 + b^2$$
$$c^2 = 15^2 + 25^2$$
$$c^2 = 225 + 625$$
$$c^2 = 850$$
c is approximately 29 inches, since $29 \times 29 = 841$.

6. **(2) $12\frac{1}{2}$** Use the Pythagorean Theorem:
$$c^2 = a^2 + b^2$$
$$c^2 = \left(7\frac{1}{2}\right)^2 + 10^2$$
$$c^2 = 56\frac{1}{4} + 100$$
$$c^2 = 156\frac{1}{4}$$
$$c = 12\frac{1}{2}$$

7. **(2) 15°.** A right triangle has a 90° angle and two acute angles. The sum of the angles in any triangle is 180°. Set up an equation, where x equals the measure of the smaller angle and $5x$ equals the measure of the larger acute angle.
$$90° + x + 5x = 180°$$
$$90° + 6x = 180°$$
$$6x = 90°$$
$$x = 15°$$

8. **(1) They are alternate exterior angles.** Angles 4 and 5 are on alternate sides of the transversal t and are on the outside of the parallel lines P and M.

9. **(5) $m\angle 3 = 135°$** Since $m\angle 8$ is 45°, $m\angle 4$ must be 135°. Since $\angle 4$ and $\angle 3$ are supplementary, $m\angle 3$ must be 45° also.

10. **(4) $\angle 7$** $\angle 7$ is on the same side of the transversal and is in the same position in regard to the parallel lines.

11. **(2) 22 ft** Set up a proportion:
$$\frac{\text{shadow of post}}{\text{actual post}} = \frac{\text{shadow of pole}}{\text{actual pole}}$$
$$\frac{4\frac{1}{2}}{3} = \frac{33}{x}$$
$$4\frac{1}{2}x = 99 \qquad x = 22 \text{ ft}$$

12. **(2)** $\frac{AB}{AC} = \frac{FB}{GC}$ Corresponding sides of similar triangles have equal ratios.

13. **(3) 1,500** Find the volume of one candle:
$$V = \frac{1}{3}Ah$$
$$= \frac{1}{3}(4.5)(5)$$
$$= 7.5 \text{ cu in}$$
Find wax needed to make 200 candles:
$$(7.5)\,200 = 1{,}500 \text{ cu in}$$

14. **(1) ∠6 and ∠2** Angle 6 is supplementary to ∠8. So, ∠6 = 180° − 50° = 130°. Since l and m are parallel lines intersected by a transversal, ∠2 is congruent to ∠6. Thus, ∠6 and ∠2 both measure 130°.

15. **(5) Not enough information is given.** While ∠AED appears to be obtuse, there is not enough information given to be able to come to that conclusion. Remember: appearance is not enough to reach a conclusion.

16. **(1) $m\angle ABC = 55°$** The sum of the angles of a triangle is 180° and △ABC is isosceles because two sides are equal. Then, $m\angle C = m\angle B$ because the angles opposite the congruent sides in an isosceles triangle are equal.
$$m\angle A + m\angle B + m\angle C = 180°$$
$$70° + m\angle B + m\angle B = 180°$$
$$2m\angle B = 180° - 70°$$
$$m\angle B = 55°$$
Remember that angles can be named using the vertex only or the vertex as the middle letter.

17. **(4) 13 ft** Use the Pythagorean Theorem: (the wire is the hypotenuse).
$$c^2 = a^2 + b^2$$
$$c^2 = 5^2 + 12^2$$
$$c^2 = 25 + 144$$
$$c^2 = 169$$
$$c = 13$$

18. **(3) ∠AHG** The angles are alternate exterior angles.

19. **(3) 1,400 sq ft**
Use the formula:
$$V = \frac{1}{3}Ah$$
$$82{,}600 = \frac{1}{3}A(177)$$
$$82{,}600 = 59A$$
$$1{,}400 = A$$

20. **(3) Box Z has the greatest volume.**
Multiply length times width times height to find the volume of each box.
Box X: $7.6 \times 5 \times 10 = 380$ cu in
Box Y: $8 \times 4.5 \times 10 = 360$ cu in
Box Z: $7 \times 5.5 \times 10 = 385$ cu in

21. **(2) △TUR** ∠U is a right angle. △TUR is the only answer option which contains ∠U.

22. **(3) a scalene triangle** No sides of the triangle are equal.

23. **(3) three** △RUV, △RUT, and △RUS are right triangles.

24. **(4) > 6 < 7 in high** The volume formula is $\frac{1}{3} \times A \times h$, where $A = 3$ in $\times$ 3 in = 9 sq in and h is unknown: $21 = \frac{1}{3} \times 9 \times h$; $21 = 3h$. The height (h) is 7 inches. The tallest bottle that can fit is > 6 < 7.

25. **(2) $\overline{AC} \cong \overline{AE}$** We can only assume what is shown in the figure and what is told specifically. Thus we cannot assume that $\overline{AB} \cong \overline{BC} \cong \overline{CD}$, nor that any pair of corresponding sides are congruent. $\overline{AC} \cong \overline{AE}$ because they are congruent sides of the known isosceles triangle.

26. **(3) 75°** The sum of the angles is 180°.
Let $m\angle C = x$: $25° + 80° + x = 180°$
$$x = 75°$$

27. **(4) the supplement of ∠BAC** $\overline{AB}$ is parallel to $\overline{DE}$. $\overline{AD}$ transverses $\overline{AB}$ and $\overline{DE}$. Interior angles on the same side of a transversal are supplementary.

28. **(1) 105°** ∠BCD is supplementary to ∠ACB which is 75° (see item 26). 180° − 75° = 105°.

GED Cumulative Review: Mathematics (page 637)

1. **(5) $18\frac{2}{3}$** Multiply $\frac{4\frac{2}{3} \text{ yd}}{\text{cover}} \times 4 \text{ covers} = \frac{14}{3} \times 4 = \frac{56}{3} = 18\frac{2}{3}$.

2. **(5) The maximum frequency of Model B is 100 times as great as that of Model A.** 3×10^3 is 3,000. 3×10^5 is 300,000. $\frac{\text{Model B}}{\text{Model A}} = \frac{3 \times 10^5}{3 \times 10^3} = \frac{300{,}000}{3{,}000} = 100$.

3. **(4) $502.50** Add the amounts she collected: $1,900 + $2,350 + $5,800 = $10,050; multiply by 5% (0.05): $10,050 × 0.05 = $502.50.

4. **(1) 20(5) + 12(9)** Multiply the number of students taking a particular lesson by the lesson price. Add the two products.

5. **(3) 1999** To find the number of years needed to build 80 planes at a rate of 16 planes/year, divide: 80 planes ÷ 16 planes/year = 5 years. Add: 1994 + 5 = 1999.

6. **(4) 900** Multiply 1,200 by 75%: 1,200 × 0.75 = 900.

7. **(2) B** Start at 0 and count 5 to the left on the number line.

8. **(2) 32%** Add the rates for taxes withheld and taxes owed: 24% + 3% + 4% + 1% = 32%.

9. **(3) 2.5%** Divide the amount of disability tax by her taxable income. Change the decimal to a percent. $475 ÷ $19,000 = 0.025 = 2.5%.

10. **(4) between 5 and 6 hours** Use the formula: $d = rt$. Solve for time (t) by dividing distance (d) 305 by rate (r) 55. Estimate $\frac{305}{55}$ is less than $\frac{300}{50}$ or 6.

11. **(3) 3 and 4** Estimate the square root of 14. The square of 3 is 9 and the square of 4 is 16. The square root of 14 falls between 3 and 4.

12. **(4) C and F** Cliff has worked $4\frac{1}{2}$ $\left(2 + 2\frac{1}{2}\right)$ hours of the 6 hours available. He has $1\frac{1}{2}$ hours left to work. The only combination among the options on the list that is less than $1\frac{1}{2}$ is C and F. $\left(\frac{3}{4} + \frac{1}{2} = 1\frac{1}{4}\right)$.

13. **(5) Not enough information is given.** You need to know the weight of the tomatoes in pounds, not the number of tomatoes: $\frac{79¢}{\text{pound}} \times 6$ tomatoes—the units are NOT the same, so you cannot perform this operation.

14. **(2) 15%** Divide 12 by the total number of employees (80): 12 ÷ 80 = 0.15 = 15%.

15. **(4) $\frac{1}{10}$** The ratio of buyers to total employees is $\frac{8}{80}$, which reduces to $\frac{1}{10}$.

16. **(3) 150** Use a proportion: $\frac{1 \text{ in}}{40 \text{ mi}} = \frac{3\frac{3}{4} \text{ in}}{x}$
x $= 3\frac{3}{4} \times 40 = \frac{15}{4} \times 40 = 150$

17. **(2) $112.50** Multiply $90 by 1.25.

18. **(5) (3.14)(4)²(14)** Use the formula: $V = \pi r^2 h$. If the diameter is 8 inches, the radius r is 4 inches.

19. **(5) 6(4) + 2(3)** Multiply the number of patterns of each type by the cost for each type:

~~patterns~~ $\times \frac{\$}{\text{~~pattern~~}}$. Then add the two products.

20. **(4) $\frac{2}{3}$** Divide $\frac{1}{2}$ hour by 45 $\frac{\text{minutes}}{\text{lawn}}$ $\left(\frac{3}{4} \text{ hour}\right)$. $\frac{1}{2}$ hour $÷ \frac{3}{4}$ hour/lawn $= \frac{1}{2}$ hour $\times \frac{4}{3} = \frac{2}{3}$.

21. **(4) 1,600** Multiply: $\frac{200 \text{ square feet}}{\text{~~gallon~~}} \times 8$ ~~gallons~~ = 1,600 square feet.

22. **(1) 2.062493 ×10⁶** Move the decimal 6 places to the right to multiply by 10^6.

23. **(4) 64%** 46% + 18% = 64%

24. **(5) 76%** 100% − (15% + 9%) = 76%

25. **(1) $\frac{72 + 66 + 74 + 68}{4}$** Add the scores and divide by the number of scores.

26. **(5) $480,000**
100% − 4% = 96%. Multiply:
$500,000 × 0.96 = $480,000
OR $500,000 × 4% = $500,000 × .04 = 20,000
$500,000 − $20,000 = $480,000

27. **(3) $\frac{1}{30}$** Write a ratio and reduce: $\frac{5}{150} = \frac{1}{30}$.

28. **(2) 201** Use the formula: $A = \pi r^2$. Since the diameter is 16 feet, the radius of the platform is 8 feet. So, $3.14 \times 8 \times 8 = 201$ (rounded).

29. **(1) 180** Multiply: $\frac{12 \text{ plants}}{\text{~~row~~}} \times 15$ ~~rows~~ = 180 plants.

30. **(3) 60** Find the area of Lot B: $A = lw = (90)(40) = 3,600$. The area of Lot A is $A = s^2$. Find the square root of the area (3,600) to find the length of the sides of Lot A: $6 \times 6 = 36$; since 3,600 ends in 2 zeros, multiply $6 \times 10 = 60$.

31. **(2) 26%** Divide:
18 calories $÷ \frac{70 \text{ calories}}{1 \text{ serving}} =$
18 ~~calories~~ $\times \frac{1 \text{ serving}}{70 \text{ ~~calories~~}} =$
$\frac{.257 \text{ calories}}{1} = 26\%$ of the calories are from fat.

32. **(3) $423.87** Multiply to find the sales tax $\left(6\frac{1}{2}\% = 0.065\right)$: $398 × 0.065 = $25.87. Add tax to the price of the desk: $398 + $25.87 = $423.87

33. **(4) 0.04($500) + $500** Find the increase by multiplying the cost by 4%. Then add the increase to the original cost.

34. **(5) Not enough information is given.** Use the formula for volume of a rectangular container: $V = lwh$. You have the length and

volume, but you need the height to solve for the width.

35. **(3) $5x + 5y$** Combine the x's ($6x - x = 5x$); combine the y's ($2y + 3y = 5y$).

36. **(5) $7.56** Convert $3\frac{1}{2}$ dozen.

$$\overset{6}{\underset{1}{\frac{7}{2}}} \text{ dozen} \times \frac{\overset{6}{\cancel{12}} \text{ oranges}}{\cancel{\text{dozen}}} = 42 \text{ oranges.}$$

$$\frac{6}{\$1.08} = \frac{42}{x}$$
$$6x = 42(\$1.08)$$
$$x = \frac{42(\$1.08)}{6} = \$7.56$$

37. **(1) 93** $15\%(620) = 93$

38. **(4) 60**
$$p = 3(4)(3 + 2)$$
$$p = 12(5)$$
$$p = 60$$

39. **(1) $1\frac{1}{4}x = 25$** Set up a proportion:
$$\frac{5 \text{ miles}}{1\frac{1}{4} \text{ hours}} \bowtie \frac{x \text{ miles}}{5 \text{ hours}} \quad \text{Cross multiply.}$$

40. **(5) $74 - 2(22) = 2w$** Use the formula:
$$P = 2l + 2w$$
$$74 = 2(22) + 2w$$
$$\text{So } 74 - 2(22) = 2w$$

41. **(3) $153.60** Multiply: $\frac{\$12.80}{\cancel{\text{month}}} \times 12 \, \cancel{\text{months}}$.

42. **(1) $3m - n$** Combine the m's ($2m + m = 3m$); combine the n's ($2n - 3n = -n$).

43. **(2) $p - \$24.95 - \$18.65$** Subtract both purchases from the amount of the gift certificate.

44. **(1) 3** $3z < 12$
$$z < 4$$

45. **(5) 110°** Straight angle $BAD = 180°$. Therefore, $180° - 70° = 110°$.

46. **(3) 135°** The sum of the interior angles of a triangle is 180°.
$$m\angle x + 25° + 20° = 180°$$
$$m\angle x = 135°$$

47. **(1) 72 ft** Set up a proportion:
$$\frac{\text{pole}}{\text{shadow}} = \frac{\text{building}}{\text{shadow}}$$
$$\frac{3}{5} = \frac{x}{20}$$
$$5x = 360$$
$$x = 72$$

48. **(2) 12** Find the sum of the given sides ($16 + 15 + 20 + 9 = 60$) and subtract from the perimeter, 72: ($72 - 60 = 12$).

49. **(4) 15 ft** Draw a diagram. Set up a proportion.

$$\frac{8}{6} = \frac{(8 + 12)}{x}$$
$$8x = 120$$
$$x = 15$$

50. **(4) 8** The radius of the large circle is the diameter of the small circle. ($32 \div 2 = 16$). Divide 16 by 2 to find the radius of the small circle.

51. **(5) 46** Add all the sides. The leftmost side is 8. The right inner side is 5. The base is 10(3 + 4 + 3). Thus: $3 + 5 + 4 + 5 + 3 + 8 + 10 + 8 = 46$.

52. **(5) 20 ft** Use the Pythagorean Theorem. The wire is the hypotenuse, or c^2 in the formula.
$$a^2 + b^2 = c^2$$
$$12^2 + 16^2 = c^2$$
$$144 + 256 = c^2$$
$$400 = c^2$$
$$20 = c$$

53. **(3) side $\overline{FH}$** $\angle FDE$ corresponds to $\angle GHF$ because they have the same measure. If the triangles were oriented by placing points D and H together, sides $\overline{DF}$ and $\overline{FH}$ would lie on the same line.

54. **(4) 50** Similar triangles have proportionate sides. Set up a proportion using any corresponding pair of sides.
$$\frac{\overline{FE}}{\overline{FG}} = \frac{\overline{DE}}{\overline{GH}}$$
$$\frac{40}{80} = \frac{x}{100}$$
$$50 = x$$

55. **(1) $a^2 + 9^2 = 15^2$** Use the Pythagorean Theorem on the formula page. The longest side (15) is the hypotenuse (c).

56. **(4) 90°** The sum of the internal angles of a triangle is 180°.
$$m\angle 1 + m\angle 2 + m\angle 3 = 180°$$
$$55° + 35° + m\angle 3 = 180°$$
$$m\angle 3 = 180° - 35° - 55°$$
$$m\angle 3 = 90°.$$

Simulated GED Tests

Writing Skills (page 647)

1. **(2) controversial, contradictory, and** (Sentence structure/Fragments; Mechanics/Punctuation—commas between items in series) Both sentences are fragments; combined they contain a series of three adjectives—controversial, contradictory, and emotional—that describe the subject. Items in series should be separated by commas, so option (2) is correct. Option (3) is incorrect

because and should be used only between the last two items in the series. Options (1), (4), and (5) do not correct the sentence fragments.

2. **(5) parlors is legal, but private** (Usage/Subject-verb agreement with the interrupting phrase; Mechanics/Punctuation—commas between independent clauses) The subject of the first independent clause is betting. Betting is singular, so the singular verb is is correct. Therefore, option (5) is correct and option (2) is incorrect. When a coordinate conjunction joins two sentences (independent clauses), a comma, not a semicolon, is needed before the conjunction; therefore, options (3) and (4) are incorrect.

3. **(2) change There is to There are** (Usage/Subject-verb agreement—expletive and verb tense) Option (2) is correct because the subject of the sentence is organizations, which is plural; the plural verb are is required. The paragraphs are written in present tense. Option (1) is incorrect because the past-tense were would not be consistent with the verb tense in the other sentences. Use of the pronoun they, as in option (3), is incorrect. There is no reason for the change in option (4).

4. **(3) change nevada, to Nevada** (Mechanics/Capitalization; Mechanics/Punctuation—overuse of commas) Option (3) is correct because the name of a state, Nevada, should be capitalized. Because the dependent clause is restrictive, a comma after Nevada is not needed, so option (4) is incorrect. There is no reason for the changes in options (1) and (2).

5. **(3) insert a comma after card game** (Mechanics/Punctuation—appositives) A card game, an appositive that further explains Poker, should be set off by commas; therefore, option (3) is correct and option (1) is incorrect. There is no reason for the changes in options (2) and (4).

6. **(5) no correction is necessary** (Mechanics/Capitalization; Usage/Verb tense and subject-verb agreement) The passage is written in present tense and Daydreaming is singular, so the verb is is correct, making options (2) and (3) incorrect. In options (1) and (4), Daydreaming and popular are capitalized correctly.

7. **(2) if you control it and do not** (Usage/Verb tense; Mechanics/Punctuation and capitalization) Control is present tense, which is consistent with the rest of the sentence and paragraph. Options (3) and (5) add unnecessary punctuation, and Do Not is incorrectly capitalized in option (4).

8. **(4) mood when you're** (Mechanics/Contractions) You're is a contraction meaning "you are." No ownership is expressed, so the possessive pronoun your is not correct, as in options (1) and (5). A comma is not needed because the dependent clause is restrictive, so option (2) is incorrect.

9. **(2) change will begin to begin** (Usage/Verb tense) Verb tense should be consistent in the same sentence. Need and do get are present tense. The verb will begin is future tense and should be changed to present tense begin, so options (1) and (4) are incorrect. Option (3) is incorrect because the possessive pronoun your is needed, not the contraction you're.

10. **(3) job, such as pushing a lawn mower** (Usage/Verb tense—verb forms) Only option (3) correctly joins the dependent clause to the independent clause. The verb doing in sentence 6 is present tense; the verb pushed in sentence 7 is past tense. The two verbs should be parallel in form—doing and pushing. Options (1), (2), (4), and (5) are incorrect because the verb push, though present tense, is not parallel to the verb doing.

11. **(2) daydreaming while you are** (Sentence structure/Fragment and improper subordination) Sentence 9 is a fragment, so option (1) is incorrect. The sentences should be joined to clarify the relationship between the two thoughts. Because sentence 9 becomes a dependent clause, semicolons should not be used to connect it to the independent clause. Therefore, options (3) and (5) are incorrect. Option (4) is incorrect because the possessive pronoun your cannot replace you are.

12. **(3) change when you drive a car to driving a car** (Sentence structure/Parallelism) This sentence contains a listing in which all items should be parallel. To create parallel structure, the verb in the third item of the list should also end in -ing. None of the other options results in a parallel structure.

13. **(3) Yes, anyone** (Mechanics/Punctuation—commas after introductory elements and capitalization) The word Yes is an introductory element that is not part of the main idea. It should be followed by a comma, not a semicolon as in option (5). There is no reason to capitalize anyone, as in options (2) and (4).

14. **(3) and tightening the screws in the door** (Sentence structure/Parallelism) This sentence contains three items in series. The verbs in the first two items end in -ing, so the

Simulated Test

last item should begin with tightening for parallel structure. None of the other options results in a series with parallel structure.

15. **(3) add a comma after Tricks** (Mechanics/Punctuation—appositives) The title of the reference guide is an appositive that explains which reference guide. Nonrestrictive appositives should be set off by commas. Removing the comma in option (1) would be incorrect because the appositive is not restrictive. There is no reason for the changes in options (2) and (4).

16. **(2) change is to are** (Usage/Subject-verb agreement) Preparations is plural, so the verb are is correct, as in option (2). Option (1) is incorrect because a comma is not necessary. Options (3) and (4) incorrectly change the verb to past tense.

17. **(2) messy, you will** (Sentence structure/Improper coordination and subordination) In the rewritten sentence, the word because, a subordinate conjunction, is used to connect ideas of unequal rank. When the subordinate idea comes first in the sentence, it must be followed by a comma. Semicolons are not used to join clauses of unequal rank, so options (1) and (3) are wrong. Option (4) creates a run-on. In option (5), a comma after you incorrectly separates a subject and verb.

18. **(1) change There is to There are** (Usage/Subject-verb agreement—expletive) The expletive there is not the subject of the sentence; paints is the subject. Therefore, the plural verb are is required. In options (2), (3), and (4), there is no reason to capitalize oil-base, latex, or paints.

19. **(3) remove the comma after and** (Mechanics/Punctuation—overuse of commas) The comma after and separates the two parts of a compound subject. This is an inverted sentence, in which the verb comes before the subject. There is no reason for the changes in options (1), (2), and (4).

20. **(3) one is born a handy person; the** (Sentence structure/Comma splice and run-on sentence; Usage/Verb tense) Two independent clauses must be joined either with a coordinating conjunction and a comma or with a semicolon. Therefore, options (1), (2), and (5) are incorrect. The paragraphs are written in present tense. For consistency, the past-tense was born should be changed to present-tense is born, so option (4) is incorrect.

21. **(3) disease; it** (Sentence structure/Comma splice; Mechanics/Punctuation—semicolons) Option (3) is correct because two complete ideas need to be joined either with a semicolon alone or with a comma and a coordinating conjunction. Option (1) is a comma splice. Options (2), (4), and (5) all incorrectly join the two independent clauses.

22. **(3) replace some people get emotional with emotion** (Sentence structure/Parallelism) Option (3) is correct because three items in a series should all be of parallel structure. The first two items, hysteria and ignorance, are nouns. The last item should be changed to a noun, emotion. Option (5) is incorrect because the last item is not a noun. Option (1) is incorrect because the verb must be singular to agree with the singular subject a lot. In option (2), ignorance is spelled correctly. In option (4), the noun ignorance is parallel to the other nouns in the series; ignorant is an adjective.

23. **(1) and** (Sentence structure/Improper coordination and subordination) Option (1) is correct because the connecting word and shows the relationship between the two complete ideas. Options (2), (3), (4), and (5) are incorrect because they change the relationship between the two ideas expressed in the original sentence.

24. **(1) change We to You** (Usage/Pronoun reference—pronoun shift) Option (1) is correct because the rest of the paragraph uses the pronoun you. For consistency, this sentence should use the same pronoun. Options (2) and (3) are incorrect because the rest of the paragraphs uses you. Option (4) is incorrect because get is the correct present-tense verb.

25. **(2) infected; you** (Mechanics/Punctuation; Sentence structure/Improper coordination and subordination) Option (2) is correct because two sentences can be joined either with a semicolon alone or with a comma and a coordinating conjunction. In option (1), the sentences are incorrectly joined by a semicolon and and. Option (3) creates a run-on sentence. Option (4) is incorrect because it uses a comma without a coordinating conjunction. Option (5) is wrong because there is no cause-and-effect relationship between the two sentences, as suggested by because.

26. **(4) your** (Mechanics/Possessives and contractions) Option (4) is correct because the possessive pronoun your is needed in this sentence. Option (1) is incorrect because the

word you're is a contraction meaning "you are." Option (2) is incorrect because the possessive pronoun your does not require an apostrophe. Their and my, in options (3) and (5), are pronouns that are inconsistent with those used in the rest of the paragraph.

27. **(5) no correction is necessary** (Mechanics/ Punctuation and spelling) In option (1), removing the comma after mask would be incorrect; a comma is needed to separate items in series. The adverbial clause when giving medical attention to . . . does not need a comma or a semicolon because it's second in the sentence, so options (2) and (3) are incorrect. Option (4) is incorrect because needles is spelled correctly.

28. **(3) change it's to its** (Mechanics/ Contractions) Option (3) is correct because the possessive pronoun its is needed, rather than it's, the contraction of it is. In option (1), symptoms is spelled correctly. In option (2), removing the comma after AIDS would create a run-on sentence. A comma is needed to separate the two clauses. Option (4) is incorrect because there is spelled correctly.

29. **(1) when** (Sentence structure/Improper coordination and subordination) Option (1) is correct because the word when shows the relationship between the two sentences. Options (2), (3), (4), and (5) do not properly use a subordinate conjunction to connect the dependent clause and the independent clause.

30. **(4) Hundreds** (Sentence structure/Clarity) The sentence is wordy. Eliminating the words virtually and countless makes the sentence concise; therefore, option (4) is correct. Options (1), (2), (3), and (5) do not eliminate the wordiness.

31. **(3) change they to the people** (Usage/ Pronoun reference—ambiguous reference) It is not clear whether they refers to countries or to people. Option (3) is correct because using the people eliminates the ambiguous reference. Options (1) and (2) do not clarify the pronoun reference. Option (4) is incorrect because succeed is spelled correctly.

32. **(3) change your shoulder to our shoulders** (Usage/Pronoun reference— pronoun shift) Because the first pronoun in the sentence is we, for consistency the second pronoun should be our, rather than your; therefore, option (3) is correct. There is no reason for the change in option (1). Options (2) and (4) shift to other incorrect pronouns.

33. **(5) change had gave to gave** (Usage/Verb tense—verb form) Option (5) is correct because the past-tense gave does not need a helping verb. There is no reason for the changes in options (1), (2), (3), and (4).

34. **(3) cooperation and understanding** (Mechanics/Punctuation—overuse of commas) Option (3) is correct because the conjunction and joins two nouns that are objects of the preposition of. There is no reason to use a comma or a semicolon as in the other options.

35. **(2) the free world** (Sentence structure/ Improper coordination and subordination) Option (2) is correct because this is a complex sentence and no conjunction is needed. The clauses are improperly coordinated in options (1) and (5); the ideas being joined are not of equal rank, so no coordinating conjunction is needed. Options (3) and (4) are incorrect because they result in two dependent clauses.

36. **(5) today than in** (Sentence structure/ Clarity) Than is used to compare today with the past; then is used in reference to time, so options (1) and (4) are wrong. A comma is not needed, as in option (2), because the dependent clause is restrictive. Option (3) eliminates the comparison that is meant.

37. **(1) change There is to There are** (Usage/ Subject-verb agreement) The subject of the sentence is people, which is plural, so the plural verb are is needed. There is no reason for the changes in options (2), (3), and (4).

38. **(4) However, we** (Mechanics/Capitalization and punctuation; Sentence structure/Clarity) The phrase on account of this simply makes the sentence wordy and should be eliminated. Therefore, options (1) and (2) are wrong. A comma is needed after the introductory element however, so option (3) is incorrect. There is no reason to capitalize we, as in option (5).

39. **(2) change nation, is to nation, are** (Usage/Subject-verb agreement; Mechanics/ Punctuation) The subject we is plural and requires the plural verb are. Option (1) is incorrect because the word nation is part of the phrase as a nation, which should be set off by commas. There is no reason for the changes in options (3) and (4).

40. **(3) remove the phrase back in the beginning** (Sentence structure/Clarity) Option (3) is correct because the phrase back in the beginning is unnecessary. The sentence is clearer and more concise without it, since

originally means the same. Options (1), (2), and (4) do not make the sentence clearer.

41. **(2) change social security act to Social Security Act** (Mechanics/Capitalization) Option (2) is correct because Social Security Act is the name of a particular law and should be capitalized. Option (1) is incorrect because the word act also needs to be capitalized. There is no reason for the changes in options (3) and (4).

42. **(2) those who have disabilities** (Usage/Pronoun reference—wrong relative pronoun) Option (2) is correct because who is the subject of the verb have and is correct; whom, as in options (1) and (4), is objective case and cannot be the subject. Option (3) is incorrect because the relative pronoun which does not refer to people. Option (5) is incorrect because the last item in the series must name a category of people.

43. **(3) years, and the** (Mechanics/Punctuation—commas between independent clauses) Option (3) is correct because sentences joined by a coordinating conjunction need a comma before the conjunction, not a semicolon as in options (1), (2), and (4). Option (4) is incorrect because the coordinating conjunction and should not be followed by a comma. Option (5) is incorrect because no possession is shown.

44. **(2) health care, the number** (Sentence structure/Fragment; Mechanics/Punctuation—commas after introductory elements and capitalization) Option (2) is correct because a parenthetical dependent clause should be set off with commas. Sentence 5 is a fragment. Option (3) is incorrect because a dependent clause should not be separated from an independent clause by a semicolon. Option (4) is incorrect because using while creates two fragments (two dependent clauses) with no independent clause to make a complete sentence. Option (5) is incorrect because there is no reason to capitalize health care.

45. **(3) change which to who** (Usage/Pronoun reference—wrong relative pronoun) Option (3) is correct because the relative pronoun which does not refer to people; who or whom refers to people. Who is the subject of the verb were working. Option (4) is incorrect because whom is objective case and cannot be used as the subject of a verb. There is no reason for the changes in options (1) and (2).

46. **(5) move temporarily between the words using and to** (Sentence structure/Modification) Option (5) is correct because the

adverb temporarily should be moved as close as possible to the verb it modifies, to fund. There is no reason for the changes in options (1), (2), (3), and (4).

47. **(2) youth if we want** (Mechanics/Punctuation—overuse of commas) Option (2) is correct because the dependent clause is essential to the meaning of the sentence; it should not be set off by a comma. Options (1), (3), (4), and (5) are incorrect because the commas and semicolons are used incorrectly.

48. **(1) change academy to Academy** (Mechanics/Capitalization) Option (1) is correct because Academy is part of the name of an organization and should be capitalized. There is no reason for the changes in options (2), (3), and (4).

49. **(3) An Oscar is a gold-plated** (Sentence structure/Clarity) The combination in option (3) is the most concise and clear version. Options (1), (2), and (5) are wordy and incorrectly use the comparison word like. Option (4) is incorrect because the pronoun it has no antecedent.

50. **(4) change Spring to spring** (Mechanics/Capitalization) Option (4) is correct because the names of seasons should not be capitalized. There is no reason for the changes in options (1), (2), and (3).

51. **(3) actress, and the Oscars are** (Usage/Pronoun reference—ambiguous reference and subject-verb agreement; Mechanics/Punctuation—comma between independent clauses) Option (3) is correct because it eliminates the ambiguous reference of the pronoun they. In the original sentence it is not clear whether they refers to the Oscars or to every actor and actress. Options (2) and (5) are incorrect because a semicolon is not used with the conjunction and. Option (4) is incorrect because the plural subject they requires the plural verb are.

52. **(5) no correction is necessary** (Mechanics/Punctuation—appositives) Option (5) is correct because the phrase a device that reads the prices on groceries at the checkout and records them is an appositive that further explains what a scanner is; an appositive should be set off with commas, as in the original sentence. Options (1) and (3) are incorrect because they remove these commas. There is no reason for the change in option (2). Option (4) is incorrect because an appositive is not set off with a semicolon.

53. **(4) these devices is** (Usage/Subject-verb agreement with interrupting phrase and verb tense) Because the subject of the sentence, name, is singular, the singular verb is is correct; therefore, option (4) is correct and options (1) and (2) are incorrect. The rest of the paragraph is written in present tense, so the present-tense verb is is correct. Changing the verb tense, as in options (3) and (5), is incorrect.

54. **(4) replace who with that** (Usage/Pronoun reference—wrong relative pronoun) Option (4) is correct because the relative pronoun in the sentence refers to a computer voice. The relative pronoun who refers to people; that refers to things. There is no reason for the changes in options (1), (2), and (3).

55. **(4) move on the package after spacing** (Sentence structure/Misplaced modifier) Option (4) is correct because it clarifies the meaning of the sentence. The original sentence does not make clear whether the package or the lines have different widths and spacing. There is no reason for the changes in options (1), (2), and (3).

Writing Skills Part II, The Essay (page 663)

Evaluating and scoring your essay can be done by you or by someone else. If you are taking a class, have your teacher evaluate your essay. If you are working independently, ask a friend or relative to read your essay. If this is not possible, evaluate your writing yourself. After finishing an essay, put it aside for a day. Then read it as objectively as possible. No matter who checks your writing, make sure that person follows the Scoring Guide on page 181 and uses the chart on page 187 as scoring evaluation guides.

Write the date on your completed essays and keep them together in a folder or notebook. This way, you will be able to keep track of your progress, note your strengths, and figure out areas in which you want to improve.

Social Studies (page 665)

1. **(1) marching in a pro-choice rally** (Application) The First Amendment guarantees people the right to assemble, or gather, peaceably. As long as a march or demonstration is not violent, it is protected. Options (2), (3), (4), and (5) are not issues dealt with by the First Amendment.

2. **(4) the rights of individual citizens** (Evaluation) This amendment guarantees people the freedom to worship as they choose, to speak and publish freely, and to assemble

and petition, or request, that the government hear their complaints. This is a statement of the rights of individual citizens. Options (1), (2), (3), and (5) are covered in other parts of the Constitution.

3. **(3) punishment** (Evaluation) If Americans valued either mercy or human life most highly, options (1) and (2), they would not execute people. There is no evidence in the paragraph to support option (4). Since the paragraph states that innocent people are executed, option (5) is incorrect. This leaves punishment, option (3), as the most valued.

4. **(1) an improvement in Kennedy's ability to lead a group** (Analysis) Kennedy's expressed enthusiasm for the invasion of Cuba silenced dissent in the first group. In contrast, with the second group he asked for differing opinions and potential problems. This demonstrates Kennedy's improved leadership abilities. Option (2) is incorrect because both groups belonged to the same administration. Option (3) is not supported by the information. Option (4) is not related to foreign policy. Option (5) is incorrect because these group meetings took place without increased public input.

5. **(3) the western coast of the United States** (Application) The map shows that the western coast of the United States has a higher concentration of earthquakes and volcanoes than northern Africa, option (1); eastern South America, option (2); northern Europe, option (4); or Australia, option (5).

6. **(5) Compared to dry land, the ocean floor is thin and easily pierced by the underlying hot molten rock.** (Evaluation) The map shows far more volcanoes and earthquakes occurring in oceans than on land, giving support to option (5). The map suggests nothing about "unnoticed" earthquakes, ruling out option (1). It gives no information about predicting volcanoes, so option (2) is incorrect. One cannot tell from the map how many active volcanoes there are, ruling out option (3). Nor can one tell anything about volcanic soils from the map, ruling out option (4).

7. **(1) A large earthquake will occur along the West Coast of the United States.** (Analysis) This is an area of many earthquakes and volcanoes, according to the map, so it seems possible that an earthquake will occur in that area, but we cannot be certain. Therefore, this is an opinion. It is a fact that the map shows earthquake and volcano concentrations in the Pacific Ocean, option (2), and in Central

America, option (3). It is also a fact that the map shows few earthquakes and volcanoes around the Great Lakes, option (4), and shows more earthquakes and volcanoes in the oceans than on land, option (5).

8. **(5) protection of innocent people** (Evaluation) This shows a sense of right and wrong. Many Americans could not believe that American soldiers would harm innocent people. While Americans may believe in the values named in options (1), (2), (3), and (4), these values are not mentioned in the paragraph and are irrelevant to this item.

9. **(4) tell the people that government was working for them** (Comprehension) The last sentence of the paragraph says that the fireside chats "were designed to keep the public informed and to reassure them that government was acting in their interests." The chats probably did help persuade people to support legislation, option (1), but this was not their main, or their stated, purpose. Roosevelt won the 1932 presidential election, so option (2) is incorrect. Nothing in the paragraph hints that the fireside chats were used for options (3) or (5).

10. **(4) Roosevelt's confident, personal style was almost as important as his programs** (Analysis) It is the writer's opinion that Roosevelt's personality was as important as his legislation. There is no way to prove such a statement. Options (1), (2), (3), and (5) are facts that can be proven.

11. **(1) anti-Communist sentiment among Americans** (Comprehension) President Eisenhower decided to overthrow Castro when he became convinced that Castro was allied with the Soviets. In other words, Eisenhower decided that Castro was a Communist. Anti-communism has been a major attitude in American foreign policy since 1945. Nothing in the paragraph suggests there was anti-Cuban feeling, option (2), or pressure from Cuban exiles, option (3). Nor does the paragraph say that Kennedy feared a Cuban invasion of the United States, option (4). Eisenhower was not allied with the Soviet Union, ruling out option (5).

12. **(2) make sure the governor does not have too much power** (Comprehension) If the governor can appoint officials to key positions, he or she may be tempted to choose people who will support his or her policies. Nothing in the information presented addresses options (1), (3), and (5). Option (4) may be true, but it would result from an abuse of power mentioned in option (2).

13. **(4) look for the comptroller's signature** (Analysis) The comptroller is the only person who can authorize withdrawals from the state treasury. Therefore, option (2) cannot be the first course of action. The officials in options (1), (3), and (5) are not involved in this financial transaction.

14. **(4) comptroller** (Evaluation) Option (4) is the only office in which accounting skills and knowledge of the legal system are needed. Options (1) and (3) do not list these as part of their functions. Option (2) suggests that knowledge of the law is needed, but it does not mention anything about accounting. Option (5) suggests that accounting skills are needed, but it does not mention anything about law.

15. **(1) Government should be by consent of the people.** (Analysis) Whether or not the people would elect their representatives was never an issue throughout the delegates' discussions. The disagreement was only about how many should be elected from each state. There is no information in the article that supports options (2), (3), (4), and (5).

16. **(2) fewer representatives** (Application) States elect representatives to the House of Representatives in proportion to their population. If a state loses population, it elects fewer representatives, ruling out option (4). Options (1) and (5) are incorrect because they involve senators, and the article says that each state would elect two senators, regardless of its size. Option (3) can be ruled out because it describes state, not federal, government.

17. **(2) the census, a regular count of the population** (Application) To insure that the population is accurately represented, the delegates established the government census, a count of the people every ten years. Options (1), (3), (4), and (5) are not related to the system of states' representation.

18. **(4) increase import tariffs** (Application) The government wants to protect American business, so the government will make it more difficult—that is, more expensive—to buy Hong Kong radios. Options (1), (2), and (3) would not affect the cost of goods coming into the United States. Option (5) is not an action that the government would take.

19. **(2) buy radios made in the U.S.** (Application) If more American radios were purchased, the problem faced by the businessmen pictured would not exist. Consumers would probably "buy American" if the prices were competitive

with foreign merchandise. Option (1) is too general. Option (3) is the opposite of a reasonable solution. Options (4) and (5) are avoiding the problem rather than solving it.

20. **(4) The lemming and vole population cycles affect other animals and people.** (Analysis) Options (1), (2), (3), and (5) are details that support the main idea of the paragraph.

21. **(1) live by trapping** (Comprehension) The article explains that when there are many lemmings and voles, foxes have plenty to eat and so raise more young. You can infer that Eskimos can then trap more foxes for their fur. Options (2) and (4) describe actions that Eskimos probably take when the lemming and vole populations are low. Option (3) is incorrect because the article states that the caribou move away when the lemming and vole populations are high. Option (5) is unlikely because the first sentence says that this situation exists in both the Arctic and the subarctic.

22. **(3) ecosystem—an ecological community, the relationship of living things to each other and their environment** (Application) The paragraph describes how several animals affect each other, their environment, and the people who live there. The article does not deal with people in cities or with farming, ruling out options (1) and (2). It does not show people getting used to a new environment or adapting plants and animals to their use, ruling out options (4) and (5).

23. **(5) labor and management agreed to maintain the image of round-the-clock negotiations** (Comprehension) When asked a main idea question, try to bring all the information together. In this cartoon, labor, management, and the press are all involved. Options (1) and (4) are concerned with details, not with the main idea. Options (2) and (3) are not suggested in the cartoon.

24. **(1) Because third parties get so few votes, the United States remains a two-party system.** (Comprehension) Only option (1) summarizes the information. Option (2) is only one detail from the article. Options (3), (4), and (5) are untrue, according to the information.

25. **(4) voters possibly hesitate to vote for someone they think cannot win** (Analysis) This is offered as a possible explanation; it is the writer's opinion. Option (1) was the opinion of John Quincy Adams. Options (2), (3), and (5) are facts; they could be checked independently.

26. **(3) the United States is populated largely by immigrants and their descendants** (Comprehension) The fact that more than 12 million immigrants passed through Ellis Island in a 50-year period strongly suggests that the United States has a large immigrant population. The information will not support options (1), (2), (4), and (5).

27. **(2) gives people the right to bear arms** (Comprehension) The right to bear arms is granted by the 2nd Amendment, and it is the basis of the anti-gun-control lobbyists' arguments. Options (1), (3), (4), and (5) are incorrect because they do not relate directly to guns.

28. **(2) Government controls the price of water and electricity.** (Analysis) In paragraph three the author explains that under socialism, government owns more businesses and makes the economic decisions. Option (2), then, is a more likely effect of socialism. Options (1), (3), (4), and (5) would be effects of capitalism as explained in paragraph one.

29. **(4) Government planners ask the nation's farmers to produce 10 percent more wheat this year.** (Application) Options (1), (2), (3), and (5) show private persons or groups owning businesses, responding to consumers and to prices, and seeking profits. These are characteristics of capitalism. A government directive to producers, option (4), is more characteristic of a socialist economy.

30. **(5) Many modern economies have both capitalist and socialist elements.** (Comprehension) The article says that private persons own "most" businesses under capitalism, and that government owns "more" businesses under socialism. Ownership and control are not total in either case. The article's last sentence also points out that socialist economies differ greatly from each other in amounts of government ownership and control. This supports option (5), ruling out options (1), (2), (3), and (4).

31. **(2) public safety** (Evaluation) In this situation, individuals are giving up whatever right they may have to travel freely in order to guard the public as a whole against drunk drivers, ruling out option (1). Police control, option (3), is not the issue, since it appears that the public supports their actions. Options (4) and (5) are not issues in this situation.

32. **(2) The population is increasing.** (Comprehension) The numbers in the table

show that the population was larger every time the census was taken; thus option (2) is correct. There is no evidence for Options (1) and (3). Options (4) and (5) are not true.

33. **(2) the census figures for 2000** (Application) The new census numbers would update the table. Options (1), (3), (4), and (5) are incorrect because numbers from past years would not change.

34. **(5) Married women are economically dependent on their husbands.** (Analysis) Lenders treated women as if they had no money of their own. If lenders had assumed option (1) or (2), they would have most likely given women credit. Options (3) and (4) do not explain why married women would be denied credit.

35. **(3) economic fairness** (Evaluation) The law says that it is unfair to deny a person credit based on sex or marital status. This rules out options (1) and (2). Options (4) and (5) are not related to the question of marital status.

36. **(4) Slavery existed in the border states between the Confederacy and the Union, but these states remained loyal to the Union.** (Evaluation) This is direct evidence that there were considerations other than slavery in a state's decision to support the Union or the Confederacy. Options (1), (2), (3), and (5) may or may not be true, but they do not support the fact that slavery was not the only issue of the Civil War.

37. **(5) The border states probably remained in the Union because most of their populations believed slavery was wrong.** (Analysis) This is an opinion that cannot be proved by reference to the map. Options (1), (2), (3), and (4) are facts based on the map.

38. **(3) mandatory jail terms for convicted drug dealers** (Application) The President said we must be tough on drug criminals. "Sometimes," he said, "that means tougher penalties." This supports option (3). Being "tougher" would rule out options (1), (4), and (5). He said nothing about treatment for drug addicts, ruling out option (2).

39. **(2) Drugs contribute to crime.** (Analysis) The President seemed to assume that there was a relationship between drugs and crime stating that the country will not have safe streets and neighborhoods until we are "tougher on drug criminals." Option (1) is incorrect because the quotation discussed only drug criminals and does not indicate that all

criminals take drugs. Option (3) is incorrect because according to the President, the opposite was true. Options (4) and (5) are not issues discussed in the quotation.

40. **(1) to correct the financial problems the old company had** (Analysis) The former managers or products were probably the reason for the old company's financial problems. Options (2) and (4) would not make sense. Options (3) and (5) have no support.

41. **(2) letting some employees go** (Analysis) When two companies combine operations, they need fewer employees. Option (1) is the opposite of what is likely to happen. Options (3), (4), and (5) are not likely results of a merger.

42. **(2) network of relatives and nonrelatives** (Comprehension) Large families linked by blood and other ties are a source of support for low-income families. Options (1) and (4) are characteristic of middle-income families. Option (3) refers to wealthy people's connections beyond the family; it is not a form of family. Option (5) is not mentioned in the paragraphs.

43. **(4) economic** (Evaluation) This is an economic analysis of why family forms differ in the various income brackets. The other values may also relate to the family, but they are not the values stressed by this writer.

44. **(1) cultural diversity in food, education, the media, and other aspects of life** (Application) Coming from all parts of the world, immigrants to the United States bring elements of their own cultures with them. Options (2) and (5) are incorrect because the charts give no information about where in the United States immigrants settle. Option (3) is incorrect because the pie chart shows a greater percentage of Asian immigrants. Option (4) is the opposite of what you would expect, given the diversity of the immigrant population.

45. **(2) Latin Americans make up the largest group of immigrants in the United States today.** (Evaluation) This is supported by the fact that Latin Americans made up 42.5 percent of all immigrants in 1990, the largest single group. Option (1) is contradicted by the two charts. Options (3) and (5) are incorrect because the charts give no information about immigrant life in this country. Option (4) is incorrect because the charts give percentages, not actual numbers, and give information by region, not by country.

46. **(3) African Americans as a group have a high percentage of smokers** (Comprehension) Dr. Sullivan described African Americans as "a group already bearing more than its share of smoking-related illness" and death. This suggests that a high percentage of African Americans smoke. The information does not support options (1), (2), (4), or (5).

47. **(4) Pedro has worked as a carpenter for three years and has his own tools and car.** (Application) He has one year less experience than is required, but Pedro meets more of the job requirements (experience, tools, car) than the applicants in options (1), (2), (3), and (5).

48. **(3) January 1995** (Application) During that month, you would have gotten about 102 yen per dollar, the highest exchange rate of the period shown. The other options are incorrect because the exchange rate was lower during these months.

49. **(4) The dollar's value against the yen fell steadily in February and March 1995.** (Evaluation) This is shown by the steady downward slant of the line during this period. Option (1) is incorrect because the lowest point shown is March 1995. Option (2) is incorrect because the value decreased, not increased. Option (3) is true, but it is not supported by the information, which covers only a recent six-month period. Option (5) is the opposite of what will happen if the trend continues.

50. **(2) constantly being reformed** (Comprehension) Earth's plates are said to be "moving" and "colliding" to form mountain chains. This suggests that Earth's surface is being constantly changed, supporting option (2) and ruling out option (1). Option (4) is not mentioned. The paragraph does not say how much of Earth is ocean, so option (3) is incorrect. Nor does the paragraph mention erosion, ruling out option (5).

51. **(1) redesigning and rebuilding a dangerous intersection of a U.S. highway** (Application) The letters U.S. suggest that this is part of the federal highway system, so the federal government would be responsible for it. Also, the size and complexity of such a job suggest that a larger unit of government, at least as large as the state, would probably handle it. Option (2) could be handled by the municipality. Option (4) would be handled by the county. Options (3) and (5) appear to be special district matters.

52. **(4) A person is jailed for a year before being brought to trial.** (Application) The 6th Amendment insures an accused person "a speedy trial." This appears to prohibit the situation described in option (4). Option (1) is ruled out because the 6th Amendment concerns what happens after a person is accused of a crime. The 6th Amendment does not deal with the issues in options (2), (3), and (5).

53. **(1) protection of accused people** (Evaluation) The 6th Amendment outlines those things that must be done to protect people accused of crimes. The amendment naturally protects the rights of minorities, option (3), when they are accused of crimes, but this is not the best answer. The 6th Amendment does not address the issues in options (2), (4), and (5).

54. **(3) human life** (Evaluation) The high fines of clearly valuable animals supports this conclusion. There is no evidence of attitudes toward options (1) and (2). Option (4) is incorrect because money plays no part in the transactions. Option (5) is incorrect because there is mention of raiding.

55. **(1) urban homesteaders who become owners of abandoned buildings that they fix up** (Application) In modern homesteading programs, people who fix up empty houses or apartments and live in them become owners. Option (2) is incorrect because it does not involve owning property. Option (3) is incorrect because nomads own only the possessions they take from place to place, not the places themselves. Options (4) and (5) involve traditional ways of acquiring property.

56. **(2) eventually they would own the land they claimed** (Analysis) That assumption was powerful motivation for people to move west. Options (1) and (5) are not likely because people had a good idea of the geography of the West and where land was available. Options (3) and (4) are not supported by the information.

57. **(1) Snow delays flights at Minneapolis airports.** (Analysis) The map shows snow in Minneapolis, making snow and flight delays possible. Options (2), (3), (4), and (5) are not supported by information in the map.

58. **(3) Partly cloudy skies and highs in the 70s are expected in Dallas today.** (Analysis) This statement is a fact based on a correct reading of the map's symbols. Only Dallas displays the symbols for partly cloudy

skies combined with a high temperature in the 70s. Options (1), (2), (4), and (5) are not based on the information in the map.

59. **(5) The mechanical reaper left thousands of farm workers without jobs.** (Evaluation) This is stated in the last sentence. Options (1), (2), (3), and (4) do not describe effects of the Industrial Revolution.

60. **(3) power-driven machines** (Analysis) The third sentence in the paragraph states that production increased when people started making things by power-driven machines. Options (1) and (2) are identified as the older, slower methods of production. Options (4) and (5) are two effects—not causes—of increased production.

61. **(1) prevent the making and selling of liquor** (Comprehension) The first sentence of the paragraph states the purpose of Prohibition, which "outlawed the manufacture and sale of liquor." Option (2) is the opposite of what is stated in the paragraph. Options (3) and (4) are incorrect because the purpose of Prohibition was not to amend the Constitution. Option (5) is not supported by information in the paragraph.

62. **(4) an increase in urban crime** (Analysis) The paragraph says that many people in the cities disobeyed the law. This led to an increase in urban crime. The information in the paragraph gives no evidence to support that options (1), (2), and (5) resulted from, or were effects of, Prohibition. Option (3) refers to the action by Congress that made Prohibition law.

63. **(3) Andrew Jackson invaded Florida while looking for the Seminoles.** (Analysis) This event caused the diplomatic crisis with Spain. Options (1) and (2) led to Jackson's mission, which was the immediate cause. Option (4) was the position the United States took after the crisis. Option (5) was the result, not the cause.

64. **(1) the 1763 Peace of Paris, in which France gave up the Mississippi Valley and Canada** (Application) Both these events involved the giving up of North American land by a European power. None of the other options involves the giving up of land.

Science (page 683)

1. **(4) formation of volcanoes** (Analysis) The map shows a relationship between the boundaries of colliding plates and the locations of volcanoes. Options (1), (2), (3), and (5) are not shown to have any relationship to where plates collide.

2. **(5) western South America** (Application) The map shows a high number of earthquakes and volcanoes along the western coast of this continent. The other options have only a few earthquakes and volcanoes and would not be the best areas to study.

3. **(1) Elements can be broken down into simpler substances by methods other than chemical reactions.** (Analysis) In the definition of an element, the author states that an element "cannot be broken down into simpler substances by chemical reactions." By specifically mentioning "chemical," the author implies that there are other methods that can break down elements. In fact, nuclear reactions can break down atoms of an element into smaller atoms. Option (2) is incorrect because the information about iron and oxygen is given as an example of a compound. It does not indicate that iron and oxygen are the only elements that combine into compounds. Option (3) is incorrect because it is untrue and because the article does not discuss the states of matter. Option (4) is untrue. Option (5) is incorrect because nothing in the article indicates a greater interest on the part of the author in atoms, elements, or compounds.

4. **(3) Most substances expand when heated and contract when cooled.** (Evaluation) Option (1) is incorrect because a few substances such as water expand when cooled. Options (2) and (4) are incorrect because most substances do not contract when heated. Option (5) is incorrect because substances do change in volume when heated or cooled.

5. **(4) A and B only** (Evaluation) When telephone wires expand in the heat, they become longer and sag, Statement A. When glass is suddenly heated, the quick expansion in one portion causes it to break, Statement B. Therefore, options (1) and (2) are correct but incomplete. Statement C is not true; soup, made mostly of water, acts like water when frozen and expands. Therefore, options (3) and (5) are incorrect.

6. **(1) The molecules and atoms of gases are the farthest apart and the most mobile.** (Evaluation) It takes progressively more heat to change matter from solid to liquid to gas. Therefore, it follows that gases have atoms and molecules with the most kinetic energy, moving the fastest and farthest apart. Options (2) and (3) are thus incorrect. Option (4) is also

incorrect. If the molecules and atoms always acted in the same manner, the states of matter would not differ. Option (5) is not true; the molecules and atoms of a solid move slowly.

7. **(4) gold** (Analysis) Gold is the only metal listed with a density greater than that of liquid mercury. Therefore, it is the only one that will sink in liquid mercury. Options (1), (2), (3), and (5) have densities less than that of liquid mercury, and they will float in it.

8. **(1) 24K gold** (Application) Pure gold has a density of 19.3. This is greater than the densities of the mixtures of gold and copper represented by options (2), (3), and (4), because 24-karat gold has the highest ratio of gold to copper. Option (5) is incorrect because the different karats each contain a different proportion of gold to copper, making their densities different.

9. **(3) the gravitational pull of the moon** (Comprehension) The first paragraph states that the moon's pull is the primary cause of tides. The sun's gravitational pull, option (2), has some influence but not much compared to the moon. Options (1) and (4) do not affect tides. Option (5) contributes to the movement of high tide around the world, but it is not a cause of tides.

10. **(1) The sun's gravitational pull is added to that of the moon, which increases the height of the tides.** (Analysis) When the moon and sun are in a line on one side of Earth, their gravitational forces combine and exert more pull on the oceans, increasing the height of the tides. Option (2) is incorrect because if the moon's gravitational pull were weaker, the tides would be lower. Options (3) and (4) are incorrect because the position of the three bodies does not affect rainfall or ice melting on Earth. Option (5) is not true.

11. **(2) The Doppler effect can be used to determine whether a source of sound is moving away from or toward someone.** (Evaluation) The faster the source of sound moves toward the observer, the greater the frequency of sound waves detected by the observer. Option (1) is incorrect since the Doppler effect works with other types of waves such as light waves. Nothing in the article suggests that the effect applies only to sound waves. Option (3) is incorrect because the Doppler effect is shown to work with distant sounds. Option (4) is incorrect because the frequency at which sound waves are emitted by the source never changes. It is the frequency at which they are received by the observer that changes. Option (5) is incorrect

because nothing in the passage or diagram gives information about wave interference.

12. **(4) releasing laboratory-bred sterile males** (Comprehension) This method is described as being used in the Southwest. Option (1) is incorrect because nothing is mentioned about the current use of chemical insecticides. Option (2) is incorrect because it is too expensive. Options (3) and (5) are incorrect because they involve changing the insects in the wild, not in the laboratory.

13. **(2) Treating cattle individually with chemical insecticides was too expensive.** (Evaluation) It was necessary to find a less costly way to control the screwworm. Option (1) is incorrect because the article does not say that chemical insecticides were hard to obtain; they were just too expensive to use. The article does not support option (3). Option (4) is true but was not the reason stated for deciding to try biological control methods. Option (5) is not true. Biological control methods are generally developed by scientists in well-equipped research laboratories, not on farms.

14. **(5) A, B, and C** (Analysis) The author assumes that it is important to protect an agricultural area. Changing the ecology can help the cattle industry by getting rid of a pest (Statement A). The article does not mention disadvantages because the author assumes they are not very important (Statement B). The author criticizes chemical insecticides in the case of the screwworm mostly because of the cost. The author does not say that chemical insecticides are unsuitable in general (Statement C). Therefore, options (1), (2), (3), and (4) are incorrect since they do not include all the assumptions made by the author.

15. **(2) works best on isolated insect populations** (Evaluation) The sterile-male release method described was successful on the island of Curaçao, which is a small, isolated area. When it was used on the mainland, it was less successful. Option (1) is incorrect because it is difficult to apply the method over a wide area like the southwestern United States. Option (3) is incorrect because it is too general a statement to be supported by the article. In some places, chemical insecticides may work better. Option (4) is incorrect because the article holds that the method was successful. Option (5) is incorrect because the article shows that biological control can wipe out an entire population, thereby ending the problem.

16. **(3) decrease in several generations because many fertilized eggs would be seriously defective and would die** (Evaluation) Males would have sperm that could fertilize the eggs, but the fertilized eggs would be defective. This would lower the number of healthy insects born. Options (1) and (2) are incorrect; eggs would still be fertilized, but they would not develop properly. Option (4) is incorrect because some of the eggs would not produce healthy young; the population would decrease. Option (5) is incorrect because many of the fertilized eggs would be defective, and this would not increase the population.

17. **(2) spaying animals to prevent their reproduction** (Application) Spaying animals and sterilizing male insects reduce the number of offspring the species can produce. Option (1) is incorrect because insecticides directly kill the insects and their eggs. Options (3) and (4) are incorrect because they involve adding a new species, not more of the same species. Option (5) is incorrect because it involves directly killing the pest.

18. **(3) very good condition after one minute of heavy exercise** (Comprehension) The pulse rate of the person in average condition after one minute of moderate exercise is 98 beats per minute. The chart shows that option (1) is 107 beats, option (2) is 102 beats, option (3) is 96 beats, option (4) is 111 beats, and option (5) is 114 beats. Of these, 98 beats is faster than option (3), or 96 beats.

19. **(5) There is a greater difference in the pulse rate between moderate and heavy exercise than between light and moderate exercise.** (Evaluation) For all types of subjects, the jump in pulse rate between moderate and heavy exercise is greater than the jump between light and moderate exercise. Option (1) is incorrect because the chart does not show what happens after more than one minute of exercise. Options (2) and (3) may be true, but they are not supported by the information given. Option (4) is not true; the pulse rate increases from moderate to heavy exercise.

20. **(3) rectum** (Analysis) The diagram shows the digestive system ending at the rectum. Options (1) and (2) are incorrect because the liver and the pancreas are in the middle section of the digestive system. Option (4) empties into the rectum. Option (5) is in the middle part of the alimentary canal.

21. **(2) esophagus** (Application) The esophagus passes downward through the chest. When stomach acids irritate the esophagus, the discomfort is felt in the chest. The other organs listed in options (1), (3), (4), and (5) are not in the chest. Discomfort in any of these organs would not be felt in the chest.

22. **(4) running a car engine in a closed garage** (Application) Since carbon monoxide is part of the exhaust, a car engine should not be run in an enclosed area without proper ventilation. Options (1), (2), (3), and (5) are incorrect because they involve using potentially dangerous items in the proper way, which lessens the danger involved.

23. **(5) drowsiness** (Comprehension) According to the paragraph, drowsiness is the first symptom of carbon-monoxide poisoning. Options (1), (2), (3), and (4) are therefore incorrect.

24. **(2) Particles of solids are tightly packed and transmit disturbances quickly.** (Analysis) Gases, on the other hand, have particles that are farther apart. Sound takes longer to pass from particle to particle in a gas. Option (1) may or may not be true in a given situation. Option (3) is not true. Gases transmit disturbances relatively slowly. Option (4) is not true; gases have particles that transmit sound. Option (5) is not necessarily true.

25. **(1) seeing lightning before hearing thunder** (Application) Because light travels faster than sound, lightning is seen before thunder is heard during a thunderstorm. Option (2) is incorrect because the distances are so small that light and sound are perceived at the same time. Option (3) is incorrect because neon signs do not involve sound. Options (4) and (5) are incorrect because they do not compare the speed of light and sound. They involve either light or sound.

26. **(5) erosion by the river** (Analysis) As the river gets older, it erodes the sides of its channels and starts to loop from side to side. This process widens its valley. The other options are not related to landscape formation in a river valley.

27. **(2) Oxbow lakes are found near old rivers.** (Evaluation) Two oxbow lakes are shown in the diagram of the old river. They are created when a meander of the river is cut off from the main stream. Option (1) is incorrect because the diagram does not show how rivers drain. Option (3) is incorrect because no flooding is indicated in the diagrams. Option (4) is incorrect because the diagram of an old river shows a gently sloping

valley. Option (5) is incorrect because the diagram of the old river shows no waterfall.

28. **(1) duplication of hereditary material (Interphase)** (Analysis) The division of hereditary material into two sets of chromosomes ensures that each new cell has the same chromosomes as the parent cell. (See Interphase in the cell division diagram.) Options (2), (3), (4), and (5) are aspects of the cell-division process, but they are not the direct cause of each new cell receiving a complete set of chromosomes from the parent.

29. **(3) It enters the cytoplasm.** (Analysis) The nuclear material goes into the cytoplasm, the cell material outside the nucleus. This is shown in the prophase stage. Option (1) is incorrect because the cell membrane functions as a protective surface for the cell contents. Options (2) and (4) are cell structures with other functions. Option (5) is incorrect because the nuclear membrane disappears at this stage.

30. **(4) Cover the lines with material that blocks the electromagnetic fields.** (Evaluation) This solution would enable people to continue to use electricity, which is an important source of energy in our society, without moving wires, homes, or businesses. Options (1) and (2) are not practical, since transmission lines are needed where people are located. Option (3) is not a likely solution because it would involve a complete change in the way we live. Option (5) is not only impractical and expensive, but would generate electromagnetic fields anyway.

31. **(3) The load moves upward.** (Comprehension) A downward pull on the rope results in the upward movement of the load. Option (1) is incorrect because the load moves. Option (2) is incorrect because the load moves upward. Option (4) is incorrect because it is the turn of the wheel that helps move the rope. Option (5) is incorrect because the rope does move when you pull on it.

32. **(1) A single fixed pulley changes the direction in which force must be exerted.** (Evaluation) Without a fixed pulley, the effort in lifting a load would be upward. With a fixed pulley, the effort exerted is downward. The pulley changes the direction in which effort must be exerted. Option (2) is incorrect because the single fixed pulley does change the direction in which effort must be exerted. Option (3) is incorrect because it is easier to pull downward on something with your body

weight than it is to lift something. Options (4) and (5) are incorrect because the distance in which the rope is pulled is equal to the distance in which the load is lifted.

33. **(3) are formed by sediment or soil carried by rivers from mountains to the plain** (Analysis) The diagram shows the river emerging from the mountain range and dividing into many little channels. The slowdown of the river's flow causes it to deposit the sediment it carries. Option (1) is incorrect because nothing in the diagram indicates whether the formation is new or old. Option (2) is incorrect because the diagram indicates the presence of a river, not a glacier. Options (4) and (5) cannot be assumed from the information given.

34. **(4) spreads out and slows down** (Analysis) The diagram shows the river spreading out and dividing into channels. The action of the river suddenly flowing into a flat area from the mountains causes the flow to spread out and slow. None of the other options is supported by the picture. Option (1) is incorrect because the speed of the water slows when the river reaches a flat area. The temperature is not shown. Options (2) and (3) are incorrect because the river becomes wider, not narrower. Option (5) is incorrect because nothing in the picture indicates that the stream goes underground.

35. **(2) B only** (Analysis) The chemicals in the dry cell battery may have been used up. The chemical action in a dry cell battery continues even when the switch is off. Therefore, the batteries wear out even though the item has not been used for a while. Statement A is what happens when the circuit is completed in a flashlight with good batteries. It does not explain why this flashlight did not come on. Therefore, options (1) and (4) are incorrect. Statement C is a conclusion about the relative value of the two types of batteries. There is no information in the article supporting this statement. Therefore, options (3) and (5) are incorrect.

36. **(3) An outside electric current restored the chemicals in the battery so that they could produce current again.** (Application) Option (1) is incorrect because it explains why the battery stopped working but not why it resumed working. Option (2) is not true; chemical action continues at a reduced rate. Option (4) is not true; the CD is described as being portable. Option (5) may or may not be

true, but it does not explain why the CD player started working again.

37. **(4) The life of the battery is shorter when the flashlight is left on.** (Analysis) When the circuit is complete, a dry cell battery works at current-producing levels, and the chemicals run out faster. Option (1) is incorrect because batteries do not always produce the same amount of current. Option (2) is incorrect because the question does not mention recharging. Option (3) is incorrect because the chemical reaction is faster when the flashlight is on. Option (5) is incorrect because dry cell batteries continue their chemical reaction at a reduced rate when the circuit is broken.

38. **(4) a toy truck** (Application) Batteries are most suited for portable items that cannot be plugged into an outlet. Dry cells are used for smaller toys and machines. Options (1) and (5) are incorrect because they are not portable. Options (2) and (3) also cannot be plugged in while they are operating, so batteries are suitable for them. However, cars and motorized wheelchairs are larger machines that use storage batteries, which can be recharged.

39. **(3) The car's engine generates electricity that recharges the battery as the car runs.** (Analysis) Option (1) is incorrect because the battery is the source of enough current to start the car. Options (2), (4), and (5) are incorrect because car batteries do not need external recharging, so the car would not need to be jump-started.

40. **(4) Annelida** (Application) The earthworm belongs to the phylum Annelida, which consists of soft-bodied, segmented animals that are bilaterally symmetrical, or the same on both sides. Option (1) is incorrect because the earthworm does not have a notochord. Option (2) is incorrect because Mollusca are not segmented and the earthworm does not have a shell. Option (3) is incorrect because earthworms are not covered by an external skeleton. Option (5) is incorrect because Cnidarians are not segmented.

41. **(2) Mollusca** (Application) A clam has a soft body and a hard shell, which is characteristic of animals of the phylum Mollusca. Option (1) is incorrect because the clam does not have a notochord. Option (3) is incorrect because the clam does not have a jointed external skeleton. Option (4) is incorrect because a clam has a shell, which members of the phylum Annelida do not have. Option (5) is incorrect because clams are not symmetrical around a central point.

42. **(1) Chordata** (Application) The phylum Chordata is the only one that has animals with backbones as members. All the other options are phyla whose members are invertebrates, animals without backbones.

43. **(3) Arthropoda** (Application) The grasshopper, an insect, belongs to the phylum Arthropoda, along with other animals having external jointed skeletons. None of the other phyla contain animals with external jointed skeletons.

44. **(4) HIV** (Analysis) The virus HIV is the cause of AIDS. Options (1), (2), and (3) are not causes of AIDS but activities associated with the spread of the AIDS virus. Option (5) involves substances that are produced by the body to fight HIV.

45. **(1) exposure to HIV** (Analysis) HIV antibodies are produced only in response to infection by HIV. Option (2) is incorrect because most transfused blood does not contain HIV. Options (3), (4), and (5) are symptoms of the later stages of AIDS.

46. **(1) carbon 14** (Application) The chart indicates that carbon 14 is used to estimate the age of material that was once alive, such as a human bone. Options (2), (3), (4), and (5) all have medical uses.

47. **(4) Radioactive substances have many uses.** (Evaluation) Option (1) is incorrect because the chart does not give information about the value of radioactive substances. Option (2) is incorrect because uranium 235 is also used in nuclear reactors. Option (3) is incorrect because radioactive substances are used in atomic weapons. Option (5), although true, is incorrect because the chart does not give any information about the origin of radioactive substances.

48. **(3) There must be an equal number of atoms from each element on each side of the equation.** (Analysis) If you examine the equation and the illustration, you will see that before and after the reaction there are four hydrogen atoms, four oxygen atoms, and one carbon atom. They recombine to form different substances, but their number remains the same. Option (1) is incorrect because all reactions do not produce gases. Option (2) is disproved by the information; molecules are said to be made up of atoms. Options (4) and (5) are not supported by the equation given.

49. **(1) respiratory system** (Comprehension) The second paragraph states that respiratory infections are spread by the droplets released through sneezing and coughing. Options (2), (3), (4), and (5) are incorrect because they include areas not infected by airborne pathogens.

50. **(4) A and B** (Analysis) Washing your hands is effective against many respiratory and intestinal pathogens (Statements A and B) because they can be picked up by your hands from sneezes, coughs, or excretions. Options (1) and (2) are incorrect because they are incomplete. Pathogens in the blood (Statement C) generally are spread by insects or other animals that bite and draw blood, not by contaminated hands. Therefore, options (3) and (5) are incorrect.

51. **(1) blood** (Application) Since pathogens are transmitted by means related to where they reside in the host, a pathogen transmitted by an insect bite would affect the blood. The respiratory system, skeleton, digestive system, and brain mentioned in options (2), (3), (4), and (5) are not accessible to insect bites.

52. **(3) color blindness is related to whether a person is male or female** (Analysis) Color blindness is an inherited characteristic that is linked with sex. Option (1) is not true. Options (2) and (4) are untrue, and they are also unrelated to the distribution of color blindness between the sexes. Option (5) is true under most circumstances, but it is unrelated to the greater incidence of color blindness among men.

53. **(4) railroad engineer** (Application) Since railroad engineers must be able to distinguish red from green on railroad signals, a color-blind person would not be considered for such a position. Options (1), (2), (3), and (5) involve occupations in which the ability to distinguish red from green is not essential.

54. **(4) from spring to fall** (Comprehension) The article states that ladybugs stop hunting when it gets cold and prey is hard to find. Options (1), (2), and (3) are incorrect because the article implies that ladybugs hunt during the day. Option (5) is incorrect because ladybugs are not active during the winter.

55. **(4) there are varieties of ladybugs that feed on different types of insects** (Analysis) This assumption is made when the author explains that an Australian type of ladybug was imported to California to help control the cottony cushion scale. If the American ladybugs had hunted this type of scale insect, the

Australian variety would not have been necessary. Options (1), (2), and (5) are stated explicitly in the article; therefore, they are not unstated assumptions. Option (3) is not true.

56. **(3) Many ladybugs are beneficial to humans.** (Evaluation) The article states that many varieties of ladybugs feed on plant-eating insects. The ladybugs help control the destruction of plants that are valuable to humans. Option (1) is incorrect because the article states that many, not all, varieties of ladybugs hunt insects. Option (2) is incorrect because the article describes how the Australian ladybug lays its eggs near the hatchlings' source of food. Option (4) is incorrect because ladybugs take shelter during the winter and resume hunting the next spring. This implies that they survive more than one season and thus longer than two months. Option (5) is incorrect because the article gives no information about the mating habits of ladybugs.

57. **(1) frogs burying themselves in pond bottoms for the winter** (Application) Like ladybugs, frogs hibernate during the winter and become active again in the spring. Options (2), (3), (4), and (5) are other forms of adaptation to cold weather, but they differ from the ladybug's adaptation. Migration, option (2), does not occur; ladybugs take shelter where they are. Changes in color, option (3), protect animals that continue to be active during the snowy winter. Ladybugs do not shed anything during the winter, option (4). They do not grow more protection from the cold, option (5).

58. **(4) the effects of an earthquake on a particular place** (Comprehension) The Mercalli scale rates what an earthquake does. Options (1) and (2) are incorrect since the Mercalli scale measures the effects of an earthquake, not the amplitude of seismic waves. Option (3) is only partly correct. The Mercalli scale is used not only in the area over the focus, but in surrounding areas that feel the earthquake as well. Option (5) is incorrect because the Mercalli scale measures effects, not waves.

59. **(2) the amplitude of seismic waves at the focus of an earthquake** (Comprehension) The Richter scale measures the amplitude of seismic waves where the earthquake starts. Option (1) is incorrect because the focus of an earthquake is deep in Earth's crust, not on the surface. Option (3) is incorrect because the scale measures amplitude, not direction, of seismic waves. Option (4) is incorrect because

the scale does not measure the effects of an earthquake. Option (5) is incorrect because the scale measures intensity, not distance.

60. **(1) bacteria** (Comprehension) Bacteria start the decomposition process and are later replaced by other microorganisms. Options (2), (3), and (4) are microorganisms active in the later stages of composting. Option (5) is incorrect because each organism is active at a different time.

61. **(5) plastic wrap** (Analysis) Plastic wrap is the only material listed that is not living. Options (1), (2), (3), and (4) are all from living plants or animals and so are incorrect.

62. **(1) bacteria** (Analysis) The bacteria do most of the initial decomposition of the organic matter; their removal would, in effect, stop the composting process. Options (2), (3), (4), and (5) would have a lesser impact; therefore, option (1) is correct.

63. **(4) Water flows from high elevations, such as mountains, to sea level.** (Analysis) The map shows that the watershed areas are bounded by mountainous areas, which are higher than sea level. Water flows downward. Options (1) and (2) are true but do not tell why rivers flow in a certain direction. Options (3) and (5) are untrue.

64. **(2) They saw that the Columbia River was flowing to the west.** (Application) After they crossed the Rocky Mountains, explorers saw that water was flowing toward the west, not the southeast. This change suggested that water was flowing to a western ocean, the Pacific. Option (1) would not tell the explorers anything. Option (5) is not true. Options (3) and (4) would not tell the explorers about the location of the nearest ocean.

65. **(5) thermosphere** (Application) The thermosphere is the highest layer shown. It is closest to outer space, and spacecraft would operate very efficiently in its thin air. Options (1), (2), (3), and (4) are all closer to the surface of Earth, where increasing air density would create more friction for a spacecraft.

66. **(1) The ozone layer is part of both the stratosphere and the mesosphere.** (Comprehension) The diagram shows the ozone layer starting in the upper part of the stratosphere and extending partly into the mesosphere. Option (2) is incorrect because the ozone layer does not reach the thermosphere. Option (3) is incorrect because the troposphere extends to a height of 10 miles. Option (4) is incorrect because the thermosphere extends

beyond the mesosphere, which goes up to 50 miles. Option (5) is incorrect because the troposphere is close to Earth's surface, where animals live and breathe.

Literature & the Arts (page 704)

1. **(4) he began acting out a role** (Literal Comprehension) The changes noticeable in the older Hemingway were a consequence of a fame that was based increasingly on his image instead of his writing. Lines 30–35 support this. Options (1), (2), (3), and (5) are true but are not the cause of his behavior changes.

2. **(3) introduce a discussion of Hemingway's life and style of writing** (Analysis) The first paragraph shows his style of writing and describes an important event in his life. Options (1) and (4) are not mentioned in the excerpt. The first paragraph does not criticize Hemingway's behavior, option (2), or explain why he became a celebrity, option (5).

3. **(5) an international star** (Inferential Comprehension) Because Hemingway presented himself more as a celebrity than a writer (cause), people began to think of him as a star (effect). His literary skill, option (1), took second place. Options (2), (3), and (4) are factual but are not mentioned in the excerpt.

4. **(3) an early Hemingway story** (Application) The reviewer states a preference for Hemingway's early work in the third paragraph. Options (1), (2), (4), and (5) are about Hemingway's life, which the reviewer does not favor.

5. **(2) describe what became of Hemingway in his later years** (Analysis) The reviewer is giving an opinion of Hemingway later in his life, not of his literature, so options (1) and (4) are incorrect. Publicity is not being described, so option (3) is incorrect. Option (5) describes other people's opinion of Hemingway.

6. **(4) moving into a new apartment** (Inferential Comprehension) The speaker's references to the new telephone and the new neighbor indicate that she is moving into a new apartment. There is no support for options (1), (2), (3), and (5).

7. **(1) the upstairs apartment** (Analysis) This is indicated in line 7, when the speaker introduces her neighbor. There is no support for options (2) and (5). Option (3) describes the telephone installer's mother. Option (4) has no direct evidence in the poem.

8. **(3) is new to the apartment building** (Analysis) This point is suggested by the fact

that a new phone is being installed and a neighbor comes by to get acquainted. There is no support for options (1), (2), and (5). Option (4) is incorrect because no reference is made to the speaker's feelings about chocolate cake.

9. **(3) a friend who is a librarian** (Literal Comprehension) This is stated in lines 10–12. There is no support for options (1) and (4). Options (2) and (5) may be true, but they are not directly stated in the poem.

10. **(2) the installer's wife is exhausted** (Analysis) The installer is interested in the students who are helping the speaker because he would like to get some help with his parents. The line is an expression meaning that the installer's wife works hard, not that she moves rapidly, so options (1) and (4) are incorrect. There is no support for options (3) or (5).

11. **(3) the author's happy memories of returning west from school** (Inferential Comprehension) There is no evidence for options (1), (2), and (5) in the paragraph. Option (4) is simply a supporting detail.

12. **(5) It made people aware of their regional identity.** (Inferential Comprehension) There is no evidence for options (1) and (2) in the paragraph. Options (3) and (4) are supporting details.

13. **(5) Westerners are somehow unadaptable to life in the East.** (Inferential Comprehension) Options (1) and (4) are true but are secondary to the main point. There is no evidence for options (2) and (3) in the paragraph.

14. **(2) Everyone clutched red tickets.** (Literal Comprehension) The tickets were green (line 16). Options (1), (3), (4), and (5) are all supporting details.

15. **(1) somewhat ill at ease** (Application) The narrator describes West Egg as though it were a distorted painting or a nightmare, so he would probably feel ill at ease there. The narrator is remembering West Egg, so option (2) is incorrect. Options (3), (4), and (5) refer to the middle-west, not West Egg.

16. **(3) emphasizes the cold, impersonal nature of the East** (Analysis) In the narrator's dream, no one knows or cares about one another. Options (1), (2), (4), and (5) are not supported by the excerpt.

17. **(2) a serious look at the issues facing inner-city teens** (Inferential Comprehension) This point is made by the author's description

of the struggles of the film's two lead characters. There is no evidence for options (1) or (4). The author says this film is not sensational like some Hollywood films; therefore, option (3) is incorrect. Option (5) is incorrect because the author compares only the budgets and does not imply that the films should be compared in any other way.

18. **(1) indicate how the filmmakers got close to the two boys** (Analysis) The reviewer describes the relationship to indicate the closeness that developed between the filmmakers, the boys, and their families, therefore option (2) is incorrect. There is no support for option (3). Option (4) is suggested by one of the filmmakers, but is not implied by the reviewer. Option (5) is incorrect because the excerpt did not imply that this made the film easier to complete.

19. **(4) premiered at the New York Film Festival** (Literal Comprehension) The review says that the film premiered at the Sundance Film Festival. Options (1), (2), (3), and (5) are all things that the reviewer did say.

20. **(2) The reviewer was suggesting the obstacles that the filmmakers had to overcome.** (Analysis) In the first paragraph, the odds against the success of the film are stressed. The review does not suggest that the lack of stars, a big budget, or a script makes the movie bad, option (1), or good, option (4). It is not implied that other filmmakers should do the same thing, so option (3) is incorrect. Option (5) is incorrect because line 1 states that "not too many filmmakers" face these odds.

21. **(1) succeeds in exploring the lives of people living in urban areas** (Literal Comprehension) Lines 31–32 discuss the film's examination of "inner-city struggle and survival." There is no discussion of camera techniques, so option (2) is incorrect. Option (3) is incorrect because the reviewer states no opinions about the length of the film. There is no support for options (4) and (5).

22. **(2) are not usually commercially successful** (Inferential Comprehension) This point is made by the reviewer's suggestion that this is a "stigma" which must be overcome by the film (line 11); therefore, option (1) is incorrect. There is no evidence to support options (3) and (4). While the review does compare the movie to a soap opera, it does not imply that all documentaries are like soap operas, so option (5) is incorrect.

23. **(3) Mr. Brooks would allow her more freedom** (Inferential Comprehension) Mrs. Brooks is upset because her husband has forbidden her to buy a new dress. It can be inferred that if he were to allow her some freedom, she would be happier. There is no support for option (1). Option (2) is unlikely because Mrs. Brooks and Ruby are friends. Option (4) is incorrect because it is a literal interpretation. Option (5) is not true.

24. **(1) She is worried about Mrs. Brooks's future.** (Inferential Comprehension) The thrust of Ruby's dialogue is to slow Mrs. Brooks down, to caution her, so option (2) is incorrect. There is no evidence that Ruby likes or admires Mr. Brooks, so options (3) and (5) are incorrect. There is no direct evidence for option (4).

25. **(4) does not spend money readily** (Inferential Comprehension) The evidence in the excerpt indicates that Mr. Brooks is stingy. We do not know much else about him, so option (4) is the best answer. There is no support for options (1), (2), (3), and (5).

26. **(2) bad things can result even when someone means well** (Inferential Comprehension) The excerpt suggests that even though Mr. Brooks might mean well, his actions still result in Mrs. Brooks feeling hurt and mad. There is no support for options (1) and (5). Option (3) is incorrect because Ruby's comments suggest times when Mr. Brooks has been nice. Even though option (4) may sometimes be true, there is no evidence for it in the excerpt.

27. **(1) she has thought about leaving Mr. Brooks for a long time** (Inferential Comprehension) Mrs. Brooks refers to "the last straw," implying that this decision had been building up over time. There is no evidence for options (2), (3), (4), and (5).

28. **(3) wordy but lively** (Analysis) While wordy by today's standards, the style is full of life and feeling. It is not simple, option (1); dry, option (2); solemn, option (4); or flat, option (5).

29. **(3) a disagreeable and savage animal** (Literal Comprehension) Option (1) refers to Topper; option (2) is a separate character; option (4) lists things that Scrooge is *not*; and option (5) is something Fred gives.

30. **(3) Scrooge has made them laugh by being the object of a game.** (Literal Comprehension) Everyone has laughed at Scrooge, not because they are grateful, option (2), or because they like him, options (1) and

(5). There is no evidence that the partygoers think Scrooge is dead, option (4).

31. **(1) invisible** (Inferential Comprehension) The words "unconscious company" (line 57) and "inaudible" (line 58) imply that Scrooge is not visible to the others. There is no evidence for options (2), (3), (4), and (5).

32. **(2) Scrooge will be able to change his grumpy ways** (Inferential Comprehension) The last paragraph says that Scrooge became "gay and light of heart." From the rest of the excerpt, we know that Scrooge is usually grumpy and mean. Options (1), (3), and (4), which imply that Scrooge will never change, are incorrect. There is no support for option (5) in the excerpt.

33. **(5) letter** (Analysis) The speaker is directly addressing his son, so he probably wrote him a letter. A telegram, option (1), would be much shorter. A diary entry, option (4), is private. There is no evidence in the excerpt to support options (2) and (3).

34. **(2) The speaker's relationship with Jack is deeply troubled.** (Inferential Comprehension) There is no support in the excerpt for options (1), (3), and (5). Option (4) is close to the correct answer but does not summarize the whole relationship.

35. **(2) somewhat uncomfortable trying to communicate with his son** (Analysis) The writer asks Jack to "pardon me" and says that he is "not trying to make crude jokes," thus showing his discomfort. Options (1) and (5) are not supported by the excerpt, and there is no evidence for options (3) and (4).

36. **(1) emphasizes that the writer wanted to escape into a safer world** (Analysis) The speaker has alluded to danger in the political world and possibly some kind of scandal. The reference is not to Jack, nor about the speaker's second wife, so options (4) and (5) are incorrect. There is no evidence for options (2) and (3).

37. **(4) glad** (Application) From the excerpt, we can conclude that the speaker wants to be friends with his son. Though he may not understand some of his son's choices, the father takes him seriously and says that he is not unsympathetic to him. Therefore, options (1) and (2) are incorrect. The father's tone is serious, so option (3) is incorrect. Option (5) is not supported by the excerpt.

38. **(4) not doing his chores** (Literal Comprehension) Troy believes that football is taking Cory away from his responsibilities.

There is no support for options (1) and (3). It is Troy who refuses to speak to the recruiter, so option (2) is incorrect. Option (5) is incorrect because Cory is cutting back his hours at the A&P.

39. **(3) is opposed to Cory's desire to play football** (Inferential Comprehension) Troy makes a number of arguments trying to change Cory's mind; therefore, options (1) and (2) are incorrect. There is no support for option (4). Option (5) is incorrect because it misrepresents Troy's statements.

40. **(2) go to college** (Inferential Comprehension) Cory states that he wants to play football because he sees it as an opportunity to go to college. Options (1) and (5) are Troy's desires, not Cory's. There is no evidence for option (3). While option (4) may be correct, there is no support for it in the excerpt.

41. **(3) Troy wants Cory to respect his authority.** (Analysis) The last lines of the excerpt indicate Troy's attempt to remind Cory of his authority as Cory's father. Options (1) and (2) are not directly supported by the excerpt. While the pair's exchange of words shows their difficulties in communicating with each other, Troy does show concern for Cory's future; therefore, option (4) is incorrect. The excerpt does not provide enough details to support option (5).

42. **(5) tense and full of conflict** (Analysis) The conflict between Troy and Cory over football and Cory's job produce an air of tension. No evidence is present for options (1) and (3) so they are incorrect. Although there may be elements of options (2) and (4), neither describe the overall mood.

43. **(3) People were reacting to the effects of a tornado.** (Inferential Comprehension) This covers the actions of all the people in the excerpt. Options (1), (2), (4), and (5) refer to details in the excerpt, not to the general situation.

44. **(5) did not understand why her husband had called** (Inferential Comprehension) Mrs. Miller had not worried about her husband because she did not realize there was anything to worry about. Option (1) is highly unlikely. Most people find tornadoes very frightening. There is no evidence to support options (2) and (3). Although Mrs. Miller clearly did not know about the tornado, there is no evidence that she slept through it, option (4).

45. **(3) there was danger of an explosion** (Analysis) The area demolished by the tornado was under immediate threat of explosion from escaping gas; therefore, everyone had to leave the area. Nothing in the excerpt indicates that the hotel itself is damaged by the tornado, so option (1) is incorrect. Options (2) and (5) are not sufficient reasons for evacuating the hotel. Option (4) is incorrect because it cannot be predicted where the second tornado will strike, so moving the guest to another hotel may not make them safer.

Mathematics (page 723)

1. **(3) 1999** To find the number of years needed to build 80 planes at a rate of 16 planes/year, divide: 80 planes ÷ 16 planes/year = 5 years. Add: 1994 + 5 = 1999.

2. **(4) 60 degrees** The sum of the interior angles of any triangle is 180°. Add the known angles and subtract from 180.
180 − (60 + 60) = 180 − 120 = 60.

3. **(1) 9** Set up a series of equations:
Stuart + 4 = Michela
Sofia − 3 = Stuart
If Sofia = 8, then
Stuart = 8 − 3 = 5 and Michela = 5 + 4 = 9.

4. **(4) between 11 and 12 feet** Use the Pythagorean Theorem:
$$c^2 = a^2 + b^2$$
$$12^2 = 4^2 + b^2$$
$$144 = 16 + b^2$$
$$144 − 16 = b^2$$
$$128 = b^2$$
Estimate the square root of 128. It falls between 11 and 12 ($11^2 = 121$; $12^2 = 144$.)

5. **(2) $9,500 − (0.20)($9,500)** Subtract the discount ($0.20 \times$ $9,500) from the original amount ($9,500).

6. **(4) between 7 and 8 hours** Divide 420 by 55.

7. **(4) 1999** To meet the goal, the university needs 6,000 students.
(20,000 − 14,000 = 6,000). Divide 6,000 by 1,500. It will take four years: 1995 + 4 = 1999.

8. **(3) $1,261.60** You can solve the problem using either of these equations:
1,660(100% − 24%) = x
1,660 − (1,660)(.24) = x

9. **(4) 12** Substitute and solve.
$$4x^3 − 2y$$
$$4(2^3) − (2)(10) =$$
$$4(8) − 20 =$$
$$32 − 20 = 12$$

Simulated Test

10. **(4) 32** Let x represent those who chose Plan B and $2x$ represent those who chose Plan A. Use the equation:
$$x + 2x = 48$$
$$3x = 48$$
$$\frac{3x}{3} = \frac{48}{3}$$
$$x = 16$$
$$2x = 32$$

11. **(3) 60** If 85% voted for the proposal, 15% ($100\% - 85\%$) voted against ($15\% = 0.15$).
$400 \times 0.15 = 60$

12. **(4) 38** An isosceles triangle has two sides the same length and two angles of equal measure. The equal angles are opposite the equal (congruent) sides. Side $\overline{BC}$ must be 10 feet in length, so the perimeter must be 38 feet ($10 + 10 + 18$).

13. **(1) $(3.14)(1.5)^2(5)$** Use the formula for the volume of a cylinder $V = \pi r^2 h$. Divide the diameter (3) by 2 to find the radius ($3 \div 2 = 1.5$).

14. **(4) $54** Find the lowest cost for each supply and add:

1 expense register:	$15
50 file folders:	$25
3 notebooks:	$10
6 paper rolls:	$4
	$54

15. **(3) 3,600** Use the formula for the volume of a rectangular container:
$V = lwh = (40)(9)(10) = 3,600.$

16. **(3) $300** Find 10% by moving the decimal point one place to the left: $1,500. = $150
Multiply by 2 to find 20%:
$150 \times 2 = $300.

17. **(2) 4** Divide $13\frac{1}{2}$ yards by $3\frac{3}{8}$ yards. Change to improper fractions $\left(13\frac{1}{2} = \frac{27}{2}; 3\frac{3}{8} = \frac{27}{8}\right)$. Invert $\frac{27}{8}$ and multiply. $\frac{27}{2} \div \frac{27}{8} = \frac{\overset{1}{27}}{\underset{1}{2}} \times \frac{\overset{4}{8}}{\underset{1}{27}} = 4$

18. **(5) 120** Substitute and solve.
$$x = 3a(b^2 - 8)$$
$$x = 3(5)(4^2 - 8)$$
$$x = 15(16 - 8)$$
$$x = 15(8) = 120$$

19. **(5) 10 to 12 months** The change during this period was 2 kg., more than any other change.

20. **(2) $7\frac{1}{2}$** Convert 33 inches to feet: $\frac{33}{12} = 2\frac{3}{4}$ ft
$$P = 2l + 2w$$
$$= 2\left(2\frac{3}{4}\right) + 2(1)$$
$$= 5\frac{1}{2} + 2$$
$$= 7\frac{1}{2}\text{ ft}$$

21. **(3) 396** Convert 1 foot to inches: $1 \times 12 = 12$ in
$$A = lw$$
$$= 33(12)$$
$$= 396\text{ square inches}$$

22. **(4) 11 and 12** Estimate the square root of 125: $\sqrt{121} = 11; \sqrt{144} = 12$.

23. **(4) 55** $\frac{12}{5} = \frac{132}{?}$
Cross multiply: $5 \times 132 = 660$.
Divide: $660 \div 12 = 55$.

24. **(1) 78** Find the missing lengths. Then add all the lengths to find the perimeter. The longer missing length is $12 + 9 = 21$ feet. The shorter missing length is $18 - 12 = 6$ feet. The perimeter is $18 + 9 + 6 + 12 + 12 + 21 = 78$ ft.

25. **(2) 306** Find the area of each part. Add the two amounts.
$A = lw = 12 \times 12 = 144$ square feet
$A = lw = 18 \times 9 = 162$ square feet
$144 + 162 = 306$ square feet

26. **(3) $\frac{5}{8} \times \frac{2}{5}$** You are finding the fractional part of the whole.

27. **(3) 4 and 5** The square of 4 is 16 and the square of 5 is 25; therefore, the square root of 24 must be between 4 and 5.

28. **(4) 49.5** Multiply to find how many characters will be on the 5 pages: $3,300 \times 5 = 16,500$. Set up a proportion and solve:
$$\frac{1,000}{3} = \frac{16,5000}{?}$$
Cross multiply: $3 \times 16,500 = 49,500$.
Divide: $49,500 \div 1,000 = 49.5$.

29. **(2) $3\frac{1}{4} - 2\frac{4}{5}$** You are finding the difference between two quantities.

30. **(2) 1.8592×10^4** Moving the decimal point 4 places to the right means multiplying by 10^4.

31. **(2) 44 and 49** Add the scores in the options. Only option (2) totals 93: $44 + 49 = 93$.

32. **(4) Scale: 1 in = 20 mi** Set up the ratio in the form of inches to miles:
$$\frac{2.5\text{ in}}{50\text{ mi}} = \frac{1\text{ in}}{?\text{ mi}}$$
Cross multiply: $50 \times 1 = 50$.
Divide: $50 \div 2.5 = 20$.

33. **(1) 9, 11, and 13** Add the numbers in the options. Only option (1) totals 33:
$9 + 11 + 13 = 33$.

34. **(3) 58 degrees** Since a right angle measures 90 degrees, angles 1 and 2 must add up to 90 degrees. Subtract the measure of angle 1 from $90°$ ($90° - 32° = 58°$).

35. **(2) $\frac{3}{5}$** Write the ratio and reduce:

$$\frac{\text{Fridays}}{\text{Both Days}} = \frac{9}{9+6} = \frac{9}{15} = \frac{3}{5}$$

36. **(2) 30°** $\angle S = \angle V$

37. **(3) 60°** $\angle U = 180° - (90° + 30°)$ $\angle U = 60°$

38. **(1) $(3.14)(5)^2(12)$** Use the formula $V = \pi r^2 h$. Divide the diameter (10) in half to find the radius.

39. **(5) \$8,970** They still owe $100\% - 25\% = 75\%$ ($75\% = 0.75$). $0.75 \times \$11,960 = \$8,970$.

40. **(1) $\frac{252}{900(2)}$** Use the formula $i = prt$ and solve for rate: $r = \frac{i}{pt} = \frac{252}{(900)(2)}$

41. **(2) 70°** $\angle A = 180° - (60° + 50°)$
$\angle A = 70°$
$\angle A = \angle D$
$\angle D = 70°$

42. **(5) \$90.25**
$\$9.50(5 + 3 + 1\frac{1}{2}) = \$9.50(9\frac{1}{2}) = \$90.25$

43. **(3) $\frac{1}{50}$** Write as a fraction and reduce:
$\frac{8}{400} = \frac{1}{50}$

44. **(2) A and E** Add to find out how much Linda has already spent: ($\$14.50 + \$16.80 = \$31.30$). Subtract to find out how much she has left to spend ($\$50 - \$31.30 = \$18.70$). Test each option. Only option (2), A and E, totals less than $\$18.70$ ($\$8.95 + \$9.45 = \$18.40$).

45. **(3) \$4** Round the cost of each item to the nearest whole dollar, add to find the total cost of the estimates, and subtract the total cost from \$10.
$\$1.99$ rounds to \$2.
$\$2.19$ rounds to \$2.
$\$1.14$ rounds to \$1.
$\$0.85$ rounds to \$1.
$\$2 + \$2 + \$1 + \$1 = \$6$
$\$10 - \$6 = \$4$

46. **(4) –3** Use the formula: $m = \frac{y_2 - y_1}{x_2 - x_1}$
$3 = \frac{3 - y}{3 - 1}$
$3 = \frac{3 - y}{2}$
$6 = 3 - y$
$3 = -y$
$-3 = y$

47. **(3) 6** Use this formula:
$m = \frac{y_2 - y_1}{x_2 - x_1}$

$2 = \frac{y_2 - 2}{3 - 1}$
$2 = \frac{y_2 - 2}{2}$
$4 = y_2 - 2$
$6 = y_2$

48. **(2) side $\overline{AC}$** When intersecting lines connect parallel line segments, similar triangles are formed. In the figure, $\angle B$ corresponds to $\angle D$ and $\angle A$ corresponds to $\angle E$. Therefore, side $\overline{BC}$ corresponds to side $\overline{CD}$ and side $\overline{CE}$ corresponds to side $\overline{AC}$.

49. **(3) 64** Similar triangles have proportionate sides. Set up a proportion using any pair of corresponding sides:
$\frac{\text{Side } AC}{\text{Side } CE} = \frac{\text{Side } AB}{\text{Side } DE} = \frac{15}{60} = \frac{16}{x} = \frac{1}{4} = \frac{16}{x}$
$x = 64$

50. **(5) 64** Let x represent the number of professional golfers. Use this equation:
$x + 2x = 96$
$3x = 96$
$x = 32$
The number of amateurs is $2x = 64$.

51. **(5) the length of the shadow of the street sign** You need the other shadow to set up a proportion.
$\frac{\text{height of sign}}{\text{shadow of sign}} = \frac{\text{shadow of sign}}{\text{shadow of building}}$

52. **(5) $6\frac{3}{4}$** Estimate: $2\frac{1}{4}$ is about 2.
Multiply: $3 \times 2 = 6$.
Solve: $3 \times 2\frac{1}{4} = \frac{3}{1} \times \frac{9}{4} = \frac{27}{4} = 6\frac{3}{4}$

53. **(2) 5** Estimate: 4 yards 6 inches rounds to 4 yards ($\frac{1}{2}$ yd is 18 inches). $21 \div 4$ is 5 r1. To solve change 6 inches to a fraction. 6 inches = $\frac{6}{36}$ or $\frac{1}{6}$ of a yard. Divide 21 by $4\frac{1}{6}$.

54. **(4) 15.6** The top line of the table shows the distance from Sarah's home to her daughter's day care is 1.5 miles. Reading on the bottom line of the table, from day care to work is 6.3 miles. Add the two figures: $1.5 + 6.3 = 7.8$. Multiply by 2 to find the mileage going and coming back: $7.8 \times 2 = 15.6$.

55. **(2) 60 yards** Add the areas of the patio and the pool to find the area of the fenced region. Divide by the length of the fenced region to find the width:
$4,500 + 1,500 = 6,000$
$6,000 \div 100 = 60$.

56. **(5) $a^2 + 8^2 = 10^2$** Use the Pythagorean relationship and substitute the values from the drawing.

Acknowledgments

Grateful acknowledgment is made to the following authors, agents, and publishers for permission to use copyrighted materials. Every effort has been made to trace ownership of all copyrighted material and to secure the necessary permissions to reprint. We express regret in advance for any error or omission. Any oversight will be acknowledged in future printings.

Harry Allen for an excerpt from LEGENDS, *Vibe* magazine, March, 1995. Copyright (c) 1995. Used by permission of the author. (p. 482)

American Council on Education for Test Instructions, Essay Scoring Guide, and the Math Formula Chart. Reprinted with permission of American Council on Education.

Applause Books for an excerpt from "Marty" from TELEVISION PLAYS by Paddy Chayefsky. Reprinted by permission of Applause Theatre Books, 1841 Broadway, New York, New York 10023 (212) 765-7880. (p. 428)

Louis Armstrong Educational Fund for an excerpt from LOUIS: THE LOUIS ARMSTRONG STORY, 1900-1971 by Max Jones and John Chilton. Used by permission of David Gold. (Canadian distribution rights). (p. 414)

Bantam Books for excerpt from HIGH HEARTS by Rita Mae Brown. Copyright (c) 1986 Spenkiary Productions. Used by permission of Bantam Books, a division of Bantam Doubleday Dell Publishing Group, Inc. (p. 405)

Clay Bennett for his cartoon "Lobbyists." Used by permission of Clay Bennett, North America Syndicate. (p. 316)

The Boston Globe for excerpt from "Keeping the Promise of 'Land'" by Frederic M. Biddle, from *The Boston Sunday Globe*, 2/15/95. Reprinted courtesy of *The Boston Globe*. (p. 462)

Excerpt from THE AMEN CORNER (c) 1968 by James Baldwin. Copyright renewed. Published by Vintage Books. Reprinted by permission of the James Baldwin Estate. (p. 426)

Gwendolyn Brooks for "A Song in the Front Yard" by Gwendolyn Brooks, (c) 1991 from her book BLACKS, published by Third World Press, Chicago, in 1991. (p. 237)

Cartoon Features Syndicate for cartoon captioned, "Are you sure you won't quit after a year or two to get married?" by Wyatt from The Wall Street Journal-Permission, Cartoon Features Syndicate. (p. 308)

Chatto & Windus Ltd. for excerpt from "Three Pictures"

from THE DEATH OF THE MOTH AND OTHER ESSAYS by Virginia Woolf. Reprinted by permission of the Executors of the Virginia Woolf Estate and the publisher. (p. 441). Chatto & Windus Ltd. for excerpt from CIDER WITH ROSIE by Laurie Lee. Reprinted by permission of the Executors of the Estate of Laurie Lee and the publisher. (p. 448)

Commentary magazine for excerpt from "Lord of the Ants" by Jonathan Rosen. Reprinted from *Commentary*, March 1995, by permission; all rights reserved. (p. 471)

Curtis Brown Ltd. for excerpt from A SEPARATE PEACE by John Knowles. Reprinted by permission of Curtis Brown Ltd. Copyright (c) 1959 by John Knowles, renewed 1987 by John Knowles. (p. 400)

Doubleday for excerpt from "Halfway to Dick and Jane" by Jack Agueros, copyright (c) 1971 by Doubleday, a division of Bantam Doubleday Dell Publishing Group, Inc. from THE IMMIGRANT EXPERIENCE by Thomas C. Wheeler. (p. 417). For excerpt from HOW I GOT TO BE PERFECT by Jean Kerr. Copyright (c) 1978 by Collins Productions, Inc. (p. 421). For excerpt from LONG DISTANCE LIFE by Marita Golden. Copyright (c) 1989 by Marita Golden. (p. 396). All used by permission of Doubleday, a division of Bantam Doubleday Dell Publishing Group, Inc.

Dryad Press for "Migrants" by Roderick Jellema, from SOMETHING TUGGING THE LINE, copyright by Dryad Press. Used by permission of the publisher. (p. 434)

Dutton Signet for excerpt from FENCES by August Wilson. Copyright (c) 1986 by August Wilson. Used by permission of Dutton Signet, a division of Penguin Books USA Inc. (p. 718)

Farrar, Straus & Giroux, Inc. for excerpts from "Dean of Men" from THE COLLECTED STORIES OF PETER TAYLOR by Peter Taylor. Copyright (c) 1969 by Peter Taylor. Reprinted by permission of Farrar, Straus & Giroux, Inc. (p. 716). For excerpt from 5TH OF JULY by Lanford Wilson. Copyright (c) 1978 by Lanford Wilson. Reprinted by permission of Hill and Wang, a division of Farrar, Straus & Giroux, Inc. (p. 427). "Traveling at Home" from THE COLLECTED POEMS, 1957-1982 by Wendell Berry, copyright (c) 1984 by Wendell Berry. Reprinted by permission of North Point Press, a division of Farrar, Straus & Giroux, Inc. (p. 435). "Thank You M'am" from SOMETHING IN COMMON by Langston Hughes. This story will appear in SHORT STORIES OF LANGSTON HUGHES forthcoming from Hill & Wang. Copyright (c) 1963 by Langston Hughes. Copyright renewed (c) 1991 by Arnold Rampersad and Ramona Bass. Reprinted by permission of Hill & Wang, a division of Farrar, Straus & Giroux, Inc. (p. 47)

Samuel French, Inc. for excerpt from FIVE ON THE BLACK HAND SIDE by Charlie Russell. Copyright (c) 1969 by Charlie Russell. Copyright (c) 1977 (revised and rewritten) by Charlie Russell. Reprinted by permission of Samuel French, Inc. (p. 712)

Greenhaven Press for excerpt from ANIMAL COMMUNICATION: OPPOSING VIEWPOINTS by Jacci Cole. Copyright 1989 and published and reprinted by Greenhaven Press. (p. 418)

Deborah Gregory for excerpt from "Film Producers McHenry and Jackson" from Vibe, 2/95. Used by permission of the author. (p. 475)

Harcourt Brace & Company for excerpt from "Three Pictures" from THE DEATH OF THE MOTH AND OTHER ESSAYS by Virginia Woolf, copyright 1942 by Harcourt, Brace & Company and renewed 1970 by Marjorie T. Parsons, Executrix, reprinted by permission of the publisher. (p. 441)

HarperCollins Publishers for excerpt from "Once More to the Lake" from ONE MAN'S MEAT by E. B. White. Copyright 1941 by E.B. White. Reprinted by permission of HarperCollins Publishers, Inc. (p. 442). Excerpt from "Here Is New York" from ESSAYS OF E.B. WHITE. Copyright (c) 1949 by E.B. White. Copyright renewed 1977 by E.B. White. Reprinted by permission of HarperCollins Publishers. (p. 236). Excerpt from TEACHING A STONE TO TALK by Annie Dillard. Copyright (c) 1982 by Annie Dillard. Reprinted by permission of HarperCollins Publishers. Inc. (p. 423)

HARPER'S BAZAAR for excerpt from "Film" by Polly Frost from HARPER'S BAZAAR, November 1994. Copyright (c) 1994 by Hearst Magazines. Reprinted by permission of the publisher. (p. 461)

Houghton Mifflin Company for excerpt from "Charade," NARCISSA AND OTHER FABLES by Louis Auchincloss. Copyright (c) 1983 by Louis Auchincloss. Reprinted by permission of Houghton Mifflin Company. All rights reserved. (p. 436). Excerpts from COLD SASSY TREE. Copyright (c) 1984 by Olive Ann Burns. Reprinted by permission of Ticknor & Fields/Houghton Mifflin Co. All rights reserved. (pp. 398-399, 410)

Indiana University Folklore Institute for excerpt from A BASIC GUIDE TO FIELDWORK FOR BEGINNING STUDENTS. Used by permission of the publisher. (p. 303)

King Features Syndicate for "Blondie" cartoon by Young & Drake. Reprinted with special permission of King Features Syndicate. (p. 308)

Alfred A. Knopf, Inc. for excerpt from THE YEARS OF LYNDON JOHNSON: THE PATH TO POWER by Robert A. Caro. Copyright (c) 1982 by Robert A. Caro. Reprinted by permission of Alfred A. Knopf, Inc. (p. 415). "To Be of

Use" from CIRCLES ON THE WATER by Marge Piercy. Copyright (c) 1982 by Marge Piercy. Reprinted by permission of Alfred A. Knopf, Inc. (p. 207). Excerpt from "Neighbor Rosicky" from OBSCURE DESTINIES by Willa Cather. Copyright 1932 by Willa Cather and renewed 1960 by the Executors of the Estate of Willa Cather. Reprinted by permission of Alfred A. Knopf. Inc. (p. 440)

Barbara S. Kouts Agency for "Ellis Island" from THE REMEMBERED EARTH by Joseph Bruchac. Copyright 1942. Reprinted by permission of Barbara S. Kouts for the author. (p. 437)

Stuart Krichevsky Literary Agency, Inc. for excerpt from COME NINEVEH, COME TYRE by Allen Drury. Copyright (c) by Allen Drury. Reprinted by permission of Stuart Krichevsky Literary Agency, Inc. (p. 398)

Little, Brown and Company for excerpt from THE CAT WHO CAME FOR CHRISTMAS by Cleveland Amory. Copyright (c) 1987 by Cleveland Amory; illustrations copyright (c) 1987 by Edith Allard. By permission of Little, Brown and Company. (p. 420) Excerpt from LOUIS: THE LOUIS ARMSTRONG STORY by Max Jones and John Chilton. Copyright (c) 1971 by Max Jones and John Chilton. By permission of Little, Brown and Company. (p. 414)

Donald McCaig for excerpt from "The Best Four Days in Highland County." Country Journal, Sept. 1988. Reprinted by permission of the author, Donald McCaig. (p. 419)

Richard Meryman for excerpt from ANDREW WYETH: AN INTERVIEW by Richard Meryman, May 14, 1965. Reprinted by permission of the author. (p. 479)

Shirley D. Myers for excerpt from FIFTY GREAT ARTISTS by Bernard Myers. Reprinted by permission of Shirley D. Myers. (p. 472)

The Nation magazine for "Films (Crooklyn)," by Stuart Klawans, from the June 20, 1994, issue of The Nation. Reprinted with permission from The Nation magazine. (c) 1994 The Nation Company, L.P. (p. 460)

New Directions Publishing Company for excerpt by Tennessee Williams, from ECCENTRICITIES OF A NIGHTINGALE. Copyright (c) 1948, 1964 by Tennessee Williams. Reprinted by permission of New Directions Publishing Corp. (p. 48)

The New York Times Company for excerpt from Andy Meisler, "The Man Who Keeps E.R.'s Heart Beating" 2/26/95; (p. 468); for excerpt from Veronica Chambers, The New York Times Book Review;(p. 470); for excerpt from "Psst: TV Nudging Movies Aside" by Bernard Weintrab; (p. 485); for excerpt from Maurice Herzog, "Adventure: The Unending Challenge" 10/4/53; (p. 50); for excerpt from Robert Harris, "Too Embarassed Not to Kill" 3/11/90; (p. 50); for excerpt from Frank Aitken and Edward Hilton, "Earthquake at San Francisco;" (p. 422); for excerpt from

John Russell, Art Review, 10/12/86. (p. 478). Copyright (c) 1953, 1986, 1990, 1995 by The New York Times Company. Reprinted by permission.

The New Yorker magazine for cartoon by Koren, "Have you given...world's fossil fuels are used up?" (c) 1973. *The New Yorker* magazine. (p. 249). Excerpt from "Twyla Tharp Looks Ahead and Thinks Back" by Arlene Croce from The Talk of the Town, issue of Jan 23, 1995. By permission of *The New Yorker*. (p. 474)

Newsweek magazine for excerpt from Bill Barol, "Irving Berlin: 1888-1989" 10/2/89; (p. 463); excerpt from Jack Kroll, "The Outsiders Are In" 12/25/89; (p. 477). From *Newsweek* (c) 1989, Newsweek, Inc. All rights reserved. Reprinted by permission. Excerpt from David Ansen and Peter Annin, "Battered Dreams of Glory" 10/17/94, (c) 1994 , Newsweek, Inc. All rights reserved. Reprinted by permission. (p. 710)

W. W. Norton & Company for excerpt from BLACK BETTY by Walter Mosley. Copyright (c) 1994 by Walter Mosley. Reprinted by permission of W. W. Norton & Company, Inc. (p. 409)

Harold Ober Associates for excerpt by Catherine Drinker Bowen, THE YOUNG JOHN ADAMS. Reprinted by permission of Harold Ober Associates. Copyright (c) 1949 by Catherine Drinker Bowen. Copyright renewed 1977 by Ezra Bowen. (p. 484)

Simon J. Ortiz for "Earth and Rain, the Plants & Sun." Used by permission of the author. (p.430)

The Overlook Press for "Miami" from THE BOOK OF FORTUNE by Daniel Mark Epstein. Copyright (c) 1982 by Daniel Mark Epstein. Published by The Overlook Press, Woodstock, NY 12498. Used by permission. (p. 433)

Oxford University Press for excerpt from A DOLL'S HOUSE by Henrik Ibsen, translated by James McFarlane from FOUR MAJOR PLAYS, (c) 1981. By permission of Oxford University Press, Oxford. (p. 451)

Penguin USA for excerpt from "The Dead", from DUBLINERS by James Joyce. Copyright 1916 by B.W. Heubsch. Definitive text Copyright (c) 1967 by the Estate of James Joyce. Used by permission of Viking Penguin, a division of Penguin Books USA Inc., (p. 52). Excerpt from THE GOOD APPRENTICE by Iris Murdoch. Copyright (c) 1985 by Iris Murdoch. Used by permission of Viking Penguin, a division of Penguin Books USA Inc. (p. 397). Excerpt from "The Hazards of Science", copyright (c) 1977 by Lewis Thomas, from THE MEDUSA AND THE SNAIL by Lewis Thomas. Used by permission of Viking Penguin, a division of Penguin Books USA Inc. (p. 203) Excerpt from FENCES by August Wilson. Copyright (c) 1986 by August Wilson. Used by permission of Dutton Signet, a Division of Penguin Books USA Inc. (p. 718)

Peter Porges for "Big Fish" cartoon. By permission of Peter Porges. (p. 251)

Putnam Berkley Group, Inc., for excerpt from THE UNKNOWN COUNTRY by Bruce Hutchinson, published by Coward, McCann. (p. 416)

John H. Quinn for excerpt from ISHI IN TWO WORLDS: A BIOGRAPHY OF THE LAST WILD INDIAN IN NORTH AMERICA, by Theodora Kroeber. Copyright (c) 1961 Theodora Kroeber. (c) renewal 1989 John H. Quinn. Reprinted by permission of John H. Quinn. (p. 438)

Random House, Inc. for excerpt from A RAISIN IN THE SUN by Lorraine Hansberry. Copyright (c) 1958 by Robert Nemiroff as an unpublished work. Copyright (c) 1959, 1966, 1984 by Robert Nemiroff. Reprinted by permission of Random House, Inc. (p. 450). Excerpt from RAGTIME by E.L. Doctorow. Copyright (c) 1974, 1975 by E. L. Doctorow. Reprinted by permission of Random House, Inc. (p. 407). Excerpt from THE CHILDREN'S HOUR by Lillian Hellman. Copyright (c) 1934 by Lillian Hellman Kobert and renewed 1962 by Lillian Hellman. (p. 452). Reprinted by permission of Random House, Inc. Excerpt from THE ODD COUPLE by Neil Simon. Copyright (c) 1966 and renewed 1994 by Neil Simon. Reprinted by permission of Random House, Inc. (p. 429). "Strange Season" from ALL THE NIGHT WINGS by Loren Eiseley. Copyright (c) 1979 by The Estate of Loren Eiseley. Reprinted by permission of Random House, Inc. (p. 215). Excerpt from UP IN THE OLD HOTEL by Joseph Mitchell. Copyright (c) 1992 by Joseph Mitchell. Reprinted by permission of Pantheon Books, a division of Random House, Inc. (p. 447). Excerpt from BURR: A NOVEL by Gore Vidal. By permission of Random House, Inc. (p. 404)

The Saturday Evening Post for excerpt from "Forty-five Seconds Inside a Tornado" by Ira A.J. Baden as told to Robert Parham, from MAN AGAINST NATURE. Copyright (c) 1953. Originally appeared in *The Saturday Evening Post*, July 11, 1953. By permission of *The Saturday Evening Post*. (p. 720)

Simon & Schuster, Inc. for the following excerpts: Reprinted with the permission of Simon & Schuster from THE CLUE IN THE OLD ALBUM by Carolyn Keene. Copyright (c) 1947, 1977 by Simon & Schuster. (p. 402). Reprinted with the permission of Scribner, a Division of Simon & Schuster from THE MIRACLE WORKER by William Gibson. Copyright (c) 1956, 1957 by William Gibson. Copyright (c) 1959, 1960 by Tamarack Productions, Ltd., and George S. Klein & Leo Garel as trustees under three separate deeds of trust. (p. 483). Excerpt from "A Day's Wait" with permission of Scribner, a division of Simon & Schuster, from THE COMPLETE SHORT STORIES OF ERNEST HEMINGWAY. Copyright 1933 by Charles Scribner's Sons. Copyright renewed (c) 1961 by Mary Hemingway. (p. 480). Excerpted with permission of Scribner, a Division of Simon & Schuster, from THE GREAT GATSBY (Authorized Text) by F. Scott Fitzgerald. Copyright 1925 by Charles Scribner's Sons. Copyright renewed 1953 by Frances Scott Fitzgerald Lanahan. Copyright 1991, 1992 by Eleanor Lanahan, Matthew J. Bruccoli, and Samuel J. Lanahan as Trustees u/a dated 7/3/75 created by Frances Scott Fitzgerald Smith.

(p. 708). Reprinted with the permission of Pocket Books, a Division of Simon & Schuster from LONESOME DOVE by Larry McMurtry. Copyright (c) 1985 by Larry McMurtry. (p. 406). Reprinted with the permission of Simon & Schuster from CONTACT by Carl Sagan. Copyright (c) 1985, 1986, 1987 by Carl Sagan. (p. 412). For excerpt from ON THE BEACH by Nevil Shute. (p. 411)

The Society of Authors for "The Listeners" by Walter de la Mare. By permission of The Literary Trustees of Walter de la Mare, and The Society of Authors as their representative. (p. 454)

St. Martin's Press for excerpt from HUYSMAN'S PETS by Kate Wilhelm. Copyright (c) 1986 by Kate Wilhelm. Reprinted by permission of St. Martin's Press, Inc., New York, N.Y. (p. 403)

Stanford University Press for "Carmel Point" from THE COLLECTED POETRY OF ROBINSON JEFFERS, Volume Three (1938-1962) ed. by Tim Hunt, with the permission of the publisher, Stanford University Press. (c) 1987 by Jeffers Literary Properties; (c) 1995 by the Board of Trustees of the Leland Stanford Junior University. (p. 432)

George Joseph Szabo for his "Soviet Union" cartoon. By permission of the cartoonist. (p. 265)

Time Life Syndication for excerpt from "What's Up with the Universe" by Jaroff, issue of 1/9/95, (c) 1995 Time, Inc. Reprinted by permission. (p. 464). For excerpt from "A Woman's Wit and Heart" issue of 8/24/94, (c) 1994 Time, Inc. Reprinted by permission. (p. 466). For excerpt from "Death and the Blues", issue of 4/21/95, (c) 1995 Time, Inc. Reprinted by permission. (p. 476). For excerpt from "A Quarter Century Later the Myth Endures" issue of 8/25/86, (c) 1986 Time, Inc. Reprinted by permission. (p. 704).

Universal Press Syndicate for Ben Sargent cartoon, (c) 1993 (Russian Bear). By permission of Universal Press Syndicate. (p. 268)

University of Illinois Press for "Moving In" in COLLECTED POEMS 1930-83. Copyright 1983 by Josephine Miles. Used with permission of the University of Illinois Press. (p. 706)

University of Nebraska Press. Reprinted from BLACK ELK SPEAKS, by John G. Neihardt, by permission of the University of Nebraska Press. Copyright 1932, 1959, 1972, by John G. Neihardt. Copyright (c) 1961 by the John G. Neihardt Trust. (p. 444)

USA TODAY for excerpt from "Campbell Moved by Urgency of Discord" issue of 9/2/94, copyright 1994, USA TODAY. Reprinted with permission. (p. 473). Excerpt from "Signed and Sealed, Stevie Wonder Delivers" issue of 1/9/95, copyright 1995 USA TODAY. Reprinted with permission. (p. 469)

Ed Victor, Ltd. for excerpt from THE GOOD APPRENTICE by Iris Murdoch. Copyright 1985 by Iris Murdoch. By permission of Ed Victor Ltd for Canadian distribution rights. (p. 397)

The Village Voice for excerpt from "Superfeet" by Sally M. Sommer, 10/14/86. Reprinted by permission of the author and *The Village Voice*. (p. 467)

Virginia Quarterly Review for "If a Woodchuck Could Chuck Wood", by W.D. Wetherell. Used by permission of the Virginia Quarterly Review. (p. 408)

The Washington Post Writers Group for "Non Sequitur" cartoon, "End of the Free Enterprise Zone" by Wiley. (c) 1995, Washington Post Writers Group. Reprinted with permission. (p. 280)

A.P. Watt Ltd. for excerpt from ON THE BEACH by Nevil Shute. Reprinted by permission of A. P. Watt Ltd. on behalf of the Trustees of the Estate of the Late Nevil Shute Norway. (p. 411)

Wieser & Wieser for "Calling the Child" by Karl Shapiro. By permission of Olga B. Wieser, Wieser & Wieser, Inc., agents for Karl Shapiro. (p. 481).

William Morris Agency. Excerpt from "Close Ties" reprinted by permission of the William Morris Agency, Inc. on behalf of the author. Copyright (c) 1980 by Elizabeth Diggs. All rights reserved. CAUTION: Professionals and amateurs are hereby warned that "Close Ties" is subject to a royalty. It is fully protected under the copyright laws of the United States of America, and of all countries covered by the International Copyright Union (including the Dominion of Canada and the rest of the British Commonwealth), and of all countries covered by the Pan-American Copyright Convention and the Universal Copyright Convention, and of all countries with which the United States has reciprocal copyright relations. All rights, including professional, amateur, motion picture, recitation, lecturing, public reading, radio broadcasting, television, video or sound recording, all other forms of mechanical or electronic reproduction, such as information storage and retrieval systems and photocopying, and the rights of translation into foreign languages, are strictly reserved. Particular emphasis is laid upon the matter of readings, permission for which must be secured from the Author's agent in writing. Inquiries concerning rights should be addressed to William Morris Agency, Inc.; 1325 Avenue of the Americas; New York, NY 10019; Attn: George Lane. The first professional production of "Close Ties" was by the Long Wharf Theatre, New Haven, CT on February 3, 1981. (p. 208)